DOCUMENTS
ON
AMERICAN FOREIGN
RELATIONS

VOL. VIII

JULY 1, 1945—DECEMBER 31, 1946

Edited by RAYMOND DENNETT

and ROBERT K. TURNER

PUBLISHED FOR

THE WORLD PEACE FOUNDATION

BY

PRINCETON UNIVERSITY PRESS

C-2240

Copyright, 1948, by
Princeton University Press

London: Geoffrey Cumberlege
Oxford University Press

PRINTED IN THE UNITED STATES OF AMERICA BY
THE NORWOOD PRESS: NORWOOD, MASS.

WORLD PEACE FOUNDATION
40 Mt. Vernon Street, Boston, Massachusetts
Founded in 1910

The World Peace Foundation is a non-profit organization which was founded in 1910 by Edwin Ginn, the educational publisher, for the purpose of promoting peace, justice and goodwill among nations. For many years the Foundation has sought to increase public understanding of international problems by an objective presentation of the facts of international relations. This purpose is accomplished principally through its publications and by the maintenance of a Documents Library which furnishes on request information on current international problems. Recently increased attention has been focused on the field of research and international affairs through the publication of two quarterly periodicals, *International Organization* and *Documents of International Organizations: A Selected Bibliography*, and on the field of American foreign policy through the publication of an annual series, *Documents on American Foreign Relations.*

BOARD OF TRUSTEES
HARVEY H. BUNDY, *President*

FRANK AYDELOTTE	BRUCE C. HOPPER
JAMES PHINNEY BAXTER, 3D	MANLEY O. HUDSON
PERCY W. BIDWELL	JACOB J. KAPLAN
GEORGE H. BLAKESLEE	J. GRAFTON ROGERS
LEONARD W. CRONKHITE	KENNETH C. M. SILLS
JOHN S. DICKEY	PAYSON S. WILD
CHRISTIAN A. HERTER	HENRY M. WRISTON
ALGER HISS	

GENERAL STAFF
RAYMOND DENNETT, *Director*
MARY J. MACDONALD, *Treasurer*
ROBERT K. TURNER, *Documents Service*
MARGARET L. BATES, *Editorial Associate*
BETTE DANEMAN
AVA C. SPENCER
Editorial Assistants

PREFACE

This, the eighth volume in a series published by the World Peace Foundation as a part of its contribution to a better understanding of American foreign relations, differs from previous volumes primarily in that it covers an eighteen month period (July 1, 1945 to December 31, 1946) instead of the previously normal twelve month period (July 1 to June 30). On the institution of the series, considerable emphasis was placed by the editors, and by the Trustees of the Foundation, upon the importance of publishing promptly a collection of nearly contemporaneous documents which would be of service to students and teachers; for some years it was possible to release in the last months of each year a volume containing an account of American foreign relations through the preceding June. Wartime publishing difficulties intervened, however; and, since it did not appear feasible to return to the pre-war schedule, it was decided to issue subsequent volumes on a regular calendar-year basis. The present collection, therefore, represents a transition between the two different time-periods covered in the series. It is our expectation that, in the future, the volume pertaining to American foreign policy during one calendar year will appear by late fall of the year following.

Obviously, the task of compressing into manageable form the vast flood of official documentation produced during the period covered presented unusual difficulties; neither of the editors is under any illusion that all will agree with this selection. One major decision was made early in the planning stages of the present volume: we could not include in the space available adequate documentation bearing upon the role of the United States in the negotiation of the peace treaties with Bulgaria, Hungary, Italy, Rumania and Finland without sacrificing the effective treatment of the complex problems of occupation policy, of United States participation in the United Nations and the specialized agencies or of the emergence of our post-war economic policies. There will, therefore, be a supplement to this volume, appearing in the regular series but separately titled *The First Five Peace Treaties*, which will contain, so far as is possible at the present time, a factual account of the negotiation of the treaties, their texts, and statements of American positions on the points at issue.

With a few necessary exceptions, the pattern of previous volumes has been adhered to. Chapter III has become *The Termination of the War;* Chapter IV, *American Policy Toward Former Enemy States;* Chapter V of Volume VII (*The United Nations in War*) has been omitted; a new Chapter VI (*National Defense*) has been inserted as have chapters on *Dependent Areas* (Chapter VIII) and on *Cultural Relations* (Chapter XIII). Since these changes were made necessary by the transitional nature of the period dealt with, it can be expected that a relatively consistent method of organization can be devised for the next and subsequent volumes.

The role of the United States in the activities of the United Nations has, in all cases, been dealt with topically under appropriate chapter headings.

In preparing this collection of documents we are greatly indebted to the staff of the World Peace Foundation for its cooperation and assistance. We wish to express particularly our appreciation of the contribution made by Mrs. Patricia S. Alexander and to accord recognition to Miss Margaret Bates for editorial assistance on a number of chapters. We are also indebted to Mrs. Phyllis Kalen and to Mrs. Ross Steinberger for their intelligent proofreading and checking.

RAYMOND DENNETT
ROBERT K. TURNER

May 1, 1948

CONTENTS

PREFACE v

I. PRINCIPLES AND POLICY: GENERAL STATEMENTS

(1) Statement by the Secretary of State (Byrnes) upon Taking Oath of Office, July 3, 1945 (Excerpts) . . 1
(2) Address by the President (Truman), Navy Day, New York, October 27, 1945 2
(3) Address by the Secretary of State (Byrnes) before the *New York Herald Tribune* Forum, October 31, 1945 . 7
(4) Address by the Secretary of State (Byrnes), Charleston, South Carolina, November 16, 1945 (Excerpt) . 10
(5) Annual Message of the President (Truman) to the Congress on the State of the Union, January 14, 1946 13
(6) Address by the Secretary of State (Byrnes) on the United Nations and United States Foreign Policy, February 28, 1946 (Excerpts) 21
(7) Statement by the Secretary of State (Byrnes) on the Opening Meeting of the Security Council, New York, March 26, 1946 26
(8) Address by the President (Truman), Army Day, Chicago, April 6, 1946 (Excerpt) 28
(9) Statement by the President (Truman) on the Anniversary of V-E Day, May 8, 1946 31
(10) Address by Senator Warren R. Austin (Vermont) on Peace Goals before the Foreign Policy Association, New York, June 26, 1946 (Excerpts) 31
(11) Address by the Secretary of State (Byrnes) on United States Aims and Policies in Europe, Paris, October 3, 1946 (Excerpts) 35
(12) Statement by the President (Truman) on the Bipartisan Program for Foreign Affairs, November 11, 1946 38
(13) Address by the President (Truman) before the United Nations General Assembly, October 24, 1946 (Excerpts) 40

II. CONDUCT OF FOREIGN RELATIONS

1. POWERS OF THE PRESIDENT 45

(1) Letter from the Attorney General (Clark) to the Secretary of State (Byrnes), on Validity of Commercial Aviation Agreements Executed by the President, June 18, 1946 45
(2) Letter from the Acting Attorney General (McGranery) to the Secretary of State (Byrnes), on Validity of International Agreements Executed by the President, August 20, 1946 (Excerpts) 47

2. DEPARTMENT OF STATE 49
   A. ORGANIZATION 49
   1. Office of the Secretary of State 49

CONTENTS

2. Special Assistant to the Secretary for Research and Intelligence 50
3. Office of the Under Secretary of State 51
4. Office of the Under Secretary of State for Economic Affairs 51
    (1) Statement by the Secretary of State (Byrnes) before the Committee on Foreign Affairs of the House of Representatives, June 10, 1946 (Excerpts) . . . 51
    (2) Report of the Committee on Foreign Affairs of the House of Representatives on H. R. 6646, June 11, 1946 (Excerpt) 54
    (3) An Act to Establish the Office of Under Secretary of State for Economic Affairs, Approved August 1, 1946 55
5. Office of the Counselor of the Department of State . . 56
6. Office of the Assistant Secretary for Administration . 56
7. Office of the Assistant Secretary for Congressional Relations and International Conferences. 57
8. Office of the Assistant Secretary for Public Affairs . . 57
    (1) Statement by the Assistant Secretary for Public Affairs (Benton) on His Duties and Responsibilities, September 18, 1945 59
9. Office of the Assistant Secretary for American Republic Affairs 60
10. Office of the Assistant Secretary for Occupied Areas . 60
11. Office of the Assistant Secretary for Economic Affairs . 61
12. Office of the Legal Adviser 62

B. APPROPRIATIONS 62
    (1) Comparative Statement of State Department Appropriations for 1946 and 1947 62

3. OTHER AGENCIES 63
    A. STATE-WAR-NAVY COORDINATING COMMITTEE . . . 63
        (1) Memorandum of the Secretary of State (Byrnes), the Secretary of War (Patterson) and the Secretary of the Navy (Forrestal) Defining the Authority of the State-War-Navy Coordinating Committee, October 16, 1945 64
    B. OTHER EXECUTIVE DEPARTMENTS 64
        (1) Statement by the Senate Adviser to the United States Delegation to the Conference of Twenty-One Nations (Connally), Paris, September 14, 1946 . . 65
        (2) Statement by the Senate Adviser to the United States Delegation to the Conference of Twenty-One Nations (Vandenberg), Paris, September 14, 1946 . . . 65
        (3) Statement by the President (Truman), September 20, 1946 66

4. INTERNATIONAL ORGANIZATIONS AND CONFERENCES . . 66
    A. PRIVILEGES AND IMMUNITIES OF INTERNATIONAL ORGANIZATIONS 66
        (1) An Act to Extend Certain Privileges, Exemptions, and Immunities to International Organizations and

to the Officers and Employees Thereof, and for Other Purposes, Approved December 29, 1945 . . . 67
(2) Executive Order 9698, Designating Public International Organizations Entitled to Enjoy Certain Privileges, Exemptions, and Immunities, February 19, 1946 73

B. INTERNATIONAL ORGANIZATIONS IN WHICH THE UNITED STATES PARTICIPATES, AS OF DECEMBER 31, 1946 . . 73

C. INTERNATIONAL CONFERENCES IN WHICH THE UNITED STATES PARTICIPATED, JULY 1, 1945 TO DECEMBER 31, 1946 76

5. DIPLOMATIC REPRESENTATION 81

A. FOREIGN SERVICE ACT OF 1946 81
(1) Eighth Report of the House Special Committee on Postwar Economic Policy and Planning, November 12, 1945 (Excerpt) 81
(2) An Act to Improve, Strengthen, and Expand the Foreign Service of the United States, and to Consolidate and Revise the Laws Relating to Its Administration, Approved August 13, 1946 . . . 84
(3) Statement by the President (Truman) on the Foreign Service Act of 1946, August 13, 1946 . . . 101

B. CHANGES IN FOREIGN SERVICE POSTS 102
(1) Offices Established or Reestablished during the Period from July 1, 1945 to December 31, 1946 . . 102
(2) Offices Closed during the Period from July 1, 1945 to December 31, 1946 103
(3) Changes in Rank of Offices during the Period from July 1, 1945 to December 31, 1946 104

III. THE TERMINATION OF THE WAR

1. THE JAPANESE SURRENDER 105
(1) Proclamation Defining Terms for the Japanese Surrender, Signed at Potsdam and Issued by the President of the United States (Truman) and the Prime Minister of the United Kingdom (Attlee) and Concurred in by the President of the National Government of China (Chiang), July 26, 1945 . . . 105
(2) Exchange of Notes between the Secretary of State (Byrnes) and the Swiss Chargé d'Affaires ad interim (Grässli) Regarding the Offer of Surrender from the Japanese Government 106
  (a) Note from the Swiss Chargé d'Affaires ad interim to the Secretary of State, August 10, 1945 . 106
  (b) Note from the Secretary of State to the Swiss Chargé d'Affaires ad interim, August 11, 1945 107
(3) Statement by the President (Truman) on the Japanese Acceptance of the Potsdam Declaration, Containing the Text of the Message of Acceptance from the Japanese Government, August 14, 1945 . . . 108
(4) Text of the Instrument of Surrender, Signed by Representatives of the Japanese Government and of the

CONTENTS

United Nations at War with Japan, Tokyo Bay, September 2, 1945 109
(5) Address by the President (Truman) on the Signing by Japan of the Instrument of Surrender, September 1, 1945 110

2. The Transition to Peace 111

A. THE CESSATION OF HOSTILITIES 111

(1) Proclamation by the President (Truman), Terminating the Hostilities of the Second World War, Issued December 31, 1946 112
(2) Statement by the President (Truman) on the Termination of the Hostilities of the Second World War. White House Press Release, December 31, 1946 . 112

B. DEMOBILIZATION OF THE ARMED FORCES 113

(1) Annual Message of the President (Truman) to the Congress on the State of the Union, January 14, 1946 (Excerpt) 113
(2) Demobilization Directive of January 15, 1946 . . 114
(3) Statement by General Dwight Eisenhower before a Special Meeting of Congress, January 15, 1946 (Excerpts) 116

3. Requirements and Costs of Total War 124

A. NATIONAL COSTS 124

(1) United States Battle Casualties of the Second World War 124
(2) Comparative Statement of Budgetary Receipts and Expenditures for the Fiscal Years 1947, 1946 and 1945 125

B. LEND-LEASE AND MUTUAL AID 126

1. Discontinuance of Lend-Lease Operations . . . 126

(1) White House Press Release, August 21, 1945 . . 126
(2) Message of the President (Truman) to the Congress, September 6, 1945 (Excerpt) 126

2. Lend-Lease and Mutual Aid Settlements . . . 127

(1) Agreement between the United States and the Union of Soviet Socialist Republics on the Disposition of Lend-Lease Supplies in the United States, October 15, 1945 127
(2) Joint Statement by the United States and the United Kingdom on Settlement for Lend-Lease, Reciprocal Aid, Surplus War Property and Claims, December 6, 1945 132
(3) Agreement between the United States and the United Kingdom on Lend-Lease and Reciprocal Aid Pipelines and Offsetting Arrangement, March 27, 1946 . . 134

3. Administration of Lend-Lease and Mutual Aid Fiscal Records 139

(1) Executive Order 9726, Establishing Transfer of Fiscal Functions Relating to Lend-Lease Matters from the

CONTENTS

Department of State to the Treasury Department, May 17, 1946 139

4. Summary of Lend-Lease Operations as of September 30, 1946 140

   (1) Letter from the President (Truman) Transmitting to the Congress the Twenty-Third Report on Lend-Lease Operations, December 27, 1946 140
   (2) Twenty-Third Report to Congress on Lend-Lease Operations, for the Period Ended September 30, 1946, Transmitted by the President (Truman), December 27, 1946 (Excerpts) 141
   (3) Lend-Lease Aid by Country, March 11, 1941 to September 30, 1946 154
   (4) Lend-Lease Aid by Category, March 11, 1941 to September 30, 1946 155
   (5) Reverse Lend-Lease Aid Received by the United States, by Category and Country, Cumulative to September 2, 1945, Revised as of September 30, 1946 . 156
   (6) Total Funds Made Available for Lend-Lease, Cumulative to September 30, 1946 157

C. DISPOSAL OF SURPLUS PROPERTY IN FOREIGN AREAS . . 158

   (1) Executive Order 9630, Redistributing Foreign Economic Functions and Functions with Respect to Surplus Property in Foreign Areas, September 27, 1945 (Excerpts) 159
   (2) Delegation of Authority to the Foreign Liquidation Commissioner of the Department of State. Departmental Order, October 20, 1945 . . . 161
   (3) Agreement between the United States and China for the Sale of Certain Surplus War Property, Signed at Shanghai, August 30, 1946 163
   (4) Letter from the Secretary of State (Marshall) Transmitting the Fourth Report to Congress on Foreign Surplus Disposal as of December 31, 1946, January 30, 1947 167
   (5) Summaries of Foreign Surplus Disposal as of December 31, 1946 169
       (a) By the Office of the Foreign Liquidation Commissioner 169
       (b) Total Foreign Surplus Disposal 169

4. INVESTIGATION OF THE PEARL HARBOR ATTACK . . . 169

   (1) Foreword from the Report of the Joint Congressional Committee of Investigation on Background of the Pearl Harbor Attack, Submitted July 20, 1946 . . 169
   (2) Appendix to the Report of the Joint Congressional Committee of Investigation on Summary of Investigations Conducted Prior to Congressional Inquiry, Submitted July 20, 1946 170
   (3) Report of the Army Pearl Harbor Board on Assessment of Responsibilities for the Extent of the Attack, August 29, 1945 (Excerpts) 173

(4) Statement by the President (Truman) on the Report of the Army Pearl Harbor Board on the Responsibility of the Chief of Staff (Marshall). White House Press Release, August 29, 1945 176
(5) Statement by the President (Truman) on the Report of the Army Pearl Harbor Board on the Responsibilities of the People of the United States. White House Press Release, August 30, 1945 176
(6) Senate Concurrent Resolution 27, 79th Congress, 1st Session, Establishing the Joint Congressional Committee of Investigation, Passed by the Senate, September 6, 1945, and by the House of Representatives, September 11, 1945 177
(7) Report of the Joint Congressional Committee of Investigation, Submitted July 20, 1946 (Excerpts) . 178

IV. AMERICAN POLICY TOWARD FORMER ENEMY STATES

1. POLICY TOWARD INDIVIDUAL STATES 183

   A. ITALY 183

   (1) Message from the Acting Secretary of State (Acheson) to the Mazzini Society, September 15, 1945 (Excerpt) 184
   (2) Statement by the Secretary of State (Byrnes) on United States' Interest in Italian Elections, February 11, 1946 185

   B. GERMANY 186

   1. General Policy 186

   (1) Agreement between the United States, the United Kingdom, the Union of Soviet Socialist Republics, and the Provisional Government of the French Republic on Additional Requirements to Be Imposed on Germany, Signed September 20, 1945 189
   (2) Statement of the Secretary of State (Byrnes) on the Meaning of the Potsdam Declaration for Economic Issues in Germany, December 12, 1945 (Excerpt) . 198
   (3) Exchange of Notes between the Secretary of State (Byrnes) and the Minister of Foreign Affairs of France (Bidault) on the Establishment of Central German Agencies 201
   (a) Note from the Secretary of State to the Minister of Foreign Affairs of France, February 1, 1946 . 201
   (b) Note from the Minister of Foreign Affairs of France to the Secretary of State, March 2, 1946 . 203
   (4) Draft Treaty for the Disarmament and Demilitarization of Germany, Submitted to the Council of Foreign Ministers by the Secretary of State (Byrnes), April 29, 1946 205
   (5) Statement by the Secretary of State (Byrnes) on American Policy in Establishing Central Controls for the Economic Unity of Germany, July 11, 1946 . 208
   (6) Substance of Instructions Issued to the United States Military Governor in Germany (McNarney)

on German Economic Unity. Department of State
Press Release, July 22, 1946 209
(7) Restatement of United States Policy on Germany by
the Secretary of State (Byrnes), Stuttgart, Germany,
September 6, 1946 210
(8) Memorandum of Agreement between the United
States and the United Kingdom on the Economic
Fusion of American and British Zones of Occupation
in Germany, Signed December 2, 1946 . . . 218

2. Reparations 221
(1) Statement of the Head of the United States Delegation
to the Allied Commission on Reparations (Pauley),
August 30, 1945 222
(2) Law on Vesting and Marshaling of German External
Assets, Issued by the Allied Control Council for Germany, October 30, 1945 224
(3) Final Act and Annex of the Paris Conference on
Reparation, November 9 to December 21, 1945 . . 227
(4) Anglo-Soviet-American Communiqué on the Disposal
of the German Navy. Department of State Press
Release, January 22, 1946 244
(5) Plan of the Allied Control Council for Reparations
and the Level of Postwar German Economy, March 28,
1946 244
(6) Statement of the President's Personal Representative
(Pauley) on the European Reparation Program,
July 23, 1946 (Excerpt) 249

3. Occupation Policy in the United States Zone . . . 250
(1) Exchange of Letters between the President (Truman)
and the Commander-in-Chief of the United States
Forces of Occupation in Germany (Eisenhower) on
Displaced Persons 251
 (a) Letter from the President to General Eisenhower
Transmitting the Report of the United States
Representative on the Intergovernmental Committee on Refugees (Harrison), August 31, 1945 . 251
 (b) Letter from General Eisenhower to the President,
October 8, 1945 253
(2) Letter from the President (Truman) to the Secretary
of State (Byrnes), the Secretary of War (Patterson)
and the Secretary of the Navy (Forrestal) Transmitting the Report of Byron Price on the Relations between American Forces of Occupation and the German
People, November 28, 1945 256
 (a) Report of Byron Price to the President, November 9, 1945 (Excerpts) 256
(3) Directive of the United States Military Governor for
Germany (McNarney) on the Relationship between
the Military and Civil Government in the United
States Zone Subsequent to the Adoption of the *Land*
Constitutions, Issued September 30, 1946 . . . 263

C. JAPAN 266
   1. Occupation and Control 266
      (1) United States Initial Post-Surrender Policy for Japan, August 29, 1945 267
      (2) Authority of General MacArthur as Supreme Commander for Allied Powers, September 6, 1945 . . 273
      (3) Statement of the Supreme Commander for Allied Powers (MacArthur) on Occupation Policy, September 9, 1945. 273
      (4) Agreement of Foreign Ministers on Establishing the Far Eastern Commission and the Allied Council for Japan, Moscow, December 27, 1945 275
      (5) Report of the Supreme Commander for Allied Powers (MacArthur) on the First Year of Occupation of Japan, August 29, 1946 278
   2. Japanese General Election 280
      (1) Directive of the Supreme Commander for Allied Powers (MacArthur) for General Elections in Japan, January 12, 1946 280
      (2) Exchange of Correspondence between the Far Eastern Commission and the Supreme Commander for Allied Powers (MacArthur) 280
         (a) Note from the Far Eastern Commission to the Supreme Commander for Allied Powers, March 21, 1946 280
         (b) Note from the Supreme Commander for Allied Powers to the Far Eastern Commission, March 29, 1946 281

D. AUSTRIA 283
   1. General Policy 283
      (1) Report by the Secretary of State (Byrnes) on the Latter Half of the Meeting of the Council of Foreign Ministers in Paris, June 15–July 12, 1946, Dated July 15, 1946 (Excerpt) 284
      (2) United States Policy on Status of Austria. Department of State Press Release, October 28, 1946 . . . 284
   2. German Assets and Reparations 285
      (1) Note Delivered by the Military Commissioner of the United States on the Allied Council for Austria (Clark) to the Government of Austria Regarding German Assets in Austria. Department of State Press Release, July 10, 1946 286
      (2) Communication by the Government of the Union of Soviet Socialist Republics to the Government of Austria Concerning the Potsdam Agreement, July 16, 1946 287
   3. Occupation and Control 288
      (1) Directive to the Commander in Chief of United States Forces of Occupation in Austria (Clark) Regarding the Military Government of Austria, June 27, 1945 . 290

CONTENTS

(2) Statements Summarizing the Agreements Reached by the European Advisory Commission on Control Machinery and Zones of Occupation in Austria. Department of State Press Release, August 8, 1945 . 309
  (a) Summary of the Agreement between the Governments of the United Kingdom, the United States of America, and the Union of Soviet Socialist Republics and the Provisional Government of the French Republic on Control Machinery in Austria 309
  (b) Summary of the Agreement between the Governments of the United Kingdom, the United States of America, and the Union of Soviet Socialist Republics and the Provisional Government of the French Republic on Zones of Occupation in Austria 310
(3) Statement on Recognition of Government of Austria. Department of State Press Release, January 7, 1946 . 311
(4) Agreement between the Governments of the United Kingdom, the United States of America, the Union of Soviet Socialist Republics and the Government of the French Republic on the Machinery of Control of Austria, June 28, 1946 311

4. Relations with the Austrian Government . . . 317

E. BULGARIA 317
  (1) Statement by the Secretary of State (Byrnes) Concerning Postponement of National Elections in Bulgaria. Department of State Press Release, August 25, 1945 . 318
  (2) Report of the Moscow Meeting of the Ministers of Foreign Affairs of the Union of Soviet Socialist Republics (Molotov), the United States (Byrnes) and the United Kingdom (Bevin), December 27, 1945 (Excerpt) 318
  (3) Aide-Mémoire Delivered by Counselor of the Department of State (Cohen) to the Representative of Bulgaria in Washington (Stoichew), February 22, 1946 319
    (a) Exchange of Notes between the Chargé d'Affaires of the Union of Soviet Socialist Republics (Novikov) and the Secretary of State (Byrnes) Regarding the United States Aide-Mémoire to the Government of Bulgaria of February 22, 1946 . 320
      (i) Note from the Chargé d'Affaires of the Union of Soviet Socialist Republics to the Secretary of State, March 7, 1946 320
      (ii) Note from the Secretary of State to the Chargé d'Affaires of the Union of Soviet Socialist Republics, March 10, 1946 . . 321
  (4) Exchange of Notes between the Secretary of State (Byrnes) and the Prime Minister of Bulgaria (Georgiev) 322
    (a) Note from the Secretary of State to the Prime Minister of Bulgaria, September 24, 1946 . . 322
    (b) Note from the Prime Minister of Bulgaria to the Secretary of State (Translation) 323

(5) Exchange of Letters between the United State Representative on the Allied Control Council (Robertson) and the Representative of the Union of Soviet Socialist Republics and Acting Chairman of the Council (Biryusov) 325
   (a) Letter from the United States Representative to the Representative of the Union of Soviet Socialist Republics, October 1, 1946 325
   (b) Letter from the Representative of the Union of Soviet Socialist Republics to the United States Representative, October 4, 1946 326
   (c) Letter from the United States Representative to the Representative of the Union of Soviet Socialist Republics, October 4, 1946 326

F. HUNGARY 326
(1) United States Request for Action to Halt Hungarian Economic Disintegration, Including Note from the United States Ambassador to the Union of Soviet Socialist Republics (Smith) to the Minister for Foreign Affairs of the Union of Soviet Socialist Republics (Molotov), July 23, 1946. Department of State Press Release, July 27, 1946 (Excerpts) . . . 327
(2) Note from the Vice Minister for Foreign Affairs of the Union of Soviet Socialist Republics (Dekanonozov) to the United States Ambassador to the Union of Soviet Socialist Republics (Smith), July 27, 1946 . 331

G. RUMANIA 334
(1) Statement by the Secretary of State (Byrnes). Department of State Press Release, August 22, 1945 . 335
(2) Report of the Moscow Meeting of the Ministers of Foreign Affairs of the Union of Soviet Socialist Republics (Molotov), the United States (Byrnes) and the United Kingdom (Bevin), December 27, 1945 (Excerpt) 337
(3) Recognition of Government of Rumania. Department of State Press Release, February 5, 1946 . . . 337
(4) Exchange of Notes between the Minister of Foreign Affairs of Rumania (Tatarescu) and the United States Political Representative for Rumania (Berry) on Recognition of Government of Rumania. Department of State Press Release, February 15, 1946 . . . 339
   (a) Note from the Minister of Foreign Affairs of Rumania to the United States Political Representative for Rumania, February 7, 1946 (Translation) 339
   (b) Note from the United States Political Representative for Rumania to the Minister of Foreign Affairs of Rumania, February 14, 1946 . . 339
(5) United States Position on Election Results in Rumania. Department of State Press Release, November 26, 1946 340

2. TRIAL OF WAR CRIMINALS 340
   A. UNITED NATIONS WAR CRIMES COMMISSION 340

CONTENTS

B. INTERNATIONAL MILITARY TRIBUNAL FOR EUROPE	341
(1) Agreement by the Government of the United States of America, the Provisional Government of the French Republic, the Government of the United Kingdom of Great Britain and Northern Ireland and the Government of the Union of Soviet Socialist Republics for the Prosecution and Punishment of the Major War Criminals of the European Axis, August 8, 1945	343
(2) Executive Order 9626, Appointing the Member and Alternate Member for the United States of the International Military Tribunal Established for the Trial and Punishment of the Major War Criminals of the European Axis, September 24, 1945	344
(3) Final Report to the President (Truman) from United States Chief of Council (Jackson), October 7, 1946	345
C. INTERNATIONAL MILITARY TRIBUNAL FOR THE FAR EAST	352
(1) Executive Order 9660, Conferring Certain Authority upon the Chief of Counsel (Keenan) in the Preparation and Prosecution of Charges of War Crimes against the Major Leaders of Japan and Their Principal Agents and Accessories, November 29, 1945	352
(2) Special Proclamation Establishing an International Military Tribunal for the Far East by Supreme Commander for Allied Powers (MacArthur), Tokyo, January 19, 1946	353
(3) Charter for Establishment of the International Military Tribunal for the Far East, January 19, 1946	354
3. TEATMENT OF ENEMY ALIENS	358
(1) Proclamation by the President (Truman) on Removal of Enemy Aliens, Issued July 14, 1945	359
(2) Proclamation by the President (Truman) on Removal of Enemy Aliens, Issued September 8, 1945	360
(3) Proclamation by the President (Truman) on Removal of Enemy Aliens, Issued April 10, 1946	362
V. RELIEF AND REHABILITATION	
1. RELIEF	364
A. AMERICAN PARTICIPATION IN INTERNATIONAL AGENCIES	364
1. United Nations Relief and Rehabilitation Administration	364
(1) Statement by the Assistant Secretary of State for Economic Affairs (Clayton) before the Committee on Foreign Affairs of the House of Representatives, November 14, 1945 (Excerpts)	365
(2) Joint Resolution to Enable the United States to Further Participate in the Work of the United Nations Relief and Rehabilitation Administration, Approved December 18, 1945	368
(3) Letter from the Assistant Secretary of State for Economic Affairs (Clayton) to Senator Kenneth McKellar, July 3, 1946 (Excerpts)	369

xviii   CONTENTS

    (4) Radio Address by the Acting Secretary of State (Acheson) on United States Position on UNRRA, December 8, 1946 (Excerpt) 371
    (5) Tenth Report to Congress on the Operations of UNRRA for the Period from October 31 to December 31, 1946, Submitted by the President (Truman), May 15, 1947 (Excerpts) 373
   2. Other International Organizations 375
  B. ACTION TAKEN BY THE UNITED STATES 376
    (1) Statement by the President (Truman) on the Relief and Rehabilitation Program, September 17, 1945 . 379
    (2) Statement by the President (Truman) on the World Food Crisis, February 6, 1946 381
    (3) Famine Report to the President (Truman) by the Members of the Hoover Mission, May 13, 1946 . 383
    (4) Report to the President (Truman) on 1945–46 Famine-Relief Food Shipments, Submitted by the Secretary of Agriculture (Anderson), July 8, 1946 389
 2. REFUGEES AND DISPLACED PERSONS 393
  A. INTERNATIONAL REFUGEE ORGANIZATION 393
    (1) Statement by the Representative of the United States Delegation to the United Nations (Mrs. Roosevelt) on United States Position on the International Refugee Organization, November 8, 1946 396
    (2) Constitution of the International Refugee Organization, Signed at Lake Success, New York, December 16, 1946 (Excerpts) 400
  B. ADMISSION OF REFUGEES INTO THE UNITED STATES . . 406
    (1) Executive Order 9614, Terminating the War Refugee Board, September 14, 1945 407
    (2) Statement by the President (Truman), December 22, 1945 407
     (a) Directive by the President (Truman) to the Secretaries of State (Byrnes) and War (Patterson), the Attorney General (Clark), the War Shipping Administrator (Land), the Surgeon-General of the Public Health Service (Parran) and the Director-General of UNRRA (Lehman), December 22, 1945. 410

VI. NATIONAL DEFENSE

 1. ATOMIC ENERGY 413
  A. DEVELOPMENT AND MILITARY APPLICATION 413
    (1) Statement by the Secretary of War (Stimson), August 6, 1945 413
    (2) Statement by the President (Truman), August 6, 1945 419
  B. NATIONAL CONTROL 422
    (1) Executive Order 9613, Withdrawing and Reserving for the Use of the United States Lands Containing Radio-Active Mineral Substances, September 13, 1945 . 426

CONTENTS

    (2) Message from the President (Truman) to the Congress, Requesting the Enactment of Legislation on the Control, Use and Development of Atomic Energy, October 3, 1945 426
    (3) Letter from the President (Truman) to the Chairman of the Senate Special Committee on Atomic Energy (McMahon), February 2, 1946 429
    (4) An Act for the Development and Control of Atomic Energy, Approved August 2, 1946 431
    (5) Executive Order 9816, Providing for the Transfer of Property and Personnel to the Atomic Energy Commission, December 31, 1946 454

C. THE BIKINI TESTS 455

    (1) Joint Resolution to Authorize the Use of Naval Vessels to Determine the Effect of Atomic Weapons upon Such Vessels, Approved June 25, 1946 457
    (2) Preliminary Report of the President's Evaluation Commission on the First Bikini Test, July 1, 1946. White House Press Release, July 11, 1946 . . . 458
    (3) Preliminary Report of the President's Evaluation Commission on the Second Bikini Test, July 25, 1946. Press Release, August 2, 1946 459
    (4) Announcement of the Postponement of the Third Bikini Test. White House Press Release, September 6, 1946 461

2. MAINTENANCE OF DEFENSE 461

  A. GENERAL STATEMENTS 461

    (1) Statement of the Secretary of War (Patterson) before the Committee on Military Affairs of the House of Representatives, November 8, 1945 (Excerpt) . . 461
    (2) Statement by the Secretary of State (Byrnes), March 16, 1946 (Excerpts) 463
    (3) Address by the President (Truman), Chicago, Army Day, April 6, 1946 (Excerpt) 465
    (4) Address by the Chief of Staff of the United States Army (Marshall), October 29, 1946 (Excerpts) . . 467

  B. UNIFICATION OF THE ARMED FORCES 469

    (1) Message of the President (Truman) to Congress, Recommending Legislation for the Unification of the Armed Forces, December 19, 1945 (Excerpts) . . 469
    (2) Report from the Secretary of War (Patterson) and the Secretary of the Navy (Forrestal) to the President (Truman), May 31, 1946 478
    (3) Letter from the President (Truman) to the Secretary of War (Patterson) and the Secretary of the Navy (Forrestal), June 15, 1946 (Excerpt) 483

  C. PROCUREMENT OF PERSONNEL 485
    1. Voluntary Recruitment 486
    2. Extension of Selective Service 486
        (1) Message of the President (Truman) to Congress, September 6, 1945 (Excerpt) 488

CONTENTS

  (2) Radio Address by the Secretary of War (Patterson), April 1, 1946 490
  (3) An Act to Extend the Selective Training and Service Act of 1940, As Amended, and for Other Purposes, Approved June 29, 1946 492
 3. Universal Military Training 495
  (1) Message of the President (Truman) to Congress, October 23, 1945 496
  (2) Message of the President (Truman) to Congress, December 19, 1945 (Excerpt) 502
 3. SCIENTIFIC RESEARCH AND DEVELOPMENT . . . 503
  (1) Message of the President (Truman) to Congress, September 6, 1945 (Excerpt) 504
 4. MILITARY AND NAVAL MISSIONS TO FOREIGN GOVERNMENTS 506
 5. FOREIGN INTELLIGENCE ACTIVITIES OF THE FEDERAL GOVERNMENT 506
  (1) Directive of the President (Truman) Establishing the National Intelligence Authority, January 22, 1946 . 506

VII. INTERNATIONAL PEACE AND SECURITY

 1. UNITED NATIONS 508
  A. PARTICIPATION AND MEMBERSHIP 508
   1. Ratification of the Charter of the United Nations . . 509
    (1) Message of the President (Truman) Transmitting the Charter of the United Nations to the Senate, July 2, 1945 509
    (2) Senate Resolution Ratifying the Charter of the United Nations, July 28, 1945 510
    (3) Instrument of United States Ratification of the Charter of the United Nations, Deposited August 8, 1945 511
   2. United Nations Participation Act of 1945 . . . 511
    (1) United Nations Participation Act of 1945, Approved December 20, 1945 511
   3. Acceptance of Compulsory Jurisdiction of the International Court of Justice 515
    (1) Declaration on the Part of the United States Accepting Compulsory Jurisdiction of the International Court of Justice, August 14, 1946 . . 516
  B. FINANCIAL SUPPORT 517
   (1) Statement of the United States Delegate to the United Nations (Vandenberg) on Financial Support, December 13, 1946 517
  C. SELECTION OF HEADQUARTERS 518
  D. UNITED STATES POLICY IN THE UNITED NATIONS . . . 518
   1. General 518
    (1) Statement of the President (Truman) to the General Assembly of the United Nations, October 23, 1946 (Excerpts) 519

CONTENTS

2. Admission of New Members 524
   (1) Remarks of the Deputy United States Representative on the Security Council (Johnson) in Regard to the Admission of New Members, August 28, 1946 (Excerpts) 524
3. The Question of the Veto 526
   (1) Statement by the United States Delegate to the General Assembly (Connally) on the Veto Question, November 15, 1946 (Excerpts) 526

2. REGULATION AND REDUCTION OF ARMAMENTS 530
   (1) Statement by the Representative of the Union of Soviet Socialist Republics to the United Nations Security Council (Gromyko) before the Security Council, August 29, 1946 (Excerpt) (Translation) . 532
   (2) Statement by the Representative of the Union of Soviet Socialist Republics to the United Nations General Assembly (Molotov) before the General Assembly, October 29, 1946 (Excerpts) (Translation) 533
   (3) Statement by the Senior Representative of the United States to the United Nations General Assembly (Austin) before the General Assembly, October 30, 1946 (Excerpts) 535
   (4) Resolution on Regulation and Reduction of Armaments Submitted by the United States to the Political and Security Committee of the United Nations General Assembly, November 30, 1946 536
   (5) Statement by the Representative of the United States to the United Nations General Assembly (Connally) before the Political and Security Committee, December 2, 1946 (Excerpts) 537
   (6) Statement by the Representative of the Union of Soviet Socialist Republics to the United Nations General Assembly (Molotov) before the Political and Security Committee, December 4, 1946 (Excerpts) (Translation) 538
   (7) Statement by the Senior Representative of the United States to the United Nations General Assembly (Byrnes) before the General Assembly, December 13, 1946 (Excerpts) 540
   (8) Resolution on Principles Governing the General Regulation and Reduction of Armaments, Approved by the United Nations General Assembly, December 14, 1946 542
   (9) Resolution on Principles Governing Information on Armed Forces of the United Nations, Approved by the United Nations General Assembly, December 14, 1946 544

3. INTERNATIONAL CONTROL OF ATOMIC ENERGY . . . 544
   A. INITIATION OF INTERNATIONAL CONTROLS 545
      (1) Message from the President (Truman) to the Congress, October 3, 1945 (Excerpts) 545
      (2) Agreed Declaration by the President of the United States (Truman), the Prime Minister of the United

Kingdom (Attlee) and the Prime Minister of Canada (King), Washington, November 15, 1945 . . . 547
(3) Communiqué on the Moscow Conference of Foreign Ministers, Released December 27, 1945 (Excerpt) . 548

B. UNITED NATIONS ATOMIC ENERGY COMMISSION . . . 550

(1) Statement by the Representative of the United States to the United Nations General Assembly (Connally) before the Political and Security Committee, London, January 21, 1946 (Excerpt) 550
(2) Resolution Establishing the Atomic Energy Commission, Approved by the United Nations General Assembly, January 24, 1946 551
(3) Report by the Board of Consultants to the Secretary of State's Committee on Atomic Energy, Transmitted to the Secretary of State (Byrnes), March 17, 1946 (Excerpts) 552
(4) Proposals by the Representative of the United States to the United Nations Atomic Energy Commission (Baruch), Submitted to the Commission, June 14, 1946 (Excerpts) 557
(5) Proposals by the Representative of the Union of Soviet Socialist Republics to the United Nations Atomic Energy Commission (Gromyko), Submitted to the Commission, June 19, 1946 (Translation). . 560
(6) Memoranda by the Associate Member of the United States Delegation to the United Nations Atomic Energy Commission (Eberstadt), Submitted to Subcommittee 1 of the Commission 563
   (a) Control and Development of Atomic Energy, July 2, 1946 (Excerpts) 563
   (b) Functions and Powers of Proposed Atomic Development Authority, July 5, 1946 (Excerpts) . 565
(7) Proposals by the Representative of the United States to the United Nations Atomic Energy Commission (Baruch) Regarding the Inclusion of Certain Items Among the Findings and Recommendations in the Forthcoming Report of the Commission to the Security Council, Submitted December 5, 1946 . . . 570
(8) Report of the United Nations Atomic Energy Commission to the Security Council, December 31, 1946 (Excerpts) 572

VIII. DEPENDENT AREAS

1. THE INTERNATIONAL TRUSTEESHIP SYSTEM . . . 577

A. THE TRUSTEESHIP COUNCIL AND TRUSTEESHIP AGREEMENTS 577

(1) Memorandum of the United States Delegation to the Executive Committee of the United Nations Preparatory Commission Regarding Procedure for Dealing with Trusteeship Agreements, October 2, 1945 . . 579
(2) Statement by the Alternate United States Delegate to the General Assembly (Dulles) on the United States

Position on the Establishment of the Trusteeship
System, November 7, 1946 (Excerpts) . . . 581

B. UNITED STATES TRUSTEESHIP IN THE PACIFIC . . . 584

(1) Report by the Subcommittee on Pacific Bases of the
Committee on Naval Affairs of the United States
House of Representatives, August 6, 1945 (Excerpts) 585
(2) Statement by the President (Truman) on United
States Trusteeship in the Pacific, Released to the Press
November 6, 1946 594
(3) Draft Trusteeship Agreement for the Japanese Mandated Islands under Administration of the United
States, Released to the Press November 6, 1946 . 594

2. REGIONAL ADVISORY COMMISSIONS 598

A. CARIBBEAN COMMISSION 598

(1) Letter from the President (Truman) to the President
of the Second Session of the West Indian Conference
(Taussig), held at St. Thomas, Virgin Islands of the
United States, February 21, 1946 598

3. UNITED STATES DEPENDENCIES 600

IX. TRADE AND FINANCE

1. PRINCIPLES OF POSTWAR ECONOMIC POLICY 601

A. GENERAL PRINCIPLES 601

(1) Statement by the Secretary of State (Byrnes) Submitted to the Senate Committee on Banking and
Currency, August 21, 1945 (Excerpts) . . . 601
(2) Eighth Report of the House Special Committee on
Postwar Economic Policy and Planning, November 12,
1945 (Excerpt) 602
(3) Annual Message of the President (Truman) to Congress on the State of the Union, January 14, 1946
(Excerpts) 606
(4) Address by the Under Secretary of State for Economic
Affairs (Clayton) before the Thirty-Third National
Trade Convention, New York, November 13, 1946
(Excerpts) 607

B. SPECIAL AGENCIES TO IMPLEMENT POLICY . . . 608

1. The National Advisory Council on International Monetary
and Financial Problems 609

(1) Report to the President (Truman) on the Activities
of the National Advisory Council, March 9, 1946
(Excerpt) 609

2. Committee for Financing Foreign Trade 611

(1) Statement by the Chairman of the Committee (Aldrich), July 9, 1945 611

C. FOREIGN-LENDING POLICY 612

(1) Eighth Report of the House Special Committee on
Postwar Economic Policy and Planning, November 12,
1945 (Excerpt) 613

(2) Report to the President (Truman) on the Activities of the National Advisory Council on International Monetary and Financial Problems, March 4, 1946 (Excerpts) 614

2. PARTICIPATION IN INTERNATIONAL AGENCIES 617

   A. THE INTERNATIONAL BANK AND MONETARY FUND . . 617
   (1) Address by the Chairman of the Boards of Governors of the Bank and the Fund (Snyder) at Their First Annual Meeting, Washington, September 27 to October 3, 1946, Delivered September 27, 1946 (Excerpts) 619
   (2) Report to the President (Truman) by the National Advisory Council on International Monetary and Financial Problems on Participation by the United States in the Bank and the Fund to October 31, 1946, Transmitted to the Congress, January 13, 1947 (Excerpts) 621

   B. THE INTERNATIONAL TRADE ORGANIZATION 624

   1. United States Proposals for Expansion of World Trade and Employment 624
      (1) Text of United States Proposals for Expansion of World Trade and Employment, November 1945 (Excerpt) 625
      (2) Joint Statement by the United States and the United Kingdom, December 6, 1945 627
      (3) Suggested Charter for an International Trade Organization of the United Nations, Summary of Provisions, September 20, 1946 (Excerpt) 628

   2. Preparatory Committee for an International Conference on Trade and Employment 629
      (1) Address by the United States Representative on the United Nations Economic and Social Council (Winant), February 8, 1946 (Excerpts) . . . 630
      (2) Address by the Chairman of the United States Delegation (Wilcox), London, October 17, 1946 (Excerpts) 632

   3. Export-Import Bank of Washington 635
      (1) General Statement of Policy, Released to the Press by the Export-Import Bank, September 11, 1945 (Excerpts) 637
      (2) Statement of Loans and Authorizations of the Export-Import Bank of Washington as of December 31, 1946 638
      (3) Statement of Credits Authorized by the Export-Import Bank from July 1, 1945 to December 31, 1946 . . 640

   4. Reciprocal Trade Agreements 642

   5. Anglo-American Financial and Trade Agreement . . 643
      (1) Text of the Anglo-American Financial and Trade Agreement, Signed in Washington, December 6, 1945 645
      (2) Joint Statement by the President (Truman) and the

Prime Minister of the United Kingdom (Attlee) on the Conclusion of the Anglo-American Financial and Trade Negotiations, December 6, 1945 . . . 649
(3) Message from the President (Truman) Transmitting the Agreement to the Congress, January 30, 1946 (Excerpts) 651
(4) Address by the Secretary of State (Byrnes) before the Foreign Policy Association, New York, February 11, 1946 (Excerpts) 653
(5) S. J. Resolution 138, To Implement Further the Purposes of the Bretton Woods Agreements Act by Authorizing the Secretary of the Treasury to Carry Out an Agreement with the United Kingdom, and for Other Purposes, Approved July 15, 1946 . . . 656

X. TRANSPORTATION AND COMMUNICATION

1. INTERNATIONAL AERIAL NAVIGATION 657
   A. THE CONVENTION ON INTERNATIONAL CIVIL AVIATION, SIGNED FOR THE UNITED STATES AT CHICAGO, ILLINOIS, DECEMBER 7, 1944 657
      (1) Message from the President (Truman) to the Senate, Requesting Advice and Consent to the Ratification of the Convention, June 11, 1946 657
      (2) Announcement of Withdrawal by the United States Government from the Air-Transport Agreement, Signed at Chicago, Illinois, December 7, 1944, and Accepted February 8, 1945. Department of State Press Release, July 25, 1946 659
      (3) Status of the Civil Aviation Agreements, Formulated at Chicago, Illinois, December 7, 1944, as of October 2, 1946 660
   B. PROVISIONAL INTERNATIONAL CIVIL AVIATION ORGANIZATION (PICAO) 663
   C. BILATERAL AIR-TRANSPORT AGREEMENTS CONCLUDED BY THE UNITED STATES 664
      (1) Agreement between the Government of the United States of America and the Government of the United Kingdom Relating to Air Services between Their Respective Territories, Signed at Bermuda, February 11, 1946 666
         (a) Statement by the President (Truman) on the United States-United Kingdom Air-Transport Agreement. White House Press Release, February 26, 1946 670
      (2) Chart of Bilateral Air-Transport Agreements Concluded by the Government of the United States, July 1, 1945 to December 31, 1946 671
2. MERCHANT SHIPPING 672
   A. THE UNITED MARITIME CONSULTATIVE COUNCIL . . . 672
      (1) Agreement Establishing the United Maritime Consultative Council, Adopted February 11, 1946, and Released to the Press March 11, 1946 . . . 673

B. THE INTER-GOVERNMENTAL MARITIME CONSULTATIVE ORGAN-
IZATION 675
   (1) Recommendations of the United Maritime Consulta-
tive Council to Member Governments, Adopted
October 30, 1946 676
      (a) Agreement Establishing the Provisional Maritime
Consultative Council 676

C. THE INTERNATIONAL LABOR CONFERENCE, TWENTY-EIGHTH
(MARITIME) SESSION, SEATTLE, WASHINGTON, JUNE 6 TO 29,
1946 678

3. INLAND TRANSPORT 679
  A. THE EUROPEAN CENTRAL INLAND TRANSPORT ORGANIZATION 679
   (1) Agreement Concerning the Establishment of a European Central Inland Transport Organization, Signed
at London, September 27, 1945 679
   (2) Protocol Relating to Traffic on Inland Waterways,
Signed at London, September 27, 1945 . . . 691

4. INTERNATIONAL TELECOMMUNICATIONS 692
   (1) Report by the Representative of the United States
on the Moscow Telecommunications Conference
(deWolf), September 28 to October 31, 1946. Department of State Press Release, November 8, 1946
(Excerpts) 694

XI. AGRICULTURE AND NATURAL RESOURCES

1. GENERAL 697
  A. FOOD AND AGRICULTURE ORGANIZATION OF THE UNITED
NATIONS 697
   (1) Message of the President (Truman) to the Delegates
of the United Nations Food and Agriculture Organization at Quebec, October 17, 1945 698
   (2) Statement by the United States Delegate to the Food
and Agriculture Organization Preparatory Commission
on World Food Proposals (Dodd), December 21, 1946
(Excerpts) 699
  B. INTERNATIONAL EMERGENCY FOOD COUNCIL 703
   (1) Text of the Letter of Invitation Concerning the
Establishment of an International Emergency Food
Council, Addressed by the Member Governments of
the Combined Food Board (United States, United
Kingdom and Canada) to Prospective Members of the
Council, June 3, 1946 703
  C. UNITED STATES PROPOSAL FOR CONFERENCE ON RESOURCE
CONSERVATION AND UTILIZATION 704

2. COAL 705
   (1) Agreement between the United States and Other
Powers for the Establishment of the European Coal
Organization, Signed at London, January 4, 1946 . 705

3. COFFEE 707

CONTENTS

- 4. COTTON 707
  - A. INTERNATIONAL COTTON ADVISORY COMMITTEE 707
- 5. PETROLEUM 708
  - (1) An Agreement on Petroleum between the Government of the United States of America and the Government of the United Kingdom of Great Britain and Northern Ireland, Signed in London, September 24, 1945 . . 708
- 6. RUBBER 712
  - A. RUBBER STUDY GROUP 712
  - B. TERMINATION OF RUBBER PURCHASING AGREEMENTS . . 712
- 7. SUGAR 713
  - A. INTERNATIONAL SUGAR COUNCIL 713
- 8. TIN 713
- 9. WHALING 713
- 10. WHEAT 714
  - A. INTERNATIONAL WHEAT COUNCIL 714
- 11. WOOL 715
  - A. UNITED STATES IMPORT DUTIES ON WOOL 715
    - (1) Statement by the Assistant Secretary of State (Clayton) before the Senate Special Committee to Investigate Production, Transportation and Marketing of Wool, Concerning the Effect of the Wool Market on Foreign Economic Relations, November 21, 1945 (Excerpt) 715
  - B. INTERNATIONAL WOOL TALKS AND THE ESTABLISHMENT OF THE WOOL STUDY GROUP 718

XII. LABOR AND SOCIAL PROBLEMS

- 1. LABOR PROBLEMS 720
  - A. THE INTERNATIONAL LABOR ORGANIZATION 720
- 2. SOCIAL PROBLEMS 721
  - A. THE ECONOMIC AND SOCIAL COUNCIL 721
    - 1. Human Rights 722
      - (1) Proposal by the United States for the Establishment of a Subcommission on Freedom of Information, Transmitted by the United States Delegation to the United Nations to the Secretary-General for Reference to the Commission on Human Rights, May 8, 1946 . 723
    - 2. Control of Narcotic Drugs 724
      - (1) Statement on United States Policy Relating to Opium by the Adviser to the United States Representative on the Commission on Narcotic Drugs (Morlock), Submitted to the Commission on Narcotic Drugs, September 11, 1946 (Excerpts) 726
      - (2) Statement by the United States Representative on the Commission on Narcotic Drugs (Anslinger) Regarding the Control of Narcotic Drugs in the United States

CONTENTS

Zone in Germany, Submitted to the Commission on Narcotic Drugs, December 20, 1946 (Excerpts)	730
B. HEALTH	732
1. World Health Organization	732
2. Pan American Sanitary Bureau	734
(1) Report on the Relations of the Pan American Sanitary Bureau with the World Health Organization, Approved by the Governing Board of the Pan American Union at the Session of November 6, 1946 (Excerpts)	734

XIII. CULTURAL RELATIONS

1. UNITED NATIONS EDUCATIONAL, SCIENTIFIC AND CULTURAL ORGANIZATION	737
A. UNITED STATES PARTICIPATION	737
(1) Letter from the Secretary of State (Byrnes) to Chairman of the Committee on Foreign Affairs of the House of Representatives (Bloom), April 2, 1946	738
(2) Statement by the Chairman of the United States Delegation to the London Conference on the Establishment of UNESCO (MacLeish), Submitted to the Committee on Foreign Affairs of the House of Representatives, April 3, 1946	739
(3) H. J. Resolution 305, Providing for Membership and Participation by the United States in the United Nations Educational, Scientific and Cultural Organization, and Authorizing an Appropriation Therefor, Approved July 30, 1946	740
(4) Report on the First General Conference of UNESCO by the Chairman of the United States Delegation (Benton), December 23, 1946 (Excerpts)	743
B. UNITED STATES NATIONAL COMMISSION FOR UNESCO	746
(1) Report on the First Meeting of the National Commission Concerning the Establishment of the Commission, September 1946 (Excerpts)	746
(2) Report of the National Commission on UNESCO to the Secretary of State (Byrnes), September 27, 1946 (Excerpts)	748
2. INTERNATIONAL INFORMATION SERVICE	752
(1) Statement by the Assistant Secretary of State for Public Affairs (Benton) on the Role of the International Information Service in the Conduct of Foreign Relations before the Committee on Appropriations of the House of Representatives, October 4, 1945 (Excerpts)	753
(2) Summary of Projected Activities of the International Information Service. Department of State Press Release, December 28, 1945 (Excerpt)	755
3. CULTURAL EXCHANGE PROGRAM	757
A. INTERDEPARTMENTAL COMMITTEE ON SCIENTIFIC AND CULTURAL COOPERATION	757

CONTENTS

B. THE FULBRIGHT ACT	758
(1) Statement by the Assistant Secretary of State for Public Affairs (Benton). Department of State Press Release, August 1, 1946	759
(2) An Act to Amend the Surplus Property Act of 1944 to Designate the Department of State as the Disposal Agency for Surplus Property Outside the Continental United States, Its Territories, and Possessions, and for Other Purposes, Approved August 1, 1946	761

XIV. WESTERN HEMISPHERE

1. RELATIONS WITH THE AMERICAN REPUBLICS	763
A. GENERAL	763
(1) Address by the Secretary of State (Byrnes) before the *Herald Tribune* Forum Regarding Principles of the Inter-American System, New York, October 31, 1945 (Excerpts)	763
B. POLITICAL SOLIDARITY AND DEFENSE	765
1. General	765
(1) Address by the Director of the Office of American Republic Affairs, Department of State (Briggs) at the University of Pennsylvania Concerning a Post-War Estimate of Pan American Solidarity, Philadelphia, November 20, 1945 (Excerpts)	765
2. Military Missions	768
3. Proposed Conference for the Maintenance of Continental Peace and Security	768
4. Proposed Program of Inter-American Military Cooperation	769
(1) Letter from the President (Truman) to the Congress Regarding the Inter-American Military Cooperation Act, May 6, 1946	769
C. ECONOMIC AND SOCIAL COOPERATION	771
1. Coffee	771
2. Trade with the American Republics	772
(1) Address by the Assistant Secretary of State (Braden) before the National Foreign Trade Convention Concerning Foreign Trade Reconstruction in the Americas, New York, November 14, 1945 (Excerpts)	772
2. RELATIONS WITH INDIVIDUAL COUNTRIES	775
A. ARGENTINA	775
(1) Memorandum by the United States to the American Republics on the Argentine Situation. Department of State Press Release, April 8, 1946 (Excerpts)	776
B. MEXICO	777
(1) Text of Statement by the Secretary of State (Byrnes) on Exchange of Ratifications of the Treaty Relating to the Utilization of Waters of Certain Streams, November 8, 1945	778
C. PANAMA	779

CONTENTS

3. RELATIONS WITH CANADA 779
   A. DISPOSITION OF DEFENSE INSTALLATIONS 779
   (1) Exchange of Notes between the Canadian Secretary of State for External Affairs (King) and the United States Ambassador to Canada (Atherton) Regarding Transfer of Defense Installations and Equipment, Ottawa, March 30, 1946 780
     (a) Note from the Canadian Secretary of State for External Affairs to the American Ambassador . 780
     (b) Note from the American Ambassador to the Canadian Secretary of State for External Affairs 782
   (2) Exchange of Notes between the Canadian Secretary of State for External Affairs (King) and the American Chargé d'Affaires ad interim (Clark) Regarding Amendment to the Agreement on Transfer of Defense Installations and Equipment 783
     (a) Note from the Canadian Secretary of State for External Affairs to the American Chargé d'Affaires ad interim, Ottawa, July 11, 1946 . . . 783
     (b) Note from the American Chargé d'Affaires ad interim to the Canadian Secretary of State for External Affairs, Ottawa, July 15, 1946 . . 783
   B. ST. LAWRENCE SEAWAY AND POWER PROJECT . . . 784
   (1) Statement by the Under Secretary of State (Acheson) before the Sub-Committee of the Senate Foreign Relations Committee on Legislation for the St. Lawrence Seaway and Power Project. Department of State Press Release, February 18, 1946 (Excerpts) . 784
   C. GREAT LAKES FISHERIES CONVENTION 786
   (1) Report by the Secretary of State (Byrnes) Concerning the Treaty on the Great Lakes Fisheries, April 19, 1946 (Excerpts) 786
   D. INTERPRETATION OF RUSH-BAGOT AGREEMENT . . . 788
   (1) Exchange of Notes between the Acting Secretary of State (Acheson) and the Canadian Ambassador (Wrong) Concerning Interpretation of the Rush-Bagot Agreement 789
     (a) Note from the Canadian Ambassador in Washington to the Acting Secretary of State, November 18, 1946 789
     (b) Reply from the Acting Secretary of State to the Canadian Ambassador in Washington, December 5, 1946 789

4. RELATIONS WITH ICELAND 790
   A. NEGOTIATIONS REGARDING MILITARY FACILITIES IN ICELAND 790
   (1) Note Delivered by the American Minister at Reykjavik (Dreyfus) to the Icelandic Minister for Foreign Affairs (Thors), September 19, 1946 790

XV. EASTERN ASIA AND THE PACIFIC AREA

1. GENERAL POLICY 793
    (1) Address by the Director of the Office of Far Eastern Affairs, Department of State (Vincent) before the Foreign Policy Association Forum, October 20, 1945 (Excerpts) 793
2. RELATIONS WITH CHINA 797
    A. GENERAL POLICY 797
    (1) Statement by the President (Truman) Regarding United States Policy toward China, December 16, 1945 (Excerpts) 799
    (2) Statement by the President (Truman) Regarding United States Policy toward China, December 18, 1946 (Excerpts) 801
    B. MILITARY AND FINANCIAL AID 803
    (1) Letter from the Secretary of State (Byrnes) to the Speaker of the House of Representatives (Rayburn) Recommending Enactment of H. R. 6795 Providing Military Assistance to China, June 12, 1946 (Excerpt) 804
    (2) An Act to Provide Assistance to the Republic of China in Augmenting and Maintaining a Naval Establishment, Approved July 16, 1946 804
3. RELATIONS WITH THE PHILIPPINES 805
    (1) An Act for the Rehabilitation of the Philippines, Approved April 30, 1946 (Excerpts) 807
    (2) An Act to Provide for Trade Relations between the United States and the Philippines, and for Other Purposes, Approved April 30, 1946 (Excerpts) . . 810
    (3) An Act to Provide Military Assistance to the Republic of the Philippines in Establishing and Maintaining National Security and to Form a Basis for Participation by That Government in Such Defensive Military Operations As the Future May Require, Approved June 26, 1946 817
    (4) Proclamation by the President (Truman) of the Independence of the Philippines, July 4, 1946 . . . 819
    (5) Treaty of General Relations between the United States of America and the Republic of the Philippines, Together with Accompanying Protocol, Signed at Manila, July 4, 1946 820
4. RELATIONS WITH SIAM 823
    (1) Letter from the Minister of Thailand (Pramoj) to the Secretary of State (Byrnes) Containing Text of Proclamation Issued by Regent of Thailand, August 17, 1945 823
    (2) Statement by the Secretary of State (Byrnes) Concerning United States Relations with Thailand, August 20, 1945 824
5. RELATIONS WITH THE SOVIET UNION IN THE FAR EAST . 825
    A. CHINA 825
    1. General Policy 826
    (1) Treaty of Friendship and Alliance between the Repub-

CONTENTS

lic of China and the Union of Soviet Socialist Republics, Signed at Moscow, August 14, 1945 . . . 826
   (a) Exchange of Notes between the Minister of Foreign Affairs of China (Wang) and the People's Commissar of Foreign Affairs of the Union of Soviet Socialist Republics (Molotov) Relating to the Treaty of Friendship and Alliance, August 14, 1945 828
      (i) Note from the People's Commissar of Foreign Affairs of the Union of Soviet Socialist Republics to the Minister of Foreign Affairs of China 828
      (ii) Note from the Minister of Foreign Affairs of China to the People's Commissar of Foreign Affairs of the Union of Soviet Socialist Republics 829
  (2) Report of the Meeting of Ministers of Foreign Affairs of the Union of Soviet Socialist Republics, the United States of America, and the United Kingdom, at Moscow, December 27, 1945 (Excerpt) . . . 829

2. Manchuria 830
  (1) Exchange of Notes between the Government of the United States and the Governments of China and the Union of Soviet Socialist Republics Regarding Disposition and Control of Industrial Enterprises in Manchuria 831
   (a) Note Presented to the Government of China and the Government of the Union of Soviet Socialist Republics through the American Embassies in Chungking and Moscow, on Instruction of the Secretary of State (Byrnes) of February 9, 1946 . 831
   (b) Partial Text of Reply from the Chinese Foreign Office to the Secretary of State, Released to the Press, March 5, 1946 832
  (2) Report by the United States Reparations Representative (Pauley) Concerning Industrial Conditions in Manchuria (Excerpts) 832

B. KOREA 834
  (1) Report of the Meeting of the Ministers of Foreign Affairs of the Union of Soviet Socialist Republics, the United States of America, and the United Kingdom, at Moscow, December 27, 1945 (Excerpt) . . . 836
  (2) Communiqué No. 5, of the United States-Soviet Joint Commission, Issued at Seoul, April 18, 1946 . . 837
  (3) Exchange of Letters between the Commanding General of the United States Army Forces in South Korea (Hodge) and the Commanding General of the Soviet Forces in North Korea (Chistiakov) 838
   (a) Letter from General Hodge to General Chistiakov, November 1, 1946 (Excerpt) 838
   (b) Letter from General Chistiakov to General Hodge, November 26, 1946 839
   (c) Letter from General Hodge to General Chistiakov, December 24, 1946 (Excerpts) 841

XVI. EUROPE AND WESTERN ASIA

1. RELATIONS WITH PARTICULAR EUROPEAN COUNTRIES . . . 843
   A. THE UNITED KINGDOM 843
      (1) Address by the Prime Minister of the United Kingdom (Attlee) before a Joint Session of the Congress, November 13, 1945 (Excerpt) 843
   B. THE UNION OF SOVIET SOCIALIST REPUBLICS . . . 845
      1. General 845
         (1) Order of the Day, Issued by the Chairman of the Council of People's Commissars of the Union of Soviet Socialist Republics (Stalin), April 30, 1946 (Excerpts) (Translation) 845
         (2) Interview Granted by the Chairman of the Council of People's Commissars of the Union of Soviet Socialist Republics (Stalin) to the London *Sunday Times*, September 24, 1946 846
      2. The Prosecution of the War Against Japan . . . 848
         (1) Announcement of the Soviet Declaration of War Against the Japanese Government, Made by the People's Commissar for Foreign Affairs of the Union of Soviet Socialist Republics (Molotov), August 8, 1945 848
         (2) Agreement Concerning the Entry of the Union of Soviet Socialist Republics into the War Against Japan, Signed at Yalta, the Crimea, February 11, 1945. Department of State Press Release, February 11, 1946 . . . 849
      3. Financial Relations 849
      4. Relations with Bulgaria 851
      5. Relations with Hungary 851
      6. Relations with Iran 851
         (1) Exchange of Notes between the Government of the United States and the Governments of the Union of Soviet Socialist Republics and the United Kingdom, Regarding the Withdrawal of Foreign Troops from Iran 851
             (a) Note from the Government of the United States to the Government of the Union of Soviet Socialist Republics, November 24, 1945 851
             (b) Note from the Government of the Union of Soviet Socialist Republics to the Government of the United States, November 29, 1945 (Translation) . 852
             (c) Note from the Government of the United Kingdom to the Government of the United States, Released to the Press, December 14, 1945 854
         (2) Note from the Government of the United States to the Government of the Union of Soviet Socialist Republics, Regarding the Retention of Soviet Troops in Iran, March 6, 1946 855
         (3) Resolution Adopted by the Security Council at Its Thirtieth Meeting, April 4, 1946 857

(4) Communiqué Issued by the Prime Minister of Iran (Ghavam) and the Ambassador of the Union of Soviet Socialist Republics to Iran (Sadchikov), Regarding Soviet-Iranian Negotiations, April 4, 1946 (Translation) 858

7. Relations with Rumania 859

8. Relations with Turkey 859
 (1) Note from the United States Ambassador to Turkey (Wilson) to the Minister of Foreign Affairs of Turkey (Hasan Saka), November 2, 1945 860
 (2) Exchange of Notes between the Chargé d'Affaires ad interim of the Union of Soviet Socialist Republics (Orekhov) and the Acting Secretary of State (Acheson) 861
  (a) Note from the Chargé d'Affaires ad interim of the Union of Soviet Socialist Republics to the Acting Secretary of State, August 7, 1946 . . . 861
  (b) Note from the Acting Secretary of State to the Chargé d'Affaires ad interim of the Union of Soviet Socialist Republics, August 19, 1946 . . 863
 (3) Note from the United States Ambassador to the Union of Soviet Socialist Republics (Smith) to the Commissar of Foreign Affairs of the Union of Soviet Socialist Republics (Molotov), Presented October 9, 1946 . 864

C. FRANCE 865
 (1) Declaration by the Government of the United States and the Provisional Government of the French Republic Regarding Economic and Financial Matters, Washington, May 28, 1946 865
  (a) Declaration Made in Paris by the President of the Provisional Government of the French Republic and in Washington by the President of the United States 865
  (b) Declaration on Commercial Policy and Related Matters 866
  (c) Memorandum of Understanding Regarding Settlement for Lend-Lease, Reciprocal Aid, Surplus War Property, and Claims 869

D. ALBANIA 871
 (1) Exchange of Notes between the Acting United States Representative in Tirana (Henderson) and the Premier of Albania (Hoxha) Regarding the Withdrawal of the United States Mission in Tirana 871
  (a) Note from the Acting United States Representative in Tirana to the Premier of Albania, November 5, 1946 871
  (b) Note from the Premier of Albania to the Acting United States Representative, November 14, 1945 871

E. BELGIUM 873
 (1) Joint Statement by the Governments of the United States and Belgium Concerning Arrangements on

Financial and Supply Problems, Released to the Press, October 20, 1945 873

F. CZECHOSLOVAKIA 875

(1) Exchange of Notes between the Acting Secretary of State (Acheson) and the Ambassador of Czechoslovakia (Slavik) Concerning Commercial Policy, November 14, 1946 875
 (a) Note from the Acting Secretary of State to the Ambassador of Czechoslovakia 875
 (b) Note from the Ambassador of Czechoslovakia to the Acting Secretary of State (Excerpts) . . 877

G. FINLAND 877

H. GREECE 878

1. The Greek Elections 878
 (1) Summary of the Report of the Allied Mission for Observing the Greek Elections. White House Press Release, April 11, 1946 (Excerpt) 879

2. Economic and Financial Relations 881

3. Incidents on the Greek Border 881
 (1) Resolution Establishing a Commission of Investigation of Greek Border Incidents, Adopted by the Security Council, December 19, 1946 881

I. POLAND 882

1. The Polish Elections 882
 (1) Note from the United States Ambassador to Poland (Lane) to the Polish Foreign Office Regarding Arrangements for the Polish Elections, August 19, 1946 . . 882
 (2) Note from the Ambassador of Poland (Lange) to the Acting Secretary of State (Acheson) on the Proposed Polish Elections, April 24, 1946 884
 (3) Note from the United States Chargé d'Affaires in Poland (Keith) to the Polish Foreign Office Regarding United States Position on the Polish Elections, November 22, 1946 884

2. Economic and Financial Relations 885
 (1) Exchange of Notes between the Acting Secretary of State (Acheson) and the Ambassador of Poland (Lange) Concerning Economic and Financial Cooperation, April 24, 1946 885
 (a) Note from the Acting Secretary of State to the Ambassador of Poland 885
 (b) Note from the Ambassador of Poland to the Acting Secretary of State 886

J. SPAIN 887

(1) Position of the United States, the United Kingdom and France on Relations with the Spanish Government. Department of State Press Release, March 4, 1946 888

(2) Statement by the Representative of the United States (Connally) before the Political and Security Committee of the United Nations General Assembly, October 30, 1946 (Excerpts) 889
(3) Resolution on Relations between Spain and the United Nations, Adopted by the General Assembly, December 12, 1946 890

K. SWEDEN 892
    1. Swedish-Soviet Trade Negotiations 892
        (1) Exchange of Notes between the Governments of the United States and Sweden Regarding Swedish-Soviet Trade Negotiations 892
            (a) Note from the Chargé d'Affaires of the United States to the Prime Minister of Sweden (Hansson), August 15, 1946 . . . 892
            (b) Note from the Foreign Minister of Sweden (Unden) to the Chargé d'Affaires of the United States, August 29, 1946 893

    2. Allied-Swedish Negotiations for German External Assets . 894
        (1) Statement by Representatives of the United States, the United Kingdom, France and the Royal Swedish Government Regarding the Disposition of German Assets in Sweden, July 18, 1946. 894

L. SWITZERLAND 895
    1. Allied-Swiss Negotiations for German External Assets . 895
        (1) Letter Exchanged between the Delegate of the Government of Switzerland (Stucki) and the Chiefs of the Allied Delegations, May 25, 1946 896

M. YUGOSLAVIA 897
    1. Recognition of the Federal People's Republic of Yugoslavia 897
        (1) Instructions Concerning the Recognition of the Federal People's Republic of Yugoslavia Transmitted to the United States Ambassador in Yugoslavia (Patterson). Department of State Press Release, December 22, 1945 898

    2. General Relations with Yugoslavia 899
        (1) Note from the Acting Secretary of State (Acheson) to the Chargé d'Affaires ad interim of Yugoslavia (Makiedo) Protesting Attacks by Yugoslav Forces Against United States Military Aircraft, August 21, 1946 900

2. RELATIONS WITH PARTICULAR COUNTRIES OF WESTERN ASIA 902

A. IRAN 902

B. PALESTINE 902
    1. Admission of Jewish Refugees to Palestine . . . 902
        (1) Letter from the President (Truman) to the Prime Minister of Great Britain (Attlee), August 31, 1945 . 902

CONTENTS

(2) Statement by the President (Truman) on the Palestine Situation. White House Press Release, October 4, 1946 903
(3) Exchange of Notes between the King of Saudi Arabia (Abdul-Aziz) and the President (Truman) . . 905
   (a) Note from the King of Saudi Arabia to the President, October 15, 1946 905
   (b) Note from the President to the King of Saudi Arabia, October 28, 1946 906

2. Anglo-American Committee of Inquiry 908
(1) Report of the Anglo-American Committee of Inquiry, Lausanne, Switzerland, April 20, 1946 (Excerpts) . 908

C. THE YEMEN 914
(1) Exchange of Notes between the Chief, Special United States Diplomatic Mission to the Yemen (Eddy) and the Deputy Minister of Foreign Affairs of the Yemen (Abdul Karim Mutahhar), Sana'a, May 4, 1946 . 914
   (a) Note from the Chief, Special United States Diplomatic Mission to the Yemen to the Deputy Minister of Foreign Affairs of the Yemen . . 914
   (b) Note from the Deputy Minister of Foreign Affairs of the Yemen to the Chief, Special United States Diplomatic Mission to the Yemen (Translation) . 917

APPENDIX I

PROTOCOL OF PROCEEDINGS OF THE CRIMEA CONFERENCE, FEBRUARY 4–11, 1945. DEPARTMENT OF STATE PRESS RELEASE, MARCH 24, 1947 919

APPENDIX II

PROTOCOL OF PROCEEDINGS OF THE BERLIN CONFERENCE, JULY 17–AUGUST 2, 1945. DEPARTMENT OF STATE PRESS RELEASE, MARCH 24, 1947 925

CHAPTER I

PRINCIPLES AND POLICY: GENERAL STATEMENTS

(1) *Statement by the Secretary of State (Byrnes) upon Taking Oath of Office, July 3, 1945.*[1]

[Excerpts]

I enter upon my duties as Secretary of State, deeply conscious of the great and grave responsibilities of that office.

It is the function of the State Department to advise the President in the formulation of foreign policy and to carry out the foreign policy of the United States as determined by the President and the Congress. It follows that a change in the Secretaryship of State at this time involves no change in the basic principles of our foreign policy, in the prosecution of the war and in the struggle for enduring peace, which have been charted by the late President Roosevelt and reaffirmed by President Truman.

. . . .

The making of enduring peace will depend on something more than skilled diplomacy, something more than paper treaties, something more even than the best charter the wisest statesmen can draft. Important as is diplomacy, important as are the peace settlements and the basic Charter of world peace, these cannot succeed unless backed by the will of the peoples of different lands not only to have peace but to live together as good neighbors.

Centuries ago devout men thought that they had to fight with one another to preserve their different religious beliefs. But we have learned through long and bitter experience that the only way to protect our religious beliefs is to respect and recognize the right of others to their religious beliefs.

Today there can be no doubt that the peoples of this war-ravaged earth want to live in a free and peaceful world. But the supreme task of statesmanship the world over is to help them to understand that they can have peace and freedom only if they tolerate and respect the rights of others to opinions, feelings, and ways of life which they do not and cannot share.

. . . .

[1] Department of State, *Bulletin*, XIII, p. 45.

(2) *Address by the President (Truman), Navy Day, New York, October 27, 1945.*[1]

I am grateful for the magnificent reception which you have given me today in this great city of New York. I know that it is given to me only as the representative of the gallant men and women of our naval forces, and on their behalf, as well as my own, I thank you.

New York joins the rest of the Nation in paying honor and tribute to the 4 million fighting Americans of the Navy, Marine Corps, and Coast Guard — and to the ships which carried them to victory.

On opposite sides of the world, across two oceans, our Navy opened a highway for the armies and air forces of the United States. They landed our gallant men, millions of them, on the beachheads of final triumph. Fighting from Murmansk, the English Channel, and the Tyrrhenian Sea, to Midway, Guadalcanal, Leyte Gulf, and Okinawa — they won the greatest naval victories in history. Together with their brothers in arms in the Army and Air Force, and with the men of the Merchant Marine, they have helped to win for mankind all over the world a new opportunity to live in peace and dignity — and, we hope, in security.

In the harbor and rivers of New York City and in other ports along the coasts and rivers of the country, ships of that mighty United States Navy are at anchor. I hope that you and the people everywhere will visit them and their crews, seeing for yourselves what your sons and daughters, your labor and your money, have fashioned into an invincible weapon of liberty.

The fleet, on V-J Day, consisted of 1,200 warships, more than 50,000 supporting and landing craft, and over 40,000 navy planes. By that day, ours was a sea power never before equaled in the history of the world. There were great carrier task forces capable of tracking down and sinking the enemy's fleet, beating down his airpower, and pouring destruction on his war-making industries. There were submarines which roamed the seas, invading the enemy's own ports, and destroying his shipping in all the oceans. There were amphibious forces capable of landing soldiers on beaches from Normandy to the Philippines. There were great battleships and cruisers which swept enemy ships from the seas and bombarded his shore defense almost at will.

And history will never forget that great leader who, from his first day in office, fought to reestablish a strong American Navy — who watched that Navy and all the other might of this Nation grow into an invincible force for victory — who sought to make that force an instrument for a just and lasting peace — and who gave his life in the effort — Franklin D. Roosevelt.

The roll call of the battles of this fleet reads like signposts circling the globe — on the road to final victory. North Africa, Sicily, Italy, Normandy, and southern France; Coral Sea, Midway, Guadalcanal, and the Solomons; Tarawa, Saipan, Guam, the Philippine Sea, Leyte Gulf; Iwo

[1] *Ibid.*, p. 653.

Jima, and Okinawa. Nothing which the enemy held on any coast was safe from its attack.

Now we are in the process of demobilizing our naval force. We are laying up ships. We are breaking up aircraft squadrons. We are rolling up bases and releasing officers and men. But when our demobilization is all finished as planned, the United States will still be the greatest naval power on earth.

In addition to that naval power, we shall still have one of the most powerful air forces in the world. And just the other day, so that on short notice we could mobilize a powerful and well-equipped land, sea, and air force, I asked the Congress to adopt universal training.

Why do we seek to preserve this powerful naval and air force, and establish this strong Army reserve? Why do we need them?

We have assured the world time and again — and I repeat it now — that we do not seek for ourselves one inch of territory in any place in the world. Outside of the right to establish necessary bases for our own protection, we look for nothing which belongs to any other power.

We do need this kind of armed might however, and for four principal tasks:

First, our Army, Navy, and Air Force, in collaboration with our Allies, must enforce the terms of peace imposed upon our defeated enemies.

Second, we must fulfil the military obligations which we are undertaking as a member of the United Nations Organization — to support a lasting peace, by force if necessary.

Third, we must cooperate with other American nations to preserve the territorial integrity and the political independence of the nations of the Western Hemisphere.

Fourth, in this troubled and uncertain world, our military forces must be adequate to discharge the fundamental mission laid upon them by the Constitution of the United States — to "provide for the common defense" of the United States.

These four military tasks are directed not toward war — not toward conquest — but toward peace.

We seek to use our military strength solely to preserve the peace of the world. For we now know that that is the only sure way to make our own freedom secure.

That is the basis of the foreign policy of the people of the United States.

The foreign policy of the United States is based firmly on fundamental principles of righteousness and justice. In carrying out those principles we shall firmly adhere to what we believe to be right; and we shall not give our approval to any compromise with evil.

But we know that we cannot attain perfection in this world overnight. We shall not let our search for perfection obstruct our steady progress toward international cooperation. We must be prepared to fulfil our responsibilities as best we can, within the framework of our fundamental principles, even though we recognize that we have to operate in an imperfect world.

Let me restate the fundamentals of that foreign policy of the United States:

1. We seek no territorial expansion or selfish advantage. We have no plans for aggression against any other state, large or small. We have no objective which need clash with the peaceful aims of any other nation.

2. We believe in the eventual return of sovereign rights and self-government to all peoples who have been deprived of them by force.

3. We shall approve no territorial changes in any friendly part of the world unless they accord with the freely expressed wishes of the people concerned.

4. We believe that all peoples who are prepared for self-government should be permitted to choose their own form of government by their own freely expressed choice, without interference from any foreign source. That is true in Europe, in Asia, in Africa, as well as in the Western Hemisphere.

5. By the combined and cooperative action of our war Allies, we shall help the defeated enemy states establish peaceful, democratic governments of their own free choice. And we shall try to attain a world in which Nazism, Fascism, and military aggression cannot exist.

6. We shall refuse to recognize any government imposed upon any nation by the force of any foreign power. In some cases it may be impossible to prevent forceful imposition of such a government. But the United States will not recognize any such government.

7. We believe that all nations should have the freedom of the seas and equal rights to the navigation of boundary rivers and waterways and of rivers and waterways which pass through more than one country.

8. We believe that all states which are accepted in the society of nations should have access on equal terms to the trade and the raw materials of the world.

9. We believe that the sovereign states of the Western Hemisphere, without interference from outside the Western Hemisphere, must work together as good neighbors in the solution of their common problems.

10. We believe that full economic collaboration between all nations, great and small, is essential to the improvement of living conditions all over the world, and to the establishment of freedom from fear and freedom from want.

11. We shall continue to strive to promote freedom of expression and freedom of religion throughout the peace-loving areas of the world.

12. We are convinced that the preservation of peace between nations requires a United Nations Organization composed of all the peace-loving nations of the world who are willing jointly to use force if necessary to insure peace.

That is the foreign policy which guides the United States now. That is the foreign policy with which it confidently faces the future.

It may not be put into effect tomorrow or the next day. But none the less it is our policy; and we shall seek to achieve it. It may take a long time, but it is worth waiting for, and it is worth striving to attain.

The Ten Commandments themselves have not yet been universally achieved over these thousands of years. Yet we struggle constantly to achieve them, and in many ways we come closer to them each year. Though we may meet set-backs from time to time, we shall not relent in our efforts to bring the Golden Rule into the international affairs of the world.

We are now passing through a difficult phase of international relations. Unfortunately it has always been true after past wars that the unity among Allies, forged by their common peril, has tended to wear out as the danger passed.

The world cannot afford any let-down in the united determination of the Allies in this war to accomplish a lasting peace. The world cannot afford to let the cooperative spirit of the Allies in this war disintegrate. The world simply cannot allow this to happen. The people in the United States, in Russia and Britain, in France and China, in collaboration with all other peace-loving people, must take the course of current history into their own hands and mould it in a new direction — the direction of continued cooperation. It was a common danger which united us before victory. Let it be a common hope which continues to draw us together in the years to come.

The atomic bombs that fell on Hiroshima and Nagasaki must be made a signal, not for the old process of falling apart but for a new era — an era of ever closer unity and ever closer friendship among peaceful nations.

Building a peace requires as much moral stamina as waging a war. Perhaps it requires even more, because it is so laborious and painstaking and undramatic. It requires undying patience and continuous application. But it can give us, if we stay with it, the greatest reward that there is in the whole field of human effort.

Differences of the kind that exist today among the nations that fought together so long and so valiantly for victory are not hopeless or irreconcilable. There are no conflicts of interest among the victorious powers so deeply rooted that they cannot be resolved. But their solution will require a combination of forbearance and firmness. It will require a steadfast adherence to the high principles we have enunciated. It will also require a willingness to find a common ground as to the methods of applying these principles.

Our American policy is a policy of friendly partnership with all peaceful nations, and of full support for the United Nations Organization. It is a policy that has the strong backing of the American people. It is a policy around which we can rally without fear or misgiving.

The more widely and clearly that policy is understood abroad, the better and surer will be the peace. For our own part, we must seek to understand the special problems of other nations. We must seek to understand their own legitimate urge toward security as they see it.

The immediate, the greatest threat to us is the threat of disillusionment, the danger of an insidious skepticism — a loss of faith in the effectiveness of international cooperation. Such a loss of faith would be dangerous at any time. In an atomic age it would be nothing short of disastrous.

There has been talk about the atomic bomb scrapping all navies, armies, and air forces. For the present, I think that such talk is 100 percent wrong. Today control of the seas rests in the fleets of the United States and her Allies. There is no substitute for them. We have learned the bitter lesson that the weakness of this great Republic invites men of ill-will to shake the very foundations of civilization all over the world.

What the distant future of atomic research will bring to the fleet which we honor today, no one can foretell. But the fundamental mission of the Navy has not changed. Control of our sea approaches and of the skies above them is still the key to our freedom and to our ability to help enforce the peace of the world. No enemy will ever strike us directly except across the sea. We cannot reach out to help stop and defeat an aggressor without crossing the sea. Therefore, the Navy, armed with whatever weapons science brings forth, is still dedicated to its historic task: control of the ocean approaches to our country and of the skies above them.

The atomic bomb does not alter the basic foreign policy of the United States. It makes the development and application of our policy more urgent than we could have dreamed six months ago. It means that we must be prepared to approach international problems with greater speed, with greater determination, and with greater ingenuity, in order to meet a situation for which there is no precedent.

We must find the answer to the problems created by the release of atomic energy — as we must find the answers to the many other problems of peace — in partnership with all the peoples of the United Nations. For their stake in world peace is as great as our own.

As I said in my message to the Congress, discussion of the atomic bomb with Great Britain and Canada and later with other nations cannot wait upon the formal organization of the United Nations. These discussions, looking toward a free exchange of fundamental scientific information, will be begun in the near future. But I emphasize again, as I have before, that these discussions will not be concerned with the processes of manufacturing the atomic bomb or any other instruments of war.

In our possession of this weapon, as in our possession of other new weapons, there is no threat to any nation. The world, which has seen the United States in two great recent wars, knows that full well. The possession in our hands of this new power of destruction we regard as a sacred trust. Because of our love of peace, the thoughtful people of the world know that that trust will not be violated, that it will be faithfully executed.

Indeed the highest hope of the American people is that world cooperation for peace will soon reach such a state of perfection that atomic methods of destruction can be definitely and effectively outlawed forever.

We have sought, and we will continue to seek, the attainment of that objective. We shall pursue that course with all the wisdom, patience, and determination that the God of Peace can bestow upon a people who are trying to follow in His path.

(3) *Address by the Secretary of State (Byrnes) before the* New York Herald Tribune *Forum, October 31, 1945.*[1]

The subject about which I wish to speak briefly this evening is "Neighboring Nations in One World."

It was no accident that President Roosevelt, who did so much to develop our inter-American system, did even more to develop the world community of the United Nations. For today all nations are neighbors, and although we may have special relations with our nearer neighbors in the Americas, we must remember that we and they are parts of a single, interdependent world.

When we consider the principles which govern our inter-American system as it has been worked out in recent years, it is well to remember that these principles were not always recognized by us in our relations with our neighbors. There were times, not so far distant, when we tried dollar diplomacy and intervention and were accused of Yankee imperialism.

But we have learned by experience that to have good neighbors, we must be a good neighbor.

We have discovered that understanding and good will cannot be bought and cannot be forced. They must spring spontaneously from the people. We have learned also that there can be no lasting friendship between governments unless there is understanding and good will between their peoples.

In the inter-American system the members do not interfere in the internal affairs of their neighbors nor do they brook interference in those internal affairs by others. Freedom means more than freedom to act as we would like them to act.

But we do want other people to know what our people are thinking and doing. And we want to know what other people are thinking and doing. Only with such knowledge can each people determine for itself its way of life.

We believe other nations have a right to know of our own deep attachment to the principles of democracy and human rights, our profound belief that governments must rest upon the free consent of the governed; and our firm conviction that peace and understanding among nations can best be furthered by the free exchange of ideas.

While we adhere to the policy of non-intervention, we assert that knowledge of what other people are thinking and doing brings understanding; and understanding brings tolerance and a willingness to cooperate in the adjustment of differences.

Censorship and blackouts, on the other hand, breed suspicion and distrust. And all too often this suspicion and distrust are justified. For censorship and blackouts are the handmaidens of oppression.

The policy of non-intervention in internal affairs does not mean the approval of local tyranny. Our policy is intended to protect the right of our neighbors to develop their own freedom in their own way. It is not intended to give them free reins to plot against the freedom of others.

[1] *New York Times*, November 1, 1945.

We have learned by bitter experience in the past ten years that Nazi and Fascist plans for external aggression started with tyrannies at home which were falsely defended as matters of purely local concern. We have learned that tyranny anywhere must be watched, for it may come to threaten the security of neighboring nations and soon become the concern of all nations.

If, therefore, there are developments in any country within the inter-American system which, realistically viewed, threaten our security, we consult with other members in an effort to agree upon common policies for our mutual protection.

We Americans can take genuine pride in the evolution of the good neighbor policy from what in a way were its beginnings in the Monroe Doctrine. We surely cannot and will not deny to other nations the right to develop such a policy.

Far from opposing, we have sympathized with, for example, the effort of the Soviet Union to draw into closer and more friendly association with her Central and Eastern European neighbors. We are fully aware of her special security interests in those countries and we have recognized those interests in the arrangements made for the occupation and control of the former enemy States.

We can appreciate the determination of the people of the Soviet Union that never again will they tolerate the pursuit of policies in those countries deliberately directed against the Soviet Union's security and way of life. And America will never join any groups in those countries in hostile intrigue against the Soviet Union. We are also confident that the Soviet Union would not join in hostile intrigue against us in this hemisphere.

We are concerned to promote friendship not strife among neighbors everywhere. For twice in our generation strife among neighbors has led to world conflict. Lasting peace among neighbors has its roots in spontaneous and genuine friendship. And that kind of friendship among nations depends upon mutual respect for one another.

It is our belief that all peoples should be free to choose their own form of government, a government based upon the consent of the governed and adapted to their way of life.

We have put that belief into practice in our relations with our neighbors. The Soviet Union has also declared that it does not wish to force the Soviet system on its neighbors. The whole-hearted acceptance of this principle by all the United Nations will greatly strengthen the bonds of friendship among nations everywhere.

But the point I wish to emphasize is that the policy of the good neighbor, unlike the institution of marriage, is not an exclusive arrangement. The best neighbors do not deny their neighbors the right to be friends with others.

We have learned that our security interests in this hemisphere do not require its isolation from economic and cultural relations with the rest of the world.

We have freely accepted the Charter of the United Nations, and we recognize the paramount authority of the world community. The Charter, while reserving to us and other nations the inherent right of individual and collective self-defense in case of armed attack, requires that enforcement action taken under regional arrangements be sanctioned by the Security Council of the United Nations Organization.

Moreover, we adhere strictly to the policy that cooperation among the American republics does not justify discrimination against non-American States. The American republics have practiced the policy of equal treatment for all States which respect the sovereignty and integrity of their fellow States.

Inter-American cooperation is not inconsistent with world-wide cooperation among the nations. Regional arrangements, like the Inter-American system, which respects the rights and interests of other States and fit into the world system, can become strong pillars in the structure of world peace.

But we cannot recognize regional arrangements as a substitute for a world system. To do so would not promote the common and paramount interests of all nations, large and small, in world peace.

We live in one world, and in this atomic age regional isolationism is even more dangerous than is national isolationism.

We cannot have the kind of cooperation necessary for peace in a world divided into spheres of exclusive influence and special privilege.

This was the great significance of the Moscow Declaration of 1943. That joint statement of policy pledged the world's most powerful nations to mutual cooperation in winning the war and maintaining the peace. It was a landmark in our efforts to create a world community of nations and to abandon the discredited system of international relations based upon exclusive spheres of influence.

Out of the Moscow Declaration have come the Dumbarton Oaks, Teheran, Crimea, San Francisco and Potsdam conferences. And the United Nations Organization and the London Council of Foreign Ministers were created in the spirit of that declaration.

International cooperation must — as I emphasized in my recent report on the London Council — depend upon intelligent compromise. It does not require us or any other nation to neglect its special relations with its nearer neighbors. But it does require that all neighborly relations be fitted into an organized system of international relations world-wide in scope.

The world system which we seek to create must be based on the principle of the sovereign equality of nations.

That does not mean that all nations are equal in power and in influence any more than all men are equal in power and influence. But it does mean equal respect for the individuality and sovereignty of nations, large and small. Nations, like individuals, should be equal before the law.

That principle is the cornerstone of our inter-American system as is the cornerstone of the United Nations.

Adherence to that principle in the making of the peace is necessary if we are to achieve enduring peace. For enduring peace is indivisible. It is not the exclusive concern of a few large States or a few large groups of States. It is the concern of all peoples.

Believing this, the position of the United States will continue to be that the nations, large and small, which have borne the burdens of the war must participate in making the peace.

In centuries past powerful nations for various purposes tried to divide the world among themselves. They failed, and in failing left a trail of blood through the centuries. Such efforts have even less chance of success in the modern world where all nations have become neighbors.

Today the world must take its choice. There must be one world for all of us or there will be no world for any of us.

(4) Address by the Secretary of State (Byrnes), Charleston, South Carolina, November 16, 1945.[1]

[Excerpt]

. . . . . .

Political peace and economic warfare cannot long exist together. If we are going to have peace in this world, we must learn to live together and work together. We must be able to do business together.

Nations that will not do business with one another or try to exclude one another from doing business with other countries are not likely in the long run to be good neighbors.

Trade blackouts, just as much as other types of blackouts, breed distrust and disunity. Business relations bring nations and their peoples closer together and, perhaps more than anything else, promote good-will and determination for peace.

Many of the existing restrictions on world trade result from present-day conditions and practices, largely growing out of the war.

Many countries, and not least Great Britain, had to sacrifice their foreign earning power to win the war. They have sold most of their foreign stocks and bonds, borrowed heavily abroad, let their foreign commerce go, and lost ships and factories to enemy attack.

Their needs for foreign goods are great and pressing, but they lack foreign exchange, that is, purchasing power to buy abroad. Without aid they cannot see their way to buy as they used to abroad, not to speak of the additional things they need from abroad to rehabilitate their shattered and devasted economies.

In a situation of this kind what can a country do? It can seek to borrow the foreign currencies it needs, which will enable it to apply the liberal principles of trade which must be the basis of any permanent prosperity.

Or it can draw in its belt. It can reduce the standard of living of its people, conserve in every way the foreign currencies that it finds hard to get, and transfer its foreign trade by government decree to countries whose currencies are easier to obtain.

In the latter way lies increased discrimination and the division of the commerce of the world into exclusive blocs. We cannot oppose exclusive

---

[1] Department of State, *Bulletin*, XIII, p. 783.

PRINCIPLES AND POLICY: GENERAL STATEMENTS 11

blocs if we do not help remove the conditions which impel other nations, often against their will, to create them.

We must not only oppose these exclusive trading blocs but we must also cooperate with other nations in removing conditions which breed discrimination in world trade.

Whatever foreign loans we make will of course increase the markets for American products, for in the long run the dollars we lend can be spent only in this country.

The countries devastated by the war want to get back to work. They want to get back to production which will enable them to support themselves. When they can do this, they will buy goods from us. America, in helping them, will be helping herself.

We cannot play Santa Claus to the world but we can make loans to governments whose credit is good, provided such governments will make changes in commercial policies which will make it possible for us to increase our trade with them.

In addition to loans, lend-lease settlements, and the disposal of our surplus war materials, we have been discussing with Great Britain the principle of commercial relations — principles we want to see applied by all nations in the post-war world. These are the same liberal principles which my friend and predecessor, Cordell Hull, urged for so many years.

They are based on the conviction that what matters most in trade is not the buttressing of particular competitive positions but the increase of productive employment, the increase of production, and the increase of general prosperity.

The reasons for poverty and hunger are no longer the stinginess of nature. Modern knowledge makes it technically possible for mankind to produce enough good things to go around. The world's present capacity to produce gives it the greatest opportunity in history to increase the standards of living for all peoples of the world.

Trade between countries is one of the greatest forces leading to the fuller use of these tremendously expanded productive powers. But the world will lose this opportunity to improve the lot of her peoples if their countries do not learn to trade as neighbors and friends. If we are going to have a real people's peace, world trade cannot be throttled by burdensome restrictions.

Some of these restrictions are imposed by government decree, others by private combination. They must be removed if we are to have full employment.

To do this it will be necessary to agree upon some general rules, and to apply them in detail. We shall shortly submit to the peoples of the world our views about these matters.

We intend to propose that commercial quotas and embargoes be restricted to a few really necessary cases, and that discrimination in their application be avoided.

We intend to propose that tariffs be reduced and tariff preferences be eliminated. The Trade Agreements Act is our standing offer to negotiate to that end.

We intend to propose that subsidies, in general, should be the subject of international discussion, and that subsidies on exports should be confined to exceptional cases, under general rules, as soon as the period of emergency adjustment is over.

We intend to propose that governments conducting public enterprises in foreign trade should agree to give fair treatment to the commerce of all friendly states, that they should make their purchases and sales on purely economic grounds, and that they should avoid using a monopoly of imports to give excessive protection to their own producers.

We intend to propose that international cartels and monopolies should be prevented by international action from restricting the commerce of the world.

We intend to propose that the special problems of the great primary commodities should be studied internationally, and that consuming countries should have an equal voice with producing countries in whatever decisions may be made.

We intend to propose that the efforts of all countries to maintain full and regular employment should be guided by the rule that no country should solve its domestic problems by measures that would prevent the expansion of world trade, and no country is at liberty to export its unemployment to its neighbors.

We intend to propose that an International Trade Organization be created, under the Economic and Social Council, as an integral part of the structure of the United Nations.

We intend to propose that the United Nations call an International Conference on Trade and Employment to deal with all these problems.

In preparation for that Conference we intend to go forward with actual negotiations with several countries for the reduction of trade barriers under the Reciprocal Trade Agreements Act.

Just when these negotiations will commence has not been determined. They will be announced in the usual way, as required by the act, and due notice will be given in order that all interested persons may be heard before the detailed offers to be made by the United States are settled.

Success in those negotiations will be the soundest preparation for the general conference we hope will be called by the United Nations Organization.

By proposing that the United Nations Organization appoint a commission to consider the subject of atomic energy and by proposing that the Organization likewise call a conference to enable nations to consider the problems of international trade, we demonstrate our confidence in that Organization as an effective instrumentality for world cooperation and world peace.

After the first World War we rejected the plea of Woodrow Wilson and refused to join the League of Nations. Our action contributed to the ineffectiveness of the League.

Now the situation is different. We have sponsored the United Nations Organization. We are giving it our whole-hearted and enthusiastic support. We recognize our responsibility in the affairs of the world. We shall not evade that responsibility.

With other nations of the world we shall walk hand in hand in the paths of peace in the hope that all peoples can find freedom from fear and freedom from want.

(5) *Annual Message of the President (Truman) to the Congress on the State of the Union, January 14, 1946.*[1]

[Excerpts]

. . . . . .

I. From War to Peace — The Year of Decision

In his last Message on the State of the Union, delivered one year ago, President Roosevelt said:

"This new year of 1945 can be the greatest year of achievement in human history.

"1945 can see the final ending of the Nazi-Fascist reign of terror in Europe.

"1945 can see the closing in of the forces of retribution about the center of the malignant power of imperialistic Japan.

"Most important of all — 1945 can and must see the substantial beginning of the organization of world peace."

All those hopes, and more, were fulfilled in the year 1945. It was the greatest year of achievement in human history. It saw the end of the Nazi-Fascist terror in Europe, and also the end of the malignant power of Japan. And it saw the substantial beginning of world organization for peace. These momentous events became realities because of the steadfast purpose of the United Nations and of the forces that fought for freedom under their flags. The plain fact is that civilization was saved in 1945 by the United Nations.

Our own part in this accomplishment was not the product of any single service. Those who fought on land, those who fought on the sea, and those who fought in the air deserve equal credit. They were supported by other millions in the armed forces who through no fault of their own could not go overseas and who rendered indispensable service in this country. They were supported by millions in all levels of government, including many volunteers, whose devoted public service furnished basic organization and leadership. They were also supported by the millions of Americans in private life — men and women in industry, in commerce. on the farms, and in all manner of activity on the home front — who contributed their brains and their brawn in arming, equipping, and feeding them. The country was brought through four years of peril by an effort that was truly national in character.

Everlasting tribute and gratitude will be paid by all Americans to those brave men who did not come back, who will never come back — the 330,000 who died that the Nation might live and progress. All Americans will also remain deeply conscious of the obligation owed to that larger number of soldiers, sailors, and marines who suffered wounds

[1] *Ibid.*, XIV, p. 135.

and sickness in their service. They may be certain that their sacrifice will never be forgotten or their needs neglected.

The beginning of the year 1946 finds the United States strong and deservedly confident. We have a record of enormous achievements as a democratic society in solving problems and meeting opportunities as they developed. We find ourselves possessed of immeasurable advantages — vast and varied natural resources; great plants, institutions, and other facilities; unsurpassed technological and managerial skills; an alert, resourceful, and able citizenry. We have in the United States Government rich resources in information, perspective, and facilities for doing whatever may be found necessary to do in giving support and form to the widespread and diversified efforts of all our people.

. . . . . .

Our Nation has always been a land of great opportunities for those people of the world who sought to become part of us. Now we have become a land of great responsibilities to all the people of all the world. We must squarely recognize and face the fact of those responsibilities. Advances in science, in communication, in transportation, have compressed the world into a community. The economic and political health of each member of the world community bears directly on the economic and political health of each other member.

The evolution of centuries has brought us to a new era in world history in which manifold relationships between nations must be formalized and developed in new and intricate ways.

The United Nations Organization now being established represents a minimum essential beginning. It must be developed rapidly and steadily. Its work must be amplified to fill in the whole pattern that has been outlined. Economic collaboration, for example, already charted, now must be carried on as carefully and as comprehensively as the political and security measures.

It is important that the nations come together as States in the Assembly and in the Security Council and in the other specialized assemblies and councils that have been and will be arranged. But this is not enough. Our ultimate security requires more than a process of consultation and compromise.

It requires that we begin now to develop the United Nations Organization as the representative of the world as one society. The United Nations Organization, if we have the will adequately to staff it and to make it work as it should, will provide a great voice to speak constantly and responsibly in terms of world collaboration and world well-being.

There are many new responsibilities for us as we enter into this new international era. The whole power and will and wisdom of our Government and of our people should be focused to contribute to and to influence international action. It is intricate, continuing business. Many concessions and adjustments will be required.

The spectacular progress of science in recent years makes these necessities more vivid and urgent. That progress has speeded internal development and has changed world relationships so fast that we must realize the fact of a new era. It is an era in which affairs have become complex and rich in promise. Delicate and intricate relationships, involving us all in countless ways, must be carefully considered.

. . . . .

II. THE FEDERAL PROGRAM

International Affairs

1. FOREIGN POLICY

The year 1945 brought with it the final defeat of our enemies. There lies before us now the work of building a just and enduring peace.

Our most immediate task toward that end is to deprive our enemies completely and forever of their power to start another war. Of even greater importance to the preservation of international peace is the need to preserve the wartime agreement of the United Nations and to direct it into the ways of peace.

Long before our enemies surrendered, the foundations had been laid on which to continue this unity in the peace to come. The Atlantic meeting in 1941 and the conferences at Casablanca, Quebec, Moscow, Cairo, Tehran, and Dumbarton Oaks each added a stone to the structure.

Early in 1945, at Yalta, the three major powers broadened and solidified this base of understanding. There fundamental decisions were reached concerning the occupation and control of Germany. There also a formula was arrived at for the interim government of the areas in Europe which were rapidly being wrested from Nazi control. This formula was based on the policy of the United States that people be permitted to choose their own form of government by their own freely expressed choice without interference from any foreign source.

At Potsdam, in July 1945, Marshal Stalin, Prime Ministers Churchill and Attlee, and I met to exchange views primarily with respect to Germany. As a result, agreements were reached which outlined broadly the policy to be executed by the Allied Control Council. At Potsdam there was also established a Council of Foreign Ministers which convened for the first time in London in September. The Council is about to resume its primary assignment of drawing up treaties of peace with Italy, Rumania, Bulgaria, Hungary, and Finland.

In addition to these meetings, and in accordance with the agreement at Yalta, the Foreign Ministers of Great Britain, the Soviet Union, and the United States conferred together in San Francisco last spring, in Potsdam in July, in London in September, and in Moscow in December. These meetings have been useful in promoting understanding and agreement among the three governments.

Simply to name all the international meetings and conferences is to suggest the size and complexity of the undertaking to prevent international war in which the United States has now enlisted for the duration of history.

It is encouraging to know that the common effort of the United Nations to learn to live together did not cease with the surrender of our enemies.

When difficulties arise among us, the United States does not propose to remove them by sacrificing its ideals or its vital interests. Neither do we propose, however, to ignore the ideals and vital interests of our friends.

Last February and March an Inter-American Conference on Problems of War and Peace was held in Mexico City. Among the many significant accomplishments of that Conference was an understanding that an attack by any country against any one of the sovereign American republics would be considered an act of aggression against all of them; and that if such an attack were made or threatened, the American republics would decide jointly, through consultations in which each republic has equal representation, what measures they would take for their mutual protection. This agreement stipulates that its execution shall be in full accord with the Charter of the United Nations Organization.

The first meeting of the General Assembly of the United Nations now in progress in London marks the real beginning of our bold adventure toward the preservation of world peace, to which is bound the dearest hope of men.

We have solemnly dedicated ourselves and all our will to the success of the United Nations Organization. For this reason we have sought to insure that in the peacemaking the smaller nations shall have a voice as well as the larger states. The agreement reached at Moscow last month preserves this opportunity in the making of peace with Italy, Rumania, Bulgaria, Hungary, and Finland. The United States intends to preserve it when the treaties with Germany and Japan are drawn.

It will be the continuing policy of the United States to use all its influence to foster, support, and develop the United Nations Organization in its purpose of preventing international war. If peace is to endure it must rest upon justice no less than upon power. The question is how justice among nations is best achieved. We know from day-to-day experience that the chance for a just solution is immeasurably increased when everyone directly interested is given a voice. That does not mean that each must enjoy an equal voice, but it does mean that each must be heard.

Last November, Prime Minister Attlee, Prime Minister Mackenzie King, and I announced our proposal that a commission be established within the framework of the United Nations to explore the problems of effective international control of atomic energy.

The Soviet Union, France, and China have joined us in the purpose of introducing in the General Assembly a resolution for the establishment of such a commission. Our earnest wish is that the work of this commission go forward carefully and thoroughly, but with the greatest dispatch. I have great hope for the development of mutually effective safeguards which will permit the fullest international control of this new atomic force.

I believe it possible that effective means can be developed through the

United Nations Organization to prohibit, outlaw, and prevent the use of atomic energy for destructive purposes.

The power which the United States demonstrated during the war is the fact that underlies every phase of our relations with other countries. We cannot escape the responsibility which it thrusts upon us. What we think, plan, say, and do is of profound significance to the future of every corner of the world.

The great and dominant objective of United States foreign policy is to build and preserve a just peace. The peace we seek is not peace for twenty years. It is permanent peace. At a time when massive changes are occurring with lightning speed throughout the world, it is often difficult to perceive how this central objective is best served in one isolated complex situation or another. Despite this very real difficulty, there are certain basic propositions to which the United States adheres and to which we shall continue to adhere.

One proposition is that lasting peace requires genuine understanding and active cooperation among the most powerful nations. Another is that even the support of the strongest nations cannot guarantee a peace unless it is infused with the quality of justice for all nations.

On October 27, 1945, I made, in New York City, the following public statement of my understanding of the fundamental foreign policy of the United States. I believe that policy to be in accord with the opinion of the Congress and of the people of the United States. I believe that that policy carries out our fundamental objectives.[1]

. . . .

We may not always fully succeed in our objectives. There may be instances where the attainment of those objectives is delayed. But we will not give our full sanction and approval to actions which fly in the face of these ideals.

The world has a great stake in the political and economic future of Germany. The Allied Control Council has now been in operation there for a substantial period of time. It has not met with unqualified success. The accommodation of varying views of four governments in the day-to-day civil administration of occupied territory is a challenging task. In my judgment, however, the Council has made encouraging progress in the face of most serious difficulties. It is my purpose at the earliest practicable date to transfer from military to civilian personnel the execution of United States participation in the government of occupied territory in Europe. We are determined that effective control shall be maintained in Germany until we are satisfied that the German people have regained the right to a place of honor and respect.

On the other side of the world, a method of international cooperation has recently been agreed upon for the treatment of Japan. In this pattern of control, the United States, with the full approval of its partners, has retained primary authority and primary responsibility. It will continue to do so until the Japanese people, by their own freely expressed choice, choose their own form of government.

[1] See this volume, p. 4.

Our basic policy in the Far East is to encourage the development of a strong, independent, united, and democratic China. That has been the traditional policy of the United States.

At Moscow the United States, the Union of Soviet Socialist Republics, and Great Britain agreed to further this development by supporting the efforts of the national government and non-governmental Chinese political elements in bringing about cessation of civil strife and in broadening the basis of representation in the Government. That is the policy which General Marshall is so ably executing today.

It is the purpose of the Government of the United States to proceed as rapidly as is practicable toward the restoration of the sovereignty of Korea and the establishment of a democratic government by the free choice of the people of Korea.

At the threshold of every problem which confronts us today in international affairs is the appalling devastation, hunger, sickness, and pervasive human misery that mark so many areas of the world.

By joining and participating in the work of the United Nations Relief and Rehabilitation Administration the United States has directly recognized and assumed an obligation to give such relief assistance as is practicable to millions of innocent and helpless victims of the war. The Congress has earned the gratitude of the world by generous financial contributions to the United Nations Relief and Rehabilitation Administration.

We have taken the lead, modest though it is, in facilitating under our existing immigration quotas the admission to the United States of refugees and displaced persons from Europe.

We have joined with Great Britain in the organization of a commission to study the problem of Palestine. The Commission is already at work and its recommendations will be made at an early date.

The members of the United Nations have paid us the high compliment of choosing the United States as the site of the United Nations headquarters. We shall be host in spirit as well as in fact, for nowhere does there abide a fiercer determination that this peace shall live than in the hearts of the American people.

It is the hope of all Americans that in time future historians will speak not of World War I and World War II, but of the first and last world wars.

2. FOREIGN ECONOMIC POLICY

The foreign economic policy of the United States is designed to promote our own prosperity, and at the same time to aid in the restoration and expansion of world markets and to contribute thereby to world peace and world security. We shall continue our efforts to provide relief from the devastation of war, to alleviate the sufferings of displaced persons, to assist in reconstruction and development, and to promote the expansion of world trade.

We have already joined the International Monetary Fund and the International Bank for Reconstruction and Development. We have expanded the Export-Import Bank and provided it with additional capital. The Congress has renewed the Trade Agreements Act which provides the necessary framework within which to negotiate a reduction of trade barriers on a reciprocal basis. It has given our support to the United Nations Relief and Rehabilitation Administration.

In accordance with the intentions of the Congress, lend-lease, except as to continued military lend-lease in China, was terminated upon surrender of Japan. The first of the lend-lease settlement agreements has been completed with the United Kingdom. Negotiations with other lend-lease countries are in progress. In negotiating these agreements, we intend to seek settlements which will not encumber world trade through war debts of a character that proved to be so detrimental to the stability of the world economy after the last war.

We have taken steps to dispose of the goods which on V-J Day were in the lend-lease pipe line to the various lend-lease countries and to allow them long-term credit for the purpose where necessary. We are also making arrangements under which those countries may use the lend-lease inventories in their possession and acquire surplus property abroad to assist in their economic rehabilitation and reconstruction. These goods will be accounted for at fair values.

The proposed loan to the United Kingdom, which I shall recommend to the Congress in a separate message, will contribute to easing the transition problem of one of our major partners in the war. It will enable the whole sterling area and other countries affiliated with it to resume trade on a multilateral basis. Extension of this credit will enable the United Kingdom to avoid discriminatory trade arrangements of the type which destroyed freedom of trade during the 1930's. I consider the progress toward multilateral trade which will be achieved by this agreement to be in itself sufficient warrant for the credit.

The view of this Government is that, in the longer run, our economic prosperity and the prosperity of the whole world are best served by the elimination of artificial barriers to international trade, whether in the form of unreasonable tariffs or tariff preferences or commercial quotas or embargoes or the restrictive practices of cartels.

The United States Government has issued proposals for the expansion of world trade and employment to which the Government of the United Kingdom has given its support on every important issue. These proposals are intended to form the basis for a trade and employment conference to be held in the middle of this year. If that conference is a success, I feel confident that the way will have been adequately prepared for an expanded and prosperous world trade.

We shall also continue negotiations looking to the full and equitable development of facilities for transportation and communications among nations.

The vast majority of the nations of the world have chosen to work together to achieve, on a cooperative basis, world security and world prosperity. The effort cannot succeed without full cooperation of the United States. To play our part, we must not only resolutely carry out the foreign policies we have adopted but also follow a domestic policy which will maintain full production and employment in the United

States. A serious depression here can disrupt the whole fabric of the world economy.

3. OCCUPIED COUNTRIES

The major tasks of our Military Establishment in Europe following V-E Day, and in the Pacific since the surrender of Japan, have been those of occupation and military government. In addition we have given much-needed aid to the peoples of the liberated countries.

The end of the war in Europe found Germany in a chaotic condition. Organized government had ceased to exist, transportation systems had been wrecked, cities and industrial facilities had been bombed into ruins. In addition to the tasks of occupation we had to assume all of the functions of government. Great progress has been made in the repatriation of displaced persons and of prisoners of war. Of the total of 3,500,000 displaced persons found in the United States zone only 460,000 now remain.

The extensive complications involved by the requirement of dealing with three other governments engaged in occupation and with the governments of liberated countries require intensive work and energetic cooperation. The influx of some 2 million German refugees into our zone of occupation is a pressing problem, making exacting demands upon an already overstrained internal economy.

Improvements in the European economy during 1945 have made it possible for our military authorities to relinquish to the governments of all liberated areas, or to the United Nations Relief and Rehabilitation Administration, the responsibility for the provision of food and other civilian relief supplies. The Army's responsibilities in Europe extend now only to our zones of occupation in Germany and Austria and to two small areas in northern Italy.

By contrast with Germany, in Japan we have occupied a country still possessing an organized and operating governmental system. Although severely damaged, the Japanese industrial and transportation systems have been able to insure at least a survival existence for the population. The repatriation of Japanese military and civilian personnel from overseas is proceeding as rapidly as shipping and other means permit.

In order to insure that neither Germany nor Japan will again be in a position to wage aggressive warfare, the armament-making potential of the countries is being dismantled and fundamental changes in their social and political structures are being effected. Democratic systems are being fostered to the end that the voice of the common man may be heard in the councils of his government.

For the first time in history the legal culpability of war makers is being determined. The trials now in progress in Nürnberg — and those soon to begin in Tokyo — bring before the bar of international justice those individuals who are charged with the responsibility for the sufferings of the past six years. We have high hope that this public portrayal of the guilt of these evildoers will bring wholesale and permanent revulsion on the part of the masses of our former enemies against war, militarism, aggression, and notions of race superiority.

We have won a great war — we, the nations of plain people who hate war. In the test of that war we found a strength of unity that brought us through — a strength that crushed the power of those who sought by force to deny our faith in the dignity of man.

During this trial the voices of disunity among us were silent or were subdued to an occasional whine that warned us that they were still among us. Those voices are beginning to cry aloud again. We must learn constantly to turn deaf ears to them. They are voices which foster fear and suspicion and intolerance and hate. They seek to destroy our harmony, our understanding of each other, our American tradition of "live and let live." They have become busy again, trying to set race against race, creed against creed, farmer against city dweller, worker against employer, people against their own governments. They seek only to do us mischief. They must not prevail.

It should be impossible for any man to contemplate without a sense of personal humility the tremendous events of the 12 months since the last annual Message, the great tasks that confront us, the new and huge problems of the coming months and years. Yet these very things justify the deepest confidence in the future of this Nation of free men and women.

The plain people of this country found the courage and the strength, the self-discipline, and the mutual respect to fight and to win, with the help of our allies, under God. I doubt if the tasks of the future are more difficult. But if they are, then I say that our strength and our knowledge and our understanding will be equal to those tasks.

(6) *Address by the Secretary of State (Byrnes) on the United Nations and United States Foreign Policy, February 28, 1946.*[1]

[Excerpts]

* * * * * *

During the war our goal was clear. Our goal was victory. The problems of industrial and military mobilization, it is true, were problems of the first magnitude. Production bottlenecks often seemed unbreakable, transportation difficulties and manpower shortages insurmountable. On the fighting front the combined land, sea, and air operations were heartbreaking in complexity.

These were hard tasks. Yet we were able to apply a yardstick to each proposal by asking a simple question: "Will it help to win the war?" The common goal of victory served to unite us and to give purpose and direction to our efforts.

Now that we have come into calmer waters, our relief and gratitude are mixed with uncertainty. Our goal now is permanent peace, and surely we seek it even more anxiously than we sought victory.

The difficulty is that the path to permanent peace is not so easy to see and to follow as was the path to victory.

[1] Department of State, *Bulletin*, XIV, p. 355.

When an issue is presented, we ask, "Will it help to win the peace?" When the answer is slow to come or does not come at all, we grow uneasy and apprehensive.

While we may be in doubt about many things, there are certain basic propositions on which we are clear.

One is that a just and lasting peace is not the inevitable result of victory. Rather, victory has given us the opportunity to build such a peace. And our lives depend upon whether we make the most of this opportunity.

Another thing of which we are certain is that we Americans alone cannot determine whether the world will live in peace or perish in war. Peace depends quite as much upon others as it does upon us. No nation is the complete master of its fate. We are all bound together for better or for worse.

Because we know this, we have pinned our hopes to the banner of the United Nations. And we are not content simply to take our place in that Organization. We realize that, although the dreams of the world are lodged in it, the United Nations will fail unless its members give it life by their confidence and by their determination to make it work in concrete cases and in everyday affairs.

And so I wish to talk to you about the first meetings of the United Nations. What has been said in these meetings has been said as plainly and bluntly as anything I have heard said by responsible statesmen in any private conference.

These first meetings were intended only to establish the various organs of the United Nations. But so pressing were some of the problems presented to the Security Council that they had to be dealt with before there was a chance for the Council to adopt even provisional rules of procedure.

All was not calm and peaceful at the meetings in London. There was effort to use the United Nations to advance selfish national aims. But the clash of national interests and purposes which were reflected in the debates in London was very much like the clash of local and special interests which are reflected in our national and state legislatures.

We may deprecate some of these clashes of interest. But when they exist, it is better that they should be publicly revealed. If these conflicts of interest did not appear in the forums of the United Nations, these forums would be detached from reality and in the long run turn out to be purposeless and futile.

. . . . . .

The United Nations got off to a good start. However, that does not mean it is an assured success. It simply means that the Charter will work if the peoples of the United Nations are determined to make it work. At times our Congress may make serious errors of omission and commission. Such errors are not the fault of the Congress as an institution. They are the fault of its members or of their constituents who fail to measure up to their responsibilities.

So it is with the United Nations. It will succeed only as we, the peoples of the United Nations, measure up to our responsibilities.

I should be lacking in candor if I said to you that world conditions today are sound or reassuring. All around us there is suspicion and distrust, which in turn breeds suspicion and distrust.

Some suspicions are unfounded and unreasonable. Of some others that cannot be said. That requires frank discussion between great powers of the things that give rise to suspicion. At the Moscow conference there was such frank discussion. It was helpful. But the basis of some suspicions persists and prompts me to make some comments as to our position.

We have joined with our allies in the United Nations to put an end to war. We have covenanted not to use force except in the defense of law as embodied in the purposes and principles of the Charter. We intend to live up to that covenant.

But as a great power and as a permanent member of the Security Council we have a responsibility to use our influence to see that other powers live up to their covenant. And that responsibility we also intend to meet.

Unless the great powers are prepared to act in the defense of law, the United Nations cannot prevent war. We must make it clear in advance that we do intend to act to prevent aggression, making it clear at the same time that we will not use force for any other purpose.

The great powers are given special responsibilities because they have the strength to maintain peace, if they have the will to maintain peace. Their strength in relation to one another is such that no one of them can safely break the peace if the others stand united in defense of the Charter.

The present power relationships of the great states preclude the domination of the world by any one of them. Those power relationships cannot be substantially altered by the unilateral action of any one great state without profoundly disturbing the whole structure of the United Nations.

Therefore, if we are going to do our part to maintain peace in the world we must maintain our power to do so; and we must make it clear that we will stand united with other great states in defense of the Charter.

If we are to be a great power we must act as a great power, not only in order to ensure our own security but in order to preserve the peace of the world.

Much as we desire general disarmament and much as we are prepared to participate in a general reduction of armaments, we cannot be faithful to our obligations to ourselves and to the world if we alone disarm.

While it is not in accord with our traditions to maintain a large professional standing army, we must be able and ready to provide armed contingents that may be required on short notice. We must also have a trained citizenry able and ready to supplement those armed contingents without unnecessarily prolonged training.

That is why in the interest of peace we cannot allow our military establishment to be reduced below the point required to maintain a position commensurate with our responsibilities; and that is why we must have some form of universal military training.

Our power thus maintained cannot and will not be used for aggressive purposes. Our tradition as a peace-loving, law-abiding, democratic people should be an assurance that our force will not be used except in defense of law. Our armed forces, except as they may be called into action by the Security Council, cannot be employed in war without the consent of the Congress. We need not fear their misuse unless we distrust the representatives of the people.

I am convinced that there is no reason for war between any of the great powers. Their present power relationships and interests are such that none need or should feel insecure in relation to the others, as long as each faithfully observes the purposes and principles of the Charter.

. . . .

To banish war, nations must refrain from doing the things that lead to war.

It has never been the policy of the United States in its internal affairs or in its foreign relations to regard the *status quo* as sacrosanct. The essence of our democracy is our belief in life and growth and in the right of the people to shape and mold their own destiny.

It is not in our tradition to defend the dead hand of reaction or the tyranny of privilege. We did not fight against the Nazis and Fascists who turned back the clock of civilization in order that we might stop the clock of progress.

Our diplomacy must not be negative and inert. It must be capable of adjustment and development in response to constantly changing circumstances. It must be marked by creative ideas, constructive proposals, practical and forward-looking suggestions.

Though the *status quo* is not sacred and unchangeable, we cannot overlook a unilateral gnawing away at the *status quo*. The Charter forbids aggression, and we cannot allow aggression to be accomplished by coercion or pressure or by subterfuges such as political infiltration.

When adjustments between states, large or small, are called for, we will frankly and fairly consider those adjustments on their merits and in the light of the common interests of all states, large and small, to maintain peace and security in a world based on the unity of all great powers and the dominance of none.

There are undoubtedly vitally important adjustments which will require our consideration. Some of these situations are delicate to deal with. I am convinced, however, that satisfactory solutions can be found if there is a stop to this maneuvering for strategic advantage all over the world and to the use of one adjustment as an entering wedge for further and undisclosed penetrations of power.

We must face the fact that to preserve the United Nations we cannot be indifferent — veto or no veto — to serious controversies between any of the great powers, because such controversies could affect the whole power relationship between all of the great powers.

The United States wishes to maintain friendly relations with all nations

PRINCIPLES AND POLICY: GENERAL STATEMENTS 25

and exclusive arrangements with no nation. Naturally there are some problems which concern some nations much more than other nations. That is true in regard to many problems related to inter-American affairs. That is true in regard to the control of Germany and Japan.

In our relations with the other great powers there are many problems which concern two or three of us much more than the others of us. I see no objection to conferences between the big three or the big four or the big five.

Even conferences between ourselves and the Soviet Union alone, conferences between ourselves and Britain alone, or conferences between ourselves and France or China alone, can all help to further general accord among the great powers and peace with the smaller powers.

But in such conferences, so far as the United States is concerned, we will gang up against no state. We will do nothing to break the world into exclusive blocs or spheres of influence. In this atomic age we will not seek to divide a world which is one and indivisible.

We have openly, gladly, and whole-heartedly welcomed our Soviet Ally as a great power, second to none in the family of the United Nations. We have approved many adjustments in her favor and, in the process, resolved many serious doubts in her favor.

Only an inexcusable tragedy of errors could cause serious conflict between us in the future. Despite the differences in our way of life, our people admire and respect our Allies and wish to continue to be friends and partners in a world of expanding freedom and rising standards of living.

But in the interest of world peace and in the interest of our common and traditional friendship we must make plain that the United States intends to defend the Charter.

Great powers as well as small powers have agreed under the United Nations Charter not to use force or the threat of force except in defense of law and the purposes and principles of the Charter.

We will not and cannot stand aloof if force or the threat of force is used contrary to the purposes and principles of the Charter.

We have no right to hold our troops in the territories of other sovereign states without their approval and consent freely given.

We must not unduly prolong the making of peace and continue to impose our troops upon small and impoverished states.

No power has a right to help itself to alleged enemy properties in liberated or ex-satellite countries before a reparation settlement has been agreed upon by the Allies. We have not and will not agree to any one power deciding for itself what it will take from these countries.

We must not conduct a war of nerves to achieve strategic ends.

We do not want to stumble and stagger into situations where no power intends war but no power will be able to avert war.

We must not regard the drawing of attention to situations which might endanger the peace, as an affront to the nation or nations responsible for those situations.

It is quite possible that any nation may in good faith embark on a course of conduct without fully appreciating the effects of its conduct.

We must all be willing to review our actions to preserve our common interests in the peace, which are so much more important to all of us than the differences which might divide us.

We must get back to conditions of peace. We must liquidate the terrible legacy which the war has left us. We must return our armies to their homelands. We must eliminate the breeding grounds of suspicion and fear. We must not deceive ourselves or mislead our Allies. To avoid trouble we must not allow situations to develop into incidents from which there is no retreat.

We must live by the Charter. That is the only road to peace.

To live by the Charter requires good-will and understanding on the part of all of us. We who had patience and gave confidence to one another in the most trying days of the war must have patience and give confidence to one another now.

No nation has a monopoly of virtue or of wisdom, and no nation has a right to act as if it had. Friendly nations should act as friendly nations.

Loose talk of the inevitability of war casts doubt on our own loyalty to the Charter and jeopardizes our most cherished freedoms, both at home and abroad.

There are ideological differences in the world. There always have been. But in this world there is room for many people with varying views and many governments with varying systems. None of us can foresee the far-distant future and the ultimate shape of things to come. But we are bound together as part of a common civilization.

As we view the wreckage of the war, we must realize that the urgent tasks of reconstruction, the challenging tasks of creating higher standards of living for our people, should absorb all our constructive energies.

Great states and small states must work together to build a friendlier and happier world. If we fail to work together there can be no peace, no comfort, and little hope for any of us.

(7) Statement by the Secretary of State (Byrnes) on the Opening Meeting of the Security Council, New York, March 26, 1946.[1]

This is a moment of great importance in the history of the world. With this meeting the Security Council begins, as required by the Charter, to function continuously. For this purpose the members of the Council are obligated to be represented at all times at the seat of the Organization. This is essential because it is the function of the Council to guard at all times the peace of the world.

The President of the United States has requested me to read to you the following message:

"On behalf of the people of the United States I welcome the members of the Security Council and the Secretary-General of the United Nations and their staffs to our country.

"We are greatly honored that the United Nations has chosen a site in our country for its home. We will do our best to make you feel at home.

[1] *Ibid.*, p. 567.

PRINCIPLES AND POLICY: GENERAL STATEMENTS 27

"But there can be no home anywhere for the United Nations unless the United Nations remain united and continue to work together, as they have fought together, for peace and for freedom.

"The people of the United States not only wish you success, but they pledge to you their whole-hearted cooperation to give to the United Nations the strength and the will to maintain peace and freedom in this interdependent world."

I am sure that the Governor of the State of New York and the mayor of this city will join with President Truman and me in welcoming you to our country and to your temporary headquarters in the city of New York.

It is less than 160 years ago that our 13 sovereign states entered into a union for their common defense and to promote the general welfare and to secure the blessings of liberty for themselves and their posterity. That was then an untried experiment, and many doubted whether such a union of free states could long endure. It is fitting to recall that that union also chose as its temporary abode the city of New York.

Although it was later to go through dark days of trial, that union did survive. It grew in strength and has played its part in preserving the blessings of liberty for all mankind. Let us hope that the new and broader union of states, which has also chosen New York City as its temporary abode, will likewise grow in strength and survive every crisis.

It is, I am sure, the firm resolve of the American people to uphold the Charter. I am sure this is the equally firm resolve of all the peoples of the United Nations who have joined together to preserve the peace under law.

The Charter does not sanctify ancient privilege. It does not attempt to outlaw change in an ever-changing world. It does, however, obligate all the states, large and small alike, to refrain from the use of force or threat of force, except in the defense of law.

Nations, like individuals, should do their best to adjust their disputes without resort to litigation. But no nation has the right to take the law into its own hands. If disputes cannot be settled by friendly negotiations, they must be brought before the Security Council.

That is why the Security Council must at all times be prepared to act promptly. That is why the Security Council must be prepared to function continuously. If the United Nations is to endure, there must be no excuse or need for any nation to take the law into its own hands.

Upon the Security Council rests the gravest responsibility for the maintenance of peace and security. It must of necessity deal with the problems about which nations in the past have been prepared to fight.

Upon all the members of the United Nations rests the duty to cooperate with the Council to enable it to meet its responsibility. They must be willing freely and frankly to discuss their grievances before the Council.

Questions affecting the peace of the world must not be treated as questions of honor which cannot be discussed. Questions of honor between individuals are no longer left to the ordeal of the duel. Questions of honor between nations cannot be left to the ordeal of battle.

We must live by the Charter. That is the road to peace. And the road to peace is the road the peoples of the world want to travel.

We are here to carry out their mandate. We must not let them down.

(8) *Address by the President (Truman), Army Day, Chicago, April 6, 1946.*[1]

[Excerpt]

. . . . .

For the desire for peace and freedom is the very root of our foreign policy. I stated the fundamental foreign policy of the United States in New York City on Navy Day last October and in my message to the Congress January 21, 1946. That policy remains the same today. It is based squarely upon the pursuit of peace and justice; and it definitely rejects any selfish advantage for ourselves.

The immediate objective of our foreign policy is to support the United Nations to the utmost.

It is my conviction that the Security Council of the United Nations, now meeting in New York City, is fully capable of reaching agreements between the peoples of the world — however different their traditions and philosophies, and however divergent their interests. The essential requirements to that end are that its member nations follow the dictates of justice, that they consider and respect the legitimate aspirations and needs of their fellow members.

All the citizens of the United States worthy of the honor of that citizenship are determined to preserve our democratic form of government. They will not, on the other hand, interfere in any way with the governments of other peace-loving people.

Peace is not a reward that comes automatically to those who cherish it. It must be pursued, unceasingly and unwaveringly, by every means at our command.

In the pursuit of peace, there is no single path. We must have a policy to guide our relations with every country in every part of the world. No country is so remote from us that it may not some day be involved in a matter which threatens the peace. Remember that the First World War began in Serbia; that the peace of Versailles was first broken in Manchuria; and that the Second World War began in Poland. Our foreign policy must be universal.

In the Far East our program for peace is designed to combat and remedy the conditions that made it possible for Japan to turn upon her neighbors. We have disarmed Japan, and are promoting reforms which we hope will bring into being a democratic and peaceful nation. But the control and reform of Japan is only a beginning. In the Far East, as elsewhere, we shall encourage the growth and spread of democracy and civil liberties.

In Korea we are even now working with our Soviet Allies and with Korean leaders to create a provisional democratic government. Our aim is to speed the day when Korea will again take her place as an independent and democratic nation.

[1] *Ibid.*, p. 622.

PRINCIPLES AND POLICY: GENERAL STATEMENTS

In China we are supporting a free and democratic government. Through the wise counsel of General Marshall the Chinese leaders are on the road to achieve political unity by peaceful democratic processes.

The Philippine Commonwealth, on July fourth next, will become a fully sovereign and independent nation. We hope for the peaceful settlement of the differences which have arisen between colonial peoples and colonial sovereigns in all areas.

The roots of democracy, however, will not draw much nourishment in any nation from a soil of poverty and economic distress. It is a part of our strategy of peace, therefore, to assist in the rehabilitation and development of the Far Eastern countries. We seek to encourage a quick revival of economic activity and international trade in the Far East. To do that we stand ready to extend credits and technical assistance to help build the peace.

We recognize that the Soviet Union, the British Commonwealth, and other nations have important interests in the Far East. In return we expect recognition by them that we also have an interest in maintaining peace and security in that area. We expect understanding on their part that our objectives are dedicated to the pursuit of peace; and we shall expect them to pursue the same objectives.

Turning to the Near East and Middle East, we find an area which presents grave problems. This area contains vast natural resources. It lies across the most convenient routes of land, air, and water communications. It is consequently an area of great economic and strategic importance, the nations of which are not strong enough individually or collectively to withstand powerful aggression.

It is easy to see, therefore, how the Near and Middle East might become an arena of intense rivalry between outside powers, and how such rivalry might suddenly erupt into conflict.

No country, great or small, has legitimate interests in the Near and Middle East which cannot be reconciled with the interests of other nations through the United Nations. The United Nations have a right to insist that the sovereignty and integrity of the countries of the Near and Middle East must not be threatened by coercion or penetration.

If peace is to be preserved and strengthened in this important section of the world, however, we can not be content merely to assure self-government and independence. The people of the Near and Middle East want to develop their resources, widen their educational opportunities, and raise their standards of living. The United States will do its part in helping to bring this about.

Turning to Europe, we find her suffering the terrible pangs of hunger and privation. Economic reconstruction is first of all a task for the people and the governments of Europe. Help from outside, however, will quicken the pace of reconstruction and reduce the cost in human misery. The United States is in a position to help; we are helping now; and we shall continue to help.

We shall help because we know that we ourselves cannot enjoy prosperity in a world of economic stagnation. We shall help because economic distress, anywhere in the world, is a fertile breeding ground for violent political upheaval. And we shall help because we feel it is simple humanitarianism to lend a hand to our friends and allies who are convalescing from wounds inflicted by our common enemy.

Food is Europe's most critical need. It is not enough to share our surpluses, for to share surpluses is not really to share at all. No worthy American will hesitate to reduce his own consumption of food when the food so released will avert starvation abroad.

Next to food, Europe's greatest need is for machinery and raw materials to rehabilitate her transportation systems, her mines, and her factories. We have been supplying these products to Europe on long-term credit and we shall continue to do so. Billions of dollars for reconstruction have been made available by the Congress through the Export-Import Bank and through the International Bank.

We seek to lay the groundwork of a world trading system which will strengthen and safeguard the peace. We want no return to the kind of narrow economic nationalism which poisoned international relations and undermined living standards between the two world wars.

The Congress is now considering, and I hope will soon approve, the financial agreements with Great Britain. These arrangements have not been made merely to support a faithful ally. They are of vital importance to our own country as a means of opening the channels of world trade to American enterprise.

We shall work to achieve equal opportunity in world trade, because closed economic blocs in Europe or any place in the world can only lead to impoverishment and isolation of the people who inhabit it.

We shall press for the elimination of artificial barriers to international navigation, in order that no nation, by accident of geographic location, shall be denied unrestricted access to seaports and international waterways.

The American Republics propose to settle differences between the nations of the Western Hemisphere as good neighbors by consultation in the common cause of peace and national well-being — consultation in which all of them will have equal representation. The United States intends to join with other sovereign Republics of America in a regional pact to provide a common defense against attack.

Perhaps the greatest challenge which the war has bequeathed to us is the control of atomic energy so that this vast new force may not destroy, but instead may serve, mankind. Our country has joined with all the United Nations in a determined effort to devise international action which will achieve these ends. We are pressing on steadfastly in this task. We realize that we must bring to it political imagination as great as the scientific genius which unleashed this new force. The same unswerving determination and effort which produced the release of atomic energy can and will enable mankind to live without terror and reap untold benefits from this new product of man's genius.

I am not pessimistic about the future. I have confidence that there is no international problem which cannot be solved if there are the will and the strength to solve it through the United Nations which we have all created.

PRINCIPLES AND POLICY: GENERAL STATEMENTS 31

We attained overwhelming victory in close union with the free and peaceful nations of the world. In the same kind of union with them, and with the help of the same heroic men and women who fought the war and whom we honor today, we can attain a lasting peace.

(9) *Statement by the President (Truman) on the Anniversary of V-E Day, May 8, 1946.*[1]

On the first anniversary of V-E Day the people of the United States remember with grateful pride the men and the women of the United Nations whose unstinted sacrifices made the victory possible. The year that has passed has made us realize with greater awareness the nature of their gift to this and succeeding generations. They gave us not justice but the opportunity to achieve it, not security but the opportunity to win it, not peace but the opportunity to make it. Let each of us judge for himself how well in the past year we have used what came to us at such great price.

These opportunities will not be ours forever. Unless we take advantage of them fully, quickly, and selflessly, they will slip from our grasp. A year after V-E Day, the opportunities that it brought to build a just, secure, and peaceful world are still with us. To the extent that we maintain our unity within ourselves and with other peoples, and to the extent that we dedicate ourselves wholly and unselfishly to the mighty tasks confronting us, they will become on succeeding anniversaries not narrowing but expanding vistas of the hopes of man.

(10) *Address by Senator Warren R. Austin (Vermont) on Peace Goals before the Foreign Policy Association, New York, June 26, 1946.*[2]

[Excerpts]

The following statement by Warren R. Austin, Senator from Vermont, was his first public statement after his nomination by President Truman as the United States representative to the Security Council of the United Nations.

This first anniversary of the signing of the Charter of the United Nations is fittingly celebrated by concentrating on peace goals.

They are those objectives which the nations might practically achieve together before some world leader announces them as war goals. The achievement of them through the machinery of the United Nations, developing a habit among free peoples of collaboration on a world program, would give vitality to the Charter and demonstrate that we can peacefully attain the broader objectives.

Working together patiently under God's guidance is the only way to that understanding and confidence which will make the United Nations effective.

The machinery of general international organization cannot run itself. Only men who know what they want to achieve, and who have the united support of their several peoples, can supply the energy that will make the wheels turn.

[1] *Ibid.*, p. 859.   [2] *Ibid.*, XV, p. 16.

Therefore, through national organizations of business, labor, agriculture, veterans, women, education, religion, and international relations, we strive to —

Plan a nation-wide educational program on the United Nations;

Inspire Americans, especially such citizens' organizations as the 150 conferring under the sponsorship of the Foreign Policy Association today, to look ahead and discuss what they hope to see accomplished through United Nations machinery, particularly the goals toward which they want their representatives in the various organs, commissions, and specialized agencies to work;

Relate the main lines of American foreign policy to the task of clarifying our peace goals;

Suggest a few of the specific goals on which to exercise the relatively new function of acting together internationally.

Our deeds will count, not only in the attainment of their beneficent objectives, but also in building up morale to wage peace generally.

Every strategic point gained in collaboration with our Allies in the peace struggle will bring the world nearer to the final victory over the impersonal enemies of mankind.

In warfare we have defeated the enemy. In peace we have not consolidated the victory. This will not be achieved unless the purposes and principles of the United Nations are made living motives in the souls of men.

To bring this about, two immediate steps are necessary:

The holding action to prevent threats to peace defined in article 2 of the Charter. Thus, as in the shadow of a great rock, we could enjoy the security in which the other, and corresponding step, can be taken.

Operation of the machinery in definite, specific, common enterprises.

. . . . . .

The Final Act of the Inter-American Conference on Problems of War and Peace at Mexico City, in February and March, 1945, comprehended juridical, economic, social, political, and security programs designed to preserve the independence and dignity of each member state, and to provide for determination of controversies which might arise among them. At that time, before the Charter had been formulated, the regional organization could initiate the ultimate sanction of military force in the event of a threat or act of aggression.

The Act of Chapultepec, which provided especially for reciprocal assistance and American solidarity, was so designed that it must conform to the principles and policies of the United Nations Charter subsequently to be adopted. Within the letter and spirit of the Charter which we celebrate, this benevolent organization of American republics is striving to carry into effect article 52 of the Charter, namely:

"The Members of the United Nations entering into such arrangements or constituting such agencies shall make every effort to achieve

PRINCIPLES AND POLICY: GENERAL STATEMENTS

pacific settlement of local disputes through such regional arrangements or by such regional agencies before referring them to the Security Council.

"The Security Council shall encourage the development of pacific settlement of local disputes through such regional arrangements or by such regional agencies either on the initiative of the states concerned or by reference from the Security Council."

The effect of the ratification of the Charter upon the Act of Chapultepec was principally to take away from the Union of American Republics the right of regional enforcement action without the previous authorization of the Security Council.

Thus, a threat of aggression may not now be met without first obtaining direction of the Security Council.

However, it left to the regional organization two extremely important functions:

 1st. The right and the duty to consult among themselves in order to agree upon the measures that may be advisable to take;
 2d. The inherent right of individual or collective self-defense if an armed attack should occur against a member of the United Nations, until the Security Council has taken the measures necessary to maintain international peace and security.

The system of consultation has developed in the Western Hemisphere during the past 56 years, and has gradually become a substitute for the use of armed force.

During the past year, the harmony of the Western Hemisphere has been disturbed, but no war has occurred, and none will occur.

The situation calls for the exercise of great wisdom, poise, patience, and consideration of all the various points of view. Here is an opportunity to strengthen the habit of collaboration and achieve both restoration of harmony in this hemisphere, and the strengthening of the machinery of the United Nations.

Other illustrations of goals and of public participation are the high points advanced by speakers today covering eight areas. They avoid generalities and advance highly significant and realizable objectives. Categorically, they are —

Expansion of trade and employment.
Reconstruction and development.
Human rights — freedom of information and education.
Health and social welfare.
Peaceful settlements.
United military defense.
Atomic energy — control and utilization.
Trusteeship and self-government for dependent areas.

Consideration of your time impels me to omit discussion of these goals now, notwithstanding that these, too, are objectives which the nations might practically achieve together before some world leader announces them as war goals.

Our best hope for preventing war is international collaboration on positive goals:

(1) Developing large-scale plans to which each country can contribute in terms of its ability — really investing the peaceful struggles in a cooperative program as we did in the violent struggle. The way to stay united is to get busy on common enterprises that we can agree on.

(2) Concentrating the forces and facilities we have on specific objectives that we feel confident we can take within a reasonable time — and then to apply the principles of logistics to make an effective and concerted drive. Resolutions and recommendations on principles and purposes are not enough; we must be very specific on exactly what each country can do in a plan of combined operations, organize task forces, pool resources, bring the experts and organizers of the various countries together for united effort to get things done. People can't act unless they see clearly where we are headed and what is required of them.

(3) By doing important things together at a few strategic points we will gain strength and build up morale in the peaceful struggles as we did in the war. Only by taking next steps with precision and determination will people learn to win the final victory over the impersonal enemies of mankind. There is danger in dissipating our forces on too many fronts, trying to lick tough problems with phrases and speeches. Acting together is the purpose of talking things over together. Start with the goals we most universally agree on and thus create a pattern of common action to move forward in the more controversial areas.

(4) Behind whatever programs we agree on must be a popular will and determination to risk and sacrifice and persist.

In the war we were very specific; we said we had to use inland shipping facilities to rush war materials to ports and to bring up troops; and this meant saving fuel, dim-outs, getting people to do specific things to help reach the goal. The same kind of specific thinking and planning is needed for peace goals. They have to be the accepted goals of the people — not only our people but the people of the other cooperating nations. And the people have to understand clearly why such goals are given priority attention, what it will take to realize them, what others are prepared to do and are doing.

Now that the United Nations machinery is set up, we and all the other United Nations peoples have to make up our minds what we want to accomplish with it and in what order — putting first things first. This is a challenge to all the citizen groups that have taken such an active interest in American participation in the United Nations. We're now ready to participate — to do something. What? And how? This is a challenge to the writers and broadcasters and film makers; to make the goals of peace as vivid and as urgent as the goals in the war.

Let's talk about the real things we want to do, and spend less time speculating about whether there'll be another war and what this nation or that politician may be maneuvering for.

We need a vast educational program to make the possibilities of peace goals understood and to help people to understand what they can do to cooperate.

So, this is an invitation on the first anniversary of the signing of the Charter for public participation in the setting of peace goals and the task of organizing collaboration of the nations to achieve the goals agreed upon.

Henry James talked about the moral equivalent for war. He thought it involved mobilizing people for common struggle against the common impersonal enemies. If once they could get the exhilaration of planning campaigns against disease and hunger, of collaborating in vast projects of construction and development, they might bring to bear on constructive programs all of the forces they expend in the fury of destructive warfare. In the process of working and planning together they might develop new patterns of thinking and come to understand each other.

For centuries men fought to take things away from each other in a world of low productivity and to collect tribute from the conquered. In the twentieth century the wars are started by organizers who claim they want to introduce new orders. They gain their dynamic from an appeal to the sense of national superiority. Behind all this is a powerful drive toward applying the science and "know-how" of our times, and breaking down the interfering barriers that frustrate large-scale organization and exchange. Either we do by agreement and free collaboration through the United Nations what we know is possible to give peoples everywhere opportunity to fashion their futures with twentieth-century tools, or we confront the almost inevitable task of resisting in war the attempt of another set of strong men to impose order and to organize the world as a whole.

Peace goals, then, are those objectives which the nations might practically achieve together before some world leader announces them as war goals.

We in the United States assert the belief that we can do cooperatively and by agreement what must somehow be done — that we can peacefully apply what science has taught us — that we can find ways of releasing and organizing the productive and creative powers of people on a world-wide basis through the processes of democracy. To make good on this belief, we must move quickly to collaborate with other free peoples on a program of action through the machinery of the United Nations.

(11) *Address by the Secretary of State (Byrnes) on United States Aims and Policies in Europe, Paris, October 3, 1946.*[1]

[Excerpts]

In this company I will not speak of the long and firm friendship which has existed between the people of France and the people of the United States — a friendship which existed before we attained our independence. That friendship runs so deep that we do not have to talk about it. Differ

[1] *Ibid.*, p. 665.

as we may from time to time, our two peoples always have stood and always will stand together in time of crisis. Liberty, equality, fraternity — the rights of man — are our common heritage.

Twice in my generation the soldiers of France and the soldiers of America have fought side by side in defense of their common heritage of freedom.

America is proud of her contribution to our common victory in 1945. America is proud of her contribution to our common victory in 1918. But America is not so proud of the course she followed after the victory of 1918.

In 1918 I was a follower of Woodrow Wilson. I gloried in his idealism and in the magnificent effort he made to build the peace upon the covenant of the League of Nations.

But the American people expected too much from Woodrow Wilson and supported him too little.

While he was in Paris working for peace, political opponents at home bitterly criticized his course and questioned his motives. They exaggerated and exploited the shortcomings of the Treaty of Versailles, and they belittled and besmirched what Woodrow Wilson had accomplished.

America failed to join the League of Nations. America refused to guarantee the defense of the French frontier. America allowed other countries to believe that she had no interest, and would not seriously concern herself, in what was happening in Europe, in Africa, or Asia.

But wars started, first in Asia, then in Africa, and then in Europe. Then came Pearl Harbor. America learned too late that this is one world and that she could not isolate herself from that world.

America is determined this time not to retreat into a policy of isolation. We are determined this time to cooperate in maintaining the peace. President Roosevelt this time sought to avoid the political opposition which had defeated the peace after the first World War. Then President Wilson neglected to invite the leaders of the political party in opposition to his administration to participate with him in making the peace.

President Roosevelt, on the other hand, asked the congressional leaders to participate in the peace studies being made by the Department of State shortly after our entry into the war.

At Yalta, immediately after the heads of government had agreed to call the San Francisco conference to draw up the Charter for the United Nations, President Roosevelt advised Secretary Stettinius and me that he would appoint on the Delegation to the San Francisco conference Republicans as well as Democrats, and would name Senator Vandenberg as the ranking Republican member of the Delegation.

Even before our entry into the war, President Roosevelt repudiated the idea that the United States was not interested in what takes place in Europe. Knowing from the start that the war was a war of aggression, he never asked the American people to be neutral in spirit.

Before we entered the war, he inspired the declaration of principles known as the Atlantic Charter, which was proclaimed by him and the Prime Minister of the United Kingdom on August 14, 1941.

It was President Roosevelt who at Yalta presented the declaration on liberated Europe which Generalissimo Stalin and Prime Minister Churchill accepted and which imposed a responsibility upon the three governments to continue their interest in the Balkan states and uphold the basic freedoms embodied in that declaration.

The policies inaugurated by President Roosevelt have been consistently followed by his successor, President Truman. He has consistently urged the carrying out in the liberated and ex-enemy states of Europe of the policies agreed to by the heads of government at Yalta at the instance of President Roosevelt.

President Truman continued the practice of seeking the cooperation of the leaders of both major political parties in the making of peace.

It was with the approval of President Truman that I invited Senator Vandenberg as well as Senator Connally to assist me in the drafting of the peace treaties.

And President Truman reenforced this bipartisan policy by appointing Senator Austin our representative on the Security Council of the United Nations.

The President has recently made known to the world in the most convincing manner possible that the foreign policy which was started by President Roosevelt and which has been consistently followed by President Truman will continue to be the policy of the American Government.

Because that policy is supported by Republicans as well as Democrats, it gives assurance to the world that it is our American policy and will be adhered to regardless of which political party is in power.

Because today we have such a policy I was able to say recently, with the approval of the President, and I am happy to be able to reaffirm here in France, that so long as there is an occupation army in Germany the armed forces of the United States will be in the army of occupation.

I would not want you to believe that our course in this regard is entirely unselfish. It is true that the United States wants no territory and seeks no discriminatory favors. The United States is interested in one thing above all else, a just and lasting peace.

The people of the United States did their best to stay out of two European wars on the theory that they should mind their own business and that they had no business in Europe. It did not work.

The people of the United States have discovered that when a European war starts our own peace and security inevitably become involved before the finish. They have concluded that if they must help finish every European war it would be better for them to do their part to prevent the starting of a European war.

Twice in our generation doubt as to American foreign policy has led other nations to miscalculate the consequences of their actions. Twice in our generation that doubt as to American foreign policy has not brought peace, but war.

That must not happen again.

. . . .

After every great war which has been won by the combined efforts of many nations, there has been conflict among the Allies in the making of peace. It would be folly to deny the seriousness of the conflict in viewpoints among the Allies after this war.

To ignore that conflict or minimize its seriousness will not resolve the conflict or help us along the road to peace. To exaggerate that conflict and its seriousness, on the other hand, only makes more difficult the resolution of the conflict.

I concur most heartily in the view recently expressed by Generalissimo Stalin that there is no immediate danger of war. I hope that his statement will put an end to the unwarranted charges that any nation or group of nations is seeking to encircle the Soviet Union, or that the responsible leaders of the Soviet Union so believe.

I do not believe that any responsible official of any government wants war. The world has had enough of war. The difficulty is that while no nation wants war, nations may pursue policies or courses of action which lead to war. Nations may seek political and economic advantages which they cannot obtain without war.

That is why if we wish to avoid war we must decry not only war but the things which lead to war.

Just because war is not now imminent, we must take the greatest care not to plant the seeds of a future war. We must seek *less* to defend our actions in the eyes of those who already agree with us, and *more* to defend our actions in the eyes of those who do not agree with us. But our defense must be the defense of justice and freedom, the defense of the political and economic rights not of a few privileged men or nations but of all men and all nations.

It is particularly appropriate that here in the birthplace of the doctrine of the rights of man I should reaffirm the conviction of the Government and the people of the United States that it is the right of every people to organize their own destiny through the freest possible expression of their collective will. The people of the United States believe in freedom for all men and all nations, freedom of speech, freedom of worship, freedom of assembly, freedom to progress. The people of the United States have no desire to impose their will upon any other people or to obstruct their efforts to improve their social, economic or political conditions. In our view human freedom and human progress are inseparable.

We want to give the common men and women of this world who have borne the burdens and sufferings of war a chance to enjoy the blessings of peace and freedom. We want the common men and women of this world to share in the rising standards of life which science makes possible in a free, peaceful, and friendly world.

(12) *Statement by the President (Truman) on the Bipartisan Program for Foreign Affairs, November 11, 1946.*[1]

The mid-term elections of November 5, 1946 saw the Democratic Party, for the first time in fourteen years, swept from control of both Houses of Congress. The increase in the strength of the Republican Party immediately raised questions both in the United States and particularly in foreign countries as to whether the foreign policies of the United States would be altered and

[1] *Ibid.*, p. 911.

the country would revert to one or another form of isolationism. Protection against such an eventuality had been sought throughout the period under review by associating leading members of the Republican Party, particularly Senator Vandenberg and John Foster Dulles, with every major delegation engaged in peace negotiations.

I shall devote all my energy to the discharge of my duty with a full realization of the responsibility which results from the present state of affairs. I do not claim for myself and my associates greater devotion to the welfare of our Nation than I ascribe to others of another party. We take the same oath of office. We have at one time or another been equally willing to offer our lives in the defense of our country. I shall proceed, therefore, in the belief that the members of the Congress will discharge their duties with a full realization of their responsibility.

Inevitably, issues will arise between the President and the Congress. When this occurs, we must examine our respective positions with stern and critical analysis to exclude any attempt to tamper with the public interest in order to achieve personal or partisan advantage.

The change in the majority in the Congress does not alter our domestic or foreign interests or problems. In foreign affairs we have a well-charted course to follow. Our foreign policy has been developed and executed on a bipartisan basis. I have done my best to strengthen and extend this practice. Members of both parties in and out of the Congress have participated in the inner council in preparing and in actually carrying out the foreign policies of our Government. It has been a national and not a party program. It will continue to be a national program insofar as the Secretary of State and I are concerned. I firmly believe that our Republican colleagues who have worked intelligently and cooperatively with us in the past will do so in the future.

My concern is not about those in either party who know the seriousness of the problems which confront us in our foreign affairs. Those who share great problems are united and not divided by them. My concern is lest any in either party should seek in this field an opportunity to achieve personal notoriety or partisan advantage by exploitation of the sensational or by the mere creation of controversy.

We are set upon a hard course. An effort by either the executive or the legislative branch of the Government to embarrass the other for partisan gain would bring frustration to our country. To follow the course with honor to ourselves and with benefit to our country, we must look beyond and above ourselves and our party interests for the true bearing.

As President of the United States I am guided by a simple formula: to do in all cases, from day to day, without regard to narrow political considerations, what seems to me to be best for the welfare of all our people. Our search for that welfare must always be based upon a progressive concept of government.

I shall cooperate in every proper manner with members of the Congress, and my hope and prayer is that this spirit of cooperation will be reciprocated.

To them, one and all, I pledge faith with faith, and promise to meet good-will with good-will.

(13) Address by the President (Truman) before the United Nations General Assembly, October 24, 1946.[1]

[Excerpts]

. . . . . .

This meeting of the Assembly symbolizes the abandonment by the United States of a policy of isolation.

The overwhelming majority of the American people, regardless of party, support the United Nations.

They are resolved that the United States, to the full limit of its strength, shall contribute to the establishment and maintenance of a just and lasting peace among the nations of the world.

However, I must tell you that the American people are troubled by the failure of the Allied nations to make more progress in their common search for lasting peace.

It is important to remember the intended place of the United Nations in moving toward this goal. The United Nations, as an organization, was *not* intended to settle the problems arising immediately out of the war. The United Nations *was* intended to provide the means for maintaining international peace in the future after just settlements have been made.

The settlement of these problems was deliberately consigned to negotiations among the Allies as distinguished from the United Nations. This was done in order to give the United Nations a better opportunity and a freer hand to carry out its long range task of providing peaceful means for the adjustment of future differences, some of which might arise out of the settlements made as a result of this war.

The United Nations cannot, however, fulfil adequately its own responsibilities until the peace settlements have been made and unless these settlements form a solid foundation upon which to build a permanent peace.

I submit that these settlements, and our search for everlasting peace, rest upon the four essential freedoms.

These are freedom of speech, freedom of religion, freedom from want, and freedom from fear. These are fundamental freedoms to which all the United Nations are pledged under the Charter.

To the attainment of these freedoms, everywhere in the world, through the friendly cooperation of all nations, the Government and people of the United States are dedicated.

The fourth freedom, freedom from fear, means above all else freedom from fear of war.

This freedom is attainable *now*.

Lately we have all heard talk about the possibility of another world war. Fears have been aroused all over the world.

These fears are unwarranted and unjustified.

However, rumours of war still find willing listeners in certain places. If these rumours are not checked they are sure to impede world recovery.

[1] United Nations, *Journal of the General Assembly*, No. 13, Supplement A, p. 6.

I have been reading reports from many parts of the world. These reports all agree on one major point; the people of every nation are sick of war. They know its agony and its futility. No responsible government can ignore this universal feeling.

The United States of America has no wish to make war now or in the future, upon any people anywhere in the world. The heart of our foreign policy is a sincere desire for peace. This nation will work patiently for peace by every means consistent with self-respect and security. Another world war would shatter the hopes of mankind and completely destroy civilization as we know it.

I am sure that every delegate in this hall will join me in rejecting talk of war. No nation wants war. Every nation needs peace.

To avoid war and rumours and danger of war the peoples of all countries must not only cherish peace as an ideal but they must develop means of settling conflicts between nations in accordance with principles of law and justice.

The difficulty is that it is easier to get people to agree upon peace as an ideal than to agree upon principles of law and justice or to agree to subject their own acts to the collective judgment of mankind.

But difficult as the task may be, the path along which agreement may be sought, with hope of success, is clearly defined.

In the first place, every Member of the United Nations is legally and morally bound by the Charter to keep the peace. More specifically, every Member is bound to refrain in its international relations from the threat, or use, of force against the territorial integrity or political independence of any State.

In the second place, I remind you that twenty-three Members of the United Nations have bound themselves by the Charter of the Nuremberg Tribunal to the principle that planning, initiating or waging a war of aggression is a crime against humanity for which individuals as well as States shall be tried before the bar of international justice.

The basic principles upon which we are agreed go far, but not far enough, in removing fear of war from the world. There must be agreement upon a positive, constructive course of action as well.

The people of the world know that there can be no real peace unless it is peace with justice for all. Justice for small nations and for large nations and justice for individuals without distinction as to race, creed or colour; a peace that will advance, not retard the attainment of the four freedoms.

We shall attain freedom from fear when every act of every nation, in its dealings with every other nation, brings closer to realization the other freedoms; freedom of speech, freedom of religion, and freedom from want. Along this path we can find justice for all, without distinction between the strong and the weak nations, and without discrimination among individuals.

. . . .

The United States will continue to seek settlements arising from the war that are just to all States, large and small, that uphold the human rights and fundamental freedoms to which the Charter pledges all its Members, and that do not contain the seeds of new conflicts.

A peace between the nations based on justice will make possible an early improvement in living conditions throughout the world and a quick recovery from the ravages of war. The world is crying for a just and durable peace with an intensity that must force its attainment at the earliest possible date.

If the Members of the United Nations are to act together to remove the fear of war, the first requirement is for the Allied nations to reach agreement on the peace settlements.

Propaganda that promotes distrust and misunderstanding among the Allies will not help us. Agreements designed to remove the fear of war can be reached only by the co-operation of nations to respect the legitimate interests of all States and act as good neighbours toward each other.

Lasting agreements between Allies cannot be imposed by one nation nor can they be reached at the expense of the security, independence or integrity of any nation. There must be accommodation by all the Allied nations in which mutual adjustments of lesser national interests are made in order to serve the greater interest of all in peace, security and justice.

. . . . . .

Two of the greatest obligations undertaken by the United Nations towards the removal of the fear of war remain to be fulfilled.

First we must reach an agreement establishing international controls of atomic energy that will ensure its use for peaceful purposes only, in accordance with the Assembly's unanimous resolution of last winter.

Secondly, we must reach agreements that will remove the deadly fear of other weapons of mass destruction, in accordance with the same resolution.

Each of these obligations is going to be difficult to fulfil. Their fulfilment will require the utmost in perseverance and good faith, and we cannot succeed without setting fundamental precedents in the law of nations. Each will be worth everything in perseverance and good faith that we can give to it. The future safety of the United Nations, and of every Member nation, depends upon the outcome.

On behalf of the United States I can say we are not discouraged. We shall continue to seek agreement by every possible means.

At the same time we shall also press for preparation of agreements in order that the Security Council may have at its disposal peace forces adequate to prevent acts of aggression.

The United Nations will not be able to remove the fear of war from the world unless substantial progress can be made in the next few years toward the realization of another of the four freedoms; freedom from want.

The Charter pledges the Members of the United Nations to work together toward this end. The structure of the United Nations in this field is now nearing completion, with the Economic and Social Council, its commissions and related specialized agencies. It provides more complete and effective institutions through which to work than the world has ever had before.

A great opportunity lies before us.

In these constructive tasks which concern directly the lives and welfare of human beings throughout the world, humanity and self-interest alike demand of all of us the fullest cooperation.

The United States has already demonstrated in many ways its grave concern about economic reconstruction that will repair the damage done by war.

We have participated actively in every measure taken by the United Nations toward this end. We have in addition taken such separate national action as the granting of large loans and credits and renewal of our reciprocal trade-agreements programme.

Through the establishment of the Food and Agriculture Organization, the International Bank for Reconstruction and Development and the International Monetary Fund, Members of the United Nations have proved their capacity for constructive cooperation toward common economic objectives. In addition, the International Labour Organization is being brought into relationship with the United Nations.

Now we must complete the structure. The United States attaches the highest importance to the creation of the International Trade Organization now being discussed in London by a preparatory committee.

This country wants to see, not only the rapid restoration of devastated areas, but the industrial and agricultural progress of the less well-developed areas of the world.

We believe that all nations should be able to develop a healthy economic life of their own. We believe that all peoples should be able to reap the benefits of their own labour and of their own natural resources.

There are immense possibilities in many parts of the world for industrial development and agricultural modernization.

These possibilities can be realized only by the cooperation of Members of the United Nations, helping each other on a basis of equal rights.

In the field of social reconstruction and advancement the completion of the Charter for a World Health Organization is an important step forward.

The assembly now has before it for adoption the constitution of another specialized agency in this field, the International Refugee Organization. It is essential that this organization be created in time to take over from UNRRA as early as possible in the new year the tasks of caring for and repatriating or resettling the refugees and displaced persons of Europe. There will be similar tasks, of great magnitude, in the Far East.

The United States considers this a matter of great urgency in the cause of restoring peace and in the cause of humanity itself.

I intend to urge the Congress of the United States to authorize this country to do its full part, both in financial support of the International Refugee Organization and in joining with other nations to receive those refugees who do not wish to return to their former homes for reasons of political or religious belief.

The United States believes a concerted effort must be made to break down the barriers to a free flow of information among the nations of the world.

We regard freedom of expression and freedom to receive information — the right of the people to know — as among the most important of those human rights and fundamental freedoms to which we are pledged under the United Nations Charter.

The United Nations Educational, Scientific and Cultural Organization, which is meeting in November, is a recognition of this fact. That organization is built upon the premise that since wars begin in the minds of men, the defence of peace must be constructed in the minds of men, and that a free exchange of ideas and knowledge among peoples is necessary to this task. The United States therefore attaches great importance to all activities designed to break down barriers to mutual understanding and to wider tolerance.

The United States will support the United Nations with all the resources that we possess.

The use of force or the threat of force anywhere in the world to break the peace is of direct concern to the American people.

The course of history has made us one of the stronger nations of the world. It has therefore placed upon us special responsibilities to conserve our strength and to use it rightly in a world so interdependent as our world today.

The American people recognize these special responsibilities. We shall do our best to meet them, both in the making of the peace settlements and in the fulfilment of the long-range tasks of the United Nations.

The American people look upon the United Nations not as a temporary expedient but as a permanent partnership. A partnership among the peoples of the world for their common peace and common well-being.

It must be the determined purpose of all of us to see that the United Nations lives and grows in the minds and the hearts of all peoples.

May Almighty God, in His infinite wisdom and mercy, guide us and sustain us as we seek to bring peace everlasting to the world.

With His help we shall succeed.

CHAPTER II

THE CONDUCT OF FOREIGN RELATIONS

1. POWERS OF THE PRESIDENT

(1) *Letter from the Attorney General (Clark) to the Secretary of State (Byrnes), on Validity of Commercial Aviation Agreements Executed by the President, June 18, 1946.*[1]

I refer to your request for my views concerning the validity of existing commercial aviation agreements to which the United States is a party.

The agreements in question were discussed by the President in his message to the Congress of June 11, 1946, urging ratification of the Convention on International Civil Aviation. I refer particularly to the following statement.

The Convention makes no attempt to cover controversial questions of commercial aviation rights. It leaves these questions to be settled by other international agreements, which are entirely independent of the Convention, and which provide for the reciprocal exchange of commercial air transport rights. Under authority vested in me, I have actively undertaken to consummate such agreements, in order to assure the most favorable development of international civil aviation. Naturally, agreements of this nature to which the United States is a party are consistent with the requirements of the Civil Aeronautics Act, are valid under its terms, and fully protect the public interest. Under these agreements, before foreign air carrier permits are issued by the United States to foreign airlines, they must qualify under the provisions of the Civil Aeronautics Act.

The President consulted me in connection with the above statement, and it was made with my full approval.

It is recognized that there are many classes of agreements with foreign countries which are not required to be formulated as treaties. Of particular pertinence to the question here is that class of executive agreements which are entered into in accordance with, and within the scope of, authority vested in the executive branch by legislation enacted by the Congress. Notable examples of agreements which fall within this class are postal conventions and reciprocal trade agreements.

The agreements referred to by the President in his message of June 11 were executed under the authority vested in him by the Constitution and statutes, including the Civil Aeronautics Act of 1938 (approved June 23, 1938, c. 601, 52 Stat. 973; 49 U.S.C. 401 *et seq.*). Section 802 of the act clearly anticipates the making of agreements with foreign countries concerning civil aviation, and provides that, "the Secretary of State shall advise the Authority [now Civil Aeronautics Board;

[1] Department of State, *Bulletin*, XV, p. 1070.

Reorganization Plan No. IV, 54 Stat. 1235] of, and consult with the Authority [Board] concerning, the negotiation of any agreements with foreign governments for the establishment or development of air navigation, including air routes and services."

Having anticipated the possibility of agreements with foreign countries and having prescribed the manner of arriving at such agreements, the 1938 act, in section 1102, provides that the Civil Aeronautics Board, in exercising its powers and performing its duties, "shall do so consistently with any obligation assumed by the United States in any treaty, convention, or agreement that may be in force between the United States and any foreign country." Moreover, under section 801, the President is required to make the final decision with respect to the grant or denial of a permit to a foreign carrier.

The foregoing statutory provisions make it clear that the Congress contemplated the consummation of agreements with foreign nations relating to international civil aviation.

The only argument which, so far as I know, has been advanced that existing agreements in this field are not valid is based on section 402 of the Civil Aeronautics Act of 1938. That section provides that "no foreign air carrier shall engage in foreign air transportation unless there is in force a permit issued by the Authority [Board] authorizing such carrier so to engage." Such a permit may be issued by the Board "if it finds that such carrier is fit, willing, and able properly to perform such air transportation and to conform to the provisions of this chapter and the rules, regulations, and requirements of the Authority [Board] hereunder, and that such transportation will be in the public interest." However, as I have previously indicated, any action taken by the Board is subject to approval or disapproval by the President under section 801 of the statute and, therefore, it is the President, rather than the Board, who makes the final decision.

I understand that it is the position of the Department of State that the jurisdiction of the Civil Aeronautics Board in connection with the granting of permits is not affected by any of the civil aviation agreements which have been concluded, and that the Board in each case must still decide whether the applicant carrier is a suitable airline for performance under the requested permit and whether the issuance of the permit would meet the other requirements of the statute. It is also the position of your Department that where an agreement with a foreign nation exists, the Board, pursuant to section 1102, must act "consistently with any obligation assumed by the United States" in such agreement and, therefore, within the board policy declared in the agreement. The ultimate decision, of course, under section 801, must be made by the President.

I concur in the position taken by the Department of State. None of the existing executive agreements purports to waive the necessity of proceeding under section 402 of the Civil Aeronautics Act of 1938, and I am informed that the procedure specified in that section is in fact complied with by the Civil Aeronautics Board whether or not there is in existence an agreement with the foreign country involved.

(2) *Letter from the Acting Attorney General (McGranery) to the Secretary of State (Byrnes), on Validity of International Agreements Executed by the President, August 20, 1946.*[1]

[Excerpts]

By letter dated July 9, 1946, you have asked for my opinion with respect to the following question:

Would the enclosed agreement [2] when executed by the President pursuant to authorization by a joint resolution of the Congress operate as the supreme law of the land superseding any inconsistent State or local laws with the same effect in that regard as a treaty ratified by and with the advice and consent of the Senate?

The draft agreement referred to, dated June 20, 1946, would be between the United States and the United Nations. It would create a zone in which the headquarters of the United Nations would be located, and would define, broadly, the rights, privileges and obligations of the parties in connection therewith. At its present stage of negotiation, the agreement does not specify the size of the zone or its precise location within the borders of the United States. Your letter indicates that it has not yet been determined whether the agreement will take the form of a treaty or be executed by the President pursuant to a joint resolution of the Congress.

In this connection, representatives of the United Nations have asked you whether the proposed agreement, in the event that it is authorized by a joint resolution of the Congress, would have the same binding effect as a treaty, in superseding inconsistent State and local laws. It is your view that an agreement executed by the President, pursuant to such a joint resolution, would have the effect indicated, and you desire to have my opinion in the matter. I concur fully in your position.

The question you have asked is confined to the particular agreement now before me, and does not require me to consider whether or not there are circumstances under which a given international compact must take the form of a treaty. It is sufficient to say that the proposed agreement is clearly within the constitutional authority of the Federal Government, and may, with full legal effect, be executed as a legislative executive agreement.

The Constitution of the United States expressly provides in clause 2 of Article VI that

This Constitution, and the laws of the United States which shall be made in pursuance thereof; and all treaties made, or which shall be made, under the authority of the United States, shall be the supreme law of the land; and the judges in every state shall be bound thereby, any thing in the Constitution or laws of any state to the contrary notwithstanding.

[1] *Ibid.*, p. 1068.
[2] Draft agreement between the United States and the United Nations regarding headquarters. Not reprinted here.

It is thus axiomatic that where there is a conflict between a State or local law and a treaty, the State or local law must yield. *Ware* v. *Hylton*, 3 Dall. 199, 236–237, 242–243, 282 (1796); *Asakura* v. *Seattle*, 265 U.S. 332, 341 (1924); 1 Willoughby, *The Constitutional Law of the United States* (2d ed. 1929), section 76. It is equally well established that such a State or local law must give way to a conflicting Federal statute. *Gibbons* v. *Ogden*, 9 Wheat. 1, 210–211 (1824); *Hines* v. *Davidowitz*, 312 U.S. 52, 62–68 (1941); 1 Willoughby, *op. cit. supra*. A like rule applies where the conflict is occasioned by Federal executive action authorized by an act of Congress. *Case* v. *Bowles*, 327 U.S. 92, 102, 66 Sup. Ct. 438, 443 (1946); the *Shreveport Case*, 234 U.S. 342 (1914); *Wisconsin R. R. Comm.* v. *C., B. & Q. R. R. Co.*, 257 U.S. 563 (1922); 35 Op. A. G. 110.

Since a joint resolution, approved by the President, is, plainly, a law of the United States (*Wells* v. *United States*, 257 Fed. 605, 610–611 (C. C. A. 9) (1919)), it follows that an otherwise valid joint resolution authorizing execution of the proposed agreement will supersede State or local laws inconsistent with the joint resolution or the agreement. Cases cited *supra*.

The Supreme Court has pointed out that if international understandings could be vitiated by State laws, the United States would be open to a "charge of national perfidy." *United States* v. *Belmont*, 301 U.S. 324, 331 (1937). The need for supremacy of Federal action in the field of foreign affairs is, therefore, if anything, greater than with respect to exclusively domestic concerns. *Hines* v. *Davidowitz*, 312 U.S. 52, 68 (1941).

Thus, the Supreme Court held in the *Belmont* case that the laws of New York, otherwise applicable to the disposition of a bank deposit, must yield to a conflicting Executive agreement with a foreign government executed by the President pursuant to authority vested in him by the Constitution. Mr. Justice Sutherland, speaking for the Court, said in part (331–332):

Plainly, the external powers of the United States are to be exercised without regard to state laws or policies. The supremacy of a treaty in this respect has been recognized from the beginning. . . . the same rule would result in the case of all international compacts and agreements from the very fact that complete power over international affairs is in the national government and is not and cannot be subject to any curtailment or interference on the part of the several states. Compare *United States* v. *Curtis-Wright Export Corp.*, 299 U.S. 304, 316, *et seq.* In respect of all international negotiations and compacts, and in respect of our foreign relations generally, state lines disappear. As to such purposes the State of New York does not exist. Within the field of its powers, whatever the United States rightfully undertakes, it necessarily has warrant to consummate. . . .

A similar conclusion with respect to the same Executive agreement was subsequently reached in *United States* v. *Pink*, 315 U.S. 203 (1942), in which the Supreme Court, per Mr. Justice Douglas, stated, in part, the following (230–233):

"All constitutional acts of power, whether in the executive or in the judicial department, have as much legal validity and obligation as if they proceeded from the legislature, . . ." The Federalist, No. 64. A treaty is a "Law of the Land" under the supremacy clause (Art. VI, Cl. 2) of the Constitution. Such international compacts and agreements as the Litvinov Assignment have a similar dignity. *United States* v. *Belmont, supra*, 301 U.S. at p. 331. See Corwin, The President, Office & Powers (1940), pp. 228–240.

... But state law must yield when it is inconsistent with, or impairs the policy or provisions of, a treaty or of an international compact or agreement. See *Nielsen* v. *Johnson,* 279 U.S. 47. Then, the power of a State to refuse enforcement of rights based on foreign law which runs counter to the public policy of the forum (*Griffin* v. *McCoach,* 313 U.S. 498, 506) must give way before the superior Federal policy evidenced by a treaty or international compact or agreement. *Santovincenzo* v. *Egan, supra,* 284 U.S. 30; *United States* v. *Belmont, supra.* ...

We recently stated in *Hines* v. *Davidowitz,* 312 U.S. 52, 68, that the field which affects international relations is "the one aspect of our government that from the first has been most generally conceded imperatively to demand broad national authority"; and that any state power which may exist "is restricted to the narrowest of limits." There, we were dealing with the question as to whether a state statute regulating aliens survived a similar federal statute. We held that it did not. Here, we are dealing with an exclusive federal function. If state laws and policies did not yield before the exercise of the external powers of the United States, then our foreign policy might be thwarted. These are delicate matters. If state action could defeat or alter our foreign policy, serious consequences might ensue. The nation as a whole would be held to answer if a State created difficulties with a foreign power. Cf. *Chy Lung* v. *Freeman,* 92 U.S. 275, 279–280. Certainly, the conditions for "enduring friendship" between the nations, which the policy of recognition in this instance was designed to effectuate, are not likely to flourish where, contrary to national policy, a lingering atmosphere of hostility is created by state action.

The agreement involved in the *Belmont* and *Pink* cases, and given precedence over conflicting State policy, was not predicated on an act of Congress. Hence, there can be no doubt that the proposed agreement, if executed pursuant to congressional authority, will supersede incompatible State and local laws. As the Supreme Court stated, in the *Belmont* case, "it is inconceivable" that State constitutions, State laws, and State policies "can be interposed as an obstacle to the effective operation of a federal constitutional power." (301 U.S. 324, 332.)

2. DEPARTMENT OF STATE

A. Organization

1. OFFICE OF THE SECRETARY OF STATE

On July 2, 1945, the Senate unanimously approved the appointment of James F. Byrnes to succeed Edward R. Stettinius Jr. as Secretary of State.[1] Mr. Byrnes took the oath of office and assumed his duties on the following day [2] and remained at the head of the Department of State during the whole of the period under review. Joseph C. Grew, Under Secretary of State, served as Acting Secretary during Mr. Byrnes' absence while attending the Tripartite Conference at Berlin (July 17–August 2, 1945). Dean Acheson, Mr. Grew's

---

[1] *New York Times,* July 3, 1945, p. 1.

[2] For excerpts from Mr. Byrnes' statement upon assuming office, see this volume, p. 1.

successor, served in the same capacity for the periods during which Mr. Byrnes attended two sessions of the Council of Foreign Ministers in Paris (April–July 1946) and the Paris Conference of Twenty-One Nations (July–October 1946).

2. SPECIAL ASSISTANT TO THE SECRETARY FOR RESEARCH AND INTELLIGENCE

On September 27, 1945, the Department of State announced the appointment of Col. Alfred McCormack as Special Assistant to the Secretary for research and intelligence.[1] Simultaneously with this announcement, the Department revealed that, effective October 1, the Research and Analysis Branch and the Presentation Branch of the Office of Strategic Services would be incorporated under the Special Assistant as the Interim Research and Intelligence Service.[2] The Office of Strategic Services had previously been terminated and its functions transferred to the Department of State by Executive Order on September 20, 1945.[3] The functions of the Office of War Information (established by Executive Order 9182, June 13, 1945)[4] and the information functions of the Office of Inter-American Affairs (established as the Office of Coordinator of Inter-American Affairs by Executive Order 8840, July 30, 1941)[5] which were performed abroad or were concerned with informing the peoples of other nations as to the interests of the United States were transferred to the Interim Research and Intelligence Service by Executive Order on August 31, 1945.[6] The Secretary of State established the Interim Research and Intelligence Service, to function until December 31, 1945, by Departmental Order, dated October 26 and effective October 24, 1945.[7] The position of Special Assistant in charge of research and intelligence was established on the same date, and the Special Assistant was made responsible:

(a) For advice and assistance to the Secretary with respect to the development of a coordinated program for the procuring and production of foreign intelligence needed by the Department of State.

(b) For advice and assistance to the Secretary with respect to the development of a comprehensive and coordinated foreign intelligence program for all Federal agencies concerned with that type of activity.

(c) For the direction of such organization units as are hereafter established in the Department for the procuring and production of foreign intelligence.

(d) For the direction, until December 31, 1945, of the Interim Research and Intelligence Service.

(e) For the performance of those functions of the Director of Strategic Services and of the United States Joint Chiefs of Staff, relating to the functions of the Interim Research and Intelligence Service as are transferred to the Secretary of State pursuant to Executive Order 9621 of September 20, 1945.[8]

Col. McCormack assumed his duties as Special Assistant in charge of research and intelligence on October 1, 1945[9] and continued in that capacity until his resignation on April 23, 1946,[10] when he was succeeded by William L. Langer. Mr. Langer was replaced by Col. William A. Eddy on August 1.[11]

[1] Department of State, *Bulletin*, XIII, p. 499.
[2] *Ibid.*
[3] Executive Order 9621; for the text of the Order, see *ibid.*, p. 449 or *Federal Register*, X, p. 12033.
[4] See *Documents on American Foreign Relations, IV, 1941–1942*, Boston, World Peace Foundation, p. 189 (hereinafter series cited as *Documents*).
[5] See *ibid.*, p. 329.
[6] Executive Order 9608; for the text of the Order, see Department of State, *Bulletin*, XIII, p. 307 or *Federal Register*, X, p. 11223.
[7] Departmental Order 1350; for the text of the order, see Department of State, *Bulletin*, XIII, p. 739.
[8] Departmental Order 1351; for the text of the order, see *ibid.*
[9] *Ibid.*, p. 499. [10] *Ibid.*, XIV, p. 778. [11] *Ibid.*, XV, p. 286.

THE CONDUCT OF FOREIGN RELATIONS 51

3. OFFICE OF THE UNDER SECRETARY OF STATE

On August 15, 1945, Joseph C. Grew, Under Secretary of State since December 19, 1944,[1] in a letter to President Truman requested the acceptance of his resignation from that position; President Truman acceded on August 16, 1945.[2] Dean Acheson took the oath of office as Under Secretary on August 27[3] and was confirmed in that position by the Senate, September 24, 1945.[4]

4. OFFICE OF THE UNDER SECRETARY OF STATE FOR ECONOMIC AFFAIRS

On June 3, 1946, Rep. Sol Bloom (New York) introduced in the House of Representatives H. R. 6646, "A bill to establish the office of Under Secretary of State for Economic Affairs."[5] The Bill proposed the establishment of this office for a two-year period, the holder of the office to rank immediately below the Under Secretary of State and to perform such duties as were prescribed by the Secretary of State.[6] Secretary Byrnes appeared in support of the bill before the House Committee on Foreign Affairs on June 10. During his testimony Mr. Byrnes pointed out that the House Special Committee on Postwar Economic Policy and Planning, in its eighth report,[7] had recommended the creation of an Under Secretary for Economic Policy.[8] The Bill was favorably reported on June 11, 1946,[9] and was approved by the House on July 20.[10] The Senate Committee on Foreign Relations reported the Bill favorably on July 24, 1946,[11] and the Senate gave its approval on July 29.[12] The Bill was signed by the President on August 1, 1946.

The Senate confirmed the nomination of William L. Clayton as Under Secretary of State for Economic Affairs on August 2.[13] Mr. Clayton took the oath of office and formally assumed his new duties on August 17, 1946.[14]

(1) *Statement by the Secretary of State (Byrnes) before the Committee on Foreign Affairs of the House of Representatives, June 10, 1946.*[15]

[Excerpts]

. . . .

Since the cessation of hostilities the State Department has had transferred to it a number of agencies. Among those agencies there are several related to our foreign economic activities — the administration of lend-lease affairs, the settlement of claims between our Government and other

---

[1] See *Documents, VII, 1944–1945*, p. 48.
[2] Department of State, *Bulletin*, XIII, p. 271.   [3] *Ibid.*, p. 310.   [4] *Ibid.*, p. 502.
[5] *Congressional Record*, 92, p. 6305 (Daily edition, June 3, 1946).
[6] For provisions of the approved act, see this volume, p. 55.
[7] House Report No. 1205, 79th Cong., 1st sess., p. 50.
[8] *Office of Under Secretary of State for Economic Affairs. Hearings before the Committee on Foreign Affairs, House of Representatives, Seventy-Ninth Congress, Second Session, on H. R. 6646, A Bill to Establish the Office of Under Secretary of State for Economic Affairs, June 10, 1946*, p. 1; for excerpts from Secretary Byrnes' statement before the Committee on Foreign Affairs, see below.
[9] House Report No. 2249, 79th Cong., 2d sess.; for excerpts, see this volume, p. 54.
[10] *Congressional Record*, 92, p. 9723 (Daily edition, July 20, 1946).
[11] Senate Report No. 1824, 79th Cong., 2d sess.
[12] *Congressional Record*, 92, p. 10507 (Daily edition, July 29, 1946).
[13] Department of State, *Bulletin*, XV, p. 338.
[14] *Ibid.*, p. 387.
[15] *Office of Under Secretary of State for Economic Affairs. Hearings . . ., on H. R. 6646 . . .*, cited above, p. 1.

governments, the formation of the Export-Import Bank, and the monetary fund, as well as many other activities such as establishing credit for foreign governments — and they all tend to give the Assistant Secretary in Charge of Economic Affairs more than any one man can possibly do.

He has under his supervision, for instance, aviation, communications, shipping, and those subjects impose increasing demands upon his time.

I am a member of the National Advisory Council which meets at least once a week to consider all financial matters. It is impossible for me to attend the meetings with the demands upon my time, not only here but of course abroad. The Assistant Secretary for Economic Affairs must attend those meetings. The result is that Mr. Clayton, who fills that office, has so many demands upon his time that he just cannot stand it.

I come, therefore, to ask you to be good enough to give to me this Office of Under Secretary of Economic Affairs whose tenure will be limited to two years. I do that deliberately because I would not want to see established a precedent which other departments might wish to follow, and the fact that it is temporary would make it possible for you to avoid this difficulty.

Now, if at the end of the period of two years we return to more normal conditions, the State Department may not be engaged in all of these activities which are necessarily placed in the Department now.

There is an additional reason why I ask that the position of Under Secretary for Economic Affairs be established. There are members of the Cabinet on the National Advisory Council. The representative of the State Department should be at least the Under Secretary, and only the man who is charged with the direction of foreign economic affairs can represent the Department of State there. When we are engaged in the negotiation of a credit for a foreign government, such as the French negotiations just completed, men of high rank will come from abroad. Mr. Clayton will sit in at the conference representing me, and he is an Assistant Secretary. Representatives of other departments will be there, and among them will be members of the Cabinet. It would be exceedingly helpful if the man who represents the State Department could be an Under Secretary, so that he would have rank somewhat equivalent to those with which he deals.

. . . .

Mr. Clayton has been doing a wonderful job.

An Assistant Secretary is charged with the activities that are placed under his control. Necessarily when there is a bill pending on both sides of this Capitol on some subject connected with foreign economics, the Assistant Secretary for Economic Affairs has to appear before the legislative committees. Because he has charge of reciprocal trade, members of the Senate and of the House must see him to present constituents who would not want to see one of his clerks — they must see him. When he gets through attending the sessions of the legislative committees and seeing people and attending meetings of the Food Committee with

Secretary Anderson and attending meetings with the Secretary of Commerce and the National Advisory Council and the Aviation Council and UNRRA, the rest of the time he can play out in the park.

I really think that the demands upon him exceed those of any man of my acquaintance. He has patience and has been discharging those duties in a most efficient manner.

If the office of Under Secretary were established, he could appoint someone who could have the authority perhaps in the fields of aviation and shipping and communications, and they could take some of these burdens away from him, and he would have authority to sit in at these other conferences and sign letters and see people connected with those problems.

. . . .

... In this postwar period many activities have been transferred in great part from the War and Navy Departments to the State Department. There have been other activities transferred and most of them are in this field of foreign economics. . . .

. . . .

... [T]hese activities are all new to the Department of State. Then there are the lend-lease accounts and the disposal of surplus property and the settlement of claims between governments, the granting of credits to foreign governments. Also, there is the determination of the Government's economic policy with respect to Germany and Japan. There is a great responsibility there that requires constant communication with both Germany and Japan — with our representatives there. Then there is the International Monetary Fund and the International Bank. The United Nations have an Economic and Social Council and our representatives there must have a liaison with the Department. Under the statute that you enacted the policy of the United States representative to that Council comes from the President transmitted through the Secretary of State. That is just another activity that has been added. I think that those alone would keep an Under Secretary busy.

. . . .

As to making the office permanent, there is no question that for some time, as a result of the legislation of Congress, you will have in the State Department economic questions arising out of the reciprocal trade agreements. All of us who have spent time in Congress know the result of that legislation is to keep a department busy. I am anxious to have this office created now in this period, when undoubtedly the State Department has a greater increase in its activities than any other department of the Government. From my experience in the State Department I have concluded that this would be the wise thing to do. . . .

. . . .

(2) *Report of the Committee on Foreign Affairs of the House of Representatives on H. R. 6646, June 11, 1946.*[1]

[Excerpt]

. . . . .

Purpose

The Secretary of State appeared before the committee and discussed the greatly increased number of responsibilities which had been given to the Department of State since the end of the war. To a large extent these responsibilities have related to foreign economic affairs and have been added to the already numerous functions with which the present Assistant Secretary of State for Economic Affairs has been charged. These new responsibilities include the settlement of the lend-lease accounts with foreign governments, the disposal of surplus property abroad, the settlement of numerous claims between the United States and other countries, credits to foreign governments and our economic policy with respect to Germany and Japan. In addition, the United Nations has been created, and the Economic and Social Council is in operation; the United Nations Food and Agriculture Organization, the International Monetary Fund, the International Bank for Reconstruction and Development and the United Nations Relief and Rehabilitation Administration have been established, and in the fields of aviation, shipping and telecommunications additional discussions are in prospect. This Government has also published proposals for an international conference on trade and employment.

All of these activities acquired new importance when the fighting stopped and we were free to turn to the building of a lasting peace. With all of them the present Assistant Secretary of State for Economic Affairs has a close association and attendant heavy responsibilities.

Increased Administrative Efficiency

During the next 2 years, the duties now performed by the Assistant Secretary of State for Economic Affairs will be of the greatest significance in the conduct of our foreign relations, and those duties will require the most thoughtful attention to the problems which confront us and the most careful search for appropriate solutions. The scope of the work requires the complete attention of more than one principal officer of the Department. And quite apart from the fact that the task is beyond the capacity or endurance of any single individual, it will be most helpful in the conduct of international discussions and negotiations if the principal officer of the Department of State concerned with economic affairs has a rank commensurate with his duties.

With the creation of this office, the functions and duties now assigned to the Assistant Secretary of State for Economic Affairs can be shared with the Under Secretary of State for Economic Affairs. In this way it will be possible during the next 2 years to secure adequate and full con-

[1] House Report No. 2249, 79th Cong., 2d sess.

sideration of the serious problems with which the Department of State will be faced. The term of the Office of the Under Secretary of State for Economic Affairs has been limited to 2 years because it is apparent that during that period the Secretary of State will require the assistance of an officer of this rank. It is not now contemplated that the office would be established on a permanent basis and its creation should not be considered a precedent for the establishment of a similar office in any other department. A number of the temporary war agencies have been transferred to the Department of State which makes the need for the proposed legislation unique.

The recommendation for the establishment in the Department of State of the office proposed in the resolution was first made in the Eighth Report of the Special Committee on Postwar Economic Policy and Planning of the House of Representatives. A subcommittee of this special committee had traveled extensively abroad and had devoted special consideration to our foreign economic program. It was the conclusion of that committee that an Under Secretary of State for Economic Affairs was necessary if the numerous and difficult problems involved were to be properly handled.

Conclusion

With our allies, we have successfully waged a great war, and we must devote our best efforts to the creation of a secure and lasting peace. If we are to succeed in this task, the conduct of our foreign relations must be efficient and capable. Unless the Secretary of State is authorized to have the assistants he believes are reasonably necessary it will be impossible for him to adequately represent this Government in its dealings with other countries. The establishment of the Office of Under Secretary of State for Economic Affairs will serve to focus the attention on our foreign economic program which it deserves and will provide the assistance which is necessary if the problems involved are to receive the care and vigorous analysis which they require.

(3) *An Act to Establish the Office of Under Secretary of State for Economic Affairs, Approved August 1, 1946.*[1]

Be it enacted by the Senate and House of Representatives of the United States of America in Congress assembled, That there is hereby established in the Department of State for a period of two years following the enactment and approval of this legislation by the President, the Office of Under Secretary of State for Economic Affairs, which shall be filled by appointment by the President, by and with the advice and consent of the Senate. The Under Secretary of State for Economic Affairs shall receive compensation at the rate of $10,000 a year and shall perform such duties as may be prescribed by the Secretary of State. The Under Secretary of State for Economic Affairs shall serve subject to the direction of the Secretary of State and the Under Secretary of State.

[1] Public Law 590, 79th Cong., 2d sess.

5. OFFICE OF THE COUNSELOR OF THE DEPARTMENT OF STATE

On September 5, 1945, President Truman nominated Benjamin V. Cohen to fill the office of Counselor, vacant since the death of R. Walton Moore on February 8, 1941.[1] Mr. Cohen's appointment was confirmed by the Senate on September 14, 1945.[2]

6. OFFICE OF THE ASSISTANT SECRETARY FOR ADMINISTRATION

On October 11, 1945, Frank McCarthy submitted his resignation as Assistant Secretary for Administration.[3] The following day, the Secretary of State announced the assignment of Donald S. Russell to succeed Mr. McCarthy.[4] Mr. Russell had been appointed as Assistant Secretary of State on September 5[5] and his appointment had been confirmed by the Senate on September 14, 1945.[6] Mr. Russell had assumed his duties, prior to his assignment as Assistant Secretary for Administration, on September 24.[7]

Office of Departmental Administration. By Departmental Order 1354, dated October 29 and effective November 1, 1945, there was reestablished in the Office of Departmental Administration, a Division of Communications and Records for the purpose of improving the organization of the Department "by segregating the functions relating to communications and records."[8] This new Division was made responsible "for the formulation of policies and the development and establishment of procedures and regulations governing the dispatch, receipt, and distribution of all correspondence and telegraphic communications that are transmitted via the diplomatic channels (telegraphic or diplomatic pouch) between the United States and other countries."

Office of Foreign Service. For information on the Foreign Service, see this volume, p. 81.

Office of Budget and Finance. The Office of Budget and Finance was established by Departmental Order 1359, dated and effective November 21, 1945, for the purpose of increasing the "budgetary and fiscal operations" of the Department and was made responsible for "the budgetary and fiscal policies and operations of the Department of State, including the Departmental Service, the Foreign Service, international commissions, organizations, and other bodies affiliated with the Department."[9] Certain functions of the UNRRA Operations Branch of the Office of Foreign Liquidation Commissioner were transferred to the UNRRA Division of the Office of Budget and Finance under Departmental Regulation 124.4, effective March 8, 1946.[10] Under the general director of the Office of Budget and Finance and in accordance with the policies established or approved by the Special Assistant to the Assistant Secretary for Economic Affairs, the UNRRA Division was directed to:

A. Have general responsibility for directing the various phases of the UNRRA supply operations through the facilities of U. S. Government procuring agencies.

---

[1] *New York Times,* September 6, 1945, p. 10. See also, *Documents, III, 1940–1941,* p. 758.

[2] Department of State, *Bulletin,* XIII, p. 417.

[3] *Ibid.,* p. 582.

[4] *Ibid.,* p. 558.

[5] *New York Times,* September 6, 1945, p. 10.

[6] Department of State, *Bulletin,* XIII, p. 417.

[7] *Ibid.,* p. 558.

[8] For the text of the order, see *ibid.,* p. 740.

[9] For the text of the order, see *ibid.;* p. 976.

[10] For the text of the regulation, see *ibid.,* p. 1015.

THE CONDUCT OF FOREIGN RELATIONS 57

B. Provide such assistance in regard to the formulation of policies and programs in connection with U. S. participation in UNRRA as may be requested by the Special Assistant.

C. Assist UNRRA in processing relief supply-requirements.

D. Process UNRRA requisitions for supplies to be procured from U. S. contributions to UNRRA.

E. Prepare commitment letters and other procurement documents.

F. Maintain continual liaison with UNRRA and the procuring and servicing agencies on procurement and movement of relief supplies.

G. Maintain adequate accounting and operating records.

H. Prepare periodic and special reports as required by the Special Assistant, and Government agencies and the Congress.

Office of Controls. "In the interest of security and in order to expedite the flow of essential policy information from the files of German, Italian-Fascist, and Japanese official and quasi-official organizations to interested Divisions and Offices of the Department, and to facilitate arrangements with other Allied Governments on investigative procedure for combined exploitation of enemy documents," the responsibility for the collection and processing of information from such sources was centralized, by Departmental Regulation 230.1, effective February 15, 1946, in the Division of Foreign Activity Correlation of the Office of Controls.[1]

7. OFFICE OF THE ASSISTANT SECRETARY FOR CONGRESSIONAL RELATIONS AND INTERNATIONAL CONFERENCES

The position of Assistant Secretary for Congressional Relations and International Conferences has not been filled since the resignation of Dean Acheson from that post on August 13, 1945.[2]

8. OFFICE OF THE ASSISTANT SECRETARY FOR PUBLIC AFFAIRS

Archibald MacLeish, confirmed by the Senate in his appointment as Assistant Secretary for Public Affairs on December 19, 1944,[3] submitted his resignation from that post on August 15, 1945. His resignation was accepted by the President two days later.[4] The nomination of William Benton, Acting Assistant Secretary for Public Affairs, to succeed Mr. MacLeish was sent to the Senate on September 5 [5] and confirmed by that body on September 14, 1945.[6] Mr. Benton assumed his duties on September 17.[7]

Chief among the responsibilities of the Assistant Secretary for Public Affairs is the supervision of the Office of International Information and Cultural Affairs and of the Interim International Information Service, which was established under the Assistant Secretary by Departmental Order 1337, dated and effective September 10, 1945,[8] and pursuant to the provisions of Executive Order 9608 of August 31, 1945.

The following functions were assigned the Office of International Information and Cultural Affairs by Departmental Regulation 132.10, effective December 31, 1945:

A. The promotion among foreign peoples of a better understanding of the aims, policies, and institutions of the United States.

B. The coordination of policy and action for programs of the United States in the field of international information and cultural affairs.

[1] For the text of the regulation, see *ibid.*, XIV, p. 1016.
[2] *New York Times*, August 14, 1945, p. 1.
[3] See *Documents, VII, 1944–1945*, p. 49.
[4] Department of State, *Bulletin*, XIII, p. 273.
[5] *New York Times*, September 6, 1945, p. 10.
[6] Department of State, *Bulletin*, XIII, p. 417.
[7] *Ibid.*, p. 430.
[8] For the text of the order, see *ibid.*, p. 418.

C. The dissemination abroad of information about the United States through all appropriate media.

D. The promotion of freedom of information among peoples.

E. The furtherance of the international exchange of persons, knowledge, and skills.

F. The integration with over-all United States foreign policy of the programs and objectives of other Federal Agencies involving international interchange of persons, knowledge, and skills.[1]

The functions of the divisions within the Office of International Information and Cultural Affairs were redefined by various Departmental Regulations during the period under review. The International Press and Publications Division was charged with the "formulation of operational policy with respect to, and for the conduct of, the participation of the Department in the international dissemination of information through the media of press, publications (excluding books) and related visual techniques";[2] the International Broadcasting Division was made responsible for the same functions with respect to the media of radio broadcasting;[3] and the International Motion Pictures Division performs the same functions through the medium of motion pictures.[4] The Division of International Exchange of Persons was given these same responsibilities "so far as such operations involve the exchange of students, professors, specialists, or other persons and relationships between organizations in the fields of the sciences, letters and arts."[5] The Division of Libraries and Institutes was given identical responsibilities "so far as such operations involve the establishment of, operation of, or the provision of books and other cultural materials for, libraries, cultural centers, schools, or other institutions in foreign lands and for other uses by the missions."[6] Area Divisions for Europe, the Near East and Africa, the Far East, the American Republics and the Occupied Areas were made responsible for "the initial planning of, and the general supervision of, all programs of OIC conducted in foreign lands."[7]

On June 30, 1946, the Department of State announced the transfer of the control of cultural affairs, including information, education and religion, in Germany, Austria, Japan and Korea to the Civil Affairs Division of the War Department. The Office of International Information and Cultural Affairs retained world-wide responsibility in radio operations for the occupied areas, while the Civil Affairs Division maintained policy liaison with the Office.[8]

For further information on the cultural relations program of the Department of State, see this volume, p. 752 and 757.

Under a Departmental Regulation, effective September 16, 1946,[9] the responsibility for the formulation and coordination of policy and programs concerning the public aspects of foreign relations was assigned to the Office of Public Affairs and its four subordinate divisions: Public Liaison, Public Studies, Historical Policy Research, and Publications. The Division of Public

[1] For the text of the regulation, see *ibid.*, XIV, p. 42.

[2] Departmental Regulation 132.11, effective December 31, 1945; for the text of the regulation, see *ibid.*, p. 43.

[3] Departmental Regulation 132.12, effective December 31, 1945; for the text of the regulation, see *ibid.*

[4] Departmental Regulation 132.13, effective December 31, 1945; for the text of the regulation, see *ibid.*, p. 44.

[5] Departmental Regulation 132.14, effective December 31, 1945; for the text of the regulation, see *ibid.*

[6] Departmental Regulation 132.15, effective December 31, 1945; for the text of the regulation, see *ibid.*, p. 45.

[7] Departmental Regulation 132.16, effective December 31, 1945; for the text of the regulation, see *ibid.*

[8] *New York Times*, July 1, 1946, p. 12.

[9] Departmental Regulation 132.20; for the text of the regulation, see Department of State, *Bulletin*, XV, p. 728.

Liaison maintains liaison with editors and writers, authors and publishers, radio commentators and radio networks, motion picture producers, Department and non-governmental organizations and groups for the purpose of making available, upon request, information concerning American foreign policy. The Division also makes available to Congress and other Government agencies background information, arranges speaking engagements for Department officers, and prepares replies to public-comment mail concerning foreign policy.[1] The Division of Public Studies analyzes "every available type of public expression," prepares for policy officers reports on public attitudes, advises policy officers regarding public attitudes and opinion, and makes recommendations on the basis of its analyses for the development of information policy leading to the maximum of public understanding of foreign policy questions.[2] The Division of Historical Policy Research formulates and executes "policy with respect to Departmental research in the field of American foreign policy, historically considered."[3] The Division of Publications initiates and coordinates the publication policy of the Department and executes the publication program.[4]

(1) *Statement by the Assistant Secretary for Public Affairs (Benton) on His Duties and Responsibilities, September 18, 1945.*[5]

In his Executive order of August 31, President Truman transferred to the State Department many functions of the Office of War Information and the Office of Inter-American Affairs. He said he wanted the rest of the world to "receive a full and fair picture of American life and of the aims and policies of the United States Government."

President Truman's Executive order is renewed recognition of a new factor in foreign affairs. The development of modern means of communication has brought the peoples of the world into direct contact each with the other. Foreign relations are being conducted in public to an accelerated degree. I believe it is inevitable that this trend will continue. Friendship between the leaders and the diplomats of the world is important, but it is not enough. The peoples themselves must strive to understand each other. Open and public debate — through the newspapers, the magazines, the radio, and other forms of communication between peoples — is perhaps the most important development in the history of our diplomatic efforts abroad.

The war has dramatized once more the superlative economic strength of the United States. The advent of atomic power, with American science in the forefront of research, means that we have become — temporarily at least — the most powerful military nation on earth. Such strength could easily generate suspicion and dislike abroad. Thus we face one of the great challenges of our history. Morally, spiritually, and intellectually we must rise to the responsibilities inherent in our economic and political strength. And we must make clear to all the world that we propose to use our strength, and the force of our example, constructively and in the interest of the well-being of all mankind.

[1] Departmental Regulation 132.21; for the text of the regulation, see *ibid.*
[2] Departmental Regulation 132.22; for the text of the regulation, see *ibid.*, p. 729.
[3] Departmental Regulation 132.23; for the text of the regulation, see *ibid.*
[4] Departmental Regulation 132.24; for the text of the regulation, see *ibid.*
[5] *Ibid.*, XIII, p. 430.

We must strive to interpret ourselves abroad through a program of education and of cultural exchange. Our objective as a free people must be to avoid the taint of special pleading but to aim at better understanding of our democratic processes. We must support the free press and the radio in this objective. We must seek clarification and avoid propaganda. Further, here at home we must strive for a better understanding of the other peoples of the world, with whom we want to live in peace and cannot live in peace unless we achieve mutual understanding. Our processes in foreign relations must be exposed to the insight of the common man: his conscience and intelligence must be drawn into the State Department.

It will be my privilege under Secretary Byrnes' direction to try to develop an organization within the State Department which will assist Secretary Byrnes and the Department to carry out the spirit of President Truman's directive and the plans of Secretary Byrnes for the development of our relations with all the peoples of the world.

9. OFFICE OF THE ASSISTANT SECRETARY FOR AMERICAN REPUBLIC AFFAIRS

On August 25, 1945, President Truman accepted the resignation of Nelson A. Rockefeller from the office of Assistant Secretary for American Republic Affairs and nominated to succeed him Spruille Braden, former ambassador of the United States to Argentina.[1] Confirmation of Mr. Braden's appointment was received from the Senate on September 22.[2] Mr. Braden assumed his duties on October 29, 1945.[3]

10. OFFICE OF THE ASSISTANT SECRETARY FOR OCCUPIED AREAS

President Truman accepted the resignation of J. C. Holmes as Assistant Secretary for Occupied Areas on August 17, 1945.[4] Maj. Gen. John H. Hilldring was appointed his successor on February 27, 1946,[5] and was confirmed by the Senate on April 11, 1946.[6]

The Assistant Secretary for Occupied Areas is held directly responsible to the Secretary of State for the coordination of State Department policy with respect to the occupation of Germany, Austria, Japan and Korea. In this capacity, he serves as the representative of the Department of State on the State-War-Navy Coordinating Committee [7] and as the Chairman of the Policy Committee on Arms and Armaments. The coordination of Departmental policy in occupation matters is accomplished through the Assistant Secretary and two Secretariats under his direction: the Germany-Austria Secretariat and the Japan-Korea Secretariat. Each Secretariat includes appropriate membership from the Offices of Research and Intelligence, International Information and Cultural Affairs, European Affairs, Far Eastern Affairs, Economic Security Policy, Financial and Development Policy, the Legal Adviser, and such other offices as the Chairman of the Secretariat may designate.[8] As

---

[1] *Ibid.*, p. 219; for the text of Mr. Rockefeller's letter of resignation and the texts of President Truman's and Secretary Byrnes' replies thereto, see *ibid.*
[2] *Ibid.*, p. 705.   [3] *Ibid.*, p. 714.   [4] *Ibid.*, p. 272.
[5] *Ibid.*, XIV, p. 369.   [6] *Ibid.*, p. 736.
[7] *Ibid.*, p. 1132; for information on the State-War-Navy-Coordinating Committee, see this volume, p. 63.
[8] Departmental Regulation 134.1, effective April 8, 1946; for the text of the regulation, see Department of State, *Bulletin*, XIV, p. 1132. See also *Directive on Organization and Procedure for the Development and Promulgation of United States Policy with Respect to Occupied Areas*, released to the press April 17, 1946, *ibid.*, p. 734.

Chairman of the Policy Committee on Arms and Armaments the Assistant Secretary is responsible for coordination of all Department policy in those fields. The Committee consists of a representative of the Assistant Secretary for Economic Affairs; representatives of the geographical offices of the Department; representatives of the Offices of Special Political Affairs and of Controls; and a Deputy Chairman and Executive Chairman designated by the Chairman.[1]

11. OFFICE OF THE ASSISTANT SECRETARY FOR ECONOMIC AFFAIRS

With the elevation of William Clayton to the post of Under Secretary of State for Economic Affairs,[2] Williard L. Thorp received the appointment to the position of Assistant Secretary for Economic Affairs and assumed his duties on November 15, 1946.[3]

Deputy on Financial Affairs. By a Departmental Order, dated October 19 and effective October 20, 1945,[4] there was established under the Assistant Secretary for Economic Affairs a Deputy on Financial Affairs to coordinate the work of the Office of Financial and Development Policy with that of the Office of Economic Security Policy and to coordinate the policy of the Office of Foreign Liquidation with the policy of the other two offices.

Special Assistant to the Assistant Secretary for Economic Affairs. Departmental Regulation 131.2, effective March 15, 1946,[5] assigned to the Special Assistant the following responsibilities: (1) to advise and assist the Assistant Secretary on assigned aspects of relations of the Department with other departments and agencies, international bodies, and other Government bodies; (2) to act as alternate for the Assistant Secretary on all UNRRA matters; (3) to act as primary liaison between the Department and UNRRA; (4) to establish, approve or generally guide the execution of all policies and programs of the UNRRA Division of the Office of Budget and Finance; (5) to exercise, with some exceptions, the authority and perform the functions relating to expenditure of funds and provision of supplies and services relating to United States participation in UNRRA; and (6) to execute documents on behalf of the Department relating to the discharge of the responsibility delegated to the Special Assistant in respect of UNRRA.

Office of Economic Security Policy. The Office of Economic Security Policy was established under the Assistant Secretary for Economic Affairs in order to initiate, formulate and coordinate economic security policy, including the economic aspects of the occupation of Germany, Austria, Japan and Korea.[6] The Division of Economic Security Controls deals with foreign funds or properties, export control, control and disposition of enemy property in the United States and elsewhere, prevention of concealment or flight of enemy assets and capital, protection or restoration of patents and copyrights affected by the war, administration of financial and economic controls in accordance with various Inter-American Conferences, and collection and evaluation of biographic data. The Division of German and Austrian Economic Affairs and the Division of Japanese and Korean Economic Affairs have responsibility, with regard to their respective areas, for economic and financial matters related to occupation and control of those areas, reparations, restitution, and economic and financial aspects of the peace treaties insofar as they concern their respective countries.[7]

---

[1] Departmental Regulation 183.8, effective May 20, 1946; for the text of the regulation, see *ibid.*, p. 1096.
[2] See this volume, p. 51.
[3] Department of State, *Bulletin*, XV, p. 1115.
[4] Departmental Order 1344; for the text of the order, see *ibid.*, XIII, p. 703.
[5] For the text of the regulation, see *ibid.*, XIV, p. 1015.
[6] Departmental Order 1346, dated October 19 and effective October 20, 1945; for the text of the order, see *ibid.*, XIII, p. 703.
[7] *Ibid.*

Office of Foreign Liquidation Commissioner. With the transfer of jurisdiction over surplus property to the Department of State, there was established within the Department an Interim Foreign Economic and Liquidation Service to discharge the newly acquired duties of the Department.[1] The Office of Foreign Liquidation was established at the same time [2] and the Foreign Liquidation Commissioner was given the "authority now or hereafter vested in the Secretary of State to dispose of, subject to the authority of the Surplus Property Administrator under the Surplus Property Act of 1944, all surplus property, including scrap salvage, waste materials, property captured from the enemy, and surplus property of Lend-Lease origin, in the control of or for the disposal of which the Department of State may be responsible, located in foreign areas."[3]

For further information on foreign surplus disposal, see this volume, p. 158.

12. OFFICE OF THE LEGAL ADVISER

On April 2, 1946, the Secretary of State announced the appointment of Charles Fahy, former Solicitor General and Director of the Legal Division of the Office of the Military Governor for Germany (United States), to the office of Legal Adviser of the Department of State to succeed Green H. Hackworth following the latter's election to the International Court of Justice.[4] Mr. Fahy assumed his duties on May 15 and his appointment was confirmed by the Senate on June 13, 1946.[5]

B. Appropriations

(1) *Comparative Statement of State Department Appropriations for 1946 and 1947.*[6]

Title of Appropriation	Appropriations for 1946	Appropriations for 1947	(+) Increase (−) Decrease for 1947
Department proper	$13,797,320.00	$44,437,121.00	+$30,639,801.00
Foreign Service	46,115,870.00	52,663,000.00	+6,547,130.00
Emergency Fund	17,500,000.00	9,000,000.00	−8,500,000.00
Foreign Service Buildings	1,000,000.00	1,000,000.00	
International Obligations	21,372,266.96	28,254,514.60[7]	+6,882,247.64
Cooperation with the American Republics	4,098,370.00	5,375,000.00	+1,276,630.00
Claims	22,791.06	2,783.31	−20,007.75
Totals	103,906,618.02[8]	140,732,418.91	+36,825,800.89[9]

[1] Departmental Order 1343, dated October 19 and effective October 20, 1945; for the text of the order, see *ibid.*

[2] Departmental Order 1345, dated October 19 and effective October 20, 1945; for the text of the order, see *ibid.*

[3] Departmental Order 1347, dated and effective October 20, 1945; for the text of the order, see *ibid.*, p. 704.

[4] Department of State Press Release, April 2, 1946.

[5] Department of State, *Bulletin*, XIV, p. 1097.

[6] From information furnished by the Department of State, Division of Organization and Budget.

[7] This figure does not include salaries and expenses for Philippine Rehabilitation in the amount of $47,918,000, bringing the total of appropriations for 1947 to $188,650,418.91.

[8] This figure does not include transfers from war agencies in the amount of $40,842,002, bringing the total of appropriations of 1946 to $144,748,620.02.

[9] Adjusted as shown in notes (2) and (3) the increase of 1947 appropriations over 1946 is +$43,901,798.89.

THE CONDUCT OF FOREIGN RELATIONS   63

3. OTHER AGENCIES

A. State-War-Navy Coordinating Committee [1]

The State-War-Navy Coordinating Committee was established in December, 1944 as the result of an exchange of letters between the Secretaries of the three Departments, for the purpose of "improving existing methods of obtaining for the State Department advice on politico-military matters in which all have a common interest, particularly those involving foreign policy and relations with foreign nations." The authority of the Committee, in October 1945, was defined and formalized in a memorandum signed by the three Secretaries.[2]

The Committee is composed of the Assistant Secretary of State for Occupied Areas as Chairman in all matters of occupation policy [3] or the Assistant Secretary of State for European, Far Eastern, Near Eastern and African Affairs as Chairman for matters not pertaining to occupation policy; [4] of the Assistant Secretary of War; and of the Under Secretary of the Navy. The Secretariat for the Committee consists of three officers from each of the Departments and supporting force of WAVES, WAC and civilian personnel. Subcommittees consider matters pertaining to particular geographic areas or special projects; ad hoc committees have been created for effecting collaboration between the Departments on certain phases of policy. In addition to those dealing with geographic regions there are standing subcommittees for Technical Information Security Control and for Rearmament.

Prior to the end of the war, the existence of the Committee was a confidential matter for security and other reasons.

The subjects dealt with by the Committee are not limited either as to nature or to geographic location. Although originally intended as an aid to the Department of State, the Committee has also been used by the War and Navy Departments and the Joint Chiefs of Staff for advising the military on political aspects of particular problems. The Committee has proven of value in coordinating inter-departmental views for the purpose of determining policy for presentation of United States proposals at international conferences. The Committee was also used as a means of obtaining United States viewpoints on subjects of politico-military nature brought up before the European Advisory Commission during its existence in London,[5] and similar cooperation is possible between the Committee and the Far Eastern Commission.

On August 30, 1945, President Truman transferred to the Committee the functions of the Informal Policy Committee on Germany.[6] This latter Committee had evolved in the interval between the Crimea Conference and the Potsdam Conference for the purpose of formulating policy for the control of Germany.[7] Its evolution began with a memorandum from President Roosevelt to the Secretary of State (Stettinius) on February 28, 1945 asking the Secretary to "assume the responsibility for seeing that the conclusions, exclusive of course of military matters, reached at the Crimea Conference, be carried forward." In discharging this responsibility the Secretary was instructed "to confer with other officials

---

[1] This note depends largely upon an article on the State-War-Navy Coordinating Committee, appearing in the Department of State, *Bulletin*, XIII, p. 745, which was written by Harold W. Moseley (Department of State), Col. Charles W. McCarthy (War Department) and Com. Alvin F. Richardson (Navy Department), all members of the secretariat of SWNCC.

[2] For the text of this memorandum, see this volume, p. 64.

[3] See Department of State, *Bulletin*, XIII, p. 734, for the text of the Department of State Directive of April 8, 1946, appointing the Assistant Secretary for Occupied Areas to the post. See also, *ibid.*, XV, p. 47.

[4] *Ibid.*

[5] See *Documents, VI, 1943–1944,* p. 14, 34, 184, 242; and *ibid., VII, 1944–1945,* p. 189, 351, 364.

[6] Department of State, *Bulletin*, XV, p. 292.

[7] *Ibid.*, p. 291.

of this Government on matters touching upon their respective fields."[1] The directive was communicated to the Secretaries of War, Navy, and Treasury and to the Foreign Economic Administrator on March 12, 1945.[2] The outgrowth of this exchange of directives was the Informal Policy Committee on Germany, composed of representatives of the five government agencies mentioned above, which held its first meeting on April 15, 1945. With the issuing of the communiqué from Potsdam by President Truman, Prime Minister Attlee and Premier Stalin [3] and with the determination at that conference of agreed policies for the control of Germany, the Informal Policy Committee was absorbed into the State-War-Navy Coordinating Committee.

The basis of policy upon Japanese occupation is the statement of initial postsurrender policy which was prepared by the State-War-Navy Coordinating Committee for transmittal to General MacArthur on September 6, 1945, and was released by the White House on September 22 as "United States Initial Post-Surrender Policy for Japan."[4]

(1) *Memorandum of the Secretary of State (Byrnes), the Secretary of War (Patterson) and the Secretary of the Navy (Forrestal) Defining the Authority of the State-War-Navy Coordinating Committee, October 16, 1945.*[5]

The State-War-Navy Coordinating Committee is designated as the agency to reconcile and coordinate the action to be taken by the State, War and Navy Departments on matters of common interest and, under the guidance of the Secretaries of State, War and the Navy, establish policies on politico-military questions referred to it.

Action taken by the Coordinating Committee will be construed as action taken in the names of the Secretaries of State, War and the Navy. Subject to approval of the President where appropriate, decisions of the Committee will establish the approved policy of the State, War and Navy Departments. Dissemination of the decisions of the Committee will be accomplished by the three departments for the information and guidance of all concerned and, where appropriate, with necessary instructions for action.

B. Other Executive Departments

The role of the Executive agencies other than the Department of State in the formulation of foreign policy was somewhat clarified as a result of an address delivered by the Secretary of Commerce, Henry A. Wallace, in New York on September 12, 1946. Declaring that "just two days ago, when President Truman read these words, he said that they represented the policy of his Administration."[6] Mr. Wallace, in the course of his address, presented views, particularly with regard to policy toward the Soviet Union, which almost immediately caused the Administration to deny that the address constituted "a statement of the foreign policy of this government."[7] The situation was made more significant by the fact that Mr. Wallace's talk was delivered during the Paris Conference of Twenty-One Nations at a time when, in the eyes of Congressional leaders, there should have been no division on policy at home nor any doubt as to the unity and authority of the policy enunciated by Secretary of State Byrnes in Paris.

[1] *Ibid.*   [2] *Ibid.*
[3] For the text of the Potsdam Declaration, see this volume, Appendix II.
[4] For the text of this statement, see *ibid.*, p. 267.
[5] Department of State, *Bulletin*, XIII, p. 747.
[6] *New York Times*, September 13, 1946, p. 4.
[7] *Ibid.*, September 15, 1946, p. 1.

THE CONDUCT OF FOREIGN RELATIONS   65

Announcing that there was "no change in the established foreign policy of our Government" President Truman, on September 14, said that he had "approved the right of the Secretary of Commerce to deliver the speech" but did not "intend to indicate that I approved the speech as constituting a statement of the foreign policy of this country." [1] The Department of State, at the same time, denied any knowledge of the text of the speech prior to the time it was handed to the press.

(1) *Statement by the Senate Adviser to the United States Delegation to the Conference of Twenty-One Nations (Connally), Paris, September 14, 1946.*[2]

The task of Secretary Byrnes is difficult at most.

He has performed his duties with real ability, splendid tact and remarkable patience.

He has advanced and protected United States interests, and has sought a stable and just peace.

It has been generally understood that at no time has there been any disagreement with President Truman's policy. He deserves and should have the support of the united peoples in the United States.

There is no place in our international relations either for partisan politics or for intraparty division or personal ambitions.

While we are striving desperately for peace in the world there should be no controversy or bickering or strife at home. If the United States is to speak with a persuasive and influential voice in the peace conference there must be no division behind the lines.

(2) *Statement by the Senate Adviser to the United States Delegation to the Conference of Twenty-One Nations (Vandenberg), Paris, September 14, 1946.*[3]

The authority of American foreign policy is dependent upon the degree of American unity behind it. Rightly or wrongly, Paris is doubtful of this unity this morning.

Our bi-partisan foreign policy during the last eighteen months has had overwhelming bi-partisan support in behalf of the unselfish aim for which we fought the war. Though differing in some points, most Republicans have been glad to join with most Democrats in thus presenting a united American front to the world. This is the only road to organized peace and collective security.

Those who leave this road jeopardize the very objective which they profess to embrace.

I am sure most Republicans, despite inevitable differences in some aspects, will be glad to continue to seek unity with the Administration in a bi-partisan foreign policy on a sound American basis which rejected dictatorship by anybody, which is neither hostile nor subservient to any other power on earth, and which defends human rights and fundamental freedom.

But the situation equally requires unity within the Administration itself. We can only cooperate with one Secretary of State at a time.

[1] *Ibid.*   [2] *Ibid.*   [3] *Ibid.*

(3) *Statement by the President (Truman), September 20, 1946.*[1]

The foreign policy of this country is the most important question confronting us today. Our responsibility for obtaining a just and lasting peace extends not only to the people of this country but to the nations of the world.

The people of the United States may disagree freely and publicly on any question, including that of foreign policy, but the Government of the United States must stand as a unit in its relations with the rest of the world.

I have today asked Mr. Wallace to resign from the Cabinet. It had become clear that between his views on foreign policy and those of the administration — the latter being shared, I am confident, by the great body of our citizens — there was a fundamental conflict. We could not permit this conflict to jeopardize our position in relation to other countries. I deeply regret the breaking of a long and pleasant official association, but I am sure that Mr. Wallace will be happier in the exercise of his right to present his views as a private citizen. I am confirmed in this belief by a very friendly conversation I had with Mr. Wallace on the telephone this morning.

Our foreign policy as established by the Congress, the President and the Secretary of State remains in full force and effect without change. No change in our foreign policy is contemplated. No member of the executive branch of the government will make any public statement as to foreign policy which is in conflict with our established foreign policy. Any public statement on foreign policy shall be cleared with the Department of State. In case of disagreement, the matter will be referred to me.

As I have frequently said, I have complete confidence in Mr. Byrnes and his delegation now representing this country at the Paris Peace Conference.

Mr. Byrnes consults with me often and the policies which guide him and his delegation have my full endorsement.

4. INTERNATIONAL ORGANIZATIONS AND CONFERENCES

A. Privileges and Immunities of International Organizations

Following a preliminary vote by the United Nations favoring the United States as the location of the permanent headquarters of the Organization, Rep. Robert L. Doughton (North Carolina) introduced in the House of Representatives on October 24, 1945, "A Bill to extend certain privileges, exemptions, and immunities to international organizations and to the officers and employees thereof, and for other purposes" (H.R. 4489).[2] The Bill was reported favorably without amendment by the Ways and Means Committee of the House on November 12[3] and debate in the House opened on November 20, 1945.[4] The Bill was passed by the House on the same day.[5] H. R. 4489 was referred to the Senate

[1] Department of State, *Bulletin*, XV, p. 577.
[2] *Congressional Record*, 91, p. 10197 (Daily edition, October 24, 1945).
[3] *Ibid.*, p. 10783 (Daily edition, November 12, 1945); House Report No. 1203, 79th Cong., 1st sess.
[4] *Congressional Record*, 91, p. 11041 (Daily edition, November 20, 1945).
[5] *Ibid.*, p. 11043.

THE CONDUCT OF FOREIGN RELATIONS   67

on November 23, 1945 [1] and reported favorably with amendments by the Committee on Finance on December 18, 1945.[2] The amendments submitted by Committee were agreed to by the Senate and the Bill was passed by that body on December 20, 1945.[3]

The House concurred in the Senate amendments the following day, December 21 [4] and the Bill was approved by the President on December 29, 1945.[5] Pursuant to the provisions of the Act, the President, by Executive Order of February 19, 1946,[6] designated those agencies entitled to enjoy the privileges, exemptions and immunities which the Act specified.

(1) *An Act to Extend Certain Privileges, Exemptions, and Immunities to International Organizations and to the Officers and Employees Thereof, and for Other Purposes, Approved December 29, 1945.*[7]

Be it enacted by the Senate and House of Representatives of the United States of America in Congress assembled,

TITLE I

SECTION 1. For the purposes of this title, the term "international organization" means a public international organization in which the United States participates pursuant to any treaty or under the authority of any Act of Congress authorizing such participation or making an appropriation for such participation, and which shall have been designated by the President through appropriate Executive order as being entitled to enjoy the privileges, exemptions, and immunities herein provided. The President shall be authorized, in the light of the functions performed by any such international organization, by appropriate Executive order to withhold or withdraw from any such organization or its officers or employees any of the privileges, exemptions, and immunities provided for in this title (including the amendments made by this title) or to condition or limit the enjoyment by any such organization or its officers or employees of any such privilege, exemption, or immunity. The President shall be authorized, if in his judgment such action should be justified by reason of the abuse by an international organization or its officers and employees of the privileges, exemptions, and immunities herein provided or for any other reason, at any time to revoke the designation of any international organization under this section, whereupon the international organization in question shall cease to be classed as an international organization for the purposes of this title.

[1] *Ibid.*, p. 11073 (Daily edition, November 23, 1945).
[2] *Ibid.*, p. 12417 (Daily edition, December 18, 1945); Senate Report No. 861, 79th Cong., 1st sess.
[3] *Congressional Record*, 91, p. 12609 (Daily edition, December 20, 1945).
[4] *Ibid.*, p. 12709 (Daily edition, December 21, 1945).
[5] Public Law 291, 79th Cong., 1st sess.
[6] Executive Order 9698; for the text of the Order, see this volume, p. 73.
[7] Public Law 291, 79th Cong., 1st sess.

SEC. 2. International organizations shall enjoy the status, immunities, exemptions, and privileges set forth in this section, as follows:

(*a*) International organizations shall, to the extent consistent with the instrument creating them, possess the capacity —
  (*i*) to contract;
  (*ii*) to acquire and dispose of real and personal property;
  (*iii*) to institute legal proceedings.

(*b*) International organizations, their property and their assets, wherever located, and by whomsoever held, shall enjoy the same immunity from suit and every form of judicial process as is enjoyed by foreign governments, except to the extent that such organizations may expressly waive their immunity for the purpose of any proceedings or by the terms of any contract.

(*c*) Property and assets of international organizations, wherever located and by whomsoever held, shall be immune from search, unless such immunity be expressly waived, and from confiscation. The archives of international organizations shall be inviolable.

(*d*) Insofar as concerns customs duties and internal-revenue taxes imposed upon or by reason of importation, and the procedures in connection therewith; the registration of foreign agents; and the treatment of official communications, the privileges, exemptions, and immunities to which international organizations shall be entitled shall be those accorded under similar circumstances to foreign governments.

SEC. 3. Pursuant to regulations prescribed by the Commissioner of Customs with the approval of the Secretary of the Treasury, the baggage and effects of alien officers and employees of international organizations, or of aliens designated by foreign governments to serve as their representatives in or to such organizations, or of the families, suites, and servants of such officers, employees, or representatives shall be admitted (when imported in connection with the arrival of the owner) free of customs duties and free of internal-revenue taxes imposed upon or by reason of importation.

SEC. 4. The Internal Revenue Code is hereby amended as follows:

(*a*) Effective with respect to taxable years beginning after December 31, 1943, section 116 (*c*), relating to the exclusion from gross income of income of foreign governments, is amended to read as follows:

"(*c*) INCOME OF FOREIGN GOVERNMENTS AND OF INTERNATIONAL ORGANIZATIONS. — The income of foreign governments or international organizations received from investments in the United States in stocks, bonds, or other domestic securities, owned by such foreign governments or by international organizations, or from interest on deposits in banks in the United States of moneys belonging to such foreign governments or international organizations, or from any other source within the United States."

(*b*) Effective with respect to taxable years beginning after December 31, 1943, section 116 (*h*) (1), relating to the exclusion from gross income of amounts paid employees of foreign governments, is amended to read as follows:

"(1) RULE FOR EXCLUSION. — Wages, fees, or salary of any employee of a foreign government or of an international organization or of the Commonwealth of the Philippines (including a consular or other officer, or a nondiplomatic representative), received as compensation for official services to such government, international organization, or such Commonwealth —

"(A) If such employee is not a citizen of the United States, or is a citizen of the Commonwealth of the Philippines (whether or not a citizen of the United States); and

"(B) If, in the case of an employee of a foreign government or of the Commonwealth of the Philippines, the services are of a character similar to those performed by employees of the Government of the United States in foreign countries or in the Commonwealth of the Philippines, as the case may be; and

"(C) If, in the case of an employee of a foreign government or the Commonwealth of the Philippines, the foreign government or the Commonwealth grants an equivalent exemption to employees of the Government of the United States performing similar services in such foreign country or such Commonwealth, as the case may be."

(c) Effective January 1, 1946, section 1426 (b), defining the term "employment" for the purposes of the Federal Insurance Contributions Act, is amended (1) by striking out the word "or" at the end of paragraph (14), (2) by striking out the period at the end of paragraph (15) and inserting in lieu thereof a semicolon and the word "or", and (3) by inserting at the end of the subsection the following new paragraph:

"(16) Service performed in the employ of an international organization."

(d) Effective January 1, 1946, section 1607 (c), defining the term "employment" for the purposes of the Federal Unemployment Tax Act, is amended (1) by striking out the word "or" at the end of paragraph (14), (2) by striking out the period at the end of paragraph (15) and inserting in lieu thereof a semicolon and the word "or", and (3) by inserting at the end of the subsection the following new paragraph:

"(16) Service performed in the employ of an international organization."

(e) Section 1621 (a) (5), relating to the definition of "wages" for the purpose of collection of income tax at the source, is amended by inserting after the words "foreign government" the words "or an international organization".

(f) Section 3466 (a), relating to exemption from communications taxes is amended by inserting immediately after the words "the District of Columbia" a comma and the words "or an international organization".

(g) Section 3469 (f) (1), relating to exemption from the tax on transportation of persons, is amended by inserting immediately after the words "the District of Columbia" a comma and the words "or an international organization".

(h) Section 3475 (b) (1), relating to exemption from the tax on transportation of property, is amended by inserting immediately after the words "the District of Columbia" a comma and the words "or an international organization".

(i) Section 3797 (a), relating to definitions, is amended by adding at the end thereof a new paragraph as follows:

"(18) INTERNATIONAL ORGANIZATION. — The term 'international organization' means a public international organization entitled to enjoy privileges, exemptions, and immunities as an international organization under the International Organizations Immunities Act."

SEC. 5. (a) Effective January 1, 1946, section 209 (b) of the Social Security Act, defining the term "employment" for the purposes of title II of the Act, is amended (1) by striking out the word "or" at the end of paragraph (14), (2) by striking out the period at the end of paragraph (15) and inserting in lieu thereof a semicolon and the word "or", and (3) by inserting at the end of the subsection the following new paragraph:

"(16) Service performed in the employ of an international organization entitled to enjoy privileges, exemptions, and immunities as an international organization under the International Organizations Immunities Act."

(b) No tax shall be collected under title VIII or IX of the Social Security Act or under the Federal Insurance Contributions Act or the Federal Unemployment Tax Act, with respect to services rendered prior to January 1, 1946, which are described in paragraph (16) of sections 1426 (b) and 1607 (c) of the Internal Revenue Code, as amended, and any such tax heretofore collected (including penalty and interest with respect thereto, if any) shall be refunded in accordance with the provisions of law applicable in the case of erroneous or illegal collection of the tax. No interest shall be allowed or paid on the amount of any such refund. No payment shall be made under title II of the Social Security Act with respect to services rendered prior to January 1, 1946, which are described in paragraph (16) of section 209 (b) of such Act, as amended.

SEC. 6. International organizations shall be exempt from all property taxes imposed by, or under the authority of, any Act of Congress, including such Acts as are applicable solely to the District of Columbia or the Territories.

SEC. 7. (a) Persons designated by foreign governments to serve as their representatives in or to international organizations and the officers and employees of such organizations, and members of the immediate families of such representatives, officers, and employees residing with them, other than nationals of the United States, shall, insofar as concerns laws regulating entry into and departure from the United States, alien registration and fingerprinting, and the registration of foreign agents, be entitled to the same privileges, exemptions, and immunities as are accorded under similar circumstances to officers and employees, respectively, of foreign governments, and members of their families.

(b) Representatives of foreign governments in or to international organizations and officers and employees of such organizations shall be immune from suit and legal process relating to acts performed by them in their official capacity and falling within their functions as such representatives, officers, or employees except insofar as such immunity may be waived by the foreign government or international organization concerned.

THE CONDUCT OF FOREIGN RELATIONS 71

(*c*) Section 3 of the Immigration Act approved May 26, 1924, as amended (U. S. C., title 8, sec. 203), is hereby amended by striking out the period at the end thereof and inserting in lieu thereof a comma and the following: "and (7) a representative of a foreign government in or to an international organization entitled to enjoy privileges, exemptions, and immunities as an international organization under the International Organizations Immunities Act, or an alien officer or employee of such an international organization, and the family, attendants, servants, and employees of such a representative, officer, or employee".

(*d*) Section 15 of the Immigration Act approved May 26, 1924, as amended (U. S. C., title 8, sec. 215), is hereby amended to read as follows:

"SEC. 15. The admission to the United States of an alien excepted from the class of immigrants by clause (1), (2), (3), (4), (5), (6), or (7) of section 3, or declared to be a nonquota immigrant by subdivision (*e*) of section 4, shall be for such time and under such conditions as may be by regulations prescribed (including, when deemed necessary for the classes mentioned in clause (2), (3), (4), or (6) of section 3 and subdivision (*e*) of section 4, the giving of bond with sufficient surety, in such sum and containing such conditions as may be by regulations prescribed) to insure that, at the expiration of such time or upon failure to maintain the status under which admitted, he will depart from the United States: *Provided*, That no alien who has been, or who may hereafter be, admitted into the United States under clause (1) or (7) of section 3, as an official of a foreign government, or as a member of the family of such official, or as a representative of a foreign government in or to an international organization or an officer or employee of an international organization, or as a member of the family of such representative, officer, or employee, shall be required to depart from the United States without the approval of the Secretary of State."

SEC. 8. (*a*) No person shall be entitled to the benefits of this title unless he (1) shall have been duly notified to and accepted by the Secretary of State as a representative, officer, or employee; or (2) shall have been designated by the Secretary of State, prior to formal notification and acceptance, as a prospective representative, officer, or employee; or (3) is a member of the family or suite, or servant, of one of the foregoing accepted or designated representatives, officers, or employees.

(*b*) Should the Secretary of State determine that the continued presence in the United States of any person entitled to the benefits of this title is not desirable, he shall so inform the foreign government or international organization concerned, as the case may be, and after such person shall have had a reasonable length of time, to be determined by the Secretary of State, to depart from the United States, he shall cease to be entitled to such benefits.

(*c*) No person shall, by reason of the provisions of this title, be considered as receiving diplomatic status or as receiving any of the privileges incident thereto other than such as are specifically set forth herein.

SEC. 9. The privileges, exemptions, and immunities of international organizations and of their officers and employees, and members of their families, suites, and servants, provided for in this title, shall be granted notwithstanding the fact that the similar privileges, exemptions, and immunities granted to a foreign government, its officers, or employees, may be conditioned upon the existence of reciprocity by that foreign government: *Provided,* That nothing contained in this title shall be construed as precluding the Secretary of State from withdrawing the privileges, exemptions, and immunities herein provided from persons who are nationals of any foreign country on the ground that such country is failing to accord corresponding privileges, exemptions, and immunities to citizens of the United States.

SEC. 10. This title may be cited as the "International Organizations Immunities Act".

TITLE II

SEC. 201. EXTENSION OF TIME FOR CLAIMING CREDIT OR REFUND WITH RESPECT TO WAR LOSSES.

If a claim for credit or refund under the internal revenue laws relates to an overpayment on account of the deductibility by the tax-payer of a loss in respect of property considered destroyed or seized under section 127 (*a*) of the Internal Revenue Code (relating to war losses) for a taxable year beginning in 1941 or 1942, the three-year period of limitation prescribed in section 322 (*b*) (1) of the Internal Revenue Code shall in no event expire prior to December 31, 1946. In the case of such a claim filed on or before December 31, 1946, the amount of the credit or refund may exceed the portion of the tax paid within the period provided in section 322 (*b*) (2) or (3) of such code, whichever is applicable, to the extent of the amount of the overpayment attributable to the deductibility of the loss described in this section.

SEC. 202. CONTRIBUTIONS TO PENSION TRUSTS.

(*a*) DEDUCTIONS FOR THE TAXABLE YEAR 1942 UNDER PRIOR INCOME TAX ACTS. — Section 23 (*p*) (2) of the Internal Revenue Code is amended by striking out the words "January 1, 1943" and inserting in lieu thereof "January 1, 1942", and by striking out the words "December 31, 1942" and inserting in lieu thereof "December 31, 1941".

(*b*) EFFECTIVE DATE. — The amendment made by this section shall be applicable as if it had been made as a part of section 162 (*b*) of the Revenue Act of 1942.

SEC. 203. PETITION TO THE TAX COURT OF THE UNITED STATES.

(*a*) TIME FOR FILING PETITION. — The second sentences of sections 272 (*a*) (1), 732 (*a*), 871 (*a*) (1), and 1012 (*a*) (1), respectively, of the Internal Revenue Code are amended by striking out the parenthetical expression appearing therein and inserting in lieu thereof the following: "(not counting Saturday, Sunday, or a legal holiday in the District of Columbia as the nineteenth day)".

(*b*) EFFECTIVE DATE. — The amendments made by this section shall take effect as of September 8, 1945.

THE CONDUCT OF FOREIGN RELATIONS

(2) *Executive Order 9698, Designating Public International Organizations Entitled to Enjoy Certain Privileges, Exemptions, and Immunities, February 19, 1946.*[1]

By virtue of the authority vested in me by section 1 of the International Organizations Immunities Act, approved December 29, 1945 (Public Law 291, 79th Congress),[2] and having found that the United States participates in the following-named international organizations pursuant to a treaty or under the authority of an act of Congress authorizing such participation or making an appropriation therefor, I hereby designated such organizations as public international organizations entitled to enjoy the privileges, exemptions, and immunities conferred by the said International Organizations Immunities Act:

The Food and Agriculture Organization.
The International Labor Organization.
The Pan American Union.
The United Nations.
The United Nations Relief and Rehabilitation Administration.

With respect to the designation of such other international organizations as may be entitled to the privileges, exemptions, and immunities conferred by the said Act, the Department of State is hereby designated as the agency to receive applications for the granting of such privileges, exemptions, and immunities. The Secretary of State shall require such information as he may deem necessary from the international organizations making such applications, and shall submit recommendations to the President as to whether the applicant organizations should be designated as public international organizations entitled to enjoy the privileges, exemptions, and immunities conferred by the said Act.

B. International Organizations in Which the United States Participates, as of December 31, 1946 [3]

The international organizations listed below are those in the work of which the United States is currently participating as well as those with which this Government most probably will be concerned through the responsibilities arising from wider international contacts in world affairs. American participation has taken the form of: (1) official Government delegations, (2) payment of contributions through specific appropriations or from general or emergency funds, (3) the attendance of Foreign Service Officers and (4) the attendance of technical experts. Agencies which are defunct or largely dormant and minor proposed agencies are not listed.

[1] *Federal Register*, XI, p. 1809.
[2] For the text of the International Organizations Immunities Act, see this volume, p. 67.
[3] Compiled from Department of State Publication 2699, p. 304; from a list prepared by the Department of State, Division of International Organization Affairs; and from *United States Government Manual, 1947* (First edition), p. 137.

74 DOCUMENTS ON AMERICAN FOREIGN RELATIONS

1. MULTILATERAL

A. General

Union of American Republics
United Nations

B. Agricultural

Food and Agriculture Organization of the United Nations [1]
Inter-American Committee on Agriculture
Inter-American Institute of Agricultural Sciences [1]
International Institute of Agriculture
International Society for the Study of Chemistry of the Soil [2]

C. Commerical and Financial

Emergency Economic Committee for Europe [1,3]
Inter-American Bank [4]
Inter-American Economic and Social Council
Inter-American Statistical Institute [1]
International Bank for Reconstruction and Development [1]
International Bureau for the Publication of Customs Tariffs [1]
International Institute of Statistics [1]
International Monetary Fund [1]
International Trade Organization [4]
International Union for the Protection of Industrial Property [1]

D. Commodity

Combined Coal Committee [3]
Combined Rubber Committee
Combined Textile Committee [3]
Combined Tin Committee [3]
Combined Working Party on European Food Supplies [3]
European Coal Organization [1,3]
Four Party Supply Committee for the Netherlands [3]
Inter-American Coffee Board [1]
International Committee on Coal-Mining Industry [3]
International Emergency Food Council [3]
International Sugar Council [1]
International Tin Committee
International Wheat Council [1]
North American Council on Fishery Investigations [2]
Rubber Study Group [1]

E. Educational, Scientific and Cultural

Central Bureau of the International Map of the World on the Millionth Scale [1]
International Astronomical Union [1]
International Bureau for Technical Education [2]
International Bureau of Education [1,2]
International Bureau of Weights and Measures [1]
International Commission for Radiological Protection
International Council of Scientific Unions [1]
International Geographical Union [2]
International Geological Congresses [2]
International Hydrographic Bureau [1]
International Meteorological Organization [1]
International Physiological Laboratories on Monte Rosa
International Scientific Radio Union
International Union of Biological Sciences [2]
International Union of Chemistry
International Union of Geodesy and Geophysics [1,5]
International Union of Physics [2]
Pan American Columbian Society
Pan American Institute of Geography and History [1]
Permanent General Secretariat of the Inter-American Caribbean Union
United Nations Educational, Scientific and Cultural Organization
United Nations International Standards Organization [4]

F. Political and Legal

Advisory Commission to Rumania [3]
Allied Advisory Council for Italy [3]

---

[1] Appropriations.   [2] Technical experts.   [3] Temporary or war.   [4] Proposed.
[5] The following associations and commissions are parts of the International Union of Geodesy and Geophysics: International Association of Geodesy; International Association of Magnetism (Geomagnetism) and Electricity; International Association of Meteorology; International Association of Oceanography; International Association of Scientific Hydrology; International Association of Seismology; International Association of Vulcanology; International Commission on Continental and Oceanic Structure; International Commission on Snow and Glaciers; International Commission on Subterranean Waters.

THE CONDUCT OF FOREIGN RELATIONS

Allied Commission for Austria [3]
Allied Commission for Italy [3]
Allied Commission on Reparations [1] [3]
Allied Control Commission for Bulgaria [3]
Allied Control Commission for Hungary [3]
Allied Control Commission for Rumania [3]
Allied Control Council for Germany [3]
Allied Council for Japan [3]
Allied Swiss-German External Assets Liquidation Commission [3]
Allied Mission to Observe the Greek Election [3]
Committee of Control at Tangier [1]
Council of Foreign Ministers [1]
Emergency Advisory Committee for Political Defense [1] [3]
Far Eastern Commission [3]
Inter-Allied Reparation Agency [3]
Inter-American Defense Board [3]
Inter-American Juridical Committee [3]
International Court of Justice
International Military Tribunal [1] [3]
International Military Tribunal for the Far East [3]
Interparliamentary Union for the Promotion of International Arbitration [1]
Mediterranean Commission [3]
Permanent Court of Arbitration
United Nations War Crimes Commission [1] [3]

G. Social and Health

American International Institute for the Protection of Childhood [1]
Caribbean Commission [1]
Institute of Inter-American Affairs [1]
Inter-American Commission of Women [1]
Inter-American Committee on Social Security
Inter-American Indian Institute [1]
Intergovernmental Committee on Refugees [1] [3]
International Central Office for the Control of Liquor Traffic in Africa
International Commission for the Decennial Revision of the International Lists of Diseases and Causes of Death
International Committee of Military Medicine and Pharmacy [2]
International Criminal Police Commission [1]
International Hospital Association [2]
International Labor Organization [1]

International Office of Public Health [1]
International Penal and Penitentiary Commission [1]
International Refugee Organization [4]
Pan American Sanitary Bureau [1]
Permanent Central Opium Board [1]
Supervisory Body, established by the Convention for limiting the manufacture and regulating the distribution of narcotic drugs (1931) [1]
United Nations Relief and Rehabilitation Administration [1] [3]
World Health Organization [4]

H. Transport and Communications

Engineering Committee of the North American Regional Broadcasting Conference
European Central Inland Transport Organization [1]
Inter-American Radio Office [1]
International Civil Aviation Organization [4]
International Commission for the Maintenance of the Lighthouse at Cape Spartel [1]
International Commission on the Rhine River [1]
International Ice Patrol and Ice Observation Service [1]
International Shipping Organization [4]
International Technical Committee of Aerial Legal Experts [1]
International Telecommunications Union [1]
Pan American Highway Confederation [2]
Pan American Railway Congress [2]
Pei-ho Conservancy Board
Permanent International Association of Navigation Congresses [1]
Permanent International Association of Road Congresses [1]
Permanent South American Railway Congress Association
Postal Union of the Americas and Spain [1]
Provisional International Civil Aviation Organization [1] [3]
Special International Committee on Radio Static
Technical Advisory Committee on Inland Transport [3]
Transatlantic Air Services Safety Organization
United Maritime Consultative Council [3]
Universal Postal Union [1]
Whang-pu Conservancy Board

[1] Appropriations. [2] Technical experts. [3] Temporary or war. [4] Proposed.

2. BILATERAL

A. Agricultural
Mexican-United States Agricultural Commission

B. Commercial and Financial
British-American Joint Patent Interchange Commission [3]
International Screwthread Commission
Mexican-American Industrial Commission

C. Commodity
Anglo-American Rice Commission
International Fisheries Commission (United States and Canada) [1]
International Pacific Salmon Fisheries Commission [1]
Joint Hide Control Office (United States and Great Britain) [1,3]
Munitions Assignments Board [1,3]

D. Political and Legal
(1) *Boundary*
   International Boundary Commission (United States, Canada and Alaska) [1]
   International Boundary Commission (United States and Canada) [1]
   International Boundary and Water Commission (United States and Mexico) [1]
(2) *Commissions of Inquiry*
   Albania; Australia; Austria; Belgium; Bolivia; Brazil; Bulgaria; Canada; Chile; China; Czechoslovakia; Denmark and Iceland; Ecuador; Egypt; Estonia; Ethiopia; Finland; France; Germany; Great Britain; Greece; Hungary; Iceland; Italy; Latvia; Liberia; Lithuania; Luxembourg; the Netherlands; New Zealand; Norway; Paraguay; Peru; Poland; Portugal; Rumania; Spain; Sweden; Switzerland; Union of South Africa; Union of Soviet Socialist Republics; Uruguay; Venezuela; and Yugoslavia
(3) *Conciliation Commissions*
   Costa Rica; Guatemala; Honduras; Nicaragua; and El Salvador
(4) *Miscellaneous*
   Canton (Condominium)
   Combined Chiefs of Staff [1,3]
   Filipino Rehabilitation Commission [3]
   Joint Brazilian-United States Defense Commission [1,3]
   Joint Commission on Korea [1]
   Joint Mexican-United States Defense Commission [1,3]
   Permanent Joint Board on Defense (United States and Canada) [3]

E. Social and Health
Gorgas Memorial Institute of Tropical and Preventive Medicine [1]

F. Transport and Communications
Alaskan International Highway Commission [1]
Interdepartmental Committee on Resumption of Communications with Liberated Areas [1,3]
International Joint Commission (United States and Canada)
Joint Aircraft Committee [1,3]
Trans-Isthmian Joint Highway Board [1,3]

C. International Conferences in Which the United States Participated, July 1, 1945 to December 31, 1946 [5]

The following list includes the more important conferences in which the Government of the United States participated during the period under review. Certain small, technical meetings, subcommittee meetings and conferences of limited interest have been omitted.

Date of Meeting	Conference	Place
July 23–28, 1945	Permanent Inter-American Committee on Social Security, Second Session	Mexico City

[1] Appropriations.   [2] Technical experts.   [3] Temporary or war.   [4] Proposed.
[5] Compiled from a list prepared by the Department of State, Division of International Conferences.

THE CONDUCT OF FOREIGN RELATIONS 77

Date of Meeting	Conference	Place
July 24–August 7, 1945	Third Inter-American Conference on Agriculture	Caracas
July 26, 1945	Anglo-American Caribbean Commission, Seventh Meeting	Washington
August 3, 1945	International Sugar Council	London
August 7–25, 1945	United Nations Relief and Rehabilitation Administration, Third Session of the Council	London
August 15–30, 1945	Provisional International Civil Aviation Organization, First Session of the Interim Council	Montreal
August 16–October 27, 1945	Executive Committee of the Preparatory Commission of the United Nations	London
August 31–September 1, 1945	International Wheat Council, Eighth and Ninth Sessions	London
September 11–October 2, 1945	Council of Foreign Ministers, First Session	London
October 6–November 1, 1945	Food and Agriculture Organization of the United Nations, First Session of the Conference	Quebec
October 10–14, 1945	Governing Body of the International Labor Office, Ninety-Sixth Session	Paris
October 12 and November 5, 1945	European Central Inland Transport Organization, First Session of the Council	London
October 15–November 30, 1945	Provisional International Civil Aviation Organization, Second Session of the Interim Council	Montreal
November 1–16, 1945	United Nations Conference for the Establishment of an Educational, Scientific and Cultural Organization	London
November 6–7, 1945	Governing Body of the International Labor Office, Ninety-Seventh Session	Paris
November 9–December 21, 1945	Paris Conference on Reparation	Paris
November 15–December 1, 1945	Maritime Preparatory Technical Conference of the International Labor Organization	Copenhagen
November 16–19, 1945	Preparatory Commission of the United Nations Educational, Scientific and Cultural Organization	London
November 19–23, 1945	Rubber Study Group, Second Meeting	London
November 20–22, 1945	Intergovernmental Committee on Refugees, Fifth Plenary Session	Paris
November 21–December 4, 1945	Bermuda Telecommunications Conference	Hamilton
November 24–December 24, 1945	Preparatory Commission of the United Nations, Second Session	London
December 10, 1945	European Central Inland Transport Organization, Second Session of the Council	London

Date of Meeting	Conference	Place
December 16–26, 1945	Council of Foreign Ministers	Moscow
January 4–April 20, 1946	Anglo-American Committee of Inquiry	Washington, London, American Zone of Germany, Czechoslovakia, Paris, French Zones of Germany and Austria, Berlin, Poland, British Zone of Germany, Vienna, American Zone of Austria, British Zone of Austria, Italy, Cairo, Palestine, Damascus, Baghdad, Amman, Lausanne
January 10, 1946	International Wheat Council, Tenth Session	Washington
January 10–February 14, 1946	United Nations General Assembly, First Part of the First Session	London
January 15–February 11, 1946	Anglo-American Civil Aviation Conference	Hamilton
January 18, 1946	Preparatory Commission of the United Nations Educational, Scientific and Cultural Organization	London
January 21–February 25, 1946	Provisional International Civil Aviation Organization, Third Session of the Interim Council	Montreal
January 22–29, 1946	International Technical Committee of Aerial Legal Experts (CITEJA), Fourteenth Plenary Session	Paris
January 30, 1946	European Central Inland Transport Organization, Third Session of the Council	London
February 5, 1946	International Sugar Council	London
February 11–13, 1945	Preparatory Commission of the United Nations Educational, Scientific and Cultural Organization	London
February 21–March 13, 1946	West Indian Conference, Second Session	St. Thomas
February 23–March 15, 1946	Caribbean Commission, First Meeting	St. Thomas
February 27, 1946	International Wheat Council, Eleventh Session	Washington
March 8–18, 1946	International Monetary Fund and International Bank for Reconstruction and Development, Inaugural Meetings of the Boards of Governors	Savannah
March 15–19, 1946	United Nations Relief and Rehabilitation Administration, Fourth Session of the Council	Atlantic City
April 2– June 5, 1946	Provisional International Civil Aviation Organization, Fourth Session of the Interim Council	Montreal

THE CONDUCT OF FOREIGN RELATIONS 79

Date of Meeting	Conference	Place
April 12, 1946	European Central Inland Transport Organization, Fourth (Special) Session of the Council	London
April 25–May 15, 1946	Council of Foreign Ministers, Second Session (First Part)	Paris
May 7–14, 1946	International Cotton Advisory Committee, Fifth Meeting	Washington
May 20–27, 1946	United Nations Food and Agriculture Organization, Special Meeting on Urgent Food Problems	Washington
May 21–June 7, 1946	Provisional International Civil Aviation Organization, First Interim Assembly	Montreal
May 23–27, 1946	Governing Body of the International Labor Office, Ninety-Eighth Session	Montreal
June 6–29, 1946	International Labor Conference, Twenty-Eighth (Maritime) Session	Seattle
June 15–July 12, 1946	Council of Foreign Ministers, Second Session (Second Part)	Paris
June 17–28, 1946	Provisional International Civil Aviation Organization, Fifth Session of the Interim Council	Montreal
June 18–24, 1946	United Maritime Consultative Council, First Session	Amsterdam
June 19–July 22, 1946	International Health Conference	New York
July 5–13, 1946	Preparatory Commission of the United Nations Educational, Scientific and Cultural Organization	London
July 8–9, 1946	International Institute of Agriculture, General Assembly	Rome
July 8–15, 1946	Caribbean Commission, Second Meeting	Washington
July 15, 1946	International Wheat Council, Twelfth Session	Washington
July 15, 1946	International Sugar Council	London
July 19–23, 1946	World Health Organization, First Meeting of the Interim Commission	New York
July 29–October 15, 1946	Paris Conference of Twenty-One Nations	Paris
August 5–7, 1946	United Nations Relief and Rehabilitation Administration, Fifth Session of the Council	Geneva
August 19, 1946	International Wheat Council, Thirteenth Session	Washington
August 19–21, 1946	United Nations Educational, Scientific and Cultural Organization, Executive Committee	London
September 2–13, 1946	Food and Agriculture Organization, Second Session of the Conference	Copenhagen
September 4–November 18, 1946	Provisional International Civil Aviation Organization, Sixth Session of the Interim Council	Montreal
September 16–18, 1946	Governing Body of the International Labor Office, Ninety-Ninth Session	Montreal
September 19–October 9, 1946	International Labor Conference, Twenty-Ninth Session	Montreal

Date of Meeting	Conference	Place
September 26–October 3, 1946	International Monetary Fund and International Bank for Reconstruction and Development, First Annual Meeting of the Boards of Governors	Washington
September 28–October 21, 1946	Five-Power Preliminary Telecommunications Conference	Moscow
October 1–3, 1946	Executive Committee of the United Nations Educational, Scientific and Cultural Organization	Paris
October 7–8, 1946	Governing Body of the International Labor Office, One-Hundredth Session	Montreal
October 8–12, 1946	Conference on Tin	London
October 14–15, 1946	International Emergency Food Council	Washington
October 15–November 26, 1946	Preparatory Committee for the International Conference on Trade and Employment	London
October 22–29, 1946	International Committee on Weights and Measures	Paris
October 23–December 14, 1946	United Nations General Assembly, Second Part of the First Session	Flushing Meadows
October 24, 1946 continuing	Inter-Allied Trade Board for Japan	Washington
October 24–30, 1946	United Maritime Consultative Council, Second Meeting	Washington
October 28, 1946–January 24, 1947	Food and Agriculture Organization, Preparatory Commission to Study World Food Board Proposals	Washington
November 4–13, 1946	World Health Organization, Second Session of the Interim Commission	Geneva
November 4–December 11, 1946	Council of Foreign Ministers, Third Session	New York
November 14–15, 1946	Preparatory Commission of the United Nations Educational, Scientific and Cultural Organization	Paris
November 14–17, 1946	International Technical Committee of Aerial Legal Experts, Fifteenth Session	Cairo
November 19–December 10, 1946	United Nations Educational, Scientific and Cultural Organization, First Session of the General Conference	Paris
November 25–28, 1946	Rubber Study Group	The Hague
December 2–12, 1946	Inter-American Commission of Women, First Annual Assembly	Washington
December 10–13, 1946	United Nations Relief and Rehabilitation Administration, Sixth Session of the Council	Washington
December 10–16, 1946	Caribbean Commission, Third Meeting	Curaçao
December 16–18, 1946	Food and Agriculture Organization, Executive Board	Washington
December 16–20, 1946	Intergovernmental Committee on Refugees, Sixth Plenary Session	London
December 18–19, 1946	European Central Inland Transport Organization, Sixth Session of the Council	Paris
December 19, 1946	International Children's Emergency Fund, Executive Board	Lake Success

… THE CONDUCT OF FOREIGN RELATIONS

5. DIPLOMATIC REPRESENTATION

A. Foreign Service Act of 1946

The increased responsibilities of the Foreign Service in implementing United States policy of "collaboration by this Government on an unprecedented scale in achieving and maintaining peace, in rehabilitating and democratizing the nations freed from Axis domination, and in bringing about stability and prosperity"[1] caused considerable attention to be focused on the question of reorganizing the Service during the period under review. On August 7, 1945, members of the Subcommittee on Appropriations for the Department of State of the House of Representatives sailed for Europe to survey, in cooperation with the Department of State, the Foreign Service establishments in that area;[2] and certain weaknesses within the Service were pointed out and recommendations of corrective measures included in the Eighth Report of the House Special Committee on Postwar Economic Policy and Planning.[3]

Accordingly there was introduced in the House of Representatives on July 8, 1946, by Rep. John W. Kee (Virginia) H. R. 6967, "A bill to improve, strengthen, and expand the Foreign Service of the United States and to consolidate and revise the laws relating to its administration."[4] The Bill was favorably reported with amendments by the Committee on Foreign Affairs on July 12,[5] and was passed by the House on July 20.[6] The Senate passed H. R. 6967 instead of its own Senate-sponsored reorganization measure (S.2451) on July 29, 1946[7] and the Bill was enacted into law on August 13, 1946.[8]

(1) *Eighth Report of the House Special Committee on Postwar Economic Policy and Planning, November 12, 1945.*[9]

[Excerpt]

. . . .

IV. INSTRUMENTS OF AMERICAN FOREIGN POLICY AND ORGANIZATION OF THE FOREIGN SERVICE

The organization of the Department of State in Washington is weakened in the judgment of the committee in two respects in its foreign service:

1. The career service of the United States is not put upon a basis of comparable attraction in allowances, as well as in salaries, to hold the best talents in the foreign service. Comparable grades and responsibilities of the foreign service were found to be less well remunerated and with less rapid promotion in the foreign service than in the permanent departments in Washington and on a much less adequate basis

---

[1] Letter from the Secretary of State (Stettinius) to the Chairman of the Subcommittee on Appropriations for the Department of State of the House of Representatives (Rabaut), March 13, 1945. Department of State, *Bulletin*, XIII, p. 201.
[2] *Ibid.*
[3] House Report No. 1205, 79th Cong., 1st sess.
[4] *Congressional Record*, 92, p. 8560 (Daily edition, July 8, 1946).
[5] House Report No. 2508, 79th Cong., 2d sess.
[6] *Congressional Record*, 92, p. 9717 (Daily edition, July 20, 1946).
[7] *Ibid.*, p. 10494 (Daily edition, July 29, 1946).
[8] Public Law 724, 79th Cong., 2d sess.; for excerpts from the text of the Foreign Service Act of 1946, see this volume, p. 84.
[9] House Report No. 1205, 79th Cong., 1st sess., p. 49.

in the same respects than the temporary war agencies. The committee strongly urges the consideration of Congress for strengthening the usefulness of the career service by insisting in its appropriations to the Department of State on a recognition of the more expensive living conditions abroad and appropriate salaries and retirement allowances. The type of information obtained and the execution of foreign economic policies must depend upon the caliber of the personnel retained in the foreign service.

2. The second general point is the lack of appropriate scope for promotion in the economic sides of the foreign service of the United States and the consequent tendency of officers to prefer appointments in the political side of the foreign service, rather than in the economic side. Missions in the most important European capitals, where the Russian and British Governments were represented by a very large staff and by the top-ranking officials both in service and in pay, were found to be restricted in scope and in the rewards available for distinguished service to our diplomats who were on the commercial and economic side of the legation or embassy staff. The committee would like to pay tribute to the devotion of many Americans who have loyally served their country for the greater part of their lives abroad under these difficult conditions and the high caliber of the representation which we found. It was nevertheless recognized that in many missions it would be difficult, if not impossible, to retain in the foreign service of the United States not only the higher-ranking personnel but the clerical staffs and research workers and special officers in postwar conditions. It seems to the committee of critical importance to make the foreign service of the United States rank in its ability and consequent influence with that of Great Britain, Russia, France, and other countries. Special attention should be paid to the improvement of the foreign service and in particular its economic and information branches.

As the Office of War Information and presumably the Foreign Economic Administration are dissolved, some portion of the better personnel and a great part of the activities of these agencies should be incorporated into the regular foreign service of the United States.

In the organization of the department in Washington it seems to the committee that there is a lack of control within the hands of the State Department proper of many aspects of the foreign policy of the United States. It is recognized that interdepartmental relationships with the Treasury, Agriculture, and Commerce and in some instances with the Department of the Interior and other specially interested agencies, require clearance with the heads of these departments. It seems, however, to the committee that the organization of a parallel to the British Department of Overseas Trade would be a natural development for the growing importance of foreign trade to the United States. (It would also incorporate the control of the Export-Import Bank and bring under its head a considerable part of the activities of the Bureau of Foreign and Domestic Commerce.)

The committee regards it as imperative that American foreign economic policies should be guided from a single center of responsibility which logically is the Department of State, since our economic foreign policy is our strongest bargaining weapon in setting political policies. The granting of loans, the disposal of foreign surplus property (which the committee notes has already been put in the Department of State for policy guidance), the distribution of relief, and the actual channeling of trade, all require to be made a part of the single and clearly defined economic foreign policy. At the same time, the development of trade relations and the placing of business abroad, both for exports and imports, needs a more aggressive policy than can normally be followed under the guidance of the Department of State alone. The committee therefore recommends to the executive agencies consideration of closer coordination of the implementation of foreign economic policy under the policy guidance of the Department of State.

The committee feels that legislative sanction should be given to the creation of an Under Secretary of State for Foreign Economic Policy who would report directly to the Secretary of State. He should coordinate the aspects of trade promotion that now come under the Department of Commerce, of loans, whether of Treasury or of the Export-Import Bank; of foreign agricultural trade coming under the Department of Agriculture; and foreign mineral trade promotion coming under the Department of the Interior. It is not proposed to alter the present location of these functions in the departments concerned but to give legislative sanction for clearing the assistant secretaries in each department concerned with these foreign economic aspects of the Department with the Under Secretary of State for Foreign Economic Policy. It is in the highest degree important that the closest working relationships be established by the assistant secretaries of the various departments with the Under Secretary of State for Foreign Economic Policy. It is, therefore, felt that he should be consulted in all instances as to the acceptability of the persons appointed to this function in the departments concerned. He should also act as chairman, with ultimate powers of making the binding decisions, of a policy committee composed of the assistant secretaries of the departments previously mentioned to pass on the matters of foreign economic policy.

It is not the proper function of the Department of State itself to undertake the promotional aspects of trade policy, but it is essential that the formulation of foreign economic policy should in every way encourage and afford legitimate protection to American economic interests abroad. It is particularly important to have one policy carried out in this field rather than conflicting policies. The committee feels that the Under Secretary of State for Foreign Economic Policy, reporting directly to the Secretary of State on this whole area, is the logical official to carry out this responsibility.

An awakened interest on the part of the entire business community and of the Nation in the stake of the United States in foreign trade should be accompanied by an appropriate recognition of the increased importance of the agencies of government which promote and protect this trade.

The international trade organization, already treated in the summary of conclusions at some length, can become an instrument for American foreign policy in reaching and maintaining agreements to remove trade barriers and restrictions. It may also serve to scrutinize on an international scale cartel policies and commodity agreements. The committee heartily endorses the initiative of the Departments of State and of Commerce to this end.

(2) *An Act to Improve, Strengthen, and Expand the Foreign Service of the United States and to Consolidate and Revise the Laws Relating to its Administration, Approved August 13, 1946.*[1]

Be it enacted by the Senate and House of Representatives of the United States of America in Congress assembled,

TITLE I — SHORT TITLE, OBJECTIVES AND DEFINITIONS

Part A — Short Title

Sec. 101. Titles I to X, inclusive, of this Act may be cited as the "Foreign Service Act of 1946".

Part B — Objectives

Sec. 111. The Congress hereby declares that the objectives of this Act are to develop and strengthen the Foreign Service of the United States so as —

(1) to enable the Foreign Service effectively to serve abroad the interests of the United States;

(2) to insure that the officers and employees of the Foreign Service are broadly representative of the American people and are aware of and fully informed in respect to current trends in American life;

(3) to enable the Foreign Service adequately to fulfill the functions devolving on it by reason of the transfer to the Department of State of functions heretofore performed by other Government agencies;

(4) to provide improvements in the recruitment and training of the personnel of the Foreign Service;

(5) to provide that promotions leading to positions of authority and responsibility shall be on the basis of merit and to insure the selection on an impartial basis of outstanding persons for such positions;

(6) to provide for the temporary appointment or assignment to the Foreign Service of representative and outstanding citizens of the United States possessing special skills and abilities;

(7) to provide salaries, allowances, and benefits that will permit the Foreign Service to draw its personnel from all walks of American life and to appoint persons to the highest positions in the Service solely on the basis of their demonstrated ability;

(8) to provide a flexible and comprehensive framework for the direction of the Foreign Service in accordance with modern practices in public administration; and

(9) to codify into one Act all provisions of law relating to the administration of the Foreign Service.

[1] Public Law 724, 79th Cong., 2d sess.

THE CONDUCT OF FOREIGN RELATIONS

Part C — Definitions

Sec. 121. When used in this Act, the term —
(1) "Service" means the Foreign Service of the United States;
(2) "Secretary" means the Secretary of State;
(3) "Department" means the Department of State;
(4) "Government agency" means any executive department, board, bureau, commission, or other agency in the executive branch of the Federal Government, or any corporation wholly owned (either directly or through one or more corporations) by the United States;
(5) "Government" means the Government of the United States of America;
(6) "Continental United States" means the States and the District of Columbia;
(7) "Abroad" means all areas not included in the continental United States as defined in paragraph (6) of this section;
(8) "Principal officer" means the officer in charge of an embassy, legation, or other diplomatic mission or of a consulate general, consulate, or vice consulate of the United States; and
(9) "Chief of mission" means a principal officer appointed by the President, by and with the advice and consent of the Senate, to be in charge of an embassy or legation or other diplomatic mission of the United States, or any person assigned under the terms of this Act to be minister resident, chargé d'affaires, commissioner, or diplomatic agent.

. . . .

TITLE III — DUTIES

Part A — General Duties

COMPLIANCE WITH TERMS OF STATUTES, INTERNATIONAL AGREEMENTS, AND EXECUTIVE ORDERS

Sec. 301. Officers and employees of the Service shall, under the direction of the Secretary, represent abroad the interests of the United States and shall perform the duties and comply with the obligations resulting from the nature of their appointments or assignments or imposed on them by the terms of any law or by any order or regulation issued pursuant to law or by any international agreement to which the United States is a party.

DUTIES FOR WHICH REGULATIONS MAY BE PRESCRIBED

Sec. 302. The Secretary shall, except in an instance where the authority is specifically vested in the President, have authority to prescribe regulations not inconsistent with the Constitution and the laws of the United States in relation to the duties, functions, and obligations of officers and employees of the Service and the administration of the Service.

DELEGATION OF AUTHORITY TO PRESCRIBE REGULATIONS

Sec. 303. In cases where authority to prescribe regulations relating to the Service or the duties and obligations of officers and employees of the Service is specifically vested in the President by the terms of this or any other Act, the President may, nevertheless, authorize the Secretary to prescribe such regulations.

Part B — Services for Government Agencies and Other Establishments of the Government

Sec. 311. The officers and employees of the Service shall, under such regulations as the President may prescribe, perform duties and functions in behalf of any Government agency or any other establishment of the Government requiring their services, including those in the legislative and judicial branches, but the absence of such regulations shall not preclude officers and employees of the Service from acting for and on behalf of any such Government agency or establishment whenever it shall, through the Department, request their services.

TITLE IV — CATEGORIES AND SALARIES OF PERSONNEL

Part A — Categories of Personnel

Sec. 401. The personnel of the Service shall consist of the following categories of officers and employees:

(1) Chiefs of mission, who shall be appointed or assigned in accordance with the provisions of section 501;

(2) Foreign Service officers, who shall be appointed in accordance with section 511, including those serving as chiefs of mission;

(3) Foreign Service Reserve officers, who shall be assigned to the Service on a temporary basis from Government agencies or appointed on a temporary basis from outside the Government in accordance with the provisions of section 522, in order to make available to the Service such specialized skills as may from time to time be required;

(4) Foreign Service staff officers and employees, who shall be appointed in accordance with the provisions of section 531 and who shall include all personnel who are citizens of the United States, not comprehended under paragraphs (1), (2), (3), and (6) of this section, and who shall occupy positions with technical, administrative, fiscal, clerical, or custodial responsibilities.

(5) Alien clerks and employees, who shall be appointed in accordance with the provisions of section 541; and

(6) Consular agents, who shall be appointed in accordance with the provisions of section 551.

Part B — Salaries

CHIEFS OF MISSION

Sec. 411. The President shall for salary purposes classify into four classes the positions which are to be occupied by chiefs of mission.

THE CONDUCT OF FOREIGN RELATIONS 87

The per annum salaries of chiefs of mission within each class shall be as follows: Class 1, $25,000 per annum; class 2, $20,000; class 3, $17,500; and class 4, $15,000.

FOREIGN SERVICE OFFICERS

SEC. 412. There shall be seven classes of Foreign Service officers, including the class of career minister. The per annum salary of a career minister shall be $13,500. The per annum salaries of Foreign Service officers within each of the other classes shall be as follows:
 Class 1, $12,000, $12,400, $12,800, $13,200, $13,500;
 Class 2, $10,000, $10,350, $10,700, $11,050, $11,400, $11,750, $11,900;
 Class 3, $8,000, $8,300, $8,600, $8,900, $9,200, $9,500, $9,800, $9,900;
 Class 4, $6,000, $6,300, $6,600, $6,900, $7,200, $7,500, $7,800, $7,900;
 Class 5, $4,500, $4,700, $4,900, $5,100, $5,300, $5,500, $5,700, $5,900;
 Class 6, $3,300, $3,500, $3,700, $3,900, $4,100, $4,300, $4,400.

SALARIES AT WHICH FOREIGN SERVICE OFFICERS MAY BE APPOINTED

SEC. 413. (a) A person appointed as a Foreign Service officer of class 6 shall receive salary at that one of the rates provided for that class by section 412 which the Secretary shall, taking into consideration his age, qualifications, and experience, determine to be appropriate for him to receive.

(b) A person appointed as a Foreign Service officer of classes 1 through 5, inclusive, shall receive salary at the minimum rate provided for the class to which he has been appointed.

FOREIGN SERVICE RESERVE OFFICERS

SEC. 414. (a) There shall be six classes of Foreign Service Reserve officers, referred to hereafter as Reserve officers, which classes shall correspond to classes 1 to 6 of Foreign Service officers.

(b) A Reserve officer shall receive salary at any one of the rates provided for the class to which he is appointed or assigned in accordance with the provisions of section 523.

(c) A person assigned as a Reserve officer from any Government agency shall receive his salary from appropriations provided for the Department during the period of his service as a Reserve officer.

FOREIGN SERVICE STAFF OFFICERS AND EMPLOYEES

SEC. 415. There shall be twenty-two classes of Foreign Service staff officers and employees, referred to hereafter as staff officers and employees. The per annum rates of salary of staff officers and employees within each class shall be as follows:
 Class 1, $8,820, $9,120, $9,420, $9,720, $10,000;
 Class 2, $8,100, $8,340, $8,580, $8,820, $9,120;
 Class 3, $7,380, $7,620, $7,860, $8,100, $8,340;
 Class 4, $6,660, $6,900, $7,140, $7,380, $7,620;
 Class 5, $6,120, $6,300, $6,480, $6,660, $6,900, $7,140;

Class 6, $5,580, $5,760, $5,940, $6,120, $6,300, $6,480;
Class 7, $5,040, $5,220, $5,400, $5,580, $5,760, $5,940;
Class 8, $4,500 $4,680, $4,860, $5,040, $5,220, $5,400;
Class 9, $3,960, $4,140, $4,320, $4,500, $4,680, $4,860;
Class 10, $3,600, $3,720, $3,840, $3,960, $4,140, $4,320, $4,500;
Class 11, $3,240, $3,360, $3,480, $3,600, $3,720, $3,840, $3,960;
Class 12, $2,880, $3,000, $3,120 $3,240, $3,360, $3,480, $3,600;
Class 13, $2,520, $2,640, $2,760, $2,880, $3,000, $3,120, $3,240;
Class 14, $2,160, $2,280, $2,400, $2,520, $2,640, $2,760, $2,880;
Class 15, $1,980, $2,040, $2,100, $2,160, $2,280, $2,400, $2,520;
Class 16, $1,800, $1,860, $1,920, $1,980, $2,040, $2,100, $2,160;
Class 17, $1,620, $1,680, $1,740, $1,800, $1,860, $1,920, $1,980;
Class 18, $1,440, $1,500, $1,560, $1,620, $1,680, $1,740, $1,800;
Class 19, $1,260, $1,320, $1,380, $1,440, $1,500, $1,560, $1,620;
Class 20, $1,080, $1,140, $1,200, $1,260, $1,320, $1,380, $1,440;
Class 21, $900, $960, $1,020, $1,080, $1,140, $1,200, $1,260;
Class 22, $720, $780, $840, $900, $960, $1,020, $1,080.

SALARIES AT WHICH FOREIGN SERVICE STAFF OFFICERS AND EMPLOYEES MAY BE APPOINTED

SEC. 416. A person appointed as a staff officer or employee shall receive salary at the minimum rate provided for the class to which appointed except as otherwise provided in accordance with the provisions of part E of this title.

SALARIES OF ALIEN CLERKS AND EMPLOYEES

SEC. 417. The salary or compensation of an alien clerk or employee shall be fixed by the Secretary in accordance with such regulations as he shall prescribe and, as soon as practicable, in accordance with the provisions of section 444 (b). The salary or compensation of an alien clerk or employee fixed on a per annum basis may, notwithstanding the provisions of any other law, be payable on a weekly or biweekly basis. When a one- or two-week pay period of such a clerk or employee begins in one fiscal year and ends in another, the gross amount of the earnings for such pay period may be regarded as a charge against the appropriation or allotment current at the end of such pay period.

SALARIES OF CONSULAR AGENTS

SEC. 418. The salary or compensation of a consular agent shall be fixed by the Secretary in accordance with such regulations as he shall prescribe and, as soon as practicable, in accordance with the provisions of section 445.

PART C — SALARIES OF OFFICERS TEMPORARILY IN CHARGE AS CHARGÉS D'AFFAIRES AD INTERIM

SEC. 421. For such time as any Foreign Service officer shall be authorized to act as chargé d'affaires ad interim at the post to which he is assigned, he shall receive, in addition to his basic salary as Foreign Service officer, compensation equal to that portion of the difference between such salary and the basic salary provided for the chief of mission as the Secretary may determine to be appropriate.

AS OFFICERS IN CHARGE OF CONSULATES GENERAL OR CONSULATES

SEC. 422. For such time as any Foreign Service officer or any consul or vice consul who is not a Foreign Service officer is temporarily in charge of a consulate general or consulate during the absence or incapacity of the principal officer, he shall receive, in addition to his basic salary as Foreign Service officer or consul or vice consul, compensation equal to that portion which the Secretary shall determine to be appropriate of the difference between such salary and the basic salary provided for the principal officer, or, if there be none, of the former principal officer.

TITLE V — APPOINTMENTS AND ASSIGNMENTS

PART A — PRINCIPAL DIPLOMATIC REPRESENTATIVES

APPOINTMENTS

SEC. 501. (a) The President shall, by and with the advice and consent of the Senate, appoint ambassadors and ministers, including career ministers.

(b) The President may, in his discretion, assign any Foreign Service officer to serve as minister resident, chargé d'affaires, commissioner, or diplomatic agent for such period as the public interest may require.

LISTS OF FOREIGN SERVICE OFFICERS QUALIFIED TO BE CAREER MINISTERS OR CHIEFS OF MISSION TO BE FURNISHED TO THE PRESIDENT

SEC. 502. (a) The Secretary shall, on the basis of recommendations made by the Board of the Foreign Service, from time to time furnish the President with the names of Foreign Service officers qualified for appointment to the class of career minister together with pertinent information about such officers, but no person shall be appointed into the class of career minister who has not been appointed to serve as a chief of mission or appointed or assigned to serve in a position which, in the opinion of the Secretary, is of comparable importance. A list of such positions shall from time to time be published by the Secretary.

(b) The Secretary shall also, on the basis of recommendations made by the Board of the Foreign Service, from time to time furnish the President with the names of Foreign Service officers qualified for appointment or assignment as chief of mission, together with pertinent information about such officers, in order to assist the President in selecting qualified candidates for appointment or assignment in such capacity.

Part B — Foreign Service Officers

APPOINTMENTS

Sec. 511. The President shall appoint Foreign Service officers by and with the advice and consent of the Senate. All appointments of Foreign Service officers shall be by appointment to a class and not to a particular post.

COMMISSIONS

Sec. 512. Foreign Service officers may be commissioned as diplomatic or consular officers or both and all official acts of such officers while serving under diplomatic or consular commissions shall be performed under their respective commissions as diplomatic or consular officers.

LIMITS OF CONSULAR DISTRICTS

Sec. 513. The Secretary shall define the limits of consular districts.

ASSIGNMENTS AND TRANSFERS

Sec. 514. A Foreign Service officer, commissioned as a diplomatic or consular officer, may be assigned by the Secretary to serve in any diplomatic position other than that of chief of mission or in any consular position, and he may also be assigned to serve in any other capacity in which he is eligible to serve under the terms of this or any other Act. He may be transferred from one post to another by order of the Secretary as the interests of the Service may require.

CITIZENSHIP REQUIREMENTS

Sec. 515. No person shall be eligible for appointment as a Foreign Service officer unless he is a citizen of the United States and has been such for at least ten years.

ADMISSION TO CLASS 6

Sec. 516. No person shall be eligible for appointment as a Foreign Service officer of class 6 unless he has passed such written, oral, physical, and other examinations as the Board of Examiners for the Foreign Service may prescribe to determine his fitness and aptitude for the work of the Service and has demonstrated his loyalty to the Government of the United States and his attachment to the principles of the Constitution. The Secretary shall furnish the President with the names of those persons who have passed such examinations and are eligible for appointment as Foreign Service officers of class 6.

ADMISSION TO CLASSES 1, 2, 3, 4, AND 5 WITHOUT PRIOR SERVICE IN CLASS 6

Sec. 517. A person who has not served in class 6 shall not be eligible for appointment as a Foreign Service officer of classes 1 to 5, inclusive, unless he has passed such written, oral, physical, and other examinations as the Board of Examiners for the Foreign Service may prescribe to determine his fitness and aptitude for the work of the Service; demonstrated his loyalty to the Government of the United States and his attachment to the principles of the Constitution; and rendered at least four years of actual service immediately prior to appointment in a position of responsibility in the Service or in the Department or both, except that, if he has reached the age of thirty-one years, the requirement as to service may be reduced to three years. The Secretary shall furnish the President with the names of those persons who shall have passed such examinations and are eligible for appointment as Foreign Service officers of classes 1 to 5, inclusive. The Secretary shall, taking into consideration the age, qualifications, and experience of each candidate for appointment, recommend the class to which he shall be appointed in accordance with the provisions of this section.

ADMISSION TO THE CLASS OF CAREER MINISTER

SEC. 518. No person shall be eligible for appointment to the class of career minister who is not a Foreign Service officer.

REASSIGNMENT TO FOREIGN SERVICE OF FORMER AMBASSADORS AND MINISTERS

SEC. 519. If, within three months of the date of the termination of his services as chief of mission and of any period of authorized leave, a Foreign Service officer has not again been appointed or assigned as chief of mission or assigned in accordance with the provisions of section 514, he shall be retired from the Service and receive retirement benefits in accordance with the provisions of section 821.

REINSTATEMENT AND RECALL OF FOREIGN SERVICE OFFICERS

SEC. 520. (a) The President may, by and with the advice and consent of the Senate, reappoint to the Service a former Foreign Service officer who has been separated from the Service by reason of appointment to some other position in the Government service and who has served continuously in the Government up to the time of reinstatement. The Secretary shall, taking into consideration the qualifications and experience of each candidate for reappointment and the rank of his contemporaries in the Service, recommend the class to which he shall be reappointed in accordance with the provisions of this section.

(b) Whenever the Secretary shall determine an emergency to exist, the Secretary may recall any retired Foreign Service officer temporarily to active service.

PART C — FOREIGN SERVICE RESERVE OFFICERS

ESTABLISHMENT OF RESERVE

SEC. 521. In accordance with the terms of this Act and under such regulations as the Secretary shall prescribe, there shall be organized and maintained a Foreign Service Reserve, referred to hereafter as the Reserve.

APPOINTMENTS AND ASSIGNMENTS TO THE RESERVE

SEC. 522. Whenever the services of a person who is a citizen of the United States and who has been such for at least five years are required by the Service, the Secretary may —

(1) appoint as a Reserve officer for nonconsecutive periods of not more than four years each, a person not in the employ of the Government whom the Board of the Foreign Service shall deem to have outstanding qualifications of a specialized character; and

(2) assign as a Reserve officer for nonconsecutive periods of not more than four years each a person regularly employed in any Government agency, subject, in the case of an employee of a Government agency other than the Department of State, to the consent of the head of the agency concerned.

APPOINTMENT OR ASSIGNMENT TO A CLASS

SEC. 523. A Reserve officer, appointed or assigned to active duty, shall be appointed or assigned to a class and not to a particular post, and such an officer may be assigned to posts and may be transferred from one post to another by order of the Secretary as the interests of the Service may require. The class to which he shall be appointed or assigned shall depend on his age, qualifications, and experience.

COMMISSIONS

SEC. 524. Whenever the Secretary shall deem it in the interests of the Service that a Reserve officer shall serve in a diplomatic or consular capacity, he may recommend to the President that such officer be commissioned as a diplomatic or consular officer or both. The President may, by and with the advice and consent of the Senate, commission such officer as a diplomatic or consular officer or both, and all official acts of such an officer while serving under a diplomatic or consular commission shall be performed under his commission as a diplomatic or consular officer. In all other cases, appropriate rank and status, analogous to that of Foreign Service officers engaged in work of comparable importance shall be provided to permit Reserve officers to carry out their duties effectively.

ACTIVE DUTY

SEC. 525. The Secretary shall by regulation define the period during which a Reserve officer shall be considered as being on active duty.

BENEFITS

SEC. 526. A Reserve officer shall, except as otherwise provided in regulations which the Secretary may prescribe, receive all the allowances, privileges, and benefits which Foreign Service officers are entitled to receive in accordance with the provisions of title IX.

REAPPOINTMENT OR REASSIGNMENT OF RESERVE OFFICERS

SEC. 527. A person who has served as a Reserve officer may not be reappointed or reassigned to active duty until the expiration of a period of time equal to his preceding tour of duty or until the expiration of a year, whichever is the shorter.

REINSTATEMENT OF RESERVE OFFICERS

SEC. 528. Upon the termination of the assignment of a Reserve officer assigned from any Government agency, such person shall be entitled to reinstatement in the Government agency by which he is regularly employed in the same position he occupied at the time of assignment, or in a corresponding or higher position. Upon reinstatement he shall receive the within-grade salary advancements he would have been entitled to receive had he remained in the position in which he is regularly employed under subsection (*d*), section 7, of the Classification Act of 1923, as amended, or any corresponding provision of law applicable to the position in which he is serving. A certificate of the Secretary that such person has met the standards required for the efficient conduct of the work of the Foreign Service shall satisfy any requirements as to the holding of minimum ratings as a prerequisite to the receipt of such salary advancements.

PART H — ASSIGNMENT OF FOREIGN SERVICE PERSONNEL

ASSIGNMENTS TO ANY GOVERNMENT AGENCY

SEC. 571. (*a*) Any officer or employee of the Service may, in the discretion of the Director General, be assigned or detailed for duty in any Government agency, such an assignment or combination of assignments to be for a period of not more than four years. He may not again be assigned for duty in a Government agency until the expiration of a period of time equal to his preceding tour of duty on such assignment or until the expiration of two years, whichever is the shorter.

(*b*) A Foreign Service officer may be appointed as Director General or Deputy Director General, notwithstanding the provisions of the last sentence of paragraph (*a*) of this section, but any such officer may not serve longer than four years in such position or positions and upon the completion of such service may not again be assigned to a position in the Department until the expiration of a period of time equal to his tour of duty as Director General or Deputy Director General or until the expiration of two years, whichever is shorter.

(*c*) If a Foreign Service officer shall be appointed by the President, by and with the advice and consent of the Senate, to a position in the Department, the period of his service in such capacity shall be construed as constituting an assignment for duty in the Department within the meaning of paragraph (*a*) of this section and such person shall not, by virtue of the acceptance of such an assignment, lose his status as a Foreign Service officer. Service in such a position shall not, however, be subject to the limitations concerning the duration of an assignment or concerning reassignment contained in that paragraph.

(*d*) If the basic minimum salary of the position to which an officer or employee of the Service is assigned pursuant to the terms of this section is higher than the salary such officer or employee is entitled to receive as an officer or employee of the Service, such officer or employee shall, during the period such difference in salary exists, receive the salary of the position in which he is serving in lieu of his salary as an officer or employee of the Service. Any salary paid under the provisions of this section shall be paid from appropriations made available for the payment of salaries of officers and employees of the Service and shall be the salary on the basis of which computations and payments shall be made in accordance with the provisions of title VIII.

COMPULSORY SERVICE OF FOREIGN SERVICE OFFICERS IN THE CONTINENTAL UNITED STATES

SEC. 572. Every Foreign Service officer shall, during his first fifteen years of service in such capacity, be assigned for duty in the continental United States in accordance with the provisions of section 571 for periods totaling not less than three years.

ASSIGNMENT FOR CONSULTATION OR INSTRUCTION

SEC. 573. (*a*) Any officer or employee of the Service may, in the discretion of the Secretary, be assigned or detailed to any Government agency for consultation or specific instruction either at the commencement, during the course of, or at the close of the period of his official service; and any such detail or assignment, if not more than four months in duration, shall not be considered as an assignment within the meaning of section 571.

(*b*) Any officer or employee of the Service may be assigned or detailed for special instruction or training at or with public or private nonprofit institutions; trade, labor, agricultural, or scientific associations; or commercial firms.

ASSIGNMENT TO TRADE, LABOR, AGRICULTURAL, SCIENTIFIC, OR OTHER CONFERENCES

SEC. 574. An officer or employee of the Service may, in the discretion of the Secretary, be assigned or detailed for duty with domestic or international trade, labor, agricultural, scientific, or other conferences, congresses, or gatherings, including those whose place of meeting is in the continental United States; or for other special duties, including temporary details under commission not at his post or in the Department.

ASSIGNMENTS TO FOREIGN GOVERNMENTS

SEC. 575. The Secretary may, in his discretion, assign or detail an officer or employee of the Service for temporary service to or in cooperation with the government of another country in accordance with the provisions of the Act of May 25, 1938, as amended (52 Stat. 442; 53 Stat. 652; 5 U. S. C. 118e).

ASSIGNMENTS TO INTERNATIONAL ORGANIZATIONS

Sec. 576. The Secretary may, in his discretion, assign or detail an officer or employee of the Service for temporary service to or in cooperation with an international organization in which the United States participates under the same conditions as those governing the assignment or detail of officers or employees of the Service to the government of another country in accordance with the provisions of the Act of May 25, 1938, as amended (52 Stat. 442; 53 Stat. 652; 5 U. S. C. 118e).

ASSIGNMENT OR DETAIL TO THE UNITED STATES NOT TO AFFECT PERSONNEL CEILINGS

Sec. 577. An officer or employee of the Service assigned or detailed to the continental United States in accordance with the provisions of this Act shall not be counted as a civilian employee within the meaning of section 607 of the Federal Employees' Pay Act of 1945, as amended by section 14 of the Federal Employees' Pay Act of 1946.

TITLE VI — PERSONNEL ADMINISTRATION

. . . .

Part C — Promotion of Foreign Service Officers and Foreign Service Reserve Officers

PROMOTION OF FOREIGN SERVICE OFFICERS BY SELECTION

Sec. 621. All promotions of Foreign Service officers shall be made by the President, in accordance with such regulations as he may prescribe, by appointment to a higher class, by and with the advice and consent of the Senate. Promotion shall be by selection on the basis of merit.

ELIGIBILITY

Sec. 622. The Secretary shall, by regulation, determine the minimum period Foreign Service officers must serve in each class and a standard for performance for each class which they must meet in order to become eligible for promotion to a higher class. In the event the Director General shall certify to the Board of the Foreign Service that a Foreign Service officer has rendered extraordinarily meritorious service, the Board of the Foreign Service may recommend to the Secretary that such officer shall not be required to serve such minimum period in class as a prerequisite to promotion, and the Secretary may exempt such officer from such requirement.

RECOMMENDATIONS FOR PROMOTION

Sec. 623. The Secretary is authorized to establish, with the advice of the Board of the Foreign Service, selection boards to evaluate the performance of Foreign Service officers, and upon the basis of their findings the Secretary shall make recommendations to the President for the promotion of Foreign Service officers. No person assigned to serve on any such board shall serve in such capacity for any two consecutive years.

PROMOTION OF FOREIGN SERVICE RESERVE OFFICERS

SEC. 624. Any Reserve officer may receive promotions from one class to a next higher class in accordance with regulations prescribed by the Secretary.

IN-CLASS PROMOTIONS OF FOREIGN SERVICE OFFICERS AND RESERVE OFFICERS

SEC. 625. Any Foreign Service officer or any Reserve officer, whose services meet the standards required for the efficient conduct of the work of the Foreign Service and who shall have been in a given class for a continuous period of nine months or more, shall, on the first day of each fiscal year, receive an increase in salary to the next higher rate for the class in which he is serving. The Secretary is authorized to grant to a Foreign Service officer or a Reserve officer, in any class, additional increases in salary within the salary range established for the class in which he is serving, based upon especially meritorious service.

. . . . . .

TITLE VII — THE FOREIGN SERVICE INSTITUTE

ESTABLISHMENT OF THE INSTITUTE

SEC. 701. The Secretary shall, in order to furnish training and instruction to officers and employees of the Service and of the Department and to other officers and employees of the Government for whom training and instruction in the field of foreign relations is necessary, and in order to promote and foster programs of study incidental to such training, establish a Foreign Service Institute, hereinafter called the Institute.

THE DIRECTOR OF THE INSTITUTE — APPOINTMENT, SALARY, AND DUTIES

SEC. 702. The head of the Institute, who shall be known as its Director, shall be appointed by the Secretary. The Director shall, under the general supervision of the Director General and under such regulations as the Secretary may prescribe, establish the basic procedures to be followed by the Institute; plan and provide for the general nature of the training and instruction to be furnished at the Institute; correlate the training and instruction to be furnished at the Institute with the training activities of the Department and other Government agencies and with courses given at private institutions that are designed or may serve to furnish training and instruction to officers and employees of the Service; encourage and foster such programs outside of the Institute as will be complementary to those of the Institute; and take such other action as may be required for the proper administration of the Institute.

AID TO NONPROFIT INSTITUTIONS

SEC. 703. The Secretary may, within the limits of such appropriations as may be made specifically therefor, make grants or furnish such other gratuitous assistance as he may deem necessary or advisable to nonprofit institutions cooperating with the Institute in any of the programs conducted by the Director by authority of this title.

APPOINTMENT, ASSIGNMENT, AND DETAIL TO THE INSTITUTE

SEC. 704. (a) The Secretary may appoint to the faculty or staff of the Institute on a full- or part-time basis such personnel as he may deem necessary to carry out the provisions of this title in accordance with the provisions of the civil-service laws and regulations and the Classification Act of 1923, as amended, except that, when deemed necessary by the Secretary for the effective administration of this title, personnel may be appointed without regard to such laws and regulations, but any person so appointed shall receive a salary at one of the rates provided by the Classification Act of 1923, as amended. All appointments to the faculty or staff of the Institute shall be made without regard to political affiliations and shall be made solely on the basis of demonstrated interest in, and capacity to promote, the purposes of the Institute.

(b) The Secretary may, under such regulations as he may prescribe and on a full- or part-time basis, assign or detail officers and employees of the Service to serve on the faculty or staff of the Institute or to receive training at the Institute.

(c) The Secretary may, under such regulations as he may prescribe and on a full- or part-time basis, assign or detail any officer or employee of the Department, and, with the consent of the head of the Government agency concerned, any other officer or employee of the Government, to serve on the faculty or staff of the Institute, or to receive training. During the period of his assignment or detail, such officer or employee shall be considered as remaining in the position from which assigned.

(d) It shall be the duty of the Director to make recommendations to the Secretary with regard to the appointment, assignment, or detail of persons to serve on the faculty or staff of the Institute, and the Secretary shall in each case take such recommendations into consideration in making such appointments, assignments, or details.

INSTRUCTION AND EDUCATION AT OTHER LOCALITIES THAN THE INSTITUTE

SEC. 705. The Secretary may, under such regulations as he may prescribe, pay the tuition and other expenses of officers and employees of the Service, assigned or detailed in accordance with the provisions of section 573 (b) for special instruction or training at or with public or private nonprofit institutions, trade, labor, agricultural, or scientific associations, or commercial firms.

ENDOWMENTS AND GIFTS TO THE INSTITUTE

SEC. 706. The Secretary may accept, receive, hold, and administer gifts, bequests, or devices of money, securities, or property made for the benefit of, or in connection with, the Foreign Service Institute in accordance with part C of title X.

ACQUISITION OF REAL PROPERTY FOR THE INSTITUTE

SEC. 707. The Secretary may, in the name of the United States, acquire such real property as may be necessary for the operation and maintenance of the Institute and, without regard to section 3709 of the Revised Statues, such other property and equipment as may be necessary for its operation and maintenance.

. . . . . .

TITLE IX — ALLOWANCES AND BENEFITS

PART A — ALLOWANCES AND SPECIAL ALLOTMENTS

QUARTERS, COST OF LIVING, AND REPRESENTATION ALLOWANCES

SEC. 901. In accordance with such regulations as the President may prescribe and notwithstanding the provisions of section 1765 of the Revised Statues (5 U. S. C. 70), the Secretary is authorized to grant to any officer or employee of the Service who is a citizen of the United States —

(1) allowances, wherever Government owned or rented quarters are not available, for living quarters, heat, light, fuel, gas, and electricity, including allowances for the cost of lodging at temporary quarters, incurred by an officer or employee of the Service and the members of his family upon first arrival at a new post, for a period not in excess of three months after such first arrival or until the occupation of residence quarters, whichever period shall be shorter, up to but not in excess of the aggregate amount of the per diem that would be allowable to such officer or employee for himself and the members of his family for such period if they were in travel status;

(2) cost-of-living allowances, whenever the Secretary shall determine —

(i) that the cost of living at a post abroad is proportionately so high that an allowance is necessary to enable an officer or employee of the Service at such post to carry on his work efficiently;

(ii) that extraordinary and necessary expenses, not otherwise compensated for, are incurred by an officer or employee of the Service incident to the establishment of his residence at his post of assignment;

(iii) that an allowance is necessary to assist an officer or employee of the Service who is compelled by reason of dangerous, notably unhealthful, or excessively adverse living conditions at his post abroad or for the convenience of the Government to meet the additional expense of maintaining his wife and minor children elsewhere than in the country of his assignment;

(3) allowances in order to provide for the proper representation of the United States by officers or employees of the Service.

ALLOTMENT FOR OFFICIAL RESIDENCE OF CHIEF AMERICAN REPRESENTATIVES

SEC. 902. The Secretary may, under such regulations as he may prescribe, make an allotment of funds to any post to defray the unusual expenses incident to the operation and maintenance of an official residence suitable for the chief representative of the United States at that post.

ACCOUNTING FOR ALLOWANCES

SEC. 903. All such allowances and allotments shall be accounted for to the Secretary in such manner and under such rules and regulations as the President may prescribe. The Secretary shall report all such expenditures annually to the Congress with the budget estimates of the Department.

PART B — TRAVEL AND RELATED EXPENSES

GENERAL PROVISIONS

SEC. 911. The Secretary may, under such regulations as he shall prescribe, pay —

(1) the travel expenses of officers and employees of the Service, including expenses incurred while traveling pursuant to orders issued by the Secretary in accordance with the provisions of section 933 with regard to the granting of home leave;

(2) the travel expenses of the members of the family of an officer or employee of the Service when proceeding to or returning from his post of duty; accompanying him on authorized home leave; or otherwise traveling in accordance with authority granted pursuant to the terms of this or any other Act;

(3) the cost of transporting the furniture and household and personal effects of an officer or employee of the Service to his successive posts of duty and, on the termination of his services, to the place where he will reside;

(4) the cost of storing the furniture and household and personal effects of an officer or employee of the Service who is absent under orders from his usual post of duty, or who is assigned to a post to which, because of emergency conditions, he cannot take or at which he is unable to use, his furniture and household and personal effects;

(5) the cost of storing the furniture and household and personal effects of an officer or employee of the Service on first arrival at a post for a period not in excess of three months after such first arrival at such post or until the establishment of residence quarters, whichever shall be shorter;

(6) the travel expenses of the members of the family and the cost of transporting the personal effects and automobile of an officer or employee of the Service, whenever the travel of such officer or employee is occasioned by changes in the seat of the government whose capital is his post;

(7) the travel expenses and transportation costs incident to the removal of the members of the family of an officer or employee of the Service and his furniture and household and personal effects, including automobiles, from a post at which, because of the prevalence of disturbed conditions, there is imminent danger to life and property, and the return of such persons, furniture, and effects to such post upon the cessation of such conditions; or to such other post as may in the meantime have become the post to which such officer or employee has been assigned.

(8) the cost of preparing and transporting to their former homes in the continental United States or to a place not more distant, the remains of an officer or employee of the Service who is a citizen of the United States and of the members of his family who may die abroad or while in travel status.

. . . .

TITLE X — MISCELLANEOUS

Part A — Prohibitions

AGAINST UNIFORMS

Sec. 1001. An officer or employee of the Service holding a position of responsibility in the Service shall not wear any uniform except such as may be authorized by law or such as a military commander may require civilians to wear in a theater of military operations.

AGAINST ACCEPTING PRESENTS

Sec. 1002. An officer or employee of the Service shall not ask or, without the consent of the Congress, receive, for himself or any other person, any present, emolument, pecuniary favor, office, or title from any foreign government. A chief of mission or other principal officer may, however, under such regulations as the President may prescribe, accept gifts made to the United States or to any political subdivision thereof by the government to which he is accredited or from which he holds an exequatur.

AGAINST ENGAGING IN BUSINESS ABROAD

Sec. 1003. An officer or employee of the Service shall not, while holding office, transact or be interested in any business or engage for profit in any profession in the country or countries to which he is assigned abroad in his own name or in the name or through the agency of any other person, except as authorized by the Secretary.

THE CONDUCT OF FOREIGN RELATIONS

AGAINST CORRESPONDENCE ON AFFAIRS OF FOREIGN GOVERNMENTS

SEC. 1004. (a) An officer or employee of the Service shall not correspond in regard to the public affairs of any foreign government except with the proper officers of the United States, except as authorized by the Secretary.

(b) An officer or employee of the Service shall not recommend any person for employment in any position of trust or profit under the government of the country to which he is detailed or assigned, except as authorized by the Secretary.

AGAINST POLITICAL, RACIAL, RELIGIOUS, OR COLOR DISCRIMINATION

SEC. 1005. In carrying out the provisions of this Act, no political test shall be required and none shall be taken into consideration, nor shall there be any discrimination against any person on account of race, creed, or color.

. . . .

CONTINUANCE IN FORCE OF EXISTING RULES, REGULATIONS, AND EXECUTIVE ORDERS

SEC. 1135. Notwithstanding the provisions of this Act, existing rules, regulations of or applicable to the Service, and Executive orders shall remain in effect until revoked or rescinded or until modified or superseded by regulations made in accordance with the provisions of this Act, unless clearly inconsistent with the provisions of this Act.

PART E — EFFECTIVE DATE OF ACT

SEC. 1141. The effective date of this Act shall be three months following the date of its enactment.

(3) *Statement by the President (Truman) on the Foreign Service Act of 1946, August 13, 1946.*[1]

It is significant that this bill (H. R. 6967, "to improve, strengthen, and expand the Foreign Service of the United States and to consolidate and revise the laws relating to its administration") comes to me for signature at just the time that the efforts of Secretary Byrnes at the Peace Conference are demonstrating how great a stake the United States has in world affairs. While we strive to reach international agreement on the large and confused issues, we can make progress by trying to perfect those instruments of international relations, which it lies in our power to improve. This administration is doing everything possible to back up our participation in the United Nations and its ancillary organizations, and in the International Bank and the International Monetary Fund. This Foreign Service legislation is consistent with all our efforts in this field. It seeks to make the Service as efficient an instrument of our foreign policy as possible and to make our efforts to win the peace that much more effective.

[1] Department of State, *Bulletin*, XV, p. 386.

The traditional responsibilities of the Foreign Service have increased in complexity and importance and many new duties have been added as a result of the inclusion in the Department of State of some of the functions of wartime agencies. The efficient performance of this service is now more vital to the Government and individual American citizens than before the war. It must keep our Government informed with the greatest foresight and accuracy; it must make effective our policies in great countries and small; it must protect our citizens abroad in a troubled world and must promote our commerce under conditions of trade still influenced by the war and subject to controls not always familiar to the private trader.

The Foreign Service is now functioning as best it can on an outmoded plan laid down in 1924. In this bill we create a "new model" service. One of the basic reforms is a revision of the salary structure so that a man without independent means can serve his country as an Ambassador or Minister or in any Foreign Service position as effectively as a wealthy man. At the same time that the bill improves compensation it subjects the Service to more rigid requirements in regard to promotion and training; it seeks to keep our diplomats and consuls from losing touch with American life and thought by providing more frequent and varied assignments in this country; and it tries to make the Service truly representative of the whole Government and people by making it possible for the best qualified men and women in the country, in or out of the Government, to have tours of duty with the Foreign Service in any of its ranks.

We hope to speed the success of our foreign policy by improving its instruments. For a country situated as we are, only the best possible Foreign Service will suffice; this new act will, I hope, provide the foundations on which we can build such a service.

B. Changes in Foreign Service Posts

(1) *Offices Established or Reestablished during the Period from July 1, 1945 to December 31, 1946.*[1]

Post	Rank	Date
Amsterdam, Netherlands	CG	July 2, 1945 (R)
Antilla, Cuba	C	June 7, 1945
Arequipa, Peru	CA	July 1, 1946
Bangkok, Siam	L	January 5, 1946 (R)
Batavia, Java	CG	October 21, 1945 (R)
Bremen, Germany	C	April 2, 1946 (R)
Bremerhaven, Germany	VC	October 21, 1946
Budapest, Hungary	L	January 26, 1946 (R)
Canton, China	CG	November 15, 1945 (R)
Caserta, Italy	USPA	(Opened 1945)
Chungking, China	C	April 26, 1946

[1] Compiled from information furnished by the Department of State, Division of Foreign Service Administration. Key to symbols used:
C — Consulate
CA — Consular Agency
CG — Consulate General
E — Embassy
L — Legation
M — Mission
USM — U. S. Mission
USPA — U. S. Political Adviser
VC — Vice Consulate

THE CONDUCT OF FOREIGN RELATIONS

Post	Rank	Date
Dairen, China	C	April 7, 1946 (R)
Frankfort on the Main, Germany	CG	March 1, 1946 (R)
Gdansk, Poland	C	May 7, 1946
The Hague, Netherlands	E	August 29, 1945 (R)
Hamburg, Germany	CG	March 1, 1946 (R)
Hankow, China	CG	November 15, 1945 (R)
Hong Kong	CG	October 14, 1945 (R)
Iquitos, Peru	CA	February 25, 1946
Krakow, Poland	C	July 1, 1946
Limerick, Ireland (Moved from Foynes)	C	May 1, 1946
Manaos, Brazil	CA	June 18, 1946
Manila, Philippine Islands	E	July 4, 1946
Mukden, China	CG	March 20, 1946 (R)
Munich, Germany	CG	March 1, 1946 (R)
Nanking, China (Moved from Chungking)	E	April 24, 1946
Patras, Greece	C	c. July 10, 1945 (R)
Peiping, China	C	January 1, 1946
Poznan, Poland	C	January 26, 1946
Rangoon, Burma	CG	November 2, 1945 (R)
Saigon, French Indochina	C	February 19, 1946 (R)
San Pedro Sula, Honduras (Moved from Puerto Cortes)	C	December 1, 1946
Seoul, Korea	USPA	c. September 9, 1945
(Consular Section established)		August 28, 1946
Shanghai, China	CG	September 13, 1945 (R)
Singapore	CG	October 6, 1945 (R)
Strasbourg, France	C	March 23, 1946 (R)
Stuttgart, Germany	C	March 1, 1946 (R)
Taipei, Taiwan, China	C	April 11, 1946 (R)
Tientsin, China	CG	October 7, 1945 (R)
Tokyo, Japan	USPA	September 22, 1945
Tsingtao, China	C	November 27, 1945 (R)
Trieste, Italy	USPA	June 28, 1946
Turin, Italy	C	January 27, 1946 (R)
Vienna, Austria	USM	August 22, 1945 (R)
Warsaw, Poland	E	July 31, 1945 (R)
Yokahama, Japan	USPA	September or October 1945
Zagreb, Yugoslavia	C	May 9, 1946 (R)

(2) *Offices Closed during the Period from July 1, 1945 to December 31, 1946.*[1]

Post	Rank	Date
Acapulco, Mexico	VC	September 15, 1945
Adana, Turkey	C	July 4, 1945
Antilla, Cuba	C	February 1, 1946
Arequipa, Peru	VC	June 30, 1946
Arica, Chile	VC	April 5, 1946

[1] Compiled from information furnished by the Department of State, Division of Foreign Service Administration. Key to symbols used:
C — Consulate   E — Embassy   USM — U. S. Mission
CA — Consular Agency   L — Legation   USPA — U. S. Political Adviser
CG — Consulate General   M — Mission   VC — Vice Consulate

Post	Rank	Date
Beira, Mozambique, Africa	C	c. December 30, 1945
Bello Horizonte, Brazil	C	December 4, 1946
Brazzaville, French Equatorial Africa	CG	July 13, 1946
Cienfuegos, Cuba	C	September 15, 1945
Curitiba, Brazil	VC	October 25, 1946
Djibouti, French Somali Coast, Africa	CA	December 15, 1946
Durango, Mexico	C	July 11, 1946
Foynes, Ireland (Moved to Limerick)	C	April 30, 1946
Freetown, Sierra Leone, Africa	CA	October 15, 1946
Galway, Ireland	CA	December 31, 1945
Horta, Fayal, Azores	C	June 30, 1946
Iskenderûn, Turkey	C	July 8, 1945
Las Palmas, Canary Islands	C	September 30, 1946
Lugano, Switzerland	C	March 31, 1946
Malmo, Sweden	C	March 24, 1946
Manaos, Brazil	VC	June 28, 1946
Manzanillo, Mexico	VC	June 6, 1946
Oran, Algeria	C	May 9, 1946
Peiping, China	E	December 31, 1945
Puerto Cortes, Honduras (Moved to San Pedro Sula)	C	November 30, 1946
Punta Arenas, Chile	VC	November 30, 1946
Puntarenas, Costa Rica	VC	November 15, 1946
San Sebastian, Spain	C	September 30, 1946
Suez, Egypt	C	March 31, 1946
Tapachula, Mexico	VC	June 25, 1946
Tirana, Albania	USM	November 14, 1946

(3) *Changes in Rank of Offices during the Period from July 1, 1945 to December 31, 1946.*[1]

Post	Rank	Changed to	Date
Baghdad, Iraq	L	E	December 28, 1946
Bombay, India	C	CG	July 1, 1945
Budapest, Hungary	USM	L	June 26, 1946
Cairo, Egypt	L	E	October 10, 1946
Canberra, Australia	L	E	July 19, 1946
Casablanca, Morocco	C	CG	May 4, 1946
Goteborg, Sweden	C	CG	July 24, 1946
Helsinki, Finland	USM	L	September 1, 1945
Kingston, Jamaica	C	CG	July 20, 1946
Kunming, China	CG	C	August 26, 1946
Milan, Italy	C	CG	September 1, 1945
New Delhi, India	M	E	November 1, 1946
Saigon, French Indochina	C	CG	May 23, 1946
Tsingtao, China	C	CG	August 31, 1946
Tunis, Tunisia	C	CG	May 22, 1946
Vienna, Austria	USM	L	September 7, 1946

[1] Compiled from information furnished by the Department of State, Division of Foreign Service Administration. Key to symbols used:
C — Consulate
CA — Consular Agency
CG — Consulate General
E — Embassy
L — Legation
M — Mission
USM — U. S. Mission
USPA — U. S. Political Adviser
VC — Vice Consulate

CHAPTER III

THE TERMINATION OF THE WAR

1. THE JAPANESE SURRENDER

(1) *Proclamation Defining Terms for the Japanese Surrender, Signed at Potsdam and Issued by the President of the United States (Truman) and the Prime Minister of the United Kingdom (Attlee) and Concurred in by the President of the National Government of China (Chiang), July 26, 1945.*[1]

(1) We — the President of the United States, the President of the National Government of the Republic of China, and the Prime Minister of Great Britain, representing the hundreds of millions of our countrymen, have conferred and agree that Japan shall be given an opportunity to end this war.

(2) The prodigious land, sea and air forces of the United States, the British Empire and of China, many times reinforced by their armies and air fleets from the west, are poised to strike the final blows upon Japan. This military power is sustained and inspired by the determination of all the Allied Nations to prosecute the war against Japan until she ceases to resist.

(3) The result of the futile and senseless German resistance to the might of the aroused free peoples of the world stands forth in awful clarity as an example to the people of Japan. The might that now converges on Japan is immeasurably greater than that which, when applied to the resisting Nazis, necessarily laid waste to the lands, the industry and the method of life of the whole German people. The full application of our military power, backed by our resolve, *will* mean the inevitable and complete destruction of the Japanese armed forces and just as inevitably the utter devastation of the Japanese homeland.

(4) The time has come for Japan to decide whether she will continue to be controlled by those self-willed militaristic advisers whose unintelligent calculations have brought the Empire of Japan to the threshold of annihilation, or whether she will follow the path of reason.

(5) Following are our terms. We will not deviate from them. There are no alternatives. We shall brook no delay.

(6) There must be eliminated for all time the authority and influence of those who have deceived and misled the people of Japan into embarking on world conquest, for we insist that a new order of peace, security and justice will be impossible until irresponsible militarism is driven from the world.

[1] Department of State, *Bulletin*, XIII, p. 137. See also, Department of State Publication 2671, Far Eastern Series 17, p. 53.

(7) Until such a new order is established *and* until there is convincing proof that Japan's war-making power is destroyed, points in Japanese territory to be designated by the Allies shall be occupied to secure the achievement of the basic objectives we are here setting forth.

(8) The terms of the Cairo Declaration shall be carried out and Japanese sovereignty shall be limited to the islands of Honshu, Hokkaido, Kyushu, Shikoku and such minor islands as we determine.

(9) The Japanese military forces, after being completely disarmed, shall be permitted to return to their homes with the opportunity to lead peaceful and productive lives.

(10) We do not intend that the Japanese shall be enslaved as a race or destroyed as a nation, but stern justice shall be meted out to all war criminals, including those who have visited cruelties upon our prisoners. The Japanese Government shall remove all obstacles to the revival and strengthening of democratic tendencies among the Japanese people. Freedom of speech, of religion, and of thought, as well as respect for the fundamental human rights shall be established.

(11) Japan shall be permitted to maintain such industries as will sustain her economy and permit the exaction of just reparations in kind, but not those which would enable her to re-arm for war. To this end, access to, as distinguished from control of, raw materials shall be permitted. Eventual Japanese participation in world trade relations shall be permitted.

(12) The occupying forces of the Allies shall be withdrawn from Japan as soon as these objectives have been accomplished and there has been established in accordance with the freely expressed will of the Japanese people a peacefully inclined and responsible government.

(13) We call upon the government of Japan to proclaim now that unconditional surrender of all Japanese armed forces, and to provide proper and adequate assurances of their good faith in such action. The alternative for Japan is prompt and utter destruction.

(2) *Exchange of Notes between the Secretary of State (Byrnes) and the Swiss Chargé d'Affaires ad interim (Grässli) Regarding the Offer of Surrender from the Japanese Government.*[1]

(a) *Note from the Swiss Chargé d'Affaires ad interim to the Secretary of State, August 10, 1945.*

I have the honor to inform you that the Japanese Minister to Switzerland, upon instructions received from his Government, has requested the Swiss Political Department to advise the Government of the United States of America of the following:

In obedience to the gracious command of His Majesty the Emperor who, ever anxious to enhance the cause of world peace, desires earnestly to bring about a speedy termination of hostilities with a view to saving mankind from the calamities to be imposed upon them by further continuation of the war, the Japanese

[1] Department of State, *Bulletin*, XIII, p. 205. See also, Department of State Publication 2671, Far Eastern Series 17, p. 56.

Government several weeks ago asked the Soviet Government, with which neutral relations then prevailed, to render good offices in restoring peace vis-à-vis the enemy powers. Unfortunately, these efforts in the interest of peace having failed, the Japanese Government in conformity with the august wish of His Majesty to restore the general peace and desiring to put an end to the untold sufferings entailed by war as quickly as possible, have decided upon the following.

The Japanese Government are ready to accept the terms enumerated in the joint declaration which was issued at Potsdam on July 26th, 1945, by the heads of the Governments of the United States, Great Britain, and China, and later subscribed by the Soviet Government, with the understanding that the said declaration does not comprise any demand which prejudices the prerogatives of His Majesty as a Sovereign Ruler.

The Japanese Government sincerely hope that this understanding is warranted and desire keenly that an explicit indication to that effect will be speedily forthcoming.

In transmitting the above message the Japanese Minister added that his Government begs the Government of the United States to forward its answer through the intermediary of Switzerland. Similar requests are being transmitted to the Governments of Great Britain and the Union of Soviet Socialist Republics through the intermediary of Sweden, as well as to the Government of China through the intermediary of Switzerland. The Chinese Minister at Berne has already been informed of the foregoing through the channel of the Swiss Political Department.

Please be assured that I am at your disposal at any time to accept for and forward to my Government the reply of the Government of the United States.

(b) *Note from the Secretary of State to the Swiss Chargé d'Affaires ad interim, August 11, 1945.*

I have the honor to acknowledge receipt of your note of August 10, and in reply to inform you that the President of the United States has directed me to send to you for transmission by your Government to the Japanese Government the following message on behalf of the Governments of the United States, the United Kingdom, the Union of Soviet Socialist Republics, and China:

With regard to the Japanese Government's message accepting the terms of the Potsdam proclamation but containing the statement, "with the understanding that the said declaration does not comprise any demand which prejudices the prerogatives of His Majesty as a sovereign ruler," our position is as follows:

From the moment of surrender the authority of the Emperor and the Japanese Government to rule the state shall be subject to the Supreme Commander of the Allied powers who will take such steps as he deems proper to effectuate the surrender terms.

The Emperor will be required to authorize and ensure the signature by the Government of Japan and the Japanese Imperial General Headquarters of the surrender terms necessary to carry out the provisions of the Potsdam Declaration, and shall issue his commands to all the Japanese military, naval and air authorities and to all the forces under their control wherever located to cease active operations and to surrender their arms, and to issue such other orders as the Supreme Commander may require to give effect to the surrender terms.

Immediately upon the surrender the Japanese Government shall transport prisoners of war and civilian internees to places of safety, as directed, where they can quickly be placed aboard Allied transports.

The ultimate form of government of Japan shall, in accordance with the Potsdam Declaration, be established by the freely expressed will of the Japanese people.

The armed forces of the Allied Powers will remain in Japan until the purposes set forth in the Potsdam Declaration are achieved.

(3) *Statement by the President (Truman) on the Japanese Acceptance of the Potsdam Declaration, Containing the Text of the Message of Acceptance from the Japanese Government, August 14, 1945.*[1]

I have received this afternoon a message from the Japanese Government in reply to the message forwarded to that Government by the Secretary of State on August 11. I deem this reply a full acceptance of the Potsdam Declaration which specifies the unconditional surrender of Japan. In the reply there is no qualification.

Arrangements are now being made for the formal signing of surrender terms at the earliest possible moment.

General Douglas MacArthur has been appointed the Supreme Allied Commander to receive the Japanese surrender. Great Britain, Russia, and China will be represented by high-ranking officers.

Meantime, the Allied armed forces have been ordered to suspend offensive action.

The proclamation of V-J Day must wait upon the formal signing of the surrender terms by Japan.

Following is the Japanese Government's message accepting our terms:

"Communication of the Japanese Government of August 14, 1945, addressed to the Governments of the United States, Great Britain, the Soviet Union, and China:

"With reference to the Japanese Government's note of August 10 regarding their acceptance of the provisions of the Potsdam declaration and the reply of the Governments of the United States, Great Britain, the Soviet Union, and China sent by American Secretary of State Byrnes under the date of August 11, the Japanese Government have the honor to communicate to the Governments of the four powers as follows:

"1. His Majesty the Emperor has issued an Imperial rescript regarding Japan's acceptance of the provisions of the Potsdam declaration.

"2. His Majesty the Emperor is prepared to authorize and ensure the signature by his Government and the Imperial General Headquarters of the necessary terms for carrying out the provisions of the Potsdam declaration. His Majesty is also prepared to issue his commands to all the military, naval, and air authorities of Japan and all the forces under their control wherever located to cease active operations, to surrender arms and to issue such other orders as may be required by the Supreme Commander of the Allied Forces for the execution of the above-mentioned terms."

[1] Department of State, *Bulletin*, XIII, p. 255. See also, Department of State Publication 2671, Far Eastern Series 17, p. 59.

(4) *Text of the Instrument of Surrender, Signed by Representatives of the Japanese Government and of the United Nations at War with Japan, Tokyo Bay, September 2, 1945.*[1]

We, acting by command of and in behalf of the Emperor of Japan, the Japanese Government and the Japanese Imperial General Headquarters, hereby accept the provisions set forth in the declaration issued by the heads of the Governments of the United States, China and Great Britain on 26 July 1945, at Potsdam, and subsequently adhered to by the Union of Soviet Socialist Republics, which four powers are hereafter referred to as the Allied Powers.

We hereby proclaim the unconditional surrender to the Allied Powers of the Japanese Imperial General Headquarters and of all Japanese armed forces and all armed forces under Japanese control wherever situated.

We hereby command all Japanese forces wherever situated and the Japanese people to cease hostilities forthwith, to preserve and save from damage all ships, aircraft, and military and civil property and to comply with all requirements which may be imposed by the Supreme Commander for the Allied Powers or by agencies of the Japanese Government at his direction.

We hereby command the Japanese Imperial General Headquarters to issue at once orders to the Commanders of all Japanese forces and all forces under Japanese control wherever situated to surrender unconditionally themselves and all forces under their control.

We hereby command all civil, military and naval officials to obey and enforce all proclamations, orders and directives deemed by the Supreme Commander for the Allied Powers to be proper to effectuate this surrender and issued by him or under his authority and we direct all such officials to remain at their posts and to continue to perform their non-combatant duties unless specifically relieved by him or under his authority.

We hereby undertake for the Emperor, the Japanese Government and their successors to carry out the provisions of the Potsdam Declaration in good faith, and to issue whatever orders and take whatever action may be required by the Supreme Commander for the Allied Powers or by any other designated representative of the Allied Powers for the purpose of giving effect to that Declaration.

We hereby command the Japanese Imperial Government and the Japanese Imperial General Headquarters at once to liberate all allied prisoners of war and civilian internees now under Japanese control and to provide for their protection, care, maintenance and immediate transportation to places as directed.

The authority of the Emperor and the Japanese Government to rule

---

[1] Department of State, *Executive Agreement Series* 493. See also, Department of State, *Bulletin*, XIII, p. 364; and Department of State Publication 2671, Far Eastern Series 17, p. 62.

110   DOCUMENTS ON AMERICAN FOREIGN RELATIONS

the state shall be subject to the Supreme Commander for the Allied Powers who will take such steps as he deems proper to effectuate these terms of surrender.

Signed at Tokyo Bay, Japan at 0908 I on the second day of September, 1945.

[Here follow the signatures of the representatives of the Japanese Government and of the Japanese Imperial General Headquarters.]

Accepted at Tokyo Bay, Japan at 0908 I on the second day of September, 1945, for the United States, Republic of China, United Kingdom and the Union of Soviet Socialist Republics, and in the interests of the other United Nations at war with Japan.

[Here follow the signatures of the Supreme Commander for the Allied Powers and of the representatives of the United Nations at war with Japan.]

(5) *Address by the President (Truman) on the Signing by Japan of the Instrument of Surrender, September 1, 1945.*[1]

The thoughts and hopes of all America — indeed of all the civilized world — are centered tonight on the battleship *Missouri*. There on that small piece of American soil anchored in Tokyo Harbor the Japanese have just officially laid down their arms. They have signed terms of unconditional surrender.

Four years ago the thoughts and fears of the whole civilized world were centered on another piece of American soil — Pearl Harbor. The mighty threat to civilization which began there is now laid at rest. It was a long road to Tokyo — and a bloody one.

We shall not forget Pearl Harbor.

The Japanese militarists will not forget the U. S. S. *Missouri*.

The evil done by the Japanese warlords can never be repaired or forgotten. But their power to destroy and kill has been taken from them. Their Armies and what is left of their Navy are now impotent.

To all of us there comes first a sense of gratitude to Almighty God who sustained us and our Allies in the dark days of grave danger, Who made us to grow from weakness into the strongest fighting force in history, and Who now has seen us overcome the forces of tyranny that sought to destroy His civilization.

God grant that in our pride of the hour we may not forget the hard tasks that are still before us; that we may approach these with the same courage, zeal, and patience with which we faced the trials and problems of the past four years.

Our first thoughts of course — thoughts of gratefulness and deep obligation — go out to those of our loved ones who have been killed or maimed in this terrible war. On land and sea and in the air, American

[1] Department of State, *Bulletin*, XIII, p. 299. See also, Department of State Publication 2671, Far Eastern Series 17, p. 65.

THE TERMINATION OF THE WAR

men and women have given their lives so that this day of ultimate victory might come and assure the survival of a civilized world. No victory can make good their loss.

We think of those whom death in this war has hurt, taking from them husbands, sons, brothers, and sisters whom they loved. No victory can bring back the faces they longed to see.

And so on V-J Day we take renewed faith and pride in our own way of life. We have had our day of rejoicing over this victory. We have had our day of prayer and devotion. Now let us set aside V-J Day as one of renewed consecration to the principles which have made us the strongest Nation on earth and which, in this war, we have striven so mightily to preserve.

Those principles provide the faith, the hope, and the opportunity which help men to improve themselves and their lot. Liberty does not make all men perfect nor all society secure. But it has provided more solid progress and happiness and decency for more people than any other philosophy of government in history. And this day has shown again that it provides the greatest strength and the greatest power which man has ever reached.

We know that under it we can meet the hard problems of peace which have come upon us. A free people with free Allies, who can develop an atomic bomb, can use the same skill and energy and determination to overcome all the difficulties ahead.

Victory always has its burdens and its responsibilities as well as its rejoicing.

But we face the future and all its dangers with great confidence and great hope. America can build for itself a future of employment and security. Together with the United Nations it can build a world of peace founded on justice and fair dealing and tolerance.

As President of the United States, I proclaim Sunday, September 2, 1945 to be V-J Day — the day of formal surrender by Japan. It is not yet the day for the formal proclamation of the end of the war or of the cessation of hostilities. But it is a day which we Americans shall always remember as a day of retribution — as we remember that other day, the day of infamy.

From this day we move forward. We move toward a new era of security at home. With the other United Nations we move toward a new and better world of peace and international good-will and cooperation.

God's help has brought us to this day of victory. With His help we will attain that peace and prosperity for ourselves and all the world in the years ahead.

2. THE TRANSITION TO PEACE

A. The Cessation of Hostilities

On December 31, 1946, President Truman issued a proclamation establishing the cessation of hostilities, effective as of twelve o'clock noon, of that day. An accompanying statement by the President called particular attention to the fact that this Proclamation in no way served to terminate the states either of emergency or of war.

(1) *Proclamation by the President (Truman), Terminating the Hostilities of the Second World War, Issued December 31, 1946.*[1]

With God's help this nation and our allies, through sacrifice and devotion, courage and perseverance, wrung final and unconditional surrender from our enemies. Thereafter, we, together with the other United Nations, set about building a world in which justice shall replace force. With spirit, through faith, with a determination that there shall be no more wars of aggression calculated to enslave the peoples of the world and destroy their civilization, and with the guidance of Almighty Providence great gains have been made in translating military victory into permanent peace. Although a state of war still exists, it is at this time possible to declare, and I find it to be in the public interest to declare, that hostilities have terminated.

Now, THEREFORE, I, HARRY S. TRUMAN, President of the United States of America, do hereby proclaim the cessation of hostilities of World War II, effective twelve o'clock noon, December 31, 1946.

IN WITNESS WHEREOF, I have hereunto set my hand and caused the seal of the United States of America to be affixed.

[SEAL] DONE at the City of Washington this 31st day of December in the year of our Lord nineteen hundred and forty-six, and of the Independence of the United States of America the one hundred and seventy-first.

(2) *Statement by the President (Truman) on the Termination of the Hostilities of the Second World War. White House Press Release, December 31, 1946.*[2]

I have today issued a proclamation terminating the period of hostilities of World War II, as of 12 o'clock noon today, December 31, 1946.

Under the law, a number of war and emergency statutes cease to be effective upon the issuance of this proclamation. It is my belief that the time has come when such a declaration can properly be made, and that it is in the public interest to make it. Most of the powers affected by the proclamation need no longer be exercised by the executive branch of the Government. This is entirely in keeping with the policies which I have consistently followed, in an effort to bring our economy and our Government back to a peacetime basis as quickly as possible.

The proclamation terminates Government powers under some 20 statutes immediately upon its issuance. It terminates Government powers under some 33 others at a later date, generally at the end of 6 months from the date of the proclamation. This follows as a result of provisions made by the Congress when the legislation was originally passed. In a few instances the statutes affected by the proclamation give the Government certain powers which in my opinion are desirable in peacetime, or for the remainder of the period of reconversion. In these

---

[1] Department of State, *Bulletin*, XVI, p. 77. See also, Proclamation 2714, *Federal Register*, XII, p.1.

[2] Department of State, *Bulletin*, XVI, p. 77.

instances, recommendations will be made to the Congress for additional legislation.

It should be noted that the proclamation does not terminate the states of emergency declared by President Roosevelt on September 8, 1939, and May 27, 1941. Nor does today's action have the effect of terminating the state of war itself. It terminates merely the period of hostilities. With respect to the termination of the national emergency and the state of war I shall make recommendations to the Congress in the near future.

B. Demobilization of the Armed Forces

(1) *Annual Message of the President (Truman) to the Congress on the State of the Union, January 14, 1946.*[1]

[Excerpt]

. . . . . .

4. DEMOBILIZATION OF OUR ARMED FORCES

The cessation of active campaigning does not mean that we can completely disband our fighting forces. For their sake and for the sake of their loved ones at home, I wish that we could. But we still have the task of clinching the victories we have won — of making certain that Germany and Japan can never again wage aggressive warfare, that they will not again have the means to bring on another world war. The performance of that task requires that, together with our allies, we occupy the hostile areas, complete the disarmament of our enemies, and take the necessary measures to see to it that they do not rearm.

As quickly as possible, we are bringing about the reduction of our armed services to the size required for these tasks of occupation and disarmament. The Army and the Navy are following both length-of-service and point systems as far as possible in releasing men and women from the service. The points are based chiefly on length and character of service, and on the existence of dependents.

Over 5 million from the Army have already passed through the separation centers.

The Navy, including the Marine Corps and the Coast Guard, has discharged over one and a half million.

Of the 12 million men and women serving in the Army and Navy at the time of the surrender of Germany, one-half have already been released. The greater part of these had to be brought back to this country from distant parts of the world.

Of course, there are cases of individual hardship in retention of personnel in the service. There will be in the future. No system of such size can operate to perfection. But the systems are founded on fairness and justice, and they are working at full speed. We shall try to avoid mistakes, injustices, and hardship — as far as humanly possible.

We have already reached the point where shipping is no longer the bottleneck in the return of troops from the European theater. The

[1] *Ibid.*, XIV, p. 141.

governing factor now has become the requirement for troops in sufficient strength to carry out their missions.

In a few months the same situation will exist in the Pacific. By the end of June, 9 out of 10 who were serving in the armed forces on V–E day will have been released. Demobilization will continue thereafter, but at a slower rate, determined by our military responsibilities.

Our national safety and the security of the world will require substantial armed forces, particularly in overseas service. At the same time it is imperative that we relieve those who have already done their duty, and that we relieve them as fast as we can. To do that, the Army and the Navy are conducting recruiting drives with considerable success.

The Army has obtained nearly 400,000 volunteers in the past four months, and the Navy has obtained 80,000. Eighty percent of these volunteers for the regular service have come from those already with the the colors. The Congress has made it possible to offer valuable inducements to those who are eligible for enlistment. Every effort will be made to enlist the required number of young men.

The War and Navy Departments now estimate that by a year from now we still will need a strength of about 2 million, including officers, for the armed forces — Army, Navy, and Air. I have reviewed their estimates and believe that the safety of the Nation will require the maintenance of an armed strength of this size for the calendar year that is before us.

In case the campaign for volunteers does not produce that number, it will be necessary by additional legislation to extend the Selective Service Act beyond May 16, the date of expiration under existing law. That is the only way we can get the men and bring back our veterans. Action along this line should not be postponed beyond March, in order to avoid uncertainty and disruption.

. . . . . .

(2) *Demobilization Directive of January 15, 1946.*[1]

To:

CG USFET, Main Frankfurt, Germany.
CINCAFPAC advance Tokyo, Japan.
CG IBT, New Delhi, India.
CG USF China Theatre, Shanghai, China (pass to Secretary of War).
CG USF Middle East, Cairo, Egypt.
CG MTO, Caserta, Italy.

1. Effective immediately, the following will govern the demobilization of the Army until June 30, 1946:

A. By April 30, 1946, the following will be separated from the Army or aboard ship returning home:

1. All enlisted men (except volunteers) with forty-five points as of Sept. 2, 1945, or with thirty months service as of April 30, 1946.

[1] *New York Times*, January 16, 1946, p. 15. See also, *Congressional Record*, 92, p. A97 (Daily edition, January 17, 1946).

THE TERMINATION OF THE WAR

2. All enlisted Wac (except volunteers) with twenty-four months service as of April 30, 1946.
3. All male officers (except Regular Army, volunteers, and medical department officers) with sixty-seven points as of Sept. 2, 1945, or forty-five months service as of April 30, 1946.
4. All Wac officers (except volunteers) with thirty-six months length of service as of April 30, 1946.

B. By June 30, 1946, the following will be separated from the Army or aboard ship returning home:
1. All enlisted men (except volunteers) with forty points as of Sept. 2, 1945, or with twenty-four months service as of June 30, 1946.
2. All male officers (except Regular Army, volunteers, and medical department officers) with sixty-five points as of Sept. 2, 1945, or with forty-two months service as of June 30, 1946.
3. Separate instructions covering the discharge of Wac personnel, officer and enlisted, for the period after April 30 will be issued by the War Department.

C. Medical Corps officers will be demobilized by separate criteria established by the War Department.

D. As soon as the tabulation of the desires of officers according to category as prescribed in War Department circular 366, 1945, has been made further instructions on their separation will follow.

E. It is emphasized, repeat emphasized, that release of all personnel will follow the principle of priority of release for those with highest points and longest length of service, particularly combat.

2. Computation of length of service will include total active commissions and enlisted honorable service, continuous or interrupted, since Sept. 16, 1940. Time lost under AW 107 will not be included.

3. Eligibility for separation of personnel made eligible by previously published criteria is not affected by this message. Such personnel will be given priority for separation over personnel demobilized in accordance with Paragraph 1 above.

4. The term "volunteers" as used herein includes enlisted personnel who have volunteered under provisions of Change 2 of RR 1-1 or who have enlisted in the Regular Army. Officer volunteers are those who sign certificates under War Department Circular 366, 1945, as Category I, II, or III, or Category IV until date specified in the certificate.

5. Scarce category personnel who appear in Circular 321, WD, 1945, and in Circular 382, WD, 1945, may be retained in the service until replaced provided they are utilized in their speciality, but in no case longer than six months beyond date upon which they would be discharged under these instructions.

6. The above constitutes the War Department program of demobilization for the period until June 30, 1946. Z/I (Zone of the Interior) and theater commanders are responsible for the immediate release of every individual for whom there is no military need, and for releasing officers and men in sufficient time to carry out these instructions.

However, no individual will be discharged under this directive with less service or smaller scores than set forth herein. The bulk of the men made eligible for discharge by this order should be discharged in the early part of the periods January to April and May to June, respectively. Theatre commanders will notify War Department without delay of revised shipping requirements by month through June.

(3) *Statement by General Dwight Eisenhower before a Special Meeting of Congress, January 15, 1946.*[1]

[Excerpts]

. . . . . .

There is no mystery in demobilization. There are no hidden ball plays. Long before our victory in Europe, General Marshall approved a master plan which has served and still serves as the basis of establishing priority of men for discharge. In any job as big as this one there are bound to be modifications made in the light of experience. But I assure you that I have made and intend to make no changes in the basic plan. The plan was simply this: to discharge men as quickly as possible and to the limit of available shipping with priority on those with the longest and hardest service — that is, with the most points. These criteria were to govern until we reached the point where minimum personnel requirements to do the jobs in hand were threatened by the rate of discharge. We have been in the business of discharging veterans from the Army under the point system for eight months, with the system at full blast for the past four months since V–J Day. Men have been discharged so fast that the five millionth passed through one of the separation centers last week.

We used shipping to the utmost and secured the complete cooperation of the Navy in our zeal to get every man and woman back from overseas who could be spared. There is no longer any shortage of transports, and the shipping people assure me they will have vessels where and when we need them to bring troops home. The fact is that we worked so fast that about ten days ago we had to slow the pace so that the work of our forces in Europe and the Pacific would not suffer too much from lack of manpower. The announcement of that slow-down was what touched off the fireworks.

. . . . . .

Primarily, two underlying causes are responsible for the present confusion, which for a time has quite evidently exceeded the power of any information program to control. The first is that the Nation's release from the urgency of war started an emotional wave to get men out of the Army. . . . The second cause of our present discontent arises, I believe, from the almost incredible speed with which the War Department moved in bringing men home from V–J Day to the close of the year. . . .

. . . . . .

If we were to continue shipping men home at the rate we reached during the past few months, about April we would have nothing left but a woefully inadequate number of volunteers — we would literally have "run out of Army." That is the reason for the slow-down. There is no change in policy; there is no change in plan. We have merely reached a point in the pursuance of our plans and policies which we knew we must face when the time came. That time is now. We took all possible steps to meet inescapable needs without slowing the pace of demobilization. We pressed the recruiting campaign to the utmost in order to bring volunteers into the Army who could take the place of those over-

[1] *Ibid.*, p. A91–97.

seas. We urged that positive steps be taken to provide us our full quotas of 50,000 men monthly through the Selective Service System. We required all theater commanders overseas to institute the most searching drive to cut down their estimates in manpower needed for occupation duties, for supply, and for the extensive personnel required to close up overseas depots, ports, warehouses, bases. We had also to cooperate with the designated disposal agencies in disposing of Government property as expeditiously as possible while still taking all necessary precautions to protect it. Similar instructions were issued to all commanders at home.

. . . .

Now, understand this — the men who do not need replacement when their jobs are finished will come home immediately. So far as possible this will be in the order of their point scores and length of service. These will be the surplus men, the men available for discharge. But if we are not to disintegrate our occupation forces certain men must be kept until trained replacements are available or their job finished.

. . . .

One thing right here on this matter of replacements which I believe is generally misunderstood is why, if we recruit 5,000 men today, we cannot release 5,000 men from the Army tomorrow, or next week, or next month. The answer is quite simple when you analyze the problem. So far as essential jobs in the theater are concerned, the recruits become available not when they enlist but only when they arrive overseas, trained to take over their assignments. If an 18-year-old enlists or is inducted through selective service in this country, he goes off to a camp for three months to learn the rudiments of being a soldier.

If a trained man already in the Army chooses to volunteer for regular enlistment, he is entitled to a furlough in the United States which will make him useless as a replacement until he returns. Any way you work it, there is bound to be a lag of three to six months in this replacement business. It cannot be avoided. The men who enlist or are drafted between now and next July will not be available in time to solve the immediate problem before us, even if there were enough of them. They are the effective replacements for men to be discharged three to six months from now. The lack of replacements facing the Army now is due to the shortage of selective-service men and the volunteers of the last six months in 1945. Because they did not come in fast enough, we must slow down our discharge rate now.

The people at home must understand this, too. Acceptance of the need for keeping large numbers of men overseas at the present time lies, I believe, in an understanding of all the necessary tasks they must perform. . . .

. . . .

Start with our primary and continuing mission of occupation duties. Troops assigned to this work supervise the German and Austrian Governments. It is a complex job. . . . In our zones in those two unhappy countries the Army is responsible for supervising all the headaches of a change-over from war to peace, with the added directive that we must make certain these people are so disarmed, both economically and in a military sense, that they cannot make war again. Reconversion measures in those two countries are enormously complicated by devastation. . . . It requires a great many men to supervise the local governments in our zone in Germany and Austria with a civilian population of over 15,000,000. However much you may delegate local work to Germans, you still have the responsibility for policing these people, their industry, trade, and commerce, food and agriculture, education, finance, telephone and telegraph and transportation. . . .

. . . .

Then there is the extensive intelligence and counterintelligence work required to carry out the work of denazification and pacification. This includes a constant watch for subversive activities, evaluation and processing of Nazi documents, supervision of civilian censorship, and the conduct of counterintelligence which alone is expected to result in the arrest of an over-all total of 500,000 persons. Unquestionably, many prominent Nazis are still at large because of a shortage of trained counterintelligence personnel.

* * * * * *

Discipline in this respect has a wider significance than the simple protection of the lives of American soldiers and of Government stores. Our example in maintaining law and order throughout the conquered countries will have the most far-reaching effect in hastening the pacification of the German people. If, through curtailment of manpower, lawlessness and contempt for the American brand of justice should be permitted to develop, it would not only hurt our progress in Germany but would weaken our prestige throughout Europe. Quickly, our commanders and forces would be in an impossible position.

In addition to these operations, recruits from this country, who have already been given their basic training as soldiers, must be further trained in occupation duties after arrival. This means that experienced men from the occupation force must be detailed to instruct them — another drain on the over-all manpower assigned to this work.

These duties have taken no account of the men who must be assigned to the procurement, storage, and distribution of supplies. Besides the normal function of supplying the military forces, General McNarney's theater has the responsibility of providing for such agencies as United Nations Relief and Rehabilitation Administration and the Foreign Liquidation Commission. The problem is complicated by the limited amount of rail transportation. Although civilians are employed as much as possible, there are limits to the effectiveness of their use. In order to reduce stealing in a land where goods are very scarce, civilians are usually worked in depot areas where they can be closely supervised. . . .

The task of providing communications throughout the United States zone was greatly hampered by the damaged and chaotic condition in which the established lines of communication were found when we took over. These facilities must provide not only for the occupational forces but for the minimum needs of the civilian population. Considerable construction of bridges and, to a lesser extent, of highways and waterways is necessary. Civilian labor under military supervision is utilized in construction, but because of the technical nature of the work our own Signal Corps troops are required to perform maintenance on signal communication facilities. German civilians are operating such ground transport as exists, under our Army's supervision. The system of air transport must be operated entirely by our troops.

Of considerable importance is the disposal of United States property remaining in the theater, as well as the storage and orderly destruction of captured enemy material. . . .

. . . A great deal of effort has gone into the roll-up and concentration of this property, but there still remains a vast amount to be done.

Regardless of whether this property is stored for the use of our occupation forces, returned to the United States for current and future needs of the Army, in process of being declared surplus, or already declared surplus but not disposed of by the disposal agencies, the Army has the complete responsibility for care, maintenance, protection, delivery, and fiscal accounting for such property. These responsibilities also apply to captured enemy property. . . .

That is a very brief and a very rough summary of the present duties of troops engaged on the strictly military duties incident to occupation. This work now requires the assignment of some 298,000 American troops. General McNarney's estimate is that by next July 1, their number may be cut to 171,000, of which 98,000 will be performing the duties of supervising the German Government and population and 73,000 will be performing the direct supply requirements of this force. The figure includes the considerable number who carry on constant occupational negotiations with British, Russian, and French members of allied control councils.

Another of our duties is the guarding, screening, supervision, administration, and eventual release of enemy personnel held by United States forces. . . .

The care of displaced persons has been an enormous problem from the time of our entry into Germany. The repatriation of millions of these individuals has already been carried out with sympathy and high regard for the humanitarian nature of the problem involved. . . .

Numbers of our troops are also engaged in the emergency program of providing supplies in Germany and Austria to minimize starvation, disease and disorder among the civilian population. In Austria we are also helping to sustain vital economic projects on a minimum scale. Before the winter is over the distribution of emergency food supplies will undoubtedly become necessary.

At the present time some 50,000 of our men are directly concerned in control and direction of prisoners of war and displaced persons. By July 1, 1946, their number will have been reduced by half — to 25,000.

Some 111,000 service troops are now assigned to the European theater, to take care of the needs of the occupation force and troops engaged in winding up our surplus property installations. . . . Our troops are scattered over a wide area. Lack of the usual civilian facilities has placed unusual burdens on the service units. These service units must also carry on a limited amount of construction and considerable maintenance work. This includes airfields, laundries, American Red Cross installations for the recreation of troops, winterized billets, and hospitals. Maintenance is constantly necessary in all the ports. Prisoners of war and local civilian labor are largely used in this work under our military supervision, but the problems are so extensive that thousands of Americans are required for these jobs.

Last in this category I mention the Graves Registration Service, which involves the location, identification, concentration, care and disposition of the remains of our heroic dead. . . .

At present, as I have said, some 111,000 troops are assigned to these various service missions. By July 1, 1946, General McNarney expects to have cut this total to 61,000.

There is a final manpower category for the theater consisting of men temporarily unavailable for duty which the Army calls ineffectives, for want of a better word. This lumps together individuals who may be charged against the theater roster but are actually not, for one reason or another, performing any part of its duties. In this category are troops who are being moved in order to be discharged or to replace those troops; men on sick leave, pass, and recreation; men in schools, in confinement, or in transit to station; men absent from the theater on rest, recuperation, and rehabilitation; men on furlough in the United States after re-enlisting in the theater. The total number of these individuals on January 1 was about 163,000. This number will be cut to 50,000 by July 1.

. . . .

Within the broad categories I have indicated I believe you may imagine the thousands of daily tasks which must be performed by thousands of men. I know, and you know, that many of them are homesick men. But there is a job to be finished. Although our Allies are carrying a heavy load, Americans have assumed the definite commitment and the responsibility of carrying out their own share. To the Army has been delegated the principal job in performing this work. The work cannot be done without men. Remember, this is your Army — not the War Department's Army and not the generals' Army. It belongs to the country — to the Congress and the people. It carries out their wishes and their orders.

Let's turn now to the Pacific, where similar heavy responsibilities are being carried out by troops under command of General MacArthur. In addition to occupation duties, closing up supply bases, ports, dumps, etc., and the disposal of great stores of property assembled for the invasion of Japan, this theater has an additional duty in occupying bases which our troops seized in the island campaigns during the advance toward the home islands. The build-up of supply, concentrated in Hawaii and in the Philippines, was well along when the Japs gave up. As a matter of fact, our tonnage of supplies in the Philippines actually increased after the close of hostilities in the Pacific, due to the great number of ships nearing port and our uncertainty at that time of what our needs would be when we landed in Japan. While the majority of these ships were coming from the United States, many others of them carried supplies redeployed from Europe and other inactive theaters to support the invasion of Japan scheduled for November 1945.

General MacArthur has reported 7,000,000 tons of supplies as being on hand January 1 in the Pacific theater. The duties our troops are performing out there are almost exactly similar to those I have described for the European theater. Our occupation functions involve most of the islands captured from the Japanese as well as Japan proper. We have a force in Korea. We are still accepting the surrender of Japanese troops in the Philippines, Ryukyus and other localities, long after their nation had surrendered.

... The supply system, operating over thousands of miles, is a formidable problem in the Pacific. The Army is exerting every effort to maintain a never-ending flow of fresh foods to all bases and areas where our forces are located, but transport by air, water, and land is made difficult by great distances.

. . . .

A great part of the work our men are now doing on many of those small Pacific islands whose conquest made savage headlines for a brief spell two and three years ago, is concerned with the disposition of property. . . .

Then the war itself ended, and all need for these bases ceased. The business of "closing out" these bits of temporary American soil began. Our troops commenced to "roll them up," in the phrase the soldiers use.

This process of rolling up our bases occupies the time of a great many soldiers in the Pacific. These islands have been piled high with American goods, brought in to push our soldiers along the seaway to Tokyo. This is Government property, and now these things which the Army no longer needs must be disposed of through the proper disposal agency. They must be inventoried, inspected, packed, and guarded until the Army's responsibility is discharged..

But out in the Pacific there is an enemy of property far more dangerous than thieves. It is the tropical elements which mildew and rot and destroy unless the utmost precaution is used. Trained and disciplined soldiers are needed for this work, men who know their jobs and who feel a sense of responsibility for the preservation of this property while it remains in the hands of the Army.

. . . .

The property-disposal problem is a definite part of this nation's mission in the Pacific. It is my responsibility, it is the soldier's responsibility out there — in the end, it is your responsibility, as members of the Congress, to the American people. Except where necessary for health, safety, or security, we do not have the authority to abandon this property; it must be taken off our hands by properly constituted civil authority. It is one of the incompatibles defying unrestricted rate of demobilization. It will continue to be a charge against our military manpower until it is liquidated.

. . . .

I will not go into the service functions of our Pacific troops in detail, since in most particulars they parallel those I described for the European theater, complicated by long supply lines, the tropical enemy, and difficulties of transport within many areas. But I should like to say a special word about the mission of our troops in the Philippines. . . . As a result of the war the Philippines were left without an effective police force and the splendid Philippine Scout organizations were practically destroyed. Now armed bands of guerrillas roam the hills, bent on pilferage which only our active presence controls. We are now engaged in recruiting a force of 50,000 Filipinos to replace a comparable number of our men in the Philippines and elsewhere in the Pacific, but it will be many months before this force becomes effective enough to accept the responsibility of policing the islands. It is our clear obligation to assist until that time arrives. In addition to this activity, American troops have here also the familiar task of liquidating the bases and immense stores of Government property which were assembled at a time when these islands were our principal forward base for the planned assault on Japan's home islands. With the exception of air and supply bases on Luzon and Leyte, our Philippine bases and supply points will be progressively reduced and closed out by July 1, 1946. On January 1 we had approximately 279,000 troops in the Philippines. These will be reduced as rapidly as possible to a garrison of approximately 79,000 which will be needed on July 1 to carry out our continuing responsibilities there.

· · · · · ·

What I have said of the Pacific and of Europe applies to all the other areas overseas where we have American troops and property. The same problems exist in varying degrees in all theaters, and in the last analysis, we must rely on the professional judgment and ability of our theater commanders to find the solutions. I have the utmost confidence in them.

I have spoken to you thus fully of the situation and the mission of our forces overseas because only in the light of all these jobs, which complete the commitments and obligations placed on the Army by higher authority, is it possible to understand the continuing necessity of adjusting the demobilization program to the job in hand.

These foreign commitments and obligations cannot be met, our demobilization cannot continue in an orderly fashion, we cannot carry on the business of our far-flung forces unless we keep a proportionate force on duty in the United States during this interim period. . . .

· · · · · · ·

The question may well be asked — and it has been — if you have 2,000,000 men in this country now and are cutting these to 654,000 by next July, why not send some of the difference overseas to replace veterans who might then come home? That is exactly what we are doing. All of the replacements going overseas are carried as strength in this country until they arrive at a foreign port. But there is no economy in sending a man overseas if he is so close to eligibility for discharge that we should have to turn him right around and send him back. Nor is there any sound reason for keeping him in the Army if we no longer have a job for him here. So we discharge him. I realize that it is a source of irritation to veterans overseas to have a man discharged in this country with fewer points than the veteran over there. From his angle, it is rank injustice. But from the point of view of the country the only realistic and practical decision is to let him out. We can't make an omelet the size of this demobilization job without breaking a few eggs.

I have described for you the composition and duties of our January 1 Army of 4,200,000 and of our Army of 1,500,000 as it will be next July 1. Our present problem lies wholly between these two figures.

· · · · · · ·

. . . In order to insure this and to make clear to every man in the Army exactly where he stands, the War Department has issued an order to all major commanders. It is appended in full to the statement.[1] The salient points affecting enlisted men are:

(1) By April 30, 1946, all enlisted men (except volunteers) with forty-five points as of September 2, 1945, or with thirty months service as of April 30, 1946, will be separated from the Army or aboard ship returning home.

(2) By June 30, 1946, all enlisted men (except volunteers) with forty points as of September 2, 1945, or with twenty-four months' service as of June 30, 1946, will be separated from the Army or aboard ship returning home.

Whether or not these criteria can continue to be observed after July 1 depends directly upon the rate of inflow. Failing the necessary monthly intake either these criteria will have to be abandoned or competent authority — I presume the Congress itself — will have to relieve the Army of its vitally important mission. None of us can escape the realization that this will be a most fateful decision, therefore let me repeat at once that the commitment I now make is limited to July 1, 1946.

Now let me talk of the replacement rate itself. Present estimates are based on past performance of Selective Service and our recruiting service. Only if future rates keep pace can the Army's rock-bottom requirements of 1,500,000 men in the service on July 1 be met. Let me examine these data for you. First, as to Selective Service: In July, the Army received 88,000 men through induction. In August, with the capitulation of Japan at hand and with the consequent easing of pressure by local boards, this figure fell to 55,000. Beginning with September, the Army arbitrarily reduced its monthly call to a total of 50,000. In September we actually received through Selective Service 41,000; in October, 37,000; in November, 35,000; and in December only 21,000.

As to enlistment, the Personnel Procurement Service, consisting of over 10,000 officers and men, is exclusively concerned with obtaining the maximum number of enlistments from every source — men in the service, those who have had previous service and now discharged, and from the vast number of men in civilian life who are eligible to serve. The most stringent orders are in effect to stress to the utmost all the inducements for enlistment which the Congress so recently authorized. Through the press and radio, a most comprehensive program of advertising has been launched. In November, when this program actually got into full swing, all previous records were broken when the Army enlisted 185,000. In December this number dropped off to 131,000. By January 1, our enlistments totaled slightly less than 400,000, but of this number approximately forty-four percent are men who have enlisted for the minimum periods of one year or eighteen months service. . . . Our enlistment record has been good, but, taken together with selective service, it has not been high enough to provide required replacements. We shall continue to push this enlistment program, but only if selective service is able to provide the 50,000 men per month we are asking for will the 1,500,000-man Army be guaranteed under our present discharge policy.

Let me make clear that the basic figure of 1,500,000 has no connection with the permanent peacetime Military Establishment. In this regard, I should like to dispel once and for all the confusion which apparently exists in the minds of many in the meaning of the term, "post-war Army." The Army that won the war needs no definition, apology, or justification by me or anyone else. Its record speaks for it. It was the finest military organization the world has ever seen. It was perfectly adapted in quantity and quality to the tasks assigned it. In the accomplishment of these tasks it covered itself with everlasting glory.

But that Army no longer exists! Most of the long-service combat veterans are already back in civilian life. They are largely among the 5,000,000 who have already been discharged. As I said before, we are particularly concerned about the combat man still in service.

What we have today is the remnant of that combat Army in a state of reorganization and reduction to an interim Army assigned an entirely different mission

---

[1] See this volume, p. 114.

or task. It is still a World War II task, but is not yet a task for a permanent peacetime Regular Army. It is the task of reconversion and of "securing the peace." When we have secured the peace, and liquidated our emergency tasks, we shall then have a third task — to preserve the peace. This is the long-term, continuing peacetime mission of the Army. It will be the job of our permanent peacetime Military Establishment. The size and composition of that establishment are, of course, up to you.

But that is not the issue here. We are not talking about our permanent peacetime Military Establishment but the establishment to do the job now in hand. I know of no responsible officer who would not infinitely prefer to have both our present interim Army as well as our future Regular Army on a 100-percent voluntary basis at the earliest possible moment. . . .

Now just where does this leave us? On V–E Day we had 8,300,000 troops. We have already discharged 5,000,000 and by July 1 we shall have discharged another 2,750,000 men who were in the Army the day Germany collapsed. This leaves but half a million or so of the V–E Day men. Except for veteran volunteers, this is all that will be left of our own V–E Day Army on July 1, 1946, less than fourteen months after the last shot was fired in Europe. All the rest will be recruits. It is with this relatively untrained Army in the throes of reconversion that we must undertake the grave tasks still ahead.

This has been the most rapid and broad-scale demobilization in history. I consider our July 1 figure to be almost without a safety factor. It is a risk which, under any other circumstances than the vastly appealing one of reuniting men with their families, I should be unwilling to take.

The order on two and a half-year men means the release of 2,200,000 by the end of April. It takes an estimated 500,000 men now in the Pacific, 400,000 in Europe, 400,000 from other areas overseas or already en route home, 900,000 now on duty in this country. This order has not been issued without the gravest consideration. . . .

. . . If we are not relieved of the still huge supplies of Government property entrusted to our custody overseas, we shall have no choice but to abandon them where they lie. But even if you gentlemen should approve such action on the choice between two evils, I know you would not tolerate the reduction of occupational forces below the levels required by General MacArthur and General McNarney to carry out their duties. There is no possible doubling up of work load which could enable us to accomplish that part of our present mission with fewer men. If that situation should develop, you gentlemen will have to decide what we must do. Other functions would have to be abandoned, too, with tragic results. Pared down to the bone, the Army air, ground, and service troops are still just able to discharge the duties I have outlined to you. We can function with no less. For my part, I can assure you that the Army will continue to carry out faithfully its planned reduction through the coming months, in accordance with the directive I have read to you. In the light of its terms, there will no longer be any useful purpose in such demonstrations as our troops have conducted during the past week in various areas around the world. . . .

During the war in Europe I had the heavy responsibility of sending into action the gallant sons of America, knowing full well that many would not come back alive. That is a commander's responsibility in a time of impelling need to defeat a menacing enemy. I did everything in my power to insure a sound plan of action and to implement this plan with the necessary troops and matériel to keep our losses at a minimum. Throughout this campaign the welfare and best interests of our men were always close to the hearts of their commanders of every grade. I regard the responsibility placed upon me in the current situation as a continuation of what I bore during the war. Along with that responsibility I carry the same vital interest in the welfare of our men and the same determination to see that their interests are fully weighed and protected. In no question involving the GI will I ever appear except as his friend and his advocate, although I may be of the "brass." I feel confident that when the reasons for the change in pace in the demobilization program are recognized by our soldiers and they have the full knowledge of their outlook for the next six months, they will accept, with that mature judgment Americans always show, their own responsibility for finishing the job. The time has now arrived to replace hysteria with calm judgment and sound discipline.

. . . . . .

One last thought I would like to leave with you. The War Department has no intention of abandoning the mission assigned to it by the Government, the Congress, and the people of the United States, so long as we have the troops to accomplish it. . . . We want to bring home quickly any man that has borne the brunt of battle and replace him, when necessary, by a man who has not.

My sole purpose, which I am certain you share, is that the Army which did so much to win the victory will be left fit to preserve it.

3. REQUIREMENTS AND COSTS OF TOTAL WAR

A. National Costs

(1) *United States Battle Casualties of the Second World War.*

Branch of Service	Dead	Missing
Army [1]	237,049 [2]	26,911 [3]
Navy [4]	62,484 [5]	64 [6]
Marine Corps [4]	24,446 [7]	33 [6]
Coast Guard [4]	1,912 [8]	0

[1] From information furnished by the War Department, the Adjutant General's Office, February 19, 1947.

[2] Figure as of June 30, 1945, including: 175,407 killed in action; 26,706 died of wounds; 23,042 declared dead; 11,894 died while classified as missing in action or prisoners of war.

[3] Figure as of June 30, 1945, including as missing in action 1,204 whose exact status is unknown.

[4] From information furnished by the Navy Department, Executive Office of the Secretary, Office of Public Information, February 10, 1947. Including aviation casualties.

[5] Figure as of January 1, 1947, including 13,049 casualties suffered in the United States.

[6] Figure as of January 1, 1947.

[7] Figure as of January 1, 1947, including 2,650 casualties suffered in the United States.

[8] Figure as of January 1, 1947, including 874 casualties suffered in the United States.

(2) Comparative Statement of Budgetary Receipts and Expenditures for the Fiscal Years 1947, 1946 and 1945.[1]

(In millions of dollars)

Classification	1947 (Estimated)	1946 (Actual)	1945 (Actual)
Receipts:			
Internal revenue:			
Income and profits taxes	27,134	30,885	35,173
Employment taxes	1,941	1,701	1,780
Miscellaneous internal revenue [2]	8,013	7,725	6,949
Customs	496	435	355
Other receipts [3]	4,001	3,493	3,483
Total receipts	41,585	44,239	47,740
Less:			
Net appropriations to Federal Old-Age and Survivors Insurance Trust Fund	1,355	1,201	1,283
Net receipts	40,230	43,038	46,457
Expenditures:			
War and defense activities:			
War Department	7,654	27,800	50,337
Navy Department	5,116	15,161	30,047
Armed Forces Leave Act of 1946:			
Bonds	1,900	—	—
Cash			
Miscellaneous war and defense activities	3,456	5,581	9,645
Total	18,126	48,542	90,029
Veterans' Administration, interest on public debt, and refunds of taxes and duties:			
Veterans' Administration [4][5]	7,518	4,253	2,060
Interest on the public debt	4,950	4,722	3,617
Refunds of taxes and duties	2,117	3,027	1,707
Total	14,585	12,002	7,384
International finance:			
Bretton Woods Agreements Act:			
International Bank	476	159	—
International Monetary Fund	950	—	—
Export-Import Bank — capital stock	325	674	—
Credit to United Kingdom	1,500	—	—
Total	3,251	833	—
Aid to agriculture [4]	1,680	980	762
Social security program [4][6]	1,234	852	815
Public works	1,257	407	323
Other general expenditures [4]	2,555	1,403	1,093
Reserve for contingencies	10		
Government corporations (wholly owned), etc. (net):			
Reconstruction Finance Corporation:			
War and defense activities	161	328	472
Other		− 23	− 288
Commodity Credit Corporation	− 790	− 1,044	470
Other	454	− 566	− 662
Total	− 175	− 1,305	− 7
Total expenditures	42,523	63,714	100,397
Net budgetary deficit (−) or surplus (+)	− 2,293	− 20,676	− 53,941

[1] Compiled from United States Treasury Department. Office of the Secretary. *Treasury Bulletin*, January 1947, p. 2.
[2] Includes chiefly alcoholic beverages taxes, tobacco taxes, manufacturers' and retailers' excise taxes, and estate taxes.
[3] Includes deposits resulting from the renegotiation of war contracts. On the basis of covering warrants, such deposits were as follows: fiscal year 1945, $2,041 million and fiscal year 1946, $1,063 million. Deposits are estimated at $408 million for fiscal year 1947.
[4] Includes transfers to trust accounts, etc.
[5] Includes expenditures for public works undertaken by Veterans' Administration.
[6] Includes railroad retirement and railroad unemployment activities and excludes expenditures made by Department of Labor, U. S. Employment Service under authority of the Social Security Act.

B. Lend-Lease and Mutual Aid

[See *Documents, III, 1940–1941*, p. 246, 711–736; *ibid., IV, 1941–1942*, p. 169–179, 225–239, 535–536, 542, 592–598, 605–607; *ibid., V, 1942–1943*, p. 105–132, 215–248, 364–366; *ibid., VI, 1943–1944*, p. 50, 118–137, 216–223; and *ibid., VII, 1944–1945*, p. 137–160, 301–345.]

1. DISCONTINUANCE OF LEND–LEASE OPERATIONS

(1) *White House Press Release, August 21, 1945.*[1]

The President has directed the Foreign Economic Administrator to take steps immediately to discontinue all lend-lease operations and to notify foreign governments receiving lend-lease of this action.

The President also directs that all outstanding contracts for lend-lease be canceled, except where Allied governments are willing to agree to take them over or where it is in the interest of the United States to complete them.

The Foreign Economic Administrator furthermore is instructed to negotiate with Allied governments for possible procurement by them of lend-lease inventories now in stockpile and in process of delivery.

If the military needs lend-lease supplies for the movement of troops or for occupation purposes the military will be responsible for procurement.

It is estimated that uncompleted contracts for non-munitions and finished goods in this country not yet transferred to lend-lease countries amount to about 2 billion dollars and that lend-lease supplies in stockpile abroad amount to between 1 and 1½ billion dollars.

(2) *Message of the President (Truman) to the Congress, September 6, 1945.*[2]

[Excerpt]

. . . .

18. LEND-LEASE AND POST-WAR RECONSTRUCTION

With the arrival of V–J Day lend-lease aid has practically come to an end. It was always understood that it would come to an end at that time. Immediately after Japan accepted the terms of unconditional surrender, I instructed the Foreign Economic Administrator to advise promptly all governments that deliveries of supplies under lend-lease would cease on V–J Day.[3]

I also directed the Administrator in advance of the actual termination of lend-lease deliveries on V–J Day to enter into immediate negotiations with the receiving governments for the purchase of all goods in the pipeline or in storage. These negotiations are proceeding satisfactorily.

In due time we must consider the settlement of the lend-lease obligations which have been incurred during the course of the war. We must

---

[1] Department of State, *Bulletin*, XIII, p. 284.
[2] *Ibid.*, p. 359.
[3] See this volume, above.

THE TERMINATION OF THE WAR   127

recognize that it will not be possible for our Allies to pay us dollars for the overwhelming portion of the lend-lease obligations which they have incurred. But this does not mean that all lend-lease obligations are to be canceled. We shall seek under the procedure prescribed in the Lend-Lease Act and in subsequent agreements with other governments to achieve settlements of our wartime lend-lease relations which will permit generally a sound world-wide economy and will contribute to international peace and our own national security.

. . . .

2. LEND-LEASE AND MUTUAL AID SETTLEMENTS

(1) *Agreement between the United States and the Union of Soviet Socialist Republics on the Disposition of Lend-Lease Supplies in the United States, October 15, 1945.*[1]

The Government of the United States and the Government of the Union of Soviet Socialist Republics, in order to provide for the orderly disposition in their mutual interests of the undelivered articles which were in inventory or procurement in the United States, prior to the cessation of active military operations against the common enemy, for the purpose of providing war aid to the Union of Soviet Socialist Republics under the act of Congress of March 11, 1941, as amended, agree as follows:

ARTICLE I

All articles and services undertaken to be provided by the Government of the United States under this agreement shall be made available under the authority and subject to the terms and conditions of the act of Congress of March 11, 1941, as amended, and any acts supplementary thereto.

ARTICLE II

Within such periods as may be authorized by law, the Government of the United States undertakes to transfer to the Government of the Union of Soviet Socialist Republics, and the Government of the Union of Soviet Socialist Republics agrees to accept subject to the right of inspection referred to in article V, those articles which are or will be available to the Government of the United States for transfer to the Government of the Union of Soviet Socialist Republics out of articles that are included in the requisitions set forth in schedule I–A or in the categories of articles set forth in schedule I–B and that were in inventory or procurement in the United States for the purpose of providing war aid to the Union of Soviet Socialist Republics, but were not transferred, prior to the date of the signature of this agreement.

The Government of the Union Soviet of Republics undertakes to pay the Government of the United States in dollars, for the articles

[1] *Twenty-First Report to Congress on Lend-Lease Operations, for the Period Ended September 30, 1945,* p. 48.

transferred to the Government of the Union of Soviet Socialist Republics under this article, an amount to be determined as set forth in schedule II, and interest thereon, according to the terms and conditions set out in that schedule. The obligation of the Government of the Union of Soviet Socialist Republics to make payment in dollars in accordance with the terms of this agreement may be discharged by the delivery of gold, which will be valued at the buying price for gold provided in the provisional regulations issued under the Gold Reserve Act of 1934 as the same may be in effect at the time of each delivery.

Schedule I–A, Schedule I–B, and Schedule II, which are annexed hereto, are made a part of this Agreement.

Article III

Changes may be made from time to time by mutual agreement of the parties in the list of requisitions and categories in schedule I–A and schedule I–B.

The Government of the Union of Soviet Socialist Republics shall be released from its obligation to accept articles under the provisions of article II upon payment to the Government of the United States of any net losses to the Government of the United States, including contract cancellation charges, resulting from the determination of the Government of the Union of Soviet Socialist Republics not to accept such articles.

The Government of the Union of Soviet Socialist Republics reserves the right, without payment as provided in the foregoing paragraph, not to accept articles which cannot be made available by the Government of the United States in complete units as specified in the approved requisitions or written requests of the Government of the Union of Soviet Socialist Republics, or in the offerings made by the United States Government, relating to such articles and units.

Article IV

Within such periods as may be authorized by law, the Government of the United States undertakes to aid in the movement to the Union of Soviet Socialist Republics of the articles provided under article II by furnishing American flag shipping and related services so far as it deems necessary to supplement Soviet flag shipping and so far as it is consistent with the national interest of the United States, and the Government of the Union of Soviet Socialist Republics agrees to pay the Government of the United States for such shipping and related services as may be made available under the provisions of this article in an amount and on terms and conditions set forth in schedule II.

Article V

The Government of the United States will, in lieu of granting any warranty express or implied with respect to articles transferred to the Union of Soviet Socialist Republics, assign to the Government of the Union of Soviet Socialist Republics any assignable rights which it may have against the suppliers, inland carriers, or other private contracting agencies for breach of warranty, or any assignable claims for loss of or damage to articles prior to transfer to the Government of the Union of Soviet Socialist Republics. The Government of the Union of Soviet Socialist Republics shall have the right of inspection of articles prior to delivery. The Government of the United States undertakes to use its best efforts to provide appropriate assistance to the Government of the Union of Soviet Socialist Republics to effectuate a satisfactory settlement with the suppliers, inland carriers, or other private contracting agencies of any claims of the Government of the Union of Soviet Socialist Republics covered by the aforesaid assignment.

The Government of the United States agrees that the provisions of article V of the Mutual Aid Agreement of June 11, 1942, shall not apply to supplies made available to the Government of the Union of Soviet Socialist Republics under the provisions of article II of this agreement.

ARTICLE VI

The provisions of this agreement shall not apply to those articles which the Government of the Union of Soviet Socialist Republics has agreed to purchase and the United States Government has agreed to transfer under the terms and conditions of the letter dated May 30, 1945, from the Foreign Economic Administrator to the Chairman of the Government Purchasing Commission of the Soviet Union in the United States.

Nothing in this agreement shall modify or otherwise affect the final determination, under the act of March 11, 1941, as amended, and the Mutual Aid Agreement between the two Governments of June 11, 1942, of the terms and conditions upon which the Government of the Union of Soviet Socialist Republics has received aid except for the articles and services made available under the provisions of this agreement.

ARTICLE VII

This agreement shall take effect as from this day's date.

In witness whereof the undersigned, duly authorized by their respective Governments, have signed the present agreement in duplicate in Washington on the 15th day of October 1945.

For the Government of the United States:
(Signed)   LEO T. CROWLEY.

For the Government of the Union of Soviet Socialist Republics:
(Signed)   LEONID G. RUDENKO.

SCHEDULE I

(Schedule I–A and Schedule I–B contain voluminous detailed information concerning the materials and equipment to be supplied under the Agreement.)

SCHEDULE II

The terms and conditions upon which articles are to be transferred and shipping and related services rendered by the Government of the United States to the Government of the Union of Soviet Socialist Republics under the provisions of this Agreement are as follows:

A. *Definitions.* — 1. The term "contract price" means the contract price f. o. b. point of origin, or the price computed by the United States Government f. o. b. point of origin in cases in which contracts are written on terms other than f. o. b. point of origin (confirmed by proper documents), which is paid by the United States Government to the contractor. The contract price shall be evidenced by a specific contract in cases where specific contracts have been entered into by a United States Government procurement agency in pursuance of an approved requisition or other written request of the Soviet Government Purchasing Commission or to fulfill offerings made by the United States to the Union of Soviet Socialist Republics for the war programs of the Union of Soviet Socialist Republics. In cases where articles so requested or offered are not procured on contracts placed by a U. S. Government procurement agency in part or in whole specifically for the Union of Soviet Socialist Republics but are procured by a United States Government procurement agency on general war supply contracts without specification of the particular ultimate recipient or recipients, the contract price shall be the average contract price (as computed by the United States Government) f. o. b. point of origin paid by the United States Government procurement agency for similar articles.

2. The term "the fair value of the articles" means: (*a*) In the case of nonfoodstuffs, in the aggregate, the contract price less 10 percent of such contract price; (*b*) In the case of foodstuffs, the price (as computed by the United States Government) at which the United States Government sells similar articles in similar quantities in the United States to other foreign governments at or about the time of transfer to the Union of Soviet Socialist Republics.

3. The term "Inland point of origin" means the factory in the case of articles in production or under contract for production at the time of the signing of this agreement and in the case of articles completed at the time of the signing of this agreement the point at which such articles are then situated or their immediate next destination if the articles are in transit.

B. Unless otherwise provided by mutual agreement, transfers of articles to the Government of the Union of Soviet Socialist Republics shall take place, in the case of nonfoodstuffs, immediately upon delivery of the articles at the inland point of origin, and in the case of foodstuffs, immediately upon the loading of the articles on board ocean vessels in a United States port, and title and risk of loss with respect to articles shall pass upon transfer to the Government of the Union of Soviet Socialist Republics; provided, that any article which shall not have been transferred to the Government of the Union of Soviet Socialist Republics as above set forth prior to 3 months following the time of the signing of this agreement or 3 months following the time of notice to the Government of the Union of Soviet Socialist Republics of the availability of the articles, whichever is the later, shall be deemed to be transferred to the Government of the Union of Soviet Socialist Republics upon such date, and the Government of the Union of Soviet Socialist Republics shall thereafter assume complete financial responsibility for the articles.

All articles made available shall be properly packed or prepared to meet the requirements of ocean shipping. The invoice delivered by the Government of the United States as certified by authorized officials of the Government of the Union of Soviet Socialist Republics with respect to articles transferred under article II shall be final. The Government of the Union of Soviet Socialist Republics shall, with respect to foodstuffs transferred, supply the Government of the United States with the necessary number of ship manifests and signed-on-board bills of lading with related invoices, packing lists, and other documents, whenever the foodstuffs are transported on a vessel not under the control of an agency of the Government of the United States.

C. The amount which the Government of the Union of Soviet Socialist Republics shall pay the Government of the United States, for articles transferred under the provisions of article II of this agreement, shall be the sum of the following items set forth in subparagraphs 1 and 2:

1. The fair value of the articles.
2. The costs incurred subsequent to transfer for storage, inland transportation, inland accessorial charges, and port accessorial charges normally incurred by cargo in accordance with the custom of the port.

In the case of nonfoodstuffs, such costs shall be evidenced by bills of lading, warehouse receipts or other appropriate invoices which shall be certified by the Government of the Union of Soviet Socialist Republics to represent true charges. Upon presentation of such documents to the Government of the United States by the Government of the Union of Soviet Socialist Republics the Government of the United States will pay the carrier, warehouse or other contracting agency, as the case may be. The Government of the Union of Soviet Socialist Republics undertakes to identify by marking on the bill of lading, warehouse receipt, or other documents involved, the requisition and contract numbers and shipping marks or a description of the articles covered by such documents.

In the case of foodstuffs, such cost is included in the fair value of the article determined in accordance with subparagraph (1) above.

D. The amount which the Government of the Union of Soviet Socialist Republics shall pay the Government of the United States for shipping and related services made available under the provisions of article IV of this agreement shall be determined on the basis of applicable rates established by the Government of the United States, which shall be subject to acceptance by the Government of the Union of Soviet Socialist Republics.

E. Payment of the total amount determined as set forth above in paragraphs C and D shall be made by the Government of the Union of Soviet Socialist Republics, on or before July 1, 1975, in 22 annual installments, the first of which shall become due and payable on July 1, 1954.

The amounts of the annual installments shall be as follows: each of the first 4 installments shall be in an amount equal to 2.5 percent of the amount determined as set forth above; each of the second 4 installments shall be 3.5 percent of said determined amount; each of the third 4 installments shall be 4.5 percent of said determined amount; each of the fourth 4 installments shall be 5.5 percent of said determined amount; and each of the last 6 installments shall be 6 percent of said determined amount.

Nothing herein shall be construed to prevent the Government of the Union of Soviet Socialist Republics from anticipating the payment of any of the installments, or any part thereof, set forth above.

If by agreement of both Governments it is determined that, because of extraordinary and adverse economic conditions arising during the course of payment, the payment of a due installment would not be in the joint interest of the United States and the Union of Soviet Socialist Republics, payment may be postponed for an agreed upon period.

Interest on the unpaid balance of the total amount determined as set forth above in paragraphs C and D shall be paid by the Government of the Union of Soviet Socialist Republics at a fixed rate of $2\frac{3}{8}$ percent per annum accruing from July 1, 1946. Interest shall be payable annually, the first payment to be made July 1, 1947.

(2) *Joint Statement by the United States and the United Kingdom on Settlement for Lend-Lease, Reciprocal Aid, Surplus War Property and Claims, December, 6, 1945.*[1]

1. The Governments of the United States and the United Kingdom have reached an understanding for the settlement of Lend-Lease and Reciprocal Aid, for the acquisition of United States Army and Navy surplus property, and the United States interest in installations, located in the United Kingdom, and for the final settlement of the financial claims of each government against the other arising out of the conduct of the war. Specific agreements necessary to implement these understandings, setting forth the terms in detail, and consistent herewith, are in the course of preparation and will shortly be completed.

2. This settlement for Lend-Lease and Reciprocal Aid will be complete and final. In arriving at this settlement both Governments have taken full cognizance of the benefits already received by them in the defeat of their common enemies. They have also taken full cognizance of the general obligations assumed by them in Article VII of the Mutual Aid Agreement of February 23, 1942,[2] and the understandings agreed upon this day with regard to commercial policy. Pursuant to this settlement, both Governments will continue to discuss arrangements for agreed action for the attainment of the economic objectives referred to in Article VII of the Mutual Aid Agreement. The Governments expect in these discussions to reach specific conclusions at an early date with respect to urgent problems such as those in the field of telecommunica-

---

[1] Department of State, *Treaties and Other International Acts Series* 1509, p. 46.
[2] See *Documents, IV, 1941–1942*, p. 235.

tions and civil aviation. In the light of all the foregoing, both Governments agree that no further benefits will be sought as consideration for Lend-Lease and Reciprocal Aid.

3. The net sum due from the United Kingdom to the United States for the settlement of Lend-Lease and Reciprocal Aid, for the acquisition of surplus property, and the United States interest in installations, located in the United Kingdom, and for the settlement of claims shall be $650,000,000 subject to the accounting adjustment referred to below. This amount consists of (a) a net sum of $118,000,000 representing the difference between the amount of the services and supplies furnished or to be furnished by each Government to the other Government after V-J Day through Lend-Lease and Reciprocal Aid channels, less the net sum due to the United Kingdom under the claims settlement, and (b) a net sum of $532,000,000 for all other Lend-Lease and Reciprocal Aid items, and for surplus property, and the United States interest in installations, located in the United Kingdom and owned by the United States Government. The actual amounts due to the respective Governments for items included in (a) above other than claims will, however, be ascertained by accounting in due course, and the total sum of $650,000,000 will be adjusted for any difference between the sum of $118,000,000 mentioned above and the actual sum found to be due. All new transactions between the two Governments after December 31, 1945, will be settled by cash payment.

4. The total liability found to be due to the Government of the United States will be discharged on the same terms as those specified in the Financial Agreement concluded this day for the discharge of the credit provided therein.

5. In addition to the financial payments referred to above, the two Governments have agreed upon the following:

(a) Appropriate non-discriminatory treatment will be extended to United States nationals in the use and disposition of installations in which there is a United States interest;

(b) Appropriate settlements for the Lend-Lease interest in installations other than in the United Kingdom and the Colonial Dependencies will be made on disposal of the installations;

(c) The United States reserves its right of recapture of any Lend-Lease articles held by United Kingdom Armed Forces, but the United States has indicated that it does not intend to exercise generally this right of recapture;

(d) Disposals for military use to forces other than the United Kingdom Armed Forces of Lend-Lease articles held by the United Kingdom Armed Forces at V-J Day, and disposals for civilian use other than in the United Kingdom and the Colonial Dependencies of such Lend-Lease articles, will be made only with the consent of the United States Government and any net proceeds will be paid to the United States Government. The United Kingdom Government agrees that except to a very limited extent it will not release for civilian use in, or export from, the United Kingdom and the Colonial Dependencies Lend-Lease articles held by the United Kingdom Armed Forces.

(e) The Government of the United Kingdom will use its best endeavors to prevent the export to the United States of any surplus property transferred in accordance with this understanding.

6. The Government of the United Kingdom agrees that, when requested by the Government of the United States from time to time prior to December 31, 1951, it will transfer, in cash, pounds sterling to an aggregate dollar value not in excess of $50,000,000, at the exchange rates prevailing at the times of transfer, to be credited against the dollar payments due to the Government of the United States as principal under this settlement. The Government of the United States will use these pounds sterling exclusively to acquire land or to acquire or construct buildings in the United Kingdom and the Colonial Dependencies for the use of the Government of the United States, and for carrying out educational programs in accordance with agreements to be concluded between the two Governments.

7. The arrangements set out in this statement are without prejudice to any settlements concerning Lend-Lease and Reciprocal Aid which may be negotiated between the Government of the United States and the Governments of Australia, New Zealand, the Union of South Africa, and India.

(3) *Agreement between the United States and the United Kingdom on Lend-Lease and Reciprocal Aid Pipelines and Offsetting Arrangement, March 27, 1946.*[1]

In accordance with their JOINT STATEMENT REGARDING SETTLEMENT FOR LEND-LEASE, RECIPROCAL AID, SURPLUS WAR PROPERTY AND CLAIMS, dated December 6, 1945,[2] the Governments of the United States and of the United Kingdom have reached agreement as set forth below regarding settlement for articles and services furnished after September 1, 1945 to either Government through lend-lease and reciprocal aid channels and regarding other matters covered by the offsetting arrangement described in paragraph 3 (a) of the Joint Statement. In general this agreement covers certain articles and services which were intended for supply through mutual aid channels but which, on September 2, 1945, had not been made available to the recipient Government.

A. PROVISION OF CERTAIN MILITARY AND NAVAL SUPPLIES AND SERVICES AS BETWEEN ARMED FORCES

1. Straight mutual aid between the Governments of the United States and of the United Kingdom was terminated generally on September 2, 1945, with certain exceptions (which include the provision of military and naval supplies and services referred to in paragraph 2 of this section).

2. In accordance with standing directives, the United States War and Navy Departments have had discretion, in the period after September 2,

[1] Department of State, *Treaties and Other International Acts Series* 1509, p. 5.
[2] See this volume, p. 132.

1945, to continue to make supplies and services available to the United Kingdom Armed Forces on a straight lend-lease basis in certain specified circumstances. Similarly United Kingdom military and air commanders in the areas under the South East Asia Command and under the United States Army Forces in the Pacific Theatre, and United Kingdom naval commanders in all theatres, have had discretion to make supplies and services available to United States Armed Forces on a straight reciprocal aid basis in similar circumstances. Supplies and services furnished on the above basis are excepted from the arrangements outlined below.

3. It has been agreed that accounts will be rendered in due course for supplies and services (other than any furnished on a straight lend-lease or reciprocal aid basis) furnished by the United States and United Kingdom Armed Forces to each other during the period from September 2, 1945 to December 31, 1945, inclusive, and that such accounts will be settled under the offsetting arrangement referred to in section E of this Agreement. Any such supplies and services furnished after December 31, 1945 (other than any furnished on a straight lend-lease or reciprocal aid basis or covered under section B of this Agreement) will be for cash settlement between the two Governments. Petroleum products designated for withdrawal by either Government from its share of stocks held by the other Government under the Agreement relating to Petroleum concluded this day (No. VI) [1] are not covered by this paragraph.

B. LEND-LEASE

1. The lend-lease pipeline consists of such of the following articles as the Government of the United Kingdom selected for transfer to it after September 1, 1945 as evidenced by a designation duly made by representatives of the Government of the United Kingdom, together with the services specified below:

(*a*) Articles and services covered by United Kingdom requisitions filed with the Foreign Economic Administration or its successor (other than articles under procurement through the United States Department of Agriculture covered by subparagraph (*b*) hereof) which were under contract, or were completed, but had not been transferred on September 2, 1945.

(*b*) Foodstuffs, services and other materials under procurement through the United States Department of Agriculture to the extent of

    (*i*) all firm allocations, emergency allocations, and tentative fourth quarter 1945 allocations in effect as of August 18, 1945 for United Kingdom programs;

    (*ii*) the shares which, after August 18, 1945, were apportioned to the United Kingdom programs out of the quantities for which the Foreign Economic Administration had theretofore incurred procurement obligations but had not made suballocations to claimants; and

---

[1] Not reprinted here. See Department of State, *Treaties and Other International Acts Series* 1509, p. 27, for the text of the Agreement.

(iii) the quantities under United Kingdom requisitions, determined to have been active as of August 18, 1945, for commodities not controlled by United States allocation.

(c) (i) Naval supplies available in inventory or under contract which, as of September 2, 1945, were covered by formal United Kingdom requisitions or earmarked against approved requirements placed directly with the United States Navy Department.

(ii) Military supplies available in United States War Department inventories which, as of September 2, 1945, were covered by formal requisitions or earmarked against approved requirements placed directly with the War Department.

(iii) Military and naval maintenance spares issued against requisitions placed during the period from September 2, 1945 to December 31, 1945, inclusive, with the United States War or Navy Department by the Government of the United Kingdom under standing United States Government directives (other than spares issued under section A, paragraph 2 of this Agreement).

(d) Inland transportation, storage, handling and services incidental thereto, furnished in the United States during the period from September 2, 1945 to December 31, 1945, inclusive, with respect to certain materials under the control of the Government of the United Kingdom, to the extent such services were originally requisitioned by that Government prior to September 2, 1945, as modified by later requisition.

(e) Transportation provided out of lend-lease funds for United Kingdom personnel or cargo on United States flag civilian airlines during the period from September 2, 1945 to December 31, 1945, inclusive.

(f) Shipping services and supplies described in part I of the Annex to this Agreement.

(g) Petroleum products in accordance with the Agreement relating to Petroleum concluded this day (No. VI).

2. (a) The Government of the United States agrees to complete as early as possible the transfer of articles in the lend-lease pipeline (both civilian and military), in the quantities and according to the specifications and other conditions, except as to time of delivery, set forth in the requisitions or comparable documents submitted by the Government of the United Kingdom, to the extent that such articles are or will be available to the Government of the United States for transfer to the Government of the United Kingdom and subject to the conditions set forth in this Agreement. The Government of the United States may, however, in exceptional cases, decline to complete the transfer of articles in the lend-lease pipeline, when it determines that such transfer would be contrary to its national interests. The Government of the United Kingdom agrees to accept the transfer of articles in the lend-lease pipeline (both civilian and military) and to settle for such articles under the offsetting arrangement. The Government of the United Kingdom may, however, in exceptional cases, decline to accept articles which it has designated for transfer, but agrees in that event to settle under the offsetting arrange-

ment for the costs (including costs of contract cancellations) incurred by the Government of the United States in connection with such articles, less the value of such articles to the Government of the United States or the proceeds realized from their disposal.

(b) Unless otherwise provided by mutual agreement, transfer of articles in the lend-lease pipeline shall be deemed to have taken place immediately upon loading of the articles on board ocean vessel in a United States port, or on board aircraft preparatory to flight from the United States, and title to such articles shall pass at the time of such loading; provided that risk of loss not recoverable from the supplier, carrier or other third party shall be assumed by the Government of the United Kingdom

  (i) with respect to articles specifically contracted for under United Kingdom requisitions, upon shipment from the factory or other premises of the supplier;

  (ii) with respect to articles covered by paragraph 1(b) of this section, upon delivery f. a. s.; and

  (iii) with respect to all other articles, upon shipment from warehouse or United States Government depot.

Any articles that shall not have been transferred as provided in this paragraph prior to midnight on December 31, 1946 or 6 months after receipt by the Government of the United Kingdom of notice of availability, whichever is later, shall be deemed to have been transferred as of such later date.

3. The amount which the Government of the United Kingdom agrees to pay by means of the offsetting arrangement for articles and services in the lend-lease pipeline (other than (a) shipping services and supplies, which for this purpose will be dealt with in accordance with part I of the Annex to this Agreement, and (b) petroleum products, which for this purpose will be dealt with in accordance with the Agreement relating to Petroleum concluded this day (No. VI)) will be the amount determined by the Government of the United States as the cost to it of such articles and services. The general basis of costing by the Government of the United States has been the subject of full consultation with the appropriate United Kingdom authorities.

C. Reciprocal Aid

1. (a) Certain supplies and services of types which before V-J Day were made available to the Government of the United States under reciprocal aid have continued to be furnished without current payment, and settlement for such supplies and services furnished during the period from September 2, 1945 to December 31, 1945, inclusive (other than any furnished on a straight reciprocal aid basis under section A, paragraph 2 of this Agreement) will be made under the offsetting arrangement. Any services rendered or supplies made available after midnight on December 31, 1945 (other than any furnished on a straight reciprocal aid basis under section A paragraph 2 of this Agreement) will be for cash settlement.

(b) In the case of bulk commodities for import into the United States on a "Government-to-Government" basis the offsetting arrangement will apply to all such commodities of types which before V-J Day were made available to the Government of the United States on reciprocal aid, entered on ocean bill of lading during the period from September 2, 1945 to December 31, 1945, inclusive. All commodities entered on ocean bill of lading after the latter date will be for cash settlement. Transfer to the Government of the United States shall be deemed to have taken place immediately upon loading of the articles on board ocean vessel. Title and risk of loss with respect to such articles shall pass at the time of such loading.

(c) In the case of bulk commodities for import into the United States for which the Government of the United States itself makes payment in the first instance, the offsetting arrangement will not apply, and the Government of the United Kingdom will not reimburse the Government of the United States for any such commodities entered on ocean bill of lading after midnight on September 1, 1945. The Government of the United Kingdom will reimburse the Government of the United States in cash for commodities covered by approved requisitions for reimbursement under reciprocal aid entered on ocean bill of lading prior to midnight on September 1, 1945 in accordance with the practice previously followed.

2. The amount which the Government of the United States agrees to pay by means of the offsetting arrangement for articles and services in the reciprocal aid pipeline (other than (a) shipping services and supplies, which for this purpose will be dealt with in accordance with Part II of the Annex to this Agreement, and (b) petroleum products, which for this purpose will be dealt with in accordance with the Agreement relating to Petroleum concluded this day (No. VI)) will be the amount determined by the Government of the United Kingdom as the cost to it of such articles and services. The general basis of costing by the Government of the United Kingdom has been the subject of full consultation with the appropriate United States authorities.

D. Tort Claims

The amounts paid by the Governments of the United States and of the United Kingdom in settlement of certain claims described in the Agreement relating to Tort Claims concluded this day (No. IX)[1] shall be included in the offsetting arrangement.

E. Offsetting Arrangement

The Joint Statement of December 6, 1945 contemplated that the total amounts due for certain supplies and services furnished after September 1, 1945 through lend-lease and reciprocal aid channels to the Governments of the United Kingdom and of the United States respectively, would be offset in order finally to compute the net sum due from the Government of the United Kingdom to the Government of the United States in accordance with paragraph 3 of the Joint Statement. The sum

---

[1] Not reprinted here. See *ibid.*, p. 45.

of $118,000,000 appearing in paragraph 3 (*a*) of the Joint Statement represented the best estimate then obtainable of the net amount which would be due to the Government of the United States under paragraph 3 (*a*), after deducting the net sum due to the Government of the United Kingdom under the claims settlement. The net sum due to the Government of the United Kingdom under the Agreement on Settlement of Intergovernmental Claims concluded this day (No. II) [1] has been finally computed at $53,020,000.

The supplies and services to be brought into this offsetting arrangement are those so specified in this Agreement. The total amounts due for such supplies and services will be computed in accordance with the principles set forth in this Agreement.

An agreed accounting procedure shall be established for the computation of the net sum due under this offsetting arrangement.

3. ADMINISTRATION OF LEND-LEASE AND MUTUAL AID FISCAL RECORDS

(1) *Executive Order 9726, Establishing Transfer of Fiscal Functions Relating to Lend-Lease Matters from the Department of State to the Treasury Department, May 17, 1946.*[2]

By virtue of the authority vested in me by the Constitution and the statutes, including the act of March 11, 1941, as amended, entitled "An Act further To Promote the Defense of the United States, and for Other Purposes" (55 Stat. 31), and as President of the United States, it is hereby ordered as follows:

1. All functions with respect to the maintenance of accounts and other fiscal records relating to lend-lease and reverse lend-lease matters under the said act of March 11, 1941 (hereinafter referred to as the act), are transferred from the Department of State to the Treasury Department and shall be administered under the supervision and direction of the Secretary of the Treasury. The Department of State shall continue to administer all other functions relating to the administration of the act which are now under the jurisdiction of that Department.

2. In carrying out the purposes and provisions of paragraph 1 of this order, the Treasury Department:

(*a*) Shall perform all necessary fiscal functions and maintain all necessary fiscal records and prepare all required reports pertaining to the act, except that until such date as the Director of the Bureau of the Budget shall determine, the Secretary of State shall prepare for the President the reports required under section 5 (*b*) of the act.

(*b*) Shall furnish the Department of State with such information and reports concerning lend-lease operations as may be requested by such Department, including information as to the status of funds.

(*c*) In accordance with the request of the Secretary of State, shall make additional allocations to procurement agencies of the Government of available funds, and shall bill, collect, and account for funds from foreign governments and others, under the act.

[1] Not reprinted here. See *ibid.*, p. 13.   [2] *Federal Register*, XI, p. 5437.

(d) After consultation with the Department of State, shall revoke excess allocations in the hands of procurement agencies and return such funds to the master account.

(e) May act through the personnel transferred hereunder or through such other personnel of the Treasury Department as the Secretary of the Treasury may designate.

3. There is transferred to the Treasury Department so much as the Director of the Bureau of the Budget shall determine to relate primarily to the functions transferred by this order of the records, personnel, and property of the Department of State and of the unexpended balances of the funds of the Department of State available or to be made available for use in connection with the administration of the functions transferred by this order.

4. The Department of State shall provide the Treasury Department with two certified copies of all agreements relating to lend-lease settlements and with two copies of all other documents and correspondence which in any way affect lend-lease accounting records.

5. The Secretary of State and the Secretary of the Treasury shall from time to time jointly recommend to the Director of the Bureau of the Budget amounts by which lend-lease appropriations may be rescinded or placed in reserve.

6. All prior regulations, rulings, and directives relating to the functions transferred by this order shall remain in effect except as hereafter amended or revoked by the Secretary of the Treasury. To the extent authorized by law, the Secretary of the Treasury may issue such additional regulations and instructions as he may deem necessary to carry out this order.

7. All provisions of prior Executive orders and of prior instructions to any Federal agency in conflict with this order are amended accordingly.

8. This order shall become effective at the close of business on May 31, 1946.

4. SUMMARY OF LEND-LEASE OPERATIONS AS OF SEPTEMBER 30, 1946

(1) *Letter from the President (Truman) Transmitting to the Congress the Twenty-Third Report on Lend-Lease Operations, December 27, 1946.*[1]

I am transmitting herewith to the Congress the twenty-third report of operations under the Lend-Lease Act.

Lend-lease operations since V–J Day have been limited largely to negotiating final settlement agreements and to certain other liquidation activities. The principal liquidation activity has related to the substantial quantities of lend-lease supplies which were in inventory or procurement in the United States at the time that direct lend-lease aid was terminated. Steps were taken immediately to sell to lend-lease countries the supplies which had been procured or contracted for on their behalf. Such sales agreements were entered into with 13 countries, the total amount aggregating almost $1,200,000,000. Most of these supplies have

[1] Department of State, *Bulletin*, XVI, p. 32.

already been shipped and the remainder will be transferred to the recipient countries as rapidly as possible. This report discusses the terms and provisions of the sales agreements.

In the period covered by this report, agreements on final settlement for lend-lease and reciprocal aid have been signed with the Governments of France, Belgium, Turkey, Australia, New Zealand, and India. Detailed accounts of these agreements are contained in this report. The first settlement agreement was negotiated with the United Kingdom and was discussed in the twenty-second report.

Final settlements have been signed with countries which received 70 percent of total lend-lease aid. Countries with which agreements remain to be negotiated include the U.S.S.R., China, Greece, the Netherlands, Norway, and the Union of South Africa. Preliminary discussions concerning settlements are now in progress with several of these countries.

In the negotiation of the settlements the objective has been to carry out the provisions of Article VII of the Master Lend-Lease Agreements with various countries, which provide that ". . . the terms and conditions thereof shall be such as not to burden commerce between the two countries but to promote mutually advantageous economic relations between them and the betterment of world-wide economic relations." Viewed in the light of the objectives of the Lend-Lease Act and the Master Agreements, I believe that the settlements which have been worked out not only are highly satisfactory to the United States in the financial sense but also serve the long-range interests of this country by providing one of the foundations of economic stability in the postwar world.

Although the value of lend-lease can never be satisfactorily measured in monetary terms, I think it should be noted that return to the United States from lend-lease through September 30, 1946 exceeded 10 billion dollars, including reverse lend-lease aid, cash payments for goods and services furnished under lend-lease, payment made or to be made under the final settlement agreements, and the sale of supplies in inventory or procurement.

Negotiation of the remainder of the final lend-lease settlements, fiscal activities in connection with the payments due under the various agreements, and the recording and reporting of fiscal operations are the principal continuing lend-lease functions.

(2) *Twenty-Third Report to Congress on Lend-Lease Operations, for the Period Ended September 30, 1946, Transmitted by the President (Truman), December 27, 1946.*[1]

[Excerpts]

CHAPTER 1

LEND–LEASE SETTLEMENTS

The negotiation of final settlement agreements with the various lend-lease countries is progressing as rapidly as discussions with representatives of the several governments can be initiated and agreement reached. Discussions with several countries have been in progress at all times since the first negotiations

[1] Department of State Publication 2707.

started over a year ago. The final settlement with the United Kingdom, which closed the most complex of our wartime supply arrangements, was described in the Twenty-Second Report to Congress on Lend-Lease Operations. Since the signing of the final agreement and subsidiary understandings with the United Kingdom, there have been completed final settlements with France,[1] India,[2] Australia,[3] New Zealand,[4] Belgium,[5] and Turkey.[6] Lend-lease aid to these countries and the United Kingdom constituted about 70 percent of all aid rendered to our Allies under lend-lease. Brief descriptions of the settlements with those countries follow in this chapter and texts of the agreements appear in the Appendixes of this report.[7]

In all these agreements, the same general principles have been followed as in the settlement with the United Kingdom. Under these principles, the lend-lease countries and the United States each pay for and receive full title to lend-lease and reciprocal aid articles of postwar civilian utility in their possession as of VJ-day, while military items are left in the possession of recipient governments, without payment, but subject to a right of recapture. In most of the agreements, the United States has undertaken to complete delivery of certain lend-lease articles which were in the process of procurement as of VJ-day, and the lend-lease governments agree to pay for these pipeline articles under appropriate terms, as set forth in the agreements. In some cases, the settlement agreements have also covered sales of surplus Army and Navy material, and all of the agreements so far concluded have contained provisions for the settlement of outstanding claims between the two governments arising out of the war.

At the present time, settlement negotiations are actively in progress with South Africa, Norway, Greece, and the Netherlands. The Soviet Union has been invited to open negotiations. Final settlements remain to be discussed with representatives of the Governments of Yugoslavia, Poland, and Czechoslovakia. Preparation for such discussions has been made, but it has not as yet been possible to start active negotiations.

The lend-lease account with Canada is considered closed. During the war Canada paid for all supplies and material procured in the United States, even the items which were procured through the lend-lease mechanism. Accordingly, there remains nothing to be settled. Lend-lease relations with various of the Latin-American countries were on somewhat the same basis. Under the agreements with those countries, lend-lease military supplies were delivered in return for a commitment to pay amounts stipulated in the agreements. Except in a few cases, such as Brazil, which received a substantial amount of lend-lease aid through supplies and services made available to the Brazilian Expeditionary Force while it served overseas with United States troops, only relatively minor matters remain to be settled with the other American Republics.[8]

No final settlement negotiations have been started with China, as our lend-lease relations with that country are still in a fluid state, as described in Chapter 2 of this report.

FRANCE

The lend-lease settlement agreement with France was concluded on May 28, 1946. In addition to finally disposing of the accounts for lend-lease and recip-

[1] See Department of State, *Bulletin*, XIV, p. 1127.
[2] See Department of State, *Treaties and Other International Acts Series* 1532.
[3] See *ibid*. 1528.
[4] See *ibid*. 1536.
[5] See Department of State Press Release 668, September 24, 1946.
[6] See Department of State, *Treaties and Other International Acts Series* 1541.
[7] Appendices not reprinted here.
[8] A settlement with Brazil for the disposition of lend-lease supplies in the United States was signed at Washington, June 28, 1946. For the text, see *ibid*. 1537.

rocal aid, the agreement, which is printed in Appendix IV,[1] settled all outstanding claims between the two governments arising out of the war. On the balance of these accounts and claims France undertook to pay $420,000,000. Also included was a sale for $300,000,000 of the bulk of the remaining United States Army and Navy surplus property in France and certain French overseas territories, which has been separately reported to the Congress. Concurrently, credit of $650,-000,000 for France was made available through the Export-Import Bank. At the same time and as an integral part of the same transaction, the two governments signed a declaration on steps to be taken toward expansion of world trade and an understanding on related commercial policy matters. In other words, a complete and final lend-lease settlement was arrived at and to this was coupled the satisfactory disposition of a number of other subjects, which should eliminate many sources of potential dispute between the two governments and should, in the language of the Master Lend-Lease Agreement, "promote mutually advantageous economic relations between them and the betterment of worldwide economic relations." This agreement consolidated the financial terms of all previous lend-lease supply agreements between the two governments.

The negotiations for the over-all settlement were conducted on the United States side under the supervision of the members of the National Advisory Council on International Monetary and Financial Problems, which was established by Congress in Public Law 171, Seventy-ninth Congress.[2] The basic principles underlying the settlement were laid down by this committee. The chief principles of the lend-lease portion of the settlement were:

1. No payment was required for goods originally transferred under straight lend-lease and lost, destroyed or consumed in the course of the war. As in the British settlement, these are regarded as part of the price of victory for which there should be no later financial charge. France, however, agreed to make payment on account of lend-lease goods of civilian utility remaining in her hands at VJ-day and goods thereafter delivered under the lend-lease supply agreement of February 28, 1945.

For their part, the French made no charge for the cost of goods and services furnished to the United States as reverse lend-lease before VJ-day. Moreover, France suggested no adjustment for such goods in United States hands at VJ-day, it being understood that the goods furnished were for current consumption and without substantial post-war civilian value.

2. The settlement was to the fullest possible extent final and not subject to later accounting adjustments, which enables both governments to avoid the need for continuing for many years the relatively minor adjustment of accounts and to foreclose so far as possible future disputes of detail. This was not possible as to certain deliveries of goods, chiefly post VJ-day transfers, for which France assumed obligation to pay, and with respect to this category it was agreed that the books would remain open so that final payment would be on the basis of actual deliveries. However, the area left open for future accounting adjustments was substantially reduced, so that future complicated negotiations will be largely eliminated.

3. The United States share of so-called Plan A supplies furnished to France was treated in the same way as consumed lend-lease goods in the general settlement. Plan A was the program under which, after the Normandy landings, supplies needed for the minimum support of civilians to prevent disease and unrest in liberated areas behind the allied lines were furnished jointly by the United States, Britain, and Canada. The original program called for eventual payment by France and other countries receiving benefits under Plan A. In view of the similarity of these supplies to those furnished under lend-lease and the fact that during this whole period most countries receiving Plan A supplies were themselves furnishing goods

---

[1] Not reprinted here. See Department of State, *Bulletin*, XIV, p. 1127, for the text of the agreement.

[2] See this volume, p. 609.

and services to the United States and allied areas on straight reciprocal aid were persuasive reasons for treating them in the settlement as consumed lend-lease goods.

Other features of the lend-lease settlement agreement with France followed generally the pattern of the British settlement. All known types of war-connected claims between the two governments were reviewed. Some were left to be disposed of in accordance with arrangements previously agreed to; some were resolved in the course of the negotiations; and it was agreed that any others would be released and not afterward asserted. In this connection, France agreed to assume claims arising out of acts of United States military and other personnel in French territory and other claims based on United States use for war purposes of French-owned patents and tangible property in the United States. An involved group of shipping claims of both governments was also disposed of, arising out of the chartering by the United States on various terms of a number of French vessels, as well as the loss of the liner *Normandie*.

The United States reserved the right to recapture lend-lease property held by French armed forces, except for petroleum products and certain non-combat aircraft, which were purchased by France. It is not contemplated that this recapture right will be generally exercised, except for such naval and merchant vessels as must under existing statutes and agreements be returned to the United States. United States consent is required for any retransfers by the French armed forces for military use, and for retransfers for civilian use outside French territory. Proceeds of any retransfers of materials subject to recapture are to be paid to the United States.

After allowance for all claims of the types referred to above, and after credit for $232,000,000 already paid by France for goods supplied through lend-lease procedures, the lend-lease settlement figure stood at $420,000,000, subject to adjustment for those post VJ-day transfers previously referred to. Interest at 2 percent runs from July 1, 1946, the first payment being due on July 1, 1947. Principal is payable over 30 years, beginning July 1, 1951. Of the total sum due, the United States has the option of taking $15,000,000 in real estate and $10,000,000 in francs to be used to acquire or improve real estate or carry on educational programs of the type contemplated in the Fulbright Act (Public Law 584, Seventy-ninth Cong.).[1]

In summary, the dollar figures of the lend-lease account and settlement are as follows, it being again emphasized that the amounts are approximations or estimates.

The United States furnished lend-lease aid to France in all categories of some $3,235,000,000, and the United States share of Plan A deliveries to France has been estimated at $130,000,000. On her part, France supplied reverse lend-lease of some $868,000,000, assumed settlement of a variety of claims against the United States valued at close to $50,000,000, paid $232,000,000, and agreed to pay about $420,000,000.

The French settlement represents an equitable adjustment of the contributions of both countries to the success of the combined cause, carries out the provisions and intent of the Lend-Lease Act and the Master Agreements concluded under its authority, and conforms with the principles heretofore expounded in reports to the Congress on lend-lease operations.

INDIA

The final settlement with India for lend-lease, reciprocal aid, and surplus war property located in India, and for financial claims of each government against the other arising as a result of World War II, was signed on May 16, 1946. The text of the settlement agreement appears as Appendix V.[2]

[1] See *ibid.*, p. 758.
[2] Not reprinted here. See Department of State, *Treaties and Other International Acts Series* 1532, for the text of the settlement.

The lend-lease settlement with India was complicated by the fact that India formed a supply base for the Southeast Asia Command during the war. As a result, a very large quantity of lend-lease supplies shipped to India was actually for the use of the United Kingdom armed forces. Because of the greater urgency of other wartime operations, the work of maintaining records was subordinated and it was not always possible to determine what supplies were properly chargeable to the Government of India. An exact figure, therefore, of the total amount of lend-lease aid chargeable to India could not be compiled. In the settlement negotiations, however, it was recognized that precise figures on lend-lease aid, or of reciprocal aid, were not vital to a settlement based on the principles that had been generally applied to lend-lease settlements in accordance with the formula adopted by the National Advisory Council.

Because of the highly industrialized economy of the United States as contrasted with the economy of India, lend-lease aid largely comprised finished military and industrial equipment and machinery, while India furnished raw materials to the United States under reverse lend-lease. Consequently, on VJ-day the United States had consumed most of the reverse lend-lease articles received from India, while India had in its possession a considerable quantity of equipment that would be useful in its postwar civilian economy. It was recognized, however, that each government had contributed approximately equally to the war effort of the other under lend-lease and reverse lend-lease.

In the final agreement, it was determined that no payment would be made by either government for lend-lease and reciprocal aid items made available to the other government. Each government obtained full title to the civilian-type lend-lease articles remaining in its possession or in the pipeline as of VJ-day, while lend-lease military articles remained subject to recapture by the United States.

The Government of India, in consideration of the over-all settlement, assumed responsibility for the settlement and payment of claims against the Government of the United States or members of the United States armed forces arising from acts or omissions occurring before June 1, 1946.

The settlement agreement did not alter the obligation of the Government of India to return to the United States an amount of silver bullion equivalent to the quantity transferred under lend-lease, which obligation was the same as that assumed by both governments with respect to lend-lease transfers of silver bullion. The amount of silver bullion to be returned in accordance with this undertaking is 226 million ounces which cost the United States about $160,-000,000. This is to be returned within 5 years after the end of the emergency, as determined by the President, but this period may be extended for 2 years, by agreement of the Governments of the United States and India, if the conditions of the world supply of silver make it advisable.

AUSTRALIA

The final settlement of the lend-lease and reverse lend-lease accounts was signed by the United States and Australia on June 7, 1946. As in the case of some of the other settlements, the agreement included a disposal of surplus property and a settlement of outstanding claims between the two governments. The lend-lease and reciprocal aid accounts were closed by agreement that no payment would be made by either government for the articles and services used in the achievement of the common victory. Provision was made for payment by the Australians for certain United States Army and Navy surpluses in the Pacific area, at a price of $6,500,000. Australia also agreed, in accordance with a commitment made prior to the end of hostilities, to pay for the postwar value of certain lend-lease machine tools located in Australia, for the postwar value of certain other items of capital equipment transferred under lend-lease, and for a number of non-combat aircraft and spares remaining in Australia. The total agreed payment, including the surplus purchase, amounted to $27,000,000, of which $7,000,000 is to be made available in Australian currency for the acquisition of real estate, the construction of United States Government buildings and improvements thereon, and for the furtherance of cultural relationships of mutual benefit to the two countries. The Australian Government paid $20,000,000, as called for in this settlement, on September 6, 1946.

The extent of Australia's contribution to the war effort of the allied nations, measured in sacrifice of manpower and of material, is well known. As part of this contribution, Australia provided large quantities of food and war material to the United States forces in the Southwest Pacific area. General MacArthur's headquarters were located in Australia and Australian territories for approximately 3 years. The value of foodstuffs, supplies, buildings and other installations, services, and labor supplied to the United States armed forces under reciprocal aid amounted to $888,000,000 as of September 2, 1945. Lend-lease exports from the United States to Australia during the war aggregated $1,220,000,000, which does not include the cost of shipping and other services supplied to Australia under lend-lease. Both of these figures, however, are of questionable value in determining the true extent of lend-lease and reciprocal aid. The materials turned over by the Australian Government represented an enormous saving in shipping for the United States, which is not reflected in the reported value of reciprocal aid. Similarly, the value of having the enormous productive capacity of the United States available to our Allies cannot be measured in money. On balance, the contribution made by Australia, a country having a population of about 7 million, approximately equaled that of the United States to Australia, and the settlement agreement was negotiated with that equivalence in mind.

As part of the settlement, Australia assumed the responsibility for the settlement and payment of all claims against the Government of the United States or members of the United States armed forces arising from acts or omissions occurring before June 30, 1946, in the course of the military duties of members of United States armed forces in Australia. This undertaking was of considerable value to the United States, in view of the relief it gave to us from the burden of maintaining a sufficient force in Australia to arrange for the settlement of outstanding claims. It enabled the United States to redeploy a number of officers and men who would otherwise have been forced to remain in Australia for an indefinite period in connection with this work.

In accordance with general practice, the two governments agreed that the obligations assumed by Australia at the time of the transfer of silver under lend-lease for industrial and coinage purposes during the war were not affected by the settlement agreement. In accordance with such obligations, Australia will return to the United States within 5 years of the end of the emergency silver equal in value to approximately $7,000,000. This period may be extended for 2 years by agreement of the two governments, if the conditions of the world silver supply make it advisable.

Following the principle of the settlement that both governments had made approximately equal contributions under lend-lease and reverse lend-lease, the lend-lease and reciprocal aid pipelines were considered paid for and were to be delivered by each government without further payment. The lend-lease pipeline consisted of approximately $17,000,000 worth of material for which contracts had been let or, in the case of agricultural commodities, which were under allocation as of VJ-day. The reverse lend-lease pipeline, having about the same value, consisted of articles and services supplied to the United States armed forces in Australia after VJ-day.

The full text of the agreement is printed as Appendix VI of this report.[1]

NEW ZEALAND

An agreement was signed on July 10, 1946 by the United States and New Zealand covering settlement of lend-lease and reciprocal aid and providing for the sale of certain surplus war property and for the settlement of outstanding claims between the two governments. Under this settlement, no payment was to be made by either government to the other with respect to lend-lease or reciprocal aid articles. This agreement was based on recognition of the approxi-

[1] Not reprinted here. See *ibid.* 1528, for the text of the agreement.

mately equal contribution of both governments to each other in the form of lend-lease and reciprocal aid.

The reported figures of lend-lease and reciprocal aid were approximately $250,000,000 on both sides. Because of the disparity in prices between the two countries and the impossibility of giving a dollar value to such matters as the saving in shipping space and the advantage gained from the availability of the enormous productive facilities of the United States, a settlement based on an even balancing of accounts was readily agreed upon.

The final agreement, which is printed in Appendix VII of this report,[1] called for funds to be made available by New Zealand in an amount equivalent to approximately $5,500,000 in consideration of the transfer of certain United States Army and Navy surpluses, surplus air navigation equipment, certain lend-lease noncombat aircraft and spares located in the Pacific area. The funds may be used by the United States in New Zealand currency for the acquisition of real estate and Government buildings in New Zealand and, pursuant to the provisions of the Fulbright Act, for the furtherance of cultural relations of mutual benefit to the two countries.[2] If agreement on such uses is not reached after 3 years, payment of any residue of these funds will be made in dollars.

As part of the settlement, New Zealand agreed to assume responsibility for the settlement and payment of all claims against the Government of the United States or members of the United States armed forces arising from acts or omissions of members of the United States armed forces occurring in New Zealand before June 30, 1946. By assuming the financial and administrative burden of settling these claims, New Zealand relieved the United States of the burden of maintaining sufficient officers and men in New Zealand to handle such settlements.

BELGIUM

The lend-lease settlement with Belgium, signed on September 24, 1946, dealt with all accounts arising out of the war, provided for a bulk transfer of United States surplus property in Belgium, and modified an interim lend-lease arrangement made in October 1945. This settlement was based upon reported lend-lease transfers by the United States of $114,000,000, reverse lend-lease aid to United States forces in Belgium, Luxembourg, and the Belgian Congo aggregating $204,800,000, and a Plan A (civilian supplies furnished under the military relief program) contribution by the United States to Belgium and Luxembourg approximately equal to the $90,000,000 by which reverse lend-lease exceeded lend-lease aid. Luxembourg was included in these accounts because of its close economic relations with Belgium, and it concurred in the settlement insofar as it was concerned. The text of the agreement is printed as Appendix VIII.[3]

The two governments agreed in the over-all settlement that their contributions to each other in the common war effort through lend-lease, reciprocal aid, and Plan A (civilian supplies furnished under the military relief program) were substantially in balance and that accordingly no further benefits would be sought by either government from the other on these accounts. Belgium agreed to pay $18,000,000 for surplus property previously designated for transfer to Belgium — payment to be partly in dollars and partly in funds for educational programs, real estate, and the assumption of claims. In addition, the settlement provided that all United States surplus property in Belgium remaining unsold on October 1, 1946, or declared surplus thereafter (except nondemilitarized combat material and certain other reserved items) should pass to Belgium under an undertaking by Belgium to sell it and turn over one-half of the gross proceeds to the United States in dollars. The date of October 1, 1946, was selected to give this country an adequate opportunity to meet the demands of other markets for its surplus property located in Belgium. The amounts due from Belgium for these transfers

[1] Not reprinted here. See *ibid.* 1536, for the text of the agreement.
[2] See this volume, p. 758.
[3] Not reprinted here. See Department of State Press Release 668, September 24, 1946.

of surplus are payable in 30 annual installments beginning July 1, 1947, with interest at 2⅜ percent, subject to certain provisions for accelerated payments. The United States, on its part, agreed to pay in cash for supplies and services furnished by the Belgian Government after September 2, 1945.

TURKEY

The lend-lease settlement agreement with Turkey was signed in Ankara on May 7, 1946. The agreement covered only the lend-lease account and financial claims between the two governments, inasmuch as surpluses in Turkey had been disposed of in prior agreements. The settlement called for cash payment by Turkey of $4,500,000, representing the residual value of lend-lease equipment of postwar civilian utility located in Turkey. This equipment, consisting of railroad rolling stock and industrial capital goods, had an original cost value of $5,728,000. Military items remaining in the possession of the Turkish Government are subject to a continuing right of recapture by the United States, although it is not intended that such right will be generally exercised.

The amount of straight lend-lease aid received by Turkey from the United States directly and through retransfers is estimated at $90,000,000, plus an amount aggregating approximately $5,000,000 for which the Turkish Government paid cash prior to delivery. Straight lend-lease aid was limited to military supplies, while the articles for which cash was paid were civilian items such as agricultural machinery, trucks, and industrial equipment. A large volume of the material destined for Turkey when exported from the United States was diverted to more urgent war needs before its arrival in Turkey. The amount of aid actually received by Turkey is not as great as the amount reported as exported to that country.

In accordance with the terms of the final agreement, the text of which appears in Appendix IX of this report,[1] Turkey paid $4,500,000 to the United States within 30 days after the effective date of the agreement. Turkey became the first country which received a substantial quantity of lend-lease aid to agree with this Government on an immediate cash liquidation of its entire financial obligation for lend-lease supplies. This closed a transaction which represented an investment by the United States, as part of the Allies' world-wide war effort, in the strengthening of a small country's ability to resist Axis pressure. Turkey's defiance of threatened German attack was made possible largely by the efforts of the United States and the United Kingdom to build up Turkey's military potential and to sustain her economy in the face of wartime disruption.

CHAPTER 2

LEND–LEASE AID TO CHINA

Although China was the first of the major nations to feel the weight of Axis aggression, lend-lease aid was slow to reach her. It had been determined by the President and his military advisers that the principal allied effort in the early stages of the war would be directed to the European Theater. After the German menace had been checked and a substantial share of the allied effort could be diverted to the Asiatic Theater, the Japanese had succeeded in establishing an almost airtight blockade of China, and the only supply facilities open to our Chinese ally were the hazardous Burma Road and the so-called hump route over the treacherous Himalayas from Assam to Yunnan. Consequently, by VJ-day only some $870,000,000 worth of lend-lease supplies had reached China. The end of hostilities, moreover, found China on the verge of collapse. Chinese sovereignty had to be reasserted over the rich coastal provinces which for years had been under Japanese occupation, and upward of 3,000,000 potentially dangerous Japanese, including approximately 1,250,000 Japanese troops, remained

[1] Not reprinted here. See Department of State, *Treaties and Other International Acts Series* 1541, for the text of the agreement.

to be taken into custody and repatriated. These special circumstances prompted the President to authorize the continuance of military lend-lease aid beyond the date of the termination of hostilities. Total military lend-lease, both pre and post VJ-day, amounted to about $1,565,000,000. There remain in operation certain minor military lend-lease programs, including supplies for the Chinese forces participating in the occupation of Japan and specialized training services. Aid since June 30, 1946 is by agreement, being furnished on a reimbursable basis.

On VJ-day there was in procurement or awaiting shipment in this country nearly $50,000,000 worth of goods intended for China. This amount included a high percentage of supplies sorely needed for the reconstruction of China's civilian economy. On September 29, 1945 China undertook to accept delivery of this material in its pipeline on conditions subject to later determination. The first vessel carrying pipeline goods sailed from New York on November 16, 1945 and by September 30, 1946, a total of $40,117,000 worth of goods had been shipped. On June 14, 1946 an agreement was signed at Washington whereby China committed herself to the payment in 30 annual installments beginning July 1, 1947, of the contract price of the articles transferred plus $7\frac{1}{2}$ percent to cover storage and inland transportation plus the actual cost of ocean freight. Interest was provided for at the rate of $2\frac{3}{8}$ percent per annum.

The texts of the pipeline and military aid agreements are printed as Appendixes X and XII.[1]

CHAPTER 3

PIPELINE OPERATIONS

Promptly upon the surrender of Japan, the United States Government determined that lend-lease, as it had been conducted during the active war period, should cease.[2] However, in view of the relatively sudden termination of hostilities, there were still on order for, or under allocation to, foreign governments vast amounts of civilian type industrial and agricultural commodities, intended for transfer under the Lend-Lease Act.

It was evident that a sudden termination of lend-lease deliveries would have worked considerable hardship upon the many nations which, as part of the overall wartime strategy of the Allies, had been made dependent upon United States supply lines for the essentials of their civilian economies. Through no fault of their own they would have been deprived for an indefinite period of time — until their regular commercial channels could be established — of the essential civilian goods which they had been induced to rely on securing from United States production.

At the same time, an abrupt discontinuance of lend-lease transfers of civilian goods would have had a markedly detrimental effect on the internal economy of the United States. In the case of partially finished goods heavy cancellation charges would have been incurred, and finished goods, in many cases built to foreign specifications and therefore of no particular value to United States consumers, would have had to be disposed of through domestic surplus property channels at substantial losses. Apart from the financial burden thus cast upon the United States Government, economic recovery would have been retarded in this country through the widespread discharge of factory and port workers engaged in the production and shipment of lend-lease goods, and the flooding of our domestic market with civilian type lend-lease goods sold at surplus prices would have seriously disturbed our effort toward reconversion to a peacetime production basis.

In order to avoid these unfortunate consequences of an abrupt termination of lend-lease production, the United States offered to the various lend-lease recipient countries an opportunity to acquire, on reasonable credit payment

[1] Not reprinted here. See *ibid*. 1533, for the text of the agreement.
[2] See this volume, p. 126.

terms, any or all of the civilian type lend-lease goods on order for them on VJ-day, September 2, 1945. In the case of industrial articles, goods "on order" meant goods for which contracts had been placed with suppliers by the United States procurement agencies; in the case of agricultural goods, "on order" meant commodities up to amounts already allocated for the third quarter, and tentatively allocated for the fourth quarter, of 1945. The goods selected by the various lend-lease countries pursuant to these offers are commonly known as pipeline goods.

The total value of pipeline goods selected, by countries, is shown in the following table.

Recipient Country	Estimated Amount (Millions of Dollars)
United Kingdom and Colonies	350
Australia	17
New Zealand	7
India	2
U. S. S. R.	244
France	400
Belgium	56
The Netherlands	63
China	48
Brazil	2
Total *	1,189

* Not including Chile, Cuba and Peru.

At the time the pipeline offers were made it was considered probable that deliveries could be completed in regular course some time relatively early in 1946. However, no final delivery date was specified in any of the pipeline contracts, since under Section 3 (c) of the Lend-Lease Act as amended by Public Law No. 31, Seventy-ninth Congress, the powers of the President to carry out contracts or agreements made with foreign governments before July 1, 1946, are continued until July 1, 1949, a date amply distant to permit completion of deliveries.

The pipeline deliveries have for the most part already been accomplished. The pipeline of agricultural commodities, measured by allocations rather than by contracts to supply specified items, is being terminated completely as of December 31, 1946. However, of the industrial pipeline, goods of a value ranging from $15,000,000 to $30,000,000, depending on the effects of the recent coal strike, will still remain undelivered on December 31, 1946, due to unforeseen delays caused by such factors as material shortages, strikes, and adverse weather conditions.

The terms of the pipeline agreements made with foreign governments are such as to require the delivery of these goods even though such delivery cannot be made before the end of the calendar year. The Congress in the Third Deficiency Appropriation Act, 1946, placed a limitation on the use of the funds appropriated by that act to the Treasury for administrative expenses incident to the pipelines, prohibiting the use of any such funds for expenses incident to the shipment of the pipeline goods after December 31, 1946. In view of the importance of fulfilling commitments which the United States has made to other governments, and the desirability of avoiding financial loss from contract cancellation charges and from the sale of surplus equipment at depreciated values, arrangements are contemplated which will make possible the remaining pipeline deliveries in a manner consistent with the existing legislation.

. . . .

Administration

During the period covered by this report the administration of the Lend-Lease Act has been in the Department of State, having been transferred to that Department from the Foreign Economic Administration by Executive Order 9630, effective October 20, 1945.[1] Effective the same day the authority of the Secretary of State to administer the act was delegated to Mr. Thomas B. McCabe, Foreign Liquidation Commissioner.[2] Upon Mr. McCabe's resignation from Government service on September 20, 1946, the administration of the act was delegated to Mr. Chester T. Lane as Lend-Lease Administrator. Mr. Lane, as Deputy Foreign Liquidation Commissioner, had since January 14, 1946, been in charge of lend-lease operations under Mr. McCabe's general supervision.[3]

Chapter 4
FISCAL OPERATIONS

An important operation from the beginning of the lend-lease program has been the collection of amounts due to the United States resulting from various types of lend-lease transactions. These transactions include cash reimbursement lend-lease requisitions, transfers upon agreement by the recipient government to pay the landed cost of the articles, and various 3 (c) or pipeline agreements.

As described in the Twenty-First Report to Congress, many lend-lease articles were transferred under requisitions in which the recipient governments agreed to reimburse the United States in full for the cost of the articles. Although it has been the general practice to require cash to be deposited at the time of clearance of these cash reimbursement requisitions, it has not always been possible to ascertain the exact cost of the articles prior to completion of procurement and shipment. As a result, extensive accounting and billing operations are required in order to assure that the amount due the United States is collected. This function was transferred to the Treasury Department by Executive Order 9726 of May 17, 1946.[4] More than $300,000,000 has been advanced by foreign governments and used to finance the procurement of articles for those governments.

The final accounting for amounts due under requisitions in which the foreign governments agreed to pay the full landed cost of the articles transferred is also the responsibility of the Office of Lend-Lease Fiscal Operations of the Treasury Department. Because of financial and budgetary problems existing in various countries, the collection of these amounts has occasionally been delayed, and in some cases extensive refunding operations have been necessary in order to assure ultimate payment to the United States. In addition, auditing and accounting operations, similar to those arising under cash reimbursement requisitions, are necessary. Up to the present time collection for transfers under these transactions have exceeded $800,000,000.

Another operation, which has resulted in the collection of approximately $200,000,000, is the sale of raw materials received by the United States from foreign governments under reciprocal aid. These articles were brought to the United States by the U. S. Commercial Company and sold through regular trade channels in this country. The proceeds are added to the sums received from foreign governments in consideration of lend-lease aid rendered. A considerable amount of accounting remains in this operation. Part of the reverse lend-lease deliveries is handled on what is called a "government to private" basis. Under this arrangement the United States Government agency buys the material from private dealers abroad. After delivery in the United States, a statement is prepared by the Office of Lend-Lease Fiscal Operations of the Treasury Department and forwarded to the foreign government for reimbursement.

[1] See *ibid.*, p. 159.
[2] See *ibid.*, p. 161.
[3] For further information on foreign surplus disposal, see *ibid.*, p. 158.
[4] See *ibid.*, p. 139.

When paid for in this manner, the value of the goods is recorded as reverse lend-lease aid to the United States.

Since the beginning of the lend-lease program, cash reimbursement and related lend-lease transactions have resulted in collections of more than $1,300,000,000.

Under the 3 (c) and other pipeline agreements, some of which have been incorporated in the final lend-lease settlement agreements, collections from the various lend-lease governments may reach $2,000,000,000 more. Under settlement agreements already concluded, $1,035,000,000 will be paid to the United States. Before this sum is finally paid to the United States, it will be necessary for the Treasury Department to prepare periodic billings showing the exact amounts due under all the agreements requiring extensive auditing of procurement accounts and vouchers for storage and other incidental expenses, and frequent conferences with representatives of the United States agencies and of foreign governments.

CHAPTER 5

LEND–LEASE AID

Total lend-lease aid reported from the beginning of the program on March 11, 1941, through September 30, 1946, amounted to $50,692,000,000.[1] This total amount includes, in addition to the lend-lease aid supplied directly to our Allies during the war, the following items: Pipeline shipments since VJ-day, sold on long-term credit, $1,150,000,000; production facilities in the United States erected with lend-lease funds, $720,000,000; and transfers to United States agencies of goods originally procured with lend-lease funds, $748,000,000.

Limited transfers of goods and services classified as lend-lease aid have been made since September 30. These have included a relatively small quantity of goods sold under the pipeline agreements and which had not been transferred as of that date.

In the period from VJ-day, on September 2, 1945, through September 30, 1946, lend-lease aid amounted to $2,113,000,000. Approximately one-half of this amount represented goods in the so-called pipeline, as defined in Chapter 3 of this report. Such goods were sold to the lend-lease countries on long-term credit terms. The value of goods transferred under these sales agreements is included in the lend-lease aid totals, even though the United States is being paid for them. The remainder of lend-lease aid in the period subsequent to VJ-day consisted largely of field transfers by the United States Army to the Chinese forces, shipping services prior to November 1, 1945, and certain transfers to relieve hardship in devastated areas.

The British Empire received 65 percent of the total lend-lease aid charged to foreign governments and the U. S. S. R. received 23 percent. These two countries with France and China combined received nearly 98 percent of the total. China was the principal recipient of lend-lease aid in the post-VJ-day period. Statistics by country are given in Table 2, page 27.[2]

Total aid through September 30, 1946, amounted to $50,692,000,000, compared with total funds made available for lend-lease of more than $66,000,000,000. (See Appendix I, page 32.) [3]

Lend-lease settlements had been made as of September 30, 1946, with countries which had received aid amounting to more than $34,000,000,000, or approximately 70 percent of the total aid charged to foreign governments. As a result of these agreements the United States is receiving payments, to be made over extended periods, totaling $1,035,000,000. That represents part of the direct realization to the United States from lend-lease, which also includes cash payments by foreign governments for articles received under lend-lease amounting to $1,033,000,000; reverse lend-lease aid received by the United States during

[1] See *ibid.*, p. 154, for tabulation of lend-lease operations as of September 30, 1946.
[2] See *ibid.*
[3] See *ibid.*, p. 157.

the war valued at $7,819,000,000; and additional sales of goods in the pipeline. The total of these items exceeds 10 billion dollars. In addition to the amount realized to date, settlements remaining to be negotiated with foreign governments will result in the realization of a substantial sum. Lend-leased items returned and to be returned will raise the return from lend-lease still higher.

SUPPLY PROGRAM FOR ITALY

During the military campaign in Italy, the War Department, in conjunction with other allied armies, provided food and medical supplies to the people of Italy in quantities intended to prevent disease and unrest. This was regarded as a military necessity. In addition, certain industrial rehabilitation supplies, equally important to the maintenance of civilian morale during the campaign, were sent to Italy at the request of the War Department. After the European campaign was over the War Department believed that the continuation of these shipments was not a proper function of the War Department, but it was evident to all the United States Government agencies concerned that continued shipments of food and basic supplies to Italy were necessary if a complete economic collapse was to be avoided.

Because such a collapse would adversely affect our troops still in Italy and also our long-term economic and political aims in the country, Mr. Leo T. Crowley, Administrator of the Foreign Economic Administration, and Mr. John J. McCloy, Assistant Secretary of War, on June 15, 1945, jointly proposed to the subcommittee of the House Committee on Appropriations that $100,000,000 of lend-lease funds be earmarked for basic supplies for Italy. Together with supplies already purchased by the War Department, these articles would serve as an interim measure to maintain the flow of essential supplies through December 31, 1945, by which time long-term provision of assistance to Italy could be arranged. The supplies acquired through the use of these lend-lease funds were to be transferred to the War Department for subsequent distribution. An additional $40,000,000 was allocated for the expense of shipping supplies to Italy.

Under this program, called the YB program, the United States, between September 1945 and June 1946, shipped almost 3,000,000 short tons of wheat, flour, coal, petroleum products, cotton, and other food and industrial supplies, at a cost of $136,000,000, including freight.

Concurrently with the YB program, industrial supplies and machinery were shipped to Italy under the Troop Pay or YT program. The purchase and shipment of supplies for this program were financed out of a special dollar account established by the Italian Government in the United States Treasury, to which was credited the net dollar equivalent of Italian lire given to our troops in Italy for their pay. Under this program 423,000 tons of miscellaneous industrial supplies, with a landed cost of $73,000,000, were shipped to Italy. Although no United States Government funds were used for this program, it was managed through the same mechanism as the program financed with lend-lease funds.

(3) Lend-Lease Aid by Country, March 11, 1941 to September 30, 1946.[1]

COUNTRY	In Thousands of Dollars		
	Mar. 11, 1941 to VJ-day (Sept. 2, 1945)	Sept. 2, 1945 to Sept. 30, 1946	Total, Mar. 11, 1941, to Sept. 30, 1946
British Empire	30,949,870	442,491	31,392,361
Union of Soviet Socialist Republics	11,058,833	239,050	11,297,883
France and Possessions	2,842,082	391,777	3,233,859
China	870,435	694,263	1,564,698
Netherlands and Possessions	182,000	66,896	248,896
Belgium	90,278	68,320	158,598
Greece	71,697	3,907	75,604
Norway	45,820	6,683	52,503
Yugoslavia	32,000	36	32,036
Turkey	27,397	60	27,457
Saudi Arabia	14,988	2,543	17,531
Poland	16,874	80	16,954
Liberia	7,237	0	7,237
Ethiopia	5,152	100	5,252
Iran	4,798	0	4,798
Iceland	4,797	12	4,809
Egypt	1,016	44	1,060
Czechoslovakia	349	154	503
Iraq	4	0	4
American Republics:			
Argentina	0	0	0
Bolivia	5,155	456	5,611
Brazil	326,913	4,738	331,651
Chile	21,499	381	21,880
Colombia	8,120	7	8,127
Costa Rica	155	0	155
Cuba	6,083	10	6,093
Dominican Republic	1,594	20	1,614
Ecuador	6,979	562	7,541
Guatemala	1,779	0	1,779
Haiti	1,437	6	1,443
Honduras	374	0	374
Mexico	38,468	149	38,617
Nicaragua	902	0	902
Panama	84	0	84
Paraguay	1,963	2	1,965
Peru	18,553	480	19,033
Salvador	894	0	894
Uruguay	7,132	9	7,141
Venezuela	4,407	11	4,418
Not charged by country	1,900,805	189,939	2,090,744
Total Lend-Lease Aid	48,578,923	2,113,186	50,692,109

[1] Compiled from *Twenty-Third Report to Congress on Lend-Lease Operations, for the Period Ended September 30, 1946*, Department of State Publication 2707, p. 27.

(4) Lend-Lease Aid by Category, March 11, 1941 to September 30, 1946.[1]

Category	Amount (In Thousands of Dollars)	Category	Amount (In Thousands of Dollars)
Ordnance	1,433,601	Industrial equipment and commodities:	
Ammunition	2,957,410	Machine tools	888,484
		Agricultural implements	102,305
Aircraft:		Electrical equipment and supplies	421,868
Bombers	2,692,592	Railroad equipment and supplies	545,564
Pursuit and fighters	1,783,824	Iron and steel	1,224,883
Other planes	844,417	Copper and brass	248,118
Total	5,320,833	Aluminum	162,662
		Silver	293,006
		Other metals and minerals	519,641
Aeronautical material:		Fertilizers	20,961
Spare engines and parts	1,146,868	Other chemicals	299,384
Propellers and parts	245,010	Rubber and rubber products	107,034
Other equipment	1,855,840	Textiles and clothing	198,960
Total	3,247,718	Timber products	238,774
		Other equipment and commodities	3,088,979
Ordnance vehicles and parts		Total	8,360,623
Tanks	2,595,067		
Other ordnance vehicles	848,786	Food:	
Spare engines and parts	338,100	Dairy products and eggs	1,749,690
Total	3,781,953	Meat and fish	2,010,640
		Fruits and vegetables	522,320
		Grains and cereals	302,428
Motor vehicles and parts:		Sugar	225,677
Trucks	1,829,758	Lard, fats, and oils	645,389
Automobiles	2,275	Other foodstuffs	372,572
Other vehicles and parts	714,902	Total	5,828,716
Total	2,546,935		
		Other agricultural products:	
		Cotton	519,487
		Tobacco	272,112
Watercraft:		Seeds	50,139
Combatant vessels	1,663,846	Other products	11,175
Naval auxiliary and small craft	994,989	Total	852,913
Merchant vessels	899,302	Total transfers	45,007,229
Other equipage, services, supplies, materials	499,305	Services rendered	3,594,136
Total	4,057,442	Lend-lease costs not charged to foreign governments:	
		Production facilities in the United States	720,388
Petroleum products	2,731,199	Transfers to Federal agencies	747,683
Military clothing	639,036	Losses on inventories and facilities	11,763
Signal equipment and supplies	1,236,888	Administrative expenses	35,486
Engineer equipment and supplies	808,648	Miscellaneous charges	575,424
Chemical warfare equipment	236,551	Total	2,090,744
Other military equipment and supplies	966,763	Total Lend-Lease Aid	50,692,109

[1] *Ibid.*, p. 28.

(5) Reverse Lend-Lease Aid Received by the United States, by Category and Country, Cumulative to September 2, 1945, Revised as of September 30, 1946.[1]

Category	Amount (In Thousands of Dollars)
Capital installations	1,664,915
Foodstuffs	512,875
Clothing	91,089
Petroleum and coal products	1,684,629
Air force supplies and equipment	474,622
Other military supplies and equipment	1,189,739
Shipping and other transportation	1,349,421
Other services	504,744
Raw materials and food shipped to the United States	347,288
Total	7,819,322

Country	Amount (In Thousands of Dollars)
United Kingdom	4,975,478
Fiji Islands	9,482
Nigeria	3,087
Gold Coast	7,496
Other Colonies	6,988
Total from United Kingdom	5,002,531
Australia	888,440
New Zealand	251,732
India	608,500
Union of South Africa	870
Total from British Empire	6,752,073
France	760,696
French Africa	107,085
Belgium	182,603
Belgian Congo	339
Luxembourg	8,273
Netherlands	1,133
Netherlands — Curaçao and Surinam	1,235
China	3,672
U. S. S. R.	2,213
Total	7,819,322

[1] Ibid., p. 30.

(6) Total Funds Made Available for Lend-Lease, Cumulative to September 30, 1946.[1]

I. Lend-Lease Appropriations to the President

First Lend-Lease Appropriation (March 27, 1941)	$7,000,000,000
Second Lend-Lease Appropriation (October 28, 1941)	5,985,000,000
Third Lend-Lease Appropriation (March 5, 1942)	5,425,000,000
Fourth Lend-Lease Appropriation (June 14, 1943)	6,273,629,000
Fifth Lend-Lease Appropriation (June 30, 1944)	3,538,869,000
Sixth Lend-Lease Appropriation (July 5, 1945)	2,475,000,000
Total	$30,697,498,000

Deduct:

Rescission of appropriations (February 19, 1946)	$1,739,561,000
Rescission of appropriations (May 27, 1946)	945,000,000
Rescission of appropriations (July 23, 1946)	672,000,000
Transfer to Treasury Department (Coast Guard)	12,966,000
Transfer to UNRRA	385,000,000
Reserve for postwar price support of agriculture	500,000,000
Total deductions	$4,254,527,000
Net appropriations available for lend-lease	$26,442,971,000

II. Transfers Authorized from Other Appropriations

Acts appropriating funds to the War and Navy Departments provided that defense articles, information and services procured from such funds could be transferred under lend-lease up to specified maximum amounts, which are shown below:

War Department:	
Third Supplemental, 1942	$2,000,000,000
Fourth Supplemental, 1942	4,000,000,000
Fifth Supplemental, 1942	11,250,000,000
Sixth Supplemental, 1942	2,220,000,000
Military Appropriation Act, 1943	12,700,000,000
Navy Department: Second Supplemental, 1943	3,000,000,000
Departments Other Than War: Third Supplemental, 1942	800,000,000
Total	$35,970,000,000

In addition to the foregoing, Congress with certain limitations authorized the leasing of ships of the Navy and merchant ships constructed with funds appropriated to the Maritime Commission without any numerical limitation as to dollar value or the number of such ships which may be leased. (See for example, Public Law 1, 78th Cong., approved February 19, 1943, and Public Law 11, 78th Cong., approved March 18, 1943.)

III. Total Funds Made Available for Lend-Lease

Maximum provided, as of September 30, 1946 (not including the leasing of ships) (total of I and II)	$62,412,971,000

[1] *Ibid.*, p. 32.

IV. Disposition of funds

Obligations and expenditures:
Lend-lease appropriations	$25,988,759,000
War Department	19,348,763,000
Navy Department	4,615,790,000
Maritime Commission (War Shipping Administration)	620,647,000
Coast Guard	12,966,000
Total	$50,586,925,000 [1]

C. Disposal of Surplus Property in Foreign Areas

The sudden termination of the war in the Pacific on September 2, 1945, found vast quantities of military equipment and matériel, the property of the United States Government, in storage or in use in many widely-scattered foreign areas. In many instances, the return and salvage of this surplus property was rendered impractical by distance and its comparative uselessness to this country in time of peace. This situation had been anticipated in December, 1944, with the establishment by the War and Navy Departments of the Office of Army-Navy Liquidation Commissioner. The Commissioner was given the responsibility of liquidating these surplus supplies so as to prevent their complete loss to this country in terms of their original monetary value.[2] In accordance with a later executive order of the President, the organization for foreign surplus disposal was transferred to and continued under the Foreign Liquidation Commissioner of the Department of State.[3] At the end of the period under review, bulk sales to ten foreign governments accounted for 75 percent of the total sales of surplus property, figured on an original-cost basis.[4] In accordance with the UNRRA Participation Appropriation Act of 1945 quantities of surplus were transferred to UNRRA as a part of the contribution of the United States to that organization.[5] In some instances dollar obligations of the United States to other countries for expenses incurred during the recent war were cancelled as part payment for surplus purchases.[6] A $100,000,000 transfer of surplus property to the Commonwealth of the Philippines was provided by the Philippine Rehabilitation Act[7] and incorporated in the bulk sale of surplus to the Philippine Government.[8] In addition to dollar purchases and transfers, credit agreements were negotiated as a basis for further transfer of surplus without immediate payment in dollars or local currencies; to December 31, 1946, arrangements of this type provided for total credits of $1,104,000,000.[9] Bulk sales were also included as a part of the over-all settlement of war accounts, as in the case of the United Kingdom and France. Through the provisions of the Fulbright Act, surplus disposals contributed to the exchange of students between the United States

---

[1] The net difference between this figure and the reported total amount of lend-lease aid (see this volume, p. 154) is accounted for by the aid supplied from foreign government funds, the reissues of returned lend-lease articles, and the excess of obligations of funds over the amount of aid rendered.

[2] *Report to Congress on Foreign Surplus Disposal, April 1946*, Department of State Publication 2518, p. 9.

[3] Executive Order 9630, September 27, 1945; for text, see this volume, p. 159.

[4] *Report to Congress on Foreign Surplus Disposal, January 1947*, Department of State Publication 2722, p. 9.

[5] For total transfers to UNRRA as of December 31, 1946, see this volume, p. 169.

[6] *Report to Congress on Foreign Surplus Disposal, January 1947*, cited above, p. 10.

[7] For the text of this Act, see this volume, p. 807.

[8] *Report to Congress on Foreign Surplus Disposal, January 1947*, cited above, p. 27.

[9] *Ibid.*; for the text of the Revised Standard Form of Dollar Credit Agreement, under which such arrangements are negotiated, see *ibid.*, Appendix II.

and other countries, in the interest of international understanding;[1] amounts were made available for this purpose to Australia, Belgium, China, Egypt, France, Italy, New Zealand, Philippines and the United Kingdom.[2] Rights and interests of American airlines abroad were also considered in the sale of surplus property, and bilateral air agreements were concluded with all countries to which significant quantities of surplus were sold.[3]

(1) *Executive Order 9630, Redistributing Foreign Economic Functions and Functions with Respect to Surplus Property in Foreign Areas, September 27, 1945.*[4]

[Excerpts]

By virtue of the authority vested in me by the Constitution and Statutes, including Title I of the First War Powers Act, 1941, and as President of the United States, and Commander in Chief of the Army and the Navy, it is hereby ordered as follows:

Part I

1. The Foreign Economic Administration established by Executive Order No. 9380 of September 25, 1943, hereinafter referred to as the Administration, and its agencies except as otherwise provided in this order, and the office of the Administrator of the Foreign Economic Administration, are terminated and disposition shall be made of the affairs thereof according to the provisions of this Part.

2. There are transferred to the Department of State all functions of the Administration and of its agencies with respect to:

(*a*) The administration of the Act of March 11, 1941, as amended, entitled "An Act further to promote the defense of the United States and for other purposes."

(*b*) The participation by the United States in the United Nations Relief and Rehabilitation Administration, as defined in Executive Order No. 9453 of July 6, 1944.

(*c*) Activities in liberated areas with respect to supplying the requirements of and procuring materials in such areas under paragraph 4 of the said Executive Order No. 9380.

(*d*) The gathering, analysis, and reporting of economic and commercial information, insofar as such functions are performed abroad.

(*e*) The planning of measures for the control of occupied territories.

(*f*) The administration of Allocation No. 42/3–98 of February 1, 1943 from the appropriation, "Emergency Fund for the President, National Defense, 1942 and 1943."

· · · · · · ·

---

[1] See this volume, p. 758.
[2] *Report to Congress on Foreign Surplus Disposal, January 1947*, cited above, p. 31.
[3] *Ibid.*, p. 35. For further information on bilateral air agreements negotiated by the United States, see this volume, p. 671.
[4] Department of State, *Bulletin*, XIII, p. 491; *Federal Register*, X, p. 12245.

Part II

7. For the purpose of unifying the disposition of foreign property owned by the United States in foreign areas under a single agency acting in conformity with the foreign policy of the United States and with the Surplus Property Act of 1944, and consonant with the transfer of such disposition function under paragraph 2 (*a*) hereof and the designation of the Department of State, pursuant to the provisions of the Surplus Property Act of 1944, as a disposal agency for all surplus property in foreign areas, excepting certain vessels, there are transferred to the Department of State all functions of the Army-Navy Liquidation Commissioner (under whatever authority, including War Department Memorandum No. 850–45, dated January 27, 1945 and letter of the Secretary of the Navy dated February 1, 1945) and all functions of the War Department and the Navy Department relating to the disposition abroad of property captured from the enemy. So much of the functions of the Secretary of War and the Secretary of the Navy as relates thereto is transferred to the Secretary of State. The office of Army-Navy Liquidation Commissioner is abolished.

8. The War Department and the Navy Department shall each store, care for, handle, deliver and keep the fiscal and other accounts for all property declared to be surplus in foreign areas, including property captured from the enemy, and shall also furnish such personnel, transportation and administrative services or facilities as may be required for foreign disposal. The provisions of this paragraph shall be carried out without reimbursement from the Department of State for the services rendered. As used in this order, the words "foreign areas" mean areas outside the continental United States, its territories and possessions.

9. The Secretary of War and the Secretary of the Navy are authorized to detail officers and enlisted persons of the military and naval establishments, respectively, to the Department of State to assist it in the discharge of its duties under this Part or of any duties delegated to it under the Surplus Property Act of 1944, and any such officer or enlisted person shall, while so detailed, retain and be entitled to the rights, benefits, promotions and status of an officer or enlisted person of the establishment from which he was detailed.

Part III

10. There are transferred to the respective agencies to which functions are transferred by this order, for use in connection with the functions so transferred, so much as the Director of the Bureau of the Budget shall determine to relate to such functions, respectively, of the records, property, civilian personnel, and funds of the Administration and its agencies (including funds appropriated to the President for carrying out functions administered by the Administration) and of the War Department and of the Navy Department. Such further measures and dispositions as may be determined by the Director of the Bureau of the Budget to be necessary to effectuate the transfers and abolitions provided for in this order shall be carried out in such manner as the Director may direct and by such agencies as he may designate.

11. The head of each agency to which functions are transferred by this order may, in the interest of efficient administration, assign such of the functions transferred to such head or to his agency by this order as he shall determine to such officers and agencies under his jurisdiction as he shall designate.

12. All prior regulations, rulings, and other directives relating to any function transferred by this order shall remain in effect except as they are in conflict with this order or are hereafter amended or revoked under proper authority.

13. All provisions of prior Executive orders and of prior instruments of any Federal agency in conflict with this order are amended accordingly. Each transfer of functions provided for in this order shall be effective on such date, not later than December 31, 1945, as shall be designated jointly by the Director of the Bureau of the Budget and the head of the agency to which the function is transferred. Pending such designations the officers and agencies from whom functions are transferred under this order shall continue to administer their respective functions.

(2) *Delegation of Authority to the Foreign Liquidation Commissioner of the Department of State. Departmental Order, October 20, 1945.*[1]

Pursuant to the provisions of the Surplus Property Act of 1944 (58 Stat. 765), Surplus Property Board Revised Regulation 8 dated September 25, 1945 (10 F.R. 12452), designating the Department of State as the disposal agency for all surplus property located in foreign areas, excepting certain vessels, and Executive Order 9630, dated September 27, 1945 (10 F.R. 12245),[2] transferring to the Department of State all functions of the Army-Navy Liquidation Commissioner, and all functions of the War Department and the Navy Department relating to the disposition abroad of property captured from the enemy, and transferring to the Secretary of State so much of the functions of the Secretary of War and the Secretary of the Navy as related thereto, it is hereby ordered that:

1. There is hereby delegated, as herein provided, to the Foreign Liquidation Commissioner the authority now or hereafter vested in the Secretary of State or the Department of State to dispose of, subject to the authority of the Surplus Property Administrator under the Surplus Property Act of 1944, all surplus property, including scrap, salvage, waste materials, property captured from the enemy, and surplus property of Lend-Lease origin, in the control of or for the disposal of which the Department of State may be responsible, located in foreign areas.

2. The Foreign Liquidation Commissioner will exercise the authority hereby delegated under the general supervision of, and in conformity with such directions, orders, or instructions as may from time to time be issued by, the Secretary of State in the execution of the foreign policies of the United States, and he will report to the Secretary of State through the Assistant Secretary of State for Economic Affairs.

[1] Departmental Order 1347, dated and effective October 20, 1945; Department of State, *Bulletin*, XIII, p. 704. [2] See this volume, p. 159.

3. Provisions of law and regulations requiring owning agencies to file with the Department of State, as the disposal agency, declarations of surplus real and personal properties located in foreign areas, shall be complied with by filing in such manner as the Foreign Liquidation Commissioner may direct.

4. The Foreign Liquidation Commissioner is authorized, with the approval of the Assistant Secretary for Economic Affairs, to designate:

(*a*) One or more Deputy Commissioners who may in the order prescribed in the instrument of appointment exercise all of the authority and perform all of the functions hereunder of the Commissioner in his absence, and one or more assistant Commissioners who may in the order prescribed in the instrument of appointment exercise all of the authority and perform all of the functions of Commissioner hereunder in the absence of the Commissioner and the Deputy Commissioners;

(*b*) Field Commissioners, Deputy Representatives, Officers, and Assistants;

(*c*) In such representative capacities as may be deemed necessary, such officers and enlisted personnel of military or naval establishments as may be detailed to the Department of State pursuant to Executive Order 9630 of September 27, 1945 (10 F.R. 12245).

5. The Foreign Liquidation Commissioner or his local representatives are authorized to call upon the War and Navy Departments, and the military commander of any Theater of Operations, command, department or base in foreign areas and the Naval Commander of any area, several areas or fleet, or the Commandant of a Naval District, in foreign areas for the assignment within his Command to the local representative of the Commissioner, of such military and Naval personnel, transportation, and administrative services, or facilities as may be required to be furnished by them pursuant to paragraphs 8 and 9 of Executive Order 9630, dated September 27, 1945 (10 F.R. 12245).

6. The Commissioner is authorized, with the approval of the Assistant Secretary for Economic Affairs, to redelegate and authorize successive redelegations of all or any part of his authority and functions hereunder to such Deputy Commissioners, Assistant Commissioners, Field Commissioners, Deputy Representatives, Officers, Assistants, and to any United States Government agency, with the consent of such agency, or subject to such conditions, directions and restrictions as may be prescribed by the Commissioner or his authorized representatives, either in the instrument of delegation, or otherwise from time to time, to a person under the complete control of such Government agency.

7. Such personnel as may be necessary to enable the Commissioner to carry out his functions shall be supplied by the Division of Departmental Personnel and the Division of Foreign Service Personnel.

8. The Foreign Liquidation Commissioner will maintain records of all his transactions and require that such records be kept by each foreign representative in the form and manner prescribed by him.

9. This Order is effective as of the close of business October 20, 1945.

THE TERMINATION OF THE WAR 163

(3) *Agreement between the United States and China for the Sale of Certain Surplus War Property, Signed at Shanghai, August 30, 1946.*[1]

This agreement between the Government of the United States of America, hereinafter called "UNITED STATES", and the Government of the Republic of China, hereinafter called "CHINA",

WITNESSETH:

WHEREAS, the cessation of active military operations in the War with Japan has rendered surplus to the needs of the United States quantities of its property now situated in the Western Pacific Area, and

WHEREAS, such surplus property available for sale to China represents an estimated aggregate procurement cost of approximately Five Hundred Million Dollars ($500,000,000) in movables and Eighty-Four Million Dollars ($84,000,000) in fixed installations, of which over one-half has already been declared surplus, and

WHEREAS the Congress of the United States has, by the Surplus Property Act of 1944, as amended, authorized the disposal of the surplus property of the United States; and the Foreign Liquidation Commissioner has been charged with responsibility for that disposal in the Western Pacific Area, and

WHEREAS the prosecution of the War with Japan caused widespread damage and loss in China, and

WHEREAS it is the policy of the United States, as declared in the Surplus Property Act, to establish and develop foreign markets and promote mutually advantageous economic relations between the United States and other countries by the orderly disposition of surplus property in other countries, and to dispose of surplus property as promptly as feasible without fostering monopoly or restraint of trade.

NOW, THEREFORE, in consideration of the premises and the mutual agreements and convenants hereinafter stated, it is agreed:

ARTICLE 1. *Property Sold.*

That by these presents the United States sells and China buys all that property owned by the United States on the date hereof but surplus to its needs in China, Okinawa, Guam, Saipan, Tinian, Eniwetok, Marcus, Kwajalein, Los Negros, Ulithi, Majuro, Makin, Manus, Peleliu, Finschhaven, Iwo Jima, Wake and Roi, except aircraft, nondemilitarized combat material, ships and other maritime equipment, and fixed installations outside Chinese Territory, subject, however, to the limitations following:

(1) That the United States owning agency, as defined in the Surplus Property Act, shall be the sole determining agency as to what property is surplus to the needs of the United States, and

(2) No property is sold hereby which is already under contract or firm commitment for sale or transfer. All information available as to

[1] *Report to Congress on Foreign Surplus Disposal, October 1946*, Department of State Publication 2655, Appendix I. This agreement is typical of those governing bulk sales of surplus property.

such property shall be furnished on request of China by appropriate United States representatives.

ARTICLE 2. *Transfer of Possession.*

  a. That the right to possession of the property sold under Article 1 hereof shall, after declaration to the Foreign Liquidation Commissioner for disposal as surplus, pass to China upon either (1) the surrender by the United States and the acceptance by China of physical possession, or (2) the passage of sixty (60) days' time after a notice to China that specified property is available for transfer, whichever shall first occur. That such notice shall be deemed to have been duly given when delivered in writing to the Office of the Director of the Board of Supplies or its successor, in Shanghai, China, and shall be deemed sufficient if it either generally describes the property available or generally describes the location thereof.

  b. That until right to possession passes to China pursuant to paragraph *a* of this Article, the United States shall continue to have custody and control of the property sold, and shall give said property the same care and protection as is accorded its own property of like character.

  c. That after the right to possession with respect to specified property has passed to China pursuant to paragraph *a*, all responsibility, risk of loss, and liability for the care, custody, protection and maintenance of such property shall be upon China, including rents and liabilities for the storage thereof and damages and claims of any nature arising out of or incident to the ownership of such property and China shall indemnify and hold the United States harmless from any such responsibilities, risks, liabilities, rents, damages and claims.

  d. That China shall take the necessary steps to ensure that its personnel engaged in the custody or handling of the property sold outside the territory of China, comply with all orders, rules and regulations of the owning agency of the United States having jusridiction of the territory where the property is located, and shall, within sixty (60) days after removal of the property, repatriate all non-citizens of the United States engaged in the custody or handling of the property sold, in default of which the United States is authorized to accomplish repatriation for China's account.

  e. That the owning agency of the United States shall make property available for visual inspection before the transfer of right to possession.

ARTICLE 3. *Handling.*

  a. That all storage, crating, conditioning, handling, loading and transportation of the property sold shall be arranged and paid for by China, and that all of such property shall be removed within a period of twenty-two (22) months from the date hereof, or a period of six (6) months after China acquires right to possession of the property, whichever shall later expire. That in the event of China's failure to remove the said property within the specified period, the United States is authorized to remove, destroy or otherwise dispose of the property for China's account.

b. The Board of Supplies being convinced of the value to China of obtaining expert technical assistance in connection with this operation; that China proposes to employ an established American firm or firms acting under the direction of the Board of Supplies to coordinate the over-all operation of packing, outloading the property from the islands, rehabilitating, shipping to China, unloading and moving the property to storage in China in conjunction with Chinese personnel and that China shall afford to such firm such personnel, facilities, support, resources and other assistance as it may require in order to accomplish the removal to China of the property sold within the time specified.

c. That the United States shall forthwith make a payment of Thirty Million Dollars ($30,000,000) on its Yuan obligations to China for use by China in accomplishing the transfer of the property sold hereby in manner following:

(1) The sum of Twenty-Five Million Dollars ($25,000,000) to be deposited in a special account in the United States to the credit of China subject to appropriate withdrawal restrictions guaranteeing the payment of charter hire of United States flag vessels, and thereafter the payment of dollar obligations to the United States arising from this agreement, and

(2) The sum of Five Million Dollars ($5,000,000) to be deposited in a second special account in the United States to the credit of China subject to withdrawal restrictions guaranteeing the payment of the fees of the engineering firm employed pursuant to paragraph *b* of this Article, the reimbursement of expenses incurred by the United States under this agreement, the cost of services and materials furnished China by agencies of the United States on an agreed compensatory basis in connection with the transfer operation and dollar obligations to a limit of Two Million Dollars ($2,000,000) incurred in the United States for the purchase of materials and parts needed initially to rehabilitate the property sold.

That when the transfer (by which is meant the removal of the property from non-Chinese territory) has been completed, the uncommitted balance of both accounts shall pass to China. That to the extent that the sums so deposited are insufficient to cover the United States dollar costs of the transfer, China shall make available, as required, the necessary United States dollars.

ARTICLE 4. *Distribution.*

That China shall utilize to the greatest extent possible established commercial distribution channels for the resale of property sold hereby and that United States distributors established in China shall have an equal opportunity to bid for and to obtain such property. That China shall recognize normal distribution practices including the marketing wherever practicable of name-brand products through the established agencies for such products.

ARTICLE 5. *Warranties.*

That the United States warrants title to the property sold and that in lieu of any other warranty or undertaking as to the kind, size, weight, quantity, quality, character, value, description, condition or fitness for use of the property sold, it is understood that if a material disparity is found to exist between the property sold to China hereunder and the consideration given therefor by China hereunder, the two Governments will consult together to fix an appropriate adjustment in the price paid.

ARTICLE 6. *Money Consideration.*

a. That China hereby releases and acquits the United States of the balance of the United States obligations to China for Yuan and Taiwan Yen advances to and expenditures on behalf of the United States and its Armed Forces in China to the date hereof; the said balance being understood to be the total of the Yuan and Taiwan Yen debt less (1) payments made by the United States to date, including the payment provided for in paragraph *c* of Article 3 hereof, and (2) certain obligations of China to the United States specifically agreed to be offset against the Yuan debt, and hereby agreed to total Seventy Four Million Dollars ($74,000,000), and identified as:

(*a*) The Calcutta Stockpile sale at approximately Twenty Five Million Dollars ($25,000,000),

(*b*) The Hogan Project at approximately Six Million Dollars ($6,000,000),

(*c*) The Small Ship program, totalling about Twenty Eight Million Dollars ($28,000,000), of which about Twelve Million Dollars ($12,000,000) has been delivered and Sixteen Million Dollars ($16,000,000) remains to be delivered,

(*d*) The down payment on the United States Army's West China sale of Five Million Dollars ($5,000,000), and

(*e*) Miscellaneous small sales of about Ten Million Dollars ($10,000,000).

b. That China shall make available to the United States the equivalent of Fifty Five Million Dollars ($55,000,000) United States dollars in manner following:

(1) The equivalent of Twenty Million Dollars ($20,000,000), to be available for the implementation of agreements between the United States and China for research, instruction and other educational activities under the terms of section 32 (*b*) of the Surplus Property Act of 1944, as amended, and

(2) The equivalent of Thirty Five Million Dollars ($35,000,000) to be available for the payment of United States governmental expenses in China at a rate not exceeding the equivalent of Two Million Dollars ($2,000,000) a year, and for the purchase of designated real estate and improvements to real estate for the use and benefit of the United States which China agrees promptly to make available at prices to be agreed upon by the Governments.

ARTICLE 7. *Miscellaneous Provisions.*

a. That in connection with the fixed installations and the weather station and communication service equipment in China which is sold to

China hereunder, and as additional consideration therefor, China shall undertake by separate agreement in the usual form to operate and maintain weather and communication services in a manner, to an extent and within limits to be negotiated.

b. That China shall use its best endeavors to insure that property not now in the United States transferred pursuant to this agreement shall not be imported into the United States in the same or substantially the same form, if such property was originally produced in the United States and is readily identifiable as such, unless such property is to be imported into the United States on consignment to a person or firm in the United States for the purpose of reconditioning for re-export, or by a member of the United States Army Forces for his personal use.

c. That no duty, tax, excise, or other governmental exaction is included in the price, and if any such duty, tax, excise or governmental exaction is levied or found to be payable, China shall pay such sum in addition to the purchase price of the property sold. The United States represents that no duties, taxes, excises, or other governmental exactions are due to the Government of the United States.

d. That this agreement is without prejudice to the final settlement of accounts between the United States and China arising out of the War and that China will undertake negotiations for such final settlement at Washington as soon as possible.

e. That the United States owning agencies shall from time to time designate by location quantities of scrap as they become available and upon acceptance by China by location title and right to possession thereto shall pass to China without further consideration. Such scrap shall be subject to the provisions of Article 3.

f. That in the event any surplus property is available in the Philippine Islands after fulfilling the requirements of the Government of the Republic of the Philippines and its nationals, as well as the requirements of certain other governments to which credit has been extended, then the residual surplus property in the Philippine Islands shall be offered to China for acceptance within thirty (30) days at a price and on terms to be determined by the office of the Foreign Liquidation Commissioner in Manila.

IN WITNESS WHEREOF the undersigned, duly authorized by their respective Governments, have signed the present agreement at Shanghai on the thirtieth day of August 1946.

(4) *Letter from the Secretary of State (Marshall) Transmitting the Fourth Report to Congress on Foreign Surplus Disposal as of December 31, 1946, January 30, 1947.*[1]

In accordance with section 24 of the Surplus Property Act of 1944 there is transmitted herewith the fourth report of the Department

---

[1] *Report to Congress on Foreign Surplus Disposal, January 1947,* cited above, p. 5.

of State on the disposal of United States surplus property in foreign areas. Incorporated therein is the report required from the Foreign Liquidation Commissioner by section 202 of the Philippine Rehabilitation Act of 1946 concerning the administration of Title II of that act.

Surplus property with an original cost of $6,800,000,000 had been sold by December 31, 1946, with a total realization to the United States of $1,590,000,000. Sales made on a cash basis for dollars, or their equivalent, accounted for one-fourth of the total realization. The remaining sales were made for foreign currencies or under dollar credits.

There still remained for sale or other disposal at the end of 1946 property with an original cost of $1,365,000,000 already declared surplus. It is estimated that future declarations will amount to approximately two billion dollars. This estimate is tentative and subject to change as it is impossible to forecast months in advance what the exact requirements of our own forces will be.

Considerable progress has been made in the exchange of foreign surpluses for real estate needed by United States diplomatic missions and in the use of surplus property in implementing the Fulbright Act. That act provides for the use of foreign currency receipts from surplus sales to finance studies and research of American citizens abroad and to pay the transportation of foreign students to the United States.[1]

During the past quarter an energetic sales program was continued and arrangements were made for the efficient, prompt, and economical delivery of and final accounting for the property sold to the Governments of China, the Philippines, Italy, and Belgium in the preceding quarter.

It now appears, as a result of several developments, that the salable surplus yet to be declared is greater than preliminary estimates indicated. Some of these developments are mentioned in this report. It has not been possible at this time, however, to include estimates of either the original cost or realization to be obtained on returned lend-lease equipment or reparations plants, ships, and other equipment. While these additional disposals will delay the close-out of overseas disposal operations, the ultimate result — a larger dollar recovery to the taxpayers of their wartime outlays — is certainly desirable.

The sale of our overseas surplus property to war-ravaged countries has been a major factor in their rehabilitation and has contributed to the economic recovery prerequisite to the inauguration of a lasting peace. The use abroad of these products of American industry and agriculture will do much to foster postwar trade and the economic stability of the world.

[1] See this volume, p. 758.

(5) *Summaries of Foreign Surplus Disposal as of December 31, 1946.*

(a) *By the Office of the Foreign Liquidation Commissioner.*[1]

	Original Cost	Realization from Disposal
Surplus Declarations [2]	$8,805,882,000	
Sales	6,803,995,000	$1,589,558,000
Transfers to UNRRA [3]	128,424,000	85,703,000
Donations and Abandonments	467,018,000	
Military Program Disposals	37,609,000	2,957,000
Total Disposal	$7,437,046,000	$1,678,218,000
Balance for Disposal	1,368,836,000	

(b) *Total Foreign Surplus Disposal.*[4]

	Original Cost	Realization from Disposal
Disposal by OFLC	$7,437,046,000	$1,678,218,000
Direct Sales by Army	128,255,000	61,288,000
Direct Sales by Navy	71,168,000	22,687,000
Scrap Sales by Army		37,321,000
Scrap Sales by Navy		237,000
Total Disposal	$7,636,469,000	$1,799,751,000

4. INVESTIGATION OF THE PEARL HARBOR ATTACK

(1) *Foreword from the Report of the Joint Congressional Committee of Investigation on Background of the Pearl Harbor Attack, Submitted July 20, 1946.*[5]

On Sunday morning, December 7, 1941, the United States and Japan were at peace. Japanese ambassadors were in Washington in conversation with our diplomatic officials looking to a general settlement of differences in the Pacific.

At 7:55 A.M. (Hawaiian time) over 300 Japanese planes launched from 6 aircraft carriers attacked the island of Oahu and the American Pacific Fleet at Pearl Harbor in the Territory of Hawaii. Within a period of less

---

[1] *Report to Congress on Foreign Surplus Disposal, January 1947*, cited above, p. 8.

[2] Declarations of surplus property by the owning agencies to the Foreign Liquidation Commissioner, excluding withdrawals.

[3] Nonremunerative transfers under section 202 of UNRRA Participation Appropriation Act.

[4] *Ibid.*, p. 9.

[5] *Investigation of the Pearl Harbor Attack. Report of the Joint Committee on the Investigation of the Pearl Harbor Attack. Congress of the United States, pursuant to S. Con. Res. 27, 79th Congress. A Concurrent Resolution to Investigate the Attack on Pearl Harbor on December 7, 1941, and Events and Circumstance Relating Thereto*, Senate Document No. 244, 79th Cong., 2d sess., p. XI.

than 2 hours our military and naval forces suffered a total of 3,435 casualties in personnel and the loss of or severe damage to: 188 planes of all types, 8 battleships, 3 light cruisers, and 4 miscellaneous vessels.

The attack was well planned and skillfully executed. The Japanese raiders withdrew from the attack and were recovered by the carriers without the latter being detected, having suffered losses of less than 100 in personnel, 29 planes, and 5 midget submarines which had been dispatched from mother craft that coordinated their attack with that of the planes.

One hour after Japanese air and naval forces had struck the Territory of Hawaii the emissaries of Japan delivered to the Secretary of State a reply to a recent American note, a reply containing no suggestion of attack by Japan upon the United States. With the benefit of information now available it is known that the Japanese military had planned for many weeks the unprovoked and ambitious act of December 7.

The Pyrrhic victory of having executed the attack with surprise, cunning, and deceit belongs to the war lords of Japan whose dreams of conquest were buried in the ashes of Hiroshima and Nagasaki. History will properly place responsibility for Pearl Harbor upon the military clique dominating the people of Japan at the time. Indeed, this responsibility Premier Tojo himself has already assumed.

We come today, over 4 years after the event, not to detract from this responsibility but to record for posterity the facts of the disaster. In another sense we seek to find lessons to avoid pitfalls in the future, to evolve constructive suggestions for the protection of our national security, and to determine whether there were failures in our own military and naval establishments which in any measure may have contributed to the extent and intensity of the disaster.

(2) *Appendix to the Report of the Joint Congressional Committee of Investigation on Summary of Investigations Conducted Prior to Congressional Inquiry, Submitted July 20, 1946.*[1]

The Roberts Commission

The Roberts Commission was organized under an Executive order, dated December 18, 1941, of President Franklin D. Roosevelt, which defined the duties of the Commission thus: "To ascertain and report the facts relating to the attack made by Japanese armed forces upon the Territory of Hawaii on December 7, 1941. The purposes of the required inquiry and report are to provide bases for sound decisions whether any derelictions of duty or errors of judgment on the part of United States Army or Navy personnel contributed to such successes as were achieved by the enemy on the occasion mentioned; and, if so, what these derelictions or errors were, and who were responsible therefor." This inquiry was commenced on December 18, 1941, and was concluded on January 23, 1942. The record of its proceedings and exhibits covers 2,173 printed pages. Members of the Commission were Mr. Justice Owen J. Roberts,

[1] *Ibid.*, Appendix A, p. 269.

United States Supreme Court, Chairman; Admiral William H. Standley, United States Navy, retired; Rear Adm. Joseph M. Reeves, United States Navy, retired; Maj. Gen. Frank R. McCoy, United States Army, retired; and Brig. Gen. Joseph T. McNarney, United States Army.

The Hart Inquiry

The inquiry conducted by Admiral Thomas C. Hart, United States Navy, retired, was initiated by precept dated February 12, 1944, from Secretary of the Navy Frank Knox to Admiral Hart "For an Examination of Witnesses and the Taking of Testimony Pertinent to the Japanese Attack on Pearl Harbor, Territory of Hawaii." The precept stated ". . . Whereas certain members of the naval forces, who have knowledge pertinent to the foregoing matters, are now or soon may be on dangerous assignments at great distances from the United States . . . it is now deemed necessary, in order to prevent evidence being lost by death or unavoidable absence of those certain members of the naval forces, that their testimony, pertinent to the aforesaid Japanese attack, be recorded and preserved, . . ." This inquiry was commenced on February 12, 1944, and was concluded on June 15, 1944. The record of its proceedings and exhibits covers 565 printed pages.

The Army Pearl Harbor Board

The Army Pearl Harbor Board was appointed pursuant to the provisions of Public Law 339, Seventy-eighth Congress, approved June 13, 1944, and by order dated July 8, 1944, of The Adjutant General, War Department. The board was directed "to ascertain and report the facts relating to the attack made by Japanese armed forces upon the Territory of Hawaii on December 7, 1941, and to make such recommendations as it may deem proper." The board held sessions beginning July 20, 1944, and concluded its investigation on October 20, 1944. The record of its proceedings and exhibits covers 3,357 printed pages. Members of the board were Lt. Gen. George Grunert, president; Maj. Gen. Henry D. Russell and Maj. Gen. Walter A. Frank.

The Navy Court of Inquiry

The Navy Court of Inquiry was appointed pursuant to the provisions of Public Law 339, Seventy-eighth Congress, approved June 13, 1944, and by order dated July 13, 1944, of the Secretary of the Navy James Forrestal. The court was ordered to thoroughly "inquire into the attack made by Japanese armed forces on Pearl Harbor, Territory of Hawaii, on 7 December 1941 . . . and will include in its findings a full statement of the facts it may deem to be established. The court will further give its opinion as to whether any offenses have been committed or serious blame incurred on the part of any person or persons in the naval service, and in case its opinion be that offenses have been committed or serious blame incurred, will specifically recommend what further proceedings should be had." The court held sessions beginning July 24, 1944, and concluded its inquiry on October 19, 1944. The record of its proceedings and exhibits covers 1,397 printed pages. Members of the court were Admiral Orin G. Murfin, retired, president; Admiral Edward C. Kalbfus, retired, and Vice Adm. Adolphus Andrews, retired.

The Clarke Inquiry

The investigation conducted by Col. Carter W. Clarke "regarding the manner in which certain Top Secret communications were handled" was pursuant to oral instructions of Gen. George C. Marshall, Chief of Staff, United States Army. Colonel Clarke was appointed by Maj. Gen. Clayton Bissell, Chief of the Military Intelligence Division, War Department, under authority of a letter dated September 9, 1944, from The Adjutant General. This investigation was conducted from September 14 to 16, 1944, and from July 13 to August 4, 1945. Testimony was taken concerning the handling of intercepted Japanese messages known as Magic, the handling of intelligence material by the Military Intelligence Division, War Department, and the handling of the message sent by General Marshall to Lt. Gen. Walter C. Short at Hawaii on the morning of December 7, 1941. The record of the proceedings of this investigation, together with its exhibits, covers 225 printed pages.

The Clausen Investigation

Secretary of War Henry L. Stimson announced on December 1, 1944, that the report of the Army Pearl Harbor board had been submitted to him, and that: "In accordance with the opinion of the Judge Advocate General, I have decided that my own investigation should be further continued until all the facts are made as clear as possible, and until the testimony of every witness in possession of material facts can be obtained, and I have given the necessary directions to accomplish this result." By memorandum dated February 6, 1945, for Army personnel concerned, Secretary Stimson stated that "Pursuant to my directions and in accordance with my public statement of 1 December 1944, Major Henry C. Clausen, JAGD, is conducting for me the investigation supplementary to the proceedings of the Army Pearl Harbor Board." This investigation was commenced on November 23, 1944 and was concluded on September 12, 1945. The record of its proceedings and exhibits covers 695 printed pages.

The Hewitt Inquiry

The inquiry conducted by Admiral H. Kent Hewitt, United States Navy, was initiated under precept dated May 2, 1945, from Secretary of the Navy James Forrestal to conduct "Further investigation of facts pertinent to the Japanese attack on Pearl Harbor, Territory of Hawaii, on 7 December 1941." The precept stated that upon review of the evidence obtained by the examinations conducted by Admiral Thomas C. Hart and by the Navy Court of Inquiry, "the Secretary (of Navy) has found that there were errors of judgment on the part of certain officers in the Naval Service, both at Pearl Harbor and at Washington. The Secretary has further found that the previous investigations have not exhausted all possible evidence. Accordingly he has decided that the investigation directed by Public Law 339 of the 78th Congress should be further continued until the testimony of every witness in possession of material facts can be obtained and all possible evidence exhausted. . . . You are hereby detailed to make a study of the enclosures (Proceedings of Hart Inquiry and Navy Court of Inquiry) and then to conduct such further investigation, including the examination of any additional persons who may have knowledge of the facts pertinent to the said Japanese attack, and to reexamine any such person who has been previously examined, as may appear necessary, and to record the testimony given thereby." This inquiry commenced on May 14, 1945, and was concluded on July 11, 1945. The record of its proceedings and exhibits covers 1,342 printed pages.

(3) *Report of the Army Pearl Harbor Board on Assessment of Responsibilities for the Extent of the Attack, August 29, 1945.*[1]

[Excerpts]

* * * * * *

1. The Secretary of State — The Honorable Cordell Hull. The action of the Secretary of State in delivering the counter-proposals of November 26, 1941, was used by the Japanese as the signal to begin the war by the attack on Pearl Harbor. To the extent that it hastened such attack it was in conflict with the efforts of the War and Navy Departments to gain time for preparations for war. However, war with Japan was inevitable and imminent because of irreconcilable disagreements between the Japanese Empire and the American Government.

2. The Chief of Staff of the Army, Gen. George C. Marshall, failed in his relations with the Hawaiian Department in the following particulars:

(a) To keep the commanding general of the Hawaiian Department fully advised of the growing tenseness of the Japanese situation which indicated an increasing necessity for better preparation for war, of which information he had an abundance and Short had little.

(b) To send additional instructions to the commanding general of the Hawaiian Department on November 28, 1941, when evidently he failed to realize the import of General Short's reply of November 27, which indicated clearly that General Short had misunderstood and misconstrued the message of November 27, and had not adequately alerted his command for war.

(c) To get to General Short on the evening of December 6 and on the early morning of December 7, the critical information indicating an almost immediate break with Japan, though there was ample time to have accomplished this.

(d) To investigate and determine the state of readiness of the Hawaiian command between November 27 and December 7, 1941, despite the impending threat of war.

[1] *New York Times*, August 30, 1945, p. 1.

3. Chief of the war plans division, War Department general staff, Maj. Gen. Leonard T. Gerow, failed in his duties in the following particulars:

(a) To keep the commanding general, Hawaiian Department, adequately informed on the impending war situation by making available to him the substance of the data being delivered to the war plans division by the assistant chief of staff, G–2 (intelligence).

(b) To send to the commanding general of the Hawaiian Department on November 27, 1941, a clear, concise directive; on the contrary he approved the message of November 27, 1941, which contained confusing statements.

(c) To realize that the state of readiness reported in Short's reply to the November 27 message was not a state of readiness for war, and he failed to take corrective action.

(d) To take the required steps to implement the existing joint plans and agreements between the Army and Navy to insure the functioning of the two services in the manner contemplated.

4. Commanding general of the Hawaiian Department, General Short, failed in his duties in the following particulars:

(a) To place his command in a state of readiness for war in the face of a war warning by adopting an alert against sabotage only. The information which he had was incomplete and confusing but it was sufficient to warn him of the tense relations between our Government and the Japanese Empire and that hostilities might be momentarily expected. This required that he guard against surprise to the extent possible and make ready his command so that it might be employed to the maximum and in time against the worst form of attack that the enemy might launch.

(b) To reach or attempt to reach an agreement with the admiral commanding the Pacific Fleet and the admiral commanding the Fourteenth Naval District for implementing the joint Army and Navy plans and agreements then in existence which provided for joint action by the two services. One of the methods by which they might have become operative was through the joint agreement of the responsible commanders.

(c) To inform himself of the effectiveness of the long-distance reconnaissance being conducted by the Navy.

(d) To replace inefficient staff officers.

. . . .

The responsibility apparently assumed by the Secretary of State (and we have no other proof that anyone else assumed the responsibility finally and definitely) was to determine when the United States would reach the impasse with Japan.

He was doubtless aware of the fact that no action taken by him should be tantamount to a declaration of war. That responsibility rests with Congress. It is important to observe that the President of the United States had been very careful, according to the testimony of the Secretary of War, to be sure that the United States did nothing that could be considered an overt act or an act of war against the Japanese.

. . . .

The intentions of the War Department not to precipitate war, as far as the War Department was concerned, are clear and unmistakable. The messages sent to the Hawaiian Department show this to be a fact. The Navy apparently had the same idea because many of their messages likewise so indicate the situation and the Hawaiian Department was given the benefit of those messages.

Short was never informed of the Secretary of State's action in delivering the "ten points" counter-proposals. He testified he first saw or heard of that document after the White Papers were published.

The message of November 27th did not convey to Short what it was meant to convey by the people who drafted it. While confusing, it contained information and instructions the significance of which should have been appreciated by Short and his staff.

The two Navy messages of October 16 and 24, both of which cautioned against precipitation of an incident, could have added to Short's confusion in interpreting the message.

The impression that the avoidance of war was paramount was heightened by the messages immediately following the one of the 27th.

From November 28 until the message that was received after the attack, Short received no other word by the courier, letter, radio, or otherwise.

These acts of omission and commission on the part of the War Department undoubtedly played their part in the failure to put the Hawaiian Department in a proper state of defense.

. . . .

The Japanese Navy was lost to us for considerable periods in those months prior to the outbreak of war. The task force which made the attack on December 7, 1941, left home ports, assembled at Tankan Bay, and notwithstanding that it was a relatively large convoy, sailed for thousands of miles without being discovered. Part of its aircraft was in flight for the targets at Pearl Harbor and on Oahu before we knew of its existence. Its detection was primarily a naval job, but obviously the Army was intensely interested.

The Japanese armed forces knew everything about us. We knew little about them. This was a problem for all our intelligence agencies. This should not come to pass again.

. . . .

Aside from the letters and telegrams sent throughout 1941 to General Short (and there were no letters from General Marshall to General Short after November 1, 1941), no action after November 1, 1941, appears to have been taken by way of communications or inspections, or full report of any sort, to reveal whether General Short was doing anything, whether he was doing it correctly, what his problems were, and what help could have been given him.

The War Plans Division took no action when Short put the alert No. 1 into operation and so reported. It took no steps to stop the use of the Hawaiian Department as a training station and put it on a combat basis. It took no steps to find out if the Hawaiian defenses were being implemented and built according to schedule and right priorities.

. . . . .

(4) *Statement by the President (Truman) on the Report of the Army Pearl Harbor Board on the Responsibility of the Chief of Staff (Marshall). White House Press Release, August 29, 1945.*[1]

I have here reports on the Pearl Harbor disaster. One is from the Army, and one is from the Navy. The Navy report gives a "Finding of Facts" by a Navy Court of Inquiry. Attached to this "Finding of Facts" are indorsements by the Judge Advocate General of the Navy, Rear Admiral T. L. Gatch; Admiral E. J. King, Chief of Naval Operations; and the Secretary of the Navy. You will find a summation of the findings in the final indorsement by the Secretary of the Navy at the end of the document.

From the Army we have the report of the Army Pearl Harbor Board and, bound separately, a statement by the Secretary of War. Certain criticisms of the Chief of Staff, General Marshall, appear in the report of the Army Pearl Harbor Board. You will notice in the Secretary's statement, beginning on page 19, that he takes sharp issue with this criticism of General Marshall, stating that the criticism "is entirely unjustified". The conclusion of the Secretary of War is that General Marshall acted throughout this matter with his usual "great skill, energy and efficiency". I associate myself whole-heartedly with this expression by the Secretary of War.

Indeed I have the fullest confidence in the skill, energy, and efficiency of all our war leaders, both Army and Navy.

(5) *Statement by the President (Truman) on the Report of the Army Pearl Harbor Board on the Responsibilities of the People of the United States. White House Press Release, August 30, 1945.*[2]

I have read it [the Pearl Harbor reports] very carefully, and I came to the conclusion that the whole thing is the result of the policy which the country itself pursued. The country was not ready for preparedness. Every time the President made an effort to get a preparedness program through the Congress, it was stifled. Whenever the President made a statement about the necessity of preparedness, he was vilified for doing it. I think the country is as much to blame as any individual in this final situation that developed in Pearl Harbor.

---

[1] Department of State, *Bulletin*, XIII, p. 302.
[2] *Ibid.*, p. 303.

(6) *Senate Concurrent Resolution 27, 79th Congress, 1st Session, Establishing the Joint Congressional Committee of Investigation, Passed by the Senate, September 6, 1945, and by the House of Representatives, September 11, 1945.*[1]

Resolved by the Senate (*the House of Representatives concurring*), That there is hereby established a joint committee on the investigation of the Pearl Harbor attack, to be composed of five Members of the Senate (not more than three of whom shall be members of the majority party), to be appointed by the President pro tempore, and five Members of the House of Representatives (not more than three of whom shall be members of the majority party), to be appointed by the Speaker of the House. Vacancies in the membership of the committee shall not affect the power of the remaining members to execute the functions of the committee, and shall be filled in the same manner as in the case of the original selection. The committee shall select a chairman and a vice chairman from among its members.

SEC. 2. The committee shall make a full and complete investigation of the facts relating to the events and circumstances leading up to or following the attack made by Japanese armed forces upon Pearl Harbor in the Territory of Hawaii on December 7, 1941 and shall report to the Senate and the House of Representatives not later than January 3, 1946, the results of its investigation, together with such recommendations as it may deem advisable.

SEC. 3. The testimony of any person in the armed services, and the fact that such person testified before the joint committee herein provided for, shall not be used against him in any court proceedings, or held against him in examining his military status for credits in the service to which he belongs.

SEC. 4. (*a*) The committee, or any duly authorized subcommittee thereof, is authorized to sit and act at such places and times during the sessions, recesses, and adjourned periods of the Seventy-ninth Congress (prior to January 3, 1946), to require by subpoena or otherwise the attendance of such witnesses and the production of such books, papers, and documents, to administer such oaths, to take such testimony, to procure such printing and binding, and to make such expenditures as it deems advisable. The cost of stenographic services to report such hearings shall not be in excess of 25 cents per hundred words.

(*b*) The committee is empowered to appoint and fix the compensation of such experts, consultants, and clerical and stenographic assistants as it deems necessary, but the compensation so fixed shall not exceed the compensation prescribed under the Classification Act of 1923, as amended, for comparable duties.

(*c*) The expenses of the committee, which shall not exceed $25,000, shall be paid one-half from the contingent fund of the Senate and one-half from the contingent fund of the House of Representatives, upon vouchers signed by the chairman.

---

[1] ... *Report of the Joint Committee on the Investigation of the Pearl Harbor Attack. Congress of the United States* ..., cited above, p. XIII.

(7) Report of the Joint Congressional Committee of Investigation, Submitted July 20, 1946.[1]

[Excerpts]

. . . . . .

On 70 days subsequent to November 15 and prior to and including May 31, 1945, open hearings were conducted in the course of which some 15,000 pages of testimony were taken and a total of 183 exhibits received incident to an examination of 43 witnesses.

Of assistance to the committee and its work were the testimony and exhibits of seven prior investigations concerning the Pearl Harbor attack, including inquiries conducted by the Roberts Commission, Admiral Thomas C. Hart, the Army Pearl Harbor Board, the Navy Court of Inquiry, Col. Carter W. Clarke, Maj. Henry C. Clausen, and Admiral H. Kent Hewitt. For purposes of convenient reference there has been set forth in appendix A to this report a statement concerning the scope and character of each of these prior proceedings, the records of which total 9,754 printed pages of testimony from 318 witnesses and the attendant 469 exhibits. The records of these proceedings have been incorporated as exhibits to the record of the committee which encompasses approximately 10,000,000 words.

All witnesses appeared under oath and were afforded the fullest opportunity to offer any and all information which was regarded as having any relationship whatever to the disaster. In the course of examination by committee counsel and the committee members themselves, an effort was made to elicit all facts having an immediate or remote bearing on the tragedy of December 7, 1941. It is believed the committee has succeeded through its record in preserving for posterity the material facts concerning the disaster.

The figures and witnesses in the drama of Pearl Harbor ran the gamut of officials of the executive branch of the Government. The principal personalities in the picture were the President of the United States, Franklin D. Roosevelt; the Secretary of State, Cordell Hull; the Secretary of War, Henry L. Stimson; the Secretary of Navy, Frank Knox; the Chief of Staff, George C. Marshall; the Chief of Naval Operations, Harold R. Stark; the commander in chief of the Pacific Fleet, Husband E. Kimmel; and the commanding general of the Hawaiian Department, Walter C. Short. In appendix B to this report there are set forth the names and positions of the ranking Army and Navy officials in Washington and at Hawaii at the time of the attack along with the principal witnesses in the various proceedings.

The committee's investigation has extended to the files of all pertinent branches of the Government. Instructions in this regard from the President of the United States, Harry S. Truman, to various departments will be found in appendix C to this report. The committee through its counsel requested Miss Grace Tully, custodian of the files of the late President Roosevelt, to furnish the committee all papers in these files

[1] *Ibid.*, p. xiv.

for the year 1941 relating to Japan, the imminence of war in the Pacific, and the general Far Eastern developments. She furnished such papers in response to this request as she considered might be involved and stood ready to testify before the committee at any time.

All parties in interest have attested to the fact that they have been afforded a full, fair, and impartial public hearing before the committee. All witnesses who retained counsel — Admiral Stark, Admiral Kimmel, and General Short — were given the opportunity to be examined by their counsel if they so desired, and to submit questions to committee counsel to be asked other witnesses.

The following action was not taken by the committee for the reasons indicated:

(1) Former Secretary of War Henry L. Stimson was not called before the committee as a witness for the reason that his health would not permit. Mr. Stimson did, however, submit a statement under oath for the committee's consideration and the answers supplied by him to interrogatories propounded were considered by the committee. He supplied the portions of his personal diary requested by committee counsel and informed the committee that the portions of his diary now in evidence are the only portions thereof having any relationship to the Pearl Harbor investigation.

(2) Former Ambassador to Japan Joseph Grew appeared before the committee as a witness and testified to material appearing in his personal diary having a relationship to the events and circumstances of the Pearl Harbor attack. On the basis of his personal representation that no additional material pertinent to the subject of the committee's inquiry appeared in his diary beyond that to which he had testified, the committee did not formally request or otherwise seek to require the production of Mr. Grew's complete diary.

(3) A request by one member of the committee for the appearance of the former Prime Minister of England, Mr. Winston Churchill, was disapproved by a majority of the committee. At the time Mr. Churchill was a guest in the United States and it was not felt that he should with propriety be requested to appear as a witness.

(4) A request by one member of the committee for production by the State Department of all papers relating to the so-called Tyler Kent case was disapproved by a majority of the committee. The State Department had advised that these papers were in no way pertinent to the subject of the committee's inquiry, and, additionally, members of the committee had discussed the question with Mr. Kent who advised that he possessed no facts that would in any way have relationship to the Pearl Harbor attack.

Former Secretary of State Cordell Hull appeared before the committee but was forced to retire by reason of failing health before completion of the examination by all members of the committee. Mr. Hull subsequently responded to interrogatories propounded by the committee.

The committee has conceived its duty to be not only that of indicating the nature and scope of responsibility for the disaster but also of recording the pertinent considerations relating to the greatest defeat in our military and naval history. Only through a reasonable amount of detail is it possible to place events and responsibilities in their proper perspective and give to the Nation a genuine appreciation of the salient facts concerning Pearl Harbor. For this reason our report is of somewhat greater length than was initially believed necessary. It is to be recalled in this connection, however, that the over-all record of the committee comprehends some ten million words. It was felt therefore that the story of the antecedent, contemporaneous, and succeeding events attending the disaster could not be properly encompassed within a report any more concise than that herewith submitted.

We believe there is much to be learned of a constructive character as a result of the Japanese attack from the standpoint of legislation and, additionally, for guidance in avoiding the possibility of another military disaster such as Pearl Harbor. Accordingly, in the section devoted to recommendations there are set forth, in addition to the recommendations proper, a series of principles, based on errors revealed by the investigation, which are being commended to our military and naval services for their consideration and possible assistance.

Our report does not purport to set forth or refer to all of the enormous volume of testimony and evidence adduced in the course of the Pearl Harbor investigation. It is believed, however, that the material facts relevant to the disaster have been outlined in the report. The committee's record and the records of all prior investigations have been printed and are available for review and study. It is to be borne in mind that the findings and conclusions are based on the facts presently in our record after an exhaustive investigation.

. . . .

Conclusions With Respect to Responsibilities [1]

1. The December 7, 1941, attack on Pearl Harbor was an unprovoked act of aggression by the Empire of Japan. The treacherous attack was planned and launched while Japanese ambassadors, instructed with characteristic duplicity, were carrying on the pretense of negotiations with the Government of the United States with a view to an amicable settlement of differences in the Pacific.

2. The ultimate responsibility for the attack and its results rests upon Japan, an attack that was well planned and skillfully executed. Contributing to the effectiveness of the attack was a powerful striking force, much more powerful than it had been thought the Japanese were able to employ in a single tactical venture at such distance and under such circumstances.

3. The diplomatic policies and actions of the United States provided no justifiable provocation whatever for the attack by Japan on this Nation. The Secretary of State fully informed both the War and Navy Departments of diplomatic developments and, in a timely and forceful manner, clearly pointed out to these Departments that relations between

[1] *Ibid.*, Part V., p. 251.

THE TERMINATION OF THE WAR

the United States and Japan had passed beyond the stage of diplomacy and were in the hands of the military.

4. The committee has found no evidence to support the charges, made before and during the hearings, that the President, the Secretary of State, the Secretary of War, or the Secretary of Navy tricked, provoked, incited, cajoled, or coerced Japan into attacking this Nation in order that a declaration of war might be more easily obtained from the Congress. On the contrary, all evidence conclusively points to the fact that they discharged their responsibilities with distinction, ability, and foresight and in keeping with the highest traditions of our fundamental foreign policy.

5. The President, the Secretary of State, and high Government officials made every possible effort, without sacrificing our national honor and endangering our security, to avert war with Japan.

6. The disaster of Pearl Harbor was the failure, with attendant increase in personnel and material losses, of the Army and the Navy to institute measures designed to detect an approaching hostile force, to effect a state of readiness commensurate with the realization that war was at hand, and to employ every facility at their command in repelling the Japanese.

7. Virtually everyone was surprised that Japan struck the Fleet at Pearl Harbor at the time that she did. Yet officers, both in Washington and Hawaii, were fully conscious of the danger from air attack; they realized this form of attack on Pearl Harbor by Japan was at least a possibility; and they were adequately informed of the imminence of war.

8. Specifically, the Hawaiian commands failed —

(a) To discharge their responsibilities in the light of the warnings received from Washington, other information possessed by them, and the principle of command by mutual cooperation.

(b) To integrate and coordinate their facilities for defense and to alert properly the Army and Navy establishments in Hawaii, particularly in the light of the warnings and intelligence available to them during the period November 27 to December 7, 1941.

(c) To effect liaison on a basis designed to acquaint each of them with the operations of the other, which was necessary to their joint security, and to exchange fully all significant intelligence.

(d) To maintain a more effective reconnaissance within the limits of their equipment.

(e) To effect a state of readiness throughout the Army and Navy establishments designed to meet all possible attacks.

(f) To employ the facilities, matériel, and personnel at their command, which were adequate at least to have greatly minimized the effects of the attack, in repelling the Japanese raiders.

(g) To appreciate the significance of intelligence and other information available to them.

9. The errors made by the Hawaiian commands were errors of judgment and not derelictions of duty.

10. The War Plans Division of the War Department failed to discharge its direct responsibility to advise the commanding general he

had not properly alerted the Hawaiian Department when the latter, pursuant to instructions, had reported action taken in a message that was not satisfactorily responsive to the original directive.

11. The Intelligence and War Plans Divisions of the War and Navy Departments failed:

(a) To give careful and thoughtful consideration to the intercepted messages from Tokyo to Honolulu of September 24, November 15, and November 20 (the harbor berthing plan and related dispatches) and to raise a question as to their significance. Since they indicated a particular interest in the Pacific Fleet's base this intelligence should have been appreciated and supplied the Hawaiian commanders for their assistance, along with other information available to them, in making their estimate of the situation.

(b) To be properly on the *qui vive* to receive the "one o'clock" intercept and to recognize in the message the fact that some Japanese military action would very possibly occur somewhere at 1 P.M., December 7. If properly appreciated, this intelligence should have suggested a dispatch to all Pacific outpost commanders supplying this information, as General Marshall attempted to do immediately upon seeing it.

12. Notwithstanding the fact that there were officers on twenty-four hour watch, the Committee believes that under all of the evidence the War and Navy Departments were not sufficiently alerted on December 6 and 7, 1941, in view of the imminence of war.

* * * * * * *

CHAPTER IV

AMERICAN POLICY TOWARD FORMER ENEMY STATES

1. POLICY TOWARD INDIVIDUAL STATES

A. Italy

[On United States policy with respect to territorial questions and the making of the peace, see *The First Five Peace Treaties. Supplement: Documents, VIII, 1945–1946*.]

[For developments from the invasion of Sicily by Allied forces in July, 1943, to the liberation of Rome in June, 1944, see *Documents, VI, 1943–1944*, pp. 160–183. For the period from June 4, 1944 to the formation of the Parri government on June 19, 1945, see *Documents, VII, 1944–1945*, p. 161–180.]

During the period under review, Italy was faced by a series of difficult and grave problems which gave rise to a number of crises. Domestically, the new government had to cope with a serious food shortage, which did not ease until the spring of 1946 and with the form and structure of the new Italian state. In the international sphere, the most important problems centered around the drafting of the final peace treaty, which involved the usually tense issue of the future of Trieste. Signor Parri's government, composed of representatives of the Christian Democratic (Sgr. de Gasperi), Communist (Sgr. Togliatti), Liberal (Sgr. Riuz) and Socialist (Barbareschi) Parties, with Sgr. Nenni and Sgr. Brosio as vice-premiers,[1] lasted until December 9, 1945, but collapsed with the withdrawal of the ministers of the Liberal and Labour Democrat Parties because of the refusal of Signor Parri to widen the coalition government by including other groups.[2] During this period Italy joined the war against Japan on July 14, 1945,[3] saw the removal of Allied control over export trade (except in the cases of the United States and the Soviet Union) on August 1, 1945,[4] and concluded a commercial treaty with Switzerland (August 7).[5]

Signor de Gasperi, representing the Christian Democratic Party, then formed a cabinet in which each of the six major parties held three portfolios,[6] and which was pledged to convene a Constituent Assembly in the spring of 1946 to determine the future form of the Italian government.[7] In the light of an apparently growing opposition to the monarchy, King Victor Emmanuel III abdicated the throne on May 9, 1946, and his son became King Humbert II. The law, approved by the Cabinet, omitted the usual phrase "by the grace of God and the will of the people" in favor of designating the new monarch merely as "King of Italy."[8] On June 2, 1946, polling took place for parliamentary elections and for a referendum regarding the monarchy. On June 18 the Court of Cassation announced that the vote for a republic was 12,717,923, for the monarchy, 10,719,284, with 1,498,136 blank or spoiled ballots.[9] King Humbert had left Italy on June 13, after having previously agreed to abide by the results of the referendum. The final figures for the election of the Constituent Assembly gave the Christian

[1] *Chronology of International Events and Documents*, I, p. 6.
[2] *Ibid.*, p. 224.   [3] *Ibid.*, p. 50.   [4] *Ibid.*, p. 63.   [5] *Ibid.*, p. 89.   [6] *Ibid.*, p. 285.
[7] *New York Times*, December 11, 1945; for text of the Decree Law establishing the provisions for the Constituent Assembly, see *United States and Italy, 1936–1946, Documentary Record*, Department of State Publication 2669, p. 233.
[8] *New York Times*, May 11, 1946.
[9] *Chronology of International Events and Documents*, II, p. 353.

Democrats 207 seats, the Socialists 115, Communists 104, Homo Qualanque 30, Republicans 23, the Union of Right Wing parties 41, Monarchist *bloc* 16, and Actionists 7. The Constituent Assembly met on June 25, 1946 and elected Signor de Nicola President of the Republic of Italy by 396 votes to 72 for two other candidates.[1] Signor de Gasperi continued as Prime Minister with a cabinet of 10 Christian Democrats, 4 Socialists, 4 Communists, 2 Republicans and 1 Independent. This cabinet continued in power with minor changes for the balance of the period under review.

Although rioting broke out in various parts of Italy in this eighteen-month period because of the economic situation, there was a gradual improvement within the country. A full scale UNRRA program in 1946 was supplemented by trade agreements or commercial treaties with France (February 9, 1946),[2] Spain (January 10, 1946),[3] Poland (October 10, 1946), by an Export-Import Bank Loan of $25,000,000 for the purchase of raw cotton,[4] by the devaluation of the lira,[5] and by the receipt of a first quota of $51,000,000 from the United States to cover occupation costs.[6] The year's end, however, found the economic situation still far from normal with an estimated deficit of 400 milliard lira and a floating debt of 778 milliard lira.[7]

(1) *Message from the Acting Secretary of State (Acheson) to the Mazzini Society, September 15, 1945.*[8]

[Excerpt]

. . . . . .

It is the policy of the American Government to welcome the efforts of Italy to wipe out the Fascist past and to work for such conditions of peace as will enable Italy to reassume her rightful place in the comity of nations. Along with our chief Allies, we look forward to the time when Italy will be a member of the United Nations. It is the hope of the American Government that the negotiations now started in London will speedily prepare the way for Italy to regain her historic international ties and position.

The policy of the American Government is also directed to aid the economic and political rehabilitation of Italy. It is in our own interest to grant such aid. This cannot, however, be economic aid on the simple order of charity. It must be such as at a critical time will enable the Italian people to get back on their own feet; it must be essentially granting the opportunity for them to rebuild their devastated agriculture, industry, and commerce.

So too in the political reconstruction of Italy, our policy is the Italian people should have full opportunity to rebuild their own house. We have welcomed the declarations of the present Italian leaders of their intention to reconstruct the government on a democratic basis. But it is the Italian people and government who must perform this task if it is to be accomplished. By its very nature democracy cannot be imposed on a people from without. It cannot be imposed on a people or country by

---

[1] *Ibid.*, p. 381.
[2] *Ibid.*, p. 96.
[3] *Ibid.*, p. 42.   [4] *Ibid.*, p. 212.   [5] *Ibid.*, p. 67.   [6] *Ibid.*, p. 778.   [7] *Ibid.*, p. 588.
[8] Department of State, *Bulletin*, XIII, p. 391.

a central government operating from the top down — from the capital to the village. While the United States has aided in purging Italy of Fascist personnel and Fascist institutions, and given its support to the removal of restrictions on a free press, on free discussion, and on free association — these steps are merely preliminary. They furnish only the opportunity for rebuilding a democratic Italy. The structure must be built by the Italian people.

Democracy depends on respect for the worth of the individual; it depends on respect for differences and on recognition of the rights of political opponents. We Americans are a mixed people embracing strains from all the nations of Europe. We live in peace with each other, not through the domination of any one class, element, or group but through a tolerance of differences. Our democratic political system functions, and functions well, because all of us prefer peaceful solutions and compromises rather than a resort to force.

Our democracy is not the result of orders and decrees from Washington. It has its roots in the towns, counties, and cities where citizens manage their own affairs through their elected representatives. Through the States it extends to the Federal Government. Our habits of self-government begin in the local units. The American people feel competent to direct and ultimately to control their Federal Government because of their constant practice in managing their own local affairs.

Now that the war in Europe is over, and the Italian people face the positive task of rebuilding a democratic system, we hope to see them begin at the grass roots with free and fair elections, and reestablish through elected mayors and councils the control over their immediate affairs.

To regain the democratic habits and ways of life, to maintain the spirit of tolerance essential for democracy, and to reintroduce elective officials in the units most directly affecting the average citizen — these are the immediate tasks of the Italian people. We in America cannot force these things upon them. We can and we do wish them well in their task.

(2) *Statement by the Secretary of State (Byrnes) on United States' Interest in Italian Elections, February 11, 1946.*[1]

The United States Government is keenly interested in the coming Italian elections, during which the people will elect a Constituent Assembly to carry out the grave task of drafting a new constitution.

Our interest in the elections of an Italian Constituent Assembly is easy to explain. Even before our armies landed on Italian soil to rid Italy of Fascist and Nazi oppression, we pledged the Italian people a free government. That pledge was solemnly renewed in the Joint Declaration of October 13, 1943, which stated that "nothing can detract from the absolute and untrammelled right of the people of Italy by constitutional means to decide on the democratic form of government they will eventually have."

[1] *Ibid.*, XIV, p. 298.

Italy has given much to western civilization. What we call communal liberties, the liberty of the citizen to appoint his leaders and to hold them responsible, found their expression in the Italian *comuni* of long ago. The Italian Constituent Assembly will have a delicate and an imposing task in giving a constitution to a country known as the Mother of Law. In that task it will have our best wishes and our encouragement.

B. Germany

1. GENERAL POLICY

The period under review opened with the Potsdam Declaration of a joint Big Three policy toward Germany and closed with Secretary Byrnes' Stuttgart speech, which was followed by the formal agreement unifying the British and American zones. Although efforts were made to clothe the bi-zonal agreement with consistency to Potsdam, it was quite apparent that American policy in the eighteen-month period had gone through a nearly complete cycle from close cooperation with the Soviet Union to a reluctant decision that such cooperation was difficult if not impossible.[1]

The Potsdam Declaration[2] summarized the agreement reached by President Truman, Generalissimo Stalin and Prime Minister Attlee, who had taken Mr. Churchill's place at the Conference table where the latter's government was overthrown in the British general election. In addition to establishing a Control Council in Germany, composed of representatives of the United States, the United Kingdom, the Soviet Union and France, with specified responsibilities, the Declaration outlined political and, especially, economic provisions which were in general conformity to JSC 1067,[3] the basic directive issued by the Joint Chiefs of Staff to General Eisenhower in April 1945. This earlier directive, the Potsdam Declaration, and the agreement signed by the United States, United Kingdom, Soviet Union and France on September 20, 1945,[4] setting up certain additional requirements to be imposed on Germany, emphasized "disarmament, de-industrialization, denazification, decentralization, reparations and the care of displaced persons,"[5] measures which were largely corrective in their nature and designed to curb Germany's political or economic capacity for waging another war. Further, the original plans envisaged the simultaneous application of these principles in each of the four zones by each of the four occupying Powers.

Some joint progress was made, particularly in regard to denazification, de-industrialization and the problems of reparations agreements and deliveries. The Control Council passed laws providing for the termination of Nazi organizations,[6] reorganizing the German judicial system,[7] and creating a German External Assets Commission[8] which was vested with title to any property outside Germany owned or controlled by any person of German nationality inside Germany.

---

[1] This note is substantially based upon the following studies: Wolfers, Arnold. *United States Policy Toward Germany.* Yale Institute of International Studies, February 1947; Hadsel, Winifred N. "The Ruhr: Object of Allied Rivalries." *Foreign Policy Reports*, XXII, No. 13 (September 15, 1946); and Dean, Vera Micheles. "U. S. Policy in Europe." *Ibid.*, XXI, No. 21 (January 15, 1946).

[2] For section of the Potsdam declaration relating to occupation of Germany, see this volume, Appendix II.

[3] See *Documents, VII, 1944–1945*, p. 193.

[4] See this volume, p. 189.

[5] Wolfers, cited above.

[6] Allied Secretariat. *Official Gazette of the Control Council for Germany.* Berlin, No. 1 (October 29, 1945), p. 19.

[7] *Ibid.*, No. 2 (November, 1945), p. 26.

[8] See this volume, p. 224.

Further, the Council, which operated on the basis of unanimity, issued a series of additional laws and decrees dissolving German Armed forces, punishing persons guilty of war crimes, and seizing the property of the I. G. Farben interests.

The Control Council found it easier to agree upon such fundamentally punitive measures as these than upon some of the constructive aspects of Potsdam envisaged as parallel steps to be undertaken by the occupying authorities. Difficulties arose not because of disagreement as to the objectives of occupation — to prevent Germany from again becoming a major military power — but as to the method to achieve the objective. Great Britain, with an eye to an important market for British goods, favored a policy leading to an industrial recovery for Germany which would fall short of creating a dangerous military potential. The French and Russians wanted, first, reparations, and second, to secure their own borders against any future resurgence of German military power. The United States, equally concerned about a German military revival, wanted an economic system which would work and which would eventually relieve the United States of responsibility for maintaining a subsistence standard of living for the Germans.[1] These differing emphases on method were underscored by the practical and immediate consequences of administering occupation zones which varied considerably in economic resources. The British zone, which lacked a sufficiency of foodstuffs, had 30% of the population, resources and production of Germany including 75% of the hard coal reserves and production with an equal percentage of the steel production. The Soviet zone had a pre-war exportable surplus of foodstuffs, large supplies of brown coal and water power, but contained as well most of the iron- and steel-finishing industries which were dependent upon the iron and steel production of the British zone for their raw and semi-finished materials. The American zone contained about 20% of the population and productivity of pre-war Germany, but most of this production was of a light-industry type and there existed a deficiency of foodstuffs. The French zone had less than a tenth of the population, resources or productivity of pre-war Germany, although it contained the important Saar area which normally was a source of about 17% of the hard coal and 12% of the steel production.[2] Under these circumstances, failure to achieve economic unity for the whole country could only result in the intensification of the economic problems of each separate zone.

Although American concern for a greater emphasis upon the constructive steps to be initiated for reconstituting a healthy German state were foreshadowed by Secretary of State Byrnes' comments upon the Memorandum on the Reparations Settlement and the Peacetime Economy of Germany, issued December 12, 1945, the United States joined in carrying forward two programs stemming from the Potsdam decisions: it participated in and became a signatory to the Paris Agreement on Reparation of January 14, 1946, which created the Inter-Allied Reparations Agency;[3] it also agreed to the so-called "level of industry" plan of March 28, 1946[4] by which the four occupying authorities planned to implement both the agreements on reparations and the long range policy of preventing the resurgence of German industry. In the United States zone some 156 German plants were confirmed for reparations, 24 of which were allocated as "advance reparations." From these latter, a total of 11,000 tons of reparations equipment were made available at the port of Bremen for transshipment to the Soviet Union by August 1, 1946.[5]

[1] Dean, cited above, p. 290.
[2] Hoffman, L. A. "Germany: Zones of Occupation." Department of State, *Bulletin*, XIV, p. 599–607.
[3] See this volume, p. 227.
[4] *Ibid.*, p. 244.
[5] Office of Military Government for Germany (U.S.). *A Year of Potsdam, The German Economy Since the Surrender*, p. 35–37.

By the spring of 1946, however, American concern about the failure to achieve the economic unification of Germany had increased to such a point that by May 4 the Deputy Military Governor of the American zone (Lt. Gen. Lucius D. Clay) stopped the further dismantling of reparations plants, except the 24 marked as advance reparations, "pending definite assurance that the provisions for treating Germany as an economic unit as specified in the Potsdam Declaration and the Reparations Plan will actually be put into effect."[1] This specific decision was merely a reflection of a much broader problem, partially economic but partially — perhaps even primarily[2] — political in nature.

German industrial recovery hinged upon coal production, most of which came from the Ruhr area in the British zone of occupation. At no point in the period under review did coal production exceed 50% of the pre-war level of 10.5 million tons monthly, and for most of the period it was less than 33%. The British blamed poor production on a food shortage, estimated to cost the British tax payers, for the zones of Germany and Austria, $320,000,000 for the period 1946-47, and which both American and British officials felt could be materially aided by prompt economic unification making available the exportable food surpluses in the Soviet zone.[3] The economics of the situation were complicated, however, by (a) a Russian desire to establish firmly a pro-Soviet political organization in their area and (b) by French refusal to agree to central German administrative organs until the western boundaries of Germany had been finally determined, coupled with French irritation at the small allocations of Ruhr coal received from the British.[4]

All of these problems were affected, and in some degree aggravated, by the fact that peace negotiations were proceeding in the various meetings of the Council of Foreign Ministers.[5] The United States sought in March 1946 to persuade the French to abandon their opposition to central administration,[6] and in April, at the Council of Foreign Ministers Meeting, attempted, through the medium of a proposed four power pact, to gain approval for what had amounted to an over-all agreement on demilitarization and disarmament policies.[7] Both of these attempts failed.

These economic and political difficulties were magnified when the Soviet Union sought popular political support in Germany through the floating of two trial balloons: (1) German communist propaganda that firm support of the German Communist Party would aid in securing a revision of the eastern boundary with Poland; and, (2) Foreign Minister V. M. Molotov's attack on July 10, 1946, of the "agrarianization" of Germany, which was coupled with what appeared to be proposals for less punitive treatment.[8]

The Russian bid for German support, coupled with the cool reception given the four power pact proposal, gave rise to the speech of Secretary of State James F. Byrnes at Stuttgart on September 6, 1946,[9] and was followed in December by the formal agreement on the unification of the United States and British zones. As a matter of fact, formal bi-zonal consultation between British and American officials to establish common living standards, rations, and import policies began on September 4, 1946.[10]

[1] *Ibid.*, p. 45.
[2] Wolfers, cited above, p. 7.
[3] Hadsel, cited above, p. 160.
[4] *Ibid.*
[5] For details, see *The First Five Peace Treaties. Supplement: Documents, VIII, 1945–1946.*
[6] For text of Byrnes-Bidault exchange of notes, see this volume, p. 201.
[7] For text, see *ibid.*, p. 205.
[8] Wolfers, cited above, p. 8; for text of Molotov speech, see *New York Times*, July 11, 1946.
[9] For text, see this volume, p. 210.
[10] Office of Military Government for Germany (U.S.). *Monthly Report of the Military Governor*, 1–30 September 1946, No. 15, p. 1.

(1) *Agreement between the United States, the United Kingdom, the Union of Soviet Socialist Republics, and the Provisional Government of the French Republic on Additional Requirements to Be Imposed on Germany, Signed September 20, 1945.*[1]

We, the Allied Representatives, Commanders-in-Chief of the forces of occupation of the United Kingdom, the United States of America, the Union of Soviet Socialist Republics and the French Republic, pursuant to the Declaration regarding the defeat of Germany, signed at Berlin on 5th June, 1945,[2] hereby announce certain additional requirements arising from the complete defeat and unconditional surrender of Germany with which Germany must comply, as follows: —

Section I

1. All German land, naval and air forces, the S.S., S.A., S.D. and Gestapo, with all their organizations, staffs and institutions, including the General Staff, the Officers' Corps, Reserve Corps, military schools, war veterans' organizations and all other military and quasi-military organizations, together with all clubs and associations which serve to keep alive the military tradition in Germany, shall be completely and finally abolished in accordance with methods and procedures to be laid down by the Allied Representatives.

2. All forms of military training, military propaganda and military activities of whatever nature, on the part of the German people, are prohibited, as well as the formation of any organization initiated to further any aspect of military training and the formation of war veterans' organizations or other groups which might develop military characteristics or which are designed to carry on the German military tradition, whether such organizations or groups purport to be political, educational, religious, social, athletic or recreational or of any other nature.

Section II

3. (*a*) German authorities and officials in all territories outside the frontiers of Germany as they existed on 31st December, 1937, and in any areas within those frontiers indicated at any time by the Allied Representatives, will comply with such instructions as to withdrawing therefrom as they may receive from the Allied Representatives.

(*b*) The German authorities will issue the necessary instructions and will make the necessary arrangements for the reception and maintenance in Germany of all German civilian inhabitants of the territories or areas concerned, whose evacuation may be ordered by the Allied Representatives.

(*c*) Withdrawals and evacuations under sub-paragraphs (*a*) and (*b*) above will take place at such times and under such conditions as the Allied Representatives may direct.

---

[1] Department of State, *Bulletin*, XIII, p. 515.
[2] See *Documents, VII, 1944–1945,* p. 217.

4. In the territories and areas referred to in paragraph 3 above, there shall immediately be, on the part of all forces under German command and of German authorities and civilians, a complete cessation of all measures of coercion or forced labor and of all measures involving injury to life or limb. There shall similarly cease all measures of requisitioning, seizure, removal, concealment or destruction of property. In particular, the withdrawals and evacuations mentioned in paragraph 3 above will be carried out without damage to or removal of persons or property not affected by the orders of the Allied Representatives. The Allied Representatives will determine what personal property and effects may be taken by persons evacuated under paragraph 3 above.

Section III

5. The Allied Representatives will regulate all matters affecting Germany's relations with other countries. No foreign obligations, undertakings or commitments of any kind will be assumed or entered into by or on behalf of German authorities or nationals without the sanction of the Allied Representatives.

6. The Allied Representatives will give directions concerning the abrogation, bringing into force, revival or application of any treaty, convention or other international agreement, or any part or provision thereof, to which Germany is or has been a party.

7. (a) In virtue of the unconditional surrender of Germany, and as of the date of such surrender, the diplomatic, consular, commercial and other relations of the German State with other States have ceased to exist.

(b) Diplomatic, consular, commercial and other officials and members of service missions in Germany of countries at war with any of the four Powers will be dealt with as the Allied Representatives may prescribe. The Allied Representatives may require the withdrawal from Germany of neutral diplomatic, consular, commercial and other officials and members of neutral service missions.

(c) All German diplomatic, consular, commercial and other officials and members of German service missions abroad are hereby recalled. The control and disposal of the buildings, property and archives of all German diplomatic and other agencies abroad will be prescribed by the Allied Representatives.

8. (a) German nationals will, pending further instructions, be prevented from leaving German territory except as authorized or directed by the Allied Representatives.

(b) German authorities and nationals will comply with any directions issued by the Allied Representatives for the recall of German nationals resident abroad, and for the reception in Germany of any persons whom the Allied Representatives may designate.

9. The German authorities and people will take all appropriate steps to ensure the safety, maintenance and welfare of persons not of German nationality and of their property and the property of foreign States.

Section IV

10. The German authorities will place at the disposal of the Allied Representatives the whole of the German inter-communication system (including all military and civilian postal and telecommunication systems and facilities and connected matters), and will comply with any instructions given by the Allied Representatives for placing such inter-communication systems under the complete control of the Allied Representatives. The German authorities will comply with any instructions given by the Allied Representatives with a view to the establishment by the Allied Representatives of such censorship and control of postal and telecommunication and of documents and other articles carried by persons or otherwise conveyed and of all other forms of inter-communication as the Allied Representatives may think fit.

11. The German authorities will comply with all directions which the Allied Representatives may give regarding the use, control and censorship of all media for influencing expression and opinions, including broadcasting, press and publications, advertising, films and public performances, entertainments, and exhibitions of all kinds.

Section V

12. The Allied Representatives will exercise such control as they deem necessary over all or any part or aspect of German finance, agriculture (including forestry) production and mining, public utilities, industry, trade, distribution and economy generally, internal and external, and over all related or ancillary matters, including the direction or prohibition of the manufacture, production, construction, treatment, use and disposal of any buildings, establishments, installations, public or private works, plant, equipment, products, materials, stocks, or resources. Detailed statements of the subjects to which the present provision applies, together with the requirements of the Allied Representatives in regard thereto, will from time to time be communicated to the German authorities.

13. (*a*) The manufacture, production and construction, and the acquisition from outside Germany, of war material and of such other products, used in connection with such manufacture, production or construction, as the Allied Representatives may specify, and the import, export and transit thereof, are prohibited, except as directed by the Allied Representatives.

(*b*) The German authorities will immediately place at the disposal of the Allied Representatives all research, experiment, development and design directly or indirectly relating to war or the production of war material, whether in government or private establishments, factories, technological institutions or elsewhere.

14. (*a*) The property, assets, rights, titles and interests (whether situated inside or outside Germany) of the German State, its political subdivisions, the German Central Bank, State or semi-State, provincial, municipal or local authorities or Nazi organizations, and those situated

outside Germany of any person resident or carrying on business in Germany, will not be disposed of in any way whatever without the sanction of the Allied Representatives. The property, assets, rights, titles and interests (whether situated inside or outside Germany), of such private companies, corporations, trusts, cartels, firms, partnerships and associations as may be designated by the Allied Representatives will not be disposed of in any way whatever without the sanction of the Allied Representatives.

(b) The German authorities will furnish full information about the property, assets, rights, titles and interests referred to in sub-paragraph (a) above, and will comply with such directions as the Allied Representatives may give as to their transfer and disposal. Without prejudice to any further demands which may be made in this connection, the German authorities will hold at the disposal of the Allied Representatives for delivery to them at such times and places as they may direct all securities, certificates, deeds or other documents of title held by any of the institutions or bodies mentioned in sub-paragraph (a) above or by any person subject to German law, and relating to property, assets, rights, titles and interests situated in the territories of the United Nations, including any shares, stocks, debentures or other obligations of any company incorporated in accordance with the laws of any of the United Nations.

(c) Property, assets, rights, titles and interests situated inside Germany will not be removed outside Germany or be transferred or disposed of to any person resident or carrying on business outside Germany without the sanction of the Allied Representatives.

(d) Nothing in sub-paragraphs (a) and (b) above shall, as regards property, assets, rights, titles and interests situated inside Germany, be deemed to prevent sales or transfers to persons resident in Germany for the purpose of maintaining or carrying on the day-to-day national life, economy and administration, subject to the provisions of sub-paragraph 19 (b) and (c) below and to the provisions of the Declaration or of any proclamations, orders, ordinances or instructions issued thereunder.

15. (a) The German authorities and all persons in Germany will hand over to the Allied Representatives all gold and silver, in coin or bullion forms, and all platinum in bullion form, situated in Germany, and all such coin and bullion situated outside Germany as is possessed by or held on behalf of any of the institutions or bodies mentioned in sub-paragraph 14 (a) above or any person resident or carrying on business in Germany.

(b) The German authorities and all persons in Germany will hand over in full to the Allied Representatives all foreign notes and coins in the possession of any German authority, or of any corporation, association or individual resident or carrying on business in Germany, and all monetary tokens issued or prepared for issue by Germany in the territories formerly occupied by her or elsewhere.

16. (a) All property, assets, rights, titles and interests in Germany held for or belonging to any country against which any of the United Nations is carrying on hostilities, or held for or belonging to the nationals

of any such country, or of any persons resident or carrying on business therein, will be taken under control and will be preserved pending further instructions.

(b) All property, assets, rights, titles and interests in Germany held for or belonging to private individuals, private enterprises and companies of those countries, other than Germany and the countries referred to in sub-paragraph (a) above, which have at any time since the 1st September, 1939, been at war with any of the United Nations, will be taken under control and will be preserved pending further instructions.

(c) The German authorities will take all necessary steps to ensure the execution of the provisions of sub-paragraphs (a) and (b) above, will comply with any instructions given by the Allied Representatives for that purpose, and will afford all necessary information and facilities in connection therewith.

17. (a) There shall, on the part of the German authorities and people, be no concealment, destruction, scuttling, or dismantling of, removal or transfer of, nor damage to, ships, transport, ports or harbours, nor to any form of building, establishment, installation, device, means of production, supply, distribution or communication, plant, equipment, currency, stocks or resources, or, in general, public or private works, utilities or facilities of any kind, wherever situated.

(b) There shall be no destruction, removal, concealment, suppression or alteration of any documents, records, patents, drawings, specifications, plans or information, of any nature, affected by the provisions of this document. They shall be kept intact in their present locations until further directions are given. The German authorities will afford all information and facilities as required by the Allied Representatives in connection therewith.

(c) Any measures already ordered, undertaken or begun contrary to the provisions of sub-paragraphs (a) and (b) above will be immediately countermanded or discontinued. All stocks, equipment, plant, records, patents, documents, drawings, specifications, plans or other material already concealed within or outside Germany will forthwith be declared and will be dealt with as the Allied Representatives may direct.

(d) Subject to the provisions of the Declaration or any proclamations, orders, ordinances, or instructions issued thereunder, the German authorities and people will be responsible for the preservation, safeguarding and upkeep of all forms of property and materials affected by any of the said provisions.

(e) All transport material, stores, equipment, plant, establishments, installations, devices and property generally, which are liable to be surrendered or delivered under the Declaration or any proclamations, orders, ordinances or instructions issued thereunder, will be handed over intact and in good condition, or subject only to ordinary wear and tear and to any damage caused during the continuance of hostilities which it has proved impossible to make good.

18. There shall be no financial, commercial or other intercourse with, or dealings with or for the benefit of, countries at war with any of the

United Nations, or territories occupied by such countries, or with any other country or person specified by the Allied Representatives.

SECTION VI

19. (a) The German authorities will carry out, for the benefit of the United Nations, such measures of restitution, reinstatement, restoration, reparation, reconstruction, relief and rehabilitation as the Allied Representatives may prescribe. For these purposes the German authorities will effect or procure the surrender or transfer of such property, assets, rights, titles and interests, effect such deliveries and carry out such repair, building and construction work, whether in Germany or elsewhere, and will provide such transport, plant equipment and materials of all kinds, labour, personnel and specialist and other services, for use in Germany or elsewhere, as the Allied Representatives may direct.

(b) The German authorities will also comply with all such directions as the Allied Representatives may give relating to property, assets, rights, titles and interests located in Germany belonging to any one of the United Nations or its nationals or having so belonged at, or at any time since, the outbreak of war between Germany and that Nation, or since the occupation of any part of its territories by Germany. The German authorities will be responsible for safeguarding, maintaining, and preventing the dissipation of, all such property, assets, rights, titles and interests, and for handing them over intact at the demand of the Allied Representatives. For these purposes the German authorities will afford all information and facilities required for tracing any property, assets, rights, titles or interests.

(c) All persons in Germany in whose possession such property, assets, rights, titles and interests may be, shall be personally responsible for reporting them and for safeguarding them until they are handed over in such manner as may be prescribed.

20. The German authorities will supply free of cost such German currency as the Allied Representatives may require, and will withdraw and redeem in German currency, within such time limits and on such terms as the Allied Representatives may specify, all holdings in German territory of currencies issued by the Allied Representatives during military operations or occupation, and will hand over the currencies so withdrawn free of cost to the Allied Representatives.

21. The German authorities will comply with all such directions as may be issued by the Allied Representatives for defraying the costs of the provisioning, maintenance, pay, accommodation and transport of the forces and agencies stationed in Germany by authority of the Allied Representatives, the costs of executing the requirements of unconditional surrender, and payment for any relief in whatever form it may be provided by the United Nations.

22. The Allied Representatives will take and make unrestricted use (whether inside or outside Germany) of any articles referred to in paragraph 12 above, which the Allied Representatives may require in connection with the conduct of hostilities against any country with which any of their respective Governments is at war.

Section VII

23. (a) No merchant ship, including fishing or other craft, shall put to sea from any German port except as may be sanctioned or directed by the Allied Representatives. German ships in ports outside Germany shall remain in port and those at sea shall proceed to the nearest German or United Nations port and there remain, pending instructions from the Allied Representatives.

(b) All German merchant shipping, including tonnage under construction or repair, will be made available to the Allied Representatives for such use and on such terms as they may prescribe.

(c) Foreign merchant shipping in German service or under German control will likewise be made available to the Allied Representatives for such use and on such terms as they may prescribe. In the case of such foreign merchant vessels which are of neutral registration, the German authorities will take all such steps as may be required by the Allied Representatives to transfer or cause to be transferred to the Allied Representatives all rights relative thereto.

(d) All transfer to any other flag, service or control, of the vessels covered by sub-paragraphs (b) and (c) above, is prohibited, except as may be directed by the Allied Representatives.

24. Any existing options to repurchase or reacquire or to resume control of vessels sold or otherwise transferred or chartered by Germany during the war will be exercised as directed by the Allied Representatives. Such vessels will be made available for use by the Allied Representatives in the same manner as the vessels covered by sub-paragraphs 23 (b) and (c) above.

25. (a) The crews of all German merchant vessels or merchant vessels in German service or under German control will remain on board and will be maintained by the German authorities pending further instructions from the Allied Representatives regarding their future employment.

(b) Cargoes on board any such vessels will be disposed of in accordance with instructions given to the German authorities by the Allied Representatives.

26. (a) Merchant ships, including fishing and other craft of the United Nations (or of any country which has broken off diplomatic relations with Germany) which are in German hands, wherever such ships may be, will be surrendered to the Allied Representatives regardless of whether title has been transferred as the result of prize court proceedings or otherwise. All such ships will be surrendered in good repair and in seaworthy condition in ports and at times to be specified by the Allied Representatives, for disposal as directed by them.

(b) The German authorities will take all such steps as may be directed by the Allied Representatives to effect or complete transfers of title to such ships regardless of whether the title has been transferred as the result of prize court proceedings or otherwise. They will secure the discontinuance of any arrests of, or proceedings against, such ships in neutral ports.

27. The German authorities will comply with any instructions given by the Allied Representatives for the destruction, dispersal, salvaging, reclamation or raising of wrecked, stranded, derelict, or sunken vessels, wherever they may be situated. Such vessels salvaged, reclaimed or raised shall be dealt with as the Allied Representatives direct.

28. The German authorities will place at the unrestricted disposal of the Allied Representatives the entire German shipping, shipbuilding and ship repair industries, and all matters and facilities directly or indirectly relative or ancillary thereto, and will provide the requisite labour and specialist services. The requirements of the Allied Representatives will be specified in instructions which will from time to time be communicated to the German authorities.

Section VIII

29. The German authorities will place at the unrestricted disposal of the Allied Representatives the whole of the German inland transport system (road, rail, air and waterways) and all connected material, plant and equipment, and all repair, construction, labour, servicing and running facilities, in accordance with the instructions issued by the Allied Representatives.

30. The production in Germany and the possession, maintenance or operation by Germans of any aircraft of any kind or any parts thereof, are prohibited.

31. All German rights in international transport bodies or organizations, and in relation to the use of transport and the movement of traffic in other countries and the use in Germany of the transport of other countries, will be exercised in accordance with the directions of the Allied Representatives.

32. All facilities for the generation, transmission and distribution of power, including establishments for the manufacture and repair of such facilities, will be placed under the complete control of the Allied Representatives, to be used for such purposes as they may designate.

Section IX

33. The German authorities will comply with all such directions as the Allied Representatives may give for the regulation of movements of population and for controlling travel or removal on the part of persons in Germany.

34. No person may leave or enter Germany without a permit issued by the Allied Representatives or on their authority.

35. The German authorities will comply with all such directions as the Allied Representatives may give for the repatriation of persons not of German nationality in or passing through Germany, their property and effects, and for facilitating the movements of refugees and displaced persons.

Section X

36. The German authorities will furnish any information and documents, and will secure the attendance of any witnesses, required by the Allied Representatives for the trial of

(*a*) the principal Nazi leaders as specified by the Allied Representatives and all persons from time to time named or designated by rank, office or employment by the Allied Representatives as being suspected of having committed, ordered or abetted war crimes or analogous offences;

(*b*) any national of any of the United Nations who is alleged to have committed an offence against his national law and who may at any time be named or designated by rank, office or employment by the Allied Representatives;

and will give all other aid and assistance for these purposes.

37. The German authorities will comply with any directions given by the Allied Representatives in regard to the property of any person referred to in sub-paragraph 36 (*a*) and (*b*) above, such as its seizure, custody or surrender.

Section XI

38. The National Socialist German Workers' Party (NSDAP) is completely and finally abolished and declared to be illegal.

39. The German authorities will comply promptly with such directions as the Allied Representatives may issue for the abolition of the National Socialist Party and of its subordinate organizations, affiliated associations and supervised organizations, and of all Nazi public institutions created as instruments of Nazi domination, and of such other organizations as may be regarded as a threat to the security of the Allied forces or to international peace, and for prohibiting their revival in any form; for the dismissal and internment of Nazi personnel; for the control or seizure of Nazi property and funds; and for the suppression of Nazi ideology and teaching.

40. The German authorities and German nationals will not allow the existence of any secret organizations.

41. The German authorities will comply with such directions as the Allied Representatives may issue for the repeal of Nazi legislation and for the reform of German law and of the German legal, judicial, administrative, police and educational systems, including the replacement of their personnel.

42. (*a*) The German authorities will comply with such directions as the Allied Representatives may issue for the rescinding of German legislation involving discrimination on grounds of race, colour, creed, language or political opinions and for the cancellation of all legal or other disabilities resulting therefrom.

(*b*) The German authorities will comply with such directions as the Allied Representatives may issue regarding the property, assets, rights, titles and interests of persons affected by legislation involving discrimination on grounds of race, colour, creed, language or political opinions.

43. No person shall be prosecuted or molested by the German authorities or by German nationals on grounds of race, colour, creed, language or political opinions, or on account of any dealings or sympathies with the United Nations, including the performance of any action calculated to facilitate the execution of the Declaration or of any proclamations, orders, ordinances or instructions issued thereunder.

44. In any proceedings before any German Court or authority judicial notice shall be taken of the provisions of the Declaration and of all proclamations, orders, ordinances and instructions issued thereunder, which shall override any provisions of German law inconsistent therewith.

Section XII

45. Without prejudice to any specific obligations contained in the provisions of the Declaration or any proclamations, orders, ordinances or instructions issued thereunder, the German authorities and any other person in a position to do so will furnish or cause to be furnished all such information and documents of every kind, public and private, as the Allied Representatives may require.

46. The German authorities will likewise produce for interrogation and employment by the Allied Representatives upon demand any and all persons whose knowledge and experience would be useful to the Allied Representatives.

47. The Allied Representatives will have access at all times to any building, installation, establishment, property or area, and any of the contents thereof, for the purposes of the Declaration or any proclamations, orders, ordinances or instructions issued thereunder, and in particular for the purposes of safeguarding, inspecting, copying or obtaining any of the desired documents and information. The German authorities will give all necessary facilities and assistance for this purpose, including the service of all specialist staff, including archivists.

Section XIII

48. In the event of any doubt as to the meaning or interpretation of any term or expression in the Declaration and in any proclamations, orders, ordinances and instructions issued thereunder, the decision of the Allied Representatives shall be final.

(2) *Statement of the Secretary of State (Byrnes) on the Meaning of the Potsdam Declaration for Economic Issues in Germany, December 12, 1945.*[1]

[Excerpt]

· · · · · · ·

The position of Germany in the present world picture must be looked at broadly against the whole background of recent history. For six years Germany has ruthlessly imposed war and destruction on Europe

---

[1] Department of State, *Bulletin*, XIII, p. 964.

and the world. The Nazis who ruled there for more than a decade are now defeated, discredited, and have been or are being rooted from positions of power. The final stages of war caused vast movements of Germans within their own country, and peace has permitted the return to their homes of millions of foreign laborers who had been enslaved in German mines and factories. The insistence of the Nazis on continuing the war to the bitter end caused enormous destruction to German cities, transport facilities, and other capital of the country. These are the basic reasons for the present position of Germany, a position for which the Germans themselves are primarily responsible. German industrial production will for some time be low and her people ill-fed even if there were no occupation and no reparations program.

The Potsdam Declaration involves three stages in the return of Germany to normal economic conditions. The first covers the German economy from the surrender of the armed forces last May to at least the end of the present winter. In this interval our broad purposes are to insure that our policy in Germany makes the maximum possible contribution to recovery in areas recently liberated from Germany and, positively, to set up a structure that will provide for the future recovery of Germany in conformity with the principles agreed at Potsdam.

Within these broad objectives four principal immediate aims are these:

First, to increase to the greatest possible extent the export of coal from Germany to liberated areas. The rate of economic recovery in Europe depends upon the coal supplies available over this winter; and it is our intention to maintain the policy of hastening the recovery of liberated areas, even at the cost of delaying recovery in Germany.

Second, to use the months before spring to set up and to set into motion, in conjunction with our Allies, the machinery necessary to execute the reparations and disarmament programs laid down and agreed at Potsdam. A considerable part of the statement just issued[1] is directed to making clear the technical basis on which we believe the reparations calculation should be made. This calculation, which requires definition of the initial post-war German economy, must be completed before February 2, 1946.

Third, to set up German administrative agencies which would operate under close policy control of the occupying authorities in the fields of finance, transport, communications, foreign trade, and industry. Such agencies, explicitly required by the terms of the Potsdam agreement, must operate if Germany is to be treated as an economic unit, and if we are to move forward to German recovery and to the eventual termination of military occupation.

Fourth, to prevent mass starvation in Germany. Throughout Europe there are many areas where the level of diet is at or close to starvation. In terms of world supply and of food shipments from the United States, liberated areas must enjoy a higher priority than Germany throughout this first post-war winter. The United States policy, in collaboration

---

[1] Not reprinted here. For text, see *ibid.*, p. 960.

with its Allies, is to see that sufficient food is available in Germany to avoid mass starvation. At the moment the calory level for the normal German consumer has been established at 1,550 per day. This requires substantial imports of foodstuffs into Germany, especially of wheat; and for its own zones of Germany and Berlin the United States is now importing wheat to achieve this level. The bulk of the German population has been eating more than 1,550 calories daily, either because they can supplement the ration from foodstuffs available in the countryside, or because their work justifies a ration level higher than that of the normal consumer, as in the case of coal miners. In the major cities, and especially Berlin, however, a food problem exists and is particularly severe during the winter months. One thousand, five hundred and fifty calories is not sufficient to sustain in health a population over a long period of time, but as a basic level for the normal consumer it should prevent mass starvation in Germany this winter. If a higher level for the normal consumer is judged to be required and if it is justified by food standards in liberated areas, the ration level in Germany may be raised by agreement among the four occupying powers.

In short, this will be an exceedingly hard winter for Germany, although only slightly more difficult than for certain of the liberated areas. A softening of American policy toward the feeding of German civilians and toward the allocation of coal exports from Germany, while it would ease the difficult task of the four occupying authorities, could largely be at the expense of the liberated areas. We are, however, constructively preparing for the second stage in German economic policy, which should begin some time next spring.

In this second stage it is envisaged that Germany will gradually recover. Simultaneously with the removal of plants under reparation, plants will be earmarked for retention; and, as fuel and raw materials become available, German industry which is permitted to remain will be gradually reactivated and the broken transport system revived. Although coal exports from Germany will continue, the probable expansion in coal output should permit larger allocations in coal to the German economy, after the end of the winter. German industrial production will then increase and German exports should begin to approach a level where they can finance necessary imports and gradually to repay the occupying powers for their outlays in the present emergency period.

The third stage of economic development will follow after the period of reparation removals which under the terms of the Potsdam Declaration must be completed by February 2, 1948. The resources left to Germany at that time will be available to promote improvement of the German standard of living to a level equal to that of the rest of continental Europe other than the Soviet Union and the United Kingdom. Housing and transport will recover more rapidly than in the previous stages of economic development. In general, the German people will during this period recover control over their economy subject to such residual limitations as the occupying powers decide to impose. These limitations, which will be determined by agreement among the occupying powers, should, in the opinion of this Government, be designed solely to prevent

German rearmament and not to restrict or reduce the German standard of living.

In all these stages it must be borne in mind that the present occupying powers, as well as many other nations, have suffered severely from German aggression, have played a large role in the German defeat, and have an enduring interest in the post-war settlement of Germany. The settlement agreed at Potsdam requires the shifting of boundaries in the East, and the movement of several million Germans from other countries. That settlement also requires, in the interests of European rehabilitation and security, the removal from Germany of a large part of the industrial war-making capacity, which never served the German civilian but which, from 1933 on, served to prepare for war and to make war. In the words of the Potsdam Declaration:

It is not the intention of the Allies to destroy or enslave the German people. It is the intention of the Allies that the German people be given the opportunity to prepare for the eventual reconstruction of their life on a democratic and peaceful basis. If their own efforts are steadily directed to this end, it will be possible for them in due course to take their place among the free and peaceful peoples of the world.

(3) *Exchange of Notes between the Secretary of State (Byrnes) and the Minister of Foreign Affairs of France (Bidault) on the Establishment of Central German Agencies.*[1]

(a) *Note from the Secretary of State to the Minister of Foreign Affairs of France, February 1, 1946.*

I should be most grateful if you could see your way clear to review the French attitude on the establishment of central German agencies. In doing this, I should like to ask you to take into account the following considerations:

I believe, as a result of our close cooperation in the European Advisory Commission in planning the occupation of Germany and in our day-to-day relationships with the French representatives on the Control Council, that the basic ideas of the French and American Governments on the political principles which govern the treatment of Germany in the occupation period are not far apart. I am certain that our reiterated intention to destroy German militarism and Nazism and our joint measures to accomplish the complete disarmament of Germany have received the complete approval of the French Government. I know that we are in accord on the political premise that the administration of affairs in Germany should be directed toward a decentralization of German governmental structure and the development of local administrations based upon democratic principles. Furthermore, I am sure you will agree that the time has not yet come to reestablish any central German Government and that the occupation of Germany under the prevailing agreements is expected to continue for an indefinite period. I should like you

[1] *Ibid.*, XIV, p. 440.

to know that I fully appreciate the natural desire of your Government to prevent the resurgence of a militant and aggressive Germany. Lying next to Germany as France does, I can readily understand the desire of the French Government to effect territorial changes which, in its opinion, will form the basis of security against Germany. Therefore, I can understand the reasons which have prompted the French Government, acting under the unanimity rule of the Control Council to prevent the establishment of central German administrative departments.

On the other hand, the central German agencies proposed will be operating under the direction of the Control Council, in which the French Government has full participation. The Control Council is directed so to manage affairs in Germany that the former highly centralized governmental structure of the German Reich will be abolished and replaced by a much looser structure. It does not seem to me that this theory is incompatible with the establishment of certain central administrative departments which will enable the Control Council to equalize and make uniform the treatment of Germany in many important aspects. Even under a loosely-federated form of Government it would seem to be indispensable eventually to permit the establishment of central agencies in the fields of finance, transport, communications, foreign trade and the control of German industry. Otherwise, we may have a situation in which it will become impossible to administer Germany as an economic unit and to effect that reduction of German war potential which we both agree is essential.

I should also like you to know that in my opinion the establishment of certain central German agencies does not prejudice the eventual consideration of Germany's western frontier. This problem is an enormously complicated one which will no doubt be the subject of extended exchanges of views between the Allies. We have not as yet begun our joint labors on the conclusion of a peace treaty with Germany and I think you will agree the time has not yet come to do so. The greatest security which France and all of the United Nations have against Germany is indeed a continued occupation of the German Reich. We all hope that this occupation will result in a Germany which is incapable for an indefinite future of waging war, but the problems of this occupation are enormously complex and it is indispensable that the four occupying powers should collaborate in executing the purposes of the occupation. The American, British and Soviet Governments have all agreed that the establishment of central German agencies is required for the purposes of this occupation. They have further agreed that such agencies will be under the direction of the Control Council.

Last, but not least, it seems to me that we must view the functioning of the Control Council as a test of the ability of the four Allies represented thereon to work together in the post-war world. Failure of the Council would mean failure of Allied cooperation and would be so regarded in the world at large.

I, therefore, express the earnest hope that the French Government will reconsider its attitude in this matter and will, by so doing, facilitate the development of the common Allied policy in Germany.

(b) *Note from the Minister of Foreign Affairs of France to the Secretary of State, March 2, 1946.*

By a communication dated February 6, you were good enough to inform me of your desire to have me re-examine the position taken by the French Government on the subject of the creation of central German agencies.

You reviewed for me on this occasion the principles on which American policy toward Germany is founded: The destruction of German militarism and Nazism, the complete disarmament of Germany, the greatest possible decentralization of the German structure, and the development of local administrations with a democratic character. You indicated that the time has not come to re-establish a central German government and that the occupation of Germany under the prevailing arrangements is expected to continue for an indefinite period. Finally you expressed your full comprehension of the French Government's desire to assure against further German aggressions and for this reason to effect territorial changes in neighboring frontier regions.

I am happy to verify the agreement of our governments on these principles and to take note of this understanding. After all, I have the feeling that, since in the last analysis it is a question of strengthening democracy and guaranteeing security, which are matters of concern common to all the United Nations, a fundamental agreement has never ceased to exist between our governments. The divergence of views appears only over the practical measures to be taken to assure the effective application of our common ideas.

The French Government for its part, if it considers, in agreement with the American Government, the prolonged occupation of Germany as the best guarantee of security, nonetheless cannot ignore the fact that this occupation will eventually end. Even at this time the French Government is preoccupied with the measures which must be taken to avoid the possibility that Germany shall become again a menace to peace when the occupation shall have ended. It seems to it, given the human potential of this country, that the German menace will exist as long as a German Government, perhaps favored by a relaxation of international vigilance such as occurred between the Two World Wars, has at its disposal the necessary industrial resources to reconstitute its military power. The experience of the last twenty-five years has made it clear that territorial clauses are the last that revisionist states question. Those clauses also may be easily implemented by an effective and precise international guarantee. For these reasons, the French Government proposes that the separation of certain regions from German sovereignty characterize (*marqué*) the irrevocable nature of the limitations imposed on German potentialities and render it, in fact, irrevocable.

These preoccupations are known to your government. You tell me you understand them. You nonetheless judge that they present an enormously complicated problem; that — for the present — the occupation assures us security; that this occupation in itself presents very complex questions; that the treatment of these questions (in this instance the creation of central German agencies) does not prejudice the terms of a future territorial settlement and therefore should be not delayed by a study of these terms.

Whatever be the importance, complexity and urgency of the questions posed by the occupation and administration of Germany, the French Government does not think that the occupation powers should, to facilitate their immediate task, compromise the guarantees of the future. It is not a simple concern for logic which leads the government to desire that before re-establishing German administrative services, the four powers will reach agreement on the extent of future German territory. In fact, to the French Government it would appear that even if the frontiers remain theoretically open to future settlement, the establishment of central German services having their own right of decision, having ramifications in all the territory actually under control and exercising direct action everywhere by their agents will be generally considered, particularly by the German population, as prejudicing future settlements. Furthermore, the manner in which this same problem has been treated in the past will reinforce this impression and finally this impression itself will make subsequent territorial modifications on which the powers may agree more difficult.

Moreover the experience of the years just after the First World War showed that the most active and successful adversaries of any kind of decentralization of the Reich were precisely the local agents of the central German administration.

For all these reasons, the French Government continues to feel that, if the occupying powers intend to follow a policy of decentralization they should not begin to establish extended (*tentacularies*) administrations having independent authority. The French Government could not in any case agree to the extension of the authority of such administrations to the Ruhr, Rhineland or even more to the Saar.

This does not mean that my government does not recognize the necessity of coordinating the activities of the various zones. It considers, however, that this coordinating role belongs to the inter-Allied Council and that the Council, under present conditions, should alone retain the power of making decisions, these decisions to continue to be presented, as necessary, to the local German administrations through the Allied authorities in each zone. As a matter of fact, this position would seem to be close to that which you yourself take in stating that the time has not yet arrived to establish any sort of central German Government.

If it is only a question, as I understand it, of facilitating the examination of technical questions coming under the competence of the inter-Allied Council and of assuring better coordination in the governing of the four zones by the authorities charged with their administration, it would not seem necessary to weaken the rules recalled above to obtain this result. It would suffice for the Council, without changing present practice, to obtain the collaboration of the German technical administrations in the preparation and support of the Council's policy.

The French Government would not object that the establishment of services of this nature and the definition of their duties should be examined by representatives of the four governments.

Moreover, whatever may be the complexity of the problem of the western frontiers of Germany and the future regime of the Rhine-Westphalian region, my government, whose views were presented in the memorandum submitted to the Council of Ministers for Foreign Affairs on September 13, and subsequently explained by the Chief of the French delegation on the 26th of that month, feels it must point out that no reply has been received up to this date in spite of the visits of M. Alphand to Moscow. It hopes that these proposals which the governments primarily interested have had the time to study in all their phases, may also be submitted to joint discussion.

It therefore suggests that a four-party conference be called as soon as possible for the examination of both the question of central German administrations and that of western Germany. If the idea of such a conference should be approved by the Government of the United States and the two other governments — to whom a similar proposal has been made — the French Government would be happy to receive any suggestions regarding the conditions under which such a conference might be organized. It feels that an appropriate setting would be the Conference of Ministers for Foreign Affairs which, in accordance with the resolution adopted at its meeting of September 26, is the proper body having competence for the discussion of these matters. The French Government is, however, ready to examine any other method of examination which might be presented to it.

(4) *Draft Treaty for the Disarmament and Demilitarization of Germany, Submitted to the Council of Foreign Ministers by the Secretary of State (Byrnes), April 29, 1946.*[1]

PREAMBLE

On June 5, 1945, the Government of the United States, the Union of Soviet Socialist Republics, the United Kingdom, and the French Republic declared their intention to effect the total disarmament and demobilization of Germany. In substantial measure this intention has already been fulfilled. Nothing shall prevent or delay the completion of the process. It remains to ensure that the total disarmament and demilitarization of Germany will be enforced as long as the peace and security of the world may require. Only this assurance will permit the nations of Europe and the world to return single-mindedly to the habits of peace. To achieve this objective, the Governments of the United States, the Union of Soviet Socialist Republics, the United Kingdom, and the French Republic agree to engage in the common undertaking defined in this treaty.

[1] *Ibid.*, p. 815.

Article I.

The high contracting parties agree that they shall take steps jointly to ensure that:

(a) All German armed forces, including land, air, anti-aircraft and naval forces, all para-military forces, such as the SS, the SA and the Gestapo, and all organizations auxiliary to the foregoing shall be and shall remain completely disarmed, demobilized and disbanded.

(b) The German general staff and the staffs of any para-military organizations shall be and shall remain disbanded.

(c) No German military or para-military organization in any form or guise shall be permitted in Germany.

(d) The manufacture, production, or importation of military equipment in Germany shall be prevented. In particular, the high contracting parties shall prevent the manufacture, production, or importation of:

(1) All arms, ammunition, explosives, military equipment, military stores and supplies and other implements of war of all kinds;

(2) All fissionable materials for any purpose, except under conditions approved by the high contracting parties;

(3) All naval vessels of all classes, both surface and submarine, and auxiliary naval-craft;

(4) All aircraft of all kinds, aviation equipment and devices, and equipment for anti-aircraft defense.

(e) The establishment, utilization or operation for military purposes of any of the following shall be prevented:

(1) All military structures, installations and establishments, including but not limited to military air fields, seaplane bases and naval bases, military and naval storage depots, permanent and temporary land and coast fortifications, fortresses and other fortified areas;

(2) All factories, plants, shops, research institutions, laboratories, testing stations, technical data, patents, plans, drawings and inventions, designed or intended to produce or to facilitate the production of items listed in paragraph (d) above.

(f) Under conditions which may be established by the high contracting parties, the demilitarization and disarmament required by this article shall be subject of the following exceptions and to no others:

(1) The formation and employment of such detachments of German civil police, and their equipment with such types and quantities of imported small arms, as may be essential to the maintenance of public security; and

(2) The importation of minimum quantities of those items listed in paragraph (d) (1) above, such as explosives or ingredients of explosives, which may be essential for purposes of construction, mining, agriculture or for other peaceful purposes.

Article II.

To implement the disarmament and demilitarization provisions set forth in Article I, the high contracting parties agree that they shall make provision for a system of quadripartite inspection, which shall become operative upon the termination of the Allied occupation of Germany. This system of inspection shall be conducted through a Commission of Control to be established by the high contracting parties on a quadripartite basis. The Commission of Control, through its officers and agents, shall conduct, in any and all parts of German territory, such inspections, inquiries and investigations as it may deem necessary to determine whether the disarmament and demilitarization provisions set forth in Article I are being observed.

Article III.

The high contracting parties agree that for the duration of the period of Allied occupation of Germany, they shall, through the Allied Control Council and in their respective zones, enforce strictly the disarmament and demilitarization provisions set forth in Article I. They agree further that the express acceptance by Germany of the provisions of Articles I and II shall be an essential condition to the termination of Allied occupation of German territory.

Article IV.

The Commission of Control provided for in Article II shall keep the high contracting parties and the Security Council of the United Nations informed of the results of the inspections, inquiries and investigations authorized by that article. The Commission of Control shall submit a report to the high contracting parties whenever in the opinion of a majority of the members of the Commission, it has reason to believe that a violation of the disarmament and demilitarization provisions of Article I has occurred or is about to occur. In conjunction with such report the Commission shall submit a recommendation for action on the part of the high contracting parties which appears appropriate to a majority of the members of the Commission. Upon receipt of such report and recommendations, the high contracting parties will, by common agreement, take such prompt action — including action by air, sea or land forces — as may be necessary to assure the immediate cessation or prevention of such violation or attempted violation. The high contracting parties shall immediately report to the Security Council of the United Nations the action taken or to be taken.

The high contracting parties agree, that, within six months of the effective date of this treaty, they shall consult for the purpose of negotiating special quadripartite agreements which shall provide in the greatest practicable detail for inspection, inquiry and investigation by the Commission of Control, for the numbers and types of forces which each party shall make available for purposes of this treaty, for their degree of readiness and general location, and for the nature of the facilities and assistance which each shall provide. Such special quadripartite agreements shall be subject to ratification by the high contracting parties in accordance with their respective constitutional processes.

ARTICLE V.

This treaty shall be ratified by the high contracting parties in accordance with their respective constitutional processes. The ratifications shall be deposited with the government of (blank), which shall notify all the high contracting parties of each deposit.

This treaty shall come into force upon the deposit of ratifications by each of the high contracting parties. This treaty shall remain in force for a period of 25 years from its effective date. The high contracting parties agree to consult six months before the date of expiration of this treaty for the purpose of determining whether the interests of international peace and security require its renewal, with or without modification, or whether the German people have so far progressed in the reconstruction of their life on a democratic and peaceful basis that the continued imposition of the controls defined herein is no longer necessary.

(5) *Statement by the Secretary of State (Byrnes) on American Policy in Establishing Central Controls for the Economic Unity of Germany, July 11, 1946.*[1]

The following statement was made by the Secretary of State during the closing days of the Paris meeting of the Council of Foreign Ministers when some preliminary discussion of the terms of the peace treaty with Germany occurred. On July 29, 1946, the Department of State announced that the British Government "accepted in principle" Secretary Byrnes' offer to treat the two zones as an economic unit.[2]

I hope that we can avoid the situation outlined by Mr. Bevin. I still hope that my colleagues at this meeting will agree to the establishment of central German administrative agencies necessary to secure economic unity in Germany.

The United States will agree that the Saar region be excluded from the authority of these central agencies so that it can be administered as at present by the French Government until the western boundaries are finally determined.

If the Council cannot agree upon central administrative agencies, then the United States, as a last resort, makes another suggestion. At present no zone of Germany can be regarded as fully self-sustaining. Treatment of any two zones as an economic unit would improve conditions in both zones.

Recently officials of the United States zone have met with officials of the United Kingdom zone to discuss agricultural policies. Meetings have been held between German economic officials from Soviet and United States zones during which agreement was reached with the approval of military governments for the exchange of some products.

Pending agreement among the four powers to implement the Potsdam Agreement requiring administration of Germany as an economic unit, the United States will join with any other occupying government in Germany for the treatment of our respective zones as an economic unit.

[1] Department of State Publication 2630, European Series 15, p. 148.
[2] Department of State, *Bulletin*, XV, p. 266.

We are prepared to instruct our military representatives in Germany to proceed immediately with the representatives of any other occupying government to establish German administrative machinery for the administration of our zones as an economic unit.

It is the view of the United States delegation that such arrangement could be accomplished without interference with the existing quadripartite government of Germany. The proposed arrangement should at all times be open on equal terms for participation of any government which did not elect to participate in the beginning. This proposal is not intended to divide Germany, but on the contrary to expedite its treatment as an economic unit.

We cannot continue to administer Germany in four air-tight compartments, preventing, as I stated a few days ago, exchange between the four zones of goods, communications and even ideas. The condition of the present situation will result in inflation and economic paralysis. It will result in increased costs to the occupying powers and unnecessary suffering to the German people.

The United States is unwilling to share responsibility for continuance of such conditions. We feel it our duty to exhaust every effort to secure the cooperation of the occupying powers in administering Germany as an economic unit.

(6) *Substance of Instructions Issued to the United States Military Governor in Germany (McNarney) on German Economic Unity. Department of State Press Release, July 22, 1946.*[1]

The Department of State made public on July 22 the substance of the instructions by the Secretary of State to Gen. Joseph T. McNarney, American Military Governor in Germany, as to steps to be taken leading toward economic unity of the occupation zones in Germany.

The instructions stated that the U. S. Government believes that Germany cannot continue to be administered in four airtight compartments without free economic interchange and said further that the continuation of the present situation will lead inevitably to economic paralysis in Germany. "The United States Government is therefore not willing to permit this creeping paralysis," the instructions declared, "when it may be possible to attain economic unity between some of the zones as a prelude to economic unity for Germany as a whole."

In proposing economic unity, the Secretary advised that it was not the intention of the United States to divide Germany but to expedite its treatment as an economic unit, and General McNarney was authorized and requested if the U. S. proposals were not accepted by all participating representatives to seek negotiations at once with occupation authorities of any zone or zones to effect the treatment of such zones as an economic unit.

Mr. Byrnes' instructions said further that whatever arrangements are made with one government are open on equal terms to governments of other zones at any time they are prepared to participate.

[1] *Ibid.*, p. 227.

The U. S. zonal authorities are instructed to join with those of any other zone or zones in measures for the treatment of their respective zones as an economic unit, pending agreement by the Four Powers for the application of the Potsdam decision regarding treatment of all Germany as a single economic unit and attainment of a balanced economy throughout Germany.

The Department said that General McNarney was also authorized "to cooperate with any or all of the other three occupying governments in establishing appropriate administrative arrangements to this end." These essential arrangements, Mr. Byrnes advised, would be established in such fields as finance, transportation, communications, industry, and foreign trade "in such a way as to obtain economic unification of the zones concerned and to be capable of development upon adherence of all four zones into central German administrative departments, headed by State secretaries provided in the Potsdam Decision."

With regard to the French zone, it was announced that General McNarney was authorized by the Secretary of State to negotiate with French representatives on the basis of excluding the Saar territory from any arrangements for economic unity that may be agreed upon.

(7) *Restatement of United States Policy on Germany by the Secretary of State (Byrnes), Stuttgart, Germany, September 6, 1946.*[1]

I have come to Germany to learn at first hand the problems involved in the reconstruction of Germany and to discuss with our representatives the views of the United States Government as to some of the problems confronting us.

We in the United States have given considerable time and attention to these problems because upon their proper solution will depend not only the future well-being of Germany but the future well-being of Europe.

We have learned, whether we like it or not, that we live in one world, from which world we cannot isolate ourselves. We have learned that peace and well-being are indivisible and that our peace and well-being cannot be purchased at the price of the peace or the well-being of any other country.

I hope that the German people will never again make the mistake of believing that because the American people are peace-loving they will sit back hoping for peace if any nation uses force or the threat of force to acquire dominion over other peoples and other governments.

In 1917 the United States was forced into the first World War. After that war we refused to join the League of Nations. We thought we could stay out of Europe's wars, and we lost interest in the affairs of Europe. That did not keep us from being forced into a second world war.

We will not again make that mistake. We intend to continue our interest in the affairs of Europe and of the world. We have helped to organize the United Nations. We believe it will stop aggressor nations

[1] *Ibid.*, p. 496.

from starting wars. Because we believe it, we intend to support the United Nations organization with all the power and resources we possess.

The American people want peace. They have long since ceased to talk of a hard or a soft peace for Germany. This never has been the real issue. What we want is a lasting peace. We will oppose soft measures which invite the breaking of the peace.

In agreeing at Potsdam that Germany should be disarmed and demilitarized and in proposing that the four major powers should by treaty jointly undertake to see that Germany is kept disarmed and demilitarized for a generation, the United States was not unmindful of the responsibility resting upon it and its major Allies to maintain and enforce peace under the law.

Freedom from militarism will give the German people the opportunity, if they will but seize it, to apply their great energies and abilities to the works of peace. It will give them the opportunity to show themselves worthy of the respect and friendship of peace-loving nations, and in time, to take an honorable place among the members of the United Nations.

It is not in the interest of the German people or in the interest of world peace that Germany should become a pawn or a partner in a military struggle for power between the East and the West.

German militarism and Nazism have devastated twice in our generation the lands of Germany's neighbors. It is fair and just that Germany should do her part to repair that devastation. Most of the victims of Nazi aggression were before the war less well off than Germany. They should not be expected by Germany to bear, unaided, the major costs of Nazi aggression.

The United States, therefore, is prepared to carry out fully the principles outlined in the Potsdam Agreement on demilitarization and reparations. However, there should be changes in the levels of industry agreed upon by the Allied Control Commission if Germany is not to be administered as an economic unit as the Potsdam Agreement contemplates and requires.

The basis of the Potsdam Agreement was that, as part of a combined program of demilitarization and reparations, Germany's war potential should be reduced by elimination and removal of her war industries and the reduction and removal of heavy industrial plants. It was contemplated this should be done to the point that Germany would be left with levels of industry capable of maintaining in Germany average European living standards without assistance from other countries.

The plants so to be removed were to be delivered as reparations to the Allies. The plants to be removed from the Soviet zone would go to the Soviet Union and Poland and the plants to be removed from the western zones would go in part to the Soviet Union but in the main to the western Allies. Provision was also made for the distribution of Germany's foreign assets among the Allies.

After considerable discussion the Allies agreed upon levels to which the principal German industries should be reduced in order to carry out the Potsdam Agreement. These levels were agreed to upon the assumption that the indigenous resources of Germany were to be available for distribution on an equitable basis for all of the Germans in Germany and that products not necessary for use in Germany would be available for export in order to pay for necessary imports.

In fixing the levels of industry no allowance was made for reparations from current production. Reparations from current production would be wholly incompatible with the levels of industry now established under the Potsdam Agreement.

Obviously, higher levels of industry would have had to be fixed if reparations from current production were contemplated. The levels of industry fixed are only sufficient to enable the German people to become self-supporting and to maintain living standards approximating the average European living conditions.

That principle involves serious hardships for the German people, but it only requires them to share the hardships which Nazi aggression imposed on the average European.

The German people were not denied, however, the possibility of improving their lot by hard work over the years. Industrial growth and progress were not denied them. Being obliged to start again like the people of other devastated countries, with a peacetime economy not able to provide them more than the average European standard, the German people were not to be denied the right to use such savings as they might be able to accumulate by hard work and frugal living to build up their industries for peaceful purposes.

That was the principle of reparations to which President Truman agreed at Potsdam. And the United States will not agree to the taking from Germany of greater reparations than was provided by the Potsdam Agreement.

The carrying out of the Potsdam Agreement has, however, been obstructed by the failure of the Allied Control Council to take the necessary steps to enable the German economy to function as an economic unit. Essential central German administrative departments have not been established, although they are expressly required by the Potsdam Agreement.

The equitable distribution of essential commodities between the several zones so as to produce a balanced economy throughout Germany and reduce the need for imports has not been arranged, although that too is expressly required by the Potsdam Agreement.

The working out of a balanced economy throughout Germany to provide the necessary means to pay for approved imports has not been accomplished, although that too is expressly required by the Potsdam Agreement.

The United States is firmly of the belief that Germany should be administered as an economic unit and that zonal barriers should be completely obliterated so far as the economic life and activity in Germany are concerned.

The conditions which now exist in Germany make it impossible for industrial production to reach the levels which the occupying powers agreed were essential for a minimum German peacetime economy. Obviously, if the agreed levels of industry are to be reached, we cannot continue to restrict the free exchange of commodities, persons, and ideas throughout Germany. The barriers between the four zones of Germany are far more difficult to surmount than those between normal independent states.

The time has come when the zonal boundaries should be regarded as defining only the areas to be occupied for security purposes by the armed forces of the occupying powers and not as self-contained economic or political units.

That was the course of development envisaged by the Potsdam Agreement, and that is the course of development which the American Government intends to follow to the full limit of its authority. It has formally announced that it is its intention to unify the economy of its own zone with any or all of the other zones willing to participate in the unification.

So far only the British Government has agreed to let its zone participate. We deeply appreciate their cooperation. Of course, this policy of unification is not intended to exclude the governments not now willing to join. The unification will be open to them at any time they wish to join.

We favor the economic unification of Germany. If complete unification cannot be secured, we shall do everything in our power to secure the maximum possible unification.

Important as the economic unification is for the recovery of Germany and of Europe, the German people must recognize that the basic cause of their suffering and distress is the war which the Nazi dictatorship brought upon the world.

But just because suffering and distress in Germany are inevitable, the American Government is unwilling to accept responsibility for the needless aggravation of economic distress that is caused by the failure of the Allied Control Council to agree to give the German people a chance to solve some of their most urgent economic problems.

So far as many vital questions are concerned, the Control Council is neither governing Germany nor allowing Germany to govern itself.

A common financial policy is essential for the successful rehabilitation of Germany. Runaway inflation accompanied by economic paralysis is almost certain to develop unless there is a common financial policy directed to the control of inflation. A program of drastic fiscal reform to reduce currency and monetary claims, to revise the debt structure, and to place Germany on a sound financial basis is urgently required.

The United States has worked hard to develop such a program, but fully coordinated measures must be accepted and applied uniformly to all zones if ruinous inflation is to be prevented. A central agency of finance is obviously necessary to carry out any such program effectively.

It is also essential that transportation, communications, and postal services should be organized throughout Germany without regard to zonal barriers. The nation-wide organization of these public services was contemplated by the Potsdam Agreement. Twelve months have passed and nothing has been done.

Germany needs all the food she can produce. Before the war she could not produce enough food for her population. The area of Germany has been reduced. The population in Silesia, for instance, has been forced back into a restricted Germany. Armies of occupation and displaced persons increase demands while the lack of farm machinery and fertilizer reduces supplies. To secure the greatest possible production of food and the most effective use and distribution of the food that can be produced, a central administrative department for agriculture should be set up and allowed to function without delay.

Similarly, there is urgent need for the setting up of a central German administrative agency for industry and foreign trade. While Germany must be prepared to share her coal and steel with the liberated countries of Europe dependent upon those supplies, Germany must be enabled to use her skills and her energies to increase her industrial production and to organize the most effective use of her raw materials.

Germany must be given a chance to export goods in order to import enough to make her economy self-sustaining. Germany is a part of Europe, and recovery in Europe, and particularly in the states adjoining Germany, will be slow indeed if Germany with her great resources of iron and coal is turned into a poorhouse.

When the ruthless Nazi dictatorship was forced to surrender unconditionally, there was no German government with which the Allies could deal. The Allies had temporarily to take over the responsibilities of the shattered German state, which the Nazi dictatorship had cut off from any genuine accountability to the German people. The Allies could not leave the leaders or minions of Nazism in key positions ready to reassert their evil influence at the first opportunity. They had to go.

But it never was the intention of the American Government to deny to the German people the right to manage their own internal affairs as soon as they were able to do so in a democratic way with genuine respect for human rights and fundamental freedoms.

The Potsdam Agreement, concluded only a few months after the surrender, bound the occupying powers to restore local self-government and to introduce elective and representative principles into the regional, provincial, and state administration as rapidly as was consistent with military security and the purposes of the military occupation.

The principal purposes of the military occupation were and are to demilitarize and de-Nazify Germany but not to raise artificial barriers to the efforts of the German people to resume their peacetime economic life.

The Nazi war criminals were to be punished for the suffering they brought to the world. The policy of reparations and industrial disarmament prescribed in the Potsdam Agreement was to be carried out. But the purpose of the occupation did not contemplate a prolonged foreign dictatorship of Germany's peacetime economy or a prolonged foreign dictatorship of Germany's internal political life. The Potsdam Agreement expressly bound the occupying powers to start building a political democracy from the ground up.

The Potsdam Agreement did not provide that there should never be a central German government; it merely provided that for the time being there should be no central German government. Certainly this only meant that no central government should be established until some sort of democracy was rooted in the soil of Germany and some sense of local responsibility developed.

The Potsdam Agreement wisely provided that administration of the affairs of Germany should be directed toward decentralization of the political structure and the development of local responsibility. This was not intended to prevent progress toward a central government with the powers necessary to deal with matters which would be dealt with on a nation-wide basis. But it was intended to prevent the establishment of a strong central government dominating the German people instead of being responsible to their democratic will.

It is the view of the American Government that the German people throughout Germany, under proper safeguards, should now be given the primary responsibility for the running of their own affairs.

More than a year has passed since hostilities ceased. The millions of German people should not be forced to live in doubt as to their fate. It is the view of the American Government that the Allies should, without delay, make clear to the German people the essential terms of the peace settlement which they expect the German people to accept and observe. It is our view that the German people should now be permitted and helped to make the necessary preparations for setting up of a democratic German government which can accept and observe these terms.

From now on the thoughtful people of the world will judge Allied action in Germany not by Allied promises but by Allied performances. The American Government has supported and will continue to support the necessary measures to de-Nazify and demilitarize Germany, but it does not believe that large armies of foreign soldiers or alien bureaucrats, however well motivated and disciplined, are in the long run the most reliable guardians of another country's democracy.

All that the Allied governments can and should do is to lay down the rules under which German democracy can govern itself. The Allied occupation forces should be limited to the number sufficient to see that those rules are obeyed.

But of course the question for us will be: What force is needed to make certain that Germany does not rearm as it did after the first World War? Our proposal for a treaty with the major powers to enforce for 25 or even 40 years the demilitarization plan finally agreed upon in the peace settlement would have made possible a smaller army of occupation. For enforcement we could rely more upon a force of trained inspectors and less upon infantry.

For instance, if an automobile factory, in violation of the treaty, converted its machinery to the production of weapons of war, inspectors would report it to the Allied Control Council. They would call upon the German Government to stop the production and punish the offender. If the German Government failed to comply then the Allied nations would take steps to enforce compliance by the German Government. Unfortunately our proposal for a treaty was not agreed to.

Security forces will probably have to remain in Germany for a long period. I want no misunderstanding. We will not shirk our duty. We are not withdrawing. We are staying here. As long as there is an occupation army in Germany, American armed forces will be part of that occupation army.

The United States favors the early establishment of a provisional German government for Germany. Progress has been made in the American zone in developing local and state self-government in Germany, and the American Government believes similar progress is possible in all zones.

It is the view of the American Government that the provisional government should not be handpicked by other governments. It should be a German national council composed of the democratically responsible minister presidents or other chief officials of the several states or provinces which have been established in each of the four zones.

Subject to the reserved authority of the Allied Control Council, the German National Council should be responsible for the proper functioning of the central administrative agencies. Those agencies should have adequate power to assure the administration of Germany as an economic unit, as was contemplated by the Potsdam Agreement.

The German National Council should also be charged with the preparation of a draft of a federal constitution for Germany which, among other things, should insure the democratic character of the new Germany and the human rights and fundamental freedoms of all its inhabitants.

After approval in principle by the Allied Control Council, the proposed constitution should be submitted to an elected convention for final drafting and then submitted to the German people for ratification.

While we shall insist that Germany observe the principles of peace, good-neighborliness, and humanity, we do not want Germany to become the satellite of any power or powers or to live under a dictatorship, foreign or domestic. The American people hope to see peaceful, democratic Germans become and remain free and independent.

Austria has already been recognized as a free and independent country. Her temporary and forced union with Germany was not a happy event for either country, and the United States is convinced that it is in the interest of both countries and the peace of Europe that they should pursue their separate ways.

At Potsdam specific areas which were part of Germany were provisionally assigned to the Soviet Union and to Poland, subject to the final decisions of the Peace Conference. At that time these areas were being held by the Soviet and Polish armies. We were told that Germans in large numbers were fleeing from these areas and that it would in fact, because of the feelings aroused by the war, be difficult to reorganize the economic life of these areas if they were not administered as integral parts in the one case of the Soviet Union and in the other case of Poland.

The heads of government agreed to support at the peace settlement the proposal of the Soviet Government concerning the ultimate transfer to the Soviet Union of the city of Königsberg and the area adjacent to it. Unless the Soviet Government changes its views on the subject we will certainly stand by our agreement.

With regard to Silesia and other eastern German areas, the assignment of this territory to Poland by Russia for administrative purposes had taken place before the Potsdam meeting. The heads of government agreed that, pending the final determination of Poland's western frontier, Silesia and other eastern German areas should be under the administration of the Polish state and for such purposes should not be considered as a part of the Soviet zone of occupation in Germany. However, as the Protocol of the Potsdam Conference makes clear, the heads of government did not agree to support at the peace settlement the cession of this particular area.

The Soviets and the Poles suffered greatly at the hands of Hitler's invading armies. As a result of the agreement at Yalta, Poland ceded to the Soviet Union territory east of the Curzon Line. Because of this, Poland asked for revision of her northern and western frontiers. The United States will support a revision of these frontiers in Poland's favor. However, the extent of the area to be ceded to Poland must be determined when the final settlement is agreed upon.

The United States does not feel that it can deny to France, which has been invaded three times by Germany in 70 years, its claim to the Saar territory, whose economy has long been closely linked with France. Of course, if the Saar territory is integrated with France she should readjust her reparation claims against Germany.

Except as here indicated, the United States will not support any encroachment on territory which is indisputably German or any division of Germany which is not genuinely desired by the people concerned. So far as the United States is aware the people of the Ruhr and the Rhineland desire to remain united with the rest of Germany. And the United States is not going to oppose their desire.

While the people of the Ruhr were the last to succumb to Nazism, without the resources of the Ruhr Nazism could never have threatened the world. Never again must those resources be used for destructive purposes. They must be used to rebuild a free, peaceful Germany and a free, peaceful Europe.

The United States will favor such control over the whole of Germany, including the Ruhr and the Rhineland, as may be necessary for security purposes. It will help to enforce those controls. But it will not favor any controls that would subject the Ruhr and the Rhineland to political domination or manipulation of outside powers.

The German people are now feeling the devastating effects of the war which Hitler and his minions brought upon the world. Other people felt those devastating effects long before they were brought home to the people of Germany.

The German people must realize that it was Hitler and his minions who tortured and exterminated innocent men, women, and children and sought with German arms to dominate and degrade the world. It was the massed, angered forces of humanity which had to fight their way into Germany to give the world the hope of freedom and peace.

The American people who fought for freedom have no desire to enslave the German people. The freedom Americans believe in and fought for is a freedom which must be shared with all willing to respect the freedom of others.

The United States has returned to Germany practically all prisoners of war that were in the United States. We are taking prompt steps to return German prisoners of war in our custody in other parts of the world.

The United States cannot relieve Germany from the hardships inflicted upon her by the war her leaders started. But the United States has no desire to increase those hardships or to deny the German people an opportunity to work their way out of those hardships so long as they respect human freedom and follow the paths of peace.

The American people want to return the government of Germany to the German people. The American people want to help the German people to win their way back to an honorable place among the free and peace-loving nations of the world.

(8) *Memorandum of Agreement between the United States and the United Kingdom on the Economic Fusion of American and British Zones of Occupation in Germany, Signed December 2, 1946.*[1]

Representatives of the two Governments have met at Washington to discuss the questions arising out of the economic fusion of their zones of occupation in Germany. They have taken as the basis of their discussion the fact that the aim of the two Governments is to achieve the economic unity of Germany as a whole, in accordance with the agreement reached at Potsdam on 2nd August, 1945. The arrangements set out hereunder, for the United States and United Kingdom Zones, should be regarded as the first step towards the achievement of the economic unity of Germany as a whole in accordance with that agreement. The two Governments are ready at any time to enter into discussions with either of the other occupying powers with a view to the extension of these arrangements to their zones of occupation.

On this basis, agreement has been reached on the following paragraphs:—

1. *Date of inception.* This agreement for the economic fusion of the two zones shall take effect on 1st January, 1947.

2. *Pooling of resources.* The two zones shall be treated as a single area for all economic purposes. The indigenous resources of the area and all imports into the area, including food, shall be pooled in order to produce a common standard of living.

3. *German administrative agencies.* The United States and United Kingdom Commanders-in-Chief are responsible for setting up under their joint control the German administrative agencies necessary to the economic unification of the two zones.

4. *Agency for foreign trade.* Responsibility for foreign trade will rest initially with the Joint Export-Import Agency (United States-United Kingdom) or such other agency as may be established by the two Commanders-in-Chief. This responsibility shall be transferred to the German administrative agency for foreign trade under joint supervision to the maximum extent permitted by the restrictions existing in foreign

---

[1] Department of State, *Treaties and Other International Acts Series* 1575.

countries at any given period. (All references in this agreement to the Joint Export-Import Agency shall apply to this agency or to any agency established by the two Commanders-in-Chief to succeed it.)

5. *Basis of economic planning.* The aim of the two Governments is the achievement by the end of 1949 of a self-sustaining economy for the area.

6. *Sharing of financial responsibility.* Subject to the provision of the necessary appropriations, the Governments of the United States and the United Kingdom will become responsible on an equal basis for costs of approved imports brought into account after 31st December, 1946 (including stocks on hand financed by the respective Governments), insofar as those cannot be paid for from other sources, in accordance with the following provisions:—

(a) For this purpose the imports of the area shall be divided into two categories: those imports required to prevent disease and unrest (Category A), which are financed in decreasing amounts by appropriated funds; and those further imports (including raw materials), however financed, which will be required if the economic state of the area is to recover to an extent sufficient to achieve the aim laid down in paragraph 5 of this Agreement (Category B).

(b) It is the intention of the two Governments that the full cost of Category A imports shall be defrayed as soon as possible, subject to sub-paragraph (c) below, from the proceeds of exports. Any portion of the cost of Category A imports which is not met by export proceeds will be defrayed by the two Governments in equal shares from appropriated funds.

(c) The proceeds of exports from the area shall be collected by the Joint Export-Import Agency and shall be used primarily for the provision of Category B imports until there is a surplus of export proceeds over the cost of these imports.

(d) In order to provide funds to procure Category B imports:—

(i) The Government of the United Kingdom will make available to the Joint Export-Import Agency the sum of $29,300,000 in settlement of the understanding reached in September, 1945, for the pooling of the proceeds of exports from the two zones in proportion to import expenditures, which shall be credited to the United States contribution.

(ii) In addition to this sum the accumulated proceeds of exports from the United States Zone (estimated at $14,500,000), will be made available to the Joint Export-Import Agency for the purchase of Category B imports.

(iii) The Government of the United Kingdom will provide Category B goods at the request of the Joint Export-Import Agency to a value equal to that of the United States contribution under sub-paragraphs (i) and (ii) above.

(iv) The Governments of the United States and the United Kingdom will make available to the Joint Export-Import Agency in like amounts their respective shares of the sum to be used for financing purchases of essential commodities for the German economy under the provisions, and upon ratification by the Government of Sweden, of the accord dated 18th July, 1946, between the Governments of the United States, the United Kingdom and France on the one hand and of Sweden on the other.

(v) Any further sums which are agreed by the Joint Export-Import Agency to be required for the purchase of Category B imports shall be provided by the two Governments on an equal basis in such manner as they may agree. To the extent that either Government advances sums for the purchase of raw materials for processing and re-export on special terms as regards security and repayment, the other Government may advance equal sums on similar terms.

(e) The costs incurred by the two Governments for their two zones before 1st January, 1947, and for the area thereafter, shall be recovered from future German exports in the shortest practicable time consistent with the rebuilding of the German economy on healthy non-aggressive lines.

7. *Relaxation of barriers to trade.* With a view to facilitating the expansion of German exports, barriers in the way of trade with Germany should be removed as rapidly as world conditions permit. To the same end the establishment of an exchange value for the mark should be undertaken as soon as this is practicable; financial reform should be effected in Germany at an early date; and the exchange of full technical and business communications between Germany and other countries should be facilitated as soon as possible. Potential buyers of German goods should be provided access to both zones to the full extent that facilities permit, and normal business channels should be restored as soon as possible.

8. *Procurement.* The determination of import requirements shall be the responsibility of the Joint Export-Import Agency. The procurement of these requirements shall be dealt with as follows:—

(i) Procurement of Category A imports to the extent that they are financed from appropriated funds of either Government shall be the responsibility of that Government.

(ii) Procurement of Category B imports and of Category A imports to the extent that they are not financed by appropriated funds shall be the responsibility of the Joint Export-Import Agency, with such assistance from the two Governments as may be desired.

Unless otherwise agreed, subject to the provisions of this paragraph, procurement shall be from the most economical source of supply. However, the sources shall be selected to the fullest extent practicable so as to minimize the drain on the dollar resources of the United Kingdom.

The two Governments will establish a joint committee in Washington with the following responsibilities:—

(a) In the case of commodities in short supply, to support the requirements of the Joint Export-Import Agency before the appropriate authorities.

(b) To determine, where necessary, sources of supply and to designate procurement agencies having regard to the financial responsibilities and exchange resources of the two Governments.

With respect to sub-paragraph (a) above, the two Governments agree to assist the committee in obtaining the requirements of the Joint Export-Import Agency having regard to all other legitimate claims on available world supply.

With respect to sub-paragraph (b) above, where the financial responsibility rests with one Government, and the designated source of supply is the territory under the authority of the other Government, the latter, if so requested, will accept responsibility for procuring those supplies as agent for the former.

9. *Currency and banking arrangements.* The Bipartite Finance Committee (United States-United Kingdom) will be authorized to open accounts with approved banks of the countries in which the Joint Export-Import Agency is operating, provided that agreements are negotiated with those countries for credit balances to be transferred on demand into dollars or sterling. The Bipartite Finance Committee will be authorised to accept payment of balances in either dollars or sterling, whichever, in the judgment of the Joint Export-Import Agency, may be better utilized in financing essential imports.

10. *Food.* The two Governments will support, to the full extent that appropriated and other funds will permit, an increase in the present ration standard to 1800 calories for the normal consumer as soon as the world food supply permits. This standard is accepted as the minimum which will support a reasonable economic recovery in Germany. However, in view of the current world food supply, a ration standard of 1550 calories for the normal consumer must be accepted at present.

11. *Imports for displaced persons.* Subject to any international arrangements which may subsequently be made for the maintenance of displaced persons, the maintenance of displaced persons within both zones from the German economy shall not exceed the maintenance of German citizens from this economy. Supplementary rations and other benefits which may be provided for displaced persons in excess of those available to German citizens must be brought in to Germany without cost to the German economy.

12. *Duration.* It is the intention of the two Governments that this agreement shall govern their mutual arrangements for the economic administration of the area pending agreement for the treatment of Germany as an economic unit or until amended by mutual agreement. It shall be reviewed at yearly intervals.

2. REPARATIONS

Provision was made at the Yalta Conference for the appointment of an Allied Commission on Reparation [1] to determine the methods and extent of the dam-

---

[1] See this volume, Appendix I.

ages to be sought from the Axis Powers. The Commission met for its first session in Moscow on June 21, 1945, remained in continuous meetings until July 14th when the Commission transferred its activities to Potsdam. Its work was reviewed by President Truman, Generalissimo Stalin and Prime Minister Attlee and formed the basis of the recommendations on reparations included in the Potsdam Declaration.[1] The Commission resumed its meetings on August 15, 1945 in Moscow, and moved later to Berlin to be in closer touch with the Allied Control Council. Members of the Commission included representatives of the Soviet Union, the United Kingdom, and the United States, with France joining later by virtue of its sharing in the administration of German territory. Mr. Edwin W. Pauley, Personal Representative of President Truman, was the first American member of the Commission and served until after the Potsdam Conference. He was succeeded on October 28, 1945 by James W. Angell.[2] Although the Commission was never formally abolished, its work was absorbed by the Inter-Allied Reparations Agency established in the Final Act of the Reparation Conference held in Paris from November 9 to December 21, 1945.[3]

(1) *Statement of the Head of the United States Delegation to the Allied Commission on Reparations (Pauley), August 30, 1945.*[4]

In the agreement on German reparations, terms of which were approved at the "Big Three" conference and announced in the Berlin communiqué of August 2, we believe a sound base has been laid for the accomplishment of three major American aims. These are:

1. In the interest of world security, to take out of Germany through the reparations program that part of her industry which would enable her again to make war. This we have regarded throughout the negotiations as of prime importance to the American people.

2. To agree, first among the three great powers and then with their other allies, on a fair division of removable industrial equipment and other German assets, so as to compensate as far as possible for the losses suffered by all nations on the basis of damage sustained and contribution to victory over the aggressor.

3. To assess a just and proper burden of reparation which the German nation can pay without depriving the German people of the means of subsistence at an agreed level; in other words, to spare our own or any other country the necessity of becoming a permanent contributor to the support of the German people.

Among the objectives of the United States, these three were uppermost before the conference at Moscow began. In the program agreed upon with the United Kingdom and the Soviet Union, they are now adopted as basic policies.

While we return with a feeling of keen satisfaction in the fact that the shaping of the whole program of reparations is in accord with the will of the American people, we recognize a problem of such magnitude is never wholly solved, nor can a program of such far-reaching economic consequences ever be guaranteed in all details at the time of its formulation.

We believe we have avoided the errors that rendered the settlement

[1] *Ibid.*, Appendix II.
[2] Department of State, *Bulletin*, XIII, p. 688.
[3] Department of State Publication 2699, p. 145.
[4] Department of State, *Bulletin*, XIII, p. 308.

after World War I a failure. We are not going to rebuild a strong Germany in order to pay reparations. We are giving out no blank checks without knowing what is in the bank. We are dealing in things which we have at hand or which we know we shall have. Where we have steel mills, we are dealing in existing steel capacity, not in hypothetical or unearned dollar values.

I wish to emphasize that the reparations plan is thoroughly workable and as agreed at the Tripartite Conference it embraces all the basic policies required for active administration. For this administration the responsibility rests solely with the occupying authorities. I have complete confidence that the military authorities know and will perform that responsibility.

Final settlement should be speeded by the feature of the plan which places the program for removal of industrial equipment on a zonal basis, instead of lumping the removals from all of Germany and then attempting to divide them equitably.

The system that we have adopted takes into account the same solid realities that were recognized in dividing Germany into zones of armed occupation, rather than setting up some scheme of over-all occupation, with a pooling of the several armed forces.

Under the plan as adopted the actual payment of reparations will be handled by "the Government of Germany," that is by the occupying powers.

Each power will be responsible for its own zone, on reparations removals, as it is on everything else, and the Zone Commanders will work together through the Control Council to maintain uniform reparation removal policies for Germany as a whole, as provided in the Berlin Agreement.

Thus, under the reparation plan as adopted at Berlin, the Control Council determines what and how much is unnecessary for a peace economy in Germany and can therefore be taken out as reparations in accordance with "common policies in regard to reparation and removal of war potential," to quote the language of Article III, paragraph 14 (*f*) of the Berlin Agreement.

The method of paying reparations, that is the method of Administration, rests equally on the zones because the occupation government is set up by zones and it is this occupation government which must manage the German economy and manage to pay the required reparation levies.

The primary problem left for negotiation in the reparation program is the determination of the percentage shares of claimant nations other than the Soviet Union and Poland. The machinery for doing this job has been agreed upon and is now in motion. Claimant nations other than the Soviet Union and Poland have been invited to file their claims for reparations. At an early date to be fixed, probably in October, it is hoped that a meeting of representatives of the several claimant nations will be convened at some convenient place in Western Europe, the purpose of which will be to arrive at the percentage shares of all the allied nations other than the USSR and Poland, the shares of which have been determined already. In the meantime, there is no reason why deliveries of German industrial equipment and goods and commodities urgently needed by our European allies for rehabilitation and relief purposes cannot be made by the Zone Commanders.

To the Soviet Union, which in turn undertakes to settle the claim of Poland, an apportionment has already been made, both through the agreement under which each of the occupying powers takes out industrial equipment properly determined to be removable from its own zone of occupation, and by the allotment to the Soviet Union of ten per cent of such removables from the western zones and an additional fifteen per cent to be compensated by the return to the occupying powers of the western zones of equivalent values in coal, food and other commodities.

This leaves seventy-five percent of the removable industrial equipment in the western zones — the industrial heart of Germany — available for reparations to the United States, United Kingdom, and their other allies.

With respect to the amount of, and time limit on, annual recurring reparations — reparations extracted in the form of current production from year to year — no decision can be made until the character and amount of removals of industrial capital equipment have been determined by the Allied Control Council and the future economy of Germany is more clearly defined.

There is also under consideration the creation of a permanent reparations agency, the primary function of which would be the allocation, among the claimant nations, of reparations determined to be available by the Allied Control Council. It is contemplated that on this body each of the claimant nations would have a representative.

(2) *Law on Vesting and Marshaling of German External Assets, Issued by the Allied Control Council for Germany, October 30, 1945.*[1]

The Allied Control Council for Germany was established by proclamation of August 30, 1945, signed by General Dwight D. Eisenhower for the United States, Lt. General B. H. Robertson for the United Kingdom, General L. Koeltz for France and Marshal Zhukov for the Soviet Union, pursuant to decisions of the Yalta Conference and the Declaration Regarding the Defeat of Germany issued on June 5, 1945.[2] By its terms of reference the Council consisted of the four Commanders-in-Chief of each occupation zone who, acting on the basis of unanimity, exercised supreme authority in Germany. The total value of the external assets affected by the following law was estimated at two billion dollars. At the end of the period under review, the Allied Governments were attempting to secure unqualified recognition of this law by the neutral countries.[3]

Whereas the Control Council is determined to assume control of all German assets abroad and to divest the said assets of their German ownership with the intention thereby of promoting international peace and collective security by the elimination of German war potentials.

Now, therefore, the Control Council, in accordance with the decisions

[1] *Ibid.*, XIV, p. 283.
[2] Allied Secretariat. *Official Gazette of the Control Council for Germany.* Berlin, No. 1 (October 29, 1945), p. 5; for details concerning the work of the Council for this period, see *International Organization,* I, p. 167.
[3] Department of State Publication 2630, p. 21.

of the Potsdam Conference and the political and economic principles by which it is necessary to be guided in dealing with this problem, enacts as follows:

Article 1. A German External Property Commission (hereinafter referred to as "the Commission") composed of representatives of the four occupying powers in Germany is hereby constituted.

For the purpose of carrying out the provisions of this law the Commission is constituted as an intergovernmental agency of the Control Council vested with all the necessary powers and authority.

Article 2. All rights, titles and interests in respect of any property outside Germany which is owned or controlled by any person of German nationality inside Germany are hereby vested in the Commission.

Article 3. All rights, titles and interests in respect of any property outside Germany which is owned or controlled by any person of German nationality outside of Germany or by any branch of any business or corporation or other legal entity organized under the laws of Germany or having its principal place of business in Germany are hereby vested in the Commission.

For the purpose of this article the term "any person of German nationality outside Germany" shall apply only to a person who has enjoyed full rights of German citizenship under Reich law at any time since 1 September 1939 and who has at any time since 1 September 1939 been within any territory then under the control of the Reich Government, but shall not apply to any citizen of any country annexed or claimed to have been annexed by Germany since 31 December 1937.

Article 4. The Commission has power by unanimous agreement from time to time to add to the categories of persons to be affected by Articles Two and Three of this law unless such addition is vetoed by the Control Council within thirty days of agreement by the Commission.

Article 5. The question of whether or not any compensation shall be paid to any person whose right, title or interest in any property has been vested in accordance with this law will be decided at such time and in such manner as the Control Council may in the future determine.

Article 6. The right, title and interest to all property, title to which has been vested in the Commission, under this law, or the proceeds of such property, shall be held by the Commission and disposed of pursuant to such further directives as the Control Council may issue from time to time.

Article 7. In addition to the general powers contained in Article One of this law the Commission shall be vested with the following specific powers which it may exercise directly or through any agency which it deems appropriate:

(*a*) To do all acts which it deems necessary or appropriate to obtain possession or control over all property, the right, title or interest in which is vested in the Commission under this law;

(*b*) To operate, control and otherwise exercise complete dominion over all such property, including where this is essential to the preservation of the value represented by the property, the sale, liquidation or other disposal thereof subject to the provisions of Article Six;

(c) To require the keeping of full records, and to seize or require the production of any books of account, records, contracts, letters, papers relating to any property affected by this law and to compel the attendance of witnesses and to require the furnishing of full information regarding such property;

(d) To require information, evidence and records with regard to any property outside Germany, in whole or in part, of all persons covered by Articles Two and Three hereof.

Article 8. The work within any zone of occupation of marshalling and recording the evidence with respect to Germany's external assets shall be the responsibility of the Commander-in-Chief for that zone.

The Commission may request zone commanders to conduct certain investigations either alone or in conjunction with investigations being conducted in other zones, and further, may itself conduct joint investigations in cases where the evidence is contained in more than one zone subject to the authority of the Commander-in-Chief in any zone in which such joint investigation is being conducted.

Article 9. Articles Two and Three of this law shall not apply to assets subject to the jurisdiction of the United Kingdom, British Dominions, India, colonies and possessions, the Union of Soviet Socialist Republics, the United States, France and any other United Nations determined by the Control Council.

Article 10. For the purpose of this law:

(a) The term "person" shall include any natural person or collective person or any juridical person or entity under public or private law having legal capacity to acquire, use, control or dispose of property or interests therein; and any government, including all political sub-divisions, public corporations, agencies and any instrumentalities thereof. Any juridical person or entity which is organized under the laws of, or has its principal place of business in Germany, shall be deemed to be a person of German nationality within the meaning of Article Two hereof.

(b) The term "property" shall include all movable and immovable property and all rights and interests in or claims to such property whether matured or not, including all property, rights, interests or claims transferred to or held by third parties as nominees or trustees and all property, rights, interests or claims transferred by way of gift or otherwise or for consideration, expressed or implied, but not including the rights or interests of third parties to a bona fide sale for full consideration, and shall include but shall not be limited to buildings and lands, goods, wares and merchandise, chattels, coin, bullion, currency, deposits, accounts or debts, shares, claims, bills of lading, warehouse receipts, all kinds of financial instruments whether expressed in reichsmarks or in any foreign currency, evidences of indebtedness or ownership of property, contracts, judgments, rights in or with respect to patents, copyrights, trademarks, etc. and in general, property of any nature whatsoever.

Article 11. It shall be an offense:

(a) For any person whose property is affected by this law to do or to attempt to do any act or make any omission in derogation of the title or interest of the Commission under Articles Two and Three, or

(b) To assist or conspire with any other person to do or to attempt to do any such act or make such omissions as are specified in this article.

Article 12. Any person violating any provision of this law shall be liable to criminal prosecution.

Article 13. All provisions of laws or decrees or parts thereof which are contradictory to any one of the provisions of this law or of any law or decree issued under the provisions of this law are hereby declared null and void.

(3) *Final Act and Annex of the Paris Conference on Reparation, November 9 to December 21, 1945.*[1]

At the invitation of the United States, the United Kingdom and France, the eighteen nation Conference on Reparation was in session in Paris from November 9 to December 21, 1945. Representatives attended from Albania, Australia, Belgium, Canada, Czechoslovakia, Denmark, Egypt, Greece, India, Luxembourg, The Netherlands, New Zealand, Norway, the Union of South Africa, and Yugoslavia. James W. Angell, the United States representative on the Allied Commission on Reparations for Germany was the United States delegate. The draft Agreement approved as the Final Act became effective January 14, 1946, at which time the Inter-Allied Reparation Agency came into existence. Mr. D. Maynard Phelps served as the first United States delegate to IARA until late February, 1946, when he was followed by Mr. Russell H. Dorr.[2]

CONFERENCE RECOMMENDATION

The Paris Conference on Reparation, which has met from 9 November 1945 to 21 December 1945, recommends that the Governments represented at the Conference should sign in Paris as soon as possible an Agreement on Reparation from Germany, on the Establishment of an Inter-Allied Reparation Agency and on the Restitution of Monetary Gold in the terms set forth below.

DRAFT AGREEMENT ON REPARATION FROM GERMANY, ON THE ESTABLISHMENT OF AN INTER-ALLIED REPARATION AGENCY AND ON THE RESTITUTION OF MONETARY GOLD

The Governments of ALBANIA, The UNITED STATES OF AMERICA, AUSTRALIA, BELGIUM, CANADA, DENMARK, EGYPT, FRANCE, The UNITED KINGDOM OF GREAT BRITIAN AND NORTHERN IRELAND, GREECE, INDIA, LUXEMBOURG, NORWAY, NEW ZEALAND, The NETHERLANDS, CZECHOSLOVAKIA, The UNION OF SOUTH AFRICA and YUGOSLAVIA, in order to obtain an equitable distribution among themselves of the total assets which, in accordance with the provisions of this Agreement and the Provisions agreed upon at Potsdam on 1 August 1945 between the Governments of the United States of America, the United Kingdom of Great Britain and Northern Ireland and the Union of Soviet Socialist Republics, are or may be declared to be available as reparation from

[1] Department of State, *Bulletin*, XIV, p. 114.
[2] Department of State Publication 2584, European Series 12, p. 1 and 7.

Germany (hereinafter referred to as German reparation), in order to establish an Inter-Allied Reparation Agency, and to settle an equitable procedure for the restitution of monetary gold,

HAVE AGREED as follows:

PART I. GERMAN REPARATION

Article 1. Shares in Reparation.

A. German reparation (exclusive of the funds to be allocated under Article 8 of Part I of this Agreement) shall be divided into the following categories:

Category A, which shall include all forms of German reparation except those included in Category B,

Category B, which shall include industrial and other capital equipment removed from Germany, and merchant ships and inland water transport.

B. Each Signatory Government shall be entitled to the percentage share of the total value of Category A and the percentage share of the total value of Category B set out for that Government in the Table of Shares set forth below:

TABLE OF SHARES

COUNTRY	CATEGORY A	CATEGORY B
Albania	.05	.35
United States of America	28.00	11.80
Australia	.70	.95
Belgium	2.70	4.50
Canada	3.50	1.50
Denmark	.25	.35
Egypt	.05	.20
France	16.00	22.80
United Kingdom	28.00	27.80
Greece	2.70	4.35
India	2.00	2.90
Luxembourg	.15	.40
Norway	1.30	1.90
New Zealand	.40	.60
Netherlands	3.90	5.60
Czechoslovakia	3.00	4.30
Union of South Africa (*o*)	.70	.10
Yugoslavia	6.60	9.60
TOTAL	100.00	100.00

(*o*) The government of the Union of South Africa has undertaken to waive its claims to the extent necessary to reduce its percentage share of Category B to the figure of 0.1 per cent but is entitled, in disposing of German enemy assets within its jurisdiction, to charge the net value of such assets against its percentage share of Category A and a percentage share under Category B of 0.1 per cent.

C. Subject to the provisions of paragraph D below, each Signatory Government shall be entitled to receive its share of merchant ships determined in accordance with Article 5 of Part I of this Agreement, provided that its receipts of merchant ships do not exceed in value its share in Category B as a whole.

Subject to the provisions of paragraph D below, each Signatory Government shall also be entitled to its Category A percentage share in German assets in countries which remained neutral in the war against Germany.

The distribution among the Signatory Governments of forms of German reparation other than merchant ships, inland water transport and German assets in countries which remained neutral in the war against Germany shall be guided by the principles set forth in Article 4 of Part I of this Agreement.

D. If a Signatory Government receives more than its percentage share of certain types of assets in either Category A or Category B, its receipts of other types of assets in that Category shall be reduced so as to ensure that it shall not receive more than its share in that Category as a whole.

E. No Signatory Government shall receive more than its percentage share of either Category A or Category B as a whole by surrendering any part of its percentage share of the other Category, except that with respect to German enemy assets within its own jurisdiction, any Signatory Government shall be permitted to charge any excess of such assets over its Category A percentage share of total German enemy assets within the jurisdiction of the Signatory Governments either to its receipts in Category A or to its receipts in Category B or in part to each Category.

F. The Inter-Allied Reparation Agency, to be established in accordance with Part II of this Agreement, shall charge the reparation account of each Signatory Government for the German assets within that Government's jurisdiction over a period of five years. The charges at the date of the entry into force of this Agreement shall be not less than 20 per cent of the net value of such assets (as defined in Article 6 of Part I of this Agreement) as then estimated, at the beginning of the second year thereafter not less than 25 per cent of the balance as then estimated, at the beginning of the third year not less than $33\frac{1}{3}$ per cent of the balance as then estimated, at the beginning of the fourth year not less than 50 per cent of the balance as then estimated, at the beginning of the fifth year not less than 90 per cent of the balance as then estimated, and at the end of the fifth year the entire remainder of the total amount actually realized.

G. The following exceptions to paragraphs D and E above shall apply in the case of a Signatory Government whose share in Category B is less than its share in Category A:

(*i*) Receipts of merchant ships by any such Government shall not reduce its percentage share in other types of assets in Category B, except to the extent that such receipts exceed the value obtained when that Government's Category A percentage is applied to the total value of merchant ships.

(*ii*) Any excess of German assets within the jurisdiction of such Government over its Category A percentage share of the total of German assets within the jurisdiction of Signatory Governments as a whole shall be charged first to the additional share in Category B to which that Government would be entitled if its share in Category B were determined by applying its Category A percentage to the forms of German reparation in Category B.

H. If any Signatory Government renounces its shares or part of its shares in German reparation as set out in the above Table of Shares, or if it withdraws from the Inter-Allied Reparation Agency at a time when all or part of its shares in German reparation remain unsatisfied, the shares or part thereof thus renounced or remaining shall be distributed rateably among the other Signatory Governments.

Article 2. Settlement of Claims against Germany.

A. The Signatory Governments agree among themselves that their respective shares of reparation, as determined by the present Agreement, shall be regarded by each of them as covering all its claims and those of its nationals against the former German Government and its Agencies, of a governmental or private nature, arising out of the war (which are not otherwise provided for), including costs of German occupation, credits acquired during occupation on clearing accounts and claims against the Reichskreditkassen.

B. The provisions of paragraph A above are without prejudice to:

(*i*) The determination at the proper time of the forms, duration or total amount of reparation to be made by Germany;

(*ii*) The right which each Signatory Government may have with respect to the final settlement of German reparation; and

(*iii*) Any political, territorial or other demands which any Signatory Government may put forward with respect to the peace settlement with Germany.

C. Notwithstanding anything in the provisions of paragraph A above, the present Agreement shall not be considered as affecting:

(*i*) The obligation of the appropriate authorities in Germany to secure at a future date the discharge of claims against Germany and German nationals arising out of contracts and other obligations entered into, and rights acquired, before the existence of a state of war between Germany and the Signatory Government concerned or before the occupation of its territory by Germany, whichever was earlier;

(*ii*) The claims of Social Insurance Agencies of the Signatory Governments or the claims of their nationals against the Social Insurance Agencies of the former German Government; and

(*iii*) Banknotes of the Reichsbank and the Rentenbank, it being understood that their realization shall not have the result of reducing improperly the amount of reparation and shall not be effected without the approval of the Control Council for Germany.

D. Notwithstanding the provisions of paragraph A of this Article, the Signatory Governments agree that, so far as they are concerned, the Czechoslovak Government will be entitled to draw upon the Giro Account of the National Bank of Czechoslovakia at the Reichsbank, should such action be decided upon by the Czechoslovak Government and be approved by the Control Council for Germany, in connection with the movement from Czechoslovakia to Germany of former Czechoslovak nationals.

Article 3. Waiver of Claims Regarding Property Allocated as Reparation.

Each of the Signatory Governments agrees that it will not assert, initiate actions in international tribunals in respect of, or give diplomatic support to claims on behalf of itself or those persons entitled to its protection against any other Signatory Government or its nationals in respect of property received by that Government as reparation with the approval of the Control Council for Germany.

Article 4. General Principles for the Allocation of Industrial and other Capital Equipment.

A. No Signatory Government shall request the allocation to it as reparation of any industrial or other capital equipment removed from Germany except for use in its own territory or for use by its own nationals outside its own territory.

B. In submitting requests to the Inter-Allied Reparation Agency, the Signatory Governments should endeavour to submit comprehensive programs of requests for related groups of items, rather than requests for isolated items or small groups of items. It is recognized that the work of the Secretariat of the Agency will be more effective, the more comprehensive the programs which Signatory Governments submit to it.

C. In the allocation by the Inter-Allied Reparation Agency of items declared available for reparation (other than merchant ships, inland water transport and German assets in countries which remained neutral in the war against Germany), the following general principles shall serve as guides:

(*i*) Any item or related group of items in which a claimant country has a substantial prewar financial interest shall be allocated to that country if it so desires. Where two or more claimants have such substantial interests in a particular item or group of items, the criteria stated below shall guide the allocation.

(*ii*) If the allocation between competing claimants is not determined by paragraph (*i*), attention shall be given, among other relevant factors, to the following considerations:

    (*a*) The urgency of each claimant country's needs for the item or items to rehabilitate, reconstruct or restore to full activity the claimant country's economy;

    (*b*) The extent to which the item or items would replace property which was destroyed, damaged or looted in the war, or requires replacement because of excessive wear in war production, and which is important to the claimant country's economy;

    (*c*) The relation of the item or items to the general pattern of the claimant country's prewar economic life and to programs for its postwar economic adjustment or development;

    (*d*) The requirements of countries whose reparation shares are small but which are in need of certain specific items or categories of items.

(*iii*) In making allocations a reasonable balance shall be maintained among the rates at which the reparation shares of the several claimant Governments are satisfied, subject to such temporary exceptions as are justified by the considerations under paragraph (*ii*) (*a*) above.

Article 5. General Principles for the Allocation of Merchant Ships and Inland Water Transport.

A. (*i*) German merchant ships available for distribution as reparation among the Signatory Governments shall be distributed among them in proportion to the respective over-all losses of merchant shipping, on a gross tonnage basis, of the Signatory Governments and their nationals through acts of war. It is recognized that transfers of merchant ships by the United Kingdom and United States Governments to other Governments are subject to such final approvals by the legislatures of the United Kingdom and United States of America as may be required.

(*ii*) A special committee, composed of representatives of the Signatory Governments, shall be appointed by the Assembly of the Inter-Allied Reparation Agency to make recommendations concerning the determination of such losses and the allocation of German merchant ships available for distribution.

(*iii*) The value of German merchant ships for reparation accounting purposes shall be the value determined by the Tri-partite Merchant Marine Commission in terms of 1938 prices in Germany plus 15 per cent, with an allowance for depreciation.

B. Recognizing that some countries have special need for inland water transport, the distribution of inland water transport shall be dealt with by a special committee appointed by the Assembly of the Inter-Allied Reparation Agency in the event that inland water transport becomes available at a future time as reparation for the Signatory Governments. The valuation of inland water transport will be made on the basis adopted for the valuation of merchant ships or on an equitable basis in relation to that adopted for merchant ships.

Article 6. German Extended Assets.

A. Each Signatory Government shall, under such procedures as it may choose, hold or dispose of German enemy assets within its jurisdiction in manners designed to preclude their return to German ownership or control and shall charge against its reparation share such assets (net of accrued taxes, liens, expenses of administration, other *in rem* charges against specific items and legitimate contract claims against the German former owners of such assets).

B. The Signatory Governments shall give to the Inter-Allied Reparation Agency all information for which it asks as to the value of such assets and the amounts realized from time to time by their liquidation.

C. German assets in those countries which remained neutral in the war against Germany shall be removed from German ownership or control and liquidated or disposed of in accordance with the authority of France, the United Kingdom and the United States of America, pursuant to arrangements to be negotiated with the neutrals by these countries. The net proceeds of liquidation or disposition shall be made available to the Inter-Allied Reparation Agency for distribution on reparation account.

D. In applying the provisions of paragraph A above, assets which were the property of a country which is a member of the United Nations or its nationals who were not nationals of Germany at the time of the occupation or annexation of this country by Germany, or of its entry into war, shall not be charged to its reparation account. It is understood that this provision in no way prejudges any questions which may arise as regards assets which were not the property of a national of the country concerned at the time of the latter's occupation or annexation by Germany or of its entry into war.

E. The German enemy assets to be charged against reparation shares shall include assets which are in reality German enemy assets, despite the fact that the nominal owner of such assets is not a German enemy.

Each Signatory Government shall enact legislation or take other appropriate steps, if it has not already done so, to render null and void all transfers made, after the occupation of its territory or its entry into war, for the fraudulent purpose of cloaking German enemy interests, and thus saving them harmless from the effect of control measures regarding German enemy interests.

F. The Assembly of the Inter-Allied Reparation Agency shall set up a Committee of Experts in matters of enemy property custodianship in order to overcome practical difficulties of law and interpretation which may arise. The Committee should in particular guard against schemes which might result in effecting fictitious or other transactions designed to favour enemy interests, or to reduce improperly the amount of assets which might be allocated to reparation.

Article 7. Captured Supplies.

The value of supplies and other materials susceptible of civilian use captured from the German Armed Forces in areas outside Germany and delivered to Signatory Governments shall be charged against their reparation shares in so far as such supplies and materials have not been or are not in the future either paid for or delivered under arrangements precluding any charge. It is recognised that transfers of such supplies and material by the United Kingdom and United States Governments to other Governments are subject to such final approval by the legislature of the United Kingdom or the United States of America as may be required.

Article 8. Allocation of a Reparation Share to Non-repatriable Victims of German Action.

In recognition of the fact that large numbers of persons have suffered heavily at the hands of the Nazis and now stand in dire need of aid to promote their rehabilitation but will be unable to claim the assistance of any Government receiving reparation from Germany, the Governments of the United States of America, France, the United Kingdom, Czechoslovakia and Yugoslavia, in consultation with the Inter-Governmental

Committee on Refugees, shall as soon as possible work out in common agreement a plan on the following general lines:

A. A share of reparation consisting of all the non-monetary gold found by the Allied Armed Forces in Germany and in addition a sum not exceeding 25 million dollars shall be allocated for the rehabilitation and resettlement of non-repatriable victims of German action.

B. The sum of 25 million dollars shall be met from a portion of the proceeds of German assets in neutral countries which are available for reparation.

C. Governments of neutral countries shall be requested to make available for this purpose (in addition to the sum of 25 million dollars) assets in such countries of victims of Nazi action who have since died and left no heirs.

D. The persons eligible for aid under the plan in question shall be restricted to true victims of Nazi persecution and to their immediate families and dependents, in the following classes:

(*i*) Refugees from Nazi Germany or Austria who require aid and cannot be returned to their countries within a reasonable time because of prevailing conditions;

(*ii*) German and Austrian nationals now resident in Germany or Austria in exceptional cases in which it is reasonable on grounds of humanity to assist such persons to emigrate and providing they emigrate to other countries within a reasonable period;

(*iii*) Nationals of countries formerly occupied by the Germans who cannot be repatriated or are not in a position to be repatriated within a reasonable time. In order to concentrate aid on the most needy and deserving refugees and to exclude persons whose loyalty to the United Nations is or was doubtful, aid shall be restricted to nationals or former nationals of previously occupied countries who were victims of Nazi concentration camps or of concentration camps established by regimes under Nazi influence but not including persons who have been confined only in prisoners of war camps.

E. The sums made available under paragraphs A and B above shall be administered by the Inter-Governmental Committee on Refugees or by a United Nations Agency to which appropriate functions of the Inter-Governmental Committee may in the future be transferred. The sums made available under paragraph C above shall be administered for the general purposes referred to in this Article under a program of administration to be formulated by the five Governments named above.

F. The non-monetary gold found in Germany shall be placed at the disposal of the Inter-Governmental Committee on Refugees as soon as a plan has been worked out as provided above.

G. The Inter-Governmental Committee on Refugees shall have power to carry out the purposes of the fund through appropriate public and private field organisations.

H. The fund shall be used, not for the compensation of individual victims, but to further the rehabilitation or resettlement of persons in the eligible classes.

I. Nothing in this Article shall be considered to prejudice the claims which individual refugees may have against a future German Government, except to the amount of the benefits that such refugees may have received from the sources referred to in paragraphs A and C above.

Part II. Inter-Allied Reparation Agency

Article 1. Establishment of the Agency.

The Governments signatory to the present Agreement hereby establish an Inter-Allied Reparation Agency (hereinafter referred to as the "Agency"). Each Government shall appoint a Delegate to the Agency and shall also be entitled to appoint an Alternate who, in the absence of the Delegate, shall be entitled to exercise all the functions and rights of the Delegate.

Article 2. Functions of the Agency.

A. The Agency shall allocate German reparation among the Signatory Governments in accordance with the provisions of this Agreement and of any other agreements from time to time in force among the Signatory Governments. For this purpose, the Agency shall be the medium through which the Signatory Governments receive information concerning, and express their wishes in regard to, items available as reparation.

B. The Agency shall deal with all questions relating to the restitution to a Signatory Government of property situated in one of the Western Zones of Germany which may be referred to it by the Commander of that Zone (acting on behalf of his Government), in agreement with the claimant Signatory Government or Governments, without prejudice, however, to the settlement of such questions by the Signatory Governments concerned either by agreement or arbitration.

Article 3. Internal Organization of the Agency.

A. The organs of the Agency shall be the Assembly and the Secretariat.

B. The Assembly shall consist of the Delegates and shall be presided over by the President of the Agency. The President of the Agency shall be the Delegate of the Government of France.

C. The Secretariat shall be under the direction of a Secretary General, assisted by two Deputy Secretaries General. The Secretary General and the two Deputy Secretaries General shall be appointed by the Governments of France, the United States of America and the United Kingdom. The Secretariat shall be international in character. It shall act for the Agency and not for the individual Signatory Governments.

Article 4. Functions of the Secretariat.

The Secretariat shall have the following functions;

A. To prepare and submit to the Assembly programs for the allocation of German reparations;

B. To maintain detailed accounts of assets available for, and of assets distributed as, German reparation;

C. To prepare and submit to the Assembly the budget of the Agency;

D. To perform such other administrative functions as may be required.

Article 5. Functions of the Assembly.

Subject to the provisions of Articles 4 and 7 of Part II of this Agreement, the Assembly shall allocate German reparation among the Signatory Governments in conformity with the provisions of this Agreement and of any other agreements from time to time in force among the Signatory Governments. It shall also approve the budget of the Agency and shall perform such other functions as are consistent with the provisions of this Agreement.

Article 6. Voting in the Assembly.

Except as otherwise provided in this Agreement, each Delegate shall have one vote. Decisions in the Assembly shall be taken by a majority of the votes cast.

Article 7. Appeal from Decisions of the Assembly.

A. When the Assembly has not agreed to a claim presented by a Delegate that an item should be allocated to his Government, the Assembly shall, at the request of that Delegate and within the time limit prescribed by the Assembly, refer the question to arbitration. Such reference shall suspend the effect of the decision of the Assembly on that item.

B. The Delegates of the Governments claiming an item referred to arbitration under paragraph A above shall select an Arbitrator from among the other Delegates. If agreement cannot be reached upon the selection of an Arbitrator, the United States Delegate shall either act as Arbitrator or appoint as Arbitrator another Delegate from among the Delegates whose Governments are not claiming the item. If the United States Government is one of the claimant Governments, the President of the Agency shall appoint as Arbitrator a Delegate whose Government is not a claimant Government.

Article 8. Powers of the Arbitrator.

When the question of the allocation of any item is referred to arbitration under Article 7 of Part II of this Agreement, the Arbitrator shall have authority to make final allocation of the item among the claimant Governments. The Arbitrator may, at his discretion, refer the item to the Secretariat for further study. He may also, at his discretion, require the Secretariat to resubmit the item to the Assembly.

Article 9. Expenses.

A. The salaries and expenses of the Delegates and of their staffs shall be paid by their own Governments.

B. The common expenses of the Agency shall be met from the funds of the Agency. For the first two years from the date of the establishment of the Agency, these funds shall be contributed in proportion to the percentage shares of the Signatory Governments in Category B — and thereafter in proportion to their percentage shares in Category A.

C. Each Signatory Government shall contribute its share in the budget of the Agency for each budgetary period (as determined by the Assembly) at the beginning of that period; provided that each Government shall, when this Agreement is signed on its behalf, contribute a sum equivalent to not less than its Category B percentage share of £50,000 and shall, within three months thereafter, contribute the balance of its share in the budget of the Agency for the budgetary period in which this Agreement is signed on its behalf.

D. All contributions by the Signatory Governments shall be made in Belgian francs or such other currency or currencies as the Agency may require.

Article 10. Voting on the Budget.

In considering the budget of the Agency for any budgetary period, the vote of each Delegate in the Assembly shall be proportional to the share of the budget for that period payable by his Government.

Article 11. Official Languages.

The official languages of the Agency shall be English and French.

Article 12. Officers of the Agency.

The seat of the Agency shall be in Brussels. The Agency shall maintain liaison officers in such other places as the Assembly, after obtaining the necessary consents, may decide.

Article 13. Withdrawal.

Any Signatory Government, other than a Government which is responsible for the control of a part of German territory, may withdraw from the Agency after written notice to the Secretariat.

Article 14. Amendments and Termination.

This Part II of the Agreement can be amended or the Agency terminated by a decision in the Assembly of the majority of the Delegates voting, provided that the Delegates forming the majority represent Governments whose shares constitute collectively not less than 80 per cent of the aggregate of the percentage shares in Category A.

Article 15. Legal Capacity. Immunities and Privileges.

The Agency shall enjoy in the territory of each Signatory Government such legal capacity and such privileges, immunities and facilities, as may be necessary for the exercise of its functions and the fulfilment of its purposes. The representatives of the Signatory Governments and the officials of the Agency shall enjoy such privileges and immunities as are necessary for the independent exercise of their functions in connection with the Agency.

Part III. Restitution of Monetary Gold

Single Article.

A. All the monetary gold found in Germany by the Allied Forces and that referred to in paragraph G below (including gold coins, except those of numismatic or historical value, which shall be restored directly if identifiable) shall be pooled for distribution as restitution among the countries participating in the pool in proportion to their respective losses of gold through looting or by wrongful removal to Germany.

B. Without prejudice to claims by way of reparation for unrestored gold, the portion of monetary gold thus accruing to each country participating in the pool shall be accepted by that country in full satisfaction of all claims against Germany for restitution of monetary gold.

C. A proportional share of the gold shall be allocated to each country concerned which adheres to this arrangement for the restitution of monetary gold and which can establish that a definite amount of monetary gold belonging to it was looted by Germany or, at any time after March 12th, 1938, was wrongfully removed into German territory.

D. The question of the eventual participation of countries not represented at the Conference (other than Germany but including Austria and Italy) in the above-mentioned distribution shall be reserved, and the equivalent of the total shares which these countries would receive, if they were eventually admitted to participate, shall be set aside to be disposed of at a later date in such manner as may be decided by the Allied Governments concerned.

E. The various countries participating in the pool shall supply to the Governments of the United States of America, France and the United Kingdom, as the occupying Powers concerned, detailed and verifiable data regarding the gold losses suffered through looting by, or removal to, Germany.

F. The Governments of the United States of America, France and the United Kingdom shall take appropriate steps within the Zones of Germany occupied by them respectively to implement distribution in accordance with the foregoing provisions.

G. Any monetary gold which may be recovered from a third country to which it was transferred from Germany shall be distributed in accordance with this arrangement for the restitution of monetary gold.

Part IV. Entry into Force and Signature.

Article 1. Entry into Force.

This Agreement shall be open for signature on behalf of any Government represented at the Paris Conference on Reparation. As soon as it has been signed on behalf of Governments collectively entitled to not less than 80 per cent of the aggregate of shares in Category A of German reparation, it shall come into force among such Signatory Governments. The Agreement shall thereafter be in force among such Governments and those Governments on whose behalf it is subsequently signed.

Article 2. Signature.

The signature of each contracting Government shall be deemed to mean that the effect of the present Agreement extends to the colonies and overseas territories of such Government, and to territories under its protection of suzerainty or over which it at present exercises a mandate.

In witness whereof, the undersigned, duly authorized by their respective Governments, have signed in Paris the present Agreement, in the English and the French languages, the two texts being equally authentic, in a single original, which shall be deposited in the Archives of the Government of The French Republic, a certified copy thereof being furnished by that Government to each Signatory Government.

—— for the Government of ——
194 .

—— for the Government of ——
194 .

UNANIMOUS RESOLUTIONS BY THE CONFERENCE

The Conference has also unanimously agreed to include the following Resolutions in the Final Act:

1. German Assets in the Neutral Countries.

The Conference unanimously resolves that the countries which remained neutral in the war against Germany should be prevailed upon by all suitable means to recognize the reasons of justice and of international security policy which motivate the Powers exercising supreme authority in Germany and the other Powers participating in this Conference in their efforts to extirpate the German holdings in the neutral countries.

2. Gold transferred to the Neutral Countries.

The Conference unanimously resolves that, in conformity with the policy expressed by the United Nations Declaration Against Axis Acts of Dispossession of January 5th, 1943 and the United Nations Declaration on Gold of February 22nd, 1944, the countries which remained neutral in the war against Germany be prevailed upon to make available for distribution in accordance with Part III of the foregoing Agreement all looted gold transferred into their territories from Germany.

3. Equality of Treatment regarding Compensation for War Damage.

The Conference unanimously resolves that, in the administration of reconstruction or compensation benefits for war damage to property, the treatment accorded by each Signatory Government to physical persons who are nationals and to legal persons who are nationals of or are owned by nationals of any other Signatory Government, so far as they have not been compensated after the war for the same property under any other form or on any other occasion shall be in principle not less favourable than that which the Signatory Government accords to its own nationals. In view of the fact that there are many special problems of reciprocity related to this principle, it is recognized that in certain cases the actual implementation of the principle cannot be achieved except through special agreements between Signatory Governments.

Reference to the Annex to the Final Act.

During the course of the Conference, statements were made by certain Delegates, in the terms set out in the attached Annex, concerning matters not within the competence of the Conference but having a close relation with its work. The Delegates whose Governments are represented on the Control Council for Germany undertook to bring those statements to the notice of their respective Governments.

In witness whereof, the undersigned have signed the present Final Act of the Paris Conference on Reparation.

Done in Paris on December 21, 1945, in the English and French languages, the two texts being equally authentic, in a single original, which shall be deposited in the Archives of the Government of the French Republic, certified copies thereof, being furnished by that Government to all the Governments represented at that Conference.

—— Delegate of the Government of ——
—— Delegate of the Government of ——

ANNEX.

1. Resolution on the subject of Restitution.

The Albanian, Belgian, Czechoslovak, Danish, French, Greek, Indian, Luxembourg, Netherlands and Yugoslav Delegates agree to accept as the basis of a restitution policy the following principles:

(a) The question of the restitution of property removed by the Germans from the Allied countries must be examined in all cases in the light of the United Nations Declaration of January 5th, 1943.

(b) In general, restitution should be confined to identifiable goods which (i) existed at the time of occupation of the country concerned, and were removed with or without payment; (ii) were produced during the occupation and obtained by an act of force.

(c) In cases where articles removed by the enemy cannot be identified, the claim for replacement should be part of the general reparation claim of the country concerned.

(d) As an exception to the above principles, objects (including books, manuscripts and documents) of an artistic, historical, scientific (excluding equipment of an industrial character), educational or religious character which have been looted by the enemy occupying Power shall, so far as possible, be replaced by equivalent objects if they are not restored.

(e) With respect to the restitution of looted goods which were produced during the occupation and which are still in the hands of German concerns or residents of Germany, the burden of proof of the original ownership of the goods shall rest on the claimants and the burden of proof that the goods were acquired by a regular contract shall rest on the holders.

(*f*) All necessary facilities under the auspices of the Commanders-in-Chief of the occupied Zones shall be given to the Allied States to send expert missions into Germany to search for looted property and to identify, store and remove it to its country of origin.

(*g*) German holders of looted property shall be compelled to declare it to the control authorities; stringent penalties shall be attached to infractions of this obligation.

2. Resolution on Reparation from Existing Stocks and Current Production.

The Delegates of Albania, Belgium, Czechoslovakia, Denmark, Egypt, France, Greece, India, Luxembourg, the Netherlands, Norway and Yugoslavia,

In view of the decision of the Crimea Conference that Germany shall make compensation to the greatest possible extent for the losses and suffering which she has inflicted on the United Nations,

Considering that it will not be possible to satisfy the diverse needs of the Governments entitled to reparation unless the assets to be allocated are sufficiently varied in nature and the methods of allocation are sufficiently flexible,

Express the hope that no category of economic resources in excess of Germany's requirements as defined in Part III, article 15 of the Potsdam Declaration, due account being taken of article 19 of the same Part, shall in principle be excluded from the assets, the sum total of which should serve to meet the reparation claims of the Signatory Governments.

It thus follows that certain special needs of different countries will not be met without recourse, in particular, to German existing stocks, current production and services, as well as Soviet reciprocal deliveries under Part IV of the Potsdam Declaration.

It goes without saying that the foregoing shall be without prejudice to the necessity of achieving the economic disarmament of Germany.

The above-named Delegates would therefore deem it of advantage were the Control Council to furnish the Inter-Allied Reparation Agency with lists of existing stocks, goods from current production and services, as such stocks, goods or services become available as reparation. The Agency should, at all times, be in a position to advise the Control Council of the special needs of the different Signatory Governments.

3. Resolution regarding Property in Germany belonging to United Nations or their nationals.

The Delegates of Albania, Belgium, Czechoslovakia, France, Greece, Luxembourg, the Netherlands, Norway and Yugoslavia, taking into account the fact that the burden of reparation should fall on the German people, recommend that the following rules be observed regarding the allocation as reparation of property (other than ships) situated in Germany:

(*a*) To determine the proportion of German property available as reparation, account shall be taken of the sum total of property actually constituting the German economy, including assets belonging to a

United Nation or to its nationals, but excluding looted property, which is to be restored.

(b) In general, property belonging legitimately to a United Nation or to its nationals, whether wholly owned or in the form of a shareholding of more than 48 percent, shall so far as possible be excluded from the part of German property considered to be available as reparation.

(c) The Control Council shall determine the cases in which minority shareholdings of a United Nation or its nationals shall be treated as forming part of the property of a German juridical person and therefore having the same status as that juridical person.

(d) The foregoing provisions do not in any way prejudice the removal or destruction of concerns controlled by interests of a United Nation or of its nationals when this is necessary for security reasons.

(e) In cases where an asset which is the legitimate property of one of the United Nations or its nationals has been allocated as reparation, or destroyed, particularly in the cases referred to in paragraphs b, c, and d above, equitable compensation to the extent of the full value of this asset shall be granted by the Control Council to the United Nation concerned as a charge on the German economy. This compensation shall, when possible, take the form of a shareholding of equal value in German assets of a similar character which have not been allocated as reparation.

(f) In order to ensure that the property in Germany of persons declared by one of the United Nations to be collaborators or traitors shall be taken from them, the Control Council shall give effect in Germany to legislative measures and juridical decisions by courts of the United Nation concerned in regard to collaborators or traitors who are nationals of that United Nation or were nationals of that United Nation at the date of its occupation or annexation by Germany or entry into the war. The Control Council shall give to the Government of such United Nation facilities to take title to and possession of such assets and to dispose of them.

4. Resolution on Captured War Materiel.

The Delegates of Albania, Belgium, Denmark, Luxembourg, the Netherlands, Norway, Czechoslovakia and Yugoslavia, taking account of the fact that part of the war materiel seized by the Allied Armies in Germany is of no use to these Armies but would, on the other hand, be of use to other Allied countries recommend:

(a) That, subject to Resolution 1 of this Annex on the subject of restitution, war materiel which was taken in the Western Zones of Germany and which has neither been put to any use nor destroyed as being of no value, and which is not needed by the Armies of Occupation or is in excess of their requirements, shall be put at the disposal of countries which have a right to receive reparation from the Western Zones of Germany, and;

(b) That the competent authorities shall determine the available types and quantities of this materiel and shall submit lists to the Inter-Allied Reparation Agency, which shall proceed in accordance with the provisions of Part II of the above Agreement.

5. Resolution on German Assets in the Julian March and the Dodecanese.

The Delegates of Greece, the United Kingdom and Yugoslavia (being the Delegates of the countries primarily concerned), agree that:

(a) The German assets in Venezia Giulia (Julian March) and in the Dodecanese shall be taken into custody by the military authorities in occupation of those parts of the territory which they now occupy, until the territorial questions have been decided; and

(b) As soon as a decision on the territorial questions has been reached, the liquidation of the assets shall be undertaken in conformity with the provisions of Paragraph A of Article 6 of Part I of the foregoing Agreement by the countries whose sovereignty over the disputed territories has been recognized.

6. Resolution on Costs relating to Goods Delivered from Germany as Reparation.

The Delegates of Albania, Australia, Belgium, Canada, Denmark, Egypt, France, Greece, India, Luxembourg, Norway, New Zealand, the Netherlands, Czechoslovakia and Yugoslavia, recommend that the costs of dismantling, packing, transporting, handling, loading and all other costs of a general nature relating to goods to be delivered from Germany as reparation, until the goods in question have passed the German frontier, and expenditure incurred in Germany for the account of the Inter-Allied Reparation Agency or of the Delegates of the Agency should, in so far as they are payable in a currency which is legal tender in Germany, be paid as a charge on the German economy.

7. Resolution on the Property of War Criminals.

The Delegates of Albania, Belgium, France, Luxembourg, Czechoslovakia and Yugoslavia express the view that:

(a) The legislation in force in Germany against German war criminals should provide for the confiscation of the property in Germany of those criminals, if it does not do so already;

(b) The property so confiscated, except such as is already available as reparation or restitution, should be liquidated by the Control Council and the net proceeds of the liquidation paid to the Inter-Allied Reparation Agency for division according to the principles set out in the foregoing Agreement.

8. Resolution on Recourse to the International Court of Justice.

The Delegates of Albania, Australia, Belgium, Denmark, France, Luxembourg, the Netherlands, Norway, Czechoslovakia and Yugoslavia recommend that:

Subject to the provisions of Article 3 of Part I of the foregoing Agreement, the Signatory Governments agree to have recourse to the International Court of Justice for the solution of every conflict of law or of competence arising out of the provisions of the foregoing Agreement which has not been submitted by the parties concerned to amicable solution or arbitration.

(4) *Anglo-Soviet-American Communiqué on the Disposal of the German Navy. Department of State Press Release, January 22, 1946.*[1]

One. It was decided at the Berlin Conference that operable surface units of the German fleet including units which could be made operable within a specified time together with 30 U-boats should be divided equally between the Three Powers and that the remainder of the German fleet should be destroyed.

Two. The Tripartite Naval Commission was accordingly appointed to make recommendations to implement this decision and it has recently reported to the governments of the Three Powers. Its report is now under consideration by these governments but its recommendation on allocation of the main units has been accepted and their division between the Three Powers is now being made.

Three. Surplus U-boats in United Kingdom ports have been sunk in accordance with this agreement.

(5) *Plan of the Allied Control Council for Reparations and the Level of Postwar German Economy, March 28, 1946.*[2]

Allied Control Authority

The plan for reparations and the level of post-war German economy in accordance with the Berlin protocol:

1. In accordance with the Berlin protocol the Allied Control Council is to determine the amount and character of the industrial capital equipment unnecessary for the German peace economy and therefore available for reparations. The guiding principles regarding the plan for reparations and the level of the post-war German economy, in accordance with the Berlin protocol, are:

(*a*) Elimination of the German war potential and the industrial disarmament of Germany.

(*b*) Payment of reparations to the countries which had suffered from German aggression.

(*c*) Development of agriculture and peaceful industries.

(*d*) Maintenance in Germany of average living standards not exceeding the average standard of living of European countries (excluding the United Kingdom and the Union of Soviet Socialist Republics).

(*e*) Retention in Germany, after payment of reparations, of sufficient resources to enable her to maintain herself without external assistance.

2. In accordance with these principles, the basic elements of the plan have been accepted. The assumptions of the plan are:

(*a*) That the population of post-war Germany will be 66.5 millions.

(*b*) That Germany will be treated as a single economic unit.

(*c*) That exports from Germany will be acceptable in the international markets.

---

[1] Department of State, *Bulletin*, XIV, p. 173.
[2] *Ibid.* p. 636.

FORMER ENEMY STATES

Prohibited Industries

1. In order to eliminate Germany's war potential, the production of arms, ammunition, and implements of war as well as all types of aircraft and sea-going ships is prohibited and will be prevented.

2. All industrial capital equipment for the production of the following items is to be eliminated:
 (a) Synthetic gasoline and oil.
 (b) Synthetic rubber.
 (c) Synthetic ammonia.
 (d) Ball and taper-roller bearings.
 (e) Heavy machine tools of certain types.
 (f) Heavy tractors.
 (g) Primary aluminum.
 (h) Magnesium.
 (i) Beryllium.
 (j) Vanadium produced from Thomas Slags.
 (k) Radioactive materials.
 (l) Hydrogen peroxide above 50 percent strength.
 (m) Specific war chemicals and gases.
 (n) Radio transmitting equipment.

Facilities for the production of synthetic gasoline and oil, synthetic ammonia and synthetic rubber, and ball and taper-roller bearings will be temporarily retained to meet domestic requirements until the necessary imports are available and can be paid for.

Restricted Industries, Metallurgical Industries

1. Steel.
 (a) The production capacity of the steel industry to be left in Germany should be 7,500,000 ingot tons. This figure to be subject to review for further reduction should this appear necessary.
 (b) The allowable production of steel in Germany should not exceed 5,800,000 ingot tons in any future year without the specific approval of the Allied Control Council, but this figure will be subject to annual review by the Control Council.
 (c) The steel plants to be left in Germany under the above program should, as far as practicable, be the older ones.

2. Non-ferrous metals. The annual consumption of non-ferrous metals (including exports of products containing these metals) is fixed at the following quantities:

Copper	140,000 tons
Zinc	135,000 tons
Lead	120,000 tons
Tin	8,000 tons
Nickel	1,750 tons

Chemical Industries

1. Basic chemicals. In the basic-chemical industries there will be retained 40 percent of the 1936 production capacity (measured by sales

in 1936 values). This group includes the following basic chemicals: nitrogen, phosphate, calcium carbide, sulphuric acid, alkalies, and chlorine. In addition, to obtain the required quantities of fertilizer for agriculture, existing capacity for the production of nitrogen through the synthetic-ammonia process will be retained until the necessary imports of nitrogen are available and can be paid for.

2. Other chemicals. Capacity will be retained for the group of other chemical production in the amount of 70 percent of the 1936 production capacity (measured by sales in 1936 values). This group includes chemicals for building supplies, consumer-goods items, plastics, industrial supplies, and other miscellaneous chemical products.

3. Dyestuffs, pharmaceuticals, and synthetic fibers. In the pharmaceutical industry there will be retained capacity for the annual production of 80 percent of the 1936 production (measured by sales in 1936 values). Capacity will be retained to produce annually 36,000 tons of dyestuffs and 185,000 tons of synthetic fibers.

Machine Manufacturing and Engineering

1. Machine tools. For the machine-tool industry there will be retained 11.4 percent of 1938 capacity, with additional restrictions on the type and size of machine tools which may be produced.

2. Heavy engineering. In the heavy-engineering industries there will be retained 31 percent of 1938 capacity. These industries produce metallurgical equipment, heavy mining machinery, material-handling plants, heavy power equipment (boilers and turbines, prime movers, heavy compressors, and turboblowers and turbopumps).

3. Other mechanical engineering. In other mechanical-engineering industries there will be retained 50 percent of 1938 capacity. This group produces constructional equipment, textile machinery, consumer-goods equipment, engineering small tools, food-processing equipment, woodworking machines, and other machines and apparatus.

4. Electroengineering. In the electroengineering industries there will be retained 50 percent of 1938 production capacity (based on sales in 1936 values). Capacity to produce heavy electrical equipment is to be reduced to 30 percent of 1938 production or 40,000,000 reichsmarks (1936 value). Heavy electrical equipment is defined as generators and converters, 6,000 kw. and over; high-tension switch gear; and large transformers, 1,500 kva. and over. Electroengineering, other than heavy electrical equipment, includes electric lamps and light fittings, installation materials, electric heating and domestic appliances, cables and wires, telephone and telegraph apparatus, domestic radios, and other electrical equipment. Export of specified types of radio receiving sets is forbidden.

Transport Engineering

1. Transportation industry.

(*a*) In the automotive industry capacity will be retained to produce annually 80,000 automobiles, including 40,000 passenger cars, 40,000 trucks, and 4,000 light road tractors.

(b) Capacity will be retained to produce annually 10,000 motorcycles with cylinder sizes between 60 and 250 cc. Production of motorcycles with cylinder sizes of more than 250 cc. is prohibited.

(c) In the locomotive industry available capacity will be used exclusively for the repair of the existing stock of locomotives in order to build up a pool of 15,000 locomotives in 1949. A decision will be made later as to the production of new locomotives after 1949.

(d) Sufficient capacity will be retained to produce annually 30,000 freight cars, 1,350 passenger coaches, and 400 luggage vans.

2. Agricultural machinery. To permit maximization of agriculture, capacity will be retained for an annual production of 10,000 light agricultural tractors. Existing capacity for the production of other agricultural equipment, estimated at 80 percent of 1938 levels, is to be retained, subject to restrictions on the type and power of the equipment which may be produced.

3. Spare parts. In estimating capacities there will be taken into account the production of normal quantities of spare parts for transport and agricultural machinery.

4. Optics and precision instruments. Capacity will be retained to produce precision instruments in the value of 340,000,000 reichsmarks (1936 value), of which 220,000,000 reichsmarks is estimated as required for domestic use and 120,000,000 reichsmarks for export. A further limitation for this industry is possible, subject to the recommendation of the Committee for the Liquidation of German War Potential.

Mining Industries

1. Coal. Until the Control Council otherwise decides, coal production will be maximized as far as mining supplies and transport will allow. The minimum production is estimated at 155,000,000 tons (hard coal equivalent), including at least 45,000,000 tons for export. The necessary supplies and services to this end will be arranged to give the maximum production of coal.

2. Potash. The production of potash is estimated at over 100 percent of the 1938 level.

Electric Power

There will be retained an installed capacity of 9,000,000 kw.

Cement

Capacity will be retained to produce 8,000,000 tons of cement annually.

Other Industries

1. The estimated levels of the following industries have been calculated as shown as necessary for the German economy in 1949:

(a) Rubber. 50,000 tons, including 20,000 tons from reclaimed rubber and 30,000 tons from imports.

(b) Pulp, paper, and printing. 2,129,000 tons, based on 26 kg. per head per annum in 1949 plus 400,000 tons for export.

(c) Textiles and clothing industries. 665,000 tons of fiber, based on 10 kg. per head for 1949 and including 2 kg. for export.

(d) Boots and shoes. 113,000,000 pairs, based on 1.7 pairs per head in 1949 (figure excludes needs of occupying forces).

Production may exceed the above estimates in this paragraph (other industries) unless otherwise determined by the Control Council.

2. Building. No level will be determined for 1949. The industry will be free to develop within the limits of available resources and the licensing system.

3. Building-materials industries (including cement). Existing capacity will be retained. Production will be in accordance with building licensing and export requirements.

4. Other unrestricted industries. For the following industries no levels have been determined for 1949. These industries are free to develop within the limitations of available resources. These industries are as follows:

(a) Furniture and woodwork.
(b) Flat glass, bottle glass, and domestic glass.
(c) Ceramics.
(d) Bicycles.
(e) Motorbicycles under 60 cc.
(f) Potash.

General Level of Industry

It is estimated that the general effect of the plan is a reduction in the level of industry as a whole to a figure about 50 or 55 percent of the prewar level in 1938 (excluding building and building-materials industries).

Exports and Imports

The following agreement has been reached with respect to exports and imports:

(a) That the value of exports from Germany shall be planned as 3,000,000,000 reichsmarks (1936 value) for 1949, and that sufficient industrial capacity shall be retained to produce goods to this value and to cover the internal requirements in Germany in accordance with the Potsdam Declaration.

(b) That approved imports will not exceed 3,000,000,000 reichsmarks (1936 value), as compared with 4,200,000,000 reichsmarks in 1936.

(c) That of the total proceeds for exports it is estimated that not more than 1,500,000,000 reichsmarks can be utilized to pay for imports of food and fodder if this will be required, with the understanding that, after all imports approved by the Control Council are paid for, any portion of that sum not needed for food and fodder will be used to pay for costs of occupation, and services such as transport, insurance, etc.

Determination of Capacities Available for Reparations

1. After the approval of this plan, the existing capacities of the separate branches of production shall be determined, and a list of enterprises available for reparations shall be compiled.

2. After decisions have been given on the matters now referred to the coordinating committee, the Economic Directorate would propose to prepare the final plan embodying these decisions and including a description of the various features of the plan, such as: disarmament, reparations, postwar German economy, and the German balance of trade.

(6) *Statement of the President's Personal Representative (Pauley) on the European Reparation Program, July 23, 1946.*[1]

[Excerpt]

. . . .

The reparations program under the Potsdam Agreement has not been working satisfactorily, as has already been reported by Secretary James F. Byrnes.[2] This failure has been due in part to the reluctance of certain countries to treat Germany as a single economic unit as agreed at Potsdam.

The original reparations program called for removal of German war potential by shipping out of Germany the excess industrial capacity which was created for war, and distributing these removables to the devastated Allied countries so as to speed up their recovery and help them to become stronger bulwarks of world peace.

Though many plants have been removed from Germany under this program, in accordance with detailed plans drawn last spring the whole program is now held up because no zone commander can go forward until he knows whether Germany is in reality to be treated as a single economic unit, as was agreed at Potsdam, or whether he must plan to run his zone as an independent economy. Obviously, the amount and kind of machinery which should be removed as surplus will differ under the two systems.

Unless the occupying powers can get together in a whole-hearted effort to carry out the Potsdam Agreement, we may find ourselves repeating the tragic blunders of World War I.

After World War I the Allies, including the United States, financed the rebuilding of the very German war-machine which was used against us in World War II. We lost sight of the main goal — removing German war potential.

We can and we must avoid these mistakes this time. We must see to it that the nations of the world do not play the fatal game of power politics with Germany and place her in the position where she can offer the might of Europe to the highest bidder.

The Potsdam Agreement is the guaranty against such a tragedy. It is to be hoped that no one nation or group of nations will force a renunciation of the Potsdam Agreement.

The Conference on German-Owned Patents, convened on the invitation of the United States, France, and the United Kingdom, met in Paris from July 15 to July 27, 1946 to consider a draft accord agreed upon by the three sponsoring governments. The accord followed, in general terms, the practice followed by

[1] *Ibid.*, XV, p. 233.   [2] *Ibid.*, XIII, p. 153.

the United States, which had been, under the direction of the Alien Property Custodian, to make German-owned patents freely available on a royalty-free non-exclusive licensing basis to American business firms.[1]

Twelve countries participated: Australia, Belgium, Canada, Czechoslovakia, Denmark, France, Luxembourg, the Netherlands, Norway, Union of South Africa, United Kingdom, and France. Disagreement arose on the proposed draft when several of the countries occupied by Germany wished to reserve the right to issue licenses for a three year transitional period to licensees undertaking to manufacture within their own territory. The final draft had no reference to the transitional period, and the four opposed countries — Belgium, Denmark, Luxembourg, and Norway — reserved their positions. The Agreement was signed by the United States, United Kingdom, France and the Netherlands and was to come into effect when accepted by three additional governments. By a resolution passed by the eight governments in favor of the accord, their representatives were to support in the Inter-Allied Reparations Agency a proposal that the value of German rights or interest in any patent should not be charged against their reparations account if the patent were made available without royalty in the manner proposed in the accord.

For text of agreement, see Department of State, *Bulletin*, XV, p. 300.

3. OCCUPATION POLICY IN THE UNITED STATES ZONE

The American Zone of occupation in Germany comprised portions of the former German states of Baden, Württemberg, Hesse and the province of Hesse-Nassau although the dividing line between the French and American Zones cut through traditional German administrative units. In addition, the United States had responsibility for the so-called Bremen Enclave and for the American district of Berlin. Responsibility for the administration of these areas rested with the Office of Military Government for Germany, which was headed for most of the period under review by Lt. Gen. Lucius D. Clay, the Deputy Military Governor, who served under General Joseph T. McNarney, Commanding General of the United States Forces, European Theater.[2]

Coordination of general political policy with the day to day administrative functions of military government was accomplished by the State-War-Navy Coordinating Committee, created in December, 1944, and chaired after April, 1946, by John H. Hilldring, Assistant Secretary of State for Occupied Areas. Policy problems arising in Germany were sent, via the War Department, to the Department of State where policy decisions were made, if necessary cleared through SWNCC, and instructions transmitted to the Office of the Military Governor by the War Department.[3] In Germany, General Clay was assisted by a force of some 6,000 officers and enlisted men stationed in Berlin, in Bremen, in the three state capitals of Bavaria, Württemberg-Baden, and Greater Hesse (created out of the portions of Hesse and Hesse-Nassau lying in the American Zone), and in each of the counties.

Occupation authorities were faced with both immediate and long-range problems. Both were, to a degree, controlled by the general policy decisions taken at Potsdam and by the agreements reached in the Allied Control Council, but these directives permitted of considerable latitude in interpretation with the result that both political and economic progress varied from zone to zone. Where no joint directives existed, the American Military Governor was, of course, bound by the policy decisions embodied in JCS 1067.[4] The immediate problems, in addition to the maintenance of order, consisted of establishing a food rationing system, starting coal production to ward off illnesses anticipated for the winter of 1945–46, handling the problem of the literally hundreds of

---

[1] The material in this summary is based upon an article by Bennett Boskey, "The Conference on German-Owned Patents," *ibid.*, XV, p. 297.

[2] The material in this note is based on *American Policy in Occupied Areas*, Department of State Publication 2794.

[3] *Ibid.*, p. 6. [4] For text, see *Documents, VII, 1944–1945*, p. 193.

thousands of displaced persons left in the wake of the Nazi labor camp system, and in general setting in motion the machinery which would bring order into the area. Apart from the question of reparations, which was handled at a higher political level, the major long range problems facing the occupation authorities were the twin ones of denazification and decentralization on the one hand and the "development of local responsibility" on the other, the latter of which was to be undertaken through the encouragement of "autonomy in regional, local and municipal agencies of German administration." [1]

After the consolidation of Hesse and Hesse-Nassau in September, 1945, the American zone consisted of the three States (*Länder*) of Bavaria, Württemberg-Baden, and Greater Hesse. Below the level of the *Land* came, in order, a varying number of *Regierungsbezirke* (administrative districts), *Kreise* (counties) and *Gemeinde* (communities). According to plans developed in September, 1945, greater administrative responsibility was gradually to be placed in the hands of Germans by terminating the functional responsibilities of the Military Government detachments at the *Landkreis* and *Stadtkreis* levels by November 15, 1945, and at the *Regierungsbezirk* level by December 15, 1945, but continuing general supervisory functions until April, 1946. At the same time, local elections, beginning in January and ending in May, 1946, took place on ascending levels from the *Gemeinde* to the *Landkreise* and *Stadtkreise* and provided local elected officials who were given increasing responsibility over local government. This evolution of local self-government was paralleled by the appointment of constitutional commissions at the *Land* level by each Minister-President. These commissions drafted constitutions which were submitted at Constitutional Assemblies whose members were elected on June 30, 1946. The Constitutions were accepted by the Office of Military Government in October, 1946, approved by the Constitutional Assemblies in the same month, and ratified by special elections in late November and early December in the three *Länder*, at which representatives to the respective *Landtage* were also elected. The Constitutions were approved by percentages ranging from 65% to 68.8% of those voting.[2]

To assure coordination of the policies of the three *Länder*, American authorities established the *Länderrat*, or Council of States, on October 17, 1945, composed of the Minister-Presidents of the three States plus the Mayor of Bremen on matters affecting his area. By May, 1946, the *Länderrat* was given authority to take independent action on certain matters without obtaining prior approval of Military Government authorities. The *Länderrat*, however, was not a zonal government in any sense since its directives had to be implemented by independent action taken by the individual Minister-Presidents or, in the later period, by the individual *Landtage*.

(1) *Exchange of Letters between the President (Truman) and the Commander-in-Chief of the United States Forces of Occupation in Germany (Eisenhower) on Displaced Persons.*

(a) *Letter from the President to General Eisenhower Transmitting the Report of the United States Representative on the Intergovernmental Committee on Refugees (Harrison), August 31, 1945.*[3]

I have received and considered the report of Mr. Earl G. Harrison, our representative on the Intergovernmental Committee on Refugees, upon his mission to inquire into the conditions and needs of displaced persons in Germany who may be stateless or non-repatriable, particu-

[1] *Ibid.*, paragraph 3c, p. 194.
[2] Office of Military Government for Germany (U. S.). *Constitutions of Bavaria, Hesse and Württemberg-Baden*, February 15, 1947, p. 2.
[3] Department of State, *Bulletin*, XIII, p. 455.

larly Jews. I am sending you a copy of that report.¹ I have also had a long conference with him on the same subject matter.

While Mr. Harrison makes due allowance for the fact that during the early days of liberation the huge task of mass repatriation required main attention, he reports conditions which now exist and which require prompt remedy. These conditions, I know, are not in conformity with policies promulgated by SHAEF, now Combined Displaced Persons Executive. But they are what actually exists in the field. In other words, the policies are not being carried out by some of your subordinate officers.

For example, military government officers have been authorized and even directed to requisition billeting facilities from the German population for the benefit of displaced persons. Yet, from this report, this has not been done on any wide scale. Apparently it is being taken for granted that all displaced persons, irrespective of their former persecution or the likelihood that their repatriation or resettlement will be delayed, must remain in camps — many of which are overcrowded and heavily guarded. Some of these camps are the very ones where these people were herded together, starved, tortured and made to witness the death of their fellow-inmates and friends and relatives. The announced policy has been to give such persons preference over the German civilian population in housing. But the practice seems to be quite another thing.

We must intensify our efforts to get these people out of camps and into decent houses until they can be repatriated or evacuated. These houses should be requisitioned from the German civilian population. That is one way to implement the Potsdam policy that the German people "cannot escape responsibility for what they have brought upon themselves."

I quote this paragraph with particular reference to the Jews among the displaced persons:

As matters now stand, we appear to be treating the Jews as the Nazis treated them except that we do not exterminate them. They are in concentration camps in large numbers under our military guard instead of S.S. troops. One is led to wonder whether the German people, seeing this, are not supposing that we are following or at least condoning Nazi policy.

You will find in the report other illustrations of what I mean.

I hope you will adopt the suggestion that a more extensive plan of field visitation by appropriate Army Group Headquarters be instituted, so that the humane policies which have been enunciated are not permitted to be ignored in the field. Most of the conditions now existing in displaced persons camps would quickly be remedied if through inspection tours they came to your attention or to the attention of your supervisory officers.

I know you will agree with me that we have a particular responsibility toward these victims of persecution and tyranny who are in our zone. We must make clear to the German people that we thoroughly abhor the Nazi policies of hatred and persecution. We have no better opportunity

---

¹ Not reprinted here. For text, see *ibid.*, p. 456.

FORMER ENEMY STATES 253

to demonstrate this than by the manner in which we ourselves actually treat the survivors remaining in Germany.

I hope you will report to me as soon as possible the steps you have been able to take to clean up the conditions mentioned in the report.

I am communicating directly with the British Government in an effort to have the doors of Palestine opened to such of these displaced persons as wish to go there.

(b) Letter from General Eisenhower to the President, October 8, 1945.[1]

This is my full report on matters pertaining to the care and welfare of the Jewish victims of Nazi persecution within the United States Zone of Germany. It deals with conditions reported by Mr. Earl G. Harrison, U.S. Representative on Inter-Governmental Committee on Refugees, which was forwarded to me under cover of your letter of 31 August 1945.

Since Mr. Harrison's visit in July many changes have taken place with respect to the condition of Jewish and other displaced persons. Except for temporarily crowded conditions, the result of shifts between established centers and an influx of persons into centers as winter approaches, housing is on a reasonable basis. Nevertheless, efforts to improve their condition continue unabated. Subordinate commanders are under orders to requisition German houses, grounds, and other facilities without hesitation for this purpose.

The housing problem must be seen in full perspective. This winter the villages and towns in the U.S. Zone of Germany will be required to house more than twice their normal population. One million and a half German air raid refugees who were evacuated into Southwestern Germany, together with some 600,000 Germans, Volksdeutsche and Sudetens who fled from Poland, New Poland, Czechoslovakia and Yugoslavia before the advancing Red Armies have created a condition of congestion in the U.S. Zone which forces the most careful conservation of housing space. At this moment the U.S. Zone is under orders to absorb 152,000 more Germans from Austria. Added to this influx of population, there is the loss of housing in bombed-out cities, averaging well over 50 percent; the necessity for billeting large numbers of our troops; and the accommodation required for prisoners of war. The resulting housing shortage is not merely acute, but desperate. Notwithstanding this situation, in my recent inspections and those made by my staff of Jewish centers, although crowded conditions were found, in nearly every instance more than the 30 square feet per person of floor space required for our soldiers was available.

Displaced persons have absolute preference over Germans for housing, but the requirements of the distribution of supplies, the provision of medical care, and the need for welfare activities make it desirable that displaced persons be sufficiently concentrated so that these services may be performed efficiently by the limited supervisory personnel and transport at our disposal. Thus, considerable use has been made of large

[1] *Ibid.*, p. 607.

installations such as brick barracks, apartment blocks and other public buildings in preference to scattered individual billets.

Special centers have been established for Jewish displaced persons. In the latter part of June, the Armies were directed to collect into special assembly centers displaced persons who did not wish to or who could not be repatriated. On 25 July 1945, Dr. Rabbi Israel Goldstein, President of the United Jewish Appeal, recommended that non-repatriable Jews be separated from other stateless people, and placed in exclusively Jewish centers. As a result, the American Joint Distribution Committee was called upon to supervise the establishment of these centers. This policy was reiterated and expanded on 22 August. Special Jewish centers were established for "those Jews who are without nationality or those not Soviet citizens who do not desire to return to their country of origin".

At the time of Mr. Harrison's report there were perhaps 1,000 Jews still in their former concentration camps. These were too sick to be moved at that time. No Jewish or other displaced persons have been housed in these places longer than was absolutely necessary for medical quarantine and recovery from acute illness. It has always been our practice, not just our policy, to remove these victims with the utmost speed from concentration camps.

The assertion that our military guards are now substituting for S.S. troops is definitely misleading. One reason for limiting the numbers permitted to leave our assembly centers was depredation and banditry by displaced persons themselves. Despite all precautions, more than 2,000 of them died from drinking methylated alcohol and other types of poisonous liquor. Many others died by violence or were injured while circulating outside our assembly centers. Perhaps then we were overzealous in our surveillance. However, my present policy is expressed in a letter to subordinate commanders wherein I said:

> Necessary guarding should be done by displaced persons themselves on the volunteer system and without arms. Military supervisors may be employed, but will not be used as sentries except in emergency. Everything should be done to encourage displaced persons to understand that they have been freed from tyranny, and that the supervision exercised over them is merely that necessary for their own protection and well-being, and to facilitate essential maintenance.

I feel that we have problems of shelter and surveillance in hand. Of equal importance is the provision of sufficient and appetizing food. In the past, a 2,000-calorie minimum diet was prescribed for all displaced persons in approved centers. Our field inspections have shown that in many places this scale was consistently exceeded, but there have also been sporadic instances where it was not met. Three or four thousand persons of the persecuted categories, including German Jews, in the American Zone have returned to their home communities. Many are there making a genuine effort to re-establish themselves. Until recently there has been no clear-cut system of assuring adequate food for this group, although in most cases they have been given double rations.

I have recently raised the daily caloric food value per person for ordinary displaced persons in approved centers to 2,300, and for racial, religious and political persecutees to a minimum of 2,500. Feeding standards have also been prescribed and sufficient Red Cross food parcels and imported Civil Affairs/Military Government foodstuffs are on hand to supplement indigenous supplies and meet requisitions to maintain these standards. We are now issuing a directive that those Jews and other persecuted persons who choose and are able to return to their communities will receive a minimum ration of 2,500 calories per day, as well as clothing and shoes, the same as those in centers.

Clothing and shoes are available in adequate amounts and of suitable types. Uniformly excellent medical attention is available to all Jewish people in our centers where they have generally adequate sanitary facilities. UNRRA and AJDC staffs, which are administering an increasing number of our centers, are becoming efficient, and are making it possible for these people to enjoy spiritually uplifting religious programs as well as schooling for children.

It is freely admitted that there is need for improvement. The schools need more books; leisure-time and welfare activities must be further developed; paid employment outside the centers needs to be fostered; additional quantities of furniture, bedding and fuel must be obtained. We have made progress in re-uniting families, but postal communications between displaced persons and their relatives and friends cannot yet be inaugurated; roads and walks must be improved in anticipation of continuing wet weather. We are conscious of these problems, we are working on them, and we have expert advice of UNRRA, of Jewish Agencies, and of our chaplains.

In certain instances we have fallen below standard, but I should like to point out that a whole army has been faced with the intricate problems of readjusting from combat to mass repatriation, and then to the present static phase with its unique welfare problems. Anticipating this phase, I have fostered since before D–Day the development of UNRRA so that persons of professional competence in that organization might take over greater responsibilities, and release our combat men and officers from this most difficult work.

You can expect our continued activity to meet the needs of persecuted people. Perfection never will be attained, Mr. President, but real and honest efforts are being made to provide suitable living conditions for these persecuted people until they can be permanently resettled in other areas.

Mr. Harrison's report gives little regard to the problems faced, the real success attained in saving the lives of thousands of Jewish and other concentration camp victims and repatriating those who could and wished to be repatriated, and the progress made in two months to bring these unfortunates who remained under our jurisdiction from the depths of physical degeneration to a condition of health and essential comfort. I have personally been witness to the expressed gratitude of many of these people for these things.

On December 8, 1945, the Department of State announced that the Allied Control Council for Germany on November 20 had approved a plan for the transfer of the German population to be moved from Austria, Czechoslovakia, Hungary and Poland into the four occupied zones of Germany. Of the 3,500,000 Germans in Poland, two million were to be admitted into the Soviet and the remainder into the British zone; of the 2,500,000 Germans in Czechoslovakia, 1,750,000 were destined for the American and 750,000 for the Soviet zones; half a million Germans in Hungary were to be admitted into the American zone; and 150 Germans from Austria were to be sent to the French zone, with all transfers to be completed by August 1, 1946. Opposition on the part of Hungary to a Czechoslovakian proposal to exchange its Hungarian-speaking minority for a Slovak-speaking minority in Hungary brought the comment from the State Department that "Where such problems affect Hungary, we would regard them as proper subjects, in the first instance, for mutual agreement between Hungary and the neighboring states directly concerned, and ultimately, for consideration or review in connection with the peace settlement with Hungary." [1]

(2) *Letter from the President (Truman) to the Secretary of State (Byrnes), the Secretary of War (Patterson) and the Secretary of the Navy (Forrestal) Transmitting the Report of Byron Price on the Relations between American Forces of Occupation and the German People, November 28, 1945.*[2]

I am enclosing a copy of the report of Byron Price dated November 9. I asked Mr. Price to go to Germany to study the relationship between the American Forces of Occupation and the German people.

Mr. Price, as you know, is an able and experienced observer, and I believe that his report is worthy of the most careful consideration. You will note that the Price report embodies eight specific suggestions.

It is requested that the Secretaries of State, War and Navy give careful consideration to this report, with a view to taking whatever joint action may be indicated.

(a) *Report of Byron Price to the President, November 9, 1945.*

[Excerpts]

This report is submitted in response to your request of August 30 that I survey "the general subject of relations between the American Forces of Occupation and the German people" so that you might have the benefit of a wholly detached view of this highly important situation.

. . . .

Considering all of the difficulties, which few people in this country are in a position to understand, General Eisenhower and his staff have done better than a good job governing the German population of the American Zone. Mistakes have been made and some confusions persist, but in general relations with the mass of Germans are on a sound basis. In so large and complex an operation no one should ask for perfect results in so short a time unless he expects miracles.

. . . .

It may possibly be helpful to you in meeting the responsibility if I state the principal problems bluntly, as I see them.

[1] *Ibid.*, p. 937.   [2] *Ibid.*, p. 885.

The entire basic structure of Military Government in Germany, including the Potsdam Declaration, should be reexamined in the light of experience and new conditions.

The United States must decide whether we mean to finish the job competently, and provide the tools, the determination and the funds requisite to that purpose, or withdraw.

We must decide whether we are going to permit starvation, with attendant epidemics and disorders, in the American Zone, or ship the food to prevent it.

We must decide whether obstructions raised by the French Government, which have deadlocked the four-power Control Council at Berlin, are to be permitted to defeat the underlying purposes of Allied policy.

We have reached the stage where we must determine much more specifically what we are going to do about minor hirelings of the Nazi Party and its satellite agencies, and how far we are going in destroying the industrial structure of Germany.

Not of least importance, it must be decided how fast and how far the Government is to go in changing from military to civilian control in Germany. Really competent civilian administrative personnel and advice must be provided from within the present governmental establishment at Washington if any such changeover is to have a chance of succeeding.

The urgency of these decisions is deepened not only by the continuing four-power deadlock at Berlin, but by the approach of winter. The next few months will be the critical months. They will determine whether the American Government, in its first large-scale attempt at governing a conquered people, is to succeed, or fail, or abandon the effort.

. . . .

Despite these and other handicaps, order and comparative tranquillity have been reestablished within six months throughout an American Zone having 18,000,000 inhabitants, so that the present crime rate actually is lower than in the United States. Demilitarization has been largely achieved. Nazism has been completely uprooted from the government service, and to a large degree from private industry. Dismantling of industrial plants not needed for peacetime German economy has begun. Firm ceilings have been put on prices and wages to cope with a still-dangerous trend toward inflation. Transportation and communications are being revived within limits, and the food control program is working as well as possible under the circumstances.

Elementary schools have been reopened throughout the entire Zone, and provided with new textbooks free of Nazi propaganda. A few seminaries and professional colleges also are opening, but 80 percent of the experienced teachers were Nazis, and a shortage of qualified substitutes leaves many gaps in the reconstituted educational system. At the end of October a score of newspapers and several magazines were being published in the Zone, most of them by Germans under license and the remainder by the Army. Radio broadcasting had been restored, and a considerable number of theaters and concert halls licensed; but slow progress had been made in the reopening of motion picture theaters.

A comprehensive public health program had been inaugurated to guard against epidemics. Newly-organized political parties and labor unions were giving German citizens actual experience in the ways of democracy.

. . . .

Notwithstanding the punishments Germans now suffer, and those still before them, there is no apparent realization of collective guilt for the unspeakable crimes committed by the German nation or for the unforgivable anguish and suffering spread by Germany throughout the world. One young German, who professed only hatred for Nazism, referred to Germany repeatedly in conversation as having been "drawn into the war". Thousands of beautiful and essential highway and railway bridges throughout Germany were demolished by the German Army in retreat; but German blame for that destruction is very often directed against the Allies. Intelligence reports indicate clearly that all of our propaganda effort to instill a sense of collective German guilt has fallen flat.

Similarly, our efforts to kindle democratic aspirations have produced but indifferent results. Few Germans understand the language of democracy, and such terms as "home rule" and "collective bargaining" confuse great numbers of the population and leave them skeptical. There is widespread and apparently genuine questioning of any political system where more than one name appears on the election ballot. Doubtless many are trying to understand, even if they fail to do so. Political meetings are often well attended, but principally by the older Germans. In at least one case, where several thousands were present, less than one percent were under 25 years of age. The field that should be most fertile for the development of political initiative and social independence thus appears actually the most sterile. The Hitler Youth has been disbanded as an organization but groups of its former members have made themselves a major problem of the occupation.

The German's traditional aversion to thinking for himself is not the only handicap to the full development of political activity. Many Germans ask why, if we really believe in self-government, we bar from the list of candidates all Nazis, although they not infrequently are the strongest leaders in the community. The answer is well understood by Americans, but not by Germans. Many others, seeing some 80,000 Nazi Party members behind prison bars in the American Zone alone, are chary of ever aligning themselves hereafter with any political party whatever. And the greatest drawback of all is the inescapable fact that the average German today is too busy trying merely to exist to find time for politics. Possibly some of these barriers may be removed once the German communities have had the actual experience of voting in the local elections which are to begin immediately after the first of the year.

. . . .

German survival has been also the expressed desire of Allied statesmen. Since the German surrender this purpose has been reiterated in the Potsdam Declaration, which provides that Germany is to be treated as a single economic unit, and allowed to have sufficient resources to "subsist without external assistance." I understand these pronouncements to represent, not an expression of sympathy or pity for a people who have outraged every law of decency and civilization, but a practical recognition that if Germany were to become an economic void, or the seat of starvation, epidemic and revolution, she would remain a menace to the peace and prosperity of the entire world.

Because I know it is your desire to safeguard that policy during the critical months immediately ahead, I submit for your consideration the following suggestions to help maintain sound relations between Military Government in Germany and the German people:

1. The necessity for breaking the present deadlock in the Control Council at Berlin is so important that use of the full force and prestige of American diplomatic power to that end is fully warranted.

Repeated attempts have been made to set up common policies so that the German railways, the German postal service and other essential facilities could be operated as integral national systems. All of these attempts have failed, due almost entirely to the rigid opposition of the French.

As a result of the French attitude, Germany is not being treated as an economic unit. Instead what is happening amounts, to speak plainly, to the economic dismemberment of Germany. This is a reversal of basic objectives and, I believe, a certain step toward future international friction.

If France is really bent on the dismemberment of Germany, as her acts indicate, she should be made to acknowledge that policy before the world and not permitted to hide behind the opposite pronouncements of the Potsdam Declaration. Our own policies should then be reexamined accordingly.

2. The proposed change-over of Military Government from Army to Civilian Control will be advantageous only if the very highest type of civilian administrators can be assigned to Germany. Second-raters not only would fail, but would involve this Government in untold new difficulty.

As individuals and executives, the Army officers now in charge of Military Government are a highly capable group of men. The only point in making a change would be to rid Military Government of the complicated Army forms and procedures, which were created for a vastly different purpose and are not sufficiently pliable to be adaptable to civil affairs. It is not the men in charge, but "the Army system," with its necessary devotion to rank, channelization and precise regimentation, which does not fit the needs of the situation.

In my opinion no change to top Civilian Control should take place earlier than June 1, 1946, the date originally recommended by General Eisenhower. The intervening time is none too long to permit a sufficient number of civilian replacements to be assembled and given the requisite training and experience on the ground in Germany.

Intensive planning should begin at once. Steps should be taken to remove any existing barriers to installation of a Civilian Governor or

High Commissioner, whether such barriers exist in international agreements or in legislative or budgetary restrictions.

It is probable that the new civilian officials will have to be recruited largely from among experienced specialists already in the Government Service in this country. Those chosen to head departments in the Military Government should have rank and pay comparable to Undersecretaries in Washington; and it should be the definite responsibility of every Cabinet Member and Agency Head to interest himself in the problem, to comb the specialized personnel of his branch of Government, and to see that fully-qualified officials, not cast-offs, are provided. To facilitate the handling of diplomatic aspects, one Assistant Secretary of State might well be designated to supervise all communications relating to Military Government in the occupied areas abroad.

Substitution of civilian personnel in Germany should have limits. I suggest that some Military Government officials, such as those in charge of public safety and some of those in the lowest rank, in direct touch with the German people locally, should remain in uniform.

Selection of the new civilian chief of Military Government must be made by the President with great care if the experiment is to succeed. The appointment should under no circumstances have partisan political implications. An ideal choice would be an army officer of proven judgment and administrative ability, with a known military background in the European theater during this war, who would be willing to serve in a civilian capacity and administer according to civilian formulas.

Special efforts should be made also to retain the services of as many as possible of the officers trained in Military Government and now serving there. In these ranks are many highly valuable men.

3. The highest-level instructions issued to Military Government from Washington are in need of revision in the light of experience.

The present basic instrument of Military Government is a 72-page directive from the Joint Chiefs of Staff in Washington (JCS 1067), together with various annexes and amendments. It was drafted originally in the Pentagon Building in the first months of 1945, long before anyone knew when the victory would come or what form it would take.

Yet the detailed provisions of this imposing document still fall with untold force upon General Eisenhower's officers, now long experienced in the actual business of dealing with the Germans.

The whole collection of orders and instructions could profitably be rewritten into a few hundred words of general principles.

4. The food situation in Germany still merits urgent attention.

My understanding is that present plans contemplate a basic ration of 1550 calories and that proposals for an increase have been rejected in Washington.

I know of no competent medical authority who would regard a ration of 1550 calories as satisfactory, or who considers that present rationing in Germany is adequate for a people who are expected to work, and have no heat at home and no way to reach their places of employment except by walking. The medical evidence is clear that deficiencies of food already are resulting in widespread dangerous loss of weight and in alarming reaction to disease.

If starvation comes, as now seems likely, epidemics and rioting will not be far behind. The approved medical ration to prevent starvation is 2000 calories, and there is no likelihood that such a ration would permit the bombed-out, freezing, pedestrian Germans to live anything like as well as the European average. To provide such a ration would require additional food exports from the United States, on credit.

A ration adequate to prevent starvation would not mean being soft with the German people. It would represent protection to our own occupation troops against disease and disorder, and decency toward our Allies of Western Europe, themselves undernourished and easily susceptible to disease.

5. No one who remembers the criminal record of Nazism will quarrel with the policy of stamping out the Nazi Party utterly and removing all its members from places of influence or profit in German life.

But Germany will not be rebuilt to peaceful and decent dimensions in a day. Too much haste in the inauguration of sweeping reform has never failed to lead to confusion and error, if not to reaction.

De-Nazification of private industry has gone further and faster in the American Zone than in any other part of Germany. The railroads, which are needed to deliver essential supplies, the communications system and other essential facilities have been handicapped greatly by abrupt removal of Nazis from key positions and installation of inexperienced substitutes.

During this initial period when the clock is being started again, and particularly during the critical months of the coming winter, Military Government should be given greater leeway to decide locally in Germany, when and how de-Nazification in essential services can best be effected.

6. The supervision of the German press, radio, motion pictures and other media of public information and entertainment has been generally well handled, but some changes seem desirable in view of changing conditions.

Many Germans regard the newspapers published under American direction as keyed to so lofty a pitch of democratic idealism as to be understandable to the masses. It is desirable that the acts of Military Government be presented and interpreted so far as possible from the viewpoint of ultimate benefit to the ordinary German, rather than from the viewpoint of Military Government itself.

The present practice of "screening" spot information coming into Germany from the outside world should be discontinued. Such censorship only defeats its own purpose, since the information is currently available to the German people from British or other nearby radio stations. Suppression in the German press or on the German radio raises the question how our policy differs from that of Goebbels.

In general, the German press and radio should have freedom of opinion also, but the publication of anti-democratic propaganda should not be permitted.

Our own propaganda needs to be given an increasingly positive character, in contrast to the long-continued attempt to impress the Germans of their collective guilt, which from now on will do more harm than good. A story circulates among the Germans to the effect that one radio listener who followed the Allied broadcasts throughout the war because they gave him hope, has now put away his receiver because he hears only condemnation and abuse.

We can win converts to democracy only if we again find a way of instilling hope — hope that Germany again can rise from the dust and become a respected nation if she will devote herself to peace and tolerance, and decent ways of life.

It is most desirable that a better arrangement be worked out to eliminate bottlenecks and assure an adequate supply of American motion picture films for the American Zone.

More books in tune with democratic concepts ought to be available to German booksellers, possibly from stock prepared by the Provost Marshal General for use in German prisoner of war camps in this country.

I am convinced that better results would be attained in all of these matters if the Information Control branch, which supervises publications, broadcasting and theaters, and which certainly is a highly important arm of military government, were made an integral part of the Military Government establishment, instead of operating independently. I am informed that steps to effect such a change are now in process.

7. Thus far there is no evidence of an organized underground resistance in the American Zone, acts of hostility being largely confined to small-time local depredations. But caution cannot be relaxed.

The former Hitler Youth — young people of their teens — are potentially the most dangerous single element of the population. It may be hoped that the current effort to organize these crooked-minded children into non-military societies and clubs after the American fashion will help turn them away from idleness and subversion.

It must be remembered, however, that many natural ties bind the Hitler Youth to the millions of recently-discharged German soldiers, to criminal elements among displaced persons, and to the increasing company of Nazis-out-of-office.

The suffering sure to come with winter may be expected to bring into the open whatever threat of real disorder and rebellion may now lie buried beneath the surface.

This is the wrong time to permit General Eisenhower's armed forces in Germany to be decimated and robbed of military effectiveness by demobilization.

8. Every additional day's delay in bringing arrested Nazis to justice weakens the position of Military Government.

There is widespread surprise among Germans that even the highest Nazi officials, held at Nürnberg under international jurisdiction as war criminals, are still awaiting trial.

The Nürnberg trials are not, of course, the responsibility of the Army. However, an additional 80,000 lesser members of the Nazi Party are in prison at the instance of Military Government. Military authorities do not feel that these cases can be tried until dependable precedents have been set at Nürnberg.

Wherever the responsibility lies, the failure to set up adequate tribunals and dispose of pending charges more promptly does not improve relations with a German people who traditionally respect only firm and swift authority.

I have confined this memorandum to matters which I felt were so important that they should be brought to your personal attention. I submitted a number of suggestions on additional subjects directly to General Eisenhower and General Clay in Germany, and am also putting myself at the disposal of the responsible officials of the War Department.

(3) *Directive of the United States Military Governor for Germany (McNarney) on the Relationship between the Military and Civil Government in the United States Zone Subsequent to the Adoption of the* Land *Constitutions, Issued September 30, 1946.*[1]

1. U.S. policy requires that the German people be permitted increasingly to govern themselves. The elections held in the U.S. Zone in 1946, and the constitutions which have been adopted are implementations of this policy. The subsequent operation of both Civil and Military Governments will be based upon this objective.

2. *Adoption of Land Constitutions Will Change Civil-Military Government Relations.* The adoption of constitutions in the Laender of the U.S. Zone marks the beginning of a new period in the relationships between Military and Civil Government. All military and civil authorities must clearly understand those relationships.

3. *Specific Restrictions Which Will Continue to Be Imposed Upon Civil Governments.* While self-government is the object of U.S. Military Government policy, it must nevertheless be understood that there are certain restrictions which will continue to apply to the actions of all levels of civil government in the U.S. Zone. The basic occupation policies announced from time to time, as in the case of the Berlin Protocol and Secretary of State Byrnes' Stuttgart speech, will, of course, continue to be enforced by Military Government. Furthermore, the specific restrictions set forth below must be considered as superior to the authority of any German governmental agency, and to both statutory and constitutional law. Those restrictions are:

a. All international agreements regarding Germany which have been or may be concluded;

b. All present and future quadripartite policy decisions, laws and regulations;

c. All basic policy decisions of the U.S.-British Bipartite Board affecting the fields of central agencies;

d. The rights of an occupying power under international law to maintain an occupying force within the zone, to preserve peace and order, to reassume at any time full occupation powers in the event the purposes of the occupation are jeopardized;

[1] Office of Military Government for Germany (U.S.). *Constitutions of Bavaria, Hesse and Württemberg-Baden,* February 15, 1947, p. 3.

e. The specific occupation purposes of the U.S. Government which, in addition to those set forth above, shall consist of the following basic tenets:
  (1) *Democracy* — All levels of German government in the U.S. Zone must be democratic to the extent that:
    (*a*) All political power is recognized as originating with the people and subject to their control;
    (*b*) Those who exercise political power are obliged to regularly renew their mandates by frequent references of their programs and leadership to popular elections;
    (*c*) Popular elections are conducted under competitive conditions in which not less than two effectively competing political parties submit their programs and candidates for public review;
    (*d*) Political parties must be democratic in character and must be recognized as voluntary associations of citizens clearly distinguished from, rather than identified with, the instrumentalities of government;
    (*e*) The basic rights of the individual including free speech, freedom of religious preference, the rights of assembly, freedom of political association, and other equally basic rights of free men are recognized and guaranteed;
    (*f*) Control over the instrumentalities of public opinion, such as the radio and press, must be diffused and kept free from governmental domination;
    (*g*) The rule of law is recognized as the individual's greatest single protection against a capricious and willful expression of governmental power.
  (2) German governmental systems must provide for a judiciary independent of the legislative and executive arms in general and of the police activity in particular. U.S. policy does not demand the rigid separation of legislative and executive powers. It has no objection to the cabinet or parliamentary type of government in which the executive and legislative branches are inter-dependent. Where a governmental system does provide for a separation of the executive and legislative, there must be no provision which would enable the executive to rule without the approval and consent of the legislative branch.
  (3) *Intergovernmental Distribution of Powers* — German governmental structure shall be federal in character (Bundesstaat), and the constituent units thereof shall be States (Staaten not Laender). The functions of government shall be decentralized within that structure to the maximum degree consistent with the modern economic life. U.S. policy concerning the relationships between levels of government requires that:
    (*a*) All political power is recognized as originating with the people and subject to their control;
    (*b*) Power shall be granted by the people primarily to the States (Staaten), and subsequently only in specifically enumerated and limited instances to a federal government;

    (c) All other grants of governmental power by the people shall be made to the States;

    (d) All powers not granted by the people shall be reserved to the people;

    (e) A substantial number of functions shall be delegated by the States to the local governments. These should include all functions which may be effectively determined and administered by local governments;

    (f) Governmental powers may not be delegated to private or quasi-public economic bodies;

    (g) Pending the establishment of a federal government, the popularly responsible governments and Landtage of the States shall act as the people's agents for the conferring of powers requiring central execution upon such transitional federal or central body or bodies as may be agreed upon by civil government and military government, or as may be directed by the latter.

  (4) *Economic Unity* — Economic unity through the establishment of German central administrative agencies, particularly in trade, industry, food and agriculture, finance, transportation, and communications, is a controlling objective of our occupation. Pending quadripartite agreement for the establishment of such agencies, the U.S. Government offered to join with any one or two of the other occupying powers in the establishment of such administrative agencies to cover such zones as would accept. The administrative agencies now established for the British and U.S. Zones are an important step toward the economic unity agreed to by the occupying powers at Potsdam. Accordingly, the furtherance of their successful operations is a major policy of the U.S. occupation. When agreement is reached with either or both of the other powers for the establishment of German administrative agencies covering the wider areas involved, the implementation of such agreements will constitute a part of the fundamental policy of the U.S. occupation.

  f. All limitations upon governmental action which may be set out as specific qualifications to the approval of the State constitutions;

  g. Such proclamations, laws, enactments, orders, and instructions of U.S. occupation authorities as continue in force or shall hereafter be promulgated.

  4. *Subsequent Functions of Military Government Will Be Limited to:* Subsequent to the adoption of these constitutions, Military Government will obtain its objective by means of:

    a. Observation, inspection, reporting and advising;

    b. Disapproval of only such economic, social and political and governmental activity as it may find to clearly violate those objectives;

    c. Removal of public officials whose public activities are in violation of those objectives;

    d. The establishment of full Military Government controls in any area in the U.S. Zone where the objectives of the occupation as herein defined or provided for may be endangered;

e. Military Government courts;

f. Direct administration of such activities as demilitarization and reparations which cannot be assumed entirely by German civil governmental agencies but which are necessitated by international agreements, quadripartite action, or U.S. occupation policy.

5. Subsequent directives will implement the foregoing statements insofar as modifications or revisions in Military Government practices may be required.

6. The Land Directors of Military Government will advise the appropriate German officials of the content of this directive. It is desirable that the widest possible distribution of both civil and military authorities be given it. However, the directive will be considered a restricted document to be used for information of Military Government only until you are subsequently authorized to release it.

C. Japan

1. OCCUPATION AND CONTROL

For details on the surrender of Japan and the termination of the war, see this volume, p. 105.

The method adopted for the occupation of Japan differed markedly from that established in Germany, partially because the majority of troops which were used to defeat the Japanese were American. General Douglas MacArthur, designated as Supreme Commander of the Allied Powers, and referred to, with his headquarters, as SCAP, became the director of Allied occupation policy. As early as August 21, 1945, the United States had submitted to the Governments of China, Great Britain, and the Soviet Union a proposal for a Far Eastern Advisory Commission[1] to be composed of representatives of these powers plus France, Canada, Australia, India and the Philippine Commonwealth. Although the commission held meetings starting on October 30, 1945, the refusal of the Soviet Union to participate led to a compromise proposal adopted at the Moscow meeting of Foreign Ministers, December 12–26, 1945, by which there was established in Washington a Far Eastern Commission composed of representatives of the same powers as had made up the Far Eastern Advisory Commission, and in Tokyo an Allied council composed of SCAP as chairman with the representatives of the USSR, one from China, and one representing jointly Great Britain, Australia, New Zealand and India.[2] The first meeting of the Far Eastern Commission was held in Washington, D. C. on February 26, 1946.[3]

While the final form of international control of Japan was in the process of agreement, however, General MacArthur was actually in Japan and faced with immediate administrative and policy problems. His activities in this period were within the terms of reference of the United States Initial Post Surrender Policy for Japan,[4] a directive prepared by the State-War-Navy Coordinating Committee.[5] Under the terms of this document, together with subsequent directives issued by the Far Eastern Commission, SCAP set about a series of fundamental reforms in both the political and economic structure of Japan. It should be noted, however, that the Allied Council for Japan "has played no significant part in setting the course of the occupation" and the Far Eastern Commission,

---

[1] For text, see *Occupation of Japan, Policy and Progress,* Department of State Publication 2671, Far Eastern Series 17, p. 67.

[2] *Ibid.*, p. 6; for text of Moscow Agreement, see this volume, p. 275.

[3] *International Organization,* I, p. 177.

[4] For text, see this volume, p. 267.

[5] For details on SWNCC, see *ibid.*, p. 63.

although following an independent course "on some questions" has "for the most part formalized and internationalized existing United States policies."[1]

(1) *United States Initial Post-Surrender Policy for Japan, August 29, 1945.*[2]

Purpose of This Document

This document is a statement of general initial policy relating to Japan after surrender. It has been approved by the President and distributed to the Supreme Commander for the Allied Powers and to appropriate U. S. departments and agencies for their guidance. It does not deal with all matters relating to the occupation of Japan requiring policy determinations. Such matters as are not included or are not fully covered herein have been or will be dealt with separately.

Part I — Ultimate Objectives

The ultimate objectives of the United States in regard to Japan, to which policies in the initial period must conform, are:

(*a*) To insure that Japan will not again become a menace to the United States or to the peace and security of the world.

(*b*) To bring about the eventual establishment of a peaceful and responsible government which will respect the rights of other states and will support the objectives of the United States as reflected in the ideals and principles of the Charter of the United Nations. The United States desires that this government should conform as closely as may be to principles of democratic self-government but it is not the responsibility of the Allied Powers to impose upon Japan any form of government not supported by the freely expressed will of the people.

These objectives will be achieved by the following principal means:

(*a*) Japan's sovereignty will be limited to the islands of Honshu, Hokkaido, Kyushu, Shikoku and such minor outlying islands as may be determined, in accordance with the Cairo Declaration and other agreements to which the United States is or may be a party.

(*b*) Japan will be completely disarmed and demilitarized. The authority of the militarists and the influence of militarism will be totally eliminated from her political, economic, and social life. Institutions expressive of the spirit of militarism and aggression will be vigorously suppressed.

(*c*) The Japanese people shall be encouraged to develop a desire for individual liberties and respect for fundamental human rights, particularly the freedoms of religion, assembly, speech, and the press. They shall also be encouraged to form democratic and representative organizations.

(*d*) The Japanese people shall be afforded opportunity to develop for themselves an economy which will permit the peacetime requirements of the population to be met.

[1] Rosinger, Lawrence K. "The Occupation of Japan." *Foreign Policy Reports*, XXIII, No. 5 (May 15, 1947), p. 50.

[2] *Occupation of Japan, Policy and Progress*, cited above, p. 73; Department of State, *Bulletin*, XIII, p. 423.

Part II — Allied Authority

1. *Military Occupation*

There will be a military occupation of the Japanese home islands to carry into effect the surrender terms and further the achievement of the ultimate objectives stated above. The occupation shall have the character of an operation in behalf of the principal allied powers acting in the interests of the United Nations at war with Japan. For that reason, participation of the forces of other nations that have taken a leading part in the war against Japan will be welcomed and expected. The occupation forces will be under the command of a Supreme Commander designated by the United States.

Although every effort will be made, by consultation and by constitution of appropriate advisory bodies, to establish policies for the conduct of the occupation and the control of Japan which will satisfy the principal Allied powers, in the event of any differences of opinion among them, the policies of the United States will govern.

2. *Relationship to Japanese Government*

The authority of the Emperor and the Japanese Government will be subject to the Supreme Commander, who will possess all powers necessary to effectuate the surrender terms and to carry out the policies established for the conduct of the occupation and the control of Japan.

In view of the present character of Japanese society and the desire of the United States to attain its objectives with a minimum commitment of its forces and resources, the Supreme Commander will exercise his authority through Japanese governmental machinery and agencies, including the Emperor, to the extent that this satisfactorily furthers United States objectives. The Japanese Government will be permitted, under his instructions, to exercise the normal powers of government in matters of domestic administration. This policy, however, will be subject to the right and duty of the Supreme Commander to require changes in governmental machinery or personnel or to act directly if the Emperor or other Japanese authority does not satisfactorily meet the requirements of the Supreme Commander in effectuating the surrender terms. This policy, moreover, does not commit the Supreme Commander to support the Emperor or any other Japanese governmental authority in opposition to evolutionary changes looking toward the attainment of United States objectives. The policy is to use the existing form of Government in Japan, not to support it. Changes in the form of Government initiated by the Japanese people or government in the direction of modifying its feudal and authoritarian tendencies are to be permitted and favored. In the event that the effectuation of such changes involves the use of force by the Japanese people or government against persons opposed thereto, the Supreme Commander should intervene only where necessary to ensure the security of his forces and the attainment of all other objectives of the occupation.

3. *Publicity as to Policies*

The Japanese people, and the world at large, shall be kept fully informed of the objectives and policies of the occupation, and of progress made in their fulfilment.

Part III — Political

1. *Disarmament and Demilitarization*

Disarmament and demilitarization are the primary tasks of the military occupation and shall be carried out promptly and with determination. Every effort shall be made to bring home to the Japanese people the part played by the military and naval leaders, and those who collaborated with them, in bringing about the existing and future distress of the people.

Japan is not to have an army, navy, air force, secret police organization, or any civil aviation. Japan's ground, air and naval forces shall be disarmed and disbanded and the Japanese Imperial General Headquarters, the General Staff and all secret police organizations shall be dissolved. Military and naval matériel, military and naval vessels and military and naval installations, and military, naval and civilian aircraft shall be surrendered and shall be disposed of as required by the Supreme Commander.

High officials of the Japanese Imperial General Headquarters, and General Staff, other high military and naval officials of the Japanese Government, leaders of ultra-nationalist amd militarist organizations and other important exponents of militarism and aggression will be taken into custody and held for future disposition. Persons who have been active exponents of militarism and militant nationalism will be removed and excluded from public office and from any other position of public or substantial private responsibility. Ultra-nationalistic or militaristic social, political, professional and commercial societies and institutions will be dissolved and prohibited.

Militarism and ultra-nationalism, in doctrine and practice, including para-military training, shall be eliminated from the educational system. Former career military and naval officers, both commissioned and non-commissioned, and all other exponents of militarism and ultra-nationalism shall be excluded from supervisory and teaching positions.

2. *War Criminals*

Persons charged by the Supreme Commander or appropriate United Nations agencies with being war criminals, including those charged with having visited cruelties upon United Nations prisoners or other nationals, shall be arrested, tried and, if convicted, punished. Those wanted by another of the United Nations for offenses against its nationals, shall, if not wanted for trial or as witnesses or otherwise by the Supreme Commander, be turned over to the custody of such other nation.

3. *Encouragement of Desire for Individual Liberties and Democratic Processes*

Freedom of religious worship shall be proclaimed promptly on occupation. At the same time it should be made plain to the Japanese that ultra-nationalistic and militaristic organizations and movements will not be permitted to hide behind the cloak of religion.

The Japanese people shall be afforded opportunity and encouraged to become familiar with the history, institutions, culture, and the accomplishments of the United States and the other democracies. Association of personnel of the occupation forces with the Japanese population should be controlled, only to the extent necessary, to further the policies and objectives of the occupation.

Democratic political parties, with rights of assembly and public discussion, shall be encouraged, subject to the necessity for maintaining the security of the occupying forces.

Laws, decrees and regulations which establish discriminations on ground of race, nationality, creed or political opinion shall be abrogated; those which conflict with the objectives and policies outlined in this document shall be repealed, suspended or amended as required; and agencies charged specifically with their enforcement shall be abolished or appropriately modified. Persons unjustly confined by Japanese authority on political grounds shall be released. The judicial, legal and police systems shall be reformed as soon as practicable to conform to the policies set forth in Articles 1 and 3 of this Part III and thereafter shall be progressively influenced, to protect individual liberties and civil rights.

Part IV — Economic

1. *Economic Demilitarization*

The existing economic basis of Japanese military strength must be destroyed and not permitted to revive.

Therefore, a program will be enforced containing the following elements, among others; the immediate cessation and future prohibition of all goods designed for the equipment, maintenance, or use of any military force or establishment; the imposition of a ban upon any specialized facilities for the production or repair of implements of war, including naval vessels and all forms of aircraft; the institution of a system of inspection and control over selected elements in Japanese economic activity to prevent concealed or disguised military preparation; the elimination in Japan of those selected industries or branches of production whose chief value to Japan is in preparing for war; the prohibition of specialized research and instruction directed to the development of war-making power; and the limitation of the size and character of Japan's heavy industries to its future peaceful requirements, and restriction of Japanese merchant shipping to the extent required to accomplish the objectives of demilitarization.

The eventual disposition of those existing production facilities within Japan which are to be eliminated in accord with this program, as between conversion to other uses, transfer abroad, and scrapping will be determined after inventory. Pending decision, facilities readily convertible for civilian production should not be destroyed, except in emergency situations.

2. *Promotion of Democratic Forces*

Encouragement shall be given and favor shown to the development of organizations in labor, industry, and agriculture, organized on a democratic basis. Policies shall be favored which permit a wide distribution of income and of the ownership of the means of production and trade.

Those forms of economic activity, organization and leadership shall be favored that are deemed likely to strengthen the peaceful disposition of the Japanese people, and to make it difficult to command or direct economic activity in support of military ends.

To this end it shall be the policy of the Supreme Commander:

(a) To prohibit the retention in or selection for places of importance in the economic field of individuals who do not direct future Japanese economic effort solely towards peaceful ends; and

(b) To favor a program for the dissolution of the large industrial and banking combinations which have exercised control of a great part of Japan's trade and industry.

3. *Resumption of Peaceful Economic Activity*

The policies of Japan have brought down upon the people great economic destruction and confronted them with the prospect of economic difficulty and suffering. The plight of Japan is the direct outcome of its own behavior, and the Allies will not undertake the burden of repairing the damage. It can be repaired only if the Japanese people renounce all military aims and apply themselves diligently and with single purpose to the ways of peaceful living. It will be necessary for them to undertake physical reconstruction, deeply to reform the nature and direction of their economic activities and institutions, and to find useful employment for their people along lines adapted to and devoted to peace. The Allies have no intention of imposing conditions which would prevent the accomplishment of these tasks in due time.

Japan will be expected to provide goods and services to meet the needs of the occupying forces to the extent that this can be effected without causing starvation, widespread disease and acute physical distress.

The Japanese authorities will be expected, and if necessary directed, to maintain, develop and enforce programs that serve the following purposes:

(a) To avoid acute economic distress.

(b) To assure just and impartial distribution of available supplies.

(c) To meet the requirements for reparations deliveries agreed upon by the Allied Governments.

(d) To facilitate the restoration of Japanese economy so that the reasonable peaceful requirements of the population can be satisfied.

In this connection, the Japanese authorities on their own responsibility shall be permitted to establish and administer controls over economic activities, including essential national public services, finance, banking, and production and distribution of essential commodities, subject to the approval and review of the Supreme Commander in order to assure their conformity with the objectives of the occupation.

4. *Reparations and Restitution*

REPARATIONS

Reparations for Japanese aggression shall be made:

(a) Through the transfer — as may be determined by the appropriate Allied authorities — of Japanese property located outside of the territories to be retained by Japan.

(b) Through the transfer of such goods or existing capital equipment and facilities as are not necessary for a peaceful Japanese economy or the supplying of the occupying forces. Exports other than those directed to be shipped on reparation account or as restitution may be made only to those recipients who agree to provide necessary imports in exchange or agree to pay for such exports in foreign exchange. No form of reparation shall be exacted which will interfere with or prejudice the program for Japan's demilitarization.

RESTITUTION

Full and prompt restitution will be required of all identifiable looted property.

5. *Fiscal, Monetary, and Banking Policies*

The Japanese authorities will remain responsible for the management and direction of the domestic fiscal, monetary, and credit policies subject to the approval and review of the Supreme Commander.

6. *International Trade and Financial Relations*

Japan shall be permitted eventually to resume normal trade relations with the rest of the world. During occupation and under suitable controls, Japan will be permitted to purchase from foreign countries raw materials and other goods that it may need for peaceful purposes, and to export goods to pay for approved imports.

Control is to be maintained over all imports and exports of goods, and foreign exchange and financial transactions. Both the policies followed in the exercise of these controls and their actual administration shall be subject to the approval and supervision of the Supreme Commander in order to make sure that they are not contrary to the policies of the occupying authorities, and in particular that all foreign purchasing power that Japan may acquire is utilized only for essential needs.

7. *Japanese Property Located Abroad*

Existing Japanese external assets and existing Japanese assets located in territories detached from Japan under the terms of surrender, including assets owned in whole or part by the Imperial Household and Government, shall be revealed to the occupying authorities and held for disposition according to the decision of the Allied authorities.

8. Equality of Opportunity for Foreign Enterprise within Japan

The Japanese authorities shall not give, or permit any Japanese business organization to give, exclusive or preferential opportunity or terms to the enterprise of any foreign country, or cede to such enterprise control of any important branch of economic activity.

9. Imperial Household Property

Imperial Household property shall not be exempted from any action necessary to carry out the objectives of the occupation.

(2) Authority of General MacArthur as Supreme Commander for Allied Powers, September 6, 1945.[1]

The text of a message transmitted on September 6 through the Joint Chiefs of Staff to General MacArthur follows. It was prepared jointly by the Department of State, the War Department, and the Navy Department and approved by the President on September 6. The message is a statement clarifying the authority which General MacArthur is to exercise in his position as Supreme Commander for the Allied powers.

1. The authority of the Emperor and the Japanese Government to rule the State is subordinate to you as Supreme Commander for the Allied powers. You will exercise your authority as you deem proper to carry out your mission. Our relations with Japan do not rest on a contractual basis, but on an unconditional surrender. Since your authority is supreme, you will not entertain any question on the part of the Japanese as to its scope.

2. Control of Japan shall be exercised through the Japanese Government to the extent that such an arrangement produces satisfactory results. This does not prejudice your right to act directly if required. You may enforce the orders issued by you by the employment of such measures as you deem necessary, including the use of force.

3. The statement of intentions contained in the Potsdam Declaration will be given full effect. It will not be given effect, however, because we consider ourselves bound in a contractual relationship with Japan as a result of that document. It will be respected and given effect because the Potsdam Declaration forms a part of our policy stated in good faith with relation to Japan and with relation to peace and security in the Far East.

(3) Statement of the Supreme Commander for Allied Powers (MacArthur) on Occupation Policy, September 9, 1945.[2]

At the time of the Japanese capitulation, the plans for the invasion of the Japanese homeland were in their final stages. Included in those plans were provisions for military government. It is obvious that this was necessary because an invasion destroys, impairs or sweeps before it organized government.

The plans for the occupation of Japan in the event of capitulations were based on the unconditional surrender provision included in the Potsdam Declaration.

---

[1] *Occupation of Japan, Policy and Progress*, cited above, p. 88.
[2] *New York Times*, September 10, 1945.

The Allied note to the Swiss Government signed by Secretary of State James F. Byrnes on August 11, 1945 contains the following:

With regards to the Japanese Government message accepting the terms of the Potsdam Proclamation, but containing the statement "with the understanding that said declaration does not comprise any demand which prejudices the prerogatives of His Majesty as sovereign ruler," our position is as follows: From the moment of surrender, the authority of the Emperor and of the Japanese Government to rule the state shall be subject to the Supreme Commander for the Allied Powers, who will take such steps as he deems proper to effectuate the surrender terms.

This note also includes the following:

The ultimate form of government of Japan shall, in accordance with the Potsdam Declaration, be established by the freely established will of the Japanese people. The armed forces of the Allied powers will remain in Japan until the purposes set forth in the Potsdam Declaration are achieved.

This note was acceptable to the Japanese Government, and since the date of surrender, the authority of the Emperor and the Japanese Government to rule the State has been subject to the Supreme Commander for the Allied Powers. The Japanese Government is apparently making every effort to execute the instructions of the surrender document, of General Order No. 1 and of General Order No. 2. Therefore, at the present time, the Supreme Commander for the Allied Powers is controlling the Government of Japan along the following lines;

I

The instrument of surrender is being enforced.

II

(A) The Supreme Commander for the Allied Powers will issue all necessary instructions to the Japanese Emperor or to the Imperial Government, and every opportunity will be given the Government and the Japanese people to carry out such instructions without further compulsion. If necessary, however, the Supreme Commander for the Allied Powers will issue appropriate orders to the Army and corps commanders indicating action to be taken by them to secure the obedience by the agencies of the Imperial Government or by the Japanese people within the areas of their commands. In other words, the occupation forces will act principally as an agency upon which the Supreme Commander for the Allied Powers may call, if necessary, to secure compliance with his instructions to the Japanese Imperial Government.

(B) The existing Japanese economy will be controlled only to the extent necessary to achieve the objectives of the United Nations.

(C) The civilian population will be treated by the occupying forces in such a way as to develop respect for and confidence in the United Nations and their representatives and encourage cooperation in the accomplishment of desired objectives. They will be required to obey all laws, proclamations, orders and regulations issued by the Japanese Imperial Government pursuant to the directives of the Supreme Commander for the Allied Powers. They will be completely free from all unwarranted interference with their individual liberty and property rights.

III

Among the post-war objectives of the United Nations are:

(A) Abolition of militarism and militant nationalism in Japan.

(B) The encouragement, subject to the necessity for maintaining military security, of liberal tendencies and processes such as the freedom of religion, press, speech and assembly.

(C) Creation of conditions that will insure that Japan will not again become a menace to the peace and security of the world, and that will permit the eventual emergence of a Government that will respect the rights of other nations and Japan's international obligations.

(4) *Agreement of Foreign Ministers on Establishing the Far Eastern Commission and the Allied Council for Japan, Moscow, December 27, 1945.*[1]

FAR EASTERN COMMISSION AND ALLIED COUNCIL FOR JAPAN

A. Far Eastern Commission

Agreement was reached, with the concurrence of China, for the establishment of a Far Eastern Commission to take the place of the Far Eastern Advisory Commission. The Terms of Reference for the Far Eastern Commission are as follows:

I. Establishment of the Commission

A Far Eastern Commission is hereby established composed of the representatives of the Union of Soviet Socialist Republics, United Kingdom, United States, China, France, the Netherlands, Canada, Australia, New Zealand, India, and the Philippine Commonwealth.

II. Functions

A. The functions of the Far Eastern Commission shall be:

1. To formulate the policies, principles, and standards in conformity with which the fulfillment by Japan of its obligations under the Terms of Surrender may be accomplished.

2. To review, on the request of any member, any directive issued to the Supreme Commander for the Allied Powers or any action taken by the Supreme Commander involving policy decisions within the jurisdiction of the Commission.

3. To consider such other matters as may be assigned to it by agreement among the participating Governments reached in accordance with the voting procedure provided for in Article V-2 hereunder.

[1] *Occupation of Japan, Policy and Progress,* cited above, p. 69.

B. The Commission shall not make recommendations with regard to the conduct of military operations nor with regard to territorial adjustments.

C. The Commission in its activities will proceed from the fact that there has been formed an Allied Council for Japan and will respect existing control machinery in Japan, including the chain of command from the United States Government to the Supreme Commander and the Supreme Commander's command of occupation forces.

III. Functions of the United States Government

1. The United States Government shall prepare directives in accordance with policy decisions of the Commission and shall transmit them to the Supreme Commander through the appropriate United States Government agency. The Supreme Commander shall be charged with the implementation of the directives which express the policy decisions of the Commission.

2. If the Commission decides that any directive or action reviewed in accordance with Article II–A–2 should be modified, its decision shall be regarded as a policy decision.

3. The United States Government may issue interim directives to the Supreme Commander pending action by the Commission whenever urgent matters arise not covered by policies already formulated by the Commission; provided that any directives dealing with fundamental changes in the Japanese constitutional structure or in the regime of control, or dealing with a change in the Japanese Government as a whole will be issued only following consultation and following the attainment of agreement in the Far Eastern Commission.

4. All directives issued shall be filed with the Commission.

IV. Other Methods of Consultation

The establishment of the Commission shall not preclude the use of other methods of consultation on Far Eastern issues by the participating Governments.

V. Composition

1. The Far Eastern Commission shall consist of one representative of each of the States party to this agreement. The membership of the Commission may be increased by agreement among the participating Powers as conditions warrant by the addition of representatives of other United Nations in the Far East or having territories therein. The Commission shall provide for full and adequate consultations, as occasion may require, with representatives of the United Nations not members of the Commission in regard to matters before the Commission which are of particular concern to such nations.

2. The Commission may take action by less than unanimous vote provided that action shall have the concurrence of at least a majority of all the representatives including the representatives of the four following

Powers: United States, United Kingdom, Union of Soviet Socialist Republics and China.

VI. *Location and Organization*

1. The Far Eastern Commission shall have its headquarters in Washington. It may meet at other places as occasion requires, including Tokyo, if and when it deems it desirable to do so. It may make such arrangements through the Chairman as may be practicable for consultation with the Supreme Commander for the Allied Powers.

2. Each representative on the Commission may be accompanied by an appropriate staff comprising both civilian and military representation.

3. The Commission shall organize its secretariat, appoint such committees as may be deemed advisable, and otherwise perfect its organization and procedure.

VII. *Termination*

The Far Eastern Commission shall cease to function when a decision to that effect is taken by the concurrence of at least a majority of all the representatives including the representatives of the four following Powers: United States, United Kingdom, Union of Soviet Socialist Republics and China. Prior to the termination of its functions the Commission shall transfer to any interim or permanent security organization of which the participating governments are members those functions which may appropriately be transferred.

It was agreed that the Government of the United States on behalf of the four Powers should present the Terms of Reference to the other Governments specified in Article I and invite them to participate in the Commission on the revised basis.

B. ALLIED COUNCIL FOR JAPAN

The following agreement was also reached, with the concurrence of China, for the establishment of an Allied Council for Japan:

1. There shall be established an Allied Council with its seat in Tokyo under the chairmanship of the Supreme Commander for the Allied Powers (or his Deputy) for the purpose of consulting with and advising the Supreme Commander in regard to the implementation of the Terms of Surrender, the occupation and control of Japan, and of directives supplementary thereto; and for the purpose of exercising the control authority herein granted.

2. The membership of the Allied Council shall consist of the Supreme Commander (or his Deputy) who shall be Chairman and United States member; a Union of Soviet Socialist Republics member; a Chinese member; and a member representing jointly the United Kingdom, Australia, New Zealand, and India.

3. Each member shall be entitled to have an appropriate staff consisting of military and civilian advisers.

4. The Allied Council shall meet not less often than once every two weeks.

5. The Supreme Commander shall issue all orders for the implementation of the Terms of Surrender, the occupation and control of Japan, and directives supplementary thereto. In all cases action will be carried out under and through the Supreme Commander who is the sole executive authority for the Allied Powers in Japan. He will consult and advise with the Council in advance of the issuance of orders on matters of substance, the exigencies of the situation permitting. His decisions upon these matters shall be controlling.

6. If, regarding the implementation of policy decisions of the Far Eastern Commission on questions concerning a change in the regime of control, fundamental changes in the Japanese constitutional structure, and a change in the Japanese Government as a whole, a member of the Council disagrees with the Supreme Commander (or his Deputy), the Supreme Commander will withhold the issuance of orders on these questions pending agreement thereon in the Far Eastern Commission.

7. In cases of necessity the Supreme Commander may take decisions concerning the change of individual Ministers of the Japanese Government, or concerning the filling of vacancies created by the resignation of individual cabinet members, after appropriate preliminary consultation with the representatives of the other Allied Powers on the Allied Council.

(5) *Report of the Supreme Commander for Allied Powers (MacArthur) on the First Year of Occupation of Japan, August 29, 1946.*[1]

First and above all else, the gigantic military machine of the Japanese Empire has been completely destroyed. Its fighting power had been temporarily nullified in the war, but a tremendous military organization, manned by millions, still remained at the time of the surrender. Its liquidation required the disarming, demobilization and disposition of approximately 4,000,000 organized and armed men in the home islands and 2,500,000 abroad. In addition, it was necessary to retrieve from overseas approximately 2,000,000 civilians and to repatriate to their homelands from Japan 1,000,000 Allied nationals.

Within the early weeks of the occupation, Japanese soldiers in the home islands were disbanded and returned to peaceful pursuits. Today, after a single year, the remnants of the overseas forces, scattered over thousands of miles, are streaming home and the work of repatriation is drawing to a close. Nine million have been processed in this time. For magnitude, thoroughness, speed and precision, this has constituted a demobilization and repatriation which has no precedent in history.

To insure further the destruction of Japan's war making power, thousands of military and civil aircraft and millions of weapons of various calibers, with vast quantities of ammunition, have been seized and disposed of; remnants of the Japanese navy have been taken over and are being destroyed or held for Allied division; and every element of Japanese industry utilized for or capable of adjustment to the making of implements of war has been either destroyed or brought under our complete control. Thus from a material standpoint also, Japan's war making power and potential is ended.

[1] Department of State, *Bulletin*, XV, p. 460.

Rapid and effective strides have been made in reshaping the Japanese Government to conform to the principles inherent in a democratic state so that the people might readjust their lives to compose a truly democratic society. A new constitution has been evolved after many months of widespread public interest and unrestricted debate which, submitted to the people by the Emperor and Government of Japan, is now in the process of democratic legislative action toward adoption of amendment. Designed effectively to curb abuse of power by individual, class or government, it places sovereignty squarely in the hands of the people upon whom it bestows the full measure of human freedom. The masses of Japan are no longer regimented — no longer enslaved. The Japanese citizen no longer cringes in the presence of police or other public authority; his home has become his castle, free from unwarranted intrusion, observation or violence; he registers his opinion on public issues, uncontrolled except by his own conscience; he enjoys the right of assembly and petition; he worships as he chooses, in accordance with his individual religious faith; he enjoys the untrammeled right, individually or collectively with his fellow workers, to demand correction of unjust labor practices and conditions; and Japanese children, 18,000,000 of whom are presently enrolled, enjoy the right to liberal and free education in 40,000 public schools, now open and dedicated to the study of the arts and sciences and the historical truth and the development of enlightened thought.

Electoral discrimination has been removed, and the electoral base expanded by reducing the age limit from 25 years to 19 and enfranchising the women of Japan. The general election held on April 10, 1946 was a vivid demonstration of democracy on the march. A far greater number of those eligible to vote participated in this election than in any other election in Japanese history. The women of Japan took their newly gained franchise as a serious obligation, sharply broke from their traditional retirement within the family circle, and elected 39 women members of the house of representatives, an accomplishment without precedent in political history.

Reform has been instituted in every element of the governmental structure and in every phase of government administrative procedure, to root out existing evils of entrenched bureaucracy which inevitably lead to totalitarian controls. Those who in past preached the doctrine of militarism, expansionism and intense nationalism, and shaped the policies responsible for Japan's collapse, have been purged and barred from governmental service to afford the people a new leadership.

To dislodge the economic hold which certain vested interests have long had over Japanese economy, the corporate and personal resources of the 14 major families, including the four big Zaibatsu groups, with approximately 1,200 firms linked in this system, are being liquidated. All principal officers and influential members of this industrial empire are being ousted. Thus the economic stranglehold upon the people in restriction of free enterprise, made possible by close alliance between Government and concentrated wealth, is being inexorably broken.

Striking at the roots of feudalism, an agrarian reform program, now under way, will enable about 2,000,000 tenant farmers of Japan to purchase the lands they now work. Shaped to break down the large land holdings into 2½- to 10-acre parcels, with their disposal provided for under conditions which will permit their ready acquisition, this program will correct one of the notorious evils which has long plagued individual economy and held in serfdom the underprivileged agricultural workers of Japan.

The task is by no means complete, but a decisive advance toward the achievement of our major objectives has been made.

2. JAPANESE GENERAL ELECTION

The decision of SCAP to hold a general election in Japan brought forth a series of questions from the Far Eastern Commission as to the desirability of acting so quickly after surrender.

(1) *Directive of the Supreme Commander for Allied Powers (MacArthur) for General Elections in Japan, January 12, 1946.*[1]

1. You are hereby authorized to hold a general election of members of the House of Representatives, fixing the date of election not earlier than 15 March 1946.

2. It is of greatest importance that every step possible be taken looking toward a free and untrammelled expression of the people's will in this election. To such end you will give fullest publicity to the penal provisions of the law, and will take such steps as may be necessary to ensure their vigorous enforcement, to preserve inviolate the secrecy of the ballot, and to further such other safeguards as may from time to time be communicated to you by the Supreme Commander.

(2) *Exchange of Correspondence between the Far Eastern Commission and the Supreme Commander for Allied Powers (MacArthur).*[2]

(a) *Note from the Far Eastern Commission to the Supreme Commander for Allied Powers, March 21, 1946.*

The Far Eastern Commission has given some short preliminary and tentative consideration to the position that may arise after the forthcoming Japanese elections. Having regard to the established position throughout the country of the more reactionary political parties, and to the very short period available to the parties of a more liberal tendency to circulate their views and organize support, the members of the Commission are not without the apprehension that the holding of the election at such an early date may well give a decisive advantage to the reactionary parties and thus create the embarrassment of a Japanese Government elected in terms of the Potsdam Declaration "in accordance with the freely expressed will of the Japanese people," which might not, in fact, truly represent their wishes, and with which it might prove impossible for the Supreme Command to cooperate. From another point

---

[1] *Occupation of Japan, Policy and Progress*, cited above, p. 136. [2] *Ibid.*

of view, the Commission feels the difficulty of expecting a fully instructed, intelligent and authoritative expression of the views of the Japanese people on their political future during this uncertain period when the whole of the future economic structure of Japan is still in doubt, and when a proportion of the electorate must necessarily be disfranchised owing to absence. Finally, the issue of the draft Constitution, of which you have approved, makes the Constitution at this late stage an election issue, upon which there can be little time for consideration by the Japanese people, and at the same time may give an undue political advantage to the political party preferring this Constitution.

The Far Eastern Commission would be most grateful if the Supreme Commander could let them have a very early expression of his views generally, and in particular on the following questions:

1. Does the Supreme Commander share the apprehensions expressed above?

2. If so, would he consider it possible and desirable to require a further postponement of the Japanese elections, and in that case, for what period?

3. If the Supreme Commander should not consider a further postponement desirable at this late date, would he express his views on the desirability, as an alternative, of publicly prescribing that the forthcoming election will be regarded as a test of the ability of Japan to produce a responsible and democratic government in full accordance with the wishes of the people and that further elections will be held at a later date?

(b) *Note from the Supreme Commander for Allied Powers to the Far Eastern Commission, March 29, 1946.*

The basis of occupational policy is the utilization of the Japanese Government to the fullest extent, under SCAP supervision and control. This is only possible through a functioning legislative body to enact new laws required to implement SCAP directives and to provide for routine governmental business. The alternative is government by Imperial Edict which denies to the Japanese People the right to participate in their own domestic affairs. Such emphasis upon the power of the Emperor would obviously be both undemocratic and unwise and would negative the basic principles envisaged at Potsdam, which we have proclaimed and are meticulously following. The present Diet is completely unsatisfactory because of its war attaint and its unrepresentative character, having been elected in 1942 under Tojo's control. It is imperative that a more representative body be organized at the earliest possible date. The urgent requirements of the present situation demand an expression of popular will. The results of the election will serve to define more clearly the political picture, to clarify political issues and political parties and to indicate the nature and trend of popular opinion. It will also provide for popular participation in the determination of major questions. The suffrage base has been greatly broadened through the lowering of the minimum age requirement and the removal of restrictions on sex.

By the application of the purge directive of January 4th 90 per centum of the members of the present Diet, as well as many other persons holding high government office in the war administration, have been removed from government service and barred from public office or activity as officers of political parties. No political group has hereby suffered so greatly as the reactionaries. Every candidate for the New Diet, of whom there are over 3000, has been screened for affiliation or association with militarism and ultra-nationalism. Many reforms in the electoral system have been accomplished. The election laws are now sufficiently democratic to provide ample opportunity for a free expression of the popular will. The campaign and the election are being carefully watched and closely studied by the forces under my command, with the objective of verifying the democratic nature of the electoral process.

It is probable that the new Diet will be the most truly responsive body to the will of the people that has ever served Japan and will provide the basis for a much more representative cabinet. Under any circumstances it will certainly be a great improvement over the last Diet along democratic and liberal lines. There is no ground for supposition that the reactionary party will secure a greater advantage as a result of the election at this time than at a later date. Political activity is now widespread. Any postponement of the election would inevitably result in greater advantage to the more experienced and better organized reactionary group severely crippled by the purge order who would thereby be provided the opportunity to regroup and strengthen.

Any postponement would certainly be misunderstood by the Japanese People, and would have a profound adverse reaction upon the purposes and success of the occupation. Should the results of the election prove disadvantageous to the purposes of the occupation, the remedy is always in my power to require the dissolution of the Diet and the holding of a new election under such provisions as are deemed necessary.

The Commission expressed the following view: "Finally, the issue of the draft Constitution, of which you have approved, makes the Constitution at this late stage an election issue, upon which there can be little time for consideration by the Japanese people, and at the same time may give an undue political advantage to the political party preferring this Constitution."

The Commission seems to be laboring under a confusion of thought in believing that the constitution has been put forth by any particular party. The Cabinet itself does not represent any party. The Prime Minister, Shidehara, is completely independent and has no party affiliations whatsoever. All parties in Japan, except the Communistic Party, overwhelmingly favor the proposed constitution, which represents the work of men from many different groups and many different affiliations. It has created confidence in the Cabinet but cannot be regarded as an appreciable factor in the elections as practically every candidate except the Communists supports it. My own approval of it will have no slightest effect in any way on the election returns of any party or any candidate.

In reply to your three specific questions in the last paragraph of your message my answers are:

1. *Question:* Does the Supreme Commander share the apprehensions expressed above?
Answer: No.
2. *Question:* If so, would he consider it possible and desirable to require a further postponement of the Japanese elections, and in that case for what period?
Answer: No.
3. *Question:* If the Supreme Commander should not consider a further postponement desirable at this late date, would he express his views on the desirability, as an alternative, of publicly prescribing that the forthcoming election will be regarded as a test of the ability of Japan to produce a responsible and democratic government in full accordance with the wishes of the people and that further elections will be held at a later date?
Answer: The suggested statement seems wholly unnecessary. The conditions it would announce are inherent in the situation and are completely understood, as I can require dissolution of the Diet and call for another election at any time.

D. Austria

1. GENERAL POLICY

Allied reconstruction of a liberated Austria was anticipated in the Moscow Declaration of November 1, 1943,[1] which was drawn up by the United States, the Soviet Union and the United Kingdom and accepted by the French Committee of National Liberation on November 16, 1943. The four powers were agreed that Austria, forcibly annexed by Germany, was to be liberated from German domination. Since that time United States policy consistently centered on adherence to the following basic objectives: "(1) Reestablishment of Austria as a free and independent state in fulfilment of the Moscow Declaration of November 1, 1943; (2) Creation of conditions for the maintenance of a democratic state and society in Austria; (3) Assurance to Austria of a basis for a healthy economic structure which will enable Austria to become independent of outside relief in the shortest possible time; (4) Restoration of Austria in the community of nations with a status of equality with other members." [2]

The problem of the Austrian peace treaty was raised several times during the various meetings of the Council of Foreign Ministers. It was the consistent policy of the United States to urge immediate attention to the Austrian peace treaty, as exemplified in the statement of Secretary Byrnes in his report on the first part of the Paris Meeting of Foreign Ministers: [3]

"It is particularly important that we press forward vigorously with the Austrian treaty. The Moscow Declaration on Austria contemplated that Austria should be regarded more as a liberated than as a satellite country. It was urged at Potsdam that no reparations would be taken from her.[4] She was one of the first countries in Central Europe to have free elections following the liberation. The continuance of foreign troops in Austria is an undue burden on her economy." [5]

Despite emphasis on the importance of an Austrian peace treaty by Secretary Byrnes at that time, the Soviet representative declined to discuss it. Subsequent

[1] For statement on Austria, see *Documents, VI, 1943–1944*, p. 231.
[2] Department of State Publication 2794, p. 23.
[3] Department of State Publication 2774, European Series 24, p. 88.
[4] For section of the Potsdam declaration regarding Austrian reparations, see this volume, Appendix II.
[5] Department of State Publication 2774, European Series 24, p. 94.

consideration of Austria resulted in the decision at the New York Meeting of the Council of Foreign Ministers (November 4–December 12, 1946) to authorize appointment of special deputies to start drafting a treaty with Austria.

For details on Austrian treaty negotiations and the problem of freedom of navigation on the Danube, see *The First Five Peace Treaties. Supplement: Documents, VIII, 1945–1946.*

(1) *Report by the Secretary of State (Byrnes) on the Latter Half of the Meeting of the Council of Foreign Ministers in Paris, June 15–July 12, 1946, Dated July 15, 1946.*[1]

[Excerpt]

. . . .

Finally we came to a discussion of the Austrian problem. On June 1, I had circulated a proposed draft treaty recognizing the independence of Austria and providing for the withdrawal of the occupying troops. The British also had submitted a draft for consideration. I asked that the Deputies be directed to prepare the treaty.

The Soviets submitted a counterproposal calling first for further action to insure the de-Nazification of Austria and the removal of a large number of displaced persons from Austria whom they regarded as unfriendly to them.

The British and French were willing to join us in submitting to the Deputies the consideration of the treaty and in requesting the Control Council to investigate and report on the progress of de-Nazification and on the problem of the displaced persons. But the Soviets were unwilling to agree to the Deputies' taking up the Austrian treaty until more tangible action was taken on these other two problems.

. . . .

(2) *United States Policy on Status of Austria. Department of State Press Release, October 28, 1946.*[2]

The Department of State considers that the visit to the United States of Dr. Karl Gruber, Foreign Minister of the Austrian Federal Republic, represents an appropriate occasion to reaffirm United States policy with respect to the status of Austria.

During the period following the first World War, the United States Government steadily encouraged the development of a free and independent Austrian state based on democratic principles, and viewed with strong disapproval all Nazi attempts to force Austria into the German Reich. The attitude of the United States toward the military occupation of Austria by Germany and its formal incorporation in the German Reich in 1938 was guided by this consideration and by the well-established policy of the United States toward the acquisition of territory by force. While, as a practical matter, the United States was obliged in its effort to protect American interests to take certain administrative measures based upon the situation created by the *Anschluss*, this Government consistently avoided any step which might be considered to constitute *de jure* recognition of the annexation of Austria by Germany.

In his radio address on May 27, 1941, President Roosevelt referred

[1] *Ibid.*, p. 109.   [2] Department of State, *Bulletin*, XV, p. 864.

repeatedly to the seizure of Austria, and described the Austrians as the first of a series of peoples enslaved by Hitler in his march of conquest. Secretary Hull stated at a press conference on July 27, 1942 that "this Government has never taken the position that Austria was legally absorbed into the German Reich." In various wartime administrative measures in the United States, such as the freezing of assets, Selective Service, and registration of aliens, Austrian nationals were included in a separate category from the German or were assimilated to the nationals of countries which Germany seized or occupied by force.

The United States has accordingly regarded Austria as a country liberated from forcible domination by Nazi Germany, and not as an ex-enemy state or a state at war with the United States during the second World War. The Department of State believes that this view has received diplomatic recognition through the Moscow Declaration on Austria and the Declaration issued at Algiers on November 16, 1943 by the French Committee of National Liberation concerning the independence of Austria. In accordance with the objectives set forth in the Moscow Declaration to see reestablished a free and independent Austria, an Austrian Government was formed after free elections were held on November 25, 1945. This Austrian Government was recognized by the four powers represented on the Allied Council, as announced simultaneously on January 7, 1946 in Vienna and the capitals of these states. In its meeting of April 25, 1946 the Allied Council, moreover, considered a statement of the United States Government's policy in Austria made by General Mark Clark, and expressed its general agreement with section I, "Status of Austria," in which the United States maintained that since Austria has been liberated from Nazi domination it should be treated as a liberated area.

In the opinion of the Department of State, the judgment of the International Military Tribunal rendered at Nürnberg on September 30–October 1, 1946 gave further international confirmation to this view of Austria's status by defining the invasion of that country as an aggressive act — "a premeditated aggressive step in furthering the plan to wage aggressive wars against other countries." The Nürnberg judgment also states that "Austria was in fact seized by Germany in the month of March 1938".

In order to clarify the attitude of the United States Government in this matter, the United States Government recognizes Austria for all purposes, including legal and administrative, as a liberated country comparable in status to other liberated areas and entitled to the same treatment, subject only to the controls reserved to the occupying powers in the new agreement on control machinery in Austria of June 28, 1946. The United States Government believes that the international acts mentioned above are adequate reason for all members of the United Nations to regard Austria as a liberated country.

2. GERMAN ASSETS AND REPARATIONS

The tripartite Potsdam Agreement provided that: "The Governments of the United Kingdom and the United States of America renounce their claims in respect of reparations to shares of German enterprises which are located in the eastern zone of occupation in Germany, as well as to German foreign assets in Bulgaria, Finland, Hungary, Rumania and Eastern Austria." [1] The indefinite terminology of this clause led to prolonged discussion and differences of opinion, particularly between the United States and the USSR, concerning the meaning of German "assets" in eastern Austria. At various times the American State Department defined German assets as those properties owned by Germany before 1938 or actually imported into the various countries at a later date; assets acquired under duress or forcible appropriation were not regarded as German. The USSR, on the other hand, maintained a more inclusive definition of German assets, interpreting "assets" as not only physical properties but shares in Austrian industries held by head offices in Vienna.[2] Russian claims to much of Austrian heavy industry, shipping and oil resources were countered by British and American charges that such demands contradicted not only the Moscow Declaration but also the United Nations Declaration in London in 1943 that acquirement of property by Germany under duress would not be recognized.

The problem of German assets in eastern Austria remained a major factor in occupation policy discussions throughout the period under review. On July 6, 1946, Russian occupation authorities issued an order requiring surrender to them of all former German property in eastern Austria. Gen. Mark W. Clark, United States representative on the Allied Control Council, warned that only German external assets within the meaning of the Potsdam Declaration were to be surrendered.[3] On July 10, Chancellor Leopold Figl, through Gen. Clark, received a message from President Truman [4] stating that the United States would not recognize any definition of "German assets" which did not conform to the United Nations Declaration of 1943 and the Moscow Declaration of the same year, and that the United States Government was prepared to turn over to the Austrian Government as trustees all German assets in the American Zone. On July 16, a Soviet note to the Austrian Government [5] indicated some concession to the American interpretation of the Potsdam Agreement by stipulating that Austrian Government or private property taken over after the Anschluss by Germany without compensation or transferred to Germans by violence should be returned to former owners; however, the note placed on the Austrian Government the responsibility of proving duress to the satisfaction of Soviet occupation authorities.

As the year 1946 ended there was some hope that Austria and Russia were approaching a compromise on the question of former German property through an arrangement enabling Austria to purchase properties that the USSR possessed, although there was no certainty that the Russians would finally accept the principle of Austria's right of repurchase. Russia's repeated offer to surrender a considerable portion of the properties they claimed under the Potsdam Agreement in return for Austrian recognition of USSR ownership of certain remaining properties was not accepted by the Austrian Government.

(1) *Note Delivered by the Military Commissioner of the United States on the Allied Council for Austria (Clark) to the Government of Austria Regarding German Assets in Austria. Department of State Press Release, July 10, 1946.*[6]

The President of the United States as one of the signers of the Potsdam Agreement has directed me to inform the Austrian Government that the United States Government is now prepared to enter into negotiations with other Allied Governments and with the Austrian Government look-

---

[1] *Ibid.*, XIII, p. 157; see this volume, Appendix II.
[2] *New York Times*, September 16, 1945, p. 24. See also, *ibid.*, November 22, 1945, p. 16.
[3] *Ibid.*, July 7, 1946, p. 1.   [4] See this volume, below.
[5] See *ibid.*, p. 287.   [6] Department of State, *Bulletin*, XV, p. 123.

ing towards the renunciation of the United States share in German assets in Austria as part of a general settlement of German assets in Austria.

While these negotiations are underway the United States Government now agrees to turn over to the Austrian Government as trustee all German assets physically located in the United States zone. It assures the Austrian Government that such assets may immediately be used for purposes of reconstruction in Austria without fear of removal of the plant and equipment from the United States zone in Austria but with the question of ownership to be resolved later.

The United States Government also wishes to make clear that it will recognize no physical transfer of property as conforming to the terms of the Potsdam Agreement which does not also conform to the terms of the United Nations Declaration on forced transfer for January 1943 and which does not leave to Austria the sovereign control of an independent country over the resources within its borders which was envisaged in the Moscow Declaration of 1943.

(2) *Communication by the Government of the Union of Soviet Socialist Republics to the Government of Austria Concerning the Potsdam Agreement, July 16, 1946.*[1]

By order of the Commander in Chief of the Soviet occupational forces in Austria and in accordance with your request which you expressed in conversation with the Commander in Chief on July 15, 1946, I send you the following Soviet settlement of German assets in Austria:

1. The Soviet command considers transferred into the property of the Soviet Union all German titles and assets in East Austria (*a*) which were such before March 15, 1938 (*b*) which by any means whatever passed over to Germany from her Allied states and satellites after, as well as before 1938 (*c*) which passed over to Germany and German citizens and associations after March 15, 1938 on a unilateral [purchase-sale] basis from firms of citizens of neutral and United Nations, as well as from Austrian owners.

Note: If in the latter case the element of violence or incomplete payment is established [confirmed by documents], the Soviet command will, in such case, either go about returning the assets to their former owner on condition that reparation be made to the Soviet command for all sums received by the latter from Germans or, vice versa, may agree in the event of retaining to itself the rights of ownership to pay the difference to the former owner between sum actually received by him and the real value of property, according to its condition on the day of negotiations.

In both cases, accounts will be effected in currency or goods at prices corresponding to the real value received by the owner at the time of property transfer.

(*d*) All rights, reacquired by German firms and private persons after 1938, to the exploitation of the natural wealth of country and all enterprises that came into existence and were developed after this year on the basis of German investments;

[1] *New York Times*, July 21, 1946, p. 26.

(e) Patents and trademarks of German legal and physical persons;

(f) Deposits and securities of all possible types in Austrian financial credit institutions belonging to German legal and physical persons;

(g) Property of German imperial public organizations and private property of German citizens. In so far as it is not proved that it had been taken away by means of violence from its old owners.

2. State, community and other property which belonged to the Austrian state or Austrian citizens before March 15, 1938, and later passed over into the hands of the German state or German citizens without any compensation. Whatever in the course of the amalgamation of State credit or other institutions, or in course of Aryanization, must be returned to owners who had possession of it before the Anschluss.

An exception in the given case is that of voluntary transfer and increase of capital at the expense of German investments.

3. OCCUPATION AND CONTROL

Initial informal planning for Austrian occupation by the Combined Chiefs of Staff provided that control of Austria should center under the Mediterranean command since it was expected that forces could be more easily provided from the Italian theater. Following the organization of the European Advisory Commission early in 1944, American, British and Soviet delegates began exchange of views and consideration of occupation policy, and by March, 1945, the European Advisory Commission (EAC) had made arrangements for the four-power occupation of Austria within 1937 frontiers. Changes in military strategy during April, 1945, resulted in the transfer of United States responsibility in Austrian occupation from the Mediterranean to the European theater of operations; consequently, the SHAEF military-government staff began work on directives for U. S. military-government personnel in Austria, while the EAC continued plans for Austria on a national level.[1] Headquarters, United States Forces in Austria (USFA), was organized in May, and Gen. Mark W. Clark was designated as United States member of the Allied Council of the Allied Commission for Austria. Command of U. S. occupation forces was taken over by USFA in July, and in August, 1945, headquarters were moved from Italy to Salzburg.

Shortly after a joint British, French and American party had submitted a report on occupation arrangements, EAC agreements were concluded on July 4, 1945, thereby setting up control machinery and providing for quadripartite zonal administration on July 9.

During the first meetings of the Allied Council in September, 1945, the four Commanders-in-Chief reached decisions which included (1) the promise of an increase in rations, (2) restoration of freedom of railway and road transport and telegraph and telephone communications, (3) official approval of the renewal of political activities of the three democratic political parties in Austria. On October 20, 1945, the Allied Council authorized extension throughout Austria of the power of the Provisional Government (set up by the Soviets under Dr. Karl Renner in April, 1945, and reconstituted by the Austrian Provincial Conference in September, 1945), subject to Allied Council control.[2]

After Austrian elections were held on November 25, 1945, the Federal Government was organized with Dr. Karl Renner as Federal President and Leopold Figl as Federal Chancellor. Recognition was extended to the Republic on January 7, 1946, and thereafter the four occupying powers exchanged representatives with the Austrian Government.

[1] For details of the beginnings of military government in Austria, see Department of State Publication 2794, p. 24.
[2] *Ibid.*, p. 27.

On April 9, Russian occupation authorities agreed to give UNRRA a 30 day supply of food to help meet the Austrian food need. American and British authorities had previously started the agency with a 90 day food supply.[1] On May 10, the Russian authorities decided to reduce their occupation costs to the extent that future costs divided among the four powers would not exceed 35 percent of the Austrian budget. A further reduction to 15 percent of the budget after January 1, 1947, was obtained by the Allied Council on December 3.[2]

The control machinery agreement of July 4, 1945, provided for the formulation of a new agreement after a freely elected Austrian Government was recognized by the occupying powers. Subsequently, the new agreement was completed with quadripartite approval, and it was signed in Vienna on June 28, 1946, thereby reducing the authority of the Allied Council and increasing the responsibility of the Austrian Government. Under this agreement zonal restrictions were removed on the movement of Austrian goods and citizens, functions of the Allied Council were made supervisory rather than administrative and Austrian laws (except constitutional provisions) and international agreements (except those with the four occupying powers) entered into effect 31 days after passage unless unanimously disapproved by the Allied Council.[3]

On July 26, over Soviet protests, the Austrian Parliament passed a nationalization law which applied to a number of Soviet claimed industries. This move was regarded as an effort to force Russia to free Austrian economy from its control by extending compensation in place of Russian controlled property.[4] Nationalization debate in the Allied Council resulted in approval of the law under conditions which excluded application to all important Allied holdings until the USSR agreed to apply the law to Soviet claimed property.[5]

Major decisions reached in Allied Council meetings by the end of 1946 included (1) agreement on the Prohibitory (Denazification) Law which had been submitted by the Austrian Government, (2) agreement on the unhampered movement of indigenous resources between all four zones and pooling of imported foodstuffs, and (3) extension to the Austrian Government of authority to conclude trade transactions with all foreign countries except Germany on condition that the Government submit to the Allied Council each month a list of such transactions as it makes.[6] During December the Allied Council and the Austrian Government worked out a detailed four year production and control program to enter into effect in 1947. The program, to be financed by loans, grants and exports during 1947, was planned in order to give coal, electricity and oil priorities to industries vital to exports.[7]

Machinery for the coordination of Department of State policy dealing with Austria was provided through the Germany-Austria secretariat (responsible to Assistant Secretary of State for occupied areas, Maj. Gen. John H. Hilldring) which included members from offices of the Department concerned with occupation affairs. Under the chairmanship of James J. Riddleberger, Chief of the Division of Central European Affairs, the secretariat met twice a week to consider matters of policy which had been referred from the field or initiated by members of the secretariat. Special divisions of Department offices responsible for the formulation of policy with regard to Germany and Austria were represented, and officers of other divisions were invited to attend when matters of special interest to them were under consideration.[8]

---

[1] *New York Times*, April 11, 1946, p. 4.
[2] *Ibid.*, May 11, 1946, p. 12.
[3] *Ibid.*, June 29, 1946, p. 7.
[4] *Ibid.*, August 12, 1946, p. 1.
[5] *Ibid.*, September 11, 1946, p. 16.
[6] Military Government in Austria. *Report of the United States Commissioner*, No. 14, December, 1946.
[7] *New York Times*, December 17, 1946, p. 13.
[8] Department of State, *Bulletin*, XV, p. 47, 291. See also, this volume, p. 60.

(1) *Directive to the Commander in Chief of United States Forces of Occupation in Austria (Clark) Regarding the Military Government of Austria, June 27, 1945.*[1]

1. *The Purpose and Scope of this Directive:*

  a. This directive is issued to you as Commanding General of the United States forces of occupation in Austria. As such you will serve as United States member of the Allied Council of the Allied Commission for Austria and will also be responsible for the administration of military government in the zone or zones assigned to the United States for purposes of occupation and administration. It outlines the basic policies which will guide you in those two capacities after the termination of the combined command in Austria. Supplemental directives will be issued to you by the Joint Chiefs of Staff as may be required.

  b. As a member of the Allied Council you will urge the adoption by the other occupying powers of the principles and policies set forth in this directive and, pending Allied Council agreement, you will follow them in your zone. It is anticipated that substantially similar directives will be issued to the Commanders in Chief of the United Kingdom, the Union of Soviet Socialist Republics, and French forces of occupation.

  c. In the event that recognition is given by the four governments to a provisional national government of Austria, such government should be delegated authority in appropriate matters to conduct public affairs in accordance with the principles set forth in this directive or agreed upon by the occupying powers. Such delegation, however, shall be subject to the authority of the occupying powers and to their responsibility to see that their policies are in fact carried out.

  d. Any provisional national government of Austria which is not recognized by all of the four Governments of the occupying powers shall not be treated by you as possessing any authority. Only individuals who recognize your supreme authority in your zone will be utilized by you in administration.

PART I. GENERAL AND POLITICAL

2. *The Basis of Military Government:*

  a. The rights, power and status of the military government in Austria prior to the unconditional surrender and total defeat of Germany, were based upon the military occupation of Austria and the decision of the occupying powers to reestablish an independent Austrian state. Thereafter the rights, powers and status are based, in addition, upon such surrender or defeat. The Text of the Instrument of Unconditional Surrender of Germany published as a separate document has been made available to you. You will assure that the policies set forth in that Instrument are carried out in your zone of occupation insofar as they are applicable in Austria even though the defeat of Germany is not followed by a formal signing of the Instrument.

  b. Subject to the provisions of paragraph 3 below, you are, by virtue

[1] Department of State, *Bulletin*, XIII, p. 661.

of your position, clothed with supreme legislative, executive, and judicial authority in the areas occupied by forces under your command. This authority will be broadly construed and includes authority to take all measures deemed by you necessary, appropriate or desirable in relation to military exigencies and the objectives set forth in this and other directives.

c. You will issue a proclamation continuing in force such proclamations, orders and instructions as may have heretofore been issued by Allied Commanders in your zone, subject to such changes as you may determine. Authorizations of action by the Supreme Allied Commander, Mediterranean, or by the Supreme Commander, Allied Expeditionary Force, may be considered as applicable to you unless inconsistent with this or other directives.

3. *The Allied Council and Zones of Occupation:*

a. The four Commanders in Chief, acting jointly, will constitute the Allied Council which will exercise supreme authority in Austria. The United States proposal for an agreement on the organization of the Control Machinery in Austria published as a separate document has been made available to you. When approved by the occupying powers, the text of the agreement on Control Machinery in Austria will be furnished you. For purposes of administration of military government, Austria will be divided into four zones of occupation. When the occupying powers have agreed upon the zones of occupation in Austria, the text of the protocol in that regard will be furnished you.

b. The authority of the Allied Council to formulate policy and procedures and administrative relationships with respect to matters affecting Austria as a whole will be paramount throughout Austria. This authority shall be broadly construed to the end that, through maximum uniformity of policy and procedures throughout Austria, the establishment of an independent Austrian Government may be accelerated. In your capacity as a member of the Allied Council, you will seek maximum agreement with respect to policy and maximum uniformity of action by the Commanders in Chief in their respective zones of occupation. You will carry out and support in your zone the policies agreed upon in the Allied Council. In the absence of such agreed policies you will act in accordance with this and other directives of the Joint Chiefs of Staff.

c. The Allied Council should cooperate with the Control Council in Germany in effecting the severance of all political and administrative connections between Austria and Germany, and the elimination of German economic and financial influences in Austria. You will in every way possible assist the accomplishment of this purpose.

d. The Allied Council should adopt procedures to effectuate, and you will facilitate in your zone, the equitable distribution of essential commodities between the zones. In the absence of a conflicting policy of the Allied Council, you may deal directly with one or more zone commanders on matters of special concern to such zones.

e. Pending the formulation in the Allied Council of uniform policies and procedures with respect to travel and movement of persons to and from Austria, no persons shall be permitted to cross the Austrian frontier in your zone except for specific purposes approved by you.

f. The military government personnel in your zone, including those dealing with regional and local branches of the departments of any central Austrian administrative machinery, shall be selected by your authority except that liaison officers may be furnished by the Commanders of the other three zones. The respective Commanders in Chief shall have exclusive jurisdiction throughout the whole of Austria over the members of the armed forces under their command and over the civilians who accompany them.

4. *Basic Objectives of Military Government in Austria:*

a. You will be chiefly concerned in the initial stages of military government with the elimination of German domination and Nazi influences. Consistently with this purpose, you will be guided at every step by the necessity to ensure the reconstruction of Austria as a free, independent and democratic state. It will be essential therefore that every measure be undertaken from the early stages of occupation with this objective in mind.

b. The Allied Council should, as soon as it is established, proclaim the complete political and administrative separation of Austria from Germany, and the intention of the occupying powers to pave the way for the reestablishment of Austria as an independent democratic state. You will make it clear to the Austrian people that military occupation of Austria is intended principally (1) to aid Allied military operations and the strict enforcement of the applicable provisions of the German unconditional surrender instrument in Austria; (2) to eliminate Nazism, Pan-Germanism, militarism, and other forces opposed to the democratic reconstitution of Austria; (3) to cooperate with the Control Council for Germany in the application and enforcement of measures designed to prevent the recurrence of German aggression; (4) to establish Allied Control over the use and disposition of German property in Austria; (5) to effect the complete political and administrative separation of Austria from Germany and free Austria from Nazi and German economic and financial influences; (6) to facilitate the development of a sound Austrian economy devoted to peaceful pursuits and not vitally dependent upon German supplies, markets and technical and financial assistance; and (7) to foster the restoration of local self-government and the establishment of an Austrian central government freely elected by the Austrian people themselves. Other objectives of the occupation will be to apprehend war criminals, to care for and repatriate displaced persons and prisoners-of-war who are members of the armed forces of the United Nations, and to carry out approved programs of reparation and restitution insofar as these are applicable to Austria.

c. You will assure that there is no fraternization by your troops with any German elements remaining in Austria. While in the initial period of occupation the relationship of the troops to the Austrian civil population will be distant and aloof but courteous, a progressively more friendly relationship may be permitted as experience justifies.

5. *Denazification:*

a. A Proclamation dissolving the Nazi Party, its formations, affiliated associations and supervised organizations, and all Nazi public institutions which were set up as instruments of Party domination, and prohibiting their revival in any form, should be promulgated by the Allied Council. You will assure the prompt effectuation of that policy in your zone and will make every effort to prevent the reconstitution of any such organization in underground, disguised or secret form. Responsibility for continuing desirable non-political social services of dissolved Party Organizations may be transferred by the Governing Body to appropriate central agencies and by you to appropriate local agencies.

b. All laws which extended the political structure of National Socialism to Austria or otherwise brought about the destruction of the Austrian state or which established discriminations on grounds of race, nationality, creed, or political opinion should be abrogated by the Allied Council. You will render them inoperative in your zone.

c. All members of the Nazi Party who were German nationals prior to March 13, 1938, Germans who entered Austria after that date, and other Germans directly connected with the Nazi exploitation of Austria will immediately be removed from government positions and all other categories of employment listed below, and will be expelled from Austria in accordance with paragraph 21. All Austrian members of the Nazi Party who have been more than nominal participants in its activities, all active supporters of Nazism and other persons hostile to Allied purposes will be removed and excluded from public office and from positions of importance in quasi-public and private enterprises such as (1) civic, economic, and labor organizations, (2) corporations and other organizations in which the German Government or subdivisions have a major financial interest, (3) industry, commerce, agriculture, and finance, (4) education, and (5) the press, publishing houses and other agencies disseminating news and propaganda. Persons are to be treated as more than nominal participants in Party activities and as active supporters of Nazism when they have (1) held office or otherwise been active at any level from local to national in the Party and its subordinate organizations, (2) authorized or participated affirmatively in any Nazi crimes, racial persecutions or discriminations, (3) been avowed believers in Nazi doctrines, or (4) voluntarily given substantial moral or material support or political assistance of any kind to the Nazi Party or Nazi officials and leaders. No such persons shall be retained in any of the categories of employment listed above because of administrative necessity, convenience or expediency.

d. Property, real and personal, owned or controlled by the Nazi Party, its formations, affiliated associations and supervised organizations, and by all persons subject to arrest under the provisions of paragraph 7 below, and found within your zone will be taken under your control pending a decision by the Allied Council or higher authority as to its eventual disposition.

e. All archives, monuments and museums of Nazi inception, or which are devoted to the perpetuation of militarism, will be taken under your control and their properties held pending decision as to their disposition by the Allied Council.

f. You will make special efforts to preserve from destruction and take under your control records, plans, books, documents, papers, files, and scientific, industrial and other information and data belonging to or controlled by the following:

(1) The central German Government and its subdivisions, the offices of the Reichsstatthalter, the former Austrian state and its subdivisions, German and Austrian military organizations, organizations engaged in military research, and such other governmental agencies as may be deemed advisable;

(2) The Nazi Party, its formations, affiliated associations and supervised organizations;

(3) All police organizations, including security and political police;

(4) Important economic organizations and industrial establishments including those controlled by the Nazi Party or its personnel;

(5) Institutes and special bureaus devoting themselves to racial, political, militaristic or similar research or propaganda.

6. *Elimination of pre-Nazi Fascist Influences:*

a. You will remove and exclude from the positions enumerated in sub-paragraph 5 *c* above all persons who took an active and prominent part in the undemocratic measures of the pre-Nazi Fascist regime or in any of its para-military organizations such as the Heimwehr and the Ostmaerkische Sturmscharen.

b. You will prevent the revival of any organization seeking to restore the pre-Nazi Fascist regime.

7. *Suspected War Criminals and Security Arrests:*

a. You will search out, arrest, and hold, pending receipt by you of further instructions as to their disposition, Adolf Hitler, his chief Nazi associates, other war criminals, and all persons who have participated in planning or carrying out Nazi enterprises involving or resulting in atrocities or war crimes.

b. All persons who if permitted to remain at large would endanger the accomplishment of your objectives will also be arrested and held in custody until their disposition is otherwise determined by an appropriate semi-judicial body to be established by you.

[Note: There follows at this point in the directive a detailed list of categories of Nazi war criminals and others who are to be arrested. Some of these have not yet been found. It is considered that to publish the categories at this time would put the individuals concerned on notice and would interfere with their apprehension and punishment, where appropriate. The list of categories is, therefore, withheld from publication for the present.]

If in the light of conditions which you encounter in Austria you believe that it is not immediately feasible to subject certain persons within these categories to this treatment, you should report your reasons and recommendations to your Government through the Joint Chiefs of Staff. If you believe it desirable, you may postpone the arrest of those whose cases you have reported, pending a decision communicated to you by the Joint Chiefs of Staff. In no event shall any differentiation be made between or special consideration be accorded to person arrested, either as to manner of arrest, or conditions of detention, upon the basis of wealth or political, industrial, or other rank or position. In your discretion you may make such exception as you deem advisable for intelligence or other military reasons.

8. *Demilitarization:*

a. In your zone you will assure that all units of the German armed forces including para-military organizations are dissolved as such and that their personnel are promptly disarmed and controlled in accordance with the policies and procedures set forth in the Instrument of Unconditional Surrender of Germany or in other directives which may be issued to you. Prior to their final disposition you will arrest and hold all military personnel who are included under the provisions of paragraph 7. Subject to military considerations and priority to be accorded repatriation of United Nations nationals, the Allied Council should cooperate with the Control Council for Germany in arranging the early repatriation or other disposition of German members of the German armed forces, including para-military organizations, found within Austria. The two Allied agencies should likewise concert the prompt return to Austria of Austrian members of the German armed forces found within Germany, except those held as active Nazis, suspected war criminals, or for other reasons.

b. The Allied Council should proclaim, and in your zone you will effectuate, the total dissolution of all military and para-military organizations together with all associations which might serve to keep alive militarism in Austria.

c. All persons who have actively supported organizations promoting militarism or who have been active proponents of militaristic doctrines will be removed and excluded from any of the categories of employment listed in sub-paragraph 5 *c.*

d. You will seize or destroy all arms, ammunition and implements of war, including all aircraft, military and civil, and stop the production thereof.

9. *Police:*

With the exception of the Kriminalpolizei (Criminal Police), all elements of the Sicherheitspolizei (Security Police), e.g., Geheime Staatspolizei (Gestapo), and the Sicherheitsdienst der S.S. will be abolished. Criminal and ordinary police will be purged of Nazi personnel and utilized under the control and supervision of the military government.

10. *Administration of Justice:*

a. All extraordinary courts, including the Volksgerichtshof (People's Court) and the Sondergerichte (Special Courts), and all courts and tribunals of the Nazi Party and of its formations, affiliated associations and supervised organizations will be abolished immediately.

b. All ordinary criminal, civil and administrative courts, except those previously re-established by Allied authority, will be closed. After the elimination of all Nazi or other objectionable features and personnel you will permit those which are to exercise jurisdiction within the boundaries of your zone to resume operations under such regulations, supervision and control as you may consider appropriate. Courts which are to exercise jurisdiction over territory extending beyond the boundaries of your zone will be reopened only with the express authorization of the Allied Council and under its regulation, supervision and control. The power to review and veto decisions of German and Austrian courts shall be included within the power of supervision and control.

11. *Political Prisoners:*

Subject to military security and to the interests of the individuals concerned, you will release all persons found within your zone who have been detained or placed in custody on grounds of race, nationality, creed or political opinion and treat them as displaced persons. You should make provision for the review of convictions of alleged criminal offenses about which there may be substantial suspicion of racial, religious or political persecution, and in which sentences of imprisonment have not been fully served by persons imprisoned within your zone.

12. *Reconstitution of an Administrative System:*

a. As soon as Nazi and Fascist influences have been eliminated from public offices in Austria, the reconstitution of Austrian administrative agencies shall be carried out in such a way as not to prejudice the political and constitutional future of Austria. The Allied Council should be responsible for the early establishment of such nation-wide administrative and judicial machinery as may be required to facilitate the uniform execution of its policy throughout Austria, to ensure freedom of transit and communication to and between the separate zones of occupation, and to lay the foundation for the restoration of an Austrian national administrative system. Administrative officials with powers extending throughout Austria should be appointed only by or under the authority of the Allied Council.

b. The formal abrogation of the Anschluss (Act of March 13, 1938) will not be considered as reestablishing the legal and constitutional system of Austria as it existed prior to that event. Such portions of earlier Austrian legislation or of Reich legislation relating to Austria may be retained or restored to force as is deemed appropriate for the purposes of military government and the reconstitution of Austria on a democratic basis. In so far as it may prove desirable to utilize constitutional laws for Austrian administration, suitable provisions of the Austrian Constitution of 1920, as amended in 1925 and 1929, should be applied.

c. You will assure the severance of all connections between regional (Gau) and local agencies on the one hand and Reich administrative agencies on the other, and will reconstitute Austrian Provincial (Land) and local administration at the earliest possible moment. You may utilize such agencies of the present regional and local administrations as may be deemed useful.

13. *Restoration of Regional and Local Self-Government:*

As a member of the Allied Council, you will urge the restoration of regional and local self-government throughout Austria at the earliest possible moment. In the absence of agreement, you will facilitate the holding of elections to local and regional public office within your zone. If prior to or during occupation, local and regional popular councils or similar organs appear, they may be granted temporary recognition pending approval by the Allied Council and be utilized in administration in the event that they possess popular support and are free from Nazi or Fascist sympathizers and affiliations.

14. *Establishment of Independent Austrian Government:*

The Allied Council should, and in your zone you will, make it clear to the Austrian people that the Allied Powers do not intend through military government to appoint or establish a national government for Austria but will aid the Austrian people themselves to prepare for the election of a national assembly by democratic means. The Austrian people will be free to determine their own form of government provided the new regime be democratic in character and assume appropriate internal and international responsibilities and obligations.

15. *Political Activity and Civil Rights:*

a. At the earliest possible moment you will permit such political activity and organization by democratic groups as neither threatens military security nor presents substantial danger of public disorder nor engenders suspicion and disunity among the United Nations.

b. You will prohibit the propagation in any form of Nazi, Fascists, militaristic, and pan-German doctrines.

c. To the extent that military interests are not prejudiced and subject to the provisions of the two preceding subparagraphs and paragraph 16, you will permit freedom of speech, assembly, press, association, and religious worship.

d. For purposes of military government you may consider as Austrian citizens all persons who held Austrian citizenship on or before March 13, 1938, or who would have automatically acquired citizenship by operation of the law of Austria in force on March 13, 1938. The acts of July 30, 1925 and August 16, 1933 should not be considered as depriving of citizenship Austrians who have entered the service of foreign states or who have taken up arms against the Reich since 1938. German laws purporting to affect Austrian citizenship should be ignored.

16. *Public Relations and Control of Public Information:*

As a member of the Allied Council you will endeavor to obtain agreement for uniform or coordinated policies with respect to (*a*) control of public information media in Austria, (*b*) accrediting of foreign correspondents, (c) press censorship, and (d) issuance of official news communiques dealing with matters within the jurisdiction of the Allied Council. United States policies in these matters will be sent to you separately and you will be guided by these in your negotiations in the Allied Council.

17. *Education:*

   a. You will initially close all schools and universities except those previously re-established by Allied authority. The closure of Nazi educational institutions, such as Adolf Hitler Schulen, Napolas and Ordensburgen, and of Nazi organizations within other educational institutions, will be permanent.

   b. A coordinated system of control over Austrian education and an affirmative program of reorientation will be established designed completely to eliminate Nazi, Fascists and militaristic doctrines and to encourage the development of democratic ideas.

   c. You will permit the reopening of elementary (Volksschulen), middle (Hauptschulen), and vocational (Berufsschulen) schools at the earliest possible date after Nazi and other objectionable personnel has been eliminated. Textbooks and curricula which are not free of Nazi, Fascists and militaristic doctrines shall not be used. The Allied Council should assure that programs are devised for the early reopening of secondary schools, universities and other institutions of higher learning. After Nazi and other objectionable personnel and features have been eliminated and pending the formulation of such programs by the Allied Council, you may formulate and put into effect an interim program within your zone and, in any case, you will encourage the reopening of such institutions and departments which offer training which you consider immediately essential or useful in the administration of military government and the purposes of the occupation.

   d. It is not intended that the military government will intervene in questions concerning denominational control of Austrian schools, or in religious instruction in Austrian schools, except in so far as may be necessary to ensure that religious instruction and administration of such schools conform to such Allied regulations as are or may be established pertaining to purging of personnel and curricula.

18. *Religious Affairs:*

   a. The Allied Council should leave to the Austrian churchmen of the respective faiths the revision of the constitutions, rituals or internal relationships of purely ecclesiastical bodies.

   b. You will protect freedom of religious belief and worship.

   c. You will refrain from intervening in matters concerning religious instruction in schools, the establishment or continuation of denominational schools and the re-establishment of ecclesiastical control of any publicly supported schools.

   d. You will take necessary measures to protect churches, shrines, church schools, and other ecclesiastical property from damage and from any treatment which lacks respect for their religious character.

e. You may permit religious bodies to conduct appropriate youth, sports, and welfare activities and to receive contributions for such purposes.

f. Subject to the provisions of paragraph 15, you will permit the establishment or revival of religious periodicals and the publication of other religious literature.

19. *Treatment of Displaced Persons and Refugees in Austria:*

a. Subject to any international agreements and to the agreed policies of the Allied Council, you will undertake the repatriation, return to former residence or resettlement of displaced persons who are (1) nationals of the United Nations and of neutral states, (2) stateless persons, (3) nationals of enemy or former enemy countries who have been persecuted by the enemy for reasons of race, nationality, creed or political opinion, (4) nationals of Italy, as rapidly as military considerations and arrangements with their respective governments permit. Due consideration will be given to the wishes of the individuals involved, and preference will be accorded to nationals of the United Nations and persons freed from concentration camps or other places of detention.

b. You will establish or maintain centers for the assembly and repatriation, resettlement or return of the foregoing displaced persons. Subject to the general control and responsibility of military government, existing Austrian agencies will be required to maintain essential supply and other services for them, including adequate food, shelter, clothing and medical care.

c. Subject to your general control, you will hold existing Austrian agencies responsible for the care and disposition of refugees and those displaced persons who are nationals of Germany or former enemy countries not otherwise provided herein. You will facilitate their repatriation, or return, subject to whatever control you may deem necessary, as rapidly as military considerations and appropriate arrangements with authorities in their respective home countries permit.

d. Subject to agreed policies of the Allied Council, you will determine the extent to which UNRRA, the Inter-Governmental Committee on Refugees, or other civilian agencies will participate in handling displaced persons and refugees.

e. You will accord liaison on matters connected with displaced persons to representatives of each of the other Occupying Powers accredited therefor by their respective Commander in Chief and to representatives of any of the United Nations and neutral states and of Italy accredited therefor by the Allied Council or other competent authority. You will arrange for such representatives to have access to displaced persons who are nationals of their countries and are authorized to permit them to use the facilities of their governments for purposes of repatriation.

f. The term "displaced persons" includes (1) non-Austrian civilian nationals who have been obliged to leave their own countries or to remain in Austria by reason of the war, (2) stateless persons, and (3) persons who have been persecuted by the enemy for reasons of race, nationality, creed or political opinion. The term "refugees" includes Austrian civilian nationals within Austria who are temporarily homeless because of military operations, or are residing at some distance from their homes for reasons related to the war.

20. *Return of Austrian Civilians to Austria:*

In accordance with military considerations and appropriate arrangements with authorities in sending countries, you will cooperate in rapid repatriation of Austrian civilian nationals outside Austria, exclusive of active Nazis and persons suspected of having committed war crimes or held for other reasons.

21. *The Removal of German Officials and Civilians from Austria:*

a. All German officials, members of the Nazi Party who were German nationals prior to March 13, 1938, Germans who entered Austria after that date and other Germans directly connected with the Nazi exploitation of Austria, except those whom it may be desirable to hold for security or other reasons, should be expelled from Austria. The Allied Council should consult with the Control Council in Germany regarding the removal to Germany of such persons. Removal will be effected at the earliest time consistent with the availability of transport facilities and with the prospect of orderly absorption into Germany.

b. Subject to instructions issued by the Allied Council in accordance with the provisions of the subparagraph *a* above, you will in your zone take all practicable measures to facilitate and expedite the removal to Germany of all German officials and of German citizens to be repatriated.

22. *Diplomatic and Consular Officials and Properties:*

All diplomatic and consular officials of countries with which any one of the United Nations has been at war since December 31, 1937 will be taken into protective custody and held for further disposition. The diplomatic and consular property and records belonging to such countries or governments and to their official personnel will be seized and secured if not found in the custody of a protecting power.

23. *Arts and Archives:*

Subject to the provisions of paragraph 5 above, you will make all reasonable efforts to preserve historical archives, museums, libraries and works of art.

Part II. Economic

General Economic Provisions

24. The Allied Council should ensure the direction of the Austrian economy in such a way as to carry out the objectives set forth in paragraph 4 *b* of this directive and should establish centralized control and administration of the Austrian economy to the extent necessary to achieve the maximum utilization of Austrian resources and equitable distribution of essential goods and services and to obtain uniformity of policies and operation throughout Austria.

You will urge the establishment of such centralized control and administration and, pending agreement in the Allied Council, you will take such measures in your own zone as are necessary to carry out the provisions of this directive.

25. To the maximum extent possible without jeopardizing the successful execution of measures required to implement the objectives outlined in paragraph 4 *b* of this directive, Austrian authorities and agencies should be used, subject to such supervision as is necessary to ensure that they carry out their task. For this purpose appropriate authority should be given to Austrian agencies and administrative services, subject to strict observance of the provisions of this directive regarding denazification and dissolution or prohibition of Nazi and Fascist organizations, institutions, principles, features and practices.

26. You will preserve all significant records pertaining to important economic, financial and research organizations and activities. You will institute or assure the maintenance of such statistical records and reports as may be necessary to carry out the objectives of this directive.

27. You will initiate appropriate surveys which may assist you in achieving the objectives of the occupation. In particular, you will promptly undertake surveys of supplies, equipment and resources in your zone. You will endeavor to obtain prompt agreement in the Allied Council to similar surveys in the other zones of occupation and urge appropriate steps to coordinate the methods and results of these and other future surveys undertaken in the various zones. You will keep the Allied Council and your government currently apprised of the information obtained by means of intermediate reports or otherwise.

Responsibility for Supplies from U. S. Military Sources

28. Imports of supplies from U. S. Military supply sources, for which you will assume responsibility, will be limited to the basic essentials necessary in your zone (*a*) to avoid disease and unrest which might endanger the occupying forces and (*b*) for the care of displaced persons. Imports will be undertaken only after maximum utilization of indigenous supplies.

Agriculture, Industry and Internal Commerce

29. You will make maximum use of supplies and resources available within Austria and you will require the Austrians to use all means at their disposal to maximize the production of foodstuffs and other essential goods and to establish as rapidly as possible effective rationing and other machinery for the distribution thereof. You will urge upon the Allied Council that uniform ration scales be applied throughout Austria.

30. The Allied Council should assure to the maximum possible extent the free movement and equitable distribution of goods and services throughout Austria.

31. The Allied Council should facilitate emergency repair and construction for the minimum housing needs of the civil population and restoration of transportation and communications services and public utilities essential to the objectives outlined in paragraph 4 *b*.

32. In order to supplement the measures taken by the Control Council in Germany for the industrial disarmament of Germany and pending final decision as to the steps necessary in Austria to eliminate Germany's war potential, you should, in cooperation with the other zone commanders, take steps to

a. prevent the production, acquisition and development of all arms, ammunition and implements of war, including all types of aircraft, and all parts, components and ingredients specially designed or produced for incorporation therein;

b. seize and safeguard, pending instructions as to disposal, all facilities which are specially designed or adapted to the production of the items mentioned in *a* and cannot be converted to non-military production, using in such conversion only materials and equipment readily available and not emanating from Germany;

c. take an inventory of all German-owned plant and equipment in Austria, and all plant and equipment regardless of ownership erected or expanded in Austria subsequent to Anschluss, in the following industries: iron mining; steel and ferro-alloys; armaments (including aircraft); machinery (including automotive vehicles, agricultural machinery, locomotives and rolling stock, bearings and other special components, electrical machinery, and general industrial equipment); electronic equipment; electric power; non-ferrous metals, including light metals; rubber and oil, including synthetic rubber and oil; wood pulp; synthetic fibers; instruments; optical glass; chemicals (including pharmaceuticals and plastics) and photographic equipment; in order that the Allied Council may determine what portion of it is redundant to the development of a sound peacetime Austrian economy and make recommendations to the governments of the occupying powers regarding the treatment of these industries;

d. prevent large-scale exportation of light metals pending subsequent instructions on the policy to be followed regarding the Austrian light metals industry;

e. prevent the construction of plant capacity for the production of synthetic oil and rubber; and establish procedures, in consultation with the Control Council for Germany, for reviewing any projected construction of new or expanded capacity for materials the production of which is prohibited or limited in Germany as a measure of industrial disarmament, in order to ensure that such expansion is not for the purpose of evading controls in Germany;

f. close initially all laboratories, research institutions and similar technical organizations except those considered necessary for the protection of public health and safety, and provide for the maintenance and security of physical facilities where deemed necessary and for the detention of such personnel as are of interest to technological and counterintelligence investigations. After the provisions of paragraphs 5, 6, 7 and 8 (*c*) have been applied, the reopening of laboratories, research institutions and similar organizations should be permitted under license and periodic supervision, in accordance with policies which will be communicated to you.

33. Without prejudice to the possible eventual transfer of equipment or production on reparation account in accordance with any Allied agreements which may be reached, the Allied Council should facilitate the conversion of industrial facilities to non-military production. In such conversion it will be your policy to give priority to the production of essential goods and equipment in short supply.

34. The Allied Council should assure that all semi-official or quasi-public business and trade organizations of an authoritarian character are abolished and that any organizations of commerce, industry, agriculture and handicrafts which the Austrians may wish to establish are based on democratic principles.

35. The Allied Council should adopt a policy prohibiting cartels or other private business arrangements and cartel-like organizations including those of public or quasi-public character, such as the Wirtschaftsgruppen, which provide for the regulation of marketing conditions, including production, prices, exclusive exchange of technical information and processes, and allocation of sales territories. Such necessary public functions as have been discharged by these organizations should be absorbed as rapidly as possible by approved public agencies. Pending agreement in the Allied Council, you should take no action in your own zone with regard to this paragraph.

36. The Allied Council should adopt policies designed to prevent or restrain inflation of a character or dimension which would endanger accomplishment of the objectives of the occupation. The Allied Council in particular should direct and empower Austrian authorities to maintain or establish controls over prices and wages and to take the fiscal and financial measures necessary to this end.

Labor, Health and Social Insurance

37. The Allied Council should permit the self-organization of employees along democratic lines, subject to such safeguards as may be necessary to prevent the perpetuation or revival of Nazi, Fascist or militarist influence under any guise or the continuation of any group hostile to the objectives and operations of the occupying forces. The Allied Council should permit free collective bargaining between employees and employers regarding wages, hours, and working conditions and the establishment of machinery for the settlement of industrial disputes. Collective bargaining shall be within the framework of such wage, hour and other controls as may be instituted or revived.

38. The Allied Council should permit the retention or reestablishment of health services and facilities and non-discriminatory systems of social insurance and poor relief.

Reparation and Restitution

39. As a member of the Allied Council and as zone commander you will ensure that the programs of reparation and restitution embodied in Allied agreements are carried out in so far as they are applicable in Austria. The Allied Council should cooperate with the Control Council in Germany for this purpose. You should urge the Allied Council to an

agreement that, until appropriate Allied authorities formulate reparation and restitution program for application in Austria,

    a. no removals should be permitted on reparation account; and

    b. restitution to other countries should be confined to identifiable looted works of art, books, archives and other cultural property.

Foreign Trade

40. The Allied Council should take prompt steps to re-establish Austrian customs autonomy subject to the provisions of paragraph 51 and establish centralized control over all trade in goods and services with foreign countries.

41. In the control of foreign trade the objectives of the Allied Council should be (*a*) to obtain as much as possible of Austria's essential imports through regular trade; (*b*) encourage the development by Austrians as rapidly as possible of foreign markets and sources of supply; and (*c*) to promote the orientation of Austrian trade away from Germany.

The Allied Council should seek to obtain from sources other than military supply sources any imports essential to the achievement of the objectives set forth in this directive. Arrangements may be made with appropriate authorities in Germany for the importation of essential supplies from Germany, whenever in your judgment such supplies cannot be readily obtained from other sources.

The Allied Council should favor the conclusion of such arrangements for the exchange of Austrian goods and services with those of foreign countries including the development of entrepôt trade, as will aid in the revival of the Austrian economy on a sound basis and will not prejudice the eventual development of trade on a multilateral basis.

The Allied Council in cooperation with the Austrian authorities, should make a survey of Austrian foreign exchange resources and of the possibilities for foreign markets and sources of supply for Austrian industry and trade to serve as the basis of a program for the development of a sound economy. You will communicate to your government through the Joint Chiefs of Staff the results of such a survey, together with such recommendations as you may deem appropriate.

42. The Allied Council should adopt a policy which would forbid participation of Austrian firms in international cartels or other restrictive contracts and arrangements, and should order the prompt termination of all existing Austrian participation in such cartels, contracts and arrangements. Pending agreement in the Allied Council, you should take no action in your own zone with regard to this paragraph.

Part III. Financial

General Provisions

43. The Allied Council should adopt, for application throughout Austria, uniform financial measures which are necessary to the accomplishment of the objectives stated in paragraph 4 (*b*) of this directive and which are in conformity with the principles and policies set forth below. You will urge the establishment of centralized administration of such

measures to the extent necessary to achieve these objectives and, pending agreement in the Allied Council, you will adopt such necessary measures in your own zone as are in conformity with the provisions of this directive.

44. In the administration of financial matters you will follow the principles set forth in paragraph 25 of this directive.

45. You will maintain such accounts and records as may be necessary to reflect the financial operations of the military government in your zone, and you will provide the Allied Council with such information as it may require, including information in connection with the use of currency by your forces, any governmental settlements, occupation costs, and other expenditures arising out of operations or activities involving participation of your forces.

46. You will take measures to safeguard books and records of all public and private banks and other financial institutions.

47. Subject to any agreed policies of the Allied Council, you are authorized to take the following steps:

a. to prohibit, or to prescribe regulations regarding transfers or other dealings in private or public securities or real estate or other property;

b. to close banks, insurance companies and other financial institutions for a period long enough for you to introduce satisfactory control, to ascertain their cash position, to apply the provisions of paragraphs 5, 6, 7 and 8 (*c*) of this directive, and to issue instructions for the determination of accounts and assets to be blocked under paragraph 55 below;

c. to close stock and commodity exchanges and similar institutions for such periods as you deem appropriate and apply the provisions of paragraphs 5, 6, 7 and 8 (*c*) of this directive;

d. to establish a general or limited moratorium, or moratoria, to the extent necessary to carry out the objectives stated in this directive. In particular, it may prove desirable to prevent foreclosures of mortgages and the exercise of similar remedies by creditors against individuals and small business enterprises;

e. to issue regulations prescribing the purposes for which credit may be extended and the terms and conditions governing the extension of credit;

f. to put into effect such further financial measures as you deem necessary to accomplish the purposes stated in this directive.

48. The Allied Council should designate a suitable bank, preferably the former Vienna Branch of the Reichsbank, to perform under its direction central banking functions. Simultaneously, all connections between such designated bank and institutions or persons in Germany should be severed in accordance with paragraph 57 of this directive. When satisfied that this bank is under adequate control, the Allied Council may, by ensuring that credits are made available only in schillings through the zone commanders or authorized issuing banks or agencies, place such bank in a position to finance other banks or other financial institutions for the conduct of approved business.

Pending the designation of such a bank by the Allied Council, you may designate a bank in your zone to perform similar functions under your direct control and supervision and subject to the conditions specified above.

In an emergency you are also authorized to make direct advances, in schillings only, to other financial institutions.

Currency

49. The Allied Council should regulate and control the issue and volume of currency in Austria in accordance with the following provisions:

a. United States forces and other Allied forces within Austria will use only Allied military schillings for pay of troops and other military requirements. Allied military schillings will be declared legal tender in Austria. As long as Reichsmarks are legal tender in Austria, Allied military schillings will circulate in Austria interchangeably with Reichsmarks at a rate of one Allied military schilling for one Reichsmark. Reichskreditkassenscheine and other military currency issued by the Germans will not be legal tender in Austria;

b. without authorization by the Allied Council, no Austrian governmental or private banks or agencies will be permitted to issue banknotes or currency;

c. appropriate Austrian authorities should, to the maximum extent possible, be required by the Allied Council to make funds available free of cost in amounts sufficient to meet all expenses of the forces of occupation, including the cost of Allied military government, the pay of Allied military personnel, and to the extent that compensation is made therefor the cost of such private property as may be requisitioned, seized, or otherwise acquired by Allied authorities for reparation or restitution purposes;

d. as soon as administratively practicable, a general conversion into Allied Military schillings of the Reichsmark and Rentenmark currency circulated in Austria should be undertaken by the Allied Council or by you in coordination with the other zone commanders.

You will receive separate instructions relative to the currency which you will use in the event that for any reason adequate supplies of Allied Military schillings are not available.

You will not announce or establish, until receipt of further instructions, any general rate of exchange between the Allied Military schilling on the one hand and the U. S. dollar and other currencies on the other. However, the rate of exchange to be used exclusively for pay of troops and military accounting purposes will be ten Allied Military schillings for one U. S. dollar.

Public Finance

50. Subject to any agreed policies of the Allied Council, you will take such action as may be necessary to insure that all laws and practices relating to taxation or other fields of finance, which discriminate for or against any persons because of race, nationality, creed or political opinion, will be amended, suspended or abrogated to the extent necessary to eliminate such discrimination. Consistent with the foregoing purpose,

the Austrian authorities should be required to take such action in the field of taxation as is necessary to assure an adequate inflow of revenues. Any public revenue in Austria previously collected by the German government may be used for approved public expenditures.

51. Pending the determination of the long-range Austrian customs and trade policy, the Austrian authorities may impose duties on imports for revenue purposes. Duties for other purposes should only be imposed with the approval of the Allied Council. No duties will be imposed on imports for military account or for the account of such relief agencies as may be designated.

52. Subject to any agreed policies of the Allied Council, you will prohibit:

a. the payment to ex-soldiers of all military pensions, or other emoluments or benefits, except compensation for physical disability limiting the recipient's ability to work at rates which are no higher than the lowest of those for comparable physical disability arising from non-military causes;

b. the payment of all public or private pensions or other emoluments or benefits granted or conferred

(1) by reason of membership in or services to the former Nazi party, its formations, affiliated associations or supervised organizations or any pre-Nazi Fascist organizations, such as the Heimwehr and the Ostmärkische Sturnscharen;

(2) to any person who has been removed from an office or position in accordance with paragraphs 5, 6 and 8 (*c*); and

(3) to any person arrested and detained in accordance with paragraph 7 during the term of his arrest, or permanently, in case of his subsequent conviction.

53. The Allied Council should exercise general control and supervision over the expenditures of public funds to the extent necessary to achieve the purposes of the occupation.

54. The Allied Council should promptly initiate a survey for the purpose of ascertaining (*a*) the amount of the German government debt held in Austria, (*b*) the amount of all outstanding internal public debts in Austria, and (*c*) the fiscal position of Austria. You will promptly submit recommendations concerning the treatment of these debts, taking into consideration the effect on Austrian public credit of policies on this matter.

Property Control

55. Subject to any agreed policies of the Allied Council, you will impound or block all gold, silver, currencies, securities accounts in financial institutions, credits, valuable papers, and all other assets falling within the following categories:

a. Property owned or controlled, directly or indirectly, in whole or in part, by any of the following:

(1) the governments, nationals or residents of the German Reich, Italy, Bulgaria, Rumania, Hungary, Finland and Japan, including those of territories occupied by them;

(2) the Austrian State, the municipal and provincial government and all governmental authorities within Austria, including their agencies and instrumentalities;

(3) the Nazi party, its formations, affiliated associations and supervised organizations, its officials, leading members and supporters;

(4) all organizations, clubs or other associations prohibited or dissolved by military government;

(5) absentee owners, including United Nations and neutral governments;

(6) any institution dedicated to public worship, charity education or the arts and sciences, which has been used by the Nazi party to further its interests or to cloak its activities;

(7) persons subject to arrest under the provisions of paragraph 7, and all other persons specified by military government by inclusion in lists or otherwise;

b. Property which has been the subject of transfer under duress, or wrongful acts of confiscation, disposition or spoliation, whether pursuant to legislation or by procedures purporting to follow forms of law or otherwise;

c. Works of art or cultural material of value or importance, regardless of the ownership thereof.

You will take such action as will ensure that any impounded or blocked assets will be dealt with only as permitted under licenses or other instructions which you may issue. In the case particularly of property blocked under *a* (2) above, you will proceed to adopt licensing measures which, while maintaining such property under surveillance, would permit its use in consonance with this directive. Property taken from Austrians under the conditions stated in *b* above should be restored as promptly as possible, subject to appropriate safeguards to prevent the cloaking of Nazi, German or militaristic influence.

The Allied Council should seek out and reduce to the possession and control of a special agency all property interests of any type and description owned either directly or indirectly by Germany or a national or a resident thereof.

External Financial and Property Relations

56. All foreign exchange transactions, including those arising out of exports and imports, shall be controlled for the purpose of achieving the objectives set forth in this directive. To effectuate such objectives the Allied Council should

a. seek out and reduce to the possession and control of a special agency all Austrian (public and private) foreign exchange and external assets of every kind and description located within or outside Austria;

b. prohibit, except as authorized by regulation or license, all dealings in gold, silver, foreign exchange, and all foreign exchange transactions of any kind;

c. make available any foreign exchange proceeds of exports for payment of imports necessary to the accomplishment of the objectives set forth in this directive and authorize no other outlay of foreign exchange assets except for purposes approved by the Allied Council or other appropriate authority;

d. establish effective controls with respect to all foreign exchange transactions, including:

(1) transactions as to property between persons inside Austria and persons outside Austria;

(2) transactions involving obligations owned by or to become due from any person in Austria to any person outside Austria; and

(3) transactions involving the importation or exportation from Austria of any currency, foreign exchange asset or other form of property.

57. The Allied Council should, in cooperation with the Control Council in Germany, take steps necessary to sever all managerial and other organizational connections of banks, including postal banking offices, and all other business enterprises located in Austria with banks and business enterprises or persons located in Germany.

(2) *Statements Summarizing the Agreements Reached by the European Advisory Commission on Control Machinery and Zones of Occupation in Austria. Department of State Press Release, August 8, 1945.*[1]

(a) *Summary of the Agreement between the Governments of the United Kingdom, the United States of America, and the Union of Soviet Socialist Republics and the Provisional Government of the French Republic on Control Machinery in Austria.*

The Allied Control Machinery in Austria will consist of an Allied Council, an Executive Committee, and staffs appointed by the four Governments concerned, the whole organization being known as the Allied Commission for Austria.

The primary tasks of the Allied Commission for Austria will be:

to achieve the separation of Austria from Germany;

to secure the establishment, as soon as possible, of a central Austrian administrative machine;

to prepare the way for the establishment of a freely elected Austrian Government;

meanwhile to provide for the administration of Austria to be carried on satisfactorily.

The Allied Council will consist of four Military Commissioners who will jointly exercise supreme authority in Austria in respect of matters affecting Austria as a whole. Subject to this, each Military Commissioner in his capacity as Commander in Chief of the forces of occupation furnished by his Government will exercise full authority in the zone occupied by those forces.

The Allied Council, whose decisions should be unanimous, will initiate plans and reach decisions on the chief questions affecting Austria as a whole and will insure appropriate uniformity of action in the zones of occupation.

[1] *Ibid.*, p. 221.

The functions of the Executive Committee and the staffs will be to advise the Allied Council and carry out its decisions.

As soon as departments of a central Austrian administration are in a position to operate satisfactorily they will be directed to assume their respective functions as regards Austria as a whole, and will fulfil them under the control of the Allied Commission.

The administration of the city of Vienna will be directed by an inter-Allied governing authority which will operate under the general direction of the Allied Council and will consist of four Commandants. They will be assisted by a Technical Staff which will supervise and control the activities of the local organs.

Liaison with other United Nations governments chiefly interested will be insured by the appointment by such governments of Military Missions, which may include civilian members, to the Allied Council.

United Nations organizations will, if admitted by the Allied Council to operate in Austria, be subordinate to the Allied Commission and answerable to it.

(b) *Summary of the Agreement between the Governments of the United Kingdom, the United States of America, and the Union of Soviet Socialist Republics and the Provisional Government of the French Republic on Zones of Occupation in Austria.*

1. Austria within its 1937 frontiers will, for purposes of occupation, be divided into four zones, one to be allotted to each power as follows:

The northeastern (Soviet) zone will consist of the province of Lower Austria, with the exception of the City of Vienna, that part of the province of Upper Austria situated on the left bank of the Danube, and the province of Burgenland.

The northwestern (United States) zone will consist of the province of Salzburg and that part of the province of Upper Austria situated on the right bank of the Danube.

The western (French) zone will consist of the provinces of Tyrol and Vorarlberg.

The southern (United Kingdom) zone will consist of the province of Carinthia, including Ost-Tyrol, and the province of Styria, except the area of the Burgenland.

2. The city of Vienna within its 1937 boundaries will be jointly occupied by the armed forces of the four powers, and its administration will be directed by an inter-Allied governing authority consisting of four Commandants appointed by their respective Commanders in Chief.

The district of the Innere Stadt will be occupied by armed forces of the four powers;

The districts of Leopoldstadt, Brigittenau, Floridsdorf, Wieden, and Favoriten will be occupied by armed forces of the Soviet Union;

The districts of Neubau, Josefstadt, Hernals, Alsergrund, Währing, and Döbling will be occupied by armed forces of the United States of America;

The districts of Mariahilf, Penzing, Fünfhaus (including the district of Rudolfsheim), and Ottakring will be occupied by armed forces of the French Republic;

The districts of Hietzing, Margareten, Meidling, Landstrasse, and Simmering will be occupied by armed forces of the United Kingdom.

(3) Statement on Recognition of Government of Austria. Department of State Press Release, January 7, 1946.[1]

In accordance with the resolution of December 18, 1945 of the Allied Council in Austria, the members of the Council unanimously recommended to their respective governments that the Austrian Government formed by Chancellor Leopold Figl as a result of the mandate received in the elections of November 25, 1945 be recognized by the states represented on the Council. The recognition of the Austrian Government has been approved by the President, and the United States member of the Allied Council has been instructed to notify the Austrian Government to this effect. The President has in addition sent the following telegram to Dr. Karl Renner on the occasion of his election to the presidency of the Austrian Republic:

I wish to extend to you my sincere congratulations on your election as President of the Austrian Republic and my best wishes in your task of completing the liberation of Austria and the revival of an independent and democratic state. I can assure you that the people of the United States will wish to assist Austria in this endeavor.

The recognition of the Austrian Government by the United States in no way affects the supreme authority of the Allied Council. The Council will continue to operate in carrying out the Allied objectives in Austria. As the Council proceeds with its task of eliminating Nazi influences and institutions in Austria, and assisting in the reconstruction of democratic life, it is hoped that a large-scale reduction may be made in the number of occupation troops of the four states and that Austria may progressively acquire the status of an independent state. The United States Government also hopes that an Austrian agent will arrive soon in Washington to discuss matters of mutual interest which do not affect the supreme authority of the Allied Council.

(4) Agreement between the Governments of the United Kingdom, the United States of America, the Union of Soviet Socialist Republics and the Government of the French Republic on the Machinery of Control in Austria, June 28, 1946.[2]

The Governments of the United Kingdom of Great Britain and Northern Ireland, the United States of America, the Union of Soviet Socialist Republics and the Government of the French Republic (hereinafter called the Four Powers);

In view of the declaration issued at Moscow on 1st November, 1943, in the name of the Governments of the United Kingdom, the United States of America and the Union of Soviet Socialist Republics, whereby

---

[1] *Ibid.*, XIV, p. 81.   [2] *Ibid.*, XV, p. 175.

the three Governments announced their agreement that Austria should be liberated from German domination, and declared that they wished to see reestablished a free and independent Austria, and in view of the subsequent declaration issued at Algiers on 16th November, 1943 by the French Committee of National Liberation concerning the independence of Austria;

Considering it necessary, in view of the establishment, as a result of free elections held in Austria on 25th November, 1945, of an Austrian Government recognized by the Four Powers, to redefine the nature and extent of the authority of the Austrian Government and of the functions of the Allied organization and forces in Austria and thereby to give effect to Article 14 of the Agreement signed in the European Advisory Commission on 4th July, 1945;

Have agreed as follows:

ARTICLE 1

The authority of the Austrian Government shall extend fully throughout Austria, subject only to the following reservations:

(*a*) The Austrian Government and all subordinate Austrian authorities shall carry out such directions as they may receive from the Allied Commission;

(*b*) In regard to the matters specified in Article 5 below neither the Austrian Government nor any subordinate Austrian authority shall take action without the prior written consent of the Allied Commission.

ARTICLE 2

(*a*) The Allied organization in Austria shall consist of

(*i*) an Allied Council, consisting of four High Commissioners, one appointed by each of the Four Powers;

(*ii*) an Executive Committee, consisting of one high ranking representative of each of the High Commissioners;

(*iii*) Staffs appointed respectively by the Four Powers, the whole organization being known as the Allied Commission for Austria.

(*b*) (*i*) The authority of the Allied Commission in matters affecting Austria as a whole shall be exercised by the Allied Council or the Executive Committee or the Staffs appointed by the Four Powers when acting jointly.

(*ii*) The High Commissioners shall within their respective zones ensure the execution of the decisions of the Allied Commission and supervise the execution of the directions of the central Austrian authorities.

(*iii*) The High Commissioners shall also ensure within their respective zones that the actions of the Austrian provincial authorities deriving from their autonomous functions do not conflict with the policy of the Allied Commission.

(*c*) The Allied Commission shall act only through the Austrian Government or other appropriate Austrian authorities except:

(*i*) to maintain law and order if the Austrian authorities are unable to do so;

(*ii*) if the Austrian Government or other appropriate Austrian authorities do not carry out directions received from the Allied Commission;

(*iii*) where, in the case of any of the subjects detailed in Article 5 below, the Allied Commission acts directly.

(*d*) In the absence of action by the Allied Council, the four several High Commissioners may act independently in their respective zones in any matter covered by subparagraphs (*i*) and (*ii*) of paragraph (*c*) of this Article and by Article 5, and in any matter in respect of which power is conferred on them by the agreement to be made under Article 8 (*a*) of the agreement.

(*e*) Forces of occupation furnished by the Four Powers will be stationed in the respective zones of occupation in Austria and Vienna as defined in the Agreement on Zones of Occupation in Austria and the administration of the City of Vienna, signed in the European Advisory Commission on 9th July, 1945. Decisions of the Allied Council which require implementation by the forces of occupation will be implemented by the latter in accordance with instructions from their respective High Commissioners.

Article 3

The primary tasks of the Allied Commission for Austria shall be:

(*a*) To ensure the enforcement in Austria of the provisions of the Declaration on the Defeat of Germany signed at Berlin on 5th June, 1945;

(*b*) To complete the separation of Austria from Germany, and to maintain the independent existence and integrity of the Austrian State, and pending the final definition of its frontiers to ensure respect for them as they were on 31st December, 1937;

(*c*) To assist the Austrian Government to recreate a sound and democratic national life based on an efficient administration, stable economic and financial conditions and respect of law and order;

(*d*) To assist the freely elected Government of Austria to assume as quickly as possible full control of the affairs of state in Austria;

(*e*) To ensure the institution of a progressive long-term educational program designed to eradicate all traces of Nazi ideology and to instill into Austrian youth democratic principles.

Article 4

(*a*) In order to facilitate the full exercise of the Austrian Government's authority equally in all zones and to promote the economic unity of Austria, the Allied Council will from the date of signature of this Agreement ensure the removal of all remaining restrictions on the movement within Austria of persons, goods, or other traffic, except such as may be specifically prescribed by the Allied Council or required in frontier areas for the maintenance of effective control of international movements. The zonal boundaries will then have no other effect than as boundaries of the spheres of authority and responsibility of the respective High Commissioners and the location of occupation troops.

(*b*) The Austrian Government may organize a customs and frontier administration, and the Allied Commission will take steps as soon as practicable to transfer to it customs and travel control functions concerning Austria which do not interfere with the military needs of the occupation forces.

ARTICLE 5

The following are the matters in regard to which the Allied Commission may act directly as provided in Article 2 (*c*) (*iii*) above:

(*i*) Demilitarization and disarmament (military, economic, industrial, technical and scientific).

(*ii*) The protection and security of the Allied forces in Austria, and the fulfilment of their military needs in accordance with the Agreement to be negotiated under Article 8 (*a*).

(*iii*) The protection, care and restitution of property belonging to the Governments of any of the United Nations or their nationals.

(*iv*) The disposal of German property in accordance with the existing agreements between the Allies.

(*v*) The care and evacuation of, and exercise of judicial authority over prisoners of war and displaced persons.

(*vi*) The control of travel into and out of Austria until Austrian travel controls can be established.

(*vii*) (*a*) The tracing, arrest and handing-over of any person wanted by one of the Four Powers or by the International Court for War Crimes and Crimes against Humanity.

(*b*) The tracing, arrest and handing-over of any person wanted by other United Nations for the crimes specified in the preceding paragraph and included in the lists of the United Nations Commission for War Crimes.

The Austrian Government will remain competent to try any other person accused of such crimes and coming within its jurisdiction, subject to the Allied Council's right of control over prosecution and punishment for such crimes.

ARTICLE 6

(*a*) All legislative measures, as defined by the Allied Council, and international agreements which the Austrian Government wishes to make except agreements with one of the 4 Powers, shall, before they take effect or are published in the State Gazette be submitted by the Austrian Government to the Allied Council. In the case of constitutional laws, the written approval of the Allied Council is required, before any such law may be published and put into effect. In the case of all other legislative measures and international agreements it may be assumed that the Allied Council has given its approval if within thirty-one days of the time of receipt by the Allied Commission it has not informed the Austrian Government that it objects to a legislative measure or an international agreement. Such legislative measure or international agreement may then be published and put into effect. The Austrian Government will inform the Allied Council of all international agreements entered into with one or more of the 4 Powers.

(*b*) The Allied Council may at any time inform the Austrian Government or the appropriate Austrian authority of its disapproval of any of the Legislative measures or administrative actions of the Government or of such authority, and may direct that the action in question shall be cancelled or amended.

Article 7

The Austrian Government is free to establish diplomatic and consular relations with the Governments of the United Nations. The establishment of diplomatic and consular relations with other Governments shall be subject to the prior approval of the Allied Council. Diplomatic Missions in Vienna shall have the right to communicate directly with the Allied Council. Military Missions accredited to the Allied Council shall be withdrawn as soon as their respective Governments establish diplomatic relations with the Austrian Government, and in any case within two months of the signature of this agreement.

Article 8

(a) A further agreement between the Four Powers shall be drawn up and communicated to the Austrian Government as soon as possible, and within three months of this day's date defining the immunities of the members of the Allied Commission and of the forces in Austria of the Four Powers and the rights they shall enjoy to ensure their security and protection and the fulfilment of their military needs.

(b) Pending the conclusion of the further agreement required by Article 8 (a) the existing rights and immunities of members of the Allied Commission and of the forces in Austria of the Four Powers, deriving either from the Declaration on the Defeat of Germany or from the powers of a Commander-in-Chief in the field, shall remain unimpaired.

Article 9

(a) Members of the Allied Council, the Executive Committee and other staffs appointed by each of the Four Powers as part of the Allied Commission may be either civilian or military.

(b) Each of the Four Powers may appoint as its High Commissioner either the Commander-in-Chief of its forces in Austria or its diplomatic or political representative in Austria or such other official as it may care to nominate.

(c) Each High Commissioner may appoint a deputy to act for him in his absence.

(d) A High Commissioner may be assisted in the Allied Council by a political adviser and/or a military adviser who may be respectively the diplomatic or political representative of his Government in Vienna or the Commander-in-Chief of the forces in Austria of his Government.

(e) The Allied Council shall meet at least twice in each month or at the request of any member.

Article 10

(a) Members of the Executive Committee shall, when necessary, attend meetings of the Allied Council;

(b) The Executive Committee shall act on behalf of the Allied Council in matters delegated to it by the Council;

(c) The Executive Committee shall ensure that the decisions of the Allied Council and its own decisions are carried out;

(d) The Executive Committee shall coordinate the activities of the Staffs of the Allied Commission.

Article 11

(a) The staffs of the Allied Commission in Vienna shall be organized in Divisions matching one or more of the Austrian Ministries or Departments with the addition of certain Divisions not corresponding to any Austrian Ministry or Department. The List of Divisions is given in Annex I to this Agreement; this organization may be changed at any time by the Allied Council;

(b) The Divisions shall maintain contact with the appropriate Departments of the Austrian Government and shall take such action and issue such directions as are within the policy approved by the Allied Council or the Executive Committee;

(c) The Divisions shall report as necessary to the Executive Committee;

(d) At the Head of each Division there shall be four Directors, one from each of the Four Powers, to be collectively known as the Directorate of that Division. Directors of Divisions or their representatives may attend meetings of the Allied Council or of the Executive Committee in which matters affecting the work of their Divisions are being discussed. The four officials acting as the head of each Division may appoint such temporary sub-committees as they deem desirable.

Article 12

The decisions of the Allied Council, Executive Committee, and other constituted bodies of the Allied Commission shall be unanimous.

The Chairmanship of the Allied Council, Executive Committee and Directorates shall be held in rotation.

Article 13

The existing Inter-Allied Command in Vienna, formerly known as the Kommendatura, shall continue to act as the instrument of the Allied Commission for affairs concerning Vienna as a whole until its functions in connection with civil administration can be handed over to the Vienna Municipality. These will be handed over progressively and as rapidly as possible. The form of supervision which will then be applied will be decided by the Allied Council. Meanwhile the Vienna Inter-Allied Command shall have the same relation to the Municipal Administration of Vienna as the Allied Commission has to the Austrian Government.

Article 14

The present Agreement shall come into operation as from this day's date and shall remain in force until it is revised or abrogated by agreement between the Four Powers. On the coming into effect of the present Agreement the Agreement signed in the European Advisory Commission on 4th July 1945, shall be abrogated. The Four Powers shall consult together not more than six months from this day's date with a view to its revision.

In witness whereof the present Agreement has been signed on behalf of each of the Four Powers by its High Commissioner in Austria.

Done this twenty-eighth day of June 1946 at Vienna in quadruplicate in English, in French and in Russian each text being equally authentic. A translation into German shall be agreed between the four High Commissioners and communicated by them as soon as possible to the Austrian Government.

4. RELATIONS WITH THE AUSTRIAN GOVERNMENT

During January 1946, the United States took the following steps regarding relations with Austria: (1) On January 9, the Department of State announced the lifting of a ban on granting exit permits for Austrian refugees who wished to return to their country; (2) On January 21, John G. Erhardt was appointed United States Political Representative to the Austrian Government with personal rank of Minister; he was also designated to serve as Political Adviser to Gen. Mark Clark in Vienna pending modification of control machinery; (3) The President approved the designation by the Austrian Government of Ludwig Kleinwaechter as Austrian Representative in the United States authorized to deal with relations between the United States and Austria not affecting the authority of the Allied Council.[1]

On May 3, 1946, the Department of State announced that a dollar credit arrangement of 10 million dollars had been completed with Austria for the purchase of American surplus property abroad, thus enabling utilization of American surplus property for the reconstruction of Austria. The arrangement represented a "credit ceiling" and all credit arrangements concluded by the Office of the Foreign Liquidation Commissioner provided for a rate of interest of $2\frac{3}{8}$ percent per annum payable annually with the principal to be made in annual installments.[2]

E. Bulgaria

The agreement concerning an armistice between Bulgaria and the governments of the United States, the Soviet Union and the United Kingdom was signed at Moscow, October 28, 1944.[3] Terms of the agreement provided that, until a peace treaty was signed with Bulgaria, an Allied Control Commission was to regulate and supervise the execution of the armistice provisions. This Control Commission was to be under the chairmanship of the Soviet Union with participation by representatives of the United States and the United Kingdom.

In view of the provisions of paragraph X of the Potsdam Agreement,[4] concerning the conclusion of peace treaties with "recognized democratic governments," the Department of State, in August, 1945, instructed the United States Political Representative in Bulgaria (Maynard Barnes) to express to the Bulgarian Government the attitude of the United States regarding the Bulgarian elections scheduled for August 26, 1945.

"The United States Government has been desirous of recognizing and establishing diplomatic relations with a provisional Bulgarian government which would be representative of all important elements of democratic opinion and which would arrange for free and untrammeled elections under conditions which would safeguard the free expression of political views and the free exercise of political rights.

[1] *Ibid.*, XIV, p. 73, 177.
[2] *Ibid.*, p. 818.
[3] For text of the agreement, see *Documents, VII, 1944–1945*, p. 239.
[4] Department of State, *Bulletin*, XIII, p. 153, 159; see this volume, Appendix II.

"The information available to the United States Government has not satisfied it that the existing provisional Bulgarian Government is adequately representative of the important elements of democratic opinion or that the existing government has arranged for the scheduled elections to take place under conditions which will allow and insure the effective participation therein, free from the fear of force and intimidation, of all democratic elements.

"In the opinion of the United States Government the effective participation of all important democratic elements in the forthcoming election is essential to facilitate the conclusion of a peace treaty with a recognized democratic government. . . ."[1]

On August 25, 1945, the Bulgarian Government announced indefinite postponement of the general election as a result of a recommendation by the Allied Control Commission.

In the text of an *aide-mémoire*[2] transmitted by Benjamin V. Cohen, Counselor of the Department of State, to Lt. Gen. Vladimir Stoichew, Bulgarian representative in Washington, the position of the United States was clarified with regard to decisions concerning Bulgaria taken at the meeting of Foreign Ministers in Moscow in December, 1945. An exchange of notes between the Governments of the United States and the Soviet Union resulted.[3]

For details of peace treaty negotiations concerning Bulgaria, see *The First Five Peace Treaties. Supplement: Documents, VIII, 1945–1946.*

(1) **Statement by the Secretary of State (Byrnes) Concerning Postponement of National Elections in Bulgaria. Department of State Press Release, August 25, 1945.**[4]

I am gratified to learn that the Bulgarian Government has announced the postponement of the national elections originally scheduled for August 26.

This decision should make it possible for the Bulgarian people, at a later date, to choose in free elections a fully representative government which will be able to conclude a treaty of peace and to reestablish normal relations with the United States.

It is especially gratifying to me that the representatives in Sofia of the Soviet Union, British and United States Governments were unanimously in accord with the decision of the Bulgarian Government. This is a striking demonstration of the unity of purpose of the three nations to work together to assist the liberated peoples of Europe in the establishment of democratic governments of their own choice.

(2) **Report of the Moscow Meeting of the Ministers of Foreign Affairs of the Union of Soviet Socialist Republics (Molotov), the United States (Byrnes) and the United Kingdom (Bevin), December 27, 1945.**[5]

[Excerpt]

. . . . . .

VI. BULGARIA

It is understood by the three Governments that the Soviet Government takes upon itself the mission of giving friendly advice to the

---

[1] Department of State, *Bulletin*, XIII, p. 274. [2] See this volume, p. 319.
[3] See *ibid.*, p. 320. [4] Department of State, *Bulletin*, XIII, p. 283. [5] *Ibid.*, p. 1031.

Bulgarian Government with regard to the desirability of the inclusion in the Bulgarian Government of the Fatherland Front, now being formed, of an additional two representatives of other democratic groups, who (a) are truly representative of the groups of the parties which are not participating in the Government, and (b) are really suitable and will work loyally with the Government.

As soon as the Governments of the United States of America and the United Kingdom are convinced that this friendly advice has been accepted by the Bulgarian Government and the said additional representatives have been included in its body, the Government of the United States and the Government of the United Kingdom will recognize the Bulgarian Government, with which the Government of the Soviet Union already has diplomatic relations.

. . . .

(3) Aide-Mémoire *Delivered by Counselor of the Department of State (Cohen) to the Representative of Bulgaria in Washington (Stoichew), February 22, 1946.*[1]

In view of the misunderstanding which appears to exist in certain quarters in Bulgaria as to the position of the United States Government in regard to the decisions concerning Bulgaria taken at the meeting of Foreign Ministers in Moscow in December, 1945,[2] the United States Government desires that the following statement of its views in the matter, which have been made known to the Soviet and British Governments, be brought to the attention of the Bulgarian Government:

It is the United States Government's interpretation of the Moscow decision that the Bulgarian Government and opposition should be urged to find a mutually acceptable basis for the participation in the present Bulgarian Government of two truly representative members of the opposition parties. It was never the understanding of the United States Government that pressure was to be exerted on the opposition to nominate two candidates for *pro forma* inclusion into the Government without regard to the conditions of their participation. Although the Moscow agreement did not set forth any specific conditions for the inclusion of the two representatives of the opposition, it did, in the view of the United States Government, anticipate that the participation of these representatives would be on the basis of conditions mutually agreeable to both the Bulgarian Government and the opposition.

It was and is the earnest hope of the United States Government that, meeting in a spirit of conciliation, representatives of the Bulgarian Government and of the opposition could and would agree to work together on a mutually acceptable basis which would enable two truly representative members of the opposition parties to participate in the Government.

[1] *Ibid.*, XIV, p. 447.
[2] For text of decision, see this volume, p. 318.

(a) *Exchange of Notes between the Chargé d'Affaires of the Union of Soviet Socialist Republics (Novikov) and the Secretary of State (Byrnes) Regarding the United States* Aide-Mémoire *to the Government of Bulgaria of February 22, 1946.*

(i) *Note from the Chargé d'Affaires of the Union of Soviet Socialist Republics to the Secretary of State, March 7, 1946.*[1]

In connection with the memorandum presented by the State Department to the Bulgarian political representative in the United States on February 22, the Soviet Government has instructed me to communicate the following:

The memorandum states that the Moscow agreement provided that the participation of the two Opposition representatives should be based on conditions mutually acceptable both to the Bulgarian Government and the Opposition.

Actually, the decision of the Three-Minister Conference in Moscow in December, 1945, stipulated only two conditions. These conditions were that the two representatives of democratic groups to be included additionally in the Bulgarian Government should:

A. Really represent the groups of parties not participating in the Government, and

B. Really be suitable and work loyally with the Government.

No other conditions were stipulated in the Moscow Conference decision on Bulgaria.

In view of the above the Soviet Government finds it necessary to state the following:

1. The statement made by the United States Government to the Bulgarian Government on February 22 does not conform to the decision reached in Moscow on Bulgaria, since the Moscow Conference decision says nothing about the opposition representative joining the Bulgarian Government on the basis of any "mutually acceptable condition."

2. The statement made by the United States Government infringes the Moscow decision of the three Ministers inasmuch as this statement put forward a new condition for participation of opposition representatives in the Bulgarian Government, a condition not provided for in that decision.

3. The Soviet Government has before now drawn the attention of the United States Government to the fact that the United States representative in Bulgaria, Mr. Barnes, has systematically instigated the Bulgarian Opposition not to act in accordance with the Three-Minister decision, but to put forward new conditions for joining the Bulgarian Government, conditions not provided for by the Moscow Conference. The statement made by the United States Government to the Bulgarian Government on February 22 is actuated by the same purpose as Mr. Barnes' action and is only calculated to encourage the representatives of the Bulgarian Opposition to resist the decision of the Three-Minister conference.

Thus, far from taking steps to further fulfillment of the decision

[1] *New York Times*, March 9, 1946, p. 1.

reached by the Moscow conference of the Three Ministers, the Government of the United States by this statement of February 22 impels the Opposition to sabotage the decision taken at the Moscow conference with a United States representative participating.

In fact, also to be noticed is that the United States Government made the statement unilaterally, without any attempt at preliminary coordination of this step with the other Governments concerned which had been a party of the decision concerning Bulgaria.

The Soviet Government notifies the Government of the United States that it had thought it necessary to inform the Government of Bulgaria of its present statement inasmuch as the United States Government statement of February 22 was brought to the notice of the Bulgarian Government.

(ii) *Note from the Secretary of State to the Chargé d'Affaires of the Union of Soviet Socialist Republics, March 10, 1946.*[1]

I acknowledge the receipt of your communication of March 7, 1946 with reference to an *aide-mémoire* delivered by this Government to the Political Representative of Bulgaria in the United States on February 22, 1946.

I have taken note of the comments of your Government in this connection, particularly the charges that this action by the United States Government is in violation of the decision in regard to Bulgaria taken by the three Foreign Ministers at Moscow in December 1945, and that the United States Government is encouraging the representatives of the Bulgarian opposition "to resist" the Moscow decision. The Soviet Government also states that the presentation of that *aide-mémoire* was a unilateral step taken without prior coordination with other interested Governments which participated in the Moscow Decision.

As indicated in the *aide-mémoire* under reference, the United States Government was motivated in this matter by a desire to correct a misunderstanding which appeared to exist in various quarters in Bulgaria as to the position of the United States Government in regard to the Moscow decision concerning Bulgaria. The Moscow Agreement provided for procedures looking toward inclusion of two representatives of other democratic groups in the Bulgarian Government. These were to be truly representative of the parties not included in the Government, and to be really suitable and work loyally with the Government. It did not occur to the Government of the United States, nor does it now seem conceivable, that such participation would be or should be on terms other than those mutually acceptable to the participants. Otherwise the participation would be upon a basis acceptable only to the participants on one side. Plainly the participation was not to be *pro forma* or created by pressure. It was and is the earnest hope of the United States Government that, meeting in a spirit of conciliation, the Bulgarian Government and the opposition would be able to find a mutually acceptable basis for the implementation of the Moscow Decision.

[1] Department of State, *Bulletin*, XIV, p. 485.

It is therefore with considerable surprise that the United States Government learns that its statement to the Bulgarian Government of so fundamental and simple a proposition is regarded by the Soviet Government as a departure from the agreement. As understood by this Government that statement is the very essence of the agreement.

With reference to the Soviet Government's contention that this step was taken unilaterally and without prior coordination with other interested Governments, the United States Government desires to call the attention of the Soviet Government to the conversations held in London on February 16, 1946 between Mr. Cohen, Counselor of the Department of State, and Mr. Vyshinski, Vice Commissar for Foreign Affairs of the Soviet Union. On that occasion Mr. Cohen on instructions informed the Soviet Government of the views of the United States Government in this matter as subsequently set forth in the *aide-mémoire* of February 22. Similar conversations were held by Mr. Cohen in London with the British Government.

Concerning the statement by the Soviet Government that the United States Government's *aide-mémoire* constitutes encouragement to the representatives of the Bulgarian opposition "to resist" the Moscow Decision and that the same tendency has previously been shown by the United States Representative in Bulgaria, the United States Government has at no time taken any action in this matter which could be interpreted as inconsistent with the friendly spirit of cooperation which motivated its agreement to that decision. The activities of the United States Representative in Bulgaria have been under the instructions he has received from his Government directed toward impressing upon all parties in Bulgaria the need for this same spirit of cooperation. It is the sincere desire of the United States Government that in this spirit an implementation of the Moscow Agreement regarding Bulgaria will be achieved.

(4) *Exchange of Notes between the Secretary of State (Byrnes) and the Prime Minister of Bulgaria (Georgiev).*[1]

(a) Note from the Secretary of State to the Prime Minister of Bulgaria, September 24, 1946.

Since our conversation on August 27 about political conditions in your country and the problem those conditions create for the United States in signing peace with Bulgaria, I have given considerable thought to Bulgaro-United States relations.

I had hoped that implementation of the program set forth in the aide memoire handed by you to Mr. Barnes on August 31 for my information would go far to dissipate the problems that I discussed with you. As I told you, it is my belief that implementation of the Moscow Agreement to enlarge the basis of the Bulgarian Government by the inclusion of two representative leaders of the Opposition before the elections on October 27 for the Grand National Assembly would be the most effective means of assuring widespread acceptance of election results. While I have as yet

[1] *Ibid.*, XV, p. 818.

perceived no signs of an effort on the part of the Bulgarian Government since your return to Sofia to put the Moscow Agreement into effect before the elections, I still hope that such efforts will be made.

I have decided to follow up our conversation in Paris with this letter because of my sincere desire to do everything possible myself to assure in the case of Bulgaria fulfillment of the hopes that were entertained and expressed by President Roosevelt, Marshal Stalin, and Prime Minister Churchill, the representatives of the three great Allies at Yalta. I feel that I should also tell you that I have instructed General Robertson to request of the Acting President of the Allied Control Commission that all party leaders in Bulgaria be heard by the Commission on the subject of the forthcoming elections for the Grand National Assembly and general political conditions in the country. General Robertson will request a special meeting of the Allied Control Commission to consider what steps along the following lines might be taken by the Commission further to assure free elections for the Grand National Assembly:

(1) freedom of press, radio, and assembly for the Opposition;
(2) non-interference of the militia, either with candidates or voters, except to maintain law and order;
(3) release of political prisoners, or open formulation of charges against them;
(4) elimination of any possible threat of post-election retaliation for political reasons.

I am sure you will understand my motives in writing you as frankly as I have and that in this connection you will recall my words on the subject of the difficulty that present-day conditions in your country present to the United States with respect to the resumption and development of friendly relations between our two peoples and Governments.

(b) Note from the Prime Minister of Bulgaria to the Secretary of State.

[Translation]

I have the honor to acknowledge the receipt of your letter of September 24. I am especially grateful for the solicitude which you have shown in the interest of a solution that would clear the way to the renewal and development of friendly relations between the Governments of the United States and Bulgaria, as well as between the Bulgarian people and the noble people of the United States toward whom we have always entertained deep gratitude and respect.

I am able to make the following explanatory comment on the contents of your letter:

On August 27 in the conversation which we had, I explained to you orally the impediments to the realization in practice of the Moscow Agreement for the enlargement of the Bulgarian Government by the inclusion of two representative leaders of the opposition. I confirm anew that the responsibility does not rest with the Government. As it was then, so it is now. There are no factors in the situation that might combine to the realization of the Moscow Agreement.

Because of this, in its intention to normalize its relations with the opposition, especially after your conversation with President V. Kolaroff, the Government decided to seek a solution in another direction; namely through holding elections for the Grand National Assembly, the date of which has been set for October 27. These elections will permit the entire Bulgarian people, Government and opposition, to send representatives to the Constituent Assembly. The results of these elections will determine the composition of the future government and will indicate the manner of settlement of relations between the Government and the opposition.

The Bulgarian Government, which has enjoyed popular support since September 9, has decided to hold entirely free elections, which are to reflect the true will of the people. With regard to this, it has taken dispositions calculated fully to realize the measures which you also recommend in your letter to me. In connection with these recommendations, I should point out the following:

One. Freedom of the press in our country within the limits of existing law is fully assured. At this moment three opposition newspapers appear without hindrance as the organs of three opposition parties, namely newspapers *Narodno Zemedelsko Zname, Svoboden Narod,* and *Zname.* In these newspapers expression is freely given to opposition views and to fairly exacting criticism of the Government.

The Government has given its agreement that all political parties, including the opposition, may expound their election platforms over the state radio.

As concerns the right of assembly of the opposition, they have never been forbidden to gather or assemble, and such meetings are held throughout the country. In this period of the electoral campaigns these meetings are primarily private, but in several localities public gatherings have already been held, and the possibility of holding such gatherings elsewhere is assured.

Two. All basic laws, and especially the electoral law, forbid the militia in our country interfering or exerting influence in the choice of candidates for popular representatives, or in the exercise of the electoral rights of Bulgarian citizens. In addition, the Government has made clear through its most authorized representatives to all officials of the militia and the administration and to the whole country that the militia will have only one obligation before and during elections; namely, to assure order and freedom for every citizen to vote as he chooses.

Three. In good time the Government, immediately after the proclamation of the Peoples Republic, with a view to creating the indispensable psychological conditions for free exercise of the electoral right of Bulgarian citizens, liberated all persons detained on political grounds and against whom there was no basis for formulation of charges of infringement of existing laws. Simultaneously about 1,700 persons who had been condemned by the Peoples Courts for Fascist activities up to September 9, 1944 were released from prison, and sentences of all remaining ones were considerably reduced. I informed you of the achievements in this direction in my letter of September 21.

At present 737 persons in all are interned in the labor-educational institutions of the entire country. Of these only 6 percent, around 45 persons, are adherents of opposition parties, Agrarians (Petkov), Socialists (Lulchev), Democrats (Mushanov), Anarchists (Girginov).

Their detention is not political abuse but is due to the accusations formulated against them for infringement of the administration laws as well as regulations in connection with the conditions for applying the armistice agreement. The remaining 94 are persons with Fascist tendencies, morally depraved persons, and idlers detained on basic existing laws.

Four. All of the measures mentioned up to this point which the Bulgarian Government undertook to assure order and freedom in the forthcoming elections, as well as all further measures that will be undertaken in this same direction, such as the creation of electoral control and supervisory committees with the participation of the opposition parties, to which the opposition has already consented, will constitute sufficient guarantee for the removal of any menace whatever of post-election reprisals on political grounds.

Proof of this sufficiency of guarantee is also the fact that the opposition parties have registered lists of candidates throughout the country. Official data show that parties of Fatherland Front have posted 99 lists, united opposition parties, Agrarians and Socialists, 18 lists, Democrats, 35 lists. Besides another eight lists have been posted by other opposition groups, which facts lead to the conclusion that political conditions are favorable for a free electoral contest.

In advising you of the above I thank you once again, Your Excellency, for the frankness with which you bring up and discuss questions that interest and concern me as well, and I take this opportunity to assure you with the same frankness that I and the Bulgarian Government will do everything necessary so that the Bulgarian people may freely express their will on October 27.

(5) *Exchange of Letters between the United States Representative on the Allied Control Council (Robertson) and the Representative of the Union of Soviet Socialist Republics and Acting Chairman of the Council (Biryusov).*[1]

(a) *Letter from the United States Representative to the Representative of the Union of Soviet Socialist Republics, October 1, 1946.*

I have been directed by the United States Secretary of State, James F. Byrnes, to request a special meeting of the Allied Control Commission to consider what steps along the following lines might be taken by the Commission further to assure free elections for the Bulgarian Grand National Assembly on October 27: (1) Freedom of the press, radio and assembly for the opposition; (2) non-interference of the militia either with candidates or voters except to maintain law and order; (3) release of political prisoners or open formulation of charges against them; (4) elimination of any possible threat of post election retaliation for political reasons. I am also instructed to request that all political

[1] *Ibid.*, p. 820.

leaders in Bulgaria be heard by the Commission on the subject of the forthcoming elections.

In view of the importance of the subject and the urgency of early action, I request that the regular plenary session of the Commission scheduled for October 3 be converted into a special session with yourself presiding. I have conferred with General Oxley who is agreeable to the postponement of the agenda for that meeting to some later date. I have been requested by Mr. Byrnes to keep him informed telegraphically of developments. Under these circumstances, I feel that I must inform him at once as to whether you are agreeable to convoking a special meeting on October 3 in place of the regularly scheduled plenary meeting.

(b) Letter from the Representative of the Union of Soviet Socialist Republics to the United States Representative, October 4, 1946.

I am very much surprised at your request of calling a special meeting of the Allied Control Commission for discussing the measures which should be taken, according to your opinion, by the Commission for the guarantee of free elections to the Grand National Assembly scheduled for October 27, 1946.

It should be known to you that the guarantee of free elections is the prerogative of the Bulgarian Government which in that respect has done everything necessary, which is attested in particular by the decision of opposition parties, published on September 14 and 19, who boycotted elections of November 18 last year, in regards to participation in the election to the Grand National Assembly.

Therefore, the discussion of questions raised by you in the Commission and even more, the taking of any kind of measures by the Commission would be in violation of these prerogatives and a rude interference in the internal affairs of Bulgaria. On the other hand, the Commission cannot consider these questions, as they do not come under its jurisdiction, as determined by the Armistice Agreement with Bulgaria.

(c) Letter from the United States Representative to the Representative of the Union of Soviet Socialist Republics, October 4, 1946.

I have just received your letter No. 3316, October 4, 1946, in reply to mine (No. A-834, October 1, 1946) requesting a special meeting of the Allied Control Commission to consider means of assuring free elections for the Grand National Assembly on October 27. I cannot agree with any of the conclusions arrived at in your letter. I am therefore telegraphing the contents of your letter to Mr. Byrnes with the request that he take such steps in the circumstances as he may consider necessary.

F. Hungary

On January 20, 1945, Hungary signed an armistice with the United States, United Kingdom and the Soviet Union, which provided for the establishment in Hungary of an Allied Control Commission, under the chairmanship of the

Soviet Union, with the participation of the United Kingdom and the United States.[1]

The Potsdam Conference of July 17 to August 2, 1945, provided that revision of the procedures of the Allied Control Commissions in Rumania, Bulgaria and Hungary could be undertaken, taking into account the interests of the United Kingdom, the United States and the Soviet Union.[2] The Potsdam Agreement further provided for orderly transfer of German populations in Hungary.[3]

On September 22, 1945, the United States Representative in Hungary, H. F. Arthur Schoenfeld, delivered a note to the Hungarian Foreign Minister which expressed the willingness of the United States to establish diplomatic relations and negotiate a treaty with the provisional government of Hungary if that government would give assurance of a free election for a representative government and provide for freedom of political expression. The reply of the Hungarian Foreign Minister, forwarded to the United States Representative in Budapest on September 25, 1945, stated that the provisional National Government of Hungary was in a position to offer full guarantee to the United States concerning conditions set forth in the note of September 22.[4]

On November 2, 1945, the United States Government approved the appointment of Aladar de Szegedy-Maszak as Envoy Extraordinary and Minister Plenipotentiary from Hungary to the United States.

On June 19, 1945, the State Department announced that $32,000,000 in Hungarian gold taken by the Germans and held by American forces in Germany would be returned to the Hungarian Government.

For details on Hungarian peace treaty negotiations, see *The First Five Peace Treaties. Supplement: Documents, VIII, 1945–1946.*

(1) *United States Request for Action to Halt Hungarian Economic Disintegration, Including Note from the United States Ambassador to the Union of Soviet Socialist Republics (Smith) to the Minister for Foreign Affairs of the Union of Soviet Socialist Republics (Molotov), July 23, 1946. Department of State Press Release, July 27, 1946.*[5]

[Excerpts]

In the Crimea Declaration on Liberated Europe, the heads of government of the Union of Soviet Socialist Republics, Great Britain, and the United States undertook "to concert during the temporary period of instability in liberated Europe the policies of their three governments in assisting the peoples liberated from the domination of Nazi Germany and the peoples of the former Axis satellite states of Europe to solve by democratic means their pressing political and economic problems."

In following closely the economic-recovery problems of the countries of Europe, the United States Government became seriously concerned several months ago over the alarming deterioration of the Hungarian economy. This concern has mounted in the intervening months, during which the Hungarian economic situation has become progressively worse, culminating in the present chaotic inflation.

Since December 1945 the United States Government has taken the initiative in proposing that the Soviet Union, Great Britain, and the United States consider means whereby the three powers, as contemplated

---

[1] For text of the agreement concerning the armistice with Hungary, see *Documents, VII, 1944–1945*, p. 244.
[2] See this volume, Appendix II.
[3] Department of State, *Bulletin*, XIII, p. 160.
[4] *Ibid.*, p. 478.   [5] *Ibid.*, XV, p. 229.

in the Crimea Declaration, could assist Hungary to rebuild its shattered economy. These proposals, however, have been rejected by the Soviet Government.

In a meeting of the Allied Control Commission in Budapest in December 1945 the United States Representative recommended the establishment of a subcommittee of the Control Commission to consider questions of Hungarian industry, finance, and economics. This approach was unavailing.

Subsequently, in a note to the Soviet Government on March 2, 1946, this Government again raised the issue by reviewing the grave economic plight of Hungary by calling attention to the over-burdening of that country with reparations, requisitions, and the costs of maintaining large occupation forces, and by requesting the Soviet Government to instruct its Representatives in Hungary to concert at an early date with the United States and British Representatives there in devising a program which would bring to an end the process of disintegration in Hungary and at the same time provide a framework within which the rehabilitation of the country and its reintegration with the general European economy might be accomplished.

In a reply dated April 21 A. Y. Vyshinski, the Soviet Deputy Foreign Minister, rejected the United States proposal on the ground that the working out of an economic rehabilitation plan for Hungary fell within the competence of the Hungarian Government. Mr. Vyshinski also denied that the cost to Hungary of Soviet reparations and occupation was in any way responsible for the deterioration of economic conditions in Hungary and alleged that the failure of the United States to return to Hungary from the U. S.-occupied zones in Germany and Austria displaced property estimated in value at $3,000,000,000 was one of the principal reasons for Hungary's present economic difficulties.

In connection with this exchange of notes concerning the economic situation in Hungary, the American Ambassador in Moscow, upon instructions from this Government, has now delivered a further note to the Soviet Government under date of July 23, 1946, the text of which is as follows:

My Government has directed me to communicate to you the following reply to Mr. Vyshinski's letter of April 21, 1946, relating to the economic situation of Hungary:

My Government is unable to agree with the Soviet Government that "the fulfillment by Hungary of its reparations obligations and the presence of occupation troops in Hungary do not and cannot exercise any serious influence on the economic situation of the country."

My Government wishes to bring to the attention of the Soviet Government the fact that half of the current output of Hungarian manufacturing industry, which is operating at only one-third of the pre-war level, is absorbed by reparations and other requirements of the occupying power. In the case of heavy industry, coal, iron, metal and machine production, which is very urgently required for Hungary's rehabilitation, reparations alone absorb between 80 and 90 percent of the current output. Except for some bridge and railway construction necessary to facilitate the movement of goods, Hungarian heavy industry is producing practically nothing for domestic requirements.

. . . . . .

My Government has noted that in the opinion of the Soviet Government "the real reasons for the severe economic and financial situation in Hungary are the expenditures incurred by her in the war against the United Nations and the ravaging of the country by the Germans and the former Hungarian rulers." I am instructed to mention for the information of the Soviet Government that, on the basis of reliable estimates, it has been calculated that the total war damage to Hungarian manufacturing industry, including removals, amounted to $345,000,000 of which $124,200,000 was due to removals by Soviet forces.

Note has also been taken of the view of the Soviet Government that "one of the main reasons for the difficult economic situation in Hungary . . . is the fact that a large quantity of Hungarian property and valuables continues to this day to remain in the American zone of occupation on the territory of Austria and southern Germany where this property was shipped by the Salaszy Government during the period of the advance of the troops of the Red Army." The Soviet Government mentions a figure of about three billion dollars as the estimated value of this property.

In connection with this estimate I am instructed to direct the attention of the Soviet Government to official Hungarian statistics, which estimate all Hungarian war damages attributed to Germans and Nyilas, including destruction within the country and removals from the country, and including damage to real estate, at $1,250,000,000. Since the property removed from Hungary is only a part of this total, and since only a part of the removed property ever reached the American zones, it is clear that the estimate cited by the Soviet Government is grossly exaggerated. This conclusion is indicated also by the fact that the Hungarian Government's estimate of total national wealth in 1943, excluding houses and buildings, amounted to only $4,400,000,000.

Since the Hungarian Government is only now, at the request of my Government, in the course of preparing complete lists of Hungarian property believed to be located in the American zones of Germany and Austria, my Government is not yet in a position accurately to determine the total value of such property. The most important single item of Hungarian property in the American zones appears, however, to be the gold which was removed from Hungary to Austria by former officials of the Hungarian National Bank, and which the United States Government understands amounts to approximately $32,000,000.

With respect to the status of Hungarian property located in the American zones of Germany and Austria, the Soviet Government will be interested to learn that my Government has notified the Hungarian Government of its intention to return to Hungary the looted gold in its custody, and to expedite restitution of identifiable looted property. Restitution of commercial inland water craft on the Danube will be deferred pending the outcome of discussions between the United States military authorities and the Soviet authorities in Vienna with a view toward establishing principles of freedom of movement of vessels on the Danube under the flags which they now fly without danger of seizure. This program of restitution is in accordance with and in implementation of the statement made by the Secretary of State to the Hungarian Premier in Washington.

As pointed out in the original letter of March 2, 1946, the United States Government, at the time of the signing of the Hungarian Armistice, reserved the right to reopen the question of Hungarian reparations. My Government agreed to the Armistice as a means of facilitating the speedy termination of hostilities. It believed that with careful management, Hungary might have been able to pay $300,000,000 in reparations. It did not foresee that Hungary's production capacity and national income would be cut to half or less in the space of a few months, and that the reparations payable by Hungary in 1945, for example, would equal 24 percent of the national income. Likewise it did not foresee that Hungary would be required to surrender large quantities of goods and services over and above its reparations obligations.

My Government has noted the position taken by the Soviet Government with respect to the formulation by the Soviet Union, the United Kingdom, and the United States, of a program which would assist the rehabilitation of Hungary and its reintegration with the general economy of Europe. The Soviet Government may be assured that it is not the policy of the Government of United States to force acceptance by Hungary of any economic program. The United States, in proposing tripartite discussion of an economic program for Hungary, had in mind the discussion of aid and assistance which the three powers could give to Hungary, once the economic obligations of that country were carefully defined and scheduled so as to permit their discharge without depriving the people of Hungary of their means of livelihood. The United States has no desire to impose a plan for Hungary's economy, but does desire to lend assistance to Hungary through a concert of policies such as was envisaged in the declaration made by the three powers at the Crimea Conference.

Hungarian Government officials have, in fact, requested such assistance of the three powers. The Hungarian Finance Minister submitted to the Soviet economic adviser of the Control Commission a report on the Hungarian economic and financial situation under date of December 3, 1945. This report concluded with the following statement:

"The only way that we can see out of our serious financial and economic difficulties is a plan of reconstruction, to be carried out with the assistance of the Allied Powers, the objective of which would be to raise production to a substantially higher level than at present, and restore equilibrium in the country's economic and financial affairs.

"Since, however, we cannot work out a plan of reconstruction until it is known what support we may count upon from the Allied Powers, there is an urgent necessity that the Allied Powers should send a commission which, with the cooperation of the Hungarian Government, would examine the economic and financial situation of the country and the methods by which assistance could be given. We should expect from the work of the commission a statement of what measures and what foreign assistance is necessary, in the present economic state of the country, with its present burdens and requirements, in order that the country may recover economically and be able to meet the triple obligation arising from reparations, other obligations under the Armistice Agreement and pre-war foreign debts."

The Soviet Chairman of the Control Commission refused to accept or to consider this report, nor would he agree to a proposal of the United States representative that there be established a subcommittee of the Control Commission to discuss questions of Hungarian industry, finance, and economics.

. . . .

I am instructed again to call attention to the obligation freely undertaken by the Soviet Union at the Yalta Conference, in which the three heads of state agreed "to concert the policies of their three Governments in assisting . . . the peoples of the former Axis satellite states of Europe to solve by democratic means their pressing political and economic problems."

Pursuant to this agreement, the United States Government again requests that instructions be sent to the Soviet representative in Hungary to concert with the American and British representatives there in halting the present economic disintegration and to provide a framework within which the rehabilitation of that country, and its early reintegration with the general economy of Europe, will be possible. Finally, an immediate consideration is that the prompt issuance of such instructions would have a salutary effect on the financial stabilization program which the Hungarian Government is initiating on August 1, and in the interest of which the United States Government is returning to Hungary monetary gold reported to be valued at about $32,000,000.

(2) *Note from the Vice Minister for Foreign Affairs of the Union of Soviet Socialist Republics (Dekanonozov) to the United States Ambassador to the Union of Soviet Socialist Republics (Smith), July 27, 1946.*[1]

In connection with your letter of July 22, 1946 addressed to Minister of Foreign Affairs V. M. Molotov regarding the economic situation of Hungary and the payment by Hungary of reparations to the Soviet Union, I consider it necessary to draw your attention to the fact that the data cited in your letter and the conclusions which you draw on the basis of this data do not correspond to reality.

In your letter you maintain that the difficulties observed at present in the economic life of Hungary are allegedly the result of the fact that the bulk of the current production of Hungarian industry is being consumed by reparations and by the satisfaction of other demands, as you express it, of the occupying power. You assert, moreover, that reparations consume from 80–90 percent of the production of heavy industry, including the production of iron, metal and machines. You add, that, moreover, from the supplies of the urban population the Red Army allegedly received from Hungary during the first months of 1945 "almost all the supplies of meat, one sixth of the wheat and rye, more than one quarter of the vegetables, almost three quarters of the supply of lard," etc., and that thus reparations paid by Hungary, on the one hand, and the above withdrawals for the supply of the Red Army on the other hand, are the cause of the grievous economic situation of Hungary. The unfoundedness of such an assertion cannot fail to strike any unprejudiced person, particularly if one takes into account the fact that the entire sum of Hungarian reparations deliveries to the Soviet Union for 1945 did not exceed $10,000,000, that is, constitutes a quite insignificant sum. This fact alone is sufficient to demonstrate the complete lack of foundation of the assertion in your letter that the bulk of Hungarian production is being consumed by reparations.

The extent of the unfoundedness of these assertions is apparent from the fact that the Hungarian Government addressing on May 28 of this year, a request to the Soviet Government to fix a plan for reparations deliveries for 1946–53 itself fixed the amount of these deliveries for 1946 as $21,800,000. Under these circumstances the statement to the effect

[1] *Ibid.*, p. 263.

that the reparations obligations of Hungary are excessive, "crushing" and so on is deprived of any foundation.

The Soviet Government, taking into account the economic difficulties of Hungary, already a year ago made considerable concessions to the Hungarian Government, extending the term of reparation deliveries to eight years from six years, prescribed by the armistice agreement. The Soviet Government fully satisfied also the above request of the Hungarian Government for further concessions to Hungary regarding reparations, fully accepting the plan proposed by the Hungarian Government on May 28 for further reparations deliveries to the Soviet Union. According to this plan, reparations deliveries for 1946 are fixed at a sum of $21,800,000; for 1947, 23,000,000; for 1948, 25,000,000; for 1949–53, 30,000,000 annually. At the same time the Soviet Government released Hungary from payment of a fine of 6,000,000 for non-fulfillment on time of reparations deliveries in the first year in which the reparations agreement was in force. To the above must be added, that according to the Soviet-Hungarian trade agreement, Hungary received from the Soviet Union in the past year 1945, goods to the amount of $6,300,000, while at the same time Hungary itself delivered to the Soviet Union goods only to the amount of $26,600. If, thus, there are taken into account goods received by Hungary from the Soviet Union to the value of 6,300,000, then, in the account, it turns out that all Hungarian deliveries for the Soviet Union do not exceed $3,700,000.

In your letter you state that the American Government agreeing to the conditions of the armistice with Hungary did not foresee that "the productive power of Hungary and its national income would be reduced by half or even more in the course of a few months and that, for example, reparations subject to payment by Hungary in 1945 would equal 24 percent of the national income." For a statement of this sort there are no foundations of reality. The above cited data prove fully convincingly that the extent of reparations pointed out in your letter, subject to delivery by Hungary in 1945 to no extent correspond to the real scope of these deliveries, constituting an entirely insignificant amount.

This is the real state of affairs regarding taking of reparations from Hungary for the benefit of the Soviet Union.

The situation also is the same with regard to the data on the supplying the Red Army at the expense of the Hungarian economy cited in your letter, particularly the data regarding wheat, rye, oats, meats, etc. All these data are entirely incorrect. In reality the Soviet forces received not more than three percent of the total amount of these cultures of the 1945 harvest and of fats not more than eight percent by head of swine. The Hungarian Government did not make deliveries of industrial products for the Red Army, with exception of fuel and a certain amount of commissary supplies.

Citing its data, the Government of the U. S. made use of clearly incorrect information which can only create confusion.

It is impossible not to note the quite arbitrary characterization contained in your letter of the economic *situation* of Hungary. The data at the disposal of the Soviet Government do not confirm this characterization. In reality the capacity of the industrial enterprises of Hungary curtailed as the result of the war to 60 percent of the prewar level, had by the middle of July 1946 risen to 70–85 percent in the production of pig iron, steel, rolled metal and machine building and to 85–90 percent in light industry. If the output of industrial production in Hungary in 1945 constituted 30–35 percent of the prewar level at the present time, the output of production has been brought to 60 percent of the prewar level. Thus, despite the existing difficulties, Hungary, since the termination of the war, has increased the productive capacity of its industry by 20–25 percent and by 25–30 percent the output of industrial production. These successes have been achieved despite the fact that the Germans and the followers of Szalshai carried off to Germany a large quantity of the most valuable industrial equipment and raw materials which, like the removed Hungarian gold, fell into the hands of the American Government and to the present time has still not been returned to Hungary. Such a situation, deriving from the policy carried out by the American authorities creates extremely difficult economic conditions for Hungary and is in complete contradiction with the statements of the U. S. Government regarding the necessity of accelerating the economic restoration of Hungary. In your letter of July 22 it is stated that the information regarding the amount of Hungarian property carried off by the Germans and the followers of Szalshai which is already for the second year in the American zone of occupation is exaggerated. But the American Government, as you state, is still preparing lists of Hungarian property plundered and carried away to Germany and Austria and has still not determined the value of this property. The Hungarian Prime Minister Ferenc Nagy in his statement in Parliament on February 7 of the present year declared that the Hungarian Government had registered the property located in the American zone of occupation of Germany and Austria at more than 2 billion. Besides this, the Hungarian Prime Minister added that as the property which had been carried away came to light this sum would reach about 3 billion. This fully corresponds to the figure of 3 million indicated in the note of the Soviet Government of April 21, 1946.

Speaking of the economic situation of Hungary, it is impossible not to note that despite the difficulties existing in this sphere, a number of new factory shops and plants have also been restored and reequipped. It is worth noting such facts as the construction of a new plant for the production of machine tools, the new "Reniks Electric Resistance Plant", and a number of shops for the production of automobile pistons, the reconstruction of the tractor shop in the "Hoferstrans" plant, the restoration and reequipping of various shops in the "Rossman", "Kozma", and other plants. The expansion of the aluminum rolling and wares plant, large scale work on the reequipping of the "Hans" electro mechanical plant. All these facts indicate that the process of the restoration of industry is proceeding in Hungary and that the reparations obligations in Hungary are in no way hindering this process. In the same way is refuted the assertion contained in your letter that the bulk of Hungarian production of current output is allegedly being consumed by reparations and that nothing remains for the restoration of Hungarian economy and for the internal needs of Hungary. Such an assertion is refuted also by the fact that during the second half of 1945 almost 50 percent of the entire rolled metal output went to the needs of Hungarian economy.

In your letter of July 22 there is contained the entirely incorrect assertion that the Soviet authorities have allegedly removed in Hungary industrial equipment in the amount of $124,000,000. Such statements do not have any foundation and only elicit surprise with regard to the sources of the information which has been utilized in this connection. The Soviet forces removed from Hungary as trophy equipment certain military enterprises of a value not exceeding $11,000,000.

With regard to the proposal of the American Government that the representatives of the Soviet Union, U. S. and Great Britain in the Control Commission jointly work out a plan for the economic restoration of Hungary, the Soviet Government as before, considers this proposal not acceptable inasmuch as was pointed out in the letter of the Ministry of Foreign Affairs of April 21, the working of such a plan belongs exclusively to the competence of the Hungarian Government.

G. Rumania

On September 12, 1944, Rumania signed armistice terms with the United States, the Soviet Union and the United Kingdom, which established an Allied Control Commission, under the chairmanship of the Soviet Union, acting for the Allied Powers. The Commission was to function until peace was concluded with Rumania.[1]

The Potsdam Agreement (July 17 to August 2, 1945) made provision for revision of the procedures of the Allied Control Commissions in Rumania, Bulgaria and Hungary, taking into account the interests of the United Kingdom, the United States and the Soviet Union.[2]

Following a communication from King Michael of Rumania asking for advice on reorganization of his government, the Moscow Conference of the three Foreign Ministers, in December, 1945, authorized a Commission composed of A. Y. Vyshinski, Mr. Harriman and Sir A. Clark Kerr to consult with King Michael and members of the present Rumanian government with a view to broadening the Rumanian government. The King was advised that one member of the National Peasant Party and one member of the Liberal Party should be included in the government.[3] After reorganization the Rumanian government was directed to declare free elections as soon as possible on the basis of secret ballot and with participation of democratic and anti-fascist parties. The government was to give assurances of freedom of the press, speech, religion and association.

On May 27, 1946, the United States protested against the non-fulfilment of the assurances given by the Rumanian government in January, 1946, to the above-mentioned tripartite Commission. The text of the note delivered by the Representative of the United States in Rumania, Burton Y. Berry, to the Rumanian Minister for Foreign Affairs, included the following statements:[4]

[1] For terms of the armistice with Rumania, see *Documents, VII, 1944–1945*, p. 231.

[2] For Potsdam provision on revised Allied Control Commission procedure in Rumania, Bulgaria, and Hungary, see this volume, Appendix II.

[3] See *ibid.*, p. 337; for Communiqué on the Moscow Conference of the Three Foreign Ministers, see Department of State, *Bulletin*, XIII, p. 1027.

[4] *Ibid.*, XIV, p. 1007.

"Upon instructions from my Government, I wish to draw to your Government's attention two aspects of political life in Rumania that are giving concern to the Government of the United States. First, the fact that no election law has been promulgated or date set for the elections, and, secondly, the abuses of the freedoms and particularly the increasing frequency of actions of violence which mock at the application of the freedoms guaranteed by the Rumanian Government through its acceptance of the Moscow decisions.

"It is now more than four months since the reorganization of the Government and not only has no date been fixed for the elections but no electoral law for such elections has been promulgated. This situation, incompatible with the Moscow decisions, gives the impression that the Government is procrastinating in the fulfilment of its promise.

. . . .

"Accordingly, it is believed that a different impression will be attained through prompt action on the part of the Rumanian Government in implementing the assurances given the Allied Commission in January by promulgating an electoral law and setting a date for elections, at the same time taking adequate measures during this period prior to elections that all democratic parties may put forward their candidates with the assurance that the freedoms set forth in the Moscow decisions apply equally to members of all such parties."

In a subsequent note of October 28, 1946,[1] from the Representative of the United States to the Rumanian Minister for Foreign Affairs, G. Tatarescu, the United States took cognizance of the promulgation by the Rumanian government of an electoral law, of registration of the Rumanian electorate and of announcement of a date for general legislative elections, but expressed concern that the elections would not be of the free character assured by the Rumanian government in its acceptance of the Moscow Conference decisions.

For details on Rumanian treaty negotiations, see *The First Five Peace Treaties. Supplement: Documents, VIII, 1945–1946.*

(1) Statement by the Secretary of State (Byrnes). Department of State Press Release, August 22, 1945.[2]

The United States representative on the Allied Control Commission in Bucharest has transmitted to this Government a communication from the King of Rumania, who has explained that he is sending similar notes to Air Vice Marshal Stevenson for the Government of the United Kingdom and to General Susaikov for the Government of the Union of Soviet Socialist Republics. The King's communication states that he has taken into consideration the report of the Conference of Berlin in accordance with which a recognized democratic government constituted a condition in order that Rumania might conclude the necessary treaties of peace with the three principal Allied powers and in order that Rumania might obtain the support of these powers for admission into the Organization of the United Nations; and that he has further taken into account the position of the Governments of the United States and of Great Britain in respect of the present composition of the Rumanian Government.

The King further stated that in accordance with the constitutional procedure of Rumania he proceeded to consult the political leaders concerning the situation, the majority of whom pronounced themselves in

[1] *Ibid.*, XV, p. 851.   [2] *Ibid.*, XIII, p. 280.

favor of the formation of a government under conditions which would permit of its recognition by the principal Allied powers, the conclusion of the necessary treaties, and the admission of Rumania as a member of the United Nations.

The King explained that in consequence he then asked the Prime Minister to make easier the realization of a solution in this sense through the resignation of the present cabinet. It appears that the formation of this government was not possible because the Prime Minister did not act upon this invitation. The King has therefore requested the Government of the Union of Soviet Socialist Republics, the Government of the United States, and the Government of Great Britain, in conformity with the decisions taken at the Crimea Conference and in application of the common responsibilities which they have proclaimed, to lend their assistance with a view to the formation of a government which, according to the report of the Conference of Berlin, might be recognized by the three principal Allied powers, thereby placing Rumania in a position to conclude the treaties of peace and to be admitted into the Organization of the United Nations.

The Government of the United States has already expressed the hope that the political situation in Rumania would develop in such a way as to permit it to establish diplomatic relations with Rumania, which were not, however, possible at the present time in view of the fact the provisional government as it was constituted under Groza was not adequately representative of all important elements of democratic opinion.

The report of the Crimea Conference of February 11, 1945 provided that:

The establishment of order in Europe and the rebuilding of national economic life must be achieved by processes which will enable the liberated peoples to destroy the last vestiges of Nazism and Fascism and to create democratic institutions of their own choice. . . .

To foster the conditions in which the liberated peoples may exercise these rights, the three governments will jointly assist the people in any European liberated state or former Axis satellite state in Europe where in their judgment conditions require (A) to establish conditions of internal peace; . . . (C) to form interim governmental authorities broadly representative of all democratic elements in the population and pledged to the earliest possible establishment through free elections of governments responsive to the will of the people. . . .

In conformity with the decision of the Conference to concert during the temporary period of instability in liberated Europe the policies of the three Governments, this Government is prepared to consult with respect to the existing situation in Rumania with the Governments of Great Britain and the Union of Soviet Socialist Republics on the measures necessary to discharge the responsibilities set forth in the declaration as quoted above. This consultation should take place at the earliest time convenient to the other two Governments and at any place which is deemed satisfactory to them. Pending the results of such consultation, this Government is confident that the necessary instructions will be sent to the representatives of the three Governments on the Control Commission to refrain from any action which might complicate the solution of this problem.

We have communicated to the British and Soviet Governments the readiness of this Government to undertake the consultation suggested.

(2) *Report of the Moscow Meeting of the Ministers of Foreign Affairs of the Union of Soviet Socialist Republics (Molotov), the United States (Byrnes) and the United Kingdom (Bevin), December 27, 1945.*[1]

[Excerpt]

. . . .

V. RUMANIA

The three Governments are prepared to give King Michael the advice for which he has asked in his letter of August 21, 1945, on the broadening of the Rumanian Government. The King should be advised that one member of the National Peasant Party and one member of the Liberal Party should be included in the Government. The Commission referred to below shall satisfy itself that

(a) they are truly representative members of the groups of the Parties not represented in the Government;

(b) they are suitable and will work loyally with the Government.

The three Governments take note that the Rumanian Government thus reorganized should declare that free and unfettered elections will be held as soon as possible on the basis of universal and secret ballot. All democratic and anti-fascist parties should have the right to take part in these elections and to put forward candidates. The reorganized Government should give assurances concerning the grant of freedom of the press, speech, religion and association.

A. Y. Vyshinski, Mr. Harriman, and Sir A. Clark Kerr are authorized as a Commission to proceed to Bucharest immediately to consult with King Michael and members of the present Government with a view to the execution of the above-mentioned tasks.

As soon as these tasks are accomplished and the required assurances have been received, the Government of Rumania, with which the Soviet Government maintains diplomatic relations, will be recognized by the Government of the United States of America and the Government of the United Kingdom.

. . . .

(3) *Recognition of Government of Rumania. Department of State Press Release, February 5, 1946.*[2]

In accordance with the agreement in regard to Rumania reached by the Foreign Ministers of the Union of Soviet Socialist Republics, the United Kingdom, and the United States at their meeting in Moscow from December 16 to December 26, 1945, a commission comprised of A. Y.

[1] *Ibid.*, p. 1031. [2] *Ibid.*, XIV, p. 256.

Vyshinsky, Ambassador W. Averell Harriman, and Sir A. Clark Kerr has consulted with King Michael and members of the present Government of Rumania in Bucharest. As a result of these discussions and in fulfilment of the provisions of the Moscow Agreement, (1) representatives of the National Peasant Party and the Liberal Party have been included in the Rumanian Government; (2) the Government thus reorganized has declared that free and unfettered elections in which all democratic and anti-Fascist parties will have the right to take part and put forward candidates will be held as soon as possible on the basis of universal and secret ballot; and (3) the Government has also given assurances concerning the grant of freedom of the press, speech, religion, and association.

In the circumstances, the United States Political Representative in Rumania, acting under instructions of the Secretary of State, on February 5, 1946 transmitted to the President of the Council of Ministers of the Rumanian Government the following note:

The Government of the United States of America has taken note of the communication of January 8, 1946, addressed to Ambassador William Averell Harriman by the President of the Council of Ministers, Dr. Petru Groza, enclosing a declaration of the Rumanian Government, made at a meeting of the Council of Ministers on January 8. According to this declaration the Council of Ministers considered it indispensable that —

One. General elections should be held in the shortest time possible.

Two. The freedom of these elections shall be assured. They shall be held on the basis of universal suffrage and secret ballot with the participation of all democratic and anti-Fascist parties which shall have the right to present candidates.

Three. Freedom of the press, speech, religion and assembly shall be assured.

The Government of the United States has been advised of the conversation which took place on January 9th between the President of the Council of Ministers, and the American and British Ambassadors. It has taken note of the oral explanation of the aforementioned declaration which the President of the Council of Ministers made to the American and British Ambassadors in this conversation to the effect that:

One. All political parties represented in the Rumanian Government shall have the right to participate in the elections and to put forward candidates.

Two. The examination of the balloting procedure and counting of the ballots shall take place in the presence of representatives of all the political parties represented in the Government.

Three. All political parties represented in the Government shall be accorded equitable broadcasting facilities for the presentation of their political views.

Four. All political parties represented in the Government shall have equal rights to print, publish and distribute their own newspapers and political publications. Newsprint shall be distributed to them on a fair and equitable basis.

Five. All political parties represented in the Government shall have the right to organize associations and hold meetings. They shall be allowed premises for this purpose.

Six. The Council of Ministers will consult with the representatives of the political parties in order to reach agreement concerning the grant of freedom of the press and speech as well as on questions relating to the drafting of the electoral law and the conduct of the elections.

The Government of the United States has taken note of the statement contained in the declaration of the Rumanian Government that the Ministries of Interior, Justice, Cults and Propaganda will be charged with the implementation of the decisions contained in the declaration. It understands from the statement of the President of the Council that these Ministries will not act on their own responsibility but under the close control of the Government as a whole. Although these Ministries will be charged with the technical implementation of these decisions, the Rumanian Government as reconstituted will bear the primary responsibility for their fulfillment and for safeguarding the interests of all the participating parties.

As for the decision to hold elections in the shortest time possible, the Government of the United States confidently expects that arrangements will be undertaken with despatch and would hope that it may be possible to hold the elections at the end of April or early in May of this year.

On the basis of the assurances contained in the declaration of the Rumanian Government and on the understanding that the oral statement of the President of the Council of Ministers, as set forth above, reflects the intentions of the Rumanian Government, the Government of the United States is prepared to recognize the Government of Rumania.

(4) *Exchange of Notes between the Minister of Foreign Affairs of Rumania (Tatarescu) and the United States Political Representative for Rumania (Berry) on Recognition of Government of Rumania. Department of State Press Release, February 15, 1946.*[1]

(*a*) *Note from the Minister of Foreign Affairs of Rumania to the United States Political Representative for Rumania, February 7, 1946.*

[Translation]

I have the honor to acknowledge the receipt of your letter addressed to His Excellency the President of the Council of Ministers, Dr. Petre Groza, on February 5, 1946, in which you notified that the United States Government are prepared toward recognition to the Roumanian Government.

The Roumanian Government received this notification with the deepest satisfaction and I believe that it will constitute the beginning of the resumption of the old relations of friendship and cooperation which existed between our countries.

At the same time, the Roumanian Government express their wish to be put in the position to proceed at the earliest date to the reestablishment of our diplomatic relations, by the appointment of a Roumanian representative in Washington.

(*b*) *Note from the United States Political Representative for Rumania to the Minister of Foreign Affairs of Rumania, February 14, 1946.*

My Government has been pleased to receive the communication of February 7, 1946 from the Minister for Foreign Affairs which my Government considers happily confirms the United States Government's understanding of the assurances received from the Rumanian Govern-

[1] *Ibid.*, p. 298.

ment in execution of the decisions taken at Moscow. In the circumstances the United States Government is prepared to entertain a request for its agreement to the appointment of a Rumanian Envoy Extraordinary and Minister Plenipotentiary to the United States.

(5) *United States Position on Election Results in Rumania. Department of State Press Release, November 26, 1946.*[1]

At the Crimea conference in 1945 the Governments of the United States, the Union of Soviet Socialist Republics, and the United Kingdom agreed jointly to assist the people of liberated Europe with a view to the earliest possible establishment through free elections of governments responsive to the will of those people. Subsequently, pursuant to agreement reached at Moscow in December 1945 between the same powers, representatives of the three Governments met in Rumania and obtained assurances from the Rumanian Government that the latter would hold free and unfettered elections as soon as possible on the basis of universal and secret ballot.

The Rumanian Government held elections on November 19, 1946. The Department of State has now received extensive reports concerning the conduct of those elections, and the information contained therein makes it abundantly clear that, as a result of manipulations of the electoral registers, the procedures followed in conducting the balloting and the counting of votes, as well as by intimidation through terrorism of large democratic elements of the electorate, the franchise was on that occasion effectively denied to important sections of the population. Consequently, the United States Government cannot regard those elections as a compliance by the Rumanian Government with the assurances it gave the United States, United Kingdom, and Union of Soviet Socialist Republics Governments in implementation of the Moscow decision.

2. TRIAL OF WAR CRIMINALS

A. United Nations War Crimes Commission

Following the Inter-Allied Declaration on Punishment of War Crimes [2] and repeated resolutions for retribution upon those responsible for such crimes, the President announced, on October 7, 1942, the intention of the United States Government to provide for the surrender to the United Nations of war criminals at the close of the war. After a meeting of representatives from interested governments at the British Foreign Office in London, the War Crimes Commission was established on October 20, 1943.[3] From January 1944 to April 10, 1946, the Commission held 103 meetings.

[1] *Ibid.*, XV, p. 1057.
[2] The signing of the Inter-Allied Declaration on Punishment of War Crimes took place in London on January 13, 1942, with the following nations participating: Belgium, Czechoslovakia, Greece, Luxembourg, the Netherlands, Norway, Poland, Yugoslavia and the Free French National Committee. Great Britain, the Dominions (except Ireland), China, the Union of Soviet Socialist Republics and the United States sent observers.
[3] *Ibid.*, IX, p. 3.

FORMER ENEMY STATES

Composed of seventeen members, representing the governments of Australia, Belgium, Canada, China, Czechoslovakia, Denmark, France, Greece, India, Luxembourg, the Netherlands, New Zealand, Norway, Poland, the United Kingdom, the United States and Yugoslavia, the United Nations War Crimes Commission acted principally as a fact-finding and advisory body. The chief purpose was to investigate war crimes committed against nationals of the United Nations. Its many functions included the recording of available testimony, reporting to the various governments cases in which crimes were committed, identifying the persons responsible, preparing lists of war criminals on the basis of evidence submitted by national war crimes offices of the United Nations, and drawing up charges against such criminals.

In order to carry out the work of investigation, a number of committees were appointed, and a Far Eastern and Pacific subcommission was created to examine information pertaining to Japanese war criminals. Representatives from national war crimes offices conferred with the Commission whenever necessary in order to coordinate activities.

The War Crimes Branch, Civil Affairs Division of the War Department, collaborating with the State Department and Navy Department, collected information on war crimes for submission to the War Crimes Commission.[1]

On May 4, 1946, the President accepted the resignation of Lt. Col. Joseph V. Hodgson as United States Commissioner of the United Nations War Crimes Commission.

Of the 1108 war criminals tried in Europe by October 31, 1946, 413 were sentenced to death, 485 imprisoned and 210 declared not guilty; 1350 were tried in the Far East and of these 384 were sentenced to death, 704 imprisoned and 262 acquitted.[2]

B. International Military Tribunal for Europe

An Agreement signed at London on August 8, 1945, by the governments of the United States, France, the United Kingdom and the Union of Soviet Socialist Republics resulted in the formation of an International Military Tribunal for the prosecution and punishment of the major war criminals of the European Axis.

The Charter of the International Military Tribunal,[3] attached to the Agreement, provided that the body was to consist of one judge and one alternate from each of the four powers, that decisions were to be taken by majority vote (in case of an evenly divided vote the vote of the President was to be decisive) and that convictions and sentences were to be imposed by affirmative votes of at least three members of the Tribunal.

Jurisdiction of the Tribunal covered (1) crimes against the peace. ("Planning, preparation, initiation, or waging a war of aggression or a war in violation of international treaties, agreements, or assurances, or participation in a common plan or conspiracy for the accomplishment of any of the foregoing.") (2) war crimes. ("Namely, violations of the laws or customs of war. Such violations shall include, but not be limited to, murder, ill treatment, or deportation to slave labor or for any other purpose of civilian population of or in occupied territory, murder or ill treatment of prisoners of war or persons on the seas, killing of hostages, plunder of public or private property, wanton destruction of cities, towns, or villages, or devastation not justified by military necessity."); and (3) crimes against humanity. ("Namely, murder, extermination, enslave-

[1] *International Agencies in which the United States Participates,* Department of State Publication 2699, p. 174.

[2] Wright, Quincy. "The Law of the Nuremberg Trial." *The American Journal of International Law,* Vol. 41, No. 1, p. 39 n.

[3] Department of State, *Bulletin,* XIII, p. 223.

ment, deportation, and other inhumane acts committed against any civilian population before or during the war or persecutions on political, racial, or religious grounds in execution of or in connection with any crime within the jurisdiction of the Tribunal, whether or not in violation of the domestic law of the country where perpetrated.")

The Tribunal consisted of Lord Justice Geoffery Lawrence (Great Britain), Francis Biddle (United States), Major General I. T. Nikitchenko (Union of Soviet Socialist Republics), and Donnedieu de Vabres (France). The body convened for its first meeting in Berlin on October 18, 1945, to receive the indictment from the Committee of Chief Prosecutors, composed of Justice Robert H. Jackson (United States), Sir Hartley Shawcross (Great Britain), François de Menthon (France) and General R. A. Rudenko (Union of Soviet Socialist Republics).[1]

The trial at Nuremberg proceeded from November 20, 1945 to October 1, 1946, conducted in four languages. Of the 24 Nazi leaders indicted on two or more counts, 21 defendants were present during the trial. Gustave Krupp von Bohlen was too ill to be tried and Martin Bormann was tried *in absentia*. Robert Ley committed suicide while in custody.

The indictment included the following counts: (1) Count One — The Common Plan or Conspiracy, (2) Count Two — Crimes Against Peace, (3) Count Three — War Crimes and (4) Count Four — Crimes Against Humanity. The Court sustained 52 of the 76 counts in the indictment against the defendants.

With respect to individual defendants, the following results were announced by the Tribunal on October 1, 1946: Schacht, Von Papen and Fritzsche were acquitted; Goering (guilty on all four counts), Ribbentrop (guilty on all four counts), Keitel (guilty on all four counts), Rosenberg (guilty on all four counts), Kaltenbrunner (guilty of war crimes and crimes against humanity), Frank (guilty of war crimes and crimes against humanity), Frick (guilty of crimes against the peace, war crimes and crimes against humanity), Streicher (guilty of crimes against humanity), Sauckel (guilty of war crimes and crimes against humanity), Jodl (guilty on all four counts), Bormann (guilty of war crimes and crimes against humanity), Seyss-Inquart (guilty of crimes against the peace, war crimes and crimes against humanity) were sentenced to hang; Hess (guilty of conspiracy and crimes against the peace), Funk (guilty of crimes against the peace, war crimes and crimes against humanity), Raeder (guilty of crimes against the peace, conspiracy and war crimes) were sentenced to life imprisonment; Schirach (guilty of crimes against humanity) and Speer (guilty of war crimes and crimes against humanity) were sentenced to twenty years' imprisonment; von Neurath (guilty on all four counts) was sentenced to fifteen years' imprisonment; Doenitz (guilty of crimes against the peace and war crimes) was sentenced to ten years' imprisonment.

The SS (Black Shirts), the SD, the Gestapo and the Leadership Corps of the Nazi Party were found criminal. The SA (Brown Shirts), the Reich Cabinet and the General Staff and High Command were acquitted.[2]

President Truman accepted the resignation of Justice Robert H. Jackson as Chief Counsel for the United States on October 17, 1946 and the resignation of Francis Biddle as United States Member of the International Military Tribunal on November 17, 1946.[3]

For section of the Potsdam declaration regarding war criminals, see this volume, Appendix II.

[1] *Trial of War Criminals*, Department of State Publication 2420; Department of State, *Bulletin*, XIII, p. 850; and *ibid.*, XV, p. 364. See also, Wright, cited above, p. 38.
[2] The Soviet Judge dissented from the acquittal.
[3] Department of State, *Bulletin*, XV, p. 954.

(1) *Agreement by the Government of the United States of America, the Provisional Government of the French Republic, the Government of the United Kingdom of Great Britain and Northern Ireland and the Government of the Union of Soviet Socialist Republics for the Prosecution and Punishment of the Major War Criminals of the European Axis, August 8, 1945.*[1]

Whereas the United Nations have from time to time made declarations of their intention that war criminals shall be brought to justice;

And whereas the Moscow Declaration of the 30th October 1943 on German atrocities in occupied Europe stated that those German officers and men and members of the Nazi party who have been responsible for or have taken a consenting part in atrocities and crimes will be sent back to the countries in which their abominable deeds were done in order that they may be judged and punished according to the laws of these liberated countries and of the free governments that will be created therein;

And whereas this declaration was stated to be without prejudice to the case of major criminals whose offenses have no particular geographic location and who will be punished by the joint decision of the Governments of the Allies;

Now, therefore, the Government of the United States of America, the Provisional Government of the French Republic, the Government of the United Kingdom of Great Britain and Northern Ireland, and the Government of the Union of Soviet Socialist Republics (hereinafter called "the signatories") acting in the interests of all the United Nations and by their representatives duly authorized thereto have concluded this agreement.

Article 1. There shall be established, after consultation with the Control Council for Germany, an International Military Tribunal for the trial of war criminals whose offenses have no particular geographical location, whether they be accused individually or in their capacity as members of organizations or groups or in both capacities.

Article 2. The constitution, jurisdiction, and functions of the International Military Tribunal shall be those set out in the charter annexed to this agreement, which Charter shall form an integral part of this agreement.

Article 3. Each of the signatories shall take the necessary steps to make available for the investigation of the charges and trial the major war criminals detained by them who are to be tried by the International Military Tribunal. The signatories shall also use their best endeavors to make available for investigation of the charges against, and the trial before the International Military Tribunal, such of the major war criminals as are not in the territories of any of the signatories.

Article 4. Nothing in this agreement shall prejudice the provisions established by the Moscow Declaration concerning the return of war criminals to the countries where they committed their crimes.

[1] *Ibid.*, XIII, p. 222.

Article 5. Any Government of the United Nations may adhere to this agreement by notice given through the diplomatic channel to the Government of the United Kingdom, who shall inform the other signatory and adhering Governments of each such adherence.

Article 6. Nothing in this agreement shall prejudice the jurisdiction or the powers of any national or occupation court established or to be established in any Allied territory or in Germany for the trial of war criminals.

Article 7. This agreement shall come into force on the day of signature and shall remain in force for the period of one year and shall continue thereafter, subject to the right of any signatory to give, through the diplomatic channel, one month's notice of intention to terminate it. Such termination shall not prejudice any proceedings already taken or any findings already made in pursuance of this agreement.

In witness whereof the undersigned have signed the present agreement.

Done in quadruplicate in London this eighth day of August, 1945, each in English, French, and Russian and each text to have equal authenticity.

(2) *Executive Order 9626, Appointing the Member and Alternate Member for the United States of the International Military Tribunal Established for the Trial and Punishment of the Major War Criminals of the European Axis, September 24, 1945.*[1]

By virtue of the authority vested in me by the Constitution and the statutes, and as President of the United States and Commander in Chief of the Army and Navy of the United States, it is ordered as follows:

1. In accordance with Article II of the Charter of the International Military Tribunal established by the Government of the United States of America, the Provisional Government of the French Republic, the Government of the United Kingdom of Great Britain and Northern Ireland, and the Government of the Union of Soviet Socialist Republics for the trial and punishment of the major war criminals of the European Axis, pursuant to their agreement of August 8, 1945, I hereby appoint Francis Biddle of Pennsylvania to be the Member for the United States of the International Military Tribunal and John J. Parker of North Carolina to be the Alternate Member for the United States of the International Military Tribunal.

2. The Member for the United States of the International Military Tribunal shall receive such compensation and allowance for expenses as may be determined by the Secretary of State. The Alternate Member shall serve without compensation but shall receive such allowance for expenses as may be authorized by the Secretary of State.

3. The Secretary of State, the Secretary of War, the Attorney General, and the Secretary of the Navy are authorized to provide appropriate assistance to the Member and the Alternate Member in the performance of their duties hereunder and may assign or detail such personnel, including members of the armed forces, as may be requested for the purpose.

[1] *Ibid.*, p. 488.

(3) *Final Report to the President (Truman) from United States Chief of Council (Jackson), October 7, 1946.*[1]

I have the honor to report as to the duties which you delegated to me on May 2, 1945 in connection with the prosecution of major Nazi war criminals.

The International Military Tribunal sitting at Nurnberg, Germany on 30 September and 1 October, 1946 rendered judgment in the first international criminal assizes in history. It found 19 of the 22 defendants guilty on one or more of the counts of the Indictment, and acquitted 3. It sentenced 12 to death by hanging, 3 to imprisonment for life, and the four others to terms of 10 to 20 years imprisonment.

The Tribunal also declared 4 Nazi organizations to have been criminal in character. These are: The Leadership Corps of the Nazi Party; *Die Schutzstaffeln*, known as the SS; *Die Sicherheitsdienst*, known as the SD; and *Die Geheimstaatspolizie*, known as the Gestapo, or Secret State Police. It declined to make that finding as to *Die Sturmabteilungen*, known as the SA; the *Reichscabinet*, and the General Staff and High Command. The latter was solely because the structure of the particular group was considered by the Tribunal to be too loose to constitute a coherent "group" or "organization," and was not because of any doubt of its criminality in war plotting. In its judgment the Tribunal condemned the officers who performed General Staff and High Command functions as "a ruthless military caste" and said they were "responsible in large measure for the miseries and suffering that have fallen on millions of men, women and children. They have been a disgrace to the honorable profession of arms." This finding should dispose of any fear that we were prosecuting soldiers just because they fought for their country and lost, but otherwise the failure to hold the General Staff to be a criminal organization is regrettable.

The magnitude of the task which, with this judgment, has been brought to conclusion may be suggested statistically: The trial began on November 20, 1945 and occupied 216 days of trial time. 33 witnesses were called and examined for the prosecution. 61 witnesses and 19 defendants testified for the defense; 143 additional witnesses gave testimony by interrogatories for the defense. The proceedings were conducted and recorded in four languages — English, German, French, and Russian — and daily transcripts in the language of his choice was provided for each prosecuting staff and all counsel for defendants. The English transcript of the proceedings covers over 17,000 pages. All proceedings were sound-reported in the original language used.

In preparation for the trial over 100,000 captured German documents were screened or examined and about 10,000 were selected for intensive examination as having probable evidentiary value. Of these, about 4,000 were translated into four languages and used, in whole or in part, in the trial as exhibits. Millions of feet of captured moving picture film were examined and over 100,000 feet brought to Nurnberg. Relevant

[1] *Ibid.*, XV, p. 771.

sections were prepared and introduced as exhibits. Over 25,000 captured still photographs were brought to Nurnberg, together with Hitler's personal photographer who took most of them. More than 1,800 were selected and prepared for use as exhibits. The Tribunal, in its judgment, states, "The case, therefore, against the defendants rests in large measure on documents of their own making, the authenticity of which has not been challenged except in one or two cases." The English translations of most of the documents are now being published by the Departments of State and War in eight volumes and will be a valuable and permanent source for the war history. As soon as funds are available, additional volumes will be published so that the entire documentary aspect of the trial — prosecution and defense — will be readily available.

As authorized by your Executive Order, it was my policy to borrow professional help from Government Departments and agencies so far as possible. The War Department was the heaviest contributor, but many loans were also made by the State, Justice, and Navy Departments and, early, by the Office of Strategic Services. All have responded generously to my requests for assistance. The United States staff directly engaged on the case at Nurnberg, including lawyers, secretaries, interpreters, translators, and clerical help numbered at its peak 654, 365 being civilians and 289 military personnel. British, Soviet and French delegations aggregated approximately the same number. Nineteen adhering nations also sent representatives, which added thirty to fifty persons to those actively interested in the case. The press and radio had a maximum of 249 accredited representatives who reported the proceedings to all parts of the world. During the trial over 60,000 visitors' permits were issued, but there is a considerable and unknown amount of duplication as a visitor was required to have a separate permit for each session attended. Guests included leading statesmen, jurists, and lawyers, military and naval officers, writers, and invited representative Germans.

On the United States fell the obligations of host nation at Nurnberg. The staffs of all nations, the press, and visitors were provided for by the United States Army. It was done in a ruined city and among an enemy population. Utilities, communications, transport, and housing had been destroyed. The Courthouse was untenantable until extensively repaired. The Army provided air and rail transportation, operated a motor pool for local transportation, set up local and long distance communications service for all delegations and the press, and billeted all engaged in the work. It operated messes and furnished food for all, the Courthouse cafeteria often serving as many as 1,500 lunches on Court days. The United States also provided security for prisoners, judges, and prosecution, furnished administrative services, and provided such facilities as photostat, mimeograph, and sound recording. Over 30,000 photostats, about fifty million pages of typed matter, and more than 4,000 record discs were produced. The Army also met indirect requirements such as dispensary and hospital, shipping, postal, post exchange, and other servicing. It was necessary to set up for this personnel every facility not only for working, but for living as well, for the community itself afforded nothing. The Theatre Commander and his staff, Military Government officials, area commanders and their staffs, and troops were cordially and tirelessly cooperative in meeting our heavy requirements under unusual difficulties and had the commendation, not only of the American staff, but of all others.

It is safe to say that no litigation approaching this in magnitude has ever been attempted. I trust my pride will be pardonable in pointing out that this gigantic trial was organized and ready to start the evidence on November 20, 1945 — less than seven months after I was appointed and after the surrender of Germany. It was concluded in less time than many litigations in the regularly established Courts of this country which proceed in one language instead of four. If it were not that the comparison might be deemed invidious, I could cite many anti-trust actions, rate cases, original cases, in the United States Supreme Court, and other large litigations that have taken much longer to try.

In this connection it should be noted that we decided to install facilities for simultaneous interpretation of the proceedings into four languages. This was done against the advice of professional interpreters of the old school that it "would not work." It does work, and without it the trial could not have been accomplished in this time, if at all. To have had three successive translations of each question, and then three of each answer, and to have had each speech redelivered three times in different languages after the first delivery finished, would have been an intolerable waste of time. The system we used makes one almost unaware of the language barrier so rapidly is every word made available in each language.

II.

Although my personal undertaking is at an end, any report would be incomplete and misleading which failed to take account of the general war crimes work that remains undone and the heavy burden that falls to successors in this work. A very large number of Germans who have participated in the crimes remains unpunished. There are many industrialists, militarists, politicians, diplomats, and police officials whose guilt does not differ from those who have been convicted except that their parts were at lower levels and have been less conspicuous.

Under your Executive Order of January 16, 1946, the war crimes functions devolve upon Military Government upon my retirement. At the time this order was signed it was agreed between Military Government and myself that I would at once name Brigadier General Telford Taylor as deputy in charge of preparing subsequent proceedings, and that upon my retirement he would be named to take over the war crimes prosecution on behalf of Military Government. He has assembled a staff and prepared a program of prosecutions against representatives of all the important segments of the Third Reich including a considerable number of industrialists and financiers, leading cabinet ministers, top SS and police officials, and militarists. Careful analysis is being made of the Tribunal's decision to determine any effects of the acquittal of Schacht and Von Papen upon this plan of prosecution of industrialists and financiers who are clearly subject to prosecution on such specific charges as the use of slave labor.

The unsettled question is by what method these should be tried. The most expeditious method of trial and the one that will cost the United States the least in money and in manpower is that each of the occupying powers assume responsibility for the trial within its own zone of the prisoners in its own custody. Most of these defendants can be charged with single and specific crimes which will not involve a repetition of the whole history of the Nazi conspiracy. The trials can be conducted in two languages instead of four, and since all of the judges in any one trial would be of a single legal system no time would be lost adjusting different systems of procedure.

A four-power, four-language international trial is inevitably the slowest and most costly method of procedure. The chief purposes of this extraordinary and difficult method of trial have been largely accomplished, as I shall later point out.

There is neither moral nor legal obligation on the United States to undertake another trial of this character. While the International Agreement makes provision for a second trial, minutes of the negotiations will show that I was at all times candid to the point of being blunt in telling the conference that the United States would accept one trial of the top criminals to suffice to document the war and to establish the principles for which we contended, and that we would make no commitment to engage in another.

It has been suggested by some of our Allies that another international trial of industrialists be held. The United States proposed to try in the first trial not only Alfried Krupp, but several other industrialists and cartel officials. Our proposal was defeated by the unanimous vote of our three Allies. After indictment, when it appeared that the elder Krupp was too ill to be tried, the United States immediately moved that Alfried Krupp be added as a defendant and tried for the crimes which he had committed as chief owner and president of the Krupp armament works. This was likewise defeated by the Combined vote of all our Allies. Later, the Soviet and French joined in a motion to include Krupp, but it was denied by the Tribunal. This is not recited in criticism of my associates; it was their view that the number of defendants was already sufficiently large and that to add others would delay or prolong the trial. However, if they were unwilling to take the additional time necessary to try industrialists in this case, it does not create an obligation on the United States to assume the burdens of a second international trial.

The quickest and most satisfactory results will be obtained, in my opinion, from immediate commencement of our own cases according to plans which General Taylor has worked out in the event that such is your decision. Of course, appropriate notifications should be given to the nations associated with us in the first trial.

Another item of unfinished business concerns the permanent custody of captured documents. In the hands of the prosecution and of various agencies there are large numbers of documents in addition to those that have been used which have not been examined or translated but which probably contain much valuable information. These are the property of the United States. They should be collected, classified, and indexed. Some of them may hold special interest for particular agencies; all of them should be available ultimately to the public. Unless some one qualified agency, such as the Library of Congress, is made responsible for this work and authorized to take custody on behalf of the United States, there is considerable danger that these documents will become scattered, destroyed, or buried in specialized archives. The matter is of such importance as to warrant calling it to your attention.

III.

The vital question in which you and the country are interested is whether the results of this trial justify this heavy expenditure of effort. While the sentences imposed upon individuals hold dramatic interest, and while the acquittals, especially of Schacht and Von Papen, are regrettable, the importance of this case is not measurable in terms of the personal fate of any of the defendants who were already broken and discredited men. We are too close to the trial to appraise its long-range effects. The only criterion of success presently applicable is the short-range test as to whether we have done what we set out to do. This was outlined in my report to you on June 7, 1945. By this standard we have succeeded.

The importance of the trial lies in the principles to which the Four Powers became committed by the Agreement, by their participation in the prosecution, and by the judgment rendered by the Tribunal. What has been accomplished may be summarized as follows:

1. We negotiated and concluded an Agreement with the four dominant powers of the earth, signed at London on August 8, 1945, which for the first time made explicit and unambiguous what was theretofore, as the Tribunal has declared, implicit in International Law, namely, that to prepare, incite, or wage a war of aggression, or to conspire with others to do so, is a crime against international society, and that to persecute, oppress, or do violence to individuals or minorities on political, racial, or religious grounds in connection with such a war, or to exterminate, enslave, or deport civilian populations, is an international crime, and that for the commission of such crimes individuals are responsible. This Agreement also won the adherence of nineteen additional nations and represents the combined judgments of the overwhelming majority of civilized people. It is a basic charter in the International Law of the future.

2. We have also incorporated its principles into a judicial precedent. "The power of the precedent," Mr. Justice Cardozo said, "is the power of the beaten path." One of the chief obstacles to this trial was the lack of a beaten path. A judgment such as has been rendered shifts the power of the precedent to the support of these rules of law. No one can hereafter deny or fail to know that the principles on which the Nazi leaders are adjudged to forfeit their lives constitute law — and law with a sanction.

3. The Agreement devised a workable procedure for the trial of crimes which reconciled the basic conflicts in Anglo-American, French, and Soviet procedures. In matters of procedure, legal systems differ more than in substantive law. But the Charter set up a few simple rules which assured all of the elements of fair and full hearing, including counsel for the defense. Representatives of the Four Powers, both on the Bench and at the Prosecutors' tables, have had to carry out that Agreement in day-to-day cooperation for more than a year. The law is a contentious profession and a litigation offers countless occasions for differences even among lawyers who represent the same clients and are trained in a single system of law. When we add the diversities of interests that exist among our four nations, and the differences in tradition, viewpoint and language, it will be seen that our cooperation was beset with real difficulties. My colleagues, representing the United Kingdom, France, and the Soviet Union, exemplified the best professional tradition of their countries and have earned our gratitude for the patience, generosity, good will and professional ability which they brought to the task. It would be idle to pretend that we have not had moments of difference and vexation, but the steadfast purpose of all delegations that this first international trial should prove the possibility of successful international cooperation in use of the litigation process, always overcame transient irritations.

4. In a world torn with hatreds and suspicions, where passions are stirred by the "frantic boast and foolish word," the Four Powers have given the example of submitting their grievances against these men to a dispassionate inquiry on legal evidence. The atmosphere of the Tribunal never failed to make a strong and favorable impression on visitors from all parts of the world because of its calmness and the patience and attentiveness of every Member and Alternate on the Tribunal. The nations have given the example of leaving punishment of individuals to the determination of independent judges, guided by principles of law, after hearing all of the evidence for the defense as well as the prosecution. It is not too much to hope that this example of full and fair hearing, and tranquil and discriminating judgment will do something toward strengthening the processes of justice in many countries.

5. We have documented from German sources the Nazi aggressions, persecutions, and atrocities with such authenticity and in such detail that there can be no responsible denial of these crimes in the future and no tradition of martyrdom of the Nazi leaders can arise among informed people. No history of this era can be entitled to authority which fails to take into account the record of Nurnberg. While an effort was made by Goering and others to portray themselves as "glowing patriots," their admitted crimes of violence and meanness, of greed and graft, leave no ground for future admiration of their characters and their fate leaves no incentive to emulation of their examples.

6. It has been well said that this trial is the world's first post mortem examination of a totalitarian regime. In this trial, the Nazis themselves with Machiavellian shamelessness exposed their methods of subverting people's liberties and establishing their dictatorship. The record is a merciless exposé of the cruel and sordid methods by which a militant

minority seized power, suppressed opposition, set up secret political police and concentration camps. They resorted to legal devices such as "protective custody," which Goering frankly said meant the arrest of people not because they had committed any crime but because of acts it was suspected they might commit if left at liberty. They destroyed all judicial remedies for the citizen and all protections against terrorism. The record discloses the early symptoms of dictatorship and shows that it is only in its incipient stages that it can be brought under control. And the testimony records the German example that the destruction of opposition produces eventual deterioration in the government that does it. By progressive intolerance a dictatorship by its very nature becomes so arbitrary that it cannot tolerate opposition, even when it consists merely of the correction of misinformation or the communication to its highest officers of unwelcome intelligence. It was really the recoil of the Nazi blows at liberty that destroyed the Nazi regime. They struck down freedom of speech and press and other freedoms which pass as ordinary civil rights with us, so thoroughly that not even its highest officers dared to warn the people or the Fuehrer that they were taking the road to destruction. The Nurnberg trial has put that handwriting on the wall for the oppressor as well as the oppressed to read.

Of course, it would be extravagant to claim that agreements or trials of this character can make aggressive war or persecution of minorities impossible, just as it would be extravagant to claim that our federal laws make federal crime impossible. But we cannot doubt that they strengthen the bulwarks of peace and tolerance. The four nations through their prosecutors and through their representatives on the Tribunal, have enunciated standards of conduct which bring new hope to men of good will and from which future statesmen will not lightly depart. These standards by which the Germans have been condemned will become the condemnation of any nation that is faithless to them.

By the Agreement and this trial we have put International Law squarely on the side of peace as against aggressive warfare, and on the side of humanity as against persecution. In the present depressing world outlook it is possible that the Nurnberg trial may constitute the most important moral advance to grow out of this war. The trial and decision by which the four nations have forfeited the lives of some of the most powerful political and military leaders of Germany because they have violated fundamental International Law, do more than anything in our time to give to International Law what Woodrow Wilson described as "the kind of vitality it can only have if it is a real expression of our moral judgment."

I hereby resign my commission as your representative and Chief of Counsel for the United States. In its execution I have had the help of many able men and women, too many to mention individually, who have made personal sacrifice to carry on a work in which they earnestly believed. I also want to express deep personal appreciation for this opportunity to do what I believe to be a constructive work for the peace of the world and for the better protection of persecuted peoples. It was, perhaps, the greatest opportunity ever presented to an American lawyer. In pursuit of it many mistakes have been made and many inadequacies must be confessed. I am consoled by the fact that in proceedings of this novelty, errors and missteps may also be instructive to the future.

C. International Military Tribunal for the Far East

In the Proclamation defining terms for Japanese surrender (Potsdam Declaration), issued on July 26, 1945, by the United States, United Kingdom and China, provision was made for punishment of Japanese war criminals, "including those who have visited cruelties upon our prisoners." [1]

The International Military Tribunal for the Far East was established on January 19, 1946, by a Special Proclamation issued by the Supreme Commander for Allied Powers, Douglas MacArthur, and implemented by the Charter of the International Tribunal.[2]

The Charter specified that the Tribunal was to consist of not less than six members nor more than eleven members, appointed by the Supreme Commander from the names submitted by the signatories to the Instrument of Surrender, India and the Philippines.

Jurisdiction of the Tribunal covered the categories of (1) crimes against peace, (2) conventional war crimes and (3) crimes against humanity. The Tribunal consisted of representatives from Australia, Canada, China, Great Britain, the Netherlands, New Zealand, the Union of Soviet Socialist Republics, United States, France, India, and the Philippines.[3] Judge John P. Higgins represented the United States on the Tribunal. Joseph B. Keenan, Chief of Counsel, acted on behalf of the United States in the prosecution of war crimes charges against the major Japanese war criminals.[4]

Twenty-eight military and political leaders of Japan during the period from January 1, 1938 to September 2, 1945 were named in a 55 count indictment [5] presented on April 29, 1946 to the International Military Tribunal by United States Chief of Counsel. The accused were: Sadao Araki, Kenji Dohihara, Kingoro Hashimoto, Shunroku Hata, Kiichiro Hiranuma, Koki Hirota, Naoki Hoshino, Seishiro Itagaki, Okinori Kaya, Koichi Kido, Heitaro Kimura, Kuniaki Koiso, Iwane Matsui, Yosuke Matsuoka, Jiro Minami, Akira Muto, Osami Nagano, Takasumi Oka, Shumei Okawa, Hiroshi Oshima, Kenryo Sato, Mamoru Shigemitsu, Shigetaro Shimada, Toshio Shiratori, Teiichi Suzuki, Shigenori Togo, Hideki Tojo, Yoshijiro Umezu.

(1) *Executive Order 9660, Conferring Certain Authority upon the Chief of Counsel (Keenan) in the Preparation and Prosecution of Charges of War Crimes against the Major Leaders of Japan and Their Principal Agents and Accessories, November 29, 1945.*[6]

By virtue of the authority vested in me by the Constitution and the statutes as President of the United States and as Commander in Chief of the Army and the Navy, and to enable Joseph B. Keenan, as Chief of Counsel in the preparation and prosecution of charges of war crimes against the major leaders of Japan and their principal agents and acces-

---

[1] Department of State Publication 2423, p. 28; see this volume, p. 105.

[2] Amended April 26, 1946; Department of State, *Bulletin*, XIV, p. 361, 890.

[3] *Trial of Japanese War Criminals*, Department of State Publication 2613.

[4] The prosecution included Associate Counsels from Australia, Canada, China, Great Britain, the Netherlands, New Zealand, Union of Soviet Socialist Republics, France, India and the Philippines.

[5] Department of State, *Bulletin*, XIV, p. 846.

[6] *Ibid.*, XIII, p. 898.

sories (hereinafter referred to as Chief of Counsel), to perform effectively his functions and duties, it is hereby ordered as follows:

1. The Chief of Counsel is authorized to select and recommend to the President or to the head of any executive department, independent establishment, or other federal agency, necessary personnel to assist him in the performance of his duties. The head of each executive department, independent establishment, and other federal agency is authorized to assist the Chief of Counsel in the performance of his duties and to employ such personnel and make such expenditures, within the limits of the appropriations now or hereafter available for the purpose, as the Chief of Counsel may deem necessary for the accomplishment of his duties, and to make available, assign, or detail for duty with the Chief of Counsel such members of the armed forces and other personnel as may be requested by the Chief of Counsel.

2. The Chief of Counsel shall receive such compensation and allowances for expenses as may be authorized by the Secretary of War.

3. The Chief of Counsel is authorized to cooperate with, and to receive the assistance of, any foreign Government to the extent deemed necessary by him for the accomplishment of his duties.

(2) Special Proclamation Establishing an International Military Tribunal for the Far East by Supreme Commander for Allied Powers (MacArthur), Tokyo, January 19, 1946.[1]

WHEREAS, the United States and the Nations allied therewith in opposing the illegal wars of aggression of the Axis Nations, have from time to time made declarations of their intentions that war criminals should be brought to justice;

WHEREAS, the Governments of the Allied Powers at war with Japan on the 26th July 1945 at Potsdam, declared as one of the terms of surrender that stern justice shall be meted out to all war criminals including those who have visited cruelties upon our prisoners;

WHEREAS, by the Instrument of Surrender of Japan executed at Tokyo Bay, Japan, on the 2nd September 1945, the signatories for Japan, by command of and in behalf of the Emperor and the Japanese Government, accepted the terms set forth in such Declaration at Potsdam;

WHEREAS, by such Instrument of Surrender, the authority of the Emperor and the Japanese Government to rule the state of Japan is made subject to the Supreme Commander for the Allied Powers, who is authorized to take such steps as he deems proper to effectuate the terms of surrender;

WHEREAS, the undersigned has been designated by the Allied Powers as Supreme Commander for the Allied Powers to carry into effect the general surrender of the Japanese armed forces;

WHEREAS, the Governments of the United States, Great Britain and Russia at the Moscow Conference, 26th December 1945, having considered the effectuation by Japan of the Terms of Surrender, with the

[1] *Ibid.*, XIV, p. 361.

concurrence of China have agreed that the Supreme Commander shall issue all Orders for the implementation of the Terms of Surrender.

Now, THEREFORE, I, Douglas MacArthur, as Supreme Commander for the Allied Powers, by virtue of the authority so conferred upon me, in order to implement the Term of Surrender which requires the meting out of stern justice to war criminals, do order and provide as follows:

Article 1. There shall be established an International Military Tribunal for the Far East for the trial of those persons charged individually, or as members of organizations, or in both capacities, with offenses which include crimes against peace.

Article 2. The Constitution, jurisdiction and functions of this Tribunal are those set forth in the Charter of the International Military Tribunal for the Far East, approved by me this day.

Article 3. Nothing in this Order shall prejudice the jurisdiction of any other international, national or occupation court, commission or other tribunal established or to be established in Japan or in any territory of a United Nation with which Japan has been at war, for the trial of war criminals.

Given under my hand at Tokyo, this 19th day of January, 1946.

(3) *Charter for the Establishment of the International Military Tribunal for the Far East, January 19, 1946.*[1]

I. CONSTITUTION OF TRIBUNAL.

ARTICLE 1. TRIBUNAL ESTABLISHED. The International Military Tribunal for the Far East is hereby established for the just and prompt trial and punishment of the major war criminals in the Far East. The permanent seat of the Tribunal is in Tokyo.

ARTICLE 2. MEMBERS. The Tribunal shall consist of not less than six members nor more than eleven members, appointed by the Supreme Commander for the Allied Powers from the names submitted by the Signatories to the Instrument of Surrender, India, and the Commonwealth of the Philippines.

ARTICLE 3. OFFICERS AND SECRETARIAT.

(a) *President.* The Supreme Commander for the Allied Powers shall appoint a Member to be President of the Tribunal.

(b) *Secretariat.*

(1) The Secretariat of the Tribunal shall be composed of a General Secretary to be appointed by the Supreme Commander for the Allied Powers and such assistant secretaries, clerks, interpreters, and other personnel as may be necessary.

(2) The General Secretary shall organize and direct the work of the Secretariat.

(3) The Secretariat shall receive all documents addressed to the Tribunal, maintain the records of the Tribunal, provide necessary clerical

[1] *Occupation of Japan, Policy and Progress,* cited above, p. 147.

services to the Tribunal and its Members, and perform such other duties as may be designated by the Tribunal.

ARTICLE 4. CONVENING AND QUORUM, VOTING AND ABSENCE.

(a) *Convening and Quorum.* When as many as six members of the Tribunal are present, they may convene the Tribunal in formal session. The presence of a majority of all members shall be necessary to constitute a quorum.

(b) *Voting.* All decisions and judgments of this Tribunal, including convictions and sentences, shall be by a majority vote of those Members of the Tribunal present. In case the votes are evenly divided, the vote of the President shall be decisive.

(c) *Absence.* If a member at any time is absent and afterwards is able to be present, he shall take part in all subsequent proceedings; unless he declares in open court that he is disqualified by reason of insufficient familiarity with the proceedings which took place in his absence.

II. JURISDICTION AND GENERAL PROVISIONS

ARTICLE 5. JURISDICTION OVER PERSONS AND OFFENSES. The Tribunal shall have the power to try and punish Far Eastern war criminals who as individuals or as members of organizations are charged with offenses which include Crimes against Peace.

The following acts, or any of them, are crimes coming within the jurisdiction of the Tribunal for which there shall be individual responsibility:

(a) *Crimes against Peace:* Namely, the planning, preparation, initiation or waging of a declared or undeclared war of aggression, or a war in violation of international law, treaties, agreements or assurances, or participation in a common plan or conspiracy for the accomplishment of any of the foregoing:

(b) *Conventional War Crimes:* Namely, violations of the laws or customs of war:

(c) *Crimes against Humanity:* Namely, murder, extermination, enslavement, deportation, and other inhumane acts committed against any civilian population, before or during the war, or persecutions on political or racial grounds in execution of or in connection with any crime within the jurisdiction of the Tribunal, whether or not in violation of the domestic law of the country where perpetrated. Leaders, organizers, instigators and accomplices participating in the formulation or execution of a common plan or conspiracy to commit any of the foregoing crimes are responsible for all acts performed by any person in execution of such plan.

ARTICLE 6. RESPONSIBILITY OF ACCUSED. Neither the official position, at any time, of an accused, nor the fact that an accused acted pursuant to order of his government or of a superior shall, of itself, be sufficient to free such accused from responsibility for any crime with which he is charged, but such circumstances may be considered in mitigation of punishment if the Tribunal determines that justice so requires.

ARTICLE 7. RULES OF PROCEDURE. The Tribunal may draft and amend rules of procedure consistent with the fundamental provisions of this Charter.

ARTICLE 8. COUNSEL.

(a) *Chief of Counsel.* The Chief of Counsel designated by the Supreme Commander for the Allied Powers is responsible for the investigation and prosecution of charges against war criminals within the jurisdiction of this Tribunal, and will render such legal assistance to the Supreme Commander as is appropriate.

(b) *Associate Counsel.* Any United Nation with which Japan has been at war may appoint an Associate Counsel to assist the Chief of Counsel.

III. FAIR TRIAL FOR ACCUSED

ARTICLE 9. PROCEDURE FOR FAIR TRIAL. In order to insure fair trial for the accused the following procedure shall be followed:

(a) *Indictment.* The indictment shall consist of a plain, concise, and adequate statement of each offense charged. Each accused shall be furnished, in adequate time for defense, a copy of the indictment, including any amendment, and of this Charter, in a language understood by the accused.

(b) *Language.* The trial and related proceedings shall be conducted in English and in the language of the accused. Translations of documents and other papers shall be provided as needed and requested.

(c) *Counsel for Accused.* Each accused shall have the right to be represented by counsel of his own selection, subject to the disapproval of such counsel at any time by the Tribunal. The accused shall file with the General Secretary of the Tribunal the name of his counsel. If an accused is not represented by counsel and in open court requests the appointment of counsel, the Tribunal shall designate counsel for him. In the absence of such request the Tribunal may appoint counsel for an accused if in its judgment such appointment is necessary to provide for a fair trial.

(d) *Evidence for Defense.* An accused shall have the right, through himself or through his counsel (but not through both), to conduct his defense, including the right to examine any witness, subject to such reasonable restrictions as the Tribunal may determine.

(e) *Production of Evidence for the Defense.* An accused may apply in writing to the Tribunal for the production of witnesses or of documents. The application shall state where the witness or document is thought to be located. It shall also state the facts proposed to be proved by the witness or the document and the relevancy of such facts to the defense. If the Tribunal grants the application the Tribunal shall be given such aid in obtaining production of the evidence as the circumstances require.

ARTICLE 10. APPLICATIONS AND MOTIONS BEFORE TRIAL. All motions, applications, or other requests addressed to the Tribunal prior to the commencement of trial shall be made in writing and filed with the General Secretary of the Tribunal for action by the Tribunal.

IV. Powers of Tribunal and Conduct of Trial

Article 11. Powers. The Tribunal shall have the power

(a) To summon witnesses to the trial, to require them to attend and testify, and to question them,

(b) To interrogate each accused and to permit comment on his refusal to answer any question,

(c) To require the production of documents and other evidentiary material,

(d) To require of each witness an oath, affirmation, or such declaration as is customary in the country of the witness, and to administer oaths,

(e) To appoint officers for the carrying out of any task designated by the Tribunal, including the power to have evidence taken on commission.

Article 12. Conduct of Trial. The Tribunal shall

(a) Confine the trial strictly to an expeditious hearing of the issues raised by the charges,

(b) Take strict measures to prevent any action which would cause any unreasonable delay and rule out irrelevant issues and statements of any kind whatsoever,

(c) Provide for the maintenance of order at the trial and deal summarily with any contumacy, imposing appropriate punishment, including exclusion of any accused or his counsel from some or all further proceedings, but without prejudice to the determination of the charges,

(d) Determine the mental and physical capacity of any accused to proceed to trial.

Article 13. Evidence.

(a) *Admissibility.* The Tribunal shall not be bound by technical rules of evidence. It shall adopt and apply to the greatest possible extent expeditious and non-technical procedure, and shall admit any evidence which it deems to have probative value. All purported admissions or statements of the accused are admissible.

(b) *Relevance.* The Tribunal may require to be informed of the nature of any evidence before it is offered in order to rule upon the relevance.

(c) *Specific evidence admissible.* In particular, and without limiting in any way the scope of the foregoing general rules, the following evidence may be admitted:

(1) A document, regardless of its security classification and without proof of its issuance or signature, which appears to the Tribunal to have been signed or issued by any officer, department, agency or member of the armed forces of any government.

(2) A report which appears to the Tribunal to have been signed or issued by the International Red Cross or a member thereof, or by a doctor of medicine or any medical service personnel, or by an investigator or intelligence officer, or by any other person who appears to the Tribunal to have personal knowledge of the matters contained in the report.

(3) An affidavit, deposition or other signed statement.

(4) A diary, letter or other document, including sworn or unsworn statements which appear to the Tribunal to contain information relating to the charge.

(5) A copy of a document or other secondary evidence of its contents, if the original is not immediately available.

(d) *Judicial Notice.* The Tribunal shall neither require proof of facts of common knowledge, nor of the authenticity of official government documents and reports of any nation nor of the proceedings, records and findings of military or other agencies of any of the United Nations.

(e) *Records, Exhibits and Documents.* The transcript of the proceedings, and exhibits and documents submitted to the Tribunal, will be filed with the General Secretary of the Tribunal and will constitute part of the Record.

ARTICLE 14. PLACE OF TRIAL. The first trial will be held at Tokyo and any subsequent trials will be held at such places as the Tribunal decides.

ARTICLE 15. COURSE OF TRIAL PROCEEDINGS. The proceedings of the Trial will take the following course:

(a) The indictment will be read in court unless the reading is waived by all accused.

(b) The Tribunal will ask each accused whether he pleads "guilty" or "not guilty."

(c) The prosecution and each accused (by counsel only, if represented) may make a concise opening statement.

(d) The prosecution and defense may offer evidence and the admissibility of the same shall be determined by the Tribunal.

(e) The prosecution and each accused (by counsel only, if represented) may examine each witness and each accused who gives testimony.

(f) Accused (by counsel only, if represented) may address the Tribunal.

(g) The prosecution may address the Tribunal.

(h) The Tribunal will deliver judgment and pronounce sentence.

V. JUDGMENT AND SENTENCE

ARTICLE 16. PENALTY. The Tribunal shall have the power to impose upon an accused, on conviction, death or such other punishment as shall be determined by it to be just.

ARTICLE 17. JUDGMENT AND REVIEW. The judgment will be announced in open court and will give the reasons on which it is based. The record of the trial will be transmitted directly to the Supreme Commander for the Allied Powers for his action thereon. A sentence will be carried out in accordance with the order of the Supreme Commander for the Allied Powers, who may at any time reduce or otherwise alter the sentence except to increase its severity.

3. TREATMENT OF ENEMY ALIENS

Shortly after the entry of the United States into the Second World War, groups of enemy aliens residing in this country and judged to be dangerous to the national welfare were interned with a view to later repatriation. Certain other groups of enemy nations, considered a threat to hemispheric security, were also deported to this country from other American republics for internment. During the war a large proportion of these persons were repatriated, at their own request or with their consent, in exchange for American nationals interned by the enemy. A considerable number, however, refused to return to their native countries, preferring, instead, to re-establish themselves in Latin America or to remain here. To handle these latter cases, President Truman, on July 14, 1945, empowered the Attorney General to require the removal of such persons from the United States.[1] The President further implemented this by later proclamations of September 8, 1945,[2] and April 10, 1946.[3] During the same period, there was established, by a Departmental order effective October 24, 1945, under Assistant Secretary of State Braden, an Alien Enemy Control Section within the Department of State,[4] establishing "an orderly procedure for disposing of these cases on an individual basis in accordance with standards to be approved by the Secretary."[5] In establishing this section, the Department of State announced that, "The over-all objective of this program is to accomplish the purposes of Resolution VII[6] of the Mexico City Conference, especially 'to prevent Axis-inspired elements from securing or regaining vantage points from which to disturb or threaten the security or welfare of an [American] Republic.'" The Department, in carrying out this policy, has cooperated closely with the other American Republics.

(1) Proclamation by the President (Truman) on Removal of Enemy Aliens, Issued July 14, 1945.[7]

WHEREAS section 4067 of the Revised Statutes of the United States (50 U.S.C. 21) provides:

Whenever there is a declared war between the United States and any foreign nation or government, or any invasion or predatory incursion is perpetrated, attempted, or threatened against the territory of the United States by any foreign nation or government, and the President makes public proclamation of the event, all natives, citizens, denizens, or subjects of the hostile nation or government, being of the age of fourteen years and upward, who shall be within the United States and not actually naturalized, shall be liable to be apprehended, restrained, secured, and removed as alien enemies. The President is authorized, in any such event, by his proclamation thereof, or other public act, to direct the conduct to be observed, on the part of the United States, toward the aliens who become so liable; the manner and degree of the restraint to which they shall be subject and in what cases, and upon what security their residence shall be permitted, and to provide for the removal of those who, not being permitted to reside within the United States, refuse or neglect to depart therefrom; and to establish any other regulations which are found necessary in the premises and for the public safety;

---

[1] For the text of this Proclamation, see this volume, below.
[2] *Ibid.*, p. 360.
[3] *Ibid.*, p. 362.
[4] Departmental Order 1352, dated October 26, 1945, and effective October 24, 1945; Department of State, *Bulletin*, XIII, p. 738.
[5] Department of State Press Release, November 2, 1945; Department of State, *Bulletin*, XIII, p. 737.
[6] *Ibid.*; for the text of Resolution VII of the Mexico City Conference, see *Documents, VII, 1944–1945*, p. 713.
[7] Proclamation 2655; Department of State, *Bulletin*, XIII, p. 107; *Federal Register*, X, p. 8947.

WHEREAS sections 4068, 4069, and 4070 of the Revised Statutes of the United States (50 U.S.C. 22, 23, 24) make further provision relative to alien enemies;

WHEREAS the Congress by joint resolutions approved by the President on December 8 and 11, 1941, and June 5, 1942, declared the existence of a state of war between the United States and the Governments of Japan, Germany, Italy, Bulgaria, Hungary, and Rumania;

WHEREAS by Proclamation No. 2525 of December 7, 1941, Proclamations Nos. 2526 and 2527 of December 8, 1941, Proclamation No. 2533 of December 29, 1941, Proclamation No. 2537 of January 14, 1942, and Proclamation No. 2563 of July 17, 1942, the President prescribed and proclaimed certain regulations governing the conduct of alien enemies; and

WHEREAS I find it necessary in the interest of national defense and public safety to prescribe regulations additional and supplemental to such regulations:

Now, THEREFORE, I, HARRY S. TRUMAN, President of the United States of America, acting under and by virtue of the authority vested in me by the Constitution of the United States and the aforesaid sections of the Revised Statutes of the United States, do hereby prescribe and proclaim the following regulations, additional and supplemental to those prescribed by the aforesaid proclamations:

All alien enemies now or hereafter interned within the continental limits of the United States pursuant to the aforesaid proclamations of the President of the United States who shall be deemed by the Attorney General to be dangerous to the public peace and safety of the United States because they have adhered to the aforesaid enemy governments or to the principles of government thereof shall be subject upon the order of the Attorney General to removal from the United States and may be required to depart therefrom in accordance with such regulations as he may prescribe.

IN WITNESS WHEREOF, I have hereunto set my hand and caused the seal of the United States to be affixed.

DONE at the City of Washington this 14th day of July in the year of our Lord nineteen hundred and forty-five and of the Independence of the United States of America the one hundred and seventieth.

[SEAL]

(2) *Proclamation by the President (Truman) on Removal of Enemy Aliens, Issued September 8, 1945.*[1]

WHEREAS section 4067 of the Revised Statutes of the United States (50 U.S.C. 21) makes provision relative to the restraint and removal from the United States of alien enemies in the interest of the public safety;

WHEREAS the Congress by joint resolution approved by the President on December 8 and 11, 1941, and June 5, 1942, declared the existence of a state of war between the United States on the one hand and Japan, Germany, Italy, Bulgaria, Hungary, and Rumania on the other hand;

[1] Proclamation 2662; Department of State, *Bulletin*, XIII, p. 361; *Federal Register*, X, p. 11635.

WHEREAS in accordance with Resolution XVII of the Conference of Foreign Ministers at Rio de Janeiro adopted on January 28, 1942, and subsequently by undertakings based upon Resolution XX of the Emergency Advisory Committee for Political Defense adopted at Montevideo on May 21, 1943, there has been assumed by the Government of the United States responsibility for the restraint and repatriation of certain dangerous alien enemies sent to the United States from other of the American republics in the interest of the security of the Western Hemisphere;

WHEREAS by Resolution VII of the Inter-American Conference on Problems of War and Peace adopted at Mexico City on March 8, 1945, the American republics recommended the adoption of measures to prevent any person whose deportation was deemed necessary for reasons of security of the continent from further residing in this hemisphere, if such residence would be prejudicial to the future security or welfare of the Americas;

WHEREAS I find it necessary in the light of the commitments of the Government and in the interest of national defense and public safety to prescribe regulations additional and supplemental to all other regulations affecting the restraint and removal of alien enemies in order to cover the case of the persons above referred to:

Now, THEREFORE, I, Harry S. Truman, President of the United States of America, acting under and by virtue of the authority vested in me by the Constitution of the United States and the aforesaid section of the Revised Statutes of the United States, do hereby prescribe and proclaim the following regulations, additional and supplemental to all other regulations affecting the restraint and removal of Alien enemies:

All alien enemies now within the continental limits of the United States (1) who were sent here from other American republics for restraint and repatriation pursuant to international commitments of the United States Government and for the security of the United States and its associated powers and (2) who are within the territory of the United States without admission under the immigration laws are, if their continued residence in the Western Hemisphere is deemed by the Secretary of State prejudicial to the future security or welfare of the Americas as prescribed in Resolution VII of the Inter-American Conference on Problems of War and Peace, subject upon the order of the Secretary of State to removal to destinations outside the limits of the Western Hemisphere in territory of the enemy governments to which or to the principles of which they have adhered. The Department of Justice and all other appropriate agencies of the United States Government are directed to render assistance to the Secretary of State in the prompt effectuation of such orders of removal.

IN WITNESS WHEREOF, I have hereunto set my hand and caused the seal of the United States of America to be affixed.

DONE at the City of Washington this eighth day of September in the year of our Lord nineteen hundred and forty-five and of the
[SEAL] Independence of the United States of America the one hundred and seventieth.

(3) *Proclamation by the President (Truman) on Removal of Enemy Aliens, Issued April 10, 1946.*[1]

WHEREAS sections 4067 and 4068 of the Revised Statutes of the United States (50 U.S.C. 21 and 22) make provision relative to the restraint and removal from the United States of alien enemies in the interest of the public safety; and

WHEREAS the Congress by joint resolutions approved by the President on December 8 and 11, 1941, and June 5, 1942, declared the existence of a state of war between the United States on the one hand and Japan, Germany, Italy, Bulgaria, Hungary, and Rumania on the other hand; and

WHEREAS in accordance with Resolution XVII of the Conference of Foreign Ministers at Rio de Janeiro adopted on January 28, 1942, and subsequently by undertakings based upon Resolution XX of the Emergency Advisory Committee for Political Defense adopted at Montevideo on May 21, 1943, there has been assumed by the Government of the United States responsibility for the restraint and repatriation of certain dangerous alien enemies brought to the United States from other of the American republics in the interest of the security of the Western Hemispheres; and

WHEREAS by Resolution VII of the Inter-American Conference on Problems of War and Peace adopted at Mexico City on March 8, 1945, the American republics recommended the adoption of measures to prevent any person whose deportation should be deemed necessary for reasons of security of the continent from further residing in this hemisphere, if such residence would be prejudicial to the future security or welfare of the Americas; and

WHEREAS I find it necessary in the light of the commitments of the Government and in the interest of national defense and public safety to prescribe regulations additional and supplemental to all other regulations affecting the restraint and removal of alien enemies:

NOW, THEREFORE, I, HARRY S. TRUMAN, President of the United States of America, acting under and by virtue of the authority vested in me by the Constitution of the United States and the aforesaid sections of the Revised Statutes of the United States, do hereby prescribe and proclaim the following regulations, additional and supplemental to all other regulations affecting the restraint and removal of alien enemies:

1. All alien enemies within the continental limits of the United States brought here from other American republics after December 7, 1941, who are within the territory of the United States without admission under the immigration laws, shall, if their continued residence in the Western Hemisphere is deemed by the Secretary of State to be prejudicial to the future security or welfare of the Americas, be subject upon the order of the Secretary of State to removal from the United States and may be required to depart therefrom in accordance with such regulations as the Secretary of State may prescribe.

[1] Proclamation 2685; *Federal Register*, XI, p. 4079.

2. In all cases in which the Secretary of State shall have ordered the removal of an alien enemy under the authority of this proclamation or in which the Attorney General shall have ordered the removal of an alien enemy under the authority of Proclamation No. 2655 of July 14, 1945, thirty days shall be considered, and is hereby declared to be a reasonable time for such alien enemy to effect the recovery, disposal, and removal of his goods and effects, and for his departure.

3. This proclamation supersedes Proclamation No. 2662 of September 8, 1945, entitled "Removal of Alien Enemies."

IN WITNESS WHEREOF, I have hereunto set my hand and cause the seal of the United States of America to be affixed.

DONE at the City of Washington this 10th day of April in the year of our Lord nineteen hundred and forty-six, and of the Independence of the United States of America the one hundred and seventieth.

[SEAL]

CHAPTER V

RELIEF AND REHABILITATION

1. RELIEF

A. American Participation in International Agencies

1. UNITED NATIONS RELIEF AND REHABILITATION ADMINISTRATION

[See *Documents, VI, 1943–1944*, p. 248–314; *VII, 1944–1945*, p. 370–86.]

Following the termination of hostilities, UNRRA entered upon a period of greatly increased activity in providing relief supplies and services to peoples of areas liberated from the enemy. By the end of 1946, however, plans were already in progress for the liquidation of the Administration, with the scheduling of last relief shipments and the termination of displaced persons activities set for June 30, 1947.[1]

Council sessions of the Administration held in London in August, 1945, and Atlantic City in March, 1946, were concerned mainly with the critical food shortage and consequent difficulties in meeting overseas commitments, and with further contributions for UNRRA operations by member governments. Resolutions requesting the governments to take stringent measures to conserve food and to make more available for export were passed by the Council,[2] which also asked for a second contribution of one percent of its national income for 1943 from each state which had not been occupied by the enemy.[3] At the London session the Council voted to extend aid to Italy and Austria, following a United States proposal.[4]

Continued United States participation in the work of UNRRA was authorized by Public Law 262, 79th Congress, which provided for a United States contribution of $1,350,000,000, bringing total United States appropriations to UNRRA to $2,700,000,000, or approximately 73 percent of its total resources. An amendment attached to the Third Deficiency Appropriation Bill, appropriating the last $465,000,000 of this amount, by the House of Representatives, would have made the United States' contribution to UNRRA for aid in any country contingent upon that country's agreement not to censor reports of American press representatives concerning the distribution and use of UNRRA supplies. This rider, the so-called Dirksen amendment,[5] was eliminated by the Senate and the conference committee following a State Department declaration that such a move would be a "grave mistake."

The fifth and sixth Council sessions of UNRRA, held in Geneva in August, 1946, and Washington in December, 1946, considered primarily the adoption of policies concerning the termination of the organization, and transfer of its functions to the United Nations, the World Health Organization, the International Refugee Organization, and the International Children's Emergency Fund. At the sessions sharp debate arose regarding establishment of an international organization to continue UNRRA's relief work; this was continued at

---

[1] Resolution 114.
[2] United Nations Relief and Rehabilitation Administration. *A Compilation of the Resolutions on Policy, Third and Fourth Sessions of the UNRRA Council.* Washington, 1946, p. 31, 36, 40.
[3] *Ibid.*, p. 23.
[4] *New York Times*, August 25, 1945.
[5] For text of amendment, see *ibid.*, June 28, 1946, p. 1.

the second part of the first session of the General Assembly of the United Nations, meeting in New York in October, 1946.

Although it had formerly strongly advocated continuation of UNRRA and an international solution of relief questions, the United States at these sessions took a position firmly opposing creation of an international relief organization or fund, as had been suggested by Fiorello H. La Guardia, who had become UNRRA Director-General following the resignation of Herbert H. Lehman in March, 1946.[1] Arguing against this plan, which would have created an emergency fund to finance essential food requirements for importing countries, and which would have been operative until the 1947 harvest, the United States representative in the Assembly (Adlai Stevenson) stated that there was no longer any need for international relief action, and proposed instead a plan of bilateral action which provided for informal consultation among governments to coordinate relief programs.[2] Although every other nation favored continued international handling of the relief problem, a compromise Canadian proposal, based on a United States-United Kingdom-Brazilian draft, was eventually approved by the Assembly, and a Special Technical Committee on Relief Needs after Termination of UNRRA, composed of experts on finance and foreign trade, was created.

At the sixth Council session also considerable dispute arose over a United States proposal that the country programs approved by the Central Committee in June, 1946, should be reviewed and, if desirable, modified. The United States position was that the Central Committee had expressly reserved the right of review, that conditions had changed so that the programs once considered feasible no longer were so, because approved supplies could not be procured within time limits fixed by Congressional legislation, and because needs of certain countries had not been foreseen; this point of view was opposed by other delegations and by the Director-General, who maintained that approval of programs represented commitments to the countries concerned, and that a resolution of the fifth Council session bound the Administration to "make every effort to complete procurement and shipments against approved programs of operation within the dates specified...."[3] After intermittent debate, the Council adopted Resolution 114, which provided that no changes of program should be made except when circumstances warranted, and extended termination dates of UNRRA shipments. The Council also made provision for a seventh session to be convened prior to June 30, 1947, unless the Central Committee should unanimously agree it was unnecessary, and accepted the resignation of Director-General Fiorello H. La Guardia. Major-General Lowell W. Rooks, who had served as Deputy-Director-General, was appointed to succeed him.

For questions concerning UNRRA as it affected American foreign relations with other nations, see chapters in this volume dealing with American relations with China, Poland, Yugoslavia, and the Union of Soviet Socialist Republics.

(1) *Statement by the Assistant Secretary of State for Economic Affairs (Clayton) before the Committee on Foreign Affairs of the House of Representatives, November 14, 1945.*[4]

[Excerpts]

The commencement of these hearings on a new authorization by Congress for United States participation in the work of UNRRA is a reminder to me of the support and cooperation which we have received

---

[1] United Nations General Assembly, Document A/C.2/38, November 11, 1946.
[2] *Journal of the United Nations*, No. 34, Supplement 2, p. 57.
[3] United Nations Relief and Rehabilitation Administration. *A Compilation of Resolutions on Policy, Fifth Session of the UNRRA Council.* Geneva, 1946, p. 13.
[4] Department of State, *Bulletin*, XIII, p. 809.

from this Committee in attempting to solve this whole vast problem of relief and rehabilitation in the war-devastated areas. I was very gratified when the Chairman informed me last July that your Subcommittee would participate in the UNRRA Council deliberations. While the members of this group were in London during August I think they were able to gain for themselves some impression of the magnitude of the problems facing the national delegations to the Third Council Session, and the UNRRA Administration itself. Other members of this Committee had an opportunity during the summer to see UNRRA at work in the field as an international relief operation. Therefore, most of us are approaching these deliberations with a sense of the urgency and the importance of the continuance of this country's support for UNRRA.

. . . . . .

UNRRA had been subject to considerable criticism for delay and administrative bungling in getting started. It had been competing unsuccessfully with military operations and other wartime activities for competent personnel and for the supplies and facilities which were necessary to do its job effectively. So long as total war continued in the Pacific, I knew UNRRA would have to face a continuation of these difficulties. These obstacles, however, were largely removed by the surrender of Japan which occurred in the course of the Council's deliberations.

The end of hostilities in Europe three months prior to the Council meeting had already burdened UNRRA with many other problems of relief and rehabilitation. Our armies and those of our Allies, which had been carrying the major burden of civilian supply to western Europe and the Mediterranean countries, were quite rightfully eager to shift that responsibility as soon as possible. A similar situation developed in eastern Europe where all supply and transport were necessarily under the control of the Soviet military command until victory over Germany was achieved. Then and then only could civilian governments and agencies begin to undertake their share of the work. We therefore realized that UNRRA, in the course of the summer, was entering upon the period of full-scale operations. It was the only functioning relief organization able to take over from the military and the only instrument through which all the European countries, as well as the other United Nations, could concert their common interests in helping to restore some semblance of economic order to that continent.

The urgency of the relief and rehabilitation problem in the Far East was equally apparent. The abrupt end of the war with Japan posed the immediate problem of relief for occupied China, a world responsibility for which no agency was sufficiently prepared except UNRRA. Although UNRRA of course had not anticipated beginning actual operations in the Far East on such short notice, it had established many months previously a mission in China which was working closely with the Chinese National Relief and Rehabilitation Agency. Not only had the plans for relief distribution been tentatively agreed upon but also preliminary screening of a target program for China had been completed and was before the Council for consideration. The fact that UNRRA's plans and personnel were so well prepared to assume immediate operating responsibilities made it easy for the Council to agree provisionally on the scope of UNRRA activities and expenditures in China, pending a further review when the mission on the spot could make reports of actual conditions.

The United States Delegation to the Council meeting, on which I was fortunate in having broad and competent representation from all the interested agencies of this Government, as well as from the Congress, reached early agreement on several objectives. We decided that the needs of all the liberated areas which were not to be under the continuing control of the military and which had insufficient foreign-exchange resources to purchase essential relief supplies abroad could best be met through a single channel. The use of any agency other than UNRRA for these new responsibilities would have meant creating a competing unilateral relief organization, which would have immediately indicated to the world that we doubted the feasibility of international cooperation. We therefore agreed to seek extension of UNRRA operations to Italy and Austria in Europe, and to Korea and Formosa in the Far East.

. . . .

The Delegation was also aware of the concern in many quarters that UNRRA might be undertaking rehabilitation responsibilities for a longer term than that originally envisaged. We concluded that if a cut-off date for UNRRA operations were established, the receiving countries would have a greater incentive to maximize their indigenous production of relief supplies. The Delegation therefore agreed to recommend a stoppage of UNRRA shipments to Europe not later than the end of 1946, and a similar stoppage of shipments to the Far East not later than three months thereafter.

In reviewing the criticisms which had been leveled at UNRRA in the past and the corrective measures that might be taken to improve participation in UNRRA activities by member nations, the United States Delegation felt that the governments concerned should take a more active interest in furnishing supplies, services, and competent personnel to UNRRA. We also decided that it would be desirable for the Director General to have the assistance and advice of the Council, through the Central Committee, in determining equitable distribution of UNRRA's resources among the various receiving countries.

. . . .

As the record will show, and as most of you are aware, we succeeded in attaining all of our objectives at the Council meeting in London. In many instances, agreement was not reached with the member nations without considerable debate and in some instances only after major differences of opinion had been resolved. Nevertheless, agreement was reached on a basis which I believe was in the interests of the United States and also in the interests of UNRRA and all member nations.

The very fact that such a meeting of the minds was achieved is a most encouraging sign that international cooperation on matters of common concern is possible.

I feel that the recommendations of the London Council meeting, which are financially embodied in the new legislation being considered by this Committee, represent a program which is in our best interests. I believe this Committee's examination of the problem before us will justify my sincere conviction that we are asking Congress to do what is right and necessary as our share of world relief and rehabilitation.

. . . .

We, as a nation, have committed ourselves to international cooperation and collaboration. UNRRA is the first operating experiment in the implementation of this policy. I have recognized difficulties and weaknesses in the UNRRA administration, which are also recognized by the Director General, Governor Lehman, and I will do all in my power as this Government's representative on the Council to help overcome or correct them. Any alternative method for giving relief and rehabilitation assistance to countries without sufficient foreign-exchange and credit resources to meet the problem themselves is, to my mind, unthinkable and impractical.

(2) *Joint Resolution to Enable the United States to Further Participate in the Work of the United Nations Relief and Rehabilitation Administration, Approved December 18, 1945.*[1]

Be it enacted by the Senate and House of Representatives of the United States of America in Congress assembled, That the joint resolution of March 28, 1944, entitled "Joint resolution to enable the United States to participate in the work of the United Nations relief and rehabilitation organization", is amended in the following respect:

(1) The first section is amended by striking out "$1,350,000,000" and inserting in lieu thereof "$2,700,000,000".

(2) Section 9 is amended by striking out "1946" and inserting in lieu thereof "1947".

(3) Add a new section 8 (a):

"8 (a) In adopting this joint resolution the Congress does so with the following recommendations:

"A. That the United States member of the control committee of the United Nations Relief and Rehabilitation Administration is hereby requested, by appropriate resolutions or agreements, to secure favorable action by that committee or by the United Nations Relief and Rehabilitation Administration Council to attain the following objectives:

"(1) That all trade agreements and all barter agreements of a recipient country with other nations, together with satisfactory information on all exports from, and imports into, such country, whether for governmental or private account, will be made available to the United Nations Relief and Rehabilitation Administration.

"(2) That each recipient country shall supply accredited United

[1] Public Law 262, 79th Cong., 1st sess.

Nations Relief and Rehabilitation Administration personnel with all necessary facilities, credentials, documents, and safe conduct in carrying out the objectives of the United Nations Relief and Rehabilitation Administration agreement, including all necessary inspections and investigations.

"(3) That the Administration, if it determines such a course to be desirable, will be permitted, during the period of its operations in a recipient country, to retain title to all motor-transport equipment supplied by the Administration and will also be permitted to route such equipment and to direct the use of the fuel and lubricants supplied by the Administration.

"B. That the President is hereby requested, through appropriate channels, to facilitate the admission to recipient countries of properly accredited members of the American press and radio in order that they be permitted to report without censorship on the utilization and distribution of United Nations Relief and Rehabilitation Administration supplies and services."

(3) *Letter from the Assistant Secretary of State for Economic Affairs (Clayton) to Senator Kenneth McKellar, July 3, 1946.*[1]

[Excerpts]

Since the fundamental objective of our foreign policy is to create conditions in the world under which we can live in friendship and peace with all nations, I am gravely concerned about the action recently taken in the House of Representatives in adopting the so-called Dirksen Amendment to the Third Deficiency Appropriation Bill.

This Amendment, as you know, would deny use of the U. S. contribution to UNRRA for aid to any country which refused to agree not to censor the reports of American press representatives concerning the distribution and use of UNRRA supplies. As the record of the debate in the House of Representatives will show, this Amendment was directed at the Soviet Union. This action was taken in consequence of a reply received from the Soviet Government, in answer to a request by the President that that Government undertake to permit reporting, with respect to UNRRA operations, free of the censorship rules which have been established in Soviet territories. The President made his request pursuant to the direction of Congress as expressed in Public Laws 259 and 262, 79th Congress.

I should like to take this opportunity to give you my views on this matter. At the outset let me say that I believe no one is more firmly convinced than the Secretary and I that the free interchange of information between the peoples and countries of the world is essential to the creation of a secure peace. We in the Department of State are constantly seeking to achieve this objective. My concern about the Dirksen Amendment therefore is not because I do not seek the freedom of information which I feel certain the House had in mind when it approved this Amendment, but because I feel that its passage would achieve precisely the opposite result.

[1] Department of State, *Bulletin*, XV, p. 35.

One of the reasons why we are so concerned to promote the free interchange of information between countries is that only by such a process will the common people of all countries come to know and appreciate the achievements and points of view of each other. I believe from all I can discover that the UNRRA program in the two Soviet Republics is serving most effectively to promote the accomplishment of these objectives.

. . . . . .

This whole issue, of course, has a far wider significance than its effect on the UNRRA program. I feel sure that adoption of the Amendment would seriously complicate all our relations with the Soviet Union and would, without achieving any tangible benefit for us, make far more difficult negotiations on many other issues.

. . . . . .

I would like to point out further, that all of the members of UNRRA, in approving the UNRRA agreement, subscribed to the policies and regulations governing its operations which had been set up by mutual agreement. If each of the contributing members should now by its own unilateral action attempt to establish new and special conditions, the operation of UNRRA would become impossible. There is no question but that the UNRRA Council and the UNRRA Administration have taken steps to assure adequate observation and complete reporting without censorship by UNRRA missions and by press representatives with respect to all matters of concern to UNRRA in the two Soviet Republics.

There is one other point which seems to me of great significance. One of our important concerns today is to demonstrate that international organizations can succeed in dealing with matters which affect the interests of all nations. This is not an easy task, as recent experience clearly proves, and we have made less progress at it than we had hoped for. Every success we do have, however, by showing that success can be achieved, tends to develop confidence in international organizations generally, and thus promotes success in other cases. Conversely every failure has the opposite effect. With all the difficulties which have beset UNRRA and with all the differences of opinion that have developed from time to time, nevertheless it cannot be denied that it is one of the international organizations that has succeeded, on the whole, in accomplishing the objectives for which it was designed. It has effectively brought relief to millions of people in the war-devastated areas, it has produced vast good will for this country and for the other contributing countries, it has increased contacts between citizens of all nations and promoted knowledge and understanding of each other among peoples throughout the world. It has demonstrated the fact that men of many different nations can work together successfully to solve a world-wide problem. It would be a tragic thing, in this critical period in international affairs, with UNRRA so close to the end of its period of operations, to destroy in large part the effect which UNRRA has had in promoting confidence and understanding between nations and to turn its success as an operating international organization into failure during the last months of its existence. I should very much regret to see such an outcome of an international effort which, otherwise, has such bright prospects of confounding those who doubt that any attempt at cooperation by nations in a common cause is possible.

I apologize for having burdened you with such a long discussion of this subject, but it is, in my opinion, of such vital importance in the whole field of our foreign relations that I must put before you fully the considerations which I believe would make the adoption of the Dirksen Amendment a very grave mistake.

(4) *Radio Address by the Acting Secretary of State (Acheson) on United States Position on UNRRA, December 8, 1946.*[1]

[Excerpt]

. . . .

The United States Government is pressing forward in the United Nations with an international organization to care for, repatriate, or resettle refugees. This is because the facts warrant such an organization. But the United States does not believe that post-UNRRA relief should be conducted by an UNRRA type of organization.

It is now quite evident that many countries, which, when liberated, had no organized machinery for procuring and shipping needed supplies are now able to perform these services for themselves. The sooner these countries take over the complete responsibility for their own buying and shipping the better it will be for them and for everybody concerned. When a country can do these things for itself, it can usually do them better and cheaper than any international organization which may be set up for that purpose.

UNRRA's other function was the provision of foreign money to countries which lacked the means to pay for food and other imported supplies.

A moment's reflection should convince anyone that there has been a vast improvement in this field also.

Most of the liberated countries are gradually regaining their export trade.

In addition to this normal method of providing foreign purchasing power, the United States and other countries have by loans and otherwise added enormously to the foreign-exchange resources of the world.

In the past 18 months, the United States Government alone has supplied foreign exchange in the following important particulars: 3 billions of dollars through loans by the Export-Import Bank, $3\frac{3}{4}$ billions of dollars' credit to the British Government which will be spent all over the world, 6 billions of dollars as the United States contribution to the Bretton Woods institutions, several billions of dollars' credit for financing lend-lease inventories and pipelines and the sale abroad of surplus property on credit. Thus, including contributions to UNRRA, the United States Government has made available a total of nearly 20 billion dollars to assist in restoring and stabilizing the economies of other countries.

[1] *Ibid.*, p. 1007.

Many other countries have contributed to the capital of the International Bank for Reconstruction and Development and to the International Monetary Fund. Indeed, these two institutions will have at their disposal some 15 billions of dollars with which to give assistance to United Nations countries having need of such assistance for reconstruction, development, and the stabilization of their currencies. These two international financial institutions have now been organized and are ready for operation.

It will thus be seen that measures have been definitely taken for the provision of a total of about 30 billion dollars of foreign exchange.

It has been charged that the United States is abandoning international cooperation in refusing to participate in relief on an international basis. It has also been charged that the United States intends to use food as a political weapon.

The plan of the United States for continuation of such relief as may be necessary in 1947 is very simple.

It should be remembered that comparatively few countries will continue to require relief after the early months of 1947 when UNRRA completes its task. There will probably be only three or four countries in Europe which can qualify as requiring free relief in order to avoid suffering and hardship.

The United States proposal is that each nation should immediately consider what it can contribute to the common 1947 relief effort. The Administration will recommend to Congress a generous appropriation for this purpose. Each country should discuss its plans with others, both those planning to help and those needing help, to obtain their views and to coordinate its activities with all others concerned. The Secretariat of the United Nations should be used as a clearing house by all such countries. The United States would keep the Secretary-General fully informed of what it is doing, and others should do the same.

In this manner, nations receiving free relief must prove their need for it, and they can be held to a much closer and fairer accountability of the use of food and other free supplies. Those in power will be compelled to distribute relief food on the basis of need. They will not be allowed to feed their political supporters and starve their political opponents.

The people of the United States and the Congress of the United States have made up their minds that the relief problems of the near future are not of a character which would warrant grants of enormous sums of money from the United States Treasury under conditions which would leave little or no effective control by the grantor of these funds.

The people of the United States are determined that they will not send free shipments of great quantities of food, trucks, tractors, and other supplies of all kinds, many of which they desperately need themselves, to countries which are diverting their manpower and facilities away from the production of the necessities of life which they are asking others to supply.

If the American people can be led to believe that this policy constitutes the use of food as a political weapon, then they do not deserve their reputation for native shrewdness and common sense.

RELIEF AND REHABILITATION 373

(5) *Tenth Report to Congress on the Operations of UNRRA for the Period from October 31 to December 31, 1946, Submitted by the President (Truman), May 15, 1947.*[1]

[Excerpts]

The bulk of UNRRA's funds is derived from the United States contribution, which, as of December 31, 1946, constituted 73 percent of all the funds received by UNRRA. Proportionate contributions have also been authorized or made available by 29 of UNRRA's 31 other noninvaded member governments. Based on UNRRA Council resolutions 14 and 80, requesting two successive contributions from each noninvaded member government, each contribution is equal to one percent of the amount determined by the member government to have been its national income for the year ending nearest June 30, 1943.

Payment of the total $2,700,000,000 contributed by the United States to UNRRA was completed in July 1946. Following the general pattern of all UNRRA contributions, approximately 90 percent of the contribution was in nonconvertible funds (to be spent within the contributing country) and approximately 10 percent in convertible funds (usable in foreign exchange).

As of the end of December UNRRA had committed all of the United States contribution of $2,700,000,000 except $85,412,038. Eighty-six percent ($73,711,228) of these uncommitted funds are nonconvertible, $64,896,927 remaining with the United States under an arrangement permitting requisitions to be drawn against them, and the remaining $8,814,301 being paid to UNRRA. The $11,700,810 in convertible funds has been paid over to UNRRA.

The UNRRA program budget of U. S. funds included $1,951,341,253 for supply purposes in the United States, exclusive of purchases from free funds. Of this amount, $919,767,987 was for food, $273,523,792 for clothing, textiles, and footwear, $272,282,704 for industrial-rehabilitation supplies, $182,042,267 for agricultural-rehabilitation supplies, and $84,961,754 for medical and sanitation supplies.

The distribution of the funds over the various budget items has been altered somewhat from the budget as shown for September 30. An increase of over 16 million dollars has been effected in the supply program, the increase in the food budget of over 84 million dollars being offset by a reduction of more than 16 million dollars in the amount budgeted for medical and sanitation supplies, a reduction of almost 32 million dollars for United States property located overseas, and the elimination of the Director General's reserve of 30 million dollars. The amount budgeted for services is 18 million dollars less than that shown in September, reflecting primarily the decrease of over 16 million dollars in the amount budgeted for ocean transportation. The amount budgeted for transfer to UNRRA shows an over-all increase of 2 million dollars, the increase of nearly 20 million in the amount shown for transfer to UNRRA for the currency fund to finance purchases outside the United States offsetting

[1] House Document No. 254, 80th Cong., 1st sess., p. 12.

(a) Status of Appropriations for the United States Participation in the Work of UNRRA as of December 31, 1946.[1]

Classification	UNRRA Program Budget	Allocations[a]	Obligations	Expenditures
Supplies:				
Clothing, textiles, and footwear	$273,523,792	$263,192,745.09	$259,473,296.86	$181,943,578.55
Food	919,767,987	874,982,481.10	874,982,481.10	630,286,067.64
Agricultural-rehabilitation supplies	182,042,267	162,636,632.76	148,913,240.79	78,194,715.95
Industrial-rehabilitation supplies	272,282,704	237,971,232.34	225,929,922.38	122,038,011.63
Medical and sanitation supplies	84,961,754	69,772,252.84	52,943,612.65	34,958,229.49
U. S. property located overseas	203,562,749	272,107,043.71	272,107,043.71	110,787,316.05
Reserve for accessorial costs	(b)	40,763,383.33	39,955,007.94	12,918,410.93
Unallotted allocations		26,207,485.87		
Program unspecified	15,200,000			
Total	1,951,341,253	1,947,633,257.04	1,874,304,605.43	1,171,126,330.24
Services:				
Ocean transportation	425,393,501	316,672,685.00	314,941,810.03	288,562,760.88
Relief and rehabilitation	2,109,851	1,811,964.65	1,692,202.78	1,638,908.82
Administrative expenses	15,848,100	11,101,053.96	9,592,265.37	9,058,685.23
Total	443,351,452	329,585,703.61	326,226,278.18	299,260,354.93
Funds transferred to UNRRA:				
Currency fund to finance purchases outside the U. S.	223,412,871	211,185,739.00	211,185,739.00	211,185,739.00
Other (administrative expenses, relief and rehabilitation services, etc.)	81,894,424	55,147,126.11	55,147,126.11	55,147,126.11
Total	305,307,295	266,332,865.11	266,332,865.11	266,332,865.11
Grand Total	2,700,000,000	2,543,551,825.76	2,466,863,748.72	1,736,719,550.28

Note: The amounts shown as obligations are subject to possible adjustments upon the receipt of documents and reports not now available.
[a] This column comprises allocations made to U. S. procuring and servicing agencies and also funds reserved for later allocation.
[b] Accessorial costs have been distributed to the supply program.
[1] Ibid., Appendix, Table A-1, p. 19.

the 17.5-million reduction programmed for transfer to meet administrative expenses, relief and rehabilitation service costs, etc.

* * * * * * *

UNRRA has taken utmost advantage of the United States-owned military surpluses which became available both in the United States and overseas at the end of the war. As of December 31, 1946, UNRRA had committed $416,704,341 to the Federal procurement agencies handling the disposal of military surpluses. Of this, $228,317,200 was committed for overseas surpluses, and $188,387,141 for military surpluses in the United States.

* * * * * *

2. OTHER INTERNATIONAL ORGANIZATIONS

Although the United Nations Relief and Rehabilitation Administration was the principal international agency concerned with problems of relief and reconstruction, a number of other intergovernmental organizations were created during 1945 and 1946 to deal with specific problems within this field, or to take over certain activities upon the termination of UNRRA. These included several agencies of the United Nations, the Food and Agriculture Organization, the International Emergency Food Council, the Emergency Economic Committee for Europe, the European Coal Organization, and the European Central Inland Transport Organization.

Following a resolution of the first part of the first session of the General Assembly of the United Nations, urging publication of full information on the world food position and future outlook, the Food and Agriculture Organization of the United Nations called a Special Meeting on Urgent Food Problems, which met May 20, 1946, in Washington, D. C. The meeting recommended the creation of a widely-representative International Emergency Food Council to replace the Combined Food Board (although the life of this group had just been extended by the three member nations),[1] and the Council came into being on June 20, 1946, when 19 countries accepted the invitation of Canada, the United States and the United Kingdom to form the new organization.[2]

Working closely with FAO and IEFC was the Emergency Economic Committee for Europe, formed in London on May 28, 1945, by nine Allied governments, including the United States. Although essentially an advisory body with no executive function, the Committee created a number of subcommittees and working parties to deal with specific problems; the Food and Agriculture Subcommittee and the Standing Committee on Starvation Conditions cooperated with UNRRA and FAO on European food questions, and a Combined Working Party on European Food Supplies was organized by the three groups.[3]

Also concerned with rehabilitation were the European Coal Organization, which was established provisionally in May, 1945, to promote the supply and equitable distribution of coal and coal-mining supplies and equipment,[4] and the

---

[1] Provision for continuation of the Board had been made by a joint statement issued by President Truman and the Prime Ministers of Canada and Great Britain on May 8, 1946. Department of State, *Bulletin*, XIV, p. 861. For organization and work of the Board, see *Documents, VI, 1943–1944*, p. 240; *ibid., VII, 1944–1945*, p. 367.

[2] Food and Agriculture Organization of the United Nations. *Report of the Special Meeting on Urgent Food Problems.* Washington, June 6, 1946, report of committee III. For further information on the work of the Food and Agriculture Organization, see this volume, p. 697.

[3] Emergency Economic Committee for Europe. *Report by the Secretary-General.* London, August 1, 1946, p. 3.

[4] The Organization was established on a permanent basis on January 1, 1946. Department of State, *Treaties and Other International Acts Series* 1508.

European Central Inland Transport Organization, created on September 27, 1945, to expedite the movement of relief and other priority traffic on the European mainland, and to give technical assistance to member governments on transport problems.[1] In both of these organizations, the United States became an active member because of its position as an occupying power in Germany.

Agencies of the United Nations which considered relief questions included the General Assembly, the Economic and Social Council, and several subsidiary bodies: the Economic and Employment Commission, the Temporary Subcommission on the Economic Reconstruction of Devastated Areas, and the International Children's Emergency Fund. A resolution passed by the second part of the first session of the General Assembly urged governments and international agencies to adopt measures to help overcome the deficit in foodstuffs during 1947, and asked regulation of international consumption. The Assembly also considered plans for a United Nations Emergency Food Fund and for international relief cooperation following the termination of UNRRA.[2]

The Temporary Subcommission on the Economic Reconstruction of Devastated Areas, created by the Economic and Social Council at its first session, considered both long and short range requirements for rehabilitation of devastated areas, and made recommendations for international action.[3] It endorsed proposals for establishment of economic commissions for Europe and the Far East, to consider reconstruction of these areas on wide regional rather than narrow national lines, which had originally been made by the United States, the United Kingdom, and Poland, and following Assembly approval, these two commissions were created by the Economic and Social Council at its fourth session in April, 1947. Another agency, the International Children's Emergency Fund, was established by the Assembly on the suggestion of UNRRA, and early in 1947 began the work of assisting the rehabilitation of children and adolescents of countries which had been victims of aggression.[4]

Other international attempts to settle world relief problems during 1946 included the Emergency Conference on European Cereals, which convened in London on April 2, 1946, following report by the Combined Food Board that an eleven-million ton gap existed between world wheat supplies and world needs. The eighteen-nation food parley urged increased allocation of grains for export by the four surplus producing countries, the United States, Canada, Australia, and Argentina, and stressed the importance of world conservation measures.[5]

B. Action Taken by the United States

Following the statement by President Truman, on his return from the Potsdam Conference, that the United States could not afford to let Europe go cold and hungry if it hoped for world-wide peace, the United States undertook a program of greatly increased relief shipment overseas, in an attempt to fill essential world needs for coal, transportation, and food. While a large part of the relief supplies from the United States were channelled through UNRRA,[6] an effort was also made to stimulate direct shipments to needy countries.

On September 17, 1945, President Truman announced that the United States Government was in a position to fill the principal relief requests of the European nations during the remainder of 1945, and stated that for the first time relief

[1] Department of State, *Executive Agreement Series* 494.

[2] For consideration by the Assembly of post-UNRRA relief needs, see this volume, p. 365.

[3] For reports by the subcommission, see United Nations Economic and Social Council, Documents E/156, September 20, 1946, and E/307, March 4, 1947.

[4] For composition of the fund and its administration, see United Nations General Assembly, Document A/230, December 9, 1946.

[5] *New York Times*, April 4, 1946.

[6] For discussion of United States participation in UNRRA and chart of appropriation for its work, see this volume, p. 364.

shipments were not being limited either by lack of supplies or shipping facilities, but by the financial problem involved in working out credits for European governments and in securing additional funds for UNRRA.[1] Mr. Truman emphasized, however, that the meeting of these requests did not guarantee that the people of Europe would reach even a minimum level of subsistence, and early in 1946 the American Government renewed efforts to increase exports. On January 25, a Presidential directive noted the establishment of a Movement Coordinating Committee, under the chairmanship of John W. Snyder, Director of the Office of War Mobilization and Reconversion, to "make certain that we attain maximum shipments of wheat as well as coal to liberated countries." [2] The committee was empowered when necessary to establish export priorities.

As shortage of relief supplies, particularly food, became more evident, more stringent measures were ordered by the Government. On February 6, 1946, President Truman instructed the appropriate Government agencies to put into effect a number of emergency measures, and asked for the support of the American people in fulfilling a nine-point conservation program; at the same time the President requested ex-President Herbert Hoover to draft proposals on domestic control measures, and the Emergency Food Administration and the National Famine Emergency Committee were created.[3] The first group, headed by Secretary of Agriculture Clinton P. Anderson, was in charge of administration of emergency measures ordered in this country. The second group consisted of 125 civic leaders with Chester Davis, former War Food Administrator, as chairman of its Executive Committee.

On March 17, Mr. Hoover, honorary chairman of the Famine Emergency Committee, and eight food experts began a 50,000-mile journey to 38 countries. The purpose of the mission was both to mobilize the support of the American public for the Government's emergency food program, and to try to find wheat supplies to fill the 11-million ton world deficit reported by the Combined Food Board,[4] the allocating authority for the world food supply. At the Emergency Conference on European Cereals, meeting in London on April 2, the United States pledged export of six million tons or 255 million bushels of wheat during the first six months of 1946, in an attempt to help meet this deficit.[5] Despite this pledge, which represented one-third of the 1945–46 grain crop, United States wheat shipments ran 650,000 tons in arrears in the first four months of 1946.[6]

Early in April other measures to increase exports were taken, with inauguration by the Department of Agriculture of a plan of grain deliveries and payments designed to move grain out of storage.[7] A program of voluntary rationing and contributions for relief was also undertaken with creation of the Emergency Food Collection campaign, under the direction of Secretary of Commerce Henry A. Wallace, while an amendment to the Trading with the Enemy Act authorized the shipment of relief supplies to countries with whom the United States was still technically at war.[8]

Speeches by Mr. Truman, Mr. Hoover, and Fiorello H. La Guardia, Director-General of UNRRA, on April 19 appealed to the American people to take further steps to relieve the critical food shortage, and six administrative orders, supplementing the President's program, tightened Government controls over the production and diversion of foodstuffs and their transportation overseas.[9] Nevertheless, Under Secretary of State Dean Acheson reported that April wheat shipments were 55 per cent in arrears and that May food relief commitments lagged

---

[1] For text of Mr. Truman's statement, see *ibid.*, p. 379.
[2] Department of State, *Bulletin*, XIV, p. 151.
[3] *New York Times*, March 17, 1946, p. 24.
[4] *Ibid.*, June 29, 1946.
[5] Department of State, *Bulletin*, XIV, p. 832.
[6] *New York Times*, May 27, 1946, p. 26.
[7] *Ibid.*, April 3, 1946, p. 6.
[8] Public Law 382, 79th Cong., 2d sess.
[9] Department of State, *Bulletin*, XIV, p. 834.

66 per cent behind the quotas pledged by the United States at the Emergency Conference on European Cereals. Mr. Acheson predicted a five-year food crisis and urged more stringent Federal action, including actual seizure of current grain production, to meet the promised export schedule,[1] while Chester Davis of the NFEC demanded resumption of rationing.[2] An offer of the British Government to ration bread, however, if the United States would do the same, was not accepted, and opposition of Secretary of Agriculture Anderson to these suggested controls led to a White House conference on April 29, at which no further measures were taken.[3] Secretary of Agriculture Anderson later proposed a program for 1946–47 which would prevent repetition of the 1946 crisis, and predicted that unless emergency governmental measures were continued a serious food shortage would again plague the world in the winter of 1946–47.[4]

The report of the Hoover mission, submitted on May 13, 1946,[5] announced the success of the mission in locating further grain supplies, with consequent reduction of the world wheat deficit to 3.6 million tons. The report charted a monthly schedule of supply shipments from the United States through September 30, 1946, when it was estimated that the worst part of the food crisis would be ended.

On May 17, United States-United Kingdom cooperation in attempting to bridge this remaining gap resulted in the drawing up of a set of basic principles to guide the two governments in their efforts to solve the crisis, following consultations between American officials and Mr. Herbert Morrison, Lord President of the Council.[6] At the same time the British Government offered to the Combined Food Board 200,000 tons of cereals from its "pipeline" reserves, and the two governments established a temporary Anglo-American Rice Commission to assist the Siamese Government in rice production and export.[7]

By June 26, Mr. Snyder was able to report to the President that the United States would fully meet its half-year goal of six million tons of food grains, although final shipments would not leave United States ports until after the first of July, and that some 250 million additional bushels of grain were scheduled for export during the crop year beginning July 1.[8] The next day Herbert Hoover, in a radio address before the Canadian Parliament which closed his report on the world food situation, declared that the 3.6 million ton gap in minimum supplies had been closed, due largely to greater exports from the Latin-American nations and the adoption of conservation measures in the United States and Canada. Mr. Hoover warned, however, that stringent measures to conserve food must continue and that an uninterrupted stream of overseas supplies must be kept up.[9] A report by Mr. Anderson on July 8 announced that the United States had met its commitments on relief shipments, and had, in the case of food grains, even exceeded them; again, however, continuing needs were stressed.[10]

With change in United States policy toward UNRRA and international relief cooperation,[11] increasing emphasis was put, during the latter half of 1946, on development of an overall program of United States relief to needy nations abroad. In September, President Truman created the Cabinet Committee on World Food Programs, consisting of the Secretaries of Agriculture, State, and Commerce, to coordinate the activities of the United States in shipping food abroad, while in December, on recommendation of this committee, he established

---

[1] *New York Times,* April 27, 1946, p. 1.
[2] *Ibid.,* April 17, 1946.
[3] *Ibid.,* April 30, 1946.
[4] *Ibid.,* May 15, 1946.
[5] For text of the report, see this volume, p. 383.
[6] Department of State, *Bulletin,* XIV, p. 895.
[7] *Ibid.,* p. 863.
[8] *Ibid.,* XV, p. 31.
[9] *New York Times,* June 29, 1946, p. 1.
[10] For text of the report, see this volume, p. 389.
[11] See *ibid.,* p. 364.

the Office of the Coordinator of Emergency Exports, under Capt. Granville Conway, to supervise all export transportation and shipping activities.[1]

On December 8, 1946, Mr. Acheson further amplified United States policy on relief for 1946–47, and indicated that it would be based on four fundamental points: (1) that every nation should consider what it can contribute to relief, and there should be discussion of these plans, using the Secretariat of the United Nations as a clearing house; (2) that nations receiving relief must prove their need, and promise distribution on the basis of need; (3) that relief problems did not warrant enormous grants of money without effective control by the grantor; and (4) that nations which diverted to their armies manpower that could be producing the necessities of life would not be entitled to relief.[2]

(1) *Statement by the President (Truman) on the Relief and Rehabilitation Program, September 17, 1945.*[3]

The United States Government is now in a position to fulfil the main requests of Europe — with the exception of sugar, fats, and oils — from this date until January 1 as these requests have been stated to it by the governments of the liberated countries and by UNRRA.

Provision of the supplies thus requested does not, however, mean that the civilian populations of Europe will reach even a minimum level of subsistence, and much suffering may be expected during the coming winter in certain areas of the Continent.

The limiting factor in meeting the minimum needs of the liberated peoples is no longer one of shipping. For the moment, in the case of most commodities, it is no longer a problem of supply. Today it is primarily a twofold financial problem: first, to work out credits or other financial arrangements with the European governments; second, to make additional funds available to UNRRA for emergency relief.

This Government is bending every effort to find solutions to this problem, in cooperation with the respective claimants, with a view to increasing the flow of urgently needed supplies. Pending such settlements this Government is taking necessary measures in relation to production, distribution, and shipping of supplies to insure a broad, equitable, and continuous flow of current stocks and new production of relief and rehabilitation supplies for liberated areas, which it is anticipated will be required, in addition to those quantities which they have already requisitioned. One purpose of such measures is to prevent the dissipation of available supplies in domestic channels where they are not essential.

When I returned from Potsdam I said, "If we let Europe go cold and hungry, we may lose some of the foundations of order on which the hope for world-wide peace must rest. We must help to the limits of our strength. And we will." That pledge, made not only to our Allies but to the American people, must be kept. It should be made perfectly clear that, contrary to the belief of many, relaxation of rationing on the home front is not a factor in the allocation of relief supplies to Europe. The Department of Agriculture reports that, despite the release of cheese from rationing controls and the possible relaxation of domestic meat

---

[1] *New York Times*, July 6, 1947.
[2] For text of Mr. Acheson's statement, see this volume, p. 371.
[3] Department of State, *Bulletin*, XIII, p. 428.

rationing, we have sufficient quantities of meat and dairy products to fulfil the requirements placed upon us by UNRRA and the paying governments for the last quarter of the year. Furthermore, should UNRRA secure the additional financial resources it so urgently needs and the paying governments conclude more satisfactory financial arrangements, again raising the problem of supply, both the Department of Agriculture and the War Production Board have the authority to issue set-aside orders on specific quantities of commodities purchased, regardless of whether they are rationed, to insure deliveries abroad. This does not mean that it may not become necessary to resume ration controls of certain items if they become so short in supply that such controls are required to insure more equitable distribution.

The most desperate needs of the liberated people are for coal, transportation, and food, in that order of priority. Other commodities urgently required include hides and leather, cotton, wool, textiles, soap, farm equipment, including fertilizer and seeds, repair parts and machinery, medical supplies, and a general list of raw materials. The items which are causing major concern because of world-wide shortages are coal, sugar and fats, hides and leather, textiles, and a few of the raw materials, in minor quantities. Locomotives constitute a special and acute problem because of the time factor involved in their manufacture.

Coal presents not only the most serious but the most complicated problem. Once self-sufficient in this commodity, Europe is now without the labor, the food, the transportation, the housing, and the machinery needed to restore production quickly to its pre-war level. The Allied Control Commission is making every effort to speed the resumption of German production in order to supply the liberated areas, but despite considerable progress the people of these areas face a winter of extreme hardship.

The United States is now shipping approximately 1,400,000 tons of coal to Europe a month. For the period ending January 1 the goal is 8,000,000 tons, or slightly more than one percent of our domestic production. The limiting factor is not primarily one of supply but of inland transportation facilities both here and abroad.

The Department of Agriculture reports that shipments of food to the paying governments and UNRRA during the last quarter of this year will include approximately these quantities:

150 million pounds of meat and meat products
70 million bushels of wheat
28 thousand short tons of raw sugar
90 million pounds of dried peas and beans
13 million pounds of lard

In addition, the Department of Agriculture is prepared to ship the following supplies of dairy products, in at least these quantities, as soon as financial arrangements have been satisfactorily completed:

60 million pounds of cheese
200 million pounds of evaporated milk

25 million pounds of dry whole-milk powder
80 million pounds of dry skim-milk powder
15 million pounds of condensed milk

It should be remembered that these supplies will serve not to improve but only to sustain the diet of the liberated peoples, which remains below the minimum level of subsistence. In some cases the doubling of these food shipments waits only upon the conclusion of satisfactory financial arrangements.

This Government has abundant evidence that the American people are aware of the suffering among our Allies. They have also made plain their determination that this country shall do its full part, along with other supplying nations, in helping to restore health and strength to those who fought at our side both in Europe and in the Far East. It is an American responsibility not only to our friends, but to ourselves, to see that this job is done and done quickly.

(2) *Statement by the President (Truman) on the World Food Crisis, February 6, 1946.*[1]

For the world as a whole, a food crisis has developed which may prove to be the worst in modern times. More people face starvation and even actual death for want of food today than in any war year and perhaps more than in all the war years combined.

The United States and other countries have moved food into war-torn countries in record amounts, but there has been a constantly widening gap between essential minimum needs and available supplies.

Although this country enjoyed a near-record production of food and a record crop of wheat, the wheat crops of Europe and North Africa and the rice crops of the Far East have proved to be much shorter than anticipated; in fact some areas have experienced the shortest crops in fifty years because of extreme droughts and the disruption of war.

We in this country have been consuming about 3,300 calories per person per day. In contrast, more than 125 million people in Europe will have to subsist on less than 2,000 calories a day; 28 million will get less than 1,500 calories a day and in some parts of Europe, large groups will receive as little as 1,000 calories.

Under these circumstances it is apparent that only through superhuman efforts can mass starvation be prevented. In recognition of this situation Great Britain only yesterday announced cuts in rations of fats and a return to the dark wartime loaf of bread.

I am sure that the American people are in favor of carrying their share of the burden.

Accordingly, I have instructed the appropriate agencies of the Government to put into effect a number of emergency measures designed to help meet critically urgent needs to the greatest possible extent in the shortest possible time. The cooperation of every man, woman and child, the food trades and industries, the transportation industry, and others

[1] *Ibid.*, XIV, p. 246.

will be needed to make these measures effective. I know the conscience of the American people will not permit them to withhold or stint their cooperation while their fellow men in other lands suffer and die.

The measures to be taken are as follows:

1. The appropriate agencies of this Government will immediately inaugurate a vigorous campaign to secure the full cooperation of all consumers in conserving food, particularly bread. Additional emphasis will be placed upon the cooperation of bakers and retailers in reducing waste of bread in distribution channels.

2. The use of wheat in the direct production of alcohol and beer will be discontinued; the use of other grains for the production of beverage alcohol will be limited, beginning March 1, to five days' consumption a month; and the use of other grains for the production of beer will be limited to an aggregate quantity equal to that used for this purpose in 1940 which was 30 percent less than the quantity used in 1945. This will save for food about 20 million bushels of grain by June 30, 1946.

3. The wheat flour extraction rate (the quantity of flour produced from each bushel of wheat) will be raised to 80 percent for the duration of the emergency. Also, steps will be taken to limit the distribution of flour to amounts essential for current civilian distribution. This will save about 25 million bushels of wheat during the first half of 1946.

4. The Department of Agriculture will control millers' inventories of wheat, and bakers' and distributors' inventories of flour. The inventory controls will be designed to maintain the wheat and flour being held for civilian use at the minimum necessary for distribution purposes.

5. Specific preference will be given to the rail movement of wheat, corn, meat, and other essential foods in order promptly to export maximum quantities to the destinations where most needed.

6. The Department of Agriculture will exercise direct control over exports of wheat and flour to facilitate movement to destinations of greatest need.

7. Necessary steps will be taken to export during this calendar year, 375,000 tons of fats and oils, 1.6 billion pounds of meat, of which one billion pounds is to be made available during the first half of 1946, and to increase the exports of dairy products, particularly cheese and evaporated milk.

8. The War and Navy Departments already have aided materially the movement of Philippine copra (the raw material from which cocoanut oil is produced) by releasing 200 LCM and J boats for the inter-island trade in the Philippines. These Departments and the War Shipping Administration will take immediate steps to make available the additional ships needed for this purpose.

The Secretaries of War and Navy will release for the movement of food to Europe all refrigerated ships not essential to the maintenance of the flow of food to the armed forces.

9. The Department of Agriculture will develop additional ways in which grain now being used in the feeding of livestock and poultry could be conserved for use as human food. These steps may include means to obtain the rapid marketing of heavy hogs, preferably all those over 225 pounds, and of beef cattle with a moderate rather than a high degree

of finish; to encourage the culling of poultry flocks; to prevent excessive chick production; and to encourage more economical feeding of dairy cattle. Regulations to limit wheat inventories of feed manufacturers and to restrict the use of wheat in feed will be prepared.

We are requesting the cooperation of retailers and other distributors in informally rationing commodities that will be in scarce supply for the months immediately ahead. Actual reductions in the volume of distribution may be suggested, with the obligations placed on the industry involved to handle distribution equitably. I believe that with the wholehearted cooperation of food manufacturers, wholesalers, and retailers the job can be done.

The measures which I have directed will no doubt cause some inconvenience to many of us. Millers and bakers, for example, will have to adapt their operations to produce and to use flour of a higher extraction rate while consumers may not be able to get exactly the kind of bread that many prefer. We will not have as large a selection of meats, cheese, evaporated milk, ice cream, margarine, and salad dressing as we may like. However, these inconveniences will be a small price to pay for saving lives, mitigating suffering in liberated countries, and helping to establish a firmer foundation for peace.

In attempting to alleviate the shortages abroad, this country will adhere to the policy of giving preference to the liberated peoples and to those who have fought beside us, but we shall also do our utmost to prevent starvation among our former enemies.

I am confident that every citizen will cooperate wholeheartedly in the complete and immediate mobilization of this country's tremendous resources to win this world-wide war against mass starvation.

(3) *Famine Report to the President (Truman) by the Members of the Hoover Mission, May 13, 1946.*[1]

We have completed your instructions to survey the principal nations affected by food shortages which have resulted, or may result, in widespread famine; to evaluate the minimum needs of these areas until the next harvest; and to discover such additional food resources as possible. In accordance with your instructions, we have also presented the American point of view on the food problem to these nations and the interest and understanding of our people in their plight. Finally, we have constantly advised American officials and the American public as to the situation as we found it.

We have traveled some 35,000 miles, visited twenty-two countries which have a deficiency of food, and informed ourselves of the situation in several others. The only country of large reported deficiency we did not visit was the Union of South Africa. We visited five self-sufficient or surplus countries and informed ourselves of the situation in other consequential surplus nations.

The dominant need of the world in this crisis is cereals, particularly wheat and rice. There is great need of fats and special food for children, but as cereals can furnish 85 percent of an emergency diet, we considered

[1] *Ibid.*, p. 897.

cereal requirements were the first concern, and the best indicator. If a foundation of bread can be assured, and as much fats and children's food as possible, mass starvation can be prevented.

At the time of our departure, the Combined Food Board's estimate of the available cereal supplies from surplus countries showed a deficit as compared with stated requirements of 11,000,000 tons, or 43 percent.

Requirements — We attach hereto (Table I) a country-by-country, month-by-month minimum program of required cereal imports to the deficit and famine areas from May 1st to September 30th.

These programs represent a considerable reduction from the hitherto stated requirements of the various nations. The amounts have in most cases been agreed upon by their governments. In the case of China, we regret to say our program is less than minimum need but is all, or more, than can be transported inland to the famine areas. The totals are:

Europe	8,390,000 tons
Latin America	1,000,000 tons
South Africa and New Zealand	198,000 tons
Middle East	100,000 tons
Indian Ocean area	2,886,000 tons
Pacific Ocean area	1,910,000 tons
TOTAL	14,484,000 tons

Of course, every country would be better off if more could be furnished.

Supplies — We have found some increases in supplies possible during the crisis through development of certain new sources of supply; through additional loans of cereals from early-crop countries which may not themselves have annual surpluses; through substitution of other cereals for wheat and rice; and as a result of conservation up to this time.

Our estimate (Table II) of Probable Supplies as of May 1st to September 30th are:

From	
United States	4,220,000 tons
Canada	2,300,000 tons
Australia	992,000 tons
United Kingdom	200,000 tons
Argentine	2,375,000 tons
Brazil	200,000 tons
Other Western Hemisphere States	40,000 tons
Burma	75,000 tons
Siam	195,000 tons
Russia to France	300,000 tons
TOTAL	10,897,000 tons

Therefore the gap in supplies between May 1st and September 30th can be reduced to about 3,600,000 tons, as against an 11,000,000 tons gap in the earlier appraisals.

In addition to the above supplies there is a "possible" about 1,500,000 tons more, as indicated in Table III.

We are confident that if until the end of August, there can be further vigorous conservation in surplus countries, mainly wheats and fats, and more energetic cooperation between nations, the remaining deficit can be largely overcome. The cooperation of Russia and the Latin American States would greatly aid in meeting the problem. If mass starvation is to be prevented it will require constant effort.

It is of interest to note that the quantities which are provided by UNRRA as charity comprise about 20 percent of the world's cereal needs, whereas nations representing 80 percent are being financed by the importing countries themselves. But the need in these latter is no less urgent.

You will recognize that these statements are estimates. They, however, comprise a reasonable basis upon which to formulate policies.

We wish to express our especial appreciation of the unfailing aid and courtesy of the Secretaries of Agriculture, State and War, and the American officials abroad. We are also deeply indebted to Generals George and Saville of the Air Transport Command, their efficient crews, and for their provisions for our comfort and safety.

TABLE I

Cereal Requirements (Including Rice)

EUROPE

Minimum Arrivals Required During Crisis Period

(Loadings at seaboard about 30 days earlier)

Based on not to exceed 300 grams cereals per person per day

Country	Population Millions	(Thousands of Tons)					
		May	June	July	Aug.	Sept.	Total
* France	39.1	350	350	350	350	350	1,750
* North Africa	12.0	100	—	—	—	—	100
* Italy	41.5	225	225	225	100	—	775
* Switzerland	4.2	—	—	30	30	30	90
* Czechoslovakia	13.5	60	60	60	60	50	290
* Poland	23.5	85	85	85	85	—	340
* Finland	3.8	—	—	25	40	40	105
* Norway	3.0	—	—	—	30	30	60
* United Kingdom	47.5	400	400	400	400	400	2,000
* Belgium	8.0	60	60	60	60	60	300
* Holland	9.0	—	—	—	—	80	80
* Germany:							
Am. Zone	18.0	50	50	50	65	60	275
Br. Zone	23.3	180	180	180	180	180	900
Fr. Zone	6.0	30	45	45	45	30	195
Russ. Zone		Data unknown					
* Austria	7.0	30	55	55	55	30	225
Spain	26.0	60	60	60	60	—	240
Portugal	8.0	30	30	30	30	—	120
Albania	1.0	5	5	5	5	—	20
* Yugoslavia	16.0	50	50	50	50	50	250
* Greece	7.5	55	55	55	55	55	275
Europe Totals	317.9	1,770	1,710	1,765	1,700	1,445	8,390

* Visited by the Mission.

LATIN AMERICA

Country or Province	Population Millions	(Thousands of Tons)					
		May	June	July	Aug.	Sept.	Total
Latin-America	—	200	200	200	200	200	1,000

NEW ZEALAND AND SOUTH AFRICA

New Zealand	—	—	9	9	0	0	18
South Africa	—	40	40	40	30	30	180
	—	40	49	49	30	30	198

NEAR EAST

Near East	—	20	20	20	20	20	100

INDIAN OCEAN

(Loadings from Eastern Hemisphere 1 month and Western Hemisphere 2 months earlier)

* INDIA (Provinces affected):							
Bombay	22.0	—	55	85	95	95	330
Mysore	7.6	14	25	25	25	25	114
Madras	51.4	210	170	170	170	170	890
Tranv	6.5	18	10	10	10	10	58
Cochin	1.5	8	7	7	7	7	36
Deccan	2.9	43	19	19	19	19	119
Behar	37.9	19	14	20	20	20	93
Un. Provinces	57.6	24	—	—	60	60	144
Bengal	61.3	—	—	90	106	106	302
Other	—	50	50	50	50	50	250
Ceylon	7.0	60	60	60	60	60	300
Malaya & Straits Settlements	3.6	50	50	50	50	50	250
TOTAL	—	496	460	586	672	672	2,886

PACIFIC OCEAN

* Philippines	14.0	12	12	12	12	12	60
* China [a]	220.0	120	150	200	200	200	870
* Japan	75.0	50	250	270	200	100	870
* Korea [b]	14.0	15	30	45	10	10	110
		197	442	527	422	322	1,910
GRAND TOTAL	—	2,723	2,881	3,147	3,044	2,689	14,484

[a] Utmost capacity of inland transportation.
[b] American Zone.
* Visited by the Mission.

SURPLUS OR SELF-SUFFICIENT COUNTRIES

Country	Population Millions	(Thousands of Tons)					
		May	June	July	Aug.	Sept.	Total
*Sweden	6.2						
*Denmark	3.8						
Hungary	9.1						
Rumania	12.1						
Bulgaria	6.5						
*Egypt	17.3						
*Iraq	4.0						
*Siam	14.0						
Total	73.0						

*Visited by the Mission.

TABLE II

Possible World Cereal Supplies from Surplus Areas (May 1 to Sept. 30)

Source	Second Quarter Loadings (April-May-June)			Loadings in July and August			Total
	(Thousands of Tons)						
	Wheat	Coarse grains	Rice	Wheat	Coarse grains	Rice	
U.S.A.	2,200	500	20	1,400	100	—	4,220
Canada	1,650	150	—	400	100	—	2,300
Australia	700	—	17	275	—	—	992
United Kingdom	200	—	—	—	—	—	200
Argentine	500	800	—	275	800	—	2,375
Brazil	—	50	60	—	50	40	200
Other Western Hemisphere States	—	—	40	—	—	—	40
Burma	—	—	40	—	—	35	75
Siam	—	—	75	—	—	120	195
Russia to France	150	—	—	150	—	—	300
	5,400	1,500	252	2,500	1,050	195	10,897
Grand Total: (Wheat — 7,900; Coarse grains — 2,550; Rice — 447)							10,897

TABLE III
Further Supplies Possible

Source	Second Quarter Loadings (April-May-June)			Loadings in July and August				Remarks
	(Thousands of Tons)							
	Wheat	Coarse grains	Rice	Wheat	Coarse grains	Rice	Total	
Indo-China	—	—	50	—	—	50	50	
Iraq	—	125	—	—	100	—	225	
India	—	—	—	—	200	—	200	Surplus Provinces.
Punjab and Sind	100	—	—	100	—	—	200	Could be borrowed.
Egypt	30	—	10	50	—	25	115	Could be borrowed.
United Kingdom	300	—	—	—	—	—	300	Released stocks.
Russia to France	75	—	—	—	—	—	75	
Siam	—	—	—	—	—	200	200	
	505	125	60	150	300	225	1,365	
Iraq (dates)	—	—	—	—	—	—	140	
							1,505	

TABLE IV
Provisional Balance Sheet of World Requirements and Supplies
(Thousands of tons)

Minimum Cereal Requirements		
Europe	8,390	
Latin-America	1,000	
Southern British Empire	198	
Middle East	100	
Indian Ocean	2,886	
Pacific Ocean	1,910	14,484
Cereal Supplies Probable		
April-May-June Loadings	7,202	
July-August Loadings	3,695	10,897
Deficit Probable . . . 3,587 tons or 24 percent		
Further Possible Cereal Supplies	1,505	

TABLE V

Comparison of the Combined Food Board Balance Sheet of March 1, 1946 (retrospective to Jan. 1, 1946) and Hoover Mission Balance Sheet as of May 1st, 1946

	(Thousands of Tons)			
	Stated Requirements	Estimated Supplies	Deficit	Deficit Percent
Combined Food Board Jan. 1–Sept. 1	25,900	14,900	11,000	42.5
Shipments to May 1	7,000	7,000		
Original Balance as at May 1	18,900	7,900	11,000	58
As Revised by Hoover Mission: May 1–Sept. 1	14,484	10,900	3,587	24
	− 4,000	+ 3,000	− 7,413	

Thus, the requirements were revised downward by 4,000,000 tons and the supplies revised upward, through new sources developed, effect of conservation, drafts on earlier crops in some countries, etc., 3,000,000 tons.

The estimated gap as of May 1st, 3,600,000 tons.

(4) *Report to the President (Truman) on 1945–46 Famine-Relief Food Shipments, Submitted by the Secretary of Agriculture (Anderson), July 8, 1946.*[1]

The United States exported more than $16\frac{1}{2}$ million long tons of foodstuffs during the year which ended June 30. The great bulk of these shipments went to war-devastated countries where starvation threatened. These exports from the United States were by far the greatest contribution made to the world's hungry during this first year of reconstruction.

The 400 million bushel "bread" grain export commitment for the year was met by June 30. Wheat and flour exports (10,336,000 tons), plus the corn and corn products shipped after May 1 from stocks acquired under the corn "bonus" plan, reached a total of 401 million bushels.

Of the total bread grain exports, 5,556,000 tons were shipped from January 1 through June 30. In addition, enough wheat, flour, corn and corn products was at ports on July 1, ready for ship loading, to bring the total above the six million ton (225 million bushel) "goal" for the half-year period. This means that the full goal totals will have left our shores and be on the way to hunger areas as soon as ships can be loaded and cleared — probably by the middle of the month. During June alone, our bread grain exports totaled about one and one-half million tons — a record for a similar period.

Meeting this full goal means actual shipment of 417 million bushels for the year. The excess of 17 million bushels above our commitments will not be deducted from the planned export of up to 250 million bushels of wheat during the 1946–47 year.

[1] *Ibid.*, XV., p. 119.

The real extent of this accomplishment in grain export is brought out by the fact that the amount shipped is nearly double the original requirement for the year which was presented to the Combined Food Board a year ago. At that time, it was thought that we would be called upon to export only about six million tons (225 million bushels) for the entire year.

Adding rice, oats, rye and barley to the "bread" grains of the specific commitments, brings the total of all grains exported during the year to 11,747,000 long tons — by far the largest volume in the total food shipments. Grains, high in calories per unit and easily handled, were the greatest need of the hungry nations.

Second in importance for relief and in the amounts shipped were fats and oils, dairy products, and meats. The totals for the year were: dairy products, 764,000 tons; meats, 614,000 tons; and fats and oils, 356,000 tons.

In addition to these major commodities, a total of more than 3,200,000 tons of other foodstuffs were exported during the year. These exports included dry beans and peas, potatoes and sweet potatoes, fruits and vegetables, sugar, eggs, and canned fish.

Our great contribution in meeting world food shortages may be measured by the fact that of all food distributed from United States supplies in 1945-46, one out of every six pounds went overseas. By major commodity groups, we sent foreign countries more than 40 percent of the wheat that was distributed from our supplies during the year, more than 35 percent of the rice, more than 20 percent of the cheese, more than 10 percent of the fats and oils, and about 6 percent of the meat.

The Need

It is not necessary to review in detail the needs that prompted us as a country to carry through this tremendous world feeding program. In your call for emergency action last February 6, and in many other messages, you as President outlined these needs clearly. We have all understood that the ravages of war left literally hundreds of millions of our fellow men in very real danger of starvation. We have known that droughts cut down production in many parts of the world, increasing the demands upon those countries fortunate enough to have continued large crop production. And we have also known that hunger is a fertile ground for anarchy, and not for the building of a stable world and a durable peace.

Cooperative Effort

It has been against this background of urgent need that this Government has driven through to reach export quotas. That they have been reached in practically all cases is a tribute to the teamwork of all groups involved. Our farmers not only produced record or near record crops for one more year, but they also cooperated in getting wheat and other commodities to market when the emergency became acute. The processing, distribution, and transportation industries have all made magnificent records in handling the foodstuffs which were being shipped to

RELIEF AND REHABILITATION

foreign countries. Our consumers, seriously inconvenienced at times when their favorite foods disappeared from grocers' shelves, have in general accepted the situation with a minimum of complaint. They have known that the food they could not buy today was on its way to maintain life and health in some war-torn country.

While the Department of Agriculture has had the major responsibility for procuring the food, and for instituting many of the emergency measures which were necessary to make it available, the job could not have been done without the efficient cooperation of many other government agencies. The Inter-Departmental Transportation Committee directed a coordinated effort which broke grain shipping records during recent weeks. Great credit is due the War Shipping Administration, the Interstate Commerce Commission, and the Office of Defense Transportation for the work they did in making transportation available. Your Famine Emergency Committee has suggested constructive over-all steps needed in the campaign effort, and has helped materially in informing the nation of the urgent need for food from the United States.

EMERGENCY MEASURES

Many emergency measures and special regulations were necessary in order to meet our export commitments and complete the programs. The Department of Agriculture ordered set-asides for Government purchase of a number of commodities. It was necessary to limit the use of wheat and other grains in livestock feeding, and to limit the amount of flour available for human consumption. The special "bonus" programs for wheat and corn were necessary in order to get grain to market in time to meet shipping schedules.

CONTINUING NEEDS

While it can be reported that we are nearing the end of the most urgent crisis for this year, and that the worst of the immediate dangers of famine have been forestalled, serious food needs abroad will continue for some time. Devastated countries cannot return to normal in a single year. When this year's harvests are completed for the northern hemisphere, we shall know a good deal more about the situation. In the meantime, we must continue relief shipments and be ready to meet at least the minimum future needs.

The Department of Agriculture has already announced that by continuing conservation and wise use of supplies at home up to 250 million bushels of wheat can be made available for export during the 1946–47 year. Tentative plans are also being made for our shipments of other major commodities.

COMMODITY SHIPMENTS IN 1945–46

Grains — A year ago it was indicated that the United States would be called on to export about 225 million bushels of wheat during 1945–46. Later, in the fall, the total was raised to 325 million. By December, UNRRA, France, and other claimants had been forced to raise their estimates of minimum requirements several times, and the United States agreed to undertake the export of a record total of 400 million bushels during the year. At that time advance estimates placed wheat and flour exports at 175 million bushels for the last six months of 1945. We therefore set a goal of 225 million for the January–June 1946 period, to bring the total for the year to the 400 million bushel commitment.

Later reports show that 192 million bushels of wheat and flour were actually shipped before January 1, leaving only 208 million to reach the 400 total. We chose, however, to stick to the 225 million bushel (six million ton) "goal" figure which had already been announced. In effect, therefore, we have been working against a 400 million bushel commitment for the year, and a 417 million bushel goal. We knew from the first that all we could ship would not be enough to meet all needs, and we therefore have made every effort to exceed the commitment.

We have now passed the 400 million commitment, and will very soon reach the 417 million bushel goal.

Meats — It is estimated that approximately 614,000 long tons of meat and meat products were actually shipped to foreign claimants during the 12 months, not including shipments to U. S. territories. This compares with the stated 1946 calendar year goal of 714,000 long tons. During the past 12 months, procurement activities were complicated by such factors as work stoppages in production, and shortages in supply during at least part of the year. The 1945–46 shipments represented 5.9 percent of total U. S. meat output during the year.

Of the 614,000 total which went for export, approximately 379,000 tons were procured by the Department of Agriculture, while 215,000 tons came from military stocks for such outlets as UNRRA and U. S. military civilian feeding. In addition, about 20,000 tons were exported commercially.

UNRRA received nearly half the total 614,000 tons shipped to foreign claimants, exports to this outlet accounting for 288,000 tons. Virtually all of the meat which went to UNRRA was for European destinations. Of the total 614,000 tons of meat exported, 588,000 tons went to Europe, including the countries served by UNRRA. The remainder was exported to outlets in the Far East, Latin American republics, and others.

Fats and Oils — High on the list of food products needed for foreign relief feeding and for other essential exports were fats and oils. It was recognized at the beginning of the 1945–46 year that we would be faced with a continuing world shortage of these commodities. Appraisal of the situation after the end of the war in the Pacific indicated little alleviation of the tight supply for some months to come. Sources in that area had been devastated by the war, and re-establishment of supplies has taken more time than had been anticipated. The situation called for the most efficient management of available world supplies, including those from U. S. sources.

According to our estimates, it is indicated that actual shipments to the outlets for which allocations were established reached slightly more than 356,000 long tons of edible fats and oils. The goal for the 1946 calendar year was set at 347,000 tons, or 375,000 tons including both edible and inedible products.

Of the 356,000 long tons exported, 268,000 went to Europe, with the remainder going to countries in the Far East, to Latin American republics, and others. Approximately 73,000 tons, or 27 percent of the total which went to Europe, was for UNRRA. Other large recipients included: the United Kingdom and British Services Overseas, France and French North Africa.

Dairy products — Measured against a tight supply situation in the U. S. was the pressure of record demand — both from the need for these products in foreign relief programs, and from U. S. civilians. Tentative plans for exports, implemented by allocations, were drawn up for the 1945–46 year. The products most in demand for foreign use are cheese, and condensed, evaporated, and dried milk.

The estimated export shipments are indicated to be 764,000 long tons. The shipments represent 28 percent of total distribution of these products in the fiscal year.

Of the approximately 764,000 long tons exported during the 12-month period, about 88 percent, or 669,000 tons, went to European countries. Shipments to UNRRA — in the amount of 316,000 tons — made up 44 percent of all shipments to Europe. The United Kingdom and British Services Overseas were the next largest recipients, followed by such countries as France and French North Africa, and Belgium. Relatively small shipments went to the Far East, and other outlets.

The table on page 394 gives the preliminary report on exports during the year, by major food groups and by destination.

A report to the President by the Cabinet Committee on World Food Programs, submitted on July 1, 1947, indicated that in the period from July to December, 1946, the United States exported 141,000 long tons of meat, and 100,000 long tons of fats and oils. From July, 1946, through June, 1947, the United States sent overseas 563 million bushels of wheat and 493,000 tons of dairy products.[1]

2. REFUGEES AND DISPLACED PERSONS[2]

A. International Refugee Organization

At the time of the end of hostilities, three international organizations, the military occupation authorities, and a number of voluntary agencies were concerned with the problem of refugees and displaced persons. During the latter part of 1945 and throughout 1946 a series of attempts were made to coordinate the programs of the different authorities and organizations, and plans for the creation of an International Refugee Organization were laid.

Under the original agreement which brought it into being, and by the terms of a number of policy resolutions adopted at several sessions of its Council, the United Nations Relief and Rehabilitation Administration had direct responsibility for refugees and displaced persons in Europe and certain categories of persons in the Middle East and Asia.[3] UNRRA placed emphasis on repatriation of persons in its care, while upholding the principle that they should not be forced to return to places of former residence. By December 31, 1946, the Administration, with assistance from military authorities and home countries, had repatriated from Germany, Austria, and Italy 7,050,606 displaced persons.

[1] *New York Times*, July 6, 1947.
[2] For information on United States policy regarding refugees and displaced persons in Germany, see this volume, p. 251.
[3] See *Documents, VI, 1943–1944*, p. 251; *ibid., VII, 1944–1945*, p. 386.

TABLE I

Food Exports [a] from the United States by Destination, Fiscal Year 1945–46 (Preliminary)

(In thousands of long tons)

Destination	Total	Wheat and Flour (Grain Equiv.) [b]	Other Grains (Grain Equiv.) [c]	Fats and Oils (Product Weight) [d]	Meat (Carcass Weight Equiv.)	Dairy Products [e]	Other Foods [f]
	1	2	3	4	5	6	7
Total food exports	16,700	10,336	1,411	356	614	764	3,219
Europe — Total	11,647	7,454	655	268	588	669	2,013
UNRRA [h]	3,951	2,624	227	73	288	311	428
U. S. Military civilian feeding	2,351	1,535	64	13	16	43	680
France and French North Africa	1,959	1,408	80	61	60	47	303
Belgium	779	541	74	19	48	33	64
Netherlands	394	304	17	11	27	21	14
Norway	68	12	30	4	1	0	21
U.K. and B.S.O.	1,086	306	26	69	99	196	390
U.S.S.R.	123	36	11	8	46	5	17
Other Europe	936	688	126	10	3	13	96
Far East — Total	1,400	879	346 [i]	4	5	29	137
UNRRA	164	127	37 [i]	0	0	(g)	0
U. S. Military civilian feeding	573	427	120	0	0	0	26
Philippines	315	160	78	1	1	23	52
India	300	164	84	0	0	0	46
Netherlands East Indies	48	1	27	0	4	(g)	13
Latin American Republics	1,384	936	243	3	10	14	129
Other exports	2,269	1,067	167	52	11	52	940

[a] Excludes shipments to U. S. Territories except for wheat and flour, amounting to approximately 4 million bushels wheat equivalent.
[b] Excludes other wheat products which are less than one half of one percent of total exports.
[c] Includes corn and corn products, rice, oats, rye, and barley, including malt.
[d] Total edible use including a very small quantity of butter. Includes oil equivalent of soybeans shipped as beans and of peanuts shipped to UNRRA.
[e] Includes cheese, condensed, evaporated, and dried milk.
[f] Includes sugar, beans and peas, fish, eggs, poultry, vegetables, fruits, sirups, soups, tea, coffee, cocoa, etc.   [g] Less than 500 tons.
[h] May include some food for UNRRA in the Far East.   [i] May include a small quantity of rice for UNRRA in Europe.

UNRRA figures at the time indicated that more than 1,000,000 persons, most of whom were "non-repatriables," remained in Europe; of these about 700,000 were receiving UNRRA aid.[1]

Also concerned with the problem were the reorganized Intergovernmental Committee on Refugees,[2] which on July 16, 1946, announced its decision to extend its mandate to include emigration services on behalf of non-repatriable refugees of Germany, Austria, and Italy,[3] and the Office of the High Commissioner of Refugees under the Protection of the League of Nations, which cared for refugees from World War I. The Intergovernmental Committee sponsored an International Conference on Travel Documents in London from October 8 to 15, 1946, which drew up a travel document for the use of stateless persons and those not under the protection of any government;[4] it also administered certain German funds made available by the Final Act of the Paris Conference on Reparations for the benefit of non-repatriable victims of German action.[5]

With the liquidation of UNRRA planned for December 31, 1946, and the end of League refugee activities set for the same date, conversations were begun in the fall of 1945 looking toward the final solution of the problem of refugees and displaced persons. At the Fifth Plenary Session of the Intergovernmental Committee in November, 1945, representatives of the United Kingdom and the United States indicated that the whole question should be referred to the United Nations, and organs of the United Nations undertook its discussion soon after their formation in January, 1946.

At meetings of the General Assembly, as well as at later sessions of other organs which considered the question, the United States took the position that displaced persons should have the right to decide whether or not they wished to return to their countries of origin. This point of view was consistently opposed by the Soviet Union, which questioned the whole idea of international action, sought to prohibit anti-repatriation propaganda in displaced persons camps, and favored the cutting off of aid to persons who refused to be repatriated. While the United States position was generally upheld, a resolution passed by the General Assembly noted (1) that the problem was international in scope, (2) that only war criminals, quislings, and traitors should be compelled to return to their countries of origin, and (3) that the main task concerning displaced persons was to encourage and assist in every way their early return to countries of origin.[6]

The problem was referred by the first part of the first session of the Assembly to the Economic and Social Council, which considered it in February, 1946, and which created a Special Committee on Refugees and Displaced Persons. Following a United States proposal, the committee, which met in London from April 8 to June 1, 1946, recommended the establishment of a specialized international agency within the framework of the United Nations, to deal with the problem.[7] Discussion continued at the second and third sessions of the Economic and Social Council; the Council transmitted both a draft constitution and suggestions for the creation of an interim Preparatory Commission to the second part of the first session of the General Assembly, since months of discussion and delay in reaching agreement on the basic principles of the new organization

[1] United Nations Relief and Rehabilitation Administration, *Report of the Director-General to the Council for the Period 1 October 1946 to 31 December 1946*, DGR-11, Washington, 1947, p. 55, 57.

[2] See *Documents, VII, 1944–1945*; p. 389.

[3] Intergovernmental Committee on Refugees, *The Future of the Problem of Refugees and Displaced Persons*, London, October, 1946, p. 16.

[4] Intergovernmental Committee on Refugees, *Preparatory Documents Concerning the Adoption of an Identity and Travel Document for Refugees Coming within the Mandate of the Intergovernmental Committee*, London, 1946.

[5] For text of the act, see *The Distribution of Reparation from Germany*, Department of State Publication 2584.

[6] United Nations, *Journal of the General Assembly*, No. 34, Supplement A, p. 663.

[7] United Nations Economic and Social Council, Document E/REF/75, June 1, 1946.

indicated that it would not be ready to assume its functions at the time of the liquidation of UNRRA, even though UNRRA's displaced persons operations had been extended until June 30, 1947.[1]

After further discussion and disagreement at the Assembly, the Constitution was finally approved on December 15, 1946, by a vote of 30 to 5 with 18 abstentions. The United States signed the Constitution and the agreement on interim measures on December 16.[2]

As envisaged in its constitution, the International Refugee Organization was to consist of a General Council, the ultimate policy-making body, in which each member had one representative and one vote, an Executive Committee of nine members chosen for two-year terms by the Council, and a Secretariat headed by a Director-General. The Council meets regularly once a year, or specially as convened by the Executive Committee or one-third of its members; the Executive Committee meets twice a month. The Organization was scheduled to come into existence when the membership was accepted by governments of 15 states with a quota of not less than 75 percent of the first year's operational budget of $151,060,000; of this amount, the United States was scheduled to contribute 45.75 percent.[3]

At the time of its creation, the Organization was to take over the functions of UNRRA and the Intergovernmental Committee, which had on January 1, 1947, assumed responsibility for persons previously cared for by the League of Nations.[4]

(1) *Statement by the Representative of the United States Delegation to the United Nations (Mrs. Roosevelt) on United States Position on the International Refugee Organization, November 8, 1946.*[5]

To begin with, Mr. Chairman, I should like to state very briefly the position of the United States on this International Refugee Organization, which will care for and help to rehabilitate nearly a million people from Europe and the Far East. As long as they are refugees and displaced persons they constitute a threat to peace and good relations among governments.

The maintenance in camps of these persons leads to deterioration among them as human beings and is an economic waste for all the nations of the world. We, in the United States, feel this most keenly, since from practically all the countries where they come from we have received citizens who have built up our nation. Therefore, the United States supports the principles of the General Assembly resolution of February 12, 1946 namely:

(*a*) The problem is international in character.

(*b*) There shall be no compulsory repatriation.

(*c*) Action taken by IRO must not interfere with existing international arrangements for apprehension of war criminals, Quislings, and traitors. This is being done by military occupation forces and is not the responsibility of this new organization.

As a consequence we support the draft constitution of the IRO which reflects the foregoing principles.

The United States has supported the principles advocated by my

[1] United Nations Relief and Rehabilitation Administration, *Journal of the Fifth Session of the Council*, No. 10, August 15, 1946.

[2] *New York Times*, December 17, 1946.

[3] Annex II to the Constitution.

[4] From information furnished by the American Resident Representative.

[5] Department of State, *Bulletin*, XV, p. 935.

colleague from the U.S.S.R. which is proved by the numbers of people that have been repatriated from the United States zone. However, it would be foreign to our conception of democracy to force repatriation on any human being. Three and one-half million persons have been repatriated from the United States zone, but our people will always believe in the right of asylum and complete freedom of choice.

The Pilgrims, the Huguenots, and the Germans of 1848 came to us in search of political and religious freedom and a wider economic opportunity. They built the United States.

These people now in displaced-persons camps are kin to those early settlers of ours, and many of them might have relatives in the United States.

My Government urges the participation in the IRO as members by all peace-loving nations. There is no question but that this participation will entail financial sacrifices by all participating governments. For a time it will be a heavy burden, but in the long run it will be an economy and well worth the cost.

The finances of our organization will be considered in committee 5, where the financial burden will be allotted to the participating governments, so that the cost will be equitably shared by all, and each government will pay according to the standards laid down by committee 5.

In the interest of brevity I shall comment at this time only on some of the essential points in Mr. Vyshinsky's speech of Wednesday, leaving other points for comment when we discuss the draft constitution article by article.

First of all I should like to say that Mr. Vyshinsky's view that no assistance should be given to those who for valid reasons decide not to return to their countries of origin is inconsistent with the unanimous decision of the General Assembly in the resolution on displaced persons of February 12, 1946. That clearly provides that these persons shall become the concern of the International Refugee Organization.

Mr. Vyshinsky says that this problem is very simple. It can be solved by repatriating all the displaced persons. In fact, those who do not wish to be repatriated must fall into this category. I think this point of view fails to take into consideration the facts of political change in countries of origin which have created fears in the minds of the million persons, who remain, of such a nature that they choose miserable life in camps in preference to the risks of repatriation.

Our colleague from Poland mentioned that since arrangements had been made to give people food allowances after their return home the numbers going home had increased. I think he is quite right that the fear of an economic situation has deterred a number of people from taking the risk of repatriation, but not all of them are actuated by consideration of the economic situation in their country of origin.

Seven million people have already been repatriated; repatriation is still proceeding. One thousand Poles are leaving the U.S. zones of Germany and Austria daily. The military administration which accomplished this result can hardly be held solely responsible for the failure of the last million to return.

It was a new point, I think, which Mr. Vyshinsky raised when he presented his position that those who do not choose to return to their countries of origin shall not be resettled, shall receive no aid towards settling somewhere else. This leaves them with the prospect of spending the rest of their lives in assembly centers as long as the IRO supports them or else of facing starvation. They obviously cannot be left in assembly centers to their own devices. They would continue as an irritant in good relations between friendly governments and contribute to delay in the restoration of peace and order which is the concern of all governments. There is no reason why they should become wanderers if instead they can be given an opportunity for resettlement in some country which has a future to offer them.

By another provision of the General Assembly resolution of February, 1946, which, I think, Mr. Vyshinsky must have forgotten, no action taken shall be of such a character as to interfere in any way with the surrender and punishment of war criminals, Quislings, and traitors in conformity with international arrangements or agreements. These arrangements, however, are the responsibility of other government bodies, including the military authorities.

I can tell you very briefly how arrangements for the apprehension of Quislings works out under the U. S. occupational authorities. U. S. officials are continuously engaged in screening the refugee personnel to locate Quislings or those who for other reasons are not entitled to be given asylum. When special complaints are received from other governments they are made by the governments' liaison officers with the United States Forces, European Theater. USFET thereupon makes an investigation through Army channels. If the investigation appears to substantiate the complaint, the case goes before a board of officers, which makes the final determination. This method of procedure has in general been satisfactory; but it must be emphasized that this committee here is not, and should not, be the form for debate as to its effectiveness. It is not our function here to discuss the adequacy of these arrangements or the performance under them. We are concerned with final decisions on the draft of the constitution of IRO. This draft clearly excludes from the benefits of the organization war criminals, Quislings, and traitors. We can hope that such persons will be entirely eliminated by the time the IRO begins to function.

Mr. Vyshinsky spoke of members of various military groups. The military character of different groups and their members, we think, has been greatly exaggerated. They are the concern of the military authorities, however, and will be handled by them. Those who fought with the Germans and collaborated with them are clearly excluded from assistance from the IRO in the constitution before us. I have asked that the U. S. military authorities supply me with a report on each of the incidents complained of by Mr. Vyshinsky where the U. S. is concerned, and I shall report these findings in writing to the committee, if it so desires, as soon as they are available.

Now we come to the point which Mr. Vyshinsky made that all propaganda should be suppressed in the camps. He challenges us on the point that under the guise of freedom of expression propaganda hostile to the countries of origin is tolerated. On this point I am afraid we hold very different ideas. But this does not preclude cooperation between us. We, in the United States, tolerate opposition provided it does not extend to the point of advocacy of the overthrow of government by force. Unless the right of opposition is conceded, it seems to me that there is very little possibility that countries with differing conceptions of democracy can live together without friction in the same world. Much progress has been made to date in dealing with this problem of propaganda within the framework of these divergent views. With patience and understanding we can achieve still further progress in this direction.

Mr. Vyshinsky objects to the inclusion of certain categories of refugees and displaced persons.

One group consists of those who, as a result of events subsequent to the outbreak of the second World War, are unable or unwilling to avail themselves of the protection of the governments of their countries of nationality or of former nationality.

This paragraph covers those who for political reasons, territorial changes, or changes of sovereignty are unable to return to their country. That paragraph is in annex 1, part 1, section A, paragraph 2. I regret that Mr. Vyshinsky cannot confirm the agreement reached at the last session of the Economic and Social Council on this point. We consider it essential that the paragraph be retained. But since he asked who these people are, I should like out of my own experience to mention a few. I visited two camps near Frankfurt, where the majority of people had come from Estonia, Latvia, and Lithuania. I have received innumerable petitions. My mail today carried three from people in different countries, who, because changes had come in the types of government in their countries, felt that they did not wish to return. That does not mean that they do not love their country; it simply means that they prefer the country as it was before they left it. That country they feel no longer belongs to them. I gather that Mr. Vyshinsky felt that anyone who did not wish to return under the present form of government must of necessity be Fascist. I talked to a great many of these people who do not strike me as Fascist, and the assumption that people do not wish to return to the country of their origin because those countries are now under what is called a democratic form of government does not seem to allow for certain differences in the understanding of the word *democracy*. As Mr. Vyshinsky uses it, it would seem that democracy is synonymous with Soviet, or at least a fairly similar conception of political and economic questions. Under that formula I am very sure that he would accept some of the other nations in the world who consider themselves democracies and who are as willing to die for their beliefs as are the people of the Soviet Union.

Mr. Vyshinsky also objected to certain exceptions to the general rule that those who had voluntarily assisted the enemy are excluded from the concern of the IRO. The intent of the exemptions is to cover those who were forced to perform slave labor or who may have rendered humanitarian assistance, such as assistance to wounded civilians.

Mr. Vyshinsky proposes to exclude all those who assisted in any manner. Under such language those merely present in any occupied area forced by necessity of survival to perform any form of work or service within the German economy would be considered to have assisted the enemy and would thus be excluded. This would result in cruel hardship on many. We can, however, discuss the point at greater length later.

I sincerely regret having to speak in opposition to some of Mr. Vyshinsky's views. But he will recall that in London there were some things which because of the fundamental beliefs I hold, I had to stand on. I felt strongly about them then and I still do. This does not mean that Mr. Vyshinsky cannot hold to his basic beliefs as well and still achieve with us a solution. This solution can be reached if we are both willing in these fields to try for a spirit of cooperation and a realistic approach to our problems. It is essential to the peace of the world that we wipe out some of our resentments as well as our fears. I hope that as time goes on our two great nations may grow to understand each other and to accept our different viewpoints on certain questions.

(2) Constitution of the International Refugee Organization, Signed at Lake Success, New York, December 16, 1946.[1]

[Excerpts]

PREAMBLE

The Governments accepting this Constitution,
RECOGNIZING:

that genuine refugees and displaced persons constitute an urgent problem which is international in scope and character;

that as regards displaced persons, the main task to be performed is to encourage and assist in every way possible their early return to their country of origin;

that genuine refugees and displaced persons should be assisted by international action, either to return to their countries of nationality or former habitual residence, or to find new homes elsewhere, under the conditions provided for in this Constitution; or in the case of Spanish Republicans, to establish themselves temporarily in order to enable them to return to Spain when the present Falangist regime is succeeded by a democratic regime;

that re-settlement and re-establishment of refugees and displaced persons be contemplated only in cases indicated clearly in the Constitution;

that genuine refugees and displaced persons, until such time as their repatriation or re-settlement and re-establishment is effectively completed, should be protected in their rights and legitimate interests, should receive care and assistance and, as far as possible, should be put to useful employment in order to avoid the evil and anti-social consequences of continued idleness; and

that the expenses of repatriation to the extent practicable should be charged to Germany and Japan for persons displaced by those Powers from countries occupied by them:

[1] United Nations General Assembly, Document A/284, January 14, 1947.

HAVE AGREED:

for the accomplishment of the foregoing purposes in the shortest possible time, to establish and do hereby establish a non-permanent organization to be called the International Refugee Organization, a specialized agency to be brought into relationship with the United Nations, and accordingly

HAVE ACCEPTED THE FOLLOWING ARTICLES:

ARTICLE 1

Mandate

The mandate of the Organization shall extend to refugees and displaced persons in accordance with the principles, definitions and conditions set forth in Annex I, which is attached to and made an integral part of this Constitution.

ARTICLE 2

Functions and Powers

1. The functions of the Organization to be carried out in accordance with the purposes and the principles of the Charter of the United Nations, shall be: the repatriation; the identification, registration and classification; the care and assistance; the legal and political protection; the transport; and the resettlement and re-establishment, in countries able and willing to receive them, of persons who are the concern of the Organization under the provisions of Annex I. Such functions shall be exercised with a view:

(a) to encouraging and assisting in every way possible the early return to their country of nationality, or former habitual residence, of those persons who are the concern of the Organization, having regard to the principles laid down in the resolution on refugees and displaced persons adopted by the General Assembly of the United Nations on 12 February 1946 (Annex III) and to the principles set forth in the Preamble, and to promoting this by all possible means, in particular by providing them with material assistance, adequate food for a period of three months from the time of their departure from their present places of residence provided they are returning to a country suffering as a result of enemy occupation during the war, and provided such food shall be distributed under the auspices of the Organization; and the necessary clothing and means of transportation; and

(b) with respect to persons for whom repatriation does not take place under paragraph 1 (a) of this article to facilitating:

  (i) their re-establishment in countries of temporary residence;
  (ii) the emigration to, re-settlement and re-establishment in other countries of individuals or family units; and
  (iii) as may be necessary and practicable within available resources and subject to the relevant financial regulations, the investigation, promotion or execution of projects of group re-settlement or large-scale re-settlement.

(c) with respect to Spanish Republicans to assisting them to establish themselves temporarily until the time when a democratic regime in Spain is established.

. . . . . .

ARTICLE 15

Relationship with Authorities of Countries of Location of Refugees and Displaced Persons

The relationship of the Organization with the Governments or administrations of countries in which displaced persons or refugees are located, and the conditions under which it will operate in such countries, shall be determined by agreements to be negotiated by it with such Governments or administrations in accordance with the terms of this Constitution.

. . . . . .

ANNEX I. DEFINITIONS

General Principles

1. The following general principles constitute an integral part of the definitions as laid down in Parts I and II of this Annex.

(a) The main object of the Organization will be to bring about a rapid and positive solution of the problem of *bona fide* refugees and displaced persons, which shall be just and equitable to all concerned.

(b) The main task concerning displaced persons is to encourage and assist in every way possible their early return to their countries of origin, having regard to the principles laid down in paragraph (c) (ii) of the resolution adopted by the General Assembly of the United Nations on 12 February 1946 regarding the problem of refugees (Annex III).

(c) As laid down in the resolution adopted by the Economic and Social Council on 16 February 1946, no international assistance should be given to traitors, quislings and war criminals, and nothing should be done to prevent in any way their surrender and punishment.

(d) It should be the concern of the Organization to ensure that its assistance is not exploited in order to encourage subversive or hostile activities directed against the Government of any of the United Nations.

(e) It should be the concern of the Organization to ensure that its assistance is not exploited by persons in the case of whom it is clear that they are unwilling to return to their countries of origin because they prefer idleness to facing the hardships of helping in the reconstruction of their countries, or by persons who intend to settle in other countries for purely economic reasons, thus qualifying as emigrants.

(f) On the other hand it should equally be the concern of the Organization to ensure that no *bona fide* and deserving refugee or displaced person is deprived of such assistance as it may be in a position to offer.

(g) The Organization should endeavour to carry out its functions in such a way as to avoid disturbing friendly relations between nations. In the pursuit of this objective, the Organization should exercise special care in cases in which the re-establishment or re-settlement of refugees or displaced persons might be contemplated, either in countries contiguous to their respective countries of origin or in non-self-governing countries. The Organization should give due weight, among other factors, to any evidence of genuine apprehension and concern felt in regard to such plans, in the former case, by the country of origin of the persons involved, or, in the latter case, by the indigenous population of the non-self-governing country in question.

2. To ensure the impartial and equitable application of the above principles and of the terms of the definition which follows, some special system of semi-judicial machinery should be created, with appropriate constitution, procedure and terms of reference.

PART I

Refugees and Displaced Persons within the Meaning of the Resolution Adopted by the Economic and Social Council of the United Nations on 16 February 1946

Section A — Definition of Refugees

1. Subject to the provisions of sections C and D and of Part II of this Annex, the term "refugee" applies to a person who has left, or who is outside of, his country of nationality or of former habitual residence, and who, whether or not he had retained his nationality, belongs to one of the following categories:

(a) victims of the nazi or fascist regimes or of regimes which took part on their side in the second world war, or of the quisling or similar regimes which assisted them against the United Nations, whether enjoying international status as refugees or not;

(b) Spanish Republicans and other victims of the Falangist regime in Spain, whether enjoying international status as refugees or not;

(c) persons who were considered refugees before the outbreak of the second world war, for reasons of race, religion, nationality or political opinion.

2. Subject to the provisions of sections C and D and of Part II of this Annex regarding the exclusion of certain categories of persons, including war criminals, quislings and traitors, from the benefits of the Organization, the term "refugee" also applies to a person, other than a displaced person as defined in section B of this Annex, who is outside of his country of nationality or former habitual residence, and who, as a result of events subsequent to the outbreak of the second world war, is unable or unwilling to avail himself of the protection of the Government of his country of nationality or former nationality.

3. Subject to the provisions of Section D and of Part II of this Annex, the term "refugee" also applies to persons who, having resided in Germany or Austria, and being of Jewish origin or foreigners or stateless persons, were victims of Nazi persecution and were detained in, or were obliged to flee from, and were subsequently returned to, one of those

countries as a result of enemy action, or of war circumstances, and have not yet been firmly resettled therein.

4. The term "refugee" also applies to unaccompanied children who are war orphans or whose parents have disappeared and who are outside their countries of origin. Such children, 16 years of age or under, shall be given all possible priority assistance, including, normally, assistance in repatriation in the case of those whose nationality can be determined.

SECTION B — Definition of Displaced Persons

The term "displaced person" applies to a person who, as a result of the actions of the authorities of the regimes mentioned in Part I, Section A, paragraph 1 (a) of this Annex has been deported from, or has been obliged to leave, his country of nationality or of former habitual residence, such as persons who were compelled to undertake forced labour or who were deported for racial, religious or political reasons. Displaced persons will only fall within the mandate of the Organization subject to the provision of Sections C and D of Part I and to the provisions of Part II of this Annex. If the reasons for their displacement have ceased to exist, they should be repatriated as soon as possible in accordance with article 2, paragraph 1 (a) of this Constitution, and subject to the provision of paragraph (c), sub-paragraphs (ii) and (iii) of the General Assembly resolution of 12 February 1946 regarding the problem of refugees (Annex III).

SECTION C — Conditions under which "Refugees" and "Displaced Persons" will become the concern of the Organization

1. In the case of all the above categories except those mentioned in Section A, paragraphs 1 (b) and 3 of this Annex, persons will become the concern of the Organization in the sense of the resolution adopted by the Economic and Social Council on 16 February 1946 if they can be repatriated, and the help of the Organization is required in order to provide for their repatriation, or if they have definitely, in complete freedom and after receiving full knowledge of the facts, including adequate information from the Governments of their countries of nationality or former habitual residence, expressed valid objections to returning to those countries.

(a) The following should be considered as valid objections:
(i) persecution, or fear, based on reasonable grounds of persecution because of race, religion, nationality or political opinions, provided these opinions are not in conflict with the principles of the United Nations, as laid down in the Preamble of the Charter of the United Nations;
(ii) objections of a political nature judged by the Organization to be "valid," as contemplated in paragraph 8 (a) of the report of the Third Committee of the General Assembly as adopted by the Assembly on 12 February 1946.

(*iii*) in the case of persons falling within the category mentioned in section A, paragraphs 1 (*a*) and 1 (*c*) compelling family reasons arising out of previous persecution, or, compelling reasons of infirmity or illness.

(*b*) The following shall normally be considered "adequate information": information regarding conditions in the countries of nationality of the refugees and displaced persons concerned, communicated to them directly by representatives of the Governments of these countries, who shall be given every facility for visiting camps and assembly centres of refugees and displaced persons in order to place such information before them.

2. In the case of all refugees falling within the terms of Section A, paragraph 1 (*b*) of this Annex, persons will become the concern of the Organization in the sense of the resolution adopted by the Economic and Social Council of the United Nations on 16 February 1946, so long as the Falangist regime in Spain continues. Should that regime be replaced by a democratic regime they will have to produce valid objections against returning to Spain corresponding to those indicated in paragraph 1 (*a*) of this section.

SECTION D — Circumstances in which Refugees and Displaced Persons will cease to be the Concern of the Organization

Refugees or displaced persons will cease to be the concern of the Organization:

(*a*) when they have returned to the countries of their nationality in United Nations territory unless their former habitual residence to which they wish to return is outside their country of nationality; or

(*b*) when they have acquired a new nationality; or

(*c*) when they have, in the determination of the Organization become otherwise firmly established; or

(*d*) when they have unreasonably refused to accept the proposals of the Organization for their re-settlement or repatriation; or

(*e*) when they are making no substantial effort towards earning their living when it is possible for them to do so, or when they are exploiting the assistance of the Organization.

PART II

Persons who will not be the concern of the Organization

1. War criminals, quislings and traitors.
2. Any other persons who can be shown:

(*a*) to have assisted the enemy in persecuting civil populations of countries, Members of the United Nations: or

(*b*) to have voluntarily assisted the enemy forces since the outbreak of the second world war in their operations against the United Nations.

3. Ordinary criminals who are extraditable by treaty.
4. Persons of German ethnic origin, whether German nationals or members of German minorities in other countries, who:

(*a*) have been or may be transferred to Germany from other countries;

(b) have been, during the second world war, evacuated from Germany to other countries;

(c) have fled from, or into, Germany, or from their places of residence into countries other than Germany in order to avoid falling into the hands of Allied armies.

5. Persons who are in receipt of financial support and protection from their country of nationality, unless their country of nationality requests international assistance for them.

6. Persons who, since the end of hostilities in the second world war:

(a) have participated in any organization having as one of its purposes the overthrow by armed force of the Government of their country of origin, being a Member of the United Nations; or the overthrow by armed force of the Government of any other Member of the United Nations, or have participated in any terrorist organization;

(b) have become leaders of movements hostile to the Government of their country of origin being a Member of the United Nations or sponsors of movements encouraging refugees not to return to their country of origin;

(c) at the time of application for assistance, are in the military or civil service of a foreign State.

. . . .

B. Admission of Refugees into the United States

While urging the creation of an international agency to deal with the problem of refugees and displaced persons, the United States also made an attempt to facilitate admission to this country of displaced persons who might be eligible for entry under existing immigration laws.

On September 14, 1945, an Executive Order by President Truman provided for the dissolution of the War Refugee Board, which had been established in January, 1944, to bring relief to persecuted minorities in Europe.[1] The President stated that the Board had fulfilled its function in saving the lives of hundreds of thousands of victims of Nazi oppression, although he pointed out that the saving of these lives would have been in vain unless immediate steps were taken for a humane, international solution of the problem of their resettlement.[2]

In a statement by the President on December 22, 1945, the United States announced a policy of expediting admission of displaced persons and refugees from Europe. A directive of the same date to interested government agencies established an interdepartmental committee, under the chairmanship of the Commissioner of Immigration and Naturalization, to supervise implementation of this policy.[3] A report to the President by the Acting Commissioner of Immigration and Naturalization, T. B. Shoemaker, on August 7, 1946, noted the arrival in the United States of a number of displaced persons whose entry had been sponsored by voluntary organizations, as provided for in the Presidential directive.[4]

On December 19, 1946, however, President Truman announced that, despite attempts to facilitate their entry, only 4,767 persons had been admitted by October 21, and foreseeable sailings in 1946 would bring in only another 683 persons.[5]

[1] See *Documents, VI, 1943–1944*, p. 306.
[2] Department of State, *Bulletin*, XIII, p. 416.
[3] For text of statement and directive, see this volume, p. 410.
[4] Department of State, *Bulletin*, XV, p. 381.
[5] *Ibid.*, p. 1184.

(1) Executive Order 9614, Terminating the War Refugee Board, September 14, 1945.[1]

By virtue of the authority vested in me by the Constitution and the statutes of the United States it is hereby ordered as follows:

The War Refugee Board, established in the Executive Office of the President by Executive Order No. 9417 of January 22, 1944, is hereby terminated.

The Secretary of the Treasury is authorized and directed (1) to liquidate all of the activities and obligations, and wind up all of the affairs, of the Board as rapidly as practicable, and not later than June 30, 1946; (2) to utilize therefor such of the personnel, property, records, and unexpended appropriations of the Board as may be necessary; and (3), consonant with applicable law and regulations and at such times as may be appropriate, to separate the personnel from the service of the Board and to dispose of its property and records.

This order shall become effective at the close of business September 15, 1945.

(2) Statement by the President (Truman), December 22, 1945.[2]

The war has brought in its wake an appalling dislocation of populations in Europe. Many humanitarian organizations, including the United Nations Relief and Rehabilitation Administration, are doing their utmost to solve the multitude of problems arising in connection with this dislocation of hundreds of thousands of persons. Every effort is being made to return the displaced persons and refugees in the various countries of Europe to their former homes. The great difficulty is that so many of these persons have no homes to which they may return. The immensity of the problem of displaced persons and refugees is almost beyond comprehension.

A number of countries in Europe, including Switzerland, Sweden, France, and England, are working toward its solution. The United States shares the responsibility to relieve the suffering. To the extent that our present immigration laws permit, everything possible should be done at once to facilitate the entrance of some of these displaced persons and refugees into the United States.

In this way we may do something to relieve human misery and set an example to the other countries of the world which are able to receive some of these war sufferers. I feel that it is essential that we do this ourselves to show our good faith in requesting other nations to open their doors for this purpose.

Most of these persons are natives of central and eastern Europe and the Balkans. The immigration quotas for all these countries for one year total approximately 39,000, two thirds of which are allotted to Germany. Under the law, in any single month the number of visas issued cannot exceed 10 percent of the annual quota. This means that from now on only about 3,900 visas can be issued each month to persons who are natives of these countries.

[1] *Ibid.*, XIII, p. 416. [2] *Ibid.*, p. 981.

Very few persons from Europe have migrated to the United States during the war years. In the fiscal year 1942, only 10 percent of the immigration quotas was used; in 1943, 5 percent; in 1944, 6 percent; and in 1945, 7 percent. As of November 30, 1945, the end of the fifth month of the present fiscal year, only about 10 percent of the quotas for the European countries has been used. These unused quotas however do not accumulate through the years, and I do not intend to ask the Congress to change this rule.

The factors chiefly responsible for these low immigration figures were restraints imposed by the enemy, transportation difficulties, and the absence of consular facilities. Most of those Europeans who have been admitted to the United States during the last five years were persons who left Europe prior to the war, and thereafter entered here from non-European countries.

I consider that common decency and the fundamental comradeship of all human beings require us to do what lies within our power to see that our established immigration quotas are used in order to reduce human suffering. I am taking the necessary steps to see that this is done as quickly as possible.

Of the displaced persons and refugees whose entrance into the United States we will permit under this plan, it is hoped that the majority will be orphaned children. The provisions of law prohibiting the entry of persons likely to become public charges will be strictly observed. Responsible welfare organizations now at work in this field will guarantee that these children will not become public charges. Similar guaranties have or will be made on behalf of adult persons. The record of these welfare organizations throughout the past years has been excellent, and I am informed that no persons admitted under their sponsorship have ever become charges on their communities. Moreover, many of the immigrants will have close family ties in the United States and will receive the assistance of their relatives until they are in a position to provide for themselves.

These relatives or organizations will also advance the necessary visa fees and travel fare. Where the necessary funds for travel fare and visa fees have not been advanced by a welfare organization or relative, the individual applicant must meet these costs. In this way the transportation of these immigrants across the Atlantic will not cost the American taxpayers a single dollar.

In order to enter the United States it is necessary to obtain a visa from a consular officer of the Department of State. As everyone knows, a great many of our consular establishments all over the world were disrupted and their operations suspended when the war came. It is physically impossible to reopen and to restaff all of them overnight. Consequently it is necessary to choose the area in which to concentrate our immediate efforts. This is a painful necessity because it requires us to make an almost impossible choice among degrees of misery. But if we refrain from making a choice because it will necessarily be arbitrary, no choice will ever be made, and we shall end by helping no one.

The decision has been made, therefore, to concentrate our immediate efforts in the American zones of occupation in Europe. This is not intended however entirely to exclude issuance of visas in other parts of the world.

In our zones in Europe there are citizens of every major European country. Visas issued to displaced persons and refugees will be charged, according to law, to the countries of their origin. They will be distributed fairly among persons of all faiths, creeds, and nationalities.

It is intended that, as soon as practicable, regular consular facilities will be reestablished in every part of the world, and the usual, orderly methods of registering and reviewing visa applications will be resumed. The pressing need, however, is to act now in a way that will produce immediate and tangible results. I hope that by early spring adequate consular facilities will be in operation in our zones in Europe, so that immigration can begin immediately upon the availability of ships.

I am informed that there are various measures now pending before the Congress which would either prohibit or severely reduce further immigration. I hope that such legislation will not be passed. This period of unspeakable human distress is not the time for us to close or to narrow our gates. I wish to emphasize, however, that any effort to bring relief to these displaced persons and refugees must and will be strictly within the limits of the present quotas as imposed by law.

There is one particular matter involving a relatively small number of aliens. President Roosevelt, in an endeavor to assist in handling displaced persons and refugees during the war and upon the recommendation of the War Refugee Board, directed that a group of about 1,000 displaced persons be removed from refugee camps in Italy and settled temporarily in a War Relocation Camp near Oswego, N. Y. Shortly thereafter, President Roosevelt informed the Congress that these persons would be returned to their homelands after the war.

Upon the basis of a careful survey by the Department of State and the Immigration and Naturalization Service, it has been determined that if these persons were now applying for admission to the United States most of them would be admissible under the immigration laws. In the circumstances, it would be inhumane and wasteful to require these people to go all the way back to Europe merely for the purpose of applying there for immigration visas and returning to the United States. Many of them have close relatives, including sons and daughters, who are citizens of the United States and who have served and are serving honorably in the armed forces of our country. I am therefore directing the Secretary of State and the Attorney General to adjust the immigration status of the members of this group who may wish to remain here, in strict accordance with existing laws and regulations.

The number of persons at the Oswego camp is, however, comparatively small. Our major task is to facilitate the entry into the United States of displaced persons and refugees still in Europe. To meet this larger problem, I am directing the Secretary of State, the Attorney General, the Secretary of War, the War Shipping Administration, and the Surgeon General of the Public Health Service to proceed at once to take all appropriate steps to expedite the quota immigration of displaced persons and refugees from Europe to the United States. Representatives of these officials will depart for Europe very soon to prepare detailed plans for the prompt execution of this project.

The attached directive has been issued by me to the responsible Government agencies to carry out this policy. I wish to emphasize, above all, that nothing in this directive will deprive a single American soldier or his wife or children of a berth on a vessel homeward bound, or delay their return.

This is the opportunity for America to set an example for the rest of the world in cooperation towards alleviating human misery.

(a) *Directive by the President (Truman) to the Secretaries of State (Byrnes) and War (Patterson), the Attorney General (Clark), the War Shipping Administrator (Land), the Surgeon-General of the Public Health Service (Parran) and the Director-General of UNRRA (Lehman), December 22, 1945.*[1]

The grave dislocation of populations in Europe resulting from the war has produced human suffering that the people of the United States cannot and will not ignore. This Government should take every possible measure to facilitate full immigration to the United States under existing quota laws.

The war has most seriously disrupted our normal facilities for handling immigration matters in many parts of the world. At the same time, the demands upon those facilities have increased many-fold. It is, therefore, necessary that immigration under the quotas be resumed initially in the areas of greatest need. I, therefore, direct the Secretary of State, the Secretary of War, the Attorney General, the Surgeon General of the Public Health Service, the War Shipping Administrator, and other appropriate officials to take the following action:

The Secretary of State is directed to establish with the utmost despatch consular facilities at or near displaced person and refugee assembly center areas in the American zones of occupation. It shall be the responsibility of these consular officers, in conjunction with the Immigrant Inspectors, to determine as quickly as possible the eligibility of the applicants for visas and admission to the United States. For this purpose the Secretary will, if necessary, divert the personnel and funds of his Department from other functions in order to insure the most expeditious handling of this operation. In cooperation with the Attorney General, he shall appoint as temporary vice-consuls, authorized to issue visas, such officers of the Immigration and Naturalization Service as can be made available for this program. Within the limits of administrative discretion, the officers of the Department of State assigned to this program shall make every effort to simplify and to hasten the process of issuing visas. If necessary, blocs of visa numbers may be assigned to each of the emergency consular establishments. Each such bloc may be used to meet the applications filed at the consular establishment to

[1] *Ibid.*, p. 983.

which the bloc is assigned. It is not intended however entirely to exclude the issuance of visas in other parts of the world.

Visas should be distributed fairly among persons of all faiths, creeds and nationalities. I desire that special attention be devoted to orphaned children to whom it is hoped the majority of visas will be issued.

With respect to the requirement of law that visas may not be issued to applicants likely to become public charges after admission to the United States, the Secretary of State shall cooperate with the Immigration and Naturalization Service in perfecting appropriate arrangements with welfare organizations in the United States which may be prepared to guarantee financial support to successful applicants. This may be accomplished by corporate affidavit or by any means deemed appropriate and practicable.

The Secretary of War, subject to limitations imposed by the Congress on War Department appropriations, will give such help as is practicable in:

(a) Furnishing information to appropriate consular officers and Immigrant Inspectors to facilitate in the selection of applicants for visas; and

(b) Assisting until other facilities suffice in:
  (1) Transporting immigrants to a European port;
  (2) Feeding, housing and providing medical care to such immigrants until embarked; and

(c) Making available office facilities, billets, messes, and transportation for Department of State, Department of Justice, and United Nations Relief and Rehabilitation Administration personnel connected with this work, where practicable and requiring no out-of-pocket expenditure by the War Department and when other suitable facilities are not available.

The Attorney General, through the Immigration and Naturalization Service, will assign personnel to duty in the American zones of occupation to make the immigration inspections, to assist consular officers of the Department of State in connection with the issuance of visas, and to take the necessary steps to settle the cases of those aliens presently interned at Oswego through appropriate statutory and administrative processes.

The Administrator of the War Shipping Administration will make the necessary arrangements for water transportation from the port of embarkation in Europe to the United States subject to the provision that the movement of immigrants will in no way interfere with the scheduled return of service personnel and their spouses and children from the European theater.

The Surgeon General of the Public Health Service will assign to duty in the American zones of occupation the necessary personnel to conduct the mental and physical examinations of prospective immigrants prescribed in the immigration laws.

The Director General of the United Nations Relief and Rehabilitation Administration will be requested to provide all possible aid to the United States authorities in preparing these people for transportation to the United States and to assist in their care, particularly in the cases of children in transit and others needing special attention.

In order to insure the effective execution of this program, the Secretary of State, the Secretary of War, the Attorney General, War Shipping Administrator and the Surgeon General of the Public Health Service shall appoint representatives to serve as members of an interdepartmental committee under the Chairmanship of the Commissioner of Immigration and Naturalization.

CHAPTER VI

NATIONAL DEFENSE

1. ATOMIC ENERGY

A. Development and Military Application

(1) *Statement by the Secretary of War (Stimson), August 6, 1945.*[1]

The recent use of the atomic bomb over Japan, which was today made known by the President, is the culmination of years of herculean effort on the part of science and industry working in cooperation with the military authorities. This development, which was carried forward by the many thousand participants with the utmost energy and the very highest sense of national duty, with the greatest secrecy and the most imperative of time schedules, probably represents the greatest achievement of the combined efforts of science, industry, labor and the military in all history.

The military weapon which has been forged from the products of this vast undertaking has an explosive force such as to stagger the imagination. Improvements will be forthcoming shortly which will increase by several fold the present effectiveness. But more important for the long-range implications of this new weapon is the possibility that another scale of magnitude will be evolved after considerable research and development.

The scientists are confident that over a period of many years atomic bombs may well be developed which will be much more powerful than the atomic bombs now at hand. It is abundantly clear that the possession of this weapon by the United States even in its present form should prove a tremendous aid in the shortening of the war against Japan.

The requirements of security do not permit of any revelation at this time of the exact methods by which the bombs are produced or of the nature of their action. However, in accord with its policy of keeping the people of the nation as completely informed as is consistent with national security, the War Department wishes to make known at this time, at least in broad dimension, the story behind this tremendous weapon which has been developed so effectively to hasten the end of the war. Other statements will be released which will give further details concerning the scientific and production aspects of the project and will give proper recognition to the scientists, technicians and the men of industry and labor who have made this weapon possible.

[1] *New York Times*, August 7, 1945, p. 4.

I

The chain of scientific discoveries which has led to the atomic bomb began at the turn of the century when radioactivity was discovered. Until 1939 work in this field was world-wide, being carried on particularly in the United States, the United Kingdom, Germany, France, Italy and Denmark.

Before the lights went out over Europe and the advent of war imposed security restrictions, the fundamental scientific knowledge concerning atomic energy from which has been developed the atomic bomb now in use by the United States was widely known in many countries, both Allied and Axis.

The war, however, ended the exchange of scientific information on this subject and, with the exception of the United Kingdom and Canada, the status of work in this field in other countries is not fully known, but we are convinced that Japan will not be in a position to use an atomic bomb in this war. While it is known that Germany was working feverishly in an attempt to develop such a weapon, her complete defeat and occupation has now removed that source of danger. Thus it was evident when the war began that the development of atomic energy for war purposes would occur in the near future and it was a question of which nations would control the discovery.

A large number of American scientists were pressing forward the boundaries of scientific knowledge in this fertile new field at the time when American science was mobilized for war. Work on atomic fission was also in progress in the United Kingdom when the war began in Europe. A close connection was maintained between the British investigations and the work here, with a pooling of information on this as on other matters of scientific research of importance for military purposes.

It was later agreed between President Roosevelt and Prime Minister Churchill that the project would be most quickly and effectively brought to fruition if all effort were concentrated in the United States, thus insuring intimate collaboration and also avoiding duplication. As a consequence of this decision, a number of British scientists who had been working on this problem were transferred here in late 1943, and they have from that time participated in the development of the project in the United States.

II

Late in 1939 the possibility of using atomic energy for military purposes was brought to the attention of President Roosevelt. He appointed a committee to survey the problem. Research which had been conducted on a small scale with Navy funds was put on a full-scale basis as a result of the recommendations of various scientific committees. At the end of 1941 the decision was made to go all-out on research work and the project was put under the direction of a group of eminent American scientists in the Office of Scientific Research and Development, with all projects in operation being placed under contract with the OSRD.

Dr. Vannevar Bush, director of OSRD, reported directly to the President on major developments. Meanwhile, President Roosevelt appointed a general policy group, which consisted of former Vice President Henry A. Wallace, Secretary of War Henry L. Stimson, General George C. Marshall, Dr. James B. Conant and Dr. Bush.

In June, 1942, this group recommended a great expansion of the work and the transfer of the major part of the program to the War Department. These recommendations were approved by President Roosevelt and put into effect. Maj. Gen. Leslie R. Groves was appointed by the Secretary of War to take complete executive charge of the program and was made directly responsible to him and the chief of staff.

In order to secure continuing consideration of the military aspects of the program, the President's general policy group appointed a military policy committee consisting of Dr. Bush as chairman, with Dr. Conant as his alternate, Lieut. Gen. Wilhelm D. Styer, and Rear Admiral William R. Purnell. This committee was charged with the responsibility of considering and planning military policy relating to the program including the development and manufacture of material, the production of atomic fission bombs, and their use as a weapon.

Although there were still numerous unsolved problems concerning the several theoretically possible methods of producing explosive material, nevertheless, in view of the tremendous pressure of time it was decided in December, 1942, to proceed with the construction of large-scale plants. Two of these are located at the Clinton Engineer Works in Tennessee and a third is located at the Hanford Engineer Works in the State of Washington. The decision to embark on large-scale production at such an early stage was, of course, a gamble, but as is so necessary in war, a calculated risk was taken and the risk paid off.

The Clinton Engineer Works is located on a Government reservation of some 59,000 acres eighteen miles west of Knoxville, Tennessee. The large size and isolated location of this site was made necessary by the need for security and for safety against possible, but then unknown, hazards. A Government-owned and operated city, named Oak Ridge, was established within the reservation to accommodate the people working on the project. They live under normal conditions in modest houses, dormitories, hutments and trailers and have for their use all the religious, recreational, educational, medical and other facilities of a modern small city. The total population of Oak Ridge is approximately 78,000 and consists of construction workers and plant operators and their immediate families; others live in immediately surrounding communities.

The Hanford Engineer Works is located on a Government reservation of 430,000 acres in an isolated area fifteen miles northwest of Pasco, Washington. Here is situated a Government-owned and operated town called Richland with a population of approximately 17,000, consisting of plant operators and their immediate families. As in the case of the site in Tennessee, consideration of security and safety necessitated placing this site in an isolated area. Living conditions in Richland are similar to those in Oak Ridge.

A special laboratory dealing with the many technical problems involved in putting the components together into an effective bomb is located in an isolated area in the vicinity of Santa Fe, New Mexico.

This laboratory has been planned, organized, and directed by Dr. J. Robert Oppenheimer. The development of the bomb itself has been largely due to his genius and the inspiration and leadership he has given to his associates.

Certain other manufacturing plants much smaller in scale are located in the United States and in Canada for essential production of needed materials. Laboratories at the Universities of Columbia, Chicago, and California, Iowa State College and at other schools, as well as certain industrial laboratories, have contributed materially in carrying on research and in developing special equipment, materials, and processes for the project. A laboratory has been established in Canada and a pilot plant for the manufacture of material is being built. This work is being carried on by the Canadian Government with assistance from, and appropriate liaison with, the United States and the United Kingdom.

While space does not permit of a complete listing of the industrial concerns which have contributed so signally to the success of the project, mention should be made of a few. The du Pont de Nemours Company designed and constructed the Hanford installations in Washington and operate them.

A special subsidiary of the M. W. Kellogg Company of New York designed one of the plants at Clinton, which was constructed by the J. A. Jones Company and is operated by the Union Carbide and Carbon Company. The second plant at Clinton was designed and constructed by the Stone and Webster Engineering Corporation of Boston and is operated by the Tennessee Eastman Company.

Equipment was supplied by almost all of the important firms in the United States, including Allis-Chalmers, Chrysler, General Electric and Westinghouse. These are only a few of the literally thousands of firms, both large and small, which have contributed to the success of the program. It is hoped that one day it will be possible to reveal in greater detail the contributions made by industry to the successful development of this weapon.

Behind these concrete achievements lie the tremendous contributions of American science. No praise is too great for the unstinting efforts, brilliant achievements, and complete devotion to the national interest of the scientists of this country. Nowhere else in the world has science performed so successfully in time of war. All the men of science who have cooperated effectively with industry and the military authorities in bringing the project to fruition merit the very highest expression of gratitude from the people of the nation.

In the War Department the main responsibility for the successful prosecution of the program rests with Maj. Gen. Leslie R. Groves. His record of performance in securing the effective development of this weapon for our armed forces in so short a period of time has been truly outstanding and merits the very highest commendation.

III

From the outset extraordinary secrecy and security measures have surrounded the project. This was personally ordered by President

Roosevelt and his orders have been strictly complied with. The work has been completely compartmentalized so that while many thousands of people have been associated with the program in one way or another no one has been given more information concerning it than was absolutely necessary to his particular job. As a result only a few highly placed persons in Government and science know the entire story.

It was inevitable, of course, that public curiosity would be aroused concerning so large a project and that citizens would make inquiries of members of Congress. In such instances the members of Congress have been most cooperative and have accepted in good faith the statement of the War Department that military security precluded any disclosure of detailed information.

In the appropriation of funds, the Congress has accepted the assurances of the Secretary of War and the Chief of Staff that the appropriations made were absolutely essential to national security. The War Department is confident that the Congress will agree that its faith was not a mistake. Because it has not been possible for Congress to keep a close check on the expenditure of the funds appropriated for the project which to June 30, 1945, amounted to $1,950,000,000, key scientific phases of the work have been reviewed from time to time by eminently qualified scientists and industrial leaders in order to be certain that the expenditures were warranted by the potentialities of the program.

The press and radio of the nation, as in so many other instances, have complied whole-heartedly with the requests of the Office of Censorship that publicity on any phase of this subject be suppressed.

IV

In order to bring the project to fruition as quickly as possible, it was decided in August, 1943, to establish a combined policy committee with the following membership:

Secretary of War Henry L. Stimson, Dr. Vannevar Bush and Dr. James B. Conant, for the United States; Field Marshal Sir John Dill and Col. J. J. Llewellin, for the United Kingdom, and Mr. C. D. Howe, for Canada. Colonel Llewellin was replaced by Sir Roland I. Campbell in December, 1943, and the latter, in turn, by the Earl of Halifax. The late Field Marshal Sir John Dill was replaced by Field Marshal Sir Henry Maitland Wilson early in 1945. The committee is responsible for the broad direction of the project as between the countries.

Interchange of information has been provided for within certain limits. In the field of scientific research and development full interchange is maintained between those working in the same sections of the field; in matters of design, construction and operation of large-scale plants information is exchanged only when such exchange will hasten the completion of weapons for use in the present war. All these arrangements are subject to the approval of the combined policy committee.

The United States members have made as their scientific adviser Dr. Richard C. Tolman; the British members, Sir James Chadwick, and the Canadian member, Dean C. J. Mackenzie.

It was early recognized that in order to make certain that this tremendous weapon would not fall into the hands of the enemy prompt action should be taken to control patents in the field and to secure control over the ore which is indispensable to the process. Substantial patent control has been accomplished by the United States, the United Kingdom and Canada. In each country all personnel engaged in the work, both scientific and industrial, are required to assign their entire rights to any inventions in this field to their respective Governments. Arrangements have been made for appropriate patent exchange in instances where inventions are made by nationals of one country working in the territory of another.

Such patent rights, interests, and titles as are exchangeable, however, are held in a fiduciary sense subject to settlement at a later date on mutually satisfactory terms.

All patent actions taken are surrounded by all safeguards necessary for the security of the project. At the present stage of development of the science of atomic fission, uranium is the ore essential to the production of the weapon. Steps have been taken, and continue to be taken, to assure us of adequate supplies of this mineral.

V

Atomic fission holds great promise for sweeping development by which our civilization may be enriched when peace comes, but the overriding necessities of war have precluded the full exploration of peacetime applications of this new knowledge. With the evidence presently at hand, however, it appears inevitable that many useful contributions to the well-being of mankind will ultimately flow from these discoveries when the world situation makes it possible for science and industry to concentrate on these aspects.

The fact that atomic energy can now be released on a large scale in an atomic bomb raises the question of the prospect of using this energy for peaceful industrial purposes. Already in the source of producing one of the elements much energy is being released, not explosively but in regulated amounts. This energy, however, is in the form of heat at a temperature too low to make practicable the operation of a conventional power plant.

It will be a matter of much further research and development to design machines for the conversion of atomic energy into useful power. How long this will take no one can predict but it will certainly be a period of many years. Furthermore, there are many economic considerations to be taken into account before we can say to what extent atomic energy will supplant coal, oil, and water as fundamental sources of power in industry in this or any other country. We are at the threshold of a new industrial art which will take many years and much expenditure of money to develop.

Because of the widespread knowledge and interest in this subject even before the war, there is no possibility of avoiding the risks inherent in this knowledge by any long-term policy of secrecy. Mindful of these considerations as well as the grave problems that arise concerning the control of the weapon and the implications of this science for the peace of the world, the Secretary of War, with the approval of the President, has appointed an interim committee to consider these matters. Membership of the committee is as follows:

The Secretary of War, chairman; the Hon. James F. Byrnes, now Secretary of State; the Hon. Ralph A. Bard, former Under-Secretary of the Navy; the Hon. William L. Clayton, Assistant Secretary of State; Dr. Vannevar Bush, director of the Office of Scientific Research and Development and president of the Carnegie Institution of Washington; Dr. James B. Conant, chairman of the National Defense Research Committee and president of Harvard University; Dr. Karl T. Compton, chief of the Office of Field Service in the Office of Scientific Research and Development and president of the Massachusetts Institute of Technology; and Mr. George L. Harrison, special consultant to the Secretary of War and president of the New York Life Insurance Company. Mr. Harrison is alternate chairman of the committee.

The committee is charged with the responsibility of formulating recommendations to the President concerning the post-war organization that should be established to direct and control the future course of the United States in this field both with regard to the research and developmental aspects of the entire field and to its military applications. It will make recommendations with regard to the problems of both national and international control.

In its consideration of these questions, the committee has had the benefit of the views of the scientists who have participated in the project. These views have been brought to the attention of the committee by an advisory group selected from the leading physicists of the country who have been most active on this subject. This group is composed of Dr. J. R. Oppenheimer, Dr. E. O. Lawrence, Dr. A. H. Compton, and Dr. Enrico Fermi. The interim committee has also consulted the representatives of those industries which have been most closely connected with the multitude of problems that have been faced in the production phases of the project.

Every effort is being bent toward assuring that this weapon and the new field of science that stands behind it will be employed wisely in the interests of the security of the peace-loving nations and the well-being of the world.

(2) *Statement by the President (Truman), August 6, 1945.*[1]

Sixteen hours ago an American airplane dropped one bomb on Hiroshima, an important Japanese Army base. That bomb had more power than 20,000 tons of TNT. It had more than two thousand times the blast power of the British "Grand Slam" which is the largest bomb ever yet used in the history of warfare.

The Japanese began the war from the air at Pearl Harbor. They have been repaid manyfold. And the end is not yet. With this bomb we have

[1] *Ibid.*

now added a new and revolutionary increase in destruction to supplement the growing power of our armed forces. In their present form these bombs are now in production and even more powerful forms are in development.

It is an atomic bomb. It is a harnessing of the basic power of the universe. The force from which the sun draws its powers has been loosed against those who brought war to the Far East.

Before 1939, it was the accepted belief of scientists that it was theoretically possible to release atomic energy. But no one knew any practical method of doing it. By 1942, however, we knew that the Germans were working feverishly to find a way to add atomic energy to the other engines of war with which they hoped to enslave the world. But they failed. We may be grateful to Providence that the Germans got the V-1's and the V-2's late and in limited quantities and even more grateful that they did not get the atomic bomb at all.

The battle of the laboratories held fateful risks for us as well as the battles of the air, land and sea, and we have now won the battle of the laboratories as we have won the other battles.

Beginning in 1940, before Pearl Harbor, scientific knowledge useful in war was pooled between the United States and Great Britain, and many priceless helps to our victories have come from that arrangement. Under that general policy the research on the atomic bomb was begun. With American and British scientists working together, we entered the race of discovery against the Germans.

The United States had available a large number of scientists of distinction in the many needed areas of knowledge. It had the tremendous industrial and financial resources necessary for the project and they could be devoted to it without undue impairment of other vital war work. In the United States the laboratory work and the production plants, on which a substantial start had already been made, would be out of reach of enemy bombing, while at the time Britain was exposed to constant air attack and was still threatened with the possibility of invasion.

For these reasons Prime Minister Churchill and President Roosevelt agreed that it was wise to carry on the project here. We now have two great plants and many lesser works devoted to the production of atomic power. Employment during peak construction numbered 125,000 and over 65,000 individuals are even now engaged in operating the plants. Many have worked there for two and a half years. Few know what they have been producing. They see great quantities of material going in and they see nothing coming out of these plants, for the physical size of the explosive charge is exceedingly small. We have spent two billion dollars on the greatest scientific gamble in history — and won.

But the greatest marvel is not the size of the enterprise, its secrecy, or its costs, but the achievement of scientific brains in putting together infinitely complex pieces of knowledge held by many men in different fields of science into a workable plan. And hardly less marvelous has been the capacity of industry to design, and of labor to operate, the machines and methods to do things never done before so that the brain child of many minds came forth in physical shape and performed as it was supposed to do.

Both science and industry worked under the direction of the United States Army, which achieved a unique success in managing so diverse a problem in the advancement of knowledge in an amazingly short time. It is doubtful if such another combination could be got together in the world. What has been done is the greatest achievement of organized science in history. It was done under high pressure and without failure.

We are now prepared to obliterate more rapidly and completely every productive enterprise the Japanese have above ground in any city. We shall destroy their docks, their factories and their communications. Let there be no mistake; we shall completely destroy Japan's power to make war.

It was to spare the Japanese people from utter destruction that the ultimatum of July 26 was issued at Potsdam. Their leaders promptly rejected that ultimatum. If they do not now accept our terms they may expect a rain of ruin from the air, the like of which has never been seen on this earth. Behind this air attack will follow sea and land forces in such numbers and power as they have not yet seen and with the fighting skill of which they are already well aware.

The Secretary of War, who has kept in personal touch with all phases of the project, will immediately make public a statement giving further details.[1]

His statement will give facts concerning the sites at Oak Ridge, near Knoxville, Tennessee, and at Richland, near Pasco, Washington, and an installation near Santa Fé, New Mexico. Although the workers at the sites have been making materials to be used in producing the greatest destructive force in history they have not themselves been in danger beyond that of many other occupations, for the utmost care has been taken for their safety.

The fact that we can release atomic energy ushers in a new era in man's understanding of nature's forces. Atomic energy may, in the future, supplement the power that now comes from coal, oil and falling water, but at present it cannot be produced on a basis to compete with them commercially. Before that comes there must be a long period of intensive research.

It has never been the habit of the scientists of this country or the policy of this Government to withhold from the world scientific knowledge. Normally, therefore, everything about this work with atomic energy would be made public.

But under present circumstances it is not intended to divulge the terminal processes of production or all the military applications, pending further examination of possible methods of protecting us and the rest of the world from the danger of sudden destruction.

I shall recommend that the Congress of the United States consider promptly the establishment of an appropriate commission to control the production and use of atomic power within the United States.[2] I shall give further consideration and make further recommendations to the Congress as to how atomic power can become a powerful and forceful influence toward the maintenance of world peace.

---

[1] See this volume, p. 413.   [2] *Ibid.*, p. 422.

B. National Control

In his statement of August 6, 1945, in which he announced the use of the atomic bomb upon Hiroshima, President Truman declared that he would "recommend that the Congress . . . consider promptly the establishment of an appropriate commission to control the production and use of atomic power within the United States" and that he would make "further recommendations to the Congress as to how atomic power can become a powerful and forceful influence towards the maintenance of world peace."[1] Until such time as the Congress might take action, the President, on September 13, 1945, by Executive Order, withdrew and reserved for the use of the United States Government all lands containing radio-active mineral substances.[2] The recommendations of the President were subsequently transmitted to the Congress on October 3, 1945.[3]

Prior to the President's message, Senator Brien McMahon (Connecticut), on September 6, 1945, introduced Senate Bill S. 1359.[4] This Bill dealt not only with measures of national control but also made provision for a system of international control and inspection under the Security Council of the United Nations.[5] The Bill proposed the establishment of a board of high government officials to supervise and license the development, research and use of atomic energy, and the empowering of this board and of the United States delegation to the United Nations to supply information, subject to Congressional approval, to the Security Council. Also provided for was the "use by the Security Council [of atomic energy] in preserving collective security, in exchange for an agreement by all other nations, to place in a common pool, controlled by the Council, all their respective scientific knowledge and secrets bearing upon the production and use of armaments and weapons of war" as well as "the free, untrammeled and complete right of access and inspection by the Security Council of all the plants, laboratories, and operations relating to research, development, manufacture, and production of armaments and munitions of war," this latter provision to be stipulated as an integral part of any international agreement such as the one referred to above.[6]

Also on September 6, 1945, Senator Arthur Vandenberg (Michigan) offered what he termed a "slightly different approach to the same subject."[7] Expressing the opinion that he was "not quite sure that Congress itself can best approach the problem through the consideration of a specific bill" and "not clear that we have yet reached the point when such an approach would be a logical one," Senator Vandenberg submitted a concurrent resolution (S. Con. Res. 28) for the creation of a joint congressional committee to make a "full and complete" study and investigation with respect to the development and control of the atomic bomb.[8] The Vandenberg Resolution was referred to the Committee on Foreign Relations, along with the McMahon Bill, with the understanding that, because of the national aspects of their subject matter, both would go later for consideration by the Interstate Commerce Committee.[9] The Resolution, having gone through Committee, was reported back to the Senate with amendments and, as amended, passed by the Senate on September 27.[10]

Following the reading of the President's message of October 3, dispute arose in the Senate as to the committee or committees which might properly claim

---

[1] For the text of the President's statement, see *ibid.*, p. 419.
[2] For the text of the Executive Order, see *ibid.*, p. 426.
[3] For the text of the President's message to Congress, see *ibid.*
[4] *Congressional Record*, 91, p. 8502 (Daily edition, September 6, 1945).
[5] *Ibid.*, p. 8504. For information on the international control of atomic energy, see this volume, p. 544.
[6] *Congressional Record*, 91, p. 8504 (Daily edition, September 6, 1945).
[7] *Ibid.*
[8] *Ibid.*; for the text of the resolution, see *ibid.*, p. 8505.
[9] *Ibid.*
[10] *Ibid.*, p. 9212 (Daily edition, September 27, 1945); for the text of the Resolution as amended, see *ibid.*

jurisdiction over matters pertaining to atomic energy. The debate raised the question of the creation of a special committee to which all measures concerned with atomic energy might in the future be submitted, and was temporarily resolved by a decision to delay consideration of the Presidential message until such time as agreement was reached on committee jurisdiction.[1] At the close of the debate on committee jurisdiction, Senator Edwin Johnson (Colorado) introduced a bill (S. 1463) intended to carry out the recommendations which the President had made to the Congress.[2] At the same time, Rep. Andrew May (Kentucky) introduced in the House of Representatives H. R. 4288, which was referred to the House Committee on Military Affairs.

In an attempt to break the deadlock on committee jurisdiction, Senator McMahon introduced in the Senate, October 9, 1945, a resolution (S. Res. 179) providing for a special committee on atomic energy to be composed of nine members of the Senate and "to make a full, complete, and continuing study and investigation with respect to problems relating to the development, use, and control of atomic energy" to which "all bills and resolutions introduced in the Senate, and all bills and resolutions from the House of Representatives, proposing legislation relating to the development, use, and control of atomic energy shall be referred."[3] The Resolution was reported from Senate committees with amendment on October 18, 1945.[4] Amended on the floor of the Senate to raise the membership of the Special Committee from nine to eleven, the Resolution was agreed to on October 22.[5] On October 29, the McMahon Bill and the Johnson Bill were referred to the Special Committee on Atomic Energy, established pursuant to the McMahon Resolution.[6]

On November 1, 1945, Rep. May introduced a second bill for the development and control of atomic energy (H. R. 4566). The Bill was referred to the House Committee on Military Affairs[7] from which it was reported on November 5 without amendment (House Report No. 1186) and submitted for consideration by the Committee of the Whole House on the State of the Union.[8]

The Special Committee on Atomic Energy opened hearings on November 27, 1945. An impressive array of scientific, industrial and military talent was summoned before the Committee during the course of the hearings. Among the scientists who testified were Dr. Harold C. Urey, Professor of Chemistry at the University of Chicago and director of the SAM Laboratory, the code designation for the laboratory at Columbia University where research was conducted on the diffusion process for the separation of uranium isotopes and for the production of heavy water and other materials used in the development of the atomic bomb; Dr. Vannevar Bush, director of the Office of Scientific Research and Development and chairman of the President's Military Policy Committee with which all major programs and policies with regard to plant construction in the Manhattan District were reviewed; Dr. J. R. Oppenheimer, Professor of Physics at the California Institute of Technology and director of the Los Alamos laboratory near Alamogordo, New Mexico; and Dr. Louis N. Ridenour, representing the Federation of American Scientists. Industry was heard in the testament of Frank R. Condon, formerly of the Stone and Webster Engineering Corporation and H. E. Thompson, vice president of the Carbide and Carbon Chemicals Corporations. Maj. Gen. Leslie R. Groves, Commanding Officer of the Manhattan District, U. S. Engineering; Vice Admiral W. H. P. Blandy, Deputy Chief, Naval Operations for Special Weapons; Gen. Thomas F. Farrell; and Maj. Alexander P. Sikorsky were among those speaking for the military.

[1] *Ibid.*, p. 9478 (Daily edition, October 3, 1945).
[2] *Ibid.*, p. 9479; for the text of the Bill, see *ibid.*, p. 9482.
[3] *Ibid.*, p. 9626 (Daily edition, October 9, 1945).
[4] *Ibid.*, p. 9917 (Daily edition, October 18, 1945).
[5] *Ibid.*, p. 10048 (Daily edition, October 27, 1945).
[6] *Ibid.*, p. 10271 (Daily edition, October 29, 1945).
[7] *Ibid.*, p. 10477 (Daily edition, November 1, 1945).
[8] *Ibid.*, p. 10563 (Daily edition, November 5, 1945).

On December 20, 1945, Senator McMahon introduced a second bill, S. 1717, which was sent immediately to the Senate Special Committee.[1] The Hearings on S. 1717 were opened by the Special Committee on January 22, 1946. Meanwhile, the May-Johnson Bill, sponsored by the War Department, had been the subject of wide-spread criticism in hearings before the House Committee on Military Affairs; chief among these criticisms was the allegation that the Bill granted to the government powers so broad, transcendent and dangerous and provided secrecy so rigid as to hamper research in the field of nuclear physics.[2] Appearing before the Special Committee with regard to the McMahon Bill, Secretary of the Navy Forrestal urged that no power be given the President to remove members of the proposed Atomic Energy Commission and urged the inclusion as *ex officio* members of the Commission the Secretaries of State, War and Navy.[3] In support of his first contention, Secretary Forrestal testified:

"Prestige of the Commission is established by the caliber of its membership. We [the Navy] think that members serving, to quote the language of the bill, 'at the pleasure of the President,' would carry a connotation of impermanence which would not be desirable and would also limit the dependence of the membership.

"We think the outstanding scientific and industrial leaders might be unwilling to serve on these terms." [4]

Stressing the need for military representation on the Commission, he asserted that, unless atomic weapons were abolished in the interim, the War and Navy Departments should share with the Commission the responsibility for military application of atomic energy until 1950.[5]

While the hearings were in progress, President Truman approved the early substitution of civilian control for military guardianship as soon as Congress fixed the necessary responsibility for control. President Truman's views were set forth in a letter of February 2, 1946 to Senator McMahon.[6]

The Special Committee, on March 12, made public its agreement on the first of the amendments it was to propose to the McMahon Bill. The amendment, sponsored by Senator Vandenberg, proposed the establishment of a Military Liaison Committee to review military application and common defense and security measures contemplated by the Atomic Energy Commission but, according to Senator Vandenberg, left "total and final authority over every phase of atomic energy in the hands of civilians." The Commission itself was to remain exclusively civilian in character. The Liaison Committee would be appointed by the President from the Army and Navy and would have access to the full proceedings of the Commission. The final settlement of differences between the Committee and the Commission would be left to the President.[7] The announcement of this amendment, a compromise between the purely civilian control provisions of the McMahon Bill and the more militaristic controls of the May Bill, however, evoked such protest from civic and scientific organizations who feared military domination of the controls established that, on the following day, Senator Vandenberg re-submitted the amendment to the whole committee which backed it by a 10 to 1 vote.[8] Two days later, another amendment, proposed by Senator Hart to counterbalance the full effect of the Vandenberg amendment, was approved by the Special Committee. The Hart Amendment authorized the appointment by the President of an advisory

[1] *Ibid.*, p. 12582 (Daily edition, December 20, 1945).

[2] *New York Times*, January 23, 1946, p. 10.

[3] *Atomic Energy Act of 1946. Hearings before the Special Committee on Atomic Energy. United States Senate, Seventy-Ninth Congress, Second Session on S. 1717. A Bill for the Development and Control of Atomic Energy.* Part 1, January 22 and 23, 1946, p. 72.

[4] *Ibid.*, p. 71.

[5] *Ibid.*, p. 73.

[6] For the text of the President's letter, see this volume, p. 429.

[7] *New York Times*, March 13, 1946, p. 1.

[8] *Ibid.*, March 14, 1946, p. 13.

body of nine civilians to assist the Atomic Energy Commission.[1] On April 2, 1946, the Special Committee unanimously passed a revision of the Vandenberg amendment narrowing the jurisdiction of the Military Liaison Committee so as to exclude measures pertaining to common defense and security and to retain only military application of atomic energy. The Committee, to be appointed by the President and to have the right of direct appeal to him under the original proposal, was now to be appointed by the Secretaries of War and Navy with indirect appeal to the President through the respective Secretaries.[2]

On April 11, S. 1717, as modified by both the revised Vandenberg amendment and the Hart amendment, was unanimously accepted by the Special Committee.[3] The Bill was reported favorably to the Senate on April 19, 1946 (Senate Report No. 1211) and debate opened on June 1, 1946. With several minor amendments from the floor the Bill was passed by the Senate on June 1[4] and sent to the House for approval on June 5.[5] The House Committee on Military Affairs reported the McMahon Bill, with amendments, on July 10, 1946 (House Report No. 2478) and referred it for discussion to the Committee of the Whole House on the State of the Union.[6] Discussion opened July 17. The three major amendments proposed by the Military Affairs Committee provided: (1) that at least one and no more than two of the members of Atomic Energy Commission should be representatives (later amended by the House to read "members") of the armed forces, (2) that the Director of the Division of Military Application should also be a member of the armed forces, and (3) that the armed forces be permitted to maintain with the approval of the President their own independent manufacturing facilities for atomic weapons. The three amendments were subsequently approved by the House.[7] The Bill, as amended, was passed by the House on July 20.[8]

The Bill as amended and approved by the House was laid before the Senate on July 22. The House amendments were read and, on a motion by Senator McMahon, rejected. Senators McMahon, Johnson, Russell, Austin, and Vandenberg, were appointed conferees on the part of the Senate for a conference with the House to reach agreement on disputed portions of the amended bill.[9] Representatives May, Thomason, Brooks, Clason, and Thomas, conferred on the part of the House.[10] Mr. Brooks was later replaced by Mr. Durham.[11] The Conference report (House Report No. 2670) was submitted to the House on July 25 and to the Senate on the following day. Both Houses adopted the report on July 26.[12] On July 29, the Bill was signed by the Speaker of the House and by the President *pro tempore* of the Senate.[13]

President Truman signed the "Atomic Energy Act of 1946" on August 2, 1946, making it law and creating a civilian dominated Commission for the control and development of atomic energy within the United States.[14] On October 28, he announced the appointment of the members of the Atomic Energy Commission: David E. Lilienthal, chairman; Robert F. Bacher; Sumner T. Pike; Lewis L. Strauss; and William W. Waymack.[15] On December 11, 1946, the Com-

[1] *Ibid.*, March 16, 1946, p. 5.
[2] *Ibid.*, April 3, 1946, p. 1.
[3] *Ibid.*, April 12, 1946, p. 1.
[4] *Congressional Record*, 91, p. 6212 (Daily edition, June 1, 1946).
[5] *Ibid.*, p. 6470 (Daily edition, June 5, 1946).
[6] *Ibid.*, p. 8732 (Daily edition, July 10, 1946).
[7] *Ibid.*, p. 9505-9 (Daily edition, July 18, 1946).
[8] *Ibid.*, p. 9690 (Daily edition, July 20, 1946).
[9] *Ibid.*, p. 9738 (Daily edition, July 22, 1946).
[10] *Ibid.*, p. 9802.
[11] *Ibid.*, p. 10071 (Daily edition, July 25, 1946).
[12] *Ibid.*, p. 10303 and 10331 (Daily edition, July 26, 1946).
[13] *Ibid.*, p. 10474 and 10553 (Daily edition, July 29, 1946).
[14] *New York Times*, August 2, 1946, p. 7; for the text of the Atomic Energy Act of 1946, see this volume, p. 431.
[15] For the text of the President's announcement, see *New York Times*, October 29, 1946, p. 3.

mission announced that it would formally assume responsibility and control of the Army's atom bomb project on January 1, 1947, following extensive conferences with the War Department on administrative and legal details, loan of military personnel and security problems.[1]

The composition of the General Advisory Committee was announced by the President on December 12, 1946: James Bryant Conant, president of Harvard University; Lee A. DuBridge, president of the California Institute of Technology; Dr. Enrico Fermi, Professor of Physics at the University of Chicago; Dr. I. I. Rabi, Professor of Physics at Columbia University; Dr. J. R. Oppenheimer; Hartley Rose, vice president and chief engineer of the United Fruit Company; Glenn T. Seaborg, Professor of Chemistry at the University of California; Cyril S. Smith, director of the Institute of Metals, University of Chicago; and Hood Worthington, chemical engineer for E. I. DuPont de Nemours and Company.[2]

By Executive Order, on the afternoon of December 31, 1946, President Truman transferred, effective as of January 1, 1947, the control of the Army's Manhattan District to the Atomic Energy Commission.[3]

(1) *Executive Order 9613, Withdrawing and Reserving for the Use of the United States Lands Containing Radio-Active Mineral Substances, September 13, 1945.*[4]

By virtue of the authority vested in me as President of the United States, it is hereby ordered as follows:

1. Subject to valid existing rights, all public lands of the United States, including Alaska, which contain deposits of radio-active mineral substances, and all deposits of such substances, are hereby withdrawn from sale and all other forms of disposal under the public-land laws, including the mining laws, and reserved for the use of the United States.

2. So far as not in conflict with existing law, all lands in the United States, its territories or possessions, heretofore acquired by the United States, which contain deposits of radio-active mineral substances owned by the United States are hereby reserved from sale, and all leases, licenses, or other authorizations of whatever kind hereafter granted to occupy or use such lands, shall reserve to the United States the right, at any and all times, to enter upon such lands, and mine and remove such mineral substances; and all such lands hereafter acquired by the United States shall become subject to the provisions of this paragraph upon their acquisition; *Provided*, That no reservation under this paragraph shall interfere with the use of the lands established or indicated by any act of Congress.

(2) *Message from the President (Truman) to the Congress, Requesting the Enactment of Legislation on the Control, Use and Development of Atomic Energy, October 3, 1945.*[5]

Almost 2 months have passed since the atomic bomb was used against Japan. That bomb did not win the war, but it certainly shortened the war. We know that it saved the lives of untold thousands of American and Allied soldiers who would otherwise have been killed in battle.

---

[1] *Ibid.*, December 12, 1946, p. 2.   [2] *Ibid.*, December 13, 1946, p. 2.
[3] For the text of the Executive Order, see below.
[4] *Federal Register*, X, p. 11789.   [5] House Document No. 301, 79th Cong., 1st sess.

The discovery of the means of releasing atomic energy began a new era in the history of civilization. The scientific and industrial knowledge on which this discovery rests does not relate merely to another weapon. It may some day prove to be more revolutionary in the development of human society than the invention of the wheel, the use of metals, or the steam or internal combustion engine.

Never in history has society been confronted with a power so full of potential danger and at the same time so full of promise for the future of man and for the peace of the world. I think I express the faith of the American people when I say that we can use the knowledge we have won, not for the devastation of war, but for the future welfare of humanity.

To accomplish that objective we must proceed along two fronts — the domestic and the international.

The first and most urgent step is the determination of our domestic policy for the control, use, and development of atomic energy within the United States.

We cannot postpone decisions in this field. The enormous investment which we made to produce the bomb has given us the two vast industrial plants in Washington and Tennessee, and the many associated works throughout the country. It has brought together a vast organization of scientists, executives, industrial engineers, and skilled workers — a national asset of inestimable value.

The powers which the Congress wisely gave to the Government to wage war were adequate to permit the creation and development of this enterprise as a war project. Now that our enemies have surrendered, we should take immediate action to provide for the future use of this huge investment in brains and plant. I am informed that many of the people on whom depend the continued successful operation of the plants and the further development of atomic knowledge, are getting ready to return to their normal pursuits. In many cases these people are considering leaving the project largely because of uncertainty concerning future national policy in this field. Prompt action to establish national policy will go a long way toward keeping a strong organization intact.

It is equally necessary to direct future research and to establish control of the basic raw materials essential to the development of this power whether it is to be used for purposes of peace or war. Atomic force in ignorant or evil hands could inflict untold disaster upon the Nation and the world. Society cannot hope even to protect itself — much less to realize the benefits of the discovery — unless prompt action is taken to guard against the hazards of misuse.

I therefore urge, as a first measure in a program of utilizing our knowledge for the benefit of society, that the Congress enact legislation to fix a policy with respect to our existing plants, and to control all sources of atomic energy and all activities connected with its development and use in the United States.

The legislation should give jurisdiction for these purposes to an Atomic Energy Commission with members appointed by the President, with the advice and consent of the Senate.

The Congress should lay down the basic principles for all the activities of the Commission, the objectives of which should be the promotion of the national welfare, securing the national defense, safeguarding world peace, and the acquisition of further knowledge concerning atomic energy.

The people of the United States know that the overwhelming power we have developed in this war is due in large measure to American science and American industry, consisting of management and labor. We believe that our science and industry owe their strength to the spirit of free inquiry and the spirit of free enterprise that characterize our country. The Commission, therefore, in carrying out its functions should interfere as little as possible with private research and private enterprise, and should use as much as possible existing institutions and agencies. The observance of this policy is our best guaranty of maintaining the preeminence in science and industry upon which our national well-being depends.

All land and mineral deposits owned by the United States which constitute sources of atomic energy, and all stock piles of materials from which such energy may be derived, and all plants or other property of the United States connected with its development and use should be transferred to the supervision and control of the Commission.

The Commission should be authorized to acquire at a fair price, by purchase or by condemnation, any minerals or other materials from which the sources of atomic energy can be derived, and also any land containing such minerals or materials, which are not already owned by the United States.

The power to purchase should include real and personal property outside the limits of the United States.

The Commission should also be authorized to conduct all necessary research, experimentation, and operations for the further development and use of atomic energy for military, industrial, scientific, or medical purposes. In these activities it should, of course, use existing private and public institutions and agencies to the fullest practicable extent.

Under appropriate safeguards the Commission should also be permitted to license any property available to the Commission for research, development, and exploitation in the field of atomic energy. Among other things such licensing should be conditioned, of course, upon a policy of widespread distribution of peacetime products on equitable terms which will prevent monopoly.

In order to establish effective control and security, it should be declared unlawful to produce or use the substances comprising the sources of atomic energy or to import or export them except under conditions prescribed by the Commission.

Finally, the Commission should be authorized to establish security regulations governing the handling of all information, material, and equipment under its jurisdiction. Suitable penalties should be prescribed for violating the security regulations of the Commission or any of the other terms of the act.

The measures which I have suggested may seem drastic and far-reaching but the discovery with which we are dealing involves forces of nature too dangerous to fit into any of our usual concepts.

The other phase of the problem is the question of the international control and development of this newly discovered energy.

In international relations, as in domestic affairs, the release of atomic energy constitutes a new force too revolutionary to consider in the framework of old ideas. We can no longer rely on the slow progress of time to develop a program of control among nations. Civilization demands that we shall reach at the earliest possible date a satisfactory arrangement for the control of this discovery in order that it may become a powerful and forceful influence toward the maintenance of world peace instead of an instrument of destruction.

Scientific opinion appears to be practically unanimous that the essential theoretical knowledge upon which the discovery is based is already widely known. There is also substantial agreement that foreign research can come abreast of our present theoretical knowledge in time.

The hope of civilization lies in international arrangements looking, if possible, to the renunciation of the use and development of the atomic bomb, and directing and encouraging the use of atomic energy and all future scientific information toward peaceful and humanitarian ends. The difficulties in working out such arrangements are great. The alternative to overcoming these difficulties, however, may be a desperate armament race which might well end in disaster. Discussion of the international problem cannot be safely delayed until the United Nations Organization is functioning and in a position adequately to deal with it.

I, therefore, propose to initiate discussions first with our associates in this discovery, Great Britain and Canada, and then with other nations, in an effort to effect agreement on the conditions under which cooperation might replace rivalry in the field of atomic power.

I desire to emphasize that these discussions will not be concerned with disclosures relating to the manufacturing processes leading to the production of the atomic bomb itself. They will constitute an effort to work out arrangements covering the terms under which international collaboration and exchange of scientific information might safely proceed.

The outcome of the discussions will be reported to the Congress as soon as possible, and any resulting agreements requiring congressional action will be submitted to the Congress.

But regardless of the course of discussions in the international field, I believe it is essential that legislation along the lines I have indicated be adopted as promptly as possible to insure the necessary research in, and development and control of, the production and use of atomic energy.

(3) *Letter from the President (Truman) to the Chairman of the Senate Special Committee on Atomic Energy (McMahon), February 2, 1946.*[1]

You have requested my views on S. 1717, a bill for the domestic development and control of atomic energy. I wish to give you my thoughts at this time because I consider the subject of paramount importance and urgency, both from the standpoint of our welfare at home and that of achieving a durable peace throughout the world.

[1] *New York Times*, February 3, 1946, p. 7.

I appreciate the thorough and impartial manner in which atomic energy hearings have been held before your committee. I believe that the hearings, in keeping with democratic tradition, have aided the people in obtaining a clearer insight into the problems which such legislation must meet.

You will recall that I sent a special message to the Congress on October 3, 1945, calling for legislation to fix a policy for the domestic control of atomic energy. Since then I have given considerable time to the further study of this most difficult subject. I have had the advantage of additional technical information and expressions of public opinion developed at the hearings. With this background I feel prepared to recommend in greater detail than before what I believe to be the essential elements of sound atomic energy legislation:

(1) A commission established by the Congress for the control of atomic energy should be composed exclusively of civilians. This should not be interpreted to disqualify former military personnel from membership, and is in accord with established American principles embodied in our statutes since 1870. I would prefer a three-man commission in lieu of a larger group, which administrative experience has shown unwieldy. It is essential that the members of the commission be full-time Government employees.

(2) The Government must be the exclusive owner and producer of fissionable materials. (Fissionable materials are, of course to be, distinguished from source materials from which fissionable materials may be derived. By fissionable materials, I mean such as U–235, or plutonium, or any substance enriched in these beyond its natural state.) It follows that there should be no private patents in this field of exclusive Government activity.

The disadvantages of Government monopoly are small compared to the danger of permitting anyone other than the Government to own or produce these crucial substances, the use of which affects the safety of the entire nation. The benefits of atomic energy are the heritage of the people: they should be distributed as widely as possible.

(3) Consistent with these principles it is essential that devices utilizing atomic energy be made fully available for private development through compulsory, non-exclusive licensing of private patents, and regulation of royalty fees to insure their reasonableness. These provisions will assure widespread distribution of the benefits of atomic energy while preserving the royalty incentive to maintain the interest of private enterprise.

(4) In my message of October 3, I wrote: "Our science and industry owe their strength to the spirit of free inquiry and the spirit of free enterprise that characterize our country. . . . (This) is our best guaranty of maintaining the preeminence in science and industry upon which our national well-being depends."

Legislation in this field must assure genuine freedom to conduct independent research and must guarantee that controls over the dissemination of information will not stifle scientific progress.

Atomic energy legislation should also insure coordination between the research activities of the commission and those of the proposed National Science Foundation, now under consideration by the Congress.

(5) Each of the foregoing provisions for domestic control of atomic energy will contribute materially to the achievement of a safe, effective international arrangement making possible the ultimate use of atomic energy for exclusively peaceful and humanitarian ends. The commission should be in a position to carry out at once any international agreements relating to inspection, control of the production of fissionable materials, dissemination of information, and similar areas of international action.

I feel that it is a matter of urgency that sound domestic legislation on atomic energy be enacted with utmost speed. Domestic and international issues of the first importance wait upon this action.

To your committee, pioneers in legislation of vast promise for our people and all people, there beckons a place of honor in history.

(4) *An Act for the Development and Control of Atomic Energy, Approved August 2, 1946.*[1]

Be it enacted by the Senate and House of Representatives of the United States of America in Congress assembled,

DECLARATION OF POLICY

SECTION 1. (a) FINDINGS AND DECLARATION. — Research and experimentation in the field of nuclear chain reaction have attained the stage at which the release of atomic energy on a large scale is practical. The significance of the atomic bomb for military purposes is evident. The effect of the use of atomic energy for civilian purposes upon the social, economic, and political structures of today cannot now be determined. It is a field in which unknown factors are involved. Therefore, any legislation will necessarily be subject to revision from time to time. It is reasonable to anticipate, however, that tapping this new source of energy will cause profound changes in our present way of life. Accordingly, it is hereby declared to be the policy of the people of the United States that, subject at all times to the paramount objective of assuring the common defense and security, the development and utilization of atomic energy shall, so far as practicable, be directed toward improving the public welfare, increasing the standard of living, strengthening free competition in private enterprise, and promoting world peace.

(b) PURPOSE OF ACT. — It is the purpose of this Act to effectuate the policies set out in section 1 (a) by providing, among others, for the following major programs relating to atomic energy:

(1) A program of assisting and fostering private research and development to encourage maximum scientific progress;

(2) A program for the control of scientific and technical information which will permit the dissemination of such information to encourage

[1] Public Law 585, 79th Cong., 2d sess.

scientific progress, and for the sharing on a reciprocal basis of information concerning the practical industrial application of atomic energy as soon as effective and enforceable safeguards against its use for destructive purposes can be devised;

(3) A program of federally conducted research and development to assure the Government of adequate scientific and technical accomplishment;

(4) A program for Government control of the production, ownership, and use of fissionable material to assure the common defense and security and to insure the broadest possible exploitation of the fields; and

(5) A program of administration which will be consistent with the foregoing policies and with international arrangements made by the United States, and which will enable the Congress to be currently informed so as to take further legislative action as may hereafter be appropriate.

ORGANIZATION

SEC. 2. (a) ATOMIC ENERGY COMMISSION. —

(1) There is hereby established an Atomic Energy Commission (herein called the Commission), which shall be composed of five members. Three members shall constitute a quorum of the Commission. The President shall designate one member as Chairman of the Commission.

(2) Members of the Commission shall be appointed by the President, by and with the advice and consent of the Senate. In submitting any nomination to the Senate, the President shall set forth the experience and the qualifications of the nominee. The term of office of each member of the Commission taking office prior to the expiration of two years after the date of enactment of this Act shall expire upon the expiration of such two years. The term of office of each member of the Commission taking office after the expiration of two years from the date of enactment of this Act shall be five years, except that (A) the terms of office of the members first taking office after the expiration of two years from the date of enactment of this Act shall expire, as designated by the President at the time of appointment, one at the end of three years, one at the end of four years, one at the end of five years, one at the end of six years, and one at the end of seven years, after the date of enactment of this Act; and (B) any member appointed to fill a vacancy occurring prior to the expiration of the term for which his predecessor was appointed, shall be appointed for the remainder of such term. Any member of the Commission may be removed by the President for inefficiency, neglect of duty, or malfeasance in office. Each member, except the Chairman, shall receive compensation at the rate of $15,000 per annum; and the Chairman shall receive compensation at the rate of $17,500 per annum. No member of the Commission shall engage in any other business, vocation, or employment than that of serving as a member of the Commission.

(3) The principal office of the Commission shall be in the District of Columbia, but the Commission or any duly authorized representative may exercise any or all of its powers in any place. The Commission shall

hold such meetings, conduct such hearings, and receive such reports as may be necessary to enable it to carry out the provisions of this Act.

(4) There are hereby established within the Commission —

(A) a General Manager, who shall discharge such of the administrative and executive functions of the Commission as the Commission may direct. The General Manager shall be appointed by the President by and with the advice and consent of the Senate, and shall receive compensation at the rate of $15,000 per annum. The Commission may make recommendations to the President with respect to the appointment or removal of the General Manager.

(B) a Division of Research, a Division of Production, a Division of Engineering, and a Division of Military Application. Each division shall be under the direction of a Director who shall be appointed by the Commission, and shall receive compensation at the rate of $14,000 per annum. The Director of the Division of Military Application shall be a member of the armed forces. The Commission shall require each such division to exercise such of the Commission's powers under this Act as the Commission may determine, except that the authority granted under section 3 (a) of this act shall not be exercised by the Division of Research.

(b) GENERAL ADVISORY COMMITTEE. — There shall be a General Advisory Committee to advise the Commission on scientific and technical matters relating to materials, production, and research and development, to be composed of nine members, who shall be appointed from civilian life by the President. Each member shall hold office for a term of six years, except that (1) any member appointed to fill a vacancy occurring prior to the expiration of the term for which his predecessor was appointed, shall be appointed for the remainder of such term; and (2) the terms of office of the members first taking office after the date of the enactment of this Act shall expire, as designated by the President at the time of appointment, three at the end of two years, three at the end of four years, and three at the end of six years, after the date of the enactment of this Act. The Committee shall designate one of its own members as Chairman. The Committee shall meet at least four times in every calendar year. The members of the Committee shall receive a per diem compensation of $50 for each day spent in meetings or conferences, and all members shall receive their necessary traveling or other expenses while engaged in the work of the Committee.

(c) MILITARY LIAISON COMMITTEE. — There shall be a Military Liaison Committee consisting of representatives of the Departments of War and Navy, detailed or assigned thereto, without additional compensation, by the Secretaries of War and Navy in such number as they may determine. The Commission shall advise and consult with the Committee on all atomic energy matters which the Committee deems to relate to military applications, including the development, manufacture, use, and storage of bombs, the allocation of fissionable material for military research, and the control of information relating to the manufacture or utilization of atomic weapons. The Commission shall keep the Committee fully informed of all such matters before it and the Committee shall keep the Commission fully informed of all atomic energy activities of the War and Navy Departments. The Committee shall have authority to make written recommendations to the Commission on matters relating to military applications from time to time as it may deem appropriate. If the Committee at any time concludes that any action, proposed action, or failure to act of the Commission on such matters is adverse to the responsibilities of the Departments of War or Navy, derived from the Constitution, laws, and treaties, the Committee may refer such action, proposed action, or failure to act to the Secretaries of War and Navy. If either Secretary concurs, he may refer the matter to the President, whose decision shall be final.

(d) APPOINTMENT OF ARMY AND NAVY OFFICERS. — Notwithstanding the provisions of section 1222 of the Revised Statutes (U. S. C., 1940 edition, title 10, sec. 576), section 212 of the Act entitled "An Act making appropriations for the Legislative Branch of the Government for the fiscal year ending June 30, 1933, and for other purposes," approved June 30, 1932, as amended (U. S. C., 1940 edition, title 5, sec. 59a), section 2 of the Act entitled "An Act making appropriations for the legislative, executive, and judicial expenses of the Government for the fiscal year ending June thirtieth, eighteen hundred and ninety-five, and for other purposes," approved July 31, 1894, as amended (U. S. C., 1940 edition, title 5, sec. 62), or any other law, any active or retired officer of the Army or the Navy may serve as Director of the Division of Military Application established by subsection (a) (4) (B) of this section, without prejudice to his commissioned status as such officer. Any such officer serving as Director of the Division of Military Application shall receive, in addition to his pay from the United States as such officer, an amount equal to the difference between such pay and the compensation prescribed in subsection (a) (4) (B) of this section.

RESEARCH

SEC. 3. (a) RESEARCH ASSISTANCE. — The Commission is directed to exercise its powers in such manner as to insure the continued conduct of research and development activities in the fields specified below by private or public institutions or persons and to assist in the acquisition of an ever-expanding fund of theoretical and practical knowledge in such fields. To this end the Commission is authorized and directed to make arrangements (including contracts, agreements, and loans) for the conduct of research and development activities relating to —

(1) nuclear processes;
(2) the theory and production of atomic energy, including processes, materials, and devices related to such production;
(3) utilization of fissionable and radioactive materials for medical, biological, health, or military purposes;
(4) utilization of fissionable and radioactive materials and processes entailed in the production of such materials for all other purposes, including industrial uses; and
(5) the protection of health during research and production activities.

NATIONAL DEFENSE 435

The Commission may make such arrangements without regard to the provisions of section 3709 of the Revised Statutes (U. S. C., title 41, sec. 5) upon certification by the Commission that such action is necessary in the interest of the common defense and security, or upon a showing that advertising is not reasonably practicable, and may make partial and advance payments under such arrangements, and may make available for use in connection therewith such of its equipment and facilities as it may deem desirable. Such arrangements shall contain such provisions to protect health, to minimize danger from explosion and other hazards to life or property, and to require the reporting and to permit the inspection of work performed thereunder, as the Commission may determine; but shall not contain any provisions or conditions which prevent the dissemination of scientific or technical information, except to the extent such dissemination is prohibited by law.

(b) RESEARCH BY THE COMMISSION. — The Commission is authorized and directed to conduct, through its own facilities, activities and studies of the types specified in subsection (a) above.

PRODUCTION OF FISSIONABLE MATERIAL

SEC. 4. (a) DEFINITION. — As used in this Act, the term "produce", when used in relation to fissionable material, means to manufacture, produce, or refine fissionable material, as distinguished from source materials as defined in section 5 (b) (1), or to separate fissionable material from other substances in which such material may be contained or to produce new fissionable material.

(b) PROHIBITION. — It shall be unlawful for any person to own any facilities for the production of fissionable material or for any person to produce fissionable material, except to the extent authorized by subsection (c).

(c) OWNERSHIP AND OPERATION OF PRODUCTION FACILITIES. —

(1) OWNERSHIP OF PRODUCTION FACILITIES. — The Commission, as agent of and on behalf of the United States, shall be the exclusive owner of all facilities for the production of fissionable material other than facilities which (A) are useful in the conduct of research and development activities in the fields specified in section 3, and (B) do not, in the opinion of the Commission, have a potential production rate adequate to enable the operator of such facilities to produce within a reasonable period of time a sufficient quantity of fissionable material to produce an atomic bomb or any other atomic weapon.

(2) OPERATION OF THE COMMISSION'S PRODUCTION FACILITIES. — The Commission is authorized and directed to produce or to provide for the production of fissionable material in its own facilities. To the extent deemed necessary, the Commission is authorized to make, or to continue in effect, contracts with persons obligating them to produce fissionable material in facilities owned by the Commission. The Commission is also authorized to enter into research and development contracts authorizing the contractor to produce fissionable material in facilities owned by the Commission to the extent that the produc-

tion of such fissionable material may be incident to the conduct of research and development activities under such contracts. Any contract entered into under this section shall contain provisions (A) prohibiting the contractor with the Commission from subcontracting any part of the work he is obligated to perform under the contract, except as authorized by the Commission, and (B) obligating the contractor to make such reports to the Commission as it may deem appropriate with respect to his activities under the contract, to submit to frequent inspection by employees of the Commission of all such activities, and to comply with all safety and security regulations which may be prescribed by the Commission. Any contract made under the provisions of this paragraph may be made without regard to the provisions of section 3709 of the Revised Statutes (U. S. C., title 41, sec. 5) upon certification by the Commission that such action is necessary in the interest of the common defense and security, or upon a showing that advertising is not reasonably practicable, and partial and advance payments may be made under such contracts. The President shall determine at least once each year the quantities of fissionable material to be produced under this paragraph.

(3) OPERATION OF OTHER PRODUCTION FACILITIES. — Fissionable material may be produced in the conduct of research and development activities in facilities which, under paragraph (1) above, are not required to be owned by the Commission.

(d) IRRADIATION OF MATERIALS. — For the purpose of increasing the supply of radioactive materials, the Commission and persons lawfully producing or utilizing fissionable material are authorized to expose materials of any kind to the radiation incident to the processes of producing or utilizing fissionable material.

(e) MANUFACTURE OF PRODUCTION FACILITIES. — Unless authorized by a license issued by the Commission, no person may manufacture, produce, transfer, or acquire any facilities for the production of fissionable material. Licenses shall be issued in accordance with such procedures as the Commission may by regulation establish and shall be issued in accordance with such standards and upon such conditions as will restrict the production and distribution of such facilities to effectuate the policies and purposes of this Act. Nothing in this section shall be deemed to require a license for such manufacture, production, transfer, or acquisition incident to or for the conduct of research or development activities in the United States of the types specified in section 3, or to prohibit the Commission from manufacturing or producing such facilities for its own use.

CONTROL OF MATERIALS

SEC. 5. (a) FISSIONABLE MATERIALS. —

(1) DEFINITION. — As used in this Act, the term "fissionable material" means plutonium, uranium enriched in the isotope 235, any other material which the Commission determines to be capable of releasing substantial quantities of energy through nuclear chain reaction of the

material, or any material artificially enriched by any of the foregoing; but does not include source materials, as defined in section 5 (*b*) (1).

(2) GOVERNMENT OWNERSHIP OF ALL FISSIONABLE MATERIAL. — All right, title and interest within or under the jurisdiction of the United States, in or to any fissionable material, now or hereafter produced, shall be the property of the Commission, and shall be deemed to be vested in the Commission by virtue of this Act. Any person owning any interest in any fissionable material at the time of the enactment of this Act, or owning any interest in any material at the time when such material is hereafter determined to be a fissionable material, or who lawfully produces any fissionable material incident to privately financed research or development activities, shall be paid just compensation therefor. The Commission may, by action consistent with the provisions of paragraph (4) below, authorize any such person to retain possession of such fissionable material, but no person shall have any title in or to any fissionable material.

(3) PROHIBITION. — It shall be unlawful for any person, after sixty days from the effective date of this Act to (A) possess or transfer any fissionable material, except as authorized by the Commission, or (B) export from or import into the United States any fissionable material, or (C) directly or indirectly engage in the production of any fissionable material outside of the United States.

(4) DISTRIBUTION OF FISSIONABLE MATERIAL. — Without prejudice to its continued ownership thereof, the Commission is authorized to distribute fissionable material owned by it, with or without charge, to applicants requesting such material (A) for the conduct of research or development activities either independently or under contract or other arrangement with the Commission, (B) for use in medical therapy, or (C) for use pursuant to a license issued under the authority of section 7. Such material shall be distributed in such quantities and on such terms that no applicant will be enabled to obtain an amount sufficient to construct a bomb or other military weapon. The Commission is directed to distribute sufficient fissionable material to permit the conduct of widespread independent research and development activity, to the maximum extent practicable. In determining the quantities of fissionable material to be distributed, the Commission shall make such provisions for its own needs and for the conservation of fissionable material as it may determine to be necessary in the national interest for the future development of atomic energy. The Commission shall not distribute any material to any applicant, and shall recall any distributed material from any applicant, who is not equipped to observe or who fails to observe such safety standards to protect health and to minimize danger from explosion or other hazard to life or property as may be established by the Commission, or who uses such material in violation of law or regulation of the Commission or in a manner other than as disclosed in the application therefor.

(5) The Commission is authorized to purchase or otherwise acquire any fissionable material or any interest therein outside the United States, or any interest in facilities for the production of fissionable material, or in real property on which such facilities are located, without regard to

the provisions of section 3709 of the Revised Statutes (U. S. C., title 41, sec. 5) upon certification by the Commission that such action is necessary in the interest of the common defense and security, or upon a showing that advertising is not reasonably practicable, and partial and advance payments may be made under contracts for such purposes. The Commission is further authorized to take, requisition, or condemn, or otherwise acquire any interest in such facilities or real property, and just compensation shall be made therefor.

(b) SOURCE MATERIALS. —

(1) DEFINITION. — As used in this Act, the term "source material" means uranium, thorium, or any other material which is determined by the Commission, with the approval of the President, to be peculiarly essential to the production of fissionable materials; but includes ores only if they contain one or more of the foregoing materials in such concentration as the Commission may by regulation determine from time to time.

(2) LICENSE FOR TRANSFERS REQUIRED. — Unless authorized by a license issued by the Commission, no person may transfer or deliver, receive possession of or title to, or export from the United States any source material after removal from its place of deposit in nature, except that licenses shall not be required for quantities of source materials which, in the opinion of the Commission, are unimportant.

(3) ISSUANCE OF LICENSES. — The Commission shall establish such standards for the issuance, refusal, or revocation of licenses as it may deem necessary to assure adequate source materials for production, research, or development activities pursuant to this Act or to prevent the use of such materials in a manner inconsistent with the national welfare. Licenses shall be issued in accordance with such procedures as the Commission may by regulation establish.

(4) REPORTING. — The Commission is authorized to issue such regulations or orders requiring reports of ownership, possession, extraction, refining, shipment, or other handling of source materials as it may deem necessary, except that such reports shall not be required with respect to (A) any source material prior to removal from its place of deposit in nature, or (B) quantities of source materials which in the opinion of the Commission are unimportant or the reporting of which will discourage independent prospecting for new deposits.

(5) ACQUISITION. — The Commission is authorized and directed to purchase, take, requisition, condemn, or otherwise acquire, supplies of source materials or any interest in real property containing deposits of source materials to the extent it deems necessary to effectuate the provisions of this Act. Any purchase made under this paragraph may be made without regard to the provisions of section 3709 of the Revised Statutes (U. S. C., title 41, sec. 5) upon certification by the Commission that such action is necessary in the interest of the common defense and security, or upon a showing that advertising is not reasonably practicable, and partial and advance payments may be made thereunder. The Commission may establish guaranteed prices for all source materials delivered to it within a specified time. Just compensation shall be made for any property taken, requisitioned, or condemned under this paragraph.

(6) EXPLORATION. — The Commission is authorized to conduct and enter into contracts for the conduct of exploratory operations, investigations, and inspections to determine the location, extent, mode of occurrence, use, or conditions of deposits or supplies of source materials, making just compensation for any damage or injury occasioned thereby. Such exploratory operations may be conducted only with the consent of the owner, but such investigations and inspections may be conducted with or without such consent.

(7) PUBLIC LANDS. — All uranium, thorium, and all other materials determined pursuant to paragraph (1) of this subsection to be peculiarly essential to the production of fissionable material, contained, in whatever concentration, in deposits in the public lands are hereby reserved for the use of the United States subject to valid claims, rights, or privileges existing on the date of the enactment of this Act: *Provided, however,* That no individual, corporation, partnership, or association, which had any part, directly or indirectly, in the development of the atomic bomb project, may benefit by any location, entry, or settlement upon the public domain made after such individual, corporation, partnership, or association took part in such project, if such individual, corporation, partnership, or association, by reason of having had such part in the development of the atomic bomb project, acquired confidential official information as to the existence of deposits of such uranium, thorium, or other materials in the specific lands upon which such location, entry, or settlement is made, and subsequent to the date of the enactment of this Act made such location, entry, or settlement or caused the same to be made for his, its, or their benefit. The Secretary of the Interior shall cause to be inserted in every patent, conveyance, lease, permit, or other authorization hereby granted to use the public lands or their mineral resources, under any of which there might result the extraction of any materials so reserved, a reservation to the United States of all such materials, whether or not of commercial value, together with the right of the United States through its authorized agents or representatives at any time to enter upon the land and prospect for, mine, and remove the same, making just compensation for any damage or injury occasioned thereby. Any lands so patented, conveyed, leased, or otherwise disposed of may be used, and any rights under any such permit or authorization may be exercised, as if no reservation of such materials had been made under this subsection; except that, when such use results in the extraction of any such material from the land in quantities which may not be transferred or delivered without a license under this subsection, such material shall be the property of the Commission and the Commission may require delivery of such material to it by any possessor thereof after such material has been separated as such from the ores in which it was contained. If the Commission requires the delivery of such material to it, it shall pay to the person mining or extracting the same, or to such other person as the Commission determines to be entitled thereto, such sums, including profits, as the Commission deems fair and reasonable for the discovery, mining, development, production, extraction, and other services performed with respect to such material prior to such delivery, but such payment shall not include any amount on account of the value

of such material before removal from its place of deposit in nature. If the Commission does not require delivery of such material to it, the reservation made pursuant to this paragraph shall be of no further force or effect.

(c) BYPRODUCT MATERIALS. —

(1) DEFINITION. — As used in this Act, the term "byproduct material" means any radioactive material (except fissionable material) yielded in or made radioactive by exposure to the radiation incident to the processes of producing or utilizing fissionable material.

(2) DISTRIBUTION. — The Commission is authorized to distribute, with or without charge, byproduct materials to applicants seeking such materials for research or development activity, medical therapy, industrial uses, or such other useful applications as may be developed. In distributing such materials, the Commission shall give preference to applicants proposing to use such materials in the conduct of research and development activity or medical therapy. The Commission shall not distribute any byproduct materials to any applicant, and shall recall any distributed materials from any applicant, who is not equipped to observe or who fails to observe such safety standards to protect health as may be established by the Commission or who uses such materials in violation of law or regulation of the Commission or in a manner other than as disclosed in the application therefor.

(d) GENERAL PROVISIONS. — The Commission shall not —

(1) distribute any fissionable material to (A) any person for a use which is not under or within the jurisdiction of the United States, (B) any foreign government, or (C) any person within the United States if, in the opinion of the Commission, the distribution of such fissionable material to such person would be inimical to the common defense and security.

(2) license any person to transfer or deliver, receive possession of or title to, or export from the United States any source material if, in the opinion of the Commission, the issuance of a license to such person for such purpose would be inimical to the common defense and security.

MILITARY APPLICATIONS OF ATOMIC ENERGY

SEC. 6 (a) AUTHORITY. — The Commission is authorized to —

(1) conduct experiments and do research and development work in the military application of atomic energy; and

(2) engage in the production of atomic bombs, atomic bomb parts, or other military weapons utilizing fissionable materials; except that such activities shall be carried on only to the extent that the express consent and direction of the President of the United States has been obtained, which consent and direction shall be obtained at least once each year.

The President from time to time may direct the Commission (1) to deliver such quantities of fissionable materials or weapons to the armed forces for such use as he deems necessary in the interest of national defense or (2) to authorize the armed forces to manufacture, produce, or acquire any equipment or device utilizing fissionable material or atomic energy as a military weapon.

(b) PROHIBITION. — It shall be unlawful for any person to manufacture, produce, transfer, or acquire any equipment or device utilizing fissionable material or atomic energy as a military weapon, except as may be authorized by the Commission. Nothing in this subsection shall be deemed to modify the provisions of section 4 of this Act, or to prohibit research activities in respect of military weapons, or to permit the export of any such equipment or device.

UTILIZATION OF ATOMIC ENERGY

SEC. 7. (a) LICENSE REQUIRED. — It shall be unlawful, except as provided in sections 5 (a) (4) (A) or (B) or 6 (a), for any person to manufacture, produce, or export any equipment or device utilizing fissionable material or atomic energy or to utilize fissionable material or atomic energy with or without such equipment or device, except under and in accordance with a license issued by the Commission authorizing such manufacture, production, export, or utilization. No license may permit any such activity if fissionable material is produced incident to such activity, except as provided in sections 3 and 4. Nothing in this section shall be deemed to require a license for the conduct of research or development activities relating to the manufacture of such equipment or devices or the utilization of fissionable material or atomic energy, or for the manufacture or use of equipment or devices for medical therapy.

(b) REPORT TO CONGRESS. — Whenever in its opinion any industrial, commercial, or nonmilitary use of fissionable material or atomic energy has been sufficiently developed to be of practical value, the Commission shall prepare a report to the President stating all the facts with respect to such use, the Commission's estimate of the social, political, economic, and international effects of such use and the Commission's recommendations for necessary or desirable supplemental legislation. The President shall then transmit this report to the Congress together with his recommendations. No license for any manufacture, production, export, or use shall be issued by the Commission under this section until after (1) a report with respect to such manufacture, production, export, or use has been filed with the Congress; and (2) a period of ninety days in which the Congress was in session has elapsed after the report has been so filed. In computing such period of ninety days, there shall be excluded the days on which either House is not in session because of an adjournment of more than three days.

(c) ISSUANCE OF LICENSES. — After such ninety-day period, unless hereafter prohibited by law, the Commission may license such manufacture, production, export, or use in accordance with such procedures and subject to such conditions as it may by regulation establish to effectuate the provisions of this Act. The Commission is authorized and directed to issue licenses on a nonexclusive basis and to supply to the extent available appropriate quantities of fissionable material to licensees (1) whose proposed activities will serve some useful purpose proportionate to the quantities of fissionable material to be consumed; (2) who are equipped to observe such safety standards to protect health and to minimize danger from explosion or other hazard to life or property as the Commission may establish; and (3) who agree to make available to the Commission such technical information and data concerning their activities pursuant to such licenses as the Commission may determine necessary to encourage similar activities by as many licensees as possible. Each such license shall be issued for a specified period, shall be revocable at any time by the Commission in accordance with such procedures as the Commission may establish, and may be renewed upon the expiration of such period. Where activities under any license might serve to maintain or to foster the growth of monopoly, restraint of trade, unlawful competition, or other trade position inimical to the entry of new, freely competitive enterprises in the field, the Commission is authorized and directed to refuse to issue such license or to establish such conditions to prevent these results as the Commission, in consultation with the Attorney General, may determine. The Commission shall report promptly to the Attorney General any information it may have with respect to any utilization of fissionable material or atomic energy which appears to have these results. No license may be given to any person for activities which are not under or within the jurisdiction of the United States, to any foreign government, or to any person within the United States if, in the opinion of the Commission, the issuance of a license to such person would be inimical to the common defense and security.

(d) BYPRODUCT POWER. — If energy which may be utilized is produced in the production of fissionable material, such energy may be used by the Commission, transferred to other Government agencies, or sold to public or private utilities under contracts providing for reasonable resale prices.

INTERNATIONAL ARRANGEMENTS

SEC. 8. (a) DEFINITION. — As used in this Act, the term "international arrangement" shall mean any treaty approved by the Senate or international agreement hereafter approved by the Congress, during the time such treaty or agreement is in full force and effect.

(b) EFFECT OF INTERNATIONAL ARRANGEMENTS. — Any provision of this Act or any action of the Commission to the extent that it conflicts with the provisions of any international arrangement made after the date of enactment of this Act shall be deemed to be of no further force or effect.

(c) POLICIES CONTAINED IN INTERNATIONAL ARRANGEMENTS. — In the performance of its functions under this Act, the Commission shall give maximum effect to the policies contained in any such international arrangement.

PROPERTY OF THE COMMISSION

SEC. 9. (a) The President shall direct the transfer to the Commission of all interests owned by the United States or any Government agency in the following property:

(1) All fissionable material; all atomic weapons and parts thereof;

all facilities, equipment, and materials for the processing, production, or utilization of fissionable material or atomic energy; all processes and technical information of any kind, and the source thereof (including data, drawings, specifications, patents, patent applications, and other sources (relating to the processing, production, or utilization of fissionable material or atomic energy; and all contracts, agreements, leases, patents, applications for patents, inventions and discoveries (whether patented or unpatented), and other rights of any kind concerning any such items;

(2) All facilities, equipment, and materials, devoted primarily to atomic energy research and development; and

(3) Such other property owned by or in the custody or control of the Manhattan Engineer District or other Government agencies as the President may determine.

(b) In order to render financial assistance to those States and localities in which the activities of the Commission are carried on and in which the Commission has acquired property previously subject to State and local taxation, the Commission is authorized to make payments to State and local governments in lieu of property taxes. Such payments may be in the amounts, at the times, and upon the terms the Commission deems appropriate, but the Commission shall be guided by the policy of not making payments in excess of the taxes which would have been payable for such property in the condition in which it was acquired, except in cases where special burdens have been cast upon the State or local government by activities of the Commission, the Manhattan Engineer District or their agents. In any such case, any benefit accruing to the State or local government by reason of such activities shall be considered in determining the amount of the payment. The Commission, and the property, activities, and income of the Commission, are hereby expressly exempted from taxation in any manner or form by any State, county, municipality, or any subdivision thereof.

CONTROL OF INFORMATION

SEC. 10. (a) POLICY. — It shall be the policy of the Commission to control the dissemination of restricted data in such a manner as to assure the common defense and security. Consistent with such policy, the Commission shall be guided by the following principles:

(1) That until Congress declares by joint resolution that effective and enforceable international safeguards against the use of atomic energy for destructive purposes have been established, there shall be no exchange of information with other nations with respect to the use of atomic energy for industrial purposes; and

(2) That the dissemination of scientific and technical information relating to atomic energy should be permitted and encouraged so as to provide that free interchange of ideas and criticisms which is essential to scientific progress.

(b) RESTRICTIONS. —

(1) The term "restricted data" as used in this section means all data concerning the manufacture or utilization of atomic weapons, the pro-

duction of fissionable material, or the use of fissionable material in the production of power, but shall not include any data which the Commission from time to time determines may be published without adversely affecting the common defense and security.

(2) Whoever, lawfully or unlawfully, having possession of, access to, control over, or being entrusted with, any document, writing, sketch, photograph, plan, model, instrument, appliance, note or information involving or incorporating restricted data —

(A) communicates, transmits, or discloses the same to any individual or person, or attempts or conspires to do any of the foregoing, with intent to injure the United States or with intent to secure an advantage to any foreign nation, upon conviction thereof, shall be punished by death or imprisonment for life (but the penalty of death or imprisonment for life may be imposed only upon recommendation of the jury and only in cases where the offense was committed with intent to injure the United States); or by a fine of not more than $20,000 or imprisonment for not more than twenty years, or both;

(B) communicates, transmits, or discloses the same to any individual or person, or attempts or conspires to do any of the foregoing, with reason to believe such data will be utilized to injure the United States or to secure an advantage to any foreign nation, shall, upon conviction, be punished by a fine of not more than $10,000 or imprisonment for not more than ten years, or both.

(3) Whoever, with intent to injure the United States or with intent to secure an advantage to any foreign nation, acquires or attempts or conspires to acquire any document, writing, sketch, photograph, plan, model, instrument, appliance, note or information involving or incorporating restricted data shall, upon conviction thereof, be punished by death or imprisonment for life (but the penalty of death or imprisonment for life may be imposed only upon recommendation of the jury and only in cases where the offense was committed with intent to injure the United States); or by a fine of not more than $20,000 or imprisonment for not more than twenty years, or both.

(4) Whoever, with intent to injure the United States or with intent to secure an advantage to any foreign nation, removes, conceals, tampers with, alters, mutilates, or destroys any document, writing, sketch, photograph, plan, model, instrument, appliance, or note involving or incorporating restricted data and used by any individual or person in connection with the production of fissionable material, or research or development relating to atomic energy, conducted by the United States, or financed in whole or in part by Federal funds, or conducted with the aid of fissionable material, shall be punished by death or imprisonment for life (but the penalty of death or imprisonment for life may be imposed only upon recommendation of the jury and only in cases where the offense was committed with intent to injure the United States); or by a fine of not more than $20,000 or imprisonment for not more than twenty years or both.

(5) (A) No person shall be prosecuted for any violation under this section unless and until the Attorney General of the United States has advised the Commission with respect to such prosecution and no such

NATIONAL DEFENSE 445

prosecution shall be commenced except upon the express direction of the Attorney General of the United States.

(B) (*i*) No arrangement shall be made under section 3, no contract shall be made or continued in effect under section 4, and no license shall be issued under section 4 (*e*) or 7, unless the person with whom such arrangement is made, the contractor or prospective contractor, or the prospective licensee agrees in writing not to permit any individual to have access to restricted data until the Federal Bureau of Investigation shall have made an investigation and report to the Commission on the character, associations, and loyalty of such individual and the Commission shall have determined that permitting such person to have access to restricted data will not endanger the common defense or security.

(*ii*) Except as authorized by the Commission in case of emergency, no individual shall be employed by the Commission until the Federal Bureau of Investigation shall have made an investigation and report to the Commission on the character, associations, and loyalty of such individual.

(*iii*) Notwithstanding the provisions of subparagraphs (*i*) and (*ii*), during such period of time after the enactment of this Act as may be necessary to make the investigation, report, and determination required by such paragraphs, (*a*) any individual who was permitted access to restricted data by the Manhattan Engineer District may be permitted access to restricted data and (*b*) the Commission may employ any individual who was employed by the Manhattan Engineer District.

(*iv*) To protect against the unlawful dissemination of restricted data and to safeguard facilities, equipment, materials, and other property of the Commission, the President shall have authority to utilize the services of any Government agency to the extent he may deem necessary or desirable.

(C) All violations of this Act shall be investigated by the Federal Bureau of Investigation of the Department of Justice.

(6) This section shall not exclude the applicable provisions of any other laws, except that no Government agency shall take any action under such other laws inconsistent with the provisions of this section.

(*c*) INSPECTIONS, RECORDS, AND REPORTS. — The Commission is —

(1) authorized by regulation or order to require such reports and the keeping of such records with respect to, and to provide for such inspections of, activities and studies of types specified in section 3 and of activities under licenses issued pursuant to section 7 as may be necessary to effectuate the purposes of this Act;

(2) authorized and directed by regulation or order to require regular reports and records with respect to, and to provide for frequent inspections of, the production of fissionable material in the conduct of research and development activities.

PATENTS AND INVENTIONS

SEC. 11. (*a*) PRODUCTION AND MILITARY UTILIZATION. —

(1) No patent shall hereafter be granted for any invention or discovery which is useful solely in the production of fissionable material

or in the utilization of fissionable material or atomic energy for a military weapon. Any patent granted for any such invention or discovery is hereby revoked, and just compensation shall be made therefor.

(2) No patents hereafter granted shall confer any rights with respect to any invention or discovery to the extent that such invention or discovery is used in the production of fissionable material or in the utilization of fissionable material or atomic energy for a military weapon. Any rights conferred by any patent heretofore granted for any invention or discovery are hereby revoked to the extent that such invention or discovery is so used, and just compensation shall be made therefor.

(3) Any person who has made or hereafter makes any invention or discovery useful in the production of fissionable material or in the utilization of fissionable material or atomic energy for a military weapon shall file with the Commission a report containing a complete description thereof, unless such invention or discovery is described in an application for a patent filed in the Patent Office by such person within the time required for the filing of such report. The report covering any such invention or discovery shall be filed on or before whichever of the following is the latest: (A) The sixtieth day after the date of enactment of this Act; (B) the sixtieth day after the completion of such invention or discovery; or (C) the sixtieth day after such person first discovers or first has reason to believe that such invention or discovery is useful in such production or utilization.

(*b*) USE OF INVENTIONS FOR RESEARCH. — No patent hereafter granted shall confer any rights with respect to any invention or discovery to the extent that such invention or discovery is used in the conduct or research or development activities in the fields specified in section 3. Any rights conferred by any patent heretofore granted for any invention or discovery are hereby revoked to the extent that such invention or discovery is so used, and just compensation shall be made therefor.

(*c*) NONMILITARY UTILIZATION. —

(1) It shall be the duty of the Commission to declare any patent to be affected with the public interest if (A) the invention or discovery covered by the patent utilizes or is essential in the utilization of fissionable material or atomic energy; and (B) the licensing of such invention or discovery under this subsection is necessary to effectuate the policies and purposes of this Act.

(2) Whenever any patent has been declared, pursuant to paragraph (1), to be affected with the public interest —

(A) The Commission is hereby licensed to use the invention or discovery covered by such patent in performing any of its powers under this Act; and

(B) Any person to whom a license has been issued under section 7 is hereby licensed to use the invention or discovery covered by such patent to the extent such invention or discovery is used by him in carrying on the activities authorized by his license under section 7.

The owner of the patent shall be entitled to a reasonable royalty fee for any use of an invention or discovery licensed by this subsection. Such royalty fee may be agreed upon by such owner and the licensee, or in the absence of such agreement shall be determined by the Commission.

(3) No court shall have jurisdiction or power to stay, restrain, or otherwise enjoin the use of any invention or discovery by a licensee, to the extent that such use is licensed by paragraph (2) above, on the ground of infringement of any patent. If in any action for infringement against such licensee the court shall determine that the defendant is exercising such license, the measure of damages shall be the royalty fee determined pursuant to this section, together with such costs, interest, and reasonable attorney's fees as may be fixed by the court. If no royalty fee has been determined, the court shall stay the proceeding until the royalty fee is determined pursuant to this section. If any such licensee shall fail to pay such royalty fee, the patentee may bring action in any court of competent jurisdiction for such royalty fee, together with such costs, interest, and reasonable attorney's fees as may be fixed by the court.

(d) ACQUISITION OF PATENTS. — The Commission is authorized to purchase, or to take, requisition, or condemn, and make just compensation for, (1) any invention or discovery which is useful in the production of fissionable material or in the utilization of fissionable material or atomic energy for a military weapon, or which utilizes or is essential in the utilization of fissionable material or atomic energy, or (2) any patent or patent application covering any such invention or discovery. The Commissioner of Patents shall notify the Commission of all applications for patents heretofore or hereafter filed which in his opinion disclose such inventions or discoveries and shall provide the Commission access to all such applications.

(e) COMPENSATION AWARDS, AND ROYALTIES. —

(1) PATENT COMPENSATION BOARD. — The Commission shall designate a Patent Compensation Board, consisting of two or more employees of the Commission, to consider applications under this subsection.

(2) ELIGIBILITY. —

(A) Any owner of a patent licensed under subsection (c) (2) or any licensee thereunder may make application to the Commission for the determination of a reasonable royalty fee in accordance with such procedures as it by regulation may establish.

(B) Any person seeking to obtain the just compensation provided in subsections (a), (b), or (d) shall make application therefor to the Commission in accordance with such procedures as it may by regulation establish.

(C) Any person making any invention or discovery useful in the production of fissionable material or in the utilization of fissionable material or atomic energy for a military weapon who is not entitled to compensation therefor under subsection (a) and who has complied with subsection (a) (3) above may make application to the Commission for, and the Commission may grant, an award.

(D) Any person making application under this subsection shall have the right to be represented by counsel.

(3) STANDARDS. —

(A) In determining such reasonable royalty fee, the Commission shall take into consideration any defense, general or special, that might be pleaded by a defendant in an action for infringement, the extent to which, if any, such patent was developed through federally financed research, the degree of utility, novelty, and importance of the invention or discovery, and may consider the cost to the owner of the patent of developing such invention or discovery or acquiring such patent.

(B) In determining what constitutes just compensation under subsection (*a*), (*b*), or (*d*) above, the Commission shall take into account the considerations set forth in paragraph (A) above, and the actual use of such invention or discovery, and may determine that such compensation be paid in periodic payments or in a lump sum.

(C) In determining the amount of any award under paragraph (2) (C) of this subsection, the Commission shall take into account the considerations set forth in paragraph (A) above, and the actual use of such invention or discovery. Awards so made may be paid by the Commission in periodic payments or in a lump sum.

(4) JUDICIAL REVIEW. — Any person aggrieved by any determination of the Commission of an award or of a reasonable royalty fee may obtain a review of such determination in the Court of Appeals for the District of Columbia by filing in such court, within thirty days after notice of such determination, a written petition praying that such determination be set aside. A copy of such petition shall be forthwith served upon the Commission and thereupon the Commission shall file with the court a certified transcript of the entire record in the proceeding, including the findings and conclusions upon which the determination was based. Upon the filing of such transcript the court shall have exclusive jurisdiction upon the record certified to it to affirm the determination in its entirety or set it aside and remand it to the Commission for further proceedings. The findings of the Commission as to the facts, if supported by substantial evidence, shall be conclusive. The court's judgment shall be final, subject, however, to review by the Supreme Court of the United States upon writ of certiorari on petition therefor under section 240 of the Judicial Code (U. S. C., title 28, sec. 347), by the Commission or any party to the court proceeding.

GENERAL AUTHORITY

SEC. 12. (*a*) In the performance of its functions the Commission is authorized to —

(1) establish advisory boards to advise with and make recommendations to the Commission on legislation, policies, administration, research, and other matters;

(2) establish by regulation or order such standards and instructions to govern the possession and use of fissionable and byproduct materials as the Commission may deem necessary or desirable to protect health or to minimize danger from explosions and other hazards to life or property;

(3) make such studies and investigations, obtain such information, and hold such hearings as the Commission may deem necessary or proper to assist it in exercising any authority provided in this Act, or in the administration or enforcement of this Act, or any regulations or orders issued thereunder. For such purposes the Commission is

authorized to administer oaths and affirmations, and by subpena to require any person to appear and testify, or to appear and produce documents, or both, at any designated place. No person shall be excused from complying with any requirements under this paragraph because of his privilege against self-incrimination, but the immunity provisions of the Compulsory Testimony Act of February 11, 1893 (U. S. C., title 49, sec. 46), shall apply with respect to any individual who specifically claims such privilege. Witnesses subpenaed under this subsection shall be paid the same fees and mileage as are paid witnesses in the district courts of the United States;

(4) appoint and fix the compensation of such officers and employees as may be necessary to carry out the functions of the Commission. Such officers and employees shall be appointed in accordance with the civil-service laws and their compensation fixed in accordance with the Classification Act of 1923, as amended, except that to the extent the Commission deems such action necessary to the discharge of its responsibilities, personnel may be employed and their compensation fixed without regard to such laws. The Commission shall make adequate provision for administrative review of any determination to dismiss any employee;

(5) acquire such materials, property, equipment, and facilities, establish or construct such buildings and facilities, and modify such buildings and facilities from time to time as it may deem necessary, and construct, acquire, provide, or arrange for such facilities and services (at project sites where such facilities and services are not available) for the housing, health, safety, welfare, and recreation of personnel employed by the Commission as it may deem necessary;

(6) with the consent of the agency concerned, utilize or employ the services or personnel of any Government agency or any State or local government, or voluntary or uncompensated personnel, to perform such functions on its behalf as may appear desirable;

(7) acquire, purchase, lease, and hold real and personal property as agent of and on behalf of the United States and to sell, lease, grant, and dispose of such real and personal property as provided in this Act; and

(8) without regard to the provisions of the Surplus Property Act of 1944 or any other law, make such disposition as it may deem desirable of (A) radioactive materials, and (B) any other property the special disposition of which is, in the opinion of the Commission, in the interest of the national security.

(b) SECURITY. — The President may, in advance, exempt any specific action of the Commission in a particular matter from the provisions of law relating to contracts whenever he determines that such action is essential in the interest of the common defense and security.

(c) ADVISORY COMMITTEES. — The members of the General Advisory Committee established pursuant to section 2 (b) and the members of advisory boards established pursuant to subsection (a) (1) of this section may serve as such without regard to the provisions of sections 109 and 113 of the Criminal Code (18 U. S. C., secs. 198 and 203) or section 19 (e) of the Contract Settlement Act of 1944, except insofar as such sections may prohibit any such member from receiving compensation in respect of any particular matter which directly involves the Commission or in which the Commission is directly interested.

COMPENSATION FOR PRIVATE PROPERTY ACQUIRED

SEC. 13. (a) The United States shall make just compensation for any property or interests therein taken or requisitioned pursuant to sections 5 and 11. The Commission shall determine such compensation. If the compensation so determined is unsatisfactory to the person entitled thereto, such person shall be paid 50 per centum of the amount so determined, and shall be entitled to sue the United States in the Court of Claims or in any district court of the United States in the manner provided by sections 24 (20) and 145 of the Judicial Code to recover such further sum as added to said 50 per centum will make up such amount as will be just compensation.

(b) In the exercise of the rights of eminent domain and condemnation, proceedings may be instituted under the Act of August 1, 1888 (U. S. C., title 40, sec. 257), or any other applicable Federal statute. Upon or after the filing of the condemnation petition, immediate possession may be taken and the property may be occupied, used, and improved for the purposes of this Act, notwithstanding any other law. Real property acquired by purchase, donation, or other means of transfer may also be occupied, used, and improved for the purposes of this Act, prior to approval of title by the Attorney General.

JUDICIAL REVIEW AND ADMINISTRATIVE PROCEDURE

SEC. 14. (a) Notwithstanding the provisions of section 12 of the Administrative Procedure Act (Public Law 404, Seventy-ninth Congress, approved June 11, 1946) which provide when such Act shall take effect, section 10 of such Act (relating to judicial review) shall be applicable, upon the enactment of this Act, to any agency action under the authority of this Act or by any agency created by or under the provisions of this Act.

(b) Except as provided in subsection (a), no provision of this Act shall be held to supersede or modify the provisions of the Administrative Procedure Act.

(c) As used in this section the terms "agency action" and "agency" shall have the same meaning as is assigned to such terms in the Administrative Procedure Act.

JOINT COMMITTEE ON ATOMIC ENERGY

SEC. 15. (a) There is hereby established a Joint Committee on Atomic Energy to be composed of nine Members of the Senate to be appointed by the President of the Senate, and nine Members of the House of Representatives to be appointed by the Speaker of the House of Representatives. In each instance not more than five members shall be members of the same political party.

(b) The joint committee shall make continuing studies of the activities of the Atomic Energy Commission and of problems relating to the development, use, and control of atomic energy. The Commission shall keep the joint committee fully and currently informed with respect to the Commission's activities. All bills, resolutions, and other matters in the Senate or the House of Representatives relating primarily to the Commission or to the development, use, or control of atomic energy shall be referred to the joint committee. The members of the joint committee who are Members of the Senate shall from time to time report to the Senate, and the members of the joint committee who are Members of the House of Representatives shall from time to time report to the House, by bill or otherwise, their recommendations with respect to matters within the jurisdiction of their respective Houses which are (1) referred to the joint committee or (2) otherwise within the jurisdiction of the joint committee.

(c) Vacancies in the membership of the joint committee shall not affect the power of the remaining members to execute the functions of the joint committee, and shall be filled in the same manner as in the case of the original selection. The joint committee shall select a chairman and a vice chairman from among its members.

(d) The joint committee, or any duly authorized subcommittee thereof, is authorized to hold such hearings, to sit and act at such places and times, to require, by subpena or otherwise, the attendance of such witnesses and the production of such books, papers, and documents, to administer such oaths, to take such testimony, to procure such printing and binding, and to make such expenditures as it deems advisable. The cost of stenographic services to report such hearings shall not be in excess of 25 cents per hundred words. The provisions of section 102 to 104, inclusive, of the Revised Statutes shall apply in case of any failure of any witness to comply with a subpena or to testify when summoned under authority of this section.

(e) The joint committee is empowered to appoint and fix the compensation of such experts, consultants, technicians, and clerical and stenographic assistants as it deems necessary and advisable, but the compensation so fixed shall not exceed the compensation prescribed under the Classification Act of 1923, as amended, for comparable duties. The committee is authorized to utilize the services, information, facilities, and personnel of the departments and establishments of the Government.

ENFORCEMENT

SEC. 16. (a) Whoever willfully violates, attempts to violate, or conspires to violate, any provision of sections 4 (b), 4 (e), 5 (a) (3), or 6 (b) shall, upon conviction thereof, be punished by a fine of not more than $10,000 or by imprisonment for not more than five years, or both, except that whoever commits such an offense with intent to injure the United States or with intent to secure an advantage to any foreign nation shall, upon conviction thereof, be punished by death or imprisonment for life (but the penalty of death or imprisonment for life may be imposed only upon recommendation of the jury and only in cases where the offense was committed with intent to injure the United States); or by a fine of not more than $20,000 or by imprisonment for not more than twenty years, or both.

(b) Whoever willfully violates, attempts to violate, or conspires to violate, any provision of this Act other than those specified in subsection (a) and other than section 10 (b), or of any regulation or order prescribed or issued under sections 5 (b) (4), 10 (c), or 12 (a) (2), shall, upon conviction thereof, be punished by a fine of not more than $5,000 or by imprisonment for not more than two years, or both, except that whoever commits such an offense with intent to injure the United States or with intent to secure an advantage to any foreign nation shall, upon conviction thereof, be punished by a fine of not more than $20,000 or by imprisonment for not more than twenty years, or both.

(c) Whenever in the judgment of the Commission any person has engaged or is about to engage in any acts or practices which constitute or will constitute a violation of any provision of this Act, or any regulation or order issued thereunder, it may make application to the appropriate court for an order enjoining such acts or practices, or for an order enforcing compliance with such provision, and upon a showing by the Commission that such person has engaged or is about to engage in any such acts or practices a permanent or temporary injunction, restraining order, or other order may be granted.

(d) In case of failure or refusal to obey a subpena served upon any person pursuant to section 12 (a) (3), the district court for any district in which such person is found or resides or transacts business, upon application by the Commission, shall have jurisdiction to issue an order requiring such person to appear and give testimony or to appear and produce documents, or both, in accordance with the subpena; and any failure to obey such order of the court may be punished by such court as a contempt thereof.

REPORTS

SEC. 17. The Commission shall submit to the Congress, in January and July of each year, a report concerning the activities of the Commission. The Commission shall include in such report, and shall at such other times as it deems desirable submit to the Congress, such recommendations for additional legislation as the Commission deems necessary or desirable.

DEFINITIONS

SEC. 18. As used in this Act —
(a) The term "atomic energy" shall be construed to mean all forms of energy released in the course of or as a result of nuclear fission or nuclear transformation.
(b) The term "Government agency" means any executive department, commission, independent establishment, corporation wholly or partly owned by the United States which is an instrumentality of the United States, board, bureau, division, service, office, officer, authority, admin-

istration, or other establishment, in the executive branch of the Government.

(c) The term "person" means any individual, corporation, partnership, firm, association, trust, estate, public or private institution, group, the United States or any agency thereof, any government other than the United States, any political subdivision of any such government, and any legal successor, representative, agent, or agency of the foregoing, or other entity, but shall not include the Commission or officers or employees of the Commission in the exercise of duly authorized functions.

(d) The term "United States," when used in a geographical sense, includes all Territories and possessions of the United States and the Canal Zone.

(e) The term "research and development" means theoretical analysis, exploration, and experimentation, and the extension of investigative findings and theories of a scientific or technical nature into practical application for experimental and demonstration purposes, including the experimental production and testing of models, devices, equipment, materials, and processes.

(f) The term "equipment or device utilizing fissionable material or atomic energy" shall be construed to mean any equipment or device capable of making use of fissionable material or peculiarly adapted for making use of atomic energy and any important component part especially designed for such equipment or devices, as determined by the Commission.

(g) The term "facilities for the production of fissionable material" shall be construed to mean any equipment or device capable of such production and any important component part especially designed for such equipment or devices, as determined by the Commission.

APPROPRIATIONS

SEC. 19. There are hereby authorized to be appropriated such sums as may be necessary and appropriate to carry out the provisions and purposes of this Act. The Acts appropriating such sums may appropriate specified portions thereof to be accounted for upon the certification of the Commission only. Funds appropriated to the Commission shall, if obligated by contract during the fiscal year for which appropriated, remain available for expenditure for four years following the expiration of the fiscal year for which appropriated. After such four-year period, the unexpended balances of appropriations shall be carried to the surplus fund and covered into the Treasury.

SEPARABILITY OF PROVISIONS

SEC. 20. If any provision of this Act, or the application of such provision to any person or circumstances, is held invalid, the remainder of this Act or the application of such provision to persons or circumstances other than those as to which it is held invalid, shall not be affected thereby.

SHORT TITLE

SEC. 21. This Act may be cited as the "Atomic Energy Act of 1946."

(5) Executive Order 9816, Providing for the Transfer of Property and Personnel to the Atomic Energy Commission, December 31, 1946.[1]

By virtue of the authority vested in me by the Constitution and the statutes, including the Atomic Energy Act of 1946, and as President of the United States and Commander in Chief of the Army and the Navy, it is hereby ordered and directed as follows:

1. There are transferred to the Atomic Energy Commission all interests owned by the United States or any Government agency in the following property:

(a) All fissionable material; all atomic weapons and parts thereof; all facilities, equipment, and materials for the processing, production, or utilization of fissionable material or atomic energy; all processes and technical information of any kind, and the source thereof (including data, drawings, specifications, patents, patent applications, and other sources) relating to the processing, production, or utilization of fissionable material or atomic energy; and all contracts, agreements, leases, patents, applications for patents, inventions and discoveries (whether patented or unpatented), and other rights of any kind concerning any such items.

(b) All facilities, equipment, and materials, devoted primarily to atomic energy research and development.

2. There also are transferred to the Atomic Energy Commission all property, real or personal, tangible or intangible, including records, owned by or in the possession, custody or control of the Manhattan Engineer District, War Department, in addition to the property described in paragraph 1 above. Specific items of such property, including records, may be excepted from transfer to the Commission in the following manner:

(a) The Secretary of War shall notify the Commission in writing as to the specific items of property or records he wishes to except; and

(b) If after full examination of the facts by the Commission, it concurs in the exception, those specific items of property or records shall be excepted from transfer to the Commission; or

(c) If after full examination of the facts by the Commission, it does not concur in the exception, the matter shall be referred to the President for decision.

3. The Atomic Energy Commission shall exercise full jurisdiction over all interests and property transferred to the Commission in paragraphs 1 and 2 above, in accordance with the provisions of the Atomic Energy Act of 1946.

4. Any Government agency is authorized to transfer to the Atomic Energy Commission, at the request of the Commission, any property, real or personal, tangible or intangible, acquired or used by such Government agency in connection with any of the property or interests transferred to the Commission by paragraphs 1 and 2 above.

5. Each Government agency shall supply the Atomic Energy Commission with a report on, and an accounting and inventory of, all interests

---
[1] *Federal Register*, XII, p. 37.

and property, described in paragraphs 1, 2 and 4 above, owned by or in the possession, custody or control of such Government agency, the form and detail of such report, accounting and inventory, to be determined by mutual agreement, or, in case of nonagreement, by the Director of the Bureau of the Budget.

6. (*a*) There also are transferred to the Atomic Energy Commission, all civilian officers and employees of the Manhattan Engineer District, War Department, except that the Commission and the Secretary of War may by mutual agreement exclude any of such personnel from transfer to the Commission.

(*b*) The military and naval personnel heretofore assigned or detailed to the Manhattan Engineer District, War Department, shall continue to be made available to the Commission, for military and naval duty, in similar manner, without prejudice to the military or naval status of such personnel, for such periods of time as may be agreed mutually by the Commission and the Secretary of War or the Secretary of the Navy.

7. The assistance and the services, personal or other, including the use of property, heretofore made available by any Government agency to the Manhattan Engineer District, War Department, shall be made available to the Atomic Energy Commission for the same purposes as heretofore and under the arrangements now existing until terminated after 30 days' notice given by the Commission or by the Government agency concerned in each case.

8. The Commission is authorized to exercise all the powers and functions vested in the Secretary of War by Executive Order No. 9001, of December 27, 1941, as amended, in so far as they relate to contracts heretofore made by or hereby transferred to the Commission.

9. Such further measures and dispositions as may be determined by the Atomic Energy Commission and any Government agency concerned to be necessary to effectuate the transfers authorized or directed by this order shall be carried out in such manner as the Director of the Bureau of the Budget may direct and by such agencies as he may designate.

10. This order shall be effective as of midnight, December 31, 1946.

C. The Bikini Tests

The first official disclosure of the details of the atom bomb tests held at Bikini Atoll was made by Vice Admiral William H. P. Blandy before the Senate's Special Committee on Atomic Energy, on January 24, 1946. In order to give Congressional sanction to the proposed experiments, Representative Carl Vinson (Georgia), Chairman of the Committee on Naval Affairs of the House of Representatives, introduced, on January 28, a Joint Resolution (H. J. Res. 307) authorizing the use of naval vessels in the tests. The Resolution was committed to the House Committee on Naval Affairs and, amended to "insure that no release of information pertaining to these tests shall be made to foreign governments or nationals except such as the Secretaries [of War and of the Navy] may determine to be not prejudicial to the best interest of the United States," was reported favorably to the House on February 1.[1]

[1] House Report No. 1514, 79th Cong., 2d sess.

On February 7, Senator Brien MacMahon, Chairman of the Senate's Special Committee and sponsor of the MacMahon Bill for the control of atomic energy,[1] announced his proposal to President Truman that "an independent commission of outstanding scientists and engineers be appointed" to evaluate the results of the tests.[2] President Truman accepted this proposal, February 18.[3]

Plans and preparations for the tests, tentatively scheduled for early May and July, were carried out under the direction of the Joint Chiefs of Staff. Admiral Blandy was designated commander of Joint Task Force One, the combined personnel of the navy, army, air force and scientific groups responsible for the actual performance of the experiment.

The Vinson Resolution, as amended and approved by the House of Representatives, was transmitted to the Senate where, on March 19, hearings were held before the Committee on Naval Affairs. With slight amendments, the Resolution was favorably reported the following day.[4]

On March 23, President Truman announced that the actual conduct of "Operations Crossroads" would be delayed "about six weeks" since "a large number of Congressmen have expressed a desire to witness both these tests but owing to the heavy legislative schedule would be prevented from doing so if the tests were held on the dates originally fixed."[5] This announcement was immediately followed by a move in the Senate, led by Senator Huffman to prohibit the tests altogether, on the ground that the world did "not need further evidence of the atomic bomb's effectiveness."[6] Despite this announcement, the President, on March 25, named the membership of the civilian Evaluation Commission proposed by Senator MacMahon. The Commission included: Senators Carl Hatch and Leverett Saltonstall; Representatives Andrew May and Walter G. Andrews; Dr. Karl T. Compton, President, Massachusetts Institute of Technology; Bradley Dewey, Rubber Director, War Production Board; Dr. J. R. Oppenheimer, Professor of Physics, University of California, and pioneer in the field of nuclear physics; William S. Newel, President, Bath Iron Works Corporation, Bath, Maine; and Fred Searles, Jr., Special Assistant to the Secretary of State.[7] Rep. May was later replaced by Rep. Chet Holifield. Senator Huffman's proposal to cancel the tests completely was, in the meantime, gaining further support in the Senate. Senator Walsh, Chairman of the Senate Committee on Naval Affairs, saw "no objection to the [Huffman] resolution", and indicated that he might re-open the hearings on the Vinson Resolution which was at that time on the Senate Calendar awaiting call. Senator Huffman, stating that "this is no time for martial gestures", suggested postponement of the tests "until the cause of international cooperation for a firm and lasting peace has been given every opportunity to succeed." Senator Scott Lucas backed Senators Walsh and Huffman and asked the Senate to consider "the reaction in the United States if another nation held the atomic bomb in monopoly and conducted experiments such as are now projected."[8] President Truman, however, on April 12, affirmed the plans for the tests.[9] At the same time, the Vinson Resolution was re-committed to the Senate Naval Affairs Committee and further hearings were held. The Resolution was favorably reported on April 24, with an amendment limiting to thirty-three the number of combatant ships to be employed as targets.[10] The Resolution was subsequently approved, June 25.[11]

After considerable discussion and debate, it was decided that foreign observers, representing the members of the United Nations Atomic Energy Commission,

[1] See this volume, p. 422.
[2] *New York Times*, February 8, 1946, p. 12.
[3] *Ibid.*, February 19, 1946, p. 1.
[4] Senate Report No. 1071, 79th Cong., 2d sess.
[5] Department of State, *Bulletin*, XIV, p. 560.
[6] *New York Times*, March 24, 1946, p. 1.
[7] Department of State, *Bulletin*, *ibid.*
[8] *New York Times*, March 30, 1946, p. 1.
[9] Department of State, *Bulletin*, XIV, p. 667.
[10] Senate Report No. 1238, 79th Cong., 2d sess.
[11] For the text of the Resolution as approved, see this volume, p. 457.

should be invited to witness the tests.[1] The nations invited by the Department of State on May 7 included: Australia, Brazil, Canada, China, Egypt, France, Mexico, the Netherlands, Poland, the Union of Soviet Socialist Republics and the United Kingdom.[2] On June 19, an invitation was also extended to Trygve Lie, Secretary General of the United Nations.[3]

The first test, an air drop over the target fleet assembled in Bikini lagoon, was made on July 1; and the second, an underwater detonation at shallow depth, followed on July 25.[4] The third test, an underwater detonation at great depth, was indefinitely postponed according to an announcement by the President on September 6.[5]

(1) *Joint Resolution to Authorize the Use of Naval Vessels to Determine the Effect of Atomic Weapons upon Such Vessels, Approved June 25, 1946.*[6]

Resolved by the Senate and House of Representatives of the United States of America in Congress assembled, That the Secretary of the Navy, with the approval of the President, is authorized to employ vessels of the Navy as targets for purposes of test and experimentation in determining the effect of atomic weapons upon such vessels.

SEC. 2. After employment pursuant to authority contained in section 1 of this Act vessels may, in the discretion of the Secretary of the Navy or such other person as may be designated by him, be —

(a) sunk if considered unseaworthy; or

(b) retained with or without repair for further test and experimentation, for further naval use, or for other disposition in accordance with other provisions of law.

SEC. 3. The number of combatant vessels, exclusive of those received from foreign governments, which may be employed as targets for the purposes set forth in section 1 of this joint resolution, is limited to thirty-three. The term "combatant vessels" for purposes of this section is defined as naval vessels of the following categories: Battleships, cruisers, aircraft carriers, destroyers, and submarines.

SEC. 4. The Secretaries of War and of the Navy shall take such measures as they deem necessary to safeguard the information, observations, findings, conclusions, and recommendations pertaining to and resulting from these tests and which are of a military nature as would normally be attached to any other vital military information or military secret.

SEC. 4A. The President, in his discretion, may appoint an advisory board to cooperate with the Secretaries of War and of the Navy in the conduct of these tests, to undertake an independent study of the tests and to submit its observations, findings, conclusions, and recommendations to the Secretaries of War and of the Navy. This advisory board shall be composed of —

(a) five civilians, one of whom shall be designated as chairman of the advisory board;

[1] *New York Times,* January 30, 1946, p. 12.
[2] Department of State, *Bulletin,* XIV, p. 864.
[3] *Ibid.,* p. 1130.
[4] For the texts of the preliminary reports of the President's Evaluation Commission, see this volume, p. 458 and 459.
[5] For the text of the President's announcement, see *ibid.,* p. 461.
[6] Public Law 442, 79th Cong., 2d sess.

(b) three naval officers, at least one of whom shall be a naval aviator; and

(c) three Army officers, at least one of whom shall be an Army aviator.

SEC. 5. Such provisions of this joint resolution as relate to the employment of vessels of the Navy as targets shall terminate two years after the date of its enactment into law.

(2) *Preliminary Report of the President's Evaluation Commission on the First Bikini Test, July 1, 1946. White House Press Release, July 11, 1946.*[1]

Your Evaluation Commission, divided between positions at sea and in the air, witnessed the First Bikini Test, at 33 seconds after 9:00 A.M. local time on July 1st, and has since completed a survey of the damage. The Second Test, wherein the bomb will be exploded under water, will in some respects be of even greater interest, for it will have no precedent.

The report of your Commission required by its directive of May 18th must await the assembling of considerable data deriving from instrumental and photographic measurements and analysis of fission product samples. However, we believe that it lies within the scope of your directive and may be of possible assistance to you, to submit, now, the following brief observations made from the layman's point of view, but with such accuracy as is presently available:

1. The organization and execution of the operation was magnificently handled and has commanded our continuous admiration. The bomb was dropped under favorable weather conditions about 30 seconds after the time set. The greatest credit is due Admiral Blandy and the officers and enlisted personnel of both services who, with scientists and other civilians, have served and are serving under him with a display of team work that must be seen to be fully appreciated.

2. Their conservatively safe distance from the burst led many observers to entertain an initial opinion that the bomb employed was somewhat under par. It is now, however, safe to state that the energy was of the same order of magnitude as in the case of previous atomic detonations, between the highest and lowest of this bomb's three predecessors.

3. The accuracy of the drop was such that the explosion occurred within the area included within the allowance for the probable error of the elevation of drop, and detonation was probably within 100 feet of the chosen altitude. Nevertheless, the explosion actually occurred several hundred yards west of a point directly above the target ship *Nevada* and therefore entirely west of the closely spaced array of capital ships.

4. There were 90 targets anchored in the lagoon when the bomb exploded. These were not in battle formation but were placed in positions to give the largest amount of desired technical information with especially close concentration around the center target point. Those ships anchored a mile or more from the point of drop largely escaped injury. Those within a mile were sunk or suffered damage

[1] Department of State, *Bulletin*, XV, p. 115.

varying with the distance from the point of detonation and with the type of ship construction. On explosion, a destroyer and two transports sank promptly. A second destroyer and the Japanese cruiser *Sakawa* sank within twenty-seven hours. The light carrier *Independence* was gutted with fire and resultant explosions. The submarine *Skate* was heavily damaged and later towed away. All of these were near the point of explosion. The other ships, including the only two capital ships which were within one-half mile of the detonation, received damage that would require more or less complete overhaul and in most cases repair at major bases before they could again be used for combat. A study of this damage will point the way to changes in design which should minimize damage from blast and heat. Beyond these ships there was extensive damage to superstructure, radar, and fire control. Had the ships within the damage area been manned, casualties and psychological injuries would have required a large percentage of replacements. Until the readings of complex instruments and the future life history of animals within the ships have been determined no accurate appraisal of potential damage to humans within the ships can be made.

5. No wave or blast damage could be noticed on Bikini Island, which is approximately three miles from the point of detonation.

6. We are of the unanimous opinion that the first test amply justified the expenditure required to conduct it and that the second test is equally desirable and necessary. You made a wise decision when you approved the plans for these tests and they have been carried out with extraordinary skill, diligence and ingenuity. The test just completed has again proven that the atomic bomb is a weapon of terrific power when used on land or sea.

(3) **Preliminary Report of the President's Evaluation Commission on the Second Bikini Test, July 25, 1946. Press Release, August 2, 1946.**[1]

Your acknowledgment on July 7th of our preliminary report on the first test at Bikini was much appreciated.

The second test was conducted in the same area, July 25 local time, and on the same target ships less those sunk in the first test. The bomb was exploded under a moderate depth of water at 8:30 a. m. local time, on schedule. Weather conditions were perfect. Seven members of your committee witnessed the results from the USS *Haven* stationed 11 miles from the point where the bomb exploded. There was no requirement of dark glasses for this test, and the target ships were readily visible to the naked eye and easily distinguishable with the aid of binoculars.

Our previous report endeavored to express our appreciation of the cooperation, assistance and unfailing courtesy extended by Admiral Blandy and by the officers and enlisted men and civilian scientific personnel of Joint Task Force One. Throughout, this attitude of interest and diligence has remained at the same high level, and the effect of longer observation of operations and better acquaintance with officers and men

[1] *Ibid.*, p. 272.

has been to convince us that you and the people of the United States can place the utmost reliance on the fairness, thoroughness and real effort for the maximum of honest information which has characterized these tests. This disposition has expedited and lightened our task in complying with your directive. These tests have consistently adhered to the stated purpose of the mission: "Primarily to determine the effects of the atomic bomb on naval vessels in order to gain information of value to the national defense."

In the interval between tests the target ships were redeployed in respect to the point chosen for the second explosion, so as to furnish maximum scientific and technical information from expected results.

When the bomb exploded, the battleship *Arkansas*, nearest to the center of impact, and three other smaller ships sank at once. The aircraft carrier *Saratoga*, also placed close by, sank $7\frac{1}{2}$ hours later. As soon as radioactivity lessened sufficiently to permit safe operations, the destroyer *Hughes* and the attack transport *Fallon* were beached to prevent their possible sinking. Of the eight submarines involved, six were submerged. Several of these appear to be injured and one at least has gone to the bottom. The two on the surface are not noticeably injured. All but a few of the target ships were drenched with radioactive sea water, and all within the zone of evident damage are still unsafe to board. It is estimated that the radioactivity dispersed in the water was the equivalent to that from many hundred tons of radium.

We believe that interesting distinctions between the general results of the two explosions can even now be drawn without the risk of serious error. Both explosions sank several ships. From the limited observation we have thus far been able to make, the ships remaining afloat within the damage area appear to have been more seriously damaged by the aerial explosion than by the submarine explosion. The damage to ships in the first test might have been far greater if the bomb had exploded directly over the target ship, the *Nevada*.

In the first test much of the personnel within the ships would have received fatal doses of neutrons and gamma rays from the first deadly flash. On the other hand, the deadly effects of persistent radioactivity would have been much more severe in the second test. Had the target array been manned, it seems clear that casualties and both physical and psychological injury to personnel would have been very great. Rescue and attention to casualties would be difficult and dangerous. Within 2,000 yards of explosion, ships would probably have been inoperative and a lapse of weeks might well ensue before relatively undamaged ships could again be used in combat.

The second bomb caused a deluge of water loaded with deadly radioactive elements over an area that embraced 90 percent of the target array. Such results might be as disastrous to the fleet as results of the first test, although in part for different reasons. An enemy possessed of two or more bombs might well so dispose them as to create simultaneously the deadly features of both tests. Such tactics might effectively dispose of a fleet for many months; for example, consider a Pearl Harbor attack on these lines.

The results of both tests are already under study by the Bureau of Ships and will undoubtedly point the way to changes in ships' size, design and structure, both above and below the water line. Such changes can offer increased immunity to flash and blast effect, but protection from catastrophe by deadly gamma and neutron radiations lies rather in wide spacing of task forces and decentralization of navy yards, repair and loading facilities, of ships within ports, and amongst all available harbors. We are convinced distance is the best defense.

As was demonstrated by the terrible havoc wrought at Hiroshima and Nagasaki, the Bikini tests strongly indicate that future wars employing atomic bombs may well destroy nations and change present standards of civilization. To us who have witnessed the devastating effects of these tests, it is evident that if there is to be any security or safety in the world, war must be eliminated as a means of settling differences among nations.

(4) *Announcement of the Postponement of the Third Bikini Test. White House Press Release, September 6, 1946.*[1]

In view of the successful completion of the first two atomic-bomb tests of Operation Crossroads and the information derived therefrom, the Joint Chiefs of Staff have concluded that the third explosion, test "C", should not be conducted in the near future. The information obtained from tests "A" and "B", together with the knowledge derived from the original experimental test in New Mexico and from study of the results of the explosions in Hiroshima and Nagasaki, will enable our scientific and military experts to make a proper evaluation of the effects of this weapon.

The additional information of value expected to result from test "C" is such that the Joint Chiefs of Staff do not feel that completion of this test in the near future is justified.

The Joint Chiefs of Staff are extremely gratified by the conduct and results of the atomic-bomb tests and consider the entire operation an unqualified success.

The invaluable assistance of the civilian scientific personnel and the inter-service cooperation toward a common end were major factors in achieving this success.

2. MAINTENANCE OF DEFENSE

A. General Statements

(1) *Statement of the Secretary of War (Patterson) before the Committee on Military Affairs of the House of Representatives, November 8, 1945.*[2]

[Excerpt]

. . . . . .

There is unanimous agreement among the men who led our troops to victory in World War II that our plans for a future emergency must be based on the following assumptions:

1. The United States will be the first target of attack.

[1] *Ibid.*, p. 508.
[2] *Universal Military Training. Hearings before the Committee on Military Affairs, House of Representatives, Seventy-Ninth Congress, First Session on H. R. 515 . . ., Part I*, p. 3.

2. The attack may come with lightning speed and may make use of weapons of great power and guided missiles launched at great distance from our coasts and sighted with electronic devices of extreme accuracy.

3. Our ability to survive may depend not only on our ability to retaliate in kind but even more on our ability to mount an immediate counteroffensive that will enable us to establish control of the enemy's launching sites and production facilities.

4. Time will be the most important element. In the war just ended a quarter of a million American fighting men gave their lives on foreign battlefields. If war comes again more than that number of men, women and children may be wiped out in a single day in their own homes. There will be no time in which to prepare for the successful defense of our country if we wait until we are in danger.

I do not make these statements to be melodramatic. They represent the sober conclusions of the War Department's studies and they indicate the essential requirements of a military program that will enable the United States to discharge its obligations to itself and to the cause of world peace until such time as we are able to place sole reliance in international commitments to outlaw war.

To be realistic, such a military program must include the following elements:

First, an alert and integrated intelligence service that will keep us informed of hostile moves anywhere in the world, whether these be military, economic, political or scientific, and that will assist us in keeping abreast of new developments in warfare. The primary aim of this service would be to anticipate an attack and thus help us avert it or minimize its initial impact.

Second, an intensive program of scientific research and development designed to insure for us continued leadership in the perfection of new weapons and defensive devices, so that our military forces will always be equipped to strike back with more devastating weapons than an enemy can direct against us and so that we can provide the most effective protection for our troops and our home population.

Third, an industrial mobilization program under which we would have at all times an initial supply of the most modern instruments of war and widely dispersed plants ready at a moment's notice to produce additional weapons of the newest design. These plants would have to be tooled up in peacetime, and arrangements for staffing them, from production managers to janitors, would also have to be made in advance. Similarly, the program must provide for a strategic stock pile of critical materials and for the swiftest conversion of private industrial facilities to war use in an emergency.

Fourth, and basic to all the others, trained military manpower to use the weapons developed by our scientists and produced by our factories. The more technological advancement we attain in our weapons, the more trained men we shall need to operate them, the more specialized training they will require, and the less time we shall have for such training after war comes. Instantaneous attack demands equally swift counterattack, utilizing all the Nation's power and resources.

(2) *Statement by the Secretary of State (Byrnes), March 16, 1946.*[1]

[Excerpts]

We Americans love peace. We are a nation of civilians, not soldiers. It is fundamental to our system of government that military authority be subordinated to civilian authority.

Even in the midst of total war, we have maintained this principle. The American soldiers and sailors who made military history from New Caledonia to Tokyo and from North Africa to Berlin were not professional soldiers and sailors. They were civilians in uniform.

This is a fine tradition. Having preserved it in war, we should not relinquish it in peace.

The problem is how to reconcile our civilian traditions with the necessity to maintain our military strength at a level to match our responsibilities in the world.

No nation is more willing than the United States to participate in any reasonable plan for the general reduction of armaments. But while other nations remain armed, the United States, in the interest of world peace, cannot disarm.

Between 1918 and 1941 there grew up in this country an important body of pacifist sentiment. The dominant theme of this movement was that the way to end war was not to prepare for war. It was argued that plain men the world over hated war and that there would be no more war if all these plain men simply refused ever to fight again.

If the United States were to scrap all its armaments and completely demobilize its army and navy, it was said, the force of its example would compel the rest of the world to follow suit. The peaceful instinct which underlay this point of view is an admirable one. The trouble with the idea is that it does not work.

. . . .

Today there is grave danger that the sense of relief which accompanies the end of the war may cause us once again to do unwittingly what we would never do consciously.

No one in or out of government desires to extend for a single day more than is necessary the enforced separation of men from their families and from their peacetime business or employment.

But those who bear the responsibility for the security and welfare of the nation are alarmed at the possibility that sufficient numbers of physically fit men will not be available to replace those who have earned the right to return to their homes.

This is true now while the Selective Service Act is still in effect. If the Act is permitted to expire on May 15 of this year, the situation will become critical. It is imperative that the Act be extended at least for the period in which the Army and the Navy have the multiple responsibility for the occupation of Germany and Japan, for the protection of

[1] Department of State, *Bulletin*, XIV, p. 481.

our surpluses overseas, for the continuing defense of the United States, and for the fulfilment of our commitments under the Charter.

It is even more important, in the long run, that we have at all times a reserve of trained men who can be called upon in case of need.

. . . .

. . . Consequently, the people of the United States have a right to know the purposes to which this reserve military strength might some day be put. This is a fair question. It deserves a fair answer.

The answer is simple. The United States is committed to the support of the Charter of the United Nations. Should the occasion arise, our military strength will be used to support the purposes and principles of the Charter.

I cannot emphasize too strongly that the United States looks to the United Nations as the path to enduring peace.

We do not propose to seek security in an alliance with the Soviet Union against Great Britain, or in an alliance with Great Britain against the Soviet Union.

We propose to stand with the United Nations in our efforts to secure equal justice for all nations and special privilege for no nation.

We must maintain our strength, therefore, for the primary purpose of preserving and using our influence in support of the Charter of the United Nations. We will not use our strength for aggressive purposes. Neither will we use it to support tyranny or special privilege.

. . . .

After every great war there comes a period of anticlimax and disillusionment. Those who fight together expect, when the fighting is over, too much from one another and are inclined to give too little to one another.

Those who have won the victory expect the millennium and feel that they should have the fruits of victory without further effort.

They forget that victory in war can only give the opportunity that would otherwise be denied, to live and work for the fruits of peace and freedom.

Having been forced to fight for military victory, they sometimes think that whatever they want should be taken by force instead of making their claims the basis for peaceful negotiation.

It takes time to pass from the psychology of war to the psychology of peace. We must have patience, as well as firmness. We must keep our feet on the ground. We cannot afford to lose our tempers.

I am deeply convinced that the peoples who fought together for freedom want to live together in peace. I am deeply convinced that the peoples of the United Nations are sincerely committed to the Charter.

There are always some of little faith; some who still believe that they cannot get their due except by force. There are others who still believe that ancient privilege will yield to nothing but force of arms.

But with firmness in the right not as we alone see it, but as the aggregate sentiments of mankind see it, and with patience and understanding we must and shall achieve a just and enduring peace for ourselves and all nations.

(3) *Address by the President (Truman), Chicago, Army Day, April 6, 1946.*[1]

[Excerpt]

. . . .

The United States today is a strong nation; there is none stronger. This is not a boast. It is a fact which calls for solemn thought and due humility. It means that with such strength we have to assume the leadership and accept responsibility. It would be a tragic breach of national duty and international faith if, consciously or carelessly, we permitted ourselves ever to be unprepared to fulfill that responsibility.

We still have much to do. We are determined to remain strong.

We still have all the duties of the armies of occupation. We still have to do our share in supervising former enemy governments, enforcing the peace terms, disarming and repatriating enemy troops, taking care of hundreds of thousands of displaced persons. We still have to service and supply all our troops overseas. We still have to protect and preserve American property all over the world. We still have to destroy the war material and the war-making industries of our enemies.

But far and above all those things, we must remain strong because only so long as we remain strong can we ensure peace in the world. Peace has to be built on power for good. Justice and good-will and good deeds are not enough. We cannot on one day proclaim our intention to prevent unjust aggression and tyranny in the world, and on the next day call for the immediate scrapping of our military might.

We must remain strong, not because we plan or want to impose our views upon the world by force. We do not want to make war upon any nation. We must remain strong in order to retain our leadership, and, with all our resources, exercise that leadership on behalf of a world of peace and harmony among all nations and all peoples. This is not only our moral duty; it is a firm obligation which we have undertaken as a member of the United Nations.

From the military point of view, how can we best maintain this strength and leadership? I have, during the past year, given what I consider appropriate answers to that question, to the Congress and to the nation. Because time passes quickly, and because delay is itself a process of decay, I emphasize those answers again today.

They are: First, unification of all our armed services in a single department; second, temporary extension of the Selective Service Act; and third, universal training.

Unification does not mean subordination of any branch of the service. It does not mean loss of identity. It means just what the word says — unification. It means a concentration and cohesion of our best military

[1] *New York Times*, April 7, 1946, p. 29.

thought and our best military resources, geared to maximum efficiency. It means using our experience in World War II for the peace of the world.

I hope that the second objective will very soon be achieved in the Congress — the temporary extension of the Selective Service Act. We won the war; we must now make the victory secure. Victorious nations cannot, on the surrender of a vicious and dangerous enemy, turn their backs and go home. Wars are different from baseball games where, at the end of the game, the teams get dressed and leave the park. In wars, the victors must make sure that there will not be a recurrence of enemy aggression and tyranny. Tyranny must be rooted out from the very soul of the enemy nation before we can say the war is really won.

The American people recognize that fact. But the process is a long and exacting one. It requires an army of many men. And that army of many men can be continuously and adequately supplied for another year only by the Selective Service Act.

If that act is not extended beyond the next month, when it will otherwise expire, we face these alternatives: Either we shall have to keep men indefinitely in foreign lands who, by reason of long service, are justly entitled to come home to their families; or we shall have to turn our backs upon the enemy before the victory is finally assured.

Justice to the men still in the armed forces, justice to all our people and to civilization itself, forbids the choice of either of these alternatives. The Congress, I am sure, will not choose either one of them.

The third essential of a strong America is a program of universal training. Let us understand this clearly. Universal training is not conscription. It does not mean that our young men would have to serve in the Army or Navy for any period during peacetime. They remain citizens and civilians unless the Congress declares an emergency and calls upon them to serve in the armed forces with other citizens.

What is proposed is that each individual be trained and fitted by his nation to take his place if war unhappily should ever come again.

It is no answer to say that we do not need a large army in the atomic age. No one knows yet precisely what we shall need — in terms of infantry, artillery, pilots, paratroopers, ships, radar, planes, rockets or bombs.

We do know this: modern war calls for the total mobilization of all men and all energies. We know, too, that we are not likely again to be given two years or more by heroic Allies to get ready. Next time — if there must be a next time — we are likely to be the first target.

And so on short notice, each man must be ready to take his place and go forward — not at the end of a few months, or a few years, but immediately. Otherwise it may be too late.

There is only one way that each man can be ready. And that way is by training ahead of the time. He will not be trained to do things which are obsolete. He will be trained to do only whatever is required in modern warfare. A nation like ours whose responsibility is leadership against tyranny and oppression surely cannot expect less of its people than that they be made ready to fight or to work to preserve that nation.

Unification of the armed forces, temporary extension of the Selective

Service Act, and a universal training program — those are the foundation stones which hold the promise of a strong nation. They are essential if we are to maintain our leadership on the road to peace and freedom.

. . . .

(4) *Address by the Chief of Staff of the United States Army (Marshall), October 29, 1946.*[1]

[Excerpts]

. . . .

Just a few months ago the world was completely convinced of the strength and courage of the United States. Now they see us falling back into our familiar peacetime habits. They witness the tremendous enthusiasm with which we mount demobilization and reconversion, but they see as yet no concrete evidence that we are determined to hold what we have won — permanently. Are we already at this early date inviting that same international disrespect that prevailed before this war? Are we throwing away today what a million Americans died or were mutilated to achieve? Are we already shirking the responsibility of the victory?

This business of dissipating the political benefits that a nation may derive from victory is in the American tradition. It is quite understandable in a nation that runs its own affairs, because there is no easy way to get big things done on this earth. The victory was hard won. It will require a great deal of effort and sacrifice to fulfill our responsibilities of that victory, to achieve the future we recently talked about so freely.

We must somehow get it clear in our thinking that the fulfilment of our responsibilities is not some vague mumbo jumbo. It requires positive active effort and sacrifice, and above all it is a continuing process. We cannot do it in one step and then have done with it. Even if the United States now adopts a sound program in its relationships with the rest of the world, the program will be worthless unless we continue to support it year in and year out.

For example, after the last war the Congress enacted the Defense Act of 1920. It was not the best program we could have found but it was generally sound and would have been a long, forward step had it been implemented through the years. It wasn't. Hardly before the President's signature on the Defense Act had dried the act was emasculated by an appropriation measure which reduced the strength of the Army from the 297,000 men just authorized to 160,000 men. The following year this appropriation was further cut by 25 per cent to a little more than a quarter of the sum recommended by the War Department at the conclusion of World War I. Within a few years Congress had thus completely reversed itself on the policy of maintaining a respectable military posture, not by meeting the issue head-on but by refusing to appropriate the money necessary to carry it out. The Army at home and abroad fell to the woefully inadequate strength of 130,000 men.

It was argued then and it will soon be argued again that the nation's economy could not stand such military expenditures. Is not that absurd

[1] *Ibid.*, October 30, 1946, p. 6.

if you consider that the country's economy can better stand expenditures for national security than it can stand defeat or even a victory with consequent debt of more than three hundred billions?

. . . .

I sincerely believe that if we had given our security its proper attention the Axis nations would not have started the war. Millions of men and women, Europeans, Asiatics and Americans, who perished in battle by disease, starvation and brutality, in the past five years, might be alive today, had we faced the world in righteous strength instead of careless weakness. The enemy counted on us to go ahead with our pleasures, ignoring the threat to our lives and our very freedom. We proved them wrong but in the end, it cost us a million casualties and astronomical sums of money to restore our security and rightful position in the world. Had we not had Allies to buy us time, our own efforts great as they finally were, might easily have been too late.

The War Department has made several recommendations to Congress on how we can best go about maintaining our strength in the future at a cost within our financial means. These recommendations have been questioned, usually by groups looking for an easy way out. I have opposed dogmatism all my life and think for a military man it can be a fatal mental disease, but I must say here tonight with all the emphasis I can command — there is no easy way. The American people will do well to give sober thought to their fateful problem.

. . . .

I cannot escape the conclusion that the possibilities of atomic explosion make it more imperative than ever before that the United States keep itself militarily strong and use this strength to promote cooperative world order.

No one can forsee unerringly into the future but it is not hard to predict that supersonic atomic rockets will have a profound influence on any war that ever again has to be fought. But, rather than decrease the necessity for our preparation both in manpower and material, this terrible new weapon will tremendously increase it.

The present public apathy regarding our military obligations for the future comes as no surprise to me. Three years ago here in New York at a meeting of the Academy of Political Science, just twenty-four hours after our landing in Africa in the first step toward liberation of Europe, I closed my remarks with this comment, which seems even more appropriate to this day and hour.

My particular interest at this time in your affairs rests on the fact that after a war a democracy like ours usually throws to the winds whatever scientific approach has been developed in the conduct of the war. This is a historical fact. It is the result of the immediate postwar aversion of the people to everything military, and of the imperative demand of the taxpayer for relief from the burden imposed by the huge war debt.

We are in a terrible war and our every interest should be devoted to winning the war in the shortest possible time. However, in view of your interest in the science of government and the intimate relationship that it bears to military requirements, I would ask your very careful consideration of these related military factors in whatever studies you make regarding the readjustments which must follow this war. The theories on the subject will have to be compressed into the realities. The attitude of the taxpayer is human and inevitable. The differing reactions of the people in the center of the country, of those along the coasts, of the people who face the Pacific, of the people who face the Atlantic, must be considered. The extreme distaste for things military to which I have already referred and which always follow an exhausting war will have to be taken into account. Then with all of these reactions, how can we so establish ourselves that we will not be doomed to a repetition of the succession of tragedies of the past thirty years? We must take the nations of the world as they are, the human passions and prejudices of peoples as they exist, and find some way to secure for us a free America in a peaceful world.

That statement was made three years ago while our troops were still pouring ashore at Casablanca and Algiers. I submit that it represents rather accurately the emotional state of mind of articulate America at this particular moment.

Are we once more to seek the easy way out, to heed only the voice of the minor objector, the critic of so-called militarism, the proponent of the selfish motive? Are we to waste the victory and doom our children's children to more years of horror and destruction?

. . . . . .

B. Unification of the Armed Forces

(1) *Message of the President (Truman) to Congress, Recommending Legislation for the Unification of the Armed Forces, December 19, 1945.*[1]

[Excerpts]

In my message of September 6, 1945, I stated that I would communicate with the Congress from time to time during the current session with respect to a comprehensive and continuous program of national security. I pointed out the necessity of making timely preparation for the nation's long-range security now — while we are still mindful of what it has cost us in this war to have been unprepared.

. . . .

Today, again in the interests of national security and world peace, I make this further recommendation to you. I recommend that the Congress adopt legislation combining the War and Navy Departments into one single department of national defense. Such unification is another essential step — along with universal training — in the development of a comprehensive and continuous program for our future safety and for the peace and security of the world.

One of the lessons which have most clearly come from the costly and dangerous experience of this war is that there must be unified direction of land, sea and air forces at home as well as in all other parts of the world where our armed forces are serving.

[1] *Ibid.*, December 20, 1945, p. 14.

We did not have that kind of direction when we were attacked four years ago — and we certainly paid a high price for not having it.

In 1941 we had two completely independent organizations with no well-established habits of collaboration and cooperation between them. If disputes arose, if there was failure to agree on a question of planning or a question of action, only the President of the United States could make a decision effective on both. Besides, in 1941, the air power of the United States was not organized on a par with the ground and sea forces.

Our expedient for meeting these defects was the creation of the Joint Chiefs of Staff. On this committee sat the President's Chief of Staff and the chiefs of land forces, the naval forces and the air forces. Under the Joint Chiefs were organized a number of committees bringing together personnel of the three services for joint strategic planning and for coordination of operations. This kind of coordination was better than no coordination at all, but it was in no sense a unified command.

In the theatres of operation, meanwhile, we went further in the direction of unity by establishing unified commands. We came to the conclusion — soon confirmed by experience — that any extended military effort required overall coordinated control in order to get the most out of the three armed forces. Had we not early in the war adopted this principle of a unified command for operations, our efforts, no matter how heroic, might have failed.

But we never had comparable unified direction or command in Washington. And even in the field, our unity of operations was greatly impaired by the differences in training, in doctrine, in communication systems, and in supply and distribution systems, that stemmed from the division of leadership in Washington.

It is true, we were able to win in spite of these handicaps. But it is now time to take stock, to discard obsolete organizational forms and to provide for the future the soundest, the most effective and the most economical kind of structure for our armed forces of which this most powerful nation is capable.

I urge this as the best means of keeping the peace.

. . . .

We would be taking a grave risk with the national security if we did not move now to overcome permanently the present imperfections in our defense organization. However great was the need for coordination and unified command in World War II, it is sure to be greater if there is any future aggression against world peace.

Technological developments have made the armed services much more dependent upon each other than ever before. The boundaries that once separated the Army's battlefield from the Navy's battlefield have been virtually erased. If there is ever going to be another global conflict, it is sure to take place simultaneously on land and sea and in the air, with weapons of ever greater speed and range. Our combat forces must work together in one team as they have never been required to work together in the past.

We must assume, further, that another war would strike much more suddenly than the last, and that it would strike directly at the United States. We cannot expect to be given the opportunity again to experiment in organization and in ways of teamwork while the fighting proceeds. True preparedness now means prepared not alone in armaments and numbers of men but preparedness in organization also. It means establishing in peacetime the kind of military organization which will be able to meet the test of sudden attack quickly and without having to improvise radical readjustment in structure and habits.

The basic question is what organization will provide the most effective employment of our military resources in time of war and the most effective means for maintaining peace. The manner in which we make this transition in the size, composition and organization of the armed forces will determine the efficiency and cost of our national defense for many years to come.

Improvements have been made since 1941 by the President in the organization of the War and Navy Departments, under the War Powers Act. Unless the Congress acts before these powers lapse, these departments will revert to their pre-war organizational status. This would be a grievous mistake.

The Joint Chiefs of Staff are not a unified command. It is a committee which must depend for its success upon the voluntary cooperation of its member agencies. During the war period of extreme national danger there was, of course, a high degree of cooperation.

In peacetime the situation will be different. It must not be taken for granted that the Joint Chiefs of Staff as now constituted will be as effective in the apportionment of peacetime resources as they have been in the determination of war plans and in their execution. As national defense appropriations grow tighter, and conflicting interests make themselves felt in major issues of policy and strategy, unanimous agreements will become more difficult to reach.

It was obviously impossible in the midst of conflict to reorganize the armed forces of the United States along the lines here suggested. Now that our enemies have surrendered, I urge the Congress to proceed to bring about a reorganization of the management of the armed forces.

Further studies of the general problem would serve no useful purpose. There is enough evidence now at hand to demonstrate beyond question the need for a unified department. A great many of the reasons for establishing a single department have been brought out already in public discussion and in Congressional committee hearings. To me the most important reasons for combining the two existing departments are these:

1. We should have integrated strategic plans and a unified military program and budget.

With the coming of peace, it is clear that we must not only continue, but strengthen, our present facilities for integrated planning. We cannot have the sea, land and air members of our defense team working at what may turn out to be cross purposes, planning their programs on different assumptions as to the nature of the military establishment we need, and engaging in an open competition for funds.

Strategy, program and budget are all aspects of the same basic decisions. Using the advice of our scientists and our intelligence officers, we must make the wisest estimate as to the probable nature of any future attack upon us, determine accordingly how to organize and deploy our military forces, and allocate the available manpower, material and financial resources in manner consistent with the over-all plan.

Up to the present time the make-up and balance of our armed forces have not been planned as a whole. Programs and budget requests from the Army and Navy have been formulated separately, on the basis of independent concepts of mission and function.

These separate programs and budgets have not been considered together until after they have passed out of military hands and even out of the hands of the Secretaries of War and the Navy. The whole job of reconciling the divergent claims of the departments has been thrust upon the President and the Congress.

This war has demonstrated completely that the resources of this nation in manpower and in raw materials are not unlimited. To realize this is to comprehend the urgent need for finding a way to allocate these resources intelligently among the competing services. This means designing a balanced military structure reflecting a considered apportionment of responsibility among the services for the performance of a joint mission.

From experience as a member of the Congress, I know the great difficulty of appraising properly the over-all security needs of the nation from piecemeal presentations by separate departments appearing before separate Congressional committees at different times. It is only by combining the armed forces into a single department that the Congress can have the advantage of considering a single coordinated and comprehensive security program.

2. We should realize the economies that can be achieved through unified control of supply and service functions.

. . . . .

Consolidation of the departments will, for example, reduce the volume of supplies that need to be procured. Supply requirements, for example, begin with a calculation of so many items per man to be supplied. But to this basic figure must be added margins of safety, to account for items in storage, transporation lags, breakdown in delivery, emergency demands, and so forth.

In these margins, savings can be made through unified systems of supply. As the volume handled in any supply system grows, the percentage factor which has to be added for reserves is reduced.

In the same way, both the Army and the Navy must add a margin of safety to their requirements for production plants, depots, hospitals, air training fields and other types of construction common to both services. When the requirements are pooled, the total amount of margin may be reduced.

The same is true of personnel. Each service must add a margin of safety in estimating its requirements for doctors, nurses, skilled mechanics and other types of specialists. The total margin is greater if the computations are made separately. Another source of economy will be the pooling of facilities and personnel in localities where at present both services have to operate, but where from the nature of the circumstances facilities and personnel are not fully used.

Other examples of duplication could be cited. Business men have to deal with separate buyers, who may use separate specifications for items which could as well have the same specifications. Separate inspectors are stationed in their plants.

During this war, instances occurred where the purchase of all available quantities of certain items by one service resulted in acute shortages in the other service. Parallel transportation and storage systems required extra overhead.

As the war progressed, it is true that increased cooperation reduced the extent of waste and conflict. But voluntary cooperation in such matters can never be expected to be fully effective. A single authority at the top would inevitably achieve a greater degree of economy than would be obtained under divided direction.

3. We should adopt the organizational structure best suited to fostering coordination between the military and the remainder of the Government.

Our military policy and program are only a part of a total national program aimed at achieving our national objectives of security and peace. This total program has many aspects, and many agencies of the Government must participate in its execution.

Our military policy, for example, should be completely consistent with our foreign policy. It should be designed to support and reflect our commitments to the United Nations Organization. It should be adjusted according to the success or lack of success of our diplomacy. It should reflect our fullest knowledge of the capabilities and intentions of other powers. Likewise, our foreign policy should take into account our military capabilities and the strategic power of our armed forces.

A total security program has still other major aspects. A military program, standing alone, is useless. It must be supported in peacetime by planning for industrial mobilization and for development of industrial and raw material resources where these are insufficient.

Programs of scientific research must be developed for military purposes, and their results woven into the defense program. The findings of our intelligence service must be applied to all of these.

Formulation and execution of a comprehensive and consistent national program embracing all these activities are extremely difficult tasks. They are made more difficult the greater the number of departments and agencies whose policies and programs have to be coordinated at the top level of the executive branch. They are simplified as the number of these agencies can be reduced.

The consolidation of the War and Navy Departments would greatly facilitate the ease and speed with which the armed forces and the other departments could exchange views and come to agreement on matters of common concern. It would minimize the extent to which interservice differences have to be discussed and settled by the civilian leaders whose main concern should be the more fundamental job of building over-all national policy.

4. We should provide the strongest means for civilian control of the military.

Civilian control of the military establishment — one of the most fundamental of our democratic concepts — would be strengthened if the President and the Congress had but one Cabinet member with clear and primary responsibility for the exercise of that control. When the military establishment is divided between two civilian secretaries, each is limited necessarily to a restricted view of the military establishment.

Consequently, on many fundamental issues where the civilian point of view should be controlling, the Secretaries of the two departments are cast in the role of partisans of their respective services, and real civilian control can be exercised by no one except the President or the Congress.

. . . . . .

There is no basis for the fear that such an organization would lodge too much power in a single individual — that the concentration of so much military power would lead to militarism. There is no basis for such fear as long as the traditional policy of the United States is followed that a civilian, subject to the President, the Congress and the will of the people, be placed at the head of this department.

The safety of the democracy of the United States lies in the solid good sense and unshakable conviction of the American people. They need have no fear that their democratic liberties will be imperiled so long as they continue fulfilling their duties of citizenship.

5. We should organize to provide parity for air power. Air power has been developed to a point where its responsibilities are equal to those of land and sea power, and its contribution to our strategic planning is as great. In operation, air power receives its separate assignment in the execution of an over-all plan. These facts were finally recognized in this war in the organizational parity which was granted to air power within our principal unified commands.

Parity for air power can be achieved in one department or in three, but not in two. As between one department and three, the former is infinitely to be preferred. The advantages of a single department are indeed much clearer when the alternative is seen to be three departments rather than the present two.

The existence of three departments would complicate tremendously every problem of coordination that now exists between the War and Navy Departments, and between the services and the rest of the Government.

The Cabinet is not merely a collection of executives administering different governmental functions. It is a body whose combined judgment the President uses to formulate the fundamental policies of the Administration. In such a group, which is designed to develop teamwork wisdom on all subjects that affect the political life of the country, it would be inappropriate and unbalanced to have three members representing three different instruments of national defense.

The President, as Commander in Chief, should not personally have to coordinate the Army and Navy and Air Force. With all the other problems before him, the President cannot be expected to balance either the organization, the training or the practice of the several branches of national defense. He should be able to rely for that coordination upon civilian hands at the Cabinet level.

6. We should establish the most advantageous framework for a unified system of training for combined operations of land, sea and air.

Whatever the form which any future war may take, we know that the men of our separate services will have to work together in many kinds of combinations for many purposes. The Pacific campaign of the recent war is an outstanding example of common and joint effort among land, sea and air forces. Despite its successes, that campaign proved that there is not adequate understanding among the officers and men of any service of the capabilities, the uses, the procedures and the limitations of the other services.

This understanding is not something that can be created overnight whenever a combined operation is planned and a task force organized. The way men act in combat is determined by the sum total of all their previous training, indoctrination and experience.

What we seek is a structure which can best produce an integrated training program, carry on merged training activities where that is appropriate, and permit officers to be assigned in such a way that an individual officer will learn firsthand of other services besides the one in which he has specialized. The organizational framework most conducive to this kind of unified training and doctrine is a unified department.

7. He should allocate systematically our limited resources for scientific research.

No aspect of military preparedness is more important than scientific research. Given the limited amount of scientific talent that will be available for military purposes, we must systematically apply that talent to research in the most promising lines and on the weapons with the greatest potentiality, regardless of the service in which these weapons will be used. We cannot afford to waste any of our scientific resources in duplication of effort.

This does not mean that all Army and Navy laboratories would be immediately or even ultimately consolidated. The objectives should be to preserve initiative and enterprise while eliminating duplication and misdirected effort. This can be accomplished only if we have an organizational structure which will permit fixing responsibility at the top for coordination among the services.

8. We should have unity of command in outlying bases.

All military authority at each of our outlying bases should be placed under a single commander who will have clear responsibility for security, who can be held clearly accountable, and whose orders come from a single authority in Washington. Reconnaissance planes, radar sets, and intelligence and counter-intelligence measures at a United States outpost are not intended to serve separate services for different purposes. Unification of the services offers a far greater guarantee of continued unity in the field than does our present organization.

9. We should have consistent and equitable personnel policies.

There have been differences in personnel policies between the Army and the Navy during the war. They began with competitive recruitment for certain types of persons and continued in almost every phase of personnel administration. In rates of promotion, in ways of selecting officers, in the utilization of reserve officers, in awards and decorations, in allowances and in point systems for discharge, the two services have followed different policies.

This inconsistency is highly undesirable. It will be reduced to a minimum under a unified organization.

Any bill which is enacted to carry out these recommendations cannot provide immediately the ultimate organization plan to accomplish unification. It can only prescribe the general organization of the authorities at the top levels of the unified department.

I recommend that the reorganization of the armed services be along the following broad lines:

(1) There should be a single department of national defense. This department should be charged with the full responsibility for armed national security. It should consist of the armed and civilian forces that are now included within the War and Navy Departments.

(2) The head of this department should be a civilian, a member of the President's Cabinet, to be designated as the Secretary of National Defense. Under him there should be a civilian undersecretary and several civilian assistant secretaries.

(3) There should be three coordinated branches of the Department of National Defense: one for the land forces, one for the naval forces and one for the air forces, each under an assistant secretary. The Navy should, of course, retain its own carrier-, ship- and water-based aviation, which has proved so necessary for efficient fleet operation. And, of course, the Marine Corps should be continued as an integral part of the Navy.

(4) The undersecretary and the remaining assistant secretaries should be available for assignment to whatever duties the President and the Secretary may determine from time to time.

(5) The President and the Secretary should be provided with ample authority to establish central coordinating and service organizations, both military and civilian, where these are found to be necessary. Some of these might be placed under assistant secretaries, some might be organized as central service organizations and some might be organized in a top military staff to integrate the military leadership of the department.

I do not believe that we can specify at this time the exact nature of these organizations. They must be developed over a period of time by the President and the Secretary as a normal part of their executive responsibilities. Sufficient strength in these department-wide elements of the department, as opposed to the separate service elements, will insure that real unification is ultimately obtained. The President and the Secretary should not be limited in their authority to establish department-wide coordinating and service organizations.

(6) There should be a chief of staff of the Department of National

Defense. There should also be a commander for each of the three component branches — Army, Navy, and Air.

(7) The Chief of Staff and the commanders of the three coordinate branches of the department should together constitute an advisory body to the Secretary of National Defense and to the President. There should be nothing to prevent the President, the Secretary, and other civilian authorities from communicating with the commanders of any of the components of the department on such vital matters as basic military strategy and policy and the division of the budget.

Furthermore, the key staff positions in the department should be filled with officers drawn from all the services, so that the thinking of the department would not be dominated by any one or two of the services.

As an additional precaution, it would be wise if the post of Chief of Staff were rotated among the several services, whenever practicable and advisable, at least during the period of evolution of the new unified department. The tenure of the individual officer designated to serve as Chief of Staff should be relatively short — two or three years — and should not, except in time of a war emergency declared by the Congress, be extended beyond that period.

Unification of the services must be looked upon as a long-term job. We all recognize that there will be many complications and difficulties. Legislation of the character outlined will provide us with the objective, and with the initial means whereby forward-looking leadership in the department, both military and civilian, can bring real unification into being.

Unification is much more than a matter of organization. It will require new viewpoints, new doctrine, and new habits of thinking throughout the departmental structure. But in the comparative leisure of peacetime, and utilizing the skill and experience of our staff and field commanders who brought us victory, we should start at once to achieve the most efficient instrument of national safety.

Once a unified department has been established, other steps necessary to the formulation of a comprehensive national security program can be taken with greater ease. Much more than a beginning has already been made in achieving consistent political and military policy through the establishment of the State-War-Navy coordinating committee.[1]

With respect to military research, I have in a previous message to the Congress proposed the establishment of a Federal research agency, among whose responsibilities should be the promotion and coordination of fundamental research pertaining to the defense and security of the nation.[2] The development of a coordinated Government-wide intelligence system is in process. As the advisability of additional action to insure a broad and coordinated program of national security becomes clear, I shall make appropriate recommendations or take the necessary action to that end.

The American people have all been enlightened and gratified by the free discussion which has taken place within the services and before the committees of the Senate and the House of Representatives.

[1] See this volume, p. 63.   [2] See *ibid.*, p. 503.

The Congress, the people and the President have benefited from a clarification of the issues that could have been provided in no other way.

But however strong the opposition that has been expressed by some of our outstanding senior officers and civilians, I can assure the Congress that once unification has been determined upon as the policy of this nation, there is no officer or civilian in any service who will not contribute his utmost to make the unification a success.

I make these recommendations in the full realization that we are undertaking a task of greatest difficulty. But I am certain that when the task is accomplished we shall have a military establishment far better adapted to carrying out its share of our national program for achieving peace and security.

The Bill (S. 2044) which was drafted by a subcommittee of the Senate Committee on Military Affairs in response to the President's message proposed: (1) the creation of a single Department of Common Defense; (2) the appointment of civilian assistants to the Secretary of Common Defense in the capacities of Secretaries (without Cabinet status) for each of the three parallel military components, Air, Navy and Army; (3) the designation of a Chief of Staff of Common Defense as principal military adviser to the President and the Secretary of Common Defense; (4) the establishment of the United States Air Force on precisely equal status with that of the Army and Navy; (5) the designation of the commanding officers of the three military components as Commanding General, United States Army; Chief of Naval Operations, United States Navy; and Commanding General, United States Air Force; (6) retention of the Joint Staff composed of the commanding officers of the three component units and the Secretary of Common Defense; (7) joint treatment and complete coordination as among the three components in recruitment, promotion, reserves, awards and decorations, demobilization, discharge and all matters affecting the morale of officers and enlisted men; (8) reorganization of the Department of Common Defense on the basis of continuing experience by the President under the provisions of the Reorganization Act of 1945; (9) the creation of a Council of Common Defense, headed by the Secretary of State and including the Secretary of Common Defense and the Chairman of the National Security Resources Board (also established by the Bill), for the coordination of over-all policies in the international and military fields, the assessment and appraisal of the objectives, commitments and risks of the United States in relation to actual and potential military power, and the recommendation to the executive departments and other Governmental agencies of courses of action deemed necessary to implement its decisions on defense policy; and (10) the creation of a National Security Resources Board and Central Intelligence Agency, the former to establish and keep up to date policies and programs for the maximum use of the nation's resources in men, materials and facilities and the latter, as a subordinate part of the Council of Common Defense, to compile, analyze, evaluate, and disseminate information gathered by all Government agencies, including the military services.

(2) *Report from the Secretary of War (Patterson) and the Secretary of the Navy (Forrestal) to the President (Truman), May 31, 1946.*[1]

When the effort at unification of the armed forces became deadlocked over differences existing between the Army and Navy on the question, President Truman requested the respective Secretaries to attempt settlement of these differences and to report to him as to how these conflicts might best be resolved.

[1] *Congressional Record*, 92, p. 7571 (Daily edition, June 25, 1946).

Pursuant to your instructions, we have reviewed the major elements involved in establishing a greater measure of unification among our national security organizations, with a view to defining those matters upon which we agree and those upon which we differ. While we regret our inability to bridge completely the gap between us, we are pleased to be able to report a considerable area of agreement. Sincere efforts to expand it were made by both of us.

For your convenience, we outline below those matters upon which agreement exists and those upon which we are unable to agree. The order of presentation is not intended to indicate the relative importance of the various items.

I. Agreement exists on the following matters:

1. Council of Common Defense

To integrate our foreign and military policies and to enable the military services and other agencies of Government to cooperate more effectively in matters involving our national security. The membership of this council should consist of the Secretary of State, the civilian head of the Military Establishment (if there be a single military department), the civilian heads of the military services, and the Chairman of the National Security Resources Board, referred to below.

2. National Security Resources Board

To establish, and keep up to date, policies and programs for the maximum use of the Nation's resources in support of our national security. It should operate under the council and be composed of representatives of the military services and of other appropriate agencies.

3. The Joint Chiefs of Staff

To formulate strategic plans, to assign logistic responsibilities to the services in support thereof, to integrate the military programs, to make recommendations for integration of the military budget, and to provide for the strategic direction of the United States military forces.

4. No Single Military Chief of Staff

In the opinion of the War Department, the Military Establishment should contain a single military Chief of Staff, who would serve as principal military adviser, available to offer advice when differences of opinion arise among the military heads of the several services. The Navy feels that the Joint Chiefs of Staff should be the highest source of military advice. The War Department is willing to omit the feature of a single Chief of Staff.

5. Central Intelligence Agency

To compile, analyze, and evaluate information gathered by various Government agencies, including the military, and to furnish such information to the national security council and to other Government agencies entitled thereto. It should operate under the council. An organization along these lines, established by Executive order, already exists.

6. PROCUREMENT AND SUPPLY

There should be an agency to prevent wasteful competition in the field of military supply and procurement through joint planning and coordination of procurement, production, and distribution. If there should be a single military department, this agency should be within the department.

7. RESEARCH AGENCIES

There should be an agency to coordinate the scientific research and development of the military services. If there should be a single military department, this agency should be within the department. The existence of such an agency would not remove the need for an over-all Central Research Agency.

8. MILITARY EDUCATION AND TRAINING

There should be an agency to review periodically the several systems of education and training of personnel of the military services and to adjust them into an integrated program. If there should be a single military department, this agency should be within the department.

As to the agencies mentioned in 6, 7, and 8 above, the War Department believes that these agencies will not be fully effective except as agencies within a single department. The Navy, on the other hand, believes that they will be more fully effective under a coordinated organization than under a single military department.

II. We are unable to agree on the following matters:

1. SINGLE MILITARY DEPARTMENT

WAR DEPARTMENT VIEW	NAVY DEPARTMENT VIEW
The Military Establishment should be set up as a single entity, headed by a civilian of Cabinet rank with authority and responsibility for the several services. The administration and supervision of the services should, however, so far as possible, be delegated to their respective heads in order that each service may have as much freedom of development as possible and in order that the traditions and prestige of each be not impaired. (Only if there is this unity of structure, headed by an individual with power of decision, can we achieve action where there is now inaction, con-	The Navy favors unification, but in a less drastic and extreme form. It believes that serious disadvantages will result from combining the military services into one department. It would involve sacrifices of sound administrative autonomy and essential service morale. The Navy recognizes the need for a greater measure of integration than now exists not only between the military departments but among all agencies of Government responsible for our national security. A single military department falls short of meeting these objectives.

NATIONAL DEFENSE

WAR DEPARTMENT VIEW—*Continued*

certed policy where there is now disjointed policy, and economy of manpower, resources, and money where there is now waste of them all. Any organization which does not facilitate prompt decision and prompt action thereon, totally ignores scientific development and the nature of modern war. The military security of the United States is a single objective. Accomplishment of this single objective with the greatest economy and efficiency demands unity of direction.)

NAVY DEPARTMENT VIEW—*Continued*

While the Navy feels that the measures upon which agreement exists, as set forth above, would fully meet the needs of present conditions, it sees certain advantages in placing a Presidential Deputy with clearly defined powers of decision over specified matters at the head of the Council of Common Defense. From this as a starting point it should be possible to move forward such further measures of unification as become advisable, based on further experience.

The Secretary of the Navy recommends to the President, in view of the wide area of agreement which presently exists, that legislation be enacted at once giving statutory effect to those matters on which there is agreement. These steps will of themselves constitute a very substantial advance over our pre-war, and even our present, organization for national security. If they are put into effect, it will be possible, in the opinion of the Secretary of the Navy, to meet the nine specific objectives set forth in the President's message to the Congress on December 19, 1945. Further consideration and study can then be given to the remaining questions on which there is wide and general divergence of view between, and outside of, the military departments.

2. THREE COORDINATE BRANCHES

WAR DEPARTMENT VIEW

The Military Establishment should contain three coordinate branches — naval, ground, and air. Each should have a civilian head and a military commander. These officials should have access to the President, but not Cabinet rank since this would be in derogation of the position of the civilian head of the Military Establishment. As was stated above, the three branches should be given as much autonomy as possible. (Our experience in the last war clearly indicates that parity for the Air Forces and the operation of all three services as a team are essential to our national security. Everything that we know of the future points to an increase rather than a decrease in the decisive role of air power.)

NAVY DEPARTMENT VIEW

The Navy feels that our national security requires maintenance of the integrity of the Navy Department, headed by a civilian Secretary of Cabinet rank. Naval aviation, together with surface and subsurface components, have been soundly integrated within the Navy. The Navy feels that similar integration by the Army of its air and ground forces would be in the best interest of our national security.

However, if the alternatives were three military departments or one, the Navy would prefer three departments.

3. Aviation

WAR DEPARTMENT VIEW

Responsibility for the development, procurement, maintenance, and operations of the military air resources of the United States should be a function of the Air Forces with the following exceptions, in which cases these responsibilities should be vested in the United States Navy: (*a*) Ship, carrier, and water-based aircraft essential to naval operations including those of the United States Marine Corps. (*b*) Land-type aircraft necessary for essential internal administration and for air transport over routes of sole interest to naval forces and where the requirements cannot be met by normal air transport facilities. (*c*) Land-type aircraft necessary for the training of personnel for (*a*) and (*b*) above.

(The Nation cannot afford the luxury of several completely self-sufficient services. The war demonstrated that they must be complementary — mutually supporting. With respect to landplanes, there are no purely naval functions which justify uneconomical duplication of equipment and installations. For example, the Air Forces already performs long-range reconnaissance for the ground forces and itself. The Navy's recognized requirement for the products of long-range reconnaissance can be effectively filled by the Air Forces. As regards anti-submarine warfare, it is the view of the War Department that the experience of Army Air Forces in the last war adequately justified the belief that land-based planes operated by the Air Forces can meet this requirement.)

NAVY DEPARTMENT VIEW

The Navy has no desire either to compete with, or to dictate to, the Army Air Forces. On the other hand, the Navy feels that its experience qualifies it to judge its own aviation needs.

One reason for the Navy's strong conviction against a single department is the continued efforts of the Army Air Forces to restrict and limit naval aviation. The Navy knows that these efforts, if successful, would seriously impair our sea power and jeopardize our national security.

To accomplish its fundamental purpose, the Navy needs a certain number of landplanes for naval reconnaissance, anti-submarine warfare and protection of shipping. Experience indicates that such landplanes, to be effective, must be manned by naval personnel trained in naval warfare. Lack of such aircraft under complete naval control as to design, procurement, operations, personnel, training, and administration might be disastrous to our national security. Similarly, the Navy must have air transport essential to its needs.

4. United States Marine Corps

The Navy and the Army differ on the functions of the United States Marine Corps, as follows:

WAR DEPARTMENT VIEW

There shall be maintained as a constituent part of the naval service a balanced Fleet Marine Force including its supporting air component for —

(1) Service with the fleet in the seizure of enemy positions not involving sustained land fighting, and

(2) To continue the development of tactics, techniques, and equipment re-

NAVY DEPARTMENT VIEW

There shall be maintained as a constituent part of the naval service a balanced Fleet Marine Force including its supporting air component for —

(1) Service with the fleet in the seizure of defense of advance naval bases or for the conduct of such limited land operations as are essential to the prosecution of a naval campaign, and

WAR DEPARTMENT VIEW—*Continued*
lating to those phases of amphibious warfare which pertain to waterborne aspects of landing operations.

NAVY DEPARTMENT VIEW—*Continued*
(2) To continue the development of those aspects of amphibious operations which pertain to the tactics, techniques, and equipment employed by landing forces.

There is agreement upon other primary duties of the Marine Corps, viz.:
(1) To provide detachments and organizations for service on armed vessels of the Navy, and
(2) To provide security detachments for protection of naval property at naval stations and bases.

These matters have been explored by us with a sincere desire to comply with your wishes that the military services reach complete mutual agreement. Our failure to achieve complete unanimity is due to no reason other than that our respective views on the points of difference are as sincere as they are divergent.

(3) *Letter from the President (Truman) to the Secretary of War (Patterson) and the Secretary of the Navy (Forrestal), June 15, 1946.*[1]

[Excerpt]

. . . .

Your report of May 31 listed four items upon which you were unable to agree. An analysis of your comments contained in your report, and in the lengthy discussion which we had, discloses that the services are not nearly so far apart in their attitude toward these points as had been reported. It is my firm conviction that the determination of these questions in the manner which I present herein will result in a plan which incorporates the best features offered by the respective services.

With reference to the points upon which full agreement was not reached my position is as follows:

1. SINGLE MILITARY DEPARTMENT

There should be one Department of National Defense. It would be under the control of a civilian who would be a member of the Cabinet. Each of the services would be headed by a civilian with the title of Secretary. These secretaries would be charged with the internal administration within their own services. They would not be members of the Cabinet. Each service would retain its autonomy, subject of course to the authority and over-all control by the Secretary of National Defense. It is recognized that the services have different functions and different organizations and for these reasons the integrity of each service should be retained. The civilian secretaries of the services would be members of the Council of Common Defense and in this capacity they would have the further opportunity to represent their respective services to the fullest extent.

[1] *Ibid.*, p. 7573.

2. THREE COORDINATED SERVICES

There should be three coordinate services — the Army, Navy, and Air Force. The three services should be on a parity and should operate in a common purpose toward over-all efficiency of the National Defense under the control and supervision of the Secretary of National Defense. The secretaries of the three services should be known as Secretary for the Army, Secretary for the Navy, and Secretary for the Air Force.

3. AVIATION

The Air Force shall have the responsibility for the development, procurement, maintenance, and operation of the military air resources of the United States with the following exceptions, in which responsibility must be vested in the Navy:

(1) Ship, carrier, and water-based aircraft essential to naval operations, and aircraft of the United States Marine Corps.

(2) Land-type aircraft necessary for essential internal administration and for air transport over routes of sole interest to naval forces and where the requirements cannot be met by normal air transport facilities.

(3) Land-type aircraft necessary for the training of personnel for the aforementioned purposes.

Land-based planes for naval reconnaissance, antisubmarine warfare, and protection of shipping can and should be manned by air force personnel. If the three services are to work as a team there must be close cooperation, with interchange of personnel and special training for specific duties.

Within its proper sphere of operation, naval aviation must not be restricted but must be given every opportunity to develop its maximum usefulness.

4. UNITED STATES MARINE CORPS

There shall be maintained as a constituent part of the naval service a balanced fleet marine force including its supporting air component to perform the following functions:

(1) Service with the fleet in the seizure or defense of advanced naval bases or for the conduct of such limited land operations as are essential to the prosecution of a naval campaign.

(2) To continue the development of those aspects of amphibious operations which pertain to the tactics, technique, and equipment employed by the landing forces.

(3) To provide detachments and organizations for service on armed vessels of the Navy.

(4) To provide security detachments for protection of naval property at naval stations and bases.

It is important that the basic elements of the plan of unification be stated clearly. The 8 fundamental points agreed upon and the 4 points which are herewith decided, constitute a total of 12 basic principles that should form the framework of the program for integration.

There is no desire or intention to affect adversely the integrity of any of the services. They should perform their separate functions under the unifying direction, authority and control of the secretary of national defense. The internal administration of the three services should be preserved in order that the high morale and esprit de corps of each service can be retained.

It was gratifying to have both of you and General Eisenhower and Admiral Nimitz assure me that you would all give your wholehearted support to a plan of unification no matter what the decision would be on those points upon which you did not fully agree. I know that I can count upon all of you for full assistance in obtaining passage in the Congress of a bill containing the 12 basic elements set forth above.

Despite the personal efforts of President Truman to push the merger of the armed forces and the favorable report of the Senate Committee on Military Affairs on S. 2044, the inability of the Army and of the Navy to reach agreement on the basic principles to govern unification and the strenuous opposition on the part of several members of the Congress resulted in the adjournment of the Seventy-Ninth Congress before the question of unification had been extensively debated or S. 2044 brought before the Senate for consideration. However, the question of unification did not thereby become a dead issue. Speaking before an American Legion Convention in San Francisco on October 2, 1946 Secretary of War Patterson, at one point in his address, spoke in favor of unification as follows:

"We cannot consider national defense properly without full appreciation of air power — and we cannot attain maximum exploitation of air power unless we give the air forces parity with naval and ground forces.

"Parity achieved by creating a separate department of air would result in even greater disunity in our national defense.

"The logical solution is to create a single department to cover the armed forces and to have within that department three branches — Army, Navy, Air."[1]

With the Republican Party in the majority in Congress as a result of the elections of November, 1946 the prospect of success in unifying the armed services became more promising. The elimination from positions of control of two of the most influential Congressional opponents of the merger contribute to this outlook: Senator David I. Walsh, chairman of the Senate Committee on Naval Affairs, who failed to be re-elected; and Representative Carl Vinson, chairman of the House Committee on Naval Affairs who, although re-elected, lost his chairmanship to a Republican member.[2]

C. Procurement of Personnel

Procurement of personnel for the service branches, a problem essential to the question of maintenance of adequate defense forces in the postwar era, received the close attention of the 79th Congress. Linked to this same problem were the further questions of demobilization and replacements for men separated from the forces and of occupation responsibilities and police activities in the defeated enemy states. In order to supply the numerical requirements sufficient to meet these needs, three alternatives were brought up before the Congress. (1) the enactment of an enlistment incentive program which would attract volunteer recruits in adequate numbers; (2) an extension into peacetime of the Selective Service Act of 1940 for a period sufficient to assure adequate replacements and

---

[1] *New York Times*, October 3, 1946, p. 1.
[2] *Ibid.*, December 6, 1946, p. 19.

to permit rapid demobilization without weakening the occupation forces in Germany, Austria, Japan and Korea; and (3) the enactment of legislation providing for universal military training in peace time.

1. VOLUNTARY RECRUITMENT

On September 6, 1945, Representative Andrew J. May (Kentucky) introduced in the House of Representatives H. R. 3951, "A bill to stimulate volunteer enlistments in the Regular Military and Naval Establishments of the United States." [1] The bill was referred to the House Committee on Military Affairs from which it was reported favorably, and without amendment, on the same day.[2] As reported, the measure included provisions for a two-year enlistment period as an alternative to the regular three-year period; retirement after twenty years' service, rather than after thirty years; reenlistment in grade; a ninety-day furlough with travel pay; payment of mustering-out pay; reenlistment allowances of $50 for each year in service for men in the upper three non-commissioned pay grades, and $25 for each year for men in the lower grades; an option for men of the three upper grades to receive monetary allowances rather than quarters allowances for dependents; an extension of franking privileges for 1947; an extension of the benefits under the Servicemen's Readjustment Act of 1904, as amended (the "G-I Bill of Rights");[3] and an indefinite extension of overseas pay differential. During debate on the floor of the House further amendments providing additional inducements were accepted, including those providing that persons enlisting on or before June 1, 1945, as privates would be promoted to privates first class within six months and upon meeting War Department qualifications; permitting one-year enlistment in the Regular Army for qualified members of the Army with six months of active service; permitting the Army to enlist volunteers at seventeen years of age; providing for the payment of mustering-out pay in lump sums to enlistees; and providing reenlistment allowances of $50 for each year of service to all men in all enlisted grades. The Bill, as amended, passed the House by a vote of 341 to 0 on September 18.[4]

In action by the Senate on H. R. 3951, a proposed amendment by the Military Affairs Committee to substitute an eighteen-months' reenlistment period for those with six months' service for the original one-year provision approved by the House was rejected by the Senate on September 26. Three major amendments were accepted by the Senate: the authorization of an eighteen-months' enlistment period for civilians as well as two- and three-year enlistments, the authorization of the Secretary of War to enlist 50,000 men in the Philippine Scouts for service with the occupation forces in Japan, and the extension until July 1, 1947, of family allowances for enlistees or reenlistees. With these amendments the Senate passed the bill on September 26, 1945.[5]

The Conference Report (No. 1075) was adopted without debate by both Houses of Congress on October 4.[6] The Bill was examined and signed by the officers in each House on the same day,[7] and approved by the President on October 6, 1945.

2. EXTENSION OF SELECTIVE SERVICE

In his message to the Congress on the State of the Union on January 14, 1946 President Truman reminded the Congress that, should the campaign for volunteers for the Army and Navy fail to produce a sufficient number of men for the

[1] *Congressional Record*, 91, p. 8559 (Daily edition, September 6, 1945).
[2] House Report No. 943, 79th Cong., 1st sess.; *ibid.*
[3] Public Law 346, 78th Cong., approved June 22, 1944.
[4] *Congressional Record*, 91, p. 8864 (Daily edition, September 18, 1945).
[5] *Ibid.*, p. 9172.
[6] *Ibid.*, p. 9563 and 9609 (Daily edition, October 4, 1945).
[7] *Ibid.*, p. 9615 and 9621; for text, see Public Law 190, 79th Cong., 1st sess.

services, it would become necessary to extend the Selective Service Act beyond May 16, 1946, and that should additional legislation to this be necessary, it should be enacted during the month of March.[1] Hearings on the question of extension were opened by the Committee on Military Affairs of the Senate on March 5, 1946 and continued through April 8; the corresponding Committee of the House of Representatives conducted hearings on March 21 and 22, and again on April 3 and 4, 1946.

In a nation-wide broadcast on April 1, 1946, Secretary of War Patterson summarized the testimony which had been submitted by him and other government witnesses in support of extension of the draft.[2] His testimony had been supplemented in Congressional hearings by General Dwight D. Eisenhower, the Chief of Staff; by Secretary of the Navy Forrestal; by the Director of Selective Service, Maj. Gen. Lewis B. Hershey; and by a number of other government witnesses. Opponents of extension, meanwhile, stressed the undemocratic aspects of peace-time conscription, questioned the accuracy of the official estimates, and supported voluntary enlistment as adequate for the needs of the armed forces.

Legislation to extend the draft was reported from Committee in both Houses in April, 1946, H. R. 6064 on April 10 [3] and S. 2057 on April 11.[4] As passed by the House April 15, H. R. 6064 provided extension of the draft to February 15, 1947; made eligible for service men between the ages of 20 and 30; limited the service of inductees to eighteen months; and set ceilings of 1,070,000 for the Army, 558,000 for the Navy, and 108,000 for the Marine Corps, as of July 1, 1947.[5]

Because the Senate was preparing to debate the question of a line of credit to the United Kingdom and that of labor legislation, action on H. R. 6064 or S. 2057 in the Senate was threatened with delay beyond the expiration date of the Selective Service Act then in force, May 15, 1946. Accordingly, S. J. Res. 159, to extend the existing act until July 1, 1946, was introduced in the Senate on May 9, was given immediate consideration and passed without debate.[6] The Resolution was adopted by the House with amendments on May 13 [7] and the Senate agreed to the House amendments, although opposed by the Senate Military Affairs Committee, on May 14 [8] and the resolution was approved "reluctantly" by the President the same day.[9]

The debate in the Senate on H. R. 6064 centered principally around the reliability of the Army's estimates on manpower requirements and the necessity of drafting men at eighteen years of age. The Senate passed the Bill on June 5 after amending it to extend the age limit to include all men between 18 and 45.[10] The Conference Report No. 2319 contained the following compromises on the question of draft extension: (1) extension to March 1, 1947; (2) induction of men between 19 and 45; (3) no suspension of inductions; and (4) no alteration in the deferment provisions of the original act.[11] The Conference report passed both Houses on June 25.[12] The Bill was approved by the President on June 29, 1946.

---

[1] See this volume, p. 488.

[2] For the text of Secretary Patterson's address, see *ibid.*, p. 490.

[3] House Report No. 1923, 79th Cong., 2d sess.; *Congressional Record*, 92, p. 3552 (Daily edition, April 10, 1946).

[4] Senate Report No. 1167, 79th Cong., 2d sess.; *Congressional Record*, 92, p. 3556 (Daily edition, April 11, 1946).

[5] *Ibid.*, p. 3787 (Daily edition, April 15, 1946).

[6] *Ibid.*, p. 4800 (Daily edition, May 9, 1946).

[7] *Ibid.*, p. 5060 (Daily edition, May 13, 1946).

[8] *Ibid.*, p. 5090 (Daily edition, May 14, 1946).

[9] *Ibid.*, p. 5129 (Daily edition, May 15, 1946); Public Law 379, 79th Cong., 2d sess.

[10] *Congressional Record*, 92, p. 6462 (Daily edition, June 5, 1946).

[11] *Ibid.*, p. 7392–7394 (Daily edition, June 21, 1946).

[12] *Ibid.*, p. 7606 and 7624 (Daily edition, June 25, 1946).

(1) *Message of the President (Truman) to Congress, September 6, 1945.*[1]

[Excerpt]

. . . .

While the cruel lessons of war are fresh in every mind, it is fitting that we now undertake appropriate measures for the future security of the United States.

The times call for a broad and realistic appraisal of our military needs and obligations. This nation, and the other members of the family of nations, are facing the hazardous transition to peace economy in a world grown acutely sensitive to power.

We have charted the course to a stable world peace, but that course still remains to be sailed.

We must, of course, plan for the immediate needs of this year and the next. But we would break faith with those who won for us the victory if we should fail at the same time to adopt an integrated and long-range program for the national security.

As a sovereign nation, we must continue to be ready to defend our national integrity by maintaining and manning adequate defense establishments within this continent, at the Panama Canal, and at all our bases overseas. As a member of the Security Council of the United Nations, we must have an immediate obligation to bear a share, commensurate with our national standing, in safeguarding the future security of all peace-loving nations. As a victor in the greatest war of history, we are committed now to an armed occupation of the lands of our defeated enemies until it is assured that the principles for which we fought shall prevail in the reconstruction of those lands.

To meet these immediate obligations will require the maintenance for some time of a real measure of our present land, sea and air power.

And in this first year after victory our people have another obligation, one which is felt in almost every American home. We owe it to those now in the armed forces that they be returned to civilian life with all possible speed.

To provide the personnel necessary to meet these immediate obligations we must obtain replacements for those veterans who have already rendered long and arduous service.

We shall make every effort to raise these replacements by recruiting volunteers. To that end I ask that the Congress consider ways and means to assure the maximum success of the recruiting campaigns which have already been authorized. I suggest that legislation be enacted to remove the present restriction on eligibility for voluntary enlistment and to allow the armed forces to enlist a larger number of volunteers than is now authorized. It is further recommended that in order to enable the armed forces satisfactorily to compete in the procurement of personnel, the Congress provide suitable inducements for volunteer service in the Army and Navy.

[1] *New York Times,* September 7, 1945, p. 17.

However, in view of our extensive national commitments, I am certain, as are the War and Navy Departments, that we cannot rely on voluntary recruitment as the sole method of procuring the necessary replacements.

I, therefore, urge that the Congress continue inductions to assure replacements for these veterans, in such numbers as are not supplied by volunteers.

An unforgivable discrimination would result if, by suspending inductions now, we should favor those who have had no military service at the cost of requiring continued sacrifice from those who have already done their part.

Our first concern should be for those who have been in the armed forces for several years. They have been separated from their homes and from their loved ones. Many of them have been under constant fire and continuous danger for months and even years. We should try to avoid imposing further service upon them.

The only way that this can be done is to continue the induction of young men who as yet have not served a tour of active duty in the armed services. Only when we find that we are able to obtain a sufficient number of volunteers to fill the necessary quotas for our occupational needs can we discontinue the Selective Service system.

Of course it is entirely up to the Congress to choose the means by which we will provide and maintain the necessary strength to meet our commitments. The alternatives presented are very simple. There are no others. Either we retain men now in the service for a further indefinite period, or we provide replacements by further inductions.

As you know, I have already directed the Selective Service to cut down the number of inductions from 80,000 to 50,000 per month, and to limit them to the age group of 18 through 25.

It would seem reasonable to limit inductions hereafter to men between the ages of 18 and 25, inclusive, and fix their maximum term of service at two years.

Under the existing statute, inductees can be legally retained only for the duration of the war and a period of six months thereafter. I trust that, in any event, the Congress will not pass a resolution to the effect that the war has terminated for the purpose of this statute. To do so would give to all inducted men and temporary officers of the Army now on active duty the right to civilian status, and would create an impossible demobilization situation.

These are the military steps which it is apparent must be taken at once to meet the needs of the transition from war to peace. First things necessarily come first.

But the full needs of our national security run far beyond this immediate period of transition. We should make timely preparation for the nation's long-range security, while we are still mindful of what it has cost us in this war to have been unprepared.

It is, therefore, my intention to communicate with the Congress from time to time during the current session with respect to a comprehensive and continuous program of national security, including a universal training program, unification of the armed services and the use and control of atomic energy.

* * * * * *

(2) *Radio Address by the Secretary of War (Patterson), April 1, 1946.*[1]

The War Department has urged that the Selective Service Act be extended for 1 year beyond the present expiration date on May 15. The reasons for this position have been explained by General Eisenhower and me in open hearings before the House Military Affairs Committee. The Secretary of State and the Secretary of the Navy have also recommended extension of selective service.

The reasons why selective service should be extended are these:

Our Nation is now in a period of transition from war to peace. Active hostilities came to an end with the surrender of Germany and Japan. But we do not yet have peace. Along with our allies we are occupying those hostile countries, to disarm and demilitarize them and prevent a renewal of hostilities — in a word, to see to it that we do not have to fight the war again. We must not throw away the victory won at such heavy cost.

The Army has the task of providing the necessary forces of occupation. It has other tasks — training replacements, operating hospitals, depots and ports of embarkation, holding of key bases, caring for surplus equipment — but the prime task for the immediate future is to occupy the parts of Germany and Japan that we have agreed to occupy. We must also be prepared to furnish our share of the military forces for world peace as set by the United Nations Organization. For the time being our words are of little value in foreign relations, unless we are prepared to back them up in case of need.

How large an army does this call for? No one can say for certain, because no one can say for certain what may come up in the future. But General Eisenhower, the Chief of Staff, gives it as his best estimate that these tasks can be performed by a force of 1,550,000 men as of July 1, 1946, dropping to a strength of 1,070,000 as of July 1, 1947, and January 1, 1948. Of this strength of 1,070,000 there are needed 400,000 for the Army Air Forces and 670,000 for the Army Ground and Service Forces.

The reason why this estimated reduction of nearly 500,000 in the year between July 1, 1946, and July 1, 1947, is possible is that the work of caring for surplus equipment, it is expected, will be completed, and it is also expected more stable conditions in the occupied enemy areas will allow cuts to be made in the size of the occupying forces.

I am convinced that General Eisenhower, in making this estimate of required strength, has pared the necessary forces down to the absolute minimum. For example, the estimate allows a force of less than 200,000 for occupation of our part of Germany on July 1, 1947, an area containing 17,000,000 Germans. We cannot go below these requirements without endangering the future peace of our country.

[1] *Congressional Record*, 92, p. A1985 (Daily edition, April 3, 1946).

The problem that faces the War Department is how to make sure that the soldiers needed to make up this force (1,550,000 on July 1 of this year, shrinking to 1,070,000 a year later) will be available.

Five hundred and fifty thousand, more or less, of the men now in the Army by induction under selective service will be available for duty after July 1. Under present commitments they will be discharged as they complete 2 years of service. It would be better if they could be discharged on completing 18 months of service after October of this year.

That leaves about 1,000,000 to be recruited or inducted. It is the policy of the War Department to recruit as many as possible from volunteers for the Regular Army. We would prefer to get the entire number from the campaign for volunteers. But there is no firm assurance that we will be able to obtain that many volunteers, unless the Selective Service Act is extended beyond May 15.

We say this because of experience thus far in the present drive to get recruits. The drive got under way last October. In 6 months, down to the middle of March, we have secured 634,000 men. That is a favorable figure. But there are three features in the results of our recruiting campaign that should be pointed out. The first is that the rate of enlistments is falling off sharply. Last November the rate was 40,000 a week. At present the rate is 17,000 a week. The second feature is that 45 percent of the enlistments are for the short terms — 18 months or 1 year. That means that a large number will be entitled to discharge beginning next October and must be replaced by new men. The third feature is that a great many of the enlistments have been brought about because of the presence of the Selective Service Act on the books. If a man feels that he will be inducted under Selective Service anyway, he is likely to enlist voluntarily. There are several advantages in voluntary enlistment. This incentive to voluntary enlistment will disappear if selective service is allowed to expire in May. It is quite certain, therefore, that without extension of selective service the number of men that can be obtained as volunteers will fall off sharply in May.

General Eisenhower and I have reviewed and checked the figures again and again. As to prospects for getting the men that will be required, I can sum it up by saying that if selective service is allowed to expire in May it is our best judgment that the Army will not have the required strength over the period from July 1 of this year to January 1 of 1948. It is our best estimate that we will have a deficit, in the last 6 months of that period, amounting to 170,000 men, that instead of having 1,070,000 men at that time, we will have no more than 900,000. That is a risk that the United States cannot afford to take.

If selective service is extended, the Nation will have the definite assurance that the strength of the Army will be maintained at the figure estimated to be necessary. There is no other way of providing the Nation with that assurance. Extension of selective service, by making available the necessary manpower, will also enable us to shorten the service of nonvolunteers now in the Army to not more than 18 months, beginning in October. This is in line with the sound principle of spreading the burden of military service, rather than making those already inducted carry the whole load. Extension will also put it within our power to discharge all fathers, if Congress believes that social and economic considerations make this desirable.

Above all, extension of selective service will serve as notice to the entire world that the United States is determined to prevent another world conflict, that this country has no intention to scuttle and run.

I urge that the extension be for 1 year. Congress may at the same time provide that the maximum period of service for all men now serving by reason of induction under Selective Service and for all those who may be inducted in the future shall be 18 months. It may also provide that there shall be no inductions if the effect will be to raise the strength of the Army above the requirements, without further authorization by Congress. These safeguards will not prejudice the national safety in any way.

In urging extension for 1 year, I should add that the War Department is not attempting to put over compulsory military service for the indefinite future. We have no program of getting conscription as part of a long-range military policy. I am recommending extension of Selective Service for 1 year, simply and solely because I am convinced that our security as a Nation requires it in these unsettled times, in this period of transition from war to peace.

I can sum the case up in a few words. We have won the greatest war in our history. It remains to make sure that we do not throw away the victory that 10,000,000 soldiers fought for. We run the risk of throwing it away if we allow our Army to dwindle, this year or next year, below the modest figure set by the Chief of Staff as the requirement for gaining a permanent peace. The War Department will spare no effort to find volunteers, but who can say that enough volunteers will be found? We can say with confidence, however, that the extension of Selective Service for 1 year will provide the strength that the Army will require to preserve the peace.

(3) *An Act to Extend the Selective Training and Service Act of 1940, As Amended, and for Other Purposes, Approved June 29, 1946.*[1]

Be it enacted by the Senate and House of Representatives of the United States of America in Congress assembled, That all of the provisions of the Selective Training and Service Act of 1940, as amended, are hereby expressly reenacted, except those provisions which are hereinafter amended or repealed.

SEC. 2. (a) So much of the first sentence of section 3 (a) of the Selective Training and Service Act of 1940, as amended, as precedes the first proviso is hereby amended to read as follows:

"SEC. 3. (a) Except as otherwise provided in this Act, every male citizen of the United States, and every other male person residing in the United States, who is between the ages of nineteen and forty-five, at the time fixed for his registration, or who attains the age of nineteen after having been required to register pursuant to section 2 of this Act, shall

[1] Public Law 473, 79th Cong., 2d sess.

be liable for training and service in the land or naval forces of the United States:".

(b) The fourth proviso of the second sentence of section 3 (a) of the Selective Training and Service Act of 1940, as amended, is amended to read as follows: "*Provided further*, That on July 1, 1946, the number of men in active training or service in the Army shall not exceed one million five hundred and fifty thousand, and that this number shall be reduced consistently month by month so that the Army's strength shall not exceed one million and seventy thousand on July 1, 1947: *And provided further*, That on July 1, 1947, the number of men in active training or service in the Navy shall not exceed five hundred and fifty-eight thousand and in the Marine Corps one hundred and eight thousand: *And provided further*, That the monthly requisitions on the President under this Act by the Secretary of War and the Secretary of the Navy shall not exceed the number of men required after consideration of the actual number of voluntary enlistments during the three months preceding that month in which the requisition is made. For the purposes of the fourth and fifth provisos of the preceding sentence, no man shall be deemed to be in active training or service or to be part of the strength of the Army, Navy, or Marine Corps, if —

"(1) he is on terminal leave;

"(2) he is a member of the detachment of patients who are to be discharged or relieved from active duty without being returned to an active duty status; or

"(3) he is being processed, following completion of his period of service, for discharge or relief from active duty."

SEC. 3. Section 3 (b) of such Act, as amended, is hereby amended to read as follows:

"(b) Each man inducted on and after October 1, 1946, under the provisions of subsection (a) shall serve for a period of training and service of eighteen consecutive months (excluding time served while pursuing a course of instruction in a university, college, or other similar institution of learning), unless sooner discharged. Each man inducted prior to October 1, 1946, under the provisions of subsection (a) who shall have completed a period of training and service under this Act of eighteen months or more (excluding time served while pursuing a course of instruction in a university, college, or other similar institution of learning) shall, upon his request, on and after such date, be relieved from his period of training and service under this Act. Notwithstanding the foregoing provisions, whenever, after January 1, 1946, the Congress declares that the national interest is imperiled, such periods of training and service may be extended by the President to such time as may be necessary in the interest of national defense."

SEC. 4. Section 3 (e) of such Act, as amended, is hereby repealed.

SEC. 5. (a) Section 5 (e) (1) of such Act, as amended, is hereby amended by inserting after the first sentence thereof the following new sentence: "No person shall be deferred for employment in industry except upon the basis of his then status in an industry essential to the national health, safety, or interest."

(b) Section 5 (e) (3) of such Act, as amended, is hereby amended to read as follows:

"(3) After May 14, 1946, no individual who has a child or children dependent upon him for support, or with whom he maintains a bona fide family relationship in their home, shall be inducted without his consent for training and service under this Act. As used in this paragraph, the term 'child' includes a child legally adopted, a stepchild, a foster child, and a person who is supported in good faith by the individual in a relationship similar to that of a parent and child but such term does not include any person eighteen years of age or over unless such person is physically or mentally handicapped."

(c) Section 5 (e) of such Act, as amended, is hereby amended by adding at the end thereof the following new paragraphs:

"(4) Any man inducted under the provisions of section 3 (a) of this Act who has a child or children, as hereinabove defined, dependent upon him for support, or with whom he maintains a bona fide family relationship in their home, shall, upon his request after August 1, 1946, be relieved from his period of training and service under this Act.

"(5) No individual shall be inducted without his consent for training and service under this Act, if he has served on active duty in the land or naval forces of the United States outside the continental limits of the United States or in Alaska; or if he has served on active duty in the land or naval forces of the United States for a period of at least six months after September 16, 1940 (excluding the time that any such individual so served while pursuing a course of instruction in a university, college, or other similar institution of learning). The provisions of this paragraph shall cease to be effective during any period after January 1, 1946, when the Congress or the President shall declare that the national interest is imperiled."

SEC. 6. Section 5 (m) of such Act, as amended, is amended to read as follows:

"(m) No individuals shall be called for induction, ordered to report to induction stations, or be inducted because of their occupations, or by occupational groups, or by groups in any plant or institutions, except pursuant to a requisition by the land or naval forces for persons in needed medical professional and specialists categories."

SEC. 7. Section 16 (b) of such Act, as amended, is amended to read as follows:

"(b) The provisions of the third sentence of section 3 (a) of this Act shall become inoperative and cease to apply at 12 o'clock post-meridian on July 1, 1947. All of the other provisions of this Act, except the provisions of sections 3 (b), 3 (c), 3 (d), 8, and 16 (b), and the fourth and fifth provisos of the second sentence of section 3 (a), shall become inoperative and cease to apply at 12 o'clock post-meridian on March 31, 1947, or on such earlier date as may be specified in a concurrent resolution of the two Houses of Congress for that purpose, except as to offenses committed prior to such date. One day prior to the date of the termination of the Selective Training and Service Act of 1940, as amended, as herein or hereafter specified, all remaining functions and responsibilities of the Personnel Division established under the authority of section 8

(g) of such Act, and all records and balances of appropriations which have been utilized or are available for use in the administration of such functions of the Personnel Division of the Selective Service System, shall be transferred to such agency of the Federal Government as the Congress may designate, or, if none is so designated, to such agency of the Federal Government as the President may designate."

3. UNIVERSAL MILITARY TRAINING

The question of universal military training received Congressional attention — by no means, for the first time — early in the period under review when Rep. Joseph Martin (Massachusetts) introduced into the House of Representatives on July 17, 1945, H. Res. 325, "A resolution urging an immediate international agreement to eliminate compulsory military training from the policies and practices of all nations."[1] There was already under consideration by the Committee on Military Affairs of the House at the time the Martin Resolution was introduced, a Bill which had been submitted by Rep. Andrew May (Kentucky) on January 3, 1945, H. R. 515 which proposed for all men at the age of 18 or within four years of that time one year's military training to be followed by a year's service in the reserve or enlistment in the regular forces. The Senate had before it a companion bill, introduced by Senator Chan Gurney (South Dakota).

During November and December, 1945, and February, 1946, the House Military Affairs Committee conducted hearings on H. R. 515, during the course of which vigorous support for and equally vigorous opposition to the proposal of peacetime training were brought out. The principle received support from most of the veterans' groups as well as from official witnesses of the War Department; the strongest opponents of the Bill were the American Federation of Labor, the Committee of Industrial Workers and representatives of educational groups. Hearings on H. R. 515 were suspended on February 21, 1946, and the Committee turned its attention to the Martin Resolution.

At the conclusion of the hearings on H. Res. 325 the question of universal military training was laid aside for the more pressing problem of extension of selective service.[2] Companion bills were again introduced in the House and in the Senate to provide for universal training: H. R. 6544 by Rep. May on May 24, 1946,[3] and S. 2303 by Senator Gurney on June 6, 1946.[4] Both Bills proposed a basic training period of 16 weeks followed by 36 weeks of basic scientific course, completion of service academy training, two years in the regular forces or three years in the National Guard or organized reserve. Prior to the adjournment of the 79th Congress, however, no hearings were held on either Bill in either House, nor was any measure either for or against universal military training reported from Committee.

In October 1946 the War Department again asked for legislation to be enacted by the 80th Congress to provide six months' training for all men and the equivalent of another six months in part-time reserve service.[5] The plan was described by Secretary of War Patterson in an address before the American Legion Convention in San Francisco on October 2. Each mentally and physically fit man between the ages of 18 and 20 would be subject to one year's training unless he enlisted for three years in one of the armed services. Trainees would have the option of a full year of training instead of one of six reserve options, or could avoid the second six-month period by enlistment in one of the services or by admission to a service academy.[6] Further action on the matter of universal training must await the convening of the 80th Congress, early in January 1947.

[1] *Congressional Record*, 91, p. 7789 (Daily edition, July 17, 1945).
[2] See this volume, p. 486.
[3] *Congressional Record*, 92, p. 5791 (Daily edition, May 24, 1946).
[4] *Ibid.*, p. 6481 (Daily edition, June 6, 1946).
[5] *New York Times*, October 3, 1946, p. 1.
[6] *Ibid.*

(1) Message of the President (Truman) to Congress, October 23, 1945.[1]

In my message to the Congress of September 6, 1945, I stated that I would communicate further with respect to a long-range program of national military security for the United States. I now present to the Congress my recommendations with respect to one essential part of this program — universal training.

The United States now has a fighting strength greater than any, at any other time in our history. It is greater than that of any other nation in the world.

We are strong because of many things: our natural resources which we have so diligently developed; our great farms and mines, our factories, shipyards and industries which we have so energetically created and operated. But above all else, we are strong because of the courage and vigor and skill of a liberty-loving people who are determined that this nation shall remain forever free.

With our strength comes grave responsibility. With it must also come a continuing sense of leadership in the world for justice and peace.

For years to come the success of our efforts for a just and lasting peace will depend upon the strength of those who are determined to maintain that peace. We intend to use all our moral influence and all our physical strength to work for that kind of a peace. We can ensure such a peace only so long as we remain strong. We must face the fact that peace must be built upon power, as well as upon good will and good deeds.

Our determination to remain powerful denotes no lack of faith in the United Nations Organization. On the contrary, with all the might we have, we intend to back our obligations and commitments under the United Nations Charter.

Indeed, the sincerity of our intention to support the organization will be judged partly by our willingness to maintain the power with which to assist other peace-loving nations to enforce its authority. It is only by strength that we can impress the fact upon possible future aggressors that we will tolerate no threat to peace or liberty.

To maintain that power we must act now. The latent strength of our untrained citizenry is no longer sufficient protection. If attack should come again, there would be no time under conditions of modern war to develop that latent strength into the necessary fighting force.

Never again can we count on the luxury of time with which to arm ourselves. In any future war, the heart of the United States would be the enemy's first target. Our geographical security is now gone — gone with the advent of the robot bomb, the rocket, aircraft carriers and modern airborne armies.

The surest guaranty that no nation will dare again to attack us is to remain strong in the only kind of strength an aggressor understands — military power.

To preserve the strength of our nation, the alternative before us is clear. We can maintain a large standing army, navy and air force. Or

[1] *Ibid.*, October 24, 1945, p. 3.

we can rely upon a comparatively small regular army, navy and air force, supported by well-trained citizens, who in time of emergency could be quickly mobilized.

I recommend the second course — that we depend for our security upon comparatively small professional armed forces, reinforced by a well-trained and effectively organized citizen reserve. The backbone of our military force should be the trained citizen, who is first and foremost a civilian, and who becomes a soldier or a sailor only in time of danger — and only when the Congress considers it necessary. This plan is obviously more practical and economical. It conforms more closely to long-standing American tradition.

In such a system, however, the citizen reserve must be trained reserve. We can meet the need for a trained reserve in only one way — by universal training.

Modern war is fought by experts — from the atomic scientist in his laboratory to the fighting man with his intricate modern weapons. The day of the minute man who sprang to the flintlock hanging on his wall is over. Now it takes many months for men to become skilled in electronics, aeronautics, ballistics, meteorology and all the other sciences of modern war. If another national emergency should come there would be no time for this complicated training. Men must be trained in advance.

The sooner we can bring the maximum number of trained men into service the sooner will be the victory and the less the tragic cost. Universal training is the only means by which we can be prepared right at the start to throw our great energy and our tremendous force into the battle. After two terrible experiences in one generation we have learned that this is the way — the only way — to save human lives and material resources.

The importance of universal training has already been recognized by the Congress and the Congress has wisely taken the initiative in this program.

The select committee of the House of Representatives on post-war military policy has organized hearings and has heard extended testimony from representatives of churches, schools, labor unions, veterans' organizations, the armed services and many other groups. After careful consideration the committee has approved the broad policy of universal military training for the critical years ahead. I concur in that conclusion and strongly urge the Congress to adopt it.

In the present hour of triumph we must not forget our anguish during the days of Bataan. We must not forget the anxiety of the days of Guadalcanal. In our desire to leave the tragedy of war behind us, we must not make the same mistake that we made after the first World War, when we sank back into helplessness.

I recommend that we create a post-war military organization which will contain the following basic elements:

First — A Comparatively small Regular Army, Navy and Marine Corps;

Second — A greatly strengthened National Guard and an organized reserve for the Army, Navy and Marine Corps;

Third — A general reserve composed of all the male citizens of the United States who have received training.

The general reserve would be available for rapid mobilization in time of emergency, but it would have no obligation to serve, either in this country or abroad, unless and until called to the service by an act of Congress.

In order to provide this general reserve, I recommend to the Congress the adoption of a plan for universal military training.

Universal military training is not conscription. The opponents of training have labeled it conscription, and by so doing have confused the minds of some of our citizens. "Conscription" is compulsory service in the Army or Navy in time of peace or war. Trainees under this proposed legislation, however, would not be enrolled in any armed services. They would be civilians in training. They would be no closer to membership in the armed forces than if they had no training. Special rules and regulations would have to be adopted for their organization, discipline and welfare.

Universal training is not intended to take the place of the present selective service system. The selective service system is now being used to furnish replacements in the armed forces for the veterans of this war who are being discharged.

Only the Congress could ever draw trainees under a universal training program into the Army or the Navy. And if that time ever came, these trainees could be inducted only by a selective process, as they were inducted for World War I and World War II. The great difference between having universal training and no training, however, is that, in time of emergency, those who would be selected for actual military service would already have been basically trained.

That difference may be as much as a year's time. That difference may be the margin between the survival and the destruction of this great nation.

The emphasis in this training of our young men will not be on mere drilling. It will be on the use of all the instruments and weapons of modern warfare. The training will offer every qualified young man a chance to perfect himself in the service of his country in some military specialty.

Under the plan which I propose, provisions should be made within the armed services to help trainees improve their educational status. The year of universal training should provide ample opportunity for self-improvement. Some part of their training could be used to develop skills which would be useful in future civilian life just as such skills have been developed during the present war.

The period of training could well be used to raise the physical standards of the nation's manpower, to lower its illiteracy rate, and to develop in our young men the ideals of responsible American citizenship.

Medical examinations of young trainees would do much toward removing some of the minor disabilities which caused the rejection of so many men during this war by the Selective Service System.

The moral and spiritual welfare of our young people should be a consideration of prime importance, and, of course, facilities for worship in every faith should be available.

But the basic reason for universal training is a very simple one — to guarantee the safety and freedom of the United States against any potential aggressor. The other benefits are all by-products — useful indeed, but still by-products. The fundamental need is, and always will be, the national security of the United States and the safety of our homes and our loved ones.

Since training alone is involved, and not actual military service, no exemptions should be allowed for occupation, dependency or for any other reason except total physical disqualification.

All men should be included in the training, whether physically qualified for actual combat service or not. There should be a place into which every young American can fit in the service of our country. Some would be trained for combat, others would be trained for whatever war service they are physically and mentally qualified to perform.

I recommend that the training should be for one year. Each young man should enter training either at the age of 18 or upon his graduation from high school — whichever is later; but in any event before his twentieth birthday. A trainee who completes high school education in his seventeenth year should be eligible, with parental consent to enter the course of training.

After the first few months of training, selected trainees who are not physically qualified for military service could be trained in certain skills so that if war came, they could take their places in shipyards, munitions factories and similar industrial plants.

Upon completion of a full year's training, the trainee would become a member of the general reserve for a period of six years. After that he should be placed in a secondary reserve.

Present personnel in the Army and Navy reserves would, of course, be retained, and the new trainees would provide the source from which the reserves of the future would draw their personnel.

Commissions would be granted to qualified men who completed the course of training and who then take additional instruction in officer candidate schools, in the Reserve Officers Training Corps or Naval Reserve Officers Training Corps. Outstanding trainees could be selected after an adequate period of training, and sent to college with government financial aid, on condition that they return, after graduation and with ROTC training, as junior officers for a year or more of additional training and service.

Such a system as I have outlined would provide a democratic and efficient military force. It would be a constant bulwark in support of our government. It would constitute the backbone of defense against any possible future act of aggression.

It has been suggested in some quarters that there should be no universal training until the shape of the peace is better known, and until the military needs of this country can be estimated and our commitments under the United Nations Organization can be determined. But it is impossible today to foresee the future. It is difficult at any time to know exactly what our responsibilities will require in the way of force. We do know that if we are to have available a force when needed, the time to begin preparing is right now.

The need exists today — and it must be met today.

If, at some later time, conditions change, then the program can be re-examined and revalued. At the present time we have the necessary organization, the required camp installations and the essential equipment and training grounds immediately available for use in a training program. Once we disband and scatter the set-up, it will be much harder and more expensive to re-establish the necessary facilities.

The argument has been made that compulsory training violates traditional American concepts of liberty and democracy, and even that it would endanger our system of government by creating a powerful military caste.

The purpose of the program, however, is just the contrary. And it will have just the contrary result. The objective is not to train professional soldiers. It is to train citizens, so that if and when the Congress should declare it necessary for them to become soldiers, they could do so more quickly and more efficiently. A large trained reserve of peace-loving citizens would never go to war or encourage war, if it could be avoided.

It is no valuable, valid argument against adopting universal training at this time that there are now millions of trained veterans of this war. No fair-minded person would suggest that we continue to rely indefinitely upon those veterans. They have earned the heartfelt gratitude of all of us — and they have also earned the right to return promptly to civilian life. We must now look to our younger men to constitute the new reserve military strength of our nation.

There are some who urge that the development of rocket weapons and atomic bombs and other new weapons indicates that scientific research, rather than universal training, is the best way to safeguard our security.

It is true that, if we are to keep ahead in military preparedness, continuous research in science and new weapons is essential. That is why in my message to Congress of September 6 I urged that there be created a national research agency, one of whose major functions would be to carry on fundamental military research.

It is true that there must be a continuous exploration into new fields of science in order to keep ahead in the discovery and manufacture of new weapons. No matter what the cost, we cannot afford to fall behind in any of the new techniques of war or in the development of new weapons of destruction.

Until we are sure that our peace machinery is functioning adequately, we must relentlessly preserve our superiority on land and sea and in the air. Until that time, we must also make sure that by planning — and by actual production — we have on hand at all times sufficient weapons of the latest nature and design with which to repel any sudden attack, and with which to launch an effective counter-attack.

That is the only way we can be sure — until we are sure that there is another way.

But research, new materials and new weapons will never, by themselves, be sufficient to withstand a powerful enemy. We must have men trained to use these weapons. As our armed forces become more and more mechanized, and as they use more and more complicated weapons, we must have an ever-increasing number of trained men. Technological advances do not eliminate the need for men. They increase that need.

General of the Army George C. Marshall, in his recent report to the Secretary of War, has made this very clear. I quote from General Marshall's report:

The number of men that were involved in the delivery of the atomic bomb on Hiroshima was tremendous. First we had to have the base in the Marianas from which the plane took off. This first required preliminary operations across the vast Pacific, thousands of ships, millions of tons of supply, the heroic efforts of hundreds of thousands of men. Further, we needed the B-29's and their fighter escort which gave us control of the air over Japan. This was the result of thousands of hours of training and preparation in the United States and the energies of hundreds of thousands of men.

The effect of technology on military structure is identical to its effect on national economy. Just as the automobile replaced the horse and made work for millions of Americans, the atomic explosives will require the services of millions of men if we are compelled to employ them in fighting our battles.

This war has made it clear that the security of the nation, when challenged by an armed enemy, requires the services of virtually all able-bodied male citizens within the effective military age group.

That is the end of General Marshall's quotation.

The atomic bomb would have been useless to us unless we had developed a strong Army, Navy and Air Force with which to beat off the attacks of our foe, and then fight our way to points within striking distance of the heart of the enemy.

Assume that on December the 7th, 1941, the United States had had a supply of atomic bombs in New Mexico and Tennessee. What could we have done with them?

Assume that the United States and Japan both had a supply of the bombs on December 7, 1941. Which would have survived?

Suppose that both England and Germany had had the atomic bomb in September of 1940 during the "blitz" over England. Which country would have been destroyed?

The answer is clear that the atomic bomb is of little value without an adequate Army, air and naval force. For that kind of force is necessary to protect our shores, to overcome any attack and to enable us to move forward and direct the bomb against the enemy's own territory. Every new weapon will eventually bring some counter-defense against it. Our ability to use either a new weapon or a counter-weapon will ultimately depend upon a strong Army, Navy and Air Force, with all the millions of men needed to supply them — all quickly mobilized and adequately equipped.

Any system which is intended to guarantee our national defense will, of course, cause some inconvenience — and perhaps even some hardships — to our people. But we must balance that against the danger which we face unless we are realistic and hardheaded enough to be prepared. Today universal training is the only adequate answer we have to our problem in this troubled world.

There will be better answers, we hope, in days to come. The United States will always strive for those better answers — for the kind of tried and tested world cooperation which will make for peace and harmony among all nations. It will continue to strive to reach that period quickly. But that time has not yet arrived.

Even from those who are loudest in their opposition to universal training, there has come no other suggestion to furnish the protection and security which we must have — nothing but pious hope and dangerous wishful thinking.

I urge that the Congress pass this legislation promptly — while the danger is still fresh in our minds — while we still remember how close we came to destruction four years ago — while we can vividly recall the horrors of invasion which our Allies suffered — and while we can still see all the ravages and ruin of war.

Let us not by a short-sighted neglect of our national security betray those who come after us.

It is our solemn duty in this hour of victory to make sure that in the years to come no possible aggressor or group of aggressors can endanger the national security of the United States of America.

(2) *Message of the President (Truman) to Congress, December 19, 1945.*[1]

[Excerpt]

In my message of September 6, 1945, I stated that I would communicate with the Congress from time to time during the current session with respect to a comprehensive and continuous program of national security. I pointed out the necessity of making timely preparation for the nation's long-range security now — while we are still mindful of what it has cost us in this war to have been unprepared.

On October 23, 1945, as part of that program, there was presented for your consideration a proposal for universal military training. It was based upon the necessities of maintaining a well-trained citizenry which could be quickly mobilized in time of need in support of a small professional military establishment. Long and extensive hearings have now been held by the Congress on this recommendation. I think that the proposal, in principle, has met with the overwhelming approval of the people of the United States.

We are discharging our armed forces now at the rate of 1,500,000 a month. We can with fairness no longer look to the veterans of this war for any future military service. It is essential, therefore, that universal training be instituted at the earliest possible moment to provide a reserve upon which we can draw if, unhappily, it should become necessary. A

---

[1] *Ibid.*, December 20, 1945, p. 14.

grave responsibility will rest upon the Congress if it continues to delay this most important and urgent measure.

. . . .

———

On December 20, 1946, President Truman appointed an Advisory Commission to study the problem of universal military training. The Commission, headed by Dr. Karl Compton, President of the Massachusetts Institute of Technology, included Joseph E. Davies, Dr. Harold W. Dodds, Dr. Daniel Poling, Father E. A. Walsh, Samuel I. Rosenman, Mrs. Anna Rosenberg, C. E. Wilson and Truman K. Gibson, Jr. The President's decision to constitute the Commission was arrived at after consultation with the Secretaries of War and Navy. The Commission was asked, in letters from the President to the appointees inviting their service on the Commission, to prepare recommendations for consideration before the convening of the 80th Congress.[1]

3. SCIENTIFIC RESEARCH AND DEVELOPMENT

The experiences of the Second World War demonstrated conclusively the importance of scientific achievement as applied to warfare. This importance was underlined on July 5, 1945, in a report submitted by Dr. Vannevar Bush, Director of the Office of Scientific Research and Development. The report was made in response to a request from President Roosevelt in November 1944 for a study on the problem of Federal support for science, and was based on individual studies of the relation of science to the public welfare, the problems of medical research, the development of scientific talent and the publication of scientific information. These studies had been prepared by some fifty prominent scientists, educators and businessmen and provided the basis for the statement by Dr. Bush that:

"Legislation is necessary. It should be drafted with great care. Early action is imperative, however, if this Nation is to meet the challenge of science, and fully utilize the potentialities of science. On the wisdom with which we bring science to bear against the problems of the coming years depends in large measure our future as a nation."[2]

Subsequently, on July 23, 1945 Senator Harley M. Kilgore (West Virginia) introduced a bill "To promote the progress of science and the useful arts, to secure the national defense, to advance the national health and welfare, and for other purposes";[3] shortly before a similar bill had been submitted by Senator Warren D. Magnuson (Washington).[4] On September 6, in a message to Congress, President Truman gave his endorsement to the principles of the Bush report which these bills were designed to implement.[5]

Between October 8 and November 2, 1945 joint hearings were held on these and related bills by a subcommittee of the Military Affairs Committee of the Senate and a subcommittee of the Commerce Committee, under the chairmanship of Senators Kilgore and Magnuson, respectively.[6] During the course of the

---

[1] *A Program of National Security, May 29, 1947. Report of the President's Advisory Commission on Universal Training*, Appendix 1, p. 99.

[2] The foregoing portion of this note depends largely upon *National Security Foundation. Report on Science Legislation from the Subcommittee on War Mobilization to the Committee on Military Affairs. United States Senate . . . February 2, 1946*, Subcommittee Report No. 8, 79th Cong., 2d sess., p. 2–3.

[3] S. 1297, 79th Cong., 1st sess.; *Congressional Record*, 91, p. 8070 (Daily edition, July 23, 1945).

[4] S. 1285, 79th Cong., 1st sess.; *Congressional Record*, 91, p. 7874 (Daily edition, July 19, 1945).

[5] For the text of the President's message, see this volume, p. 504.

[6] *Hearings on Science Legislation (S. 1297 and Related Bills). Hearings before a Subcommittee of the Committee on Military Affairs, United States Senate, Seventy-Ninth Congress, First Session . . . Parts I–V*, October 8–November 2, 1945, 1196 p.

hearings one hundred of the nation's leading scientists, educators, labor leaders, industrialists and Government officials gave testimony which, with but one exception, supported the establishment of a National Science Foundation.[1] The result of these hearings and of study by the two subcommittees was a new bill, S. 1850, jointly supported by Senators Magnuson and Kilgore, reported favorably to the Committee on Military Affairs on February 27, 1946[2] and by that Committee to the Senate on April 9.[3] The report was followed on May 24 by a minority report signed by all Republican members of the Committee with the exception of Senator H. Alexander Smith (New Jersey) in which many portions of the bill were challenged.[4]

Senate debate on the disputed portions of the bill was highlighted on July 1 when Senator Smith introduced an amendment in the nature of a substitute to S. 1850.[5] The administrative set-up envisaged in the original bill was replaced in the Smith amendment by a "National Science Foundation the members of which shall be sixty outstanding men and women representative of all sections of the Nation, recognized leaders in the field of the fundamental sciences, medical sciences, engineering and education, and lay persons of recognized standing in public affairs, selected solely on the basis of established records of distinguished service without reference to any political, social or religious factors." The amendment, however, failed of passage on July 2, although several major amendments were accepted from the floor of the Senate. Among these were two amendments offered by Senator Brien McMahon (Connecticut) intended to prevent any possible conflict with the work of the Atomic Energy Commission accepted on July 2,[6] and one introduced by Senator Thomas C. Hart (Connecticut) to strike out the social sciences from the field of the proposed Foundation accepted July 3.[7]

S. 1850 as amended passed the Senate by a vote of 48 to 18 on July 3,[8] and was referred to the Committee on Interstate and Foreign Commerce of the House of Representatives on July 5.[9] The bill remained unreported from the House Committee when the seventy-ninth Congress adjourned.

(1) Message of the President (Truman) to Congress, September 6, 1945.[10]

[Excerpt]

. . . .

Progress in scientific research and development is an indispensable condition to the future welfare and security of the nation. The events of the past few years are both proof and prophecy of what science can do.

Science in this war has worked through thousands of men and women who labored selflessly and, for the most part, anonymously in the laboratories, pilot plants, and proving grounds of the nation.

Through them, science, always pushing forward the frontiers of knowledge, forged the new weapons that shortened the war.

Progress in science cannot depend alone upon brilliant inspiration or sudden flights of genius. We have recently had a dramatic demonstra-

[1] Subcommittee Report No. 8, 79th Cong., 1st sess., cited above.
[2] *Ibid.*
[3] Senate Report No. 1136, 79th Cong., 2d sess.
[4] *Ibid.*, Part 2.
[5] *Congressional Record*, 91, p. 8134 (Daily edition, July 1, 1945).
[6] *Ibid.*, p. 8243 (Daily edition, July 2, 1945).
[7] *Ibid.*, p. 8350 (Daily edition, July 3, 1945).
[8] *Ibid.*, p. 8360.
[9] *Ibid.*, p. 8464 (Daily edition, July 5, 1945).
[10] *New York Times*, September 7, 1945, p. 17.

tion of this truth. In peace and in war, progress comes slowly in small new bits, from the unremitting day-by-day labors of thousands of men and women.

No nation can maintain a position of leadership in the world of today unless it develops to the full its scientific and technological resources. No Government adequately meets its responsibilities unless it generously and intelligently supports and encourages the work of science in university, industry, and in its own laboratories.

During the war we have learned much about the methods of organizing science, and about the ways of encouraging and supporting its activities.

The development of atomic energy is a clear-cut indication of what can be accomplished by our universities, industry, and Government working together. Vast scientific fields remain to be conquered in the same way.

In order to derive the full profit in the future from what we have learned, I urge upon the Congress the early adoption of legislation for the establishment of a single Federal research agency which would discharge the following functions:

1. Promote and support fundamental research and development projects in all matters pertaining to the defense and security of the nation.

2. Promote and support research in the basic sciences and in the social sciences.

3. Promote and support research in medicine, public health, and allied fields.

4. Provide financial assistance in the form of scholarships and grants for young men and women of proved scientific ability.

5. Coordinate and control diverse scientific activities now conducted by the several departments and agencies of the Federal Government.

6. Make fully, freely, and publicly available to commerce, industry, agriculture, and academic institutions the fruits of research financed by Federal funds.

Scientific knowledge and scientific research are a complex and interrelated structure. Technological advances in one field may have great significance for another apparently unrelated. Accordingly, I urge upon the Congress the desirability of centralizing these functions in a single agency.

Although science can be coordinated and encouraged, it cannot be dictated to or regimented. Science cannot progress unless founded on the free intelligence of the scientist. I stress the fact that the Federal Research Agency here proposed should in no way impair that freedom.

Even if the Congress promptly adopts the legislation I have recommended, some months must elapse before the newly established agency could commence its operations. To fill what I hope will be only a temporary gap, I have asked the Office of Scientific Research and Development and the Research Board for National Security to continue their work.

Our economic and industrial strength, the physical well-being of our people, the achievement of full employment and full production, the future of our security, and the preservation of our principles will be determined by the extent to which we give full and sincere support to the works of science.

It is with these works that we can build the highroads to the future.

. . . . . .

4. MILITARY AND NAVAL MISSIONS TO FOREIGN GOVERNMENTS

For information on military and naval missions sent by the United States to other countries, see this volume, p. 768.

5. FOREIGN INTELLIGENCE ACTIVITIES OF THE FEDERAL GOVERNMENT

The National Intelligence Authority was established by Presidential directive on January 22, 1946.[1] The directive named as members of the Authority the Secretaries of State, War and the Navy and one other person designated by the President as his personal representatives. As of December 1, membership in the Authority included: James F. Byrnes, Secretary of State; Robert P. Patterson, Secretary of War; James Forrestal, Secretary of the Navy; Fleet Admiral William D. Leahy, Personal Representative of the President; and Lt. Gen. Hoyt S. Vandenberg, Director of Central Intelligence who participates as a non-voting member of the Authority. The Authority is assisted in its work by a Central Intelligence Group under a Director of Central Intelligence who is, in turn, advised by an Intelligence Advisory Board consisting of the heads or the principal military and civilian intelligence agencies of the Government having functions relating to the national security.[2]

(1) *Directive of the President (Truman) Establishing the National Intelligence Authority, January 22, 1946.*[3]

1. It is my desire, and I hereby direct, that all Federal foreign intelligence activities be planned, developed and coordinated so as to assure the most effective accomplishment of the intelligence mission related to the national security. I hereby designate you, together with another person to be named by me as my personal representative, as the National Intelligence Authority to accomplish this purpose.

2. Within the limits of available appropriations, you shall each from time to time assign persons and facilities from your respective Departments, which persons shall collectively form a Central Intelligence Group and shall, under the direction of a Director of Central Intelligence, assist the National Intelligence Authority. The Director of Central Intelligence shall be designated by me, shall be responsible to the National Intelligence Authority, and shall sit as a non-voting member thereof.

[1] For the text of the Presidential Directive establishing the National Intelligence Authority, see below.

[2] United States. Bureau of the Budget. Government Information Service. Division of Public Inquiries. *United States Government Manual — 1947. First Edition.* Washington, Government Printing Office, 1947, p. 83–84.

[3] Department of State, *Bulletin*, XIV, p. 174.

3. Subject to the existing law, and to the direction and control of the National Intelligence Authority, the Director of Central Intelligence shall:

a. Accomplish the correlation and evaluation of intelligence relating to the national security, and the appropriate dissemination within the Government of the resulting strategic and national policy intelligence. In so doing, full use shall be made of the staff and facilities of the intelligence agencies of your Departments.

b. Plan for the coordination of such of the activities of the intelligence agencies of your Departments as relate to the national security and recommend to the National Intelligence Authority the establishment of such over-all policies and objectives as will assure the most effective accomplishment of the national intelligence mission.

c. Perform, for the benefit of said intelligence agencies, such services of common concern as the National Intelligence Authority determines can be more efficiently accomplished centrally.

d. Perform such other functions and duties related to intelligence affecting the national security as the President and the National Intelligence Authority may from time to time direct.

4. No police, law enforcement or internal security functions shall be exercised under this directive.

5. Such intelligence received by the intelligence agencies of your Departments as may be designated by the National Intelligence Authority shall be freely available to the Director of Central Intelligence for correlation, evaluation or dissemination. To the extent approved by the National Intelligence Authority, the operations of said intelligence agencies shall be open to inspection by the Director of Central Intelligence in connection with planning functions.

6. The existing intelligence agencies of your Departments shall continue to collect, evaluate, correlate and disseminate departmental intelligence.

7. The Director of Central Intelligence shall be advised by an Intelligence Advisory Board consisting of the heads (or their representatives) of the principal military and civilian intelligence agencies of the Government having functions related to national security, as determined by the National Intelligence Authority.

8. Within the scope of existing law and Presidential directives, other departments and agencies of the executive branch of the Federal Government shall furnish such intelligence information relating to the national security as is in their possession, and as the Director of Central Intelligence may from time to time request pursuant to regulations of the National Intelligence Authority.

9. Nothing herein shall be construed to authorize the making of investigations inside the continental limits of the United States and its possessions, except as provided by law and Presidential directives.

10. In the conduct of their activities the National Intelligence Authority and the Director of Central Intelligence shall be responsible for fully protecting intelligence sources and methods.

CHAPTER VII

INTERNATIONAL PEACE AND SECURITY

1. UNITED NATIONS

[For previous material on the development of the United Nations and the evolution of United States policy toward it, see *Documents, VI, 1943–1944*, p. 315; *Documents, VII, 1944–1945*, p. 397–464; and Goodrich, Leland M. and Edvard Hambro, *Charter of the United Nations: Commentary and Documents* (Boston, World Peace Foundation, 1947, 413 p., third printing).]

In the period under review the United Nations was transformed from a paper organization described in the Charter to an actual functioning agency. Ratification of the Charter under the procedure provided in Article 110 proceeded rapidly and was completed on October 24, 1945,[1] with the United States Senate giving its approval by a vote of 89 to 2 on July 28, 1945 and formal ratification being deposited on August 8. Meetings of the Executive Committee of the Preparatory Commission and of the Commission itself were held in London from August 16 to October 27 and from November 24 to December 23, 1945, respectively, with Edward R. Stettinius, Jr. serving as American representative during most of the period and Adlai E. Stevenson serving first as deputy representative and thereafter as acting representative. They were assisted by Messrs. Benjamin Gehrig, Abe Feller, Wilder Foote and John C. Ross as alternates.[2]

By the end of 1946, the General Assembly had completed its first session, which was held in two parts, the first in London from January 10 to February 14, 1946, and the second at Lake Success and Flushing, Long Island, from October 23 to December 16, 1946; the Security Council had been in regular session from January 18, 1946; and the Economic and Social Council had held three sessions and organized its numerous subordinate committees, commissions and sub-commissions.

Since the actual details of the work on the various organs of the United Nations are summarized in *International Organization*, I, No. 1 (February, 1947) material presented in the following sections is restricted to exhibits which reveal American policy toward the more fundamental questions before the United Nations, rather than in any way attempting to present a complete picture of all the issues discussed. For American policy toward the functional activities of the United Nations, see the appropriate chapter headings in this volume.

A. Participation and Membership

President Truman appeared before the Senate in person on July 2, 1945 to submit the Charter of the United Nations for ratification. The Charter was referred to the Committee on Foreign Relations, which held hearings from July 4 to July 15, 1945,[3] and reported its recommendations on July 23, 1945. Debate on the Charter extended to July 28 when ratification occurred by a vote of 89 in favor and 2 opposed.[4] United States ratification was deposited on August 8, 1945.[5]

[1] Department of State, *Bulletin*, XIII, p. 679.
[2] *Activities of the American Delegation to the First Part of the First Session of the General Assembly of the United Nations, London, England*, House Doc. 509, 79th Cong., 2d sess., p. 1.
[3] *Congressional Record*, 91, p. 8087 (Daily edition, July 23, 1945).
[4] *Ibid.*, p. 8329 (Daily edition, July 28, 1945).
[5] Department of State, *Bulletin*, XIII, p. 214.

The only major question arising during the discussion centered around whether the subsequent agreements to be negotiated under Article 43 for the United States' contribution to the armed forces available to the United Nations were to be approved by executive agreement, by joint resolution, or by treaty.[1] Although most Senators indicated their belief that it would not be necessary to ratify such agreements in the form of a treaty, some indicated concern that the executive authority might not refer the question to Congress at all. This problem drew forth a special message from President Truman, then at Potsdam, for Senator McKellar, President, *pro tempore*, in which he stated, "When any such agreement or agreements are negotiated, it will be my purpose to ask the Congress by appropriate legislation to approve them."[2]

1. RATIFICATION OF THE CHARTER OF THE UNITED NATIONS

(1) *Message of the President (Truman) Transmitting the Charter of the United Nations to the Senate, July 2, 1945.*[3]

It is good of you to let me come back among you. You know, I am sure, how much that means to one who served so recently in this Chamber with you.

I have just brought down from the White House and have delivered to your presiding officer the Charter of the United Nations. It was signed in San Francisco on June 26, 1945 — six days ago — by the representatives of 50 nations. The Statute of the International Court of Justice is annexed to the Charter.

I am appearing to ask for the ratification of the Charter, and the Statute annexed thereto, in accordance with the Constitution.

The Charter which I bring you has been written in the name of "We the peoples of the United Nations". Those peoples — stretching all over the face of the earth — will watch our action here with great concern and high hope. For they look to this body of elected representatives of the people of the United States to take the lead in approving the Charter and Statute and pointing the way for the rest of the world.

This Charter and the principles on which it is based are not new to the United States Senate or to the House of Representatives.

Over a year and a half ago the Senate, after thorough debate, adopted the Connally resolution, which contained the essence of this Charter. It called for "a general international organization, based on the principle of the sovereign equality of all peace-loving states, and open to membership by all such states, large and small, for the maintenance of international peace and security". What I am now presenting to the Senate carries out completely this expression of national and international necessity.

Shortly before that, the House of Representatives passed the Fulbright resolution, also favoring the creation of international machinery with participation by the United States.

You and the House of Representatives thus had a hand in shaping the Dumbarton Oaks Proposals, upon which the Charter has been based.

No international document has been drawn in a greater glare of publicity than this one. It has been the subject of public comment for

[1] *Congressional Record*, 91, p. 8087–8329, *passim* (Daily editions, July 23–28, 1945).
[2] *Ibid.*, p. 8275 (Daily edition, July 28, 1945).
[3] Department of State, *Bulletin*, XIII, p. 46.

months. This wide-spread discussion has created the impression in some quarters that there were many points of disagreement among the United Nations in drafting this Charter. Naturally, much more public attention was given to the items of disagreement than to the items of agreement. The fact is that there were comparatively few points upon which there was not accord from the very beginning. Disagreement was reduced to a minimum — and related more to methods than to principle.

Whatever differences there were, were finally settled. They were settled by the traditional democratic method of free exchange of opinions and points of view.

I shall not attempt here to go into the various provisions of the Charter. They have been so thoroughly discussed that I am sure you are all familiar with them. They will be so thoroughly discussed on this floor that you and the people of the Nation will all have a complete expression of views.

In your deliberations, I hope you will consider not only the words of the Charter but also the spirit which gives it meaning and life.

The objectives of the Charter are clear.

It seeks to prevent future wars.

It seeks to settle international disputes by peaceful means and in conformity with principles of justice.

It seeks to promote world-wide progress and better standards of living.

It seeks to achieve universal respect for, and observance of, human rights and fundamental freedoms for all men and women — without distinction as to race, language or religion.

It seeks to remove the economic and social causes of international conflict and unrest.

It is the product of many hands and many influences. It comes from the reality of experience in a world where one generation has failed twice to keep the peace. The lessons of that experience have been written into the document.

The choice before the Senate is now clear. The choice is not between this Charter and something else. It is between this Charter and no Charter at all.

Improvements will come in the future as the United Nations gain experience with the machinery and methods which they have set up. For this is not a static treaty. It can be improved — and, as the years go by, it will be — just as our own Constitution has been improved.

This Charter points down the only road to enduring peace. There is no other. Let us not hesitate to join hands with the peace-loving peoples of the earth and start down that road — with firm resolve that we can and will reach our goal.

I urge ratification. I urge prompt ratification.

(2) *Senate Resolution Ratifying the Charter of the United Nations, July 28, 1945.*[1]

Resolved (two-thirds of the Senators concurring therein), that the Senate advise and consent to the ratification of Executive F (79th Cong., 1st

[1] *Congressional Record*, 91, p. 8329 (Daily edition, July 28, 1945).

sess.), the Charter of the United Nations, with the Statute of the International Court of Justice annexed thereto, formulated at the United Nations Conference on International Organization and signed at San Francisco on June 26, 1945.

(3) *Instrument of United States Ratification of the Charter of the United Nations, Deposited August 8, 1945.*[1]

HARRY S. TRUMAN

President of the United States of America

To All to Whom These Presents Shall Come, Greeting:

KNOW YE, That whereas the Charter of the United Nations, with the Statute of the International Court of Justice annexed thereto, was formulated at the United Nations Conference on International Organization and was signed in San Francisco on June 26, 1945 in the Chinese, French, Russian, English and Spanish languages by Plenipotentiaries of the United States of America and forty-nine other nations, a certified copy of which Charter, with annexed Statute, is annexed hereto;

AND WHEREAS the Senate of the United States of America by their Resolution of July 28 (legislative day of July 9), 1945, two-thirds of the Senators present concurring therein, did advise and consent to the ratification of the said Charter, with annexed Statute;

NOW, THEREFORE, be it known that I, Harry S. Truman, President of the United States of America, having seen and considered the said Charter, with annexed Statute, do hereby, in pursuance of the aforesaid advice and consent of the Senate, ratify and confirm the same and every article and clause thereof.

IN TESTIMONY WHEREOF, I have caused the Seal of the United States of America to be hereunto affixed.

DONE at the city of Washington this eighth day of August in the year of our Lord one thousand nine hundred forty-
[SEAL] five and of the Independence of the United States of America the one hundred seventieth.

HARRY S. TRUMAN

2. UNITED NATIONS PARTICIPATION ACT OF 1945

(1) *United Nations Participation Act of 1945, Approved December 20, 1945.*[2]

The debate preceding the passage of S. 1580, the "United Nations Participation Act of 1945", was almost as extensive as that on the ratification of the Charter itself. The bill as originally submitted by the Foreign Relations Committee called for Senate approval of the appointment of the United States representative and deputy representative to the Security Council but failed to require such advice and consent in regard to the American delegates to the General Assembly on the assumption that, since some of them were likely to be members of the House of Representatives, requiring Senate advice and consent might carry implications of inferiority which would be resented by members of the House.

[1] Department of State, *Bulletin*, XIII, p. 214.
[2] Public Law 264, 79th Cong., 1st sess.

Some nine amendments were offered during the debate. Senator Taft offered amendments directed (*a*) toward giving the United States representative on the Security Council instructions to act in accordance with "international law and justice" in any votes cast under Articles 39, 41 or 42 of the Charter;[1] and (*b*) toward limiting the powers of the President's authority to dispatch American troops under Article 41 to ninety days.[2] The first amendment was defeated by a vote of 40 nays to 18 yeas,[3] and second by a voice vote without roll call. Senator Donnell sought formally to insert the provision that the military agreement to be entered into was a treaty requiring the approval of two-thirds of the Senators present and voting.[4] This was defeated by 57 nays to 14 yeas.[5] Senator Wheeler's proposal to require Congressional authorization in advance of the use of troops under Article 42 was snowed under by a vote of 65 nays to 9 yeas,[6] while an additional Taft amendment instructing the United States representative to urge the limitation of armaments suffered defeat by a vote of 54 opposed to 16 in favor.

The only significant modification of the bill as introduced arose from a series of amendments introduced by Senator Milliken who argued (*a*) that there was no need to give the American representative to the Security Council the rank of Ambassador, and (*b*) that the failure to require Senate approval of the United States delegation to the General Assembly in effect "down graded" this group to the detriment of the Security Council. He therefore proposed to strike out the provision for granting ambassadorial rank for the Security Council representative (defeated by a vote of 46 nays and 17 yeas[7]) and to create a permanent delegation to the Assembly subject to appointment by and with the advice and consent of the Senate (defeated by 31 opposed to 27 in favor).[8] On the basis of debate on the latter amendment, Senator Connally modified the original bill to include provision for Senate confirmation of American representatives to the Assembly.

The bill as amended passed the Senate by a vote of 65 to 7 on December 4,[9] and was approved on December 20, 1945.

Be it enacted by the Senate and House of Representatives of the United States of America in Congress assembled, That this Act may be cited as the "United Nations Participation Act of 1945".

SEC. 2. (*a*) The President, by and with the advice and consent of the Senate, shall appoint a representative of the United States at the seat of the United Nations who shall have the rank and status of envoy extraordinary and ambassador plenipotentiary, shall receive annual compensation of $20,000, and shall hold office at the pleasure of the President. Such representative shall represent the United States in the Security Council of the United Nations and shall perform such other functions in connection with the participation of the United States in the United Nations as the President may from time to time direct.

(*b*) The President, by and with the advice and consent of the Senate, shall appoint a deputy representative of the United States to the Security Council who shall have the rank and status of envoy extraordinary and minister plenipotentiary, shall receive annual compensation of $12,000,

---

[1] *Congressional Record*, 91, p. 11218 (Daily edition, November 27, 1945).
[2] *Ibid.*, p. 11586 (Daily edition, December 4, 1945).
[3] *Ibid.*, p. 11218 (Daily edition, November 27, 1945).
[4] *Ibid.*, p. 11347 (Daily edition, November 29, 1945).
[5] *Ibid.*, p. 11487 (Daily edition, December 3, 1945).
[6] *Ibid.*, p. 11572 (Daily edition, December 4, 1945).
[7] *Ibid.*, p. 11497 (Daily edition, December 3, 1945).
[8] *Ibid.*, p. 11503.
[9] *Ibid.*, p. 11590 (Daily edition, December 4, 1945).

and shall hold office at the pleasure of the President. Such deputy representative shall represent the United States in the Security Council of the United Nations in the event of the absence or disability of the representative.

(c) The President, by and with the advice and consent of the Senate, shall designate from time to time to attend a specified session or specified sessions of the General Assembly of the United Nations not to exceed five representatives of the United States and such number of alternates as he may determine consistent with the rules of procedure of the General Assembly. One of the representatives shall be designated as the senior representative. Such representatives and alternates shall each be entitled to receive compensat on at the rate of $12,000 per annum for such period as the President may specify, except that no member of the Senate or House of Representatives or officer of the United States who is designated under this subsection as a representative of the United States or as an alternate to attend any specified session or specified sessions of the General Assembly shall be entitled to receive such compensation.

(d) The President may also appoint from time to time such other persons as he may deem necessary to represent the United States in the organs and agencies of the United Nations at such salaries, not to exceed $12,000 each per annum, as he shall determine, but the representative of the United States in the Economic and Social Council and in the Trusteeship Council of the United Nations shall be appointed only by and with the advice and consent of the Senate, except that the President may, without the advice and consent of the Senate, designate any officer of the United States to act, without additional compensation, as the representative of the United States in either such Council (A) at any specified meeting thereof in the absence or disability of the regular representative, or (B) in connection with a specified subject matter at any specified meeting of either such Council in lieu of the regular representative. The advice and consent of the Senate shall also be required for the appointment by the President of the representative of the United States in any commission that may be formed by the United Nations with respect to atomic energy or in any other commission of the United Nations to which the United States is entitled to appoint a representative.

(e) Nothing contained in this section shall preclude the President or the Secretary of State, at the direction of the President, from representing the United States at any meeting or session of any organ or agency of the United Nations.

SEC. 3. The representatives provided for in section 2 hereof, when representing the United States in the respective organs and agencies of the United Nations, shall, at all times, act in accordance with the instructions of the President transmitted by the Secretary of State unless other means of transmission is directed by the President, and such representatives shall, in accordance with such instructions, cast any and all votes under the Charter of the United Nations.

SEC. 4. The President shall, from time to time as occasion may require, but not less than once each year, make reports to the Congress of the activities of the United Nations and of the participation of the

United States therein. He shall make special current reports on decisions of the Security Council to take enforcement measures under the provisions of the Charter of the United Nations, and on the participation therein under his instructions, of the representative of the United States.

SEC. 5. (a) Notwithstanding the provisions of any other law, whenever the United States is called upon by the Security Council to apply measures which said Council has decided, pursuant to article 41 of said Charter, are to be employed to give effect to its decisions under said Charter, the President may, to the extent necessary to apply such measures, through any agency which he may designate, and under such orders, rules, and regulations as may be prescribed by him, investigate, regulate, or prohibit, in whole or in part, economic relations or rail, sea, air, postal, telegraphic, radio, and other means of communication between any foreign country or any national thereof or any person therein and the United States or any person subject to the jurisdiction thereof, or involving any property subject to the jurisdiction of the United States.

(b) Any person who willfully violates or evades or attempts to violate or evade any order, rule, or regulation issued by the President pursuant to paragraph (a) of this section shall, upon conviction, be fined not more than $10,000 or, if a natural person, be imprisoned for not more than ten years, or both; and the officer, director, or agent of any corporation who knowingly participates in such violation or evasion shall be punished by a like fine, imprisonment, or both, and any property, funds, securities, papers, or other articles or documents, or any vessel, together with her tackle, apparel, furniture, and equipment, or vehicle, concerned in such violation shall be forfeited to the United States.

SEC. 6. The President is authorized to negotiate a special agreement or agreements with the Security Council which shall be subject to the approval of the Congress by appropriate Act or joint resolution, providing for the numbers and types of armed forces, their degree of readiness and general location, and the nature of facilities and assistance, including rights of passage, to be made available to the Security Council on its call for the purpose of maintaining international peace and security in accordance with article 43 of said Charter. The President shall not be deemed to require the authorization of the Congress to make available to the Security Council on its call in order to take action under article 42 of said Charter and pursuant to such special agreement or agreements the armed forces, facilities, or assistance provided for therein: *Provided*, That nothing herein contained shall be construed as an authorization to the President by the Congress to make available to the Security Council for such purpose armed forces, facilities, or assistance in addition to the forces, facilities, and assistance provided for in such special agreement or agreements.

SEC. 7. There is hereby authorized to be appropriated annually to the Department of State, out of any money in the Treasury not otherwise appropriated, such sums as may be necessary for the payment by the United States of its share of the expenses of the United Nations as apportioned by the General Assembly in accordance with article 17 of

INTERNATIONAL PEACE AND SECURITY 515

the Charter, and for all necessary salaries and expenses of the representatives provided for in section 2 hereof, and of their appropriate staffs, including personal services in the District of Columbia and elsewhere, without regard to the civil-service and classification laws; travel expenses without regard to the Standardized Government Travel Regulations, as amended, the Subsistence Expense Act of 1926, as amended, and section 10 of the Act of March 3, 1933, and, under such rules and regulations as the Secretary of State may prescribe, travel expenses of families and transportation of effects of United States representatives and other personnel in going to and returning from their post of duty; allowances for living quarters, including heat, fuel, and light, as authorized by the Act approved June 26, 1930 (5 U. S. C. 118a); cost of living allowance under such rules and regulations as the Secretary of State may prescribe; communication services; stenographic reporting, translating, and other services, by contract, if deemed necessary, without regard to section 3709 of the Revised Statutes (41 U. S. C. 5); local transportation; equipment; transportation of things; rent of offices; printing and binding; official entertainment; stationery; purchase of newspapers, periodicals, books, and documents; and such other expenses as may be authorized by the Secretary of State.

3. ACCEPTANCE OF COMPULSORY JURISDICTION OF THE INTERNATIONAL COURT OF JUSTICE

Under paragraph 2 of Article 36 of the Statute of the International Court of Justice, Members of the United Nations might accept as compulsory the jurisdiction of the Court in all legal disputes arising from: (a) the interpretation of a treaty; (b) any questions of international law; (c) the existence of any fact which, if established, would constitute a breach of an international obligation; (d) the nature or extent of the reparation to be made for the breach of an international obligation.

During the debate in the Senate on the ratification of the Charter of the United Nations, Senator Wayne Morse introduced a resolution, later revised and submitted with bi-partisan support as S. Res. 196, by which the Senate by a two-thirds vote was asked to recognize as compulsory, *ipso facto* and without special agreement, in relation to any other state accepting the same obligation, such jurisdiction of the Court.[1]

In the period between the introduction of the Morse Resolution on November 28, 1945 and the hearings on July 11, 12 and 15, 1946 before a subcommittee composed of Senators Thomas, Hatch and Austin of the Committee on Foreign Relations, considerable general support for the resolution had been manifested by the American Society for International Law, the American Bar Association, the American Association of University Women and similar groups.[2] Both President Truman and the Secretary of State Byrnes had endorsed the proposal, although neither had indicated whether they preferred approval by the action of two-thirds of the Senate or by joint resolution by the House and Senate, as proposed by H. J. Res. 291 introduced by Representative Christian A. Herter on December 17, 1945.[3]

The Committee on Foreign Relations unanimously accepted the recommenda-

[1] *Compulsory Jurisdiction, International Court of Justice. Hearings before a Subcommittee of the Committee on Foreign Relations, United States Senate, Seventy-Ninth Congress, Second Session, on S. Res. 196*, Washington, 1946, p. 13.
[2] *Ibid., passim.*
[3] Department of State, *Bulletin*, XIV, p. 633.

tion of its subcommittee that S. Res. 196 be submitted to the Senate for approval [1] and debate on the resolution took place from July 25 to August 4, 1946. The main issue revolved around the provision of Article 36 of the Statute of the International Court of Justice that "In the event of a dispute as to whether the Court has jurisdiction, the matter shall be settled by the decision of the Court." As submitted by the Committee on Foreign Relations, S. Res. 196 excepted from the jurisdiction of the Court "disputes with regard to matters which are essentially within the domestic jurisdiction of the United States." Over the vigorous opposition of Senators Thomas and Morse, the Senate approved, by a vote of 51 to 12 [2] an amendment submitted by Senator Connally adding the words "as determined by the United States of America" to this sentence. Support for the Connally Amendment arose from an unwillingness to run any risk that the Court might declare that such matters as control of immigration were not essentially matters of domestic jurisdiction. The resolution, as amended, was approved by a vote of 60 in favor to 2 opposed on August 4, 1946,[3] declared by President Truman on August 14, 1946, and deposited with the Secretary General of the United Nations on August 26, 1946.

(1) *Declaration on the Part of the United States Accepting Compulsory Jurisdiction of the International Court of Justice, August 14, 1946.*[4]

I, Harry S. Truman, President of the United States of America, declare on behalf of the United States of America, under Article 36, paragraph 2, of the Statute of the International Court of Justice, and in accordance with the Resolution of August 2, 1946, of the Senate of the United States of America (two-thirds of the Senators present concurring therein), that the United States of America recognizes as compulsory *ipso facto* and without special agreement, in relation to any other state accepting the same obligation, the jurisdiction of the International Court of Justice in all legal disputes hereafter arising concerning

   a. the interpretation of a treaty;

   b. any question of international law;

   c. the existence of any fact which, if established, would constitute a breach of an international obligation;

   d. the nature or extent of the reparation to be made for the breach of an international obligation;

Provided, that this declaration shall not apply to

   a. disputes the solution of which the parties shall entrust to other tribunals by virtue of agreements already in existence or which may be concluded in the future; or

   b. disputes with regard to matters which are essentially within the domestic jurisdiction of the United States of America as determined by the United States of America; or

   c. disputes arising under a multilateral treaty, unless (1) all parties to the treaty affected by the decision are also parties to the case before the Court, or (2) the United States of America specially agrees to jurisdiction; and

Provided further, that this declaration shall remain in force for a period

[1] Senate Report No. 1835, 79th Cong., 2d sess.
[2] *Congressional Record*, 92, p. 10841 (Daily edition, August 2, 1946).
[3] *Ibid.*, p. 10850.
[4] Department of State, *Treaties and Other International Acts Series* 1598.

of five years and thereafter until the expiration of six months after notice may be given to terminate this declaration.

Done at Washington this fourteenth day of August 1946.

B. Financial Support

Article 17, paragraph 2 of the Charter of the United Nations specified that "The expenses of the Organization shall be borne by the Members as apportioned by the General Assembly." Discussion of the exact allocation of percentages for the 1946 and 1947 budgets occurred in the Fifth Committee (Administrative and Budgetary Questions) during the Second Part of the First Session of the General Assembly from October 23 to December 16, 1946. Senator Arthur H. Vandenberg represented the United States at these meetings.

The Committee on Contributions, appointed by the General Assembly at its First Session in London in January and February, 1946, reporting a scale of contributions based on an "ability to pay" formula, allocated 49.98 percent of the total to the United States.[1] After Senator Vandenberg had protested that this amount was too large, the Fifth Committee appointed a subcommittee composed of the representatives of Canada, China, Egypt, France, Mexico, the Netherlands, Poland, the Soviet Union, the United Kingdom, the United States and Uruguay to reconsider the apportionment.[2] As a result, the proportion given the United States was reduced to 39.89 percent of the total. The General Assembly subsequently approved a budget of $19,390,000 for 1946 and of $27,740,000 for 1947.[3]

(1) *Statement of the United States Delegate to the United Nations (Vandenberg) on Financial Support, December 13, 1946.*[4]

The Delegation of the United States is prepared to recommend to Congress that we accept as our contribution to the 1946 and 1947 Administrative Budgets and the Working Capital Fund a figure not to exceed 39.89 per cent of the total with the following distinct reservation:

(a) That under no circumstances do we consent that under normal conditions *any one nation* should pay more than $33\frac{1}{3}$ per cent in an organization of "sovereign equals."

(b) That the difference between $33\frac{1}{3}$ per cent and 39.89 per cent is voluntarily assumed by us for 1947 and for the Working Capital Fund because we recognize that normal post-war economic relationships have not yet been restored and we are willing to accept this added, temporary assessment to assist the United Nations in meeting the emergency.

The Delegation of the United States is unwilling to have any contributions figure set for 1948. It believes that since the scale reflects abnormal economic conditions, the scale should be reviewed to reflect whatever economic changes, if any, occur from year to year. It would also anticipate that other factors than so-called "relative capacity to pay" will be given hereafter the consideration they deserve as a matter of sound public policy in an international organization of "sovereign equals".

The Delegation of the United States will request that this statement be made a part of the record of the General Assembly.

[1] *New York Times*, December 12, 1946.
[2] United Nations General Assembly, Document A/274, December 13, 1946.
[3] *International Organization*, I, p. 70.
[4] United Nations General Assembly, Document A/274, December 13, 1946.

C. Selection of Headquarters

By as early as October 3, 1945, the Executive Committee of the Preparatory Commission of the United Nations had voted 9 to 3 with 2 abstentions in favor of locating the permanent headquarters in the United States.[1] This action was subsequently confirmed by the Preparatory Commission by a vote of 25 in favor to 5 opposed with 10 abstentions, and a 12 nation subcommittee was thereupon appointed to inspect various sites in the United States.[2] The subcommittee, under the chairmanship of Dr. Styoyan Gavrilovic of Yugoslavia, reported to the General Assembly on February 4, 1946, in favor of locating the permanent headquarters "near to New York City" and preferably in the North Stamford-Greenwich area.[3] The General Assembly approved this recommendation on February 14, 1946, at which time it also decided to establish interim headquarters in or near New York City.[4] Temporary facilities at Hunter College in the Bronx were occupied from March 23 to August 15, 1946, on which date the Secretariat moved to Lake Success on Long Island.

In view of the estimated costs of the acquisition of land in the North Stamford-Greenwich area, and of the opposition voiced by residents to the location of the headquarters in that area, the Permanent Headquarters Committee approved on November 14, 1946, by a vote of 39 to 2, a United States resolution that a subcommittee be appointed to investigate alternative sites in New York, San Francisco, Boston and Philadelphia and report before the conclusion of the Second Part of the First Session of the General Assembly.[5] When it became apparent that the Permanent Site Committee was not going to agree as to which of the various areas visited by the subcommittee were most suitable, the United States delegate (Senator Warren R. Austin), after having expressed preference for a site on the East coast of the United States, suggested that discussion of the matter be postponed for another year.[6]

At this juncture, Mr. John D. Rockefeller, Jr. offered the United Nations $8,500,000 for the purchase of property between 42nd and 48th Streets between First Avenue and Franklin D. Roosevelt Drive upon which he had acquired an option, provided: (a) that the City of New York agreed to acquire and give to the United Nations the remaining property in the area not covered by the option; (b) that the City of New York would give to the United Nations rights to bulkheads, and piers along the East River and rights to close the streets within the area; and (c) that the gift should be free of all taxes.[7] On December 12, 1946, the Permanent Site Committee voted to accept the offer of Mr. Rockefeller by a vote of 33 to 7 with 6 abstentions. This action was ratified by the General Assembly on December 14, 1946, by a similar vote.[8]

When it became apparent, in the fall of 1945, that there was a disposition on the part of some countries to locate the headquarters in the United States, the House and Senate on December 10 and 11, 1945, unanimously passed H. Con. Res. 75 by which the United Nations "be, and hereby are, invited to locate the seat of the United Nations within the United States of America." [9]

D. United States Policy in the United Nations
1. GENERAL

[For details of the discussions before the various organs of the United Nations and Specialized Agencies in the period under review, see *International Organization*, I (February, 1947).]

[1] Department of State, *Bulletin*, XIII, p. 563. [2] *Ibid.*, p. 1019.
[3] United Nations General Assembly, Document A/Site/2, February 4, 1946.
[4] United Nations, *Journal of the General Assembly*, No. 33, p. 650.
[5] *Ibid.*, No. 34, p. 23; for text of United States resolution, see United Nations General Assembly, Document A/Site/23/Rev. 1.
[6] *Ibid.*, Document A/Site/43. [7] *Ibid.*, Document A/Site/50.
[8] *Ibid.*, Document A/Site/51.
[9] *Congressional Record*, 91, p. 11930 and 11970 (Daily editions, December 10 and 11, 1945).

INTERNATIONAL PEACE AND SECURITY

For statements of the United States policy in regard to the Atomic Energy Commission and the Commission on Conventional Armaments, see this volume p. 530; labor and social problems, p. 720; the International Bank for Reconstruction and Development and the International Monetary Fund, p. 617; the United Nations Educational, Scientific and Cultural Organization, p. 284; the International Telecommunications Union and the International Civil Aviation Organization, p. 692, 663; the United Nations Relief and Rehabilitation Administration and the International Refugee Organization, p. 364, 373. For questions before the Security Council, see this volume as follows: Iran, p. 851; Greece, p. 881; Spain, p. 887.

(1) Statement of the President (Truman) to the General Assembly of the United Nations, October 23, 1946.[1]

[Excerpts]

The overwhelming majority of the American people, regardless of party, support the United Nations.

They are resolved that the United States, to the full limit of its strength, shall contribute to the establishment and maintenance of a just and lasting peace among the nations of the world.

However, I must tell you that the American people are troubled by the failure of the Allied nations to make more progress in their common search for lasting peace.

It is important to remember the intended place of the United Nations in moving toward this goal. The United Nations — as an organization — was *not* intended to settle the problems arising immediately out of the war. The United Nations *was* intended to provide the means for maintaining international peace in the future after just settlements have been made.

The settlement of these problems was deliberately consigned to negotiations among the Allies, as distinguished from the United Nations. This was done in order to give the United Nations a better opportunity and a freer hand to carry out its long-range task of providing peaceful means for the adjustment of future differences, some of which might arise out of the settlements made as a result of this war.

The United Nations cannot, however, fulfil adequately its own responsibilities until the peace settlements have been made and unless these settlements form a solid foundation upon which to build a permanent peace.

I submit that these settlements, and our search for everlasting peace, rest upon the four essential freedoms.

These are freedom of speech, freedom of religion, freedom from want, and freedom from fear. These are fundamental freedoms to which all the United Nations are pledged under the Charter.

To the attainment of these freedoms — everywhere in the world — through the friendly cooperation of all nations, the Government and people of the United States are dedicated.

The fourth freedom — freedom from fear — means, above all else, freedom from fear of war.

This freedom is attainable *now*.

Lately, we have all heard talk about the possibility of another world war. Fears have been aroused all over the world.

[1] Department of State, *Bulletin* XV, p. 808.

These fears are unwarranted and unjustified.

However, rumors of war still find willing listeners in certain places. If these rumors are not checked they are sure to impede world recovery.

. . . . . .

The United States of America has no wish to make war, now or in the future, upon any people anywhere in the world. The heart of our foreign policy is a sincere desire for peace. This nation will work patiently for peace by every means consistent with self-respect and security. Another world war would shatter the hopes of mankind and completely destroy civilization as we know it.

. . . . . .

To avoid war and rumors and danger of war, the peoples of all countries must not only cherish peace as an ideal but they must develop means of settling conflicts between nations in accordance with principles of law and justice.

The difficulty is that it is easier to get people to agree upon peace as an ideal than to agree upon principles of law and justice or to agree to subject their own acts to the collective judgment of mankind.

But difficult as the task may be, the path along which agreement may be sought with hope of success is clearly defined.

In the first place, every member of the United Nations is legally and morally bound by the Charter to keep the peace. More specifically, every member is bound to refrain in its international relations from the threat or use of force against the territorial integrity or political independence of any state.

In the second place, I remind you that 23 members of the United Nations have bound themselves by the Charter of the Nürnberg Tribunal to the principle that planning, initiating, or waging a war of aggression is a crime against humanity for which individuals as well as states shall be tried before the bar of international justice.

The basic principles upon which we are agreed go far, but not far enough, in removing fear of war from the world. There must be agreement upon a positive, constructive course of action as well.

. . . . . .

The war has left many parts of the world in turmoil. Differences have arisen among the Allies. It will not help us to pretend that this is not the case. But it is not necessary to exaggerate the differences.

For my part, I believe there is no difference of interest that need stand in the way of settling these problems and settling them in accordance with the principles of the United Nations Charter. Above all, we must not permit differences in economic and social systems to stand in the way of peace, either now or in the future. To permit the United Nations to be broken into irreconcilable parts by different political philosophies would bring disaster to the world.

. . . . . .

This Assembly can do much toward recreating the spirit of friendly cooperation and toward reaffirming those principles of the United Nations which must be applied to the peace settlements. It must also prepare and strengthen the United Nations for the tasks that lie ahead after the settlements have been made.

All member nations, large and small, are represented here as equals. Wisdom is not the monopoly of strength or size. Small nations can contribute equally with the large nations toward bringing constructive thought and wise judgment to bear upon the formation of collective policy.

This Assembly is the world's supreme deliberative body.

The highest obligation of this Assembly is to speak for all mankind in such a way as to promote the unity of all members in behalf of a peace that will be lasting because it is founded upon justice.

In seeking unity we should not be concerned about expressing differences freely. The United States believes that this Assembly should demonstrate the importance of freedom of speech to the cause of peace. I do not share the view of any who are fearful of the effects of free and frank discussion in the United Nations.

The United States attaches great importance to the principle of free discussion in this Assembly and in the Security Council. The free and direct exchange of arguments and information promotes understanding and therefore contributes, in the long run, to the removal of the fear of war and some of the causes of war.

The United States believes that the rule of unanimous accord among the five permanent members of the Security Council imposes upon these members a special obligation. This obligation is to seek and reach agreements that will enable them and the Security Council to fulfil the responsibilities they have assumed under the Charter toward their fellow members of the United Nations and toward the maintenance of peace.

It is essential to the future of the United Nations that the members should use the Council as a means for promoting settlement of disputes as well as for airing them. The exercise of neither veto rights nor majority rights can make peace secure. There is no substitute for agreements that are universally acceptable because they are just to all concerned. The Security Council is intended to promote that kind of agreement and it is fully qualified for that purpose.

Because it is able to function continuously, the Security Council represents a most significant development in international relations — the continuing application of the public and peaceful methods of a council chamber to the settlement of disputes between nations.

Two of the greatest obligations undertaken by the United Nations toward the removal of the fear of war remain to be fulfilled.

First, we must reach an agreement establishing international controls of atomic energy that will ensure its use for peaceful purposes only, in accordance with the Assembly's unanimous resolution of last winter.

Second, we must reach agreements that will remove the deadly fear of other weapons of mass destruction, in accordance with the same resolution.

Each of these obligations is going to be difficult to fulfil. Their fulfilment will require the utmost in perseverance and good faith, and we cannot succeed without setting fundamental precedents in the law of nations. Each will be worth everything in perseverance and good faith that we can give to it. The future safety of the United Nations, and of every member nation, depends upon the outcome.

On behalf of the United States I can say we are not discouraged. We shall continue to seek agreement by every possible means.

At the same time we shall also press for preparation of agreements in order that the Security Council may have at its disposal peace forces adequate to prevent acts of aggression.

The United Nations will not be able to remove the fear of war from the world unless substantial progress can be made in the next few years toward the realization of another of the four freedoms — freedom from want.

The Charter pledges the members of the United Nations to work together toward this end. The structure of the United Nations in this field is now nearing completion, with the Economic and Social Council, its commissions, and related specialized agencies. It provides more complete and effective institutions through which to work than the world has ever had before.

A great opportunity lies before us.

In these constructive tasks which concern directly the lives and welfare of human beings throughout the world, humanity and self-interest alike demand of all of us the fullest cooperation.

The United States has already demonstrated in many ways its grave concern about economic reconstruction that will repair the damage done by war.

We have participated actively in every measure taken by the United Nations toward this end. We have in addition taken such separate national action as the granting of large loans and credits and renewal of our reciprocal trade-agreements program.

Through the establishment of the Food and Agriculture Organization, the International Bank for Reconstruction and Development, and the International Monetary Fund, members of the United Nations have proved their capacity for constructive cooperation toward common economic objectives. In addition, the International Labor Organization is being brought into relationship with the United Nations.

Now we must complete the structure. The United States attaches the highest importance to the creation of the International Trade Organization now being discussed in London by a preparatory committee.

This country wants to see, not only the rapid restoration of devastated areas, but the industrial and agricultural progress of the less well-developed areas of the world.

We believe that all nations should be able to develop a healthy economic life of their own. We believe that all peoples should be able to reap the benefits of their own labor and of their own natural resources.

There are immense possibilities in many parts of the world for industrial development and agricultural modernization.

These possibilities can be realized only by the cooperation of members of the United Nations, helping each other on a basis of equal rights.

In the field of social reconstruction and advancement the completion of the charter for a world health organization is an important step forward.

The Assembly now has before it for adoption the constitution of another specialized agency in this field — the International Refugee Organization. It is essential that this Organization be created in time to take over from UNRRA as early as possible in the new year the tasks of caring for and repatriating or resettling the refugees and displaced persons of Europe. There will be similar tasks, of great magnitude, in the Far East.

The United States considers this a matter of great urgency in the cause of restoring peace and in the cause of humanity itself.

I intend to urge the Congress of the United States to authorize this country to do its full part both in financial support of the International Refugee Organization and in joining with other nations to receive those refugees who do not wish to return to their former homes for reasons of political or religious belief.

The United States believes a concerted effort must be made to break down the barriers to a free flow of information among the nations of the world.

We regard freedom of expression and freedom to receive information — the right of the people to know — as among the most important of those human rights and fundamental freedoms to which we are pledged under the United Nations Charter.

The United Nations Educational, Scientific and Cultural Organization, which is meeting in November, is a recognition of this fact. That Organization is built upon the premise that since wars begin in the minds of men, the defense of peace must be constructed in the minds of men, and that a free exchange of ideas and knowledge among peoples is necessary to this task. The United States therefore attaches great importance to all activities designed to break down barriers to mutual understanding and to wider tolerance.

The United States will support the United Nations with all the resources that we possess.

The use of force or the threat of force anywhere in the world to break the peace is of direct concern to the American people.

The course of history has made us one of the stronger nations of the world. It has therefore placed upon us special responsibilities to conserve our strength and to use it rightly in a world so interdependent as our world today.

The American people recognize these special responsibilities. We shall do our best to meet them, both in the making of the peace settlements and in the fulfilment of the long-range tasks of the United Nations.

The American people look upon the United Nations not as a temporary expedient but as a permanent partnership — a partnership among the peoples of the world for their common peace and common well-being.

2. ADMISSION OF NEW MEMBERS

(1) *Remarks of the Deputy United States Representative on the Security Council (Johnson) in Regard to the Admission of New Members, August 28, 1946.*[1]

[Excerpts]

Mr. President, I have no specific comments to make on the report of the Membership Committee, except to say that it seems to me to be drawn up with precision and clarity and to give an adequate review of the work and the debates in the Committee itself.

From the inception of plans for the creation of the United Nations, it has been clearly recognized that the organization should move toward universality of membership. In the world conflict which ended only a year ago, the several United Nations had a most vivid realization of the interdependence of all peoples and all parts of the world. That great coordinated effort in which the forces of the various United Nations met the enemy throughout the world was a lesson to all who took part in it.

Now, with the memories of the fighting and the sacrifices already growing dimmer, it is necessary not to forget the fundamental lesson that the interdependence of the world demands its unity in efforts to insure peace; that the talents and energies of all peoples must be united in an organized effort to this end. If they are not, those left out inevitably become a source of danger or, at best, an unused resource. If the United Nations is to be successful, no state can be left out of it any longer than is absolutely necessary.

The conference at San Francisco created the Charter. In the first part of the first session of the Assembly and the meetings of the other United Nations organs held in London at the time, the structure of the organization was substantially completed. We believe that one of the important constructive acts of the coming Assembly meetings should be the logical next step — the expansion of membership to include all presently eligible applicants. The organization cannot afford to function any longer than is absolutely necessary without the cooperation of every qualified state.

It should, in its very first year, seek as great universality as may be possible. The General Assembly will not meet again this year after the coming session. Unless, therefore, favorable action is now taken by the Council on applications before it, the organization must carry on for some time with a less representative membership than we think necessary.

My Government proposes that the Council take broad and far-sighted action to extend the membership of the United Nations now as far as is consistent with the provisions of Article 4 of the Charter. It accordingly proposes that the Council now recommend to the General Assembly the admission of all the present applicants.

We do not disguise the fact that we have misgivings about some of the applicants, especially Albania and Outer Mongolia. Our doubts and questions with regard to these applicants were fully and clearly stated

[1] *Ibid.*, p. 487.

during the proceedings of the Membership Committee. If there were among the present applicants an entity that was not a state, in the international sense, or one that lacked the governmental powers or material means of carrying out the obligations of the Charter, we would not, Mr. President, make this proposal.

In order to accelerate the achievement of universality of membership, we are prepared, on the basis we have suggested, to resolve the questions we have had in our minds as to the complete readiness of some applicants to assume the obligations of the Charter.

The essence of our proposal, Mr. President, which I have the honor to put before the Council, is that the Council now, in a spirit of fair-mindedness toward all present applicants and in the best interests of the organization, recommend that the Assembly admit them all to membership.

I have taken cognizance, Mr. President, of the letter which we have just heard from the representative of Siam. In placing before you, therefore, the resolution which I hope will have the favorable consideration of the Council, I have taken cognizance of the withdrawal of Siam, and that country is, therefore, not included in this proposed resolution.

With your permission, I should like to read the text of a short resolution which we hope will be adopted and will give effect, if the Council approves it, to the recommendations which I have just outlined.

The Security Council

Having received applications for membership submitted to the organization by Albania, the Mongolian People's Republic, Afghanistan, Trans-Jordan, Ireland, Portugal, Iceland and Sweden:

Having pursuant to its rules of procedure and to its resolution of May 17, 1946, as amended, referred the above-mentioned applications to its Membership Committee for examination and report, and

Having received and considered the Membership Committee's report, which indicates that individual consideration has been given to each application

Recommends

To the General Assembly that it admit to membership the following applicants:

Albania, Mongolian People's Republic, Afghanistan, Trans-Jordan, Ireland, Portugal, Iceland, Sweden.

. . . .

Mr. President, it is apparent from the remarks which have been made by certain of my colleagues on the United States proposal that it does not find full acceptance in the Council. I regret, therefore, to be under the necessity of saying that if the United States proposal is not carried that I shall have to reserve the position I will take on individual countries in the detailed consideration of those countries.

. . . .

Mr. President, I am agreeable to accepting the suggestion of the Delegate of the Soviet Union to withdraw my motion. I am particularly ready and willing to accept that suggestion because it comes from him, and as it is quite evident that it would be the vote of the Soviet Union which would block the passage of this resolution. I therefore withdraw it, Mr. President.

· · · · · · ·

3. THE QUESTION OF THE VETO

(1) *Statement by the United States Delegate to the General Assembly (Connally) on the Veto Question, November 15, 1946.*[1]

[Excerpts]

No problem in the United Nations attracted more attention during the period under review than that of the "veto" — the provision of Article 27, paragraph 3 of the Charter of the United Nations that the concurring votes of the five permanent members of the Security Council was required for the passage of all substantive proposals. Extensive use of the veto by the Soviet Union on the question of the admission of new members to the United Nations, and on the questions of Spain and Greece, had brought before the Second Part of the First Session of the General Assembly a series of proposals, generally from the smaller powers, suggesting methods of reforming voting procedure in the Security Council. For details, see *International Organization*, I (February, 1947).

The Committee is considering a number of resolutions relating to the "veto". It is a term that has obtained wide usage. The press constantly refers to it — it is a short and suggestive word.

The so-called "veto question" arises from the construction of the voting formula in the Charter of the United Nations. In effect, the veto does reside in the permanent members of the Security Council. However, if we consider the Yalta formula — the formula proposed by President Roosevelt at Yalta, accepted there by Prime Minister Churchill and Marshal Stalin, and incorporated into the Charter as article 27 — we must not think of it in the narrow sense of a veto. We must not ignore the history and purpose of that formula.

Let us look at paragraph 3 of that article — the paragraph that causes much of the controversy. Let us examine the rule of unanimity.

Those of you who were at San Francisco will recall how the importance of the unanimity of the great powers in preserving peace influenced our action in adopting the Charter and approving article 27. We were convinced that the great powers alone possessed the strength and military and naval resources necessary to crush aggression and to enforce peace. World War II demonstrated that fact. We were further persuaded that the powers who in unity had won the war could through unity and a common purpose win the peace. We also believed that division between the great powers over intervention or the use of force might result in war instead of peace.

Can you imagine what would happen if four of the smaller states and three of the great powers decided to use force against a state — perhaps against a great power — over the determined opposition of two permanent members of the Council? That would mean war — not the preservation of peace.

[1] *Ibid.*, p. 987.

The unanimity of the great powers on important matters is, in the opinion of the United States, essential for the successful functioning of the Security Council and for the future of the United Nations. But — the words we stress are *successful functioning*. The requirement that the permanent members must concur in a decision must not be made use of by any of them to frustrate that functioning. On the contrary, the United States believes that the permanent members of the Security Council have a special responsibility to make the Organization work, to see that the spirit and intent of the Yalta formula are fulfilled. They must remember and live up to what they said at San Francisco in the Four-Power declaration to which they all subscribed:

It must not be assumed . . . that the permanent members . . . would use their "veto" power wilfully to obstruct the operation of the Council.

. . . .

The permanent members of the Security Council are members of the United Nations before they are members of the Council. They are obligated to perform their duties to the Organization just as are all other members. Membership on the Council does not exempt them from any duties or responsibilities. Membership on the Security Council carries no title of nobility nor privilege nor preference. The permanent members of the Security Council have a heavier responsibility for the successful operation of the United Nations than those of any other organ or agency. The members of the Security Council are trustees for all the members of the United Nations. The Charter lays upon them "primary responsibility for the maintenance of international peace and security" and the members of the United Nations "agree that in carrying out its duties under this responsibility the Security Council acts on their behalf". Note the solemn statement — "under this responsibility the Security Council acts on their behalf". The responsibility of the five permanent members of the Security Council is momentous. It is tremendous. It may have the effect of shaking the very foundations of the earth. How can any member of the Security Council consider lightly or selfishly that lofty responsibility?

I shall say little about the record of the Council to date. I do wish to point out, however, that the picture is not all black. The Council's record has not been one of unrelieved frustration. Remember its successes when you are weighing the worth of the Yalta formula. Place against the exercise of the veto such items as the agreement of Britain and France to evacuate their troops from Syria and the Lebanon, and the withdrawal of Soviet forces from Iran.

So much for the background and the record of the Security Council. The question remains — what of the future? What can we do now to insure the success of the Security Council?

First, I want to say a few words about what should *not* be done. The United Nations is barely ten months old. During the short period of its existence some things have gone well and others have gone badly. There may be parts of the Charter that will prove absolutely unworkable and have to be changed ultimately. Article 27 may be one of those parts, but we do not know that now and we shall not know it for some time to come. During the first hundred years after the adoption of the Constitution of the United States and the Bill of Rights, it was amended only five times. But all that time it was growing and developing and was meeting the needs of an expanding nation. The United Nations Charter also has in it the potentialities of growth and development. The way to find out what these potentialities are is to test it, to build slowly on the foundation that we so successfully laid at San Francisco. Let us not, therefore, in haste attempt to amend the Charter. Let us profit by experience and a better understanding of the functions and obligations, powers and purposes set forth in the Charter.

On the other hand, there are certain important steps that we may take, where already we have that wide area of agreement that is so necessary for their success. It is my conviction that many of the difficulties encountered in the Security Council during the first year of its operation have been due to lack of certainty and differences of opinion regarding the practical application of the voting formula adopted at San Francisco.

. . . .

The Security Council should put in its rules of procedure as soon as possible as complete a list of procedural decisions as the Council can agree upon. This would mean that in the future, whenever a question arises as to the kind of vote that is required, the Council could in most cases solve the problem by a simple reference to the list.

There is still another matter where I believe the stage has been set for progress. There is a provision in paragraph three of article 27 of the Charter that a party to a dispute shall abstain from voting in the Security Council in decisions relating to chapter VI of the Charter — Pacific Settlement. It is perfectly clear that the purpose of this was to prevent the party from being a judge in its own cause, to establish in the Charter a principle of justice which is elementary in every legal system. We would not permit a party to a lawsuit to sit as a member of the jury.

President Roosevelt firmly believed that this principle constituted a very great contribution to the development of international organization. Its acceptance first at Yalta, and then at San Francisco, is a landmark. However, because of some technicalities which I do not intend to explore, doubts have been suggested as to whether it can be effectively applied to the operations of the Security Council.

My own view is that the requirement that a party to a dispute shall abstain from voting constitutes an exception to the general rule set forth in the preceding part of article 27. It is the considered opinion of the United States Delegation that article 27 lays down clearly and without equivocation the fundamental principle that in the field of peaceful settlement under the Charter no state shall be a judge in its own cause. No legal technicalities or mental excursions into the stratosphere should be permitted to becloud this important concept.

I was much interested, Mr. President, in what the distinguished Delegates of El Salvador and New Zealand had to say about the possibility of a permanent member abstaining from voting on a matter without vetoing it. This problem deserves very careful consideration. It would be particularly helpful with respect to the peaceful settlement of disputes if a way could be found to permit a permanent member which does not want to block action by the Council to abstain from voting.

As it stands today a great power may find itself in the utterly ridiculous situation of voting for a measure which it does not entirely approve or else blocking the wheels of justice by the unwilling use of its veto. There should be some middle ground if the machinery of peaceful settlement is to function smoothly.

If progress can be made along these lines in the Security Council, it will not accomplish everything that some would like to see accomplished. But it will help. It will ease the task of the Security Council in arriving at satisfactory decisions relating to the pacific settlement of disputes. It will eliminate many of the arguments that have at times frustrated the work of the Council. The operations of the Council will move forward more smoothly.

. . . .

The United States opposes any steps in the direction of amending the Charter. It is well known that amendment of the Charter is impossible at this time. The resolution proposed by Australia is moderate in that it deals with general objectives. We believe however that the specific recommendation that the permanent members *shall* refrain from exercising their veto power except in the cases under chapter VII of the Charter should first be considered by the permanent members of the Council.

Mr. Chairman, I would like to review briefly the position of the United States.

1. We regard the principle of unanimity as of the highest importance for the success of the United Nations.

2. We believe that the responsibility imposed upon the great powers by the Charter requires them to exert every effort to reach agreement on important issues before the Security Council.

3. We reaffirm the position we took at San Francisco that the veto should be used only in the very rare and exceptional cases.

4. We insist that the use of the veto cannot relieve any state from its fundamental obligations under the Charter.

5. We do not favor amendment of the Charter at this time, although we hope that full agreement, including of course that of the five permanent members, may make it possible in the future to modify the practice of great-power unanimity as it applies to the peaceful settlement of disputes under Chapter VI.

6. We believe that the voting formula should be clarified in the light of experience and practical need. The Security Council should embark upon this task at the earliest practicable time.

7. In particular, we believe that the Security Council should agree upon as complete a list as possible of types of decisions where the veto does not apply.

8. We believe that article 27 makes it clear that in the field of peaceful settlement no state should be a judge in its own cause.

9. The problem of great-power abstention should be carefully considered, particularly with respect to the peaceful settlement of disputes.

Mr. Chairman, digressing a moment from the written text, I want to say that while we are opposed at this time to the amendment of the Charter, we are in favor of making the Charter work. Mr. Chairman, let me issue this warning to all the members of the United Nations and to the Security Council itself. If this Charter does not work, if its functions are not properly performed, this Organization may ultimately go down in ruins. The League of Nations perished; this Organization must not perish. It must go on; it must succeed. There is beyond these doors, there is out on the far-flung reaches of the earth, a force greater than the Security Council, a force greater than the Assembly, and that is the crystallized opinion of the peoples of the world. If we cannot attain our objectives through the United Nations, that public opinion will seek another remedy.

Mr. Chairman, I would, therefore, warn all who are in authority in this Organization to stop, look, listen, and consider their high duties and responsibilities with a view to making this Organization work.

In conclusion, let me stress that members of the Security Council in good conscience do not represent in the Security Council their own governments. They represent the entire membership of the United Nations. Their right to vote is not a personal possession. They have no right to cast a vote in any narrow or nationalistic or selfish interest. At the bar of history they are responsible for administering their high functions in the interest of international peace and in the interest of the entire United Nations Organization. Any member of the Security Council who fails to perform these high functions has no proper conception of his duties and responsibilities. Those duties and responsibilities require that they be performed in accordance with the principles and purposes of the Charter and in a manner to attain its lofty objectives. Let there be no embezzlement of power by the Security Council or by any member. Standing at the highest point of the world's history, the Security Council has a magnificent opportunity to set before all living men and the generations that come after us a commanding example of high duty nobly performed. Humankind will pour out its gratitude and will bless them if they will preserve the peace of the world. May God endow it and its members with a clear vision of their duties and with a high courage to perform every obligation to the United Nations and to the world!

2. REGULATION AND REDUCTION OF ARMAMENTS

At the fifty-seventh meeting of the Security Council of the United Nations on August 29, 1946, the first step under the United Nations was made in the direction of international regulation and reduction of armaments. At the close of that meeting, the representative of the Soviet Union (Gromyko) introduced a proposal which, although not directly concerned with the problem of disarmament, was to lead to its consideration in the course of subsequent discussion. The Soviet representative proposed that the Security Council request from the

Members of the United Nations data pertaining to the location and size of such of their armed forces as were stationed in the territory of other states, exclusive of non-enemy territories.[1]

Discussion of the Soviet proposal was delayed until September 23 when debate opened as to the inclusion of the proposal on the agenda of the Security Council. While the Soviet representative maintained that the presence of the troops in question created a situation with which the Security Council under Articles 34 and 35 of the Charter of the United Nations should be concerned, both the British and Australian representatives objected to the inclusion of the item — the former because he considered it "pure propaganda" and the latter because the proposal dealt with a general world condition rather than with any particular situation. The representative of the United States (Johnson) agreed with the British and Australian representatives and saw no practical reason for discussing the matter at that time. Although Mr. Gromyko asserted that the presence of foreign troops was a source of serious anxiety to the nations concerned and of tension between the governments, other members of the Council denied the existence of any such anxiety or tension and pointed out that none of the governments in whose territory foreign troops were stationed had appealed to the Council against their presence. At the conclusion of the debate on September 24, 1946,[2] the inclusion of the Soviet proposal on the agenda was rejected.

In the plenary session of the General Assembly on October 29, 1946, the Soviet representative (Molotov), referring to the failure of the Soviet Union to bring before the Security Council for discussion the subject of information on the disposition of troops, reaffirmed his belief in the need for supplying such information to the Security Council and introduced a resolution calling for a general reduction of armaments.[3] The United States representative (Austin) supported the Soviet resolution on disarmament and indicated the willingness of this country to furnish information on the size and deployment of its armed forces, suggesting, however, that such information be extended to include all troops, both at home and abroad.[4]

On November 20, 1946, Mr. Molotov placed the Soviet resolution on disposition of troops before the Political and Security Committee of the General Assembly.[5] British amendments to the resolution proposed the extension of its scope through: (1) a preamble covering the subject of disarmament; (2) the addition of the words "military type formations" in the paragraph on number and location of troops; (3) the inclusion of a new paragraph calling for a report on uniformed personnel at home; and (4) the insertion of a new section calling for on the spot verification of reports by a committee to be established by the Security Council.[6] The Soviet resolution as amended by the United Kingdom and modified by the United States was adopted by the Committee on November 28, 1946, and referred to the General Assembly.[7]

The Political and Security Committee then turned to the consideration of the Soviet resolution on disarmament, introduced by Mr. Molotov in the plenary session of October 29, 1946.[8] By Canadian and Australian amendments, the original resolution was broadened to include: (1) negotiations of special arrangements under Article 43 of the Charter; (2) the encouragement of the completion

---

[1] For the text of the statement of the Soviet representative and of the Soviet proposal, see this volume, p. 532.

[2] For the text of the debate on the inclusion of the Soviet proposal, see United Nations Security Council, *Official Records* (1st year, 2d series), Nos. 17 and 18.

[3] For the text of Mr. Molotov's statement and of the Soviet resolution on disarmament, see this volume, p. 533.

[4] For the text of Mr. Austin's statement, see *ibid.*, p. 535.

[5] For the text of the Soviet resolution, see *Journal of the United Nations*, No. 38: Supplement 1, p. 113 (United Nations General Assembly, Document A/C.1/65, November 21, 1946).

[6] *Ibid.*, No. 42: Supplement No. 1, p. 137.

[7] United Nations General Assembly, Document A/C.1/80.

[8] United Nations General Assembly, Document A/BUR/42.

of the work of the Atomic Energy Commission; and (3) the establishment of a system of disarmament by treaty agreement which would include inspection by a Permanent International Commission of Control.[1] An American draft which combined the various proposals with a redraft of the original Soviet resolution,[2] was subsequently accepted by the Committee as the basis upon which a special subcommittee was to draft a final resolution.[3]

From December 8 to 10, 1946, the General Assembly in plenary session debated the draft resolution on information on armed forces. The rapidity of the debate and the scope of the various British and Soviet proposals and counter-proposals were such that the President of the General Assembly (Spaak) intervened to propose that the whole subject, together with the resolution itself, be referred again to the Political and Security Committee for reconsideration in the light of statements made in the course of the debate.[4]

On December 13, 1946, the subcommittee of the Political and Security Committee unanimously accepted a resolution on disarmament which was in turn accepted by the Committee and by the Assembly on the following day.[5] No agreement, however, was reached in the Political and Security Committee on the wording of the resolution relating to information on armed forces and a substitute resolution, of a general character, was placed before the General Assembly. Subsequently, an even more general substitute resolution, sponsored by the representative of Argentina, was accepted on December 14, 1946.[6]

(1) *Statement by the Representative of the Union of Soviet Socialist Republics to the United Nations Security Council (Gromyko) before the Security Council, August 29, 1946.*[7]

[Excerpt]

[Translation]

In connection with the war of the United Nations against the common enemy, Hitlerite Germany and militaristic Japan, the troops of certain Powers, Members of the United Nations, were introduced into the territory of several countries of the United Nations and of certain States that did not take part in the war, for the purpose of driving out the German and Japanese occupation forces or of preventing invasion by the troops of the Axis Powers. After these tasks had been fulfilled and the war had ended, and Germany and Japan were placed under the control of Allied occupation forces, some of the Allied forces were withdrawn from some of the above-mentioned territories.

However, according to available information, Allied troops continue to remain in the territories of a number of Members of the United Nations and other States not comprised among the former enemy territories. The presence of Allied troops for a prolonged period after the end of the war, a presence which is not called for by military neces-

[1] For the text of the Canadian and Australian amendments, see United Nations General Assembly, Documents A/C.1/81, A/C.1/81/Rev. 1 and A/C.1/82.
[2] For the text of the redrafted Soviet resolution, see United Nations General Assembly, Document A/C.1/87.
[3] For the text of the United States draft resolution, see this volume, p. 536.
[4] For summary records of the debate, see *Journal of the United Nations*, Nos. 55–57.
[5] For the text of the resolution, see this volume, p. 542.
[6] For the text of the resolution, see *ibid.*, p. 544.
[7] United Nations Security Council, *Official Records* (1st year, 2d series), No. 5, p. 141.

sity, cannot fail to give rise to a quite natural uneasiness in the peoples of those countries in which foreign troops continue to be stationed.

Moreover, world public opinion, which is concerned with the establishment of peace as soon as possible and the maintenance of general security, follows with unconcealed anxiety the situation which has been created in the above-mentioned countries.

In view of the above, the Security Council should study the question of the presence of Allied troops at the present time in the territories of Members of the United Nations and of other States, with the exception of former enemy territories. The Security Council, however, has not at its disposal information as to where precisely and in what number on the territories of Members of the United Nations and other States, with the exception of former enemy territories, troops of other Members of the United Nations still continue to remain. However, in view of the obligations placed upon the Security Council under Chapter VII of the Charter of the United Nations, the Security Council should be informed of the locations and numbers of the armed forces of Members of the United Nations in the territories in question.

Accordingly, under instructions from the Soviet Government, I make the proposal that the Security Council should adopt a resolution requiring States Members of the United Nations to submit the following information to the Security Council within two weeks:

1. At what points on the territory of Members of the United Nations or other States, with the exception of former enemy territories, and in what number, are armed forces of other Members of the United Nations stationed?

2. At what points in the above-mentioned territories are air and naval bases situated and what is the size of their garrisons belonging to the armed forces of other Member States of the United Nations?

3. The information to be provided under paragraphs 1 and 2 should refer to the situation as it existed on the first of August, 1946.

. . . .

(2) Statement by the Representative of the Union of Soviet Socialist Republics to the United Nations General Assembly (*Molotov*) before the General Assembly, October 29, 1946.[1]

[Excerpts]

[Translation]

. . . .

Under section 7 of the Charter, the Military Staff Committee has already begun to examine the question of the armed forces which the Members of the United Nations Organization shall place at the disposal of the Security Council for the maintenance of international peace and security as provided for in Article 43. In this connection it is natural that the Security Council should know the actual situation, namely where and what armed forces of the United Nations are at present stationed out-

[1] *Journal of the United Nations*, No. 18: Supplement A — A/P.V./42, p. 167.

side the confines of their countries. The submission of this information should of course be binding on all the United Nations.

For its part, the Soviet Union is prepared to submit this information to the Security Council and it does not see any reason whatsoever for the refusal of any other Member of the United Nations Organization to do the same.

. . . . . .

The United Nations Charter authorizes the General Assembly to consider the general principles of co-operation in the maintenance of international peace and security including the principles governing disarmament and the regulation of armaments (Article 11 of the Charter).

. . . . . .

It should be recognized that the time has come to adopt definite decisions to carry out these tasks. Now that the disarmament of the principal aggressive countries has been carried out and measures have been taken to restrict sharply the armaments of other ex-enemy States, the time has come to effect measures to carry out a general restriction of armaments. The adoption of these measures will at the same time enhance the confidence that the United Nations are really permeated by a desire for lasting peace. Lastly, the reduction of armaments will be a deserved blow at the expansionist strivings of those groups which have not yet sufficiently learned the lessons of the ignominious collapse of aggressors in the recent war.

On the other hand, we cannot forget that if together with the declarations of peaceful policy, some States are not only [not][1] reducing their armaments but on the contrary are increasing them both quantitatively and qualitatively, the peoples have every justification to become doubtful as to the sincerity of these peace-loving declarations.

In accordance with Article 11 of the United Nations Charter, the Soviet delegation submits for the consideration of the General Assembly the following proposal:

1. In the interests of consolidating international peace and security and in conformity with the purposes and principles of the United Nations Organization, the General Assembly considers a general reduction of armaments necessary.

2. The implementation of the decision on the reduction of armaments should include as a primary objective the banning of the manufacture and use of atomic energy for military purposes.

3. The General Assembly recommends to the Security Council to provide for the practical achievement of the objectives set forth in the above mentioned paragraphs 1 and 2.

4. The General Assembly calls upon the governments of all States to render every possible assistance to the Security Council in this responsible undertaking, the accomplishment of which conforms to the establishment of stable peace and international security and also serves the interests of the peoples by lightening their heavy economic burden caused by excessive expenditures for armaments which do not correspond to peaceful postwar conditions.

---

[1] French text reads ". . . non seulement ne limitent pas . . ."

The adoption of the decision on a general reduction of armaments and the banning of the manufacture and use of atomic energy for military purposes will indeed respond to the pacifist strivings of our people and will contribute to the development of international co-operation.

. . . .

(3) *Statement by the Senior Representative of the United States to the United Nations General Assembly (Austin) before the General Assembly, October 30, 1946.*[1]

[Excerpts]

. . . .

We welcome the confidence expressed by Mr. Molotov that unanimous agreement among all the nations both large and small can be achieved on such vital matters as the control of atomic energy and on steps to lighten the burden of armaments and military expenditures which still rests so heavily upon the peoples of the world.

The United States urges disarmament.

The United States believes that Mr. Molotov's proposal should be placed on our agenda and fully considered and discussed.

The initiative of the Soviet Union in this matter is appropriate because of its mighty armies, just as the initiative of the United States was appropriate in proposing measures to prevent the manufacture and use of atomic weapons.

. . . .

So far as Mr. Molotov's resolution concerns the regulation and reduction of other armaments, the whole world knows where the United States stands and has always stood. For 20 years before the war and in the 15 months since the fighting stopped, the United States has consistently been in the forefront of those striving to reduce the burden of armaments upon the peoples of the world. Since the end of the war in Europe and the Pacific the United States has progressively and rapidly reduced its military establishment.

After the last war we made the mistake of disarming unilaterally. We shall not repeat that mistake.

The United States is prepared to cooperate fully with all other members of the United Nations in disarmament. It advocates effective safeguards by way of inspection and other means to protect complying states against the hazards of violation and evasion.

We cannot reduce armaments merely by talking about the "regulation of armament and possible disarmament", or the "heavy economic burden caused by excessive expenditures for armaments". We cannot achieve it without positive acts which will establish the "peaceful postwar conditions" to which Mr. Molotov also referred.

Nor can a system for the regulation of armaments and possible disarmaments as contemplated in articles 11, 26, and 47 of the Charter be effectively planned except in relation to progress in the negotiation of the

[1] *Ibid.*, No. 20: Supplement A, p. 231; Department of State, *Bulletin*, XV, p. 934.

armed-forces agreements called for by article 43. At the beginning of April, four of the five members of the Military Staff Committee made specific proposals concerning the principles which should govern the negotiation of these agreements. In September the Soviet Union submitted for the first time a statement of its views on the problem.

I am happy to note that Mr. Molotov referred to the work of the Military Staff Committee. I hope it will now be possible for this Committee to make rapid progress. The conclusion of these agreements, providing the Security Council with peace forces adequate to prevent acts of aggression, is essential to carrying out the objectives of Mr. Molotov's resolution for the reduction of armaments.

Mr. Molotov also referred to article 43 in connection with the Soviet proposal concerning the presence of armed forces of the United Nations on foreign territories. He said, "In this connection it is natural that the Security Council should know the actual situation, namely, where and what armed forces of the United Nations are situated at present outside the confines of their countries. . . . For its part the Soviet Union is prepared to submit this information to the Security Council." [1]

The Government of the United States understands Mr. Molotov's statement to mean that the Soviet Union is fully prepared to report on its armed forces in ex-enemy states as well as in other foreign territories. Therefore, the United States urges prompt fulfilment of this policy. The United States has nothing to hide with regard to our armed forces at home or abroad. The United States will promptly fulfil that policy. In no case are the United States forces in friendly countries except with the consent of those countries.

It is our opinion that the proposed inquiry should include all mobilized armed forces, whether at home or abroad.

. . . . .

(4) Resolution on Regulation and Reduction of Armaments Submitted by the United States to the Political and Security Committee of the United Nations General Assembly, November 30, 1946.[2]

1. With a view to strengthening international peace and security in conformity with the purposes and principles of the United Nations, the General Assembly recognizes the necessity of an early general regulation and reduction of armaments. Accordingly, the General Assembly recommends that the Security Council give prompt consideration to working out the practical measures, according to their priority, which are essential to provide for the general regulation and reduction of armaments pursuant to international treaties and agreements and to assure that such regulation and reduction will be generally observed by all participants and not unilaterally by only some of the participants.

2. The General Assembly recognizes that essential to the general regulation and reduction of armaments is the early establishment of international control of atomic energy and other modern technological

[1] For text of Mr. Molotov's statement, see this volume, p. 533.
[2] United Nations General Assembly, Document A/C.1/90, November 30, 1946.

discoveries to ensure their use only for peaceful purposes. Accordingly, in order to ensure that the general regulation and reduction of armaments are directed towards the major weapons the General Assembly recommends that the Security Council give first consideration to the report which the Atomic Energy Commission will make to the Security Council before 31 December 1946, and facilitate the progress of the work of that Commission.

3. The General Assembly further recognizes that essential to the general regulation and reduction of armaments is the provision of practical and effective safeguards by way of inspection and other means to protect complying states against the hazards of violations and evasions. Accordingly the General Assembly recommends to the Security Council that it give prompt consideration to the working out of proposals to provide such practical and effective safeguards in connection with the control of atomic energy and other limitation or regulation of armaments.

4. The General Assembly calls upon the governments of all states to render every possible assistance to the Security Council and the Atomic Energy Commission in order to promote the establishment of international peace and collective security with the least diversion for armaments of the world's human and economic resources.

(5) *Statement by the Representative of the United States to the United Nations General Assembly (Connally) before the Political and Security Committee, December 2, 1946.*[1]

[Excerpts]

. . . .

Let me say that the United States does not believe in any partial system. We want a comprehensive system of disarmament. Our proposal does not go into the great details of these matters. It outlines merely a set of general principles. But I want to say that this system of inspection and control is absolutely fundamental. There must be adequate international control.

Mr. Molotov, a few days ago, accepted the principle of international control and inspection. How can there be international control and inspection if any member of the Security Council can rise in his seat and interpose a veto at any stage of inspection and control? That is not international; that is individual.

So that we insist that the question of effective safeguards, including inspection and all forms of adequate control, must not be subject to being blocked and destroyed by any state or group of states through the veto. We do not think that at this particular time, when there is a prospect of a subcommittee, the Assembly should undertake to go into too much detail with respect to this matter.

We further insist that the Atomic Energy Commission, which is acting by the authority of this Assembly, shall not be interfered with in

. . . .

[1] *New York Times*, December 3, 1946, p. 4.

its jurisdiction. The United States initiated and moved the creation of that commission.[1]

* * * * *

It will be observed that the Russian proposal does not mention the other weapons, such as jet-planes, such as biological warfare, such as poison gas. We think that a victim of poison gas is just as dead as if he is struck by an atomic bomb. We see no reason why one who is infected by a biological germ that kills him has any better prospect of revival and rehabilitation than one who is a victim of the atomic bomb. And we see no reason why these other deadly measures shall not be included in any plan of disarmament. We think that the victim of a jet bomb will be just as uncomfortable as if he is struck by an atomic bomb. He will not be in a position to inquire what kind of a bomb it was that hit him.

There has been some suggestion that this commission has not done a great deal. Well, it has only been in existence a relatively short time, and it has already done a great deal. It will submit its report by the thirty-first day of December of this year. It is now engaged in undertaking to solve this question. And we do not want it robbed of its authority or jurisdiction.

* * * * *

(6) Statement by the Representative of the Union of Soviet Socialist Republics to the United Nations General Assembly (Molotov) before the Political and Security Committee, December 4, 1946.[2]

[Excerpts]

[Translation]

What did the Soviet Government have in mind when it submitted the question of the general reduction of armaments to the General Assembly for consideration?

Our purpose was a very simple one. It was that the General Assembly should take the first step in solving this important problem. We considered and still consider it quite sufficient that the General Assembly should express its mind on the following three questions.

First, the General Assembly would do a great deed by declaring in a firm voice that the time has come to set about the general reduction of armaments.

Second, the General Assembly is faced with the task of expressing its mind on the question of the prohibition of atomic energy, since it is known that the menace of atomic weapons is causing great alarm among the nations.

Third, the General Assembly should recognize the necessity of establishing reliable international control over the execution of the decision for a general reduction of armaments and the prohibition of atomic weapons, so that this international control should have at its disposal means of inspection for verifying the situation in all countries.

The adoption of these three resolutions by the General Assembly would really constitute an important step forward in the cause of the general reduction of armaments. After such a resolution the Security Council should take up the task of working out concrete measures. This is the substance of the Soviet Government's proposal.

* * * * *

[1] For detailed information on the international control of atomic energy, see this volume, p. 544.

[2] *New York Times*, December 5, 1946, p. 25.

Since the Soviet plan was submitted, we have received also a number of other plans on the question of the reduction of armaments. It is necessary to mention, above all, the proposals of the Australian and Canadian delegations. Finally, in the last few days the plan of the United States of America has been submitted to us, on the subject of which Senator Connally gave his explanations on December 2.[1]

To a greater or less extent the initiative of the Soviet Union is finding support in all these plans.

It seems to us that in this respect the American plan merits particular attention.

I will not hide the fact that the American plan in its present form cannot satisfy us. We consider it to be insufficiently clear and rather one-sided. We are going to submit amendments to this plan, which express our desires.

While pursuing the aim of achieving unanimity in the resolution of the General Assembly for the general reduction of armaments, we are prepared not to insist on the plan submitted by us and express our willingness to take the American plan as a basis for further discussion. We hope that this step by the Soviet delegation will enable us to achieve unanimity so that the General Assembly, sitting in New York, may take the first step in this important cause.

Further, I wish to say a few words about the amendments which the Soviet delegation would like to make in the American plan. There are in all three amendments.

I will begin with the amendment relating to paragraph one. On the one hand, this paragraph speaks of the Security Council, which should work out practical measures for the reduction of armaments. On the other hand, the same paragraph speaks of international treaties and agreements for the reduction of armaments. The question arises, in what way will the decision on the reduction of armaments be taken: Will it be taken by concluding international conventions or by a resolution of the Security Council?

If we take the view that the reduction of armaments is to be carried out by means of international agreements, this will give rise to a good many pretexts for all sorts of delays. For this reason the Soviet delegation is of the opinion that the decision on the reduction of armaments should be taken by means of a resolution of the Security Council. It is very important that the General Assembly should adopt this point of view; then the cause of the reduction of armaments will be considerably expedited. The wording of the first paragraph must be amended accordingly.

· · · · · · ·

As you already know, the Soviet Government takes the stand that a decision of general reduction of armaments and on the prohibition of atomic weapons should be adopted by the Security Council. The adoption of such a decision offers no small difficulties. It is possible that various points of view will be expressed in the Security Council on this or that question connected with this problem. Only the attainment of unanimity in the Security Council and, above all, of unanimity between the five permanent members can guarantee the adoption of the decision to reduce armaments.

· · · · · · ·

Observance of the principle of unanimity of the five great powers is also necessary for those decisions by the Security Council referring to the establishment of a commission for control of armaments reduction, and of the prohibition of atomic weapons. But when decisions regarding the composition of the control commissions are taken and the control commissions begin their task, they will, of course, work in accordance with those rules drawn up for them by the Security Council.

It should be quite obvious that the question of the well-known principle of unanimity operating in the Security Council has no relation at all to the work of

[1] See this volume, p. 537.

the commissions themselves. Consequently, it is entirely wrong to consider the matter in the light that any government possessing the "right of veto", will be in a position to hinder the fulfillment of the control and inspections.

The control commissions are not the Security Council, and, therefore, there are no grounds whatsoever for saying that any power making use of the "right of veto" will be in a position to obstruct the course of control. Every attempt to obstruct the control or inspection carried out in accordance with the decisions taken by the Security Council will be nothing other than a violation of the decisions of the Security Council.

That is why talk about a "veto" in connection with control and inspection is devoid of foundation. Such talk cannot be understood as anything other than an attempt to substitute one question for another, as an attempt to evade a straight answer to the question raised regarding the general reduction of armaments.

Thus, we must take an important decision. The General Assembly must take the first step in dealing with problems of general reduction of armaments. We must prepare that decision and not allow any further procrastination in this matter.

The Soviet delegation hopes that the American draft and the Soviet delegation's amendments thereto will make for a good fundamental decision by the General Assembly.

(7) Statement by the Senior Representative of the United States to the United Nations General Assembly (Byrnes) before the General Assembly, December 13, 1946.[1]

[Excerpts]

. . . . . .

Ever since the close of hostilities, it has been the policy of the United States to hasten the return of conditions of peace. We want to enable the fighting men of the United Nations to return to their homes and their families. We want to give the people of all lands the chance to rebuild what the war has destroyed. There need be no concern about the willingness of the American people to do everything within their power to rid themselves and the world of the burden of excessive armaments.

. . . . . .

Effective disarmament cannot be secured by any simple mathematical rule. Demobilized divisions can be speedily recalled to the colours. But a scrapped plane or a scrapped battleship can never be recommissioned. Disarmament, to be effective, must look to the future. It is easy for us to see what folly it would have been when gun powder was discovered, to start disarming by limiting the use of the bow and arrow.

We must see to it that disarmament starts with the major weapons of mass destruction. We must see to it that disarmament is general and not unilateral. We must see to it that disarmament rests not upon general promises which are kept by some States and ignored by other States. We must see to it that disarmament is accompanied by effective safeguards by way of inspection and other means under international control which will protect complying States against the hazards of violations and evasions.

We must see to it that these safeguards are so clear and explicit that there will be no question of the right of complying States, veto or no veto, to take immediate action in defence of the rule of law. No disarmament system which leaves law-abiding States weak and helpless in the face of aggression can ever contribute to world peace and security.

. . . . . .

[1] *Journal of the United Nations*, No. 62: Supplement A — A/P.V./62, December 13, 1946, p. 638.

I am glad that the proposed resolution raises in connection with the problem of disarmament the question of the disposal of troops and the justification of their presence on foreign soil. For disarmament necessarily raises the question of the use which may be made of arms and armed forces which are not prohibited. Reducing armaments will not bring peace if the arms and armed forces that remain are used to undermine collective security.

. . . .

On V-J Day we had over five million troops overseas. We had to send with them extensive supplies and equipment which could not be disposed of overnight.

But despite the tremendous problem of liquidating our extensive overseas war activities, today we have less than 550,000 troops outside of American territory. Most of these troops are in Germany, Japan and the Japanese Islands, Korea, Austria and Venezia Guilia.

The great majority of the troops we have on the territory of the other States outside these occupation areas are supply or administrative personnel. Let me state specifically just what combat troops we have in these other States.

We have a total of 96,000 military personnel in the Philippines but only about 30,000 are combat forces, air and ground, and of these 17,000 are Philippine Scouts. These troops are in the Philippines primarily to back up our forces in Japan. Substantial reductions are contemplated in the near future.

Of the 19,000 troops we have in China, about 15,000 are combat troops and roughly one-half of these are today under orders to return home.

We have about 1,500 troops in Panama, excluding the Canal Zone. One thousand of those, composed of a small air unit and some radar air warning detachments, can be classified as combat forces. We have, of course, our normal protective forces in the Panama Canal Zone proper.

We have no combat units in countries other than those I have just mentioned.

Our military personnel in Iceland number less than 600 men. They include no combat troops. They are being withdrawn rapidly and all will be withdrawn by early April 1947, in accordance with our agreement with the Government of Iceland. The military personnel have been there only to maintain one of our air transport lines of communication with our occupation forces in Germany.

In the Azores, on the southern air transport communication line to Germany, we have about 300 men. Again there is not a single combat soldier among them. They are technicians and administrative officials. They are there under an agreement with the Government of Portugal.

Our combat troops are in North China at the request of the Chinese National Government. Their task is to assist in carrying out the terms of surrender with respect to the disarming and deportation of the Japanese. Their mission is nearly completed. Instructions have already been issued for the return of half of our forces now in China although the Chinese Government has urged that they be retained there until conditions become more stabilized.

We have made it clear that our troops will not become participants in civil strife in China. But we are eager to do our part, and we hope other States are eager to do their part, to prevent civil war in China and to promote a unified and democratic China. A free and independent China is essential to world peace and we cannot ignore or tolerate efforts upon the part of any State to retard the development of the freedom and independence of China. The United States Government repudiates the suggestion that our troops in China or elsewhere, with the consent of the States concerned, are a threat to the internal or external peace of any country.

Because the representative of the USSR has referred to our troops in China, it is fair for me to say that I am confident that the number of American troops in North China is far less than the number of USSR troops in South Manchuria, in the Port Arthur area.

. . . .

The task before us is to maintain collective security with scrupulous regard for the sovereign equality of all States. This involves more than the question of armaments and armed forces. Aggressor nations do not go to war because they are armed, but because they want to get with their arms things which other nations will not freely accord to them. Aggressor nations attack not only because they are armed but because they believe others have not the armed strength to resist them. Sovereignty can be destroyed not only by armies but by a war of nerves and by organized political penetration. World peace depends upon what is in our hearts more than upon what is written in our treaties.

Great States must strive for understandings which will not only protect their own legitimate security requirements but also the political independence and integrity of the smaller States. It is not in the interest of peace and security that the basic power relationships among great States should depend upon which political party comes to power in Iran, Greece or in China. Great States must not permit differences among themselves to tear asunder the political unity of smaller States. Then, smaller States must recognize that true collective security requires their co-operation just as much as that of the larger States. Without the co-operation of large States and small States, all of our disarmament plans are doomed to failure.

A race for armaments, a race for power is not in the interest of any country or of any people. We want to stop the race for armaments and we want to stop the race for power. We want to be partners with all nations, not to make war, but to keep the peace. We want to uphold the rule of law among nations. We want to promote the freedom and well-being of all peoples in a friendly civilized world.

(8) *Resolution on Principles Governing the General Regulation and Reduction of Armaments, Approved by the United Nations General Assembly, December 14, 1946.*[1]

1. In pursuance of Article 11 of the Charter and with a view to strengthening international peace and security in conformity with the purposes and principles of the United Nations,

The General Assembly,

Recognizes the necessity of an early general regulation and reduction of armaments and armed forces.

2. *Accordingly,*

The General Assembly,

Recommends that the Security Council give prompt consideration to formulating the practical measures, according to their priority, which are essential to provide for the general regulation and reduction of armaments and armed forces and to assure that such regulation and reduction of armaments and armed forces will be generally observed by all participants and not unilaterally by only some of the participants. The plans formulated by the Security Council shall be submitted by the Secretary-General to the Members of the United Nations for consideration at a special session of the General Assembly. The treaties or conventions approved by the General Assembly shall be submitted to the signatory States for ratification in accordance with Article 26 of the Charter.

3. As an essential step towards the urgent objective of prohibiting and eliminating from national armaments atomic and all other major weapons adaptable now and in the future to mass destruction, and the early establishment of international control of atomic energy and other

[1] *Ibid.,* No. 75: Supplement A–A/64, Add. 1, p. 827.

modern scientific discoveries and technical developments to ensure their use only for peaceful purposes,

The General Assembly,

Urges the expeditious fulfillment by the Atomic Energy Commission of its terms of reference as set forth in section 5 of the General Assembly resolution of 24 January 1946.

4. In order to ensure that the general prohibition, regulation and reduction of armaments are directed towards the major weapons of modern warfare and not merely towards the minor weapons,

The General Assembly,

Recommends that the Security Council expedite consideration of the reports which the Atomic Energy Commission will make to the Security Council and that it facilitate the work of that Commission, and also that the Security Council expedite consideration of a draft convention or conventions for the creation of an international system of control and inspection, these conventions to include the prohibition of atomic and all other major weapons adaptable now and in the future to mass destruction and the control of atomic energy to the extent necessary to ensure its use only for peaceful purposes.

5. *The General Assembly,*

Further recognizes that essential to the general regulation and reduction of armaments and armed forces, is the provision of practical and effective safeguards by way of inspection and other means to protect complying States against the hazards of violations and evasions.

Accordingly,

The General Assembly,

Recommends to the Security Council that it give prompt consideration to the working out of proposals to provide such practical and effective safeguards in connection with the control of atomic energy and the general regulation and reduction of armaments.

6. To ensure the adoption of measures for the early general regulation and reduction of armaments and armed forces, for the prohibition of the use of atomic energy for military purposes and the elimination from national armaments of atomic and all other major weapons adaptable now or in the future to mass destruction, and for the control of atomic energy to the extent necessary to ensure its use only for peaceful purposes,

There shall be established, within the framework of the Security Council, which bears the primary responsibility for the maintenance of international peace and security, an international system, as mentioned in paragraph 4, operating through special organs, which organs shall derive their powers and status from the convention or conventions under which they are established.

7. *The General Assembly,*

regarding the problem of security as closely connected with that of disarmament,

Recommends the Security Council to accelerate as much as possible the placing at its disposal of the armed forces mentioned in Article 43 of the Charter;

Recommends the Members to undertake the progressive and balanced withdrawal, taking into account the needs of occupation, of their armed forces stationed in ex-enemy territories, and the withdrawal without delay of armed forces stationed in the territories of Members without their consent freely and publicly expressed in treaties or agreement consistent with the Charter and not contradicting international agreements;

Further recommends a corresponding reduction of national armed forces, and a general progressive and balanced reduction of national armed forces.

8. Nothing herein contained shall alter or limit the resolution of the General Assembly passed on 24 January 1946, creating the Atomic Energy Commission.

9. *The General Assembly,*

Calls upon all Members of the United Nations to render every possible assistance to the Security Council and the Atomic Energy Commission in order to promote the establishment and maintenance of international peace and collective security with the least diversion for armaments of the world's human and economic resources.

(9) Resolution on Principles Governing Information on Armed Forces of the United Nations, Approved by the United Nations General Assembly, December 14, 1946.[1]

The General Assembly,

Desirous of implementing, as soon as possible, the resolution of 14 December 1946 on the principles governing the regulation and reduction of armaments,

Calls upon the Security Council to determine, as soon as possible, the information which the States Members should be called upon to furnish, in order to give effect to this resolution.

3. INTERNATIONAL CONTROL OF ATOMIC ENERGY

The subject of international measures looking to the control of atomic energy was first opened by President Truman in his message to Congress on October 3, 1945.[2] Stating that international as well as domestic controls must be considered, the President announced his intention of initiating discussion on a limited scale at first with the United Kingdom and Canada and later with other members of the United Nations in order "to effect agreement on the conditions under which co-operation might replace rivalry in the field of atomic power." These initial conversations with Prime Ministers Attlee (United Kingdom) and Mackenzie King (Canada) subsequently opened in Washington on November 10, 1945 [3] and were concluded five days later. The conversations closed with the issuance of a Joint Declaration foreshadowing the release to other nations of information on the practical application of atomic energy "just as soon as effective enforceable safeguards against its use for destructive purposes can be devised," and recommending that the problem of international control be placed before the United Nations for solution.[4]

Discussions including the Soviet Union as well as the United Kingdom and the United States were carried on during the meeting of the Council of Foreign

---

[1] *Ibid.*, No. 63: Supplement A — A/P.V./63, December 14, 1946, p. 670.

[2] For excerpts from the President's message, see this volume, p. 545.

[3] *New York Times*, November 11, 1945, p. 1.

[4] For the text of the Joint Declaration, see this volume, p. 547.

Ministers in Moscow (December 16–26, 1945) and the communiqué released at the conclusion of that meeting dealt in part with the problem of international control.[1]

Acting in accordance with the mandate of the Foreign Ministers, Secretary of State Byrnes met on January 20, 1946, during the opening sessions of the United Nations General Assembly in London, with representatives of the United Kingdom, the Soviet Union, France and China. The result of this discussion was a resolution introduced the following day before the Political and Security Committee of the General Assembly calling, in the name of the five powers and Canada, for the formation of an atomic energy control body within the framework of the United Nations.[2] The resolution rapidly received the approval of the Committee on January 21 and of the General Assembly on January 24, 1946.[3]

As a permanent member of the Security Council the United States was assured a seat on the newly organized Atomic Energy Commission. Accordingly, in order to benefit persons selected to represent the United States on the Commission, the Department of State established, on January 7, 1946, the Secretary of State's Committee on Atomic Energy to study and prepare a report on the subject of safeguards and controls necessary to protect this country against the misuse of atomic energy. Dean Acheson, Under-Secretary of State, was appointed chairman of the Committee which also included: John J. McCloy, Assistant Secretary of War; Dr. Vannevar Bush; Dr. James B. Conant, President of Harvard University; and Maj. Gen. Leslie R. Groves. A Board of Consultants was appointed on January 23 to assist the Committee in its work. The Board consisted of David E. Lilienthal, Chairman of the Tennessee Valley Authority; Chester I. Bernard, President of New Jersey Bell Telephone Company; Dr. J. R. Oppenheimer; Charles A. Thomas, Vice President of Monsanto Chemical Company; and Harry A. Winne, Vice President and Manager of the engineering apparatus department of General Motors Corporation.[4] The Board made public the results of its study in a report (Acheson-Lilienthal Report), on March 28, 1946.[5]

Mr. Bernard M. Baruch was named by President Truman as United States Representative on the Atomic Energy Commission on March 18, 1946.[6] His nomination was confirmed by the Senate on April, 5, 1946.[7]

For an account of the debate in the Atomic Energy Commission and of its work during the period under review, see *International Organization*, I, p. 99–102.

For a discussion of atomic energy control in relation to the more general problem of regulation and reduction of armaments, see this volume, p. 538.

A. Initiation of International Controls

(1) *Message from the President* (*Truman*) *to the Congress, October 3, 1945.*[8]

[Excerpts]

. . . . . .

The discovery of the means of releasing atomic energy began a new era in the history of civilization. The scientific and industrial knowledge

---

[1] For the text of that part of the Communiqué relating to atomic energy control see *ibid.*, p. 548.

[2] *New York Times*, January 21, 1947, p. 3.

[3] United Nations General Assembly, *Official Records of the First Part of the First Session of the General Assembly: First Committee, Political and Security Questions Including Regulation of Armaments. Summary Record of Meetings, 11 January–12 February, 1946*, p. 11; for the text of the resolution, see this volume, p. 551.

[4] Department of State, *Bulletin*, XIV, p. 177.

[5] For excerpts from the Acheson-Lilienthal Report, see this volume, p. 552.

[6] *New York Times*, March 19, 1946, p. 1.

[7] Department of State, *Bulletin*, XIV, p. 676.

[8] *Ibid.*, XIII, p. 514.

on which this discovery rests does not relate merely to another weapon. It may some day prove to be more revolutionary in the development of human society than the invention of the wheel, the use of metals, or the steam or internal-combustion engine.

Never in history has society been confronted with a power so full of potential danger and at the same time so full of promise for the future of man and for the peace of the world. I think I express the faith of the American people when I say that we can use the knowledge we have won, not for the devastation of war, but for the future welfare of humanity.

To accomplish that objective we must proceed along two fronts — the domestic and the international.

. . . . . .

In international relations as in domestic affairs, the release of atomic energy constitutes a new force too revolutionary to consider in the framework of old ideas. We can no longer rely on the slow progress of time to develop a program of control among nations. Civilization demands that we shall reach at the earliest possible date a satisfactory arrangement for the control of this discovery in order that it may become a powerful and forceful influence towards the maintenance of world peace instead of an instrument of destruction.

Scientific opinion appears to be practically unanimous that the essential theoretical knowledge upon which the discovery is based is already widely known. There is also substantial agreement that foreign research can come abreast of our present theoretical knowledge in time.

The hope of civilization lies in international arrangements looking, if possible, to the renunciation of the use and development of the atomic bomb, and directing and encouraging the use of atomic energy and all future scientific information toward peaceful and humanitarian ends. The difficulties in working out such arrangements are great. The alternative to overcoming these difficulties, however, may be a desperate armament race which might well end in disaster. Discussion of the international problem cannot be safely delayed until the United Nations Organization is functioning and in a position adequately to deal with it.

I therefore propose to initiate discussions, first with our associates in this discovery, Great Britain and Canada, and then with other nations, in an effort to effect agreement on the conditions under which cooperation might replace rivalry in the field of atomic power.

I desire to emphasize that these discussions will not be concerned with disclosures relating to the manufacturing processes leading to the production of the atomic bomb itself. They will constitute an effort to work out arrangements covering the terms under which international collaboration and exchange of scientific information might safely proceed.

The outcome of the discussions will be reported to the Congress as soon as possible, and any resulting agreements requiring congressional action will be submitted to the Congress.

. . . .

(2) *Agreed Declaration by the President of the United States (Truman), the Prime Minister of the United Kingdom (Attlee) and the Prime Minister of Canada (King), Washington, November 15, 1945.*[1]

THE PRESIDENT OF THE UNITED STATES, THE PRIME MINISTER OF THE UNITED KINGDOM, AND THE PRIME MINISTER OF CANADA have issued the following statement.

1. We recognize that the application of recent scientific discoveries to the methods and practice of war has placed at the disposal of mankind means of destruction hitherto unknown, against which there can be no adequate military defence, and in the employment of which no single nation can in fact have a monopoly.

2. We desire to emphasize that the responsibility for devising means to ensure that the new discoveries shall be used for the benefit of mankind, instead of as a means of destruction, rests not on our nations alone, but upon the whole civilized world. Nevertheless, the progress that we have made in the development and use of atomic energy demands that we take an initiative in the matter, and we have accordingly met together to consider the possibility of international action:
   (a) To prevent the use of atomic energy for destructive purposes
   (b) To promote the use of recent and future advances in scientific knowledge, particularly in the utilization of atomic energy, for peaceful and humanitarian ends.

3. We are aware that the only complete protection for the civilized world from the destructive use of scientific knowledge lies in the prevention of war. No system of safeguards that can be devised will of itself provide an effective guarantee against production of atomic weapons by a nation bent on aggression. Nor can we ignore the possibility of the development of other weapons, or of new methods of warfare, which may constitute as great a threat to civilization as the military use of atomic energy.

4. Representing as we do, the three countries which possess the knowledge essential to the use of atomic energy, we declare at the outset our willingness, as a first contribution, to proceed with the exchange of fundamental scientific information and the interchange of scientists and scientific literature for peaceful ends with any nation that will fully reciprocate.

5. We believe that the fruits of scientific research should be made available to all nations, and that freedom of investigation and free interchange of ideas are essential to the progress of knowledge. In pursuance of this policy, the basic scientific information essential to the development of atomic energy for peaceful purposes has already been made available to the world. It is our intention that all further information of this character that may become available from time to time shall be similarly treated. We trust that other nations will adopt the same policy, thereby creating an atmosphere of reciprocal confidence in which political agreement and cooperation will flourish.

6. We have considered the question of the disclosure of detailed information concerning the practical industrial application of atomic energy. The military exploitation of atomic energy depends, in large part, upon the same methods and processes as would be required for industrial uses.

We are not convinced that the spreading of the specialized information regarding the practical application of atomic energy, before it is possible to devise effective, reciprocal, and enforceable safeguards acceptable to all nations, would contribute to a constructive solution of the problem of the atomic bomb. On the contrary we think it might have the opposite effect. We are, however, prepared to share, on a reciprocal basis with others of the United Nations, detailed information concerning the practical industrial application of atomic energy just as soon as effective enforceable safeguards against its use for destructive purposes can be devised.

[1] *Ibid.*, p. 781.

7. In order to attain the most effective means of entirely eliminating the use of atomic energy for destructive purposes and promoting its widest use for industrial and humanitarian purposes, we are of the opinion that at the earliest practicable date a Commission should be set up under the United Nations Organization to prepare recommendations for submission to the Organization.

The Commission should be instructed to proceed with the utmost dispatch and should be authorized to submit recommendations from time to time dealing with separate phases of its work.

In particular the Commission should make specific proposals:

(a) For extending between all nations the exchange of basic scientific information for peaceful ends,

(b) For control of atomic energy to the extent necessary to ensure its use only for peaceful purposes,

(c) For the elimination from national armaments of atomic weapons and of all other major weapons adaptable to mass destruction,

(d) For effective safeguards by way of inspection and other means to protect complying states against the hazards of violations and evasions.

8. The work of the Commission should proceed by separate stages, the successful completion of each one of which will develop the necessary confidence of the world before the next stage is undertaken. Specifically it is considered that the Commission might well devote its attention first to the wide exchange of scientists and scientific information, and as a second stage to the development of full knowledge concerning natural resources of raw materials.

9. Faced with the terrible realities of the application of science to destruction, every nation will realize more urgently than before the overwhelming need to maintain the rule of law among nations and to banish the scourge of war from the earth. This can only be brought about by giving wholehearted support to the United Nations Organization, and by consolidating and extending its authority, thus creating conditions of mutual trust in which all peoples will be free to devote themselves to the arts of peace. It is our firm resolve to work without reservation to achieve these ends.

(3) *Communiqué on the Moscow Conference of Foreign Ministers, Released December 27, 1945.*[1]

[Excerpt]

. . . .

VII. THE ESTABLISHMENT BY THE UNITED NATIONS OF A COMMISSION FOR THE CONTROL OF ATOMIC ENERGY

Discussion of the subject of atomic energy related to the question of the establishment of a commission by the General Assembly of the United Nations. The Ministers of Foreign Affairs of the Union of Soviet Socialist Republics, the United States of America, and the United Kingdom have agreed to recommend, for the consideration of the General Assembly of the United Nations, the establishment by the United Nations of a commission to consider problems arising from the discovery of atomic energy and related matters. They have agreed to invite the other permanent members of the Security Council, France and China, together with Canada, to join with them in assuming the initiative in sponsoring the following resolution at the first session of the General Assembly of the United Nations in January 1946: —

[1] *Ibid.*, p. 1031.

Resolved by the General Assembly of the United Nations to establish a Commission, with the composition and competence set out hereunder, to deal with the problems raised by the discovery of atomic energy and other related matters.

I. Establishment of the Commission

A Commission is hereby established by the General Assembly with the terms of reference set out under Section V below.

II. Relations of the Commission with the Organs of the United Nations

(a) The Commission shall submit its reports and recommendations to the Security Council, and such reports and recommendations shall be made public unless the Security Council, in the interests of peace and security, otherwise directs. In the appropriate cases the Security Council should transmit these Reports to the General Assembly and the members of the United Nations, as well as to the Economic and Social Council and other Organs within the framework of the United Nations.

(b) In view of the Security Council's primary responsibility under the Charter of the United Nations for the maintenance of international peace and security, the Security Council shall issue directions to the Commission in matters affecting security. On these matters the Commission shall be accountable for its work to the Security Council.

III. Composition of the Commission

The Commission shall be composed of one representative from each of those states represented on the Security Council, and Canada when that state is not a member of the Security Council. Each representative on the Commission may have such assistance as he may desire.

IV. Rules of Procedure

The Commission shall have whatever staff it may deem necessary, and shall make recommendations for its rules of procedure to the Security Council, which shall approve them as a procedural matter.

V. Terms of Reference on the Commission

The Commission shall proceed with the utmost dispatch and inquire into all phases of the problem, and make such recommendations from time to time with respect to them as it finds possible. In particular the Commission shall make specific proposals:

(a) For extending between all nations the exchange of basic scientific information for peaceful ends;

(b) For control of atomic energy to the extent necessary to ensure its use only for peaceful purposes;

(c) For the elimination from national armaments of atomic weapons and of all other major weapons adaptable to mass destruction;

(d) For effective safeguards by way of inspection and other means to protect complying states against the hazards of violations and evasions.

The work of the Commission should proceed by separate stages, the successful completion of each of which will develop the necessary confidence of the world before the next stage is undertaken.

The Commission shall not infringe upon the responsibilities of any Organ of the United Nations, but should present recommendations for the consideration of those Organs in the performance of their tasks under the terms of the United Nations Charter.

B. United Nations Atomic Energy Commission

(1) *Statement by the Representative of the United States to the United Nations General Assembly (Connally) before the Political and Security Committee, London, January 21, 1946.*[1]

[Excerpt]

. . . .

The Commission is intended to enquire into all aspects of the problems presented by the discovery of atomic energy and by the other forces capable of use for mass destruction. Its object is to study and recommend measures which would permit and promote the use of these forces for peaceful and humanitarian purposes under security conditions which will protect the world against their use for destructive purposes. In performing its work the Commission must obviously operate within the framework of powers conferred upon the United Nations by the Charter. It is authorized to make recommendations, but not to compel action on the part of any State. Each State would be free to consider the acceptance or rejection of the Commission's recommendations in accordance with its own constitutional processes.

As Secretary of State Byrnes said on 30 December after returning from Moscow, "The four objectives set forth in the proposed resolution establishing the Commission are not intended to indicate the order in which they are to be considered. In particular it was intended and is understood that the matter of safeguards will apply to the recommendations of the Commission in relation to every phase of the subject and at every stage. Indeed, at the root of the whole matter lies the problem of providing the necessary safeguards."

The resolution recognizes the interest and deep concern of all mankind in working out a lasting solution for this profoundly important problem by providing that the Commission shall be established by the General Assembly. In this way, as President Truman recently said, "all nations will have a voice in selecting the proposed Commission."

Further, the only known use of atomic energy at present is for mass destruction on a scale unparalleled in the history of warfare. In view of the transcendent importance of the security aspect of the problems raised by the discovery of atomic energy, the resolution provides that the Commission shall submit its reports and recommendations to the Security Council. The Security Council is authorized to give directions to the Commission in matters affecting security and it may restrain

[1] United Nations General Assembly, *Official Records of the First Part of the First Session of the General Assembly: First Committee* . . ., cited above, p. 7.

publication of reports detrimental to peace and security. But such action requires the affirmative vote of seven members of the Security Council, including the concurring votes of the permanent members. It is clear, therefore, that failure of the Security Council to act cannot block the work of the Commission. It is the earnest belief of the United States Government that this resolution will enable the Commission to perform its work effectively and without delay.

The delegation of the United States strongly urges that this Committee promptly recommend that the General Assembly approve the resolution.

(2) *Resolution Establishing the Atomic Energy Commission, Approved by the United Nations General Assembly, January 24, 1946.*[1]

RESOLVED by the General Assembly of the United Nations to establish a Commission, with the composition and competence set out hereunder, to deal with the problems raised by the discovery of atomic energy and other related matters:

I. ESTABLISHMENT OF THE COMMISSION

A Commission is hereby established by the General Assembly with the terms of reference set out under Section V below.

II. RELATIONS OF THE COMMISSION WITH THE ORGANS OF THE UNITED NATIONS

(*a*) The Commission shall submit its reports and recommendations to the Security Council, and such reports and recommendations shall be made public unless the Security Council, in the interest of peace and security, otherwise directs. In the appropriate cases the Security Council should transmit these Reports to the General Assembly and the members of the United Nations, as well as to the Economic and Social Council and other Organs within the framework of the United Nations.

(*b*) In view of the Security Council's primary responsibility under the Charter of the United Nations for the maintenance of international peace and security, the Security Council shall issue directions to the Commission in matters affecting security. On these matters the Commission shall be accountable for its work to the Security Council.

III. COMPOSITION OF THE COMMISSION

The Commission shall be composed of one representative from each of those States, represented on the Security Council, and Canada when that State is not a member of the Security Council. Each representative on the Commission may have such assistance as he may desire.

IV. RULES OF PROCEDURE

The Commission shall have whatever staff it may deem necessary, and shall make recommendations for its rules of procedure to the Security Council, which shall approve them as a procedural matter.

[1] Department of State, *Bulletin*, XIV, p. 198.

V. Terms of Reference of the Commission

The Commission shall proceed with the utmost despatch and enquire into all phases of the problems, and make such recommendations from time to time with respect to them as it finds possible. In particular the Commission shall make specific proposals:

(a) For extending between all nations the exchange of basic scientific information for peaceful ends;

(b) For control of atomic energy to the extent necessary to ensure its use only for peaceful purposes;

(c) For the elimination from national armaments of atomic weapons and of all other major weapons adaptable to mass destruction;

(d) For effective safeguards by way of inspection and other means to protect complying States against the hazards of violations and evasions.

The work of the Commission should proceed by separate stages, the successful completion of each of which will develop the necessary confidence of the world before the next stage is undertaken.

The Commission shall not infringe upon the responsibilities of any Organ of the United Nations, but should present recommendations for the consideration of those Organs in the performance of their tasks under the terms of the United Nations Charter.

(3) *Report by the Board of Consultants to the Secretary of State's Committee on Atomic Energy, Transmitted to the Secretary of State (Byrnes), March 17, 1946.*[1]

[Excerpts]

* * * * *

Section II. Principal Considerations in Developing a System of Safeguards

INTRODUCTION

* * * * *

It may be helpful to summarize the characteristics that are desirable and indeed essential to an effective system of safeguards; in other words, the criteria for any adequate plan for security.

a. Such a plan must reduce to manageable proportions the problem of enforcement of an international policy against atomic warfare.

b. It must be a plan that provides unambiguous and reliable danger signals if a nation takes steps that do or may indicate the beginning of atomic warfare. Those danger signals must flash early enough to leave time adequate to permit other nations — alone or in concert — to take appropriate action.

c. The plan must be one that if carried out will provide security; but such that if it fails or the whole international situation collapses, any nation such as the United States will still be in a relatively secure position, compared to any other nation.

d. To be genuinely effective for security, the plan must be one that is not wholly negative, suppressive, and police-like. We are not dealing simply with a military or scientific problem but with a problem in statecraft and the ways of the human spirit. Therefore the plan must be one that will tend to develop the beneficial possibilities of atomic energy and encourage the growth of fundamental knowledge, stirring the constructive and imaginative impulses of men rather than

[1] Department of State Publication 2498.

merely concentrating on the defensive and negative. It should, in short, be a plan that looks to the promise of man's future well-being as well as to his security.

e. The plan must be able to cope with new dangers that may appear in the further development of this relatively new field. In an organizational sense therefore the plan must have flexibility and be readily capable of extension or contraction.

f. The plan must involve international action and minimize rivalry between nations in the dangerous aspects of atomic development.

. . . .

CHAPTER IV. THE ELIMINATION OF INTERNATIONAL RIVALRY

. . . .

It has become clear to us that if the element of rivalry between nations were removed by assignment of the intrinsically dangerous phases of the development of atomic energy to an international organization responsible to all peoples, a reliable prospect would be afforded for a system of security. For it is the element of rivalry and the impossibility of policing the resulting competition through inspection alone that make inspection unworkable as a sole means of control. With that factor of international rivalry removed, the problem becomes both hopeful and manageable.

. . . .

. . . But there is a further advantage to vesting exclusively in an international agency these activities so hazardous to world security. That advantage grows out of the nature of the development of atomic energy itself.

This is a growing and changing field. New advances in technology may be confidently expected. It therefore becomes absolutely essential that any international agency seeking to safeguard the security of the world against warlike uses of atomic energy should be in the very forefront of technical competence in this field. If the international agency is simply a police activity for only negative and repressive functions, inevitably and within a very short period of time the enforcement agency *will not know enough* to be able to recognize new elements of danger, new possibilities of evasion, or the beginnings of a course of development having dangerous and warlike ends in view.

. . . .

We have therefore reached these two conclusions: (*a*) that only if the dangerous aspects of atomic energy are taken out of national hands and placed in international hands is there any reasonable prospect of devising safeguards against the use of atomic energy for bombs, and (*b*) only if the international agency was engaged in development and operation could it possibly discharge adequately its functions as a safeguarder of the world's future.

Such a development function also seems essential in terms of attracting to the international agency the kind of scientists and technicians that this problem requires, recognizing that a mere policing, inspecting, or suppressing function would neither attract nor hold them.

. . . .

Section III. Security through International Cooperative Development

INTRODUCTION

. . . .

Summary of Proposed Plan — The proposal contemplates an international agency conducting all intrinsically dangerous operations in the nuclear field, with individual nations and their citizens free to conduct, under license and a minimum of inspection, all non-dangerous, or safe, operations.

The international agency might take any one of several forms, such as a UNO Commission, or an international corporation or authority. We shall refer to it as Atomic Development Authority. It must have authority to own and lease property, and to carry on mining, manufacturing, research, licensing, inspecting, selling, or any other necessary operations.

· · · · · ·

The proposal contemplates an international agency with exclusive jurisdiction to conduct all intrinsically dangerous operations in the field. This means all activities relating to raw materials, the construction and operation of production plants, and the conduct of research in explosives. The large field of non-dangerous and relatively non-dangerous activities would be left in national hands. These would consist of all activities in the field of research (except on explosives) and the construction and operation of non-dangerous power-producing piles. National activities in these fields would be subject to moderate controls by the international agency, exercised through licensing, rules and regulations, collaboration on design, and the like. The international agency would also maintain inspection facilities to assure that illicit operations were not occurring, primarily in the exploitation of raw materials. It would be a further function of the Atomic Development Authority continually to reexamine the boundary between dangerous and non-dangerous activities. For it must be recognized that although the field is subject to reasonable division, the dividing line is not sharp and may shift from time to time in either direction.

The development agency itself would be truly international in character. Its staff would be recruited on an international basis. Its functions would be such as to attract a calibre of personnel comparable to our own activities in raw materials during the war and our own primary production and experimental work. It would be set up as one of the subsidiary agencies of the United Nations, but it would have to be created by a convention or charter establishing its policies, functions, and authority in comprehensive terms.

· · · · ·

In the actual conduct of its operations the development organization would at all times be governed by a dual purpose, the promotion of the beneficial use of atomic energy and the maintenance of security. We believe that much can be done in a convention or charter to make these purposes concrete and explicit, to draw the line between the dangerous and the non-dangerous, to establish the principles determining the location of stockpiles and plants so that a strategic balance may be maintained among nations, to establish fair and equitable financial policies so that the contributions of nations to, and their receipt of benefits from the organization will be justly apportioned. The most careful and ingenious definitions will be required in order to accomplish these purposes.

· · · · · ·

Section IV. The Transition to International Control

When fully in operation, the plan described in the previous section would, in our opinion, provide a great measure of security against surprise attack by atomic weapons. But it will take a considerable time before the plan can be adopted, and once the nations of the world have adopted it, a still further time will be required to put the plan into operation. It is essential to consider what will be the condition of affairs during the necessary period of transition.

· · · · ·

The Position of the U. S. During the Transition

In order to have meaning, the examination of the transition period must take account of the present position of the United States in the field of atomic energy, and that position must be compared with the one that this country would occupy during the period when the plan for international action is being adopted and executed. Today's position must also be compared with the conditions that will prevail when the plan has finally been brought into full operation. We must also consider what our position would be some years hence if we were forced to abandon our present commitment for international action and pursue instead a purely national treatment of the problem.

Today the United States has a monopoly in atomic weapons. We have strategic stockpiles; we have extensive facilities for making the ingredients of atomic bombs and for making the bombs themselves; we have a large group of people skilled in the many arts which have gone into this project; we have experience and know-how obtainable only in the actual practice of making atomic weapons; we have considerable resources of raw material; and we have a broad theoretical knowledge of the field which may appear inadequate in future years, but which enables us to evaluate not only the performance of the past but also what the future is likely to hold.

It is true that some part of our monopoly we hold in common with the United Kingdom and Canada. This applies principally not to material facilities or to weapons, but to the availability of raw materials, to theoretical knowledge, and to some elements of the know-how.

. . . .

International control implies an acceptance from the outset of the fact that our monopoly can not last. It implies substituting for a competitive development of atomic armament a conscious, deliberate, and planned attempt to establish a security system among the nations of the world that would give protection against surprise attack with atomic weapons. Above all, it involves the substituting of developments which are known to the world for developments by the several nations which might well remain more or less secret, and where the very fact of secrecy would be a constant source of fear, incitement and friction.

Inherent in the adoption of any plan of international control is a probable acceleration — but only acceleration — of the rate at which our present monopoly will inevitably disappear, since our knowledge and our mastery of practical arts, and to some extent our physical installations, must ultimately be made available to an international agency in the process of establishing control.

Let us consider, for example, the plan we recommend in this report. If adopted and executed in good faith, this will have reached a reasonably full degree of operation in a period of years. At that time nearly all the factors making the present position of the United States in relation to atomic energy a preferred one will have been eliminated. For, when the plan is in full operation, no nation will be the legal owner of atomic weapons, of stockpiles of fissionable material or raw materials, or of the plants in which they can be produced. An attempt will have been made to establish a strategic balance in the geographical distribution of the internationally owned plants and stockpiles.

The security which we see in the realization of this plan lies in the fact that it averts the danger of the surprise use of atomic weapons. The seizure by one nation of installations necessary for making atomic weapons would be not only a clear signal of warlike intent, but it would leave other nations in a position — either alone or in concert — to take counter-actions. The plan, of course, has other security purposes, less tangible but none the less important. For in the very fact of cooperative effort among the nations of the world rests the hope we rightly hold for solving the problem of war itself.

. . . .

Disclosure of Information as an Essential of International Action

One of the elements in the present monopoly of the United States is knowledge. This ranges all the way from purely theoretical matters to the intimate practical details of know-how. It is generally recognized that the transmission of any part, or all, of this knowledge to another nation could provide the basis for an acceleration of a rival effort to make atomic weapons. Even that part of our knowledge which is theoretical, which can be transmitted by word of mouth, by formula, or by written note is of value in this context. If such knowledge were available to a rival undertaking it would shorten the time needed for the solution of the practical problems of making atomic weapons, by eliminating certain unworkable alternatives, by fixing more definitely design features which depend on this theoretical knowledge, and by making it possible to undertake the various steps of the program more nearly in parallel, rather than in sequence. It is not, in our opinion, possible to give a reliable estimate of how much such revelation would shorten the time needed for a successful rival effort. It is conceivable that it would not be significantly shortened. It is conceivable that it might be shortened by a year or so. For an evaluation on this point depends on information, which is not available to us, on the detailed plans and policies of such a rival undertaking, as well as on their present state of knowledge. It is, of course, clear that even with all such theoretical knowledge available, a major program, surely lasting many years, is required for the actual production of atomic weapons.

Our monopoly on knowledge cannot be, and should not be, lost at once. Here again there are limitations on the scheduling inherent in the nature of our proposals; and in the nature of the deliberations necessary for their acceptance. But even with the recognition of these limitations, there is a rather wide freedom of choice in the actual scheduling of disclosures. Here considerations of acceptability and of general political background will make a decisive contribution.

It is clear that the information, which this country alone has, can be divided more or less roughly into categories. The acceptance and operation of the plan will require divulging certain categories of this information at successive times. A schedule can outline the point at which this must occur. In particular, there is a limited category of information which should be divulged in the early meetings of the United Nations Commission discussing these problems. There is a more extensive category which must be divulged some years hence after a charter has been adopted and the Atomic Development Authority is ready to start its operations; and there are other categories that may be reserved until the Authority later undertakes some of the subsequent stages of its operations, for instance, those that involve research on weapons. We are convinced that under the plan proposed in this report such scheduling is possible, though it is clear, as we have pointed out, that many factors beyond the scope of this report, and involving the highest considerations of international policy, will be involved in such schedules. We wish to emphasize that it will involve an initial divulging of information, which is justifiable in view of the importance of early progress on the path of international cooperation.

. . . .

We wish to emphasize that the initial disclosures will place in the hands of a nation (should it be acting in bad faith) information which could lead to an acceleration of an atomic armament program. We do not regard this circumstance as in any way peculiar to the plan recommended in this report. It is inherent in the concept of international control. The adoption of any workable scheme of international control may shorten the time during which the United States has a position as favorable as it has today. We cannot be sure of this, but we must be prepared for it.

In this section we have been discussing the problem of transition to international control as it affects the security of the United States. During this transition the United States' present position of monopoly may be lost somewhat more rapidly than would be the case without international action. But without such action the monopoly would in time disappear in any event. Should the worst happen and, during the transition period, the entire effort collapse, the United States will at all times be in a favorable position with regard to atomic weapons. This favorable position will depend upon material things; less and less will it rest upon keeping nations and individuals ignorant.

When fully in operation the plan herein proposed can provide a great measure of security against surprise attack. It can do much more than that. It can create deterrents to the initiation of schemes of aggression, and it can establish patterns of cooperation among nations, the extension of which may even contribute to the solution of the problem of war itself. When the plan is in full operation there will no longer be secrets about atomic energy. We believe that this is the firmest basis of security; for in the long term there can be no international control and no international cooperation which does not presuppose an international community of knowledge.

(4) *Proposals by the Representative of the United States to the United Nations Atomic Energy Commission (Baruch), Submitted to the Commission, June 14, 1946.*[1]

[Excerpts]

. . . .

The United States proposes the creation of an International Atomic Development Authority, to which should be entrusted all phases of the development and use of atomic energy, starting with the raw material and including —
1. Managerial control or ownership of all atomic-energy activities potentially dangerous to world security.
2. Power to control, inspect, and license all other atomic activities.
3. The duty of fostering the beneficial uses of atomic energy.
4. Research and development responsibilities of an affirmative character intended to put the Authority in the forefront of atomic knowledge and thus to enable it to comprehend, and therefor to detect, misuse of atomic energy. To be effective, the Authority must itself be the world's leader in the field of atomic knowledge and development and thus supplement its legal authority with the great power inherent in possession of leadership in knowledge.

I offer this as a basis for beginning our discussion.

. . . .

When an adequate system for control of atomic energy, including the renunciation of the bomb as a weapon, has been agreed upon and put into effective operation and condign punishments set up for violations of the rules of control which are to be stigmatized as international crimes, we propose that —
1. Manufacture of atomic bombs shall stop;
2. Existing bombs shall be disposed of pursuant to the terms of the treaty; and
3. The Authority shall be in possession of full information as to the know-how for the production of atomic energy.

Let me repeat, so as to avoid misunderstanding: My country is ready to make its full contribution toward the end we seek, subject of course to our constitutional processes and to an adequate system of control becoming fully effective, as we finally work it out.

Now as to violations: In the agreement, penalties of as serious a nature as the nations may wish and as immediate and certain in their execution as possible should be fixed for —
1. Illegal possession or use of an atomic bomb;
2. Illegal possession, or separation, of atomic material suitable for use in an atomic bomb;
3. Seizure of any plant or other property belonging to or licensed by the Authority;

[1] Department of State Publication 2560, United States-United Nations Report Series No. 2.

4. Wilful interference with the activities of the Authority;

5. Creation or operation of dangerous projects in a manner contrary to, or in the absence of, a license granted by the international control body.

It would be a deception, to which I am unwilling to lend myself, were I not to say to you and to our peoples that the matter of punishment lies at the very heart of our present security system. It might as well be admitted, here and now, that the subject goes straight to the veto power contained in the Charter of the United Nations so far as it relates to the field of atomic energy. The Charter permits penalization only by concurrence of each of the five great powers — the Union of Soviet Socialist Republics, the United Kingdom, China, France, and the United States.

I want to make very plain that I am concerned here with the veto power only as it affects this particular problem. There must be no veto to protect those who violate their solemn agreements not to develop or use atomic energy for destructive purposes.

. . . .

I now submit the following measures as representing the fundamental features of a plan which would give effect to certain of the conclusions which I have epitomized.

1. General. The Authority should set up a thorough plan for control of the field of atomic energy, through various forms of ownership, dominion, licenses, operation, inspection, research, and management by competent personnel. After this is provided for, there should be as little interference as may be with the economic plans and the present private, corporate, and state relationships in the several countries involved.

2. Raw Materials. The Authority should have as one of its earliest purposes to obtain and maintain complete and accurate information on world supplies of uranium and thorium and to bring them under its dominion. The precise pattern of control for various types of deposits of such materials will have to depend upon the geological, mining, refining, and economic facts involved in different situations.

The Authority should conduct continuous surveys so that it will have the most complete knowledge of the world geology of uranium and thorium. Only after all current information on world sources of uranium and thorium is known to us all can equitable plans be made for their production, refining, and distribution.

3. Primary Production Plants. The Authority should exercise complete managerial control of the production of fissionable materials. This means that it should control and operate all plants producing fissionable materials in dangerous quantities and must own and control the product of these plants.

4. Atomic Explosives. The Authority should be given sole and exclusive right to conduct research in the field of atomic explosives. Research activities in the field of atomic explosives are essential in order that the Authority may keep in the forefront of knowledge in the field of atomic energy and fulfil the objective of preventing illicit manufacture of bombs. Only by maintaining its position as the best-informed agency will the Authority be able to determine the line between intrinsically dangerous and non-dangerous activities.

5. Strategic Distribution of Activities and Materials. The activities entrusted exclusively to the Authority because they are intrinsically dangerous to security should be distributed throughout the world. Similarly, stockpiles of raw materials and fissionable materials should not be centralized.

6. Non-Dangerous Activities. A function of the Authority should be promotion of the peacetime benefits of atomic energy.

Atomic research (except in explosives), the use of research reactors, the production of radioactive tracers by means of non-dangerous reactors, the use of such tracers, and to some extent the production of power should be open to nations and their citizens under reasonable licensing arrangements from the

Authority. Denatured materials, whose use we know also requires suitable safeguards, should be furnished for such purposes by the Authority under lease or other arrangement. Denaturing seems to have been overestimated by the public as a safety measure.

7. Definition of Dangerous and Non-Dangerous Activities. Although a reasonable dividing line can be drawn between dangerous and non-dangerous activities, it is not hard and fast. Provision should, therefore, be made to assure constant reexamination of the questions and to permit revision of the dividing line as changing conditions and new discoveries may require.

8. Operations of Dangerous Activities. Any plant dealing with uranium or thorium after it once reaches the potential of dangerous use must be not only subject to the most rigorous and competent inspection by the Authority, but its actual operation shall be under the management, supervision, and control of the Authority.

9. Inspection. By assigning intrinsically dangerous activities exclusively to the Authority, the difficulties of inspection are reduced. If the Authority is the only agency which may lawfully conduct dangerous activities, then visible operation by others than the Authority will constitute an unambiguous danger signal. Inspection will also occur in connection with the licensing functions of the Authority.

10. Freedom of Access. Adequate ingress and egress for all qualified representatives of the Authority must be assured. Many of the inspection activities of the Authority should grow out of, and be incidental to, its other functions. Important measures of inspection will be associated with the tight control of raw materials, for this is a keystone of the plan. The continuing activities of prospecting, survey, and research in relation to raw materials will be designed not only to serve the affirmative development functions of the Authority but also to assure that no surreptitious operations are conducted in the raw-materials field by nations or their citizens.

11. Personnel. The personnel of the Authority should be recruited on a basis of proven competence but also so far as possible on an international basis.

12. Progress by Stages. A primary step in the creation of the system of control is the setting forth, in comprehensive terms, of the functions, responsibilities, powers, and limitations of the Authority. Once a charter for the Authority has been adopted, the Authority and the system of control for which it will be responsible will require time to become fully organized and effective. The plan of control will, therefore, have to come into effect in successive stages. These should be specifically fixed in the charter or means should be otherwise set forth in the charter for transitions from one stage to another, as contemplated in the resolution of the United Nations Assembly which created this Commission.

13. Disclosures. In the deliberations of the United Nations Commission on Atomic Energy, the United States is prepared to make available the information essential to a reasonable understanding of the proposals which it advocates. Further disclosures must be dependent, in the interests of all, upon the effective ratification of the treaty. When the Authority is actually created, the United States will join the other nations in making available the further information essential to that organization for the performance of its functions. As the successive stages of international control are reached, the United States will be prepared to yield, to the extent required by each stage, national control of activities in this field to the Authority.

14. International Control. There will be questions about the extent of control to be allowed to national bodies, when the Authority is established. Purely national authorities for control and development of atomic energy should to the extent necessary for the effective operation of the Authority be subordinate to it. This is neither an endorsement nor a disapproval of the creation of national authorities. The Commission should evolve a clear demarcation of the scope of duties and responsibilities of such national authorities.

. . . .

(5) **Proposals by the Representative of the Union of Soviet Socialist Republics to the United Nations Atomic Energy Commission (Gromyko), Submitted to the Commission, June 19, 1946.**[1]

[Translation]

Draft International Convention to Prohibit the Production and Employment of Weapons Based on the Use of Atomic Energy for the Purpose of Mass Destruction

(Here follows a list of signatory States)

Being profoundly aware of the vast significance of the great scientific discoveries connected with the splitting of the atom and the obtaining and use of atomic energy for the purpose of promoting the welfare and raising the standard of living of the peoples of the world, as well as for the development of culture and science for the benefit of mankind;

animated by the desire to promote in every way the fullest possible utilization by all peoples of scientific discoveries in the sphere of atomic energy for the purpose of improving the conditions of life of the peoples of the world and promoting their welfare and the further progress of human culture;

fully realizing that the great scientific discoveries in the sphere of atomic energy carry with them a great danger, above all, for peaceful towns and the civilian population in the event of these discoveries being used in the form of atomic weapons for the purpose of mass destruction;

recognizing the great significance of the fact that international agreements have already prohibited the use in warfare of asphyxiating, poisonous and other similar gases, as well as all similar liquids, substances and processes, and likewise bacteriological means, rightly condemned by the public opinion of the civilized world, and considering that the international prohibition of the use of atomic weapons for the mass destruction of human beings corresponds in still greater measure to the aspirations and the conscience of the peoples of the whole world;

being firmly resolved to avert the danger of these scientific discoveries being used to the detriment and against the interests of mankind;

resolved to conclude a convention to prohibit the production and the employment of weapons based on the use of atomic energy, and for this purpose appointed as their plenipotentiaries . . . (*here follows the list of plenipotentiaries*), who, after presenting their credentials found to be in good and due form, agreed as follows:

Article 1. The high contracting parties solemnly declare that they are unanimously resolved to prohibit the production and employment of weapons based on the use of atomic energy, and for this purpose assume the following obligations:

(*a*) not to use atomic weapons in any circumstances whatsoever;

[1] United Nations Atomic Energy Commission, *Official Records*, No. 2, p. 24.

(b) to prohibit the production and storing of weapons based on the use of atomic energy;

(c) to destroy, within a period of three months from the day of entry into force of the present convention, all stocks of atomic energy weapons whether in a finished or unfinished condition.

Article 2. The high contracting parties declare that any violation of article 1 of the present convention is a most serious international crime against humanity.

Article 3. The high contracting parties shall, within a period of six months from the day of the entry into force of the present convention, pass legislation providing severe penalties for violators of the statutes of the present convention.

Article 4. The present convention shall be of indefinite duration.

Article 5. The present convention shall be open for the adhesion of any State whether a Member or non-member of the United Nations.

Article 6. The present convention shall come into force after its approval by the Security Council and after the ratification and delivery of ratification documents to the Secretary-General for safekeeping by one half of the signatory States, including all the Member States of the United Nations named in Article 23 of the Charter of the Organization.

Article 7. After the entry into force of the present convention it shall be binding on all States whether Members or non-members of the United Nations.

Article 8. The present convention, of which the Russian, Chinese, French, English and Spanish texts shall be authentic, is drawn up in one copy and shall be kept in the archives of the Secretary-General of the United Nations. The Secretary-General shall communicate certified copies to all the parties to the convention.

Concerning the organization of the work of the Atomic Energy Commission

In accordance with the resolution of the General Assembly of 24 January 1946 regarding the establishment of a commission to deal with problems raised by the discovery of atomic energy and other related matters, and in particular with article 5 of the said resolution relating to the terms of reference of the Commission, the Soviet delegation deems it necessary to propose the following plan of organization of the work of the Commission for the initial stage of its activity.

I. ESTABLISHMENT OF COMMITTEES OF THE COMMISSION

In pursuance of the aim indicated in the resolution of the General Assembly "to proceed with the utmost despatch and inquire into all phases of the problems," it appears to be necessary to set up two committees which as auxiliary organs of the Commission would ensure a thorough examination of the problem of atomic energy and the elaboration of recommendations, which the Commission must make in fulfilment of the resolution of the General Assembly and other organs of the United Nations.

It is proposed that the following committees should be set up:

Committee for the exchange of scientific information

This committee shall be set up for the purpose of carrying out the aims indicated in point (*a*) of item 5 of the resolution of the General Assembly of 24 January 1946.

The tasks of the committee shall include the elaboration of recommendations concerning practical measures for organizing the exchange of information;

(1) concerning the contents of scientific discoveries connected with the splitting of the atomic nucleus and other discoveries connected with obtaining and using atomic energy;

(2) concerning the technology and the organization of technological processes for obtaining and using atomic energy;

(3) concerning the organization and methods of industrial production of atomic energy and the use of this energy;

(4) concerning the forms, sources and locations of the raw materials necessary for obtaining atomic energy.

Committee for the prevention of the use of atomic energy to the detriment of mankind

This committee shall be set up to carry out the aims set forth in points (*b*), (*c*) and (*d*) of item 5 of the resolution of the General Assembly.

The task of the committee shall be to elaborate recommendations:

(1) concerning the drafting of an international convention for outlawing weapons based on the use of atomic energy and prohibiting the production and use of such weapons and all other similar kinds of weapons capable of being used for mass destruction;

(2) concerning the quest for and establishment of measures to prohibit the production of weapons based on the use of atomic energy and to prevent the use of atomic weapons and all other main kinds of weapons capable of being used for mass destruction;

(3) concerning the measures, systems and organization of control over the use of atomic energy and over the observance of the terms of the above-mentioned international convention for the outlawing of atomic weapons;

(4) concerning the elaboration of a system of sanctions to be applied against the unlawful use of atomic energy.

II. COMPOSITION OF THE COMMITTEES

Each committee shall be composed of one representative of each State represented in the Commission. Each representative may have assistants.

III. RULES OF PROCEDURE OF THE COMMITTEES

The rules of procedure of the committees shall be drawn up by the Commission.

(6) *Memoranda by the Associate Member of the United States Delegation to the United Nations Atomic Energy Commission (Eberstadt), Submitted to Subcommittee 1 of the Commission.*[1]

(a) *Control and Development of Atomic Energy, July 2, 1946.*

[Excerpts]

. . . .

. . . The memorandum is an attempt to outline in logical sequence a number of the more important points upon which the Commission itself will undoubtedly desire the views of this Subcommittee. It does not purport to be complete. There will certainly be many additional points requiring this Subcommittee's consideration.

A. The control and development of atomic energy must be international and should be entrusted to an agency which for present purposes is called the Atomic Development Authority.

B. The Authority would be created by a treaty, which should include a form of charter for the Authority and some very important additional provisions.

C. The preamble of the treaty should express the following principles:

1. The preservation of international peace and security in accordance with the purposes and principles stated in the Preamble and Chapter I of the Charter of the United Nations;
2. The safeguarding of all peoples against the use of atomic weapons;
3. The development and wide distribution of atomic energy and its by-products for purposes of raising the welfare and standard of life of the peoples of the world and of contributing to their science and culture; and
4. The realization of these ends through international cooperation, through an international agency for the development and control of atomic energy, and through a system of international enforcement.

D. The treaty should contain provisions:

1. Defining the relations between the Authority and the Security Council, the General Assembly, the International Court of Justice, and the other organs of the United Nations;
2. Defining the mutual rights and obligations of the several signatory States and the Authority, including the relations between the Authority and any atomic energy control agencies of the signatory States;
3. Governing the sequence and timing of the steps in the transition from the present conditions to the conditions which will prevail once the Authority is in effective control of atomic energy;
4. Specifying the time when and the conditions under which the national and private possession, manufacture, and use of atomic weapons shall be outlawed;
5. Defining the violations which shall constitute international crimes and specifying the sanctions to be employed for such violations;
6. Relating to signature, ratification, entry into force and amendment of the treaty; and
7. Concerning any necessary amendment of the charter of the United Nations

E. The charter of the Atomic Development Authority should state the following purposes of the Authority:

1. To prevent the possession, manufacture or use of atomic weapons for mass destruction;
2. To foster the beneficial, non-dangerous uses of atomic energy;
3. To have managerial control or ownership of all atomic energy activities potentially dangerous to world security;

[1] Department of State, *Bulletin*, XV, p. 96.

4. To control, inspect, and license all other atomic energy activities;
5. To engage in atomic energy research and development; and
6. To assure that the benefits derived from such research and development shall be available to the peoples of all the signatory States so long as each State and its people support the Authority and observe their obligations under the treaty and charter.

F. The charter should contain specific provisions governing topics under the following principal headings:

1. *Functions and Powers of the Atomic Development Authority.* Subject to application in the manner to be defined in the charter, the Authority should be granted the following powers:

   a. To obtain and maintain complete and exclusive control or ownership of all uranium, thorium, and other material which may be a source of atomic energy wherever present in potentially dangerous quantities whether in raw materials, by-product, processed, or other form;

   b. To conduct continuous investigations and surveys of sources of atomic energy throughout the world, in aid of the proper exercise of the foregoing and the Authority's other functions and powers;

   c. To acquire, construct, own, and exclusively operate all facilities for the production of U–235, plutonium, and such other fissionable materials as may be specified by the Authority, and to maintain supplies of fissionable materials adequate to fulfill the purposes of the Authority;

   d. To define and determine, in the manner set forth in the charter, any other facilities or activities in the field of atomic energy which would be dangerous unless controlled by the Authority, and to supervise and have complete managerial control of all such activities and facilities;

   e. To have unhindered access to, and power to control, license, and inspect all other facilities which possess, utilize or produce materials which are a source of atomic energy, and all other activities which utilize or produce, or are capable of utilizing or producing, atomic energy;

   f. To have the exclusive right of research in the field of atomic explosives;

   g. To foster and promote the non-dangerous use and wide distribution of atomic energy for beneficial purposes under licenses or other suitable arrangements established by the Authority; and

   h. Subject to the provisions of the treaty and charter, to have power to take other necessary action and to issue rules and regulations.

2. *Composition, Organization, and Location of the Atomic Development Authority.*

   a. All signatory States to be members of the Authority.
   b. Conditions upon which States not Members of the United Nations may become parties to the treaty.
   c. The Authority to be organized to function continuously.
   d. Governing Board.
      (1) Composition and qualifications.
      (2) Method of nomination and selection.
      (3) Terms of office.
      (4) Voting procedure.
      (5) Powers and duties.
      (6) Compensation.
   e. Executive management.
      (1) Number and titles of executive officers.
      (2) Qualifications and method of selection.
      (3) Terms of office.
      (4) Powers and duties.
      (5) Compensation.
   f. Staff and consultants.
   g. Subordinate boards, divisions, and other units.
   h. Location of the Authority.

INTERNATIONAL PEACE AND SECURITY 565

G. Provisions for enforcement should be included in the treaty as follows:
1. Definitions of conduct constituting violations.
2. Consequences of such violations, including the procedures to be followed in detecting, establishing, remedying or punishing such violations:
   a. Administrative action by the Authority.
      (1) Special investigations.
      (2) Revocation or denial of licenses.
      (3) Other action.
   b. Resort to judicial processes and procedures.
   c. Reference of serious violations to the Security Council of the United Nations.

H. The following additional topics should be provided for in the treaty:
1. Legal capacity and privileges and immunities of the Authority in the territory of each signatory State.
2. Privileges and immunities of officials of the Authority.
3. Accountability of the Authority and its officials, and the scope of, and procedure for, review of their actions.
4. Method of financing the Authority.
5. Procedure for determination of the prices and quotas which the Authority should employ in the sale or lease of atomic energy materials or by-products.
6. Procedure for determination of the compensation to be made by the Authority in acquiring atomic energy supplies and facilities.
7. Measures to insure adequate protection and strategic location of the premises and property of the Authority.
8. Definitions of terms used in the treaty and charter.

. . . .

(b) Functions and Powers of Proposed Atomic Development Authority, July 5, 1946.

[Excerpts]

1. A fundamental element of the United States plan for control of atomic energy [1] is an international Atomic Development Authority with the dual functions of:
   a. preventing the use of atomic energy for destructive purposes;
   b. promoting the peaceful applications of atomic energy and its by-products for the material benefit of the peoples of the world and as a contribution to their science and culture.
2. A few very basic facts afford the opportunity, and determine the pattern, for control of atomic energy. One is that the nuclear chain reaction, essential to the release of atomic energy in any form, requires the presence of uranium alone or in combination with thorium to produce fissionable material. Available knowledge indicates that this requirement is likely to prevail for a considerable time. Another important fact is that all of the initial processes in the production of these fissionable materials and certain subsequent ones are identical whether their intended use or purpose is beneficent or dangerous.

The conclusion to be drawn from these facts is that the core of any system for control of atomic energy is effective dominion over all uranium and thorium and their fissionable derivatives.

The degree of effectiveness of such controls over these fissionable materials is the measure of the success of our undertaking. To be fully effective, such controls must attach firmly to all uranium and thorium from the moment they are produced and must remain in effect so long as they exist in a state or quantity

[1] For the text of the proposals presented to the Atomic Commission by the U. S. Representative on June 14, see *ibid.*, XIV, p. 1057.

susceptible of dangerous use. Any uranium or thorium in unauthorized hands is a threat to the entire system of control and thus to the maintenance of peace.

Since the exploitation of atomic energy for peaceful purposes necessitates operations which are, in the initial stages, identical with those needed to make atomic energy available for destructive purposes, both of these functions (1*a* and 1*b* above) should be assigned to the same agency. Furthermore, an international agency with responsibilities for fostering the beneficial uses of atomic energy, as well as responsibilities for preventing its misuse, will be more effective, constructive, and workable than if it has merely duties of inspection and policing. The activities of such an agency might even result in establishing beneficial patterns of international cooperation of a new and hopeful kind.

. . . .

3. The functions and powers of the Authority will be exercised in a variety of ways and by various means. It is impossible at this time to catalogue completely the exact forms of control which the Authority will need to employ. In general, they fall into the categories of ownership, managerial control supervision, leasing, licensing, and inspection. The Authority should, of course, be given wide power and discretion as to the particular means or combinations thereof which it deems best adapted to the accomplishment of its functions.

4. Section F of the memorandum submitted to Subcommittee No. 1 by the United States Delegation on July 2, 1946, sets forth a partial list of functions and powers of the control agency.

The following, arranged in the order of presentation contained in said memorandum, is submitted, in response to the request of our Chairman, by way of explanation and amplification of the operation of these controls:

a. to obtain and maintain complete and exclusive control or ownership of all uranium, thorium, and other material which may be a source of atomic energy wherever present in potentially dangerous quantities whether in raw material, by-product, processed, or other form.

Initial control, at the source, of the basic materials on which atomic energy depends provides the fundamental basis for protection and facilitates control over all subsequent processing of these materials. Complete control of such basic materials is essential to the successful functioning of the Authority. Uranium is, so far as we now know, the only substance occurring in nature in significant quantities which can maintain a chain reaction. However, thorium, in combination with uranium or its derivative plutonium, may well be useful in manufacturing chain-reacting, fissionable material. Therefore, we propose that the Authority be empowered to exercise such measures of control over the mining and processing of both uranium and thorium, as to assure its ownership of all stocks of both of these materials.

. . . .

The Authority, in short, must have such control of mining and concentrating operations as will assure its complete and absolute ownership of all uranium and thorium actually produced. There must be no possibility of diversion from the moment the ore is removed from the ground, and the Authority must set up such actual measures of control as will assure this result.

b. To conduct continuous investigations and surveys of sources of atomic energy throughout the world, in aid of the proper exercise of the foregoing and the Authority's other functions and powers.

The Authority should have as one of its earliest purposes to obtain and maintain complete and accurate information on world supplies of uranium and thorium. Such information as is now available is admittedly inadequate. It must be made complete and accurate and so maintained. Furthermore, the Authority should be empowered to search out new deposits and to expand its knowledge of world supplies of such materials through such surveying and prospecting activities as it may deem necessary. As a result of its own efforts and from information furnished to it by others, the Authority should keep currently informed on the discovery of new deposits.

  c. To acquire, construct, own, and exclusively operate all facilities for the production of U–235, plutonium, and such other fissionable materials as may be specified by the Authority, and to maintain supplies of fissionable materials adequate to fulfill the purposes of the Authority.

. . . .

The Authority will thus have control of the locations of primary production plants and of any stockpiles of materials. The geographical distribution of such plants and stockpiles should be determined in accordance with principles to be specified in the charter.

With the Authority having the sole right to manufacture fissionable materials, any attempt by others to carry on such operations, or to seize the Authority's facilities, whatever the announced intent, would, of itself, constitute a grave violation.

Title to all fissionable materials, and final control over their use should remain at all times with the Authority.

The Authority should be empowered to use fissionable materials for peaceful purposes, and to lease such materials for use by others under conditions which it deems safe, and subject to such controls as it deems necessary.

  d. To define and determine, in the manner set forth in the charter, any other facilities or activities in the field of atomic energy which would be dangerous unless controlled by the Authority, and to supervise and have complete managerial control of all such activities and facilities.

The development of atomic energy for peaceful purposes follows in much of its course a path parallel with the development of atomic weapons. Therefore, it is essential that the Authority have complete control of all operations which might facilitate atomic weapon production. This requires that the Authority also have the power to determine, and adjust from time to time, based on increased knowledge, the dividing line between "safe" and "dangerous" activities as new conditions demand. It is important to emphasize the complicated and varying considerations involved in determining this dividing line.

Control of "dangerous" activities should be carried out to the greatest extent possible through direct operation by the Authority. An organization which is actively carrying out an operation is in a much better position to prevent diversion of material than one which merely exercises inspection and policing functions. Furthermore, while the Authority must have full power to conduct such inspection and policing activities as are necessary, the fact that it alone carries on the critical operations will reduce inspection to manageable scope, and render control of atomic energy less burdensome and irritating to nations and their citizens.

  e. To have unhindered access to, and power to control, license, and inspect all other facilities which possess, utilize, or produce materials which are a source of atomic energy, and all other activities which utilize or produce, or are capable of utilizing or producing, atomic energy.

As covered under *c* above, the Authority may lease fissionable material exclusively for peaceful purposes under proper safeguards. In all such instances, the Authority should have unhindered access to these installations and such control and opportunity for inspection as it deems necessary to prevent misuse.

. . . .

  f. To have the exclusive right of research in the field of atomic explosives.

The Authority should have the sole right to conduct research on atomic explosives. Such research is necessary in order to keep the Authority in the forefront of knowledge in this field. This exclusive right of research does not carry with it the right to stockpile atomic weapons. This is a separate matter to be dealt with in the treaty.

The above provisions assume that the treaty will include agreements forbidding any nation, its agents, instrumentalities, and citizens from engaging in research in the field of atomic explosives.

   g. To foster and promote the non-dangerous use and wide distribution of atomic energy for beneficial purposes under licenses or other suitable arrangements established by the Authority.

While it is a prime purpose of the Authority to prevent national development or use of atomic armament, it is of importance that it foster and promote to the maximum degree scientific research, engineering development, and peaceful utilization of atomic energy for the good of mankind.

To this end, the Authority should:
(1) conduct scientific research in this field with its own facilities, and should not only permit but encourage and actively assist others to carry on such work, under such conditions as it deems appropriate,
(2) encourage and assist others to conduct non-dangerous developments directed towards the useful applications of atomic energy, and the advancement of science, and should carry on enough such work with its own facilities so that it may be fully informed, and may assist others at critical points,
(3) promote the actual beneficial utilization of atomic energy. It is obviously impossible to foresee at this time what all such uses may be.

. . . .

Other important benefits of the release of atomic energy will be in directions as yet unpredictable. For this reason, among others, the charter of the Authority should give it enough flexibility and discretion so that it may adjust quickly to new conditions as they arise.

   h. Subject to the provisions of the treaty and charter, to have power to take other necessary action and to issue rules and regulations.

In order that the Authority may properly carry out its functions it should possess the following rights and privileges: (1) the unhindered use of established postal, telephone, radio communication, and telegraph facilities; (2) the right to operate its own system of radio communication exclusively for its own business; (3) the unhindered movement of its personnel in and between installations and to any other points, across and within national boundaries in connection with proper discharge of their functions; and (4) the use of transportation facilities in and between the various nations for the unhindered movement of its personnel, supplies and equipment.

5. Adequate performance of its functions by the Authority requires that national authorities for control and development of atomic energy should be subordinate to the Authority to the extent necessary for its effective operation. However, in carrying out the functions of the Authority, there should be as little interference as possible with the economic plans and the private, corporate, and state relationships in the several countries involved.

6. Obviously, the controls outlined in this memorandum cannot spring into existence full grown and complete upon the legal establishment of the Authority. The process of putting them into effect will necessarily extend over a considerable period of time. It will have to be done by stages provided in the treaty or charter and according to prearranged schedules based on sound and logical sequence leading to full and effective establishment of all controls.

7. The exercise by the Authority of the controls referred to above will call for a wide variety of administrative decisions based upon fair, sound and responsible judgments. In suggesting the conferring of these powers upon the Authority, it is not intended that their exercise by the Authority should be absolute, unlimited and free from review. Obviously, as to certain specific fields and functions to be defined in the treaty, the Authority's decisions would be final. In others they would not. It is our intention in dealing with the relation of the Authority to other elements of the United Nations to treat this phase of the subject more

fully, and also to present proposals for enforcement of the provisions of the treaty and charter as well as for sanctions for violations.

8. As a function of its control operations, the Authority should make provision for the rendering of frequent and detailed reports to the appropriate organs of the United Nations and to the constituent nations, embodying the results of its researches, new discoveries in the atomic field, the level of its material stockpiles, new locations of ores, and all other important and pertinent information. In addition, properly accredited representatives of the United Nations and of the constituent nations should be permitted, under suitable regulations, to inspect the plants, properties, records and operations of the Authority.

9. For the effective operation of the Authority in the manner contemplated, it is essential that the Authority be composed of personnel of the highest character and ability. The affirmative character of the functions of the Authority in dealing both with "dangerous" operations and the dissemination of scientific data of a beneficial nature require, and should assure, that the Authority attract such personnel.

10. Functions and powers and controls are to a certain extent reflections of the same subject from different angles. In this memorandum, devoted predominately to controls, the repressive functions of the Authority have received more attention than its functions in the stimulation of research and of the beneficial uses of atomic energy. We want to emphasize, therefore, that we lay importance upon the Authority's activities in both fields.

Mr. Eberstadt submitted a third memorandum on July 12, 1945, dealing with "Relations between the Atomic Development Authority and the Organs of the United Nations."[1] Pointing out that (1) no consideration of the problem of international control went into the framing of the United Nations Charter, (2) none of the existing organs of the United Nations possessed the powers necessary for control and development, and (3) the Authority should be given "considerable degree of finality" in its "determinations, orders and practices", the memorandum spelled out in detail the relationships which should prevail between the proposed Authority and the other bodies of the United Nations. The General Assembly should receive periodic and special reports from the Authority, should include in its discussions and recommendation matters pertaining to the Authority, and might "appropriately have a role in connection with the budget of the Authority".

The Security Council should have "full jurisdiction" over serious violations "within the area of the Authority's jurisdiction constituting a threat to the peace, breach of the peace or act of aggression" subject to the certification by the Authority of such violations. Article 51 of the Charter, stipulating "the inherent right of individual or collective self-defense if an armed attack occurs against a member of the United Nations" before the Security Council has acted "to maintain international peace and security", should be broadened to include within the concept of "armed attack" both the actual use of atomic weapons and "certain steps themselves preliminary to such action". Additional relationships between the Authority and the Security Council should include (1) the assistance of the Authority in carrying out certain decisions of the Security Council in which "the assistance of the Authority is deemed appropriate", (2) the submission to the Security Council of reports on the Authority's activities "particularly as they bear upon the maintenance of international peace and security" and (3) consultation with the Military Staff Committee on questions "relating to the military repercussions of the Authority's plans of action".

The power to request advisory opinions of the International Court of Justice, right to appear as a party in cases before it and the obligation to submit to the jurisdiction of the Court in certain legal disputes were outlined as the relationships to exist between the Authority and the Court. Mutual consultation and

[1] For the complete text of the Memorandum of July 12, see *ibid.*, XV, p. 102.

exchange of information concerning atomic energy development and control in trust territories or related to the proper administration of such territories should exist between the Authority and the Trusteeship Council.

Detailed treatment of relations between the Authority and the Secretariat was not included in the memorandum.

(7) *Proposals by the Representative of the United States to the United Nations Atomic Energy Commission (Baruch) Regarding the Inclusion of Certain Items Among the Findings and Recommendations in the Forthcoming Report of the Commission to the Security Council, Submitted December 5, 1946.*[1]

Pursuant to the resolution of this Commission passed at its meeting held November 13, 1946, the Report of the Proceedings, Findings and Recommendations of this Commission to be submitted to the Security Council by December 31, 1946, consists of three parts:

PART I, a Summary of the Proceedings together with the Records of this Commission and of its Committees and Subcommittees;
PART II, certain Findings of this Commission based upon its deliberations to date; and
PART III, certain Recommendations of this Commission based upon its Findings to date;

RESOLVED, that Part II of said report shall contain, among others, the following Findings of the Commission:

PART II. FINDINGS

Based upon the proposals and information presented to the Commission, upon the hearings, proceedings and deliberations of the Commission to date, and upon the proceedings, discussions and reports of its several committees and subcommittees, all as set forth in Part I of this report, the Commission has made the following findings:

(1) That scientifically, technologically and practically it is feasible,
  (a) to extend among "all nations the exchange of basic scientific information on atomic energy for peaceful ends",
  (b) to control "atomic energy to the extent necessary to ensure its use only for peaceful purposes",
  (c) to accomplish "the elimination from national armaments of atomic weapons", and
  (d) to provide "effective safeguards by way of inspection and other means to protect complying states against the hazards of violations and evasions".

(2) That effective control of atomic energy depends upon effective control of the production and use of uranium, thorium and their fissionable derivatives. Appropriate mechanisms of control to prevent their unauthorized diversion or clandestine production and use, including inspection, accounting, supervision, licensing and management, must be applied through the various stages of the processes from the time these minerals are severed from the ground to the time they become fissionable materials and are used.

(3) That, whether the ultimate fissionable product be destined for peaceful or destructive uses, the productive processes are identical and inseparable up to a very advanced stage of manufacture. Thus, the control of atomic energy to ensure its use for peaceful purposes, the elimination of atomic weapons from national armaments, and the provisions of effective safeguards to protect complying states against the hazards of violations and evasions must be accomplished through a single unified international system of control designed to carry out all of these related purposes.

(4) That the development and use of atomic energy are not essentially and

[1] Department of State Publication 2713, United States-United Nations Report Series No. 6.

exclusively matters of domestic concern of the individual nations, but rather have predominantly international implications and repercussions.

(5) That an effective system of control of atomic energy must be international in scope, and must be established by an enforceable multilateral agreement (herein called "the treaty") which in turn must be administered by an international agency within the United Nations, possessing adequate powers and properly organized, staffed, and equipped for the purpose.

Only by such a system of international control can the development and use of atomic energy be freed from nationalistic rivalries with consequent risks to the safety of all peoples. Only by such a system can the benefits of widespread exchange of scientific knowledge and of the peaceful uses of atomic energy be assured. Only such a system of control would merit and enjoy the confidence of the people of all nations.

(6) That an international agreement outlawing the production, possession and use of atomic weapons is an essential part of any such system of international control of atomic energy. An international convention to this effect, if standing alone, would fail (a) "to ensure" the use of atomic energy "only for peaceful purposes" and (b) to provide for "effective safeguards by way of inspection and other means to protect complying states against the hazards of violations and evasions," and thus would fail to meet the requirements of the terms of reference of the Commission. To be effective, such an agreement must be an integral part of a treaty providing for a comprehensive system of international control and must be fortified by adequate guarantees and safeguards in the form of international supervision, inspection and control adequate to ensure the carrying out of the terms of the convention and "to protect complying states against the hazards of violations and evasions."

FURTHER RESOLVED, that Part III of said report shall contain, among others, the following recommendations:

PART III. RECOMMENDATIONS

Based upon the Findings of the Commission set forth in Part II of this report the Commission makes the following Recommendations to the Security Council with respect to the matters covered by the Terms of Reference of the Commission, which recommendations are interdependent and not severable, constituting together and as a whole, the fundamental principles and basic organizational mechanisms necessary to attain the objectives set forth in the Commission's Terms of Reference.

(1) There should be a strong and comprehensive international system of control of atomic energy aimed at attaining the objectives set forth in the Commission's Terms of Reference.

(2) Such a system of international control of atomic energy should be established and its scope and functions defined by a treaty in which all of the nations members of the United Nations should be entitled to participate with the same rights and obligations. The international control system should be declared operative only when those members of the United Nations necessary to assure its success, by signing and ratifying the treaty, bind themselves to accept and support it.

(3) The treaty should include, among others, provisions

(a) Establishing, in the United Nations, an international authority (hereinafter called "the authority") possessing powers and charged with responsibility necessary and appropriate for effective administration of the terms of the treaty, and for the prompt carrying out of its day-to-day duties. Its rights, powers, and responsibilities, as well as its relations to the several organs of the United Nations, should be clearly established and defined by the treaty. Such powers should be sufficiently broad and flexible to enable the authority to deal with new developments that may hereafter arise in the field of atomic energy. In particular, the authority shall be responsible for extending among all nations the exchange of basic scientific information on atomic energy for peaceful ends, for preventing the use of atomic energy for destructive purposes and for stimulating its peaceful beneficent uses for the benefit of the people of all nations.

The authority should have positive research and developmental responsibilities in order to remain in the forefront of atomic knowledge so as to render the authority more effective in promoting the beneficent uses of atomic energy and in eliminating its destructive ones. The exclusive right to carry on atomic research for destructive purposes should be vested in the authority.

Decisions of the authority pursuant to the powers conferred upon it by the treaty should govern the operations of national agencies for the control of atomic energy. In carrying out its prescribed functions, however, the authority should interfere as little as necessary with the operations of national agencies for the control of atomic energy, or with the economic plans and the private, corporate and state relationships in the several countries.

(b) Affording the duly accredited representatives of the authority unimpeded rights of ingress, egress and access for the performance of their inspections and other duties into, from and within the territory of every participating nation, unhindered by national or local authorities.

(c) Prohibiting the manufacture, possession, and use of atomic weapons by all nations parties thereto and by all of their nationals.

(d) Providing for disposal of any existing stocks of atomic bombs.

(e) Specifying the means and methods of determining violations of its terms, stigmatizing such violations as international crimes, and establishing the nature of the measures of enforcement and punishment to be imposed upon individuals and upon nations guilty of violating its provisions.

The judicial or other processes for determination of violations of the treaty and of punishment therefor, should be swift and certain. Serious violations of the treaty should be reported immediately by the authority to the nations party to the treaty and to the Security Council. In dealing with such violations, the permanent members of the Security Council should agree not to exercise their power of veto to protect a violator of the terms of the treaty from the consequences of his wrong doing.

The provisions of the treaty would be wholly ineffectual if, in any such situations, the enforcement provisions of the treaty could be rendered nugatory by the veto of a state which has voluntarily signed the treaty.

(4) The treaty should embrace the entire program for putting the system of international control of atomic energy into effect and should provide a schedule for the completion of the transitional process over a period of time, step by step in an orderly and agreed sequence leading to the full and effective establishment of international control of atomic energy. In order that the transition may be accomplished as rapidly as possible and with safety and equity to all, this Commission should supervise the transitional process, as prescribed in the treaty, and should be empowered to determine when a particular stage or stages have been completed and subsequent ones are to commence.

(8) *Report of the United Nations Atomic Energy Commission to the Security Council, December 31, 1946.*[1]

[Excerpts]

PART II. FINDINGS

SUMMARY OF FINDINGS

1. *Safeguards Necessary to Detect and Prevent Diversion from Declared Activities*

(a) Diversion of Uranium from Declared Mines and Mills. Adequate safeguards against diversion from declared mines and mills are possible by a system

[1] Department of State Publication 2737, United States-United Nations Report Series No. 8.

of inspection, including guards, similar to normal managerial operating controls, provided that the inspectorate has unrestricted access to all equipment and operations and has facilities for independent weighing, assay, and analysis.

(b) *Diversion of Thorium from Declared Mines and Mills.* Effective control of the raw material and concentrates of thorium is possible through a system of inspection similar to that found adequate for uranium.

(c) *Diversion of Uranium and Thorium from Declared Refineries and Chemical and Metallurgical Plants.* Adequate safeguards against diversion from declared refineries and chemical and metallurgical plants are possible by a system of inspection, including guards, similar to normal managerial operating controls, provided that the inspectorate has unrestricted access to all equipment and operations and has facilities for independent weighing, assay, and analysis and provided that it has the right to require the plant to be shut down for purposes of clean-up and accounting at appropriate times and to require efficient operating procedure.

At those stages there is no fundamental difference between the processes for thorium and for uranium.

(d) *Diversion of Uranium from Declared Isotope Separation Plants.* At present it is not possible to place reliance on the method of obtaining a material balance of uranium isotopes in the case of isotope separation plants. This is one of the important reasons why there must be internal control of such plants by a director or manager and why the management must be established by and be responsible to the international control agency. Even if the material balance could be greatly improved, the inherent danger of the operation would still require management by the international control agency.

(e) *Diversion of Uranium, Thorium, and Plutonium from Declared Nuclear Reactors and Associated Chemical Extraction Plants.*

(i) At present, it is not possible to place reliance on the method of obtaining a material balance of plutonium in the case of reactors and associated chemical extraction plants. This is one of the important reasons why the chemical extraction plants and, in some cases, the reactors should be subject to internal control by a director or manager and why the management must be established by and be responsible to the international control agency. Even if the material balance could be greatly improved, the inherent danger of the operations would still require management by the international control agency.

(ii) The safeguards required for the control of reactors will depend on their size and design and especially on their content and possible rate of production of nuclear fuel. The safeguards available to the international control agency should include licensing and inspection, supervision, and management of the operation of reactors. In addition, close supervision of the design and construction of reactors is essential in all cases.

(iii) Periodic inspection, together with licensing, is an adequate safeguard in the case of small research reactors and their associated chemical plants, unless their total content of nuclear fuel or potential rate of output in any area is of military significance.

(iv) Adequate safeguards for chemical extraction plants associated with all except small research reactors are only possible through management by the international control agency.

(v) Adequate safeguards during the preparation of the high-grade or pure nuclear fuels in a suitable form for insertion in secondary reactors, and, during the storage and shipment of such fuels, are only possible through management by the international control agency.

2. *Safeguards Necessary to Ensure the Detection of Clandestine Activities*

(a) The international control agency will require broad privileges of movement and inspection, including rights to conduct surveys by ground and air. These privileges should, however, be very carefully defined to ensure against misuse.

(b) Reports and returns on relevant matters will be required from national governments.

(c) The international control agency should coordinate all relevant information to determine what areas may be suspected of containing clandestine activities.

(d) Isotope separation plants, reactors, and chemical extraction plants, as well as mines, have distinguishing features which would facilitate the detection of clandestine activities at these stages.

(e) Detection of clandestine refineries and chemical and metallurgical plants is more difficult than detection of clandestine operations at other stages in the processing of nuclear fuel.

(f) The detection of clandestine bomb manufacture as such is almost impossible; it is, therefore, vital that any unauthorized accumulation of essential nuclear fuels be prevented.

3. *Seizure*

(a) Problems relating to seizure have been considered thus far only in preliminary terms. The major questions of seizure are political rather than technical. It appears, however, that technical measures could reduce the military advantages and, therefore, the dangers of seizure.

4. *Coordination of Safeguards*

(a) In addition to material accounting at each individual step in atomic energy processes, the international control agency should provide for material-accounting checks between points of shipment and receipt of material as a means of detecting possible diversion in transit.

(b) The international control agency should control the storage and shipment of uranium and thorium materials to the degree necessary for security purposes.

(c) The international control agency should itself store and itself handle all enriched or pure nuclear fuel in transit. This does not necessarily imply ownership either of the materials or of the transit or storage facilities, questions which have not yet been discussed.

(d) Since stocks of concentrated or pure nuclear fuel are acutely dangerous, operations at successive stages in the production of atomic energy should be so scheduled that stocks of materials in transit and in storage are minimized, but without interfering unduly with the development and effectiveness of peaceful activities.

. . . .

PART III. RECOMMENDATIONS

Based upon the findings of the Commission set forth in Part II of this report the Commission makes the following recommendations to the Security Council with respect to certain of the matters covered by the terms of reference of the Commission, which recommendations are interdependent and not severable, embodying the fundamental principles and indicating the basic organizational mechanisms necessary to attain the objectives set forth in Part II, C, General Findings, paragraph 1 (a)–(d) above.

1. There should be a strong and comprehensive international system of control and inspection aimed at attaining the objectives set forth in the Commission's terms of reference.

2. Such an international system of control and inspection should be established and its scope and functions defined by a treaty or convention in which all of the nations Members of the United Nations should be entitled to participate on fair and equitable terms.

The international system of control and inspection should become operative only when those Members of the United Nations necessary to assure its success by signing and ratifying the treaty or convention have bound themselves to accept and support it.

Consideration should be given to the matter of participation by non-members of the United Nations.

3. The treaty or convention should include, among others, provisions

(a) Establishing, in the United Nations, an international control agency possessing powers and charged with responsibility necessary and appropriate for the prompt and effective discharge of the duties imposed upon it by the terms of the treaty or convention. Its rights, powers, and responsibilities, as well as its relations to the several organs of the United Nations, should be clearly established and defined by the treaty or convention. Such powers should be sufficiently broad and flexible to enable the international control agency to deal with new developments that may hereafter arise in the field of atomic energy. The treaty shall provide that the rule of unanimity of the permanent Members, which in certain circumstances exists in the Security Council, shall have no relation to the work of the international control agency. No government shall possess any right of veto over the fulfilment by the international control agency of the obligations imposed upon it by the treaty nor shall any government have the power, through the exercise of any right of veto or otherwise, to obstruct the course of control or inspection.

The international control agency shall promote among all nations the exchange of basic scientific information on atomic energy for peaceful ends, and shall be responsible for preventing the use of atomic energy for destructive purposes, and for the control of atomic energy to the extent necessary to ensure its use only for peaceful purposes.

The international control agency should have positive research and developmental responsibilities in order to remain in the forefront of atomic knowledge so as to render the international control agency more effective in promoting the beneficial uses of atomic energy and in eliminating its destructive ones. The exclusive right to carry on atomic research for destructive purposes should be vested in the international control agency.

Research in nuclear physics having a direct bearing on the use of atomic energy should be subject to appropriate safeguards established by the international control agency in accordance with the treaty or convention. Such safeguards should not interfere with the prosecution of pure scientific research, or the publication of its results, provided no dangerous use or purpose is involved.

Decisions of the international control agency pursuant to the powers conferred upon it by the treaty or convention should govern the operations of national agencies for atomic energy. In carrying out its prescribed functions, however, the international control agency should interfere as little as necessary with the operations of national agencies for atomic energy, or with the economic plans and the private, corporate, and State relationships in the several countries.

(b) Affording the duly accredited representatives of the international control agency unimpeded rights of ingress, egress, and access for the performance of their inspections and other duties into, from, and within the territory of every participating nation, unhindered by national or local authorities.

(c) Prohibiting the manufacture, possession, and use of atomic weapons by all nations parties thereto and by all persons under their jurisdiction.

(d) Providing for the disposal of any existing stocks of atomic weapons and for the proper use of nuclear fuel adaptable for use in weapons.

(e) Specifying the means and methods of determining violations of its terms, setting forth such violations as shall constitute international crimes, and establishing the nature of the measures of enforcement and punishment to be imposed upon persons and upon nations guilty of violating the terms of the treaty or convention.

The judicial or other processes for determination of violations of the treaty or convention, and of punishments therefor, should be swift and certain. Serious violations of the treaty shall be reported immediately by the international control agency to the nations parties to the treaty, to the General Assembly, and to the Security Council. Once the violations constituting international crimes have been defined and the measures of enforcement and punishment therefor agreed to in the treaty or convention, there shall be no legal right, by veto or otherwise, whereby a wilful violator of the terms of the treaty or convention shall be protected from the consequences of violation of its terms.

The enforcement and punishment provisions of the treaty or convention would be ineffectual if, in any such situations, they could be rendered nugatory by the veto of a State which had voluntarily signed the treaty.

4. In consideration of the problem of violation of the terms of the treaty or convention, it should also be borne in mind that a violation might be of so grave a character as to give rise to the inherent right of self-defense recognized in article 51 of the Charter of the United Nations.

5. The treaty or convention should embrace the entire program for putting the international system of control and inspection into effect and should provide a schedule for the completion of the transitional process over a period of time, step by step, in an orderly and agreed sequence leading to the full and effective establishment of international control of atomic energy. In order that the transition may be accomplished as rapidly as possible and with safety and equity to all, this Commission should supervise the transitional process, as prescribed in the treaty or convention, and should be empowered to determine when a particular stage or stages have been completed and subsequent ones are to commence.

. . . . . .

CHAPTER VIII

DEPENDENT AREAS

1. THE INTERNATIONAL TRUSTEESHIP SYSTEM

A. The Trusteeship Council and Trusteeship Agreements

Chapters XII and XIII of the Charter of the United Nations, which came into effect on October 24, 1945, provided for the establishment of an international trusteeship system. Based on a formula devised at the Yalta conference, this system was a voluntary one under which, by agreement among "states directly concerned", three categories of territories might be placed: (1) mandates, (2) areas detached from enemy states as a result of World War II, and (3) any other territories placed under the system by the states responsible for their administration.

At meetings of the Preparatory Commission of the United Nations and of its Executive Committee, held in the fall of 1945, considerable conflict arose over implementation of these chapters of the Charter. Discussion centered primarily around the actual organization of the Trusteeship Council, which under the Charter could not be established until trusteeship agreements had designated enough nations as administering authorities to provide a balance between administering and non-administering states. After four possible methods of dealing with this problem had been suggested, the Executive Committee on October 18, 1945, voted to recommend the establishment of a Temporary Trusteeship Committee, which would exercise the functions of the Council until its actual creation. This decision, however, was overruled by the Preparatory Commission itself on December 20, following a statement by the Soviet Union that such a committee would be unconstitutional,[1] and the delegations approved instead a Yugoslav proposal calling for the mandatory powers to announce their willingness to place their mandates under the trusteeship system.[2]

Two other trusteeship problems were also discussed by the Preparatory Commission: the powers of the Council, as expressed in the Provisional Rules of Procedure, and the definition of the "states directly concerned" referred to in Article 79 of the Charter. The British delegation had submitted draft rules based largely on those of the Permanent Mandates Commission, but the colonial powers later acceded to a number of United States suggestions which liberalized the rules.[3] These revisions did away with numerous limitations on the powers of the Council, and made it much less dependent upon the administering authorities.

Neither the Executive Committee nor the Preparatory Commission took any

---

[1] United Nations Preparatory Commission, *Committee Four: Trusteeship. Summary Record of Meetings*, p. 2. This marked a reversal of earlier Soviet position in the Executive Committee.

[2] *Report of the Preparatory Commission of the United Nations*, Document PC/20, p. 49.

[3] Cf. *ibid.*, p. 50–56; *Report by the Executive Committee to the Preparatory Commission of the United Nations*, Document PC/EX/113/Rev. 1, p. 58–63.

specific action on a definition of "states directly concerned", despite lengthy discussions during which a number of small powers repeatedly pressed for an understanding of the term, and a Yugoslav proposal that they be considered to include (1) the mandatory states, (2) the Big Five, and (3) "perhaps the neighboring powers".[1] The matter arose also at the first meetings of the General Assembly in London in January-February 1946, when John Foster Dulles, American representative on the trusteeship committee of the Assembly, stated that the question was not within its competence, and that any attempt at definition could succeed in delaying "unduly" the conclusion of trusteeship agreements.[2] An earlier American memorandum had suggested that the powers of the Assembly to revise trusteeship agreements be limited.[3]

The first step in creation of actual trust territories was taken on January 17, 1946, when British Foreign Secretary Ernest Bevin announced that Great Britain would "enter forthwith into negotiations" to place under trusteeship certain of its mandates. Australia, Belgium, France and New Zealand also stated that agreements would be drawn up for their mandates, while the Union of South Africa reserved its rights on the question of Southwest Africa until it had consulted the wishes of the inhabitants of the territory.[4]

Following approval by the twenty-first Assembly of the League of Nations of a resolution which permitted but did not oblige administering authorities to transfer mandates to the United Nations trusteeship system,[5] trusteeship agreements for eight territories — British and French Cameroons and Togoland, New Guinea, Ruanda-Urundi, Tanganyika, and Western Samoa — were submitted to the General Assembly in October, 1946. A long memorandum which stated that inhabitants of Southwest Africa favored annexation into the Union of South Africa was submitted at the same time.[6]

Consideration of these agreements again involved a definition of "states directly concerned". The Soviet Union asked for a liberal interpretation of the phrase, while the United States now maintained that the mandatory power itself was the only state directly concerned, and that its obligations for consultation were fulfilled once other states which claimed special interest had had the opportunity to submit their ideas to the mandatory power.[7] Disputes on this question, together with those over whether a territory might be administered "as an integral part" of the trustee power, and on rights to erect fortifications, develop customs unions, and grant monopolies, were never finally resolved by the Assembly. The eight agreements, as amended by the trusteeship committee, were accepted by the Assembly on December 13, 1946; the Soviet Union, however, stated that it felt the agreements were illegal since these differences had not been resolved, and announced that it would not participate in elections to the Trusteeship Council.[8]

Incorporation of Southwest Africa by the Union of South Africa was opposed by all Assembly delegations except that of the United Kingdom; the United States stated merely that data before the Assembly did not justify it in approving, "at this session",[9] annexation of the territory. A resolution expressing the

---

[1] United Nations Preparatory Commission, *Committee Four . . . Summary Record* . . ., cited above, p. 10.

[2] *Ibid.*, p. 19, 42.

[3] For text, see this volume, p. 579.

[4] United Nations General Assembly, *Official Records of the First Part of the First Session . . . Fourth Committee. Trusteeship*, p. 10–11.

[5] League of Nations, Document A/VR/7/46, p. 5.

[6] For text of the South African memorandum, see United Nations General Assembly, Document A/123, October 19, 1946.

[7] For text of the speech by the American representative, John Foster Dulles, see this volume, p. 581.

[8] United Nations General Assembly, *Official Records of the Second Part of the First Session . . .* , *Plenary Sessions*, p. 1276–84, 1321.

[9] United Nations General Assembly, Document A/C.4/61, November 16, 1946.

desire that a trusteeship agreement might be submitted by the Union was eventually adopted.[1]

Elections on December 14, 1946, resulted in the choice of Iraq and Mexico as members of the Trusteeship Council.[2] Australia, Belgium, France, New Zealand, and the United Kingdom, as administering authorities, and China, the Soviet Union and the United States, as permanent members of the Security Council, automatically gained seats on the Council.

(1) *Memorandum of the United States Delegation to the Executive Committee of the United Nations Preparatory Commission Regarding Procedure for Dealing with Trusteeship Agreements, October 2, 1945.*[3]

Negotiation of Agreements

1. The trusteeship agreements by which territories will be placed under the trusteeship system (Article 77 of the Charter) are to include the terms of trusteeship for each such territory (Article 79), the manner in which the territory will be administered, and will designate the administering authority (Article 81). The conclusion of these agreements involves two stages. In the first stage the initiative with respect to the agreements, except in the case of territories which may be administered by the United Nations itself, and their formulation, will in each case remain with the states directly concerned (Article 79).

2. In order to carry out the intent of paragraph 2 of Article 80, the General Assembly or the Security Council could, presumably, encourage the states directly concerned to expedite the initiation and formulation of agreements, and might render whatever assistance may be requested by those states with respect to the agreements. But there would appear to be no other basis for direct participation in the first stage of the negotiation of trusteeship agreements by any of the organs of the United Nations, except where direct international administration is envisaged.

Approval of Agreements

3. The second stage in the conclusion of the agreements relates to their approval by the United Nations. In this process the General Assembly or the Security Council will be directly involved in each agreement. Once agreement is reached among the states directly concerned on the terms of a trusteeship agreement, that agreement is to be submitted to the General Assembly (Article 85) or, in the case of strategic areas, to the Security Council (Article 83), for approval.

4. The appraisal of the trusteeship agreements submitted, which would form the basis for approval or rejection by the appropriate organ of the

---

[1] United Nations General Assembly, Document A/250/Add.1/Rev.1, December 12, 1946; United Nations General Assembly, *Official Records of the Second Part of the First Session* . . . , *Plenary Sessions*, p. 1327.

[2] *Ibid.*, p. 1323.

[3] *Report by the Executive Committee* . . . , cited above, p. 64.

United Nations, should be primarily based upon their consistency with the provisions of the Charter. In this connection, it would be essential that each agreement would:

(a) provide for placing the territory in question under the trusteeship system;

(b) state the terms of trusteeship, which should be so designed as to give effect to the basic objectives of the trusteeship system as set forth in Article 76;

(c) allow for the exercise by the appropriate organs of the United Nations of the functions and powers set forth in Chapters XII and XIII;

(d) be accepted by and binding upon the states directly concerned.

Procedure

5. In the case of non-strategic areas, the General Assembly, before acting upon the approval or rejection of an agreement, might, in conformity with Article 85 (2) submit the agreement to the Trusteeship Council, or, if that Council has not yet been permanently established, to the proposed Temporary Trusteeship Committee of the General Assembly for its review and advice. The Security Council could also call upon the Trusteeship Council or the Temporary Committee for similar review and advice respecting the non-military aspects of any trusteeship agreement for a strategic area.

6. In the event of the agreement being found to be consistent with the provisions of the Charter, approval would be given by a two-thirds majority of the members present and voting in the General Assembly, and with respect to strategic areas, by an affirmative vote in the Security Council of seven members including the concurring votes of the permanent members.

7. If any provision of a trusteeship agreement should be regarded by the General Assembly or the Security Council as in conflict with a provision of the Charter, it would not be approved by them and might be returned to the states directly concerned with recommendations for modifications which in the view of the General Assembly or the Security Council would make the agreement acceptable.

8. The General Assembly or the Security Council, however, may see fit to make suggestions for revision of trusteeship agreements on grounds other than their inconsistency with the Charter. Such suggestions would doubtless be seriously considered by the states directly concerned.

9. In view of the fact that when the trusteeship agreements are submitted to the United Nations they will have been formally approved by the states directly concerned, which in the case of some states may involve constitutional processes requiring to be referred to legislative bodies, it would be advisable, in the interests of expediting the conclusion of agreements, that the exercise of the power to make suggestions for revision be limited to matters of prime importance to the effective functioning of the system and to the well-being of the inhabitants of trust territories.

(2) *Statement by the Alternate United States Delegate to the General Assembly (Dulles) on the United States Position on the Establishment of the Trusteeship System, November 7, 1946.*[1]

[Excerpts]

The United States Delegation, represented here by Congressman Bloom and myself, will not at this time comment in detail upon the various substantive matters before this committee. We will primarily deal now with the matter which we deem to be most urgent, that is, the procedure which will enable the Trusteeship Council to be established at this session. However, before passing to the question of procedure, we should like to express, on behalf of the United States, appreciation of the steps which have already been taken to implement the provisions of chapter XI and chapters XII and XIII of the Charter.

. . . . . .

Five mandatory powers have now laid before the General Assembly draft terms of trusteeship for eight mandated territories. As regards these draft terms, the United States believes that most of them, in their present revised form, are generally satisfactory and that they offer a reasonable basis for implementing the trusteeship system. The United States is hopeful, therefore, that the General Assembly will find it possible to set up the Trusteeship Council at this session. However, that will not happen easily.

In this trusteeship matter we can readily fall into a morass which will so entangle us that the trusteeship provisions of the Charter will never become operative. Let us frankly admit that the Charter provisions are awkward and ambiguous. They could give rise to prolonged controversy and lead to an impasse.

. . . . . .

At the moment there are before us eight proposed trusteeship agreements, all in relation to mandated territory which is not designated as strategic. Procedure in relation to these agreements is certain in at least two respects: First, the terms of trusteeship must be agreed to by the mandatory power; secondly, the terms of the trusteeship must be approved by the General Assembly, presumably by a two-thirds vote. Whether any further procedural steps are required, and if so what, is a matter of uncertainty.

In the case of the mandated territories before us, are there states other than the mandatory whose agreement must be obtained? If so, how are these states to be determined and how should their agreement be evidenced?

It can be contended that in the situations before us only the mandatory power is "directly concerned" within the meaning of the Charter. It is true that the Charter uses the plural "states". But this cannot mean that in every case of trusteeship more than one state must agree

[1] Department of State, *Bulletin*, XV, p. 991.

as to the terms of trusteeship. If a nation which is sole sovereign over certain colonial territory is willing to put that territory under trusteeship, on conditions agreeable to two-thirds of the General Assembly, surely it is entitled to do so. Article 77 (c) speaks of "territories voluntarily placed under the system by states responsible for their administration". Clearly, in these cases the sovereign is alone the state "directly concerned". Therefore, the fact that the Charter uses the plural does not require us, in every case, to find several states whose preliminary agreement must be obtained. The word "states" obviously includes the singular as well as the plural and the Charter should be interpreted as though it read "the state or states directly concerned". Therefore, it can be powerfully argued that where the territory proposed to be placed under trusteeship is administered by a single sovereign, its agreement is the only agreement required as a prelude to Assembly action.

The American Delegation has concluded not only that such interpretation of the Charter is legally proper but that it is the fairest and most workable interpretation that can be given to the Charter.

Every other interpretation suggested will involve us in difficulties and delays. For example, it could be contended that the phrase "directly concerned" looks to legal title and that where more than one state shares the title it is the agreement of those states which must be obtained.

This would mean, in the case of the former German colonies, that the "states directly concerned" would be the "Principal Allied and Associated Powers" in whose favor Germany, under article 119 of the Treaty of Versailles, renounced all her rights and titles over her overseas possessions. These five Principal Allied and Associated Powers were: Great Britain, France, the United States, Japan, and Italy. The rights of Japan and Italy having been extinguished, Great Britain, France, and the United States could claim that, as the three remaining effective Principal Allied and Associated Powers, they and they alone should be considered the "states directly concerned" because of their joint title. Probably that claim would give rise to argument and delay.

It could be argued that the Charter test of "direct concern" is not legal but practical. Such an interpretation would open a vast field for speculation. Are the five principal powers under the United Nations Charter "states directly concerned" either because they are permanent members of the Security Council or, prospectively, permanent members of the Trusteeship Council? Can states claim to be "states directly concerned" because of geographical propinquity or because of economic or cultural or ethnic ties or perhaps merely because they take an interest in the subject? If so, what is the measuring rod? Is the geographic propinquity only that reflected by common borders, or is it enough to be within 100 miles or 1,000 miles of the trust territory? Or even 2,500 miles, as one delegation has already suggested? How much trade is necessary to justify concern on economic grounds? How close must be the ethnic and cultural ties? Such questions do not lend themselves to any clear answer. If we assume that they must all be answered before the trusteeship system is established, then there is great risk that the trusteeship system will never be established.

In the light of these considerations the United States Delegation urges that the Assembly, and this committee on its behalf, should not become involved in all these questions. We prefer a practical procedure which, in harmony with the letter and spirit of the Charter, will, as quickly as possible, permit the establishment of the trusteeship system and the giving to the inhabitants of the trust territories the benefit of that system. Concretely, we propose:

1. That a small subcommittee of this committee should be established to consider the draft trusteeship agreements before us and to negotiate on our behalf in relation to them;

2. That all states which are interested be given the opportunity promptly to submit to this subcommittee and to the mandatory power involved their suggestions regarding these proposed trusteeship agreements;

3. That after hearing such suggestions and after consultation with the subcommittee, the mandatory power concerned shall promptly advise the subcommittee as to the acceptability of those suggestions;

4. That the agreements reflecting any such modifications shall then be considered by this committee and referred by it to the General Assembly with the recommendation of this committee, in each case, as to approval or disapproval.

Under this procedure every state which is interested, whether or not technically a state "directly concerned", whether it be large or small, whether it be near or far, will have an equal opportunity to present its views. All would, however, without prejudice to any rights they may possess, now forego formal classification as being, or not being, states "directly concerned" and would forego formal signature of the preliminary agreement, accepting the verdict of a two-thirds vote of the Assembly.

If any state other than the mandatory power is a state "directly concerned", the United States has a strong, and we believe unassailable, case to be considered to be such a state. We have an interest in the title conferred under the treaties of Versailles and of Berlin. We are a permanent member of the Security Council and will be a permanent member of the Trusteeship Council when established. We have important economic interests in all the mandated areas, and in the case of the Australian and New Zealand mandates, and perhaps others, we have a concern based upon geographic and other considerations.

The United States, however, is willing to join with others in accepting a system of equality and not asserting a special position in relation to the agreements now before us. We do not want interminable and inconclusive discussion. Neither do we want an interpretation of "states directly concerned" which might import the veto system into the work of the Assembly. Accordingly, the United States, without prejudice to its legal rights and on the assumption that others will do the same, is prepared, in relation to the trusteeship agreements now before us, to agree to them in the form in which, after an exchange of views, they are submitted by the administering authority, recommended by this committee and approved by two thirds of the Assembly.

There can be, and doubtless will be, many earnest opinions with respect to what should be the terms of trusteeship agreements. No doubt many would like a special position for impressing their views. But let us remember that such a special position may be of illusory value. For under the Charter there can be no trusteeship at all without the agreement of the mandatory power. Let us also remember that if there is trustee at all, that obligatorily provides the inhabitants of the trust territories with the benefits of the Charter. By it the administering authorities are obligated, among other things, "to promote the political, economic, social, and educational advancement of the inhabitants of the trust territories, and their progressive development towards self-government or independence . . . . —" Every administering authority is by the Charter required "to encourage respect for human rights and for fundamental freedoms for all without distinction as to race, sex, language or religion . . . —"

No doubt all of us have our ideas as to how these objectives should be attained, and all of us would like to see our ideas spelled out in the trusteeship agreements. The United States Delegation, for its part, believes that the agreements now before us are susceptible of improvement. We hope that the mandatory powers will accept changes which might bring them into accord with the views of such states as may reasonably claim an interest in the subject. But the essential is to establish the Trusteeship Council and to make operative those basic obligations which are set forth in the Charter. We can proceed without excessive insistence upon the expression of particular views, knowing that the Charter itself deals with the essentials and that no one can lawfully subtract one jot or tittle from chapter XII of the Charter which will constitute the overriding constitution for the peoples of all the trust territories.

We believe that history will not judge kindly any who take a position which would in fact block the establishment of the trusteeship system and its grant to dependent peoples of the right to eventual self-government or independence. Let us have confidence in article XII of the Charter as a constitution for trusteed areas; let us trust the judgment of two thirds of the Assembly as to how that Charter should be implemented; let us assume the good faith of our fellow members who now propose trusteeship. Under these conditions this Assembly can accomplish one of its most urgent and most difficult tasks — that is to establish the trusteeship system now.

B. United States Trusteeship in the Pacific

During 1945 and 1946 the trusteeship question with which the United States was most closely concerned was the disposition of Japanese-mandated Pacific islands, which had been captured during the war by American forces and which were under military administration.

Early in 1945 considerable support was expressed for the idea of annexation, strongly advocated by Admiral Ernest J. King and other military leaders, and also backed by the Subcommittee on Pacific Bases of the House Naval Affairs Committee, which submitted a report urging the retention not only of Japanese mandated islands but of other islands in the Pacific as well.¹ This view was opposed by the State Department, which wished to abide by those clauses of the Atlantic Charter and the Cairo Declaration which repudiated territorial aggrandizement, and by the Interior Department, which administered many United States dependencies. A possibility for compromise arose with the inclusion in the Charter of the United Nations of the concept of strategic areas trusteeship.

Despite growing public pressure, however, no public announcement of American policy was made until early in 1946. After it had been urged that the United States position be announced to the General Assembly, then meeting in London, President Truman made an informal statement to his press conference on January 15.² Although his remarks were somewhat ambiguous, they indicated that the United States would place all Japanese-mandated islands under trusteeship. The President's statement, clarified and expanded by Acting Secretary of State Acheson on January 22,³ was at once condemned by Senators Byrd, Capeheart, Eastland, and Tobey, who predicted that any treaty conceding any control over the islands to the United Nations would face "very tough sledding" in the Senate.⁴

On November 6, 1946, however, President Truman formally announced that the United States was prepared to place the Japanese-mandated islands under trusteeship as a strategic area,⁵ and made public the text of the proposed agreement for the islands, which represented a compromise worked out by the State, War, and Navy Departments.⁶ Copies of the draft agreement were transmitted to members of the Security Council, New Zealand, and the Philippines. The agreement was submitted to the Security Council by the United States Representative, Warren R. Austin, on February 26, 1947.⁷

(1) *Report by the Subcommittee on Pacific Bases of the Committee on Naval Affairs of the United States House of Representatives, August 6, 1945.*⁸

[Excerpts]

III. OBSERVATIONS AND CONCLUSIONS

Any attempt to plan the future policies of the United States in the Pacific must, of course, be based on the best available knowledge. Therein lies the fundamental reason for this study and report of members of the House Naval Affairs Committee on Pacific bases. Later sections of the report contain condensed statements of relative facts about the islands of the Pacific and their people. These facts were gained either through the direct inquiry of the subcommittee or through the compilation of information by various informed authorities pursuant to the request of the subcommittee.

---

[1] For Admiral King's statement, see *New York Times*, April 5, 1945. For the report of the Subcommittee on Pacific Bases, see above.

[2] Department of State, *Bulletin*, XIV, p. 113.

[3] *Ibid.*, p. 150.

[4] *New York Times*, January 17, 1946.

[5] For the text of the President's statement, see this volume, p. 594.

[6] For the text of the draft agreement, see *ibid.*

[7] Department of State Publication 2812, United States — United Nations Information Series 18, p. 30.

[8] Report submitted to the Committee on Naval Affairs of the House of Representatives on August 6, 1945.

A. Basic Assumptions, Unknowns and Missions

Obviously, there are important factors which are not covered and cannot be presented as matters of fact. It is, therefore, necessary that some assumptions be made and clearly set forth for the purpose of the matters discussed in this report. This report is made on the following assumptions:

(1) That the charter written by the United Nations Conference on International Organization will be approved by the major powers that participated in the conference;

(2) That the United States will assume the task of preserving peace and preventing any aggressive action in the Pacific area;

(3) That this function will require the United States to maintain in the Pacific, adequate strategic bases and forces in condition of readiness prepared to execute such necessary measures as the situation demands, with clearly defined limits within which control by the armed forces of the United States will be necessary and proper; and

(4) That the United States will maintain a fleet superior to that of any other nation.

In addition to these specific assumptions, it is recognized that there are a number of unknowns which will sooner or later have to be clarified before tentative plans can be made. We must learn or decide:

(1) The nature and function of any international control, supervision and commitments;

(2) The disposition of Japanese civilian nationals now in islands under American control and in those bypassed; and

(3) The American policies of freedom of trade, tariffs, application of coastwise shipping laws, air routes, radio communications, and possible acquisition of American citizenship.

In using the preceding assumptions and our own security as a basis, it appears that our mission in the Pacific relative to bases is dual in character:

(1) The primary mission being to occupy, maintain, and defend such bases in the Pacific area as are required to insure our superiority on the sea, on the land, and in the air in order to protect the United States and its possessions against any probable enemy; and

(2) The secondary mission being to occupy the minimum of bases in the Pacific area, prepared to execute such necessary measures as required to prevent aggression in the Pacific in order to assist in maintaining world peace.

B. Factors for Consideration

In the consideration of retention of Pacific bases that have been captured, recaptured, or occupied by American armed forces through the sacrifice of American lives and through the expenditure of vast sums of money, it is necessary to evaluate the strategic, economic, and psychological factors. The problem concerns four types of islands:

(1) The Japanese mandated islands,

(2) The outlying Japanese islands,

(3) Those islands of Allied Nations on which American bases were constructed, and

(4) The prewar American islands.

Each, of course, will entail distinctive treatment, but they must all be viewed from the over-all Pacific pattern in order to make a logical approach on the designation of Pacific islands and bases to be retained by the United States.

This report does not discuss the uncaptured prewar American islands, such as Hawaii, Midway, Samoa, and Palmyra in detail, because of our obvious retention of those islands. We still regard Pearl Harbor as the American bastion in the Pacific. Because of the overwhelming logic of American dominance over the Japanese mandated islands and the outlying Japanese islands, more detailed consideration is given to these islands, the greater part of which is known as Micronesia. Suffice to say, from a legal viewpoint, Japan has forfeited all rights to her mandated islands by breaching the trust with respect to that mandate. It is our belief that the United States should take outright the Japanese mandated islands and the outlying Japanese islands. There are those who favor trusteeship of these islands. There are those who subscribe to the thesis that what is everybody's job is nobody's responsibility. Regardless of which view prevails, the United States should have the dominating control over these islands. Because of the complexity of the problem of major American bases constructed on islands of our Allied Nations in the Pacific, we are not prepared to make any conclusions other than that this country should retain very definite rights to those bases in those areas.

The subcommittee consideration of this problem goes beyond the strategic factors, because some qualitative distinction must be made as to the particular bases we wish to retain. Since it is not necessary to retain all bases from a strategic standpoint, obviously, we must select for retention those islands which are not only strategically desirable but also of greatest economic value.

Too often does the consideration of this important problem overlook the psychological factor. In other words, a base inhabited by natives, friendly to the United States, is far more valuable from the standpoint of security. While there are indications that the natives of these Pacific islands are friendly to the United States, if only because of the comparative treatment which they have received from the Japanese and Americans, the degree of that friendliness cannot be accurately evaluated at this time. More important is the necessity of the United States to cultivate the friendship of the natives of the islands it retains in the interest of future security. This psychological factor will greatly be shaped by the methods and policies adopted by the United States and the government of these islands.

To those who challenge the justification for the retention of Pacific bases by the United States we would merely cite:

(1) The loss of American lives in taking these bases;

(2) The expenditure of vast sums of American money in establishing and equipping these bases;

(3) The great dependence of the world upon the United States for maintaining peace in the Pacific and the world; and

(4) The apparent preference of the natives of these islands for the United States Government.

In other words, we will have restored peace to the Pacific almost single-handedly and if we are to be charged with the responsibility of maintaining that peace, we must be given the authority and the means by which to maintain the peace — one of the principal means being the authority over strategic islands in the Pacific.

Nor must the fact be overlooked that our retention of these islands will be predicated solely upon the desire and responsibility to maintain peace in the Pacific, rather than upon imperialism. Prewar mandates mean little to enforcement of world peace if the countries that hold them are incapable of maintaining and defending the islands. The United States must retain those islands in Micronesia and the outlying Japanese islands that it has taken — the United States must also retain Manus, Noumea, Espiritu Santo, Guadalcanal, and other islands and places on which it has erected huge American bases in the rescue of the countries below the Equator, because —

(1) With the maintenance of peace in the Pacific being primarily the responsibility of the United States, we must have the necessary authority for such responsibility;

(2) That authority means the retention of such islands and bases built by the United States; and

(3) The other nations are either too distant from these Pacific islands, or do not have the necessary strength of manpower and materials, for the maintenance and defense of these strategic islands and bases.

· · · · · · ·

2. *Economic*

Of extreme importance in these considerations is the degree of self-sufficiency or self-subsistence of these islands as stated before. The strategic strength does not reside in the multiplicity of bases. This infers distinction in values between the various Pacific bases and illustrates the influence of economic aspects upon strategic considerations. While we cannot afford to be "penny pinchers" as we were in the case of Guam prior to the war, and while we must always bear in mind that the cost of security has been more in the loss of American lives and the investment of war dollars in the establishment of bases on these islands, nevertheless, we cannot overlook the considerations of how much it will cost the United States not only to take these islands under its wing but also to maintain them.

The first message to be brought home to the American people is that whatever the maintenance cost might be in the regulation of these islands, it will represent comparatively inexpensive national insurance of continued freedom of the United States and of peace in the Pacific. The major necessary improvements on these bases have already been made during the war, so that the future expense in the retention of the bases will be that of maintenance and any necessary expansion.

Of course these bases will have to be manned but that can be done with comparatively small garrison forces. At the same time, most of the military and naval establishments on these bases can be put to practical use as training bases. Personnel necessary for the administration of training could supply the backbone of the maintenance personnel.

Because of the economic importance of these islands and because of the fundamental that the American sphere of control should be over Micronesia, a later section is devoted to the economic aspects of Micronesia and the outlying Japanese islands. The most encouraging economic aspect of the Japanese mandated islands in Micronesia is the fact that these islands are potentially capable of being self-subsisting as far as food production is concerned, and that those which are occupied by American forces at the present time are self-sufficient. It is estimated that within 12 to 18 months after the cessation of hostilities it will be possible to restore fully local food economy in these islands. In the opinion of the subcommittee, this is of prime importance because if the natives are able to provide their own food and shelter, the greater portion of economic burdens of any of these islands will have been eliminated.

Of equal encouragement and of much surprise to the subcommittee, is the fact that the Japanese have actually made a 2-to-1 profit. That is, the income from the Japanese mandated islands has been twice that of the expense of the Japanese in their administration of these islands. This is even more remarkable and encouraging in view of the fact that this 2-to-1 ratio covers (1) government expenditures, (2) the expense of the establishment and maintenance of military and naval facilities, and (3) "unusual" administrative expenditures.

While the economic resources of the Pacific islands do not appear to be great, they are believed to be adequate to support their population and to allow substantial improvement in their well-being. The United States may have to assume administrative costs but there is no reason to believe that we shall have to put the population on the dole. That would be bad for them as well as expensive for us. There is probably some room for productive ventures financed by American capital but the field is limited.

The area of arable land, character of the soil and available water supplies indicate that the production of crops for export is bound to be limited. Copra has been a money product for some of the islands. The Japanese had a small sugar development in the Mariannas but reports of it do not indicate that it is worth reviving. Although Hawaiian capital was invested in Philippine sugar centers to some extent, no ripple of interest has been evident in Hawaii with respect to possible future investment in sugar production in the Mariannas. Improved agricultural practices for production for the use of the native populations should be the immediate objective. The natives adjacent to garrison areas can doubtless find a market for perishable vegetables and fruits, thereby getting money for needed imported products.

The possibilities of commercial fishing need to be explored and the appropriate agencies of the Federal Government can be of great assistance. Since fish is the major source of protein food supply for many of the islands, commercial fisheries should only be permitted to an extent which will not interfere with this native food supply. It is not improbable, however, that canning of fish can become an industry of some value.

Natives develop crafts which produce articles for their own use and esthetic satisfaction. Such crafts should be encouraged since not only are their products useful for their intended purposes in native life but many of them can readily be marketed in Hawaii and on the mainland.

It is obvious that the greatest potential commercial uses of these islands will be in air transportation and shipping. The map which accompanied the last report which Japan made to the League of Nations shows steamship lines between the various island groups and to Japan. In the future, there will be need for some similar facilities. Whether or not they can be established and operated by American interests without governmental assistance is open to question. American costs of ship construction and operation are high and the volume of travel and trade does not now promise to be great. Yet both strategic and administrative considerations indicate that foreign control of such transportation is undesirable. This is another matter which requires further study.

3. *Psychological*

The most important psychological factor in the occupation and retention of Pacific bases by the United States is the attitude of the natives of the islands. It is encouraging that all indications are that the natives not only prefer American control, but in some instances have requested that they be placed permanently under American authority. This can stem only from the confidence of the natives in the American sense of justice and fair treatment. Such confidence has been instilled in the natives not only by the island commanders, but also by the thousands of American soldiers, sailors, and marines in their daily contacts with the natives. They have given the United States a tremendous start toward sound and strong relations with these islands.

The subcommittee is of the opinion that this impetus afforded by the servicemen can best be perpetuated through:

(1) The teaching of English to the natives;

(2) The indoctrination of the natives to the American way as soon as possible without infringing upon the customs and institutions of the natives; and

(3) The establishment of that quality of government in these islands which will encourage the maximum of self-rule.

It is a well-established fact that the greatest friendly relations exist between those who speak the same language. The phrase "we speak the same language" is often used to express a complete meeting of the minds, just as is the phrase "he is one of us." Obviously, American ideas and the American way of life can best be presented through the medium of language, and it will be through the teaching of English that we can best inculcate the American way to make the natives feel a bond of friendship gained only through their voluntary discarding of certain of their customs and institutions in favor of the American customs and institutions. If the past American island government is to be criticized in any manner, it is in its failure to teach English to the natives. This observation is made in connection with long established American islands and not with respect to the occupied Japanese mandated islands where remarkable success has been experienced in teaching the natives English. Our naval military government has found that the natives of Micronesia are on an intelligence level with the Hawaiians, and have a similar capacity to learn.

It must be emphasized that changing the customs and institutions of natives is not to be entered upon lightly or unadvisedly. There are doubtless improvements to be made in health, education, and economic well-being. Contacts with Spaniards, Germans, Japanese and Americans have already modified and changed to some extent the original customs, attitude, and occupations of the various peoples. It should be the policy of the United States that further changes operate in so far as possible to the real benefit of the natives. Changes in objectives and ways of life should be expected to come only gradually. Because democratic institutions appear to us normal and desirable, it does not follow that prematurely forcing them on a people in a far different stage of social evolution would be in their best interests and in the long run to our advantage. The changes must be voluntary, but the natives must be given every opportunity to make those changes. A real understanding of the natives entrusted to this country's care is a prerequisite to skillful and desirable administration. Such understanding requires specialized training, experience, and intensive study. Further ethnological research should be carried on as soon as possible. It will be necessary to use care that the impact of Americans on the natives will not operate to create discontent due to arousing desires which they are incapable of satisfying. But this caution and care should in no way operate to discourage the natives' voluntary emulation of the Americans.

The character of the island government raises a certain conflict of opinion. There are those who feel that military government is the only logical form for these islands due to their prime importance and use as military and naval bases. The justification for this view would appear dependent upon the degree to which an island sustains permanent military or naval facilities. The other school of thought is that the island should be governed by a civil administration, on the grounds that civilians are better trained for the administration of the government, and that military government is not democratic government.

There is a great deal to be said for military government in the many islands occupied and to be retained by the United States. In the first place, the island commanders and members of their staffs have acquired, through their occupation of these islands, a great deal of knowledge of the natives and the islands. The natives have come to know these men, and the initial barriers in this respect which might exist between a new civilian governor and the natives would be avoided through retention of the present military and naval governments in their islands.

The naval military government has done an excellent job in administration of the islands occupied during this war as contrasted to the islands where American authority has been in force for many years. There is great strength and abundance of ability in the Army and Navy military government ranks because the armed forces have drawn off the cream of the crop of young public administrators and public officials. These men possess native ability and have much experience in dealing with people — particularly in governing them.

Although there may be racial variations in human relations, there are certain fundamentals which apply to relations of all human beings. These men of the Army and Navy military government have been ingrained through public experience in dealing with people. They have been educated to maximum specialization in dealing with the natives of the islands which our forces have occupied. The most serious question with respect to the retention of Army and Navy military governments in these islands is the ability of the armed services to make the Army and Navy satisfactorily attractive as a profession to these better-qualified men who possess the desired ability, training, and experience.

On the other hand, it must be recognized that military and civilian administrative proficiencies are distinct, calling for different training, experience, and skill, and that they are directed to different objectives. It is no criticism of the lawmaker or administrator to say that he is not adapted to military commands. It is equally no criticism of the naval officer to say that civil administration is not his proper field. Every American is filled with admiration by the achievement of our fighting men and the soundness and proficiency of the strategy and tactics of those in command. Such are the more potent arguments of those who advocate that in time of peace civilian administration and military command should be separate and correlative functions.

This subcommittee is of the opinion that one of two alternate steps should be taken with respect to the government of the islands retained:

(1) Either the Navy should assign its best qualified personnel, specialists in government instead of "seagoing" officers, to island government duty; or

(2) The governing of these islands should be by civilian administrators, possibly with Army and Navy officers on their staffs.

The seagoing ability of the naval officer is certainly not a criterion of his ability to act in the capacity of island governor. It is more apt to be an indication of his undesirability to act in that capacity, because the earnest and professed desire of seagoing officers to be at sea is one of the prime traditions of the Navy. It is well known that this results very often in the dissatisfaction of a seagoing officer in his assignment to shore duty and particularly to duty as an island governor inasmuch as the naval character of his work is greatly diluted. Too often it is the case that a seagoing officer thinks of his next assignment from the very day that he takes his duties as island governor.

Another weakness of past naval-military government has been the lack of continuity in the commands of naval governments. The continuity is imperative in the governing of those islands which we retain. However, there are government specialists in the Navy, predominantly reservists, who have expressed their willingness to serve in the naval military government of the islands. A man's desire for a job is the greatest guaranty of his doing a job well.

It is the belief of the subcommittee that civil administration in all areas not within the limits of the strategic bases is an inevitable concomitant of the maintenance of such bases, and that such civil administration should be directed to the preservation and improvement of the natives. A potential compromise of the opposing views would be to place the civil administration under the Navy Department as a distinct service manned by personnel specifically selected for civil administration of dependent and undeveloped natives and reporting to the civilian heads of the Navy. This service or group might be headed by an assistant secretary, charged with responsibility for such civil administration.

Some central administrative center must be established in the Pacific for the governing of all islands retained by this country in order to effect coordination, economy, and consistency in policy and procedure. The most apparent logical sites are Honolulu and Guam, depending on whether Hawaii is granted statehood. The islands should ultimately be given their independence, as is scheduled for the Philippines, or remain territories of the United States, or be made an integral part of this country, perhaps as the "State of the American Pacific." Through the council of the United Nations, various nations holding the Pacific islands should find an effective approach to the problems common to all of the islands.

The United States has not developed a colonial policy, nor a colonial service. The terminology would probably be offensive to most Americans. Nevertheless, if the United States is to assume the responsibility for these islands, we must develop a service which is competent for such a specialized task, give it dignified status, and provide adequate compensation to attract and hold qualified personnel. Understanding of natives is not easy, and guiding their affairs requires knowledge, experience, and wisdom.

While paternalism is a word with obnoxious connotations to most Americans, it may well be an essential characteristic of our early administration of the Pacific islands. The only limitation to self-rule should be the ability of the natives to govern themselves. At the present time, they have shown great ability for self-rule at the "chief" or "headman" level, but they are dependent upon the occupation commanders or military governors for major decisions and policy. In other words, they execute the decisions of the military governors. Because of these aspects, certain activities of our future government of these islands should receive special attention — health, land, laws, and education.

There can be no argument about the promotion of health measures, for sanitary and medical services will be essential. Some excellent work has been done in the Fijis, one of our stops, in training native medical practitioners who have returned to their communities and rendered excellent service. Improved health measures will result in a population increase which may later pose new questions.

Attention must be given to land holdings. To what extent it will be found that property titles have passed to the Japanese is not now known.

Except for lands which will have to be pre-empted for military uses, a general policy should be set to preserve the land ownership for the natives. It will not in all cases be easy to determine to whom the land really belongs, and it may well be that it will be found that the plan of land usage rather than land ownership prevails in some native societies.

Because concepts of land tenure totally different from our own obtain among the natives of these islands, it is most important that specialized personnel thoroughly investigate these concepts before any attempt is made to codify the property laws. Decisions based on superficial knowledge of native property concepts have led colonial administrators into more conflicts with independent people than has any other factor during the long and generally sordid period of colonial history.

The administration of justice will doubtless raise questions requiring careful study. Native ideas of right and wrong, and what is just and unjust, will need to be considered. It would be a mistake to assume that American law can be imposed without regard to native ideas or customs. Skillful use of the chiefs in local government will greatly assist in maintaining order and promoting smooth administration.

(2) *Statement by the President (Truman) on United States Trusteeship in the Pacific, Released to the Press November 6, 1946.*[1]

The United States is prepared to place under trusteeship, with the United States as the administering authority, the Japanese Mandated Islands and any Japanese islands for which it assumes responsibilities as a result of the second World War. Insofar as the Japanese Mandated Islands are concerned, this Government is transmitting for information to the other members of the Security Council (Australia, Brazil, China, Egypt, France, Mexico, the Netherlands, Poland, the Union of Soviet Socialist Republics, and the United Kingdom) and to New Zealand and the Philippines a draft of a strategic area trusteeship agreement which sets forth the terms upon which this Government is prepared to place those islands under trusteeship. At an early date we plan to submit this draft agreement formally to the Security Council for its approval.

(3) *Draft Trusteeship Agreement for the Japanese Mandated Islands under Administration of the United States, Released to the Press November 6, 1946.*[2]

PREAMBLE

WHEREAS Article 75 of the Charter of the United Nations provides for the establishment of an international trusteeship system for the administration and supervision of such territories as may be placed thereunder by subsequent agreements; and

[1] Department of State, *Bulletin*, XV, p. 889.
[2] *Ibid*. This draft agreement for the Japanese Mandated Islands was transmitted for their information to the members of the Security Council of the United Nations and to New Zealand and the Philippines in accordance with President Truman's statement of November 6, 1946.

WHEREAS under Article 77 of the said Charter the trusteeship system may be applied to territories now held under mandate; and

WHEREAS on December 17, 1920 the Council of the League of Nations confirmed a mandate for the former German islands north of the equator to Japan, to be administered in accordance with Article 22 of the Covenant of the League of Nations; and

WHEREAS Japan, as a result of the Second World War, has ceased to exercise any authority in these islands;

Now, THEREFORE, the Security Council of the United Nations, having satisfied itself that the relevant articles of the Charter having been complied with, hereby resolves to approve the following terms of trusteeship for the Pacific Islands formerly under mandate to Japan.

Article 1. The Territory of the Pacific Islands, consisting of the islands formerly held by Japan under mandate in accordance with Article 22 of the Covenant of the League of Nations, is hereby designated as a strategic area and placed under the trusteeship system established in the Charter of the United Nations. The Territory of the Pacific Islands is hereinafter referred to as the trust territory.

Article 2. The United States of America is designated as the administering authority of the trust territory.

Article 3. The administering authority shall have full powers of administration, legislation, and jurisdiction over the territory subject to the provisions of this agreement as an integral part of the United States, and may apply to the trust territory, subject to any modifications which the administering authority may consider desirable, such of the laws of the United States as it may deem appropriate to local conditions and requirements.

Article 4. The administering authority, in discharging the obligations of trusteeship in the trust territory, shall act in accordance with the Charter of the United Nations, and the provisions of this agreement, and shall, as specified in Article 83 (2) of the Charter, apply the objectives of the international trusteeship system, as set forth in Article 76 of the Charter, to the people of the trust territory.

Article 5. In discharging its obligations under Article 76 (a) and Article 84, of the Charter, the administering authority shall ensure that the trust territory shall play its part, in accordance with the Charter of the United Nations, in the maintenance of international peace and security. To this end the administering authority shall be entitled:

(1) to establish naval, military and air bases and to erect fortifications in the trust territory;

(2) to station and employ armed forces in the territory; and

(3) to make use of volunteer forces, facilities and assistance from the trust territory in carrying out the obligations towards the Security Council undertaken in this regard by the administering authority, as well as for the local defense and the maintenance of law and order within the trust territory.

Article 6. In discharging its obligations under Article 76 (b) of the Charter, the administering authority shall:

(1) foster the development of such political institutions as are suited

to the trust territory and shall promote the development of the inhabitants of the trust territory toward self-government, and to this end shall give to the inhabitants of the trust territory a progressively increasing share in the administrative services in the territory; shall develop their participation in local government; shall give due recognition to the customs of the inhabitants in providing a system of law for the territory; and shall take other appropriate measures toward these ends;

(2) promote the economic advancement and self-sufficiency of the inhabitants and to this end shall regulate the use of natural resources; encourage the development of fisheries, agriculture, and industries; protect the inhabitants against the loss of their lands and resources; and improve the means of transportation and communication;

(3) promote the social advancement of the inhabitants, and to this end shall protect the rights and fundamental freedoms of all elements of the population without discrimination; protect the health of the inhabitants; control the traffic in arms and ammunition, opium and other dangerous drugs, and alcohol and other spiritous beverages; and institute such other regulations as may be necessary to protect the inhabitants against social abuses; and

(4) promote the educational advancement of the inhabitants, and to this end shall take steps toward the establishment of a general system of elementary education; facilitate the vocational and cultural advancement of the population; and shall encourage qualified students to pursue higher education, including training on the professional level.

Article 7. In discharging its obligations under Article 76 (*c*), of the Charter, the administering authority, subject only to the requirements of public order and security, shall guarantee to the inhabitants of the trust territory freedom of speech, of the press, and of assembly; freedom of conscience, of worship, and of religious teaching; and freedom of migration and movement.

Article 8. 1. In discharging its obligations under Article 76 (*d*) of the Charter, as defined by Article 83 (2) of the Charter, the administering authority, subject to the requirements of security, and the obligation to promote the advancement of the inhabitants, shall accord to nationals of each Member of the United Nations and to companies and associations organized in conformity with the laws of such Member, treatment in the trust territory no less favorable than that accorded therein to nationals, companies and associations of any other United Nation, except the administering authority.

2. The administering authority shall ensure equal treatment to the Members of the United Nations and their nationals in the administration of justice.

3. Nothing in this Article shall be so construed as to accord traffic rights to aircraft flying into and out of the trust territory. Such rights shall be subject to agreement between the administering authority and the state whose nationality such aircraft possesses.

4. The administering authority may negotiate and conclude commercial and other treaties and agreements with Members of the United

Nations and other states, designed to attain for the inhabitants of the trust territory treatment by the Members of the United Nations and other states no less favorable than that granted by them to the nationals of other states. The Security Council may recommend, or invite other organs of the United Nations to consider and recommend, what rights the inhabitants of the trust territory should acquire in consideration of the rights obtained by Members of the United Nations in the trust territory.

Article 9. The administering authority shall be entitled to constitute the trust territory into a customs, fiscal, or administrative union or federation with other territories under United States jurisdiction and to establish common services between such territories and the trust territory where such measures are not inconsistent with the basic objectives of the International Trusteeship System and with the terms of this agreement.

Article 10. The administering authority, acting under the provisions of Article 3 of this agreement, may accept membership in any regional advisory commission, regional authority, or technical organization, or other voluntary association of states, may cooperate with specialized international bodies, public or private, and may engage in other forms of international cooperation.

Article 11. 1. The administering authority shall take the necessary steps to provide the status of citizenship of the trust territory for the inhabitants of the trust territory.

2. The administering authority shall afford diplomatic and consular protection to inhabitants of the trust territory when outside the territorial limits of the trust territory or of the territory of the administering authority.

Article 12. The administering authority shall enact such legislation as may be necessary to place the provisions of this agreement in effect in the trust territory.

Article 13. The provisions of Articles 87 and 88 of the Charter shall be applicable to the trust territory, provided that the administering authority may determine the extent of their applicability to any areas which may from time to time be specified by it as closed for security reasons.

Article 14. The administering authority undertakes to apply in the trust territory the provisions of any international conventions and recommendations which may be appropriate to the particular circumstances of the trust territory and which would be conducive to the achievement of the basic objectives of Article 6 of this agreement.

Article 15. The terms of the present agreement shall not be altered, amended or terminated without the consent of the administering authority.

Article 16. The present agreement shall come into force when approved by the Security Council of the United Nations and by the Government of the United States after due constitutional process.

2. REGIONAL ADVISORY COMMISSIONS

A. Caribbean Commission

[For information on the activities of the Anglo-American Caribbean Commission, see *Documents*, V, *1942–1943*, p. 469–70; *ibid.*, VI, *1943–1944*, p. 597–601.]

The Anglo-American Caribbean Commission, which had been created by the Governments of the United Kingdom and the United States on March 9, 1942, as an advisory group to help solve regional economic and social problems created by the war, was enlarged in December 1945 to include France and the Netherlands as members. The status of the group, renamed the Caribbean Commission, was formalized on October 30, 1946, when the four Governments signed in Washington an agreement restating the functions and purposes of the organization.[1]

This agreement, which was designed to strengthen cooperation among the signatory powers and their Caribbean territories "with a view toward improving the economic and social well-being of the peoples of the territory", created a commission of not more than sixteen commissioners, four to be appointed by each state, and two auxiliary bodies, the Caribbean Research Council and the West Indian Conference. The commission, which meets twice a year, is a purely advisory body with no executive function, and its decisions must be unanimous. It is empowered to cooperate with non-member governments in the area and with the United Nations and the specialized agencies.

The commission sponsored the second session of the biennial West Indian Conference at St. Thomas, Virgin Islands of the United States, from February 21 to March 13, 1946. The conference, at which representatives from the fifteen Caribbean territories of the four signatory powers were present, dealt with a wide range of subjects, including the improvement of public health, education, and nutrition, agricultural diversification, and the development of local manufacturing and handicrafts.[2] Following a conference recommendation, a Caribbean Tourist Trade Conference was convened in New York on October 1, 1946, and plans for a Caribbean Tourist Development Association drawn up.[3] Cuba, the Dominican Republic and Haiti were represented at the meeting.

A central secretariat for the organization has been established at Port-of-Spain, Trinidad, B.W.I., under the direction of the first Secretary-General, Lawrence W. Cramer, a former Governor of the Virgin Islands of the United States. American Caribbean territories which are within the commission's jurisdiction are Puerto Rico and the Virgin Islands; American commissioners during 1946 were Charles W. Taussig, Chairman of the United States Section, Rexford G. Tugwell, Governor of Puerto Rico, Ralph J. Bunche, Acting Chief of the Division of Dependent Area Affairs in the Department of State and Rafael Picó.

(1) *Letter from the President (Truman) to the President of the Second Session of the West Indian Conference (Taussig), held at St. Thomas, Virgin Islands of the United States, February 21, 1946.*[4]

As you know, I have been deeply interested in the work of the Caribbean Commission, formerly the Anglo-American Caribbean Commission.

---

[1] The agreement had been initialled on July 15, 1946, but was not formally signed until October. For text of the agreement, see Department of State Publication 2812, United States-United Nations Information Series 18, pp. 64–71.

[2] *Report of the West Indian Conference, Second Session*, Department of State Publication 2615.

[3] Department of State, *Bulletin*, XV, p. 735.

[4] *Ibid.*, XIV, p. 332.

As a consequence of that interest, I am naturally most happy that the United States of America is to be the host nation at the Second Session of the West Indian Conference. I take this occasion to ask that you, in your capacity as Chairman, convey to the Conference not only my warm greetings but my sincere best wishes for a most successful Session. I further ask that you bring the following message to the Conference:

The policy of the United States with respect to the governments and peoples of the non-self-governing territories of the Caribbean region will be guided by the following basic tenets:

1. To encourage the effective application, by all practicable means, of the fundamental principles set forth in Chapter XI of the Charter of the United Nations, entitled "Declaration Regarding Non-Self-Governing Territories", to the end that the progressive development of the peoples of the region in political, economic, educational, and social matters shall be insured. This Government takes the view that members of the United Nations which have responsibilities for the administration of non-self-governing territories in this region have undertaken a solemn obligation in this respect, and notes with particular satisfaction that in all such territories the interests of the inhabitants are to be regarded as paramount.

2. To support the work of the Caribbean Commission to the end that problems of the region may be approached as a whole, and not piecemeal. Such support will strengthen this multilateral governmental organization, which offers procedures for constructively attacking regional problems. The Caribbean Commission, formerly known as the Anglo-American Caribbean Commission, has been recently expanded to include the Governments of France and the Netherlands. The Government of the United States looks with satisfaction on this expansion. It anticipates increasing participation in the work of that Commission by the peoples of the territories of the four countries concerned.

This Government looks forward to an increasing measure of self government by the people of the Virgin Islands of the United States. With respect to Puerto Rico, it has been recommended to the Congress of the United States that it provide a means by which the people of Puerto Rico might choose their form of government and ultimate status with respect to the United States.

3. To assist, by appropriate action, in carrying out the economic objectives recommended by the First Session of the West Indian Conference held at Barbados in March 1944. Steps to effectuate these objectives received Presidential approval on June 11, 1945, and were included in a Joint Statement of the Governments of the United States and of the United Kingdom later made public.

4. To support any suitable plan which would bring the non-self-governing territories of the Caribbean region into closer cooperation with each other, with a view to developing the educational, social, and cultural institutions of the region, improving the standards of living of the people, and strengthening the foundations upon which self-governing institutions may be developed.

3. UNITED STATES DEPENDENCIES

Chapter XI of the United Nations Charter, the Declaration Regarding Non-Self-Governing Territories, bound the signatory nations to "recognize the principle that the interests of the inhabitants of these territories are paramount, and accept as a sacred trust the obligation to promote to the utmost . . . the well-being of the inhabitants . . .". In accordance with this declaration, the Governments agreed to transmit regular information concerning their territories to the Secretary-General of the United Nations.

Matters concerning this transmission of information were discussed at the first part of the General Assembly's session in February, 1946, and a resolution was passed reminding Member states that Chapter XI had entered into force, despite the fact that the Trusteeship Council had not yet been created.[1] In compliance with this resolution, the United States on August 19, 1946, submitted reports on areas which it considered non-self-governing, sending to the Secretary-General the latest annual reports of the Governors of Alaska, Hawaii, Puerto Rico, and the Panama Canal Zone, together with a special report by the Navy Department on administration of Guam, American Samoa, and other island possessions in the Pacific.[2] In an accompanying note, it was pointed out that, since no criteria for selection of the areas to be covered in the reports had yet been made, the American Government had used a purely pragmatic approach in selecting these territories. Attention was called to the fact that "the territories under the administration of this Government have already attained varying degrees of self-government and that the political advancement of all these territories is a matter of special concern to the American people."[3] The Panamanian delegate to the General Assembly later protested the inclusion of the Panama Canal Zone, on the grounds that the United States did not exercise sovereignty over it.[4]

At the second part of its first session the General Assembly took note of informations on dependent territories submitted by the United States and four other nations, and voted to create an *ad hoc* committee to examine the information presented, although several of the colonial powers stated that this contravened the Charter.[5] The Assembly also considered a Philippine proposal calling for a conference of non-self-governing peoples, to be held under United Nations auspices. After considerable opposition by the colonial powers, who were supported by the United States, the Assembly merely recommended to Member nations "having or assuming responsibilities for the administration of non-self-governing territories to convene conferences of representatives of non-self-governing peoples chosen or preferably elected in such a way that the representation of the people will be ensured to the extent that the particular conditions of the territory concerned permit, in order that the letter and spirit of Chapter XI of the Charter may be accomplished and the wishes and aspirations of the non-self-governing peoples may be expressed."[6]

---

[1] United Nations General Assembly, Document A/34, February 4, 1946; United Nations General Assembly, *Official Records of the First Part of the First Session . . . , Plenary Sessions*, p. 366–76.

[2] For summary of information submitted, see United Nations General Assembly, Document A/73, October, 1946.

[3] *The United States and Non-Self-Governing Territories*, Department of State Publication 2812, United States-United Nations Information Series 18, p. 21.

[4] United Nations General Assembly, Document A/200, November 26, 1946.

[5] United Nations General Assembly, Document A/C.4/74, December 10, 1946.

[6] United Nations General Assembly, Document A/251/Add.1/Rev.1, December 12, 1946; United Nations General Assembly, *Official Records of the Second Part of the First Session . . . , Plenary Sessions*, p. 1357.

CHAPTER IX

TRADE AND FINANCE

1. PRINCIPLES OF POSTWAR ECONOMIC POLICY

A. General Principles

(1) *Statement by the Secretary of State (Byrnes) Submitted to the Senate Committee on Banking and Currency, August 21, 1945.*[1]

[Excerpts]

Peace and prosperity are the twin goals of America's post-war effort. Our international policies and our domestic policies are inseparable. Our foreign relations inevitably affect employment in the United States. Prosperity and depression in the United States just as inevitably affect our relations with the other nations of the world. The success of our international policies will thus depend in large measure upon the character of the policies which we pursue at home.

In the field of international relations we have joined in a cooperative endeavor to construct an expanding world economy based on the liberal principles of private enterprise, non-discrimination, and reduced barriers to trade. The importance which we attach to this task derives from the firm conviction that a durable peace cannot be built on an economic foundation of exclusive blocs, discriminatory policies, prohibitive barriers, autarchy, and economic warfare.

A liberal trading system is the means by which the world's productive resources can yield the maximum of material well-being to all peoples. But such a system, involving as it does a high degree of interdependence among nations, imposes special responsibilities upon those who occupy a dominant position in world trade. Such is the position of the United States.

· · · · · ·

If our economic life is to be marked by industrial instability and mass unemployment, we shall almost certainly involve others in our distress. Depressions move easily across our boundaries. If our factories should fall idle, countries that had been producing for our market would suffer a sudden contraction of demand. If we should suddenly cease our foreign lending, countries that had been buying from us would suffer a sudden shortage of exchange. Their trade would fall off and their employment would decline.

[1] Department of State, *Bulletin*, XIII, p. 279.

The fear that is felt today, in many foreign capitals, is not that America will misuse its vast economic powers but that we may fail to use them to the full. If this fear is realized, the prestige and the influence that we have earned in every part of the world will be thrown into jeopardy and the success of our proposals for world reconstruction will be imperiled.

Nations will not long adhere to liberal trading principles if they feel their own stability is threatened by the persistence of depressions which may originate outside their borders. On the contrary, they will raise new barriers to trade in an effort to insulate themselves against a troubled world. There will be a renewal of competition in restriction; trade instead of expanding will contract. In such an atmosphere the will for international cooperation on other fronts may be lost. This is the danger that must be averted if our hopes for peace and plenty are not to fail.

The United Nations have pledged themselves, in the Charter of the United Nations Organization, "to take joint and separate action in cooperation with the Organization" to achieve the economic and social purposes of the United Nations, including "higher standards of living, full employment, and conditions of economic and social progress and development". The Senate of the United States has ratified this Charter. It has subscribed to this pledge.

. . . . . .

The United States is today a bastion of democracy and private enterprise. In many countries throughout the world our political and economic creed is in conflict with ideologies which reject both of these principles. To the extent that we are able to manage our domestic affairs successfully, we shall win converts to our creed in every land.

If we are successful in realizing the enormous productive potential of our economic system we shall have a standard of living which will be the marvel of the world. A strong, stable, and prosperous America will give courage and hope to all friends of democracy abroad. The example we set will certainly affect, and may even determine, the direction of the world's political and economic development.

(2) *Eighth Report of the House Special Committee on Postwar Economic Policy and Planning, November 12, 1945.*[1]

[Excerpt]

The Special Committee of the House of Representatives on Postwar Economic Policy and Planning, under the Chairmanship of Representative William M. Colmer (Mississippi), established a subcommittee to determine to what extent the principles outlined by the Committee in its Sixth Report [2] could be applied. Following an eight-weeks' visit to Europe, beginning August 15, 1945, the subcommittee concluded that the lack of adequate holdings of foreign reserves and the war-time destruction or dislocation of export industries were forcing international trade into channels of restrictive bilateralism accompanied by exchange controls, barters, quotas and subsidies — measures counter to the announced objectives of the United States Government to liberalize world trade and finance. The subcommittee conferred with agencies of this Government, with the Allied

[1] House Report No. 1205, 79th Cong., 1st sess., p. 13.
[2] House Report No. 541, 79th Cong., 1st sess., issued May 8, 1945; see *Documents, VII, 1944–1945*, p. 581.

Control Councils and with government officials and economic experts of the countries visited. From most of these countries, the subcommittee received requests for American loans and for allocations of surplus property.[1] Of particular concern to the Committee in making this report was the method by which these requests for American currency might be applied in the substitution of multilateral clearing for bilateral bargaining.

. . . .

Longer-Range Problems

There are four principal long-run problems:

1. *An integration of American loan policy.* — As a first instance, it is necessary to protect against the granting of large-scale loans by the Export-Import Bank or any other governmental department or agency for long-range reconstruction before the nations requesting loans have shown a willingness to make available and to utilize fully the credits, resources, and stabilizing influences of the International Monetary Fund and the International Bank for Reconstruction and Development referred to the United Nations under the Bretton Woods agreements. The committee recommends that the funds of the Export-Import Bank should not be further increased beyond the present $3,500,000,000 already authorized until the Bretton Woods agreements have gone into effect.

The committee suggests that since the advantages afforded by United States loans and other settlements are our best bargaining asset in securing political and economic concessions in the interest of world stability, there should be a total integration of economic policy to this end. And particularly it is concerned to see that the rights of property of United States firms are adequately protected. The export of our best means of spreading American ideas as well as distributing American goods in nations desiring and in need of them, namely, the books, magazines, papers, and movies of this country, should be freely promoted. Furthermore, the free access of our press to all sources of information is clearly called for if real understanding is to be developed.

2. *American policies in dealing with state trading monopolies.*— While the committee recognizes the necessity of dealing through Amtorg, the Russian state trading monopoly, it feels that direct contacts between American business firms and Russian industries should be established where possible. It does not feel that completely controlled state trading for countries under Russian occupation in eastern Europe is a necessity. The protection of American property rights in these countries and a demand for establishing freer channels of individual trade should be objectives of American policy. This reasoning applies even more strongly to our dealings with the countries of western Europe.

3. *Settlement of lend-lease.* — The committee specifically urges upon the Department of State the fulfillment of the statutory intent of the Lend-Lease Act and of the agreements concluded under it:

(a) For freeing the channels of world trade in the postwar settlements before any writing off of lend-lease;

[1] For information on surplus property allocation, see this volume, p. 158.

(b) For the return of materials and property not expended in carrying out the war;

(c) The repayment by settlements in rights to control of raw materials, bases, aviation rights, sites and buildings for embassies, and other tangible and intangible assets for some part of the lend-lease aid afforded by this country.

4. *International financial stability.* — The committee suggests that the problem of balancing American exports by imports will for several years after the war require a careful reexamination of the willingness to accept gold in unlimited amounts from such systems as Russia on a purely bilateral basis. The absence of available imports from the rest of the world should not, in the judgment of the committee, lead to the repetition of the experience of the twenties and thirties when the United States accumulated much of the world's gold supplies, acquiring overbalanced holdings of this metal. If Russia's ability to produce gold is capable of large expansion, the question is raised as to what percentage of this gold should be taken into the United States in payment for future loans.

The committee suggests a thorough examination of the possibilities of accepting other minerals, capable of being cheaply and indefinitely stored, from the surplus of world production over and above the needs of commercial imports. Protection of domestic mining interests and sterilization of stocks would be needed. This method of repayment of American loans could afford valuable assistance to the nations which have large mineral resources and would build up our own depleted reserves or stock piles of those minerals which we do not ourselves produce.

Organization for Economic Foreign Policy

Finally, the committee recommends that there should be a complete reorganization of American economic foreign policy under the capable leadership of the Department of State. It feels that adequate means for implementing and promoting this foreign policy could be achieved by the creation of an Under Secretary of State for Foreign Economic Policy. It approves the allocation of policy formulation for the disposal of surplus property to the Department of State and urges that the economic information services and much of the present work of the Foreign Economic Administration, as well as the Export-Import Bank, should be brought under the same administrative organization.

The committee calls the attention of Congress, as well as the Administration, to the need for expanding the size of the foreign service and improving the attractiveness of careers in the foreign service, particularly in its economic and information branches. It feels that the allowances and opportunities for promotion in this service should be made commensurate with the scale afforded by the best foreign services of other nations and with the tremendous stake that America will have in the adequacy of the foreign service to promote and safeguard national interests abroad.

International Economic Conference. — The committee, as its final recommendation on economic policy dealing with the increase of world trade, wishes to repeat the recommendation contained in the sixth report:

In view of the importance of reducing the barriers to international trade throughout the world, the committee recommends that an international conference be called as soon as practicable to consider reduction or elimination of trade restrictions. The conference should consider not only reduction of tariffs, but also such trade controls as import quotas, export subsidies, exchange controls and other forms of state interference with the movement of goods between countries. It is not to be expected, of course, that all of the complex problems connected with a general reduction of trade barriers can be solved in a single international convention. The aim of the conference should be simply agreement upon a general policy of reduced barriers. At the same time, a permanent economic organization should be set up to deal with the specific problems of individual countries and commodities. The principal advantage of this method of reducing trade barriers is the speed with which a general world policy can be established. By means of an international conference, the broad outlines of a plan to reduce trade barriers can be determined shortly after the war has ended. There are compelling reasons why this should be done.

The committee welcomes the efforts of the American negotiators currently reported in the press to set up an international trade organization on a permanent basis to work out standards for the protection of world trade. It feels that the initiation of international conventions and treaties for the removal of trade barriers and the protection of foreign-trade interests can be greatly advanced by a permanent organization of an international character and appropriate representation from the interests concerned in every government. Every effort of the American Government should be directed toward encouraging participation in the international trade organization.

The chairman has been authorized to introduce a joint resolution to carry out this recommendation, calling upon the Department of State to take the initiative in convoking an international conference to this end.

The conclusions which emerge from these recommendations may be stated as follows:

1. Immediate relief is necessary to prevent the deterioration of Europe into anarchy, disease, and economic stagnation. This should be granted subject to the definite safeguards outlined above to protect both the interests of the peoples of Europe themselves and the interests of the United States. It should not be continued beyond such time as production can be resumed so that nations may help themselves and pay for their imports.

2. The resumption of production in all the liberated countries and, to a considerable extent, in the occupied regions, depends upon the immediate procurement of raw materials, transportation equipment, food, and fuel for which productive short-term loans offer a better way to recovery than continued relief. The sooner these economies can be aided to recovery, the sounder will be American foreign trade and the less will be the need for relief.

3. Longer-term loans for general reconstruction and recovery of the total economies will also be needed. The committee feels that countries should show good faith in their acceptance of the Bretton Woods agreements, which afford an international source of large-scale capital for these purposes, and that loans granted to them should be subject to the conditions outlined above.

The committee wishes to stress the basic economic fact that truly productive loans are themselves a major contribution to our prosperity and to the stabilization of the world economy.

. . . . . .

(3) Annual Message of the President (Truman) to Congress on the State of the Union, January 14, 1946.[1]

[Excerpts]

. . . . . .

2. FOREIGN ECONOMIC POLICY

The foreign economic policy of the United States is designed to promote our own prosperity, and at the same time to aid in the restoration and expansion of world markets and to contribute thereby to world peace and world security. We shall continue our efforts to provide relief from the devastation of war, to alleviate the sufferings of displaced persons, to assist in reconstruction and development, and to promote the expansion of world trade.

We have already joined the International Monetary Fund and the International Bank for Reconstruction and Development. We have expanded the Export-Import Bank and provided it with additional capital. The Congress has renewed the Trade Agreements Act which provides the necessary framework within which to negotiate a reduction of trade barriers on a reciprocal basis. It has given our support to the United Nations Relief and Rehabilitation Administration.

. . . . . .

The view of this Government is that, in the longer run, our economic prosperity and the prosperity of the whole world are best served by the elimination of artificial barriers to international trade, whether in the form of unreasonable tariffs or tariff preferences or commercial quotas or embargoes or the restrictive practices of cartels.

The United States Government has issued proposals for the expansion of world trade and employment to which the Government of the United Kingdom has given its support on every important issue. These proposals are intended to form the basis for a trade and employment conference to be held in the middle of this year. If that conference is a success, I feel confident that the way will have been adequately prepared for an expanded and prosperous world trade.

[1] Department of State, *Bulletin*, XIV, p. 139.

We shall also continue negotiations looking to the full and equitable development of facilities for transportation and communications among nations.

The vast majority of the nations of the world have chosen to work together to achieve, on a cooperative basis, world security and world prosperity. The effort cannot succeed without full cooperation of the United States. To play our part, we must not only resolutely carry out the foreign policies we have adopted but also follow a domestic policy which will maintain full production and employment in the United States. A serious depression here can disrupt the whole fabric of the world economy.

. . . .

(4) *Address by the Under Secretary of State for Economic Affairs (Clayton) before the Thirty-Third National Trade Convention, New York, November 13, 1946.*[1]

[Excerpts]

. . . .

The objective of the foreign economic policy of the United States Government is to lay the foundation for peace by an expansion in world economy, that is, by an increase in the production, distribution, and consumption of goods throughout the world, to the end that people everywhere may have more to eat, more to wear, and better homes in which to live.

. . . .

Measures for implementing this policy fall into two general categories:

The first relates to financial assistance to countries faced with problems of relief, reconstruction, and development.

Since the end of the war the United States Government has made available as grants for emergency relief and rehabilitation abroad about three billions of dollars. In addition, it has made available as credits for reconstruction and development in foreign countries, for the purchase of surplus property, and for the financing of lend-lease pipe-lines, inventories, etc., a total of about 17 billions of dollars. A grand total of about 20 billions of dollars. Nearly half of this sum represents contributions of the United States Government to international organizations to which other governments have also contributed substantially. It will take some time to lend and spend this money. Without this help and the hope which it has revived in the hearts of millions of people, chaos would have followed the end of the war in some countries and world recovery would undoubtedly have been retarded for many years.

The second measure designed to promote the achievement of our objectives relates to the elimination of discriminations and the reduction of tariffs and other barriers which restrict world trade and limit the production and consumption of goods.

The United States Government is moving on a broad front in this field.

. . . .

[1] *Ibid.*, XV, p. 950.

Our objective is always an expansion in world economy through an increase in the production, distribution, and consumption of goods.

Our method — international agreement.

Formerly, nations acted unilaterally in matters affecting their international trade; in doing so, they usually hurt their neighbors, the neighbors retaliated, and, in the end, everybody was hurt and everybody was mad. Hereafter, we expect that actions affecting other countries will only be taken after consultation, through the machinery of the proposed International Trade Organization.

. . . . . .

With a substantial increase in population accompanied by a 50 percent expansion in domestic economy, we need more of foreign goods of all kinds. Much larger imports of raw materials are required to feed our greatly expanded facilities for the manufacture of producer and capital goods. Our productive facilities in the consumer goods field have shown comparatively little increase in the past decade; hence, our need to import larger quantities of such goods to satisfy the demands of a prosperous and growing population.

. . . . . .

In the past, the emphasis in our foreign trade has been on exports; within the near future it will probably be on imports. This is true because of our shift from debtor to creditor, because of the depletion in our natural resources, and because of the wants of a growing and prosperous population.

No nation in modern times can long expect to enjoy a rising standard of living without increased foreign trade.

Because of our dependence upon imports of strategic metals and minerals, what happens to American-owned reserves of such materials abroad is a matter of national concern. We ask no special privileges. American enterprises in the foreign field require only equitable treatment, and the right of the free flow of their products to market.

. . . . . .

Our objective can be finally achieved only through the constant watchfulness and support of the American people. An abandonment of the program is unthinkable because it would be a step backward with serious consequences for the peace of the world.

There are only two economic roads open to us. One leads backward to the tragic mistakes all of us made following the first World War. The other leads forward to prosperity and peace.

Which road shall we take?

The answer depends on you and me and 140 million other Americans.

B. Special Agencies to Implement Policy

On July 31, 1945, participation by the United States in the International Bank for Reconstruction and Development and in the International Monetary Fund became a reality with the passage of the Bretton Woods Agreements Act.[1] In ad-

---
[1] For text of the Act, see *Documents, VII, 1944–1945*, p. 537.

dition to providing for American membership in the Bank and the Fund, the Bretton Woods Agreements Act called for the establishment of a National Advisory Council on International Monetary and Financial Problems, designed to "coordinate the policies and operations of the representatives of the United States on the Fund and the Bank and of all agencies of the Government which make or participate in making foreign loans or which engage in foreign financial, exchange or monetary transactions."

The Foreign Economic Administration announced on September 10, 1945, the removal of most governmental controls with the exception of a limited controlling and licensing regime,[1] specified in the Foreign Economic Administration Current Export Bulletin No. 276.[2]

The policy of reconversion to private commercial channels of trade was advanced with the announcement by the Department of State on May 6, 1946, that conversations had been held with fifteen governments which, as a war-time measure, had maintained purchasing missions in the United States. These governments were informed that, in the view of the United States Government, war-time purchasing missions should curtail their activities and prepare for complete termination of their work by the end of the period of transition from war to peace.[3] These conversations were consistent with the earlier action of the United States, Great Britain and Canada in dissolving the Combined Production and Resources Board and the Combined Raw Materials Board, according to an announcement made December 31, 1945.[4] On July 9, 1946, the Department of State, with the approval of the Departments of Treasury, Justice and Commerce, ceased publication of the Proclaimed List of Certain Blocked Nationals (the "American Black List") coincidentally with similar action by the British and Canadian Governments.[5]

1. THE NATIONAL ADVISORY COUNCIL ON INTERNATIONAL MONETARY AND FINANCIAL PROBLEMS

(1) *Report to the President (Truman) on the Activities of the National Advisory Council, March 9, 1946.*[6]

[Excerpt]

. . . .

As the coordinating body for foreign financial problems, the Council, from its inception, has been engaged with the financial problems of reconstruction for peace and settlement of war accounts. These problems have determined the character of the Council's work.

The end of the war found the United States involved in foreign financial operations of unprecedented scope and complexity. The war was one in which our troops traveled and fought in all parts of the world, and in which we carried out the most extensive international economic operations in our history. These operations — of supply, of foreign procurement, and of transport — brought a multitude of problems of financial settlement between the United States and many countries of the world involving disposal of surplus property abroad, lend-lease termination, and the settlement of military currency arrangements. The Council's

[1] Department of State, *Bulletin*, XIII, p. 397.
[2] For a summary of FEA Current Export Bulletin No. 276 (September 10, 1945), see *ibid.*
[3] *Ibid.*, XIV, p. 819.   [4] *Ibid.*, XIII, p. 975.   [5] *Ibid.*, XV, p. 112.
[6] House Document No. 497, 79th Cong., 2d sess., p. 3.

work, therefore, began in a period when the Government's international financial problems related to its war programs were numerous and complicated.

With the advent of peace, the Government of the United States assumed large and new international responsibilities in relief and rehabilitation, reconstruction, military occupation, and currency stabilization. Every one of these has important financial aspects. The efforts of this country, in collaboration with the other United Nations, to build a peaceful and prosperous international order involve problems as difficult and complex as those of the war.

Just as the end of the war found the United States in a position of great military and political importance in world affairs, so too our foreign economic and foreign financial policies are helping to set the pattern of future economic and financial relations among nations. The influence of the United States in international trade and finance is especially great in contrast with the weakened position of many other countries. Most of the nations of Europe and of Asia have enormous jobs of reconstruction. They need to import far more goods than ever before and their capacity to export is temporarily low.

These problems were foreseen and the United States Government took a leading part in preparing to deal with them. UNRRA was set up to assist with the immediate problems of relief and rehabilitation. The International Monetary Fund was projected to help achieve stability of exchange rates and relaxation of obstructive exchange restrictions. The International Bank for Reconstruction and Development was planned to give financial assistance for the restoration of war-damaged economies and to assist the development of backward areas. The lending power of the Export-Import Bank was expanded primarily to help bridge the gap until the International Bank could come into effective operation.

The war-devastated countries are turning to the United States for financial assistance. The requests for credits are large. The specific day-to-day decisions which have to be made on these questions are of tremendous importance to the foreign countries and to ourselves.

In the past 6 months the Council has made necessary preparations for the speedy establishment of the International Fund and the International Bank. One of the major tasks of the members of the Council and their staffs over three of these months was the negotiation with the United Kingdom of the financial agreement and the war settlement. An equally large undertaking closely associated with the first two has been the development of a program and policies for reconstruction loans. In addition, throughout the whole period the Council has given much attention and time to the consideration of the financial aspects of the war settlements with various countries. . . .

· · · · ·

The Advisory Committee on Commercial Activities in the Foreign Service, established at the request of the Departments of State and Commerce for the purpose of examining regulations and instructions on the protection and promotion of foreign trade by the Foreign Service and composed of businessmen appointed by seven national business organizations, held its first meeting on November 8, 1945, under the direction of Amos E. Taylor, Director of the Bureau of Foreign and Domestic Commerce.[1] In its First Interim Report, transmitted to the Secretaries of State and Commerce on March 8, 1946, the Advisory Committee (1) recommended a unified and enlarged Foreign Service with a greater personnel devoted to commercial and economic work abroad, (2) endorsed Policy Declaration No. V of the National Trade Convention calling for expanding volumes of imports and exports, (3) annotated the areas of greatest need for the guidance of Foreign Service officers trained in international economics and commerce, and (4) stressed the need of an increasingly effective foreign trade reporting service for American businessmen.[2]

On June 26, 1946, President Truman appointed a twelve-man committee of industrialists and bankers directed to the parallel task of financing United States foreign trade, with reference to private capital and industry.[3] The Committee for Financing Foreign Trade was chaired by Winthrop W. Aldrich and was designed to function in cooperation with the National Advisory Council on International Monetary and Financial Problems.[4]

2. COMMITTEE FOR FINANCING FOREIGN TRADE

(1) *Statement by the Chairman of the Committee (Aldrich), July 9, 1945.*[5]

In his letter appointing the Committee the President said in part:

It is of vital importance to our country and to the stabilization of the international economy, that we proceed as rapidly as possible with another of the major objectives of our reconversion program; namely to tie in our national productive capacity with the world's reconstruction requirements.

The conduct and financing of our foreign trade should be handled by private industry with the cooperation and such assistance as is necessary from the proper Government agencies.

Government loans to other governments are necessary like many other things done in war or the aftermath of war. They cannot be the continuing basis of international trade between free countries; they should be supplemented and eventually replaced by private international financing.

The Government is doing its part. The President has appointed this Committee to encourage industry and private capital to do its part.

The Department of State explained last May to the representatives of foreign governments having purchasing missions in this country that the policy of the American Government favors the use of private commercial channels in international trade and proposed that "such trading agencies should conduct their trade in accordance with usual commercial considerations."

The Government has done and is doing, through the Export-Import Bank, its part in making the wheels of trade begin to move. The Government has further subscribed to the International Bank and the Inter-

---

[1] Department of State, *Bulletin*, XIII, p. 773.
[2] *First Interim Report*, Advisory Committee on Commercial Activities in the Foreign Service, March 8, 1946.
[3] Department of State, *Bulletin*, XV, p. 33.
[4] See this volume, p. 614.
[5] Department of State, *Bulletin*, XV, p. 111.

national Fund set up under the Bretton Woods Agreement. It has in the Office of International Trade in the Department of Commerce, which is primarily concerned with foreign trade promotion, a specialized staff to study the effects of loans on the expansion of foreign trade and our domestic economy. That office has already pointed out that while there are less goods of many kinds than our own population demands, there are already some fields in which surplus capacity is looming up.

Generally speaking, the function of the Committee, as I see it, will be to devise ways and means, in cooperation with the National Advisory Council, to accomplish the following purposes:

First: to bring into orderly common effort public and private finance, through businessmen and bankers, in the foreign field;

Second: to foster the application of the productive capacity of the United States in the most effective manner possible to the needs of domestic consumption and foreign reconstruction;

Third: to promote relations between American and foreign business enterprise for the purpose of developing and maintaining foreign trade, both export and import, on a high and expanding level.

The accomplishment of these purposes would not only help in rebuilding the economy of the world but would increase and stabilize employment in this country.

The Committee will also work with the Departments of State and Commerce in connection with the trade promotion aspects of its work. The National Advisory Council, to which the Committee will make its report and recommendations and with which it will work on the lending aspects of its assignment, includes the heads of the Treasury Department, the Department of State, the Department of Commerce, the Export-Import Bank, and the Board of Governors of the Federal Reserve System.

I have just come back from attending the meetings of the Council of the International Chamber of Commerce in Paris and have set to work immediately to get the data together to provide a basis for discussions by the Committee. We shall move forward under the President's instructions just as rapidly as the magnitude of the task permits.

I had a short letter from the President last Wednesday in which he said:

I shall look to you as Chairman of the Committee to call the members together and organize the work of the Committee.

I shall lose no time in doing just that.

C. Foreign-Lending Policy

Because the period under review was largely one of transition from war to peace, the continuation of governmental action was necessary pending the restoration of private channels of international investment. In view of the world-wide demand for American products for reconstruction purposes, the United States Government was faced with the devising of a foreign-lending policy which was (1) suited to short-term reconstruction needs; (2) adapted to long-term problems of the restoration of private multilateral trade and clearing in a peaceful, unified and expanding world economy; and (3) consistent with domestic full-employment policy. To accomplish these several objectives, lending by the United States Government was serviced by such governmental agencies as the Export-Import Bank of Washington,[1] negotiated through such inter-governmental agreements as the financial agreement with the United Kingdom [2] and coordinated through participation in the International Monetary Fund and the International Bank for Reconstruction and Development.[3]

Currency and gold credits made available through these channels were subject to provisions consistent with the announced objectives of United States commercial policy. The United States Government, using the world-wide demand for the dollar as an instrument to speed conversion to fair-trading practices within an organized frame-work of international economic cooperation, was in effect following the recommendations of the Eighth Report of the House Special Committee on Postwar Economic Policy and Planning.[4]

While it was recognized that an active lending policy in the transition period would ease reconversion problems in American industry and at the same time bolster the rehabilitation work of UNRRA, United States lending policy was also geared to long-range post-transitional objectives. This policy was therefore designed to prevent the war-time measures of restrictive exchange and commercial controls from developing into a permanent postwar system of bilateral, competitive blocs which would greatly reduce the volume of world trade.

(1) *Eighth Report of the House Special Committee on Postwar Economic Policy and Planning, November 12, 1945.*[5]

[Excerpt]

. . . .

1. *Loan policies.* — The committee recommends therefore that a primary condition to be attached to all American loans should be a schedule for the repeal of the quotas, exchanges controls, except on the export of domestically owned funds attempting to flee the country; a full mobilization of the foreign assets of the countries concerned, including their private holdings abroad, with a guaranty of nondiscriminatory treatment for all business of United States citizens. Efforts to impose laws requiring management or ownership by nationals of American branch factories or enterprises are especially to be safeguarded against.

The committee assumes that all loans other than those made by the Export-Import Bank and prior to the working of the Bretton Woods agreements will come before Congress for approval and legislation. It feels that loans cannot properly be made to states which have not shown a willingness to undertake the obligations and enjoy the benefits of the Bretton Woods arrangements except for the type of loans that are to be made by the Export-Import Bank within its present authorized funds of $3,500,000,000.

In the judgment of the committee small loans by the Export-Import Bank of a constructive nature at this time, to provide for the acquisition of raw materials, fuel, shipping, and surplus property, will clear the way for long-term recovery. The committee is particularly concerned to remove the necessity for continued relief by productive loans of this character, always subject to the conditions attaching to loans and aids stated above.

[1] See this volume, p. 635.   [2] See *ibid.*, p. 643.   [3] See *ibid.*, p. 617.
[4] See below.   [5] House Report No. 1205, 79th Cong., 1st sess., p. 44.

There is a danger, of course, that the negative aspect of this report may be stressed to the effect that only the conditions attaching to loans are emphasized. The committee wishes very strongly to make it clear that in its judgment there is a real need for large-scale loans to Britain, to France, and undoubtedly to Russia also, if these countries are prepared:

(*a*) To meet the political obligations which they have undertaken including proper settlement of lend-lease;

(*b*) To work out schedules for the removal of trade barriers and to facilitate the resumption of multilateral trade;

(*c*) To give up, insofar as is compatible with their political systems, the channeling of all trade through Government sources and the retention of quotas and exchange controls after the clearing up of wartime indebtedness and taking into account the availability of capital through the Bretton Woods agreements as well as through other loans;

(*d*) To furnish the means of judging the soundness of the loans from the point of view of the employment of national resources in armament production, in coal production, and the terms of agreements with other states; as well as the permission for American journalists, technicians, and others to have full access to information regarding production facilities as well as the official statistics of the countries concerned.

The committee wishes to emphasize that it does not see how countries which refused to admit the validity of American copyright or to permit the distribution of American books, periodicals, movies and other cultural media can afford the basis for a normal economic cooperation.

In discussing postwar lending by the United States, the committee has considered primarily governmental loans. While these will undoubtedly be the predominant type of loans in the first few years after the war, it should be emphasized that governmental loans should not be made to the exclusion of private loans. As soon as sufficient stability in international affairs is achieved, it is expected that private lending will again resume its important position in international trade.

. . . .

(2) *Report to the President (Truman) on the Activities of the National Advisory Council on International Monetary and Financial Problems, March 4, 1946.*[1]

[Excerpts]

. . . . . .

Governmental Procedure for the Consideration of Foreign Loans

The Council has given considerable attention to improving the procedure for the consideration of foreign loans by this Government. There are several agencies of the Government through which foreign loans and credits can be made under existing authority. In the recent period there have been a number of requests for foreign loans which would

---

[1] House Document No. 497, 79th Cong., 2d sess., p. 7.

have required special congressional action. In the near future the International Bank will also be making dollar loans to foreign countries. In addition to the agencies which make foreign loans or extend credits, there are certain agencies of the Government which have in the past negotiated or participated in the negotiation for foreign loans or made commitments for foreign loans. Finally there are other agencies which, although not involved in making or negotiating foreign loans, are concerned with the foreign loan policy and the purposes for which the money is spent.

Before the establishment of the Council this area of work was not coordinated and there was a certain amount of confusion and overlapping. The Council has given close attention to these problems and has installed a procedure to insure the more orderly consideration of requests and proposals for foreign loans.

Under this procedure all requests and proposals for loans come to the Council before any commitment has been made by any agency of this Government. This gives the Council an opportunity to consider the loan from the standpoint of the Government's loan policy and to draw in any parts of the Government which may be concerned with special policy aspects of the proposal. This central consideration with a number of agencies participating makes for a more thorough study of the conditions precedent to a loan. It also enables the Council to decide through what instrumentality the loan or credit is to be made and what agency or agencies should participate in the negotiations.

The procedure which is now in force is described in the following action of the Council:

1. Any agency of the United States Government which receives a request for a foreign loan or which proposes to recommend that a foreign loan be made, should, when such request is received or when the proposal is formulated, so inform the National Advisory Council on International Monetary and Financial Problems through the Secretary of the Council.
2. The Council will consider the request or proposal from the standpoints of policy and coordination. The Council will communicate its action, if any, to the agency (or agencies) which is to be responsible for conducting the loan negotiations.
3. Such agency (or agencies) will conduct its negotiations for any loan in accordance with the policies of the Council, consulting the Council as to desired changes in policy.
4. When the designated agency (or agencies) has completed negotiations for a loan or otherwise taken final action, it should notify the Council and furnish copies of the contract and other documents involved.

General Financial Policy Considerations

In its consideration of foreign loans, when they are first proposed or requested, the Council considers such questions as —

    The need for a loan, as indicated by the balance of payments and foreign exchange position of the borrower;

    Ability to repay, as indicated by the economic and financial prospects of the country involved;

Alternative sources for the loan, such as the International Bank, private investors, other foreign countries; and the

Amount of the loan, involving the allocation of the limited funds available.

For these purposes, analysis is made of the country's foreign exchange position, investment position, balance of payments, gold production, debt status, volume of foreign trade and anticipated economic, financial and monetary developments.

. . . . . .

Supply Consideration and Foreign Credits

The Council's Statement of the Foreign Loan Policy of the United States Government makes it clear that the present foreign-loan activities of this Government are based upon detailed and continuing consideration of the impact of such activities on our domestic economy.

Screening by the Export-Import Bank, allocations and export control operate to prevent foreign expenditures of loan proceeds from creating undue shortages in this country.

Further to deal with these problems, the Council has established the following procedure:

In the case of all foreign loans or credits which involve exportation of goods from the United States, it shall be the responsibility of the agency which is extending the loan or credit to furnish to the Department of Commerce, at the appropriate time, information as to the amounts and types of products which are likely to be procured together with, so far as practical, a schedule of the expected dates of purchase and dates of export. The Department of Commerce will furnish the lending agency with an analysis of the significant effects of such purchases upon United States markets of these commodities, taking account of total known and foreseeable domestic and foreign demand. When the proposed foreign purchases of specific products might seriously aggravate difficult domestic supply problems, the Department of Commerce will also make recommendations to the lending agency, considering both the relative urgency of the foreign need and the impact on domestic markets. Copies of such recommendations should be forwarded to the Secretary of the National Advisory Council for the information of the members of the Council. It shall further be the responsibility of the Department of Commerce to furnish the National Advisory Council for its guidance from time to time with analyses of the effects of foreign lending by the Government and by private investors upon domestic supply conditions.

Prerequisites for Loans

The major contribution of our foreign-loan program to the welfare of the American people is the assistance of this program in reconstruction abroad and the consequent achievement of a high level of economic activity at home and abroad. However, the question has been raised as to whether in the making of foreign loans this country is making an adequate attempt to get economic, political, and financial concessions in return for the loans. No sovereign nation will in return for a loan grant concessions which impair its sovereignty, endanger its security, or arouse the opposition of its people, and, of course, the United States has no disposition to seek such concessions.

During this period the United States Government has been carrying on negotiations with foreign countries on many separate subjects, such as commercial policy, the rights of our citizens and business abroad, sale of surplus property, and the settlement of war accounts. It is appropriate that some of these matters should be joined with loan discussions, and that the attitude of the United States Government toward making a loan should in part be conditioned upon the attitude of the borrowing countries toward other matters under discussion. It is a question of judgment in each case as to which of these separate negotiations should be joined together. The Council has served as a coordinating mechanism for this purpose. A number of the Council's actions, for example, have concerned "general settlements" similar to the negotiations with the British, in which financial assistance, lend-lease, surplus property, war claims, and commercial policy discussions went forward at the same time.

. . . . . .

2. PARTICIPATION IN INTERNATIONAL AGENCIES

A. The International Bank and Monetary Fund

[See *Documents, VI, 1943–1944*, p. 331; *VII, 1944–1945*, p. 508.]

Although the International Bank for Reconstruction and Development and the International Monetary Fund were established as two autonomous organizations by the United Nations Monetary and Financial Conference, held at Bretton Woods, New Hampshire, in July, 1944, the policy of the United States Government with regard to these two institutions has been such as to make possible their treatment here as component parts of one agency.

On July 31, 1945, the Bretton Woods Agreements Act was approved, providing for United States participation in both the Bank and the Fund. The formal signing of the Agreements took place in Washington on December 27, bringing into force the two world banking institutions designed to assure stability of exchange-rates, assist nations suffering from balance of payments difficulties, and channel capital funds into internationally guaranteed developmental projects.[1] The following representatives of the United States were announced by the Secretary of State on March 4, 1946: as United States Governor jointly of the Fund and of the Bank, Fred M. Vinson, Secretary of the Treasury; as alternate to the Governor, William L. Clayton, Assistant Secretary of State; as Executive Director of the Fund, Harry D. White, Assistant Secretary of the Treasury and principal author of the "White Plan" for a "United and Associated Nations Stabilization Fund";[2] and as Executive Director of the Bank, Emilio G. Collado, Deputy on Financial Affairs to the Assistant Secretary of State for Economic Affairs.[3]

The Boards of Governors of the Bank and the Fund met in joint inaugural session at Wilmington Island, Georgia, March 8 to 18, 1946, in order to set into motion the machinery of the Fund and the Bank.[4] The agenda for this Inaugural

[1] Department of State, *Bulletin*, XIII, p. 1058.
[2] See *Documents, VI, 1943–1944*, p. 331.
[3] Department of State Press Release 149, March 4, 1946.
[4] Department of State, *Bulletin*, XIV, p. 219.

Meeting included (1) adoption of bylaws of the Fund and the Bank, (2) selection of a permanent site for the two agencies, (3) election of the seven elective directors each of the twelve executive directors of the Fund and the Bank, (4) consideration of terms and conditions of admission of new members and (5) consideration of the United States proposal permitting admission to membership during a limited period of time of signatory countries which had not ratified the Articles of Agreement of the Bank and the Fund before December 31, 1945.[1] This last item of the agenda resulted from the failure of the Soviet Union to meet the December 31, 1945, dead-line for ratification of the Articles by "original members." As a result of this failure to ratify, the Soviet Union forfeited automatic representation among the twelve executive directors of the Fund and the Bank;[2] and India, next in line with the sixth largest Fund quota and Bank subscription, obtained automatic representation on the executive boards. On March 14, 1946, the Soviet Union was granted an extension to December 31, 1946, for ratification without prejudice to her "original member" status.[3] Secretary Vinson, as Governor of the host nation to the Inaugural Session, presided as Temporary Chairman until his election as Chairman of the Board of the Fund and Bank on March 11, 1946.[4] The first meetings of the Executive Directors of the Fund and the Bank, devoted primarily to organizational matters, were held in Washington on May 6 and May 7, 1946, respectively.[5]

Eugene Meyer of the United States was elected first President of the International Bank on June 4, 1946.[6] Camille Gutt of Belgium was named as Managing Director of the Fund two days later. Mr. Meyer, on June 20, announced a schedule of calls upon member nations of the Bank for the collection of $767 millions in all types of currency by November 25, 1946.[7] This figure represented about one half of the twenty percent set aside from the total subscriptions of the Bank for direct lending operations.

The executive nominations of John W. Snyder as United States Governor of the Bank and the Fund, of George F. Luthringer as United States alternate to the Executive Director of the Fund and of John S. Hocker as alternate to the Executive Director of the Bank were confirmed by the Senate on July 3, 1946.[8]

On September 12, 1946, Camille Gutt, Managing Director of the Fund, announced that the members of the Fund had been notified to communicate, within thirty days, the par values of their currencies expressed in gold or in United States dollars and based on the rates of exchange prevalent sixty days prior to the entry into force of the Articles of Agreement for the Fund.[9] In reply to Mr. Gutt's directive, Mr. Snyder, on September 19, stated that the "par value of the dollar is fifteen and five twenty-firsts ($15\frac{5}{21}$) grains of gold nine-tenths ($\frac{9}{10}$) fine . . . based on the rate of exchange prevailing on October 28, 1945, the sixtieth day before the entry into force of the Articles of Agreement of the International Monetary Fund, [and] is identical with the weight and fineness of the United States dollar in effect on July 1, 1944, ..."[10]

The first Annual Meeting of the Boards of Governors of the Bank and the Fund were held in Washington from September 27 to October 3, 1946.[11]

[1] *Ibid.*, p. 331.
[2] *New York Times*, January 3, 1946, p. 7.
[3] *Ibid.*, March 15, 1946.
[4] Department of State, *Bulletin*, XIV, p. 478.
[5] *Ibid.*, p. 856.
[6] *Ibid.*, p. 1044.
[7] *New York Times*, June 21, 1946, p. 7.
[8] Department of State, *Bulletin*, XV, p. 65.
[9] *Ibid.*, p. 575.
[10] *Ibid.*, p. 576.
[11] International Monetary Fund, *First Annual Meeting of the Board of Governors. Report of the Executive Directors and Summary Proceedings, September 27 to October 3, 1946.* Washington, D. C., November 1946.

TRADE AND FINANCE

(1) *Address by the Chairman of the Boards of Governors of the Bank and the Fund (Snyder) at Their First Annual Meeting, Washington, September 27 to October 3, 1946, Delivered September 27, 1946.*[1]

[Excerpts]

. . . .

We are now beyond the blueprint stage of Bretton Woods. Last March at the Savannah Conference we established the basic operating structure under which these institutions of international cooperation would function. The period since the Savannah Conference has been one of building the organizations. Basic procedures and policy have been explored by the Executive Directors of the Fund and Bank and the important task of choosing key personnel has been practically completed. The election of Mr. Camille Gutt as Managing Director of the Fund and Mr. Eugene Meyer as President of the Bank has inspired confidence in the institutions whose operations they have been chosen to guide. I wish to commend the Executive Directors for their excellent work during this organizational period.

The initial period of building the structures of the Fund and Bank is at an end. From now on they will be operating agencies in their appointed fields. If I may be permitted to express the keynote of this second meeting of the Boards of Governors, it is this: *Let us lose no time in speedily activating the Fund and Bank as effective instruments in a world sorely in need of their services.*

The Fund and Bank were designed to meet both the immediate postwar and the longer term monetary and financial needs of the world.

. . . . .

It has been the privilege of the United States to offer leadership in positive action toward international peace and economic stability, through encouraging the formation of the United Nations organization, Bretton Woods and other international groups. And in furtherance of the ideals and objectives of these endeavors, the United States has been privileged to offer considerable financial aid in an earnest effort to reestablish economic equilibrium in the war-devastated countries, as well as in those countries materially affected by the effects of the war. In making this contribution, the United States has been prompted not only by its recognition of the great needs of other nations, but also because, as a member of the world family, the intelligent self-interest of the United States recognizes that all of us must move forward together.

As a part of this broad program, since V-E Day, our Export-Import Bank has made loan commitments of over $2,000,000,000, the bulk of which has been for reconstruction purposes. When the United States Congress increased the lending power of the Export-Import Bank in 1945 from $700,000,000 to $3,500,000,000, it did so not only in recognition of the world's urgent reconstruction requirements but in the ex-

---
[1] *Ibid.*, p. 32.

pectation that the International Bank would soon become the principal international lending institution. Despite the very large loan commitments already made by the Export-Import Bank and by the United States and other governments, there remain large credit needs which should be met if we are to have a stable and prosperous world. As we all know, the International Bank must now assume the primary responsibility for underwriting reconstruction loans to countries otherwise unable to borrow on reasonable terms. I am sure that all of us in the Bank are conscious of how far-reaching our operations will be, even though necessarily tempered by the distinctions between prudent lending and improvident borrowing.

. . . .

It is equally urgent that the International Monetary Fund begin full operations at an early date. During this critical period, when nations are endeavoring to restore their currencies, they need the help that the Fund is designed to provide. We all know that no government can function internally or externally without a sound currency system. Every encouragement should be given to countries to get rid of currency restrictions, wartime or otherwise, which are designed to cover up fundamental weaknesses. We must not allow the restrictive and discriminatory trade and currency practices which were forced upon many countries prior to and during the war to become permanent fixtures, of international commerce. The Fund can provide timely assistance to countries in maintaining imports while their export industries and foreign markets are being restored.

. . . .

One of the most important jobs on which the Fund is now engaged is to determine by agreement with each member country the par value of its currency. If we are to avoid the uneconomic consequences of improper exchange rates, and avoid the competitive undermining of the exchange rate structure, we must determine by cooperative action a pattern of rates which will be consistent with the maintenance of international equilibrium and stability of international currency values. An early stabilization of exchange rates at their proper levels will give encouragement to the flow of international commerce and investment, and give confidence to people everywhere in their own currencies. Everyone must realize that this is a most complicated and difficult task. The mere attempt to do this is a great pioneering step, and, although we shall undoubtedly find obstacles and resistances, I am sure we shall be successful if we have the full cooperation and the confidence of the member nations.

A function of the Fund which I want to emphasize is that of promoting common standards of fair practice in monetary and financial relations among nations. In discharging this function the Fund must be a flexible instrument capable of adjusting to changing international economic conditions. At this time I believe that our success can be measured by our development of acceptable standards to which all countries are willing to adhere. Healthy economic competition undertaken in an atmosphere of international good will is wholesome and will contribute to the expansion of international trade. Economic warfare reduces trade and creates suspicion among nations. We cannot afford to permit economic warfare to weaken the bonds which hold the United Nations together.

Among the problems with which the Boards of Governors will want to deal at this meeting is that of considering the applications for membership which have been made since the Fund and Bank came into existence. It has always been contemplated that eventually other nations would want to join. Obviously, the Fund and Bank will gain strength if the largest possible number of peace-loving nations join with us. All but six of the 44 nations represented at the Bretton Woods Conference have joined the Fund and all but seven are members of the Bank. I sincerely hope that all peace-loving countries will see their advantage in becoming members of both institutions in the very near future. Cooperation in the economic world is no less important than cooperation in the political world. It is essential to the peace and prosperity of all nations that they operate under the same fundamental rules in their business dealings with one another. The charters of the Fund and Bank are drawn broadly enough to encompass various types of economic and trading systems. In this world of rapid change and widely differing systems of economic and political organization, it is essential that we reach an agreement on common standards of fair practice in international dealings.

. . . .

(2) *Report to the President (Truman) by the National Advisory Council on International Monetary and Financial Problems on Participation by the United States in the Bank and the Fund to October 31, 1946, Transmitted to the Congress, January 13, 1947.*[1]

[Excerpts]

. . . .

III. Payments Made by the United States to the Fund and the Bank

In accordance with the articles of agreement of the fund, each government signing the agreement paid one one-hundredth of 1 percent of its total subscription to the fund in gold or United States dollars. These payments were held in a special deposit account in the Treasury until the inaugural meeting of the Board of Governors of the fund, and on March 29, 1946, they were transferred to the fund. The fund has received a total of $737,250 from these payments by members. The United States paid $275,000 to the fund under this clause.

The balance of the subscription of the United States to the fund will be paid in accordance with article III, section 3, and article XX, section 4 (c), of the agreement, which provide for full payment on or before the date when the fund begins exchange transactions. Funds for this purpose

[1] Department of State, *Bulletin*, XVI, p. 152.

have already been provided by section 7 of the Bretton Woods Agreements Act. In accordance with section 7 (c) of the Bretton Woods Agreements Act, the United States intends to exercise its option under article III, section 5, of the fund agreement, to deliver special nonnegotiable, non-interest-bearing notes of the United States payable on demand in exchange for dollars not needed by the fund for its operations.

The articles of agreement of the bank (art. XI, sec. 2 (d)) require the payment of one one-hundredth of 1 percent of the capital subscription of each member country at the time of signature of the articles. These payments were treated in the same way as the initial payments to the fund noted above. Accordingly, the United States paid the bank $317,500 under this clause. Total payments by all member countries aggregated $767,000.

Under article II, sections 7 and 8, the balance of 2 percent of the capital subscription became payable within 60 days after the bank began operations — *i.e.*, on or before August 24, 1946. The United States accordingly paid an additional $63,182,500 to the bank on June 28, 1946. The bank, in accordance with article II, sections 5, 7, and 8, called for an additional 3 percent ($95,250,000) as of June 25, 1946, payable on or before November 25, 1946. This call was likewise paid on June 28, 1946. The total paid to the bank by the United States as of October 31, 1946, amounted, therefore, to $158,750,000.

As of September 25, 1946, the bank called an additional 5 percent of the capital subscription of all members payable by November 25, 1946, and it has also given notice that it intends to make two additional calls of 5 percent each, payable by February 25, 1947, and May 26, 1947, respectively. The United States payment on each of these calls will be $158,750,000, so that a total of $635,000,000 will be paid in on capital subscription by the United States. The remainder of the United States subscription to the capital stock of the bank will not be called unless funds are needed to make payments to investors to meet obligations of the bank.

In accordance with the Bretton Woods Agreements Act, the United States will exercise its option to deliver nonnegotiable, non-interest-bearing demand notes in exchange for dollars not needed in the banks' operations, as provided in article V, section 12, of the bank agreement.

VI. Principal Actions of the Bank and Fund

A. *Admission of members*

The United States has favored the early admission to membership in the bank and fund of all peace-loving nations. The United States Government supported the extension until December 31, 1946, of the period of time during which countries represented at Bretton Woods might accept membership in these institutions on the same terms as the original signatories. During the Savannah meeting, or shortly thereafter, five members joined both the fund and the bank, viz., Cuba, Denmark,

Nicaragua, Panama, and El Salvador. The extension still applies to Australia, Haiti, Liberia, New Zealand, the Union of Soviet Socialist Republics and Venezuela. Colombia joined the fund but not the bank and is also eligible under this extension to join the bank.

The United States has also supported the admission of new members, and at the first annual meeting of the Boards of Governors in Washington applications were accepted from Italy, Lebanon, Syria, and Turkey. Quotas in the fund for the new members were fixed at this time (Italy, 180 million dollars; Lebanon, 4.5 million dollars; Syria, 6.5 million dollars; and Turkey, 43 million dollars). Subscriptions to the capital stock of the bank are in the same amount as the fund quota for each country.

B. *Revisions of quotas and subscriptions*

The Board of Governors of the fund, with the concurrence of the United States, voted during the Washington meeting to increase the quota of France in the fund from 450 million dollars to 525 million dollars, and of Paraguay from 2 million dollars to 3.5 million dollars, conditional upon application for proportionate increases in their subscriptions to the bank. The Board of Governors of the bank approved increases in the bank subscription of France to 525 million dollars and of Paraguay to 1.4 million dollars.

C. *Functions and remuneration of the executive directors*

The United States has favored a broad delegation of powers to the Boards of Executive Directors of both the bank and the fund and has supported the principle that the offices of Executive Directors (and their alternates) should be full-time positions. It is provided in the bylaws of the bank and of the fund that —

It shall be the duty of an Executive Director and his alternate to devote all the time and attention to the business of the bank [fund] that its interests require, and, between them, to be continuously available at the principal office of the bank [fund].

The Boards of Governors of the bank and of the fund decided to fix the remuneration of Executive Directors (and their alternates) on the basis of full-time service, but where a director or alternate serves only on a part-time basis his remuneration is to be prorated according to the proportion of his time devoted to the institution.

The following resolution concerning national taxes on salaries and allowances was passed at the Savannah meeting by the Boards of Governors of the bank and the fund.

Appropriate measures for the elimination or equalization of the burden of national taxes upon salaries and allowances paid by the International Bank for Reconstruction and Development [International Monetary Fund] are indispensable to the achievement of equity among its members and equality among its personnel —

Therefore —

The Board of Governors of the International Bank for Reconstruction and Development [International Monetary Fund] recommends to the members of the bank [fund] that necessary action be taken by them to exempt from national taxation salaries and allowances paid out of the budget of the bank [fund] to the President [Managing Director], the Executive Directors and their alternates and to the staff of the bank [fund].

When the Congress is again in session, the Council will give consideration to the problem raised by this resolution insofar as the United States is concerned, in the light of the similar problem which has arisen in the case of American citizens employed by the United Nations and other international bodies of which the United States is a member.

D. Other actions of the bank and fund

The articles of agreement of the bank and of the fund provide that their principal offices are to be located in the country with the largest subscription and quota, respectively. Since these institutions are intergovernmental bodies, the United States delegation favored the location of their principal offices in Washington. This view prevailed at the Savannah Conference.

. . . . . .

B. The International Trade Organization

1. UNITED STATES PROPOSALS FOR EXPANSION OF WORLD TRADE AND EMPLOYMENT

In order to assure freer patterns of world trade in the post-war period, the United States Government, in November 1945, released a series of "Proposals for Consideration by an International Conference on Trade and Employment."[1] These Proposals, formulated by a technical staff under the chairmanship of Assistant Secretary of State for Economic Affairs William L. Clayton, were designed to rid international trade of (1) restrictions imposed either by governments, private combines or cartels; (2) fear of disorder in the markets for certain primary commodities; and (3) irregularity, or fear of irregularity, in production and employment. It was emphasized that domestic full employment and a continued high level of national income were the greatest long-term contributions which the United States might make to the maintenance of full, prosperous and stable world trade. Shortly after the publication of the United States Proposals, the British Government indicated its approval of them and agreed that they should be the basis of an international trade organization functioning under the Economic and Social Council of the United Nations.[2] The final acceptance of the United States proposal was made contingent by the British upon the granting of a loan by the United States to Great Britain.[3]

Preparatory conversations were initiated in London in the spring of 1946 in anticipation of a United Nations Conference on International Trade and Employment to convene the following fall.[4] Considerable difficulty was encountered in

---

[1] For excerpts from the Proposals, see this volume, p. 625; for complete text, see Department of State Publication 2411, Conference Series 79.

[2] *New York Times*, November 7, 1945, p. 1; for text of Joint Declaration by the United States and the United Kingdom, see this volume, p. 627.

[3] See *ibid.*, p. 643.

[4] See Department of State, *Bulletin*, XIV, p. 988.

reconciling the objectives of United States commercial policy with trade restrictions already in operation in several European countries. Key trading nations, such as Great Britain, France and Czechoslovakia, were continuing centralized governmental purchasing and selling as an adjunct to nationalization of domestic industry.[1] The practical application of the principles outlined in the United States Proposals was accordingly left to the consideration of an International Conference under the auspices of the Economic and Social Council.

(1) Text of United States Proposals for Expansion of World Trade and Employment, November 1945.[2]

[Excerpt]

A. Need for International Economic Cooperation

1. Collective measures to safeguard the peoples of the world against threats to peace and to reach just settlements of disputes among nations must be based not only on international machinery to deal directly with disputes and to prevent aggression, but also on economic cooperation among nations with the object of preventing and removing economic and social maladjustments, of achieving fairness and equity in economic relations between states, and of raising the level of economic well-being among all peoples.

2. Important contributions have already been made toward the attainment of these objectives. The Food and Agriculture Organization of the United Nations has been established. An International Monetary Fund to maintain reasonable exchange stability and facilitate adjustment in the balance of payments of member countries, and an International Bank for Reconstruction and Development to provide financial resources on a cooperative basis for those purposes are awaiting the action of governments required for their establishment.

3. In order to reach the objectives of the Atlantic Charter and Article VII of the mutual-aid agreements, it is essential that the cooperative economic measures already taken or recommended be supplemented by further measures dealing directly with trade barriers and discriminations which stand in the way of an expansion of multilateral trade and by an undertaking on the part of nations to seek full employment.

4. Cooperative action with respect to trade and employment is indispensable to the success of such other measures as those dealing with monetary and exchange stability and the flow of investment capital. Effective action in regard to employment and to trade barriers and discriminations must, therefore, be taken or the whole program of international economic cooperation will fail, and an economic environment conducive to the maintenance of peaceful international relations will not be created.

B. Proposals Concerning Employment

Since high and stable levels of employment are a necessary condition for an enlarged volume of trade, and since problems of trade and employ-

---

[1] House Report No. 1205, 79th Cong., 1st sess., p. 45.
[2] Department of State, *Bulletin*, XIII, p. 918.

ment are to be considered jointly at an international conference, the following propositions are advanced.

Governing Principles

1. It is recognized that:
   a. In all countries high and stable employment is a main condition for the attainment of satisfactory levels of living.
   b. The attainment of approximately full employment by the major industrial and trading nations, and its maintenance on a reasonably assured basis, are essential to the expansion of international trade on which the full prosperity of these and other nations depends; to the full realization of the objectives of all liberal international agreements in such fields as commercial policy, commodity problems, restrictive business practices, monetary stabilization, and investment; and, therefore, to the preservation of world peace and security.
2. Domestic programs to expand employment should be consistent with realization of the purposes of liberal international agreements and compatible with the economic well-being of other nations.
3. It is recognized that the adoption of the Bretton Woods Agreements and of measures to reduce restrictions on trade will contribute substantially to the maintenance of productive employment.
4. The United Nations have pledged, in the Charter of the United Nations Organization, to take joint and separate action in cooperation with the Organization to achieve the economic and social purposes of the United Nations, including higher standards of living, full employment, and conditions of economic and social progress and development.

Effectuation of Aims

There should be an undertaking that:
1. Each of the signatory nations will take action designed to achieve and maintain full employment within its own jurisdiction, through measures appropriate to its political and economic institutions.
2. No nation will seek to maintain employment through measures which are likely to create unemployment in other countries or which are incompatible with international undertakings designed to promote an expanding volume of international trade and investment in accordance with comparative efficiencies of production.
3. Signatory nations will make arrangements, both individually and collaboratively under the general sponsorship of the Economic and Social Council of the United Nations Organization, for the collection, analysis, and exchange of information on employment problems, trends, and policies.
4. Signatory nations will, under the general sponsorship of the Economic and Social Council, consult regularly on employment problems and hold special conferences in case of threat of widespread unemployment.

C. Proposals Concerning an International Trade Organization

Need for an International Trade Organization

1. Measures designed to effect an expansion of trade are essential because of their direct contribution to maximum levels of employment, production and consumption. Since such expansion can only be attained by collective measures, in continuous operation and adaptable to economic changes, it is necessary to establish permanent machinery for international collaboration in matters affecting international commerce, with a view to continuous consultation, the provision of expert advice, the formulation of agreed policies, procedures and plans, and to the development of agreed rules of conduct in regard to matters affecting international trade.

2. It is accordingly proposed that there be created an International Trade Organization of the United Nations, the members of which would undertake to conduct their international commercial policies and relations in accordance with agreed principles to be set forth in the articles of the Organization. These principles, in order to make possible an effective expansion of world production, employment, exchange, and consumption, should:

a. Provide an equitable basis for dealing with the problems of governmental measures affecting international trade;

b. Provide for the curbing of restrictive trade practices resulting from private international business arrangements; and

c. Govern the institution and operation of inter-governmental commodity arrangements.

. . . .

(2) *Joint Statement by the United States and the United Kingdom, December 6, 1945.*[1]

The Secretary of State of the United States has made public today a document setting forth certain "Proposals for Consideration by an International Conference on Trade and Employment". These proposals have the endorsement of the Executive branch of the Government of the United States and have been submitted to other governments as a basis for discussion preliminary to the holding of such a conference.

Equally, the Government of the United Kingdom is in full agreement on all important points in these proposals and accepts them as a basis for international discussion; and it will, in common with the United States Government, use its best endeavors to bring such discussions to a successful conclusion, in the light of the views expressed by other countries.

The two Governments have also agreed upon the procedures for the international negotiation and implementation of these proposals. To this end they have undertaken to begin preliminary negotiations at an

[1] *Ibid.,* p. 912.

early date between themselves and with other countries for the purpose of developing concrete arrangements to carry out these proposals, including definitive measures for the relaxation of trade barriers of all kinds.

These negotiations will relate to tariffs and preferences, quantitative restrictions, subsidies, state trading, cartels, and other types of trade barriers treated in the document published by the United States and referred to above. The negotiations will proceed in accordance with the principles laid down in that document.

(3) Suggested Charter for an International Trade Organization of the United Nations, Summary of Provisions, September 20, 1946.[1]

[Excerpt]

On September 20, 1946, the United States Government made public more specific proposals for an International Trade Organization.[2] The draft Charter was drafted in the light of various comments on the Proposals prepared earlier by the United States and by several other nations. It was issued solely upon the responsibility of the United States and was specifically characterized as a "basis for discussion and not as a document expressing the final and fixed views of this Government."[3] The Charter was prepared in anticipation of the meeting of the Preparatory Committee for an International Conference on Trade and Employment which was to convene in London on October 15.[4]

I. NEED FOR AN ITO CHARTER

The United Nations have taken many important steps toward the creation of prosperous economic and social conditions throughout the world.

The Bretton Woods agreements are designed to promote world monetary stability and to assist in economic reconstruction and development. Other specialized agencies of the United Nations deal with food and agriculture, with emergency relief, with civil aviation, with labor, with health, and with educational and social advancement. The United Nations at San Francisco set up an Economic and Social Council to coordinate all these institutions and generally to promote conditions of economic and social progress and development which are necessary to world peace.

There still remains the need for direct action to maintain and protect employment against threats of depression, and to attack the trade barriers and discriminations which stand in the way of an expansion of the production, exchange, and consumption of goods. Such action is essential to safeguard and strengthen the whole structure of economic and social cooperation thus far built up.

It is the purpose of the suggested Charter for an International Trade Organization of the United Nations to assure that this action will be taken.

[1] *Ibid.*, XV, p. 585; for full text see Department of State Publication 2598.
[2] Department of State, *Bulletin*, XV, p. 585.
[3] For excerpts from the text of the Suggested Charter, see below.
[4] Department of State, *Bulletin*, XV, p. 585.

II. THE CHARTER AS A WHOLE

The ITO Charter seeks to accomplish four main things: (1) to promote the maintenance of employment in member countries; (2) to bring about the general relaxation and regulation of barriers to world trade, whether such barriers are imposed by governments or private organizations; (3) to provide an orderly procedure under agreed rules for the negotiation of intergovernmental commodity arrangements; and (4) to create permanent international machinery for consultation and collaboration in trade and related matters.

The provisions of the Charter are set forth in seven chapters and 79 articles, as follows:

Chapter I — Establishes the broad purposes of the International Trade Organization (art.1)

Chapter II — Regulates membership in the Organization (art. 2)

Chapter III — Provides for the maintenance of employment (arts. 3 through 7)

Chapter IV — Provides for the reduction of governmental barriers of all kinds and for the elimination of trade discriminations (arts. 8 through 33)

Chapter V — Provides for concerted action to eliminate restrictive trade practices by cartels and combines (arts. 34 through 40)

Chapter VI — Regulates the making of intergovernmental agreements to deal with surplus commodities (arts. 41 through 49)

Chapter VII — Creates the machinery for an International Trade Organization to facilitate the operation of the Charter and to promote continuing international cooperation in trade and related matters (arts. 50 through 79)

. . . .

2. PREPARATORY COMMITTEE FOR AN INTERNATIONAL CONFERENCE ON TRADE AND EMPLOYMENT

A resolution, introduced by the United States delegation to the Economic and Social Council of the United Nations on February 1, 1946, asked that the Council, in accordance with Article 62 of the Charter of the United Nations, call an international conference on trade and employment for the consideration of United States Proposals which had been made public the preceding fall.[1] Accordingly, on February 18, the Economic and Social Council adopted a resolution which declared it "essential that the cooperative economic measures already taken be supplemented by further international measures dealing directly with trade barriers and discriminations which stand in the way of an expansion of multilateral trade and by an undertaking on the part of nations to seek full employment." The resolution established a Preparatory Committee to prepare an agenda for an International Conference on Trade and Employment to meet "in the latter part of 1946, for the purpose of promoting the expansion of production, exchange and consumption of goods." As a basis for the discussions of the Preparatory Committee, the resolution recommended the following topics:

    (*a*) International agreement relating to the achievement and maintenance of high and stable levels of employment and economic activity.

[1] United Nations Economic and Social Council, Document E/4, February 1, 1946.

(b) International agreement relating to regulations, restrictions and discriminations affecting international trade.
(c) International agreement relating to restrictive business practices.
(d) International agreement relating to inter-governmental commodity arrangements.
(e) Establishment of an international trade organization, as a specialized agency of the United Nations, having responsibilities in the fields of (b), (c) and (d) above.

The Council requested that the Preparatory Committee report to a later session of the Council recommendations regarding the date and place of the Conference and the agenda, to include a draft convention. Australia, Belgium, Luxembourg, Brazil, Canada, Chile, China, Cuba, Czechoslovakia, France, India, Lebanon, Netherlands, New Zealand, Norway, South Africa, Soviet Union, the United States and the United Kingdom were named in the resolution as members of the Preparatory Committee.[1]

The Secretary-General of the United Nations, in a communication to the Economic and Social Council on May 28, announced that, due to the "scope and complexity of the preparatory work which will be necessary before the International Conference on Trade and Employment can be held", the projected Conference would be postponed until 1947. At the same time he set the date of the meeting of the Preparatory Committee as October 15 and the place of the meeting as London.[2] The following November, specific proposals of the United States Government were released, for the consideration of the Conference.[3] The members of the United States delegation to the Preparatory Committee included: as Chairman, Clair Wilcox, Director, Office of International Trade Policy, Department of State; and, as Vice Chairman, Harry C. Hawkins, Economic Counselor, American Embassy, London.[4] The Preparatory Committee ended its meeting in London on November 26, 1946.[5] A second meeting of the Preparatory Committee was scheduled for Geneva, beginning April 8, 1947.[6]

(1) *Address by the United States Representative on the United Nations Economic and Social Council (Winant), February 8, 1946.*[7]

[Excerpts]

. . . We began in the midst of the war just ended to prepare the way for working together toward common ends in the years after victory. These aims were set forth in general terms in the Atlantic Charter and in the United Nations Declaration. Article VII of our Lend-Lease Agreements with our Allies gave further expression to them. The Food and Agriculture Organization, the Fund and the Bank have since been accepted and the Economic and Social Council established. These new organizations together with the I.L.O. provide much of the machinery required for effective cooperation in the world economic field. The major piece of machinery urgently needed, which we still lack, is an organization to deal with international trade and employment.

---

[1] United Nations Economic and Social Council, Document E/22, February 16, 1946.
[2] Department of State, *Bulletin*, XIV, p. 988.
[3] See this volume, p. 624.
[4] Department of State, *Bulletin*, XV, p. 664.
[5] Department of State Publication 2728, Commercial Policy Series 98.
[6] Department of State Press Release 937, December 30, 1946.
[7] Department of State Press Release 94, February 8, 1946.

With a view to filling this important gap the Government of the United States has had a group of experts working for several years in this field. As a result of this work and of informal discussions with experts of other governments, certain proposals for the expansion of world trade and employment were published last December. It is hoped that these proposals will be considered thoughtfully by all governments and peoples and that they will serve as a basis for discussion at an international conference. As an integral part of these proposals my government has invited a group of nations to participate in negotiations for the reduction of specific trade barriers and discriminations prior to the general conference.

Turning again to the text of the resolution, I should like to emphasize its primary purpose, namely, to bring the auspices of the United Nations a project initiated long before the establishment of the Principal Organs of the United Nations. The resolution before you represents our best efforts to accomplish this shift without loss of momentum. It proposes that this Council should sponsor the convening in the latter part of this year of an International Conference on Trade and Employment and it proposes certain major chapters on the agenda for such a conference. In our view these chapter headings are sufficiently broad to cover every important aspect of international cooperation regarding trade and employment, including the question of prices on the international market. The resolution provides also for the constitution of a preparatory committee to be charged with the task of elaborating an annotated draft agenda, including a draft convention for consideration by the conference.

This preparatory committee is directed to take into account any suggestions of this Council or of any member of the United Nations that come within the broad framework of the major chapters of the agenda. I should like to stress this point. As I have indicated the United States Government on the basis of long study has published for consideration by the peoples and governments of the world certain proposals which it feels have merit. The resolution which we have submitted however does not ask this Council to adopt these rather detailed proposals as the agenda of a conference. The resolution only sets forth the problems of trade and employment on which international agreement should be sought. It will be open to all countries to bring forward their views as to the substantive content of such agreement. Until those views have been submitted to and have been considered by the preparatory committee, we believe it would be premature for the Council to adopt agenda items of a more specific character.

. . . .

Finally, the Resolution would call upon the President of the Council to confer with members of the Council and with the Secretary General with a view to reporting to a subsequent session of the Council recommendations as to what states, if any, not members of the United Nations should be invited to the Conference.

(2) *Address by the Chairman of the United States Delegation (Wilcox), London, October 17, 1946.*[1]

[Excerpts]

. . . . . .

From the project of establishing an international trade organization, I take it, there is no dissent. But with regard to details there will be many views. It would be well, therefore, at the outset, to find the fundamental principles on which all nations can agree. Of such principles, I should like to suggest five; and, with your permission, I shall state them, dogmatically, and comment briefly upon each.

The first principle is that existing barriers to international trade should be substantially reduced, so that the volume of such trade may be large — larger, certainly, than it was between the two world wars. Readier access to foreign markets is needed if nations are to earn the foreign exchange that will enable them to pay for the imports that they require. Increased trade, with greater specialization and more active competition, should enhance the productivity of labor, cut the costs of production, enlarge the output of industry, and add to the richness and diversity of daily living. More goods should flow from less effort, and levels of consumption should be heightened all around the world. A renewed sense of well-being should contribute, in turn, to domestic stability and to international peace. Abundant trade is not an end in itself; it is a means to ends that should be held in common by all mankind.

The second principle is that international trade should be multilateral rather than bilateral. Particular transactions, of course, are always bilateral; one seller deals with one buyer. But under multilateralism the pattern of trade in general is many-sided. Sellers are not compelled to confine their sales to buyers who will deliver them equivalent values in other goods. Buyers are not required to find sellers who will accept payment in goods that the buyers have produced. Traders sell where they please, exchanging goods for money, and buy where they please, exchanging money for goods. Bilateralism, by contrast, is akin to barter. Under this system, you may sell for money, but you cannot use your money to buy where you please. Your customer insists that you must buy from him if he is to buy from you. Imports are directly tied to exports, and each country must balance its accounts, not only with the world as a whole but separately with every other country with which it deals.

. . . . . .

The third principle is that international trade should be non-discriminatory. This principle would require that every nation give equal treatment to the commerce of all friendly states. It should be evident that discrimination obstructs the flow of trade, that it distorts normal relationships and prevents the most desirable division of labor, that it tends to perpetuate itself by canalizing trade and establishing vested

[1] Department of State, *Bulletin*, XV, p. 757.

interests, and finally that it shifts the emphasis in commercial relations from economics to politics. Discrimination begets bilateralism as bilateralism begets discrimination. If we are to rid ourselves of either one of them, we must rid ourselves of both.

The fourth principle is that prosperity and stability, both in industry and agriculture, are so intimately related to international trade that stabilization policies and trade policies must be consistent, each with the other. It should be recognized that the survival of progressive trade policies will depend upon the ability of nations to achieve and maintain high and stable levels of employment and upon their willingness to protect the producers of staple commodities against the sudden impact of violent change. It should be recognized, too, that the advantages of abundant trade cannot be realized if nations seek to solve their own employment problems by exporting unemployment to their neighbors, or if they attempt, over long periods, to hold the production and prices of staple commodities at levels that cannot be sustained by world demand. Programs that are directed toward the objectives of prosperity and stability, on the one hand, and abundant trade, on the other, will not often be in conflict. But when they are they must be compromised.

The fifth and final principle is that the rules that govern international commerce should be so drafted that they will apply with equal fairness and with equal force to the external trade of all nations, regardless of whether their internal economies are organized upon the basis of individualism, collectivism, or some combination of the two. The United States, among other countries, will continue to entrust the management of her industry and the conduct of her trade to private enterprise, relying primarily for guidance upon freely determined market price. Some countries have taken over the entire operation of their economies, guiding production according to the requirements of a central plan. Others have committed substantial segments of their industry and trade to public ownership under varying patterns of control. There can be no question concerning the right of every nation to adopt and to maintain, without external interference, the form of economic organization that it prefers. But it should be agreed that this diversity of economic systems need not and cannot be permitted to split the world into exclusive trading blocs. Every nation stands to gain from the widest possible movement of goods and services. Every nation should recognize an obligation to buy and sell abroad, wherever mutual advantage is to be obtained. The rules that apply to diverse trading systems must differ in detail. But they should not differ in principle. That international trade should be abundant, that it should be multilateral, that it should be non-discriminatory, that stabilization policies and trade policies should be consistent — these are propositions on which all nations, whatever their forms of economic organization, can agree.

These are the principles that the United States has sought to embody in the *Proposals for Expansion of World Trade and Employment* that it published in December of last year, and to elaborate in the *Suggested Charter for an International Trade Organization* that it circulated to other members of this Committee during the past summer and published on

September twentieth. The latter draft, in accordance with the resolution of the Economic and Social Council, has been submitted to the Council's secretariat for transmission to this Committee. We hope that it will be accepted as a working document, that it will afford a useful basis for discussion, and that it will facilitate the process of arriving at agreement on a final draft.

. . . . . .

It will doubtless be remarked, in the course of these proceedings, that the United States has not always practiced the gospel that it now presumes to preach. This I admit. But the fact that we have sinned in the past should not be taken to justify all of us in sinning in the future, to our mutual harm. Certainly, it should not be inferred that the economic strength of the United States can be attributed to the restrictions that we have imposed on our external trade. We have within our borders an area of 3,000,000 square miles, diverse resources, and a market of 140,-000,000 customers. And the founders of our republic wisely provided that this vast market should not be split by customs barriers. As for our foreign trade, I submit that our present proposals should demonstrate that we can learn from history.

It will probably be said, too, that the provisions of the *Suggested Charter*, particularly those that deal with commercial policies and restrictive business practices, are negative rather than affirmative. It is true that the work of reducing barriers to trade and eliminating discriminatory practices is negative, in the same sense in which the work of a surgeon who removes a diseased appendix is negative. But for proposing an operation that is required to restore the body economic to full health we offer no apologies. The other chapters of the Charter, however, particularly those that deal with employment policy, commodity arrangements, and the framework of an international trade organization, are scarcely to be described as negative. And the Charter as a whole is designed to make affirmative provision for the expansion of world trade.

The draft recognizes that provision must be made to enable undeveloped countries to achieve a greater diversification of their economies. And, in this connection, I wish to make it clear that the United States affirmatively seeks the early industrialization of the less developed sections of the world. We know, from experience, that more highly industrialized nations generate greater purchasing power, afford better markets, and attain higher levels of living. We have sought to promote industrialization by exporting plant, equipment, and know-how; by opening markets to countries that are in the early stages of their industrial development; by extending loans through the Export-Import Bank; by participating in the establishment of the International Bank. We recognize that public assistance may be required, in some cases, to enable new industries to get on their feet. But we believe that such aid should be confined to enterprises that will eventually be able to stand alone and that it should be provided directly, by public contributions, rather than indirectly by restraints on trade. The interests of undeveloped countries in sound industrialization cannot be served effectively by imposing arbitrary restrictions on the flow of goods and services. We believe, finally, that the Economic and Social Council and some of the specialized agencies of the United Nations, including the proposed International Trade Organization, may make affirmative contributions to the process of industrial development, and we stand ready to consider all serious proposals that are directed toward this end.

. . . .

Acting as experts, without committing their respective governments, the Preparatory Committee reached agreement on approximately 85 percent of the provisions to be included in a Charter for an International Trade Organization. The Proposed Charter stated five main objectives: (1) the maintenance of employment in Member countries; (2) the general relaxation and regulation of barriers to world trade, whether imposed by governments or by private organizations; (3) the promotion of the economic development of Member countries; (4) the provision of an orderly procedure for the negotiation of intergovernmental commodity arrangements; and (5) the creation of permanent international machinery for consultation and collaboration in trade and related fields. The principal organs of the International Trade Organization, under the Proposed Charter, were designated as the Conference, the Interim Tariff Committee, the Executive Board, the Secretariat, and three Commissions: Commission on Commercial Policy, the Commission on Business Practices and the Commodity Commission. The Conference, in which each Member state would be represented, would have the authority to make recommendations regarding any matter relating to the purposes of the Organization and would elect the members of the Executive Board. The Interim Tariff Committee would authorize Members to withhold, if necessary, tariff reductions from other Members which failed to meet their obligations to negotiate for the substantial reduction of tariffs and the elimination of preferential practices; the Committee would be composed of those Members who had already fulfilled these obligations among themselves. The Executive Board, fifteen Members elected by the Conference for three years, would be responsible for executing the policies of the Organization and for exercising powers delegated to it by the Conference. The Commissions would be composed of experts appointed by the Executive Board and would function chiefly in an advisory capacity in relation to the Board. In addition the Commissions would perform other functions assigned them by the Conference or by the Board.[1]

3. EXPORT-IMPORT BANK OF WASHINGTON

The discontinuance of lend-lease assistance with the end of hostilities in the Pacific posed for the war-devastated countries of the world the problem of securing the dollar credits necessary for the purchase of reconstruction supplies available only in the United States markets. In the United States manufacturers whose production was geared to war-time levels were faced with the alternatives of abruptly reducing their out-put to peace-time dimensions or of finding new markets for their produce.[2] A partial solution to both these problems was the Export-Import Bank Act of 1945 which increased the lending authority of the Export-Import Bank by 3.5 billions for the fiscal year 1946.[3] So great were

[1] Department of State Press Release 937 (Re-run), December 30, 1946; for the full text of the Proposed Charter, see Department of State Publication 2728.
[2] *Export-Import Bank of Washington, First Semiannual Report to Congress, July-December 1945*, p. 7.
[3] For the text of the Export-Import Bank Act of 1945, see *Documents, VII, 1944-1945*, p. 549.

the reconstruction demands for dollar credits that authorizations by the Bank from July 1, 1945 through December 31, 1946 totaled 2.25 billions, consuming all but 5.5 millions of this additional lending authority.[1] Since total applications for loans threatened to exceed the available resources of the Bank, a priority schedule was instituted based upon the urgency of the need of the borrower and upon certain other criteria.[2]

During the second half of 1945, the Banks in October of that year ear-marked a credit line of 100 million dollars for financing exports of raw cotton to European countries, in addition to its more general reconstruction loans for that period.[3] The other area principally involved in the authorizations of the Bank was Latin America; credits totaling 106 millions were advanced to Brazil, Chile, Ecuador, Mexico and Peru.[4]

During the first six months of 1946 the utilization of Export-Import Bank credits proved a major factor in the financing of the large volume of United States exports to foreign countries. While the Bank continued to supply other types of financing more characteristic of its usual functions, as in the preceding half year, commitments were chiefly to liberated and devastated countries for reconstruction purposes.[5] Total authorizations for this period were 1,157 millions.[6] New loans were also made to Brazil, Chile, Colombia, Ecuador, Mexico and Peru among the Latin American countries.

Disbursements of the Bank during the last half of 1946 consisted almost entirely of drawings against credits which had been previously authorized. With the inauguration of the International Bank for Reconstruction and Development[7] the Export-Import Bank began the termination of its program of large emergency reconstruction loans and the reversion of its activities to the types of foreign-trade financing typical of its pre-war operations. New loans for this period were consequently small.[8]

The largest single commitment made by the Bank during the period under review was to France. A loan of 5.5 millions, negotiated at the end of 1945, was supplemented in May 1946 by an additional 6.5 millions.[9] The loans were later made a part of a comprehensive agreement on economic and financial problems reached on May 28, 1946, after discussions between representatives of the Provisional French Government and of the Government of the United States.[10] A separate line of credit of 3.75 billions, extended to the United Kingdom in December 1945, removed from the Export-Import Bank the pressure of meeting British demands for dollar exchange.[11]

For the total operations of the Export-Import Bank as of December 31, 1946, see this volume, p. 638; for operations and authorizations for the period from July 1, 1945, to December 31, 1946, see p. 640.

---

[1] *Export-Import Bank of Washington, Third Semiannual Report to Congress, July–December 1946*, p. 7.
[2] *Ibid., First Semiannual Report to Congress, July–December 1945*, p. 10.
[3] *Ibid.*, p. 19.
[4] *Ibid.*
[5] *Ibid., Second Semiannual Report to Congress, January–June 1946*, p. 17.
[6] *Ibid.*, p. 15.
[7] For information on the International Bank, see this volume, p. 617.
[8] *Export-Import Bank of Washington, Third Semiannual Report to Congress, July–December 1946*, p. 20.
[9] Department of State, *Bulletin*, XIV, p. 1127.
[10] For the text of the Declaration between France and the United States on economic and financial problems, see this volume, p. 865.
[11] For information on the Anglo-American Economic and Financial Agreement, see *ibid.*, p. 643.

TRADE AND FINANCE

(1) *General Statement of Policy, Released to the Press by the Export-Import Bank, September 11, 1945.*[1]

[Excerpts]

. . . .

Since its organization in 1934, the Export-Import Bank has been guided in its lending operations by the following basic principles:

(*a*) In accordance with the statutes governing its activities, *the Bank makes only loans and guaranties which serve to promote the export and import trade of the United States*. The Bank promotes foreign trade directly by financing exports and imports as specific transactions and by financing exports in connection with development projects and programs in foreign countries. Loans of the latter type have a further indirect effect upon United States foreign trade; for they assist in building up the economies and raising the levels of income of foreign countries, which thereby become better markets for American products and better suppliers of imports to this country. Thus, the Export-Import Bank is guided in its lending policies by the demonstrated fact that the best trading partners of the United States are countries which have reached the highest state of economic development.

(*b*) In accordance with its established practice and as explicitly provided in the Export-Import Bank Act of 1945, *the Bank makes loans generally only for specific purposes*. A corollary of this principle is that disbursements under a commitment by the Bank are made only upon receipt of evidence satisfactory to the Bank that the purposes of the loan have been carried out by the borrower. Conversely, the Bank does not make lump-sum advances for use as the borrower sees fit.

(*c*) As a matter of prudent management and as required by law, *the Bank makes only loans which offer reasonable assurance of repayment*. The restriction of loans to specific purposes is an important means to this end, as is also the spread of maturities over the productive life of a project in order to facilitate repayment. Furthermore, all loan applications are carefully analyzed by the Bank's staff from the legal, engineering, and economic points of view and must be approved by its Board of Directors.

(*d*) As a general rule, *the Bank extends credit only to finance purchases of materials and equipment produced or manufactured in the United States and the technical services of American firms and individuals as distinguished from outlays for materials and labor in the borrowing country or purchases in third countries*. The reasons for doing so are principally two: (1) The limited resources of the Bank should be used with rare exceptions solely for the purpose of directly financing and facilitating United States foreign trade; (2) foreign countries should not ordinarily assume external indebtedness to finance expenditures in local currency.

(*e*) In accordance with its own rule and the express instruction of Congress, *the Bank does not compete with private capital but rather supplements and encourages it*. The activities of the Bank are confined, therefore, to dealing with certain types of risks which private banks are not

---

[1] Department of State, *Bulletin*, XIII, p. 441.

(2) *Statement of Loans and Authorizations of the Export-Import Bank of Washington as of December 31, 1946.*[1]

Country	Authorized Amount	Cancellations and Expirations	Balance Not Yet Disbursed	Amount Disbursed		Principal Repaid on Loans	Principal Outstanding on Loans
				By Eximbank	By Commercial Banks at EIB Risk		
LATIN AMERICA							
Argentina	$93,673,000.00	$93,090,000.00	$193,000.00	$39,000.00	―	$390,000.00	―
Bolivia	17,678,004.50	48,250.58	9,775,000.00	7,854,753.92	―	2,129,753.92	$5,725,000.00
Brazil	238,212,694.14	86,663,717.23	35,997,619.84	47,375,133.20	$68,176,223.87	44,392,912.86	71,158,444.21
Chile	89,756,007.84	6,688,678.30	49,524,468.26	5,841,753.44	27,701,107.84	15,539,320.83	18,003,540.45
Colombia	50,243,456.00	864,003.88	16,037,739.30	9,818,099.36	23,523,613.46	14,447,483.80	18,894,229.02
Costa Rica	8,723,456.00	1,448,392.71	15,000.00	7,035,878.62	223,728.67	417,908.84	6,841,698.45
Cuba	90,366,535.31	26,888,061.95	7,310,000.00	30,130,973.36	26,037,500.00	43,616,473.36	12,552,000.00
Dominican Republic	3,300,000.00	16,067.58	―	3,000,000.00	283,932.42	1,351,629.09	1,932,303.33
Ecuador	17,565,000.00	75,000.00	10,425,829.90	7,064,170.10	―	798,056.59	6,266,113.51
Haiti	13,350,000.00	2,670,000.00	―	10,680,000.00	―	3,010,000.00	7,670,000.00
Honduras	2,700,000.00	1,700,000.00	―	―	1,000,000.00	299,250.00	700,750.00
Mexico	104,033,965.90	5,993,308.80	42,308,732.49	35,049,291.20	20,682,633.41	10,391,076.25	45,340,848.36
Nicaragua	5,235,000.00	585,000.00	―	4,000,000.00	650,000.00	2,168,000.00	2,482,000.00
Panama	4,500,000.00	2,012,296.12	―	2,487,703.88	―	2,487,703.88	―
Paraguay	7,800,000.00	1,600,000.00	―	6,000,000.00	200,000.00	1,110,450.00	5,089,550.00
Peru	37,450,000.00	37,000,000.00	73,494.26	376,505.74	―	9,412.64	367,093.10
Salvador	1,726,000.00	250,000.00	―	1,476,000.00	―	164,463.69	1,311,536.31
Uruguay	43,585,000.00	29,211,125.00	3,659,148.84	78,875.00	10,635,851.16	118,053.19	10,596,672.97
Venezuela	41,951,000.00	36,806,921.65	―	2,445,900.00	2,698,178.35	3,448,911.50	1,695,166.85
Miscellaneous	124,378,495.91	74,766,230.75	25,000,000.00	20,044,815.02	4,567,450.14	24,190,161.43	422,103.73
TOTAL LATIN AMERICA	996,227,159.60	408,377,054.55	200,320,032.89	201,149,852.84	186,380,219.32	170,481,021.87	217,049,050.29
EUROPE							
Belgium	100,000,000.00	―	―	100,000,000.00	―	1,833,488.00	98,166,512.00
Czechoslovakia	23,741,917.60	947,473.97	7,927,844.10	―	14,866,599.53	794,443.63	14,072,155.90
Denmark	30,000,000.00	10,000,000.00	5,000,000.00	―	15,000,000.00	―	15,000,000.00
Finland	75,000,000.00	7,596,167.81	4,267,094.31	58,382,137.19	4,754,600.69	2,341,424.61	60,795,313.27
France	1,200,000,000.00	―	574,000,000.00	626,000,000.00	―	4,773,500.00	621,226,500.00
Germany	3,011,309.75	3,006,750.75	―	―	4,559.00	4,559.00	―
Greece	25,000,000.00	―	21,600,000.00	3,400,000.00	―	―	3,400,000.00
Hungary	2,375,000.00	2,375,000.00	―	―	―	―	―
Iceland	1,000,000.00	410,000.00	―	―	590,000.00	590,000.00	―
Italy	41,917,385.58	3,541,120.90	10,448,400.67	―	27,927,864.01	14,342,165.30	13,585,698.71
Latvia	1,903,000.00	1,892,217.97	―	―	10,782.03	10,782.03	―

TRADE AND FINANCE

Netherlands	$280,250,000.00		$165,000,000.00		$113,850,071.00
Norway	60,750,000.00	$10,523,388.00	50,000,000.00		
Poland	52,906,742.52	9,359,330.94	33,591,691.00	$226,612.00	$1,399,929.00
Portugal	5,500,000.00	4,229,134.35		36,177.73	226,612.00
Rumania	50,000.00	50,000.00			246,471.40
Spain	15,072,871.78	1,391,797.89	9,919,542.85		1,270,865.65
Sweden	15,000,000.00	10,889,000.00	1,270,865.65	13,568,740.83	9,709,249.18
Yugoslavia	517,667.00	517,667.00	112,333.06	4,111,000.00	13,681,073.89
Miscellaneous	50,000,000.00		50,000,000.00		4,111,000.00
TOTAL EUROPE	1,983,995,894.23	66,729,049.58	921,835,030.08	81,096,935.82	949,805,500.06
ASIA					
China	221,737,079.99	4,526,800.00	54,622,705.49	93,224,678.16	69,362,896.34
India	16,000,000.00	16,000,000.00	133,025,283.05	29,562,283.45	
Iran	1,130,000.00	667,570.61	222,398.75	240,030.64	
Iraq	100,000.00	100,000.00		462,429.39	
Netherlands Indies	100,000,000.00		100,000,000.00		
Philippine Islands	25,600,000.00	25,600,000.00	20,000,000.00		
Saudi Arabia	30,000,000.00	5,000,000.00	28,060,000.00	5,000,000.00	5,000,000.00
Turkey	38,327,860.00	10,267,860.00			
TOTAL ASIA	432,894,939.99	62,162,230.61	202,682,705.49	29,802,322.09	74,362,896.34
OTHER COUNTRIES					
Australia	1,400,000.00	1,400,000.00			
Canada	64,965,000.00	21,850,000.00	37,415,000.00	37,415,000.00	
Ethiopia	3,500,000.00		5,700,000.00	500,000.00	500,000.00
Jamaica	25,000.00	25,000.00	3,000,000.00		
Portuguese West Africa	300,000.00	235,000.00	65,000.00		65,000.00
Puerto Rico	450,000.00		450,000.00	165,000.00	285,000.00
Virgin Islands	250,000.00	250,000.00			
TOTAL OTHER COUNTRIES	70,890,000.00	23,760,000.00	8,700,000.00	38,080,000.00	350,000.00
VARIOUS COUNTRIES	8,672,684.75		5,907,398.58	2,765,286.17	92,602.42
Total authorizations	3,519,530,582.66				
Less: Advances by participants	26,849,904.09				
GRAND TOTAL	3,492,680,678.57	561,028,334.74	1,339,445,167.04	1,291,662,413.39	2,672,683.75
				300,544,763.40	350,547,127.68	1,241,660,049.11

[1] Compiled from *Export-Import Bank of Washington, Third Semiannual Report to Congress, July–December 1946*, Appendix A. All figures include "past expenses", showing the total of authorizations which were cancelled or expired without being utilized and the total of previous loans which have been repaid in full.

in a position to assume without government assistance and with other risks which they are not prepared to assume at all.

The principle of noncompetition with private lending institutions is further carried out by the readiness of the Export-Import Bank to sell paper which it has acquired and by arrangements under which the Export-Import Bank undertakes in advance to purchase from commercial banks notes arising out of specified transactions financed in the first instance by the commercial banks.

. . . .

The Export-Import Bank will not compete in any sense with the proposed International Bank for Reconstruction and Development. This will obviously be true during the period before the International Bank comes into being. It is also true with respect to short-term and medium-term credits to United States exporters and importers, because this is a field in which the International Bank will not operate. With respect to long-term loans to foreign governments, the activities of the Export-Import Bank and the policies of the United States representatives on the International Bank will be coordinated by the National Advisory Council on International Monetary and Financial Problems, as provided in the Bretton Woods Agreements Act. The making of long-term loans to private foreign companies by the Export-Import Bank and the International Bank will be coordinated in the same way.

. . . .

(3) *Statement of Credits Authorized by the Export-Import Bank from July 1, 1945 to December 31, 1946.*[1]

Country and Obligor	Amount (in Millions of Dollars)	Purpose
LATIN AMERICA		
Argentina: Agencia de Transportes Moore-McCormack, S. A.	0.19	Export of harbor barges.
Brazil:		
Lloyd Brasileiro	38.0	Export of cargo vessels.
National Department of Railways	1.93	Export of Diesel locomotives.
Panair do Brasil	3.0	Export of air transportation equipment.
Moore-McCormack (Navegação), S. A.	.11	Export of harbor barges.
Paulista Railways Co.	3.02	Export of railway equipment.
Chile:		
Chilean State Railways	1.2	Export of locomotives.
Do	2.0	Export of electrical equipment.
Do	.8	Do.
Do	5.0	Export of railway equipment.
Fomento Corp.	28.0	Export of steel-mill equipment.
Do	5.0	Export of electrical and other equipment.
Do	5.35	Export of machinery and equipment.
Colombia:		
Ferrocarril de Antioquia	.2	Export of locomotives.
Do	.32	Do.
Republic of Colombia	3.0	Export of railway equipment.

[1] *Ibid.*, Appendix B.

Country and Obligor	Amount (in Millions of Dollars)	Purpose
LATIN AMERICA — Continued		
Ecuador:		
Republic of Ecuador	1.0	Export of engineering services.
Do	.78	Highway construction, export of materials, equipment and services.
Mexico:		
United States of Mexico [1]	10.0	Highway construction, export of equipment and services.
Nacional Financiera, S. A.[1]	20.0	Export of electrical equipment.
Do	4.0	Export of railway equipment.
Fred Leighton, Inc.	.34	Import of Mexican handicraft.
Aeronautical Radio de Mexico	3.0	Purchase of ground equipment for aviation.
Peru:		
Cia. Peruana del Santa [1]	.35	Export of electrical equipment.
Do	.10	Do.
Various Latin-American countries: TACA Airways, S. A., and TACA Airways Agency, Inc.	2.0	Purchase of air-transportation equipment.
Total Latin America	138.69	
EUROPE		
Belgium:		
Kingdom of Belgium	55.0	Export of goods and services.
Do	45.0	Do.
Czechoslovakia:		
Prague Credit Bank [2]	(20.0)	Export of raw cotton.
Do	2.0	Export of tobacco.
Denmark: Kingdom of Denmark	20.0	Export of goods and services.
Finland:		
Republic of Finland	35.0	Do.
Finlands Bank [2]	(5.0)	Export of raw cotton.
France:		
Republic of France	550.0	Export of goods and services.
Do	650.0	Export of industrial equipment and raw materials.
Greece: Kingdom of Greece	25.0	Export of goods and services.
Italy: Italian commercial banks [2]	(25.0)	Export of raw cotton.
Netherlands:		
Kingdom of the Netherlands	50.0	Export of goods and services.
Do	50.0	Do.
Do	200.0	Do.
Netherlands commercial banks [2]	(10.0)	Export of raw cotton.
Norway: Kingdom of Norway	50.0	Export of goods and services.
Poland: Republic of Poland	40.0	Export of locomotives and coal cars.
Various European countries: Various European governments	100.0	Export of raw cotton.
Total Europe	1,872.0	
ASIA		
China:		
Bank of China	33.0	Do.
Republic of China	4.24	Purchase of cargo vessels.
Do	2.6	Do.
Do	8.8	Export of generating equipment and engineering services.
Do	16.65	Export of railway repair materials.
Do	1.5	Export of equipment, materials, and supplies for coal mining.
Netherlands Indies: Bank Voor Nederlandsch Indie, N. V.	100.0	Export of goods and services.
Saudi Arabia:		
Kingdom of Saudi Arabia [3]	5.0	Purchase of goods and services.
Do	25.0	Do.
Turkey:		
Turkish State Airways	3.06	Export of airport equipment.
Various American exporters	25.0	Export of machinery and equipment.
Total Asia	224.85	

See footnotes at end of table.

Country and Obligor	Amount (in Millions of Dollars)	Purpose
VARIOUS COUNTRIES		
Canada: Canadian Viscose, Ltd.	5.7	Export of textile machinery.
Ethiopia: The Ethiopian Empire	3.0	Export of capital goods and services.
Governments of various countries	5.0	Purchase of communications equipment.
Special exporter-importer credits	1.47	Various.
	15.17	
Grand total	2,250.71	

[1] Credits authorized before June 30, 1945, but not entered on the books of the bank as commitments until after that date.

[2] Allocations from the general cotton export credit of $100 million available to European countries established in October 1945 and included in the total credits authorized during the 18 months ended Dec. 31, 1946. Hence, in order to avoid double counting, none of these allocations is added into the totals shown in the table.

[3] The smaller credit was superseded by the larger credit.

4. RECIPROCAL TRADE AGREEMENTS

[See *Documents, I, 1938–1939*, p. 334; *II, 1939–1940*, p. 448; *III, 1940–1941*, p. 459; *IV, 1941–1942*, p. 603; *V, 1942–1943*, p. 616; *VI, 1943–1944*, p. 329; and *VII, 1944–1945*, p. 480.]

The Trade Agreements Act of 1934 (An Act to Amend the Tariff Act of 1930, approved June 14, 1934) was extended in 1937, 1940, 1943 and 1945.[1] With the last renewal of the Act, the authority of the President was increased to permit the reduction of particular tariff rates up to 50 percent of their level as of January 1, 1945. The bargaining power of the United States regarding barriers maintained against United States trade by other countries was, therefore, correspondingly increased; and with the end of the war an opportunity larger than ever before was presented for the effective operation of the trade-agreements program.[2] The Government made clear, however, that, as in the past, tariff reductions under the Act of 1945 would be made only after full presentation of views and careful consideration of the interest of United States producers, and always in return for corresponding concessions from other countries.[3]

Taking the lead in a move toward the reduction of tariff barriers on a worldwide scale, the United States Government in November 1945 released for consideration by the governments of other countries its *Proposals for the Expansion of World Trade and Employment*.[4] Pending action on these *Proposals* the Department of State on December 13 announced that fifteen nations had been invited to participate in negotiations for the reduction of trade barriers to be undertaken in the spring of 1946. These negotiations were to consider two objectives: (1) the preparation of projects for the consideration of a general international conference on trade and employment to convene somewhat later under the auspices of the United Nations[5] and (2) the negotiation among the participating countries of agreements aimed at the reduction of governmental barriers to trade.[6] With the adoption by the Economic and Social Council of the United Nations of a resolution calling an International Conference on Trade and Employment and con-

[1] For the text of the Act to Extend the Authority of the President under Section 350 of the Tariff Act of 1930, see *Documents, VII, 1944–1945*, p. 506.

[2] Department of State, *Bulletin*, XIV, p. 647.

[3] *Ibid.*

[4] For excerpts from the text of the United States *Proposals*, see this volume, p. 624.

[5] For information on the International Conference on Trade and Employment, see *ibid.*, p. 629.

[6] Department of State, *Bulletin*, XIII, p. 970.

stituting a Preparatory Committee to prepare its agenda, the Department of State delayed the convening of its proposed conference until after the meeting of the Preparatory Committee. Detailed discussions of the *Proposals* were, however, carried on with a number of countries, including the United Kingdom and France.[1]

Following the meeting of the Preparatory Committee in London, the Department of State gave notice of its intention to conduct trade agreements negotiations with the following countries: Australia, Belgium, Brazil, Canada, Chile, China, Cuba, Czechoslovakia, France, India, Lebanon (including negotiations on behalf of the Syro-Lebanese Customs Union), Luxembourg, the Netherlands, New Zealand, Norway, the Union of South Africa, the Soviet Union and the United Kingdom.[2]

5. ANGLO-AMERICAN FINANCIAL AND TRADE AGREEMENT

On September 14, 1945, financial and trade discussions were begun in Washington between representatives of the United States and the United Kingdom. The delegation of the United States, led by the Secretary of State Byrnes, included: William L. Clayton, Assistant Secretary of State for Economic Affairs as alternate chairman of the delegation; Fred M. Vinson, Secretary of the Treasury; Henry A. Wallace, Secretary of Commerce; Leo T. Crowley, Administrator, Foreign Economic Administration; Marriner S. Eccles, Chairman of the Board of Governors, Federal Reserve System; W. Stuart Symington, Chairman, Surplus Property Board; and Thomas B. McCabe, Army-Navy Liquidation Commissioner. The delegation of the United Kingdom, under the chairmanship of the Earl of Halifax, Ambassador to the United States, included: Lord Keynes, Adviser to the Chancellor of the Exchequer; R. H. Brand, Chief British Trade Representative in Washington; Sir Henry Self, Deputy Chairman, British Supply Council; and E. L. Hall-Patch, British Foreign Office. The agenda of the conference called for the discussion of (1) general financial problems, (2) termination and settlement of lend-lease, (3) general commercial policy and (4) disposal of surplus property abroad.[3]

At the beginning of the discussions, the key-stone of American policy was immediately made clear: if the United Kingdom was to receive the long-term, low-interest credit suggested by President Truman in order to assist British economy over an anticipated three- to six-year transition period,[4] British empire preference trade controls and economic blocs such as the sterling-area would have to be abolished completely or sharply modified. At the same time the United States expressed the desire that the 16 billion dollar debt owed by the United Kingdom to its empire and economic satellite areas be refunded and scaled down to permit repayment by the British of whatever credit was extended by the United States.[5] The British, in turn, made the following points: (1) a loan to the United Kingdom at the normal interest rate of $2\frac{3}{8}$ percent would, with funding and service charges, require the diversion of virtually all of her exports to the United States for servicing the loan;[6] (2) the British during the war not only sustained great physical losses at home but, by June 1944, had sold 4.26 billions of their investments abroad, lost 30 percent of their merchant fleet, reduced their exports 31 percent by volume and 55 percent by value as compared with 1938, and increased their overseas indebtedness by 12 billions to the end of 1944 — making the assumption of further "normal" indebtedness almost impossible;[7] (3) most of the sterling-area countries had advanced almost the whole of their

---

[1] From information furnished by the Department of State, August 15, 1946.
[2] *Ibid.*, XV, p. 909.
[3] *Ibid.*, XIII, p. 395.
[4] *Ibid.*, p. 332.
[5] *New York Times*, September 3, 1945, p. 1.
[6] *Ibid.*, September 6, 1945, p. 1.
[7] *Ibid.*, September 10, 1945, p. 11.

external resources to the British Government for war purposes with the result that they could not continue to trade freely with the rest of the world until the British position became strong enough that some part of these resources might be made available as purchasing power;[1] and (4) liberal commercial policies, as demonstrated in the extension of special assistance to Britain, would expand trade and so contribute to the earnings and prosperity of the United States as well as to that of the British Empire and of other countries. However, the granting of a loan to the British at an unusually low rate of interest posed problems for the United States inasmuch as credits amounting to some 6 billions were being sought for the Soviet Union, China, France, Poland, Belgium, Greece and several others of the United Nations at the usual interest rate of $2\frac{3}{8}$ percent, making it difficult for the United States to ask one rate of interest of one country and a different rate of another.[2]

As the conversations progressed, conformity on world trade policies emerged. With regard to export subsidies, it was agreed that tariffs, quotas, exchange controls and other instruments of economic warfare must be outlawed in accordance with Article VII of the master lend-lease agreement with Britain[3] and as required by the Bretton Woods Agreements.[4] With regard to the Bretton Woods agencies, the British warned that without dollar credits the United Kingdom would not be able to participate in the International Bank or the International Monetary Fund. The British loan therefore became the essential factor in the restoration of non-discriminatory, multilateral trade and finance and in the support by the British Government of the United States proposals for an international trade organization.[5]

A joint statement issued by President Truman and Prime Minister Attlee on December 6, 1945, marked the conclusion of the negotiations.[6] The draft Agreement resulting from these negotiations provided the United Kingdom with a line of credit of 3.75 billions, interest-free until December 31, 1951, when the interest and amortization schedules would become effective. In return, the United Kingdom agreed to "assume the obligations of multilateral trade" outlined in the Agreement; these included the making of sterling and dollar receipts freely available for current transactions in any currency area within one year of the effective date of the Agreement; the introduction of non-discriminatory exchange and import regulations; and the funding and scaling down of accumulated sterling balances. The sum of 20 billions sent to Britain as lend-lease and reciprocal aid was reduced to 650 millions dischargeable on the same basis as the loan itself; 532 millions of this figure covered items of surplus property and United States installations located in the United Kingdom.[7] In the accompanying joint statement the United Kingdom expressed full agreement with the United States *Proposals for Consideration by an International Conference on Trade and Employment*, accepting them as a basis for future international discussions.

The draft Agreement was approved by the House of Commons, December 13, 1945, by a vote of 345 to 88[8] and by the House of Lords by a vote of 90 to 8 five days later.[9] The Agreement was endorsed in the United States by the Advisory Board of the Office of War Mobilization and Reconversion in a resolution addressed to President Truman and signed by representatives of government, agri-

---

[1] *Ibid.*, September 13, 1945, p. 12.
[2] *Ibid.*, September 10, 1945, p. 1.
[3] For the text of the master lend-lease agreement with Britain, see *Documents, IV, 1941–1942*, p. 235.
[4] *New York Times*, October 12, 1945, p. 25; for the text of the Bretton Woods Agreements, see *Documents, VI, 1943–1944*, p. 331–398.
[5] *New York Times*, November 28, 1945, p. 6.
[6] See this volume, p. 649.
[7] For the text of the Anglo-American Financial and Trade Agreement, see *ibid.*, p. 645.
[8] *New York Times*, December 14, 1945, p. 1.
[9] *Ibid.*, December 19, 1945, p. 1.

TRADE AND FINANCE 645

culture, industry and labor.[1] Formal implementation of the Agreement by the Congress followed almost six months of exhaustive debate. Senate Joint Resolution 138, "To implement further the purposes of the Bretton Woods Agreements Act by authorizing the Secretary of the Treasury to carry out an agreement with the United Kingdom, and for other purposes", was introduced in the Senate on January 31, 1946,[2] following the transmittal of the Agreement by the President to Congress on the preceding day.[3] Despite determined opposition in the Congress[4] and after extensive public hearings, the Resolution was approved by the Senate by a margin of 12 votes on May 10, 1946,[5] and by the House, by a vote of 219 to 155, on July 13.[6] Presidential signature followed on July 15.[7]

The largest credit ever extended by one nation to another did not create a precedent. The report of the National Advisory Council cited the loan to Britain as a "special case", fashioned to the leading role played by the United Kingdom in world trade.

(1) *Text of the Anglo-American Financial and Trade Agreement, Signed in Washington, December 6, 1945.*[8]

It is hereby agreed between the Government of the United States of America and the Government of the United Kingdom of Great Britain and Northern Ireland as follows:

1. *Effective date of the Agreement.* The effective date of this Agreement shall be the date on which the Government of the United States notifies the Government of the United Kingdom that the Congress of the United States has made available the funds necessary to extend to the Government of the United Kingdom the line of credit in accordance with the provisions of this Agreement.

2. *Line of credit.* The Government of the United States will extend to the Government of the United Kingdom a line of credit of $3,750,000,000 which may be drawn upon at any time between the effective date of this Agreement and December 31, 1951, inclusive.

3. *Purpose of the line of credit.* The purpose of the line of credit is to facilitate purchases by the United Kingdom of goods and services in the United States, to assist the United Kingdom to meet transitional postwar deficits in its current balance of payments, to help the United Kingdom to maintain adequate reserves of gold and dollars, and to assist the Government of the United Kingdom to assume the obligations of multilateral trade, as defined in this and other agreements.

4. *Amortization and interest.*

(i) The amount of the line of credit drawn by December 31, 1951, shall be repaid in 50 annual installments beginning on December 31,

[1] Department of State, *Bulletin*, XIV, p. 436.
[2] *New York Times*, February 1, 1946, p. 5.
[3] For the text of the President's message to Congress, see this volume, p. 651.
[4] For a comprehensive discussion of the objections to the loan, see Senate Report No. 1144, 79th Cong., 2d sess., p. 15–18 and House Report No. 2289, 79th Cong., 2d sess., p. 26–31.
[5] *New York Times*, May 11, 1946, p. 1.
[6] *Ibid.*, July 14, 1946, p. 1.
[7] *Ibid.*, July 16, 1946, p. 1.
[8] Department of State, *Bulletin*, XIII, p. 907; also printed as Department of State Publication 2439, Commercial Policy Series 80.

1951, with interest at the rate of 2 percent per annum. Interest for the year 1951 shall be computed on the amount outstanding on December 31, 1951, and for each year thereafter, interest shall be computed on the amount outstanding on January 1 of each such year.

Forty-nine annual installments of principal repayments and interest shall be equal, calculated at the rate of $31,823,000 for each $1,000,000,000 of the line of credit drawn by December 31, 1951, and the fiftieth annual installment shall be at the rate of $31,840,736.65 for each such $1,000,000,000. Each installment shall consist of the full amount of the interest due and the remainder of the installment shall be the principal to be repaid in that year. Payments required by this section are subject to the provisions of section 5.

(*ii*) The Government of the United Kingdom may accelerate repayment of the amount drawn under this line of credit.

5. *Waiver of interest payments*. In any year in which the Government of the United Kingdom requests the Government of the United States to waive the amount of the interest due in the installment of that year, the Government of the United States will grant the waiver if:

(*a*) the Government of the United Kingdom finds that a waiver is necessary in view of the present and prospective conditions of international exchange and the level of its gold and foreign exchange reserves *and*

(*b*) The International Monetary Fund certifies that the income of the United Kingdom from home-produced exports plus its net income from invisible current transactions in its balance of payments was on the average over the five preceding calendar years less than the average annual amount of United Kingdom imports during 1936–8, fixed at £866 million, as such figure may be adjusted for changes in the price level of these imports. Any amount in excess of £43,750,000 released or paid in any year on account of sterling balances accumulated to the credit of overseas governments, monetary authorities and banks before the effective date of this Agreement shall be regarded as a capital transaction and therefore shall not be included in the above calculation of the net income from invisible current transactions for that year. If waiver is requested for an interest payment prior to that due in 1955, the average income shall be computed for the calendar years from 1950 through the year preceding that in which the request is made.

6. *Relation of this line of credit to other obligations*.

(*i*) It is understood that any amounts required to discharge obligations of the United Kingdom to third countries outstanding on the effective date of this Agreement will be found from resources other than this line of credit.

(*ii*) The Government of the United Kingdom will not arrange any long-term loans from governments within the British Commonwealth after December 6, 1945, and before the end of 1951 on terms more favorable to the lender than the terms of this line of credit.

(*iii*) Waiver of interest will not be requested or allowed under section 5 in any year unless the aggregate of the releases or payments in that year of sterling balances accumulated to the credit of overseas governments, monetary authorities and banks (except in the case of colonial dependencies) before the effective date of this Agreement is reduced proportionately, and unless interest payments due in that year on loans referred to in (*ii*) above are waived. The proportionate reduction of the releases or payments of sterling balances shall be calculated in relation to the aggregate released and paid in the most recent year in which waiver of interest was not requested.

(*iv*) The application of the principles set forth in this section shall be the subject of full consultation between the two governments as occasion may arise.

7. *Sterling area exchange arrangements.* The Government of the United Kingdom will complete arrangements as early as practicable and in any case not later than one year after the effective date of this Agreement, unless in exceptional cases a later date is agreed upon after consultation, under which immediately after the completion of such arrangements the sterling receipts from current transactions of all sterling area countries (apart from any receipts arising out of military expenditure by the Government of the United Kingdom prior to December 31, 1948, to the extent to which they are treated by agreement with the countries concerned on the same basis as the balances accumulated during the war) will be freely available for current transactions in any currency area without discrimination; with the result that any discrimination arising from the so-called sterling area dollar pool will be entirely removed and that each member of the sterling area will have its current sterling and dollar receipts at its free disposition for current transactions anywhere.

8. *Other exchange arrangements.*

(*i*) The Government of the United Kingdom agrees that after the effective date of this Agreement it will not apply exchange controls in such a manner as to restrict (*a*) payments or transfers in respect of products of the United States permitted to be imported into the United Kingdom or other current transactions between the two countries or (*b*) the use of sterling balances to the credit of residents of the United States arising out of current transactions. Nothing in this paragraph (*i*) shall affect the provisions of Article VII of the Articles of Agreement of the International Monetary Fund when those Articles have come into force.

(*ii*) The Governments of the United States and the United Kingdom agree that not later than one year after the effective date of this Agreement, unless in exceptional cases a later date is agreed upon after consultation, they will impose no restrictions on payments and transfers for current transactions. The obligations of this paragraph (*ii*) shall not apply:

(*a*) to balances of third countries and their nationals accumulated before this paragraph (*ii*) becomes effective; or

(*b*) to restrictions imposed in conformity with the Articles of Agreement of the International Monetary Fund, provided that the Governments of the United Kingdom and the United States will not continue to invoke the provisions of Article XIV, Section 2 of those Articles after this paragraph (*ii*) becomes effective, unless in exceptional cases after consultation they agree otherwise; or

(*c*) to restrictions imposed in connection with measures designed to uncover and dispose of assets of Germany and Japan.

(*iii*) This section and section 9, which are in anticipation of more comprehensive arrangements by multilateral agreement, shall operate until December 31, 1951.

9. *Import Arrangements.* If either the Government of the United States or the Government of the United Kingdom imposes or maintains quantitative import restrictions, such restrictions shall be administered on a basis which does not discriminate against imports from the other country in respect of any product; provided that this undertaking shall not apply in cases in which (*a*) its application would have the effect of preventing the country imposing such restrictions from utilizing, for the purchase of needed imports, inconvertible currencies accumulated up to December 31, 1946, or (*b*) there may be special necessity for the country imposing such restrictions to assist, by measures not involving a substantial departure from the general rule of non-discrimination, a country whose economy has been disrupted by war, or (*c*) either government imposes quantitative restrictions having equivalent effect to any exchange restrictions which that government is authorized to impose in conformity with Article VII of the Articles of Agreement of the International Monetary Fund. The provisions of this section shall become effective as soon as practicable but not later than December 31, 1946.

10. *Accumulated sterling balances.*

(*i*) The Government of the United Kingdom intends to make agreements with the countries concerned, varying according to the circumstances of each case, for an early settlement covering the sterling balances accumulated by sterling area and other countries prior to such settlement (together with any future receipts arising out of military expenditure by the Government of the United Kingdom to the extent to which they are treated on the same basis by agreement with the countries concerned). The settlements with the sterling area countries will be on the basis of dividing these accumulated balances into three categories (*a*) balances to be released at once and convertible into any currency for current transactions, (*b*) balances to be similarly released by installments over a period of years beginning in 1951, and (*c*) balances to be adjusted as a contribution to the settlement of war and postwar indebtedness and in recognition of the benefits which the countries concerned might be expected to gain from such a settlement. The Government of the United Kingdom will make every endeavor to secure the early completion of these arrangements.

(*ii*) In consideration of the fact that an important purpose of the present line of credit is to promote the development of multilateral trade and facilitate its early resumption on a non-discriminatory basis, the Government of the United Kingdom agrees that any sterling balances released or otherwise available for current payments will, not later than one year after the effective date of this Agreement unless in special cases a later date is agreed upon after consultation, be freely available for current transactions in any currency area without discrimination.

11. *Definitions.*

For the purposes of this Agreement:

(*i*) The term "current transactions" shall have the meaning prescribed in Article XIX (*i*) of the Articles of Agreement of the International Monetary Fund.

(*ii*) The term "sterling area" means the United Kingdom and the other territories declared by the Defence (Finance) (Definition of Sterling Area) (No. 2) Order, 1944, to be included in the sterling area, namely "the following territories excluding Canada and Newfoundland, that is to say —

(a) any Dominion,
(b) any other part of His Majesty's dominions,
(c) any territory in respect of which a mandate on behalf of the League of Nations has been accepted by His Majesty and is being exercised by His Majesty's Government in the United Kingdom or in any Dominion,
(d) any British protectorate or protected State,
(e) Egypt, the Anglo-Egyptian Sudan and Iraq,
(f) Iceland and the Faroe Islands."

12. *Consultation on Agreement.* Either government shall be entitled to approach the other for a reconsideration of any of the provisions of this Agreement, if in its opinion the prevailing conditions of international exchange justify such reconsideration, with a view to agreeing upon modifications for presentation to their respective legislatures.

Signed in duplicate at Washington, District of Columbia, this 6th day of December, 1945.

(2) *Joint Statement by the President (Truman) and the Prime Minister of the United Kingdom (Attlee) on the Conclusion of the Anglo-American Financial and Trade Negotiations, December 6, 1945.*[1]

The economic and financial discussions between officials of the United States and United Kingdom Governments meeting in Washington have now been completed.

These discussions have been concerned with the major problems affecting the basic economic and financial relations between the two countries, in the light of the provisions of article VII of the mutual-aid agreement between their Governments signed February 23, 1942.

They have covered the questions of financial assistance from the United States to the United Kingdom, the demobilization of wartime trade and monetary restrictions, the settlement of lend-lease, the disposal of surplus war property in the United Kingdom owned by the United States, and, finally, long-range commercial policies in the broad sense, embracing the fields of trade barriers and discriminations, policies

[1] Department of State, *Bulletin*, XIII, p. 905.

in respect of commodities in world surplus, cartels, an international trade organization, and international aspects of domestic measures to maintain employment.

The purpose of the discussions has been to arrive at mutually advantageous solutions of these problems which the two Governments would commend to the peoples and legislatures of the two countries and to the world as a whole.

Both sides have been fully conscious of the significance to other countries, as well as their own, of the outcome of these discussions, and they have from the beginning had continuously in view the common interest of their Governments in establishing a world trading and monetary system from which the trade of all countries can benefit and within which the trade of all countries can be conducted on a multilateral, non-discriminatory basis.

The discussions have been successful.

Agreement has been reached, subject to the approval of the legislatures of both countries, for the extension by the United States to the United Kingdom of a line of credit of $3,750,000,000 on the terms stated in the financial agreement signed this day, for the following purposes: to facilitate purchases by the United Kingdom of goods and services from the United States, to assist the United Kingdom to meet transitional post-war deficits in its current balance of payments, to help the United Kingdom to maintain adequate reserves of gold and dollars, and to assist the United Kingdom to assume the obligations of multilateral trade. This credit would make it possible for the United Kingdom to relax import and exchange controls, including exchange arrangements affecting the sterling area, and generally to move forward with the United States and other countries toward the common objective of expanded multilateral trade.

Agreement has been reached for the final settlement of lend-lease and reciprocal aid, the disposal of surplus war property in the United Kingdom owned by the United States, and the final settlement of the claims of each Government against the other arising out of the conduct of the war.

Agreement has been reached on the broad principles of commercial policy for which the two Governments will seek general international support.

These arrangements, if carried out, will put an end to the fear of an economically divided world; will make possible, throughout the world, the expansion of employment and of the production, exchange, and consumption of goods; and will bring into being, for the first time, a common code of equitable rules for the conduct of international trade policies and relations.

The realization of these proposals will depend upon the support given them by the peoples and legislatures of the United States and the United Kingdom, and where they envisage measures requiring broad international collaboration, the support of other countries.

The following documents resulting from these discussions are being issued by the two Governments:

Financial agreement.[1]
Joint statement regarding the understanding reached on commercial policy.[2]
Joint statement regarding settlement for lend-lease and reciprocal aid, surplus war property, and claims.[3]

(3) Message from the President (Truman) Transmitting the Agreement to the Congress, January 30, 1946.[4]

[Excerpts]

. . . .

It is not too much to say that the Agreement now transmitted will set the course of American and British economic relations for many years to come. In so doing it will have a decisive influence on the international trade of the whole world. Those who represented the United States in these discussions and those who represented the United Kingdom were fully aware of the fundamental nature of the problems before them. After long and careful consideration they agreed upon the arrangements which in my opinion will provide a solid foundation for the successful conduct of our economic relations with each other and with the world.

The Financial Agreement will by its terms come into operation only after the Congress has made available the funds necessary to extend to the United Kingdom the line of credit of $3,750,000,000 in accordance with the terms set forth in the Agreement. Britain needs this credit and she needs it now. It will assist her to meet the expected deficit in her balance of payments during the next six years. It will enable her to buy from the world the supplies of food and raw materials which are essential to the life and work of the British people. At the same time it will keep open a market for those surpluses of the United States which are customarily exported to the United Kingdom. These are the important short-term purposes of the credit.

But the Financial Agreement is much more than a credit. Let me repeat, its most important purpose from our point of view is to cause the removal of emergency controls exercised by the United Kingdom over its international transactions far more speedily than is required by the Bretton Woods Agreements. The Financial Agreement will enable the United Kingdom, through the prompt relaxation of exchange restrictions and discriminations, to move side by side with the United States toward the common goal of expanded world trade which means expanded production, consumption and employment and rising standards of living everywhere.

. . . .

The financial assistance which the United Kingdom would receive under the Agreement has made it possible for the two governments to

---

[1] For text of the Agreement, see this volume, p. 645.
[2] For text of the Joint Statement, see *ibid.*, p. 649.
[3] For text of the Joint Statement, see *ibid.*, p. 132.
[4] Department of State, *Bulletin*, XIV, p. 183.

agree on a specific course of action which in a short period of time will result in the removal of emergency controls over foreign exchange and discriminatory import restrictions and the reestablishment of peacetime practices designed to promote the recovery of world trade. Britain has agreed to abolish the so-called "sterling area dollar pool." She has agreed to give up most of her rights during the transition period provided for in the International Monetary Fund Agreement and thus to abandon controls over foreign exchange which she would otherwise be permitted by the terms of that Agreement to continue for a considerable period of time. In addition to the direct benefits which will flow from this stimulus to Anglo-American trade there will be the added benefits derived from the ability of other nations to relax their restrictions once the United Kingdom has led the way.

Another troublesome financial problem which has been fully and frankly discussed by the two nations is that of the sterling liabilities of Great Britain which have resulted from her large expenditures abroad during the war. In the Financial Agreement the British Government has undertaken to adjust and settle these obligations out of resources other than the American credit and has outlined its intentions with respect to their settlement. Our concern in this connection is two-fold. In the first place we want other countries which are in a position to do so to grant assistance to the United Kingdom within their means. Those which hold large sterling balances can do so by scaling them down. In the second place we want to be certain that the liquidation of these balances will not discriminate against American trade. The Financial Agreement contains a specific undertaking by the Government of the United Kingdom that no such discrimination shall result from these settlements.

The Financial Agreement also makes it possible for the United Kingdom to give wholehearted support to the Proposals for Expansion of World Trade and Employment which the United States has recently put forward as a basis for international discussions by the United Nations. In the Joint Statement on Commercial Policy published at the same time as the Financial Agreement, the United Kingdom has undertaken to support these Proposals and to use its best endeavors in cooperation with the United States to bring to a successful conclusion international discussions based upon them.

The implementation of the Financial Agreement will be a great contribution to the establishment of a permanent state of peace and prosperity. We are all aware of the dangers inherent in unchecked economic rivalry and economic warfare. These dangers can be eliminated by the firm resolution of this nation and the United Kingdom to carry forward the work which has been so well begun.

The Financial Agreement transmitted herewith means that instead of economic controversy between the two countries, the wise rules of the Bretton Woods Agreements will be fully effective much sooner than we believed possible when the Congress enacted the Bretton Woods Agreements Act. I urge that Congress act on the Financial Agreement promptly.

(4) *Address by the Secretary of State (Byrnes) before the Foreign Policy Association, New York, February 11, 1946.*[1]

[Excerpts]

. . . .

I wish to talk to you this evening about one of the most important of these difficulties and about our plan for helping to remove it. The problem I have in mind is the economic and financial dilemma into which the war has plunged Great Britain. The partial solution I am thinking about is the Anglo-American economic and financial agreements.

. . . .

We take for granted the interdependence of the national economy. The interdependence of the world economy is less apparent. But it is quite as real. Prosperity here and abroad requires the expansion both of production and of markets.

We know that we in the United States cannot reach and maintain the high level of employment we have set as our goal unless the outlets for our production are larger than they have ever been before in peacetime.

Thus Britain's difficulties in returning to normal economic intercourse are of direct concern to us. The economic agreements we have drafted to help meet those difficulties have several objectives.

We have acted first to settle the war account. Those who remember how the last war's debts haunted the world will welcome the expeditious disposal of this issue.

Our claims on Britain and Britain's claims on us for materials delivered under lend-lease and reverse lend-lease and consumed before V–J Day have been disposed of. The victory was the payment we sought for these goods.

But Britain will pay us for American surpluses remaining in the British Isles. A multitude of claims running both ways has been considered, a balance struck, and Britain has agreed to pay, with interest and over 50 years, the sum of 650 million dollars.

The provision of the agreements which has commanded the greatest public attention is the extension of a line of credit to the United Kingdom totaling $3,750,000,000. This credit may be drawn upon at any time from the date Congress approves the loan agreement until December 31, 1951. It will, of course, be used gradually.

The sums actually borrowed are to be repaid during the 50-year period beginning in 1951, with interest at 2 percent. The United Kingdom may request the United States to waive the collection of interest in any year in which British income from sales abroad and other sources is not enough to enable Great Britain to bring in imports at the average pre-war level. This is a wise provision in a contract of such long duration. It is not the course of wisdom to insist on interest payments when world-trade conditions may sometimes make such payments impossible.

[1] *Ibid.*, p. 267.

That, briefly, is the loan. To a transaction of this magnitude it is quite natural that objections should be raised.

I have heard it said, for example, that the credit will contribute to inflation in this country. If a sum of this size were all to be drawn at once and spent for scarce consumer's goods, it would indeed be serious. But that will not occur. The British certainly will conserve the funds, drawing from them only as needed between now and 1951.

. . . .

The pressure for inflation in this country is great. I would be the last to minimize the danger. But the answer lies primarily in speedy, large-scale production of the things of which we are short. Restricting the ability of foreign purchasers to buy the things we have in abundance only adds an additional handicap to our economy.

Another objection has been suggested by history. This is the assertion that the credit will never be repaid. It should be realized, however, that the circumstances surrounding this credit are entirely different from those applying to the British debt after the first World War.

First: That debt was incurred for materials largely destroyed in the fighting — goods that created no new wealth or earning power. This time we are not treating burned-out tanks as a commercial obligation. This credit is for new goods which will help create new production and new wealth. Like any good commercial loan, it helps create the means of its own payment.

Second: The earlier British debt was larger than this credit, and the interest rate was higher. The British made full payments all through the 1920's, and continued them until the great depression caused the moratorium of 1931. Even after that they made token payments in 1932 and 1933. Altogether they paid us over 2 billion dollars, principal and interest. That is not a record of intentional default.

Third: Last time we raised our tariffs in 1921, again in 1922, and again in 1930. The British could only pay us back by selling goods to us, and yet by increased tariff duties we made it harder and harder for British goods to enter this country.

Even more important, last time we and the rest of the world let the great depression happen. When it happened goods stopped moving and earnings collapsed. It was that, more than anything else, which stopped the payments on the British debt.

This time we are firmly set on a different course. We are not going to raise tariffs. The settled policy of Congress and of the President for more than 12 years has been and is to seek their gradual reduction by negotiations under the Trade Agreements Act. We are seeking to expand trade, not reduce it. And we and other countries are going to take steps to avoid a repetition of 1929.

If business activity remains high and trade large, Great Britain should have little difficulty meeting the agreed payments. If we permit another great depression to occur, we shall lose much larger values than the instalments on this credit.

The objection also is heard that, while this British credit is justified, it should not be granted because it will require us to make similar loans to other governments. With this argument I disagree.

This credit is not a precedent for anything. It is unique because the position of Britain in world trade, her need for working capital, and the effect upon world trade of her acquiring that working capital, all are unique.

Several countries do need capital to reconstruct and improve their industry and transport. The Export-Import Bank has made loans for these purposes under its existing powers and will make others, at least through 1946. By that time the International Bank for Reconstruction and Development, set up by the 34 nations signing the Bretton Woods agreement, should be ready to take over much of this activity.

Nor could a loan precedent be established by an agreement which is far more than an extension of credit; by an agreement which is an understanding on over-all commercial policy; by an agreement which thus becomes a joint advance by two of the world's largest economic units on the general problems of world trade.

I say that the agreements provide far more than an extension of credit, because they contain a pledge on Britain's part to remove as rapidly as possible the emergency controls over foreign exchange, to abolish the so-called "sterling area dollar pool", to abandon discriminatory import restrictions, to participate in next summer's negotiations for reduction of world-trade barriers, and to support the *Proposals for the Expansion of World Trade and Employment*, which our Government published last December.

In my judgment among the most significant of the benefits which flow to us from this phase of these agreements is the British commitment to support the United States trade proposals. By this commitment the British take their place at our side as our economic allies and not our economic enemies.

. . . .

If the loan is approved, we can look ahead with considerable confidence to a general reduction of tariffs and the elimination of preferences; to a minimum of quotas and embargoes; to an intelligent and restrained resort to government subsidies; to general acceptance of the rule that international business should be conducted on a business basis and not as a phase of political action.

We can look ahead also to a loosening of the grip of cartels and combines upon world commerce; to multilateral arrangements for the handling of surplus commodities; and to progressive limitation upon export restrictions and price-fixing arrangements.

The United States believes that these objectives will be best served by the establishment of an international trade organization under the Economic and Social Council of the United Nations. We believe that the international trade organization can become one of the most important foundations of a lasting peace.

The organization gives promise of becoming a strong foundation if it is to include Great Britain. Without Great Britain it might succeed, but its prospects would not be bright. Clearly we have a great stake in this program.

The British credit is a large investment undertaken to gain an even larger objective. Without it, our efforts to construct an expanding world economy may well be frustrated. With it, we shall have won the support of a powerful ally in our efforts to break down those harmful economic practices which throttle trade, perpetuate poverty, engender ill-will among nations, and sow the seeds of conflict.

. . . .

(5) **S. J. Resolution 138, To Implement Further the Purposes of the Bretton Woods Agreements Act by Authorizing the Secretary of the Treasury to Carry Out an Agreement with the United Kingdom, and for Other Purposes, Approved July 15, 1946.**[1]

Whereas in the Bretton Woods Agreements Act the Congress has declared it to be the policy of the United States "to seek to bring about further agreement and cooperation among nations and international bodies, as soon as possible, on ways and means which will best reduce obstacles to and restrictions upon international trade, eliminate unfair trade practices, promote mutually advantageous commercial relations, and otherwise facilitate the expansion and balanced growth of international trade and promote the stability of international economic relations"; and

Whereas in further implementation of the purposes of the Bretton Woods Agreements, the Governments of the United States and the United Kingdom have negotiated an agreement dated December 6, 1945, designed to expedite the achievement of stable and orderly exchange arrangements, the prompt elimination of exchange restrictions and discriminations, and other objectives of the above-mentioned policy declared by the Congress: Therefore be it

Resolved by the Senate and House of Representatives of the United States of America in Congress assembled, That the Secretary of the Treasury, in consultation with the National Advisory Council on International Monetary and Financial Problems, is hereby authorized to carry out the agreement dated December 6, 1945, between the United States and the United Kingdom which was transmitted by the President to the Congress on January 30, 1946.

SEC. 2. For the purpose of carrying out the agreement dated December 6, 1945, between the United States and the United Kingdom, the Secretary of the Treasury is authorized to use as a public-debt transaction not to exceed $3,750,000,000 of the proceeds of any securities hereafter issued under the Second Liberty Bond Act, as amended, and the purposes for which securities may be issued under that Act are extended to include such purpose. Payments to the United Kingdom under this joint resolution and pursuant to the agreement and repayments thereof shall be treated as public-debt transactions of the United States. Payments of interest to the United States under the agreement shall be covered into the Treasury as miscellaneous receipts.

[1] Public Law 509, 79th Cong., 2d sess.

CHAPTER X

TRANSPORTATION AND COMMUNICATION

1. INTERNATIONAL AERIAL NAVIGATION

A. The Convention on International Civil Aviation, Signed for the United States at Chicago, Illinois, December 7, 1944

The International Civil Aviation Conference, which met in Chicago from November 1 to December 7, 1944, with delegates of fifty-two nations attending, resulted in four conventions: (1) a Convention on International Civil Aviation; (2) an Interim Agreement on International Civil Aviation; (3) an International Air Services Transit Agreement; and (4) an International Air Transport Agreement.[1] The Interim Agreement, providing for a Provisional International Civil Aviation Organization (PICAO) to function until the establishment of a permanent organization with the coming into force of the Convention on International Civil Aviation,[2] entered into force on June 6, 1945 with the receipt by the Department of State of the twenty-sixth acceptance of the Agreement.[3] The Government of the United States had accepted this agreement as well as the International Air Transport Agreement and the International Air Services Transit Agreement on February 8, 1945.[4] Advice and consent to the ratification of the Convention on International Civil Aviation was urged by President Truman in a message to the Senate of June 11, 1946.[5] On June 19, 1946, Senator George, the chairman of the Senate Committee on Foreign Relations, reported the approval by his Committee of the Convention. The Senate, on July 25, accordingly advised and consented to its ratification; and formal ratification by the President followed on August 6, 1946.

(1) *Message from the President (Truman) to the Senate, Requesting Advice and Consent to the Ratification of the Convention, June 11, 1946.*[6]

In the autumn of 1944, at the invitation of the United States, an International Civil Aviation Conference was held in Chicago. The main purpose and chief result of this conference was the preparation of an important treaty, the International Convention on Civil Aviation. On

---

[1] For texts of these agreements, see *International Civil Aviation Conference, Chicago, Illinois, November 1 to December 7, 1944, Final Act and Related Documents*, Department of State Publication, 2282, Conference Series 64. See also, *Documents, VII, 1944–1945*, p. 572.

[2] See this volume, p. 662.

[3] For signatures and acceptances of this agreement as of October 2, 1946, see *ibid.*, p. 660.

[4] *Executive Agreements Series*, 469; for signatures and acceptances of these agreements, see this volume, p. 660. On July 25, 1946, the Department of State announced the intention of the Government of the United States to withdraw from the International Air-Transport Agreement; see *ibid.*, p. 659.

[5] See below.

[6] *Congressional Record*, 92, p. 6788–89 (Daily edition, June 6, 1946). See also, Department of State, *Bulletin*, XIV, p. 1079.

March 12, 1945, President Roosevelt referred this convention to the Senate, with a request for consideration and ratification. It has now become a matter of urgency to this Nation, and to many other nations, that the Senate act upon the convention.

The convention has two major elements: (1) It restates and codifies the accepted principles of international law pertaining to air navigation; (2) it provides for the establishment of an International Civil Aviation Organization.

The parts of the convention dealing with the principles of international air law are self-explanatory, and I feel sure that the Senate will recognize the value of the codification.

Similarly, I believe the proposed International Civil Aviation Organization will recommend itself to the Senate. The most important task of this Organization, under the terms of the Convention, will be the promotion of safety of life in the air. In this connection, it will develop international standards for airworthiness of aircraft, for competence of aviation personnel, and for operating practices and facilities on the international air routes. The organization will also study the economic problems of international air transport; and in certain instances it may be used as an instrument through which such international aviation facilities and services as airports, radio aids, and weather information could be internationally financed.

The organization will come into existence on a permanent basis when the convention has been ratified by 26 governments. It will have its headquarters in Montreal, Canada. Meanwhile, as is accepted practice in such undertakings, and in accordance with an interim agreement, the organization has been temporarily established on a provisional basis.

The provisional organization is concerned with the same activities which will engage the permanent organization, but it lacks full powers and its life is limited. It is increasingly apparent that the establishment of the permanent organization cannot be indefinitely delayed without damage to interests vital to this and other countries. As matters stand, the safety regulations cannot be finished or made fully effective, and the economic activities remain merely exploratory. Meanwhile, as international air traffic rapidly expands, individual nations and airlines are developing their own regulations and operating practices. The guidance and authority of an actively functioning international organization is urgently needed to assure the uniform standards required for safety, efficiency, and economy.

The convention makes no attempt to cover controversial questions of commercial aviation rights. It leaves these questions to be settled by other international agreements, which are entirely independent of the convention, and which provide for the reciprocal exchange of commercial air transport rights. Under authority vested in me, I have actively undertaken to consummate such agreements, in order to assure the most favorable development of international civil aviation. Naturally, agreements of this nature to which the United States is a party are consistent with the requirements of the Civil Aeronautics Act, are valid under its terms, and fully protect the public interest. Under these agreements, before foreign air-carrier permits are issued by the United States to foreign airlines, they must qualify under the provisions of the Civil Aeronautics Act.

It is very important to the future of American aviation that the convention be promptly ratified. At the recent meeting of the provisional organization in Montreal, it was agreed that all the nations concerned would aim at March 1, 1947, as the ratification dead line. In order to make it possible for the nations as a group to meet this dead line, it is vital that the United States ratify the convention during the present session of Congress. At the present time, nine governments have already ratified the convention, but it is plain that many others are withholding action pending ratification by this country. Hope of bringing the convention into effective operation in the near future depends on prompt action by this country, which would stimulate similar early action by other governments.

We need also to consider the possibility that, if we hold back, the permanent organization may eventually be established without our participation. In that event, our airlines might be forced to operate in foreign countries under regulations which we had had no part in framing, and which might adversely affect our aircraft and air transport industries. If the interests of this country are to be fully represented in the work of the permanent organization, the United States, which sponsored the original International Civil Aviation Conference in Chicago, needs to give evidence, by prompt ratification of the convention, of continued leadership. I feel confident that the Senate will recognize this serious responsibility and notable opportunity.

(2) *Announcement of Withdrawal by the United States Government from the Air-Transport Agreement, Signed at Chicago, Illinois, December 7, 1944, and Accepted February 8, 1945. Department of State Press Release, July 25, 1946.*[1]

On February 8, 1945 the United States Government accepted as binding upon it the International Air Transport Agreement (commonly known as the Five Freedoms Agreement), which was one of the documents drawn up at the International Civil Aviation Conference held at Chicago from November 1 to December 7, 1944.

This multilateral agreement provides that each contracting state grants to the other contracting states not only the privileges of flight over its territory without landing and the privilege to land for non-traffic purposes (which are included in the International Air Transit Agreement and known as the Two Freedoms), but in addition the privileges of taking on and discharging passengers, mail, and cargo destined for or taken on in the territory of the state whose nationality the aircraft possesses and the privilege of carrying passengers, mail, and cargo between the territories of any of the contracting states. The agreement also sets forth the conditions under which the above-mentioned privileges may be exercised.

Only 15 countries have accepted the International Air Transport Agreement, and of this number only 2, besides the United States, have developed international air services to any extent. The failure of the

[1] *Ibid.*, XV, p. 236.

660 DOCUMENTS ON AMERICAN FOREIGN RELATIONS

nations principally concerned with the operation and development of air-transport services generally to accept the agreement, and the dissatisfaction with it as reflected at the meeting of the Assembly of the Provisional International Civil Aviation Organization held at Montreal, have made it clear that the agreement cannot be relied upon as an effective medium for the establishment of international air routes for operation by United States carriers. Consequently, the United States has decided to withdraw from this agreement.

In accordance with article 5 of the agreement, any contracting state may withdraw from it on one year's notice. It is the duty of the United States at once to inform all other contracting states of this decision. This Government, therefore, in accordance with article 5, will at once inform all the other states which have accepted the International Air Transport Agreement of its intention to withdraw from the agreement dating from July 25.

(3) *Status of the Civil Aviation Agreements, Formulated at Chicago, Illinois, December 7, 1944, as of October 2, 1946.*[1]

DATES OF SIGNATURES

Country	Final Act	Interim Agreement	Convention	Transit Agreement (Two Freedoms)	Transport Agreement (Five Freedoms)
Afghanistan	X[2]	X	X	X	X
Australia	X	X	X	7/4/45	—
Belgium	X	4/9/45	4/9/45	4/9/45	—
Bolivia	X	X	X	X	X
Brazil	X	5/29/45	5/29/45	—	—
Canada	X	X	X	2/10/45	—
Chile	X	X	X	X	—
China	X	X	X	—	X
Colombia	X	5/24/45	—	—	—
Costa Rica	X	3/10/45	3/10/45	3/10/45	3/10/45
Cuba	X	4/20/45	4/20/45	4/20/45	4/20/45
Czechoslovakia	X	4/18/45	4/18/45	4/18/45	—
Dominican Republic	X	X	X	—	X
Ecuador	X	X	X	X	X
Egypt	X	X	X	X	—
El Salvador	X	5/9/45	5/9/45	5/9/45	5/9/45
Ethiopia	X	3/22/45	—	3/22/45	3/22/45
France	X	X	X	X	—
Greece	X	X	X	X	—
Guatemala	X	1/30/45	1/30/45	1/30/45	1/30/45
Haiti	X	X	X	X	X
Honduras	X	X	X	X	X
Iceland	X	X	X	4/4/45	4/4/45
India	X	X	X	X	—
Iran	X	X	X	X	8/13/46
Iraq	X	X	X	X	—
Ireland	X	X	X	—	—

[1] Charts prepared by the Treaty Branch, Office of the Legal Adviser, Department of State; *ibid.*, p. 688.

[2] X indicates signatures under date of December 7, 1944.

TRANSPORTATION AND COMMUNICATION

DATES OF SIGNATURES — Continued

Country	Final Act	Interim Agreement	Convention	Transit Agreement (Two Freedoms)	Transport Agreement (Five Freedoms)
Lebanon	X	X	X	X	X [1]
Liberia	X	X	X	X	X
Luxembourg	X	7/9/45	7/9/45	7/9/45	—
Mexico	X	X	X	X	X
Netherlands	X	X	X	X	X [1]
New Zealand	X	X	X	X	—
Nicaragua	X	X	X	X	X
Norway	X	1/30/45	1/30/45	1/30/45	—
Panama	X	5/14/45	—	—	—
Paraguay	X	7/27/45	7/27/45	7/27/45	7/27/45
Peru	X	X	X	X	X
Philippines	X	X	X	X	—
Poland	X	X	X	—	—
Portugal	X	X	X	—	—
Spain	X	X	X	X	—
Sweden	X	X	X	X	X
Switzerland	X	X	7/6/45	7/6/45	—
Syria	X	X	X	7/6/45	7/6/45 [1]
Turkey	X	X	X	X	X [1]
Union of South Africa	X	6/4/45	6/4/45	6/4/45	—
United Kingdom	X	X	X	X [1]	—
United States of America	X	X	X	X	X [2]
Uruguay	X	X	X	X	X
Venezuela	X	X [1]	—	X [1]	X [1]
Yugoslavia	X	—	—	—	—
Danish Minister	X	X	X	X	X
Thaï Minister	X	X	X	X	X

SUBSEQUENT ACTION TAKEN

Country	Interim Agreement (Date of Acceptance)	Convention (Date of Deposit of Ratification or Adherence)	Transit Agreement (Date of Receipt of Note of Acceptance)	Transport Agreement (Date of Receipt of Note of Acceptance)
Afghanistan	5/16/45	—	5/17/45	5/17/45
Argentina	6/4/46	6/4/46 A[3]	6/4/46	—
Australia (*) [4]	5/19/45	—	8/28/45	—
Belgium (*)	4/17/45	—	7/19/45	—
Bolivia	5/17/46	—	—	—
Brazil (*)	5/29/45	7/8/46	—	—
Canada (*)	12/30/44	2/13/46	2/10/45	—
Chile (*)	6/4/45	—	—	—
China (*)	6/6/45	2/20/46	—	6/6/45 [5]

[1] Signature accompanied by reservation; see *ibid*.
[2] On July 25, 1946, the Government of the United States announced its intention to withdraw from this agreement; see this volume, p. 659.
[3] A indicates adherence.
[4] (*) Elected to first Interim Council.
[5] Acceptance accompanied by reservation; see Department of State, *Bulletin*, XV, p. 689.

SUBSEQUENT ACTION TAKEN — *Continued*

Country	Interim Agreement (Date of Acceptance)	Convention (Date of Deposit of Ratification or Adherence)	Transit Agreement (Date of Receipt of Note of Acceptance)	Transport Agreement (Date of Receipt of Note of Acceptance)
Colombia (*)	6/6/45	—	—	—
Costa Rica	—	—	—	—
Cuba	—	—	—	—
Czechoslovakia (*)	4/18/45	—	4/18/45	—
Denmark	11/13/45	—	—	—
Dominican Republic	1/25/46	1/25/46	—	1/25/46
Ecuador	—	—	—	—
Egypt (*)	4/26/45	—	—	—
El Salvador (*)	5/31/45	—	6/1/45	6/1/45
Ethiopia	3/22/45	—	3/22/45	3/22/45
France (*)	6/5/45	—	—	—
Greece	9/21/45	—	9/21/45	2/28/46 [1]
Guatemala	—	—	—	—
Haiti	6/2/45	—	—	—
Honduras	11/13/45	—	11/13/45	11/13/45
Iceland	6/4/45	—	—	—
India (*)	5/1/45 [1]	—	5/2/45 [1]	—
Iran	—	—	—	—
Iraq (*)	6/4/45	—	6/15/45	—
Ireland [2]	4/27/45	—	—	—
Lebanon	6/4/45	—	—	—
Liberia	3/17/45	—	3/19/45	3/19/45
Luxembourg	7/9/45	—	—	—
Mexico (*)	5/22/45	6/25/46	6/25/46	—
Netherlands (*)	1/11/45	—	1/12/45	1/12/45 [1]
New Zealand	4/18/45 [1]	—	4/19/45 [1]	—
Nicaragua	12/28/45	12/28/45	12/28/45	12/28/45
Norway (*)	1/30/45	—	1/30/45	—
Panama	—	—	—	—
Paraguay	7/27/45	1/21/46	7/27/45	7/27/45
Peru (*)	5/4/45	4/8/46	—	—
Philippines	3/22/46	—	3/22/46 [1]	—
Poland	4/6/45	4/6/45	4/6/45	—
Portugal	5/29/45	—	—	—
Spain	7/30/45	—	7/30/45	—
Sweden	7/9/45	—	11/19/45	11/19/45
Switzerland	7/6/45	—	7/6/45	—
Syria	7/6/45	—	—	—
Turkey (*)	6/6/45	12/20/45	6/6/45	6/6/45 [1]
Union of South Africa	11/30/45	—	11/30/45	—
United Kingdom (*)	5/31/45 [1]	—	5/31/45 [1]	—
United States of America (*)	2/8/45	8/9/46	2/8/45 [1]	2/8/45 [3]
Uruguay	—	—	—	—
Venezuela	3/28/46	—	3/28/46	3/28/46
Yugoslavia	—	—	—	—
Thaï Minister	—	—	—	—

[1] Acceptance accompanied by reservation; see *ibid*.

[2] Elected to first Interim Council by first Interim Assembly, June 6, 1946.

[3] The Government of the United States accepted the Transport Agreement with reservations and, on July 25, 1946, announced its intention to withdraw from that agreement; see this volume, p. 659.

B. Provisional International Civil Aviation Organization (PICAO)

Pending the deposit of the twenty-six instruments of ratification required to give effect to the Chicago Convention on International Civil Aviation,[1] an Interim Agreement established for a period of no more than three years a Provisional International Civil Aviation Organization.[2] When the Interim Council of PICAO convened for its initial session in Montreal, Canada, on August 15, 1946, the United States was represented by Dr. Edward Warner, Vice Chairman of the Civil Aeronautics Board.[3] With the election of Dr. Warner to the presidency of the Council, Mr. Gerald B. Brophy was named to replace him as the representative of the United States in that body.[4] The work of the first session was devoted primarily to the organization of the Council and to the establishment of rules of procedure for its operation.

In March, 1946, PICAO opened a series of ten scheduled regional meetings, four of which were held during the period under review. At each of these regional meetings the United States was represented. The first opened in Dublin on March 4, 1946, and was concerned with the application to the North Atlantic area of the "International Standards and Recommended Practices" approved by the Interim Council in the fields of aviation communications, rules of air and air-traffic control, landing areas and ground aids, search and rescue, and meteorological protection of international aeronautics. The conference also made plans for the operation of the facilities needed for North Atlantic air services.[5] A similar conference, devoted to the air routes of the European-Mediterranean region, was convened in Paris on April 19, 1946. Paul A. Smith, Assistant to the Director of the Coast and Geodetic Survey, U.S.C.G.S., and Charles I. Stanton, Deputy Administrator of the Civil Aeronautics Administration, were the representatives for the United States at the Paris meeting.[6] The United States acted as host to the delegates to the Caribbean Regional Air Navigation Meeting, the third of the regional conferences sponsored by PICAO, held in Washington from August 26 to September 4, 1946. Mr. Stanton was designated chairman of the United States delegation to this meeting and was elected president of the conference at its opening session.[7] The work of the conference followed, in general, lines already laid down at the two previous regional conferences at Dublin and at Paris. The fourth regional meeting dealt with the air navigation problems of the Middle East area and convened at Cairo, Egypt, on October 1, 1946. The United States delegation in this instance was headed by Glen A. Gilbert, Consultant to the Administrator of the Civil Aeronautics Administration.[8]

On May 17, 1946, President Truman announced the United States representatives to the First Annual Assembly of PICAO, which met in Montreal on May 21. The Assembly reviewed the work of the Council and of the Secretariat and broke ground for the establishment of the permanent International Civil Aviation Organization. It also discussed technical, economic and legal matters in the field of international aviation. The United States delegation consisted of: William A. M. Burden (Assistant Secretary of Commerce), who served as chairman of the delegation; L. Welch Pogue (Chairman of the Civil Aeronautics Board), who acted as vice chairman; and Harllee Branch (member of the Civil Aviation Board), Gerald B. Brophy (United States representative on the Interim Council

---

[1] For text of the Convention, see *International Civil Aviation Conference, Chicago, Illinois, November 1 to December 7, 1944, Final Act and Related Documents*, cited above. See also, *Documents, VII, 1944–1945*, p. 585.

[2] For text of the Interim Agreement, see *International Civil Aviation Conference, Chicago, Illinois, November 1 to December 7, 1944, Final Act and Related Documents*, cited above. See also, *Documents, VII, 1944–1945*, p. 572. For an analysis of PICAO and its past work, see *International Organization*, I, p. 128.

[3] Department of State, *Bulletin*, XIII, p. 108.
[4] *Ibid.*, p. 289.
[5] *Ibid.*, XIV, p. 431.
[6] *Ibid.*, p. 713.
[7] *Ibid.*, XV, p. 407.
[8] *Ibid.*, p. 574.

of PICAO), and Garrison Norton (Deputy Director of the Office of Transport and Communications Policy of the Department of State), all of whom served as delegates to the Assembly.[1]

Maj. Gen. Lawrence S. Kuter, Commanding General of the Atlantic Division of the Air Transport Command, was appointed United States representative on the Interim Council [2] following the resignation, effective June 30, 1946, of Mr. Brophy, who had served in that capacity since August, 1945.[3]

Other activities of PICAO in which the United States participated during this period included a conference on North Atlantic Ocean weather observation stations which assembled in London on September 17, and a meeting with the Special Radio Technical Division of the Air Navigation Committee in Montreal, October 30. The United States delegation to the first conference, which explored the financial and technical problems of establishing new observation stations and the coordination and operation of existing ones, was headed by J. Paul Barringer, Assistant Chief of the Aviation Division of the Department of State,[4] who also headed the technical group sent to the conference in Montreal for the formulation of plans for an international agreement for the standardization of radio equipment.[5] The PICAO conference of the Air-Traffic Control Committee, European-Mediterranean region, which was called in Paris, October 28, 1946, to complete air-traffic control plans begun at the European Air Route Services Organization Conference (the second regional conference) at Paris in April and May of that year, was also attended by United States representatives.[6]

C. Bilateral Air-Transport Agreements Concluded by the United States

In order to facilitate international air transportation and to promote the extension of world air routes, the United States, during the period under review, concluded twenty-two bilateral air-transport agreements and, by exchanges of notes, amended one which had previously been negotiated with Denmark in December 1944.[7] These agreements are easily distinguishable into two types: (1) the "Chicago standard form" agreements and (2) the "Bermuda form" agreements.

The first category of air-transport agreements follows, with such variations as are necessary for application to the respective countries with which these agreements were concluded, the recommendations resulting from the Chicago Conference on International Civil Aviation.[8] The "Form of Standard Agreement for Provisional Air Routes" particularly has been applied. The Air-Transport Agreement concluded with Portugal, December 6, 1945, is representative of "Chicago form" agreements.

The Portuguese agreement provides for exchange between the contracting governments of air rights which are to be exercised by designated airlines of each country [9] and stipulates equality of treatment and non-discriminatory practices with regard to airport charges, the imposition of customs duties and inspection fees, the exemption of certain items from such duties and fees, and the recognition by each country of the certificates of airworthiness and personnel

[1] *Ibid.*, XIV, p. 886.
[2] *Ibid.*, XV, p. 535.
[3] *Ibid.*, XIV, p. 857; for texts of letters exchanged between the President and Mr. Brophy, see White House press release dated May 6, 1946.
[4] Department of State, *Bulletin*, XV, p. 846.
[5] *Ibid.*, p. 901.
[6] *Ibid.*, p. 1101.
[7] Department of State, *Treaties and Other International Acts Series* 1519.
[8] For information on the Chicago Conference on International Civil Aviation, November 1 to December 7, 1944, see *Documents, VII, 1944–1945*, p. 560.
[9] The agreements with Iran, Italy and Saudi Arabia, all Chicago form agreements, were exceptions with respect to reciprocity. Unilateral rights are granted to the United States pending the negotiation of more formal conventions; Department of State, *Bulletin*, XV, p. 1127.

licenses issued by the other. In addition, each party agrees to comply with the laws and rules of the other pertaining to entry, clearance, immigration, passport and customs procedures, and quarantine. Criteria for the establishment of ownership and control of air services are agreed upon; the registration of pertinent agreements with the Provisional International Civil Aviation Organization (PICAO) is provided; procedure for the amendment of the Annex to the agreement is set forth; and the right of termination of the convention on one year's notice by either party is stipulated. The annexes typical of the Chicago form agreements describe in some detail the routes and traffic points specified in the agreement as having been granted to the air services of each contracting party. No restrictions are imposed upon the capacity of the air-craft or upon the number of schedules to be operated, nor is any provision made for the determination of rates. Carriage of fifth-freedom traffic, *i.e.*, international traffic, to, from, or between one or more intermediate points on the designated routes, is not limited.

Agreements of the Chicago type were concluded during the period from July 1, 1945, to December 31, 1946, by the United States with the following countries: Czechoslovakia, Denmark, Iran, Italy, Norway, Peru, Portugal, Saudi Arabia, Switzerland, and Turkey.[1]

The "Bermuda form" agreements are patterned after the United States-United Kingdom Air-Transport Agreement concluded as a result of the Bermuda Civil Aviation Conference, January 15 to February 11, 1946,[2] and represent a reconciliation of the divergent air-transport policies of one group of countries, represented by the United States, and those of another group of which the United Kingdom is representative. In the formulation of air-transport agreements the United States sought to avoid the inclusion of any restrictions or predetermined formulae with regard to the capacity of the air-craft to operate over the designated air routes, the number of frequencies, the carriage of fifth-freedom traffic and the fixing of rates. The United Kingdom, on the other hand, found regulation of these matters by specific provision desirable.

Agreements of the Bermuda type incorporate the "Chicago standard form" provisions and contain, in addition, certain further stipulations which the Chicago recommendations did not encompass. The agreement with the United Kingdom provides that disputes not amenable to bilateral settlement through consultation be submitted to the Interim Council of PICAO for an advisory report, in accordance with the provisions of Article III, Section 6 (8), of the Interim Agreement governing PICAO. A further article envisages the revision of the agreement to conform to the terms of any multilateral convention on air-transport to which the United States and the United Kingdom may subsequently become parties. The Annex to the Bermuda Agreement describes, as do the annexes to agreements of the Chicago type, the routes and traffic points granted by each party to the other. Procedure for determining rates subject to governmental review, a procedure not found in Chicago type agreements, is laid down, as is the manner of altering the specified air routes. "Change of gauge" (the procedure to be followed in the event that the onward carriage of traffic must be accomplished by an air-craft of different size from that employed on the earlier stage of the same route) is dealt with. The Bermuda Conference also produced a Final Act in which it is declared that the airlines of one country shall not unduly prejudice those of the other, and by which are established three general principles for the regulation of the carriage of "fill-up" fifth-freedom traffic.

In the application of the Bermuda model to other bilateral air-transport agreements certain changes in both form and substance necessarily occurred. The provisions of the Final Act of the Conference appear frequently in the annex to the agreement or in an accompanying protocol of signature. Rates for fifth-freedom traffic are prescribed in three of the Bermuda type agreements.[3]

[1] For dates of signature and reference as to the official texts of these agreements, see this volume, p. 671.

[2] For text of the agreement with Great Britain, see *ibid.*, p. 666. For information on the Bermuda Civil Aviation Conference, see *ibid.*

[3] With Belgium, Brazil and France.

Specific procedure for rate-fixing is omitted from five.[1] Three other agreements provide greater freedom to the parties in the settlement of disputes, permitting each government to determine in its own judgment that the conditions of the agreement or of its annex have not been fulfilled and allowing them to take immediate action appropriate thereto.[2]

Agreements of the Bermuda type have been concluded by the United States, during the period from July 1, 1945, to December 31, 1946, with the following governments: Australia, Belgium, Brazil, China, Egypt, France, Greece, India, Lebanon, New Zealand, Philippines, United Kingdom, and Uruguay.[3]

(1) *Agreement between the Government of the United States of America and the Government of the United Kingdom Relating to Air Services between Their Respective Territories, Signed at Bermuda, February 11, 1946.*[4]

During the Anglo-American economic and financial conversations of September 11 to December 6, 1945,[5] specialized problems of civil aviation presented themselves as ancillary to the liquidation of all issues outstanding between the United States and the United Kingdom. Accordingly, on January 15, 1946, delegates from both Governments inaugurated a four-weeks' Civil Air Conference at Bermuda. At the outset of the Conference, both parties reaffirmed their adherence to the principles and purposes laid down in the Chicago Convention on International Civil Aviation.[6] Following the final Plenary Session of the Conference on February 11, 1946, a joint statement was released covering the area of agreement which resolved all outstanding problems.[7] Anglo-American accord on matters of policy included: (1) governmental and inter-governmental review of rates, (2) unrestricted frequency of flights, (3) liberal fifth-freedom measures permitting transport of third-party traffic, (4) agreement on schedule of air-routes, (5) non-discriminatory commercial use of the air bases leased by the United Kingdom to the United States, (6) submission of disputes to PICAO, or to its successor, for advisory opinions. Delegates from both nations signed a Bilateral Air Transport Agreement[8] and initialed a detailed Annex appended thereto. The Conference also drafted a Final Act and Heads of an Agreement for Use by Civil Aircraft of Naval and Air Bases Leased by the United Kingdom to the United States.

THE GOVERNMENT OF THE UNITED STATES OF AMERICA AND THE GOVERNMENT OF THE UNITED KINGDOM OF GREAT BRITAIN AND NORTHERN IRELAND,

Desiring to conclude an Agreement for the purpose of promoting direct air communications as soon as possible between their respective territories,

[1] With Greece, Egypt, Lebanon, Philippines and Uruguay.
[2] With India, Australia, and New Zealand.
[3] For dates of signature and reference as to the official texts of these agreements, see *ibid.*, p. 671.
[4] Department of State, *Bulletin*, XIV, p. 586. See also, Department of State, *Treaties and Other International Acts Series* 1507.
[5] For information on the United States-United Kingdom Economic and Financial Agreement, see this volume, p. 643.
[6] See *International Civil Aviation Conference, Chicago, Illinois, November 1 to December 7, 1944, Final Act and Related Documents*, cited above. See also, *Documents, VII, 1944–1945*, p. 560.
[7] *New York Times*, February 12, 1946, p. 4.
[8] For text of Bilateral Agreement, see below.

Have accordingly appointed authorised representatives for this purpose, who have agreed as follows:—

Article 1

Each Contracting Party grants to the other Contracting Party rights to the extent described in the Annex to this Agreement for the purpose of the establishment of air services described therein or as amended in accordance with Section IV of the Annex (hereinafter referred to as "the agreed services").

Article 2

(1) The agreed services may be inaugurated immediately or at a later date at the option of the Contracting Party to whom the rights are granted, but not before (a) the Contracting Party to whom the rights have been granted has designated an air carrier or carriers for the specified route or routes, and (b) the Contracting Party granting the rights has given the appropriate operating permission to the air carrier or carriers concerned (which, subject to the provisions of paragraph (2) of this Article and of Article 6, it shall do without undue delay).

(2) The designated air carrier or carriers may be required to satisfy the aeronautical authorities of the Contracting Party granting the rights that it or they is or are qualified to fulfil the conditions prescribed by or under the laws and regulations normally applied by those authorities to the operations of commercial air carriers.

(3) In areas of military occupation, or in areas affected thereby, such inauguration will continue to be subject, where necessary, to the approval of the competent military authorities.

Article 3

(1) The charges which either of the Contracting Parties may impose, or permit to be imposed, on the designated air carrier or carriers of the other Contracting Party for the use of airports and other facilities shall not be higher than would be paid for the use of such airports and facilities by its national aircraft engaged in similar international air services.

(2) Fuel, lubricating oils and spare parts introduced into, or taken on board aircraft in, the territory of one Contracting Party by, or on behalf of, a designated air carrier of the other Contracting Party and intended solely for use by the aircraft of such carrier shall be accorded, with respect to customs duties, inspection fees or other charges imposed by the former Contracting Party, treatment not less favorable than that granted to national air carriers engaged in international air services or such carriers of the most favoured nation.

(3) Supplies of fuel, lubricating oils, spare parts, regular equipment and aircraft stores retained on board aircraft of a designated air carrier of one Contracting Party shall be exempt in the territory of the other Contracting Party from customs duties, inspection fees or similar duties or charges, even though such supplies be used by such aircraft on flights within that Territory.

Article 4

Certificates of airworthiness, certificates of competency and licenses issued or rendered valid by one Contracting Party and still in force shall be recognized as valid by the other Contracting Party for the purpose of operation of the agreed services. Each Contracting Party reserves the right, however, to refuse to recognize for the purpose of flight above its own territory, certificates of competency and licenses granted to its own nationals by another state.

Article 5

(1) The laws and regulations of one Contracting Party relating to entry into or departure from its territory of aircraft engaged in international air navigation or to the operation and navigation of such aircraft while within its territory shall apply to aircraft of the designated air carrier or carriers of the other Contracting Party.

(2) The laws and regulations of one Contracting Party relating to the entry into or departure from its territory of passengers, crew, or cargo of aircraft (such as regulations relating to entry, clearance, immigration, passports, customs and quarantine) shall be applicable to the passengers, crew or cargo of the aircraft of the designated air carrier or carriers of the other Contracting Party while in the territory of the first Contracting Party.

Article 6

Each Contracting Party reserves the right to withhold or revoke the exercise of the rights specified in the Annex to this Agreement by a carrier designated by the other Contracting Party in the event that it is not satisfied that substantial ownership and effective control of such carrier are vested in nationals of either Contracting Party, or in case of failure by the carrier to comply with the laws and regulations referred to in Article 5 hereof, or otherwise to fulfil the conditions under which the rights are granted in accordance with this Agreement and its Annex.

Article 7

This Agreement shall be registered with the Provisional International Civil Aviation Organization set up by the Interim Agreement on International Civil Aviation signed at Chicago on December 7, 1944.

Article 8

Except as otherwise provided in this Agreement or its Annex, if either of the Contracting Parties considers it desirable to modify the terms of the Annex to this Agreement, it may request consultation between the aeronautical authorities of both Contracting Parties, such consultation to begin within a period of sixty days from the date of the request. When these authorities agree on modifications to the Annex, these modifications will come into effect when they have been confirmed by an Exchange of Notes through the diplomatic channel.

Article 9

Except as otherwise provided in this Agreement or in its Annex, any dispute between the Contracting Parties relating to the interpretation or application of this Agreement or its Annex which cannot be settled through consultation shall be referred for an advisory report to the Interim Council of the Provisional International Civil Aviation Organization (in accordance with the provisions of Article III Section 6 (8) of the Interim Agreement on International Civil Aviation signed at Chicago on December 7, 1944) or its successor.

Article 10

The terms and conditions of operating rights which may have been granted previously by either Contracting Party to the other Contracting Party or to an air carrier of such other Contracting Party shall not be abrogated by the present Agreement. Except as may be modified by the present Agreement, the general principles of the air navigation arrangement between the two Contracting Parties, which was effected by an Exchange of Notes dated March 28 and April 5, 1935, shall continue in force in so far as they are applicable to scheduled international air services, until otherwise agreed by the Contracting Parties.

Article 11

If a general multilateral air Convention enters into force in relation to both Contracting Parties, the present Agreement shall be amended so as to conform with the provisions of such Convention.

Article 12

For the purposes of this Agreement and its Annex, unless the context otherwise requires:

(a) The term "aeronautical authorities" shall mean, in the case of the United States, the Civil Aeronautics Board and any person or body authorized to perform the functions presently exercised by the Board or similar functions, and, in the case of the United Kingdom, the Minister of Civil Aviation for the time being, and any person or body authorized to perform any functions presently exercised by the said Minister or similar functions.

(b) The term "designated air carriers" shall mean the air transport enterprises which the aeronautical authorities of one of the Contracting Parties have notified in writing to the aeronautical authorities of the other Contracting Party as the air carriers designated by it in accordance with Article 2 of this Agreement for the routes specified in such notification.

(c) The term "territory" shall have the meaning assigned to it by Article 2 of the Convention on International Civil Aviation signed at Chicago on December 7, 1944.

(d) The definitions contained in paragraphs (a), (b) and (d) of Article 96 of the Convention on International Civil Aviation signed at Chicago on December 7, 1944 shall apply.

Article 13

Either Contracting Party may at any time request consultation with the other with a view to initiating any amendments of this Agreement or its Annex which may be desirable in the light of experience. Pending the outcome of such consultation, it shall be open to either Party at any time to give notice to the other of its desire to terminate this Agreement. Such notice shall be simultaneously communicated to the Provisional International Civil Aviation Organisation or its successor. If such notice is given, this Agreement shall terminate twelve calendar months after the date of receipt of the notice by the other Contracting Party, unless the notice to terminate is withdrawn by agreement before the expiry of this period. In the absence of acknowledgment of receipt by the other Contracting Party notice shall be deemed to have been received fourteen days after the receipt of the notice by the Provisional International Civil Aviation Organisation or its successor.

Article 14

This Agreement, including the provisions of the Annex hereto, will come into force on the day it is signed.

IN WITNESS whereof the undersigned, being duly authorized thereto by their respective Governments, have signed the present Agreement.

DONE in duplicate this eleventh day of February Nineteen-hundred-and-forty-six at Bermuda.

(a) Statement by the President (Truman) on the United States–United Kingdom Air-Transport Agreement. White House Press Release, February 26, 1946.[1]

I want to express my satisfaction with the conclusion of an air-transport agreement with the United Kingdom at Bermuda on February 11. It is now clear that very difficult problems in specialized technical areas in the relations of the two countries can be worked out separately from the over-all financial and trade negotiations which took place during the fall. Under the Bermuda agreement there will be no control of frequencies and no control of so-called "Fifth Freedom" rights on trunk routes operated primarily for through service. It gives to the airline operators the great opportunity of using their initiative and enterprise in developing air transportation over great areas of the world's surface.

Because civil aviation involves not only problems of transportation but security, sovereignty and national prestige problems as well, the joint working out of air transport agreements between nations is a most difficult one. Many countries, naturally desirous of having air transport companies of their own, and with treasuries heavily depleted by their war efforts, have a genuine fear of the type of rate war with which the history of various forms of transportation has been so full. In the Bermuda agreement the Executive branch of the United States Government has concurred in a plan for the setting-up of machinery which should

[1] Department of State, *Bulletin*, XIV, p. 399.

protect against the type of rate war feared by so many of the countries through whose air space we desire that our airlines have the right to fly. Part of the plan for future rate control will be dependent on the granting of additional powers by the Congress of the Civil Aeronautics Board.

The major purpose of the two Governments in regard to civil air transport has now been set forth in writing and it reads:

(1) That the two Governments desire to foster and encourage the widest possible distribution of the benefits of air travel for the general good of mankind at the cheapest rates consistent with sound economic principles; and to stimulate international air travel as a means of promoting friendly understanding and good will among peoples and insuring as well the many indirect benefits of this new form of transportation to the common welfare of both countries.

I believe the results of this Conference constitute a very important forward step.

(2) *Chart of Bilateral Air-Transport Agreements Concluded by the Government of the United States, July 1, 1945, to December 31, 1946.*

COUNTRY	DATE OF SIGNATURE	OFFICIAL TEXTS
Australia (B)	December 3, 1945	*Treaties and Other International Acts Series* 1574.
Belgium (B)	April 5, 1946	*Treaties and Other International Acts Series* 1515.
Brazil (B)	September 6, 1946	Department of State press release 636, September 12, 1946.
China (B)	November 29, 1946*	*Treaties and Other International Acts Series* 1609.
Czechoslovakia (C)	January 3, 1946	*Treaties and Other International Acts Series* 1560.
Denmark (C)	October 23 and December 5, 1945 and March 21, 1946†	*Treaties and Other International Acts Series* 1519.
Egypt (B)	June 15, 1946	Department of State press release 420, June 15, 1946.
France (B)	March 27, 1946	Department of State press release 196, March 26, 1946.
Greece (B)	March 27, 1946	*Treaties and Other International Acts Series* 1626.
India (B)	November 14, 1946	*Treaties and Other International Acts Series* 1586.
Iran (C)	December 17, 1945	Confidential; not released
Italy (C)	July 16, 1945	Confidential; not released
Lebanon (B)	August 11, 1946	*Treaties and Other International Acts Series* 1632.

B indicates agreement of the Bermuda type.
C indicates agreement of the Chicago type.

* The agreement with China was initialed on this date and formally signed, following translation formalities, on December 20, 1946.

† Agreement reached by exchanges of notes amending the Agreement of December 16, 1944.

Country	Date of Signature	Official Texts
New Zealand (B)	December 3, 1946	*Treaties and Other International Acts Series* 1573.
Norway (C)	October 6, 1945	*Executive Agreement Series* 482.
Peru (C)	December 27, 1946	Department of State press release 933, December 27, 1946.
Philippines (B)	November 16, 1946	*Treaties and Other International Acts Series* 1577.
Portugal (C)	December 6, 1945	*Executive Agreement Series* 500.
Saudi Arabia (C)	January 2, 1946	Confidential; not released
Switzerland (C)	August 3, 1945	*Treaties and Other International Acts Series* 1576.
Turkey (C)	February 12, 1946	*Treaties and Other International Acts Series* 1538.
United Kingdom (B)	February 11, 1946	*Treaties and Other International Acts Series* 1507.
Uruguay (B)	December 14, 1946	Department of State press release 910, December 16, 1946.

B indicates agreement of the Bermuda type.
C indicates agreement of the Chicago type.

2. MERCHANT SHIPPING

A. The United Maritime Consultative Council

In accordance with the terms of its charter,[1] the United Maritime Authority, a war-time shipping control agency established in 1944 to replace the United Nations Combined Shipping Board, was dissolved on March 2, 1946.[2] At the final meeting of the United Maritime Executive Board, held in London, February 4 to 12, 1946,[3] recommendations were drawn up for a temporary maritime agreement to provide machinery by which the shipping of relief and rehabilitation supplies might effectively be maintained. This interim machinery was to function only until October 31, 1946, in order to deal with any difficulties and problems of international shipping arising after the dissolution of the United Maritime Authority.[4] Under the terms of this temporary agreement, an interim United Maritime Consultative Council, with powers to make recommendations and to facilitate the exchange of information, was created. The interim plan, unanimously adopted by the eighteen governments members of the United Maritime Executive Board, paralleled a proposal of the Department of State which urged a joint pooling arrangement for "surplus", the contributory nations to share in the burden of carrying relief supplies under the supervision of a central coordinating body.[5]

The first session of the Consultative Council, concluded in Amsterdam on July 24, 1946,[6] reviewed the work of the Contributory Nations Committee and of the Shipping Coordinating and Review Committee and appointed a special

---

[1] For text of the Agreement on Principles Having Reference to the Coordinated Control of Merchant Shipping, the agreement by which the United Maritime Authority was constituted, see *Documents, VII, 1944–1945*, p. 630.
[2] Department of State, *Bulletin*, XIII, p. 965.
[3] *Ibid.*, XIV, p. 292.
[4] *Ibid.*, p. 487.
[5] *New York Times*, February 2, 1946, p. 5.
[6] Department of State, *Bulletin*, XV, p. 64.

TRANSPORTATION AND COMMUNICATION 673

committee to draft a report on a proposed inter-governmental organization on shipping.[1] The second session of the Council met in Washington, from October 24 to 30, 1946.[2]

(1) *Agreement Establishing the United Maritime Consultative Council, Adopted February 11, 1946, and Released to the Press March 11, 1946.*[3]

PART "A"

1. That all nations who have regularly contributed tonnage to the common tasks shall continue to provide shipping for the common tasks of relief and rehabilitation.

Arrangements for Dry Cargo From U. S. and Canadian Loading Areas

2. That a Contributory Nations Committee consisting of representatives of nations contributing tonnage to provide shipping space for relief and rehabilitation programmes from the United States and Canada shall be established in Washington.

3. That UNRRA and liberated nations requiring assistance from the Contributory Pool referred to in (4) below, shall programme their shipping requirements and submit them to the Washington Committee established in (2) above. The procedure to be followed is set out in the Appendix.

4. That at the outset of the agreement each contributory nation shall declare to the Washington Committee the maximum and minimum monthly sailings or tonnage it will contribute for the period of the agreement. The tonnage thus contributed is referred to herein as the Contributory Pool.

Arrangements for Dry Cargo From Other Loading Areas

5. That a Co-ordinating and Review Committee representative of Nations accepting Part "A" of this agreement shall be set up in London.
This Committee:

(a) shall consider U.N.R.R.A.'s requirements for loading in areas other than the United States and Canada. The nations accepting Part "A" of this agreement recognise the necessity for meeting such requirements to the best of their ability and through their representatives on the Committee shall co-ordinate the provision of tonnage they are able to make available for these programmes.

(b) shall keep the tonnage situation in loading areas other than the United States and Canada constantly under review. Recognising the necessity for an adequate supply of tonnage for loading in these areas the nations represented shall authorise the Committee to consider and recommend the measures that should be taken to assist the fulfilment of the programmes affected in the event that normal commercial channels are failing to ensure an adequate supply of tonnage.

[1] *Ibid.*, p. 65.
[2] For work of the second session, see this volume, p. 675.
[3] Department of State, *Bulletin*, XIV, p. 488.

General

6. That nations needing shipping assistance other than that secured from the Contributory Pool, shall make suitable arrangements for the procurement of tonnage through commercial channels or may request it from other nations. The nations from whom tonnage is requested shall make all reasonable efforts to make available the requested shipping space at fair, reasonable and compensatory rates, subject to the reservation that they need not supply such tonnage if it is to be used in a manner contrary to the interests of the nation upon whom the request has been made.

APPENDIX TO PART "A"

1. To maintain without interruption the maximum flow of relief and rehabilitation cargoes from the United States and Canada, a Contributory Nations' Committee shall be established in Washington as provided in (2) of Part "A."

2. With respect to loadings from Canadian ports, the Washington Committee shall collaborate with a Canadian Sub-Committee to be established in Montreal.

3. U.N.R.R.A. and each liberated Nation requiring shipping assistance for the carriage of such cargoes, shall submit to this Committee by the 1st of each month, its total programme of cargo loadings in the United States and Canada showing the number of coal, grain or other full, bulk cargoes, and the number of general cargoes programmed for loading during the following month, and estimates in the same form for the next two months. The programme for the specific month should also show the number, nationality, and total cargo capacity of vessels already available to the programming claimant for loading during that month.

4. By the 10th of each month each contributing Nation shall notify the Committee as to the amount of tonnage that it expects to have available, such tonnage to be within the maxima and minima as agreed in accordance with (4) of Part "A," and by the 15th of each month shall confirm the actual tonnage to be supplied against the following month's requirements, such tonnage to be stated separately in liner sailings and in tramps.

5. In arranging and determining the amount of tonnage to be provided under 4 of this Appendix, individual members of the Committee shall at all times communicate direct with their respective Nations, who shall, in considering requests for tonnage to load in the United States and Canada, make every effort to avoid causing a deficiency in the supply of tonnage required for other loading areas.

6. To meet each month's berthing requirements in the United States, the Committee shall allocate all of the agreed available tonnage through the established machinery of the War Shipping Administration, so that appropriate co-ordination with respect to loading facilities, inland transportation and availability of cargoes may be secured and the maximum flow of cargo for the month achieved, together with the most efficient use of the shipping available.

Part "B"

7. That:

(A) accepting Governments should meet periodically for discussions in a United Maritime Consultative Council for the purpose of exchanging information to the end that individual governments may be enabled to frame their own policies in the post-UMA period in the light of the knowledge of the policies of other governments.

(B) the Council may undertake the consideration and study, for the purpose of making appropriate recommendations to member governments, of any problems in the international shipping field, which may be referred to it and which do not come within the terms of reference of other established governmental conferences or associations active in the field.

(C) it is the intention that the shipping industry should collaborate and assist in devising ways and means to implement the common objectives stated in (A) and (B).

(D) meetings of the Council should be held at such times and places as the Council may determine. A chairman for each meeting should be designated by the Government of the nation where such meeting is to be held. The Council should determine its own procedure.

(E) the United Maritime Consultative Council should have no executive powers.

(F) this part of the agreement should be open for acceptance by governments whether or not they accept Part "A".

Part "C"

8. That the arrangements in Part "A" and "B" shall remain in effect from 3rd March until 31st October, 1946, unless by unanimous consent of the Governments accepting the respective Parts it is decided to terminate them at an earlier date.

9. That Governments accepting the recommendations in Part "A" and/or Part "B" shall notify their acceptance to the U. S. and U. K. Governments at the earliest possible date and that, as between the Governments notifying their acceptance, the relevant recommendations shall be regarded as an agreement for the period stated in recommendation 8.

10. That other Governments requesting information should be informed of these recommendations to the end that they may participate, if they so desire, by notifying their acceptance of Part "A" and/or Part "B", in accordance with recommendation 9.

B. The Inter-Governmental Maritime Consultative Organization

The United Maritime Consultative Council [1] met for its second session in Washington, October 24 to 30, 1946, for consideration of the following topics: (1) the draft plan and report of a special committee, appointed at its first session in Amsterdam, to explore the possibilities of a world-wide inter-governmental maritime organization; (2) a reply to an inquiry from the United Nations concerning the establishment of such an organization to deal with technical matters in the realm of international shipping; (3) a review of the work of the Council

[1] See this volume, p. 672.

toward the orderly transportation of relief and rehabilitation supplies; and (4) a review of the progress made in the restoration of the normal processes of international shipping.[1] Out of the work of the second session of the Council came a series of Recommendations to Member Governments.[2] The Council urged the formation of an Inter-Governmental Maritime Consultative Council "as a permanent agency in the shipping field" and submitted to the Governments, members of the UMCC, a Draft Convention for the establishment of such an agency. In addition the Council recommended the creation of a Provisional Maritime Consultative Council to function after October 31, 1946, the date on which, by the terms of the temporary agreement establishing the UMCC, the UMCC would cease to exist. To this end, the Council submitted a second Draft Agreement. On November 21, 1946, the United States Government announced its acceptance of membership in the Provisional Council pending the further consideration of the remainder of the recommendations of the UMCC.[3]

(1) Recommendations of the United Maritime Consultative Council to Member Governments, Adopted October 30, 1946.[4]

The United Maritime Consultative Council during its second and final Session, being unanimously of the opinion that an Inter-Governmental Maritime Consultative Organization is required as a permanent agency in the shipping field, recommends to the Member Governments that —

(1) an Inter-Governmental Maritime Consultative Organization should be established as a specialized agency of the United Nations, as set forth in the draft convention for an Inter-Governmental Maritime Consultative Organization annexed hereto;

(2) each Member Government take appropriate action in requesting the Economic and Social Council to convene a conference of all interested governments for the purpose of adopting a constitution for an Inter-Governmental Maritime Consultative Organization as set forth in the annexed draft convention;

(3) in view of the fact that the United Maritime Consultative Council will cease to exist on October 31, 1946, a Provisional Maritime Consultative Council should be set up forthwith in accordance with the annexed Agreement for the establishment of a Provisional Maritime Consultative Council;

(4) government members of the United Maritime Consultative Council should accept as soon as possible the Agreement for a Provisional Maritime Consultative Council by notification to the government of the United Kingdom in accordance with Article V (1) thereof.

(a) Agreement Establishing the Provisional Maritime Consultative Council.[5]

ARTICLE I. SCOPE AND PURPOSES

The Provisional Maritime Consultative Council shall be established as a temporary organization pending the establishment of a permanent intergovernmental agency in the maritime field —

[1] Department of State, *Bulletin*, XV, p. 631.
[2] See below.
[3] Department of State, *Bulletin*, XV, p. 1002.
[4] *Ibid.*, p. 1094.
[5] *Ibid.*, p. 1098.

i. to provide machinery for cooperation among Governments in the field of Governmental regulation and practices relating to technical matters of all kinds affecting shipping engaged in international trade, and to encourage the general adoption of the highest practicable standards in matters concerning maritime safety and efficiency of navigation;

ii. to encourage the removal of all forms of discriminatory action and unnecessary restrictions by Governments affecting shipping engaged in international trade so as to promote the availability of shipping services to the commerce of the world without discrimination;

iii. to provide for the consideration by the Council of any shipping problems of an international character involving matters of general principle that may be referred to the Council by the United Nations. Matters which are suitable for settlement through the normal processes of international shipping business are not within the scope of the Council.

iv. to provide for the exchange of information among Governments on matters under consideration by the Council.

Article II. Functions

The functions of the Provisional Maritime Consultative Council, which shall be consultative and advisory, shall be —

(*a*) To consider and make recommendations on any matter within its scope as set forth in Sections (*i*) and (*ii*) of Article I.

(*b*) To consider and make recommendations on matters within its scope upon the request of any organ of the United Nations or other intergovernmental specialized agency.

(*c*) To advise on matters relating to the draft constitution for a permanent intergovernmental maritime organization.

Article III. Membership

Membership in the Council shall consist of those governments which notify the Government of the United Kingdom of their acceptance of this Agreement, being either governments members of the UMCC or governments members of the United Nations.

Article IV. Organization

(1) The Council shall consist of all Member Governments.

(2) The Council may elect an Executive Committee consisting of twelve member governments which shall exercise such functions as may be delegated to it by the Council. The Executive Committee shall not be established by the Council until at least twenty governments have accepted this agreement.

(3) The Council shall at each session determine the host government and the time for its next meeting. Upon the request of not less than four of the members the Chairman shall summon the Council for an earlier date. The Government of ——————— shall convene the first meeting of the Council at any time after March 1, 1947.

(4) The host Government arranged for each session shall designate a Chairman who shall hold office until the host Government for the next

following session has been decided, and shall provide the necessary secretariat for meetings held within its territory.

(5) Decisions of the Council shall be taken by a majority of those present and voting. Ten Members shall constitute a quorum. The Council shall otherwise determine its own rules of procedure.

ARTICLE V. ENTRY INTO FORCE

(1) This agreement shall remain open for acceptance in the archives of the Government of the United Kingdom and shall enter into force when twelve Governments, of which five shall each have a total tonnage of not less than 1,000,000 g. t. of shipping have accepted it.

(2) As soon as this agreement has come into force, a copy of the agreement together with the names of the Governments who have accepted it shall be sent by the Government of the United Kingdom to the Secretary-General of the United Nations for registration in accordance with Article 102 of the Charter of the United Nations.

ARTICLE VI. TERMINATION

This agreement shall cease to have effect upon the entry into force of a constitution for a permanent intergovernment maritime organization or if the membership falls below twelve. A member government may withdraw at any time upon six months' notice to the Government of the United Kingdom.

C. The International Labor Conference, Twenty-eighth (Maritime) Session, Seattle, Washington, June 6 to 29, 1946

Delegates representing the governments, employers and workers of twenty maritime nations, including the United States, met at Copenhagen, Denmark, in November and December of 1945 to hold preparatory discussions upon maritime problems of a social nature and to make necessary technical preparations for the further consideration of these problems at the Twenty-eighth Session of the International Labor Conference, called at Seattle, Washington, in June of 1946.[1] The Conference, attended by thirty-two of the Member States of the International Labor Organization, dealt with a nine-item agenda which had been fixed by the Governing Body of the International Labor Office and reviewed reports prepared upon the basis of the recommendations of the Copenhagen Conference.[2] The items of the agenda included such topics as social security for seafarers; crew accommodations on board ship; food and catering on board ship; entry, training and promotion of seafarers; holidays with pay for seafarers; continuous employment for seafarers; recognition of seafarers' organizations; and wages, hours of work and manning.[3] On the recommendation of the various committees, the Conference adopted nine International Labor Conventions, four recommendations and nine resolutions. In adopting a Convention on Wages, Hours and Manning, the Conference established a precedent by setting, for the first time, an international minimum wage standard.[4] The following Conventions were adopted by the Conference: (1) Convention concerning Food

[1] *Ibid.*, XIII, p. 969.
[2] *Memorandum on the International Labor Conference, 28th (Maritime) Session, Seattle, Washington, June 6–29, 1946* (International Labor Office, Montreal, 1946).
[3] *Ibid.*
[4] *Ibid.*

and Catering for Crews on Board Ship; (2) Convention concerning the Certification of Ships' Cooks; (3) Convention concerning the Medical Examination of Seafarers; (4) Convention concerning Vacation Holidays with Pay for Seafarers; (5) Convention concerning Crew Accommodation on Board Ship; (6) Convention concerning Social Security for Seafarers; (7) Convention concerning the Certification of Able Seamen; (8) Convention concerning Seafarers' Pensions; and (9) Convention concerning Wages, Hours of Work on Board Ship and Manning.[1]

3. INLAND TRANSPORT

[For information concerning the internationalization of the Danube River, see *The First Five Peace Treaties. Supplement: Documents, VIII, 1945–1946.*]

A. The European Central Inland Transport Organization

(1) *Agreement Concerning the Establishment of a European Central Inland Transport Organization, Signed at London, September 27, 1945.*[2]

WHEREAS, upon the liberation of the territories of the United Nations in Europe, and upon the occupation of the territories of the enemy in Europe, it is expedient for the fulfilment of the common military needs of the United Nations and in the interest of the social and economic progress of Europe, to provide for co-ordination both in the movement of traffic and in the allocation of transport equipment and material with a view to ensuring the best possible movement of supplies both for military forces and the civil population and the speedy repatriation of displaced persons, and also with a view to creating conditions in which the normal movement of traffic can be more rapidly resumed;

The Governments whose duly authorised representatives have signed the present Agreement

Have agreed as follows:—

ARTICLE I

There is hereby established the European Central Inland Transport Organisation, hereinafter called "the Organisation," which shall act in accordance with the provisions of the following Articles. The Organisation is established as a co-ordinating and consultative organ. Having regard to the successful completion of the war, it shall co-ordinate efforts to utilise all means of transport for the improvement of communications so as to provide for the restoration of normal conditions of economic life. It shall also provide assistance to the Allied Commanders-in-Chief and to the Occupation Authorities set up by Governments of the United Nations to maintain and improve the carrying capacity of transport.

ARTICLE II. MEMBERSHIP

The members of the Organisation shall be the Governments signatory hereto and such other Governments as may be admitted thereto by the Council.

[1] *Ibid.*   [2] Department of State, *Executive Agreement Series* 494.

Article III. Constitution

1. The Organisation shall consist of a Council and an Executive Board with the necessary headquarters, regional and local staff. The Organisation shall concert arrangements for the establishment of regional and local offices with the Member Governments in whose territory the offices are situated and/or in appropriate cases in agreement with the Allied Commander-in-Chief concerned.

The Council.

2. Each member Government shall name one representative and such alternates as may be necessary upon the Council. The Council shall, for each of its sessions, select one of its members to preside. The Council shall determine its own rules of procedure. Unless otherwise provided in this Agreement or by action of the Council, the Council shall vote by simple majority.

3. The Council shall be convened in regular session not less than twice a year by the Executive Board. It may be convened in special session whenever the Executive Board shall deem necessary and shall be convened within thirty days after request by one-third of the members of the Council.

4. The Council shall perform the functions assigned to it under this Agreement and review the work of the Organisation generally to ensure its conformity with the broad policies determined by the Council.

The Executive Board.

5. The Executive Board shall consist of seven members who shall be appointed by the Council. These seven members shall include one member nominated by each of the following Governments: the Provisional Government of the French Republic and the Governments of the Union of Soviet Socialist Republics, the United Kingdom of Great Britain and Northern Ireland and the United States of America. Each member of the Executive Board shall be provided with an alternate similarly selected, who shall act only in the absence of the member of the Executive for whom he is the alternate. The members and their alternates shall be appointed for not longer than one year. The Executive Board shall choose its own Chairman, subject to confirmation by the Council.

6. The Executive Board shall perform the executive functions assigned to the Organisation within the framework of the broad policies determined by the Council. It shall act in accordance with the ruling of the majority of its members. It shall present to the Council such reports on the performance of its functions as the Council may require.

7. The Executive Board shall appoint a chief officer who shall direct under its supervision the technical and administrative work of the Organisation in conformity with the policies of the Council and the Executive Board as determined by their decisions. This officer shall appoint the staff at headquarters and at regional and local offices, subject to the approval of the Executive Board, taking into account the exigencies of

the various branches of transport concerned. The responsibilities of the chief officer and staff shall be exclusively international in character.

8. Each member Government shall appoint one or more representatives for the purpose of consultation and communication with the Executive Board, and with the Chief Officer. Such representatives shall be fully informed by the Board and by the Chief Officer of all activities of the Organisation. Each time that any important question concerning the interests of a member Government is discussed by the Board, the representatives of that Government shall be entitled to take part in the discussions without the right of vote.

Article IV.

1. The Organisation shall have the capacity to perform any legal act appropriate to its object and purposes, including the power to acquire, hold and convey property, to enter into contracts and undertake obligations, to designate or create subordinate organs and to review their activity. The Organisation shall not, however, have power to own transport equipment and material other than for its own internal or demonstration purposes, except with the unanimous consent of the Council.

2. These powers are vested in the Council. Subject to the provisions of paragraph 2 of Article V, the Council may delegate such of these powers as it may deem necessary to the Executive Board, including the power of subdelegation. The Executive Board shall be responsible to the Council for the upkeep and administration of any property owned by the Organisation.

Article V. Finance

1. The Executive Board shall submit to the Council an initial budget and from time to time such supplementary budgets as may be required, covering the administrative expenses of the Organisation. Upon approval of a budget by the Council, the total amount approved shall be raised in such manner, or be allocated between member Governments in such proportions, as these Governments may agree. Each member Government undertakes, subject to the requirements of its constitutional procedure, promptly to contribute to the Organisation, in such currency or currencies as may be agreed by such Government with the Executive Board, its share of these expenses. Each member Government shall also provide such facilities as are required for the transfer into other currencies of sums so contributed and held by the Organisation in that Government's own currency.

2. The Organisation shall not incur any expenses, other than administrative expenses, except under authority of the Council. Proposals for such expenses shall be submitted by the Executive Board to the Council and, when approved by the Council, such expenses shall be met by contributions which one or more member Governments may agree to make or in such other manner as may be agreed between member Governments. However, the obligation of transfer into foreign currencies, as defined in paragraph 1 of this Article, does not apply to these contributions.

3. Nothing in this Agreement shall require any member Government or transport administration under its authority to perform services without remuneration.

Article VI. Scope of the Organisation

1. The Organisation shall, after giving notice of its intention, exercise its functions in any territory in Continental Europe, upon the acceptance of this Agreement by the Government of that territory and/or, in appropriate cases, provided that the Allied Commander-in-Chief concerned is satisfied that military exigencies permit and subject to such conditions as he may deem necessary.

2. In respect of any territory in Continental Europe in which any Allied Commander-in-Chief retains responsibility for the direction of the transport system, the Organisation shall on request give advice or assistance to the Allied Commander-in-Chief, and, in consultation with him, to any member Government or to other appropriate authorities of the United Nations, on any question with which it is empowered to deal under Article VII.

3. The Organisation shall treat with any of the Occupation Authorities set up by Governments of the United Nations in respect of any territory in Continental Europe in which such Occupation Authorities are exercising authority.

Article VII. Executive Functions of the Organisation

Introductory.

1. The Organisation shall carry out thorough studies of the technical and economic conditions affecting traffic of an international character and shall give to the Governments concerned with such traffic technical advice and recommendations directed to restoring and increasing the carrying capacity of the transport systems in Continental Europe and to co-ordinating the movement of traffic of common concern on these systems.

2. In case any member Government meets with difficulties in carrying out these recommendations owing to reasons of a material or economic character, the Organisation shall investigate with member Governments concerned means of practical help.

Information on Transport Equipment and Material.

3. The Organisation shall receive and collect information concerning the requirements of transport equipment and material for Continental Europe.

Realisation of Requirements for Transport Equipment and Material.

4. The Organisation shall assist the realisation of requirements of any member Government in Continental Europe for transport equipment and material.

Allocation and Distribution for Use of Transport Equipment and Material.

5. The Organisation shall, within the framework of the priorities determined by the appropriate authorities of the United Nations, determine the allocation, or distribution for use, to Governments in Continental Europe, on such conditions as it may deem necessary, of such transport equipment and material as may be made available for this purpose by the Allied Commanders-in-Chief, by Occupation Authorities, or by agencies of any one or more of the United Nations. To enable the Organisation to carry out this function effectively, it may consult with the Governments concerned on their export possibilities of, and import needs of, transport equipment and material for Continental Europe and will receive from such Governments notification of all arrangements made in respect thereto of which they have notice.

Arrangements to Make Mobile Transport Equipment and Material Available.

6. In cases where temporary emergency requirements of mobile transport equipment for carrying traffic of common concern arise and the usual arrangements for the interchange of such mobile transport equipment are inadequate, the Organisation shall arrange with member Governments concerned to make available mobile transport equipment for the purpose of meeting such requirements. Such mobile transport equipment shall be made available under arrangements made between the member Governments concerned, with the assistance of the Organisation.

Census of Transport Equipment and Material.

7. The Organisation shall at the earliest practicable time arrange through the member Governments for a census of rolling-stock in Continental Europe and of such other transport equipment and material there as may appear necessary for the proper discharge of its functions.

Identification and Restoration of Transport Equipment and Material.

8. The Organisation shall arrange, as soon as practicable, to restore to any member Government transport equipment and material belonging to it or to its nationals, found outside the territories under its authority and outside its control. Should any difficulties of identification arise, the Organisation shall arrange immediately for such special measures to be taken as may be necessary to meet them. Where such restoration would unduly prejudice the operation of essential transport, the Organisation shall work out agreements with the Governments concerned for the temporary use of transport equipment pending its restoration. The arrangements for restoration shall be made on the basis of the ownership of the property which existed before any territorial changes in Europe, resulting from Axis policy, and in accordance with any general policies which may be determined by the appropriate authorities of the United Nations regarding restoration and restitution of the property removed by the enemy.

Traffic.

9. The Organisation may make such recommendations to the appropriate authorities as it deems necessary with respect to the method of carrying out projected movements of traffic of common concern, having regard to the transport facilities available for the movement of such traffic.

10. The Organisation shall make recommendations to the Governments concerned in order to ensure the movement of traffic of common concern on all routes of transport in Continental Europe in accordance with the priorities determined by the appropriate authorities of the United Nations. In respect of traffic of military importance sponsored by the Allied Commanders-in-Chief, the appropriate authority for this purpose will be the Allied Commander-in-Chief concerned.

Charges.

11. The Organisation may work out the unification of tariffs, terms and conditions of transport and the like, applicable to traffic of an international character. It shall recommend to the Governments concerned the principles by which reasonable transport charges for traffic of common concern in Continental Europe should be fixed by them in accordance with the provisions of paragraph 9 of Article VIII. This paragraph shall not apply to military traffic under the control of any Allied Commander-in-Chief except at his request.

Rehabilitation of Transport Systems.

12. The Organisation may study the conditions of transport affecting traffic of an international character in individual countries and make recommendations to the Governments concerned as to technical measures directed to the quickest restoration of transport facilities and their most effective use, and as to the priority in which works or projects in respect of the restoration or improvement of transport facilities shall be carried out.

Operation of Transport.

13. While it remains the task of each member Government to provide for the efficient operation of the transport systems in Continental Europe for which it is responsible, the Organisation may exceptionally, at the request of any member Government, give any assistance in its power in the rehabilitation or operation of transport in any territory in Continental Europe under the authority of such Government on such conditions as may be agreed between it and the Organisation, having due regard to the rights of other member Governments.

Co-ordination of European Transport.

14. The Organisation shall work out and co-ordinate common action to secure the inauguration, maintenance, modification, resumption or, where appropriate, suppression, of international arrangements for

through working of railways and exchange of rolling-stock of the Continental European countries for carrying out international transport. In particular, it shall ensure a unified clearing system for traffic operations between the different countries in Continental Europe. In general, it shall promote where necessary the establishment of appropriate machinery for co-operation between railway administrations.

15. The Organisation shall place its services at the disposal of member Governments and make recommendations with a view to ensuring the most efficient movement of international traffic on waterways. It shall not, however, make recommendations with regard to questions concerning the régimes of the international inland waterways of Continental Europe.

16. The Organisation shall take through the Governments concerned such steps as may be practicable to facilitate international traffic of common concern in lorries and other road vehicles and the co-ordination of road and other means of transport with a view to ensuring the movement of international traffic.

17. In carrying out the functions mentioned in paragraphs 14 and 16 of this Article and in placing its services at the disposal of member Governments as described in paragraph 15 of this Article, the Organisation shall make use, to the extent practicable, of conventions in force between member Governments so as to obtain the greatest benefit therefrom for the fulfilment of this task, provided that the Organisation shall act —
   (a) in accordance with any general policies which may be determined by the appropriate authorities of the United Nations; and
   (b) with due respect for existing rights and obligations.

18. The Organisation shall make recommendations to the Governments concerned designed to promote adequate co-ordination of all European transport for the fulfilment of the common military needs of the United Nations or in the interests of traffic of an international character.

Relations with Other Agencies.

19. The Organisation shall co-operate as may be required with the appropriate authorities and agencies of any one or more of the United Nations and with international organisations.

20. The Organisation shall provide all possible assistance to the Allied Commanders-in-Chief in meeting their needs for transport facilities and improving the use of these facilities for the successful fulfilment of military requirements.

21. The Organisation shall arrange for consultation, through appropriate machinery, with representatives of persons employed in inland transport on international questions of mutual concern to the Organisation and such representatives within the field of the Organisation's activities.

Miscellaneous.

22. The Organisation may advise the Governments concerned and the appropriate authorities of the United Nations on the priority to be

given, in the interests of the rehabilitation of European transport, to the repatriation of displaced transport personnel and to workers required for the production, maintenance or repair of transport equipment and material.

23. The Organisation shall give all practicable assistance through the appropriate authorities to any member Government at its request in obtaining supplies of fuel, power, and lubricants to meet the needs of traffic of common concern, in order that that Government may fulfil its obligations under paragraph 7 of Article VIII.

Article VIII. Obligations of Member Governments

Information.

1. Every member Government, in respect of any territory which is under its authority and in the field of activity of the Organisation, shall, upon request of the Organisation, provide it with such information as is essential for the performance of its functions.

Census of Transport Equipment and Material.

2. Every member Government undertakes to co-operate fully with the Organisation in arranging any census for which provision is made in paragraph 7 of Article VII.

Identification and Restoration of Transport Equipment and Material.

3. Every member Government, in respect of any territory which is under its authority and in the field of activity of the Organisation, undertakes that —
    (*i*) It will facilitate the execution of paragraph 8 of Article VII.
    (*ii*) It will not seize: —
        (*a*) transport equipment and material in Continental Europe found outside the territories under its authority, even though such equipment and material may belong to it or to any of its nationals;
        (*b*) transport equipment and material found within territory under its authority but not belonging to it or any of its nationals;
        (*c*) transport equipment and material coming within territory under its authority as the result of arrangements made under the auspices of the Organisation for the movement of traffic of common concern;
provided, however: —
        (*i*) that every member Government shall be permitted to use equipment defined under (*b*) and (*c*) above subject to the provisions of paragraphs 5 and 8 of Article VII and, in the case of enemy or ex-enemy transport equipment and material, without prejudice to its ultimate disposal by the appropriate authorities of the United Nations; and

(ii) that nothing in this paragraph shall debar any member Government or any of its nationals from continuing the management of its or his own inland vessels.

4. The provisions of paragraph 3 of this Article shall not affect the rights of the Allied Commanders-in-Chief within any territory in respect of which the Organisation has not begun to exercise its functions under Article VII.

Traffic.

5. Every member Government undertakes to ensure by any means in its power the best possible movement of traffic of common concern in accordance with the recommendations made by the Organisation under paragraph 10 of Article VII.

6. Every member Government undertakes to provide inland vessels under its control in Continental Europe required for traffic of common concern,
   (i) in accordance with the recommendations of the Organisation generally, and
   (ii) if signatory to the Annex to this Agreement, in accordance with its terms.

Provision of Fuel, Power and Lubricants.

7. Every member Government shall take all measures necessary and practicable to ensure, in respect of the territory in Continental Europe under its authority, that adequate supplies of fuel, power and lubricants are available for traffic of common concern, provided that the Organisation has made suitable arrangements with the Government concerned.

Charges.

8. Every member Government undertakes not to levy or permit the levy of customs duties or other charges, other than transport charges, and admissible transit charges on traffic of common concern in transit through territories in Continental Europe under its authority. No discrimination shall be made in respect of import duties levied on goods of common concern, dependent on the route the goods have travelled prior to importation into the country concerned.

9. Every member Government undertakes to secure that transport charges made within territories in Continental Europe under its authority on traffic of common concern, including such traffic in transit through such territories, shall be as low and simple and as uniform with those in other territories, to which this Agreement applies, as is practicable. Every member Government shall give the fullest consideration to recommendations made by the Organisation in accordance with paragraph 11 of Article VII and report to the Organisation on the action taken.

Miscellaneous.

10. Every member Government undertakes to co-operate with the Organisation in the exercise of its functions under paragraphs 14 and 16 of Article VII.

11. Every member Government shall use its best endeavours in its relations with any other international organisations, agencies or authorities to give effect to the provisions of this Agreement.

12. Every member Government shall give the fullest consideration to any recommendations made by the Organisation in accordance with paragraphs 12, 15 and 18 of Article VII and report to the Organisation on the action taken.

13. Every member Government shall recognise the international personality and legal capacity which the Organisation possesses.

14. Every member Government shall respect the exclusively international character of the members of the Executive Board, the Chief Officer and the staff of the Organisation.

15. Every member Government shall accord to the Organisation the privileges, immunities and facilities which they grant to each other, including in particular —
   (a) immunity from every form of legal process;
   (b) exemption from taxation and customs duties; and
   (c) inviolability of premises occupied by, and of the archives and communications of the Organisation.

16. Every member Government shall accord diplomatic privileges and immunities to persons appointed by other members as their representatives in or to the Organisation, to the members of the Executive Board, and to the higher officials of the Organisation not being their own nationals.

17. Every member Government shall accord to all officials and employees of the Organisation —
   (a) immunity from suit and legal process relating to acts performed by them in their official capacity;
   (b) all such facilities for their movement, and for the execution of their functions, as are deemed necessary by the Organisation for the speedy and effective fulfilment of their official duties; and
   (c) except in the case of their own nationals, exemption from taxation of their official salaries and emoluments.

18. Every member Government shall in territory under its authority take all steps in its power to facilitate the exercise by the Organisation of any of the powers referred to in Article IV.

Article IX.

The Organisation shall be related to any general international organisation to which may be entrusted the co-ordination of the activities of international organisations with specialised responsibilities.

Article X.

1. The functions of the Organisation shall relate to all forms of transport by road, rail or waterway, within the territories of the Continent of Europe in which the Organisation operates, but not to sea-going shipping, except that the provisions of paragraph 10 of Article VII and paragraph

5 of Article VIII shall apply in respect of such shipping when employed in Continental Europe on inland waterways.

2. In regard to the handling of traffic in ports where sea-going vessels are discharged or loaded, the Organisation shall co-operate with the appropriate authorities of the member Government concerned and any shipping organisation set up by them to ensure —
- (*i*) the rapid turn-round of ships;
- (*ii*) the efficient use of port facilities in the best interests of the prompt clearance of cargo of common concern.

Article XI.

In the event of there being any direct inconsistency between the provisions of this Agreement and the provisions of any agreement already existing between any of the member Governments, the provisions of this Agreement shall, as between such member Governments, be deemed to prevail, due respect being had to the provisions of paragraph 17 of Article VII, provided, however, that nothing in this Article shall be construed to prevent member Governments from entering into agreements to facilitate the working of traffic across national frontiers.

Article XII. Definitions

1. For the purpose of this Agreement and its Annex, the definitions given in this Article have been adopted.

2. The term "inland transport" shall include all forms of transport as referred to in Article X of this Agreement.

3. The term "Continental Europe" shall mean all territories in Europe under the authority or control of member Governments, but shall not extend to territory of the United Kingdom or of the Union of Soviet Socialist Republics.

4. The term "territory under the authority of a member Government" shall be construed to mean territory in Continental Europe either under the sovereignty of a member Government or territory over which a member Government or member Governments is or are exercising authority or control.

5. The term "transport equipment and material" shall include, so far as the Executive Board deems it necessary for the execution of the functions of the Organisation:—
- (*i*) any items of fixed and mobile equipment, stores (other than fuel), plant and spares and accessories of all kinds specifically intended and required for use of transport undertakings, including equipment required for use in ports, whether ashore or afloat;
- (*ii*) equipment and material specifically intended and required for the rehabilitation, maintenance or construction of roads, railways, bridges, ports and inland waterways;
- (*iii*) major plant and tools specifically required for the repair of transport equipment and material for use by transport authorities.

6. The term "traffic of common concern" shall include —
   (i) personnel, stores, supplies or other traffic to be moved in accordance with the requirements of the Allied Commanders-in-Chief;
   (ii) displaced and other persons to be moved in accordance with the priorities determined by the appropriate United Nations authorities;
   (iii) supplies for civil needs to be moved in Continental Europe in accordance with the priorities determined by the appropriate United Nations authorities;
   (iv) property removed by the enemy.

7. The term "transport charges" shall include, in addition to freight or conveyance charges, any other incidental charges, such as tolls, port charges, charges for warehousing and handling goods in transit which may affect the cost of transport.

8. The term "admissible transit charges" means dues intended solely to defray expenses of supervision and administration entailed by the transit traffic concerned.

9. The term "Allied Commander-in-Chief" shall mean any Commander-in-Chief designated for commands on the Continent of Europe by the appropriate authorities of any of the following:—

The French Republic
The Union of Soviet Socialist Republics
The United Kingdom of Great Britain and Northern Ireland
The United States of America.

10. The term "Government" includes any Provisional Government.

Article XIII.

Until the expiry of the period of two years from this day's date, the provisions of this Agreement may be amended, suspended or terminated only by a unanimous vote of the Council. At any time after that date any provision of this Agreement may be amended, suspended or terminated by a two-thirds majority of the Council, provided that no alteration shall be made in the provisions of this Agreement so as to extend the obligations or financial liability of any member Government without that Government's consent.

Article XIV.

1. This Agreement shall come into force for each member Government on the date of signature on its behalf or of its admission to the Organisation under Article II.

2. It shall remain in force for two years from this day's date. It shall thereafter remain in force, subject to the right of any member Government, after the expiry of eighteen months from this day's date, to give six months' notice in writing to the Council of its intention to withdraw from this Agreement.

In witness whereof the undersigned, duly authorised by their respective Governments, have signed the present Agreement.

Done in London on the 27th day of September, 1945, in English, French and Russian, all three texts being equally authentic, in a single copy which shall be deposited in the archives of the Government of the United Kingdom of Great Britain and Northern Ireland, by whom certified copies shall be transmitted to all Signatory Governments.

(2) *Protocol Relating to Traffic on Inland Waterways, Signed at London, September 27, 1945.*[1]

PREAMBLE.

With a view to fulfilling, in respect to traffic on inland waterways, the obligations assumed by the member Governments under the Agreement concerning the establishment of an European Central Inland Transport Organisation (hereinafter referred to as the Agreement), and subject to the conditions set out therein, the Governments signatory hereto have agreed as follows:—

ARTICLE I.

Every Government signatory hereto undertakes to establish appropriate machinery necessary for the application of all the obligations assumed in paragraphs 5 and 6 of Article VIII of the Agreement to traffic on Inland Waterways and to appoint persons or organisations entitled to treat with the Organisation on questions of this nature.

ARTICLE II.

The Governments signatory hereto, taking into account the geographical, technical and other peculiarities connected with traffic on inland waterways and the needs of each of them in these respects, will nominate experts to be consulted by the Organisation on questions of traffic on inland waterways within the various areas of such traffic.

ARTICLE III.

For each waterways traffic area in Continental Europe, the allocation of inland shipping and, if necessary, shipping space for carrying traffic of common concern in accordance with approved programmes will be determined from time to time by the Organisation in agreement with the Governments concerned. In determining this allocation, due account shall be taken of the particulars of the vessel, its equipment and crew and of its normal traffic.

ARTICLE IV.

The terms of remuneration to be paid by the users of inland vessels for traffic of common concern shall be worked out by the Organisation in agreement with the Governments and/or the authorities concerned on a

[1] *Ibid.*

fair and reasonable basis in such a manner as to give effect to the following two principles:

(i) inland vessels of all flags performing the same services should receive the same freights;

(ii) freights with reference to paragraph 11 of Article VII shall be calculated so as to include, after providing for depreciation of the ship, a reasonable margin of profit.

ARTICLE V.

1. This Protocol shall remain open for signature in London on behalf of any member Government of the European Central Inland Transport Organisation.

2. This Protocol shall come into force for each Government signatory thereto as from the date of signature on its behalf. Any Government when signing the present Protocol may declare that its signature shall not become effective until this Protocol has been signed by certain other specified Governments.

3. This protocol shall remain in force for two years from this day's date. It shall thereafter remain in force subject to the right of any signatory Government, after the expiry of eighteen months from this day's date, to give six months' notice in writing to the Council of the European Central Inland Transport Organisation of its intention to withdraw from this Protocol.

In witness whereof the undersigned, duly authorised by their respective Governments, have signed the present Protocol.

Done in London on the 27th day of September, 1945, in English, French and Russian, all three texts being equally authentic in a single copy which shall be deposited in the archives of the Government of the United Kingdom of Great Britain and Northern Ireland, by whom certified copies shall be transmitted to all signatory Governments.

4. INTERNATIONAL TELECOMMUNICATIONS

During the period under review, the United States, through the Department of State, participated in a series of inter-governmental conferences designed to set the broad pattern of post-war telecommunications. The first of the conferences was the Third Inter-American Radio Conference which convened at Rio de Janeiro on September 3, 1945.[1] The Inter-American Arrangement Concerning Telecommunications, resulting from the Habana Inter-American Radio Conference of 1937,[2] and subsequently revised at Santiago, Chile, by the Second Inter-American Radio Conference in 1940, provided the ground-work for the Rio de Janeiro meeting. A revision of the Habana Convention submitted by the United States delegation, headed by Adolf A. Berle Jr., the United States Ambassador to Brazil, was accepted as the basis of the Final Act of the Conference. On September 27, 1945,[3] a Convention on Telecommunications was signed *ad referendum*. In addition to establishing an Office of Inter-American Telecommunications, the Convention enumerated agreed principles regarding radio frequencies, rates and arbitration procedures, and resolved that free interchange of information be maintained throughout the Hemisphere.[4]

[1] Department of State, *Bulletin*, XIII, p. 292.
[2] *Ibid.*; for text, see Department of State, *Treaty Series* 938.
[3] Department of State, *Bulletin*, XIII, p. 735. [4] *Ibid.*

On October 20, 1945,[1] the United States Government announced its acceptance of an invitation of the British Government to participate in an Empire-Wide Telecommunications Conference to be held in Bermuda, simultaneously with the Anglo-American Economic and Financial Conversations.[2] The Conference, to which the United States delegation was headed by Assistant Secretary of State James C. Dunn,[3] convened at Bermuda on November 21, 1945. Successful agreement was reached after ten days of negotiations.[4] The United States traditionally had advocated two objectives in the field of international telecommunications: (1) direct radio-telegraph circuits to foreign countries and (2) uniformly low rates for private telecommunications companies.[5] Prior to World War II, commitments of the British Commonwealth toward Cable and Wireless, Ltd., prevented the achievement of these American objectives so far as the Commonwealth was concerned, although during the war direct circuit rights were granted to the United States by the United Kingdom, Australia, New Zealand, and India.[6] Failing a permanent post-war understanding, however, termination of these war-time agreements meant a return to the pre-war system which routed messages for Asia and Africa through London. At Bermuda, accord was reached on both direct circuits and rates. The basis for a world-wide agreement, pending an anticipated international telecommunications conference, was strengthened at Bermuda; and the principle of freedom of information, adopted at Rio de Janeiro, was accepted by the British.[7]

The Second North American Regional Broadcasting Engineering Conference met in Washington from February 4 to 25, 1946, to draft an interim agreement which would extend, with some modifications, the expiring North American Regional Broadcasting Agreement of December 13, 1937. The Conference, attended by representatives of Canada, Cuba, the Dominican Republic, Mexico, the United States, and the United Kingdom in respect of the Bahamas and Newfoundland, was concerned with standard-band broadcasting and designated a three-year interim period during which scheduled preparations for the negotiation of a new Convention might be commenced.

On August 14, 1946, the United States announced its acceptance of an invitation from the Soviet Government to attend a five-power telecommunications conference in Moscow, scheduled for August 28. This Conference was planned as a preliminary to a World Plenipotentiary Telecommunications Conference to be held about April 1947. The United States, with the concurrence of Great Britain and France, requested and was granted a postponement of the Conference until after the middle of September, in order to prepare its delegation, to be headed by Francis Colt de Wolf, Chief of the Telecommunications Division of the Department of State, for departure.[8] Accordingly, delegations of the United States, the Union of Soviet Socialist Republics, Great Britain, France and China, assembled in Moscow on September 28, 1946, to consider a proposed agenda which included: (1) the time and place for convening the World Telecommunications Conference; (2) the question of provisional registration of frequencies until the entry into force of a new convention and new regulations pertaining thereto; (3) the consideration of fundamental problems of the revision of the telecommunications convention and regulations, including (a) the strengthening of the International Telecommunications Union, (b) the distribution of frequencies, (c) the strengthening of control regulations with regard to the distribution of frequencies, and (d) the possibility of a speedy entry into operation of an administration for

[1] Ibid., p. 649.
[2] For information concerning the Anglo-American Economic and Financial Conversations, see this volume, p. 643.
[3] Department of State, Bulletin, XIII, p. 862.
[4] For text of this Agreement, see Department of State, Treaties and Other International Acts Series 1518.
[5] Department of State, Bulletin, XIV, p. 59.
[6] Ibid.
[7] New York Times, January 27, 1946, p. 14.
[8] Department of State, Bulletin, XV, p. 363.

the registration of frequencies, tables of frequency distribution, and such other regulations as may be desired; and (4) preparations for special meetings in addition to the proposed World Conference.[1]

A Four-Power Broadcasting Conference, at which the United States, the Soviet Union, Great Britain and France were represented, convened in Paris on October 24, 1946, to discuss high-frequency organizational problems and the feasibility of creating a new world broadcasting organization. The Conference was concerned with such problems as they related to broadcasting only, and concentrated upon seeking unanimity of potential proposals to the World Conference with respect to high-frequency broadcast operations.[2]

The United States, although not a party to the International Telegraph Regulations nor a member of the International Telegraph Consulting Committee, received and accepted an invitation to send observers to a meeting of a special commission of the International Telegraph Consulting Committee in London, November 4 to 9, 1946. The Committee studied the application on a world-wide scale of the international telegraph rate pattern adopted at the Bermuda Telecommunications Conference of December, 1945,[3] and prepared for the resumption of the study of highly technical problems of international telegraphic operations which had been interrupted during the war.[4]

(1) *Report by the Representative of the United States on the Moscow Telecommunications Conference (de Wolf), September 28 to October 31, 1946. Department of State Press Release, November 8, 1946.*[5]

[Excerpts]

. . . . . .

At a Telecommunications Conference held in Bermuda in the fall of 1945 to settle certain outstanding questions between the United States and the British Commonwealth of Nations, it was informally agreed that it would be helpful to hold a Preliminary Five Power Telecommunications Conference, somewhat modeled on the Dumbarton Oaks Conference, to consider a basic reorganization of the existing International Telecommunications Union. I should explain that the International Telecommunications Union, which was first established at Paris in 1865, under the name of the International Telegraph Union, unlike the new Provisional International Civil Aviation Organization (PICAO) and the United Nations, has no permanent bodies which, in the interval between International Telecommunication Conferences, can effectively dispose of international telecommunication problems that may arise during such periods. Both the American and British delegations at Bermuda felt the imperative need of creating a new Telecommunications Union which would be responsive to the ever-increasing problems in the field of telecommunications, and it was further felt that the success of a union required the active participation of the U.S.S.R., it being realized that

[1] *Ibid.*, p. 459. For a report on the work of the Moscow Telecommunications Conference, see below.
[2] Department of State, *Bulletin*, XV, p. 755.
[3] For information concerning the Bermuda Telecommunications Conference, see this volume, p. 693.
[4] Department of State, *Bulletin*, XV, p. 846.
[5] Department of State Press Release 795.

while such participation in the aviation field was useful, it was absolutely essential in the field of telecommunications. I might explain here that one of the most important functions of the Union is to provide mechanisms whereby interference between radio stations is eliminated or at least greatly minimized. While such elimination obviously is essential to your enjoyment of radio programs, it is a matter of life and death when it comes to the question of communications with ships at sea and even more so with planes in the air.

At the Bermuda Telecommunications Conference it was consequently informally agreed that either the Preparatory or the main World Conference should take place in Moscow and the other in the United States. The Soviet Government was then approached and indicated a willingness to follow such a program, expressing a perference for the holding in Moscow of the preliminary conference and the convening in the United States of a World Conference.

On September 24 of this year, an American Delegation, composed of 26 representatives of government agencies and of private American companies and organizations, left Washington by plane and flew to Berlin, where a Soviet plane transported it directly to Moscow . . .

The conference decided that the next World Telecommunications Meeting should take place beginning July 1, 1947, at which time the Telecommunications Convention of Madrid would be revised to provide for an entirely new structure of the International Telecommunications Union. At the present time the Union consists merely of meetings taking place every five years and of a permanent bureau set up in Bern under the general administration of the Swiss Government. This bureau, however, has no powers whatever and for all intents and purposes is merely a registry office of radio frequencies and a publisher of service documents. All delegations present at the Moscow Conference agreed that the new Union should have an Administrative Council, composed of fifteen persons, a permanent Secretariat, and a Central Frequency Registration Board. It was also agreed that the ITU should be affiliated with the United Nations Organization and should become what is known in the Charter of the United Nations as a "specialized agency". The International Telecommunications Union, however, would retain its autonomous character and would be administered by its own council. The Central Frequency Registration Board (CFRB) is an American invention. As far as that goes, most of the other suggestions adopted by the Moscow Conference were based on American proposals. For the last three years, preparatory committees in Washington have been working on proposals for the complete reorganization of the international telecommunications administrative structure. The American proposal for the creation of a Central Frequency Registration Board, which was adopted unanimously by the Moscow Conference, may be described briefly as follows. In the past, when a country wished to use a frequency for a particular radio station, it merely notified the Bern Bureau of the fact and the latter then published the information in what is known as a Frequency List. It made no difference whether the proposed frequency would interfere with other radio stations in the rest of the world. Under the proposed set-up, a new procedure would be followed. Let us assume, for instance, that the United States wished to build a short wave radio station in Washington, with a power of 50 kilowatts and a frequency of 15,000 kilocyles. This information would be forwarded to the Central Frequency Board, on which would sit five impartial and competent radio technicians. They would examine the application of the United States to determine whether the proposed station would cause any interference to existing stations. If it did not, the frequency would be registered and would thereafter be protected from interference from any other stations in any other countries. If, on the other hand, the Board was of the opinion that the new station with its proposed frequency would cause serious interference to one or more other stations situated in other countries, it would so inform the Government of the United States and suggest that the latter select some other frequencies. However, if the United States should insist on using the frequency in question, it would so inform the Board. The latter would take note of this fact and publish the information given by the American Government in a column entitled "Notification." In these circumstances, however, no protection whatever would be given to the station by other countries and if the new station suffered interference it could not seek any remedy from any of the other members of the Telecommunications Union. This is obviously a step in the right direction, although it should be obvious that it still leaves quite a lot of latitude to the various governments since the Board does not have the power to forbid the use of a frequency which it considers would cause interference to other stations in other countries.

The Moscow Conference also agreed that there should be called in the Fall of 1947 a World High Frequency Broadcasting Conference whose purpose would be, in the first place, to assign frequencies to short wave stations all over the world and, in the second place, to establish a new World High Frequency Broadcasting Organization whose purpose would be to facilitate in every way the interchange of short wave broadcast programs between countries and eliminate causes of interference and in other ways improve the existing working of this important phase of telecommunications.

. . . .

CHAPTER XI

AGRICULTURE AND NATURAL RESOURCES

1. GENERAL

A. Food and Agriculture Organization of the United Nations

The establishment of a United Nations Interim Commission on Food and Agriculture resulted from action by the United States in calling a United Nations Conference on Food and Agriculture in May, 1943 at Hot Springs, Virginia.[1] The Interim Commission subsequently drew up a constitution for the proposed permanent Organization and submitted it to the United Nations governments for their consideration.[2] Under authorization of Public Law 174,[3] approved July 31, 1945, the United States accepted membership in the Food and Agriculture Organization (FAO) of the United Nations.

On October 16, 1945, FAO entered into official existence with the signing of the constitution at the opening session of the Organization's first Conference at Quebec, Canada;[4] at the close of the session, FAO membership included 42 countries. The Union of Soviet Socialist Republics, a member of the Interim Commission, was not a signatory country, although its delegation remained at the Conference as observers.

American efforts to cooperate with FAO were furthered on March 30, 1946, when President Truman requested coordination of government agency work on problems concerning United States participation in the Organization.

On February 11, 1946, Sir John B. Orr, Director-General of the Organization, notified the General Assembly of the United Nations that FAO planned to undertake studies and surveys of the world food problem. Acceptance of such responsibility by the Executive Committee of the Organization resulted in a Special Meeting on Urgent Food Problems, held on May 20 in Washington under the auspices of FAO. Representatives from six international agencies and 22 governments (including the United States) recommended: (1) measures for utilization of the 1946 harvest and maximum production for 1947; (2) the creation of the International Emergency Food Council to replace the Combined Food Board; (3) rapid development of the research and information service of FAO; and (4) the drawing-up by the Director-General of proposals dealing with production, distribution and consumption.

The second session of the Conference met in Copenhagen, Denmark, on September 2, 1946. Norris E. Dodd, Under Secretary of Agriculture, headed the United States delegation, and Leslie A. Wheeler, Director of the Office of Foreign Agricultural Relations, Department of Agriculture, acted as alternate. Included on the agenda were matters concerning long-term food machinery; the technical work of the Organization in agricultural production, nutrition, economics and statistics, fisheries and forestry; relations with other international and non-governmental organizations; and a preliminary report of the mission to Greece.[5] At this session the Director-General of FAO (Orr) submitted his Proposals for a World Food Board and an international reserve of food. The 47 members accepted

[1] For details on the organization of the Interim Commission on Food and Agriculture, see *Documents, VI, 1943–1944*, p. 415.

[2] For message by President Roosevelt transmitting to Congress the first report of the Interim Commission, see *ibid., VII, 1944–1945*, p. 657.

[3] See *ibid.*, p. 666.

[4] For list of members of FAO, see Food and Agriculture Organization of the United Nations, *Report of the First Session of the Conference*, Washington, January 1946.

[5] Department of State, *Bulletin*, XV, p. 491.

the general objectives of the Proposals as follows: "(a) developing and organizing production, distribution and utilization of the basic foods to provide diets on a health standard for the peoples of all countries; (b) stabilizing agricultural prices at levels fair to producers and consumers alike."

The United States favored the creation of an international committee to consider the various food proposals, including those set forth by FAO. On August 9, the State Department issued the following statement regarding world food proposals:

"As proposed by FAO, the plan is not sufficiently developed to permit this Government to determine whether it provides a promising approach to these agricultural problems. It is believed, however, that these problems are important and should be studied, and alternate solutions considered. Accordingly the Government favors creation of an international committee to analyze this and any alternate proposals and to prepare a plan for international action."[1]

In order to achieve these objectives, the Conference established a Preparatory Commission of sixteen members (including the United States) which convened at Washington on October 28, 1946.

At both the Copenhagen and Washington Conferences, controversy centered mainly around the Orr Proposals for a World Food Board. Under this plan, commodities were to be sold from a world pool reserve to needy countries at a predetermined price if the market price rose above the level established by the World Food Board. If the price fell below this level, commodities were to be purchased from surplus producing countries. As proposed, the plan envisioned a two-price system. The United States approved the purpose of the plan but noted that it would necessarily involve large expenditures and that there were certain conflicts between the plan and the proposals for an International Trade Organization; the latter provided for dealing with surplus commodities without large-scale buying and selling by an international body.

Tentative approval of the Orr Plan was given by the United States at the Copenhagen Conference. Then, in a reversal of policy, reportedly reflecting the view of the Department of State rather than that of the Department of Agriculture,[2] the United States withdrew support of the World Food Board. The American Representative (Dodd), while agreeing to the principle of international action on world food problems, set forth the following objections to the support of the Orr food proposals: (1) Government intervention in the agricultural demand and supply situation at the end of the present emergency might render ineffective the work of the Board; (2) A combination of "buffer-stock and surplus disposal operations" using a two-price system might be inadequate without control over supply; (3) Special negotiations on each commodity presented a more successful method of dealing with rapidly changing problems; (4) The United States believed it unlikely that governments would be prepared to give funds to an international agency over which they would have little control. Mr. Dodd further commented that the policy of the United States toward the International Trade Organization was to apply to its position on the World Food Board.[3]

(1) Message of the President (Truman) to the Delegates of the United Nations Food and Agriculture Organization at Quebec, October 17, 1945.[4]

My thoughts and the thoughts of the people of the United States of America today turn toward Quebec. The first conference of the Food and Agriculture Organization of the United Nations is truly a momentous occasion. It is an occasion on which the people of the United Nations begin to cultivate, if not yet to gather, the fruits of victory.

If we had not won our victory through common effort and common

[1] *Ibid.*, p. 329. [2] *New York Times*, October 29, 1946, p. 4.
[3] *Ibid.* See also, *ibid.*, September 1, 1946, p. 15. For information on the proposed International Trade Organization, see this volume, p. 624.
[4] Department of State, *Bulletin*, XIII, p. 619.

sacrifice, a meeting such as this would have been impossible. There would have been no room in the world for candor and decency and mutual helpfulness. Certainly there would have been no room for an international organization dedicated to these two simple propositions: first, that people in all parts of the world can and should have plenty of food and of other products of the farm; and second, that the world's people who draw wealth from the earth and sea can and should enjoy their fair share of the good things of life.

These are high goals. Neither the world nor any single nation has as yet even come close to achieving either. It will take time to reach them. Creation of a Food and Agriculture Organization in itself will not be enough; we must look to the patient cooperation of the family of nations through FAO and other means. But the work you are beginning at Quebec is an essential step forward, and a long one.

The world is watching your efforts for still another reason. The Food and Agriculture Organization is the first of the new permanent world organizations to grow out of the wartime cooperation of the United Nations. Its early stages, for good or ill, will do much to set the pattern for the other world organizations that must follow if we are to succeed in building a foundation for world peace and prosperity.

It is particularly fortunate that your meeting comes at this time, when some of the problems and difficulties that must inevitably follow military victory in so great a war have made themselves felt so keenly. The tasks of repairing the ravages of war and building for a saner future are tremendous. Each day it becomes clearer that in many ways we must work harder to win the peace than we did to win the war. But we know that the peace can be won. One of the major victories can be won at Quebec.

The United States is eager and proud to take its full part in your efforts. The success of this all-important first step in the life of the food and agriculture organization is the primary aim of my country's delegation. Its members come to this conference prepared to work together with the delegations of other nations for the good of all, and to bear their full share of the responsibility for a successful outcome.

Please convey my best wishes to the delegates of the host Government of the Dominion of Canada and to the delegates from the other United Nations. Much depends on your work during the days ahead. I am fully confident you will accomplish your purpose, no matter what obstacles may arise. Working together you cannot fail.

(2) *Statement by the United States Delegate to the Food and Agriculture Organization Preparatory Commission on World Food Proposals (Dodd), December 21, 1946.*[1]

[Excerpts]

In this statement, we want to bring forward for your consideration our ideas as to the direct national and international action which is

[1] Food and Agriculture Organization of the United Nations, Press Release 46, December 21, 1946.

possible upon the problem of hunger among those whose diets most desperately need improving — the vulnerable groups in all countries. We believe that international commodity agreements can be used as weapons in such a direct attack upon malnutrition and the starvation which has too often accompanied catastrophe due to drought, flood, pestilence and war. We envisage FAO as playing an essential part in bringing these weapons to bear.

. . . .

I shall not attempt, in this statement, to lay before you the details of this proposal, inasmuch as we have presented them in greater detail in a Commission document. I must be very clear about one point in putting forward our suggestions. The work of this Commission must, of course, be referred to the FAO member governments. Provisions which might be made parts of international commodity agreements must be negotiated in the future, and the agreements in turn referred to the participating governments. None of us has authority to commit his government in any way at this time.

We can say, however, that we are prepared to recommend to the Congress and the Executive branch of our Government that the United States undertake action along the lines we are suggesting here, should this be acceptable to this Commission.

. . . .

First, FAO should assist member governments of countries in this category to devise immediate measures applicable to their own circumstances. Second, FAO should keep the question before national authorities by especially requesting reports upon such immediate measures in the annual reports of member governments.

Finally, with respect either to countries having a sufficient, or an insufficient, food supply, we believe that the annual consultation among responsible national agricultural and nutritional officials, which we have suggested, will be a valuable means of stimulating and developing supplemental food programs for vulnerable groups.

Now I want to turn to the question of international aid to supplemental food programs for vulnerable groups. At Copenhagen, the member governments of FAO accepted two objectives and agreed that international machinery was necessary to achieve them. The objectives are to raise diets to a health standard and to stabilize prices of agricultural commodities at levels fair to producers and consumers.

We scarcely need to remind this commission that stabilization will also depend upon the successful stabilization of exchange rates under the Monetary Fund, the increased flow of international investment funds under the leadership of the World Bank, and the expansion of world trade under the leadership of the ITO.

To our minds, the acceptance of an objective means an obligation to work actively and positively for its achievement. The obligation rests not alone upon either exporting or importing countries. It rests upon us all.

We feel most strongly that if the exporting countries undertake the obligation of making the importing countries secure in ample supplies of food and other agricultural commodities, then it becomes the obligation of the importing countries not to restrict markets by subsidizing their production of such commodities at uneconomic levels.

We feel just as strongly that the cost involved in making available ample supplies of agricultural commodities, including supplies for supplemental food programs for vulnerable groups, must not be charged to the farmers who grow the crops through prices beaten down by burdensome surpluses. The cost is an obligation to be shared in some degree by the countries, exporter or importer, which accepted the objectives of health-standard diets and stabilized prices.

It may be argued that selling food at concession prices to support supplemental food programs for vulnerable groups in areas of insufficient total food supply will be at the cost of higher prices to commercial importers. To the extent that this may be true, it seems to us to be a way of discharging their obligation to share the costs of raising diets toward a health standard.

There is another side to the argument, however. Many exporting countries have in the past diverted from commercial markets considerable quantities of agricultural commodities. It is unfortunately possible that exporting countries may again in the future deem it necessary to make grain into alcohol, subsidize its feeding to cattle, burn it as fuel, or restrict its production in order to realize for their farmers an acceptable price for the commercially-marketed portion of their crop. The result of this would certainly not be lower prices for importing countries, nor would it be more food for the malnourished.

We would like, therefore, to suggest that this Commission recommend to FAO, and FAO to member governments and appropriate international agencies, the nature of provisions designed to help improve the diets of vulnerable groups, for consideration by the parties to commodity agreements concluded within the framework of the draft ITO Charter.

We visualize international aid in the form of food supplies supporting supplemental food programs for vulnerable groups as being appropriate in two kinds of situations.

First, areas where famine is not usually experienced may suffer catastrophe which destroys production and exhausts reserves, so that an acute temporary food shortage results. Such areas normally provide themselves with food, including supplies imported and paid for through normal commercial channels. In the emergency, the national government may well undertake to protect vulnerable groups through supplemental food programs such as school feeding or community kitchens.

In such circumstances, when FAO certified to the need of the special food program and the International Monetary Fund certified that the position of the government was such as to require international aid, food might be furnished either free or upon concessional terms, for the duration of the emergency.

Second, international aid would be appropriate in areas where a major part of the population suffers chronic malnutrition, accompanied by recurring famine, and where long-term programs looking toward permanent solution of the underlying causes of malnutrition are being undertaken.

In such circumstances, when FAO certified to the need of a special food program, and appropriate findings as to the long-term program were forthcoming, food might be furnished upon concessional terms. The aid should taper off and terminate as the ability of the area to sustain its own food programs increased.

In either case, the national government concerned should undertake substantial contributions to the special food program, and the supplemental food supplied should be a net addition to the diets of the beneficiaries, not a substitution for purchases which they would otherwise make. In either case, the benefits should be confined to members of truly vulnerable groups.

I would like to summarize as follows the provisions for supplemental food programs which should be considered in connection with international commodity agreements.

First, the intent should be that during the term of the agreement there would be available at a minimum enough of the commodity for ample and expanding normal commercial consumption, normal commercial working stocks, and an earmarked quantity for relief — gratis if necessary — in case of catastrophe. Further accumulations which occurred or were anticipated over and above these needs should be considered available to meet obligations which the parties to an agreement might undertake in connection with supplemental food programs for vulnerable groups under long-term development programs.

Second, all or any number of the exporting countries party to an agreement should be permitted to export such excess supplies on concessional terms to support supplementary food programs for vulnerable groups, such exports to be considered as outside export quotas which might pertain to commercial exports. These supplies should be offered on a substantially equal basis to all countries complying with the principles of international aid to supplementary food programs. The agreement should either provide for the concessional terms, or provide a method for prompt negotiation of concessional terms when occasion arose. Such provisions would be necessary to protect other provisions of commodity agreements.

Third, compensatory features should be considered. For example, vulnerable groups may need milk in order to balance diets, which the country cannot furnish because it cannot afford to reduce production of grain for direct human food use. The proposal is that food exporting countries temporarily furnish enough more grain to compensate for grain yield lost to direct human food use by shifting of acreage into production of milk actually furnished to vulnerable groups.

Fourth, we think it may be possible to extend to a limited number of perishable commodities the essential principles of international aid to supplemental food programs for vulnerable groups which have been outlined, in such a manner as to assist at the same time in stabilizing

AGRICULTURE AND NATURAL RESOURCES

supplies and prices in situations of expected oversupply. We recommend that the Commission study both the price stabilization and the nutritional possibilities.

. . . .

B. International Emergency Food Council

The Combined Food Board, operating through international commodity subcommittees, was regarded as a temporary agency, designed to function until the supply situation eased sufficiently to allow gradual withdrawal of controls.[1] In May 1946, during the Special Meeting on Urgent Food Problems,[2] recommendations were approved providing for the establishment of an International Emergency Food Council to replace the Combined Food Board. On June 3, in accordance with these recommendations, the United States, the United Kingdom and Canada extended invitations to prospective members of the new organization.

The Council's terms of reference outlined its functions as follows:[3] (1) to consider, investigate and formulate plans on questions of common concern relating to supply and distribution of foods, equipment and nonfood materials necessary to the production of such foods and agricultural materials and to recommend means of reconciling international differences on such questions; (2) to work in cooperation with members of the United Nations and appropriate international organizations toward the most effective utilization of food resources and to formulate plans and recommendations, in consultation with interested parties, pertaining to the best use of their food resources during the present emergency. Duration of Council activity was assured for a period extending to December 31, 1947, subject to a continuing critical supply condition.

Initial meetings of the Council, starting June 20, were attended by 20 country representatives. An expanding membership was anticipated since membership was open to any country through membership on any of the commodity committees. Dr. D. A. FitzGerald, formerly of the United States Department of Agriculture, was named Secretary-General of the Organization. United States Secretary of Agriculture Anderson served as chairman of the nine member central committee.

Since its formation the Council's work has consisted chiefly of making specific allocation recommendations for the guidance of governments and international organizations in encouraging conservation and expansion of food supplies.

(1) *Text of the Letter of Invitation Concerning the Establishment of an International Emergency Food Council, Addressed by the Member Governments of the Combined Food Board (United States, United Kingdom and Canada) to Prospective Members of the Council, June 3, 1946.*[4]

Proposals for the establishment of an International Emergency Food Council to replace the existing Combined Food Board were considered at a Special Meeting on Urgent Food Problems convened by the Director

---

[1] For information on the establishment of the Combined Food Board, see *Documents, VI, 1943–1944*, p. 240. See also, Department of State, *Bulletin*, XIII, p. 17.

[2] For information on events leading to the Special Meeting on Urgent Food Problems, see this volume, p. 375.

[3] See Food and Agriculture Organization of the United Nations, *Report of the Special Meeting on Urgent Food Problems*, Washington, June 6, 1946, p. 35.

[4] Department of State, *Bulletin*, XIV, p. 1075.

General of the Food and Agriculture Organization and held in Washington, D. C., from May 20 to May 27. As a result of discussions at that meeting, the attached recommendations were approved and submitted to all the governments concerned. It is part of these recommendations that the Governments of the United States, the United Kingdom and Canada arrange without delay for a meeting of the Combined Food Board. Accordingly, I am now writing on behalf of the Combined Food Board to invite you to appoint a representative to attend a meeting to be held on Thursday, June 20, 1946, at 2 P.M. in Washington, D. C. You will be notified shortly of the building and room in which the meeting will be held.

The purpose of the meeting is to enable the governments concerned, through their representatives, to state whether they are ready to accept the attached recommendations and thus to become members of the new International Emergency Food Council. I should therefore be glad if your representative could be authorized to state your Government's official position in regard to the proposal. If the recommendations are generally accepted, the meeting will proceed forthwith to establish the International Emergency Food Council.

It is proposed that if the International Emergency Food Council is established at the meeting on June 20 the Council should immediately thereafter hold its first session and consider a number of items of initial business. A draft agenda for the first session is attached for your information and comment.

I should be grateful if you would advise me as soon as possible whether your Government will be able to be represented at the proposed meeting and the name of your authorized representative.

Identical letters are being addressed to the diplomatic representatives in Washington of the Governments of Argentina, Australia, Belgium, Brazil, Chile, China, Cuba, Denmark, France, Greece, India, Netherlands, New Zealand, Norway, Siam, Turkey, Union of South Africa, and the USSR.

C. United States Proposal for Conference on Resource Conservation and Utilization

In a letter on September 4, 1946, to the United States Representative on the Economic and Social Council, Mr. John G. Winant, President Truman suggested that a proposal be made to the Economic and Social Council regarding an international scientific conference on the conservation and utilization of natural resources. Mr. Winant transmitted this proposal and a draft resolution [1] to that effect to the Acting President of the Council, Dr. Andrija Stampar.[2] The proposal remained on the Council's agenda for discussion throughout the period under review.

[1] United Nations Economic and Social Council, Document E/139, September 14, 1946.

[2] The resolution, not printed in this volume, can be found in *ibid.*, or in the Department of State, *Bulletin*, XV, p. 623. For a letter from President Truman to Mr. Winant regarding the proposal, see *ibid.*, p. 624.

2. COAL

(1) Agreement between the United States and Other Powers for the Establishment of the European Coal Organization, Signed at London, January 4, 1946.[1]

The problem of distributing available fuel at a time of severe shortages prompted early discussion among the Allies during 1944 and 1945 concerning a European organization to handle these and other problems of coordinating needs for equipment. At a meeting in London on May 18, 1945 the United States joined Belgium, Denmark, France, Greece, Luxembourg, the Netherlands, Norway, Turkey and the United Kingdom [2] in informal agreement on the formation of the European Coal Organization. Established under a formal agreement on January 4, 1946 which was to operate originally for one year with extension if necessary, the Organization was invested with the two main functions of assisting the increase of coal production in Europe, and recommending means of facilitating an equitable distribution among importing countries. The Organization, possessed of advisory powers only, collected and studied information on all matters pertaining to European coal supply for the use of member and interested governments.[3]

The Governments of Belgium, Denmark, France, Greece, Luxembourg, the Netherlands, Norway, Turkey, the United Kingdom of Great Britain and Northern Ireland and the United States of America, being convinced that, during the present period of general shortage of coal and of certain types of coal-mining supplies and equipment, effective co-ordination of the demand for and supply of these commodities in Europe will continue to be necessary, have agreed as follows:—

Article 1. Establishment of a European Coal Organisation.

The European Coal Organisation, hereinafter referred to as the "Organisation," is hereby formally established.

Article 2. Membership of the Organisation.

The members of the Organisation shall be the Governments on whose behalf this Agreement is signed and those other Governments which accede to the Agreement at the invitation of the Council provided for in Article 3.

Article 3. Structure of the Organisation.

1. The Organisation shall consist of a Council and a Full-time Staff.
2. The Council shall be composed of representatives of the member Governments. Each Government shall appoint one representative and may appoint an alternate representative and technical advisers.
3. The Council shall draw up its own rules of procedure and may establish such committees or other subordinate bodies as may be desirable.

[1] Department of State, *Treaties and Other International Acts Series* 1508.
[2] The Union of Soviet Socialist Republics, Czechoslovakia, Yugoslavia and Poland were invited to join the Organization; in March 1946 Poland accepted the invitation.
[3] For detailed information on fuel needs and the work of the European Coal Organization, see Department of State, *Bulletin*, XIII, p. 879.

4. The Full-time Staff shall consist of a Chairman, who shall preside in the Council, a Secretary-General, both appointed by the Council, and other necessary staff appointed by the Chairman with the approval of the Council and in accordance with conditions to be prescribed by the Council.

Article 4. Purpose of the Organisation.

1. The purpose of the Organisation is to promote the supply and equitable distribution of coal and scarce items of coal-mining supplies and equipment while safeguarding, as far as possible, the interests of both producers and consumers. With this object the Council shall keep itself constantly acquainted with and, when necessary, discuss the situation in regard to such supply and distribution, disseminate information in regard thereto, and make appropriate recommendations to the Governments concerned and to any other competent authorities.

2. To these ends the member Governments shall —
   (a) provide the Organisation, at its request, with all relevant information, in particular, information regarding production, imports, exports, consumption, stocks and requirements of coal and of coal-mining supplies and equipment, and
   (b) give their full co-operation to the Organisation in the accomplishment of its task.

Article 5. Headquarters.

The Headquarters of the Organisation shall be in London or such other place as the Council may from time to time decide.

Article 6. Relations with other Organisations, Authorities and Agencies.

1. The Organisation may establish relations with national and international organisations, authorities and agencies.

2. After the establishment of the Economic and Social Council of the United Nations, the Organisation shall communicate with that Council with the view of determining what relationship should be created between it and the Council and, in particular, whether its functions can and should be taken over by the Council.

Article 7. Administrative Expenses.

The Council shall consider and approve a budget covering the necessary administrative expenses of the Organisation. Administrative expenses shall be apportioned between and borne by the member Governments in a manner to be determined by the Council. Each member Government undertakes, subject to the requirements of its constitutional procedure, to contribute to the Organisation promptly its share of the administrative expenses so determined.

Article 8. Privileges and immunities.

1. The Organisation shall enjoy in the territories of the member Governments such privileges and immunities as are necessary for the fulfilment of its purpose.

2. Representatives of the member Governments and officials of the Organisation shall likewise enjoy in those territories such privileges and immunities as are necessary for the independent exercise of their functions.

Article 9. Definitions.

For the purposes of this Agreement:
The word "coal" shall mean all coal (whether anthracite, bituminous brown coal, lignite or other species), coke (whether produced at gas works or coke ovens), briquettes or other manufactured solid fuel and pitch for use in the manufacture of solid fuel.

The expression "coal-mining supplies and equipment" shall mean such articles, including machinery and parts thereof, as are used in the production and treatment of coal.

Article 10. Entry into force and duration of the Agreement.

This Agreement, which is drawn up in French and English, both texts being equally authoritative, shall enter into force on the 1st January, 1946, for an initial period of one year. The member Governments (or some of them) may prolong its operation for such further period as they may determine. On or after the 1st October, 1946, any member Government may give in writing to the Government of the United Kingdom notice of withdrawal from the Organisation and the Agreement shall terminate in respect of any Government by whom such notice has been given three months after the date of the receipt of the notice by the Government of the United Kingdom.

In witness whereof the undersigned, duly authorised by their respective Governments, have signed the present Agreement.

Done in London on the 4th January, 1946, in a single copy which shall be deposited with the Government of the United Kingdom and of which certified copies shall be communicated to all signatory or acceding Governments.

3. COFFEE

For information relating to the Inter-American Coffee Board, see this volume, p. 771.

4. COTTON

A. International Cotton Advisory Committee

Pursuant to a resolution adopted by the International Cotton Advisory Committee at its fourth meeting [1] in April, 1945, the International Cotton Study Group met in July, 1945, and January and February, 1946, to prepare a report for submission to the International Cotton Advisory Committee. The Group was authorized by the Committee to formulate proposals for international collaboration, based on assumptions that: (1) cooperation of governments dependent upon imports is essential to effective international action in dealing with the cotton surplus; (2) in order to obtain a reduction in excess supplies, regulation of exports, export prices and production might be required; and (3) any international action should involve expansion of cotton consumption.[2]

[1] For information on the fourth meeting of the International Cotton Advisory Committee and resolution adopted April 14, 1945, see *Documents, VII, 1944–1945*, p. 673.   [2] Department of State, *Bulletin*, XV, p. 1078.

Although unable to present a comprehensive plan at that time for such cooperation in the cotton field, the Group recommended the continuation of studies and surveys of international cotton problems. Acting upon this recommendation at the fifth meeting from May 7–14, 1946, the Committee agreed to set up an executive committee composed of representatives of twelve member governments, both cotton exporting and cotton importing countries. Mr. L. A. Wheeler, Director of the Office of Foreign Agricultural Relations of the United States Department of Agriculture and chairman of the International Cotton Advisory Committee, was asked to convene the executive committee. This committee, to be composed of representatives from Argentina, Belgium, Brazil, Canada, China, Czechoslovakia, Egypt, France, India, Peru, the United Kingdom and the United States, was directed in its terms of reference: "(1) to establish practical cooperation with the Food and Agriculture Organization of the United Nations and with other international organizations concerned with the world cotton situation; (2) to provide a medium for exchange of views in regard to current developments; (3) to develop further the work on methods of international cooperation; and (4) to create and maintain at Washington a secretariat for the purpose of supplying complete, authentic and timely statistics on world cotton production, trade, consumption, stocks, and prices." [1]

Also reporting to the fifth meeting of the Committee was a subcommittee, headed by Mr. C. D. Walker of the United States, who expressed the hope that particular attention be given to the following: "consumption of raw cotton and measures for increasing it; criteria for determining when a burdensome surplus exists; criteria for estimating efficiency of production and methods for the adjustment of production; claims of producers of special staples to be outside any scheme of quotas; basis for establishing quota shares including consideration of seasonal and shipping factors; buffer stock operations; freedom of markets in presence of a quota scheme; development of, and competition from, substitute fibers." [2]

5. PETROLEUM

(1) *An Agreement on Petroleum between the Government of the United States of America and the Government of the United Kingdom of Great Britain and Northern Ireland, Signed in London, September 24, 1945.*[3]

A revised agreement, signed by the Governments of the United Kingdom and United States, was announced on September 24, 1945. A previous Anglo-American agreement on petroleum of August 8, 1944, had not been brought into force due to opposition in the United States Senate for reasons of domestic policy.[4] Subsequent conferences between the two countries resulted in the later agreement, negotiated for the United States by the Honorable Harold L. Ickes, Secretary of the Interior and Petroleum Administrator for War; Mr. Ralph K. Davies, Deputy Petroleum Administrator; and Mr. Charles B. Rayner, Petroleum Adviser to the State Department.[5]

At the request of the Secretary of State, President Truman transmitted the agreement to the Senate on November 1, 1945, for consent to ratification. No further action was taken during the remainder of the period under review.

[1] *Ibid.*, for the final resolution of the fifth meeting of the International Cotton Advisory Committee, see *ibid.*, XIV, p. 888.

[2] *Ibid.*, p. 887.

[3] *Ibid.*, XIII, p. 481.

[4] For text of the petroleum agreement of August 8, 1944, see *Documents VII, 1944–1945*, p. 678. For an address on oil policy for the United States by Secretary of Interior Ickes, see *ibid.*, p. 683.

[5] Department of State, *Bulletin*, XIII, p. 481. See also, *ibid.*, p. 385.

Preamble: The Government of the United States of America and the Government of the United Kingdom of Great Britain and Northern Ireland, whose Nationals hold, to a substantial extent jointly, rights to explore and develop petroleum resources in other countries, recognize:

1. That ample supplies of petroleum, available in international trade to meet increasing market demands, are essential for both the security and economic well-being of nations;
2. That for the foreseeable future the petroleum resources of the world are adequate to assure the availability of such supplies;
3. That the prosperity and security of all nations require the efficient and orderly development of the international petroleum trade;
4. That the orderly development of the international petroleum trade can best be promoted by international agreement among all countries interested in the petroleum trade, whether as producers or consumers.

The two Governments have therefore decided, as a preliminary measure to the calling of an international conference to consider the negotiation of a multilateral petroleum agreement, to conclude the following agreement.

Article I:

The signatory Governments agree that the international petroleum trade in all its aspects should be conducted in an orderly manner on a worldwide basis with due regard to the considerations set forth in the preamble, and within the framework of applicable laws and concession contracts. To this end and subject always to considerations of military security and to the provisions of such arrangements for the preservation of peace and prevention of aggression as may be in force, the signatory Governments affirm the following general principles with respect to the international petroleum trade:

(A) That adequate supplies of petroleum, which shall in this agreement mean crude petroleum and its derivatives, should be accessible in international trade to the Nationals of all countries on a competitive and nondiscriminatory basis;

(B) That, in making supplies of petroleum thus accessible in international trade, the interests of producing countries should be safeguarded with a view to their economic advancement.

Article II:

In furtherance of the purposes of this agreement, the signatory Governments will so direct their efforts:

(A) That all valid concession contracts and lawfully acquired rights shall be respected and that there shall be no interference directly or indirectly with such contracts or rights;

(B) That with regard to the acquisition of exploration and development rights the principle of equal opportunity shall be respected;

(C) That the exploration for and development of petroleum resources, the construction and operation of refineries and other facilities, and the distribution of petroleum shall not be hampered by restrictions inconsistent with the purposes of this agreement.

Article III:

1. With a view to the wider adoption of the principles embodied in this agreement, the signatory governments agree that as soon as practicable they will propose to the governments of all interested producing and consuming countries the negotiation of an international petroleum agreement which *inter-alia* would establish a permanent international petroleum council.

2. To this end the signatory governments agree to formulate at an early date plans for an international conference to negotiate such a multilateral petroleum agreement. They will consult together and with other interested governments with a view to taking whatever action is necessary to prepare for the proposed conference.

Article IV:

1. Numerous problems of joint immediate interest to the signatory governments with respect to the international petroleum trade should be discussed and resolved on a co-operative interim basis if the general petroleum supply situation is not to deteriorate.

2. With this end in view, the signatory governments agree to establish an international petroleum commission to be composed of six members, three members to be appointed immediately by each government. To enable the commission to maintain close contact with the operations of the petroleum industry, the signatory governments will facilitate full and adequate consultation with their nationals engaged in the petroleum industry.

3. In furtherance of and in accordance with the purposes of this agreement, the commission shall consider problems of mutual interest to the signatory governments and their nationals, and with a view to the equitable disposition of such problems it shall be charged with the following duties and responsibilities:

(A) to study the problems of the international petroleum trade caused by dislocations resulting from war;

(B) to study past and current trends in the international petroleum trade;

(C) to study the effects of changing technology upon the international petroleum trade;

(D) to prepare periodic estimates of world demands for petroleum and of the supplies available for meeting the demands, and to report as to means by which such demands and supplies may be correlated so as to further the efficient and orderly conduct of the international petroleum trade;

(E) To make such additional reports as may be appropriate for achieving the purposes of this agreement and for the broader general understanding of the problems of the international petroleum trade.

4. The Commission shall have power to regulate its procedure and shall establish such organization as may be necessary to carry out its functions under this agreement. The expenses of the Commission shall be shared equally by the signatory governments.

Article V:

The signatory governments agree:

(A) That they will seek to obtain the collaboration of the governments of other producing and consuming countries for the realization of the purposes of this agreement, and to consult with such governments in connection with activities of the Commission;

(B) That they will assist in making available to the Commission such information as may be required for the discharge of its function.

Article VI:

The signatory governments agree:

(A) That the reports of the Commission shall be published unless in any particular case either government decides otherwise;

(B) That no provision in this agreement shall be construed to require either government to act upon any report or proposal made by the Commission, or to require the nationals of either government to comply with any report or proposal made by the Commission, whether or not the report or proposal is approved by that government.

Article VII:

The signatory governments agree:

(A) That the general purpose of this agreement is to facilitate the orderly development of the international petroleum trade, and that no provision in this agreement, with the exception of Article II, is to be construed as applying to the operation of the domestic petroleum industry within the country of either government;

(B) That nothing in this agreement shall be construed as impairing or modifying any law or regulation, or the right to enact any law or regulation, relating to the importation of petroleum into the country of either government;

(C) That, for the purposes of this article, the word "country" shall mean

(1) In relation to the Government of the United Kingdom of Great Britain and Northern Ireland, the United Kingdom, those British colonies, overseas territories, protectorates, protected states, and all mandated territories administered by that government and

(2) In relation to the Government of the United States of America, the continental United States and all territory under the jurisdiction of the United States, lists of which, as of the date of this agreement, have been exchanged.

Article VIII:

This agreement shall enter into force upon a date to be agreed upon after each government shall have notified the other of its readiness to bring the agreement into force and shall continue in force until three months after notice of termination has been given by either government or until it is superseded by the international petroleum agreement contemplated in Article III.

In witness whereof the undersigned, duly authorised thereto, have signed this agreement.

6. RUBBER

A. Rubber Study Group

The Rubber Study Group, established in 1944 by the Governments of the Netherlands, the United Kingdom and the United States as an informal study group,[1] convened in London for its second meeting on November 19, 1945, with added participation by the Government of France. Mr. Donald D. Kennedy, Chief of the International Resources Division, Department of State, and leader of the United States delegation, acted as vice-chairman. Further studies were presented for Group survey by participating governments; latest information on the synthetic industry, particularly in the United States, and reports of conditions in the rubber producing areas in the Far East were used as the basis for discussion. United States capacity for production of synthetic rubber was estimated at 1,055,000 tons per annum. Although very little information concerning rubber supplies in the Netherlands was available, there were facts to indicate that rubber estates in Indo-China and in Malaya had escaped with only slight damage. The Group agreed that although it was impossible at that time to estimate accurately the future rate of production, it was probable that supplies of natural rubber becoming available from all areas of the world during 1946 might reach 600,000 tons. On the assumption that a high level of economic activity in rubber consuming countries was to be maintained, the Group expected that the trend of consumption would continue to rise in the next few years to the maximum figure of 1,500,000 tons annually of all types of natural and synthetic rubber.[2]

The United States also participated in the third meeting of the Group, held at The Hague on November 25–28, 1946. It was then estimated that world production in 1946 amounted to 940,000 tons of synthetic rubber and 760,000 to 860,000 tons of natural rubber. Group discussion at the meeting was mainly concerned with (1) future availability of natural and synthetic rubber, (2) the possibility of future disequilibrium between the productive capacity of the world and demands for consumption, and (3) the various uses for natural and synthetic rubber. After noting the work of the Preparatory Committee of the International Conference on Trade and Employment,[3] it was felt by member representatives that expansion of the Group's membership to include countries interested in rubber production and consumption would be desirable.[4]

B. Termination of Rubber Purchasing Agreements

The Tripartite Rubber Agreement, concluded May 2, 1945, by representatives of Argentina, Brazil and the United States, was canceled by exchange of notes, effective August 29, 1946. The agreement was originally made in order to meet war demands for natural rubber, and to this end, provided for the integration of Argentina within the inter-American system covering rubber supplies.[5]

Rubber purchasing agreements with Ecuador, Haiti and Bolivia, negotiated with the United States in 1942 [6] as part of the inter-governmental rubber agreements concluded by the United States with seventeen rubber producing countries in the Western Hemisphere, expired on December 31, 1946. Upon invitation by the United States in April 1946, agreements with several of these countries were extended until June 30, 1947. Due to the end of the war and by means of the

---

[1] For information on the first meeting of the Rubber Study Group, see *Documents*, VII, *1944–1945*, p. 676.

[2] The foregoing paragraphs were based on information obtained from a report on the second meeting of the Rubber Study Group, Department of State, *Bulletin*, XIII, p. 840.

[3] See this volume, p. 629.

[4] Department of State, *Bulletin*, XV, p. 1054.

[5] *Ibid.*, p. 827.

[6] See *Documents*, V, *1942–1943*, p. 405.

AGRICULTURE AND NATURAL RESOURCES 713

mutual cancellation provisions, agreements with Guatemala, El Salvador, Honduras, British Honduras and Venezuela were terminated at various times, leaving nine agreements [1] still in effect until June 1947.[2]

7. SUGAR

A. International Sugar Council

On August 3, 1945, the International Sugar Council convened in London to consider a further extension of the International Sugar Agreement.[3] Representatives of thirteen countries, including the United States, were present. During a meeting of the Council in London on February 5, 1946, at which the United States Government was not represented, resolutions were adopted, authorizing the secretariat to prepare a draft memorandum regarding the operation of the International Sugar Agreement, and requesting the various delegations to provide statistics regarding available sugar supplies.[4]

On June 10, 1946, President Truman proclaimed a protocol of August 31, 1945 which prolonged for one year the international agreement on the regulation and marketing of sugar. On August 30, 1946, a later protocol [5] was signed by eighteen countries, including the United States, which once again extended the agreement until September 1, 1947. In this document note was taken of future revision of the agreement at an appropriate time.

8. TIN

There was international allocation of tin by the Combined Raw Materials Board during the war. Shortly after V-J day, as a method to continue tin allocations, the Combined Tin Committee, with members from the Governments of the United States, United Kingdom, France, Belgium and the Netherlands, was established at Washington. Its purpose was to ensure a fair amount of tin for each of the consuming countries.[6]

At the invitation of the United Kingdom a conference on tin was scheduled to meet in London from October 8 to 12, 1946, to study the world tin situation and consider possible intergovernmental action by producing and consuming countries. It was noted that provisions for intergovernmental study were created through the machinery of the proposed International Trade Organization.[7]

On December 10, 1946, negotiations were concluded by the United States, the United Kingdom, Australia and Siam for procuring Siamese tin and for easing the tin shortage. Terms of the agreement provided that: (1) a four member commission was to facilitate movement of Siamese tin stocks into world trade; (2) the metal was to be shipped according to the allocations of the Combined Tin Committee; (3) Siamese tin stocks were to be purchased in equal amounts by the United States and the United Kingdom; and (4) prices were to be equivalent to prices in Malaya.[8]

9. WHALING

On November 20, 1945, an International Whaling Conference was held in London, attended by representatives of Denmark, France, Mexico, the Nether-

---

[1] Nine agreements were still in effect with Peru, Colombia, Brazil, Costa Rica, Nicaragua, Panama, Mexico, British Guiana, and Trinidad and Tobago.

[2] Department of State, *Bulletin*, XVI, p. 75.

[3] For information on early protocols relating to the agreement, see *Documents*, V, *1942–1943*, p. 635.

[4] Department of State Publication 2817, Conference Series 95, p. 19.

[5] Ratification by the United States was deposited on May 20, 1947; the protocol was proclaimed by the President on May 27, 1947. See Department of State, *Treaties and Other International Acts Series* 1614.

[6] See Department of State, *Bulletin*, XV, p. 195.

[7] *Ibid.*, p. 663.   [8] *Ibid.*, p. 1186.

lands, Norway, the United States, Australia, Canada, Newfoundland, New Zealand, the Union of South Africa and the United Kingdom.[1] A resulting protocol, supplementary to the agreement of 1937, was signed on November 26, and transmitted by President Truman to the Senate on July 19, 1946, for consent to ratification.[2] Because of the continued shortage of fats and oils the Conference considered possible special measures for the 1946–1947 whaling season. It was agreed that certain provisions of the 1937 whaling agreement were to be relaxed for the following year and it was further agreed to carry over regulations similar to those contained in the 1944 protocol.[3]

Representatives of nineteen countries and observers from the Food and Agriculture Organization of the United Nations participated in an International Whaling Conference from November 20 to December 2, 1946, in Washington to consider conservation of world whale stocks. Mr. Remington Kellogg, chairman of the American Delegation, acted as chairman of the Conference. The codification and expansion of existing conservation regulations and the creation of an international whaling commission to adjust the regulations whenever necessary resulted from the final documents of the Conference, which were: (1) an international whaling protocol; (2) an international whaling convention; and (3) a final act. The regulations embodied in these final documents (open for signature until December 16) were to extend through the 1947–1948 whaling season and, in the case of the convention, through the 1948–1949 and later whaling seasons.[4]

10. WHEAT

A. International Wheat Council

At its ninth meeting on September 1, 1945 a resolution was adopted by the International Wheat Council[5] recommending that the member governments insofar as possible maintain export prices of wheat at the lowest possible levels until July 31, 1946. Because of the recognized need for broadened membership in the Council, the Governments of Belgium, Brazil, China, Denmark, France, India, Italy and the Netherlands joined the body at the twelfth session on July 15, 1946, thus enlarging its membership to thirteen countries. The Union of Soviet Socialist Republics and Yugoslavia, also invited to participate, were not present. The chairman, Mr. L. A. Wheeler (United States), reviewed the reasons for the action taken by original members of the Council to amend the Memorandum of Agreement; thereafter, the business of the session centered mainly on appointment of a preparatory committee to revise the draft convention drawn up in 1941–1942[6] for submission to an international wheat conference and to initiate studies and surveys as preparation for such a conference.[7]

The thirteenth session, held on August 19 at the United States Department of Agriculture, had as its principal agenda item the consideration of the first report of its preparatory committee. After noting the statements made by the several delegations, the Council instructed the committee to: "proceed with discussions

[1] *Ibid.*, XIII, p. 969.

[2] For text of the President's message to the Senate and the Report by Secretary of State Byrnes regarding the protocol, see *ibid.*, XV, p. 284.

[3] For text of the 1944 protocol, see *Documents, VI, 1943–1944*, p. 453. See also, Department of State, *Bulletin*, XIII, p. 872.

[4] For texts of final documents of the International Whaling Conference signed at Washington, December 2, 1946, see: Canada, Department of External Affairs, *Acts of the International Whaling Conference Held in Washington from November 20 to December 2, 1946.* Ottawa (Treaties Series 1946, No. 54), 1947.

[5] For text of the Memorandum of Agreement which established the Council, see *Documents, IV, 1941–1942*, p. 714.

[6] This convention dealt with problems of expansion of wheat trade, production control, stocks, export control, price control and a relief pool; it was never ratified, but it served as the basis for the Memorandum of Agreement.

[7] Department of State, *Bulletin*, XV, p. 359.

toward a specific proposal on the range of prices which might be recommended to governments, and thereafter to clarify the clauses on production, export quotas, and reserve stocks in response to queries raised with regard to the draft outline of the proposed international wheat agreement submitted to governments on 19th July to the end that a complete draft agreement may be submitted to the Council at the earliest possible date." [1] The preparatory committee, composed of representatives of member countries and aided by representatives of the Food and Agriculture Organization and the Economic and Social Council, met periodically from July 17 to December 9, 1946, to work on a memorandum regarding a new international wheat agreement, and during that time the committee reported twice to the Council. At its meeting in December 1946, the Council decided to consider the complete draft of a wheat agreement at the scheduled fifteenth session in January 1947.[2]

11. WOOL

A. United States Import Duties on Wool

Since the conclusion of the war period, consumption of apparel wool in the United States remained above the pre-war level and resulted in renewed interest on the part of the United States government, as well as other wool producing countries, in pricing and export policies in the liquidation of world apparel-wool stocks.[3] A Senate Special Committee to Investigate the Production, Transportation and Marketing of Wool held hearings in November and December 1945 on features of a domestic wool program. In his appearance before the Senate Committee, Assistant Secretary of State William L. Clayton expressed the view that an increase in import duty on apparel wool or the imposition of quota restrictions on imports would not conform to the spirit of American economic policy and international attempts to reduce trade barriers. Instead, he favored means which would allow domestic wool to compete with foreign wool at the duty-paid import price.

(1) *Statement by the Assistant Secretary of State (Clayton) before the Senate Special Committee to Investigate Production, Transportation and Marketing of Wool, Concerning the Effect of the Wool Market on Foreign Economic Relations, November 21, 1945.*[4]

[Excerpt]

. . . . . .

It is on this common ground of desire to promote conditions of prosperity both at home and abroad that I am glad to discuss with this Committee the problems which you are considering. The interests of the Department of State in the questions before the Committee are in general those which relate to the foreign economic relations of the United States. As I have said, a major objective of our foreign economic policy is the expansion of international trade as a means of facilitating increased production and rising standards of living in the United States and other countries. The Department is therefore concerned that all policies affecting United States foreign trade, including those relating to foreign trade in individual products, should be consistent with our broad general program of expansion.

[1] International Wheat Council Press Release, August 20, 1946.
[2] Department of State, *Bulletin*, XVI, p. 61.
[3] For a full discussion of American wool import policy, both in the pre-war and postwar periods, see *ibid.*, XV, p. 783.
[4] *Ibid.*, XIII, p. 837.

Over a longer period of years the United States has been one of the world's largest importers of wool. During the war, large stocks of wool have accumulated in the countries producing for export. Policies which affect our importation of wool are, therefore, an important phase of our foreign economic relations generally, and one in which the Department of State has a vital interest.

Earlier testimony has already brought out the fact that in the United States, early in the war, contracts for wool goods for the armed forces provided a premium for the use of domestic wool. At that time there was danger that Australia and New Zealand would be cut off as sources of supply, and it was considered wise to stimulate domestic wool production. Prices of domestic wool, as a consequence of these premium payments, rose above the duty-paid import prices of foreign wool. Ceiling prices on domestic wool were established in 1942 by the Office of Price Administration after this spread between the price of domestic and duty-paid foreign wool had developed.

Because the Commodity Credit Corporation wool-purchase program, which began April 25, 1943 and is currently scheduled to continue through June 1946, maintains prices of domestic wool at this ceiling, mills are now buying foreign wool almost exclusively to produce goods for the domestic market. The Corporation is therefore accumulating in its stocks practically all of the domestic wool output.

There is no doubt that a program is urgently needed at this time which will enable domestic wool to move into the domestic market in competition with imported wool. Further, there is the long-run problem of determining the minimum requirements of domestic wool production in the United States for national security.

The methods which have been proposed to make domestic wool available to the domestic market and maintain a minimum level of wool production fall into two broad categories. The first category includes measures to adjust prices of foreign wool in this country upward toward the support prices of domestic wool by extending controls over wool imports through an increase in the import duty, the establishment of import quotas, or the importation of foreign wool by a government agency. The second category includes measures which would enable domestic wool to be sold to domestic mills at prices competitive with the duty-paid import prices of foreign wool.

The basic objection to measures falling in the first category is that they all require the erection of new barriers to international trade at a time when it is of the utmost importance that the United States carry out the mandate which the people have given to the President through a series of acts of Congress to pursue vigorously a program for expanding world trade through the reduction of such barriers.

The imposition of restrictive import quotas or importations through a government agency would have much the same result as an increase in the import duty on wool above the present basic rate of 34 cents per clean pound. Any one of these measures would therefore fly directly in the face of the strong efforts which we are making to persuade other countries to join with us in knocking down the network of trade barriers which was strangling foreign trade of all countries, including that of the United States, in the years just preceding the war. If we want to achieve that level of prosperity at home and abroad to which the Chairman of this Committee referred, we cannot ourselves take the lead in building up new barriers to trade.

In his address to which I have already referred, the Secretary of State indicated that we shall shortly submit to the peoples of the world our views about these matters, and that we intend to propose that tariffs shall be reduced and tariff preferences be eliminated. An increase in one of our major tariff rates would be contrary to everything we are trying to do to open up the channels of international commerce.

Quotas have been one of the greatest obstacles to American exports that our trade has encountered. Their effects have been far more restrictive than have the tariffs of foreign countries. They are generally discriminatory in effect owing to the virtual impossibility of allocating quota shares to the exporting countries on an equitable basis. The Secretary of State, in his address, indicated that we intend to propose that commercial quotas and embargoes be restricted to a few really necessary cases and that discrimination in their application be avoided.

State trading, except in time of war, is utterly alien to the American way of doing business. While we do not intend to try to dictate what economic systems other countries shall have, I am sure the American people would not look with favor upon the substitution of public enterprise for private enterprise in this country. For those governments that do conduct public enterprises in foreign trade, we intend to propose that they should be operated so as to give fair treatment to the commerce of all friendly states, that they should make their purchases and sales on purely economic grounds, and that they should avoid using a monopoly of imports to give excessive protection to their own producers.

For these reasons the Department hopes that this Committee will seek measures which will enable domestic wool to compete with foreign wool in the domestic market at the duty-paid import price. To the extent that these measures may require appropriation of funds from the Federal Treasury, such expenditures should properly be regarded as a part of the cost of the war and of future national security.

The question at issue here is not whether there shall be a subsidy, but what kind of a subsidy there shall be, who shall pay it, and how much it will cost. Tariffs or other controls over imports have the purpose of increasing the price of wool in the domestic market above the world price, and thus they constitute a subsidy to the domestic producer in that his return is higher than he would otherwise receive from the sale of the product. The difference is that, if imports are restricted, the consumer pays the subsidy on all the wool consumed whether domestically produced or imported, whereas in the procedure I have favored, the subsidy is paid by the taxpayers but only on that part of domestic consumption which is domestically produced. This would appear to be a more equitable way of allocating the cost of the subsidy required to maintain the domestic production of wool at a level which is deemed, as a matter of public policy, to be in the national interest.

If we use the method of selling the domestic clip at the duty-paid import price, there must be assurances that the world price will not be depressed unreasonably by policies followed in liquidating the stocks which have accumulated during the war. This Government is therefore prepared to urge upon those countries which hold large stocks that the United States and other importing and exporting countries participate in the formulation of decisions governing liquidation policy.

Our Government is now making a frontal attack on barriers to world trade. If we erect further barriers, that action would be interpreted by all nations as evidence of lack of faith in our own policies. The reestablishment of trade patterns cannot be long delayed. Unless there is a general reduction of barriers soon, countries may be forced further to entrench themselves behind protective walls while they reconstruct and expand uneconomic industries in order to attain greater self-sufficiency. It is therefore the hope of the Department of State that the action taken by this Committee will be consistent with the foreign economic policy of this country which is directed toward the expansion of world trade.

In a letter to President Truman in January 1946 Senator Joseph C. O'Mahoney, Chairman of the Special Committee to Investigate the Production, Transportation and Marketing of Wool, urged that a constructive long-term policy on domestic wool be adopted to aid the domestic wool-growing industry. In his reply to Senator O'Mahoney, transmitting a proposed wool program [1] based on a study by the Office of War Mobilization and Reconversion, President Truman included the following comments: "In addition to such a legislative program, it would seem desirable to have the executive agencies undertake the development of an international wool agreement in collaboration with the various interested foreign governments to provide for coordinated action and more unified supervision of world wool marketing and price policies from the standpoints of producers, consumers, and international trade. I am asking the executive agencies to determine the willingness of foreign governments to participate in such undertaking. In the meantime, it is hoped that consultations can be held with foreign wool agencies which will provide for a mutual understanding of objectives and activities in selling policies." [2]

B. International Wool Talks and the Establishment of the Wool Study Group

At the invitation of the United Kingdom Government, representatives of thirteen countries, including the United States, participated in discussion of the world apparel wool situation on November 11-15, 1946 in London. There was subsequent agreement that: (1) there should be continued intergovernmental survey of the wool problems; (2) an International Wool Study Group should be established; (3) the United Kingdom government should obtain decisions of the various governments regarding the creation of a Wool Study Group by February 1, 1947. The proposed Study Group, as planned at the Conference, was to (1) study the world wool picture, (2) disseminate information regarding supply and

[1] The Seventy-Ninth Congress did not enact a wool bill before adjournment. A bill, S. 2033, with provisions similar to those of the President's program was reported favorably by the Senate Committee on Agriculture and Forestry. For a summary of the President's domestic wool program, see *ibid.*, XV, p. 788.

[2] *Ibid.*, p. 789.

demand, (3) work on solutions to unusual problems of wool trade and (4) provide advice and recommendations to participating governments.[1]

Although given a large share of attention to the formation of the Study Group, the Conference also considered fully the statistics on world stocks, production and consumption of apparel wool, and reviewed the situation for 1946–1947. Further agreement was reached on the desirability of avoiding price fluctuations, the desirability of expanding world consumption of wool and the desirability of liquidation of large stocks at reasonable and stable price levels.[2]

[1] For a report on the international wool talks, see *ibid.*, p. 1163.
[2] *Ibid.*

CHAPTER XII

LABOR AND SOCIAL PROBLEMS

1. LABOR PROBLEMS

A. The International Labor Organization

The 27th Session of the International Labor Conference, with 48 member nations represented, met in Paris, France, from October 15 to November 5, 1945, at which time the chief topic for discussion was the formulation of constitutional amendments to separate the ILO from the League of Nations and to enable the Organization to exist independently. Additional resolutions were adopted concerning (1) maintenance of high levels of employment during the period of industrial reconversion and rehabilitation, (2) a young workers' Charter and (3) minimum standards of social policy in dependent territories. Delegates representing the United States were as follows: Frances Perkins, formerly United States Secretary of Labor, and Senator Elbert D. Thomas, chairman of the Military Affairs Committee, government delegates; David Zellerbach, employers' delegate; Robert J. Watt, workers' delegate.[1]

The 28th (Maritime) Session, which dealt entirely with social policy in the maritime industry, convened in Seattle, Washington, on June 6, 1946.[2] Salient points for consideration centered around (1) the question of establishing an international minimum-wage standard, (2) problems of hours, working standards, manning procedures, crew accommodations, holidays with pay, continuation of employment and social security for seafarers. The United States Delegation included Lewis B. Schwellenbach, Secretary of Labor and Rep. Henry M. Jackson, Member of the Marine and Fisheries Committee, as government representatives; Maitland S. Pennington, as employers' representative; Harry Lundeberg, workers' representative.[3]

Prior to the Montreal meeting of the 29th Session of the International Labor Conference, a Conference Delegation on Constitutional Questions (composed of delegates from the United States, France, Great Britain, Cuba, Union of South Africa and China) drew up amendments providing for effective relationship between the International Labor Organization and the United Nations.

The 29th Session of the International Labor Conference,[4] which met at Montreal, Canada, from September 19 to October 9, 1946, was attended by representatives from 46 member states and by observers from the United Nations, the United Nations Relief and Rehabilitation Administration, the United Nations Educational, Scientific and Cultural Organization, the Intergovernmental Committee on Refugees and the Provisional International Civil Aviation Organization. The tripartite United States Delegation to the Montreal Conference included David A. Morse, Assistant Secretary of Labor, and Senator Elbert D. Thomas, as government delegates; James D. Zellerbach, as employers' delegate; Robert J. Watt, as workers' delegate.[5]

The agenda for the 29th Session covered the following six categories: (1) Director's report which dealt with immediate peace problems, international economic collaboration, the organization of employment and activities of the Organization since November 1945; (2) reports on application of conventions; (3) constitutional questions; (4) budgetary and financial matters; (5) protection of children and young workers; (6) minimum standards of social policy in dependent terri-

---

[1] Department of State, *Bulletin*, XIII, p. 470; *ibid.*, XIV, p. 668.
[2] For further information on the Maritime Session, see this volume, p. 678.
[3] Department of State, *Bulletin*, XIV, p. 993.   [4] *Ibid.*, XV, p. 1034.   [5] *Ibid.*, p. 573.

tories. With the exception of the Director's report (which was discussed during seven plenary sessions) agenda items were referred to committees which reported back to the Conference. Senator Elbert D. Thomas acted as chairman of the Committee on Minimum Standards of Social Policy in Dependent Territories.

After recommendations by the various committees, the Conference adopted an instrument for the amendment of the Organization's constitution, four international labor conventions, two recommendations and fourteen resolutions.[1]

Important amendments to the constitution were designed to (1) promote the objects set forth in the Declaration of Philadelphia, (2) delete all references to the League of Nations, (3) facilitate cooperation between the Organization and the United Nations, (4) extend greater recognition to the Governing Body, (5) change the title of Director of the International Labor Office to Director General, (6) clarify the obligations of member states in respect to conventions and recommendations and (7) empower the Governing Body to recommend measures to secure compliance with the terms of ratified conventions.

The Conference also approved a draft agreement between the United Nations and the International Labor Organization, which was subsequently accepted by the General Assembly on December 14 and signed on December 20, thus bringing the ILO into official relationship with the United Nations as a specialized agency under the coordinating authority of the Economic and Social Council.[2]

Pursuant to a decision of the Governing Body in January, 1945, the following seven major industrial committees were established to cover social and economic aspects of the various industries: Coal Mining (first meeting, December 5, 1945); Inland Transport (first meeting, December 13, 1945); Iron and Steel Production (first meeting, April 23, 1946);[3] Metal Trades (first meeting, May 2, 1946); Textiles (first meeting, November 14, 1946); Building, Civil Engineering and Public Works (first meeting, November 25, 1946); and Petroleum Production and Refining.

The Third Conference of American States members of the ILO met in Mexico City, April 1 to 16, 1946, to discuss vocational training, labor inspection, industrial relations, inflation and problems of the Indian populations. Senator Dennis Chavez and Verne A. Zimmer, Division of Labor Standards, represented the United States Government; James D. Zellerbach represented United States employers and George Meany represented United States workers.

The first post-war session of the Permanent Migration Committee of the International Labor Office took place in Montreal from August 26 to 31, 1946, attended by the following 25 governments: Australia, Argentina, Belgium, Chile, Colombia, Denmark, Dominican Republic, Ecuador, Egypt, France, Greece, India, Italy, Mexico, the Netherlands, New Zealand, Panama, Peru, Poland, Portugal, Sweden, Switzerland, United States, Uruguay and Venezuela. Canada, the United Kingdom and Yugoslavia sent observers. Three advisory members representing the United Nations, the United Nations Relief and Rehabilitation Administration and the Intergovernmental Committee on Refugees were present. Work of the Committee centered around various aspects of the migration problem and four resolutions which prepared the way for greater bilateral and multilateral international cooperation in post-war migration. Robert C. Goodwin, Director, United States Employment Service of the Department of Labor was designated as United States government member of the Committee.[4]

2. SOCIAL PROBLEMS

A. The Economic and Social Council

The Charter of the United Nations authorized the General Assembly to initiate studies and formulate recommendations for promoting international cooperation in the economic, social, cultural, educational and health fields. The Economic

---

[1] The Organization has adopted 80 conventions and 80 recommendations to date. Fifty of the conventions are in force.
[2] *Ibid.*, XVI, p. 24. [3] *Ibid.*, XV, p. 447. [4] *Ibid.*, XVI, p. 120.

and Social Council was also instructed to organize studies and make recommendations regarding international economic, social, cultural, educational, health and related matters in order to promote fundamental freedom and respect for human rights. Commissions established by the Council to further work in the social field included the Social Commission, the Commission on the Status of Women, the Narcotics Commission, the Population Commission and the Commission on Human Rights.

The Social Commission, formed as a nuclear commission by the First Session of the Economic and Social Council, submitted a report dealing with international organizations in the social field to the Second Session of the Council. Subsequently, the permanent Social Commission was established to advise the Council on all social matters outside the investigation of specialized agencies and on international agreements on social questions. The Commission on the Status of Women, formerly a sub-commission of the Commission on Human Rights, was established by the Council at its Second Session. Work of the Commission centered around (1) political rights of women, (2) survey of laws pertaining to the status of women and (3) polls to determine public opinion. The Commission on Narcotic Drugs, the first commission set up by the Economic and Social Council, was instructed to advise the Council on matters relating to control of drugs, application of necessary international agreements. The first meeting of the Narcotic Commission, from November 27 to December 15, 1946, resulted in resumption of international controls in drugs, such as limitation of production of raw materials, abolition of opium smoking in the Far East and international control of drugs not covered by existing conventions. At the Third Session of the Council, the Population Commission was authorized to deal with population problems, particularly (1) population changes, (2) migratory movements and (3) economic and social conditions pertaining to the foregoing. A nuclear Commission on Human Rights, initiated by the Economic and Social Council at its First Session, began investigation of recognition of human rights and recommended the formulation of an International Bill of Rights. Commission studies have included (1) minority protection, (2) prevention of discrimination, (3) civil liberties and (4) all matters dealing with human rights. Three subcommissions, freedom of press information, protection of minorities, and prevention of discriminations, were set up under Commission direction.

1. HUMAN RIGHTS

In the interval between the Dumbarton Oaks Conversations and the United Nations Conference on International Organization at San Francisco, efforts were made to insure that the Charter would further amplify the commitment of the Dumbarton Oaks Proposals that the promotion of human rights should be included in the Charter of the international organization. Consultants to the American Delegation at the San Francisco Conference, appointed by national groups at the invitation of the Department of State, implemented the movement by urging the American Delegation to sponsor amendments insuring the development of human rights.[1] As a result, the phrase "human rights and fundamental freedoms for all without distinction as to race, sex, language or religion" occurred several times in the Charter, and the Preamble specifically stressed the importance of fundamental rights. The Charter also provided that the General Assembly initiate studies and make recommendations for "assisting in the realization of human rights and fundamental freedoms for all without distinction as to race, sex, language, or religion" and that the Economic and Social Council "make recommendations for the purpose of promoting respect for, and observance of, human rights and fundamental freedoms for all."

On May 15, 1946, former Secretary of State Edward R. Stettinius, stated: "The provisions proposed for the Charter will not, of course, assure by themselves the realization of human rights and fundamental freedoms for all people. The provisions are not made enforceable by any international machinery. The

[1] *Ibid.*, XIV, p. 212.

responsibility rests with the member governments to carry them out. We can here make only a beginning, but I believe it is a good and substantial beginning. ... The United States Government will work actively and tirelessly, both for its own people, and — through the international Organization — for peoples generally, toward the protection and promotion of these rights and freedoms. We must be eternally vigilant against assaults upon them. We must also act affirmatively to enlarge the scope of their protection and to nourish their growth. As long as rights and freedoms are denied to some, the rights and freedoms of all are endangered. Everything possible must be done to bring to effective life not only the commission on human rights, but the other vital agencies and functions of the Economic and Social Council." [1]

International action in the field of human rights was considered so imperative that the Economic and Social Council was specifically instructed to create such a commission. The Executive Committee of the Preparatory Commission of the United Nations at London recommended that the work of the Commission center around (1) formulation of an international bill of rights, (2) formulation of recommendations for an international declaration on civil liberties, status of women, freedom of information, (3) protection of minorities, (4) prevention of discrimination and (5) matters of human rights considered essential to general welfare.

On February 16, 1946, the Economic and Social Council resolved to establish a nuclear Commission on Human Rights, which subsequently met in New York from April 29 to May 20, 1946, under the Chairmanship of Mrs. Franklin D. Roosevelt, United States Representative. Delegates from Norway, USSR, Yugoslavia, France, Belgium, Peru, China and India were members of the nuclear Commission. After approving the report of the Commission, the Economic and Social Council passed a resolution on June 21, thereby establishing a permanent Commission on Human Rights. On May 8, 1946, the United States Delegation to the United Nations transmitted to the Secretary-General a proposal for the establishment of a Subcommission on Freedom of Information.

(1) *Proposal by the United States for the Establishment of a Subcommission on Freedom of Information, Transmitted by the United States Delegation to the United Nations to the Secretary-General for Reference to the Commission on Human Rights, May 8, 1946.*[2]

The Commission on Human Rights has been directed by the Economic and Social Council to undertake among its first tasks the preparation and submission of proposals, recommendations, and reports to the Council on freedom of information.

It is the view of the Government of the United States that:

(a) material progress toward the ultimate attainment of universal freedom of information is of the utmost importance if the United Nations is to achieve the purposes for which it has been established; (b) the Commission on Human Rights will require special advice and assistance in carrying out its responsibilities toward the fulfillment of this important and complex task.

It is therefore proposed that the Commission on Human Rights recommend to the Economic and Social Council the establishment, at the Council's next session, of a Subcommission on Freedom of Information. This Subcommission should consist of from ten to fifteen members, who need not be members of the Commission on Human Rights, to be ap-

[1] *Ibid.*   [2] *Ibid.*, p. 855.

pointed by the Council and serving in an individual capacity. The following terms of reference are suggested for the Subcommission:

1. The Subcommission should submit proposals, recommendations and reports to the Commission on Human Rights regarding freedom of information. In the discharge of this function, the Subcommission should

   a. determine what rights, obligations and practices should, in the Subcommission's opinion, be included in the concept, freedom of information;

   b. consider and report on the extent to which freedom of information as thus defined is accorded to the peoples of the United Nations; and the nature and extent of obstacles thereto;

   c. examine proposals for promoting or facilitating freedom of information and eliminating obstacles thereto;

   d. make recommendations to the extent deemed appropriate for action by the United Nations, by member states, and by UNESCO and other specialized agencies;

   e. assume continuing responsibilities for discussing and preparing, with the assistance of the Secretariat, a draft provision on freedom of information to be incorporated in a bill of rights.

2. In the discharge of its functions the Subcommission should maintain close working relations with UNESCO and other specialized agencies whose activities may be related to the field of its competence.

3. The Subcommission may submit proposals to the Council, through the Commission on Human Rights, regarding its terms of reference.

2. CONTROL OF NARCOTIC DRUGS

Due to war conditions the Opium Advisory Committee which had begun preparatory work relating to a conference on the limitation of opium production was unable to hold meetings after 1940. In 1939, however, it had prepared a draft of the main articles which might be embodied in a convention for limiting the cultivation of the opium poppy and the production of raw opium. Thereafter, the United States continued the work of preparation. Following the Judd Resolution [1] adopted by the United States government on July 1, 1944, the United States wrote the governments of Afghanistan, China, Iran, Mexico, Turkey, the Union of Soviet Socialist Republics, the United Kingdom (for India and Burma) and Yugoslavia proposing a conference to draft a convention prohibiting the cultivation of the opium poppy except for medical and scientific needs. Favorable replies were received from Afghanistan, China, India, Turkey, Union of Soviet Socialist Republics and the United Kingdom.[2]

On September 21, 1943 *aide-mémoires* were delivered in Washington to the Chinese and Netherlands Ambassadors, the Minister of Portugal and the British Chargé d'Affaires [3] stating that the policy to be pursued by all American expeditionary forces under American command upon occupation of territories occupied by Japanese forces would be to seize all drugs, except those intended for medical

---

[1] See *Documents, VII, 1944–1945*, p. 694.

[2] During discussions of the Commission on Narcotic Drugs, the representatives of Iran, Mexico and Yugoslavia indicated agreement to participate in such a conference. For exchange of notes between the United States and Great Britain relating to limitation of the production of opium, see Department of State, *Bulletin*, XIV, p. 237; for similar exchange with the USSR, see *ibid.*, XIII, p. 129; with Turkey, *ibid.*, p. 63.

[3] For exchange of notes between the United States and the United Kingdom, see *ibid.*, XV, p. 1165–1170.

and scientific purposes. The United States proposed that a similar policy be extended to the expeditionary forces under allied command and that resumption of control over territories occupied by the Japanese would result in necessary legislation prohibiting the use of opium and other dangerous drugs. The governments of the Netherlands and the United Kingdom in November 1943 and the government of France in January 1944 announced their intention of adopting a policy of complete prohibition of opium smoking in their Far Eastern territories following release of these territories from enemy occupation. On May 28, 1946, Portugal issued a decree abolishing the opium monopoly in Macao.[1]

Narcotic control in the United States zone in Germany was initiated in December, 1945, and carried on by means of Opium Offices established in each of the three Laender in the zone. The German law of 1929 relating to control of narcotic drugs was reestablished after certain changes by Military Government regulations. Administration of the Opium Offices was left in the hands of German officials under the supervision of the chief narcotic-control office of the Military Government.

In line with cooperative efforts at international drug control, the United States accepted membership on the Commission on Narcotic Drugs, which was created on February 18, 1946, by the Economic and Social Council. The following resolution constitutes the terms of reference of the Commission:[2]

1. The Economic and Social Council, in order to provide machinery whereby full effect may be given to the international conventions relating to narcotic drugs, and to provide for continuous review of and progress in the international control of such drugs, establishes a Commission on Narcotic Drugs.

2. The Commission shall:
   (a) assist the Council in exercising such powers of supervision over the application of international conventions and agreements dealing with narcotic drugs as may be assumed by or conferred on the Council;
   (b) carry out such functions entrusted to the League of Nations Advisory Committee on Traffic in Opium and other Dangerous Drugs by the international conventions on narcotic drugs as the Council may find necessary to assume and continue;
   (c) advise the Council on all matters pertaining to the control of narcotic drugs, and prepare such draft international conventions as may be necessary;
   (d) consider what changes may be required in the existing machinery for the international control of narcotic drugs and submit proposals thereon to the Council;
   (e) perform such other functions relating to narcotic drugs as the Council may direct.

3. The Commission may make recommendations to the Council concerning any subcommission which it considers should be established.

4. The Commission shall be composed of fifteen Members of the United Nations, which are important producing or manufacturing countries or countries in which illicit traffic in narcotic drugs constitutes a serious social problem. The term of office of members is three years. They are eligible for reappointment.

5. The Commission is authorized by the Council to appoint in a consultative capacity, and without the right to vote, representatives of bodies created under the terms of international conventions on narcotic drugs.

6. The Council requests the following Governments to designate one representative each to constitute the Commission: Canada, China, Egypt, France, India, Iran, Mexico, Netherlands, Peru, Poland, Turkey, United Kingdom, United States of America, Union of Soviet Socialist Republics, and Yugoslavia.

---

[1] United Nations Economic and Social Council, *Official Records*, Second Year, Fourth Session, Supplement No. 1, Report of the Commission on Narcotic Drugs, New York, 1946.

[2] Department of State, *Bulletin*, XV, p. 887.

The Commission convened for the first time at Lake Success, New York, from November 27 to December 13, 1946, with an agenda which included (1) an invitation to the Permanent Central Opium Board and the Supervisory Body to be represented at the session, (2) discussion of the Commission's terms of reference, (3) transfer to the United Nations of functions previously exercised by the League of Nations, (4) limitation of the production of raw materials for drug manufacturing, (5) abolition of opium smoking in the Far East, (6) drug addiction, (7) illicit traffic, (8) future appointments to the Permanent Central Opium Board and (9) reestablishment of international control of narcotic drugs.[1] The first session was concerned mainly with problems relating to organization. After reviewing the situation since 1940 when the work of the League of Nations in narcotics was interrupted by the war, a special review was made of particular problems concerning the limitation of production of raw materials, opium-smoking in the Far East, illicit traffic and drug addiction. The Commission also gave special attention to a proposal for extended control of drugs in Japan and Korea.

With respect to the transfer to the United Nations of the powers and functions exercised by the League of Nations under the international conventions on narcotic drugs, on October 3, 1946, the Economic and Social Council approved a draft protocol amending the agreements, conventions and protocols concluded in 1912, 1925, 1931 and 1936. On November 19, 1946, the General Assembly approved this protocol; the amendments set forth in the annex were to come into force with respect to each international instrument when the majority of parties became parties to the protocol. On December 11, 1946, representatives of 36 countries signed the protocol transferring to the United Nations the functions performed by the League under the international drug conventions.

The Commission studied the arrangements to ensure continuance of the work of the Permanent Central Opium Board and the Supervisory Body and the fusion of their respective secretariats as of September, 1946. It was suggested that the Opium Board and Supervisory Body consider the possibility of establishing the seat of the two organizations near the headquarters of the United Nations.

The following representative and assistants from the United States were present at the initial meeting of the Commission: H. J. Anslinger; George A. Morlock; John W. Bulkley; Julia H. Renfrew.

(1) *Statement on United States Policy Relating to Opium by the Adviser to the United States Representative on the Commission on Narcotic Drugs (Morlock), Submitted to the Commission on Narcotic Drugs, September 11, 1946.*[2]

[Excerpts]

. . . . . .

The interest of the United States in narcotics control increased considerably soon after our annexation of the Philippine Islands in 1898, where a government monopoly for sales of opium to addicts, principally Chinese, for the satisfaction of their addiction, had been legalized prior to annexation. The Congress of the United States passed an act, approved 3 March 1905, providing "That after March first, nineteen hundred and eight, it shall be unlawful to import into the Philippine Islands opium, in whatever form, except by the Government, and for medicinal purposes only, and at no time shall it be lawful to sell opium to any native of the Philippine Islands except for medicinal purposes."

[1] *Ibid.*, XVI, p. 91.
[2] United Nations Economic and Social Council, Document E/C.S.7/8, November 26, 1946, p. 57; reprinted from the Department of State, *Bulletin*, XI, p. 48.

Recognizing that nations acting alone are unable adequately to protect themselves against the international illicit traffic in narcotic drugs, the United States decided to co-operate with other nations in the control of the legal trade in these dangerous drugs and in international efforts to suppress their abuse. It took the initiative in bringing about the first international conference on the subject, which was held in Shanghai in 1909, and later proposed the convening of the conference which resulted in the international opium convention signed at The Hague on 23 January 1912. The American Government took part in the conferences held at The Hague in 1912, in 1913, and in 1914; participated in the Second Geneva Drug Conference of 1924–25; and in the Narcotics Limitation Conference of 1931 held at Geneva; was represented by an observer at the Bangkok Conference of 1931 on Opium Smoking in the Far East, and sent delegates to the Conference for the Suppression of the Illicit Traffic in Dangerous Drugs at Geneva in 1936. In those conferences representatives of the Government of the United States clearly stated that the policy of the United States was to limit the production of the poppy plant and manufacture of narcotic drugs strictly to medical and scientific requirements and to consider use for any other purpose as abuse. The Department of State, through its representatives at international conferences and at meetings of the Opium Advisory Committee at Geneva, has constantly carried on a vigorous campaign looking to the suppression of the illicit traffic in narcotic drugs and the abuse of those drugs.

The delegates for the United States withdrew from the Geneva Drug Conference of 1925 when it became apparent that the Conference would not restrict the production of opium and coca leaves to the medicinal and scientific requirements of the world. The withdrawal of the American delegation was based on a memorandum by the chairman of the American delegation, the Honourable Stephen G. Porter, addressed to the president of the Conference on 6 February 1925. As this memorandum outlines principles of policy to which the United States has consistently adhered, it is reproduced below in full:

> On October 18, 1923, the League of Nations extended an invitation to the powers signatory to The Hague Convention, including the United States, to participate in an international conference which was called for the purpose of giving effect to the following principles, subject to reservations made by certain nations regarding smoking opium.
>
> One. If the purpose of the Hague Opium Convention is to be achieved according to its spirit and true intent it must be recognized that the use of opium products for other than medical and scientific purpose is an abuse and not legitimate.
>
> Two. In order to prevent the abuse of these products it is necessary to exercise the control of the production of raw opium in such a manner that there will be no surplus available for non-medical and non-scientific purpose.
>
> The joint resolution adopted by the Congress of the United States on May 15, 1924, authorizing our participation in the present conference, quoted the principles referred to in the preamble and expressly stipulated that the representatives of the United States shall sign no agreement which does not fulfill the conditions necessary for the suppression of the narcotic drug traffic as set forth in the preamble.

Despite more than two months of discussion and repeated adjournments it now clearly appears that the purpose for which the Conference was called cannot be accomplished. The reports of the various committees of the Conference plainly indicate that there is no likelihood under present conditions that the production of raw opium and coca leaves will be restricted to the medicinal and scientific needs of the world. In fact the nature of the reservations made show that no appreciable reduction in raw opium may be expected.

It was hoped that if the nations in whose territories the use of smoking opium is temporarily permitted would, in pursuance of the obligation undertaken under Chapter Two of the Hague Convention, adopt measures restricting the importation of raw opium for the manufacture of smoking opium or would agree to suppress the traffic within a definite period, such action would materially reduce the market for raw opium and an extensive limitation of production would inevitably follow.

Unfortunately, however, these nations with the exception of Japan are not prepared to reduce the consumption of smoking opium. Unless the producing nations agree to reduce production and prevent smuggling from their territories and then only in the event of an adequate guarantee being given that the obligations undertaken by the producing nations would be effectively and promptly fulfilled, no restriction of the production of raw opium under such conditions can be expected.

In the matter of manufactured drugs and the control of transportation an improvement over the Hague Convention is noticeable. There is, however, no likelihood of obtaining a complete control of all opium and coca leaf derivative irrespective of the measure of control provided. For manufactured drugs it is believed that by reason of the very small bulk, the ease of transportation with minimum risk of detection, and the large financial gains to be obtained from their illicit handling, such drugs and their derivatives can only be effectively controlled if the production of the raw opium and coca leaves from which they are obtained is strictly limited to medical and scientific purposes. This the Conference is unable to accomplish.

In the circumstances the delegation of the United States in pursuance of instructions received from its Government has no alternative under terms of the joint resolution authorizing participation in the conference other than to withdraw, as it could not sign the agreement which it is proposed to conclude. We desire to make it clear that withdrawal from the present conference does not mean that the United States will cease its efforts through international co-operation for the suppression of the illicit traffic in opium and other dangerous drugs. The United States recognizes that the world-wide traffic in habit-forming drugs can be suppressed only by international co-operation but believes that for the present at least greater strides in the control of the traffic may be hoped for if it should continue to work towards this end upon the basis of the Hague Convention of 1912.

The narcotic drugs which are the subject of international co-operation are the principal habit-forming ones, namely, opium and its derivatives, the coca leaf and its derivatives, and *Cannabis sativa* and its derivatives. Opium is the coagulated juice obtained from the capsules of the soporific poppy (*Papaver somniferum*). The principal derivates of opium are morphine, heroin, and codeine. The principal derivative of the coca leaf is cocaine. *Cannabis sativa* is Indian hemp, from which hashish, marihuana, and other dangerous drugs are made.

. . . .

The principal cause of illicit traffic is surplus production. The United States has been making and continues to make every effort to persuade the poppy-producing countries of the world to reduce production. For this reason the United States has discouraged the planting of the opium poppy within its territories and possessions for the production of opium and opium products, although it could easily supply its entire requirements. Nevertheless, large-scale production continues in other parts of the world. . . .

. . . . . .

The Governments of the United Kingdom and the Netherlands, after pursuing for many years a policy of gradual suppression of the use of smoking opium, decided last year to make a change in policy in view of the new conditions which will prevail in their Far Eastern territories as a consequence of the Japanese occupation. On 10 November 1943 they announced that on regaining control of their Far Eastern territories they would suppress the smoking of opium and would not re-establish the opium monopolies. This means that a market which averaged 347,036 kilogrammes of opium annually during the years 1933 to 1938 will disappear. It is obvious, therefore, that, if present world production continues at the rate of 2,400,000 kilogrammes a year, about 2,000,000 kilogrammes will remain for the satisfaction of drug addiction. The United States is anxious to prevent this surplus production, thus liberating several million souls throughout the world from the awful slavery of drug addiction.

There is immediate need for the opium-producing and consuming countries of the world to join in an international convention to limit and control the cultivation of the opium poppy and to suppress the illicit traffic in opium. The United States, as one of the principal victims, is deeply interested in and is prepared to co-operate with all nations in efforts to solve this problem.

. . . . . .

In view of the large world production of opium over and above medical needs, the United States has, whenever opportunity offered, discouraged production in this hemisphere, because new production in any areas, even if restricted and controlled, results in making an equal quantity in an old producing area available to non-medical use or to the illicit traffic. The experience of opium-producing countries is that, even with severe laws well enforced, it is extremely difficult to prevent the escape of a part of the production into the international illicit traffic and to check the spread of addiction and illegal use within the country. The history of narcotics in China, India, and Iran confirms this statement.

The United States regards the present time as propitious for the poppy-producing and narcotic-drugs-consuming countries to give serious consideration to the advisability of joining immediately after the war in a convention for the limitation and control of the cultivation of the opium poppy strictly to medicinal and scientific requirements.

(2) *Statement by the United States Representative on the Commission on Narcotic Drugs (Anslinger) Regarding the Control of Narcotic Drugs in the United States Zone in Germany, Submitted to the Commission on Narcotic Drugs, December 20, 1946.*[1]

[Excerpts]

Narcotic control in the United States Zone in Germany was initiated in December 1945. It is exercised through Opium Offices established in each of the three Laender in the Zone. They function under the Minister President and are located in the Interior Ministry, Public Health Department. So far as possible all of the reports required by the former Opium Offices have been re-established and copies are furnished to the United States Military Government. . . . Inventories required of persons authorized to handle narcotics are being received according to the provisions of the law. Administration of the Opium Offices is entirely in hands of the German officials, but their activities are supervised by the chief narcotic control office of Military Government. All interzonal transactions are examined by Military Government and none are made without approval of that Office. While each of the Opium Offices is a separate unit, uniformity is achieved by monthly meetings of the chiefs at which the Narcotic Control Officer is present.

Statistics on addiction are being collected and information on this subject will be kept in the files of the three Opium Offices. There are indications that large quantities of narcotics scattered by bombings and left behind by the retreating German armies are in the hands of unauthorized individuals at the present time and will eventually reach the black market. The re-establishment of the inspection system has revealed an increase in the number of addicts, particularly among professional people. There is a desire on the part of the authorities to provide institutional treatment for addicts, but there is a shortage of facilities for such treatments.

. . . .

The development of the control system has been slow and difficult. Each of the three Land Opium Offices had to be staffed by inexperienced personnel and an inspection service had to be re-established. After much painstaking work on the part of the American authorities, an adequate supply of narcotics in the United States Zone is being assured and the illegal traffic and drug addiction are being kept at a minimum. Efforts are being made for close co-operation between the regulating officials and the local police in connection with the investigation of violations of the narcotic laws. . . .

On the whole the control system in Germany is unsatisfactory. In order to improve the situation the United States Delegate submitted a proposal to the Allied Health Committee for the establishment of a Narcotics Control Working Party, as follows:

[1] United Nations Economic and Social Council, Document E/C.S.7/60, December 20, 1946, p. 17.

1. ... It is proposed that a Working Party be appointed to study the question of collecting certain statistics on narcotic drugs with a view to providing such statistics eventually to competent authorities designated by United Nations. Such statistics would be concerned with:
   (a) Facilities for the production of narcotic drugs in Germany.
   (b) Amounts of narcotic drugs required for medical use within Germany.
   (c) Quantities of narcotic drugs currently in the hands of legitimate dealers in Germany.
   (d) Whatever other information the Working Party may deem essential to the problem of narcotic control.
2. In the belief that such statistics can best be collected by German Civil Authorities acting under authority of the German Opium Law of 1929 and subsequent provisions, it is further proposed that this law be studied by the Working Party in order to make recommendations for:
   (a) Changes necessary to adapt said law to present circumstances.
   (b) The establishment of qualified German Civil Agencies of uniform structure throughout the Zones of Occupation to regulate trade in narcotics under the law.
   (c) The establishment of facilities for gathering and exchanging information for the suppression of illicit traffic in narcotics.
   (d) The establishment of a control office for the collection and distribution of the required information.
3. Because of existing variations among the Zones in the enforcement of the aforesaid German Opium Law, it is believed that the present distribution of narcotics is inefficient and inequitable. In those areas where drugs are needed for legitimate purposes and are not available, great hardship is caused. It is therefore further proposed that the Working Party prepare recommendations which will facilitate:
   (a) The distribution of narcotic drugs for medical or scientific needs *within* the Zones.
   (b) The legitimate trade in narcotics *between* the Zones.

It is further proposed that the Working Party make recommendations for the re-establishment and, where necessary, the expansion of facilities for the rehabilitation and cure of addicts by German Civil Agencies, and for the collection of statistics relative to the incidence of addiction in Germany.

This proposal was considered at a meeting held on 11 September 1946 at Berlin. The Allied Health Committee, after discussing the proposal, agreed (a) that a Working Party be set up; (b) that the terms of reference of the Working Party will be to consider and submit to the Health Committee proposals for the revision of the German Opium Law of 1929 with a view of adapting it to present circumstances as envisaged in the United States proposal and (c) that with the exception of the British member whose name will be submitted later, the composition of the Working Party will be the United States of America, Mr. Giuliani, U.S.S.R., Mr. Karpov and France, Mr. Vergougnon. It was agreed that the first meeting would take place on 23 September 1946. ...

It is suggested that each occupying Power, pending the establishment of centralized controls,

(1) Secure the most uniform, effective and centralized controls possible within their respective areas of responsibility;

(2) Designate an official to supervise those activities within the respective areas and to act as liaison officer with the Commission on Narcotic Drugs and with each other;

(3) Arrange for the direct and prompt exchange of information between such officials, and for the prompt transmission to the Commission on Narcotic Drugs, of pertinent information regarding illicit traffickers, seizures of contraband drugs, and potential violations, connected with traffic across national boundaries or between the respective zones of occupation; and

(4) Report to the Commission on Narcotic Drugs and to each other (*a*) the identity of the officer so designated, (*b*) the stocks of narcotics found to be available for the civilian population and the requirements which must be met, (*c*) the quantities of each drug which will be required to be imported into the respective areas from outside the country or from other zones, and (*d*) the circumstances under which such imports will be permitted and the official titles and addresses of the persons authorized to approve them.

I desire to present for the consideration of the Commission a resolution regarding the situation in Germany:

THE COMMISSION ON NARCOTIC DRUGS

To establish a narcotic control organization which will insure adequate supplies of narcotic drugs for the medicinal and scientific requirements of Germany,
To prevent illicit traffic in narcotic drugs, and
To reduce addiction,
REQUESTS the Economic and Social Council to urge the Governments of France, the United Kingdom, the Union of Soviet Socialist Republics and the United States of America to organize and establish, through their Allied Control Authority, at the earliest possible moment an effective centralized narcotics administration for all Germany.

B. Health

1. WORLD HEALTH ORGANIZATION

On February 15, 1946, at the First Session of the Economic and Social Council, a resolution was adopted, calling for an International Health Conference and providing for a Technical Preparatory Committee, composed of experts from sixteen countries, to meet in Paris, March, 1946, to prepare for the Conference.

Proposals for a draft Constitution for the proposed health organization were developed by the Department of State and Public Health Service in 1945 and early 1946, and on October 11–12, 1945, an Advisory Health Group, composed of national health and civic leaders, adopted a resolution urging the creation of an international health organization. On December 20, 1945, the Senate adopted Senate Joint Resolution 89 requesting the President to urge the United Nations to convene an international health conference for the purpose of establishing an international health organization.[1]

The Economic and Social Council appointed Dr. Thomas Parran, Surgeon General of the United States Public Health Service, to the Technical Preparatory

---

[1] *International Health Conference*, New York, N. Y., June 19 to July 22, 1946, Report of the United States Delegation Including the Final Act and Related Documents, Department of State Publication 2703, p. 1–7. For Report of the Technical Preparatory Committee, see *ibid.*, Annex 10, p. 103–127.

Committee, and also appointed Dr. James A. Doull, Chief of the Office of International Health Relations of the Public Health Service, as alternate. The initial meeting of the Committee held in Paris, March 18 to April 5, 1946, examined draft constitutional proposals, representation at the International Health Conference, the eventual creation of a World Health Organization and an annotated agenda designed to serve as a guide to the International Health Conference.

At its session in May and June, 1946, the Economic and Social Council considered the report of the Technical Preparatory Committee, and further decided to extend Conference invitations to certain states not Members of the United Nations, to the Allied Control Commissions of Germany, Japan, and Korea and to certain international organizations.

The International Health Conference met from June 19 to July 22, 1946, attended by representatives of all Members of the United Nations and by observers from 13 states not members of the United Nations, control authorities of Germany, Japan and Korea, and ten international organizations.

The Conference was concluded by the signing of the following documents: (1) the Final Act (61 states); (2) the Constitution of the World Health Organization (61 states); (3) an Arrangement establishing its Interim Commission (61 states); (4) a Protocol concerning the *Office International d'Hygiène publique* (60 states).[1] Under Constitutional terms, the World Health Organization was designated as a specialized agency to be brought into relationship with the United Nations in accordance with Article 57 of the Charter of the United Nations. The Constitution further provided for integration with the World Health Organization of existing regional intergovernmental health agencies.

Created by a resolution of the Conference, an Interim Commission, composed of eighteen states, began its work before the Conference ended and continued work thereafter under authorization of the Arrangement signed on July 22, 1946, which allowed the Commission to take over the functions of the Health Organization of the League of Nations, the *Office International d'Hygiène publique*, and special functions of UNRRA.

Pending acceptance of the Constitution of the World Health Organization by 26 Members of the United Nations, the Interim Commission was authorized to continue its activities.

The Interim Commission of the World Health Organization convened for its second session in Geneva on November 4, 1946, with representatives of the eighteen member states, except Peru and the Ukraine, present. Work of the Commission included (1) the consolidation of the administration of exchange of epidemiological information, (2) the approval of a draft agreement with the United Nations Relief and Rehabilitation Administration providing for transfer of certain UNRRA health functions to the Interim Commission, (3) the creation of expert committees to serve as nuclei for more permanent groups,[2] (4) a decision to maintain Interim Commission headquarters in New York and to establish an office in Geneva to be concerned primarily with epidemiological information services and health functions (transferred from UNRRA) in Europe. A committee was appointed to study the question of World Health Organization headquarters so that a recommendation might be made at the world health assembly.[3]

The Commission approved several basic principles pertaining to relations between the World Health Organization and other specialized agencies, which aimed at coordinating the work of experts in related fields rather than experts

---

[1] *Ibid.*, p. 1. See also, Department of State, *Bulletin*, XV, p. 453; *ibid.*, p. 756.

[2] Expert committees established by the second session were: Expert Committee on Revision of International List of Causes of Death and on the Establishment of International Lists of Causes of Morbidity; Expert Committee on Biological Standardization; Expert Committee on Pilgrimages; Expert Committee on Quarantine; Expert Committee on Narcotic Drugs; Expert Committee on Malaria.

[3] Information on the Second Session was based on an article by H. Van Zile Hyde, "Second Session of Interim Commission of World Health Organization," Department of State, *Bulletin*, XV, p. 1134.

in the same field by providing for joint committees and subcommittees. Representation on such committees was to be apportioned on the basis of the relative importance of the particular field to the agencies participating in the work of the committees. In certain instances liaison officers were to be appointed between specialized agencies with interests in common.

2. PAN AMERICAN SANITARY BUREAU

The Pan American Sanitary Bureau,[1] the oldest international health body, was created and maintained by the 21 American Republics for purposes of (1) acting as a central coordinating sanitary agency and distribution center, (2) appointing representatives to confer with health authorities of the signatory governments, (3) publishing information on vital statistics, disease status and control, public health organization, (4) stimulating scientific research and (5) facilitating exchanges of medical and health officers.[2]

The Bureau was given initial authorization by the Second International Conference of American States (1901–1902) and organized by the First Pan American Conference (1902). Further reorganization by succeeding Sanitary Conferences extended the powers of the Bureau to include consultation and action in every aspect of public health.[3]

The International Health Conference, convened by the Economic and Social Council in New York on June 19, 1946,[4] took action to provide for integration of regional health organizations, such as the Pan American Sanitary Bureau, with the World Health Organization by mutual agreement.

(1) *Report on the Relations of the Pan American Sanitary Bureau with the World Health Organization, Approved by the Governing Board of the Pan American Union at the Session of November 6, 1946.*[5]

[Excerpts]

Prior to the International Health Conference that met in New York in June, 1946, a preliminary meeting took place from March 18th to April 5th, of the same year in Paris, at which the subject of Regional Arrangements received considerable discussion. . . .

. . . .

When this matter was submitted to the Conference in New York, the United States Delegation offered the following draft project as a basis of discussion:

> Regional inter-governmental health agencies shall be integrated with or brought into relationship with the Organization by means of special agreements between the Organization and such agencies, providing that the agencies shall be transferred into offices of the Organization and that their facilities

---

[1] The Pan American Sanitary Bureau was known as the International Sanitary Bureau until 1923.

[2] Functions of the Bureau were defined by the Pan American Sanitary Code (1924), an international treaty ratified by all the 21 American Republics.

[3] *The Pan American Sanitary Bureau*, Its Organization, Functions and Activities, prepared and distributed by the Pan American Sanitary Bureau, June, 1946.

[4] See this volume, p. 732.

[5] *Report on the Relations of the Pan American Sanitary Bureau with the World Health Organization*, Presented to the Governing Board of the Pan American Union by the Committee on the Organization of the Inter-American System, Approved by the Governing Board of the Pan American Union at the Session of November 6, 1946, Annex I.

and services shall be utilized to the fullest possible extent so as to enable their gradual merging into the Organization by mutual agreement. Such agreements shall be negotiated by the Director General on behalf of the Organization and shall be subject to confirmation by the Conference.

The United States delegation also presented a draft of resolution on the establishment of relationships between the World Health Organization and the Pan American Sanitary Organization. This resolution contemplated the negotiation of an agreement between the two organizations which should embrace the following provisions:

(a) That the Pan American Sanitary Conference be expressly recognized as the appropriate body both (1) to promote programs and undertakings among the American Republics on regional health problems of common interest in continuation of its present work and in harmony with the general policies of the World Health Organization, and (2) in addition to act, when necessary, as the Regional Committee for the Organization in performing the functions set forth in paragraph 1 (b) of Chapter XII.

(b) That the existence and continuance of the Pan American Conference of National Health Directors be expressly recognized.

(c) That the Pan American Sanitary Bureau continue to serve as the administrative agency in executing the recommendations and programs of the Pan American Sanitary Conference, in whichever capacity the latter acts in initiating such programs, and that it function likewise as the Regional Office of the World Health Organization in carrying out, under the general supervision of the Director General of the latter, such projects and functions as may be decided upon by the Organization.

(d) That such appropriate special or regional programs as may be undertaken by the American Republics through the Bureau as a purely inter-American agency be financed independently of the World Health Organization; that all activities of the Bureau as a Regional Office of the Organization be financed from the budget of the Organization, and that unallocable general administrative expenses be equitably apportioned between the Organization and the Bureau.

(e) That provision be made for periodic review of the terms of the agreement to the end of making such alterations as experience may dictate to be desirable.

. . . .

A Harmonizing Subcommittee of 16 members, which included the representatives of Brazil, El Salvador, the United States, Mexico, Peru, the Dominican Republic and Venezuela, was appointed to consider the various proposals. This subcommittee drafted the formula which with minor changes was finally incorporated in the Constitution, with the approval of all the delegations, and which is couched in the following terms:

The Pan American sanitary organization represented by the Pan American Sanitary Bureau and the Pan American Sanitary Conferences, and all other inter-governmental regional health organizations in existence prior to the date of signature of this Constitution, shall in due course be integrated with the Organization. This integration shall be effected as soon as practicable through common action based on mutual consent of the competent authorities expressed through the organizations concerned.

At the New York Conference an agreement was also signed which provided for the appointment of an Interim Commission to act until the

Constitution becomes effective and the World Health Organization is established. Among other functions of that Commission is the following:

> (b) to enter into the necessary arrangements with the Pan American Sanitary Organization and other existing inter-governmental regional health organizations, with a view to giving effect to the provisions of Article 54 of the Constitution, which arrangements shall be subject to approval by the Health Assembly.

. . . .

The Interim Commission named a subcommittee of four of its members to negotiate the necessary arrangement with the Pan American Sanitary Organization in accordance with the provisions of Article 54. Such arrangement is subject to the approval of the World Health Assembly. The subcommittee is made up of the representatives of Brazil, Mexico, United States and Venezuela.

CHAPTER XIII

CULTURAL RELATIONS

1. UNITED NATIONS EDUCATIONAL, SCIENTIFIC AND CULTURAL ORGANIZATION

A. United States Participation

On March 31, 1944, the United States announced its decision to send a mission to the Ninth Meeting of the Conference of Allied Ministers of Education which was held in London on April 6, 1944, for the purpose of formulating plans for educational and cultural reconstruction and considering proposals for a United Nations organization for educational cooperation. Under the leadership of Rep. J. William Fulbright (Arkansas) the American mission participated in the general discussion and agreed on the necessity of an educational organization designed to restore cultural heritages of war devastated countries. These initial moves were supported by various educational agencies in the United States. During proceedings of the San Francisco Conference, Dean Virginia Gildersleeve, member of the American delegation, suggested further provisions for the development of educational cooperation. These cumulative preparations resulted in the inclusion in the Charter of the United Nations of principles relating to cooperation in educational and cultural fields.[1]

Shortly after the signing of the Charter, a draft proposal for a United Nations Educational and Cultural Organization was submitted to the Council of Allied Ministers of Education by the late Grayson Kefauver, United States consultant to the State Department who had remained in London after the Fulbright mission of 1944.

On October 19, 1945, Assistant Secretary of State Benton announced the composition of the United States Delegation to a conference convened in London in November, 1945, to prepare for the creation of an Educational and Cultural Organization of the United Nations, an action in harmony with the San Francisco declaration which approved the calling of such a conference.[2] Members of the Delegation included Archibald MacLeish, Chairman of the Delegation; William Benton, Assistant Secretary of State; Arthur H. Compton, Chancellor of Washington University (serving until November 13); Harlow Shapley, Director of the Harvard College Observatory (commencing November 10); Rep. Chester E. Merrow; Senator James E. Murray; George Stoddard, President of the University of Illinois; Miss C. Mildred Thompson, Dean, Vassar College.

In December, 1945, Assistant Secretary of State Benton announced the appointment of the American representatives on the Preparatory Commission of the United Nations Educational, Scientific and Cultural Organization (UNESCO): Grayson N. Kefauver, United States representative on the Preparatory Commission and member of its Executive Committee; Richard Johnson, alternate to Dr. Kefauver; Walter M. Kotschnig, Deputy Executive Secretary

[1] Article 1, Section 3; Article 55.
[2] For further information on membership of the Delegation, see Department of State, *Bulletin*, XIII, p. 625. See also, *ibid.*, p. 686.

(temporarily); Charles A. Thomson, the Department of State officer responsible for matters pertaining to UNESCO.[1]

An advisory group, appointed to gather suggestions and advice in the field of mass communications for consideration by UNESCO, included Edward W. Barrett, Chairman; Thurman L. Barnard, Don Francisco, Ferdinand Kuhn, Jr. and John Hay Whitney.[2] These special consultants advised the Department of State on matters in which radio, motion pictures and publications could cooperate with UNESCO.

Hearings before the Committee on Foreign Affairs of the House of Representatives concerning membership by the United States in UNESCO[3] were conducted in April, 1946,[4] and on July 30, 1946, Congress passed the joint resolution admitting the United States to membership in the Organization.[5]

(1) *Letter from the Secretary of State (Byrnes) to Chairman of the Committee on Foreign Affairs of the House of Representatives (Bloom), April 2, 1946.*[6]

I understand the Foreign Affairs Committee will begin hearings shortly on United States membership in the United Nations Educational, Scientific and Cultural Organization (UNESCO). I want to express to you my full and hearty support of the Organization.

In President Truman's address last June, at San Francisco, he said "we must set up an effective agency for consistent and thorough interchange of thought and ideas, for there lies the road to a better and more tolerant understanding among nations and among peoples". UNESCO is designed to fulfill the purpose outlined by the President.

I can conceive of no more important endeavour than to make the mind of man a constructive force for peace. That effort is fundamental to the success of the United Nations' Organization. We realize that world peace can be maintained only by the united efforts of all peoples. But men work together most effectively when they have learned to think together and to feel together. Without common knowledge, common agreement is difficult or impossible.

The discovery of atomic energy has made the task of the United Nations Educational, Scientific and Cultural Organization an even more imperative one. In a world where nations may arm themselves with weapons against which there is no physical defense, basic security lies in the creation of mutual trust and confidence among the peoples of the world. If UNESCO can bring that goal nearer by one step, it deserves our prompt and wholehearted participation.

---

[1] *Ibid.*, p. 1057.
[2] *Ibid.*, XIV, p. 172.
[3] *Membership and Participation by the United States in the United Nations Educational, Scientific and Cultural Organization, Hearings before the Committee on Foreign Affairs, House of Representatives, Seventy-Ninth Congress, 2d Session on H. J. Res. 305, April 3, 4 and 5, 1946.*
[4] For amendments to the Resolution providing for membership in the United Nations Educational, Scientific and Cultural Organization, see House Report No. 1927, 79th Cong., 2d sess.
[5] Public Law 565, 79th Cong., 2d sess., H. J. Res. 305; see this volume, p. 740.
[6] Department of State, *Bulletin*, XIV, p. 625.

(2) *Statement by the Chairman of the United States Delegation to the London Conference on the Establishment of UNESCO (MacLeish), Submitted to the Committee on Foreign Affairs of the House of Representatives, April 3, 1946.*[1]

I have submitted to the Secretary of State a report on the London conference, together with a summary description of the constitution of the proposed United Nations Educational, Scientific and Cultural Organization. This report is, of course, available to the committee, and I will therefore not consume the committee's time with a recapitulation of the points made. There are, however, one or two matters in connection with the London conference and the plans for the new organization to which I should like to call the committee's attention.

First, I should like to recall to the committee's mind the position of UNESCO with reference to earlier efforts in this same direction. Scientific and scholarly and cultural and educational bodies of one kind or another in the various countries of the world have established international relationships with each other over a considerable period of time. It was not, however, until the establishment of the League of Nations that an effort was made to give the international support of governments to these efforts at communication between private associations and other bodies. But even the attempt in this direction under the League fell far short of what is undertaken in the constitution of UNESCO. The activities of the League in this direction were based upon the assumption that if men of learning, scientists, teachers, were put in touch with each other on an international basis, one of the by-products of their association would be an increased understanding of each other by the peoples of the nations involved. UNESCO pushes this idea one step further. UNESCO makes international understanding its prime and immediate objective and proposes to use as means for the realization of that objective not only the association of learned men and learned societies and organizations, but popular education and the modern instruments of mass communication — newspaper, radio, motion picture. The difference between UNESCO and its predecessors is, in part, a material evolutionary difference. Men who regarded international activity in the field of education as impossible in 1919 now regard it as not only possible but essential. The real reason, however, for the greater directness of UNESCO's approach to the problem lies, in my opinion, in the new realization, now abroad in the world, that the mutual understanding of the peoples of the world is essential to the hope for peace — that in a world armed with weapons of such terrible destructiveness as those which men contrived during the last war, the only hope for peace lies in the mutual understanding not of Foreign Offices alone but of the peoples themselves. Certainly it is for this reason that the aim of UNESCO is set not at the elevated level of advanced scholarship or science but at the level of the popular education of the peoples of the world and of their communication with each other through the mass media now at their disposition.

A second point I should like to make is one which derives from my experience at London and subsequently in this country. It would be

[1] *Ibid.*, p. 629.

impossible for anyone who did not attend the London conference to form an idea, in any degree adequate, of the depth and fervor of the human hope and expectation which produced the constitution of UNESCO. A very large number of the delegates at the London conference were men and women who had played a leading part in the resistance movements of their countries under the Nazi occupation. They knew of their own personal experience what issues were at stake. They were determined that an attack should be made upon the problem of war and peace at the one level where success is possible — the level of human beings themselves who will, in the last analysis, determine which of the two alternatives will be chosen. But this fervor and hope is not limited to the men and women of Europe who suffered the full impact of the war. It is shared, as I can assure the committee, by enormous numbers of men and women in the United States who believe, and believe with conviction, that the hope of the world lies where the hope of America has always lain — in the things of the mind and of the spirit — in the education of children, and the full and just information of the citizens, and the fullest possible development of science and scholarship and the fine arts.

I have heard it said that the people of the United States were not interested in matters of education and science and culture. Nothing I have seen during my life — certainly nothing I have seen in the years of the war and the months after it — would give any support whatever to that assertion. On the contrary, I think the history of the American people and their frequent expressions of opinion have clearly demonstrated that they attach greater importance to education and science and to all those forms of human expression through which their life as a people has been developed than they attach to anything else except — if it is an exception — their religious faith.

My colleagues on the American Delegation to the London conference will be able to report to the committee on the details of the constitution. My own report to the Secretary of State, to which I have referred above, sums up my own opinions on that subject, if my own opinions are considered relevant. I cannot, however, too strongly assert my personal conviction and belief that UNESCO is not only an important part of the group of organizations which will compose the UNO, but is also an instrument of particular importance to the people of this country.

How much it will accomplish in fact will depend upon the men who staff it and the warmth with which it is supported by the member governments. The constitution drafted at London does, however, create an instrument of which use *can* be made, should the men be found and should the nations so desire.

(3) **H. J. Resolution 305, Providing for Membership and Participation by the United States in the United Nations Educational, Scientific and Cultural Organization, and Authorizing an Appropriation Therefor, Approved July 30, 1946.**[1]

Resolved by the Senate and House of Representatives of the United States of America in Congress assembled, That the President is hereby

[1] Public Law 565, 79th Cong., 2d sess.

authorized to accept membership for the United States in the United Nations Educational, Scientific, and Cultural Organization (hereinafter referred to as the "Organization"), the constitution of which was approved in London on November 16, 1945, by the United Nations Conference for the establishment of an Educational, Scientific, and Cultural Organization, and deposited in the Archives of the Government of the United Kingdom.

SEC. 2. The President by and with the consent of the Senate shall designate from time to time to attend a specified session or specified sessions of the General Conference of the Organization not to exceed five representatives of the United States and such number of alternates not to exceed five as he may determine consistent with the rules of procedure of the General Conference: *Provided, however,* That each such representative and each such alternate must be an American citizen. One of the representatives shall be designated as the senior representative. Such representatives and alternates shall each be entitled to receive compensation at such rates, not to exceed $12,000 per annum, as the President may determine, for such periods as the President may specify, except that no Member of the Senate or House of Representatives or officer of the United States who is designated under this section as a representative of the United States or as an alternate to attend any specified session or specified sessions of the General Conference shall be entitled to receive such compensation. Whenever a representative of the United States is elected by the General Conference to serve on the Executive Board, or is elected President of the General Conference and thus becomes an ex officio adviser to the Executive Board, under provision of article V of the constitution of the Organization, the President may extend the above provisions for compensation to such representative during periods of service in connection with the Executive Board.

SEC. 3. In fulfillment of article VII of the constitution of the Organization, the Secretary of State shall cause to be organized a National Commission on Educational, Scientific, and Cultural Corporation of not to exceed one hundred members. Such Commission shall be appointed by the Secretary of State and shall consist of (*a*) not more than sixty representatives of principal national, voluntary organizations interested in educational, scientific, and cultural matters; and (*b*) not more than forty outstanding persons selected by the Secretary of State, including not more than ten persons holding office under or employed by the Government of the United States, not more than fifteen representatives of the educational, scientific, and cultural interests of State and local governments, and not more than fifteen persons chosen at large. The Secretary of State is authorized to name in the first instance fifty of the principal national voluntary organizations, each of which shall be invited to designate one representative for appointment to the National Commission. Thereafter, the National Commission shall periodically review and, if deemed advisable, revise the list of such organizations designating representatives in order to achieve a desirable rotation among organizations represented. To constitute the initial Commission, one-third of the members shall be appointed to serve for a term of one year, one-third for a term of two years, and one-third or the remainder thereof for a term of three years; from thence on following, all members shall be appointed for a term of three years each, but no member shall serve more than two consecutive terms. The National Commission shall meet at least once annually. The National Commission shall designate from among its members an executive committee, and may designate such other committees as may prove necessary, to consult with the Department of State and to perform such other functions as the National Commission shall delegate to them. No member of the National Commission shall be allowed any salary or other compensation for services: *Provided, however,* That he may be paid his actual transportation expenses, and not to exceed $10 per diem in lieu of subsistence and other expenses, while away from his home in attendance upon authorized meetings or in consultation on request with the Department of State. The Department of State is authorized to provide the necessary secretariat for the Commission.

Sec. 4. That each such member of the National Commission must be an American citizen.

Sec. 5. The National Commission shall call general conferences for the discussion of matters relating to the activities of the Organization, to which conferences organized bodies actively interested in such matters shall be invited to send representatives: *Provided, however,* That the travel and maintenance of such representation shall be without expense to the Government. Such general conferences shall be held annually or biennially, as the National Commission may determine, and in such places as it may designate. They shall be attended so far as possible by the members of the National Commission and by the delegates of the United States to the General Conference of the Organization. The National Commission is further authorized to call special conferences of experts for the consideration of specific matters relating to the Organization by persons of specialized competences. Under such regulations as the Secretary of State may prescribe, the actual transportation expenses of experts attending such conferences shall be borne by the Department of State, and they shall be allowed a per diem of $10 in lieu of subsistence and other expenses, for the period of actual attendance and of necessary travel.

Sec. 6. There is hereby authorized to be appropriated annually to the Department of State, out of any money in the Treasury not otherwise appropriated, such sums as may be necessary for the payment by the United States of its share of the expenses of the Organization as apportioned by the General Conference of the Organization in accordance with article IX of the constitution of the Organization, and such additional sums as may be necessary to pay the expenses of participation by the United States in the activities of the Organization, including: (*a*) salaries of the representatives provided for in section 2 hereof, of their appropriate staffs, and of members of the secretariat of the National Commission provided for in section 3 hereof, including personal services in the District of Columbia and elsewhere, without regard to the civil-service laws and the Classification Act of 1923, as amended; (*b*) travel expenses without regard to the Standardized Government Travel Regulations, as amended, the Subsistence Expense Act of 1926, as amended, and section 10 of the Act of March 3, 1933 (U.S.C., title 5, sec. 73*b*), and, under such rules and regulations as the Secretary of State may prescribe, travel expenses of families and transportation of effects of United States representatives and other personnel in going to and returning from their post of duty; (*c*) allowances for living quarters, including heat, fuel, and light, as authorized by the Act approved June 26, 1930 (U.S.C., title 5, sec. 118*a*); (*d*) cost of living allowances under such rules and regulations as the Secretary of State may prescribe, including allowances to persons temporarily stationed abroad; (*e*) communication services; (*f*) stenographic reporting, translating, and other services, by contract, if deemed necessary, without regard to section 3709 of the Revised Statutes (U.S.C., title 41, sec. 5); (*g*) local transportation; (*h*) equipment; (*i*) transportation of things; (*j*) rent of offices; (*k*) printing and binding without regard to section 11 of the Act of March 1, 1919 (U.S.C., title 44, sec. 111), and section 3709 of the Revised Statutes (U.S.C., title 41, sec. 5); (*l*) official entertainment; (*m*) stationery; (*n*) purchase of newspapers, periodicals, books, and documents; and (*o*) such other expenses as may be authorized by the Secretary of State.

SEC. 7. Unless Congress by law authorizes such action, neither the President nor any person or agency shall on behalf of the United States approve any amendment under article XIII of the constitution of the Organization involving any new obligation for the United States.

SEC. 8. In adopting this joint resolution, it is the understanding of the Congress that the constitution of the Organization does not require, nor does this resolution authorize, the disclosure of any information or knowledge in any case in which such disclosure is prohibited by any law of the United States.

(4) *Report on the First General Conference of UNESCO by the Chairman of the United States Delegation (Benton), December 23, 1946.*[1]

[Excerpts]

. . . .

We learned in Paris the great importance that the statesmen and politicians of other countries attach to the proposed educational, scientific, and cultural activities of UNESCO. The problem within the United States is to see to it that we understand how vital it is to us as well. Potentially, UNESCO is a political force of the first magnitude. It can achieve little unless the political, economic, and military problems which now becloud the world's future are resolved. But, in a world environment which opens the doors to scientific, educational, and cultural exchanges between peoples, UNESCO can contribute mightily to the creation of a world will toward peace. It can be a major force in the security program of the United States, and in the furtherance of the broad objectives of American foreign policy — peace and prosperity among all peoples of the world.

---

[1] Department of State, *Bulletin*, XVI, p. 20.

Before the Paris meeting we had heard that some of the other nations — particularly some of the smaller nations — feared that the United States would try to dominate the conference. We were told that the small nations feared what they called "American cultural imperialism". It is the Hollywood motion picture which is feared most of all.

The American Delegation arrived in Paris determined to press for maximum use of the mass media of communication — motion pictures, radio, and the press — because they constitute a potent new instrument in the pursuit of peace. We were delighted to find other nations taking the lead on proposals which we had been prepared to advance.

In the conference subcommission on mass media, under the chairmanship of a Belgian and the vice-chairmanship of a Dane, the British, the French, the Canadians and others came forward vigorously with proposals that coincided closely with our own ideas.

Even after a rigorous effort to screen proposed projects, over 100 potential projects emerged in the final report of the conference. That was probably too many. I shall list briefly five of the major projects UNESCO has agreed to begin work on during 1947. You will see that they are immense undertakings for a young and untried organization.

First, a world-wide attack on the problem of illiteracy and the establishment of minimum standards of education everywhere. This is a revolutionary undertaking, but it lies at the heart of UNESCO's long-range effort. If UNESCO can contribute substantially to its solution, it will have justified its existence through this effort alone. Well over half the world's population is illiterate. Can the world achieve peace through understanding in the absence of the simplest tools of understanding, the ability to read and write? Illiterate men are pawns in a power struggle. They are also victims of an inequality so grave as to constitute a threat to peace. UNESCO will create a staff of its own, supplemented by experts from many nations, to recommend programs for combatting illiteracy; to develop educational materials; and to determine how best to use books, pictures, films, and radio, as well as the schoolroom.

Second, UNESCO will undertake a study of the psychological and social tensions that lead to war. When the tensions that produce unrest, suspicion, and hatred among classes, races, and peoples have been identified and described we shall know better how to attack UNESCO's central problem of promoting peace through understanding. UNESCO will seek to stimulate and coordinate research on these tensions by social scientists of many nations.

Third, an effort to reduce the barriers that now obstruct the free flow of communications among peoples. In this UNESCO will cooperate with the Commission on Human Rights of the United Nations. We know from bitter experience that even highly literate peoples, when they are cut off from a full, honest, and continuous account of developments among other peoples, can be propagandized and bullied into aggressive belligerency. UNESCO will cooperate with the United Nations in a report that will survey available facilities throughout the world for the printing of news, books, and periodicals; the production and distribution of films; and the broadcasting and reception of radio programs. The report will deal also with copyright restrictions, with the high cost of cable and wireless communication — indeed with all the restrictions on the flow of information and ideas across international boundaries, and with the suppression and distortion of information and ideas by any influence.

Fourth, and again in cooperation with the United Nations, UNESCO will explore the possibility of creating a world-wide broadcasting network under international auspices. Such a network might bring to ordinary people everywhere, and in many languages, an account of the history, the achievements, the problems, the hopes and the aspirations, the music and the literature of other peoples.

Fifth, and a very different kind of enterprise — this one in the field of science — is the proposed International Institute of the Amazon. This will bring together scientists from many nations and from many fields of science to study the problems of food, disease, and natural resources of a tropical area. The tropical areas of the world have been characterized by malnutrition and backwardness. An international attack upon this problem will offer an opportunity for cooperative action. It may open up new possibilities for the development of the tropics in such a way as to reduce future international tensions.

I have given five major examples of the scope of UNESCO and of the decisions taken at Paris. There was unanimous and enthusiastic support for the proposed projects for the exchange of students and scholars and scientists, and the exchange of books and educational films. And although UNESCO is not a relief agency, $400,000 was voted for a short-term project to stimulate public and private organizations to assist in the reconstruction of the educational systems of war-devastated countries.

I shall close on a note of hope and caution. UNESCO can become one of the most useful instruments ever devised by man. But it can fulfil its potentialities only under favorable conditions.

The winning of peace is largely a political and an economic problem. It cannot succeed unless the political and economic agencies of the United Nations succeed. It can help them to succeed. In the long run it can build a firmer foundation of understanding, making future political and economic problems easier to solve.

Do not expect too much of UNESCO too soon. UNESCO has no powers to intervene in the cultural or educational life of any nation and should not have. It must do its work chiefly through other organizations. Its operating budget for 1947 — $6,000,000 — though it is as much as many small nations could afford in this difficult period — is a pittance compared to the task and the opportunity.

The great hope of UNESCO is that its leadership will learn how to seize and fire the imagination of ordinary men and women everywhere, without producing ultimate disillusion through promising too much too fast. . . .

B. United States National Commission for UNESCO

In compliance with the provisions of Public Law 565 of the 79th Congress [1] and Article VII of the Constitution of the United Nations Educational, Scientific and Cultural Organization, the United States National Commission for UNESCO was organized by the Secretary of State for the purpose of advising the Department of State on United States participation in UNESCO.

(1) *Report on the First Meeting of the National Commission Concerning the Establishment of the Commission, September 1946.*[2]

[Excerpts]

The Department of State recommended that the U. S. National Commission be small enough for its entire membership to serve as a consultative body; further, it recommended that the National Commission consist of individuals to be selected by the Secretary of State, in order to insure the formation of a widely representative body without the express inclusion (and consequent exclusion) of particular organizations. An opposing view was strongly urged: that the Commission should give direct representation to organizations, and should be large enough to permit the inclusion of many organizations.

The structure of the National Commission, as finally prescribed by Congress, represents a compromise between these views: Section 3 of the Joint Resolution of the Senate and House of Representatives of the United States authorized the creation of a National Commission on Education, Scientific and Cultural Cooperation of not to exceed 100 members, consisting of two main categories. First, not more than 60 members were to be representatives of principal national voluntary organizations interested in educational, scientific, and cultural matters; secondly, there were to be not more than 40 additional outstanding persons, including not more than 10 persons working under or employed by the Government of the United States, not more than 15 representatives of the educational, scientific, and cultural interests of State and local governments, and not more than 15 persons chosen at large.

In the appointment of the second category of the United States Commission members indicated above, the Department of State exercises discretionary authority within the Federal, State and local, and general categories. In the first category the following procedure of selection is specified in the law. First, the Department must name 50 organizations from among the "principal national voluntary organizations interested in educational, scientific and cultural matters". Secondly, the Department invites each of these organizations to designate one representative for appointment to the National Commission. Thirdly, the National Commission itself may select an additional 10 organizations which in turn may designate representatives for appointment to the Commission. Fourthly, the National Commission itself is directed to review periodi-

---

[1] Authority to create the National Commission was given on July 30, 1946.

[2] Department of State Publication 2726, United States-United Nations Information Series 14, p. 2.

cally the list of organizations and, if deemed advisable, revise the list in order to achieve desirable rotation among the organizations represented thereon.

When the selection of organizations and individuals was determined, every effort was made to secure adequate representation of all the fields involved in UNESCO's wide variety of interests, including broad population groups and wide associations as well as those specialized bodies devoted to education, science, culture, and mass communication. The following criteria were used as a basis for the final choice in the case of organizations:

Organizations selected should be
 national;
 recognized generally in their irrespective fields as being representative and reputable;
 known to be effectively concerned with international relations in their respective fields, as indicated by history and practice;
 competent to make valuable contributions to the work of the National Commission.

While every effort was made to assure reasonable balance, the chief goal, rather than absolute equality of numbers among interested groups, was to assure that the membership of the National Commission would offer adequate facilities through which each of these particular groups might co-operate and make its contribution to UNESCO.

The law provides that to constitute the initial Commission one third of the members shall be appointed to serve for a one-year term, one third for a two-year term, and the remainder for three years. Thereafter all members are to be appointed for three-year terms, but no member shall serve more than two consecutive terms. Thus desirable rotation is further encouraged.

Members of the National Commission will not be paid for their services. Their transportation and living expenses will be paid by the Department of State while they are serving in a consultative capacity. The Department will also provide the necessary secretariat for the National Commission. The Commission is required to meet at least once annually. The law also assigns to the Commission one important function in addition to those which belong to it under the UNESCO Constitution. In the United States the National Commission is directed to call conferences for the discussion of matters relating to UNESCO. The Commission will invite all interested organized bodies to participate in large annual or biennial general conferences as the National Commission deems wise. Smaller conferences of experts for the consideration of specific matters relating to UNESCO are also authorized. In this manner the most effective possible means of liaison is provided for which will also allow for direct participation in the work of the UNESCO program by all interested organizations in addition to those which may at the time hold membership on the National Commission.

In preparation for the first meeting the Department of State invited members of the Commission residing in or near Washington to constitute themselves into a Preparatory Committee. The Preparatory Committee held two meetings, one on September 9 and another on September 18, 1946. A temporary chairman was elected and the work of the preparatory group was subdivided into preparation of an agenda for the first meeting, establishment of a working committee structure for the first meeting, and preparation of bylaws. A subcommittee was named which formulated a draft of bylaws to be submitted to the Commission as a whole.

. . . .

At the opening session, members of the Commission were introduced, and lots were drawn to determine their terms of membership. The chairman of the Preparatory Committee submitted the provisional agenda and bylaws, requested nominations in writing for 10 additional organizations, and announced the schedule of round tables and temporary committees.

A second plenary session was devoted to general discussion of the primary purposes of UNESCO. Committees on nominations, bylaws, and findings and reports were selected from among the membership to provide final recommendations in these fields to the Commission itself. The membership was further subdivided among working round tables on education, mass communications, cultural institutions, natural sciences, social sciences, humanities, and creative arts. These Committees were to consider a program of activities for UNESCO which had been prepared by the Preparatory Commission of the Organization as the chief order of business at the Paris Conference.

At the third plenary session, the committee on bylaws submitted a draft of permanent bylaws, thus eliminating the necessity for an intermediate consideration and vote on provisional bylaws; and the election of officers and members of the Executive Committee took place.[1]

(2) *Report of the National Commission on UNESCO to the Secretary of State (Byrnes), September 27, 1946.*[2]

[Excerpts]

. . . . . .

The purpose of the Organization,[3] as stated in its Constitution, is to contribute to peace and security by promoting collaboration among the nations through education, science and culture. The Organization is not conceived of, in other words, as an international undertaking to promote education and science and culture as ends in themselves, but rather, through education and science and culture, to advance the peace of the world.

In the opinion of the National Commission, the position to be taken by

[1] For Bylaws of the United States National Commission for UNESCO, see *ibid.*, p. 21–24.

[2] Department of State, *Bulletin*, XV, p. 684.

[3] United Nations Educational, Scientific and Cultural Organization.

the American Delegation in the General Conference of the Organization should be determined by this purpose. The American Delegation should support those proposals for action by the Organization which give promise of advancing directly and significantly the cause of peace through understanding. The necessity of this labor grows clearer from day to day as the effects of misunderstanding and distrust and fear upon the conduct of international relations become increasingly evident. The recognition of the fundamental community of human interests which made possible the great collaborative effort of the war has diminished with time and change, and the possibility of common effort for peace and for security has diminished with it. To restore and make increasingly articulate the intellectual and moral solidarity of mankind — to identify and analyze existing obstacles to that solidarity and to develop action which will strengthen or create forces to overcome them — is the most immediate and the most urgent need of our time.

In the opinion of the National Commission, the responsibility of the United Nations Educational, Scientific and Cultural Organization in the present crisis is so great and so pressing that the Organization should not hesitate to employ any proper means, however novel or however costly, which give promise of success. The Organization is itself a new agency, daring in purpose and novel in structure. The means it employs should be appropriate to its nature. It must serve as the cutting edge for international action. If annual military expenditures of thirteen billion dollars for the defense of the people of the United States against attack are justified, ten percent of that amount, and far more than ten percent, might well and wisely be expended to remove or greatly to reduce the danger of attack. It would be cheap insurance. In the first place, it is the consensus of military opinion that no adequate military defense against the weapons of modern warfare exists. In the second place, even if such measures were available, their cost in terms of life and suffering are so inestimably great that any action which would diminish the necessity for their use would be economical.

. . . . . .

But though the American Delegation should be prepared to think and to act boldly and imaginatively in the General Conference of UNESCO, it should never forget, in the opinion of this Commission, that it represents a people deeply and firmly committed to certain fundamental propositions bearing upon the nature and destiny of man. It should hold unwaiveringly to the absolute requirement of freedom of thought and freedom of expression as the basic means of arriving at the world understanding which is the immediate as well as the ultimate objective of the Organization's labors.

The Commission has considered a large number of proposals for action by the new Organization as developed by a Preparatory Commission established in London by the Conference of the United Nations which drafted the Constitution of the new Organization in November, 1945. These proposals will be reviewed at the meeting of the General Conference of UNESCO. Accordingly, the National Commission has considered the report of the Preparatory Commission as a point of departure and has not hesitated to develop and to advance additional or different ideas of its own. The present report of the Commission does not undertake to list in full the recommendations adopted by the National Commission in the various fields of UNESCO's activity. Many of these, specific and detailed in character, are submitted to you in a document supplemental to this report for such use as you may think wise to make of them. The Commission believes that these recommendations should be supported by the American Delegation in so far as they are not inconsistent with the general principles laid down in this report. The recommendations here listed are the recommendations to which the Commission attaches greatest over-all and present importance. They are, moreover, recommendations which, in the opinion of the Commission, best illustrate the character of the work UNESCO should undertake.

We have arranged our proposals in terms of the functions of the Organization as defined in the first Article of its Constitution. Fundamentally, the concern of the Organization is with the relations of men to each other. It approaches these relations in terms of three kinds of international collaboration. First, international collaboration for the *preservation* of men's knowledge of themselves, their world and each other; second, international collaboration for the *increase* of that knowledge through learning, science and the arts; third, international collaboration for the *dissemination* of that knowledge through education and through all the instruments of communication between the peoples of the earth in order that understanding may replace mistrust and suspicion and the fear which leads to war.

In the opinion of the Commission, the order of present urgency puts the third of these functions first. The Commission, therefore, recommends at this time only a limited number of projects in connection with the first and second activities of the Organization.

(1) *International Collaboration for the Preservation of Men's Knowledge of Themselves, Their World, and Each Other.*

Here the Commission recommends that the American Delegation advance and support proposals for action looking toward the rehabilitation of libraries, museums, scientific laboratories and educational institutions and other depositories of the materials and tools of art and learning. The Commission does not feel that it is appropriate for the Organization under its Constitution to attempt the work of reconstruction and rehabilitation itself. The Organization is, however, the only body which can probably direct a general study of needs and draft a plan of action.

(2) *International Collaboration for the Increase of Men's Knowledge of Themselves, Their World and Each Other Through Learning, Science and the Arts.*

Here the Commission feels that the American Delegation should advance and support proposals looking toward the development of conditions more favorable to the creative and investigative work of artists, scientists and scholars. Where agencies capable of improving these conditions in whole or in part already exist, the Organization should give its active support and encouragement to their undertakings and should attempt to facilitate their cooperation with each other. Furthermore, the Organization should encourage the establishment of new agencies of this character where they are needed but do not already exist.

The American Delegation should advance and support proposals for studies by the Organization of social and international tensions which create obstacles to international understanding and therefore to peace, and for action by the Organization to encourage the development of appropriate means for their elimination.

The American Delegation should advance and support proposals for the establishment of new scientific and scholarly projects for research in fields in which work can most effectively be undertaken on an international basis, as, for instance, research in meteorology, oceanography, international health, and the study of epidemic diseases.

(3) *International Collaboration for the Dissemination of Men's Knowledge of Themselves, Their World and Each Other through Education and through all the Instruments of Communication.*

The American Delegation should advance and support proposals for the establishment or the reestablishment of the means of international communication through education and through all other media where they are needed and where they are at present lacking.

The American Delegation should advance and support proposals for the establishment by the Organization, alone or in connection with the United Nations, of a world-wide radio network capable of laying down a strong and consistent signal in all major areas of the world.

The American Delegation should advance and support proposals for the removal of obstacles to the free flow of information in accordance with the report of the Committee of Consultants to the Department of State on Mass Media and UNESCO. The Commission differs, however, with the Committee of Consultants in believing that the Organization should concern itself with the quality of international communication through the mass media and should give serious study to the means by which the mass media may be of more positive and creative service to the cause of international understanding and therefore of peace. The Organization should, of course, avoid at all times any act or suggestion of censorship.

The American Delegation should advance and support proposals for action to free the channels of international communication of obstacles created by discriminatory or unduly restrictive copyright legislation, discriminatory or unfair rates, or other similar practices or laws.

The American Delegation should advance and support proposals that the Organization concern itself with the press, radio and motion pictures, and all other means of publication, reproduction and dissemination of materials, as instruments at the service of art, education, culture and scientific advancement in the labor of international understanding, and with the protection of the peoples of the world against any misuse of these media such as might result in their degradation and perversion to the point of fostering international ill-will and misunderstanding.

The American Delegation should advance and support proposals for the investigation by the Organization of methods of education for international understanding and for the development of attitudes conducive to peace. Such investigations should direct themselves to the processes by which nations organize and give practice, within their own boundaries, to their people in the arts of peaceful cooperation. They should be more than mere fact-finding investigations. They should be sociological studies of great scope and depth.

The American Delegation should advance and support proposals that the Organization call a conference in the year 1947 on the principles, policies and procedures to be followed in the preparation of textbooks and other teaching materials. This Conference should include in its membership classroom teachers from all educational levels, school administrators, writers, publishers, and other experts in the production and use of instructional materials.

The American Delegation should advance and support proposals for the exchange of students, teachers, scholars, artists, artisans, scientists, government officials, and others, active in the various fields of the Organization's work.

The American Delegation should advance and support proposals looking to the increase and improvement of the access of the masses of the people throughout the world to printed and other materials of intellectual, informational and cultural significance. The Commission believes that the American Delegation should advance and support proposals for the development by the Organization of an effective system of international inter-library loan, in original or copy, together with the development of necessary international finding lists, and arrangements to avoid duplication in abstracting and bibliographical services.

The American Delegation should advance and support proposals for the encouragement of the establishment of popular library and museum systems in those areas of the world where such systems do not now exist.

2. INTERNATIONAL INFORMATION SERVICE

The conclusion of hostilities brought a revision in overseas informational services which resulted in the abolition of the Office of War Information (established June 13, 1942) by Executive Order on August 31, 1945. OWI functions and those of the Office of Inter-American Affairs were taken over by the Interim International Information Service (IIS), a temporary agency which operated until December 31, 1945.[1]

A permanent organization, the Office of International Information and Cultural Affairs (OIC), was set up within the Department of State to absorb and continue the functions of the IIS at the expiration of its four months' existence and to carry on informational and cultural activities of the Government abroad. The following established activities of the Department of State were inherited and developed by OIC:

[1] *America — "A Full and Fair Picture", The Government's Information and Cultural Relations Program Overseas*, Revised ed., No. 2, Office of Public Affairs, Department of State, January, 1947.

"1. Those functions related to the preparation and issuance of the daily (Morse) radio bulletin. Radio service of textual, documentary and other background materials to Foreign Service officers, for their information, was started in 1935.

"2. Those functions, originally limited to this Hemisphere, related to: (*a*) travel and study grants; (*b*) exchange of professors and books; (*c*) assistance to United States cultural centers in Latin America such as libraries, institutes and schools; (*d*) the distribution in Latin America of informational motion pictures and other cultural materials. The program was to assist and supplement the work of private agencies, and was based upon an act of Congress approved August 9, 1939 entitled 'An Act to render closer and more effective the relationship between the American republics.'

"In November, 1941, the Secretary of State informed the President that the initiation of a cultural program with China was a matter of immediate concern since such a program could effectively undergird Chinese cultural and scientific activities during the period of national resistance and could build a closer understanding between China and the United States. Accordingly, in January, 1942, the cultural program was extended to China with an allocation from the President's emergency fund. There it centered largely upon: (*a*) sending American technical experts requested by the Chinese Government; (*b*) exchanging professors; (*c*) awarding study grants to Chinese students in the United States; (*d*) sending microfilm reproductions of technical and scholarly journals requested by Chinese universities.[1]

"In the spring of 1943, a careful study of field reports indicated an immediate need for the development of closer cooperation with countries of the Near East and Africa, and in July 1943 the program was further extended to those areas, again with an Emergency Fund allocation . . .

"3. Those functions of the Secretariat of the Interdepartmental Committee on Scientific and Cultural Cooperation, established early in 1938. The act of August 9, 1939 authorized not only the State Department but other agencies of the Government, as well, to carry on personal, cultural and informational exchange programs with other American republics. Coordination of all Government activity in these fields has been achieved by the Interdepartmental Committee, operating under the leadership of the State Department. Personnel of the State Department compose the Committee's Secretariat, which handles funds voted by Congress for projects carried out under the Committee's supervision. Twenty-eight agencies of the Government were represented on the Committee as of October, 1946." [2]

(1) *Statement by the Assistant Secretary of State for Public Affairs (Benton), on the Role of the International Information Service in the Conduct of Foreign Relations, before the Committee on Appropriations of the House of Representatives, October 4, 1945.*[3]

[Excerpts]

. . . .

On September 12 the Acting Secretary of State, Mr. Acheson, wrote you that the Department would determine "as promptly as possible" which of the transferred functions should be continued after the end of this year and which should be abolished. He explained that we would not be able to recommend a program for the future until we had finished our survey. He did say, however, that I would appear before you,

[1] *Ibid.*, p. 4.
[2] *Ibid.*, p. 5.
[3] Department of State, *Bulletin*, XIII, p. 593.

especially "to advise you as to the vital need of an international information service and the important role such a service will have to play in the post-war conduct of our foreign relations."

. . . . . .

America's strength, and America's good example, need to be understood beyond our borders. Our military and economic power is so great, in fact, that it is bound to lead many people and groups throughout the world to distrust us or fear us or even hate us, and not all the information work in the world can wholly prevent it. At least we can try to minimize the unfair or untruthful impressions of this country, and to see that accurate knowledge counteracts the growth of suspicion and prejudice.

The Department of State believes that a constructive program in this area is essential in the conduct of American foreign relations. It believes that we must try to give other countries what the President has called "a full and fair picture of American life and of the aims and policies of the United States Government."

Private facilities can do a very big part of the job, and, as far as I am concerned, the more the better. The soundest procedure, in my opinion, is for the State Department to determine, and to keep determining as conditions change, American needs in the various fields of overseas information — news, motion pictures, publications, and the rest — and then to support and help private industry to do everything it will and can to meet those needs. Already I am consulting with representatives of private industry in these fields, in the hope that much of the job can be taken off the Government's shoulders. The remainder of the job, with the approval of this committee and the Congress, will devolve upon the future overseas information service within the State Department.

Some of this work will be transitional and temporary, in the backwash of the war. Information has to be supplied and controlled in Germany and Japan in accordance with policy directives from Washington and the orders of our military authorities on the spot. The same is true, to a different degree, in Austria and in the city of Trieste, where American troops are part of an Allied occupation. Another example is the Army's urgent request for the help of information teams in France, to keep the good-will and understanding of the civilians in areas where great numbers of our troops are waiting for transportation home.

Vast areas in the Balkans and eastern Europe are still cut off from normal contact with America, and special efforts will be needed for some time to see that American policy and its background are presented truthfully. Still greater areas in southeastern Asia and China have just been liberated from the Japanese. For almost four years in some places, almost eight years in others, a black curtain has cut these people off from the United States and the rest of the world. The lies spread by Japan will have to be counteracted, and the truth about our country will have to be told, if we are to win and hold the respect of the people of Asia.

These are areas where emergency work has to be done right now and for some months to come. But there is also a long-term information job to be done everywhere in the world — in Latin America, in Europe, in the Middle East, the British Commonwealth, and Russia. In these areas, too, truth and not special pleading is our instrument in clarifying American policy and in presenting a frank, accurate picture of American life.

This is work that can and should be done on a modest scale. Perhaps 3 or 4 American information officers in the smaller countries, 10 to 20 in the larger, will be enough, with the help of a compact and efficient service organization at home. I would not come here today to justify this work on a basis of dollar-and-cents return, but it is only fair to say that anything which promotes good-will and understanding of our country also promotes American business abroad.

We have no intention of competing in expenditure with the information organizations of other governments, but we cannot rely on the private or governmental facilities of other countries — even of our best friends abroad — to make the world better acquainted with America as it really is.

Through the cooperative efforts of American private industry and Government, this work is going on now under the interim service that has been set up in the State Department. There can be no break in the continuity, although the scale and the scope of our information work has already been cut sharply from its wartime level, and will be cut much further before the end of the year. We can do the necessary peacetime work with far fewer people and at far less cost.

. . . .

(2) **Summary of Projected Activities of the International Information Service. Department of State Press Release, December 28, 1945.**[1]

[Excerpt]

. . . .

Plans have been completed for carrying on in foreign countries the following activities, which are regarded as necessary for a peacetime information and cultural program:

1. The exchange of students, of scholars, and of technicians and other experts with special knowledge and skills. In this the Department acts as coordinating agency for 26 Government departments and bureaus which have foreign programs. Funds voted by Congress for this purpose are handled by the Department of State as a clearing agency for these 26 departments and bureaus.

2. The maintenance and servicing of American libraries of information in 60 countries abroad.

3. A daily wireless bulletin, which will bring to diplomatic missions throughout the world the full texts, or textual excerpts, of important official pronouncements.

4. A documentary service which will supply missions abroad, by mail, with background material, biographical sketches, and documentary material relating to the United States; and a small service of still photographs, limited to pictures of Government origin.

[1] *Ibid.*, p. 1046.

5. The preparation of photo-exhibits and film strips for showing in foreign countries.

6. Continuation of the bimonthly illustrated magazine in the Russian language for distribution in Soviet Union, where privately published magazines are barred.

7. Acquiring, adapting, and scoring in foreign languages of newsreels and documentary films about the United States.

8. The maintenance of small staffs in each of 62 countries, totaling about 400 United States public-affairs officers, to provide information about the United States through all media and especially through personal contacts, and to carry on the work of American cultural relations abroad.

9. An activity in the 1947 program which deserves special mention because of the magnitude of the operation, relative to other activities, is the operation under the Department of State of short-wave broadcasting covering virtually the whole world. It has not yet been decided whether the Government will continue to operate, maintain, and program the radio transmitters in its possession, or whether these activities should be conducted through public or private corporations. The future control and operation of international radio is now being studied in the Department, and recommendations will be made to the President and Congress within the next few months. Meantime it is essential to continue the operation of short-wave radio from this country, on a scale much reduced from that of wartime years, using 18 languages instead of the 40 used in wartime and broadcasting for nighttime listeners only.

The Department's operation of short-wave broadcasting at present requires a staff of more than 500 in New York for programing and engineering and more than 400 in San Francisco, and involves the maintenance of relay stations in Algiers, Honolulu, Saipan, Manila, and in the American zone in Germany. Further reductions in this staff will be made between January 1, 1946 and June 30, 1946, down to about 850.

Some areas in the world, such as the Balkans, can be reached with news about America by no other means. The Department feels radio is playing an essential role in giving foreign peoples a better understanding of American aims, policies, and institutions.

These nine activities constitute the "permanent" or continuing part of the program which has been evolved and which is now in process of further refinement. Sixty-six United States diplomatic missions abroad where informational and cultural work are planned have been queried this month on the proposed program and on the personnel to be assigned. No mission in our Foreign Service has reported that it wants informational and cultural work ended. Of the sixty-six only four seriously question the specific proposals, one of them because of a temporary political situation in the country involved.

Information activities are planned in 22 other, smaller posts, using the part-time services of a regular Foreign Service officer.

In addition to the "permanent" program the Department plans to continue temporarily an emergency program representing essential activities which remain in the backwash of the war. Such activities may be

CULTURAL RELATIONS

continued at least through the fiscal year 1947 but are not regarded as a regular part of an overseas information program.

Foremost among these is the present responsibility of the Department of State in the occupied areas of Germany, Austria, Venezia Giulia, and Japan, as well as similar emergency work in the areas of China and southeast Asia from which the Japanese have only recently been expelled. In the cases of Germany and Austria, the Department is now called on to supply civilian specialists in the various media of communications and certain materials and services to help support them, such as news, radio programs, recordings, films, and publications. At present there are about 225 such State Department specialists in Germany, assigned to General McClure, and approximately 50 in Austria.

In the case of the Trieste area, this Government is committed to continue its cooperation with the British in information work until a peace conference can determine the future of the region. In the case of Japan, seven civilian employees have been assigned responsibilities in the information and reeducation field on General MacArthur's staff, and they now require special services from the Department, through its Office of International Information and Cultural Affairs.

3. CULTURAL EXCHANGE PROGRAM

A. Interdepartmental Committee on Scientific and Cultural Cooperation

In October 1945 the Department of State removed its wartime suspension of awards of official fellowships and travel and maintenance grants to students from the United States for study in the other American republics and encouraged postwar study or research or supervised short-term undergraduate study in foreign countries which were in a condition to receive students.[1]

Since 1938 and during the war years the Interdepartmental Committee on Scientific and Cultural Cooperation carried on the planning and execution of a long-range program to promote understanding and to coordinate the activities of departments and agencies of the Government under the leadership of the Department of State. Until December 1944 the Committee was known as the Interdepartmental Committee on Cooperation with the American Republics. William Benton, Assistant Secretary of State, acted as chairman of the Committee with William T. Stone as vice chairman and Raymund L. Zwemer as Executive Director.[2] Members of the Committee represented 36 bureaus of 12 Government agencies and received advice from experts in many and diversified fields.

Member agencies of the Committee carried on programs which were inaugurated at the request of other governments, and participated in activities which covered the cultural, technological and scientific fields in three main classifications: cooperative scientific and technical projects; exchange of experts and students; and exchange of information.[3]

Under the terms of Public Law 63 (76th Cong.) Government specialists and technicians were authorized to serve under the governments of the other American republics, the Philippines and Liberia. By June 30, 1946 more than one hundred employees of Government departments had rendered services to the American republics, the Philippines and Liberia. Governments, interested in obtaining the services of a specialist from the United States, made requests through diplomatic channels to the Department of State which then relayed the

[1] Ibid., p. 701.
[2] Department of State Publication 2622, Inter-American Series 31, p. 2.
[3] Ibid., p. 18.

requests to the most appropriate department or agency. The expert was selected and the United States could then accept from the other country reimbursement for all or part of the expenses involved.[1]

The Interdepartmental Committee participated in many cooperative scientific and technical projects such as surveys of fishery and wildlife resources; development of mineral resources, tidal observations; magnetic surveys to aid aeronautical navigation; seismological observations; maintenance of radiosonde weather stations; investigations in insect pest eradication and disease control; agricultural experiment stations; training of aircraft pilots; cooperation in child welfare programs; and studies of educational conditions in the Western Hemisphere.

In effecting its program of exchange of persons, the Interdepartmental Committee provided for a government in-service training program; exchange of hemisphere leaders, professors and specialists; grants-in-aid to assist graduate students; and student exchange as stipulated by terms of the Buenos Aires Convention for the Promotion of Inter-American Cultural Relations.[2]

In order to maintain the cultural centers founded by nationals of the countries of the Western Hemisphere and by resident United States citizens, the Interdepartmental Committee established a program of grants, administered by the Division of International Libraries and Institutes, which assisted in the maintenance of 27 independent and 20 branch cultural centers in the other republics, paid the salaries of 32 directors and 31 American teachers of English, supplied about $50,000 worth of American books and materials, and paid approximately 20 percent of operating expenses. Eight centers were operating before the war; eight were organized in 1942 and six more in 1943 and 1944. During 1945 aid was extended to centers in La Paz, Bolivia; San Jose, Costa Rica; Guatemala City, Guatemala; Medellin, Colombia; and Cochabamba, Bolivia. English teaching programs were developed in Managua, Nicaragua; Ciudad Trujillo, Dominican Republic; Montevideo, Uruguay; Barranquilla, Colombia; and Cape Haitien, Haiti. Branch centers were established in Blumenau, Joinville, and Itajai, Brazil; Temuco, Valladivia, and Valparaiso, Chile; and Ambato, Guayaquil, Riobamba, and Cuenca, Ecuador.[3]

The Interdepartmental Committee fostered exchange of information through its member agencies which made possible publication, translation and distribution of material on a wide variety of subjects.

One appropriation covered all items for cooperative programs with the other republics. The agencies participating in the Committee's program furnished the information and requests and the Executive Committee presented the annual program to the Interdepartmental Committee which in turn modified and transmitted it to the Office of Budget and Finance of the Department of State to be incorporated into the consolidated budget request for the Department.[4]

B. The Fulbright Act

After consideration of bills S. 1440 and S. 1636 [5] the Committee on Military Affairs reported favorably on the bill S. 1636 with an amendment and recommended passage of the bill as amended.[6]

The bill had the following principal objectives:

"1. To transfer to the Secretary of State with respect to the disposal abroad of surplus property all functions heretofore conferred upon the Surplus Property Administrator by the Surplus Property Act, as amended;

[1] Ibid.
[2] Ibid., p. 20.
[3] Ibid., p. 26.
[4] Ibid., p. 45.
[5] Sponsored by Senator Fulbright of Arkansas; for text of the approved act, see this volume, p. 761.
[6] Foreign Educational Benefits and Surplus Property, Report of the Committee on Military Affairs (to accompany S. 1636), p. 1.

"2. To authorize the Secretary of State to dispose of all surplus property located abroad for foreign currencies or credits, intangible rights or benefits, or the discharge of claims; and

"3. To authorize the Secretary of State to enter into agreements with foreign governments for the use of such foreign currencies or credits for the purpose of financing studies of American citizens in the institutions of higher learning located in such foreign countries." [1]

Educational provisions of S. 1636, stipulated in subsection (2) which amended section 32 (b) of the Surplus Property Act, authorized the Secretary of State to enter into agreements with any foreign government for the use of currencies or credits acquired as a result of surplus property disposal abroad in order to finance studies for American citizens in schools and institutions in such foreign countries; to use such funds to provide assistance to citizens of foreign countries who wish to study in American schools of higher learning located abroad; and to use these funds and credits to furnish transportation for foreign students who desire to enroll in American universities.[2]

(1) *Statement by the Assistant Secretary of State for Public Affairs (Benton). Department of State Press Release, August 1, 1946.*[3]

A step of great long-range significance for the advancement of international understanding was taken today when the President signed an act of Congress, introduced by Senator Fulbright of Arkansas, which authorizes the Department of State to use some of the proceeds from surplus-property sales abroad for exchanges of students and other educational activities.

The bill provides that up to $20,000,000 can be earmarked for educational exchanges with any country which buys surplus property and up to $1,000,000 can be spent each year in each country where such an agreement is made. Thus tens of millions of dollars should become available under this bill, over a period of years.

The exchange of students and scholars is, in my judgment, the surest single method, over the decades, for promoting understanding among peoples. The activities of the press, radio, and films are indispensable in the exchange of current information among countries; but the effect of current developments is often ephemeral, and news is often misunderstood for lack of background and context. The solid background acquired by those who study outside of their own countries can provide the basis for truer understanding of other peoples. The beneficent results of the Boxer Indemnity scholarships, in the relationship between the United States and China, provides one of the best examples of this.

The Department of State had already completed an agreement with Great Britain, pending congressional approval, which will provide $20,000,000 from the sale of surplus property for educational exchanges with the United Kingdom and the British colonies. Similar agreements are now being negotiated for amounts ranging from $3,000,000 to $20,000,000 in the following countries, among others: Australia, New Zealand, China, the Philippines, Burma, India, Iran, Iraq, Saudi Arabia,

[1] *Ibid.*   [2] *Ibid.*, p. 3.
[3] Department of State, *Bulletin*, XV, p. 262.

Turkey, Egypt, Greece, Italy, Austria, France, Holland, Belgium, and the Scandinavian countries.

The Fulbright bill authorizes the following types of educational activities:

(1) American students can be given grants of foreign currencies to be used to pay the cost of higher education or research in foreign countries.

(2) American professors can be given grants to give lectures in foreign institutions of higher learning.

(3) Foreign students can be given scholarships to study at American non-denominational institutions abroad such as the American University at Beirut, Syria, and Robert College at Istanbul, Turkey.

(4) Foreign students can be given funds to pay for their transportation to the United States to attend American institutions of higher learning.

It is implicit in the bill that all of these activities must be financed with foreign currencies. The bill therefore cannot authorize expenses of foreign students within the United States. The bill is designed to utilize foreign credits in many countries in lieu of American dollars for American surplus property.

The students who will benefit by this bill will be selected by a ten-man Board of Foreign Scholarships, which the bill authorizes the President to establish. The bill provides that this Board shall include representatives of the United States Office of Education, the United States Veterans Administration, state educational institutions, and privately endowed institutions. If funds are negotiated to the limit of the bill's potential, and if facilities abroad develop capable of handling the students, it is possible that 100,000 or more American students would be sent abroad under this bill in the next two or three decades.

Veterans of World War I and II will be given preference. The bill requires that "due consideration shall be given to applicants from all geographical areas of the United States." It is expected that some type of regional selection method will be devised to insure that all parts of the United States are suitably represented.

It is unlikely that any scholarships will be awarded under the authority of this act for the 1946–47 academic year. After the President has appointed the Scholarship Board, and the Board has determined the qualifications for awards, ample publicity and time should be permitted for all suitably qualified people to make application. It is hoped that the grants will be made in the spring of 1947 for the school year beginning in the autumn of 1947.

While the major effect of the Fulbright bill will be to permit thousands of American students to study abroad, we should be prepared to welcome thousands of foreign students to our shores. I look forward to the day when we shall have as many as 50,000 foreign students in this country. Senator Fulbright, the author of the bill which was signed today, has seen at first hand the importance of such student exchanges as a result of his own studies abroad, and during his tenure as president of the University of Arkansas. It is due to his understanding and his leadership that this bill has been enacted by Congress.

(2) *An Act to Amend the Surplus Property Act of 1944 to Designate the Department of State as the Disposal Agency for Surplus Property outside the Continental United States, Its Territories, and Possessions, and for Other Purposes, Approved August 1, 1946.*[1]

Be it enacted by the Senate and House of Representatives of the United States of America in Congress assembled, That section 10 of the Surplus Property Act of 1944, as amended, is hereby amended by adding a new subsection (c) to read as follows:

"(c) Except as provided in subsection (b) of this section, the Department of State shall be the sole disposal agency for surplus property located outside the continental United States, Hawaii, Alaska (including the Aleutian Islands), Puerto Rico, and the Virgin Islands, and with respect to such property the Secretary of State shall exercise the functions heretofore conferred upon the Surplus Property Administrator by Public Law 181, Seventy-ninth Congress. The Secretary of State shall, subject to the provisions of the War Mobilization and Reconversion Act of 1944, have sole responsibility for carrying out the provisions of the Surplus Property Act of 1944, with respect to surplus property located outside the continental United States, Hawaii, Alaska (including the Aleutian Islands), Puerto Rico, and the Virgin Islands."

SEC. 2. Section 32 (b) of such Act, as amended, is hereby amended to read as follows:

"(b) (1) The provisions of this Act shall be applicable to disposition of property within the United States and elsewhere, but the Secretary of State may exempt from some or all of the provisions hereof dispositions of property located outside of the continental United States, Hawaii, Alaska (including the Aleutian Islands), Puerto Rico, and the Virgin Islands, whenever he deems that such provisions would obstruct the efficient and economic disposition of such property in accordance with the objectives of this Act. In addition to the authority conferred by section 15 of this Act, the Department of State may dispose of surplus property located outside the continental United States, Hawaii, Alaska (including the Aleutian Islands), Puerto Rico, and the Virgin Islands, for foreign currencies or credits, or substantial benefits or the discharge of claims resulting from the compromise, or settlement of such claims by any Government agency in accordance with the law, whenever the Secretary of State determines that it is in the interest of the United States to do so and upon such terms and conditions as he may deem proper. Any foreign currencies or credits acquired by the Department of State pursuant to this subsection shall be administered in accordance with procedures that may from time to time be established by the Secretary of the Treasury and, if and when reduced to United States currency, shall be covered into the Treasury as miscellaneous receipts.

"(2) In carrying out the provisions of this section, the Secretary of State is hereby authorized to enter into an executive agreement or agreements with any foreign government for the use of currencies, or credits for currencies, of such government acquired as a result of such surplus

[1] Public Law 584, 79th Cong., 2d sess.

property disposals, for the purpose of providing, by the formation of foundations or otherwise, for (A) financing studies, research, instruction, and other educational activities of or for American citizens in schools and institutions of higher learning located in such foreign country, or of the citizens of such foreign country in American schools and institutions of higher learning located outside the continental United States, Hawaii, Alaska (including the Aleutian Islands), Puerto Rico, and the Virgin Islands, including payment for transportation, tuition, maintenance, and other expenses incident to scholastic activities; or (B) furnishing transportation for citizens of such foreign country who desire to attend American schools and institutions of higher learning in the continental United States, Hawaii, Alaska (including the Aleutian Islands), Puerto Rico, and the Virgin Islands, and whose attendance will not deprive citizens of the United States of an opportunity to attend such schools and institutions: *Provided, however*, That no such agreement or agreements shall provide for the use of an aggregate amount of the currencies, or credits for currencies, of any one country in excess of $20,000,000 or for the expenditure of the currencies, or credits for currencies, of any one foreign country in excess of $1,000,000 annually at the official rate of exchange for such currencies, unless otherwise authorized by Congress, nor shall any such agreement relate to any subject other than the use and expenditure of such currencies or credits for currencies for the purposes herein set forth: *Provided further*, That for the purpose of selecting students and educational institutions qualified to participate in this program, and to supervise the exchange program authorized herein, the President of the United States is hereby authorized to appoint a Board of Foreign Scholarships, consisting of ten members, who shall serve without compensation, composed of representatives of cultural, educational, student and war veterans groups, and including representatives of the United States Office of Education, the United States Veterans' Administration, State educational institutions, and privately endowed educational institutions: *And Provided further*, That in the selection of American citizens for study in foreign countries under this paragraph preference shall be given to applicants who shall have served in the military or naval forces of the United States during World War I or World War II, and due consideration shall be given to applicants from all geographical areas of the United States. The Secretary of State shall transmit to the Congress not later than the 1st day of March of each year a report of operations under this paragraph during the preceding calendar year. Such report shall include the text of any agreements which have been entered into hereunder during the preceding calendar year, and shall specify the names and addresses of American citizens who are attending schools or institutions of higher learning in foreign countries pursuant to such agreements, the names and locations of such schools and institutions, and the amounts of the currencies or credits for currencies expended for any of the purposes under this paragraph in each such foreign country during the preceding calendar year."

CHAPTER XIV

WESTERN HEMISPHERE

1. RELATIONS WITH THE AMERICAN REPUBLICS

A. General

(1) *Address by the Secretary of State (Byrnes) before the* Herald Tribune *Forum Regarding Principles of the Inter-American System, New York, October 31, 1945.*[1]

[Excerpts]

. . . .

When we consider the principles which govern our inter-American system as it has been worked out in recent years, it is well to remember that these principles were not always recognized by us in our relations with our neighbors. There were times, not so far distant, when we tried "dollar diplomacy" and intervention and were accused of "Yankee imperialism."

But we have learned by experience that to have good neighbors we must be a good neighbor.

We have discovered that understanding and good-will cannot be bought and cannot be forced. They must spring spontaneously from the people. We have learned also that there can be no lasting friendship between governments unless there is understanding and good-will between their peoples.

In the inter-American system the members do not interfere in the internal affairs of their neighbors nor do they brook interference in those internal affairs by others. Freedom means more than freedom to act as we would like them to act.

. . . .

The policy of non-intervention in internal affairs does not mean the approval of local tyranny. Our policy is intended to protect the right of our neighbors to develop their own freedom in their own way. It is not intended to give them free rein to plot against the freedom of others.

We have learned by bitter experience in the past ten years that Nazi and Fascist plans for external aggression started with tyrannies at home which were falsely defended as matters of purely local concern. We have learned that tyranny anywhere must be watched, for it may come to threaten the security of neighboring nations and soon become the concern of all nations.

[1] Department of State, *Bulletin*, XIII, p. 709.

If, therefore, there are developments in any country within the inter-American system which, realistically viewed, threaten our security, we consult with other members in an effort to agree upon common policies for our mutual protection.

We Americans can take genuine pride in the evolution of the good-neighbor policy from what, in a way, were its beginnings in the Monroe Doctrine. We surely cannot and will not deny to other nations the right to develop such a policy.

. . . . . .

But the point I wish to emphasize is that the policy of the good neighbor, unlike the institution of marriage, is not an exclusive arrangement. The best neighbors do not deny their neighbors the right to be friends with others.

We have learned that our security interests in this hemisphere do not require its isolation from economic and cultural relations with the rest of the world.

We have freely accepted the Charter of the United Nations, and we recognize the paramount authority of the world community. The Charter, while reserving to us and other nations the inherent right of individual and collective self-defense in case of armed attack, requires that enforcement action taken under regional arrangements be sanctioned by the Security Council of the United Nations Organization.

Moreover, we adhere strictly to the policy that cooperation among the American republics does not justify discrimination against non-American states. The American republics have practiced the policy of equal treatment for all states which respect the sovereignty and integrity of their fellow states.

Inter-American cooperation is not inconsistent with world-wide cooperation among the nations. Regional arrangements, like the inter-American system, which respect the rights and interests of other states and fit into the world system can become strong pillars in the structure of world peace.

But we cannot recognize regional arrangements as a substitute for a world system. To do so would not promote the common and paramount interests of all nations, large and small, in world peace.

We live in one world; and in this atomic age regional isolationism is even more dangerous than is national isolationism.

We cannot have the kind of cooperation necessary for peace in a world divided into spheres of exclusive influence and special privilege.

This was the great significance of the Moscow Declaration of 1943. That joint statement of policy pledged the world's most powerful nations to mutual cooperation in winning the war and maintaining the peace. It was a landmark in our efforts to create a world community of nations and to abandon the discredited system of international relations based upon exclusive spheres of influence.

. . . . . .

International cooperation must — as I emphasized in my recent report on the London Council — depend upon intelligent compromise. It does not require us or any other nation to neglect its special relations with its nearer neighbors. But it does require that all neighborly relations be fitted into an organized system of international relations world-wide in scope.

The world system which we seek to create must be based on the principle of the sovereign equality of nations.

That does not mean that all nations are equal in power and in influence any more than all men are equal in power and influence. But it does mean equal respect for the individuality and sovereignty of nations, large and small. Nations, like individuals, should be equal before the law.

That principle is the cornerstone of our inter-American system as it is the cornerstone of the United Nations.

. . . .

B. Political Solidarity and Defense

1. GENERAL

The Governing Board of the Pan American Union and other inter-American agencies were engaged in the preparation of projects to be submitted to the Ninth International Conference of American States. The Organic Pact on the Inter-American System [1] was forwarded to American Governments for comments on the preliminary draft pursuant to action taken by the Governing Board at its meeting of April 10, 1946. A draft of an Inter-American Peace System [2] formulated by the Inter-American Juridical Committee was forwarded to the various Governments by the Pan American Union.

(1) Address by the Director of the Office of American Republic Affairs, Department of State (Briggs) at the University of Pennsylvania Concerning a Post-War Estimate of Pan American Solidarity, Philadelphia, November 20, 1945.[3]

[Excerpts]

. . . .

Our sister republics and ourselves have been preoccupied since well before the war with the problem of security. In the nine years beginning with the Buenos Aires conference we have been perfecting, step by step, our own procedure for dealing with threats of aggression. Our progress is traceable in the series of meetings — at Lima in 1938, at Panamá in 1939 immediately following the outbreak of hostilities, at Habana in 1940 after the fall of France, and at Rio de Janeiro in 1942 — each of which represented a step forward in our search for hemisphere security. Finally, the American republics agreed in Mexico City last March that an attack *from any source* would automatically constitute an attack

---

[1] *Project of Organic Pact of the Inter-American System Submitted for the Consideration of the Governments of the American Republics by the Governing Board of the Pan American Union*, Washington, Pan American Union, 1946.

[2] *Draft of an "Inter-American Peace System" and an Accompanying Report Formulated by the Inter-American Juridical Committee*, Washington, Pan American Union, October, 1945.

[3] Department of State, *Bulletin*, XIII, p. 867.

against all, and that they would consult in the event of any threat of aggression. That agreement is known as the "Act of Chapultepec."

At an early date we expect to enter into a treaty that will put the Chapultepec agreement, a temporary wartime measure, on a permanent basis. We are now actively preparing for a conference to be held at Rio de Janeiro for the specific purpose of negotiating and signing this treaty.

The proposed agreement will be a pact of military assistance. It is the first inter-American instrument of that character that our government has been prepared to undertake. Our own suggestions, shortly to be conveyed to the host Government of Brazil and to other governments for their preliminary consideration, have been drafted with the collaboration of members of the Congress and of the War and Navy Departments. We expect to receive between now and the date when the conference convenes in Rio valuable suggestions from other governments.

The primary purpose of this treaty will be the protection of the New World and its separate member states, but the agreement will also be in harmony with the United Nations Organization.

While we are thus collaborating with our neighbors in strengthening our own machinery and in gearing it to the equipment for peace of the United Nations, the world is painfully endeavoring to emerge from a devastating conflict. A struggle of that magnitude may well be a turning-point in civilization. All peoples, regardless of the degree of their participation, have been profoundly affected. Important political, social, and economic changes may come as a result of universal war. We cannot at this juncture identify these changes, or determine to what extent reconstruction in hungry, shattered Europe and reconversion in the United States are responsive to forces generated by the war. We recognize however that this is a time of unrest, of change, of suffering, and, we solemnly hope, of rebirth.

. . . . .

It has been argued that the exercise of collective initiative is destructive to unanimity, and hence dangerous to continental solidarity. It would impair, these critics argue, the unity of the hemisphere.

The fallaciousness of this view is apparent to anyone who has taken the trouble to scrutinize the record. Unanimity among the American republics has seldom been present. It may exist as an ultimate objective — the ideal situation, if you like, in an ideal world — but unfortunately we do not yet live in an ideal world. We live in a battered universe, now groping forward and trying to find a better and more workable association.

In recent years a great deal of effort has been spent in seeking, especially at inter-American conferences, to have everyone agree upon everything. This not infrequently resulted in whittling down principles to fit the lowest unanimous denominator, so that instead of taking a vigorous forthright position which would have commanded the respect, if not the support, of all the people the American republics for the sake of twenty-one votes sometimes lowered their sights below the main target. They allowed the lowest unanimous denominator to become a low denominator in common.

. . . . . .

Notwithstanding this lack of unanimity, the nations of this hemisphere have on the whole a most enviable record. The great majority of our boundary disputes have been settled by negotiation or arbitration. The Chaco war, which threatened the peace of a whole continent, yielded solution to inter-American mediation. The use of the waters of two great rivers has just been satisfactorily adjusted by treaty. We are cooperating with our neighbors with respect to problems resulting from wartime dislocation of trade. We have pledged ourselves to collaborate in a wide variety of fields of international endeavor.

Our future may not be smooth, but at least we have evidence that we are traveling in the right direction, even though each one of us may not choose to move abreast of all of the others.

It is suggested therefore that we revise our thinking about unanimity to accord more closely with the facts. Let us agree that when we speak of continental solidarity we have discarded both the idea of simultaneous acceptance by all of the American republics and the corollary notion that there is something unusual or unworthy in the failure of everyone to see eye to eye with everyone else on a given subject. Let us instead stick to the more reasonable and attainable objective of a substantial majority, and of seeing to it at the same time that the rights of the minority are fully protected.

. . . . . .

All of this presupposes — as it must presuppose if we are to have faith in the future — that the essential basis of the inter-American relationship is a common interest in democratic ideals, as they affect internal political development and as they find expression in the conduct of international relations. We refer to those principles that enhance the dignity of man, that safeguard and preserve his freedom, and that are conducive to the attainment of orderly representative government, characterized by respect for law and fair elections.

It is conceded that some governments in this hemisphere have not come into power through democratic processes. Some have maintained their positions through other than constitutional means, or without the consent of the governed.

We do not intend to intervene to impose democracy. The peoples of those countries are primarily responsible. But we obviously feel a warmer friendship for and a greater desire to cooperate with those governments that rest on the periodically and freely expressed endorsement of the governed. With respect to other regimes, our sympathy is extended to the people themselves in their struggle for liberty.

. . . .

We believe that the people of the United States, one million of whose sons were casualties during the war, desire to profit by the experience of this costliest of lessons. We believe that the inter-American relationship, to the maintenance and further development of which our country is dedicated, demands that each nation state the facts as it sees them. We believe that by taking counsel together in an atmosphere of trust and understanding the American republics will arrive at solutions commanding the support of their peoples.

Finally, we are convinced that only through a practical application of the principles of democracy can we achieve the real solidarity of this hemisphere.

2. MILITARY MISSIONS

During the period under review agreements were concluded by the United States and various American republics concerning military, naval and air missions.[1] An agreement with Bolivia, originally signed on September 4, 1941, was renewed for a four year period from September 4, 1945. An agreement providing for an American naval mission in Brazil was extended for four years from May 7, 1946.[2] On October 14, 1946, an agreement was signed with Colombia providing for an American naval mission to Colombia for a period of four years.[3] On December 10, 1945, a four year agreement regarding an American military mission was signed with Costa Rica. A four year agreement was signed with Honduras on December 28, 1945, concerning a military mission to that country.[4] On October 7, 1946, an agreement between Peru and the United States authorized the operation of an American Army Air Forces mission to Peru for a four year period.[5] On June 3, 1946, an agreement was signed with Venezuela providing for the detail of a military mission during the subsequent two years.[6]

3. PROPOSED CONFERENCE FOR THE MAINTENANCE OF CONTINENTAL PEACE AND SECURITY

The proposed conference to give permanent form to the principles embodied in the Act of Chapultepec[7] of March 1945 was originally scheduled to meet in Rio de Janeiro on October 20, 1945. Postponement was announced early in October because, in the view of the United States Government, Argentina had failed to fulfill its obligations and commitments under the Inter-American System, in particular, those which required elimination of Axis influences from this hemisphere. Acting Secretary of State Acheson, in announcing the United States' request for postponement, further stated: "In view of recent developments in Argentina, the United States Government does not feel that it can properly negotiate or sign with the present Argentine regime a treaty of military assistance. Since the conference to be convened in Rio de Janeiro on October 20 is exclusively for the purpose of negotiating such a treaty, this Government has communicated with the host Government of Brazil, suggesting that that conference be postponed, but emphasizing that, in view of the great importance which this Government attaches to the negotiation of such a treaty, it has urged that negotiations proceed as rapidly as possible to the end of concluding and signing such a treaty in Rio de Janeiro at the earliest possible moment." [8] Despite uneasiness displayed

---

[1] For list of previous agreements, see *Documents, VII, 1944–1945*, p. 758.
[2] Department of State, *Treaties and Other International Acts Series* 1559.
[3] *Ibid.*, 1563.
[4] *Ibid.*, 1503.
[5] *Ibid.*, 1562.
[6] *Ibid.*, 1522.
[7] See *Documents, VII, 1944–1945*, p. 717.
[8] *New York Times*, October 4, 1945, p. 1.

by several Latin American countries regarding the wisdom of such action, the Governing Board of the Pan American Union decided on March 6, 1946 to consult the American republics regarding further postponement of the special conference. A majority of American Republics favored the drawing up of a defense plan to be signed whenever the Government of Argentina, under the new leadership of Juan D. Perón, carried out Argentina's defense commitments, including elimination of Axis influence from Argentina's territory. In preparation for the projected pact the Governing Board of the Pan American Union adopted a resolution (proposed by the United States) to appoint a drafting committee to reconcile the various treaty proposals.[1] On August 31, 1946, the Argentine Chamber of Deputies endorsed the Senate's action of approving the Act of Chapultepec without reservations. Hope was expressed by the United States Government that the Perón Government would act quickly to expel Nazi activities from its borders.

Although there was considerable criticism of American policy toward Argentina, the following course of action stated by Secretary of State Byrnes on April 8 was adhered to throughout the period under review: "The Government of the United States feels that it expressed the sentiments of all its sister Governments in declaring its fervent hope that when the newly elected (Argentine) Government takes office and its Congress meets, it will give prompt implementation by positive acts to its solemn commitments under the inter-American system; in particular those undertaken in the final Act of the Inter-American Conference on Problems of War and Peace. Those commitments are plain and unequivocal. They require the elimination from this Hemisphere of Axis influences which have threatened the security of the inter-American system." [2]

4. PROPOSED PROGRAM OF INTER-AMERICAN MILITARY COOPERATION

In a message to Congress on May 6, 1946, President Truman outlined a program of inter-American military cooperation.[3] Standardization of hemispheric defenses and the training and equipping of armed forces in the American system were salient features of the plan. Legislation authorizing the United States to undertake such a program was approved by the House Foreign Affairs Committee [4] but received no action in the Senate during the period under review.

(1) *Letter from the President (Truman) to the Congress Regarding the Inter-American Military Cooperation Act, May, 6 1946.*[5]

I submit herewith for the consideration of the Congress a bill to be entitled "The Inter-American Military Cooperation Act" authorizing a program of military collaboration with other American States including the training, organization, and equipment of the armed forces of those countries. I recommend that the Congress give this bill its favorable consideration and enact it.

For several years our Army and Navy have maintained cordial relations of collaboration with the armed forces of other American republics within the framework of the Good Neighbor Policy. Under authorization of the Congress, military and naval training missions have been sent

[1] *Ibid.*, April 11, 1946, p. 16.
[2] *Ibid.*, December 24, 1946, p. 8.
[3] *Ibid.*, May 7, 1946, p. 1, 2.
[4] H.R. 6326, House Report No. 2230, 79th Cong., 2d sess.; for statement of the Secretary of State before the House Foreign Affairs Committee on May 29, 1946, see Department of State, *Bulletin*, XIV, p. 1001.
[5] *Ibid.*, p. 859.

to various American republics. During the recent war, even prior to Pearl Harbor, this collaboration was intensively developed on the basis of inter-American undertakings for hemisphere defense. Training activities were expanded, and under the Lend-Lease Act limited amounts of military and naval equipment were made available to the other American republics as part of the hemisphere defense program. Forces from two of the American republics participated in combat overseas, and others joined in the defense of the shores and seas of the Americas at a time when the danger of invasion of our continents was all too great.

More recently the American republics have assumed new responsibilities, for their mutual defense and for the maintenance of peace, in the Act of Chapultepec and the Charter of the United Nations. The close collaboration of the American republics provided for in the Act of Chapultepec, the proposed treaty to be based upon that Act, and other basic inter-American documents, makes it highly desirable to standardize military organization, training methods and equipment as has been recommended by the Inter-American Defense Board.

Under the bill transmitted herewith, the Army and Navy, acting in conjunction with the Department of State, would be permitted to continue in the future a general program of collaboration with the armed forces of our sister republics with a view to facilitating the adoption of similar technical standards. Certain additional training activities, not covered by existing legislation, would be permitted. The President would also be authorized to transfer military and naval equipment to the Governments of other American States by sale or other method.

The collaboration authorized by the bill could be extended also to Canada, whose cooperation with the United States in matters affecting their common defense is of particular importance.

A special responsibility for leadership rests upon the United States in this matter because of the preponderant technical, economic and military resources of this country. There is a reasonable and limited purpose for which arms and military equipment can rightfully be made available to the other American States. This Government will not, I am sure, in any way approve of, nor will it participate in, the indiscriminate or unrestricted distribution of armaments, which would only contribute to a useless and burdensome armaments race. It does not desire that operations under this bill shall raise unnecessarily the quantitative level of armament in the American republics. To this end the bill specifies that amounts of non-standard material shall be sought in exchange for United States equipment.

It is my intention that any operations under this Bill, which the Congress may authorize, shall be in every way consistent with the wording and spirit of the United Nations Charter. The bill has been drawn up primarily to enable the American nations to carry out their obligations to cooperate in the maintenance of inter-American peace and security under the Charter and the Act of Chapultepec which is intended to be supplanted by a permanent Inter-American Treaty.

It is incumbent upon this Government to see that military developments in which we have a part are guided towards the maintenance of peace and security and that military and naval establishments are not encouraged beyond what security considerations require. In this connection the bill provides that operations thereunder are subject to any international agreement for the regulation of armaments to which the United States may become a party. In addition provision will be made for continuing coordination of the actual operations under the legislation with developing plans and policy in the field of armaments regulation.

In executing this program it will be borne in mind, moreover, that it is the policy of this Government to encourage the establishment of sound economic conditions in the other American republics which will contribute to the improvement of living standards and the advancement of social and cultural welfare. Such conditions are a prerequisite to international peace and security. Operations under the proposed legislation will be conducted with full and constant awareness that no encouragement should be given to the imposition upon other people of any useless burden of armaments which would handicap the economic improvement which all countries so strongly desire. The execution of the program authorized by the bill will also be guided by a determination to guard against placing weapons of war in the hands of any groups who may use them to oppose the peaceful and democratic principles to which the United States and other American nations have so often subscribed.

In entering into agreements with other American States for the provision of training and equipment as authorized by the bill, the purposes of this program will be made clear to each of the other governments.

C. Economic and Social Cooperation

Throughout the period under review the United States participated in several inter-American conferences dealing with economic and social affairs within the hemisphere. For a listing of such conferences, see this volume, p. 76.[1]

For information on credits authorized by the Export-Import Bank to various American republics, see this volume, p. 638.

For compilation of statistics regarding lend-lease aid to the American republics, see this volume, p. 154.

1. COFFEE

In reply to numerous communications directed to government authorities from the Fourth Pan American Coffee Conference regarding modifications or possible elimination of coffee price ceilings [2] then in effect, Acting Secretary of State Acheson suggested by letter on October 1, 1945, the methods by which the United States would consider international problems relating to coffee, namely, through the Inter-American Coffee Board,[3] or through direct negotiations with countries signatory to the Inter-American Coffee Agreement.

On January 22, 1946, President Truman transmitted a protocol to extend for a year, with certain modifications, the Inter-American Coffee Agreement; the

[1] For information on agricultural cooperation, see *ibid.*, XIII, p. 58, 409; for information on the promotion of child welfare in the American Republics, see *ibid.*, XIV, p. 428; for information on the Inter-American Conference of Experts on Copyright, see Department of State Publication 2827, Conference Series 99.

[2] For previous requests of coffee producing countries for increase in green coffee ceiling prices in March, 1945, see *Documents, VII, 1944–1945*, p. 770.

[3] The Inter-American Coffee Board was authorized in Article IX of the Inter-American Coffee Agreement, November 28, 1940.

Senate on April 11, 1946, approved the protocol, and the instrument of ratification by the United States was deposited with the Pan American Union on May 1, 1946. Although retaining the framework of the Coffee Agreement, the protocol suspended the provisions of Articles I to VIII relating to coffee quotas. Under emergency conditions, however, it provided that those Articles could again become effective if approval was given by at least 95 percent of the total vote of the Inter-American Coffee Board. The protocol further stipulated, under Article 3, that the Board continue the study of world coffee conditions and, whenever necessary, make recommendations for consideration by the governments participating in the Agreement and other interested governments; such recommendations were to take into account commodity principles and policies embodied in agreements concluded under the auspices of the United Nations.[1]

Following a recommendation made by the Inter-American Coffee Board on August 16, 1946, the signatory governments extended the Agreement for a period of one year from October 1, 1946. The protocol [2] provided for study of the coffee situation by the Inter-American Coffee Board in preparation for a possible revised agreement at some later date.

2. TRADE WITH THE AMERICAN REPUBLICS

(1) *Address by the Assistant Secretary of State (Braden) before the National Foreign Trade Convention Concerning Foreign Trade Reconstruction in the Americas, New York, November 14, 1945.*[3]

[Excerpts]

. . . .

The resources of the United States were inadequate to meet the insatiable demands of modern warfare. We needed many things — tin, rubber, petroleum, antimony, copper, food — and some of them we needed desperately.

To meet these deficiencies we turned to our southern neighbors. Because they had confidence in us and because from the very beginning we gave their civilian needs the same treatment as our own, they, for the most part, responded in a fine cooperative spirit. Thus Assistant Secretary Clayton at the Mexico City conference testified to the fact that the procurement contracts with the other American governments "were made without undue bargaining . . . [and] were on the whole performed with complete honesty and integrity; . . . the prices were fair", and "every effort was made to extend production".

It is essential that our neighbors and we continue to solve our problems through consultation in an atmosphere of mutual respect and collaboration. There can be no dictation by either party to the other. When differences arise, as they surely will, they must be settled by straightforward negotiations, by compromise, by arbitration, and always with that friendly understanding which enables one to see the other's point of view.

In the reconstruction era that unanimity of purpose which prevails in wartime will be lacking, selfish interests will more readily come to the fore, and accommodations will be more difficult, as tempers already

---

[1] Department of State, *Bulletin*, XIV, p. 867.
[2] Department of State, *Treaties and Other International Acts Series* 1605.
[3] Department of State, *Bulletin*, XIII, p. 793.

fatigued by war strains become increasingly harassed by the manifold and complicated problems which lie ahead for all.

The stern necessities of war have left to every country in this hemisphere a legacy of serious economic problems. Among these are the menace of inflation and exaggerated nationalisms, both of which are presently threatening on every side.

. . . . .

Our war procurement of raw materials from the neighboring republics in some instances caused a great expansion in production facilities. The abrupt cancellation of our purchase contracts inevitably would cause wide-spread unemployment and economic distress. Yet we could not afford to continue to buy largely in excess of our needs.

This problem was recognized in resolution XXI at the Mexico City conference, which records general agreement with our view that international trade in these basic products and strategic materials should be returned to normal commercial channels so soon as possible. At the same time that resolution provides that suitable steps shall be taken during the readjustment period to minimize the adverse consequences of "cutbacks" on the economies of the countries concerned.

We are now in process of reducing our public purchases from Latin America. As we do so, we are adhering to the letter and spirit of our undertakings at Mexico City.

. . . . .

The other American republics are normally heavily dependent on imports for their supplies of many types of manufactured goods, especially capital equipment of all varieties. Unhappily, the goods needed by our neighbors for the repair, improvement, and expansion of their economies were precisely the types most essential for prosecution of the war. Consequently, they sold to us during the war much more than we were able to sell to them, and now possess a large supply of dollars which they are eager to spend on imports. In view of the continuing shortage in the United States of many types of producers' goods, some of the other American nations are apprehensive that they may be unable to purchase a fair share of our output.

Lest there be misunderstanding on this score, I wish to emphasize that the United States Government rejects the view that the industrialization and diversification of the Latin American economies are threats to the maintenance of our own export markets in that area. The ancient mercantilist fallacy that an industrial exporting nation should strive to impede the industrialization of its overseas markets was ridiculed and exploded nearly 200 years ago by Adam Smith; but, like many mistaken theories, this one dies hard.

. . . . .

The industrialization programs of the other American republics must be considered from both a short- and a long-range point of view. In the present period, during which the demand for our output of producers' goods exceeds the supply, we are giving close and sympathetic attention to the needs of our American neighbors. Many United States manufacturers of producers' goods, eager to reestablish their export trade, are voluntarily allocating a portion of their output to meet foreign demands. In cases of unusual urgency, we still possess the authority to give limited priority assistance to the orders of foreign buyers in certain cases. Moreover, we are anxious to bring Latin American buyers into contact with our manufacturers and, where necessary, to request our factories to allocate a portion of their output for export.

With these transitional problems solved, our neighbors and we shall then be face to face with working out the longer run economic relations of the Americas with each other and with the world. We shall be too late, however, if we wait to face their problems until they are upon us. Decisions are being made today and every day which will determine our economic relations tomorrow. As we make these decisions, all of the American nations should have clearly in mind the kind of economic system which will best serve our common ends.

We believe that the best suited system of economic relationships is the one most conducive to the preservation of peace and international understanding, and which is most effective in promoting higher living standards and increased prosperity here and throughout the Americas. The two, of course, are interdependent. Rising standards of living are a powerful bulwark to the institutions of freedom and popular government, and these institutions, as we now know too well, are stones in the arch of peace. The tyrant must first place his own people in chains before he is ready to leap at the throat of a neighbor.

With these ultimate objectives in mind, it is immediately clear that neither our neighbors nor we seek to establish a Western Hemisphere economic bloc. The American nations could, perhaps, organize an exclusive system of hemispheric trading arrangements, under which commerce between the Americas and the rest of the world would be discouraged or prevented.

What would that avail us? It would sanction the formation of other exclusive economic blocs. Economic blocs of this kind must inevitably become political blocs, the emergence of which would be an ominous warning that the peace of the world was in jeopardy.

. . . . .

The sole sane alternative to a hemispheric system of discrimination and restriction is an international system of equal treatment and expansion. It is only in a world economy constructed along these lines that each nation, in the Americas and elsewhere, can realize the highest potential of its productive powers; nor is there any other basic pattern for world economic organization which produces fewer of the economic practices which engender international friction and hostility.

The achievement of these goals demands, on the part of all like-minded nations, a concerted effort to eliminate every form of economic discrimination, including preferences, multi-column tariffs, and discriminatory exchange and quota practices; to reduce substantially the tariff barriers which have throttled the trade of the world; to put an end to the restrictive practices of international cartels; to adopt a code of principles to govern the use of subsidies, commodity agreements, and other such devices; and to proscribe the use of tactics of economic aggression.

. . . . . .

No area will benefit more than the Americas from the reconstruction of world trade along liberal, non-discriminatory lines; no peoples have a greater stake in the rehabilitation of the world economy than do the peoples of all the American republics.

We want to see the Americas, then, not as an economic bloc but as an integral part of an economic whole. We desire this because of, and not in spite of, our special security interests in the Western Hemisphere; for we know of no way better to protect this hemisphere and ourselves than by helping to promote the prosperity, stability, and mutual trust and confidence of the Americas.

We ask no special rights or privileges from our neighbors, nor do we ask them to discriminate against non-American nations. We could not, of course, sit idly by while a non-American nation tried, as did the Nazis, to use its economic relations with the Americas as a cover for political intrigue and provocation; but we seek to bar from this hemisphere no nation which desires, in good faith, to engage in commerce with it.

The economic integration of the Americas with the rest of the world is not a development which we fear; on the contrary, we desire it, and we will gladly do our utmost to achieve it.

. . . . . .

2. RELATIONS WITH INDIVIDUAL COUNTRIES

A. Argentina

On August 25, 1945, President Truman accepted the resignation of Mr. Nelson A. Rockefeller as Assistant Secretary of State for American Republic Affairs and appointed Mr. Spruille Braden, Ambassador to Argentina, as his successor. In his new post Mr. Braden continued his criticism of the Argentine Government as a dictatorship and a threat to Hemispheric peace and solidarity.[1]

In October, 1945, the United States Government initiated consultation with other American Republics concerning the Argentine situation. On February 11 a Memorandum, known as the "Blue Book",[2] was delivered to representatives of other American countries for consideration. The Memorandum contained charges that the Government of Argentina had given actual support to the German war effort and was giving refuge to Nazi interests within its borders. According to the evidence presented by the Department of State, Col. Juan D. Perón, former Vice-President and candidate for the Argentine Presidency, was involved with Nazi agents and native collaborators. Shortly thereafter, Foreign Minister Juan I. Cooke answered the charges in detail and stated that the Memorandum could only be construed as a "lamentable interference in the internal political affairs of Argentina."[3]

[1] *New York Times*, August 26, 1945, p. 1; for text of a farewell address by Ambassador Braden in Buenos Aires, see *ibid.*, August 29, 1946, p. 10.

[2] Department of State Publication 2473, Inter-American Series 29, 1946.

[3] For details of the Argentine repudiation of charges contained in the Memorandum, see *New York Times*, April 18, 1946, p. 18.

On April 3, the Argentine Government consented to the appointment of George Messersmith as the new American Ambassador to that country. On June 4, Juan D. Perón was inaugurated as President of Argentina.

Upon the advice of Ambassador Messersmith, who consistently advocated a more conciliatory attitude toward Argentina, the United States agreed to release to Argentina over $600,000,000 in "frozen funds", retaining a minor part of the funds for further investigation as to whether the Nazis had any interests in the deposits.[1]

Following final approval by the Argentine Congress in August, 1946, of the United Nations Charter and the Act of Chapultepec, relations between the United States and Argentina were somewhat improved. The United States, however, remained firm in its policy of refusal to enter a Hemisphere defense pact[2] with that country while Nazi influences were still in evidence.

(1) Memorandum by the United States to the American Republics on the Argentine Situation. Department of State Press Release, April 8, 1946.[3]

[Excerpts]

1. In October 1945 this Government within the framework established by the Inter-American System initiated consultation with the other American republics concerning the Argentine situation and in connection therewith issued a memo now commonly known as the Blue Book.

2. In initiating such consultation the United States was not animated by any feeling of hostility towards the Argentine people. On the contrary it was the desire of the United States to strengthen the friendly relationships between the people of United States and the people of Argentina by bringing into the open those conditions which had caused the Government of the United States great embarrassment and concern in its relations with the then Government of Argentina. It was also the desire of the United States that the other American republics should know the conditions which caused this embarrassment and concern so that it would be clear that the United States was acting in defense and not in derogation of the principles of the inter-American system.

. . . . . .

3. The consultation respecting the Argentine situation initiated by the United States raised the question whether the proposed inter-American Mutual Assistance Treaty should be negotiated with the participation of the Farrell Government of Argentina in view of its failure to fulfill its obligations and commitments under the inter-American system.

4. To date, in the consultation respecting the Argentine situation initiated by the Government of the United States, replies have been received from less than half of the other American republics. Some of these answers entirely agree with views expressed by the United States; others emphasize the changed position resulting from the recent election. All of the Governments so far heard from join with the United States in their dedication to the following principles and objectives:

[1] *Ibid.*, June 26, 1946, p. 1.
[2] For discussion of the proposed Inter-American Defense Treaty, see this volume, p. 768.
[3] Department of State, *Bulletin*, XIV, p. 666. See also, *ibid.*, p. 285.

(1) The "unity of the peoples of America is indivisible" and "the Argentine nation is and always has been an integral part of the union of the American republics."

(2) The security of the Hemisphere is of paramount importance and will be materially enhanced by the negotiation and signature of a Mutual Assistance Treaty at the projected Rio de Janeiro Conference.

5. While it is not clear that the election will remove the conditions which prompted the Government of the United States to initiate a consultation on the Argentine situation, the Government of the United States does not believe that the people of Argentina intended to approve the continuance of conditions which would threaten the safety of the inter-American system.

6. A new constitutional government will soon be inaugurated in Argentina. The Government of the United States feels that it expresses the sentiments of all its sister governments in declaring its fervent hope that when that newly elected government takes office and its congress meets, it will give prompt implementation by positive acts to its solemn commitments under the Inter-American System, in particular, those undertaken in the Final Act of the Inter-American Conference on Problems of War and Peace. Those undertakings are plain and unequivocal. They require the elimination from this Hemisphere of Axis influences which have threatened the security of the inter-American system.

Were such unequivocal and sustained performance to ensue, the road would then be open to that "complete unity of the peoples of America", and the negotiation and signature of a Mutual Assistance Pact. But there must be deeds and not merely promises.

7. The military assistance commitments undertaken by the United States under the Act of Chapultepec will terminate with the expiration of the War Powers Act in this country. It is to the benefit of all of the American republics that a treaty of mutual assistance be negotiated and signed at the earliest possible date.

To do this, it is proposed that at the next meeting of the Governing Board of the Pan American Union a committee of its members be appointed to coordinate the five draft treaties, which have been under consideration, together with such other suggestions as may then be received, into a single document.

This document would in due course be presented to the Rio Conference.

We hope the Conference can be called to meet after the new Government of Argentina has been installed and has had a reasonable time to comply with the promises made at Mexico City. When it has complied we feel satisfied the American republics will welcome that Government's participation in the treaty of mutual assistance.

B. Mexico

On October 2, 1945, the Chargé d'Affaires ad interim of Mexico presented to the Secretary of State his Government's check for $4,085,327.45 as instalment payment due under the agreement (September 29, 1943)[1] which provided for compensation for petroleum properties expropriated by Mexico in March 1938.[2]

[1] See *Documents, VI, 1943–1944*, p. 546.   [2] Department of State, *Bulletin*, XIII, p. 553.

On November 20, 1945 the Ambassador of Mexico presented to the Secretary of State the fourth annual instalment ($2,500,000) under the claims convention concluded November 19, 1941 as settlement of certain property claims of American citizens against the Mexican Government.[1]

On November 8, 1945 Mexico and the United States exchanged instruments of ratification of the treaty and supplementary protocol between the two countries relating to utilization of the waters of the Colorado and Tijuana Rivers and the Río Grande from Fort Quitman, Texas to the Gulf of Mexico.[2] The following statement by the Secretary of State was made at the time of exchange of ratifications.

(1) *Text of Statement by the Secretary of State (Byrnes) on Exchange of Ratifications of the Treaty Relating to the Utilization of Waters of Certain Streams, November 8, 1945.*[3]

We are about to sign the protocol of the exchange of ratifications of the treaty relating to the utilization of the waters of certain streams that run along or across our common boundary.

By this act we shall bring to a successful conclusion the efforts of our Governments over a period of several decades to find a mutually acceptable solution to the problem of making an equitable division of the water supply of these rivers and at the same time providing cooperatively the means of controlling, conserving, and distributing these waters in such manner that in both countries the people and communities in these river basins will be able to carry forward their developments.

That this treaty will make possible, in each country, the maximum feasible water uses along these rivers is a tribute to the technical skill of the engineers and consultants engaged upon the complicated studies involved in this question and to the vision, the friendly cooperation, and sense of fairness of the negotiators.

Likewise, Mr. Ambassador, we have reason to be gratified at the fair and full consideration which, in accordance with our political institutions and procedures, was given to this treaty by the Senates of our two Republics, both in the hearings and in the debates.

The procedures before these two legislative bodies, together with the able assistance of the press and radio, assured every interested person and group an opportunity to be informed and to be heard in regard to the merits of this important agreement.

In signing this protocol, Mr. Ambassador, I have full confidence that this treaty which is about to become of force will constitute an historic milestone in the annals of the cordial relations between Mexico and the United States.

I am confident also, that its provisions will in the years to come assure steadily increasing well-being and prosperity to the peoples and commu-

[1] *Ibid.*, p. 871.
[2] For text of the treaty signed February 3, 1944, see *Documents, VI, 1943–1944,* p. 547; for text of supplementary protocol signed November 14, 1944, see *Documents, VII, 1944–1945,* p. 797; for exchange of notes regarding ratification, see Department of State, *Bulletin,* XIII, p. 770.
[3] *Ibid.*

nities — in either country — dependent upon these vital water resources, and that its great significance and beneficent influence will be felt far beyond our national frontiers.

C. Panama

On September 12, 1946 the Department of State released a joint statement [1] by the Governments of Panama and United States regarding the return to Panama of 71 defense sites and preparation for return of 27 others. The two Governments agreed to continue consultation on the most effective means for defense of the Panama Canal, in conformance with the objectives of the 1936 Treaty of Friendship and Cooperation and of the Defense Sites Agreement of May 18, 1942.[2]

3. RELATIONS WITH CANADA

For information on the status of civil aviation agreements formulated at Chicago, Illinois, December 7, 1944, with respect to Canada, see this volume, p. 660.

A. Disposition of Defense Installations

On February 20, 1946 Foreign Liquidation Commissioner Thomas B. McCabe revealed that strategic field offices had opened under Deputy Field Commissioners to facilitate disposal operations in Canada and the North Atlantic area. The main office was established in Washington, with field offices at Ottawa, Canada; St. John's, Newfoundland; Reykjavik, Iceland; Godthaab, Greenland. Surpluses in these areas existed mainly in Canada.[3]

By exchange of notes in March and July, 1946,[4] the Governments of the United States and Canada concluded an agreement for the purchase by Canada of certain American owned defense installations, projects, equipment and supplies for $12,000,000 (U.S.). Representatives of the office of the Field Commissioner for Foreign Liquidation for Canada and the North Atlantic Areas worked out details of the transaction for the Department of State and the President of War Assets Corporation, Canada. Installations included in the agreement were those along the Alaska Highway and Northwest Staging Route, wartime weather stations in northeastern Canada, surplus movable property reported by the American Government to War Assets Corporation and certain naval and air equipment originally provided to the United Kingdom under lend-lease. In addition, the United States made available to Canada until April 1, 1947 certain surplus equipment (to the maximum cost of $7,000,000) to be used in the training programs of Canada's armed forces.[5]

By exchange of notes signed at Ottawa on December 21, 1945 and January 3, 1946, an agreement was concluded between the two countries relating to disposition of storage and loading facilities at Prince Rupert.[6]

---

[1] *Ibid.*, XV, p. 551.
[2] See *Documents, IV, 1941–1942*, p. 344.
[3] Department of State, *Bulletin*, XIV, p. 350.
[4] For complete exchange of notes, see Department of State, *Treaties and Other International Acts Series* 1531.
[5] Department of State, *Bulletin*, XIV, p. 683; for agreement between the two countries in June 1944 regarding disposition of defense installations, see *Documents, VII, 1944–1945*, p. 804.
[6] Department of State, *Treaties and Other International Acts Series* 1565.

(1) *Exchange of Notes between the Canadian Secretary of State for External Affairs (King)* [1] *and the United States Ambassador to Canada (Atherton) Regarding Transfer of Defense Installations and Equipment, Ottawa, March 30, 1946.*[2]

(a) Note from the Canadian Secretary of State for External Affairs to the American Ambassador.

I have the honour to refer to discussions which have recently taken place between representatives of our Governments on the subject of war surpluses and related matters. It is my understanding that these representatives have agreed on the following proposals which are acceptable to the Canadian Government.

2. With regard to defence installations and equipment owned by the United States Government and located in Canada and not yet otherwise disposed of, the two Governments have found it mutually advantageous to expedite and simplify the procedure set forth in the 33rd Recommendation of the Permanent Joint Board on Defence and approved by the two Governments, while continuing to accept its underlying principles. To the extent, therefore, that this agreement is inconsistent with the exchange of notes of November 22nd and December 20th, 1944, it shall be regarded as superseding them.

3. It is agreed that for the sum of $12,000,000.00 (U.S.) the United States Government will transfer to the Canadian Government the following defence installations, projects and/or supplies and equipment connected therewith owned by the United States Government and located in Canada, the original cost price of which was approximately $59,000,-000.00 (U.S.). In each case the details are listed in appendices [3] to this note, giving approximate original costs, as follows:

(a) *Immovable Property.*
   Original cost — $27,882,825.00 — Appendix I.
(b) *Movable Property in Northwestern Canada.*
   Original cost — $16,481,811.00 — Appendix II.
(c) *Movable Property in Northeastern Canada.*
   Original cost — $197,841.00 — Appendix III.
(d) *Movable Property Heretofore Reported to Crown Assets Allocation Committee but not Sold.*
   Original cost — $9,994,650.00 — Appendix IV.
(e) *United States Navy Property Lend-leased to the United Kingdom, Declared Surplus and Left in Canada.*
   Original cost — $4,349,717.00 — Appendix V.

4. It is understood that United States forces now stationed in Canada will continue to use without cost, until their withdrawal from Canada, such immovable and movable property as they may require but which may be transferred to the Canadian Government under this agreement. Ordinary depreciation, damage, wear, tear and loss in connection with

---
[1] Signed by N. A. Robertson for the Secretary of State for External Affairs.
[2] *Ibid.*, 1531, p. 1.
[3] *Ibid.*, p. 5.

any such property will not be a charge against the United States Government.

5. The Government of the United States will retain the right to recapture certain property necessary for the use of its armed forces in an amount not to exceed 15% of the original cost value of the material listed in Appendix II, page 1, and items 10, 11, 12, 13, 14, 15, 17, 18, 19, 20 and 21 of Appendix II, page 2, totalling approximately $12,000,000.00. The United States Government will designate in writing to the Canadian Government prior to May 15th, 1946, such articles as it desires to withdraw and appropriate adjustments of the financial settlement covered in paragraph 3 will be arranged.

6. Any United States Government owned property located in Canada which is not transferred to the Canadian Government under this agreement, may be withdrawn from Canada by the United States Government or sold in Canada for United States account, either by negotiation between the two Governments or by War Assets Corporation as has been the procedure heretofore.

7. Lend Lease aircraft, aircraft parts and accessories returned to United States account from the United Kingdom and located in Canada will be disposed of in the following manner:

(a) The United States Government will indicate in writing to the Canadian Government prior to 30 May, 1946, that property it desires to recapture. The Canadian Government agrees to assist to the best of its ability the United States Government in the preparation for movement and the movement of such property.

(b) Combat type aircraft, aircraft parts and accessories, left by the United States Government in Canada, will be transferred to Canadian account for salvage without further reimbursement to the United States Government.

(c) Non-combat type aircraft, aircraft parts and accessories left by the United States Government in Canada will be transferred to the account of the Canadian Government without reimbursement to the United States Government except that when flyable non-combat type aircraft and Anson aircraft containing Lend Lease components are disposed of for use as flyable aircraft, appropriate reimbursement in respect of the Lend Lease content of such complete aircraft will be made to the United States Government by the Canadian Government. The Canadian Government further agrees that flyable non-combat type aircraft other than Ansons will not be disposed of as flyable aircraft outside of Canada without consultation between appropriate agencies of the two Governments. The United States Government agrees that in the case of proposed sales of this type it will not unreasonably withhold its agreement.

(d) It is further agreed that any similar property which may become available in Canada following May 30th, 1946, shall be dealt with in a like manner, provided that the United States Government shall give thirty days' notice from the date of such property becoming available in Canada of its intention to return such property to the United States.

8. The Canadian Government will designate an agency to coordinate

the acceptance of custody of property transferred under this agreement by the United States Government to the Canadian Government. It is understood that the United States Government will not abandon property transferred to the Canadian Government under this agreement until after having provided a reasonable opportunity for the Canadian Government to arrange for custody.

9. It is understood that this agreement does not affect existing agreements between the two countries relating to the transfer of responsibility from the United States to Canada for defence projects.

10. At the request of the Canadian Government, and in order to provide equipment necessary for the training programmes of the Canadian armed forces, the United States Government will endeavour to make available surplus military type equipment, up to April 1st, 1947, in such quantities and at such prices as may be negotiated between the two Governments up to a maximum cost of $7,000,000.00 (U.S.). The Canadian Government will make a payment on account into a suspense account of the United States Government of $7,000,000.00 (U.S.) to apply against such purchases. If the United States Government is unable to provide under this agreement the amount of equipment that the Canadian Government desires to purchase and therefore the payment on account should exceed the amount finally determined to be payable, the excess remaining in the suspense account will be returned to the Canadian Government.

11. The effective date of this agreement shall be March 31st, 1946, except that with regard to sales of movables concluded and invoiced by War Assets Corporation on or before that date, the Canadian Government will make payment to the United States Government in accordance with existing agreements. During the period in which the negotiations have been in progress, and pending the coming into force of the agreement, the United States Government has undertaken and undertakes not to remove from Canada any of the property covered by the agreement.

12. If the foregoing is acceptable to the Government of the United States, this note and your reply thereto shall be regarded as placing on record the understanding arrived at between our Governments.

(b) Note from the American Ambassador to the Canadian Secretary of State for External Affairs.

I have the honor to refer to your note No. 44 of March 30, 1946, referring to discussions which have recently taken place between representatives of our two Governments on the subject of war surpluses and related matters and setting forth therein certain proposals which they have reached and which, you state, are acceptable to the Canadian Government.

At the direction of my Government, I have the honor to state that the proposals submitted in your note under reference are acceptable to the Government of the United States and it concurs in the proposals that your note and this reply shall be regarded as placing on record the understanding arrived at between the two Governments on these matters.

(2) *Exchange of Notes between the Canadian Secretary of State for External Affairs (King)* [1] *and the American Chargé d'Affaires ad interim (Clark) Regarding Amendment to the Agreement on Transfer of Defense Installations and Equipment.*[2]

(a) *Note from the Canadian Secretary of State for External Affairs to the American Chargé d'Affaires ad interim, Ottawa, July 11, 1946.*

I have the honour to refer to my note No. 44 of March 30th and your reply of the same date placing on record the understanding arrived at between our two Governments on the subject of war surpluses and related matters.

2. As the result of subsequent discussions between officials of our two Governments, I have the honour to propose that this understanding be clarified by the addition of a proviso to paragraph 7 (*b*) of my note under reference so that it will read as follows:

(*b*) (*i*) Combat type aircraft left by the United States Government in Canada will be transferred to Canadian account for salvage without further reimbursement to the United States Government, subject to the proviso that should the Canadian Government wish to purchase any combat type aircraft for their own use then these may be so purchased by the Canadian Government, provided that appropriate reimbursement will be made to the United States Government by the Canadian Government and further provided that when such combat type aircraft are transferred to the Canadian Government, an additional payment of 5% of the sale price of the aircraft will be paid to provide reimbursement for any combat type spare parts and accessories which may be used by the Canadian Government, in accordance with para. (*ii*) below.

(*ii*) All other combat type parts and accessories will be salvaged or may be transferred to the Canadian Government for their own use without reimbursement to the U. S. Government except as provided in Para. 1 above.

3. If the foregoing is acceptable to the Government of the United States, this note and your reply thereto shall be regarded as revising the understanding contained in the exchange of notes of March 30th.

(b) *Note from the American Chargé d'Affaires ad interim to the Canadian Secretary of State for External Affairs, Ottawa, July 15, 1946.*

I have the honor to acknowledge the receipt of your note, No. 94 of July 11, 1946, concerning war surpluses and related matters, and to confirm that the additional proviso to paragraph 7 (*b*) of your note No. 44 of March 30, outlined therein, is acceptable to my Government.

It is also agreeable to my Government that your note and this reply shall be regarded as revising the understanding contained in the exchange of notes of March 30, 1946.

[1] Signed by N. A. Robertson for the Secretary of State for External Affairs.
[2] *Ibid.*, p. 11.

B. St. Lawrence Seaway and Power Project

On October 3, 1945 President Truman [1] urged "speedy approval" by Congress of the agreement of March 19, 1941 [2] between the United States and Canada for the development of the Great Lakes–St. Lawrence Basin. The legislation before Congress was introduced in both houses on October 2 as a joint resolution providing for approval of major portions of the 1941 agreement. S. J. Res. 104 was referred to the Senate Committee on Foreign Relations. In the House identical resolutions were introduced, all of which were referred to the Committee on Rivers and Harbors.[3] On June 5, 1946, the Foreign Relations Committee voted to report the resolution to the Senate. The following statement on the project was made by Under Secretary of State Acheson before the Subcommittee of the Senate Foreign Relations Committee.

(1) *Statement by the Under Secretary of State (Acheson) before the Sub-Committee of the Senate Foreign Relations Committee on Legislation for the St. Lawrence Seaway and Power Project. Department of State Press Release, February 18, 1946.*[4]

[Excerpts]

The purpose of the legislation before you is to increase the wealth of the United States by developing one of the greatest natural resources in the world, the Great Lakes–St. Lawrence Basin.

. . . . .

Secondly, the legislation would provide for the construction in the International Rapids Section of hydroelectric-power works which would convert the torrential flow of the St. Lawrence into one of the greatest sources of cheap power in the world. The single power dam to be built will have a generating capacity of 2,200,000 horsepower, half of which would be made available to Canada and half reserved to the United States. The bill before you would wisely provide that the United States share of these power facilities be turned over as a public power project to the State of New York which will share with the Federal Government in the cost of the project.

It is estimated that all of this will cost the United States some $285,-000,000 on the basis of 1941 figures, of which about one third would be paid by New York so that the total cost to the Federal Government would be something under $200,000,000. Some of the work, allocated to the United States and included in this estimate, such as the Mac-Arthur Locks, has been done since 1941, and there will be some changes in these figures as the result of price variations. The Corps of Engineers will address themselves to this point.

. . . . . .

---

[1] For the message by the President to Congress on October 3, 1945, see Department of State, *Bulletin*, XIII, 528; for exchange of telegrams between the President and Governor Dewey concerning the project, see *ibid.*, p. 489.

[2] See *Documents, III, 1940–1941*, p. 187.

[3] For details of the background and progress of the legislation, see Department of State, *Bulletin*, XIII, p. 715.

[4] *Ibid.*, XIV, p. 334.

The St. Lawrence project has been described in the Department of Commerce Survey of 1941 as "among those projects which will reduce the expenditure of human energy per unit of product produced." It will make it possible not only to cope with the transportation problems which will arise as our present Great Lakes industries call upon the outside world for more and more raw materials, but it will also help to serve other industries which may be expected to develop in this area in the next 30 years. It will enable the farmer to get more out of his wheat crop and perhaps to make his crop larger to the extent that he can economically compete in the world market. Finally, as our efforts to build up an expanding world economy are successful, the Seaway will assist us in maintaining our share of the markets of the world — and will make it physically possible to move the increased volume of trade to which we must look forward.

Added to this we shall be harnessing the waters of the International Rapids Section so that we can utilize to the fullest extent this great source of cheap electrical power. The results are incalculable in terms of increased wealth and added purchasing power for our Nation. We have already seen what the TVA, the Boulder Dam, and the Grand Coulee have done for their respective areas. The part of the United States which would be served by the St. Lawrence power development has been a power deficit area and also needs the stimulation of low-cost power. The value of water power has long been recognized in other countries. The Committee members undoubtedly have seen recent reports that water power generated in Norway will be made available across the Skagerrak for consumption in Denmark. In the Soviet Union, China, and other parts of the world, water power development is constantly increasing. We must make certain that the development of our power resources keeps pace with our industrial development. While the deepwater navigation through the St. Lawrence will promote international trade, the power made available by this project will serve the same end. Every bit of power that we add to our capacity increases our ability to use the world's raw materials and to provide the finished goods which are needed in our own and other areas. The time has come when we can no longer afford the enormous waste of wealth that is involved in our failure to harness the energy of this river.

Not least among the advantages of the St. Lawrence project will be the benefits that it will bring about also for our neighbor, Canada. For years the waters of the St. Lawrence have been a source of mutual concern to our two countries. The Canadian Government has already made important improvements in the waterway at its expense which the United States is entitled to and does utilize free of charge. The cost to Canada of the Welland Canal and certain less important improvements in the system has been about $133,000,000. It is proposed that Canada will be given credit for these expenditures in arriving at the over-all division of cost between the two countries in the construction provided in the pending agreement. Furthermore, the economic development of the Great Lakes Basin in Canada is naturally of interest to us since Canada has long been our second-best customer and we in turn are

Canada's best customer. The stronger that Canada becomes the better it is for us.

The Department of State realizes that there are interests in this country that object strongly to this program of construction. Some railroads believe that their capital investment will be prejudiced through diversion of traffic to the Seaway. Certain port cities entertain the same fear of loss of traffic. Great Lakes shipping interests believe that the entrance of ocean-going vessels into their territory will injure them economically. Coal interests allege that they will lose all or part of the Canadian markets. And power interests raise the controversial issue of public power. Other witnesses will appear in favor of the St. Lawrence project who can testify with greater authority on these matters than I. However, there is good authority for saying that these fears are unjustified. The St. Lawrence Survey of the Department of Commerce completed in 1941 indicates for example that the prospective increase in freight traffic in the United States over the next 15 years will be such as to make the St. Lawrence Seaway an absolute necessity to help in handling our ocean-bound traffic. Similarly the survey indicates that many or all of the port cities deemed to be affected will gain new traffic as the result not only of normal growth in the United States but of the industrial expansion that will be stimulated through this project.

. . . . . .

C. Great Lakes Fisheries Convention

Largely as a result of recommendations submitted by the International Board of Inquiry for the Great Lakes Fisheries [1] the United States and Canada signed a treaty on April 2, 1946 for the development and conservation of the Great Lakes fisheries. The treaty and a report by the Secretary of State were transmitted by President Truman to the Senate on April 22, 1946.

(1) *Report by the Secretary of State (Byrnes) Concerning the Treaty on the Great Lakes Fisheries, April 19, 1946.*[2]

[Excerpts]

The undersigned, the Secretary of State, has the honor to lay before the President, with a view to its transmission to the Senate to receive the advice and consent of that body to ratification, if his judgment approve thereof, a convention between the United States of America and Canada relating to the fisheries of the Great Lakes and their connecting waters, signed at Washington April 2, 1946.

The convention has been negotiated with the objective of providing for the development, protection, and conservation of the fisheries of the Great Lakes through cooperation between and joint action by the governmental agencies of the United States and Canada concerned with the administration of these fisheries.

As a means for achieving this objective, the convention provides for the establishment of an International Commission for the Great Lakes Fisheries. The establishment of the Commission will provide an effec-

[1] The Joint Board of Inquiry was appointed by the United States and Canadian Government in 1940; see *Documents, II, 1939–1940,* p. 239.
[2] Department of State, *Bulletin*, XIV, p. 823.

tive solution to the need for coordinated action by the various governments having responsibilities relating to the fisheries of the Great Lakes. At the present time, 11 governments have responsibilities relating to those fisheries — the Governments of the United States of America and Canada, the governments of the States of New York, Pennsylvania, Ohio, Michigan, Indiana, Illinois, Wisconsin, and Minnesota, and the government of the Province of Ontario — and there are in existence no effective means for coordinating their efforts to discharge these responsibilities.

. . . .

The provisions of the convention may be summarized as follows:

Article I defines the waters to which the convention applies.

Article II provides for the establishment of an International Commission for the Great Lakes Fisheries, to be composed of a United States section and a Canadian section and for the appointment of an advisory committee for each lake consisting of representatives designated by each State or Province, as the case may be, having jurisdiction on the lake. The Commission, the national sections, and the advisory committees are to be constituted in accordance with and governed by the provisions of the schedule annexed to the convention.

Article III provides that the Commission shall formulate and recommend specific research programs of observations and studies of the Great Lakes fisheries to be carried out by the appropriate agencies of the two Governments in collaboration with the States of the United States concerned and the Province of Ontario as well as with other institutions and facilities.

Article IV requires that the Commission undertake to develop a comprehensive plan for the effective management of the fishery resources of the Great Lakes for the purpose of securing the maximum use of those resources consistent with their perpetuation. This article provides also that the Commission may make regulations fixing —

(a) Open and closed seasons;
(b) Open and closed waters;
(c) The size limits for each species of fish;
(d) The time, methods, and intensity of fishing;
(e) The type and specifications of the nets, gear, and apparatus and appliances which may be used;
(f) The methods of measurement;
(g) The extent and nature of stocking operations;
(h) The introduction of new species; and
(i) Catch returns and other statistical records as may be necessary to give effect to the purposes of this convention.

Pursuant to the provisions of article IV, the United States section alone, i.e., the American members of the Commission, will act in matters relating to Lake Michigan. Regulations affecting fishing in United States waters will not become effective until approved by the President of the United States; and regulations affecting fishing in Canadian waters will not become effective until approved by the Governor General in Council. Paragraph 10 of the schedule annexed to the convention provides that regulations made and approved under article IV shall not become effective until 1 year from the date when the convention comes into force.

Article V requires that the Governments of the United States of America and Canada provide for the enforcement of the regulations in their own respective waters. It is provided, however, that in United States waters the regulations for each lake may be enforced, in the first instance, by the States bordering thereon within their respective jurisdictions. With respect to Canadian waters the regulations may be enforced in the first instance by the Province of Ontario. The Commission is required to keep itself informed as to the effectiveness of enforcement and to report to the two Governments on unsatisfactory conditions of enforcement. Upon the receipt of complaints, the Federal Government concerned agrees to take appropriate action to insure proper enforcement.

Article VI provides that nothing in the convention shall be construed as preventing any of the governments concerned from making or enforcing such laws or regulations within their respective jurisdictions as will give further protection to the fisheries of the Great Lakes provided that such laws or regulations are not inconsistent with the provisions of the convention or with the regulations made and approved thereunder.

Article VII provides for the prohibition of the shipment, transport, purchase, sale, import, or export of fish taken from the Great Lakes in violation of the regulations made and approved under the convention.

Article VIII provides that licenses to fish in the waters of the Great Lakes within the jurisdiction of any State or Province may continue to be issued by such State or Province in accordance with its laws and subject to such fees as it may fix. If licensing is necessary to give effect to the regulations of the Commission, and if any State or Province fails to establish or maintain adequate licensing, the appropriate Federal Government may take necessary measures to provide such licensing, in addition to that of the State or Province, as is required.

Article IX contains provisions regarding the enactment and enforcement of such legislation as may be necessary to give effect to the provisions of the convention and the regulations made and approved thereunder, with appropriate penalties for violations.

Article X provides for the ratification of the convention, the exchange of ratifications, and the entry into force on the date of the exchange of ratifications. This article provides also for the continuance in force of the convention for a period of 10 years and thereafter until 1 year from the day on which either of the high contracting parties shall give notice to the other high contracting party of an intention of terminating the convention.

D. Interpretation of Rush-Bagot Agreement

On December 13, 1946 the United States and Canada announced a further interpretation of the Rush-Bagot agreement of 1817 which regulated the presence of naval vessels on the Great Lakes. Although many of its provisions have since become outdated, the practice of consultation between the two countries relating to naval vessels upon the Great Lakes symbolized continued friendly relations. The following exchange of notes between the Acting Secretary of State and the Canadian Ambassador constituted a later interpretation of the agreement.

(1) *Exchange of Notes between the Acting Secretary of State (Acheson) and the Canadian Ambassador (Wrong) Concerning Interpretation of the Rush-Bagot Agreement.*[1]

(a) *Note from the Canadian Ambassador in Washington to the Acting Secretary of State, November 18, 1946.*

You will recall that the Rush-Bagot Agreement of 1817 has been the subject of discussion between our Governments on several occasions in recent years and that notes were exchanged in 1939, 1940 and 1942 relating to the application and interpretation of this Agreement. It has been recognized by both our Governments that the detailed provisions of the Rush-Bagot Agreement are not applicable to present-day conditions, but that as a symbol of friendly relations extending over a period of nearly one hundred and thirty years the Agreement possesses great historic importance. It is thus the spirit of the Agreement rather than its detailed provisions which serves to guide our Governments in matters relating to naval forces on the Great Lakes.

Discussions have taken place in the Permanent Joint Board on Defence with regard to the stationing on the Great Lakes of naval vessels for the purpose of training naval reserve personnel. The naval authorities of both our Governments regard such a course as valuable from the point of view of naval training and the Board has recorded its opinion that such action would be consistent with the spirit of existing agreements. The Canadian Government concurs in this opinion.

In order that the views of our two Governments may be placed on record, I have the honour to propose that the stationing of naval vessels on the Great Lakes for training purposes by either the Canadian Government or the United States Government shall be regarded as consistent with the spirit of the Rush-Bagot Agreement provided that full information about the number, disposition, functions and armament of such vessels shall be communicated by each Government to the other in advance of the assignment of vessels to service on the Great Lakes. If your Government concurs in this view, this note and your reply thereto shall be regarded as constituting a further interpretation of the Rush-Bagot Agreement accepted by our two Governments.

(b) *Reply from the Acting Secretary of State to the Canadian Ambassador in Washington, December 5, 1946.*

I have the honor to acknowledge the receipt of your note No. 421 of November 18, 1946, in which you advised me that your Government has proposed a further interpretation of the detailed provisions of the Rush-Bagot Agreement. My Government is in complete accord with yours as to the historic importance of this Agreement as a symbol of the friendship between our two countries and agrees that it is the spirit of this agreement which guides our Governments in matters relating to naval forces on the Great Lakes.

[1] *Ibid.*, XV, p. 1152.

I am now pleased to inform you that my Government concurs with your proposal, namely, that the stationing of naval vessels on the Great Lakes for training purposes by either the Canadian Government or the United States Government shall be regarded as consistent with the spirit of the Rush-Bagot Agreement provided that full information about the number, disposition, functions and armament of such vessels shall be communicated by each Government to the other in advance of the assignment of vessels to service on the Great Lakes.

4. RELATIONS WITH ICELAND

For status of civil aviation agreements formulated at Chicago, Illinois, with respect to Iceland, see this volume, p. 660.

A. Negotiations Regarding Military Facilities in Iceland

On October 1, 1945 the United States proposed to Iceland that negotiations be concluded making the military facilities in Iceland available for the joint use of the two countries following the war period.[1] In submitting such a proposal the United States assured the Icelandic Government that rights granted to the United States would be exercised with respect and due regard to the independence of Iceland.[2] In November 1945 the Icelandic Government replied that it was not yet ready to enter into discussions relating to the American proposals, but that it was prepared to continue discussion concerning the admission of Iceland to the United Nations.

On September 19, 1946 by means of a note delivered by the American Minister at Reykjavik to the Foreign Minister of Iceland, an agreement was proposed abrogating the defense agreement of July 1, 1941.

Accordingly, it was announced on October 25, 1946 that the return of the Keflavik airport to Iceland was provided in the United States-Icelandic agreement concluded October 7, 1946, which also brought to an end the defense of Iceland agreement of July 1, 1941. American Army personnel was withdrawn during a subsequent 180 day period, and all naval personnel was withdrawn except for a group of caretakers for Navy property.

(1) *Note Delivered by the American Minister at Reykjavik (Dreyfus) to the Icelandic Minister for Foreign Affairs (Thors), September 19, 1946.*[3]

In 1941 the Government of Iceland entrusted the protection of Iceland to the United States. The threat to the security of Iceland and the American continent then existing has been eliminated by the military defeat of the Axis forces. However, obligations arising out of the war still continue.

In view of the changed conditions and following recent conversations between Your Excellency and representatives of my Government I have the honor to propose an agreement between the Government of the United States and the Government of Iceland as follows:

[1] For information on defense of Iceland by American forces, see *Documents, IV, 1941–1942*, p. 453.
[2] Department of State, *Bulletin*, XIV, p. 773.
[3] *Ibid.*, XV, p. 583.

(1) The Government of the United States and the Government of Iceland agree to the abrogation of the defense agreement of July 1, 1941, which shall terminate upon the coming into force of the present agreement.

(2) The Keflavik area and the airfields hereinafter referred to as the airport and the immovable installations constructed thereon by the United States, which will be listed in a joint United States-Icelandic inventory to be prepared concurrently with the transfer of the airport, will be transferred to the Government of Iceland. The airport shall then become the undisputed property of the Icelandic State in fulfilment of the undertakings of the Government of the United States with respect thereto.

(3) Transit and technical stop rights at the airport will be accorded to civil aircraft of all nations which are granted such rights by the Government of Iceland.

(4) The Government of the United States will withdraw as promptly as possible United States military and naval personnel now in the city of Reykjavik and during a period of 180 days, commencing upon the coming into force of the present agreement, will progressively withdraw all other United States military and naval personnel now in Iceland.

(5) The Keflavik airport will continue to be available for use by aircraft operated by or on behalf of the Government of the United States in connection with the fulfilment of United States obligations to maintain control agencies in Germany. To this end the Government of the United States shall have the right to and may, at its expense, maintain either directly or under its responsibility the services, facilities and personnel necessary to such use. The special character of these aircraft and their personnel will be respected as far as customs, immigration and other formalities are concerned. No landing fees shall be charged such aircraft.

(6) In connection with the operation of the airport the United States will train Icelandic personnel, to the extent circumstances permit, in airport techniques to enable Iceland to assume progressively the operation of the airport to the greatest possible extent.

(7) The Government of the United States and the Government of Iceland will jointly determine operational, safety and similar regulations to govern the use of the airport by all aircraft. Such regulations shall not, however, impair the ultimate authority of the Government of Iceland with respect to the control and operation of the airport.

(8) The Government of the United States and the Government of Iceland will determine a mutually satisfactory formula for the equitable distribution between them of the cost of maintenance and operation of the airport; provided, however, that neither Government shall be obligated to incur any expense with regard to maintenance and operation of the airport which it does not deem necessary to meet its own needs.

(9) No duty or other taxes shall be charged on material, equipment, supplies or goods imported for the use of the Government of the United States or its agents under the agreement or for the use of personnel in Iceland by reason of employment pursuant to the agreement. No export tax shall be charged on the removal of such articles.

(10) No personnel of the United States resident on territory of Iceland by reason of employment pursuant to the agreement shall be liable to pay income tax on income derived from sources outside of Iceland.

(11) Upon the termination of the present agreement the Government of the United States shall have the right to remove from the airport all movable installations and equipment which have been constructed or provided by the United States or its agents after the date of the agreement, unless by agreement such installations and equipment are bought by the Government of Iceland.

(12) The agreement shall continue in effect until the obligations of the Government of the United States to maintain control agencies in Germany shall have been fulfilled; provided, however, that at any time after the lapse of five years from the coming into force of the present agreement either government may propose a review of the agreement. In such case, the two goverments shall consult as soon as possible. If no agreement is reached as a result of such consultation within a period of six months from the date of original notification either government may at any time thereafter give notice of intention to denounce the agreement, which shall then terminate twelve months from the date of such notice.

Should the Government of Iceland accept the proposals set forth above, the affirmative reply of Your Excellency shall constitute, together with this note, the agreement of the two Governments in these matters.

CHAPTER XV

EASTERN ASIA AND THE PACIFIC AREA

1. GENERAL POLICY

(1) *Address by Director of the Office of Far Eastern Affairs, Department of State (Vincent) before the Foreign Policy Association Forum, October 20, 1945.*[1]

[Excerpts]

* * * * * * *

What are the objectives of our foreign policies that I have in mind? They can be stated quite simply. They are: (1) to provide for the security of the United States and the maintenance of international peace and (2) to create in the relations among states conditions conducive to mutually beneficial commercial and cultural exchanges which will promote international welfare and understanding.

In a joint statement issued from Chungking on June 24, 1944, Generalissimo Chiang Kai-shek and Vice President Wallace enunciated an objective directly related to those I have stated. They said: "The objective of victory in the Pacific is the establishment of a democratic peace based on political and social stability deriving from government devoted to the welfare of peoples." They then, as I shall do, went on to name some policies which they considered essential to the achievement of that objective. They said: "Enduring peace in the Pacific will depend upon (1) effective, permanent demilitarization of Japan; (2) understanding, friendship, and collaboration between and among the four principal powers in the Pacific area — China, the Soviet Union, the United States and the British Commonwealth of Nations — and among all United Nations willing to share in the responsibilities of post-war international order; and (3) recognition of the fundamental right of presently dependent Asiatic peoples to self-government, and the early adoption of measures in the political, economic, and social fields to prepare those dependent peoples for self-government within a specified practical time limit." I believe there will be found in America little or no disposition to question those policies.

Our objectives in regard to the Far East can be generalized. Our policies cannot be. They must be adapted to meet divergent geographical, political, and social situations. In the Far East we have (1) a defeated and so far unregenerate Japan; (2) Korea, which is to start on the road to independence after two generations of subjection to Japan; (3) China,

[1] Department of State, *Bulletin*, XIII, p. 644.

our Ally and long-time friend, whose principal problems, now that the menace of Japan has been removed, are political unity and economic reconstruction; (4) Siam, an independent nation which has for the past five years been under the domination of Japan; and (5) the colonial area of southeast Asia under the sovereignty of our Allies.

With regard to Japan, a White House release on September 22 gave in some 15 pages a clear summary of our policy toward Japan. It was entitled "U. S. Initial Post-Surrender Policy for Japan".[1] I commend it to you. . . .

. . . . . .

This policy paper . . . was prepared in SWNCC [2] and approved by the President. A reading of the subheadings in that document will give you an idea of some of the special subjects dealt with in our papers. Those headings include such subjects as war criminals; economic demilitarization; promotion of democratic forces; fiscal, monetary, and banking policies; equality of opportunity for foreign enterprise in Japan; individual liberties and democratic processes. One of them, entitled "Relationship to Japanese Government", calls for special mention.[3]

. . . . . .

This [document], I think, makes quite clear our interpretation of the Potsdam Declaration and also quite clear for General MacArthur what his relationship is to the Japanese Government.

In Korea our policy problems are both obvious and difficult. Korea is to be separated from Japan and become an independent member of the family of nations. But Korea, after years of subjection to Japan, is not immediately prepared to exercise self-government. We therefore advocate a period of trusteeship during which Koreans will be prepared to take over the independent administration of their country. How long that will require neither you nor I can say; we will agree, however, that the briefer the period, the better.

. . . . . .

Our policy with regard to Korea is then to bring into being as quickly as possible an independent, democratic, and prosperous nation. As soon as it is feasible to do so, I should like to see American businessmen, missionaries, and cultural organizations established in Korea and contributing their share toward implementing American policies there.

In southeast Asia a situation has developed to the liking of none of us, least of all to the British, the French, the Dutch, and, I gather, to the Annamese and Indonesians. With regard to the situation in French Indochina, this Government does not question French sovereignty in that area. Our attitude toward the situation in the Dutch East Indies is similar to that in regard to French Indochina. In both these areas,

---

[1] For text, see this volume, p. 267.

[2] State-War-Navy Coordinating Committee; for detailed information on its activities, see *ibid.*, p. 63.

[3] Transmitted to General MacArthur on September 9, 1945; for text, see *ibid.*, p. 268.

however, we earnestly hope that an early agreement can be reached between representatives of the governments concerned and the Annamese and Indonesians. It is not our intention to assist or participate in forceful measures for the imposition of control by the territorial sovereigns, but we would be prepared to lend our assistance, if requested to do so, in efforts to reach peaceful agreements in these disturbed areas.

In a statement issued by Secretary Hull on March 21, 1944, entitled "Bases of the Foreign Policy of the United States", there occurs the following paragraph in regard to "dependent peoples": "There rests upon the independent nations a responsibility in relation to dependent peoples who aspire to liberty. It should be the duty of nations having political ties with such peoples . . . to help the aspiring peoples to develop materially and educationally, to prepare themselves for the duties and responsibilities of self-government, and to attain liberty." This continues to be American policy.

With regard to Siam, we have never considered ourselves at war with that nation, although the Government in control in 1942 declared war on the United States. We consider Siam an independent and sovereign nation. It is our policy to foster friendly relations with Siam and encourage the development of healthy democratic institutions and a sound economy. We advocate the "Open Door" there, as in other areas, and equality of treatment by Siam of all nations and their nationals. The British Government, which declared war on Siam in response to Siam's declaration of war on Great Britain, is now negotiating at Kandy with the Siamese an agreement to terminate the state of hostilities. We have followed these negotiations and have reason to hope that they may be successfully concluded in the near future.

Our policy toward our Ally China is clear and consistent. Our policy has been, is, and will be to encourage and assist, when we can appropriately do so, the development of a unified, strong, and cooperative nation with a government based on democratic principles and popular sovereignty. Our Ambassador, General Hurley, has worked unflaggingly for the realization of this policy. We fought side by side with China in a war against Japan which China entered four and a half years before we did. We shall continue to collaborate with China in the solution of its and our problems.

Generalissimo Chiang and Mao Tse-tung have recently announced a 12-point agreement in regard to the Kuomintang-Communist problem. No one who knows anything about conditions in China would argue that the agreement is definitive, but it allays the fears which were so lively a month ago that there would be wide-spread civil war in China, and it furnishes the framework for an adjustment of the differences between the Government, the Communists, and other non-government political groups in China.

. . . .

It is our policy to encourage and facilitate the reestablishment of American business in China. Probably not with all the speed desired, but with all the speed we can generate, we are endeavoring to get businessmen back into China for their sake and for China's sake. We want them back in Shanghai, Hong Kong, Tientsin, and other ports as quickly as possible. We are reopening consulates in these and other cities.

What I have said regarding American businessmen applies with equal force to missionaries and representatives of cultural and philanthropic organizations. We want them back in China as soon as transportation facilities and conditions in China will permit.

Some question may have arisen in your mind with regard to the dispatch of American Marines to north China. They have been sent there pursuant to military directives to serve a specific purpose, that is, to assist Chiang Kai-shek in demobilizing and repatriating Japanese troops in the area. Their stay is temporary. They will be withdrawn when they are no longer required for the purpose for which they were sent. Generalissimo Chiang has announced that the Marines would leave north China as soon as they can be relieved by Chinese Government forces. The process of relief is now in progress.

China is in a position to form a buffer or a bridge in our relations with the Soviet Union in the Far East. We will all agree, I believe, that the bridge concept is preeminently preferable, and that it should be our policy to make it a fact. I would go further and say that only through the cooperation of China, the U.S.S.R., and ourselves can the objectives of our policy in the Far East be achieved.

In August, the Chinese and Soviet Governments entered into certain agreements which we hope will stabilize the relations between those two countries. It will be our policy to cooperate with China and the Soviet Union for stability in the Far East. We will cooperate with neither of them in any policy directed against the other.

Secretary Byrnes has indicated that the United States desires cooperation with the Soviet Union on all matters of mutual concern. This attitude rests upon a recognition of the importance of amicable Soviet-American relations. We know that Russia has important interests in the Far East. We expect recognition by Russia that we also have important interests in that area. We shall, therefore, pursue policies consistent with our over-all objectives, best calculated to bring about Russian recognition of our position in the Far East and to accord fair recognition to the Russian position in that area — and further, to bring about a Russian understanding that our objectives in the Far East are in harmony with the objectives of any peacefully inclined nation.

In conclusion, let me recapitulate and pose some questions. Our objectives are (1) to provide for the security of the United States and the maintenance of international peace; (2) to create in the relations among states conditions conducive to mutually beneficial commercial and cultural exchanges which will promote international welfare and understanding; and (3) the related objective, stated by Generalissimo Chiang and Mr. Wallace, to establish a democratic peace based on political and social stability deriving from government devoted to the welfare of peoples.

But — and this is my last word, or last paragraph, I should say — we must not fall into the error of considering the implementation of these policies and the realization of these objectives as our private and exclusive job. I have described international cooperation as a policy. It is a policy — but it is, to my mind, an overriding policy. We are to be a participant in the United Nations Organization. The operation of that Organization will not, as some seem to think, furnish a substitute for national foreign policies. It should be — we should make it — a convenient, and efficient, and an effective clearing-house for national foreign policies and for their reconciliation in the interests of international security, peace, and welfare. Therefore, and in conclusion, I would strongly advocate that the policies we pursue be able to stand careful international examination. I believe those I have summarized for the Far East will do so.

2. RELATIONS WITH CHINA

For statement of loans and authorizations of Export-Import Bank, see this volume, p. 638.

For information on lend-lease aid, see this volume, p. 126.

For agreement between the United States and China for sale of certain surplus property, see this volume, p. 163.

For status of bilateral air transport agreements, see this volume, p. 671.

A. General Policy[1]

[See *Documents, VII, 1944–1945*, p. 822.]

Tension between the Chungking Government and the Chinese Communists continued throughout August 1945, as conferences were held by Generalissimo Chiang Kai-shek, Lieut. Gen. Albert C. Wedemeyer and American Ambassador Patrick J. Hurley regarding reoccupation policies in Japanese-controlled China upon surrender of Japan.

American efforts to effect an agreement between the Kuomintang and Communist groups were initiated once more as Ambassador Hurley flew to Yenan to accompany Mao Tse-tung, the Communist leader, as he returned for conferences with the Generalissimo concerning possible reconciliation. Negotiations were climaxed by a message [2] from the Generalissimo on September 3, 1945 in which he stated that "the Government is prepared to consult all leaders before the convocation of the National Assembly . . . and seek a rational settlement of other related problems." Although these words signified some measure of agreement, sporadic clashes occurred between the two forces, and on September 13 Gen. Wedemeyer stated that plans were under consideration by which American troops might be used to occupy major Chinese cities until the internal situation evidenced more stability.[3] It was understood at this time that Ambassador Hurley, although eager to see agreement reached, took the position that the settlement of the Communist issue was a Chinese matter.[4]

[1] For additional surveys of the Chinese internal conflict and American policy in that area during the period under review, see "China, Internal Disunion and the War." *The World Today*, II, p. 78; and Rosinger, L. K. "China in Ferment." *Foreign Policy Reports*, XXII, No. 20 (January 1, 1947); for information on Soviet-American relations concerning China, see this volume, p. 825.

[2] For excerpts from the Generalissimo's message, see *New York Times*, September 4, 1945, p. 3.

[3] *Ibid.*, September 14, 1945, p. 1.

[4] *Ibid.*, October 1, 1945, p. 1.

On November 27, 1945, it was announced that President Truman had accepted the resignation of Ambassador Hurley,[1] and that Gen. George C. Marshall had been named the President's special envoy to China. In a statement [2] before the Senate Committee on Foreign Relations on December 5, 1945, Secretary of State Byrnes reiterated the long range goal of the United States to promote the development of a united and democratic China. He declared that "the broad outlines of our policy in China have never been hidden or difficult to recognize."

On December 16 President Truman issued a clarifying statement on United States policy regarding China.[3]

Gen. Marshall's arrival in Nanking on December 21 revived hopes of a possible end to the country's civil war. Shortly after his arrival he communicated with both Government officials and Chinese Communist leaders. On January 5, 1946, both factions agreed to meet with Gen. Marshall for formal conferences concerning cessation of hostilities. A formal truce order [4] on January 10 heralded the announcement of a series of political and democratic reforms. The truce also provided for the establishment of Executive Headquarters, consisting of three commissioners, one a United States representative, which was to carry out agreements for ending hostilities. It was expressly stated that American participation would be limited to the purpose of assisting the Chinese members in implementing the orders.

Policies for a new coalition Government of China were approved on January 31 at a full session of the Political Consultation Conference; these policies covered the adoption of principles for reorganization and nationalization of armies, broad plans for a Constitution and plans for the composition of a national Assembly.

On February 25 a formal agreement on military reorganization and the integration of Communist forces into the National Army was signed by Kuomintang and Communist representatives and by Gen. Marshall as special United States envoy.[5] After returning to Washington in March for consultation with President Truman, Gen. Marshall issued a statement on the Chinese situation in which he appealed for American aid for that country and a policy of helping the Chinese to achieve national unity.[6]

On April 14 hostilities in Manchuria resumed and on the same date the acting three-man truce commission and commissioners of the Executive Headquarters, accompanied by Gen. Gillem and Mr. Walter S. Robertson of the United States, left for Mukden to investigate the Manchurian situation.[7]

Gen. Marshall arrived in Chungking on April 18 to resume the task of mediation between the two groups, and under his special urging, peace talks were continued on May 25. On June 6 Generalissimo Chiang Kai-shek issued an order to national troops to halt advances and attacks for a 16-day armistice in order to allow time for the working out of detailed arrangements for a lasting truce; [8] however, the so-called truce resulted only in more claims of military successes by both sides.

On July 9 Dr. J. Leighton Stuart was appointed as Ambassador to China, and shortly thereafter, he and Gen. Marshall issued a joint statement expressing pessimism as to the possibility of a general peace for China. Although efforts for conciliation were continued throughout the period under review, no lasting agreement was reached. On October 8 Gen. Marshall and Ambassador Stuart once

[1] For text of Ambassador Hurley's statement of resignation, see *ibid.*, November 28, 1945, p. 3.

[2] For complete text of the statement by Secretary Byrnes, see Department of State, *Bulletin*, XIII, p. 930.

[3] See this volume, p. 799.

[4] For text of truce order, see *New York Times*, January 11, 1946, p. 10.

[5] For details of the agreement, see *ibid.*, February 26, 1946, p. 1.

[6] Department of State, *Bulletin*, XIV, p. 484.

[7] *New York Times*, April 15, 1946, p. 1; for Chinese-Russian negotiations concerning Manchuria, see this volume, p. 825.

[8] *New York Times*, June 7, 1946, p. 8.

again announced [1] that the American proposal for a ten-day halt in hostilities had been rejected. This seemingly final break in Kuomintang-Communist relations was thought to necessitate a redefinition of American policy, which had previously been based on the hope of a coalition government. On December 18, 1946 President Truman issued a policy statement regarding China in which he indicated a continuation of American efforts to achieve unity in that country.[2]

On November 2, 1946 a Treaty of Friendship, Commerce and Navigation [3] was signed at Nanking by the United States and China.

(1) Statement by the President (Truman) Regarding United States Policy toward China, December 16, 1945.[4]

[Excerpts]

. . . .

It is the firm belief of this Government that a strong, united, and democratic China is of the utmost importance to the success of this United Nations Organization and for world peace. A China disorganized and divided either by foreign aggression, such as that undertaken by the Japanese, or by violent internal strife is an undermining influence to world stability and peace, now and in the future. The United States Government has long subscribed to the principle that the management of internal affairs is the responsibility of the peoples of the sovereign nations. Events of this century, however, would indicate that a breach of peace anywhere in the world threatens the peace of the entire world. It is thus in the most vital interest of the United States and all the United Nations that the people of China overlook no opportunity to adjust their internal differences promptly by methods of peaceful negotiation.

The Government of the United States believes it essential:

(1) That a cessation of hostilities be arranged between the armies of the National Government and the Chinese Communists and other dissident Chinese armed forces for the purpose of completing the return of all China to effective Chinese control, including the immediate evacuation of the Japanese forces.

(2) That a national conference of representatives of major political elements be arranged to develop an early solution to the present internal strife — a solution which will bring about the unification of China.

The United States and the other United Nations have recognized the present National Government of the Republic of China as the only legal government in China. It is the proper instrument to achieve the objective of a unified China.

The United States and the United Kingdom by the Cairo Declaration in 1943 and the Union of Soviet Socialist Republics by adhering to the Potsdam Declaration of last July and by the Sino-Soviet treaty [5] and agreements of August 1945 are all committed to the liberation of China,

[1] Department of State, *Bulletin*, XV, p. 723.
[2] See this volume, p. 801.
[3] For text of the treaty, see Department of State Press Release 733, November 4, 1946; for a brief summary of terms included in the treaty, see Department of State, *Bulletin*, XV, p. 866.
[4] *Ibid.*, XIII, p. 945.
[5] For text of the Sino-Soviet treaty, see this volume, p. 826.

including the return of Manchuria to Chinese control. These agreements were made with the National Government of the Republic of China.

. . . . . .

The United States recognizes and will continue to recognize the National Government of China and cooperate with it in international affairs and specifically in eliminating Japanese influence from China. The United States is convinced that a prompt arrangement for a cessation of hostilities is essential to the effective achievement of this end. United States support will not extend to United States military intervention to influence the course of any Chinese internal strife.

. . . . .

The United States is cognizant that the present National Government of China is a "one-party government" and believes that peace, unity, and democratic reform in China will be furthered if the basis of this Government is broadened to include other political elements in the country. Hence, the United States strongly advocates that the national conference of representatives of major political elements in the country agree upon arrangements which would give those elements a fair and effective representation in the Chinese National Government. It is recognized that this would require modification of the one-party "political tutelage" established as an interim arrangement in the progress of the nation toward democracy by the father of the Chinese Republic, Dr. Sun Yat-sen.

The existence of autonomous armies such as that of the Communist army is inconsistent with, and actually makes impossible, political unity in China. With the institution of a broadly representative government, autonomous armies should be eliminated as such and all armed forces in China integrated effectively into the Chinese National Army.

In line with its often expressed views regarding self-determination, the United States Government considers that the detailed steps necessary to the achievement of political unity in China must be worked out by the Chinese themselves and that intervention by any foreign government in these matters would be inappropriate. The United States Government feels, however, that China has a clear responsibility to the other United Nations to eliminate armed conflict within its territory as constituting a threat to world stability and peace — a responsibility which is shared by the National Government and all Chinese political and military groups.

As China moves toward peace and unity along the lines described above, the United States would be prepared to assist the National Government in every reasonable way to rehabilitate the country, improve the agrarian and industrial economy, and establish a military organization capable of discharging China's national and international responsibilities for the maintenance of peace and order. In furtherance of such assistance, it would be prepared to give favorable consideration to Chinese requests for credits and loans under reasonable conditions for projects which would contribute toward the development of a healthy economy throughout China and healthy trade relations between China and the United States.

(2) *Statement by the President (Truman) Regarding United States Policy toward China, December 18, 1946.*[1]

[Excerpts]

Last December I made a statement of this Government's views regarding China. We believed then, and do now, that a united and democratic China is of the utmost importance to world peace, that a broadening of the base of the National Government to make it representative of the Chinese people will further China's progress toward this goal, and that China has a clear responsibility to the other United Nations to eliminate armed conflict within its territory as constituting a threat to world stability and peace. It was made clear at Moscow last year that these views are shared by our Allies, Great Britain and the Soviet Union.[2]

. . . . . .

The policies of this Government were also made clear in my statement of last December. We recognized the National Government of the Republic of China as the legal government. We undertook to assist the Chinese Government in reoccupation of liberated areas and in disarming and repatriating the Japanese invaders. And finally, as China moved toward peace and unity along the lines mentioned, we were prepared to assist the Chinese economically and in other ways.

. . . . . .

While comprehensive large-scale aid has been delayed, this Government has completed its wartime lend-lease commitments to China. ... According to the latest figures reported, lend-lease assistance to China up to V-J Day totaled approximately $870,000,000. From V-J Day to the end of February, shortly after General Marshall's arrival, the total was approximately $600,000,000 — mostly in transportation costs. Thereafter, the program was reduced to the fulfilment of outstanding commitments, much of which was later suspended.

A considerable quantity of civilian goods has also been made available by our agreement with China for the disposal of surplus property which enabled us to liquidate a sizable indebtedness and to dispose of large quantities of surplus material. During the war the Chinese Government furnished Chinese currency to the United States Army for use in building its installations, feeding the troops, and other expenses. By the end of the war this indebtedness amounted to something like 150,000,000,000 Chinese dollars. Progressive currency inflation in China rendered it impossible to determine the exact value of the sum in United States currency.

. . . . . .

The Chinese Government canceled all but 30,000,000 United States dollars of our indebtedness for the Chinese currency, and promised to

[1] Department of State, *Bulletin*, XV, p. 1179.
[2] For section of Soviet-Anglo-American Communiqué concerning China, see this volume, p. 829.

make available the equivalent of 35,000,000 United States dollars for use in paying United States governmental expenses in China and acquiring and improving buildings and properties for our diplomatic and consular establishments. An additional sum of 20,000,000 United States dollars is also designated for the fulfilment of a cultural and educational program.

. . . . .

There has been encouraging progress in other fields, particularly the elimination of Japanese from China. The Chinese Government was responsible under an Allied agreement for the disarmament of all Japanese military personnel and for the repatriation of all Japanese civilians and military personnel from China, Formosa, and French Indo-China north of the sixteenth degree of latitude. Our Government agreed to assist the Chinese in this task. The scope of the job was tremendous. There were about 3,000,000 Japanese, nearly one half of them Army or Navy personnel, to be evacuated. . . .

. . . . .

At the end of last year, approximately 200,000 Japanese had been repatriated. They were leaving Chinese ports at a rate of about 2,500 a day. By March of this year, rapidly increased efforts on the part of the American forces and the Chinese authorities involved had increased this rate to more than 20,000 a day. By November, 2,986,438 Japanese had been evacuated and the program was considered completed. Except for indeterminate numbers of certain parts of Manchuria, only war criminals and technicians retained on an emergency basis by the Chinese Government remain. That this tremendous undertaking has been accomplished despite conflict, disrupted communications, and other difficulties will remain an outstanding example of successful American-Chinese cooperation toward a common goal.

. . . . .

Thus during the past year we have successfully assisted in the repatriation of the Japanese and have subsequently been able to bring most of our own troops home. We have afforded appropriate assistance in the reoccupation of the country from the Japanese. We have undertaken some emergency measures of economic assistance to prevent the collapse of China's economy and have liquidated our own wartime financial account with China.

. . . . .

The views expressed a year ago by this Government are valid today. The plan for political unification agreed to last February is sound. The plan for military unification of last February has been made difficult of implementation by the progress of the fighting since last April, but the general principles involved are fundamentally sound.

. . . . .

We believe that our hopes for China are identical with what the Chinese people themselves most earnestly desire. We shall therefore continue our positive and realistic policy toward China, which is based on full respect for her national sovereignty and on our traditional friendship for the Chinese people, and is designed to promote international peace.

B. Military and Financial Aid

In a letter dated June 12, 1946 to the Speaker of the House of Representatives, Secretary of State Byrnes transmitted the draft of a proposed bill to provide military advice and assistance to China in modernizing its armed forces.[1] The legislation had as its main objective the implementation of the reorganization and unification of armed forces in that country. Action on the bill was delayed throughout the period under review. However, on July 16 legislation was approved by Congress [2] which authorized the President at his discretion to provide assistance to China in such matters as naval services, training plans, technical advice, and disposal of naval vessels.

The Military Advisory Group in China, consisting of 750 American officers and men, initiated operations to assist the Chinese Government in reorganization of its Ministry of National Defense and establishment of interim schools to train military instructors. Although permanent status of the group depended on the future passage of Congressional enabling legislation, the Army and Navy branches, operating under the Wartime Powers Act, were able to carry out some organizational work.[3]

On September 29, 1945, the President announced that he was sending his Personal Representative, Edwin A. Locke Jr., to China for discussion with several Chinese officials concerning methods of utilizing the industrial experience of the United States for the benefit of Chinese reconstruction.[4] The duties of Mr. Locke covered (1) attention to the Chinese acquisition of industries in Manchuria and other liberated provinces, and (2) arrangements for terminating the work of the American Production Mission which was established in 1944 to aid the war effort. This mission had remained in close cooperation with the Chinese Government in obtaining increased production of munitions and raw materials and, since the end of the war, it had extended aid in the fields of reconversion and industrial activity.

On August 27, 1946 Assistant Secretary of War Howard C. Peterson and Thomas B. McCabe, Special Assistant to the Secretary of State and Foreign Liquidation Commissioner, issued a joint statement denying the charges that negotiations were in progress regarding sale to China of surplus military items.[5] The statement, however, revealed that discussions were in progress concerning sale of surplus property of non-military nature having an estimated value of $500,000,000, then on western Pacific islands.

In his statement of December 18, 1946, clarifying United States policy in China, President Truman described American assistance in the reoccupation of Japanese-held areas and American responsibility concerning protection of supply lines.[6]

[1] H. R. 6795, 79th Cong., 2d sess.; for text of the Secretary of State's letter, see this volume, p. 804.
[2] Public Law 512, 79th Cong., 2d sess.; see this volume, p. 804.
[3] *New York Times*, September 30, 1946, p. 7.
[4] Department of State, *Bulletin*, XIII, p. 497.
[5] *Ibid.*, XV, p. 548.
[6] See this volume, p. 801; for statement of Soviet reaction to United States military and financial aid to China, see Markov, M. "American Troops in China." *Pravda*, translated in the *Soviet Press Translations* of the Far Eastern Institute, Univ. of Washington, I, No. 2 (November 15, 1946), p. 7.

(1) *Letter from the Secretary of State (Byrnes) to the Speaker of the House of Representatives (Rayburn) Recommending Enactment of H. R. 6795 Providing Military Assistance to China, June 12, 1946.*[1]

[Excerpt]

. . . . . .

I firmly believe that the national interest, including this country's interest in the reestablishment and preservation of peace and security in Asia, requires that the United States give aid to the Republic of China by assisting that country to organize and maintain modern military forces of moderate size which will permit China to make a substantial contribution to peace in that part of the world.

The Republic of China has already requested that this Government send a mission to China to give advice and assistance in military matters. Under his wartime powers, the President has directed the War and Navy Departments to send a small advisory group to China. Missions to provide military advice and assistance have previously been sent by this country to many other countries, including Brazil, Colombia, Costa Rica, etc., under legislation enacted by the Congress in 1926 and amended in 1935 and 1942. This legislation, however, does not make provision for a mission to China and unless the draft bill or similar legislation is passed, authority for the mission to China would end with the termination of the President's wartime powers.

While the Republic of China desires to modernize its armed forces, at the present time and under existing conditions it does not possess the facilities for such development nor the technical experts who can train and reorganize the armed forces. I believe that this Government should continue to assist China, which has suffered such severe losses during the war. Our present programs of military assistance to China will be terminated under provisions of existing law after June 30, 1946, unless the proposed legislation or similar legislation is enacted. In the national interest, it is extremely important that assistance to China continue without interruption.

. . . . . .

(2) *An Act to Provide Assistance to the Republic of China in Augmenting and Maintaining a Naval Establishment, Approved July 16, 1946.*[2]

Be it enacted by the Senate and House of Representatives of the United States of America in Congress assembled, That notwithstanding the provisions of any other law, the President is authorized, whenever in his discretion the public interests render such a course advisable, or will assist in relieving United States forces of duty in China or putting the Government of the Republic of China in better position to protect or improve the safety of navigation in its waters, to provide to the Republic of China such naval services, training, plans, and technical advice as he may deem proper; and to dispose of naval vessels and craft, not to exceed

---

[1] Department of State, *Bulletin*, XV, p. 125.
[2] Public Law 512, 79th Cong., 2d sess.

two hundred and seventy-one vessels and craft under authority of this Act, which are in excess of the naval needs of the United States, floating drydocks of capacity sufficient to accommodate any vessel or craft disposed of under authority of this Act, and material necessary for the operation and maintenance of the vessels and craft disposed of under authority of this Act and for the training of the crews of such vessels and craft, to the Republic of China by sale, exchange, lease, gift, or transfer for cash, credit, or other property, with or without warranty, or upon such other terms and conditions as he may deem proper: *Provided,* That prior to the disposition under the authority of this Act of any battleship, aircraft carrier of any type, cruiser, destroyer (but not destroyer escort), or submarine the President shall first obtain the authority of the Congress in each instance: *Provided further,* That no information, plans, advice, material, documents, blueprints, or other papers, bearing a secret or top-secret classification shall be disposed of or transferred under authority of this Act.

SEC. 2. The President is authorized, upon application from the Republic of China, and whenever in his discretion the public interests render such a course advisable, to detail not to exceed one hundred officers and two hundred enlisted men of the United States Navy and Marine Corps to assist the Republic of China in naval matters: *Provided,* That United States naval or Marine Corps personnel shall not accompany Chinese troops, aircraft, or ships on other than training maneuvers or cruises: *Provided further,* That the Secretary of Navy is authorized to pay to such persons such additional compensation as may be necessary to make appropriate adjustment for increased cost of living occasioned by reason of detail to such duty: *And provided further,* That while so detailed such officers and enlisted men shall receive the pay and allowances thereunto entitled in the United States Navy or Marine Corps and shall be allowed the same credit for longevity, retirement, and for all other purposes that they would receive if they were serving with the forces of the United States.

SEC. 3. The provisions of this Act shall terminate five years after the date of its enactment.

3. RELATIONS WITH THE PHILIPPINES

[See *Documents, VI, 1943–1944,* p. 617–26; *ibid., VII, 1944–1945,* p. 828–37.]
For information concerning surplus property, see this volume, p. 809.
For status of air transport agreements, see this volume, p. 660, 672.

Following landing of American troops on Leyte on October 20, 1944, and subsequent restoration of the Commonwealth Government to its full powers and responsibilities under the 1935 Constitution, preparations continued for the complete independence of the Philippines. The Office of United States High Commissioner to the Philippines was reactivated,[1] and on September 14, 1945, the Senate confirmed the nomination of Paul V. McNutt as United States High Commissioner. A series of memoranda to several executive departments by President Truman, released on October 26, laid the basis for United States assistance to the islands,[2] and by joint resolution the Congress made provision

---
[1] Executive Order 9616, *Federal Register,* X, p. 11837.
[2] Department of State, *Bulletin,* XIII, p. 690.

for Philippine national elections.[1] These elections, held on April 23, 1946, resulted in the choice of General Manuel A. Roxas as president of the first Philippine government, and Señor Roxas came to the United States shortly afterward to confer with President Truman and other officials.

On April 30, 1946, President Truman signed two bills concerned with Philippine rehabilitation and recovery. The first of these created the Philippine War Damage Commission, and provided for the granting to Philippine claimants of $400,000,000 in war damages, disposition to the Philippine government of $100,000,000 in surplus property, and spending of $120,000,000 in rehabilitation and training projects.[2] The second bill, the Philippine Trade Act, authorized conclusion of an executive agreement providing for free trade between the United States and the Philippines until 1954, after which products would be taxed at a progressively increasing rate until 1974, when full rates would apply.[3] One section of the act also provided for special rights for American citizens in development of Philippines natural resources (a provision which would make necessary the amendment of the Philippine Constitution), while the implementation of the Rehabilitation Act was made dependent upon the signing of the executive agreement provided for in the Trade Act. In signing both bills, President Truman noted that they were "exceptional" from the standpoint of conventional American policy, but that the situation was "unprecedented".[4]

In May, the Congress passed Public Law 380, 79th Congress, which authorized the President to negotiate for retention of military bases in the Philippines, and a military assistance act became law in June.[5] American immigration and nationality laws were also amended to make possible the entry and naturalization of races indigenous to the Philippines.[6]

On July 4, 1946, President Truman proclaimed the independence of the islands. On the same day the two governments signed at Manila three agreements, two dealing with general relations between the two countries and a third incorporating the provisions of the Philippine Trade Act. The first agreement, provisional in nature, was designed to serve until ratification of the second agreement, a treaty which formally recognized the independence of the Philippines and provided for future negotiation of agreements on such topics as mutual defense, settlement of claims, extradition, etc.[7] Following consent of the Senate on July 31, the treaty was ratified by President Truman on August 16, and ratifications were exchanged in Manila on October 22, 1946. The trade agreement, amended by an exchange of notes on October 22, was proclaimed by the President on December 17, 1946, and entered into force on January 2, 1947.[8]

Other United States action regarding the Philippines, during the period under review, included passage of several acts concerning transfer of funds and securities to the Philippine treasury, provision for the retention of United States property in the Philippines and for the administration of the Trading with the Enemy Act subsequent to Philippine independence, and authorization of the Export-Import Bank to include the Philippines in its operations.[9] The United States also concluded a series of agreements with other nations concerning the special trading status of the Philippines, and the two governments created an American-Philippine Financial Commission to consider the financial and budgetary problems of the Philippines.[10] A treaty of conciliation was signed on November 16, 1946.

[1] Public Law 258, 79th Cong., 2d sess.
[2] Public Law 370, 79th Cong., 2d sess.; for excerpts, see this volume, p. 807.
[3] Public Law 371, 79th Cong., 2d sess.; for excerpts, see this volume, p. 810.
[4] Department of State, *Bulletin*, XIV, p. 822.
[5] Department of State, *Treaties and Other International Acts Series* 1568; for text, see this volume, p. 817.
[6] Public Law 483, 79th Cong., 2d sess.
[7] For text of the treaty, see this volume, p. 820.
[8] Department of State, *Treaties and Other International Acts Series* 1588.
[9] Public Laws 215, 282, 485, and 652, 79th Cong., 2d sess.
[10] Department of State, *Treaties and Other International Acts Series* 1572 and 1612.

(1) *An Act for the Rehabilitation of the Philippines, Approved April 30, 1946.*[1]

[Excerpts]

Be it enacted by the Senate and House of Representatives of the United States of America in Congress assembled, That this Act may be cited as the "Philippine Rehabilitation Act of 1946".

TITLE I — COMPENSATION FOR WAR DAMAGE

SEC. 101. (a) There is hereby established a Philippine War Damage Commission (in this title referred to as the "Commission"). The Commission shall consist of three members, to be appointed by the President of the United States, by and with the advice and consent of the Senate. One of the members of the Commission shall be a Filipino. The members of the Commission shall receive compensation at the rate of $12,000 a year. The terms of office of the members of the Commission shall expire at the time fixed in subsection (d) for winding up the affairs of the Commission. A vacancy in the membership of the Commission shall not impair the authority of the remaining two members of the Commission to exercise all of its functions. Vacancies occurring in the membership of the Commission shall be filled in the same manner as in the case of the original selection. Members of the Commission shall receive their necessary traveling and other expenses incurred in connection with their duties as such members, or a per diem allowance in lieu thereof, to be fixed by the Commission without regard to the limitation prescribed in any existing law.

. . . .

(d) The Commission shall, so far as practicable, give consideration to, but need not await, or be bound by, the recommendations of the Filipino Rehabilitation Commission (created by the Act approved June 29, 1944) with respect to Philippine war damage. The Commission shall wind up its affairs not later than two years after the expiration of the time for filing claims under this title if possible, but, in no event later than five years from the enactment of this Act.

SEC. 102. (a) The Commission is hereby authorized to make compensation to the extent hereinafter provided on account of physical loss or destruction of or damage to property in the Philippines occurring after December 7, 1941 (Philippine time), and before October 1, 1945, as a result of one or more of the following perils: (1) Enemy attack; (2) action taken by or at the request of the military, naval, or air forces of the United States to prevent such property from coming into the possession of the enemy; (3) action taken by enemy representatives, civil or military, or by the representatives of any government cooperating with the enemy; (4) action by the armed forces of the United States or other forces cooperating with the armed forces of the United States in opposing, resisting or expelling the enemy from the Philippines; (5) looting, pillage, or other lawlessness or disorder accompanying the collapse of civil authority determined by the Commission to have resulted from any of the other perils enumerated in this section or from control by enemy forces:

. . . .

Provided further, That no claim shall be approved in an aggregate amount which exceeds whichever of the following amounts, as determined by the Commission, is less: (a) The actual cash value, at the time of loss, of property lost or destroyed and the amount of the actual damage to other property of the claimant which was damaged as a direct result of the causes enumerated in this section; (b) the cost of repairing or rebuilding such lost or damaged property, or replacing the same with other property of like or similar quality: *Provided further*, That in case the aggregate amount of the claims which would be payable to any one claimant

[1] Public Law 370, 79th Cong., 2d sess., as amended by Public Law 597, 79th Cong., 2d sess.

under the foregoing provisions exceeds $500, the aggregate amount of the claims approved in favor of such claimant shall be reduced by 25 per centum of the excess over $500.

* * * * *

SEC. 103. The Commission shall make no payment under the provisions of this title —
    (a) to any enemy alien;
    (b) to any person who, by a civil or military court having jurisdiction, has been found guilty of collaborating with the enemy, or of any act involving disloyalty to the United States or the Commonwealth of the Philippines;
    (c) to any unincorporated association, trust, corporation or sociedad anonima owned or controlled by any of the persons specified in clauses (a) and (b) of this section;

* * * * *

SEC. 104. (a) No claim shall be paid unless approved by the Commission or its authorized representatives, and on account of each claim so approved the Commission may make immediate payment of (1) so much of the approved amount of the claim as does not exceed five hundred dollars or one thousand Philippine pesos, plus (2) such percentage, not in excess of 80 per centum of the remainder of the approved amount of the claim as the Commission shall make applicable to all approved claims, due consideration having been given to the total funds available for distribution. After the time for filing claims has expired, the Commission shall determine the amount of money available for the further payment of claims. Such funds shall be applied pro rata toward the payment of the unpaid balances of the amounts authorized to be paid pursuant to section 102 of this title.

(b) The Commission may, at its option, make payment, in whole or in part, of the amount payable in the case of any claim authorized to be paid under this title by replacing lost, damaged, or destroyed property with other property of like or similar kind. The amount expended for such purpose in any case, including the fair value of property transferred to the claimant, shall be deemed to have been paid to the claimant on account of his claim, and such amount shall in no case exceed the amount authorized to be paid under this title on account of such claim. The Commission is authorized to acquire such property, to have such work done, to make such contracts, and to take such other action as may be necessary for the purposes of this subsection. To accomplish the purposes of this section such surplus property of the United States, wherever located, as the President of the United States by Executive order shall direct, shall be transferred to the Commission. The Commission shall pay to the disposal agency the fair value of the property as agreed to by the Commission and the disposal agency.

(c) All of the provisions of this title shall be subject to the requirement that to the fullest extent practicable, the Commission shall require that the lost or damaged property be rebuilt, replaced, or repaired before payments of money are actually made to claimants under this title: *Provided,* That if the Commission determines it is impossible for any reason beyond the control of the claimant, or is impractical to rebuild, replace, or repair the lost or damaged property, the Commission may make payment to the claimant without making said requirement: *Provided, however,* That as a condition to the making of such payment, the Commission shall require that the whole of such payment shall be reinvested in such manner as will further the rehabilitation or economic development of the Philippines: *And provided further,* That nothing in this subsection shall preclude the partial payment of claims as the rebuilding, replacing, or repairing of the property progresses.

SEC. 105. Not later than six months after its organization, and every six months thereafter, the Commission shall make a report to the Congress concerning operations under this title.

SEC. 106. (*a*) There is hereby authorized to be appropriated, out of any money in the Treasury not otherwise appropriated, the amount of $400,000,000 for the purposes of paying compensation to the extent authorized by this title, and of such sum, not to exceed $4,000,000 shall be available to pay the expenses of the Commission.

(*b*) Any money or bullion received by the United States from the Japanese Government or the Japanese people by way of reparations or indemnity on account of war losses in the Philippines —

    (1) shall be covered into the Treasury of the United States until the value of said money or bullion so covered into the Treasury is equal to the sum of the amounts appropriated for the payment of compensation under this title and the amounts appropriated for carrying out the purposes of title III of this Act;

    (2) when the amounts covered into the Treasury under clause (1) are equal to the amounts so appropriated, the excess over the amounts so appropriated shall be used, first, to satisfy in full the balance unpaid of any approved claims under this title; second, toward the payment of any amount by which any claim was reduced under Section 102 (*a*) hereof; third, toward the satisfaction of any approved claim of the Government of the Commonwealth of the Philippines (or the Republic of the Philippines), its provinces, cities, municipalities, and instrumentalities, not compensated under this Act; and

    (3) the balance shall be covered into the Treasury of the United States.

(*c*) Notwithstanding any other provision of law, any other property received by the United States from the Japanese Government or the Japanese people, whether by way of reparations or restitution on account of war losses in the Philippines, may be transferred, by Executive order of the President of the United States, to the Commission, to be applied in kind, under such regulations as may be adopted by it, to the payment of losses or damages covered by this Act, or in such other manner as the Commission may determine to be necessary to carry out the purposes and policy of this Act.

(*d*) Nothing in this Act shall prejudice the right of any claimant not covered by this Act to recover damages from the Japanese Government or the Japanese people, by way of reparations or indemnity on account of the war, for losses not, or not fully, compensated for hereunder.

TITLE II — DISPOSAL OF SURPLUS PROPERTY

SEC. 201. In order to expedite the disposition of surplus property of the United States in the Philippines and to aid in repairing and replacing buildings (including hospitals, educational, and charitable institutions furnishing essential health, educational, and welfare services), works, utilities, equipment, or other property, owned by the Commonwealth of the Philippines, provincial governments, chartered cities or municipalities, or other governmental units in the Philippines, in cases where such government-owned buildings, works, utilities, equipment, or other property have been damaged, lost, or destroyed in the war, and otherwise to aid in facilitating the normal operations of existing governmental units in the Philippines, the Department of State, the disposal agency for the Philippines designated under the Surplus Property Act of 1944, acting through the Foreign Liquidation Commissioner (hereinafter referred to as the "Commissioner"), is hereby authorized to transfer to the Commonwealth of the Philippines (Republic of the Philippines), provincial government, chartered cities or municipalities, without reimbursement, property of the United States now or hereafter located in the Philippines and declared surplus under the Surplus Property Act of 1944, upon such terms and conditions, including the use or disposition of such property by the Commonwealth of the Philippines (Republic of the Philippines), as the Commissioner may deem appropriate to carry out the purposes of this title.

SEC. 204. No military weapons, munitions, or toxic gas shall be transferred or otherwise disposed of under section 201.

SEC. 205. The fair value of the property transferred to the Commonwealth of the Philippines (Republic of the Philippines) provincial government, chartered cities or municipalities under section 201, as estimated by the Commissioner, shall not exceed $100,000,000 in the aggregate.

. . . . .

TITLE III — RESTORATION AND IMPROVEMENT OF PUBLIC PROPERTY AND ESSENTIAL PUBLIC SERVICES

SEC. 301. As a manifestation of good will to the Filipino people, there are hereby authorized to be appropriated, out of any money in the Treasury not otherwise appropriated, (1) the sum of $120,000,000, to be allocated from time to time, but not later than the fiscal year 1950, by the President of the United States among the various programs set forth in section 302, 303, 304, and 305, and (2) such additional sums as may be necessary to carry out the purposes of sections 306 to 311, inclusive.

. . . . .

[Omitted sections 302–311 deal with restoration and improvement of public roads, port and harbor facilities, public health services, inter-island commerce and navigation, etc.]

TITLE VI — GENERAL PROVISIONS

SEC. 601. No payments under title I of this Act in excess of $500 shall be made until an executive agreement shall have been entered into between the President of the United States and the President of the Philippines, and such agreement shall have become effective according to its terms, providing for trade relations between the United States and the Philippines, and which agreement shall also provide for the same offenses, and penalties upon conviction, thereof, as are set forth in section 107 and section 108 of title I of this Act.

. . . . .

(2) *An Act to Provide for Trade Relations between the United States and the Philippines, and for Other Purposes, Approved April 30, 1946.*[1]

[Excerpts]

. . . . .

TITLE II — LAWS AND PROPOSED OBLIGATIONS OF UNITED STATES

PART 1 — CUSTOMS DUTIES

SEC. 201. FREE ENTRY OF PHILIPPINE ARTICLES.

During the period from the day after the date of the enactment of this Act to July 3, 1954, both dates inclusive, Philippine articles entered, or withdrawn from warehouse, in the United States for consumption shall be admitted into the United States free of ordinary customs duty.

SEC. 202. ORDINARY CUSTOMS DUTIES ON PHILIPPINE ARTICLES.

(a) *July 4, 1954 – July 3, 1974.* — The ordinary customs duty to be collected on Philippine articles, which during the following portions of the period from July 4, 1954, to July 3, 1974, both dates inclusive, are entered, or withdrawn from warehouse, in the United States for consumption, shall be determined by applying the following percentages of the United States duty:

[1] Public Law 371, 79th Cong., 2d sess.

(1) *July 4 to December 31, 1954.* — During the period from July 4, 1954, to December 31, 1954, both dates inclusive, 5 per centum.

(2) *Calendar year 1955.* — During the calendar year 1955, 10 per centum.

(3) *Calendar years 1956–1972.* — During each calendar year after the calendar year 1955 until and including the calendar year 1972, a percentage equal to the percentage for the preceding calendar year increased by 5 per centum of the United States duty.

(4) *Percentage after 1972.* — During the period from January 1, 1973, to July 3, 1974, both dates inclusive, 100 per centum.

(5) *Exceptions to above rules.* — The provisions of this subsection shall not be applicable to the classes of articles referred to in section 214 (a) of Part 2 of this title (relating to quotas).

(b) *Period after July 3, 1974.* — The ordinary customs duty to be collected on Philippine articles which after July 3, 1974, are entered, or withdrawn from warehouse, in the United States for consumption, shall be determined without regard to the provisions of subsection (a) of this section or of section 214.

SEC. 203. CUSTOMS DUTIES OTHER THAN ORDINARY.

Customs duties on Philippine articles, other than ordinary customs duties, shall be determined without regard to the provisions of sections 201 and 202 (a), but shall be subject to the provisions of section 204.

SEC. 204. EQUALITY IN SPECIAL IMPORT DUTIES, ETC.

(a) With respect to Philippine articles imported into the United States, no duty on or in connection with importation shall be collected or paid in an amount in excess of the duty imposed with respect to like articles which are the product of any other foreign country, or collected or paid in any amount if the duty is not imposed with respect to such like articles.

(b) As used in this section the term "duty" includes taxes, fees, charges, or exactions, imposed on or in connection with importation; but does not include internal taxes or ordinary customs duties.

SEC. 205. EQUALITY IN DUTIES ON PRODUCTS OF PHILIPPINES.

(a) With respect to products of the Philippines, which do not come within the definition of Philippine articles, imported into the United States, no duty on or in connection with importation shall be collected or paid in an amount in excess of the duty imposed with respect to like articles which are the product of any other foreign country (except Cuba), or collected or paid in any amount if the duty is not imposed with respect to such like articles which are the product of any other foreign country (except Cuba).

(b) As used in this section the term "duty" includes taxes, fees, charges, or exactions, imposed on or in connection with importation; but does not include internal taxes.

PART 2 — QUOTAS

SEC. 211. ABSOLUTE QUOTA ON SUGARS.

* * * * *

(c) *Amount of Quota.* — During the period from January 1, 1946, to July 3, 1974, both dates inclusive, the total amount of all Philippine sugars which, in any calendar year, may be entered, or withdrawn from warehouse, in the United States for consumption, shall not exceed 952,000 short tons (the equivalent of 850,000 long tons), of which not to exceed 56,000 short tons (the equivalent of 50,000 long tons) may be refined sugars; except that during the period from January 1, 1974, to July 3, 1974, both dates inclusive, such total amount shall not exceed 476,000 short tons (the equivalent of 425,000 long tons), of which not to exceed 28,000 short tons (the equivalent of 25,000 long tons) may be refined sugars.

(d) *Allocation of Quotas for Unrefined Sugars.* — The quota for unrefined sugars, including that required to manufacture the refined sugars, established by this section, shall be allocated annually to the sugar-producing mills and plantation owners in the Philippines in the calendar year 1940 whose sugars were exported to the United States during such calendar year, or their successors in interest, proportionately on the basis of their average annual production (or in the case of such a successor in interest, the average annual production of his predecessor in interest) for the calendar years 1931, 1932, and 1933, and the amount of sugars which may be so exported shall be allocated in each year between each mill and the plantation owners on the basis of the proportion of sugars to which each mill and the plantation owners are respectively entitled, in accordance with any milling agreements between them, or any extension, modification, or renewal thereof.

(e) *Allocation of Quotas for Refined Sugars.* — The quota for refined sugars established by this section shall be allocated annually to the manufacturers of refined sugars in the Philippines in the calendar year 1940 whose refined sugars were exported to the United States during such calendar year, or their successors in interest, proportionately on the basis of the amount of refined sugars produced by each such manufacturer (or in the case of such successor in interest, the amount of refined sugars produced by his predecessor in interest) which was exported to the United States during the calendar year 1940.

. . . . . .

SEC. 215. LAWS PUTTING INTO EFFECT ALLOCATIONS OF QUOTAS.

The necessary laws and regulations for putting into effect the allocation of quotas on the basis provided for in sections 211, 212, and 214, respectively, shall not be enacted by the United States, it being the purpose of this title that such laws and regulations shall be enacted by the Philippines.

. . . . . .

PART 3 — INTERNAL TAXES

SEC. 221. EQUALITY IN INTERNAL TAXES.

(a) With respect to articles which are products of the Philippines coming into the United States, or with respect to articles manufactured in the United States wholly or in part from such articles, no internal tax shall be —

(1) collected or paid in an amount in excess of the internal tax imposed with respect to like articles which are the product of the United States, or collected or paid in any amount if the internal tax is not imposed with respect to such like articles;

(2) collected or paid in an amount in excess of the internal tax imposed with respect to like articles which are the product of any other foreign country, or collected or paid in any amount if the internal tax is not imposed with respect to such like articles.

(b) Where an internal tax is imposed with respect to an article which is the product of a foreign country to compensate for an internal tax imposed (1) with respect to a like article which is the product of the United States, or (2) with respect to materials used in the production of a like article which is the product of the United States, if the amount of the internal tax which is collected and paid with respect to the article which is the product of the Philippines is not in excess of that permitted by paragraph (2) of subsection (a) such collection and payment shall not be regarded as in violation of subsection (a).

(c) This section shall not apply to the taxes imposed under section 2306, 2327, or 2356 of the Internal Revenue Code.

. . . . . .

SEC. 223. PROHIBITION OF EXPORT TAXES.

No export tax shall be imposed or collected by the United States on articles exported to the Philippines.

. . . . . .

PART 4 — IMMIGRATION

SEC. 231. CERTAIN PHILIPPINE CITIZENS GRANTED NON-QUOTA STATUS.

(a) Any citizen of the Philippines who actually resided in the United States for a continuous period of three years during the period of forty-two months ending November 30, 1941, if entering the United States during the period from July 4, 1946, to July 3, 1951, both dates inclusive, for the purpose of resuming residence in the United States, shall, for the purposes of the immigration laws, be considered a non-quota immigrant; and shall not be excluded from entry into the United States by reason of section 13 (c) of the Immigration Act of 1924, or by reason of so much of section 3 of the Immigration Act of 1917 as provides for the exclusion from admission into the United States of natives of a therein specified geographical area.

(b) After such admission as a non-quota immigrant he shall, for the purposes of the immigration and naturalization laws, be considered as lawfully admitted to the United States for permanent residence.

(c) The benefits of this section shall also apply to his wife, if a citizen of the Philippines or eligible to United States citizenship, and to his unmarried children under 18 years of age, if such wife or children are accompanying or following to join him during such period.

(d) This section shall not apply to a citizen of the Philippines admitted to the Territory of Hawaii, without an immigration or passport visa, under the provisions of paragraph (1) of section 8 (a) of the Act of March 24, 1934 (48 Stat. 456, ch. 84).

TITLE III — OBLIGATIONS OF PHILIPPINES

Part 1 — Purposes of Title

Sec. 301. Statement of Purposes of Title.

(a) *Period Until July 4, 1946.* — The following Parts and sections of this title, insofar as they are applicable to the period from the date of the enactment of this Act to July 3, 1946, both dates inclusive, are intended to, and shall, operate as statutes of the United States, binding on one of its possessions.

(b) *Period July 4, 1946–July 3, 1974.* — The following Parts and sections of this title, although expressed in statutory form, are not in any manner intended, insofar as they are applicable to the period after July 3, 1946, as an attempt on the part of the Congress of the United States to legislate for the Republic of the Philippines as a sovereign nation, but constitute a statement in precise terms of provisions —

(1) which the Government of the Philippines, on the taking effect of the executive agreement provided for in Title IV of this Act, will be obligated to observe and execute as the law of the Republic of the Philippines during the effectiveness of the agreement; except that the observance of such part of the provisions of section 341 as is in conflict with the Constitution of the Philippines will not be required under such agreement for the period prior to the amendment to the constitution referred to in section 402 (b); and

(2) which, between the proclamation of the independence of the Philippines and the date of the taking effect of such executive agreement, will, according to the policy and expectations of the Congress of the United States, be observed and executed by the Government of the Philippines.

. . . . . .

[Parts 2 and 3 duplicate for the Philippines the obligations of the United States listed in Parts 1 and 3 of Title II.]

Part 4 — Immigration

Sec. 331. Certain United States Citizens Given Non-quota Status.

Any citizen of the United States who actually resided in the Philippines for a continuous period of three years during the period of forty-two months ending November 30, 1941, if entering the Philippines during the period from July 4, 1946, to July 3, 1951, both dates inclusive, for the purpose of resuming residence in the Philippines, shall, for the purposes of the immigration laws, be considered a non-quota immigrant. After such admission as a non-quota immigrant he shall, for the purposes of the immigration and naturalization laws, be considered as lawfully admitted to the Philippines for permanent residence. The benefits of this section shall also apply to his wife, if a citizen of the United States, and to his unmarried children under 18 years of age, if such wife or children are accompanying or following to join him during such period.

SEC. 332. IMMIGRATION OF UNITED STATES CITIZENS INTO THE PHILIPPINES.

Citizens of the United States, admissible to the Philippines under the provisions required by section 402 (e) to be included as a part of the executive agreement made under Title IV, shall be entitled to enter the Philippines, in the numbers and during the periods of years, and to remain therein for the time, specified in that part of the agreement which embodies the provisions of section 402 (e).

PART 5 — MISCELLANEOUS

SEC. 341. RIGHTS OF UNITED STATES CITIZENS AND BUSINESS ENTERPRISES IN NATURAL RESOURCES.

The disposition, exploitation, development, and utilization of all agricultural, timber, and mineral lands of the public domain, waters, minerals, coal, petroleum, and other mineral oils, all forces and sources of potential energy, and other natural resources of the Philippines, and the operation of public utilities, shall, if open to any person, be open to citizens of the United States and to all forms of business enterprise owned or controlled, directly or indirectly, by United States citizens.

SEC. 342. CURRENCY STABILIZATION.

The value of Philippine currency in relation to the United States dollar shall not be changed, the convertibility of pesos into dollars shall not be suspended, and no restrictions shall be imposed on the transfer of funds from the Philippines to the United States, except by agreement with the President of the United States.

. . . .

TITLE IV — EXECUTIVE AGREEMENT BETWEEN UNITED STATES AND PHILIPPINES

SEC. 401. AUTHORIZATION OF AGREEMENT.

The President of the United States is authorized (except as hereinafter in this title otherwise provided) to enter into an executive agreement with the President of the Philippines providing for the acceptance on the part of each country of the provisions of Title II and of Title III (except Part 1) of this Act. The President of the United States is not authorized by this section to enter into such agreement unless it contains a provision that it shall not take effect —

(a) Unless and until the Congress of the Philippines accepts it by law; and

(b) Unless and until the Congress of the Philippines (in the act of acceptance, or separately) has enacted such legislation as may be necessary to make all the provisions of Parts 2, 3, 4, and 5 of Title III take effect as laws of the Philippines, except (during the period prior to the amendment to the Constitution of the Philippines referred to in subsection (b) of section 402) such provisions of section 341 as are in conflict with such constitution.

SEC. 402. OBLIGATIONS OF PHILIPPINES.

The President of the United States is not authorized by section 401 to enter into such executive agreement unless in the agreement the Government of the Philippines agrees —

(a) That the Republic of the Philippines will continue in effect as laws of the Philippines, during the effectiveness of the agreement, the provisions of Parts 2, 3, 4, and 5 of Title III, except (for the period prior to the amendment of the Constitution of the Philippines referred to in subsection (b) of this section) such part of the provisions of section 341 as is in conflict with such constitution.

(b) That the Government of the Philippines will promptly take such steps as are necessary to secure the amendment of the Constitution of the Philippines so as to permit the taking effect as laws of the Philippines of such part of the provisions of section 341 as is in conflict with such constitution before such amendment.

(c) That the Republic of the Philippines will promptly enact, and keep in effect during the effectiveness of the agreement, such legislation as may be necessary —

    (1) to supplement the legislation referred to in section 401 (b), and to implement the provisions of Parts 2, 3, 4, and 5 of Title III; and

    (2) to put and keep in effect during the effectiveness of the agreement, the allocation, reallocation, transfer, and assignment of quotas on the basis provided for in Part 2 of Title II.

(d) That the United States shall have the right to provide the basis for the allocation of the quotas established under that portion of the agreement which sets forth the provisions of section 403 (c) of this Act, and that, if the United States exercises such right, the Republic of the Philippines will promptly enact, and keep in force during the period for which each such quota is established, such legislation as is necessary to put and keep in effect, on the basis provided by the United States, the allocation of such quotas.

(e) That there shall be permitted to enter the Philippines, without regard to any numerical limitations under the laws of the Philippines, in each of the years of a specified period of years, a specified number of citizens of the United States. The number of years (which shall not be less than five) the number of citizens of the United States (which shall not be less than one thousand) entitled to be so admitted in each year, and the length of time each shall be entitled to remain in the Philippines, shall be stated in the agreement.

(f) That the value of Philippine currency in relation to the United States dollar shall not be changed, the convertibility of pesos into dollars shall not be suspended, and no restrictions shall be imposed on the transfer of funds from the Philippines to the United States, except by agreement with the President of the United States.

SEC. 403. OBLIGATIONS OF UNITED STATES.

The President of the United States is not authorized by section 401 to enter into such executive agreement unless in such agreement the Government of the United States agrees —

(a) That upon the taking effect of the agreement the provisions of Title II —

    (1) if in effect as laws of the United States at the time the agreement takes effect, shall continue in effect as laws of the United States during the effectiveness of the agreement; or

    (2) if not so in effect at the time the agreement takes effect (because suspended under section 502 of Title V) shall take effect and continue in effect as laws of the United States during the effectiveness of the agreement.

(b) That the United States will promptly enact, and keep in effect during the effectiveness of the agreement, such legislation as may be necessary to supplement and implement the provisions of Title II so continued in effect, or so made to take effect, as laws of the United States.

(c) That with respect to quotas on Philippine articles (other than the quotas established in Part 2 of Title II, and other than quotas established in conjunction with quantitative limitations, applicable to products of all foreign countries, on imports of like articles), the United States will not establish any such quota for any period before January 1, 1948; and that, for any part of the period from January 1, 1948, to July 3, 1974, both dates inclusive, it will establish such a quota only if —

    (1) the President of the United States, after investigation, finds that such Philippine articles are coming, or are likely to come, into substantial competition with like articles the product of the United States; and

    (2) the quota established for any Philippine article for any twelve-month period is not less than the amount determined by the President as the total amount of Philippine articles of such class which (during the twelve months ended on the last day of the month preceding the month in which occurs the date proclaimed by the President as the date of the beginning of the

investigation) was entered, or withdrawn from warehouse, in the United States for consumption; or, if the quota is established for any period other than a twelve-month period, is not less than a proportionate amount.

(d) That during the effectiveness of the agreement the United States will not reduce the preference of 2 cents per pound provided in section 2470 of the Internal Revenue Code (relating to processing taxes on coconut oil, etc.) with respect to articles "wholly the production of the Philippine Islands" or articles "produced wholly from materials the growth or production of the Philippine Islands"; except that it may suspend the provisions of subsection (a) (2) of such section during any period as to which the President of the United States, after consultation with the President of the Philippines, finds that adequate supplies of neither copra nor coconut oil, the product of the Philippines, are readily available for processing in the United States.

SEC. 404. TERMINATION OF AGREEMENT.

The President of the United States is not authorized by section 401 to enter into such executive agreement unless it provides —

(a) *Termination in General.* — That the agreement shall have no effect after July 3, 1974; and

(b) *Termination by Either Party.* —

(1) that the agreement may be terminated by either party at any time, upon not less than five years' notice; and

(2) that if the President of the United States or the President of the Philippines determines and proclaims that the other country has adopted or applied measures or practices which would operate to nullify or impair any right or obligation provided for in such agreement, then the agreement may be terminated upon not less than six months' notice; and

(c) *Termination or Suspension by the United States.* —

(1) that if the President of the United States determines that a reasonable time for the making of the amendment to the Constitution of the Philippines referred to in section 402 (b) has elapsed, but that such amendment has not been made, he shall so proclaim and the executive agreement shall have no effect after the date of such proclamation; and

(2) that if the President of the United States determines and proclaims, after consultation with the President of the Philippines, that the Republic of the Philippines or any of its political subdivisions or the Philippine Government is in any manner discriminating against citizens of the United States or any form of United States business enterprise, then the United States shall have the right to suspend the effectiveness of the whole or any portion of the agreement; and

(3) that if the President of the United States determines and proclaims, after consultation with the President of the Philippines, that the discrimination which was the basis for the suspension under paragraph (2) of this subsection —

(A) has ceased, the suspension effected under paragraph (2) shall end; or

(B) has not ceased after the lapse of a time determined by the President of the United States to be reasonable, then the United States shall have the right to terminate the agreement upon not less than six months' notice.

SEC. 405. EFFECT OF TERMINATION OF AGREEMENT.

Upon the termination of the agreement as provided in section 404, the provisions of Title II shall cease to have effect as laws of the United States.

SEC. 406. INTERPRETATION OF AGREEMENT.

The President of the United States is not authorized by section 401 to enter into such executive agreement unless it provides that the acceptance of the provisions of Titles II and III is on the understanding that the definitions, and provisions in the nature of definitions, contained in section 2 of Title I, shall apply in the interpretation of the provisions so accepted.

SEC. 407. TERMINATION OF AUTHORITY TO MAKE AGREEMENT.

Whenever the President of the United States determines that a reasonable time for the entering into, acceptance and taking effect, of the executive agreement has elapsed, but that such agreement has not taken effect, he shall so proclaim, and thereupon his authority to enter into such executive agreement shall terminate, and the provisions of Title II shall cease to have effect as laws of the United States.

SEC. 408. EFFECTIVE DATE OF AGREEMENT.

When the President of the United States determines that the executive agreement entered into under section 401 has been accepted by the Congress of the Philippines by law and that the Congress of the Philippines has enacted the legislation the enactment of which is, under section 401, a condition precedent to the taking effect of the agreement, he shall so proclaim, and in his proclamation specify the effective date of the agreement

. . . . .

SEC. 508. TRADE AGREEMENTS WITH THE PHILIPPINES.

Until July 4, 1974, no trade agreement shall be made with the Philippines under section 350, as amended, of the Tariff Act of 1930, unless, prior to such time, the President of the United States has made the proclamation provided for in section 407 of this Act, or the executive agreement provided for in Title IV of this Act has been terminated.

SEC. 509. RIGHTS OF THIRD COUNTRIES.

The benefits granted by this Act, and by the executive agreement provided for in Title IV, to the Philippines, Philippine articles or products, and Philippine citizens, shall not, by reason of any provision of any existing treaty or agreement with any third country, be extended to such country or its products, citizens, or subjects.

. . . . .

(3) *An Act to Provide Military Assistance to the Republic of the Philippines in Establishing and Maintaining National Security and to Form a Basis for Participation by That Government in Such Defensive Military Operations As the Future May Require, Approved June 26, 1946.*[1]

Be it enacted by the Senate and House of Representatives of the United States of America in Congress assembled, That this Act may be cited as the "Republic of the Philippines Military Assistance Act".

SEC. 2. Notwithstanding the provisions of any other law, the President is authorized, upon application by the Republic of the Philippines, and whenever in his discretion the public interest renders such course advisable, to provide: (*a*) for the instruction and training of military and naval personnel of the Republic of the Philippines; (*b*) for the maintenance, repair, and rehabilitation of military or naval equipment in the possession of the said country; and (*c*) for the transfer to the said country of any arms, ammunition, and implements of war as defined in the President's proclamation 2549 of April 9, 1942, or any superseding proclamations; any other aircraft; naval vessels except those in the category of battleships, cruisers, aircraft carriers, destroyers, and submarines; any stores, supplies, services, technical information, material, and equipment: *Provided,* That such transfer shall be consistent with military and naval requirements of the United States and with the national interest.

[1] Public Law 454, 79th Cong., 2d sess.

SEC. 3. The President is authorized to provide such assistance or transfer property or information pursuant to section 2, by sale, loan, exchange, lease, gift, or transfer for cash, credit, or other property with or without warranty and upon such other terms and conditions as he shall find proper.

SEC. 4. As a condition precedent to the receipt of any assistance, information, or property pursuant to this Act the Government of the Republic of the Philippines shall undertake (*a*) that it will not, without the consent of the President of the United States, transfer title to or possession of any property transferred to it pursuant to this Act, (*b*) that it will not permit use of any property so received or disclosure of any plan, specification, or other information pertaining thereto or any technical information furnished, by or to anyone not an officer, employee, or agent of the Republic of the Philippines, or for any purpose other than those set forth in this Act, and (*c*) that the Government of the Republic of the Philippines will make provisions comparable to those customarily made by the United States for the security of any article, plan, or information received under the terms of this Act.

SEC. 5. The President of the United States is authorized, upon application from the Republic of the Philippines, and whenever in his discretion the public interest renders such a course advisable, to detail officers and enlisted men of the Army of the United States, and the United States Navy and Marine Corps to assist that Government: *Provided*, That the officers and enlisted men so detailed are authorized to accept from the Republic of the Philippines offices and such compensation and emoluments thereunto appertaining as may be first approved by the Secretary of War, or by the Secretary of the Navy, as the case may be: *Provided further*, That such compensation may be accepted by the United States Government for remittance to the individual if in the opinion of the Secretary of War, or of the Secretary of the Navy, as the case may be, such a course appears desirable: *Provided further*, That while so detailed such officers and enlisted men shall receive, in addition to the compensation and emoluments allowed them by that Government, the pay and allowances thereto entitled in the Army of the United States, or the United States Navy, and Marine Corps, and shall be allowed the same credit for longevity, retirement, and for all other purposes that they would receive if they were serving with the forces of the United States: *And provided further*, That in addition to or in the absence of such compensation from that Government, the officers and enlisted men so detailed shall receive such additional compensation as may be determined by the Secretary of War, or the Secretary of the Navy, as the case may be, and approved by the President.

SEC. 6. There is hereby authorized to be appropriated, out of any money in the Treasury not otherwise appropriated, such sums as may be necessary to carry out the provisions of this Act: *Provided*, That articles or services furnished pursuant to the provisions of this Act shall be within the limits of appropriations made specifically for that purpose or to the extent of availability of items which are surplus to the needs of the United States Government.

SEC. 7. The President may from time to time promulgate such rules and regulations as may be necessary and proper to carry out any of the provisions of this Act; and he may exercise any power or authority conferred upon him by this Act through such department, agency, or officer as he shall direct: *Provided*, That no property shall be transferred by such department, agency, or officer pursuant to this Act except after consultation with the Secretary of State, and the Secretaries of War and Navy as their respective interests may appear.

SEC. 8. The provisions of this Act become effective on the 4th day of July 1946 and continue in effect for a period of five years.

(4) *Proclamation by the President (Truman) of the Independence of the Philippines, July 4, 1946.*[1]

WHEREAS the United States of America by the Treaty of Peace with Spain of December 10, 1898, commonly known as the Treaty of Paris, and by the Treaty with Spain of November 7, 1900, did acquire sovereignty over the Philippines, and by the Convention of January 2, 1930, with Great Britain did delimit the boundary between the Philippine Archipelago and the State of North Borneo; and

WHEREAS the United States of America has consistently and faithfully during the past forty-eight years exercised jurisdiction and control over the Philippines and its people; and

WHEREAS it has been the repeated declaration of the legislative and executive branches of the Government of the United States of America that full independence would be granted the Philippines as soon as the people of the Philippines were prepared to assume this obligation; and

WHEREAS the people of the Philippines have clearly demonstrated their capacity for self-government; and

WHEREAS the Act of Congress approved March 24, 1934, known as the Philippine Independence Act, directed that, on the 4th Day of July immediately following a ten-year transitional period leading to the independence of the Philippines, the President of the United States of America should by proclamation withdraw and surrender all rights of possession, supervision, jurisdiction, control, or sovereignty of the United States of America in and over the territory and people of the Philippines, except certain reservations therein or thereafter authorized to be made, and, on behalf of the United States of America, should recognize the independence of the Philippines:

Now, THEREFORE, I, Harry S. Truman, President of the United States of America, acting under and by virtue of the authority vested in me by the aforesaid act of Congress, do proclaim that, in accord with and subject to the reservations provided for in the applicable statutes of the United States,

The United States of America hereby withdraws and surrenders all rights of possession, supervision, jurisdiction, control, or sovereignty now existing and exercised by the United States of America in and over the territory and people of the Philippines; and,

---

[1] Department of State, *Bulletin*, XV, p. 66.

On behalf of the United States of America, I do hereby recognize the independence of the Philippines as a separate and self-governing nation and acknowledge the authority and control over the same of the government instituted by the people thereof, under the constitution now in force.

IN WITNESS WHEREOF, I have hereunto set my hand and caused the seal of the United States of America to be affixed.

DONE at the City of Washington this Fourth day of July in the year of our Lord, nineteen hundred and forty-six, and of the [SEAL] Independence of the United States of America the one hundred and seventy-first.

(5) *Treaty of General Relations between the United States of America and the Republic of the Philippines, together with Accompanying Protocol, Signed at Manila, July 4, 1946.*[1]

The United States of America and the Republic of the Philippines, being animated by the desire to cement the relations of close and long friendship existing between the two countries, and to provide for the recognition of the independence of the Republic of the Philippines as of July 4, 1946 and the relinquishment of American sovereignty over the Philippine Islands, have agreed upon the following articles:

ARTICLE I

The United States of America agrees to withdraw and surrender, and does hereby withdraw and surrender, all right of possession, supervision, jurisdiction, control or sovereignty existing and exercised by the United States of America in and over the territory and the people of the Philippine Islands, except the use of such bases, necessary appurtenances to such bases, and the rights incident thereto, as the United States of America, by agreement with the Republic of the Philippines, may deem necessary to retain for the mutual protection of the United States of America and of the Republic of the Philippines. The United States of America further agrees to recognize, and does hereby recognize, the independence of the Republic of the Philippines as a separate self-governing nation and to acknowledge, and does hereby acknowledge, the authority and control over the same of the Government instituted by the people thereof, under the Constitution of the Republic of the Philippines.

ARTICLE II

The diplomatic representatives of each country shall enjoy in the territories of the other the privileges and immunities derived from generally recognized international law and usage. The consular representatives of each country, duly provided with exequatur, will be permitted to reside in the territories of the other in the places wherein

---

[1] Department of State, *Treaties and Other International Acts Series* 1568. The treaty was ratified by President Truman on August 16 and became effective October 22, 1946.

consular representatives are by local laws permitted to reside; they shall enjoy the honorary privileges and the immunities accorded to such officers by general international usage; and they shall not be treated in a manner less favorable than similar officers of any other foreign country.

Article III

Pending the final establishment of the requisite Philippine Foreign Service establishments abroad, the United States of America and the Republic of the Philippines agree that at the request of the Republic of the Philippines the United States of America will endeavor, in so far as it may be practicable, to represent through its Foreign Service the interests of the Republic of the Philippines in countries where there is no Philippine representation. The two countries further agree that any such arrangements are to be subject to termination when in the judgment of either country such arrangements are no longer necessary.

Article IV

The Republic of the Philippines agrees to assume, and does hereby assume, all the debts and liabilities of the Philippine Islands, its provinces, cities, municipalities and instrumentalities, which shall be valid and subsisting on the date hereof. The Republic of the Philippines will make adequate provision for the necessary funds for the payment of interest on and principal of bonds issued prior to May 1, 1934 under authority of an Act of Congress of the United States of America by the Philippine Islands, or any province, city or municipality therein, and such obligations shall be a first lien on the taxes collected in the Philippines.

Article V

The United States of America and the Republic of the Philippines agree that all cases at law concerning the Government and people of the Philippines which, in accordance with Section 7 (6) of the Independence Act of 1934, are pending before the Supreme Court of the United States of America at the date of the granting of the independence of the Republic of the Philippines shall continue to be subject to the review of the Supreme Court of the United States of America for such period of time after independence as may be necessary to effectuate the disposition of the cases at hand. The contracting parties also agree that following the disposition of such cases the Supreme Court of the United States of America will cease to have the right of review of cases originating in the Philippine Islands.

Article VI

In so far as they are not covered by existing legislation, all claims of the Government of the United States of America or its nationals against the Government of the Republic of the Philippines and all claims of the Government of the Republic of the Philippines and its nationals against the Government of the United States of America shall be promptly adjusted and settled. The property rights of the United States of America and the Republic of the Philippines shall be promptly adjusted and settled by mutual agreement, and all existing property rights of citizens and corporations of the United States of America in the Republic of the Philippines and of citizens and corporations of the Republic of the Philippines in the United States of America shall be acknowledged, respected and safeguarded to the same extent as property rights of citizens and corporations of the Republic of the Philippines and of the United States of America respectively. Both Governments shall designate representatives who may in concert agree on measures best calculated to effect a satisfactory and expeditious disposal of such claims as may not be covered by existing legislation.

Article VII

The Republic of the Philippines agrees to assume all continuing obligations assumed by the United States of America under the Treaty of Peace between the United States of America and Spain concluded at Paris on the 10th day of December, 1898, by which the Philippine Islands were ceded to the United States of America, and under the Treaty between the United States of America and Spain concluded at Washington on the 7th day of November, 1900.

Article VIII

This Treaty shall enter into force on the exchange of instruments of ratification.

This Treaty shall be submitted for ratification in accordance with the constitutional procedures of the United States of America and of the Republic of the Philippines; and instruments of ratification shall be exchanged and deposited at Manila.

Signed at Manila this fourth day of July, one thousand nine hundred forty-six.

PROTOCOL

It is understood and agreed by the High Contracting Parties that this Treaty is for the purpose of recognizing the independence of the Republic of the Philippines and for the maintenance of close and harmonious relations between the two Governments.

It is understood and agreed that this Treaty does not attempt to regulate the details of arrangements between the two Governments for their mutual defense; for the establishment, termination or regulation of the rights and duties of the two countries, each with respect to the other, in the settlement of claims, as to the ownership or control of real or personal property, or as to the carrying out of provisions of law of either country; or for the settlement of rights or claims of citizens or corporations of either country with respect to or against the other.

It is understood and agreed that the conclusion and entrance into force of this Treaty is not exclusive of further treaties and executive agreements providing for the specific regulation of matters broadly covered herein.

It is understood and agreed that pending final ratification of this Treaty, the provisions of Articles II and III shall be observed by executive agreement.

Signed at Manila this fourth day of July, one thousand nine hundred forty-six.

4. RELATIONS WITH SIAM[1]

In a letter[2] dated August 17, 1945 the Minister of Thailand, M. R. Seni Pramoj, transmitted the text of a proclamation issued by the Regent of Thailand in which the declaration of war by Thailand on January 25, 1942 against the United States was declared null and void. Shortly thereafter, Secretary of State Byrnes released a statement[3] in which he welcomed this move by the Thai Government.

On September 10, 1945 the Thai Chargé d'Affaires notified the Secretary of State that his Government had discarded the term Thailand and had reverted to the name Siam or Siamese.

On September 14, 1945 the Siamese Legation informed the Secretary of State that the Siamese Government had officially notified the Japanese Government of the termination of the Pact of Alliance concluded between those two countries in 1941; announcement was made on October 1, 1945 of formal denunciation of all remaining political agreements concluded with Japan during the period of Luang Pibul's premiership.[4]

Siamese diplomatic relations with the United States and Great Britain were reestablished on January 5, 1946.[5] Subsequently, the United States recognized that treaties and other international agreements between the two countries in force prior to the outbreak of war were to continue in effect.[6]

Closer economic cooperation was reported on September 9, 1946 by the State Department in an announcement that Siam had informed the United States that it would welcome the participation of American capital in the development of mineral resources.[7]

(1) *Letter from the Minister of Thailand (Pramoj) to the Secretary of State (Byrnes) Containing Text of Proclamation Issued by Regent of Thailand, August 17, 1945.*[8]

I have the honour to communicate to Your Excellency, for the information of the United States Government, the text of the following Proclamation issued by the Regent of Thailand on August 16th, 1945, and unanimously approved on the same day by the National Assembly of Thailand.

[1] See Thompson, V. "Siam and the Great Powers." *Foreign Policy Reports*, XXI, No. 24 (March 1, 1946).
[2] See below.
[3] See this volume, p. 824.
[4] Department of State, *Bulletin*, XIII, p. 521.
[5] For release of the State Department concerning resumption of relations, see *ibid.*, XIV, p. 5.
[6] *Ibid.*, p. 178.   [7] *Ibid.*, XV, p. 550.   [8] *Ibid.*, XIII, p. 261.

Whereas Thailand had pursued a fixed policy of maintaining strict neutrality and of combating foreign aggression by all means, as is clearly evident from the enactment in B.E. 2484 (1941) of the Law "Defining the Duties of the Thais in Time of War", this fixed determination was made clear, when Japan moved her forces into Thai territory on the 8th December B.E. 2484 (1941), by acts combating aggression everywhere, and numerous soldiers, police and civilians lost their lives thereby.

This circumstance, which stands as evidence in itself, shows clearly that the declaration of war on Great Britain and the United States of America on the 25th January B.E. 2485 (1942), as well as all acts adverse to the United Nations are acts contrary to the will of the Thai people and constitute an infringement of the provisions of the Constitution and the laws of the land. The Thai people inside as well as outside the country, who were in a position to help and support the United Nations who are lovers of peace in this world, have taken action by every means to assist the United Nations as most of the United Nations are already aware. This shows once again that the will of the Thai people does not approve of the declaration of war and of acts adverse to the United Nations as already mentioned.

Now that Japan has agreed to comply with the declaration of the United States of America, Great Britain, China and the Soviet Union which was made at Potsdam, peace is restored to Thailand as is the wish of the Thai people.

The Regent, in the name of His Majesty the King, hereby openly proclaims on behalf of the Thai people that the declaration of war on the United States of America and Great Britain is null and void and not binding on the Thai people as far as the United Nations are concerned. Thailand has resolved that the good friendly relations existing with the United Nations prior to the 8th December B.E. 2484 (1941) shall be restored and Thailand is ready to cooperate fully in every way with the United Nations in the establishment of stability in the world.

As for the territories the occupancy of which Japan entrusted to Thailand, namely the States of Kelantan, Trengganu, Kedah, Perlis, Kengtung, and Muang Phan, Thailand has no desire for the territories and is ready to arrange for their delivery as soon as Great Britain is ready to take delivery thereof.

As for any other provisions of law having effects adverse to the United States of America, Great Britain, and the British Empire, their repeal will be considered hereafter. All damages of any kind resulting from those laws will be legitimately made good.

In conclusion, all the Thai people as well as aliens who are in the Thai kingdom are requested to remain in tranquility and not to commit any act which will constitute a disturbance of public order. They should hold steadfastly to the ideals which have been laid down in the resolutions of the United Nations at San Francisco.

(2) *Statement by the Secretary of State (Byrnes) Concerning United States Relations with Thailand, August 20, 1945.*[1]

The Minister of Thailand, M. R. Seni Pramoj, has communicated to the Department of State the text of the proclamation issued by the Regent of Thailand in the name of His Majesty the King on August 16. As regards Thai relations with this country, the proclamation declared null and void, as unconstitutional and contrary to the will of the Thai people, the declaration of war by Thailand on January 25, 1942 against

[1] *Ibid.*

the United States; announced Thai determination to restore the friendly relations which existed with the United Nations before the Japanese occupation; promised that repeal of laws prejudicial to our interests would be considered; assured just compensation for damages resulting from such laws; and pledged full Thai cooperation with the United Nations in establishing world stability.

The action of the Thai Government is a welcome step in American-Thai relations. The Japanese occupation of Thailand took place at the same time as the Japanese attack on Pearl Harbor. The Thai declaration of war was made seven weeks later. The Thai Government was then completely controlled by the Japanese. The American Government has always believed that the declaration did not represent the will of the Thai people. Accordingly we disregarded that declaration and have continued to recognize the Thai Minister in Washington as the Minister of Thailand, although, of course, we did not recognize the Thailand Government in Bangkok as it was under Japanese control.

Immediately following the Japanese occupation of Thailand, the Minister of Thailand in Washington organized a Free Thai movement among those Thai who were outside their country when the Japanese blow fell. The Free Thai have since contributed substantially to the Allied cause.

Soon after the Japanese occupation a resistance movement developed within Thailand. Our Government and the British Government have both given to and received from the resistance movement important aid and for some time past have been in constant communication with its leaders. For a number of months the resistance movement has been prepared to commence overt action against the Japanese. For operational reasons this Government and the British Government requested that such action be deferred. It was only because of this express request that the resistance movement did not begin open fighting for the liberation of their country before Japanese surrender made such action unnecessary.

Before the war Thailand and the United States had a long history of close friendship. We hope that friendship will be even closer in the future. During the past four years we have regarded Thailand not as an enemy but as a country to be liberated from the enemy. With that liberation now accomplished we look to the resumption by Thailand of its former place in the community of nations as a free, sovereign, and independent country.

5. RELATIONS WITH THE SOVIET UNION IN THE FAR EAST

For information concerning relations with the Soviet Union on topics other than those concerning the Far East, see this volume, p. 845.

A. China

A special agreement reached at the Yalta conference, but not made public until February 11, 1946, established the conditions upon which the Soviet Union would enter the war against Japan. *Inter alia*, the agreement provided for (1) preservation of the status quo in Outer Mongolia, and (2) restoration to the Soviet Union of certain rights in Manchuria, which had been ceded to Japan by the treaty of Portsmouth in 1904. These included internationalization of the commercial port of Dairen, lease of Port Arthur to the Soviet Union as a naval base, joint Chinese-Soviet operation of the Chinese Eastern and South Manchurian railroads, and the safeguarding in Manchuria of the "preeminent interests of the Soviet Union".

Since China was not a signatory to this agreement, it was provided that President Roosevelt would take steps to secure the concurrence of Generalissimo Chiang Kai-shek. Criticism in the United States of these provisions brought forth the statement by Secretary of State James Byrnes that the memorandum did not control relations between China and the Soviet Union, that when the agreement was signed United States armies "needed all the assistance that could come from a simultaneous attack on the Eastern front", and that he himself had not known of the agreement until September 1945.[1]

On August 14, 1945, these provisions concerning Soviet rights in eastern Asia were incorporated in a series of agreements signed by China and the Soviet Union. These agreements included a treaty of friendship and alliance between the two nations, and several special agreements which (1) made Dairen a free port and gave the Soviet Union a share in its administration, (2) provided for joint use of the naval base at Port Arthur, (3) decreed joint ownership of the Chinese Changchun Railway, and (4) established a basis for Soviet military operations in Manchuria, while recognizing Chinese sovereignty there. An exchange of notes by the two Governments on the same day settled the question of Outer Mongolia, the Chinese Government agreeing to independence for the area if a plebiscite should determine this to be the desire of the Mongolian people.[2]

United States and Soviet relations with China were considered at the Moscow Meeting of the Foreign Ministers of the United Kingdom, United States and the Soviet Union in December 1945. Foreign Minister Molotov and Secretary of State Byrnes discussed the presence of Soviet and United States armed forces in China and agreed that they should be withdrawn at the "earliest practicable moment".[3]

1. GENERAL POLICY

(1) *Treaty of Friendship and Alliance between the Republic of China and the Union of Soviet Socialist Republics, Signed at Moscow, August 14, 1945.*[4]

The President of the National Government of the Republic of China, and the Presidium of the Supreme Soviet of the U.S.S.R.,

Desirous of strengthening the friendly relations that have always existed between China and the U.S.S.R., through an alliance and good neighborly post-war collaboration,

Determined to assist each other in the struggle against aggression on the part of enemies of the United Nations in this world war, and to collaborate in the common war against Japan until her unconditional surrender,

Expressing their unswerving aspiration to cooperate in the cause of maintaining peace and security for the benefit of the peoples of both countries and of all the peace-loving nations,

---

[1] *Ibid.*, XIV, p. 282.
[2] For text of the Sino-Soviet treaty, see below; for text of other agreements, see Department of State, *Bulletin*, XIV, p. 204-8.
[3] For text of agreement, see this volume, p. 829.
[4] Department of State, *Bulletin*, XIV, p. 201.

Acting upon the principles enunciated in the joint declaration of the United Nations of January 1, 1942, in the Four Power Declaration signed in Moscow on October 30, 1943, and in the Charter of the International Organization of the United Nations.

Have decided to conclude the present Treaty to this effect and appointed as their Plenipotentiaries:

The President of the National Government of the Republic of China;
  His Excellency Dr. Wang Shih-chieh, Minister for Foreign Affairs of the Republic of China,
The Presidium of the Supreme Soviet of the U.S.S.R.;
  His Excellency Mr. V. M. Molotov, the People's Commissar of Foreign Affairs of the U.S.S.R.,

Who, after exchanging their Full Powers, found in good and due form, have agreed as follows:

Article I

The High Contracting Parties undertake in association with the other United Nations to wage war against Japan until final victory is won. The High Contracting Parties undertake mutually to render to one another all necessary military and other assistance and support in this war.

Article II

The High Contracting Parties undertake not to enter into separate negotiations with Japan and not to conclude, without mutual consent, any armistice or peace treaty either with the present Japanese Government or with any other government or authority set up in Japan which do not renounce all aggressive intentions.

Article III

The High Contracting Parties undertake after the termination of the war against Japan to take jointly all measures in their power to render impossible a repetition of aggression and violation of the peace by Japan.

In the event of one of the High Contracting Parties becoming involved in hostilities with Japan in consequence of an attack by the latter against the said Contracting Party, the other High Contracting Party shall at once give to the Contracting Party so involved in hostilities all the military and other support and assistance with the means in its power.

This article shall remain in force until such time as the organization "The United Nations" may on request of the two High Contracting Parties be charged with the responsibility for preventing further aggression by Japan.

Article IV

Each High Contracting Party undertakes not to conclude any alliance and not to take any part in any coalition directed against the other High Contracting Party.

Article V

The High Contracting Parties, having regard to the interests of the security and economic development of each of them, agree to work together in close and friendly collaboration after the coming of peace and to act according to the principles of mutual respect for their sovereignty and territorial integrity and of non-interference in the internal affairs of the other contracting party.

Article VI

The High Contracting Parties agree to render each other every possible economic assistance in the post-war period with a view to facilitating and accelerating reconstruction in both countries and to contributing to the cause of world prosperity.

Article VII

Nothing in this treaty shall be so construed as may affect the rights or obligations of the High Contracting Parties as members of the organization "The United Nations".

Article VIII

The present Treaty shall be ratified in the shortest possible time. The exchange of the instruments of ratification shall take place as soon as possible in Chungking.

The Treaty comes into force immediately upon its ratification and shall remain in force for a term of thirty years.

If neither of the High Contracting Parties has given notice, a year before the expiration of the term, of its desire to terminate the Treaty, it shall remain valid for an unlimited time, each of the High Contracting Parties being able to terminate its operation by giving notice to that effect one year in advance.

In faith whereof the Plenipotentiaries have signed the present Treaty and affixed their seals to it.

Done in Moscow, the Fourteenth August, 1945, corresponding to the Fourteenth day of the Eighth month of the Thirty-fourth year of the Chinese Republic, in two copies, each one in the Russian and Chinese languages, both texts being equally authoritative.

(a) *Exchange of Notes between the Minister of Foreign Affairs of China (Wang) and the People's Commissar of Foreign Affairs of the Union of Soviet Socialist Republics (Molotov) Relating to the Treaty of Friendship and Alliance, August 14, 1945.*[1]

(i) *Note from the People's Commissar of Foreign Affairs of the Union of Soviet Socialist Republics to the Minister of Foreign Affairs of China.*

With reference to the Treaty of Friendship and Alliance signed today between the Republic of China and the U.S.S.R., I have the honor to

---

[1] *Ibid.*, p. 204.

put on record the understanding between the High Contracting Parties as follows:

1. In accordance with the spirit of the aforementioned Treaty, and in order to put into effect its aims and purposes, the Government of the U.S.S.R. agrees to render to China moral support and aid in military supplies and other material resources, such support and aid to be entirely given to the National Govermnent as the central government of China.

2. In the course of conversations regarding Dairen and Port Arthur and regarding the joint operation of the Chinese Changchun Railway, the Government of the U.S.S.R. regarded the Three Eastern Provinces as part of China and reaffirmed its respect for China's full sovereignty over the Three Eastern Provinces and recognize their territorial and administrative integrity.

3. As for the recent developments in Sinkiang the Soviet Government confirms that, as stated in Article V of the Treaty of Friendship and Alliance, it has no intention of interfering in the internal affairs of China.

If Your Excellency will be so good as to confirm that the understanding is correct as set forth in the preceding paragraphs, the present note and Your Excellency's reply thereto will constitute a part of the aforementioned Treaty of Friendship and Alliance.

I take this opportunity to offer Your Excellency the assurances of my highest consideration.

(*ii*) *Note from the Minister of Foreign Affairs of China to the People's Commissar of Foreign Affairs of the Union of Soviet Socialist Republics.*

I have the honour to acknowledge receipt of Your Excellency's Note of today's date reading as follows:

[Here follows the text of the above note from V. M. Molotov.]

I have the honour to confirm that the understanding is correct as set forth above.

I avail myself of this opportunity to offer to Your Excellency the assurance of my highest consideration.

(2) **Report of the Meeting of Ministers of Foreign Affairs of the Union of Soviet Socialist Republics, the United States of America, and the United Kingdom, at Moscow, December 27, 1945.**[1]

[Excerpt]

. . . .

IV. China

The three Foreign Secretaries exchanged views with regard to the situation in China. They were in agreement as to the need for a unified and democratic China under the National Government, for broad par-

[1] Department of State Publication 2448, p. 15.

ticipation by democratic elements in all branches of the National Government, and for a cessation of civil strife. They reaffirmed their adherence to the policy of non-interference in the internal affairs of China.

Mr. Molotov and Mr. Byrnes had several conversations concerning Soviet and American armed forces in China.

Mr. Molotov stated that the Soviet forces had disarmed and deported Japanese troops in Manchuria but that withdrawal of Soviet forces had been postponed until February 1st at the request of the Chinese Government.

Mr. Byrnes pointed out that American forces were in north China at the request of the Chinese Government, and referred also to the primary responsibility of the United States in the implementation of the Terms of Surrender with respect to the disarming and deportation of Japanese troops. He stated that American forces would be withdrawn just as soon as this responsibility was discharged or the Chinese Government was in a position to discharge the responsibility without the assistance of American forces.

The two Foreign Secretaries were in complete accord as to the desirability of withdrawal of Soviet and American forces from China at the earliest practicable moment consistent with the discharge of their obligations and responsibilities.

. . . . . .

2. MANCHURIA

On January 16, 1946 the American press reported that since the signing of the Sino-Soviet Treaty of Friendship and Alliance of August 14, 1945 [1] Soviet negotiators in Changchun had sought additional concessions from the Chinese Government, including:

"1. Joint control over certain Japanese-developed heavy industries on the grounds that much Japanese industry here [*i.e.*, in Manchuria] was built up for war against Russia and that Russia had helped defeat Japan in Manchuria.

"2. Soviet commercial air rights and the construction of air fields throughout Manchuria.

"3. Erection of a telephone line from Dairen to Manchouli, western terminus of the Chinese Eastern Railway."[2]

Learning of these discussions, the United States sent identical notes to the Chinese and Soviet Governments, the text of which appears below. The Chinese reply also is printed below. No reply from the Soviet Government was received.

Other communications on the same subject included a Russian reply on March 4, 1946 to a United States note of February 11, a United States note from the Moscow Embassy on March 9 and a Soviet reply of April 22. The contents of this correspondence were withheld.[3] With the receipt of the Soviet reply the United States Government dropped further direct communication upon the subject, pending the results of a survey by Edwin W. Pauley, United States reparations commissioner, on conditions in Manchuria.

On December 13, announcement was made concerning the final report [4] of Ambassador Pauley regarding his Far Eastern mission. The report revealed that Manchurian industry sustained damage amounting to $858,000,000 during Russian occupancy.

[1] For text of treaty, see this volume, p. 826.
[2] *New York Times*, January 17, 1946, p. 1.
[3] *Ibid.*, March 6, 1946, p. 1; *ibid.*, April 26, 1946, p. 11.
[4] For excerpts from the report, see this volume, p. 832.

(1) *Exchange of Notes between the Government of the United States and the Governments of China and the Union of Soviet Socialist Republics Regarding Disposition and Control of Industrial Enterprises in Manchuria.*[1]

(a) *Note Presented to the Government of China and the Government of the Union of Soviet Socialist Republics through the American Embassies in Chungking and Moscow, on Instruction of the Secretary of State (Byrnes) of February 9, 1946.*

Current reports of discussions between officials of the Chinese Government and the Russian Government with regard to the disposition and control of industrial enterprises in Manchuria give concern to this Government.

The Sino-Soviet Treaty and agreements signed August 14, 1945 provide for joint Sino-Soviet control over certain trunk railways in Manchuria, but these agreements exclude reference to any similar control over industrial enterprises in Manchuria. It is the understanding of the United States Government, which was kept informed of the course of negotiations which led up to the agreements of August 1945 and which has accepted those agreements, that exclusive Sino-Soviet governmental control over Manchurian enterprise would be limited to the railways dealt with in the aforesaid agreements. It is therefore disturbing to this Government to receive reports that discussions are under way which might result in the establishment of exclusive Sino-Soviet control over industrial enterprises in Manchuria. Under present conditions, when free access to Manchuria is not open to nationals of other powers and equality of opportunity in seeking participation in the economic development of Manchuria is denied Americans and other Allied nationals, it is felt that negotiation of agreements between the Chinese and Russian Governments with regard to industries in Manchuria would be contrary to the principle of the Open Door, would constitute clear discrimination against Americans who might wish an opportunity to participate in the development of Manchurian industry, and might place American commercial interests at a distinct disadvantage in establishing future trade relations with Manchuria.

Directly related to this matter of the industries in Manchuria is the matter of reparations policy for Japan, because the major portion of the industries of Manchuria were Japanese-owned prior to the defeat of Japan. This Government considers that the ultimate disposition of Japanese external assets, such as the industries in Manchuria, is a matter of common interest and concern to those Allies who bore the major burden in defeating Japan. This Government is now preparing a general policy outline for consideration by the concerned governments with regard to Japanese reparations. It will be suggested that an Inter-Allied Reparations Commission for Japan be established, and that one of the primary functions of this Commission will be the final allocation of Japanese external assets among the various claimant nations. It would

[1] Department of State, *Bulletin*, XIV, p. 448.

seem, therefore, most inappropriate at this juncture for any final disposition to be made of Japanese external assets in Manchuria either by removal from Manchuria of such industrial assets as "war booty" or by agreement between the Russian and Chinese Governments for the control of ownership of those assets.

The Government of the United States desires to be cooperative with the Chinese and Soviet Governments in seeking a solution of the problems outlined above and it hopes that the other two Governments are animated by a similarly cooperative spirit. It would therefore appreciate being informed of any discussions which the two Governments may be having or may plan to have or any action they may have taken, in regard to the disposition or control of industrial enterprises in Manchuria and we would welcome full and frank discussion of the general problem.

(b) *Partial Text of Reply from the Chinese Foreign Office to the Secretary of State, Released to the Press, March 5, 1946.*

The Soviet Government declared in a memorandum addressed to Chinese Government on January 21, 1946 that all Japanese enterprises in the Chinese northeastern provinces which had rendered services to the Japanese Army were regarded by Soviet Union as war booty of Soviet forces. The Chinese Government considers this claim of Soviet Government as far exceeding the scope of war booty as generally recognized by international law and international usage and for this reason the two governments have not been able to reach a unanimity of views of fundamental principles involved.

In another memorandum presented to officials of the Generalissimo's Headquarters in Changchun the Soviet Government declared that it proposed to hand over to China a part of the Japanese enterprises which Soviet Union regarded as war booty while remaining enterprises (including specified coal mines, power plants, iron and steel industries, chemical industries and cement industries) were to be jointly operated by China and Soviet Union. Chinese Government on its part has found it impossible to agree to this Soviet proposal because it goes beyond provisions of the Sino-Soviet agreements of August 14, 1945 and is contrary to the aforesaid stand of Chinese Government regarding Japanese properties and enterprises in China.

(2) *Report by the United States Reparations Representative (Pauley) Concerning Industrial Conditions in Manchuria.*[1]

[Excerpts]

· · · · ·

The difference in condition of the Manchurian industrial plant between Japanese surrender and the dates the Pauley mission made its survey is appalling. How much of the wrecked condition is a direct result of Soviet removals, and how much may be ascribed to pillage, civil war, and in-

[1] *Ibid.*, XV, p. 1154. Completion of the report was announced on December 13, 1946.

direct consequences of the Soviet occupation cannot be accurately determined.

. . . .

During the years before and after Pearl Harbor, the Japanese had created in Manchuria a tremendous industrial structure which was definitely tributary to the economy of Japan.

Had this structure remained as intact as it was on the date of Soviet occupancy and had China remained peaceful, the Manchurian industrial complex could have readily been integrated with China's growing economy, and so greatly accelerated the over-all Chinese industrial development.

The large capacities in basic industries in Manchuria would have made possible a rapid absorption by China of further processing equipment removed from Japan as reparations. At the same time, this action would have lopped off from Japan one of the most important sources of strength in the Japanese war potential. It was presumed that China could fill at least partially the economic vacuum resulting from the Japanese defeat and the consequent imposed reduction of Japan's productive capacity to a peacetime level.

. . . .

United States policy has long held that all Japanese assets, whether situated in Japan proper or in other areas, were subject to removal as Allied reparations. Japanese assets in conquered areas such as the Philippines, China, including Manchuria and Korea, were to be taken from Japanese ownership and control and were to be operated for the benefit of the countries where the physical assets exist. It was considered that this primary step was necessary in order to strengthen the economies of the countries which had been victims of Japanese aggression and further to keep the facilities operating in order to prevent loss of needed production and safeguard the livelihood of the local population.

. . . .

Soviet forces entered Manchuria on August 8, 1945. Japanese resistance was confined to northern Manchuria and within a week this ended. Southern Manchuria, which contained over 80 percent of Manchurian industry, was taken practically unopposed and with little if any damage. There was ample opportunity for the orderly occupation of the entire area.

Upon their arrival, the Soviets began a systematic confiscation of food and other stock piles and in early September, started the selective removal of industrial machinery. It is apparent that they planned to complete these removals by December 3, 1945, the date originally set for the withdrawal of all Soviet military forces from Manchuria.

The term *stripping* as it has been used in the press in connection with removals from Manchuria is a misnomer. The Soviets did not take everything. They concentrated on certain categories of supplies, machinery, and equipment. In addition to taking stock piles and certain complete industrial installations, the Soviets took by far the larger part of all functioning power generating and transforming equipment, electric motors, experimental plants, laboratories, and hospitals. In machine tools, they took only the newest and best, leaving antiquated tools behind. In the old Mukden Arsenal, for example, about one third of the tools were taken, while in the new Arsenal, virtually everything was taken or demolished.

Not only were buildings and structures damaged by the removal of the equipment but the taking of some key equipment, such as generators and pumps from mines resulted in the loss of current production, and in irreparable damage to the mines by flooding. The removal of power facilities not only halted all current industrial production but also made it impossible to maintain and protect the plants themselves.

By far the greatest part of the damage to the Manchurian industrial complex occurred during the Soviet occupation and was primarily due to Soviet removals of equipment. After the Soviet withdrawal, Chinese Communist action resulted in further damage to some of the installations.

. . . .

It is generally agreed that China's first economic need is communications, principally railways, transport, and domestic shipping. Less than 10,000 miles of railway is in existence in all of China exclusive of Manchuria and less than half of that is now operable. Manchuria with its abundant natural resources and industrial plant would have been the logical point to begin the rehabilitation of China's transport. If Manchurian industry had been left intact it could also have produced the steel, machinery, and consumer goods so badly needed for restoration and for new construction in China.

China's continuing internal strife is a major factor in retarding her economic recovery. But even this cannot minimize the powerful setback which the destruction of the Manchurian industrial plant has been to Manchuria, to China, and to the Far Eastern world.

. . . .

B. Korea

[See *Documents, VII, 1944–1945*, p. 230.]

In accordance with a wartime decision which had established the 38th parallel as the boundary between American and Soviet military and naval operations, General Order No. 1 of the Supreme Commander of the Allied Powers (MacArthur) to the Japanese Government on September 2, 1945, provided for surrender of Japanese troops in Korea south of that line to United States forces, while those to the north were to surrender to Soviet forces. United States troops entered southern Korea on September 8, 1945, and the formal surrender of Japanese troops took place the following day. Soviet troops had previously occupied north Korea.

Military occupation of the country and its division into zones was regarded as a temporary expedient, in line with the decision of the Cairo Conference in December, 1943, "that in due course Korea shall be free and independent",[1] a decision which had been confirmed at the Potsdam Conference in August 1945

---

[1] For statement of the Cairo Conference, see *Documents, VI, 1943–1944*, p. 232–3.

EASTERN ASIA AND THE PACIFIC AREA 835

and again at the time of the entry of the Soviet Union into the war with Japan.[1] However, because of the political vacuum caused by removal of Japanese officials, the American commander, Lt. General John R. Hodge, found it necessary to assume major governmental responsibility in south Korea, and his attempts to maintain the unity of Korea, through negotiation with the Soviet commander in the north, were without result. On November 16, 1945, the Department of State announced that the question of reintegration and unification of Korea had been taken up with the Soviet Government in Moscow, and that the United States was "making every effort to improve the situation in Korea." [2]

Following preliminary conversations between the two Governments, the Korean question was discussed at the meeting of foreign ministers of the United Kingdom, United States and the Soviet Union in Moscow in December 1945. The ministers agreed to establish a Joint Commission of United States and Soviet representatives, to assist in the formation of a provisional Korean Government, and proposed the negotiation of a trusteeship agreement for that country, with the Soviet Union, China, the United Kingdom and the United States as trustee powers.[3] Following announcement of these decisions, stoppages of work were organized in Seoul, capital of the American zone, and street-brawls and rioting led to imposition of a curfew for Americans. The United States commander, General Hodge, told the Seoul press that the decisions did not necessarily mean trusteeship.[4]

The Moscow conference also provided for the consideration of urgent economic and administrative problems by a Joint Conference, composed of ten representatives from each Korean command, which met in Seoul from January 16 through February 5, 1946. Early discussions indicated divergent approaches to the problem, the American delegation seeking a broad solution which would bring a large amount of economic unification, while the Soviet delegation desired discussion on a limited number of topics such as flow of electric power, reestablishment of rail and auto traffic, and exchange of certain commodities and equipment. The conference reached limited agreement only in the fields of mail exchange, allocation of radio frequencies, liaison between the two commands, transportation, and movements of persons between the two zones. Implementation of even these agreements was not successful, and only those dealing with exchange of mail and military liaison teams were carried out.[5]

On March 20, 1946, the Joint Commission provided for in the Moscow Agreement convened in Seoul. At the outset of the discussions, the Soviet delegation raised the issue of "anti-trusteeship activity", and maintained that no group which had protested against the Moscow Agreement should be consulted in the formation of a provisional Korean Government; this proposal was opposed by the American delegation, since a large proportion of the population would thus be excluded from consultation. This difference in viewpoint was thought to be resolved on April 18, when the Commission agreed to Communiqué No. 5,[6] which declared willingness to consult with groups "truly democratic in their aims and methods", which would uphold the Moscow Agreement and decisions of the Joint Commission. Following approval of the communiqué, however, the Soviet delegation insisted that no party could be represented by an individual who had opposed trusteeship; this was interpreted by the United States delegation as violating the principle of freedom of speech. On May 8, 1946, the Commission adjourned *sine die*.

The following day General Hodge sent to the Soviet commander, Guard Colonel General Ivan M. Chistiakov, the first of a series of letters seeking resump-

---

[1] For statement at Potsdam, see this volume, Appendix II. For U.S.S.R. declaration of war against Japan, see *ibid.*, p. 848.
[2] Department of State, *Bulletin*, XIII, p. 812.
[3] For text of the foreign ministers' statement, see this volume, p. 836.
[4] *Chronology of International Events and Documents*, II, p. 779.
[5] *Korea's Independence*, Department of State Publication 2933, Far Eastern Series 18.
[6] For text, see this volume, p. 837.

tion of negotiations, and attempting to secure agreement on the issues of party consultation and "anti-trusteeship activity". Despite an exchange of letters which continued until January 28, 1947, these differences were not resolved and the Joint Commission remained adjourned.[1]

Pending further meetings of the Commission, the two zones continued to be separately administered by the United States and Soviet commanders. In the United States zone, a military government, paralleling in organization the Government General in Seoul, had been proclaimed on September 7, 1945; the personnel of the Government General, predominantly Japanese, was for the most part dismissed. A program to train Koreans to take over governmental activities of all kinds was launched, and Korean Advisory Councils were established on local as well as national levels in October 1945. Eventual creation of a Provisional Korean Government was sought through attempts at coalition of the major political parties.

In February 1946 a Representative Democratic Council of South Korea was organized to advise the military governor, Major General Archibald V. Lerch, in the formation of such a government, while in October a Korean Interim Legislative Assembly, composed of forty-five elected members and forty-five members appointed by the military government, was created and the first elections held. The assembly met for the first time in December 1946.[2]

(1) *Report of the Meeting of the Ministers of Foreign Affairs of the Union of Soviet Socialist Republics, the United States of America, and the United Kingdom, at Moscow, December 27, 1945.*[3]

[Excerpt]

. . . . . .

III. KOREA

1. With a view to the re-establishment of Korea as an independent state, the creation of conditions for developing the country on democratic principles and the earliest possible liquidation of the disastrous results of the protracted Japanese domination in Korea, there shall be set up a provisional Korean democratic government which shall take all the necessary steps for developing the industry, transport and agriculture of Korea and the national culture of the Korean people.

2. In order to assist the formation of a provisional Korean government and with a view to the preliminary elaboration of the appropriate measures, there shall be established a Joint Commission consisting of representatives of the United States command in southern Korea and the Soviet command in northern Korea. In preparing their proposals the Commission shall consult with the Korean democratic parties and social

[1] For texts of various letters between General Hodge and General Chistiakov, see *ibid.*, p. 838.

[2] For information concerning administration in the American zone in Korea, see Supreme Commander for the Allied Powers, *Summation of Non-Military Activities in Japan and Korea*, Nos. 1–5, September-October 1945 to February 1946, and *Summation of United States Army Military Government Activities in Korea*, Nos. 6–15, March to December 1946. Charts outlining governmental organization are contained in No. 12, September 1946. For information concerning the Soviet zone, see Washburn, J. N., "Russia Looks at Northern Korea." *Pacific Affairs*, June 1947, and two articles from *Pravda* and *Izvestia*, translated in the *Soviet Press Translations* of the Far Eastern Institute, Univ. of Washington, I, No. 4 (December 14, 1946).

[3] Department of State Publication 2448, p. 14.

organizations. The recommendations worked out by the Commission shall be presented for the consideration of the Governments of the Union of Soviet Socialist Republics, China, the United Kingdom and the United States prior to final decision by the two Governments represented on the Joint Commission.

3. It shall be the task of the Joint Commission, with the participation of the provisional Korean democratic government and of the Korean democratic organizations to work out measures also for helping and assisting (trusteeship) the political, economic and social progress of the Korean people, the development of democratic self-government and the establishment of the national independence of Korea.

The proposals of the Joint Commission shall be submitted, following consultation with the provisional Korean Government for the joint consideration of the Governments of the United States, Union of Soviet Socialist Republics, United Kingdom and China for the working out of an agreement concerning a four-power trusteeship of Korea for a period of up to five years.

4. For the consideration of urgent problems affecting both southern and northern Korea and for the elaboration of measures establishing permanent coordination in administrative-economic matters between the United States command in southern Korea and the Soviet command in northern Korea, a conference of the representatives of the United States and Soviet commands in Korea shall be convened within a period of two weeks.

. . . .

(2) *Communiqué No. 5 of the United States-Soviet Joint Commission, Issued at Seoul, April 18, 1946.*[1]

The U.S.-Soviet Joint Commission continued discussion on the question of conditions of consultation with democratic parties and social organizations. Col. Gen. T. F. Shtikov, Chief of the Soviet Delegation, was chairman on sessions held on April 8, 9, 11, and 13, 1946, in the Tuk Soo Palace, Seoul, Korea, and Maj. Gen. A. V. Arnold, chief of the U.S. delegation, was chairman at the session, April 17, 1946.

As a result of a thorough investigation and analysis of the points of view of the Soviet delegation and the delegation of the United States, the Joint Commission reached the following decision on the first point of the joint program of work covering the conditions of the consultation with democratic parties and social organizations:

DECISION

The Joint Commission will consult with Korean democratic parties and social organizations which are truly democratic in their aims and methods and which will subscribe to the following declarations:

We .... declare that we will uphold the aims of the Moscow Decision on Korea as stated in paragraph 1 of this decision, namely:

The reestablishment of Korea as an independent state, the creation of conditions for developing the country on democratic principles, and the earliest

[1] Issued at Seoul over the signatures of Col. Gen. T. F. Shtikov and Maj. Gen. A. V. Arnold. Department of State, *Bulletin*, XVI, p. 173.

possible liquidation of the disastrous results of the protracted Japanese domination in Korea. Further, we will abide by the decisions of the Joint Commission in its fulfilment of paragraph 2 of the Moscow decision in the formation of a Provisional Korean Democratic Government; further, we will cooperate with the Joint Commission in the working out by it with the participation of the Provisional Korean Democratic Government of proposals concerning measures foreseen by paragraph 3 of the Moscow decision.

Signed ....
Representing the ....
Party or Organization

The procedure for inviting representatives of Korean democratic parties and social organizations to consult with the Joint Commission is being worked out by Joint Sub-Commission No. 1. When details of the procedure are completed it will be announced publicly.

(3) *Exchange of Letters between the Commanding General of the United States Army Forces in South Korea (Hodge), and the Commanding General of the Soviet Forces in North Korea (Chistiakov).*[1]

(a) *Letter from General Hodge to General Chistiakov, November 1, 1946.*

[Excerpt]

* * * * *

For the purposes of reconciling the differences between the United States and the U.S.S.R. delegations, which are not fully resolved in your letter, I propose that the following basis of agreement for reconvening the joint U.S.–U.S.S.R. Commission be accepted by both the Soviet and American delegations with view to the early resumption of the sessions of the Joint Commission. It is agreed to interpret paragraph Two and Three of the declaration in communiqué no. 5 of the U.S.–U.S.S.R. Joint Commission dated April 17th, 1946, to mean that such individuals, parties and social organizations shall not foment or instigate mass opposition to the work of the Joint Commission or the fulfilment of the Moscow decision. Those individuals, parties, and social organizations which do foment or instigate such opposition shall be excluded from further consultation with the Joint Commission. The decision excluding such individuals, parties, and social organizations shall be by agreement of the Joint Commission.

In consideration of this interpretation of the declaration established in communiqué no. 5 of the Joint Commission, dated April 17th, 1946, both delegations agree that they will not oppose consultation with any individual, political party, or social organization which subscribes to and abides by the declaration published in joint communiqué no. 5.

In order to eliminate any possible future misunderstanding, I believe it is advisable briefly to restate the position of the United States at this time.

[1] Department of State Publication 2933, p. 26.

(A) The United States has always favored the exact fulfilment of the Moscow decision by the Joint Commission. This decision obviously includes the preparation of proposals "for the working out of an agreement concerning a Four Power trusteeship of Korea for a period of up to five years" which "shall be submitted for the joint consideration" of the Four Powers "following consultation with the provisional Korean Government". However, there is nothing in the Moscow decision which predetermines the terms or nature of a Four Power trusteeship except that it shall be a method "for helping and assisting (trusteeship) the political, economic and social progress of the Korean people, the development of democratic self-government, and the establishment of the national independence of Korea" to be worked out "with the participation of the Provisional Korean Democratic Government," and a limitation placed upon its duration.

(B) The United States has always favored the exercise of freedom of speech in Korea. The United States believes that all Korean democratic parties and social organizations should be permitted to make known their desires in the formation of their own government. The representatives of the United States see a great difference between (1) the instigation of mass opposition to the work of the Joint Commission and the fulfilment of the Moscow decision, and (2) the proper exercise of freedom of expression by Korean individuals, democratic parties, and groups concerning their wishes and desires in the formation of their own government.

On the basis of the United States' position herein stated and the suggested interpretation of paragraphs Two and Three of the declaration in communiqué no. 5 to the Joint Commission which is approved for the United States delegation, the American Command proposes that the Joint Commission resume its work without delay and I again cordially invite Soviet delegation to return to Seoul at an early date for the purpose of resuming negotiations. I shall be pleased to hear from you as early as possible in order that the necessary preliminary arrangements can be effected.

(b) *Letter from General Chistiakov to General Hodge, November 26, 1946.*

I acknowledge the receipt of your letter dated November 1, 1946.

It is with regret that I have to conclude that the conditions upon which you propose to renew the negotiations of the Joint Soviet-American Commission in substance do not differ from the position laid down in your previous letter, which, in the opinion of the Soviet delegation is in contradiction to the Moscow Decision on Korea.

Actually, you propose that the Joint Commission should consult with any person, political party or social organization which adheres to and abides by the declaration published in communiqué number 5, moreover, such persons, parties or social organizations must not and will not instigate or foment mass opposition to the work of the Joint Commission or the fulfillment of the Moscow Decision.

Thus, according to this formula, the Joint Commission must consult not only with democratic parties and social organizations which uphold the Moscow decision, but also with those parties and organizations which are hostile to this Decision. Furthermore, these latter parties and organizations are even given an opportunity to continue these activities directly against the Moscow Decision with the exception that they should not instigate or foment mass opposition to the work of the Joint Commission or the fulfillment of the Moscow Decision.

The acceptance of such proposal would appear, rather as call to reactionary parties and groups not to retreat from their hostile position towards the Moscow Decision, but merely to curtail temporarily their activities directed against this Decision so that they may have an opportunity to take part in the consultations with the Joint Commission. I must remind you that it was precisely in such manner that these parties accepted your public announcement of April 27, 1946 which contained an analogous interpretation of the agreement embodied in communiqué number 5.

The result was that the parties and organizations which had voiced their opposition to the Moscow Decision agreed to sign the declaration, but on the very second day after the termination of the work of the Joint Commission, prominent leaders of these parties and organizations again returned to an active fight against the Moscow Decision and its supporters.

There is no doubt that participation by those elements in the consultations would be utilized by them with the aim of sabotaging the fulfillment of the Moscow Decision and would only facilitate their activities in that direction. I must again declare that if we are aiming at actual and complete realization of the Moscow Decision on Korea, then, in the opinion of the Soviet delegation, it is impossible to consult on the question of methods of fulfilling this Decision with those persons, parties and organizations who voice opposition to the above mentioned Decision and who are aiming at sabotaging its fulfillment, whom, for tactical considerations, may for the period of consultation with the Joint Commission temporarily and in part limit their activities directed against the Moscow Decision in order that they may renew these activities in full force as soon as consultation with Joint Commission is terminated.

The foregoing in no way limits the freedom of Korean democratic parties, social organizations or individuals to express their position regarding the formation of the Korean Government or other questions connected with the realization of the Moscow Decision on Korea.

In my previous letter I have already directed your attention to the fact that the Soviet delegation has never made proposals directed against the freedom of individuals, parties or organizations to express anywhere their views on these questions and it is accordingly understood that any party or social organization as well as an individual Korean citizen can express similar views or present them to the Joint Commission.

Desiring to fulfill the Moscow Decision on Korea speedily and as definitely as possible, the Soviet side advances the following proposals as basis for the resumption of the work of the Joint Soviet-American Commission.

1. The Joint Commission must consult those democratic parties and organizations which uphold fully the Moscow Decision on Korea.

2. Parties or social organizations invited for consultation with the Joint Commission must not nominate for consultation those representatives who have compromised themselves by actively voicing opposition to the Moscow Decision.

3. Parties and social organizations invited for consultation with the Joint Commission must not and will not voice opposition nor will they incite others to voice opposition to the Moscow Decision and the work of the Joint Commission. If such be the case such parties and social organizations, by mutual agreement of both delegations, will be excluded from further consultations with the Joint Commission.

In the event you should agree to the foregoing proposals the Soviet delegation is prepared, without delay, to arrive in Seoul for the resumption of the negotiations of the Joint Commission.

(c) *Letter from General Hodge to General Chistiakov, December 24, 1946.*

[Excerpts]

I wish to acknowledge receipt of your letter of November 26, 1946.

. . . . . .

From a careful reading of Paragraphs II to VIII, both inclusive, the impression I receive is that the Soviet delegation believes that proposals previously submitted by the United States delegation appear to encourage "reactionary parties and groups" to continue hostile opposition to the Moscow Decision. I assure you that the United States delegation has no such intention and desires to cooperate with you in preventing such hostile opposition. Paragraphs IX and X of your letter guarantee on the part of the Soviet delegation complete freedom of expression to Korean political parties, social organizations and individuals "regarding the formation of the Korean Government and other questions connected with the realization of the Moscow Decision on Korea." The views expressed in these paragraphs are identical with the position assumed by the United States delegation.

The last three paragraphs of your letter numbered 1 to 3, although apparently in conflict with paragraphs IX and X nevertheless provide a basis for further discussion.

In view of the closeness of our position, I suggest that your proposals and the following modifications be made the basis for reconvening the Joint Commission.

Proposal number 1 to be interpreted as follows: Signing the Declaration in communiqué number 5 will be accepted as a declaration of good faith with respect to upholding fully the Moscow Decision and will make the signatory party or organization eligible for initial consultation.

Proposal number 2, I consider it the right of a declarant party or organization to appoint the representative which it believes will best present to the Joint Commission its views of the implementation of the

Moscow Decision. However, should such representative for good reason be believed to be antagonistic to the implementation of the Moscow Decision or to either of the Allied Powers, the Joint Commission may, after mutual agreement, require the declarant party to name a substitute spokesman.

Proposal number 3, it is suggested that it be reworded as follows: "Individuals, parties and social organizations invited for consultation with the Joint Commission shall not after signing the declaration contained in communiqué number 5 foment or instigate active opposition to the work of the Joint Commission or to either of the Allied Powers or the fulfillment of the Moscow Decision. Those individuals, parties and social organizations which after signing the declaration contained in communiqué number 5 do foment or instigate active opposition to the work of the Joint Commission or to either of the Allied Powers or to the fulfillment of the Moscow Decision shall be excluded from further consultation with the Joint Commission. The decision excluding such individuals, parties and social organizations shall be by agreement of the Joint Commission".

I trust that the basis proposed above will be acceptable to you and trust you will notify me so that I may make the necessary preliminary arrangements for reconvening the Joint Commission.

CHAPTER XVI

EUROPE AND WESTERN ASIA

1. RELATIONS WITH PARTICULAR EUROPEAN COUNTRIES

A. The United Kingdom

Relations between the United States and the United Kingdom for the period under review fall into three general categories: (1) those relating to the functioning of the United Nations; (2) those of a quadrilateral character relating to occupation matters and the framing of the peace treaties; and (3) those of a less general and/or bilateral nature relating to regional organizations, commodity arrangements and normal diplomatic intercourse. For the most part these have been documented elsewhere in this volume.

In the first category, information on British-United States relations within the general framework of the United Nations will be found on p. 508–530; on the International Trade Organization, p. 624; on the International Refugee Organization, p. 393; on the World Health Organization, p. 732; on regulation and reduction of armaments, p. 530; on international control of atomic energy, p. 544. Information on British-United States relations in the occupation of Germany will be found on p. 186; of Austria, p. 283; and of Japan, p. 266. Information on the punishment of war criminals and on the Far Eastern Commission will be found on p. 341 and p. 275 respectively. The activities of the Council of Foreign Ministers in framing the peace treaties with Bulgaria, Finland, Hungary, Italy and Rumania are dealt with in *The First Five Peace Treaties. Supplement: Documents, VIII, 1945–1946*. Information on British-United States relations in the third category will be found as follows: the Anglo-American Committee of Inquiry and relations concerning Palestine, p. 908 and 902, respectively; the Caribbean Commission, p. 598; financial and trade negotiations, p. 643; telecommunications and civil aviation agreements, p. 693 and 666; disposal of surplus war materials, p. 132; commodity agreements and negotiations concerning petroleum, tin and wheat, p. 708, 713 and 714; joint observance of the Greek elections, p. 878; and labor and social problems, p. 284.

(1) *Address by the Prime Minister of the United Kingdom (Attlee) before a Joint Session of the Congress, November 13, 1945.*[1]

[Excerpt]

On October 30, 1945 the White House announced the impending visit to Washington early in November of Prime Minister Clement Attlee to discuss with President Truman and with Prime Minister Mackenzie King of Canada, the problems arising from the discovery of atomic energy.[2] Mr. Attlee arrived in Washington on November 10, and informal discussions were immediately begun.[3] In the course of his visit, Mr. Attlee, on November 13, addressed a joint session of the Congress on the subject of relations between the United States and the United Kingdom.

. . . .

---

[1] *Congressional Record*, 91, p. 10788 (Daily edition, November 13, 1945).
[2] Department of State, *Bulletin*, XIII, p. 714.
[3] *Ibid.*, p. 766. For the text of the Joint Declaration issued at the conclusion of these discussions, see this volume, p. 547.

What is our attitude toward foreign affairs? We believe that we cannot make a heaven in our own country and leave a hell outside and we believe this not only from the moral basis of our movement which is founded on the brotherhood of man, without distinction of race or creed, but also from an entirely practical standpoint. We seek to raise the standard of life of our people. We can only do so by trading with the rest of the world and as good traders we wish to have prosperous customers. The advance in methods of production so strongly exemplified in the United States results in an immense output of goods and commodities of all kinds. We in our turn show the same results on a smaller scale. Yet there are hundreds of millions of people living in the world at a standard of life which is the same as they have had for a thousand years. There is ample room in the world for the products of the great industrial nations like yours and ours to raise the general levels throughout the world. We like you believe in an expansive economy and we can see no reason why the need being so great there should be any undue rivalry between us. We believe that the foundations of peace must be world prosperity and good neighborliness. That where science has placed such potential abundance before the human race we should collaborate to take advantage of it rather than scramble and fight for larger individual shares which only results in an immense increase in poverty. We recognize that our immediate task is not easy. Many a man in Britain returning from the war finds his home blitzed and his business ruined. He has to start afresh and it is a tough proposition.

As a country we are just like that man. We went all out to win the war and now have to start afresh. Like him we are facing the future with courage and a determination to win through. We have not stood up to our enemies for 6 years to be beaten by economics.

I look forward to an era of an increasing cooperation and friendship between the United States of America and Great Britain — not as being an exclusive friendship but as a contribution to the knitting together with all peoples through the United Nations Organization in the bonds of peace.

In our internal policies each will follow the course decided by the peoples' will. You will see us embarking on projects of nationalization; on wide all-embracing schemes of social insurance designed to give security to the common man. We shall be working out a planned economy. You, it may be, will continue in your more individualistic methods. It is more important that we should understand each other and other nations whose institutions differ from our own. It is essential if we are to build up a peaceful world that we should have the widest toleration recognizing that our aim is not uniformity but unity in diversity. It would be a dull world if we were all alike.

In a town there may be a great diversity of character and habit among the townsfolk. To some of my neighbors I may be drawn closely by ties of relationship or by old memories; for others I may have more sympathy through sharing their religious convictions, although perhaps I am estranged by their political views. Yet I may be on good terms with all of them and in close friendship with some. I hope to see a world as orderly as a well-run town, with citizens diverse in character but cooperating for the common good. In the British Commonwealth and Empire we offer an example of many nations, some of which have reached, others of which are approaching, full self-government. Even during the war India was given the opportunity of taking complete charge of her own affairs, and in the Colonial Empire eight or nine new constitutions have been adopted or are being worked out — all based on the extension of democratic principles. I hope that there will be even closer friendship between our great democracies. We have much in common. We have the language of Milton and Shakespeare, of Burke and Chatham, of Lincoln and Jefferson. We have the memories of comradeship in a great adventure. Above all things, we share the things of the spirit. Both of our nations hold dear the rule of law; the conception of freedom and the principles and methods of democracy; and, most vital of all, we acknowledge the validity of the moral precepts upon which our whole civilization is founded. Man's material discoveries have outpaced his moral progress. The greatest task that faces us today is to bring home to all people before it is too late that our civilization can only survive by the acceptance and practice in international relations and in our national life of the Christian principle we are all members one of another.

B. The Union of Soviet Socialist Republics

For information on Soviet-United States relations within the general framework of the United Nations, see p. 508–530; on regulation and reduction of armaments, p. 530; and on the international control of atomic energy, p. 544. Relations with the Soviet Union in the occupation of Germany are dealt with on p. 186; in the occupation of Austria, on p. 283; and in the occupation of Japan, on p. 266. The activities of the Council of Foreign Ministers in framing the peace treaties with Bulgaria, Finland, Hungary, Italy and Rumania are discussed in *The First Five Peace Treaties. Supplement: Documents, VIII, 1945–1946*. Soviet-United States relations concerning lend-lease and mutual aid settlements are described on p. 127.

Since, to a large degree, relations between the United States and the Soviet Union during the period under review centered around the policy of one or both countries with regard to a third state, information on relations with third states is included in the following section.

1. GENERAL

(1) *Order of the Day, Issued by the Chairman of the Council of People's Commissars of the Union of Soviet Socialist Republics (Stalin), April 30, 1946.*[1]

[Excerpts]

[Translation]

. . . .

In the vanguard of the struggle for peace and security marches the Soviet Union, which played an outstanding part in smashing fascism and fulfilled its great mission of liberation. The nations liberated by the Soviet Union from the Fascist yoke received an opportunity of

[1] *New York Times*, May 1, 1946, p. 1. The above text is that recorded by the Soviet monitor station in London.

building their state life on democratic foundations, of realizing their historical aspirations. On this road they find fraternal assistance on the part of the Soviet Union.

The entire world has had an opportunity to convince itself, not only of the might of the Soviet Union, but also of the fairness of its policy based on the recognition of equality of all peoples, respect for their freedom and independence.

There is no reason to doubt that in the future the Soviet Union will be true to its policy, the policy of peace and security, the policy of the equality and friendship of peoples.

. . . . . .

Upon the termination of the war, the Soviet Union started peaceful Socialist construction. The Soviet people enthusiastically set about peaceful constructive labor, which had been interrupted by the war. The law on the Five-Year Plan of restoration and development of the national economy of the U.S.S.R. in the period from 1946 to 1950, adopted by Supreme Soviet of the U.S.S.R., opens new prospects of further growth of the productive forces of our own country, the growth of her economic might, the rise of her material welfare and culture.

Developing peaceful Socialist construction, we should not forget for a single minute the intrigues of international reaction, which is hatching plans of a new war. It is necessary to remember the teaching of the great Lenin to the effect that after switching over to peaceful labor, it is necessary to be constantly vigilant, to protect as the apple of one's eye, the armed forces and defensive power of our country.

The armed forces of the Soviet Union — our land troops, air forces and navy — discharged their duty to the country in the Great Patriotic War. Now our armed forces are faced with a task of no less importance, vigilantly to guard the peace which was won and the constructive labor of the Soviet people, to be the reliable bulwark of interests of the Soviet Union.

The successful accomplishment of this honorable task is possible only on condition of further growth of military culture and military skill of the officers and men of our army, our navy and our aviation. The armed forces of the Soviet Union must daily improve their military art on the basis of experience of war, on the basis of the progress of military science and technique. Beyond any doubt, our army, our navy and our aviation will accomplish all those tasks facing them.

. . . . . .

(2) *Interview Granted by the Chairman of the Council of People's Commissars of the Union of Soviet Socialist Republics (Stalin) to the London* Sunday Times, *September 24, 1946.*[1]

Q. Do you believe in a real danger of a "new war," about which at the present time so much irresponsible talk is being carried on? What steps should be taken for preventing war if such danger exists?

[1] *Ibid.*, September 25, 1946, p. 3.

A. I do not believe in a real danger of a "new war." The noise is being raised about a "new war" mainly by military-political scouts and their few supporters from the ranks of civilian officials.

They need this noise if only (A) to frighten with the specter of war some naïve politicians from the ranks of their counter-agents and thereby aid their Governments to extract more concessions; (B) to make difficult for some time the reduction of military budgets in their countries; (C) to check demobilization of troops and thereby prevent quick growth of unemployment in their countries.

It is necessary to distinguish sharply between the noise about a "new war," which is being carried on now, and the real danger of a "new war," which does not at present exist.

Q. Do you think that Great Britain and the United States consciously are forming a "capitalistic encirclement" of the Soviet Union?

A. I do not think the ruling circles of Great Britain and the United States of America could create a "capitalistic encirclement" of the Soviet Union even if they wanted to do this, which, however, we cannot affirm.

Q. Speaking in the words Mr. Wallace used in his last speech, can England, western Europe and the United States be assured that Soviet politics in Germany will not be turned into a weapon of Russian efforts directed against western Europe?

A. I believe using Germany by the Soviet Union against western Europe and the United States of America is excluded. I believe this is excluded not only because the Soviet Union is bound by a treaty of mutual assistance against German aggression with Great Britain and France, and with the United States of America by the decisions of the Potsdam Conference of the three Great Powers; but also because the politics of using Germany against western Europe and the United States of America would mean a departure of the Soviet Union from its fundamental national interests.

Speaking briefly, the politics of the Soviet Union in the German question comes down to demilitarization and democratization of Germany. I think that demilitarization and democratization of Germany presents one of the most important guarantees for the establishment of a sound and lasting peace.

Q. What is your opinion about the accusation that the policies of Communist parties in western Europe are "dictated by Moscow?"

A. I consider this accusation absurd and to be borrowed from the bankrupt arsenal of Hitler and Goebbels.

Q. Do you believe in the possibility of a friendly and lasting collaboration of the Soviet Union and western democracy despite the existence of ideological discord, and in friendly competition between the two systems, of which Wallace spoke in his speech?

A. I do, unconditionally.

Q. During the sojourn here of the [British] Labor party delegation, you, as I understood it, expressed belief in the possibility of friendly relations between the Soviet Union and Great Britain. What could help in the establishment of these relations, which are so eagerly desired by the broad masses of the English people?

A. I really believe in the possibility of friendly relations between the Soviet Union and Great Britain. Establishment of such relations would be appreciably helped by strengthening political, trade and cultural relations between these countries.

Q. Do you believe that the quickest withdrawal of all American forces in China is vitally necessary for the future of peace?

A. Yes, I do.

Q. Do you believe that the actual monopoly possession of the atomic bomb by the United States of America is one of the principal threats to peace?

A. I do not believe the atomic bomb to be as serious a force as certain politicians are inclined to regard it. Atomic bombs are intended for intimidating weak nerves, but they cannot decide the outcome of war, since atomic bombs are by no means sufficient for this purpose. Certainly monopolist possession of the secret of the atomic bomb does create a threat, but at least two remedies exist against it:

(A) Monopolist possession of the atomic bomb cannot last long.

(B) Use of the atomic bomb will be prohibited.

Q. Do you suppose that with the further advance of the Soviet Union toward Communism the possibilities for peaceful collaboration with the outside world will not decrease in so far as this concerns the Soviet Union? Is "Communism in one country" possible?

A. I do not doubt that the possibilities for peaceful collaboration not only will not decrease, but can even increase. "Communism in one country" is fully possible, especially in such a country as the Soviet Union.

2. THE PROSECUTION OF THE WAR AGAINST JAPAN

(1) *Announcement of the Soviet Declaration of War Against the Japanese Government, Made by the People's Commissar for Foreign Affairs of the Union of Soviet Socialist Republics (Molotov), August 8, 1945.*[1]

On August 8, People's Commissar for Foreign Affairs of the U.S.S.R. Molotov received the Japanese Ambassador, Mr. Sato, and gave him, in behalf of the Soviet Government, the following for transmission to the Japanese Government:

After the defeat and capitulation of Hitlerite Germany, Japan became the only great power that still stood for the continuation of the war.

The demand of the three powers, the United States, Great Britain and China, on July 26 for the unconditional surrender of the Japanese armed forces was rejected by Japan, and thus the proposal of the Japanese Government to the Soviet Union on mediation in the war in the Far East loses all basis.

Taking into consideration the refusal of Japan to capitulate, the Allies submitted to the Soviet Government a proposal to join the war against Japanese aggression and thus shorten the duration of the war, reduce the number of victims and facilitate the speedy restoration of universal peace.

Loyal to its Allied duty, the Soviet Government has accepted the proposal of the Allies and has joined in the declaration of the Allied Powers of July 26.

[1] *Ibid.*, August 9, 1945, p. 3.

The Soviet Government considers that this policy is the only means able to bring peace nearer, free the people from further sacrifice and suffering and give the Japanese people the possibility of avoiding the dangers and destruction suffered by Germany after her refusal to capitulate unconditionally.

In view of the above, the Soviet Government declares that from tomorrow, that is from August 9, the Soviet Government will consider itself to be at war with Japan.

(2) *Agreement Concerning the Entry of the Union of Soviet Socialist Republics into the War Against Japan, Signed at Yalta, the Crimea, February 11, 1945. Department of State Press Release, February 11, 1946.*[1]

In making public this agreement the Secretary of State called attention to the fact that the Government of the Chinese Republic was not a party to the agreement and that the relations between China and the Soviet Republics are in no way controlled by this memorandum but are governed entirely by the provisions of the treaty between China and the Soviet Republics signed at Moscow on August 14, [1945] and subsequent agreements between those two Governments.[2]

The Secretary further stated that it is evident that this agreement was regarded by President Roosevelt, Prime Minister Churchill and Generalissimo Stalin as a military agreement and was marked "top secret". There was good reason for the agreement being regarded as top secret. The agreements were based upon Russia's entering the war. The Soviet military leaders advised our military leaders that Russia could not enter the war until 90 days after the surrender of Germany, that it would take them that time to move their arms to the Japanese front. At that time, February 11, 1945, our armies were attacking on the western front. They needed all the assistance that could come from a simultaneous attack from the Soviet Armies on the eastern front. Had the Japanese learned of this agreement they would have immediately attacked Russia. That would have necessitated the removal of Russian troops from the German front toward Japan at a time when Russia was starting the final drive which brought about the collapse of the German Army on that front. The removal of Russian troops at that time would have made the task of the American Armies that much more difficult and cost more lives.

The Secretary stated that he learned that an agreement had been reached on this subject on September 2 [1945], after the Japanese surrender on August 12, and at his press conference on September 4 announced the existence of an agreement.

3. FINANCIAL RELATIONS

Although little official information was released concerning negotiations for an extension of credit to the Soviet Union during the period under review, numerous reports with regard to such negotiations appeared in the press.

[1] Department of State, *Bulletin*, XIV, p. 282; for pertinent sections of the Yalta Agreement, see this volume, Appendix I.
[2] See *ibid*.

Discussions of the possibility of a loan were first reported in July 1945 as having grown out of the testimony of Leo T. Crowley, Foreign Economic Administrator and Chairman of the Board of the Export-Import Bank, before the Senate Committee on Banking and Currency with regard to the expansion of lending authority of the Export-Import Bank. While denying that application for a loan had been received from the Soviet authorities by the Bank, Mr. Crowley estimated that "in working out the proportions of credits it would be fair to assume that from $700,000,000 to $1,000,000,000 would be a reasonable amount" to be used to finance trade with the Soviet Union.[1]

The subject was again brought up in the eighth report of the House Special Committee on Postwar Economic Policy and Planning (the Colmer Report). In recognizing the Soviet Union as "potentially the greatest economic as well as political power covering the continents of Europe and Asia" and observing that "there would seem to be a real economic opportunity for extensive trade between the United States and Russia", the Committee Report outlined certain conditions upon which the extension of credit to the Soviet Union should, in its opinion, depend. These included: (1) investigation of the Soviet policy of armaments production and a comparison of that policy with that of other nations; (2) "a full and frank discussion of . . . statistics and an opportunity to scrutinize the facts upon which they are based with regard to economic production in all parts of Russia"; (3) "fulfillment of Russia's political obligations on the same terms as those of other governments"; (4) "disclosure of the terms of trade treaties made by Russia with the Eastern European countries now under Russian occupation and control"; (5) "administration of relief . . . on non-political lines and in a way that does not permit the siphoning off of supplies to Russia which will have to be replaced by the relief afforded from the United States and UNRRA sources"; and (6) "the protection of American property, including copyrights", and "full freedom of entry of reporters and the protection of rights of individuals and nations to distribute books, magazines, papers and periodicals." [2]

On March 1, 1946, the Department of State announced that the Soviet Union had been invited to enter into "over all" negotiations for a credit of $1,000,000,-000. This credit, the Department added, had been requested several months previously but, due to errors in transferring the records of the Foreign Economic Administration to the custody of the Department in September 1945, the official request had been misplaced.[3] A second invitation was dispatched to the Soviet Government in April, the Secretary of State announced on April 19. At the same time the Secretary disclosed the beliefs of the United States Government as to the topics which negotiations should cover, including: (1) the Soviet trade pacts with the Balkan nations to which the United States had objected; and (2) the Soviet attitude concerning the projected United Nations International Trade Organization, the International Bank for Reconstruction and Development and the International Monetary Fund. The United States invitation suggested that negotiations begin in May or by summer, at the latest.[4] It was reported by the press, at this time, however, that this note was not a new invitation but merely a clarification of the original note sent March 1 and an attempt to accommodate the Soviet position regarding the scope of the negotiations.[5]

The Department of State further revealed on May 23, 1946, that the Soviet reply had expressed a renewed interest in the opening of negotiations but had not resulted in agreement between the two Governments as to the topics to be discussed nor the date for beginning the discussions.[6] A third United States note, dispatched in June 1946, merely reiterated the topics which this Government wished included in the discussion.[7]

With the announcement in July 1946 that the President would not seek additional lending authority for the Export-Import Bank's operations, the impossibility of a Soviet loan for the remainder of the period under review became more definite. Further negotiations for 1946 were accordingly suspended.[8]

[1] *New York Times*, July 18, 1945, p. 1.   [2] *Ibid.*, November 12, 1945, p. 1.
[3] *Ibid.*, March 2, 1946, p. 1.   [4] *Ibid.*, April 20, 1946, p. 1.   [5] *Ibid.*, April 21, 1946, p. 17.
[6] *Ibid.*, May 24, 1946, p. 12.   [7] *Ibid.*, June 16, 1946, p. 1.   [8] *Ibid.*, July 22, 1946, p.1.

EUROPE AND WESTERN ASIA

4. RELATIONS WITH BULGARIA

For information on United States-Soviet relations concerning Bulgaria within the framework of the Allied Control Council for Bulgaria, see this volume, p. 317.

5. RELATIONS WITH HUNGARY

For information on United States-Soviet relations concerning Hungary within the framework of the Allied Control Council for Hungary, see this volume, p. 326.

6. RELATIONS WITH IRAN

(1) *Exchange of Notes between the Government of the United States and the Governments of the Union of Soviet Socialist Republics and the United Kingdom, Regarding the Withdrawal of Foreign Troops from Iran.*

(a) *Note from the Government of the United States to the Government of the Union of Soviet Socialist Republics, November 24, 1945.*[1]

The Government of Iran has informed the Government of the United States that armed uprisings have taken place in areas of northern Iran where Soviet troops are stationed; that the Iranian Government has directed certain of its armed forces to enter those areas for the purpose of reestablishing internal security and its own authority; that Soviet military commanders have refused to permit these forces to proceed; and that consequently the Iranian Government has not been able to carry out its responsibility for the maintenance of peace and order in Iranian territory.

It will be recalled that on December 1, 1943, Marshal Stalin, Prime Minister Churchill and President Roosevelt signed in Tehran a declaration in which they stated that their Governments were "at one with the Government of Iran in their desire for the maintenance of the independence, sovereignty and territorial integrity of Iran". This Government has entire confidence that the Governments of the Soviet Union and Great Britain are just as zealous as the Government of the United States meticulously to abide by the assurances contained in this declaration. In the view of this Government the fulfillment of these assurances requires that the Government of Iran should have full freedom, without interference from Soviet, British, or American military or civil authorities, to move its armed forces through Iran in such a manner as it may consider necessary in order to preserve its authority and to maintain internal security.

The Government of the United States realizes that any Soviet commanders in the areas concerned who may have prevented the free movement of Iranian forces may have been acting without the sanction of the Soviet Government. If the Soviet commanders have been acting without instructions in this matter, it is assumed that the Soviet Government is issuing to them instructions in keeping with the declaration referred to above. In any event the situation which has arisen has convinced the

---
[1] Department of State, *Bulletin*, XIII, p. 884.

American Government that it would be in the common interest for all Soviet, British, and American troops to be withdrawn immediately from Iran. As long as any of these troops remain in the territory of a friendly government, incidents and misunderstandings are likely to occur. The Government of the United States has already reduced its forces in Iran during the present year from a maximum strength of approximately 28,000 to less than 6,000. There are no American combat troops in Iran. Those who remain are engaged in activities exclusively of a service nature connected with the liquidation and disposal of military supplies and the operation of certain important communications connected with demobilization. While the immediate withdrawal of these troops will cause considerable inconvenience to this Government, nevertheless instructions are being issued to the American military authorities in Iran to take immediate steps to effect the complete withdrawal of all American forces from Iran by January 1, 1946. This Government proposes that the British and Soviet Governments issue similar instructions to their commanders and that arrangements be made immediately for the complete withdrawal of all foreign troops from Iran by January 1, 1946. Immediate steps to effect such withdrawal would dispel any doubt regarding the intentions of the three Governments to carry out the assurances given by them. In making this suggestion the Government of the United States is aware that no undertaking has been given that these troops are to be removed from Iran before March 2, 1946. On the other hand, now that hostilities have ceased, it sees no compelling reason for them to remain until that date. It is of the opinion that immediate steps to effect withdrawal by January 1 not only would obviate possible misunderstandings but would also be a fitting recognition of the notable contributions which Iran, a member in good standing of the United Nations, has made to the common war effort.

Nations such as Iran were encouraged at the United Nations Conference at San Francisco to place full trust in the friendly intentions and good will of the permanent members of the Security Council. The Government of the United States is confident that the Soviet Union and Great Britain are no less anxious than the United States, in dealing with nations such as Iran, to follow a line of action which will make it clear that the trust of these nations in the permanent members of the Security Council has not been misplaced.

Similar proposals are being made to the British Government.

(b) *Note from the Government of the Union of Soviet Socialist Republics to the Government of the United States, November 29, 1945.*[1]

[Translation]

The statement made in that communication concerning the armed uprising in northern Iran does not, according to information at the disposal of the Soviet Government, correspond to reality. The events which have taken place in recent days in Iran not only do not consti-

[1] *Ibid.*, p. 934.

tute an armed uprising but also are not directed against the Shahkin Shakh Government of Iran. Now that the declaration of the Popular Assembly of Northern Iran has been published, it is evident that this is a matter of aspirations with respect to the assurance of the democratic rights of Azerbaijanian population of northern Iran which is seeking national autonomy within the limits of the Iranian state and which has its own particular language, different from the Persian language. It is also apparent from the contents of the above-mentioned declaration of the Popular Assembly which took place in Tabriz November 20 to 21 that the Popular Assembly addressed the expression of its wishes to the Shah, the Majlis, and the Government of Iran, basing itself in this on the Iranian Constitution. The undesirable incidents which have taken place in conjunction with these recent events at various points of northern Iran have been caused by reactionary elements which have opposed the extension of national rights to the populations of northern Iran, although there is nothing in these desires of the local population which is unusual for a democratic state.

As far as the Soviet military command is concerned it has not hindered, and is not hindering, the movements of the Iranian military forces and the gendarme police units which are in the districts of northern Iran. According to information at the disposal of the Soviet Government there are in these districts of Iran one infantry regiment, two infantry brigades, two regiments of gendarme police units, the presence of which can assure order and calm in these parts. The Soviet Government opposed the dispatch of new Iranian troops to northern districts of Iran and informed the Iranian Government that the dispatch of further Iranian forces to northern Iran could cause not the cessation but the increase of the disorders and likewise bloodshed, which would compel the Soviet Government to introduce into Iran further forces of its own for the purpose of preserving order and of assuring the security of Soviet garrison. In as much as the Soviet Government considers the further introduction of Soviet forces into Iran undesirable, it took the position that the introduction of new Iranian forces into the northern province of Iran at the present time would serve no useful purpose.

As to the reference in the communication of the Government of the United States to the Three Power declaration concerning Iran December 1, 1943, the Soviet Government as far as it is concerned must state that it adheres unwaveringly to the principles of that declaration. The declaration in question, however, does not affect questions of the number of Soviet armed forces on Iranian territory just as it does not affect the question of the period of the stationing of Soviet troops in Iran. This latter is determined by another document, namely the Anglo-Soviet-Iranian Tripartite Treaty of 1942, and in connection with the stationing of its troops in Iran notwithstanding the fact that the right of introduction of Soviet troops into the territory of Iran was envisaged by the Soviet-Iranian treaty of February 26, 1941. Furthermore, as the Government of the United States is aware, the question of the time for the removal of Soviet and British troops from Iran was subject of consideration at the Council of Foreign Ministers in London as little as two months ago and was decided by exchange of letters between the Soviet and British representatives which was brought to the attention of the above-mentioned Council of Ministers and which did not find objection in any quarters. In connection with the above it should also be noted that the British Government, in its note on the Iranian question, received by the Soviet Government on November 25, does not raise the question of the removal of Soviet troops from Iran.

On the strength of the consideration set forth above with relation to Soviet troops, the Government of the Union of Soviet Socialist Republics does not see grounds for renewed consideration of the question of the time limit for the removal of these forces from Iran.

(c) Note from the Government of the United Kingdom to the Government of the United States, Released to the Press, December 14, 1945.[1]

As the United States Government will recall, His Majesty's Government suggested to the Soviet Government at the London meeting of the Foreign Ministers that the Soviet Government and His Majesty's Government should agree to withdraw by the middle of December their respective forces from the whole of Persia except certain defined zones, leaving only small parties for the disposal of surplus property and installations.

The Soviet Government were unable to accept this proposal; nonetheless, His Majesty's Government proceeded with the arrangements suggested in their proposal to the Soviet Government, and, except for small administrative parties, such British troops as now remain in Persia have been withdrawn southwards as quickly as possible and are stationed in the extreme southwest of the country.

His Majesty's Government takes the view that the Allied troops were stationed in Persia only for purposes connected with the war, and that the war being ended they should withdraw as soon as possible. Therefore, upon the receipt of the United States Government's proposal that all Allied troops should be withdrawn from Persia before the first January 1946, His Majesty's Government as a matter of urgency commenced an examination of the practicability of withdrawing their forces by that date.

The Soviet Government, having intimated to the United States Government that they are not prepared to accede to the United States Government's proposal, British military authorities are not continuing their plans to examine the details involved in arrangements for withdrawal by January 1, 1946.

His Majesty's Government entirely agree with the view that fulfillment of assurances contained in the Declaration of Tehran of December 1, 1943 requires that the Government of Iran should have full freedom to move its armed forces in such manner as it consider necessary in order to preserve its authority and maintain internal security.

[1] *Ibid.*, p. 946.

(2) *Note from the Government of the United States to the Government of the Union of Soviet Socialist Republics, Regarding the Retention of Soviet Troops in Iran, March 6, 1946.*[1]

The question of Soviet troops in Iran became a subject for international discussion when, on January 26, 1946, the Security Council of the United Nations began consideration of the dispute. In a letter of January 19, the Iranian delegation to the General Assembly of the United Nations addressed the following letter to the Acting Secretary General of the organization:

"Owing to interference of the Soviet Union, through the medium of their officials and armed forces, in the internal affairs of Iran, a situation has arisen which may lead to international friction.

"In accordance with Article 33 of the Charter of the United Nations the Iranian Government have repeatedly tried to negotiate with the Government of the Soviet Union, but have met with no success.

"Accordingly, the Iranian delegation to the General Assembly of the United Nations, on behalf of the Iranian Government, have the honour to request you, in accordance with the terms of Article 35 (1) of the Charter, to bring the matter to the attention of the Security Council so that the Council may investigate the situation and recommend appropriate terms of settlement.

"The Iranian delegation is prepared to assist the Security Council by furnishing a full statement of the facts which have given rise to the present situation, together with a copy of the relevant Treaty which binds the parties concerned." [2]

The Iranian position was elaborated at the second session of the Security Council when the Iranian representative specifically charged the Soviet Union with a violation of the Tripartite Treaty of 1942 between the Soviet Union, Iran and the United Kingdom and with a refusal to seek settlement through bilateral negotiations.[3] The Soviet delegate countered with the statement that negotiations between Iran and the Soviet Union had been concluded to the expressed satisfaction of the Iranian Government on December 1, 1945 and that, in accordance with the result of those negotiations, the presence of Soviet troops did not constitute "interference"; therefore, the Soviet representative opposed the consideration of the question by the Security Council.[4] An expressed willingness on the part of both parties to seek a solution by bilateral means led to the passage of a resolution by the Security Council on February 1, requesting both Iran and the Soviet Union to inform the Council of the results of the bilateral negotiations and stating that the Council "in the meanwhile retains the right at any time to request information on the progress of the negotiations." [5]

For a detailed account of the discussion in the Security Council concerning the Iranian Question, see *International Organization*, I, p. 74–7; or *Yearbook of the United Nations, 1946–47*, p. 327–36.

In addition to participating in the Security Council's investigation of the question, the United States Government also continued direct correspondence with the Soviet Government looking toward a peaceful solution to the dispute.

The Government of the United States has been informed that the Government of the Soviet Union has decided to retain Soviet troops in Iran after March 2, 1946, that this decision was taken without the consent of the Iranian Government, and that Soviet troops continue to remain on Iranian territory in spite of the protests of the Iranian Government. It will be recalled that in reply to a note addressed on Novem-

---

[1] *Ibid.*, XIV, p. 435.
[2] United Nations, *Journal of the Security Council*, No 2, January 24, 1946, p. 1.
[3] For a full exposition of Iranian charges against the Soviet Union, see United Nations Security Council, Document S/3, January 1946.
[4] United Nations, *Journal of the Security Council*, No. 3, January 26, 1946, p. 24–5.
[5] *Ibid.*, No. 6, February 1, 1946, p. 82.

ber 24, 1945 by the Government of the United States to the Government of the Soviet Union suggesting the immediate withdrawal of all foreign troops from Iran, the Soviet Government on November 29 stated that the period of the stationing of Soviet troops in Iran was governed by the Anglo-Soviet-Iranian Treaty of January 29, 1942.[1] The Government of the United States understood from this statement that it was the intention of the Government of the Soviet Union that all Soviet troops would be withdrawn from Iran not later than March 2, 1946, six months after the date of the signing of the instrument of surrender with Japan on September 2, 1945. This understanding was based upon Article Five of the Tripartite Treaty referred to above which states:

> The forces of the Allied Powers shall be withdrawn from Iranian territory not later than six months after all hostilities between the Allied Powers and Germany and her associates have been suspended by the conclusion of an armistice or armistices, or on the conclusion of peace between them, whichever date is the earlier.

So far as the Government of the United States is aware, this commitment was not questioned at the recent meeting of the Security Council in London which agreed that the Soviet Union and Iran should seek a solution of their differences by direct negotiation.

The decision of the Soviet Government to retain Soviet troops in Iran beyond the period stipulated by the Tripartite Treaty has created a situation with regard to which the Government of the United States, as a member of the United Nations and as a party to the Declaration Regarding Iran dated December 1, 1943, can not remain indifferent. That Declaration announced to the world that the Governments of the United States, the Union of Soviet Socialist Republics and the United Kingdom were "at one with the Government of Iran in their desire for the maintenance of the independence, sovereignty and territorial integrity of Iran". In the opinion of the Government of the United States, the maintenance of troops in Iranian territory by any one of the three signatories to that Declaration, without the consent and against the wishes of the Government of Iran, is contrary to the assurances contained in that Declaration. Furthermore it was generally accepted during the various discussions which took place at the meeting of the Security Council in London that the retention by a member of the United Nations of its troops in the territory of a country which is also a member of the United Nations, without the consent of the Government of that country, is not in accordance with the principles of the United Nations and that the withdrawal of such troops should not be made contingent upon other issues.

The Government of the United States, in the spirit of the friendly association which developed between the United States and the Soviet Union in the successful effort against the common enemy and as a fellow member of the United Nations, expresses the earnest hope that the Government of the Soviet Union will do its part, by withdrawing im-

[1] See this volume, p. 852.

mediately all Soviet forces from the territory of Iran, to promote the international confidence which is necessary for peaceful progress among the peoples of all nations.

The Government of the United States trusts that the Government of the Soviet Union, no less than itself, appreciates the heavy responsibility resting upon the great powers under the Charter to observe their obligations and to respect the sovereign rights of other states.

The Government of the United States requests that it be promptly advised of the decision of the Government of the Soviet Union which it hopes will be in accord with the views herein expressed.

On March 12, the Department of State announced that it had dispatched a further note to the Soviet Government investigating reports to the effect that during the preceding week additional Soviet forces and heavy military equipment had been moved from the Iranian-Soviet frontier in the direction of Tehran and the western border of Iran. The Department's note inquired whether such movements had taken place and, if so, the reasons therefor.[1]

(3) *Resolution Adopted by the Security Council at Its Thirtieth Meeting, April 4, 1946.*[2]

On March 26, 1946 Andrei Gromyko, the Soviet representative to the Security Council, reported briefly to the Council on negotiations between his Government and that of Iran. His report, in part, stated:

"... Negotiations between the Soviet Government and the Government of Iran have resulted in an agreement regarding the evacuation of Soviet troops still in that country. It is already known that the evacuation of these troops began some time ago, on the 2d of March. As regards the evacuation of the troops still remaining in certain zones of Iran, ... in accordance with an agreement concluded between the Soviet and Iranian Governments the evacuation of these troops began on the 24th of March, that is, two days ago, and will probably end within five or six weeks unless unforeseen circumstances arise." [3]

The following resolution was introduced by Secretary Byrnes at the thirtieth meeting of the Security Council in order to implement the action by the Council which Mr. Byrnes had suggested to the Council on March 29.[4] The resolution was adopted by the Council with nine affirmative votes.

Taking note of the statements of the Iranian Representative that the Iranian appeal to the Council arises from the presence of Soviet troops in Iran and their continued presence there beyond the date stipulated for their withdrawal in the Tripartite Treaty of January 29, 1942:

Taking note of the replies dated April 3rd of the Soviet Government and the Iranian Government pursuant to the request of the Secretary-General for information as to the status of the negotiations between the two Governments and as to whether the withdrawal of Soviet troops from Iran is conditional upon agreement on other subjects; and in particular taking note of and relying upon the assurances of the Soviet

---

[1] Department of State, *Bulletin*, XIV, p. 483.
[2] United Nations, *Journal of the Security Council*, No. 24, April 8, 1946. See also, Department of State, *Bulletin*, XIV, p. 621.
[3] *Ibid.*, p. 568.   [4] See *ibid.*, p. 620.

Government that the withdrawal of Soviet troops from Iran has already commenced; that it is the intention of the Soviet Government to proceed with the withdrawal of its troops as rapidly as possible; that the Soviet Government expects the withdrawal of all Soviet troops from the whole of Iran to be completed within five or six weeks; and that the proposals under negotiation between the Iranian Government and the Soviet Government "are not connected with the withdrawal of Soviet troops":

Being solicitous to avoid any possibility of the presence of Soviet troops in Iran being used to influence the course of the negotiations between the Governments of Iran and the Soviet Union; and recognizing that the withdrawal of all Soviet troops from the whole of Iran cannot be completed in a substantially shorter period of time than that within which the Soviet Government has declared it to be its intention to complete such withdrawal:

Resolved that the Council defer further proceedings on the Iranian appeal until May 6, at which time the Soviet Government and the Iranian Government are requested to report to the Council whether the withdrawal of all Soviet troops from the whole of Iran has been completed and at which time the Council shall consider what, if any, further proceedings on the Iranian appeal are required;

Provided, however, that if in the meantime either the Soviet Government or the Iranian Government or any member of the Security Council reports to the Secretary-General any developments which may retard or threaten to retard the prompt withdrawal of Soviet troops from Iran, in accordance with the assurances of the Soviet Union to the Council, the Secretary-General shall immediately call to the attention of the Council such reports which shall be considered as the first item on the agenda.

(4) *Communiqué Issued by the Prime Minister of Iran (Ghavam) and the Ambassador of the Union of Soviet Socialist Republics to Iran (Sadchikov), Regarding Soviet-Iranian Negotiations, April 4, 1946.*[1]

[Translation]

Negotiations begun by the Prime Minister of Iran in Moscow with leaders of the Government of the Union of Soviet Socialist Republics and continued in Teheran, after the arrival of the Soviet Ambassador, were ended April 4, 1946 (15 Farvardin 1325) and complete agreement was reached on all problems, namely:

1. Red Army troops will evacuate all Iranian territory within one and one-half months from Sunday March 24, 1946 (4th Farvardin 1325).

2. An agreement for the formation of a joint Iranian-Soviet oil company and its terms will be submitted to the fifteenth Majlis (Parliament) for its approval within seven months after March 24.

With regard to Azerbaijan, since it is internal Iranian affair, peaceful arrangements will be made between the Iranian government and the

---

[1] Embassy of the Union of Soviet Socialist Republics, *Information Bulletin*, VI, p. 299.

people of Azerbaijan for carrying out of reforms, in accordance with existing laws and in a benevolent spirit toward the people of Azerbaijan.

Pursuant to the resolution of the Security Council of April 4, the Iranian Government on May 6, 1946 began a series of reports on the withdrawal of Soviet troops from Iranian territory and on the alleged "interference" by the Soviet officials in the internal affairs of Iran. The first of these reports was communicated to the President of the Security Council on May 6, and said in part:

"Soviet troops have now been completely evacuated from the Provinces of Khorassan, Gorgan, Mazanderan and Gilan. This information is based upon investigations made by responsible officials of the Government of Iran.

"So far as the Province of Azerbaijan is concerned, the Government has been informed through other sources that the evacuation of Soviet troops from that Province has been going forward and it said will have been completed before 7 May 1946. These reports have not been verified by direct observations of officials of the Iranian Government. The reason for this is that, as previously pointed out to the Council, the Iranian Government has been unable because of the interferences complained of, to exercise effective authority within Azerbaijan since 7 November 1945, and from that time to the present has had no opportunity to ascertain through its own officials what are the conditions prevailing throughout that Province. While it is hoped that arrangements can be made which will remove the unfortunate results of the interferences complained of, it is impossible to forecast at this time with certainty what the subsequent developments will be."[1]

A second report on May 20 stated that "as a consequence of the interferences previously complained of, the Iranian Government is still prevented from exercising any effective authority in the Province of Azerbaijan and that Soviet interference in the internal affairs of Iran has not ceased." In order to investigate "reports that Soviet soldiers have been left in Azerbaijan in civilian clothes and that military equipment had been placed at the disposal of those who challenge the sovereignty and territorial integrity" of Iran, the report continued, "a commission has been appointed and is now stated to be in the city of Tabriz to make inquiries about conditions throughout the Province of Azerbaijan." The report also mentioned, but did not confirm, "reports of armed conflict" in Azerbaijan.[2]

On the following day, May 21, a third report was communicated to the Security Council based on information obtained by the Commission appointed to investigate conditions in Azerbaijan. In the course of a week's investigation in important centers such as Tabriz, Marand, Julfa, Khoy, Salmas, Maju, Rezacyeh and Mianduab, the Commission reported "that no trace whatever of Soviet troops, equipment or means of transport was found, and that according to trustworthy, local people, who were questioned in all these places, Soviet troops evacuated Azerbaijan on 6 May."[3]

7. RELATIONS WITH RUMANIA

For information on United States-Soviet relations within the framework of the Allied Control Council for Rumania, see this volume, p. 334.

8. RELATIONS WITH TURKEY

During the period under review, relations between the United States and Turkey centered for the most part around the question of the Turkish Straits and the revision of the Montreux Convention of July 20, 1936, by which the use of the Straits was regulated.[4] Under Article 29 of that Convention, the necessity for its revision at five-year intervals was recognized. The problem of revision was discussed by President Truman, Prime Minister Attlee and Generalissimo Stalin

---

[1] Department of State, *Bulletin*, XIV, p. 854.   [2] *Ibid.*, p. 941.   [3] *Ibid.*, p. 942.
[4] This note is based largely upon information taken from *The Problem of the Turkish Straits*, Department of State Publication 2752.

during the Potsdam Conference in July 1945.¹ Although no final disposition of the problem was brought about in the course of these discussions, the need for the revision of the Convention was acknowledged. American proposals to that end were transmitted to the Turkish Government in a note of November 2, 1945 commencing an involved diplomatic correspondence among the Governments of the United States, Turkey, the Soviet Union and the United Kingdom which, during the period under review, failed to resolve the conflicting viewpoints of the governments involved.

(1) *Note from the United States Ambassador to Turkey (Wilson) to the Minister of Foreign Affairs of Turkey (Hasan Saka), November 2, 1945.*²

I have the honor, under instructions of my Government, to inform Your Excellency as follows:

The American Government has given careful consideration to the Turkish Government's note of August 20, 1945, together with the *aide-memoire* attached thereto, concerning the question of the Straits.

The Turkish Government is no doubt aware that at the recent conference in Berlin, the President of the United States concurred with Premier Stalin and Prime Minister Attlee (1) that the convention of 1936 signed at Montreux regarding the régime of the Straits should be revised to meet present day conditions and (2) that the matter would be the subject of direct conversations between each of the three governments and the Turkish Government. It is the earnest hope of the Government of the United States that the problem of the control and use of the Straits can be solved in a manner which will promote international security, will show due consideration for the interests of Turkey and all Black Sea riparian powers, and will assure the free use of this important waterway to the commerce of all nations.

It is the understanding of the Government of the United States that the Montreux Convention is subject to revision in 1946. This government suggests that an international conference be held for the purpose of revising the convention in order that the régime of the Straits may be more in harmony with changed world conditions. The United States, if invited, would be pleased to participate in such a conference.

The Government of the United States is of the opinion that a revision of the Montreux Convention undertaken to meet changed world conditions should be based on the following principles:

(1) The Straits to be open to the merchant vessels of all nations at all times;

(2) The Straits to be open to the transit of the warships of Black Sea powers at all times;

(3) Save for an agreed limited tonnage in time of peace, passage through the Straits to be denied to the warships of non-Black Sea powers at all times, except with the specific consent of the Black Sea powers or except when acting under the authority of the United Nations; and

---

¹ For pertinent sections of the Potsdam Declaration, see this volume, Appendix II.
² Department of State Publication 2752, cited above, p. 47.

(4) Certain changes to modernize the Montreux Convention; such as the substitution of the United Nations system for that of the League of Nations and the elimination of Japan as a signatory.

The British and Soviet Governments are also being informed of the American Government's views set forth above.

(2) *Exchange of Notes between the Chargé d'Affaires ad interim of the Union of Soviet Socialist Republics (Orekhov) and the Acting Secretary of State (Acheson).*[1]

(a) *Note from the Chargé d'Affaires ad interim of the Union of Soviet Socialist Republics to the Acting Secretary of State, August 7, 1946.*

By direction of the Soviet Government I have the honor to communicate to you the following:

As is known, the Berlin Conference of the Three Powers on the question of the Montreux Convention adopted a resolution, whereby the three governments declared that the said convention should be revised, since it does not correspond to present conditions. At the same time the three governments agreed that this question was to be the subject of direct negotiations between each of the three powers and the Turkish Government. In accordance with this, the Soviet Government on August 7 of this year addressed to the Turkish Government a note which is transcribed below:

The Ministry of Foreign Affairs of the U. S. S. R. has the honor to inform the Turkish Government of the following:

Events which occurred during the past war clearly indicated that the regime of the Black Sea Straits, established by the Straits Convention, signed in 1936 at Montreux, does not meet the interests of the safety of the Black Sea Powers and does not insure conditions under which the use of these Straits for purposes inimical to the Black Sea Powers would be prevented.

It will suffice to mention a series of incidents during this war, when the Axis Powers directed their warships and auxiliary craft through the Straits into the Black Sea and out of the Black Sea, which in its turn gave rise to the corresponding steps and protests registered by the Soviet Government with the Turkish Government.

On July 9, 1941 the German command sent the German patrol boat *Seefalke* through the Straits into the Black Sea, which was a gross violation of the Straits Convention and called forth a protest to the Turkish Government on the part of the Soviet Government.

In August, 1941, Turkish authorities gave the Italian auxiliary war vessel *Tarvisio* permission to pass through the Straits into the Black Sea, which likewise called forth a representation on the part of the Soviet Government, calling to the attention of the Turkish Government the fact that the passage of the Italian auxiliary vessel into the Black Sea would appear to be a violation of the Straits Convention.

On November 4, 1942, the Soviet Government again called to the attention of the Turkish Government the fact that Germany planned to send to the Black Sea through the Straits auxiliary warships under the guise of merchant vessels with a total displacement of 140,000 tons. These vessels were intended for the

[1] *Ibid.*

transfer of military forces and war materials of the Axis countries into the Black Sea. In its representation, the Soviet Government emphasized the fact that "the admission of the aforementioned vessels through the Straits into the Black Sea would be an obvious violation of the Convention regarding the regime of the Straits concluded in Montreux, inasmuch as these vessels are left at the disposal of the German Government and are in reality auxiliary warships."

In June, 1944, the Soviet Government registered a protest against the fact that toward the end of May and early in June of 1944 there took place a series of passages through the straits from the Black Sea into the Aegean Sea of German warships and auxiliary warships of varying tonnage of the *Ems* (8 vessels) and *Kriegstransport* (5 vessels) types, which had taken part in the naval operations in the Black Sea.

It is obvious from the aforementioned facts that at the time of the past war with Germany and her allies, the Straits Convention did not prevent the enemy powers from using the straits for military purposes against the U. S. S. R. and other allied powers, with the Turkish Government not being able to escape the responsibility for this situation.

In view of this, the Soviet Government suggested to the Berlin Conference of the Three Powers — Great Britain, the United States of America and the Soviet Union, which took place in July and August 1945, to discuss the question that the regime of the Straits, established by the Montreux Convention, does not conform to present conditions and that it is necessary to establish a new regime of the Straits. As is known, the Berlin Conference of the Three Powers adopted a resolution consisting of the following:

(*a*) The three governments declared that the Convention regarding the Straits, concluded in Montreux, should be revised, as it does not meet the conditions of the present time;

(*b*) The three governments agreed that as the proper course the said question would be the subject of direct negotiations between each of the three powers and the Turkish Government.

The Soviet Government is also acquainted with the contents of the note of November 2, 1945 of the Government of the United States of America and with the note of the British Government of November 21, 1945 addressed to the Government of Turkey on this question.

For its own part, the Soviet Government proposes to establish for the Straits a regime, proceeding from the following principles:

(1) The Straits should be always open to the passage of merchant ships of all countries.

(2) The Straits should be always open to the passage of warships of the Black Sea powers.

(3) Passage through the Straits for warships not belonging to the Black Sea powers shall not be permitted except in cases specially provided for.

(4) The establishment of a regime of the Straits, as the sole sea passage, leading from the Black Sea and to the Black Sea, should come under the competence of Turkey and other Black Sea powers.

(5) Turkey and the Soviet Union, as the powers most interested and capable of guaranteeing freedom to commercial navigation and security in the Straits, shall organize joint means of defense of the Straits for the prevention of the utilization of the Straits by other countries for aims hostile to the Black Sea powers.

The Soviet Government is informing the governments of the United States of America and Great Britain regarding the present declaration.

The Soviet Union has directed me to bring this to the knowledge of the Government of the United States of America.

(b) *Note from the Acting Secretary of State to the Chargé d'Affaires ad interim of the Union of Soviet Socialist Republics, August 19, 1946.*

I acknowledge receipt of your note of August 7, 1946 which sets forth the text of the note addressed on the same day by the Government of the Union of Soviet Socialist Republics to the Government of the Republic of Turkey and express the appreciation of this Government for the courtesy of the Soviet Government in making this information available.

It will be recalled that the American Embassy in Moscow made available to the Soviet Government in November 1945 a copy of the note which the American Embassy in Ankara delivered to the Turkish Government on November 2, 1945.

This Government has given careful study to the views expressed by the Soviet Government in its note to the Turkish Government. It would appear from a comparison of this Government's note of November 2, 1945 with the Soviet note to the Turkish Government of August 7, 1946 that the views of the Governments of the United States and of the Soviet Union, while not in entire accord, are in general agreement with regard to the three following proposals set forth in the Soviet note:

1. The Straits should be always open to the passage of merchant ships of all countries.
2. The Straits should be always open to the passage of warships of the Black Sea powers.
3. Passage through the Straits for warships not belonging to the Black Sea powers shall not be permitted except in cases specially provided for.

The fourth proposal set forth in the Soviet note does not appear to envisage a revision of the Montreux Convention as suggested in our note to the Turkish Government of November 2, 1945, but rather the establishment of a new regime which would be confined to Turkey and the other Black Sea powers. It is the view of this Government that the regime of the Straits is a matter of concern not only to the Black Sea powers but also to other powers, including the United States. This Government cannot, therefore, agree with the Soviet view that the establishment of the regime of the Straits should come under the competence of the Black Sea powers to the exclusion of other powers.

The fifth proposal set forth in the note of the Soviet Government was that Turkey and the Soviet Union should organize joint means of defense of the Straits. It is the firm opinion of this Government that Turkey should continue to be primarily responsible for the defense of the Straits. Should the Straits become the object of attack or threat of attack by an aggressor the resulting situation would constitute a threat to international security and would clearly be a matter for action on the part of the Security Council of the United Nations.

It is observed that the note of the Soviet Government contains no reference to the United Nations. The position of the Government of the United States is that the regime of the Straits should be brought into appropriate relationship with the United Nations and should function in a manner entirely consistent with the principles and aims of the United Nations.

The Government of the United States reaffirms its willingness to participate in a conference called to revise the Montreux Convention.

(3) *Note from the United States Ambassador to the Union of Soviet Socialist Republics (Smith) to the Commissar of Foreign Affairs of the Union of Soviet Socialist Republics (Molotov), Presented October 9, 1946.*[1]

I have the honor to inform Your Excellency that my Government has studied carefully the contents of the note of the Soviet Union to Turkey of September 24 relating to the regime of the Straits.[2]

In pursuance of its policy of making clear to all interested parties its views on matters relating to the Straits, my Government has instructed me to inform you that after examining the note referred to above it continues to adhere to the position outlined in its note of August 19, 1946 to the Soviet Government.

It will be recalled that in the Protocol of the proceedings of the Potsdam Conference, signed by the U.S.S.R., Great Britain and the United States, the three Governments recognized that the Convention on the Straits concluded at Montreux should be revised as failing to meet present-day conditions. It was further agreed in the Protocol that as the next step the matter should be the subject of direct conversations between each of the three Governments and the Turkish Government.

It has been the understanding of my Government that the three Governments, in agreeing with one another that the regime of the Straits should be brought into accord with present-day conditions by means of a revision of the Montreux Convention, mutually recognized that all three signatories of the Protocol have an interest in the regime of the Straits and in any changes which might be made in that regime. My Government furthermore informed the Soviet Government in its note of August 19, that in its view the regime of the Straits is a matter of concern not only to the Black Sea powers but also to other powers, including the United States. The Soviet Government, nevertheless, in its note of September 24, apparently continues to take the position set forth in its note of August 7 to Turkey that "the establishment of a regime of the Straits . . . should come under the competence of Turkey and the other Black Sea powers". My Government does not consider that it was contemplated at the Potsdam Conference that the direct conversations which might take place between any one of the three signatory governments and the Turkish Government with regard to the regime of the Convention of the Straits concluded at Montreux should have the effect of prejudicing the participation of the other two signatory powers in the revision of the regime of the Straits. On the contrary,

---

[1] *Ibid.*, p. 59.
[2] Not reprinted here. For text, see *ibid.*, p. 50.

my Government considers that the Potsdam Agreement definitely contemplated only an exchange of views with the Turkish Government as a useful preliminary to a conference of all of the interested powers, including the United States, to consider the revision of the Montreux Convention. As stated in its note of August 19, my Government stands ready to participate in such a conference.

My Government also feels that it would be lacking in frankness if it should fail to point out again at this time, in the most friendly spirit, that in its opinion the Government of Turkey should continue to be primarily responsible for the defense of the Straits and that should the Straits become the object of attack or threat of attack by an aggressor, the resulting situation would be a matter for action on the part of the Security Council of the United Nations.

C. France

For information regarding relations between the United States and France concerning international civil aviation during the period under review, see this volume, p. 660, 662 and 671.

(1) Declarations by the Government of the United States and the Provisional Government of the French Republic Regarding Economic and Financial Matters, Washington, May 28, 1946.

On August 22, 1945, General Charles de Gaulle arrived in Washington for a discussion of future United States-French relations in the postwar period. At the conclusion of General de Gaulle's three-day visit, the following joint statement was issued by the two leaders.

Shortly after General de Gaulle's visit to Washington, official French quarters revealed that the French leader, while in this country, had requested credits of more than $1,000,000,000 to be extended in a series of three loans.[1] Actual negotiations with French representatives opened in Washington in March 1946[2] and were successfully concluded on May 28, 1946. Included among the subjects upon which agreements were reached were commercial policy, lend-lease, mutual aid and surplus property.

For further information on the activities of the Export-Import Bank as applied to France, see this volume, p. 636 and 638; for further information on lend-lease and mutual aid settlements between the two Governments, see *ibid.*, p. 142, 154 and 158.

(a) Declaration Made in Paris by the President of the Provisional Government of the French Republic and in Washington by the President of the United States.[3]

Representatives of the Provisional Government of the French Republic and the Government of the United States have met together in Washington and have discussed important economic and financial problems of common interest. These problems have included the need for foreign credits for reconstructing and modernizing the French economy, the settlement of lend-lease reciprocal aid and other war accounts, the purchase of United States surplus property situated in France and certain French overseas territories, the purchase of ships owned by the United States, and international commercial policy.

[1] *New York Times*, August 31, 1945, p. 10.
[2] *Ibid.*, March 17, 1946, p. 17.
[3] Department of State, *Bulletin*, XIV, p. 1127.

The discussions have brought out clearly the full agreement of the two Governments on cooperation in the fulfillment of the economic objectives which both Governments recognize as essential to world peace and prosperity. The well-being of the people of all nations can be advanced through a full flow of trade which enables each country to maintain higher levels of production and better standards of living. These benefits of world trade can be realized only as the markets of the world are opened to all countries on fair and equal terms. The two Governments are determined to work together in securing general international acceptance of the world trade proposals of the United States to be considered by a conference of the United Nations.

The reconstruction and modernization of the French economy will facilitate the integration of Europe in the world economy and enable France to resume her place as a great producing and trading nation. The French Delegation has presented a program for reconstructing and modernizing the economy of France. The immediate objective is to restore French production to the prewar level; the ultimate objective is to expand French production to higher levels commensurate with the technical progress of the past two decades. One requisite for the fulfillment of this program is an adequate and assured supply of coal, not only from increased French production, but also from imports of German coal. The United States Government will continue to assist France in securing an adequate supply of coal from Germany.

In the opinion of the American representatives, attainment of the objectives of increased production and trade presented by the French Delegation is necessary to the full and effective participation of France in the world economy. In furtherance of the efforts of the French people to this end, the United States has agreed to the extension of additional credits to France.

At the end of 1945 the Export-Import Bank made a loan of $550 million to France. The Board of Directors of the Export-Import Bank have now approved a new line of credit of $650 million. This action has been taken pending the time when the International Bank for Reconstruction and Development will be in full operation.

The two Governments have reached complete agreement for the final settlement of all lend-lease and reciprocal aid, including military and civilian supplies furnished by each Government to the other. They have also agreed on the acquisition of United States army and navy surplus property located in France and certain French overseas territories. Under this Agreement, credits of $720 million have been provided for the purchase of surplus property and for goods supplied to France since the end of the war.

Discussions are taking place for an additional credit, subject to the provisions of the Merchant Ship Sales Act of 1946, whereby France will acquire approximately 750,000 tons of merchant shipping owned by the Government of the United States.

The two Governments believe that the results of the discussions which have now been concluded will help France in reconstructing and modernizing the French economy and are a substantial step towards the achievement of the international economic cooperation which is the prerequisite of a peaceful and prosperous world. They welcome the support of all of the United Nations in establishing a world trading and monetary system which will assure a full flow of commerce to the benefit of the peoples of all countries.

(b) *Declaration on Commerical Policy and Related Matters.*[1]

The Government of the United States of America and the Provisional Government of the French Republic, having concluded comprehensive discussions on commercial policy and related matters, find themselves in full agreement on the general principles which they desire to see established to achieve the liberation and expansion of international trade, which they deem to be essential to the realization of world-wide prosperity and lasting peace.

[1] *Ibid.*, p. 995.

The French Government has made known to the United States Government the measures which it has taken and intends to take to make possible the attainment of this common objective. The French Government has also made known to the United States Government its plan for the reconstruction and modernization of the French economy. In accordance with the letters exchanged on November 8, 1945, the two Governments have examined this plan and have agreed that the attainment of its objectives should make possible full participation by France in the cooperative achievement of an expanding world economy.

The two Governments have studied the problems involved in the construction of a general framework for world trade and have also examined a number of specific questions relating to commercial policy and other matters which are of interest to themselves and to other countries. The following joint statement by the two Governments summarizes the understanding reached in these discussions.

I

The two Governments are in complete agreement, at all important points, on the principles expressed in the "Proposals for Consideration by an International Conference on Trade and Employment" submitted to the French Government by the Government of the United States. They have therefore resolved to continue discussions between themselves and with other like-minded countries in order to give effect to these principles in the Charter of the proposed International Trade Organization. The two Governments are of the opinion that the prior conclusion of agreements among the major trading nations of the world for the substantial reduction of tariffs and other barriers to trade and for the removal of discriminatory arrangements would contribute greatly to the success of the World Conference.

II

The French Government has advised the United States Government of the following policies:

(a) A new French tariff is being prepared which will contain *ad valorem* duties only and which will not increase the degree of protection over the level which existed prior to the war. This new tariff will serve as the level from which reciprocal reductions will be negotiated in the forthcoming multilateral conference.

(b) France has definitely abandoned its pre-war policy of protecting French producers with import quotas.

(c) The French Government has reiterated that it has abandoned the price equalization (perequation) procedure which it was compelled to use provisionally during the period prior to the revaluation of the franc in order to facilitate exports.

III

The French Government has made clear that it must maintain import controls within the framework of an import program but that it will maintain such controls only so long as they are necessary to safeguard the equilibrium of its balance of payments and to achieve in an orderly way its plan of reconstruction and modernization. The French Government will administer the issuance of import licenses under the French import program without discrimination as among foreign sources of supply as soon as France possesses, or is able to earn, sufficient free foreign exchange so that it is no longer necessary for her to make her purchases within the limits of bilateral trade and financial arrangements.

IV

The two Governments have reached a mutually satisfactory understanding on the return to private channels of trade between France and the United States. The French Government has already restored to private channels a large part of the import trade of France and its colonies, and will continue to curtail the foreign procurement activities of the Government.

French Government procurement in the United States will be limited to equipment for public corporations and agencies. For the time being, Government procurement will also be continued for a restricted list of items, such as short supply foodstuffs, steel, lumber, tires and certain medical supplies.

Temporarily, a part of French imports will be handled by associations of private traders (groupments) until the difficulties of loading, shipment, and transport of essential supplies and their distribution in France are overcome.

The French Supply Council in the United States will continue to operate on a reduced scale, engaging principally in the liquidation of outstanding contracts and governmental procurement as indicated above. It will limit its purchases to the satisfaction of essential civilian requirements; it will make the maximum practicable use of normal trade channels; it will pursue methods consistent with commercial practices and it will cease operations as soon as possible.

V

The two Governments have agreed that important benefits would accrue to both countries from a substantial expansion of French exports to the United States. They have discussed certain United States laws and regulations, which, in the opinion of the French Government, tend to hamper unduly the importation of French products into the United States. Special attention has been given to trade mark and copyright legislation, the use of geographic names related to particular products, price control of imported goods, and valuation of imported goods for the assessment of customs duties. The various agencies of the United States Government which are concerned with these matters have agreed to give careful and sympathetic consideration to the views of the French Government, and to study the possibility of altering their administrative procedures or recommending to the Congress the revision of existing legislation.

VI

The two Governments have agreed, subject to participation in the program by other important industrial nations, each to license freely and without royalty to the nationals of the other, on conditions of reciprocity, all former German-owned patents which have come into the full possession of either Government, reserving only those rights which have already been granted with respect to such patents. The two Governments believe that the general adoption of this policy will eliminate an important barrier to international trade and will contribute substantially to the achievement of expanding world economy. In accordance with these objectives, they have agreed, at some future time, jointly to consider other questions relating to German patents.

VII

The French Government will accord to American nationals who have suffered damage to their properties in France, through causes originating in the war, compensation equal to that payable to French nationals having the same types and extent of losses. The United States Government has informed the French Government that equality of treatment is accorded to French and American nationals with reference to war damages to property in the United States.

VIII

In order to provide a sound framework for the expansion of mutually beneficial economic relations between their two countries, the Governments of France and the United States have agreed to begin negotiations as soon as possible looking toward the conclusion of a modern and comprehensive Treaty of Establishment, Commerce and Navigation.

DONE at Washington, in duplicate, in the English and French languages, this 28th day of May, 1946.

(c) *Memorandum of Understanding Regarding Settlement for Lend-Lease, Reciprocal Aid, Surplus War Property, and Claims.*[1]

1. The Government of the United States of America and the Provisional Government of the French Republic have reached an understanding for the final settlement of lend-lease and reciprocal aid, and of the French obligation to the United States Government under the military supply program (Plan A); the acquisition by the French Government of certain United States Army and Navy surplus property, including installations, located in France and certain French overseas territories, and for the final settlement of other financial claims of each Government against the other arising out of the conduct of the war. In arriving at this understanding both Governments have recognized the considerations expressed in Article VII of their Preliminary Agreement of February 28, 1945, on the principles applying to mutual aid, as well as the benefits accruing to each from the contributions of both to the defeat of their common enemies. In the light of the foregoing, both Governments agree that no further benefits will be sought as consideration for lend-lease and reciprocal aid.

2. The net amount due from the French Government to the United States Government for the foregoing, including all indebtedness arising from provisions of the lend-lease and reciprocal aid agreements of February 28, 1945, is $720,000,000, made up in part of amounts now agreed upon and in part of estimated amounts subject to revision. The latter, for which the best available figures have been used pending their final determination by agreed accounting procedures, represent in the main transfers after September 1, 1945.

3. The French Government will pay interest on the net amount due to the United States Government from July 1, 1946, at the rate of two percent per annum. Such interest payments will be made annually on the first day of July of each of the years 1947 to 1950, inclusive. Beginning on July 1, 1951, interest and principal will be paid in thirty (30) equal annual installments. Each installment shall consist of the full amount of the interest due for the year preceding the July 1 on which the payment is made, and the remainder of the installment shall be the principal due in that year. Nothing herein shall be construed to prevent the French Government from anticipating the payment of any of such installments, or of any part thereof. If, by agreement of both Governments, it is determined that because of extraordinary and adverse economic conditions arising during the course of payment, the payment of any installment would not be in the joint interest of both Governments, payment may be postponed for an agreed upon period.

To the extent that the terms of payment provided in this paragraph 3 are inconsistent with those contained in previous agreements, the provisions of this paragraph shall prevail.

4. The two Governments have agreed upon arrangements and procedures for the settlement of past and future troop pay and procurement of United States Armed Forces in France and French overseas territories.

5. As and when requested by the United States Government from time to time prior to January 1, 1950, the French Government will transfer to the United States Government real property to be mutually agreed upon and not to exceed a total dollar value of $15,000,000. In addition, the French Government will provide, at the request of the United States Government, francs representing an aggregate dollar value not in excess of $10,000,000. Any francs so transferred will be furnished at the exchange rate established in conformity with procedures of the International Monetary Fund, or if no such rate exists, at the rate used in official French Government transactions at the time of such transfer. The United States Government will use francs so transferred exclusively to acquire or improve real property for United States Government use or to carry out educational programs agreed between the two Governments.

Transfers made in accordance with this paragraph 5 will be credited first to interest then due and then to installments of principal in direct order of maturity.

[1] *Ibid.*, p. 997.

6. The two Governments have also agreed upon the following:

(a) All claims and financial obligations between the two Governments arising out of the acquisition, operation, disposition or loss of French vessels and cargoes of such vessels while under United States control will be settled by the United States for $17,500,000 in accordance with the provisions of an agreement relating to the purchase by France of up to 75 Liberty ships.

(b) Both Governments express their intention of entering into a maritime claims agreement, providing for the mutual waiver of intergovernmental claims arising from maritime accidents, and for the handling by each Government of claims asserted in its courts by its nationals against the other Government and based on maritime accidents occurring prior to November 1, 1945.

(c) As part of the general settlement, the French Government has agreed to process and pay all unpaid claims of French residents against the United States Government arising out of the use or infringement in war production of patent rights held by them, out of the requisitioning by the United States Government for use in the war program of any property interest owned by French residents, and out of acts or omissions prior to July 1, 1946, in France or French overseas territories of members of the United States Armed Forces or civilian personnel attached to such Forces.

(d) During the course of the negotiations both Governments have reached agreement on the disposition of certain specific claims of one Government against the other. All other financial claims of either Government against the other, except where liability has heretofore been acknowledged and the method of computation agreed, which (1) arose out of lend-lease or reciprocal aid, or (2) otherwise arose on or after September 3, 1939, and prior to September 2, 1945, out of or incidental to the conduct of the war, not otherwise dealt with in this Memorandum of Understanding, are hereby waived.

(e) Appropriate non-discriminatory treatment will be extended by the French Government to United States nationals in the use and disposition of installations in the building of which there has been a United States Government contribution and which are transferred under this settlement.

(f) The United States Government reserves its right of recapture of any lend-lease articles held by the French Armed Forces, except petroleum products and an agreed list of non-combat aircraft. The United States Government has indicated that it does not intend to exercise generally this right of recapture, except that vessels of the United States Navy and lend-lease merchant vessels are to be returned to the United States Government unless otherwise agreed.

(g) Disposals for military use to forces other than the French Armed Forces of lend-lease articles held on September 2, 1945, or received thereafter by the French Armed Forces, and disposals for civilian use other than in France and French overseas territories of such lend-lease articles, will be made only with the consent of the United States Government and any net proceeds will be paid to the United States Government. The French Government will not, except to a very limited extent, release for civilian use in, or export from, France and French overseas territories lend-lease articles held by the French Armed Forces.

(h) Except as otherwise provided in this Memorandum of Understanding, the French Government and the United States Government receive full title to lend-lease and reciprocal aid articles respectively held as of September 2, 1945, or transferred thereafter. If any United States surplus installation not transferred under this Memorandum of Understanding contains a lend-lease interest, such lend-lease interest is retained by the United States.

(i) The United States Government will undertake to make available to the French Government part of the United States Government's share of captured German and Japanese surface naval vessels when such vessels become excess to United States needs and are no longer needed for any task connected with the implementation of the German and Japanese surrenders.

7. The two Governments agree to conclude such specific agreements as may be necessary to implement this general understanding.

8. This Memorandum of Understanding will be effective upon signature, and instruments of ratification will be exchanged as soon as possible.

DONE at Washington, in duplicate, in the English and French languages, both texts being equally authentic, this 28th day of May, 1946.

D. Albania

(1) Exchange of Notes between the Acting United States Representative in Tirana (Henderson) and the Premier of Albania (Hoxha) Regarding the Withdrawal of the United States Mission in Tirana.

In a note of November 10, 1945, the United States agreed to the establishment of official relations with the Albanian Government. In so doing this Government requested from the Albanian Government assurances "that the treaties and agreements which were in force between the United States and Albania on April 7, 1939, remain valid." [1] On August 13, 1946, the Albanian Government gave the required assurances with respect to multilateral treaties and agreements to which both Governments were parties but failed to confirm its recognition of the validity of bilateral agreements between the two Governments.[2]

(a) Note from the Acting United States Representative in Tirana to the Premier of Albania, November 5, 1946.[3]

Since arriving in Tirana on May 8, 1945, to survey conditions in Albania in connection with the question of United States recognition of the existing Albanian regime, the informal United States mission has sought to bring about mutual understanding and the establishment of diplomatic relations between the Governments of the United States and Albania.

Despite United States endeavors in this regard, and in the absence of a satisfactory response from the Albanian Government to the offer of recognition which was tendered by the United States Government in November, 1945, the mission has been unable to achieve the purposes for which it was originally sent to Albania.

In the circumstances, although my Government retains its sentiment of warm friendship for the Albanian people, it does not feel that there is any further reason for the mission to remain in Albania. The United States Mission is accordingly being withdrawn.

(b) Note from the Premier of Albania to the Acting United States Representative, November 14, 1946.[4]

[Excerpts]

I have the honor to inform you that I have received your letter dated November 5 of this year in which you inform me that, in your opinion, there is no basis for the United States of America mission to remain in Albania, that therefore the mission is recalled.

More than eighteen months have passed since the American Government addressed itself to our Government for permission to send to Albania an official American mission headed by Mr. Jacobs, who would inform the United States of America about our Government.

From our side the American mission was received with satisfaction and it received everything it required for the performance of its task.

---

[1] For the text of the United States note of November 10, 1945, see *ibid.*, XIII, p. 767.
[2] *New York Times*, November 9, 1946, p. 6.
[3] *Ibid.*
[4] Text as recorded in London from a broadcast by the Moscow radio of November 14, 1946. *Ibid.*, November 15, 1946, p. 6.

For the whole eighteen months your mission has freely traveled about the whole of Albania, our villages and towns, and has met with no obstacles in its activity — which was to bear a purely informative character connected with the recognition of our Government.

. . . . . .

The condition proposed for the recognition of our Government was not merely a "technical" question, as Mr. Jacobs wished to present it; on the contrary, facts testify that this is purely a question of principle, which the American Government has raised and utilized as a first-rate obstacle to the establishment of diplomatic relations between our countries. We have seen, unfortunately, that the American Government over this entire period has made use of the question of the treaties as an argument for opposition to all our legitimate rights won by blood, international relations.

But to the extent to which the question of the treaties is a question of principle for the American Government — and the American Government stubbornly defends this position — to that extent it is a question of principle also for us, and we also have every right to defend our position in the interests of our people.

Our Government has always endeavored to find a solution to this question, which hindered the establishment of diplomatic relations between our peoples in accordance with the sincere friendship that is demanded by the recent past of the common war and the present situations.

The Albanian people continues to harbor deep sympathies for the friendly American people. It much regrets that various reasons are put forward for hindering the further development of that friendship. Over the entire period of the negotiations on the question of the treaties, not only did the American mission fail to make every effort to find a solution for this question — but, on the contrary, its lengthy unjustified stay was taken advantage of to create ever greater difficulties in the achievement of a satisfactory decision.

The most convincing proof that the Albanian Government was always ready to solve the question of the treaties and of the recognition of the Albanian Government in a friendly way, and without hurt to the interests of either country, was our note of August 13 of this year, in which we agreed to recognize all international treaties that existed between the United States and Albania; and as far as the two or three remaining treaties of a bilateral character are concerned, we agreed to examine them immediately after the arrival of an American Ambassador in Tirana.

The Albanian people and its Government have confidence in the American people. They preserve their friendship for the American people, and express in a friendly spirit their desire to strengthen this friendship on a just and stable basis, which many persons in the United States of America State Department and in the American mission in Tirana do not reciprocate.

E. Belgium

For information on relations between the United States and Belgium during the period under review, see this volume as follows: on international civil aviation, p. 660, 661 and 671; on mutual aid settlements, p. 142, 147, 150, 154 and 157; on disposition of surplus property, p. 168; on relations with the Export-Import Bank, p. 638 and 641; and on reciprocal trade, p. 642.

(1) Joint Statement by the Governments of the United States and Belgium Concerning Arrangements on Financial and Supply Problems, Released to the Press, October 20, 1945.[1]

The Government of the United States and the Government of Belgium today announced the conclusion of arrangements with respect to certain urgent financial and supply problems created by the economic support given by Belgium to the United States armed forces and the termination of lend-lease aid to Belgium. Up to V-J Day, Belgium provided at least 90 million dollars more in goods and services as reverse lend-lease than it had received from the United States under lend-lease. This excess of reciprocal aid is largely the result of the very cooperative attitude of Belgium in unstintingly furnishing from its own limited resources whatever was requested by our armed forces after liberation. The goods and services which the Belgians provided went directly to United States troops. This aid was an important factor in the prosecution of the war against Germany, and continues to be important in the support of the United States occupation forces in Germany, and in the redeployment and evacuation of United States troops and equipment from Europe.

The excess of reciprocal aid which Belgium provided has created serious economic problems for Belgium, at a time when there were insufficient consumer supplies and when the productivity of Belgium industry was still suffering from the ravages of war and the burdens imposed upon it by the occupation.

To alleviate these economic consequences of the Belgian support of the Allied cause and to strengthen Belgium in the interest of the United States armed forces still in Europe and continuing to draw heavily on Belgian resources for transportation and other services, the United States Government has authorized that the following steps be taken:

The United States will pay dollars to Belgium, on a monthly basis, for the francs advanced to the United States Army by the Belgian Government after September 2, 1945. Heretofore these dollar payments have been made on a deferred basis except for 23 million dollars paid during the current year. As a result of the present negotiations, a further payment of 61 million dollars has already been made on account of net troop pay advances made in francs by the Belgian Government prior to September 2, 1945.

The United States has also agreed to make dollar payment for all goods and services furnished to United States armed forces after September 2, 1945. These goods and services prior to V-J Day were furnished by the Belgian Government as reciprocal aid, without charge to

[1] Department of State, *Bulletin*, XIII, p. 610.

the United States Army. As noted above, by V-J Day these goods and services exceeded by at least 90 million dollars all the lend-lease aid authorized to be given to Belgium.

In view of this excess of reciprocal aid, the United States Government has further agreed to offset against it the amounts which the Belgian Government is required to pay under the 3 (c) lend-lease agreement of April 17, 1945. The 3 (c) agreement between the United States and Belgium provides that whatever goods the United States may transfer under its terms to Belgium after V-J Day shall be paid for on a credit basis. On August 17 the President authorized the transfer of certain goods and services to Belgium under terms of this agreement following V-J Day. The amount of goods and services to be so transferred is approximately 42 million dollars. The recent action of the United States Government means that this debt will be considered to be satisfied by reason of the extent to which Belgian reverse lend-lease exceeds lend-lease heretofore provided by United States.

In addition the United States Government has authorized the transfer to Belgium of articles having civilian utility which the United States Army no longer requires for its own uses. The United States Army has substantial quantities of equipment, clothing and foodstuffs which are greatly needed by liberated areas of Europe and which would otherwise be declared surplus. There is a great deal of this kind of property in Belgium. Most important of such items are medical supplies, clothing and shoes, trucks and trailers, building materials, and reconstruction equipment and certain raw materials. Under the arrangements announced today the Belgian Government will be permitted to select up to 45 million dollars of such articles, to be transferred under straight lend-lease. The articles transferred will be of the types which were to be supplied under the 3 (c) agreement between the United States and Belgium, and their transfer to Belgium at this time will serve to improve the Belgian economic situation and to strengthen those activities of the Belgian economy which are still important to the servicing and supplying of our occupation forces and the evacuation of our troops from Europe.

These arrangements, it is felt by both Governments, will facilitate the conclusion of a final settlement of lend-lease under the master agreement. Conversations looking toward such a final settlement, which would include agreed action contemplated in article VII of the agreement, including questions of commercial policy, will be held between the two governments in the near future.

During the negotiations consideration was also given to questions pertaining to commercial policy and the desire of the United States Government that discussions be held in the immediate future on mutually advantageous measures with a view to the elimination of all forms of discriminatory treatment in international commerce, payments and investments, with the objective of expanding production and increasing employment. It is understood that the Governments of Belgium and the United States mutually agree to confer together in the near future on questions of commercial policy and, pending such a conference, to avoid the adoption of new measures affecting international trade, payments or investments which would prejudice the objective of such a conference. It was also suggested that the two governments should mutually agree to afford to each other adequate opportunity for consultation regarding such measures.

F. Czechoslovakia

On October 27, 1945, the Czechoslovak Government issued four nationalization decrees pertaining to certain industrial and financial enterprises. As a result, property of United States nationals estimated in value as between $30,000,000 and $50,000,000 was affected. Negotiations looking toward the compensation of American nationals opened in January, 1946. An exchange of notes between the two Governments of January 14, 1946 gave general assurances on the question of compensation and culminated discussions concerning commercial policy and related economic matters.[1]

The United States announced on November 9, 1945 that the withdrawal of American forces from Czechoslovakia would be completed by December 1, 1945, the date set for the withdrawal of Soviet troops from that area.[2]

A credit of $20,000,000 for the financing of cotton imports from the United States was advanced to the Prague Credit Bank by the Export-Import Bank of Washington in May, 1946.[3] Negotiations for a further credit of $50,000,000 were suspended by the Department of State, however, allegedly for three reasons: (1) the Czech nationalization of American enterprises; (2) the support by the Czechoslovak Government of Soviet charges that the United States, through its foreign lending program, was engaging in "economic imperialism"; and (3) the transfer by Czechoslovakia of surpluses to Rumania. As of November 20, 1945, these negotiations had not been resumed.[4]

For additional information on relations between the United States and Czechoslovakia during the period under review, see this volume as follows: on lend-lease and mutual aid, p. 142 and 154; and on international civil aviation, p. 660, 662 and 671.

(1) *Exchange of Notes between the Acting Secretary of State (Acheson) and the Ambassador of Czechoslovakia (Slavík) Concerning Commercial Policy, November 14, 1946.*[5]

(a) *Note from the Acting Secretary of State to the Ambassador of Czechoslovakia.*

The Government of the United States expresses its satisfaction at the successful conclusion of the discussions with the Government of Czechoslovakia concerning commercial policy, compensation for nationalized properties and related matters of mutual interest in furthering the economic relations between their two countries. These discussions have resulted in agreement by the two Governments on the following matters:

1. The two Governments affirm their continued support of the principles set forth in Article VII of the Mutual Aid Agreement of July 11,

[1] For the text of this exchange of notes, see below. For further information on the Czech nationalization program and negotiations with the United States, see Department of State, *Bulletin*, XV, p. 651 and 1027.

[2] *Ibid.*, XIII, p. 766.

[3] *Export-Import Bank of Washington: Second Semiannual Report to Congress for the Period January–June 1946.* Washington, 1946, p. 21.

[4] *New York Times*, November 21, 1946, p. 1.

[5] Department of State, *Treaties and Other International Acts Series* 1569.

1942,[1] and reiterate their desire to achieve the elimination of all forms of discriminatory treatment in international commerce, and the reduction of tariffs and other trade barriers.

2. The Government of Czechoslovakia is in accord with the general tenor of the "Proposals for Expansion of World Trade and Employment" recently transmitted to the Government of Czechoslovakia by the Government of the United States. Pending the conclusion of the negotiations at the general international conference on trade and employment contemplated by the "Proposals", the two Governments declare it to be their policy to abstain from adopting new measures which would prejudice the objectives of the conference.

3. The two Governments share the view that the conduct of international trade through the mechanism of bilateral barter, clearing, and similar agreements is generally not compatible with the maximization of benefits deriving from trade or with the goal of eliminating trade discrimination. The Government of Czechoslovakia has expressed the view, however, that the use of such agreements during the postwar transition period has been necessary, but it will direct its efforts to their abandonment and a return to multilateralism at the earliest possible date.

4. The Government of Czechoslovakia has declared that it must maintain a system of import and export controls during the postwar transition period in order to safeguard the equilibrium of its balance of payments while seeking to achieve in an orderly way its plan of economic reconstruction. The Government of Czechoslovakia will administer the issuance of import licenses without discrimination as among foreign sources of supply as soon as Czechoslovakia possesses or is able to obtain sufficient free foreign exchange so that it is no longer necessary for her to make her purchases within the limits of bilateral trade and financial agreements.

5. If the Government of either country establishes or maintains a monopoly or enterprise for the importation, exportation, purchase, sale, distribution or production of any article, or grants exclusive privileges to any enterprise to import, export, purchase, sell, distribute or produce any article, such monopoly or enterprise shall accord to the commerce of the other country fair and equitable treatment in respect of its purchases of articles the growth, produce or manufacture of foreign countries and its sales of articles destined for foreign countries. To this end the monopoly or enterprise shall, in making such purchases or sales of any article, be influenced solely by considerations, such as price, quality, marketability, transportation and terms of purchase or sale, which would ordinarily be taken into account by a private commercial enterprise interested solely in purchasing or selling such article on the most favorable terms.

6. The two Governments express their intention at the earliest practicable date to enter into negotiations looking toward the conclusion of a comprehensive treaty of friendship and commerce which will regulate to their mutual satisfaction economic relations between the two coun-

---

[1] *Ibid., Executive Agreement Series* 261.

tries. Meanwhile the two Governments have taken cognizance of the fact that each continues to accord to articles the growth, produce or manufacture of the other unconditional most-favored-nation treatment with respect to customs duties, the rules and formalities of customs, and the taxation, sale, distribution, and use within its territory of such articles consistent with provisions of the former trade agreement between the two countries dated March 7, 1938.

7. The Government of the United States and the Government of Czechoslovakia will make adequate and effective compensation to nationals of one country with respect to their rights or interests in properties which have been or may be nationalized or requisitioned by the Government of the other country. In this connection, the Government of the United States has noted with satisfaction that negotiations concerning compensation on account of such claims will shortly begin in Praha.

8. The two Governments agree to afford each other adequate opportunity for consultation regarding the matters mentioned above, and the Government of Czechoslovakia, recognizing that it is the normal practice of the Government of the United States to make public comprehensive information concerning its international economic relations, agrees to make available to the Government of the United States full information, similar in scope and character to that normally made public by the United States, concerning the international economic relations of Czechoslovakia.

The Government of the United States will be pleased to receive from the Government of Czechoslovakia a statement confirming its understanding of this agreement reached by the two Governments.

(b) *Note from the Ambassador of Czechoslovakia to the Acting Secretary of State.*

[Excerpts]

The Government of Czechoslovakia expresses its satisfaction at the successful conclusion of the discussions with the Government of the United States concerning commercial policy, compensation for nationalized properties and related matters of mutual interest in furthering the economic relations between their two countries. These discussions have resulted in agreement by the two Governments on the following matters:

. . . .

[Here follows text of agreement printed in (a) above.]

The Government of the Czechoslovak Republic is pleased to confirm by the present note its understanding of this agreement reached by the two Governments.

G. Finland

The Department of State announced on August 21, 1945, that, having concluded that "the Finnish parliamentary elections of March 1945 were freely

878 DOCUMENTS ON AMERICAN FOREIGN RELATIONS

conducted and expressed through secret ballot the democratic wishes of the Finnish people", the re-establishment of diplomatic relations between the two Governments [1] would be proposed.[2] Upon the favorable response of the Finnish Government, relations were resumed as of midnight, August 31, 1945.[3] The Finnish Minister was received in Washington on November 21.[4]

For information concerning the policy of the United States regarding Finnish membership in the United Nations, see this volume, p. 16. For information on the activities of the Export-Import Bank as applied to Finland, see *ibid.*, p. 638 and 641. The activities of the Council of Foreign Ministers in framing the peace treaty with Finland are dealt with in *The First Five Peace Treaties. Supplement: Documents, VIII, 1945–1946.*

H. Greece

For further information on relations between the United States and Greece during the period under review, see this volume as follows: on international civil aviation, p. 660, 662 and 671; and on lend-lease and mutual aid, p. 141, 142 and 154.

1. THE GREEK ELECTIONS

The Department of State, on August 20, 1945, announced that in accordance with the Yalta Agreement [5] the United States would send a commission, to cooperate with similar commissions appointed by the British and French Governments, to aid "in securing the free expression, by secret ballot, of the will of the Greek people" in the forthcoming elections.[6] This commitment was confirmed by the three Governments in a joint statement of September 19, 1945.[7] Formal provision for American participation in the observation of the elections was made by executive order on November 16, 1945.[8] Preliminary discussions among the four Governments were held in London and in various parts of Greece during December 1945,[9] and the date for the elections was ultimately set for March 31, 1946.[10] A statement on the report of the Allied commissions was released on April 11, 1946 [11] and the text of the final report was made public on May 10.[12]

The acceptance of a second invitation by the Greek Government to aid in the revision of the electoral lists prior to the September 1 election on the return of King George II was announced on June 18, 1946 — again in cooperation with the British Government.[13] A summary of the findings of the Anglo-American commission was released on August 19, 1946.[14]

Again at the invitation of the Greek Government, the United States announced on August 24, 1946, its decision to retain observers in Greece during the course of the plebiscite itself.[15]

---

[1] For information regarding the severance of diplomatic relations with Finland, see *Documents, IV, 1941–1942*, p. 642; *ibid., V, 1942–1943*, p. 589; and *ibid., VI, 1943–1944*, p. 683.
[2] Department of State, *Bulletin*, XIII, p. 283.
[3] *Ibid.*, p. 339.
[4] *Ibid.*, p. 861.
[5] See this volume, Appendix I.
[6] Department of State, *Bulletin*, XIII, p. 283.
[7] For the text of the joint statement, see *ibid.*, p. 429.
[8] For the text of Executive Order 9657, see *Federal Register*, X, p. 14243.
[9] Department of State, *Bulletin*, XIII, p. 970.
[10] *Ibid.*, XIV, p. 297.
[11] See this volume, p. 879.
[12] Department of State Publication 2522.
[13] Department of State, *Bulletin*, XIV, p. 1128.
[14] For the text of the summary, see *ibid.*, XV, p. 424.
[15] *Ibid.*, p. 425.

(1) *Summary of the Report of the Allied Mission for Observing the Greek Elections. White House Press Release, April 11, 1946.*[1]

[Excerpt]

. . . .

The Greek elections of March 31 were conducted under conditions that warranted holding them on the date selected. They were on the whole free and fair, and the results represent a true and valid verdict of the Greek people, in the considered judgment of the Allied Mission To Observe the Greek Elections.

This is the Mission's final judgment in a report to the American, British, and French Governments, made after analysis of factual information gathered in all parts of Greece by 240 trained observation teams throughout the period of pre-election campaigning, on election day, and in the few days immediately after.

The report recognizes "the present intensity of political emotions in Greece" and gives the election a favorable verdict after giving that factor in all its aspects study and consideration. If Leftist parties which boycotted the election had taken part, the single-house Parliament that was chosen would now include perhaps 20 percent, but certainly not more than 25 percent, of the representatives of those parties, but this would not have altered the general outcome, the Mission reports.

The Populist Party, a conservative party, had a majority in the popular vote and has a majority in the Parliament now. Almost all of the remaining votes and seats were won by the National Political Union, a party cooperating with the Populists, and the Liberal Party under former Premier Sophoulis.

The Allied Mission's report states that election day was peaceful and orderly, ranking well with past Greek elections and capable of standing comparison as to decorum with general elections in France, Great Britain, and America. It points out that, while some of the registration lists of voters had been completely recompiled for the election and were satisfactory, others have not been corrected by striking off the names of all the dead and others not qualified to vote. War and disorder and careless administration of electoral laws are mentioned as being responsible for this. The total registration figures are therefore inaccurate and misleading. The Mission's experts find that Greece's population is about 7,500,000, that a maximum of 1,989,000 males were qualified to be registered, and that of those 1,850,000 actually were validly registered. This was 93 percent of the eligibles. The number who voted March 31 was 1,117,000. While the presence of the names of dead or otherwise ineligible men on the uncorrected registers provided opportunity for fraud, the Mission found no evidence of such fraud on an important scale either in making up the lists of qualified voters or in plural voting. Among the specific findings of the section of scientific sampling experts of the Mission were these: For all Greece, 71 percent of the names on

[1] *Ibid.*, XIV, p. 671.

registration lists were unquestionably valid, only 13 percent were invalid, and 16 percent were of doubtful validity. Sixty percent of the number validly registered actually voted. The 40 percent who did not vote included an estimated 9.3 percent who allegedly abstained for "party" reasons, and varying percentages for other reasons not identifiable with political strategy. However, the technical analysts have allowed, in their basic estimates, for from 10 to an absolute maximum 20 percent of "party" abstention, with 15 percent as a probable maximum. The 15-percent estimate gives a total for deliberate abstainers of 280,000. But of the votes actually cast not more than 2 percent were cast illegally in the names of dead or unidentifiable persons. In other words, fraud of this kind may have been responsible for a maximum of 22,000 votes out of approximately 1,117,000 and could not have influenced general election results. Of the registered voters who did not vote, only 11,000 can be definitely regarded as having abstained because unfairly prevented from voting, the sampling staff says. Though, therefore, the Mission finds that the opportunity for fraud that was presented by the exaggerated registration lists was not exploited in this election, it recommends in its report that all registration lists in Greece, in rural as well as city areas, be completely recompiled before the opinion of the Greek people is again sought on matters of national importance, so as to remove all possible justification for fraud charges based on inaccurate registers in the future.

Some intimidation of voters both by Rightists and by Leftists was found, varying by regions and even villages. While this was general enough to be consequential on election day itself, it is regarded by the Mission as an inevitable product of Greece's experience under domestic dictatorship, under enemy occupation, and especially of the brief but desperate "civil war" between Leftist forces of the resistance movement and Greek Government forces at the end of 1944. The passions thus generated did produce intimidation in the year preceding the election. This was particularly marked against extreme Leftists in the agricultural regions of the Peloponnesus and in northwestern Greece. These conditions, says the Mission, had an important bearing on the abstention of EAM members from voting, and did have "some effect" on the election, without materially affecting the outcome.

Presence of British troops in Greece had no effect whatever on the election results, the Mission finds.

Investigation of complaints about pro-Rightists bias by police and gendarmerie led to the conclusion that the police as a whole were loyal to their duties but that some of the gendarmerie showed partisanship. This, however, had a very minor influence on the general results, the Mission says.

While under the present Greek election law abstention is illegal, its practice as party strategy is too well established by custom to permit control by legalistic means, says the Mission, and it does not feel that party abstentions this time either altered the results or represent a new and alarming element in Greek politics. The fact that abstention, although a contravention of Greek law, was countenanced by the authorities gave even dissident elements an opportunity fully to indicate their views. The Mission is convinced that its presence in Greece has a reassuring effect and contributed to orderliness.

. . . .

2. ECONOMIC AND FINANCIAL RELATIONS

Subject to certain limitations resulting, for the most part, from the limited foreign exchange resources in Greece, the resumption of private trade between the United States and Greece was announced by the two Governments on September 19, 1945.[1]

Discussions were held with a Greek economic mission in Washington from August 1 to 22, 1946. Topics of discussion included: (1) general economic, financial and reconstruction problems; (2) procurement and supply problems raised by the imminent cessation of UNRRA activities in Greece; (3) the revival of trade between the two countries through normal commercial channels; and (4) the settlement of lend-lease questions.[2] These same general problems were outlined on December 11, 1946, as the subjects of a survey to be made, at the request of the Greek Government, by an American mission under the direction of Paul Porter early in 1947.[3]

For information concerning the activities of the Export-Import Bank as applied to Greece, see this volume, p. 638 and 641.

3. INCIDENTS ON THE GREEK BORDER

For an account of the discussions of the Security Council concerning the presence of British troops in Greece and the occurrence of incidents on the Greek Frontier, see *International Organization*, I, p. 84–90 and *Yearbook of the United Nations, 1946–47*, p. 336–8, and 361–75.

A resolution concerning border violations along the Greek frontier, introduced by the United States on December 18,[4] was the basis of a resolution adopted unanimously by the Security Council on December 19.

(1) *Resolution Establishing a Commission of Investigation of Greek Border Incidents, Adopted by the Security Council, December 19, 1946.*[5]

WHEREAS, there have been presented to the Security Council oral and written statements by the Greek, Yugoslav, Albanian and Bulgarian Governments relating to disturbed conditions in Northern Greece along the frontier between Greece on the one hand and Albania, Bulgaria and Yugoslavia on the other, which conditions, in the opinion of the Council, should be investigated before the Council attempts to reach any conclusions regarding the issues involved.

Resolved: That the Security Council under Article 34 of the Charter establish a Commission of Investigation to ascertain the facts relating to the alleged border violations along the frontier between Greece on the one hand and Albania, Bulgaria and Yugoslavia on the other.

That the Commission be composed of a Representative of each of the Members of the Security Council as it will be constituted in 1947.

[1] *Ibid.*, p. 440.   [2] *Ibid.*, XV, p. 426.   [3] *Ibid.*, p. 1151.
[4] Not reprinted here. For text, see *ibid.*, p. 1172.   [5] *Ibid.*, XVI, p. 23.

That the Commission shall proceed to the area not later than January 15, 1947, and shall submit to the Security Council at the earliest possible date a report of the facts disclosed by its investigation. The Commission shall, if it deems it advisable or if requested by the Security Council, make preliminary reports to the Security Council.

That the Commission shall have authority to conduct its investigation in Northern Greece and in such places in other parts of Greece, in Albania, Bulgaria, and Yugoslavia as the Commission considers should be included in its investigation in order to elucidate the causes and nature of the above-mentioned border violations and disturbances.

That the Commission shall have the authority to call upon the Governments, officials and nationals of those countries, as well as such other sources as the Commission deems necessary, for information relevant to its investigation.

That the Security Council request the Secretary-General to communicate with the appropriate authorities of the countries named above in order to facilitate the Commission's investigation in those countries.

That each Representative on the Commission be entitled to select the personnel necessary to assist him and that, in addition, the Security Council requests the Secretary-General to provide such staff and assistance to the Commission as it deems necessary for the prompt and effective fulfillment of its task.

That the Representative of each of the Governments of Greece, Albania, Bulgaria and Yugoslavia be invited to assist in the organization of the Commission in a liaison capacity.

That the Commission be invited to make any proposals that it may deem wise for averting a repetition of border violations and disturbances in these areas.

I. Poland

1. THE POLISH ELECTIONS

(1) *Note from the United States Ambassador to Poland (Lane) to the Polish Foreign Office Regarding Arrangements for the Polish Elections, August 19, 1946.*[1]

I have been instructed by my Government to inform you that it has been glad to learn of the announcement that the Polish Provisional Government intends to promulgate electoral laws during the month of August and to hold elections early in the month of November. My Government is deeply conscious of the grave responsibility which it assumed, together with the British and Soviet Governments, by the decisions taken at the Crimea and Potsdam conferences with respect to the holding of free and unfettered elections in Poland.[2] During the conversations which were held in Moscow in June 1945 the Polish leaders agreed to the acceptance of the principles formulated at Yalta. Accordingly, the Polish Government which was then functioning in Poland was reorganized and there was created the Polish Provisional Government

---

[1] *Ibid.*, XV, p. 422.

[2] For pertinent sections of the Yalta and Potsdam Agreements, see this volume, Appendix I and Appendix II.

of National Unity, with which the Governments of the Soviet Union, Great Britain and the United States established diplomatic relations.

In departing from its traditional policy by assuming responsibilities in connection with the internal affairs of another State, my Government was motivated by the feeling that as one of the principal powers engaged in liberating the peoples of Europe from the yoke of Nazi aggression, it had a special responsibility to assist in giving the Polish people who had suffered so greatly from Nazi occupation an opportunity freely to choose the government under which they would live. My Government feels, therefore, that it has both the right and the duty to bring the following to the attention of the Polish Provisional Government of National Unity.

The United States Government considers that it had no responsibilities in connection with the referendum held in Poland on June 30. Nevertheless, as the Polish Ambassador in Washington informed my Government on April 24, 1946, this referendum was a measure preparatory to the election and the methods by which it was held bear a relation to the preparations for holding the election itself. The official representatives of the United States Government in Poland have reported that the voting in the referendum appeared to have been generally carried out in a correct and fair manner but that the methods used in tabulating the ballots and reporting the vote have given rise to charges of serious irregularities, including removal of ballot boxes from polling places in contravention of the referendum law.

It has also been brought to the attention of my Government that the Polish Labor Party charges that it was not allowed to hold its party congress and that as a result of this and administrative persecution of the party by arrests, censorship restrictions, administrative interference and other oppressive acts which have prevented normal democratic political activity, the Central Committee of the Labor Party has requested the membership of that party to suspend all political activity until such time as the attitude of the Polish Provisional Government toward the Labor Party has changed. The Polish Provisional Government is, of course, aware that one of the essential elements in the agreement for the holding of free elections in Poland is that all democratic, anti-Nazi parties shall have the right to take part and to put forward candidates. To this end it is necessary that all democratic parties be free to engage in political activity in the period preceding the elections.

Furthermore, my Government has learned with great regret that steps have been taken depriving the Polish Peasant Party of its right to assemble and to perform normal party functions at numerous points within Poland. According to reliable information the facilities which other parties enjoy in publishing electoral or party material, in using the radio for propaganda purposes and the ability to make known the views of the party through public posters and other forms of advertisement are, through censorship or other means, either denied to the Polish Peasant Party or restricted to a degree less than that accorded the parties adhering to the so-called government bloc.

In view of the foregoing, my Government wishes to emphasize its belief that *inter alia* it is essential for the carrying out of free elections that (1) all democratic and anti-Nazi parties shall be allowed to conduct election campaigns freely without arrest or threat of arrest. The parties recognized as "democratic and anti-Nazi parties" include the following: The Polish Workers Party (PPR), the Democratic Party (SD), the Polish Socialist Party (PPS), the Polish Peasant Party (PSL), the Peasant Party (SL), and the Labor Party (SP); (2) all such parties shall be represented on all electoral commissions and ballots be counted in presence of representatives of all such parties; (3) results shall be published immediately by local districts; and (4) there shall be an adequate system of appealing election disputes.

My Government is confident that the Polish Provisional Government of National Unity will take into account the views presented above in making arrangements for the elections.

(2) *Note from the Ambassador of Poland (Lange) to the Acting Secretary of State (Acheson) on the Proposed Polish Elections, April 24, 1946.*[1]

The Ambassador of Poland presents his compliments to His Excellency the Secretary of State and has the honor to communicate to him the following statement.

Certain information recently published in the press concerning the purpose of the Referendum proposed by the six Political Parties which support the Provisional Government of National Unity seems to imply that the Referendum is to be a substitute for the general elections. This is not the case. The Referendum is a measure preparatory to the election. The principal question to be submitted for decision must be clarified by popular vote before elections are held. This question is whether the future parliament is to be composed of one or two houses. This consultation is to take place this summer, by which time it is hoped that the major part of displaced citizens of Poland will be returned home. Thus, the Government will leave to the Electorate decisions on this basic constitutional issue.

The general elections will take place this year in accordance with the stipulations of Article IX: A of the Agreement of Potsdam of August 2, 1945, which notes that the Polish Provisional Government "has agreed to the holding of free and unfettered elections as soon as possible and on the basis of universal suffrage and secret ballot in which all democratic and anti-Nazi parties shall have the right to take part and to put forward candidates, and that representatives of the Allied Press shall enjoy full freedom to report to the World upon developments in Poland before and during the elections."

(3) *Note from the United States Chargé d'Affaires in Poland (Keith) to the Polish Foreign Office Regarding United States Position on the Polish Elections, November 22, 1946.*[2]

I have been instructed to inform you that my Government has taken note of the announcement that the Polish Government of National Unity has fixed January 19, 1947 as the date on which general elections will be

[1] Department of State, *Bulletin*, XV, p. 762.   [2] *Ibid.*, p. 1057.

held in Poland. In this connection, my Government recalls that Ambassador Lange's note of April 24, 1946 [1] stated that in accordance with the Potsdam Agreement of August 2, 1945, which provided that elections would be held as soon as possible, elections would take place this year. Although my Government is surprised that the Polish Government would fail, without explanation, to fulfill this formal assurance, its chief concern is not with any particular date but with the discharge of its responsibility under the decisions taken at the Crimea and Potsdam conferences with respect to the holding of free elections in Poland.

The importance which the United States Government attaches to the carrying out of these decisions has repeatedly been brought to the attention of the Polish Government. In his note of August 19, 1946,[2] to which no reply has been received, Ambassador Lane outlined certain points which the United States Government considers essential for the carrying out of free elections. In view of the disturbing reports which it has received concerning the preparations for the elections, my Government has instructed me again to inform Your Excellency that the Government of the United States expects that equal rights and facilities in the forthcoming election campaigns and in the elections themselves will be accorded to all democratic and anti-Nazi parties in accordance with the Potsdam Agreement. My Government could not otherwise regard the terms of the Yalta and Potsdam decisions as having been fulfilled.[3]

2. ECONOMIC AND FINANCIAL RELATIONS

(1) *Exchange of Notes between the Acting Secretary of State (Acheson) and the Ambassador of Poland (Lange) Concerning Economic and Financial Cooperation, April 24, 1946.*[4]

(a) *Note from the Acting Secretary of State to the Ambassador of Poland.*

The Government of the United States, desirous of aiding the people of Poland in their efforts to repair war damages and to reconstruct the Polish economy, expresses its satisfaction at the successful conclusion of the negotiations concerning the opening of credits of $40,000,000 to the Provisional Government of Poland by the Export-Import Bank of Washington, D.C., and the satisfactory conclusion of arrangements for extending credits up to $50,000,000 for the purchase by Poland of United States surplus property held abroad.

The Government of the United States hopes that these agreements will prove to be the first step toward durable and mutually beneficial economic and financial cooperation between the Governments of the two countries. It believes, however, that such cooperation can develop fully only if

[1] For the text of the note, see this volume, p. 884.
[2] For the text of the note, see *ibid.*, p. 882.
[3] For pertinent sections of the Yalta and Potsdam Agreements, see *ibid.*, Appendix I and Appendix II.
[4] Department of State, *Bulletin*, XIV, p. 761; also appears as *ibid.*, *Treaties and Other International Acts Series* 1516.

(1) a general framework is established within which economic relations between Poland and the United States can be effectively organized on the basis of principles set forth in Article VII of the Mutual Aid Agreement of July 1, 1942,[1] so as to result in the elimination of all forms of discriminatory treatment in international commerce, and the reduction of tariffs and other trade barriers;

(2) the Provisional Government of Poland is in accord with the general tenor of the "Proposals for Expansion of World Trade and Employment"[2] recently transmitted to the Provisional Government of Poland by the Government of the United States, and undertakes together with the Government of the United States to abstain, pending the participation of the two Governments in the general international conference on trade and employment contemplated by the "Proposals", from adopting new measures which would prejudice the objectives of the conference;

(3) the Provisional Government of Poland will continue to accord to nationals and corporations of the United States the treatment provided for in the Treaty of Friendship, Commerce and Consular Rights between the United States and Poland, signed June 15, 1931;[3]

(4) the Government of the United States and the Provisional Government of Poland will make both adequate and effective compensation to nationals and corporations of the other country whose properties are requisitioned or nationalized;[4]

(5) the Provisional Government of Poland and the Government of the United States agree to afford other adequate opportunity for consultation regarding the matters mentioned above, and the Provisional Government of Poland, recognizing that it s the normal practice of the Government of the United States to make public comprehensive information concerning its international economic relations, agrees to make available to the Government of the United States full information, similar in scope and character to that normally made public by the United States, concerning the international economic relations of Poland.

The Government of the United States undertakes herewith to honor and to discharge faithfully the obligations which relate to the United States specified in points (1) through (5) above, and would be pleased to receive a parallel undertaking from the Provisional Government of Poland with respect to those obligations specified in points (1) through (5) above which relate to Poland.

(b) Note from the Ambassador of Poland to the Acting Secretary of State.

The receipt is acknowledged, on behalf of the Provisional Government of Poland of your note of April 24, 1946 reading as follows:

[Here follows the text of the U. S. note printed above.]

[1] For text of the Agreement, see *Documents, V, 1942–1943*, p. 217.
[2] See this volume, p. 625.
[3] For the text of the Treaty, see Department of State, *Treaty Series* 862.
[4] For further information on the nationalization program undertaken by the Polish Government, see Department of State, *Bulletin*, XV, p. 651.

Under instructions from my Government, I have the honor to communicate to you the following:

The Provisional Government of Poland shares the views of the United States as expressed by the Secretary of State and undertakes herewith to honor and to discharge faithfully the obligations which relate to Poland specified in points (1) through (5) of the note under reference.

On May 10, 1946, Acting Secretary of State Acheson confirmed reports to the effect that the $40,000,000 credit granted to Poland by the Export-Import Bank had not been made effective. He also revealed that an additional credit for $50,000,000 extended for the purchase of surplus army supplies had been withdrawn and deliveries under it suspended. In connection with the latter credit, Mr. Acheson remarked that Poland had failed to fulfill promises undertaken at the time of its extension; he listed these as including: (1) the publication of the conditions of the loan in Poland; (2) permission for foreign correspondents to cover the forthcoming elections; and (3) the communication to the United States Government of the texts of other economic agreements negotiated by Poland. No reasons were given for the suspension of negotiations for the Export-Import Bank credit.[1]

It was announced on June 26, 1946, that the $50,000,000 credit had been restored following receipt of satisfactory assurances by the Polish Government that the unfulfilled obligations would be met.[2] With the communication of the texts of the other economic agreements in question, the Department of State further announced, on August 9, 1946, that final arrangements for the granting of the Export-Import Bank credit were being negotiated.[3] Because of an agreement with the Polish Government, however, the texts of these agreements were not made public.[4]

For information regarding lend-lease and mutual aid between the United States and Poland, see this volume, p. 142 and 154.

J. Spain

An extended series of discussions between the United States, the United Kingdom and France on relations with the Franco regime in Spain resulted, on March 4, 1946, in the announcement of an agreement on policy by the three Governments.[5] This announcement had been preceded on February 27, 1946, by a note from the French Government to the United States requesting the support of the United States Government in bringing before the United Nations Security Council the question of "certain recent developments" in Spain. The Department of State replied, in a note of March 9, 1946, that American support of the French proposal could not be given since "on the basis of its present analysis of all the facts in its possession concerning the Spanish situation . . . the Government of the United States does not believe that a situation exists, the continuance of which is likely to endanger the maintenance of international peace and security."[6] Failing American support, the French Government continued to communicate through regular diplomatic channels regarding the situation in Franco Spain.

[1] *New York Times*, May 11, 1946, p. 8; Department of State, *Bulletin*, XIV, p. 33.
[2] *Ibid.*
[3] *Ibid.*, XV, p. 335.
[4] *New York Times*, August 15, 1946, p. 8.
[5] For the text of the announcement, see this volume, p. 888.
[6] Department of State, *Bulletin*, XIV, p. 486.

The situation in Spain was ultimately brought to the attention of the Security Council at the initiative of the Polish Government in April, 1946. For a detailed account of the discussions of the "Spanish Question" within the United Nations, see *International Organization*, I, p. 49 and 81–84; and *Yearbook of the United Nations, 1946–47*, p. 345–51.

For pertinent sections of the Potsdam agreement regarding policy toward the Franco regime, see this volume, Appendix II.

For additional information concerning relations between the United States and Spain during the period under review, see this volume as follows: on international civil aviation, p. 661 and 662; and on relations with the Export-Import Bank, p. 639.

(1) *Position of the United States, the United Kingdom and France on Relations with the Spanish Government. Department of State Press Release, March 4, 1946.*[1]

The Governments of France, the United Kingdom, and the United States of America have exchanged views with regard to the present Spanish Government and their relations with that regime. It is agreed that so long as General Franco continues in control of Spain, the Spanish people cannot anticipate full and cordial association with those nations of the world which have, by common effort, brought defeat to German Nazism and Italian Fascism, which aided the present Spanish regime in its rise to power and after which the regime was patterned.

There is no intention of interfering in the internal affairs of Spain. The Spanish people themselves must in the long run work out their own destiny. In spite of the present regime's repressive measures against orderly efforts of the Spanish people to organize and give expression to their political aspirations, the three Governments are hopeful that the Spanish people will not again be subjected to the horrors and bitterness of civil strife.

On the contrary, it is hoped that leading patriotic and liberal-minded Spaniards may soon find means to bring about a peaceful withdrawal of Franco, the abolition of the Falange, and the establishment of an interim or caretaker government under which the Spanish people may have an opportunity freely to determine the type of government they wish to have and to choose their leaders. Political amnesty, return of exiled Spaniards, freedom of assembly and political association and provision for free public elections are essential. An interim government which would be and would remain dedicated to these ends should receive the recognition and support of all freedom-loving peoples.

Such recognition would include full diplomatic relations and the taking of such practical measures to assist in the solution of Spain's economic problems as may be practicable in the circumstances prevailing. Such measures are not now possible. The question of the maintenance or termination by the Governments of France, the United Kingdom, and the United States of diplomatic relations with the present Spanish regime is a matter to be decided in the light of events and after taking into account the efforts of the Spanish people to achieve their own freedom.

[1] *Ibid.*, p. 412.

(2) *Statement by the Representative of the United States (Connally) before the Political and Security Committee of the United Nations General Assembly, October 30, 1946.*[1]

[Excerpts]

* * * * *

The attitude of the United States toward the Franco regime is well known. We have made that perfectly clear at San Francisco, Potsdam, and London and on other occasions. Its fascist origins, nature, and policies are completely alien to our way of life. We reaffirm the basic concept of the inherent worth of the individual which such totalitarianism denies, and we advocate the establishment of effective democracy in all nations, where through free elections the people can select their governments and representatives.

It is for these reasons that we are unalterably opposed to the Franco regime, its totalitarian character, and its suppression of human rights and freedoms. We would like to see it replaced by a democratic government chosen by the freely expressed will of the Spanish people.

* * * * *

The proponents of a break of relations have not explained the sequence of events which they hope would follow and how these events would contribute to the desired end. For its part the United States Delegation believes that such a measure would produce no result beyond cutting off the Spanish people from communication with the rest of the world and thus making worse their present condition. More extreme coercive measures such as the application of economic sanctions against Spain would, in the long run, almost certainly produce economic and political chaos in that country. Political and economic chaos in Spain would undoubtedly lead to wide-spread civil strife. We would not desire to impose upon the General Assembly the responsibility of a course of action leading to economic and political chaos which could not be prevented from degenerating into civil war with serious international complications, which would array different Spanish factions against each other and enlist in varying degrees the support of different members of the United Nations. The United States does not believe that such conditions, particularly at a time when the economic and political reconstruction of Europe is of paramount importance, would contribute either to the development of a democratic regime in Spain or to the cause of international peace and security.

* * * * *

In conclusion, Mr. Chairman, I would like to summarize very briefly the position of the United States with respect to the Spanish question.

1. We are opposed to Franco and welcome any democratic change in Spain which protects basic human rights and freedoms.
2. We shall take part in any necessary action against the Franco regime, under the United Nations Charter, if and when this regime becomes a threat to international peace and security.

[1] *Ibid.*, XV, p. 1086.

3. Pending such an eventuality, we are opposed to coercive measures by the United Nations, such as a severance of diplomatic relations or the imposition of economic sanctions, because they would either aid Franco by uniting the Spanish people against outside interference or would precipitate the Spanish people themselves into the disaster of civil war with unknown but inevitably costly consequences.

4. We shall join in continuing to oppose the admission of the Franco regime, not only to the United Nations but to any international agencies set up at the initiative of the United Nations.

5. Finally, we believe that the Spanish people should determine their own destiny. Following the withdrawal of the Franco regime, it is our hope that they will establish a provisional government and hold a free election so that Spain may once again assume her rightful place as a member of the family of nat ons.

In yesterday's debate, Mr. Chairman, a number of delegations expressed their opposition to any action by the United Nations which might constitute intervention in the internal affairs of Spain. Let me reassure the members of the Committee on this point. The United States is fully committed to the fundamental principle of non-intervention. It is a basic tenet of our foreign policy. Our resolution in no way violates this fundamental principle. The government of Spain belongs to the Spanish people, and it is for them to determine the form of government they shall have and the people who shall administer it. We are not here proposing intervention. The United Nations in this resolution would simply explain to the Spanish people in the clearest possible terms why their country is not at present eligible for membership and full participation in the community of nations, and the conditions which they themselves must create in order to remove those obstacles.

It seems to the United States that this proposed course of action is both prudent and wise and the one most likely to accomplish the end we all desire. It is submitted for your serious consideration and we hope that it will meet with your approval.

(3) Resolution on Relations between Spain and the United Nations, Adopted by the General Assembly, December 12, 1946.[1]

The peoples of the United Nations, at San Francisco, Potsdam and London condemned the Franco regime in Spain and decided that as long as that regime remains, Spain may not be admitted to the United Nations.

The General Assembly, in its resolution of 9 February 1946, recommended that the Members of the United Nations should act in accordance with the letter and the spirit of the declarations of San Francisco and Potsdam.

The peoples of the United Nations assure the Spanish people of their enduring sympathy and of the cordial welcome awaiting them when circumstances enable them to be admitted to the United Nations.

The General Assembly recalls that in May and June 1946, the Security Council conducted an investigation of the possible further action to be

---

[1] *Ibid.*, p. 1143.

taken by the United Nations. The Sub-Committee of the Security Council charged with the investigation found unanimously:

(*a*) In origin, nature, structure and general conduct, the Franco regime is a Fascist regime patterned on, and established largely as a result of aid received from Hitler's Nazi Germany and Mussolini's Fascist Italy.

(*b*) During the long struggle of the United Nations against Hitler and Mussolini, Franco, despite continued Allied protests, gave very substantial aid to the enemy Powers. First, for example, from 1941 to 1945, the Blue Infantry Division, the Spanish Legion of Volunteers and the Salvador Air Squadron fought against Soviet Russia on the Eastern front. Second, in the summer of 1940, Spain seized Tangier in breach of international statute, and as a result of Spain maintaining a large army in Spanish Morocco, large numbers of Allied troops were immobilized in North Africa.

(*c*) Incontrovertible documentary evidence establishes that Franco was a guilty party with Hitler and Mussolini in the conspiracy to wage war against those countries which eventually in the course of the world war became banded together as the United Nations. It was part of the conspiracy that Franco's full belligerency should be postponed until a time to be mutually agreed upon.

THE GENERAL ASSEMBLY,

CONVINCED that the Franco Fascist Government of Spain, which was imposed by force upon the Spanish people with the aid of the Axis Powers and which gave material assistance to the Axis Powers in the war, does not represent the Spanish people, and by its continued control of Spain is making impossible the participation of the Spanish people with the peoples of the United Nations in international affairs;

RECOMMENDS that the Franco Government of Spain be debarred from membership in international agencies established by or brought into relationship with the United Nations, and from participation in conference or other activities which may be arranged by the United Nations or by these agencies, until a new and acceptable government is formed in Spain.

FURTHER DESIRING to secure the participation of all peace-loving peoples, including the people of Spain, in the community of nations,

RECOMMENDS that, if within a reasonable time, there is not established a government which derives its authority from the consent of the governed, committed to respect freedom of speech, religion and assembly and to the prompt holding of an election in which the Spanish people, free from force and intimidation and regardless of party, may express their will, the Security Council consider the adequate measures to be taken in order to remedy the situation;

RECOMMENDS that all Members of the United Nations immediately recall from Madrid their ambassadors and ministers plenipotentiary accredited there.

THE GENERAL ASSEMBLY FURTHER RECOMMENDS that the States Members of the Organization report to the Secretary-General and to the next session of the Assembly what action they have taken in accordance with this recommendation.

Since the United States had withdrawn its ambassador from Madrid, Mr. Norman Armour, in December 1945, no further action by the United States was required to implement the pertinent section of the Assembly resolution.

K. Sweden

For additional information concerning relations between the United States and Sweden during the period under review, see this volume as follows: on Swedish admission to the United Nations, p. 524; on international civil aviation, p. 661 and 662; and on relations with the Export-Import Bank, p. 639.

1. SWEDISH-SOVIET TRADE NEGOTIATIONS

(1) *Exchange of Notes between the Governments of the United States and Sweden Regarding Swedish-Soviet Trade Negotiations.*[1]

(a) *Note from the Chargé d'Affaires of the United States to the Prime Minister of Sweden (Hansson), August 15, 1946.*

As your Excellency is aware, the Government of the United States in December 1945 published its *Proposals for Expansion of World Trade and Employment*. A copy of this document was transmitted to your Excellency's Government. A basic principle of the Proposals is the promotion of a multilateral trading system on a non-discriminatory basis.

On February 18, 1946 the Economic and Social Council of the United Nations approved a resolution concerning the calling of an International Conference on Trade and Employment for the purpose of promoting the expansion of production and the exchange and consumption of goods. It is now expected that this Conference will be convened in the latter part of 1947. The resolution as approved by the Economic and Social Council establishes a preparatory committee, which is directed to prepare an annotated draft agenda, including a draft convention, for consideration by the Conference and suggests that this agenda include the principal topics contained in the aforementioned Proposals.

The resolution also directs the preparatory committee to submit to the Economic and Social Council recommendations concerning what states, if any, not members of the United Nations should be invited to the Conference on Trade and Employment.

It is my understanding that the Government of Sweden is at the present time engaged in the negotiation of a bilateral trade agreement with the Union of Soviet Socialist Republics which might last for five or more years, and that the quantities involved may, for particular products, absorb a substantial portion of the exports of Sweden.

The effect of such a long-term bilateral trade agreement would be to allocate specified quantities of Swedish exports for shipment to the U.S.S.R. irrespective of superior commercial opportunities which may develop in other countries. Predetermination of exports over a long period of time as to destination tends to freeze trade in a bilateral pattern thereby reducing the benefits arising from multilateral trade. Furthermore, other countries would be discriminated against in that they could not bid for and obtain a share of these Swedish exports during the period of the agreement, even though market conditions might make such transactions profitable to Swedish firms as well as to buyers in these other

[1] *Ibid.*, p. 506.

countries. Presumably, therefore, the proposed trade agreement with the U.S.S.R. might be of such a type as to prevent the Government of Sweden from assuming the obligations of the character contemplated in the Proposals.

The Government of the United States does not wish to see any peoples deprived of the opportunity to participate in the benefits of this program. Consequently it hopes that the Government of Sweden will conform to the basic principles of these Proposals in its trade agreements and will avoid entering into any agreement involving such quantities of goods for such periods of time as would make it impossible for Sweden to conform to the proposed charter of ITO in its commercial policy, and that it will at least retain its freedom of action by inserting, in any such bilateral trade agreements which it may negotiate, an appropriate clause making such agreements subject to any general agreements looking to trade expansion on a multilateral basis to which Sweden may in the future become a party. My Government on previous occasions has similarly expressed to other countries its views regarding bilateral trade agreements which involve relatively large quantities of goods for long periods of time.

The foregoing comments naturally do not refer to the extension of external credits by the Government of Sweden if the sales made pursuant to those credits are based on commercial considerations.

The views of the United States on this subject are also being communicated to the Government of the U.S.S.R.

(b) *Note from the Foreign Minister of Sweden (Unden) to the Chargé d'Affaires of the United States, August 29, 1946.*

In a note of the 15th of this month addressed to His Excellency Per Albin Hansson, Prime Minister and Minister of Foreign Affairs ad interim, recalling the initiatives taken in the international field with a view to establishing a multilateral system for commercial exchange on a non-discriminatory basis, you saw fit to present certain points of view on the commercial and financial agreement which is at present the subject of negotiations between the Swedish Government and the Government of the Union of Soviet Socialist Republics. At the same time you expressed in the name of your Government the hope that the Swedish Government will adapt its commercial policy to the general principles of the proposals published by the Government of the United States in the month of December 1945 with a view to the expansion of world commerce and full employment.

With reference to this communication I must call to your attention the numerous official declarations made by members of the Royal Government advocating the establishment of an international system of free exchange on a multilateral and non-discriminatory basis. It appears clearly from these declarations that the Swedish Government is ready to adhere to a multilateral arrangement which while facilitating the resumption of international commerce would include guarantees against national discriminatory measures in the commercial and financial field as well as in that of shipping, etc., subject however to the condition that such an arrangement would be of a truly international character, that is to say, that it would receive the approval of the principal States engaging in international trade. The Swedish Government will when the time comes take the liberty of presenting more fully its points of view on the above-mentioned American proposal.

It is in this spirit that, since the termination of hostilities in Europe, Sweden has on her part and within the limits of her capabilities striven to contribute to a rapid resumption of her foreign trade. In the present state of affairs in Europe this policy has necessarily had to be based upon a bilateral collaboration between Sweden and the various European nations with which it has commercial relations. It is, however, to be noted that as has been officially stated by Sweden, the Swedish authorities have constantly taken care that the bilateral agreements concluded or in course of negotiation between Sweden and the various foreign countries far from impeding the development of international trade should contribute to the establishment of true international collaboration in the economic field. These agreements, easy to incorporate in such an international arrangement, are also of such a nature as to favor the return of a true multilateralism in international trade.

The Swedish Government which must reserve to itself complete freedom of decision as to the opportuneness of concluding such bilateral agreements as well as of adhering to an eventual international commercial arrangement can hardly understand how the situation, being that set forth in the explanations given about Swedish commercial policy, can have given rise to conclusions of the sort contained in your Note.

The Swedish-Soviet Trade Pact was signed in Moscow on October 7, 1946.[1]

2. ALLIED-SWEDISH NEGOTIATIONS FOR GERMAN EXTERNAL ASSETS

Negotiations between representatives of the United States, Sweden, the United Kingdom and France on the disposition of German assets in Sweden were opened in Washington on May 31, 1946.[2] Successful conclusion of the discussions was announced on July 18 and an agreed statement was released by the delegations at that time.

(1) *Statement by Representatives of the United States, the United Kingdom, France and the Royal Swedish Government Regarding the Disposition of German Assets in Sweden, July 18, 1946.*[3]

German assets in Sweden, the nature and extent of which have been carefully examined, will be liquidated, in continuation of Sweden's policy of the elimination of German economic interests in Sweden.

Existing procedures for mutual exchange of information between the Allies and Sweden will be maintained. The proceeds of the liquidation of the German assets are now estimated to be approximately 375 million kroner. Of this amount 150 million, which shall be considered to be the

---

[1] *New York Times*, October 9, 1946, p. 19.
[2] Department of State, *Bulletin*, XIV, p. 992.
[3] *Ibid.*, XV, p. 174.

remainder left after clearing of these proceeds against certain Swedish claims, will be made available by the Swedish Government to be used for purchase of commodities for the German economy. These purchases, which would otherwise be at the expense of the Allies, are not limited to the Swedish market but can be made in any other country. Provision will be made by the Allies for compensation in German money of German owners concerned by these measures.

In accordance with its policy to restitute looted property, the Swedish Government agrees to restore monetary gold acquired by Sweden and proved to have been looted by Germany. Provisionally the amount now traced and to be restored is about 7 tons.

Provision will be made for equitable compensation in Germany for removals or other dispositions by the Allied authorities of property belonging to Swedish nationals or property in which there is a substantial Swedish ownership interest.

In pursuance of its policy to participate in the work of reconstruction and rehabilitation the Swedish Government proposed to make the following contributions:

(1) 50 million kroner to the Intergovernmental Committee on Refugees for use in rehabilitation and resettlement of non-repatriable victims of German action;

(2) 75 million kroner for the aid and rehabilitation of countries devastated by the war who were represented at the Paris Reparation Conference.

The Government of the United States has undertaken to unblock Swedish funds in the United States according to a procedure which is being worked out. The Allies have already eliminated the "blacklists".

Other matters of common interest have been satisfactorily settled between the negotiators.

The accord is subject to ratification by the Swedish Parliament.

Mr. Seymour Rubin represented the United States in the negotiations; Mr. Christian Valensi, France; Mr. Francis W. McCombe, the United Kingdom; and Justice Emil Sandstrom, Sweden.

L. Switzerland

For information on relations between the United States and Switzerland regarding international civil aviation during the period under review, see this volume, p. 661, 662 and 672.

1. ALLIED-SWISS NEGOTIATIONS FOR GERMAN EXTERNAL ASSETS

Negotiations between representatives of the United States, Switzerland, the United Kingdom and France regarding the disposition of German assets in Switzerland opened in Washington on March 18, 1946.[1] On May 21, agreement was announced on the disposition of German holdings in Switzerland and on gold received by Switzerland from Germany. The agreement phrased in general terms and requiring detailed implementation on a technical level provided that:

"(1) Holdings of Germans in Germany or Germans subject to repatriation will be identified and liquidated or transferred to persons acceptable to all concerned. This work will be done by a Swiss agency, which the Swiss Government will set

---
[1] Department of State, *Bulletin*, XIV, p. 955.

up. The Swiss agency will cooperate with a joint commission composed of representatives of the three Allied Governments and of Switzerland. Doubtful or controversial cases will be referred to arbitration.

"(2) The proceeds of liquidation will be divided equally between the Allies as trustees for the countries claiming reparations, and Switzerland. On their side, the Allies will turn the funds they obtain over to the Inter-Allied Reparation Agency for the rehabilitation of countries devastated or depleted by Germans. Procedure for the distribution of these funds was provided in the Paris Reparation Agreement signed in Paris in January of this year.

"(3) The Allies will accept a payment of 250,000,000 Swiss francs in consideration of which the governments signatory to the Paris Reparation Agreement will waive their claim and those of their central banks for restitution from Switzerland of monetary gold. This amount will also be divided in accordance with the Paris Reparation Agreement. The amount equals approximately $58,140,000." [1]

On May 25, 1946, letters identical in all but one respect were exchanged between the Allies and Switzerland constituting letters of agreement. The sole difference was in paragraph V "in which the Swiss delegation stated that it acted on behalf also of the Principality of Liechtenstein, whereas the Allies stated that they acted on behalf of the governments signatory to the Paris Reparation Agreement." [2]

(1) Letter Exchanged between the Delegate of the Government of Switzerland (Stucki) and the Chiefs of the Allied Delegations, May 25, 1946.[3]

In the course of the discussions which have taken place, the Allied Governments, fully recognizing Swiss sovereignty, claimed title to German property in Switzerland by reason of the capitulation of Germany and the exercise of supreme authority within Germany, and sought the return from Switzerland of gold stated to have been wrongfully taken by Germany from the occupied countries during the war and transferred to Switzerland.

The Swiss Government stated it was unable to recognize the legal basis of these claims but that it desired to contribute its share to the pacification and reconstruction of Europe, including the sending of supplies to devastated areas.

In these circumstances we have arrived at the Accord which follows:

I

1. The Swiss Compensation Office shall pursue and complete its investigations of property of every description in Switzerland owned or controlled by Germans in Germany and it shall liquidate such property. This provision shall apply equally to the property of such other persons of German nationality as are to be repatriated.

2. The Germans affected by this measure shall be indemnified in German money for the property which has been liquidated in Switzerland pursuant to this Accord. In each such case an identical rate of exchange shall be applied.

3. Switzerland will, out of funds available to it in Germany, furnish one-half of the German money necessary for this purpose.

4. The Swiss Compensation Office shall exercise the functions entrusted to it in close cooperation with a Joint Commission which shall be composed of a representative of each of the three Allied Governments, and a representative of the Swiss Government. The Joint Commission, as all interested private persons, shall have a right of appeal against the decision of the Swiss Compensation Office.

5. The Swiss Government will bear the cost of the administration and liquidation of German property.

II

1. Of the proceeds of the liquidation of property in Switzerland of Germans in Germany, 50 percent shall accrue to the Swiss Government and 50 percent shall

[1] Ibid.   [2] Ibid., p. 1121.   [3] Ibid.

be placed at the disposal of the Allies for the rehabilitation of countries devastated or depleted by the war, including the sending of supplies to famine stricken people.

2. The Government of Switzerland undertakes to place at the disposal of the three Allied Governments the amount of 250,000,000 Swiss francs payable on demand in gold in New York. The Allied Governments declare on their part that, in accepting this amount, they waive in their name and in the name of their banks of issue all claims against the Government of Switzerland and the Swiss National Bank in connection with gold acquired during the war from Germany by Switzerland. All questions relative to such gold will thus be regulated.

III

The procedures relating to the application of the present Accord are set out in the Annex.

IV

1. The Government of the United States will unblock Swiss assets in the United States. The necessary procedure will be determined without delay.
2. The Allies will discontinue without delay the "black lists" insofar as they concern Switzerland.

V

The undersigned representative of the Swiss Government declares on his part that he is acting also on behalf of the Principality of Liechtenstein.

VI

In case differences of opinion arise with regard to the application or interpretation of this Accord which cannot be settled in any other way, recourse shall be had to arbitration.

VII

This Accord and the Annex shall take effect upon their approval by the Swiss Parliament.

This Accord and the Annex have been written in English and French, both texts having the same validity.

M. Yugoslavia

For information on relations between the United States and Yugoslavia during the period under review, see also this volume, as follows: on lend-lease and mutual aid, p. 142 and 154; on international civil aviation, p. 661 and 662; and on relations with the Export-Import Bank, p. 639.

1. RECOGNITION OF THE FEDERAL PEOPLE'S REPUBLIC OF YUGOSLAVIA

The resignation of Dr. Ivan Subasitch, the Yugoslav Foreign Minister, on October 8, 1945, resulted in the collapse of the coalition regime proposed by the United States, the United Kingdom and the Soviet Union at Yalta.[1] This coalition, composed of Marshal Tito, Dr. Subasitch and a three-man regency representing the interests of King Peter, had been accepted by both Tito and Subasitch and recognized by the three powers. In receiving the recognition of the latter, the coalition had obligated itself to create an interim parliament including members of the pre-war legislature and to hold free elections. In announcing his resignation, Dr. Subasitch charged that the Tito regime had employed in Yugoslavia certain totalitarian tactics, including the maintenance of a secret underground police organization, that free elections had thus been rendered impossible and

---

[1] For pertinent sections of the Yalta Agreement, see this volume, Appendix I.

that other conditions required by the recognition of the coalition regime had not been met.[1]

On November 29, 1945, the Constituent Assembly at Belgrade declared the establishment of the Federal People's Republic of Yugoslavia and deposed the Yugoslav monarch.[2]

(1) Instructions Concerning the Recognition of the Federal People's Republic of Yugoslavia Transmitted to the United States Ambassador in Yugoslavia (Patterson). Department of State Press Release, December 22, 1945.[3]

The Yugoslav Ambassador on December 10 transmitted to the Secretary of State the following communication:

The Ambassador of Yugoslavia presents his compliments to the Honorable the Secretary of State and has the honor to notify the Government of the United States of America that the Yugoslav Constituent Assembly in the session of the 29th of November 1945, in accordance with the freely expressed will of the peoples of Yugoslavia, in the name of the people and in the name of the legal decisions taken by both houses of the Constituent Assembly, proclaimed Democratic Federative Yugoslavia a people's republic with the name "Federative People's Republic of Yugoslavia." By the same decision the monarchy has been abolished and Peter Karadjordjevic together with the entire Karadjordjevic dynasty deprived of all rights previously vested in him and in his dynasty.

On the 1st of December, 1945, the Constituent Assembly enacted the law of the Presidium of the Constituent Assembly. Under this law the Presidium of the Constituent Assembly is elected by both houses and consists of one president, six vice presidents, two secretaries and a maximum of thirty members. According to paragraph three of said law the Presidium, among other executive functions, represents inside and outside the country, the sovereignty of the people and of the state as the Federative People's Republic of Yugoslavia. The Presidium appoints the ambassadors, plenipotentiary ministers and extraordinaire envoys to foreign countries at the proposal of the Federative Government. The Presidium receives the credentials of the diplomatic representatives of foreign countries. According to paragraph six, when the Constituent Assembly becomes the regular Assembly the Presidium of the Constituent Assembly *ipso facto* becomes the Presidium of the regular Assembly. This law became effective on adoption by the Constituent Assembly the 1st of December, 1945.

In accordance with this law, the Presidium of the Constituent Assembly was elected as follows: President: Ivan Rybar, former president of the Provisional Assembly; Vice Presidents: Mosa Pijade, Filip Lakus, Josip Rus, Djuro Pucar, Dimtri Vlahov and Marko Vujacic; Secretary: Mile Perunicic.

The following reply dated December 22 has now been communicated to the Ambassador:

The Acting Secretary of State presents his compliments to His Excellency the Ambassador of Yugoslavia and has the honor to inform the Ambassador that the United States Government, having taken note of the contents of the Ambassador's communication no. A. Br. 1070 of December 10, 1945, recognizes

[1] *New York Times*, October 16, 1945, p. 1.
[2] *Ibid.*, November 30, 1945, p. 1.
[3] Department of State, *Bulletin*, XIII, p. 1020.

the changes which have taken place in the constitution of Yugoslavia and the establishment of a republic under the name "Federative People's Republic of Yugoslavia" in accordance with decisions of the Constituent Assembly referred to therein.

It is assumed that, pursuant to international custom, the new Yugoslavia Government will, as a member of the family of nations and as one which has subscribed to the principles of the Declaration by the United Nations, accept responsibility for Yugoslavia's international obligations, and be disposed to confirm its continued recognition of the existing treaties and agreements between the United States and Yugoslavia. Upon receipt of assurances in this sense, the United States Government is prepared to proceed with the issuance of appropriate letters of credence accrediting the United States Ambassador in Belgrade to the new Yugoslav regime.

Mindful of the obligations which it assumed at Yalta, the United States Government has consistently made known its attitude that the people of Yugoslavia are entitled to expect the effective implementation of the guarantees of personal freedom, freedom from fear, liberty of conscience, freedom of speech, liberty of the press and freedom of assembly and association contained in the agreement between Marshal Tito and Dr. Subasic underlying the Yalta Declaration and to have an opportunity to express their will in a free and untrammeled election. In view of conditions existing in Yugoslavia, it cannot be said that those guarantees of freedom have been honored nor that the elections conducted on November 11 provided opportunity for a free choice of the people's representatives. In the circumstances the United States Government desires that it be understood that the establishment of diplomatic relations with the present regime in Yugoslavia should not be interpreted as implying approval of the policies of the regime, its methods of assuming control or its failure to implement the guarantees of personal freedom promised its people. You should make it quite clear to the authorities and people of Yugoslavia that we entertain only the friendliest sentiments toward the peoples of the country and that it is our anticipation that the evolution of events will provide developments which will make possible those relations — both political and economic — between the peoples of Yugoslavia and the United States which we on our part most urgently desire to see.

The Department of State received the desired assurances regarding the acceptance of Yugoslavia's international obligations, requested in its note of December 22, 1945, on April 2, 1946.[1] The Ambassador of Yugoslavia presented his credentials and was received by the President on July 18, 1946.[2]

2. GENERAL RELATIONS WITH YUGOSLAVIA

Throughout the period under review, the United States maintained almost continuous diplomatic correspondence with the Yugoslav Government on the guarantee of civil rights in Yugoslavia both to United States nationals residing there and to Yugoslav nationals.

A voluminous exchange of notes occurred over the capture and trial of General Draja Mikhailovich, Minister of War of the Royal Yugolsav Government and

[1] *Ibid.*, XIV, p. 728. [2] *Ibid.*, XV, p. 180.

resistance leader during the Axis occupation of Yugoslavia whom the Tito regime charged with collaboration with the enemy. This correspondence extended through the spring and summer of 1946. Requests by the United States Government to furnish testimony in behalf of Gen. Mikhailovich were rejected by the Yugoslav Government [1] as were all attempts on the part of this Government to intervene on behalf of Archbishop Stepinac, similarly charged with treason and collaboration by the Yugoslav Government.

On July 24, 1946, the Department of State announced that the Yugoslav authorities had prevented claimants to American citizenship from communicating with the United States Embassy in Belgrade and had, in some cases, deprived them of their identification papers. The Department reported that an estimated 500 to 2,500 United States citizens were involved.[2] A further exchange of notes between the two Governments dealt with reports that the Yugoslav Government had employed United States nationals "at forced labor".[3]

(1) *Note from the Acting Secretary of State (Acheson) to the Chargé d'Affaires ad interim of Yugoslavia (Makiedo) Protesting Attacks by Yugoslav Forces Against United States Military Aircraft, August 21, 1946.*[4]

Serious consequences resulted from alleged Yugoslav attacks upon two United States military planes during the summer of 1946 and from the death or detention of their personnel at the hands of Yugoslav authorities. Repeated protests from the United States Government [5] resulted, on August 21, 1946, in an ultimatum demanding satisfaction from the Yugoslav Government.[6] Delivery of the ultimatum was immediately followed in this country by consultations between Secretary of State Byrnes and United States military officials.[7] The release by the Yugoslav Government on August 22 of the personnel involved in the first attack caused the Department of State, on August 24, 1946, to announce that the terms of the ultimatum had been met, although the United States reserved the right to decide whether the dispute should be brought before the United Nations Security Council, pending receipt of further evidence and depending upon "the efforts of the Yugoslav Government to right the wrong done".[8]

On August 30, 1946, Acting Secretary of State Acheson announced that the United States would claim indemnity for the loss of life and damages sustained in the two attacks.[9] The indemnity figure was subsequently set at an announced figure of less than $400,000 and accepted by the Yugoslav Government.

The American Embassy in Belgrade has informed me of the contents of the message received from the Yugoslav Foreign Office on August 20.[10] The replies of the Yugoslav Government to our inquiries are wholly unsatisfactory to the government and shocking to the people of the United States.

[1] For the texts of the notes exchanged on the trial of Mikhailovich, see *ibid.*, XIV, p. 634, 669 and 909.
[2] Department of State, *Bulletin*, XV, p. 232.
[3] For the text of the correspondence exchanged on the subject of treatment of United States nationals by the Yugoslav Government, see *ibid.*, p. 764.
[4] *Ibid.*, p. 417.
[5] For the text of the correspondence exchanged between the United States and Yugoslavia, see *ibid.*, p. 409, 415, 416, 417, 418, 501 and 725.
[6] For the text of the ultimatum, see below.
[7] *New York Times*, August 22, 1946, p. 1.
[8] *Ibid.*, August 25, 1946, p. 1.
[9] *Ibid.*, August 31, 1946, p. 1.
[10] Not reprinted here.

Your government expresses regret because of what you call an unhappy "accident." Your government is aware that this was no accident; that a fighter plane of your government deliberately fired upon a passenger plane of the United States Government. Your government states that one reason for the "accident" was that since August 10th there have been forty-four instances where American planes flew over Yugoslav territory. The records show that since August 10 the total number of flights scheduled for that route was only thirty-two. These flights were made under instructions to avoid flying over Yugoslav territory and if in any instance a plane was over Yugoslav territory it was only because the pilot was forced by bad weather outside of the corridor.

But this attack of August 19th was not the first. On August 9 a United States passenger plane while in the vicinity of Klagenfurt was fired upon by a fighter plane of the Yugoslav Government. It was forced to make a crash landing. When it landed, the crew and passengers were taken into custody by Yugoslav authorities and are still held as prisoners of the Yugoslav Government.

For some days the representative of the United States Government was unable to communicate with these American citizens. Finally he was permitted to do so but only in the presence of the military authorities of Yugoslavia. Twelve days have passed and these American citizens are still held by Yugoslavia.

The message now received from our representative indicates that on the 19th of August when this second passenger plane was fired upon, some if not all, of the occupants were killed. They met their death not by "accident" but by the deliberate acts of Yugoslav authorities. The excuse given for taking the lives of these American citizens is that the plane in which they were travelling was a few kilometers inside of Yugoslav territory. Your government asserts that for twelve minutes prior to the attack the pilot of the plane was "invited" to land. At the time you claim the pilot was "invited" to land the records at Klagenfurt show the pilot advised the Klagenfurt station that he was over Klagenfurt, which is well outside of Yugoslav territory, and was all right.

These outrageous acts have been perpetrated by a government that professes to be a friendly nation. Until we have had opportunity to confer with the survivors of these two attacks and we receive such other evidence as is available, we make no statement as to the exact location of the two planes when they were attacked.

Regardless of whether the planes were a short distance within or without the corridor, they were unarmed passenger planes en route to Udine, in Italy. Their flight in no way constituted a threat to the sovereignty of Yugoslavia. The use of force by Yugoslavia under the circumstances was without the slighest justification in international law, was clearly inconsistent with relations between friendly states, and was a plain violation of the obligations resting upon Yugoslavia under the Charter of the United Nations not to use force except in self-defense. At no time did the Yugoslav Government advise the United States Government that if one of its planes should, because of weather conditions, be forced a mile or two outside of the corridor or, because of mechanical troubles, should find itself outside of that corridor, the Yugoslav Government would shoot to death the occupants of the plane. The deliberate firing without warning on the unarmed passenger planes of a friendly nation is in the judgment of the United States an offense against the law of nations and the principles of humanity.

Therefore the Government of the United States demands that you immediately release the occupants of these planes now in your custody and that you insure their safe passage beyond the borders of Yugoslavia.

The Government of the United States also demands that its representatives be permitted to communicate with any of the occupants of the two planes who are still alive.

If within forty-eight hours from the receipt of this note by the Yugoslav Government these demands are complied with, the United States Government will determine its course in the light of the evidence then secured and the efforts of the Yugoslav Government to right the wrong done.

If, however, within that time these demands are not complied with, the United States Government will call upon the Security Council of the United Nations to meet promptly and to take appropriate action.

During the period under review, friction between the United States and Yugoslavia resulted from the presence of occupation forces of both countries in the Venezia-Giulia area. Clashes between border patrols occurred at least twice during the period,[1] and protests were received by the United States authorities against alleged mistreatment of Yugoslav nationals in the American zone of occupation.[2]

2. RELATIONS WITH PARTICULAR COUNTRIES OF WESTERN ASIA

A. Iran

For information concerning United States policy with regard to Soviet-Iranian relations, see this volume, p. 851.

B. Palestine

1. ADMISSION OF JEWISH REFUGEES TO PALESTINE

(1) *Letter from the President (Truman) to the Prime Minister of Great Britain (Attlee), August 31, 1945.*[3]

Because of the natural interest of this Government in the present condition and future fate of those displaced persons in Germany who may prove to be stateless or non-repatriable, we recently sent Mr. Earl G. Harrison to inquire into the situation.

Mr. Harrison was formerly the United States Commissioner of Immigration and Naturalization, and is now the Representative of this Gov-

---

[1] For the texts of the United States notes concerning border skirmishes and protesting the unauthorized entry of Yugoslav forces into the United States occupation zone (Zone A), see Department of State, *Bulletin*, XV, p. 414 and 676.

[2] For the text of the United States reply to this protest, see *ibid.*, p. 579.

[3] *Ibid.*, XIII, p. 790.

ernment on the Intergovernmental Committee on Refugees. The United Kingdom and the United States, as you know, have taken an active interest in the work of this Committee.

Instructions were given to Mr. Harrison to inquire particularly into the problems and needs of the Jewish refugees among the displaced persons. Mr. Harrison visited not only the American zone in Germany, but spent some time also in the British zone where he was extended every courtesy by the 21st Army Headquarters.

I have now received his report.[1] In view of our conversations at Potsdam I am sure that you will find certain portions of the report interesting. I am, therefore, sending you a copy.

I should like to call your attention to the conclusions and recommendations appearing on page 8 and the following pages — especially the references to Palestine. It appears that the available certificates for immigration to Palestine will be exhausted in the near future. It is suggested that the granting of an additional one hundred thousand of such certificates would contribute greatly to a sound solution for the future of Jews still in Germany and Austria, and for other Jewish refugees who do not wish to remain where they are or who for understandable reasons do not desire to return to their countries of origin.

On the basis of this and other information which has come to me I concur in the belief that no other single matter is so important for those who have known the horrors of concentration camps for over a decade as is the future of immigration possibilities into Palestine. The number of such persons who wish immigration to Palestine or who would qualify for admission there is, unfortunately, no longer as large as it was before the Nazis began their extermination program. As I said to you in Potsdam, the American people, as a whole, firmly believe that immigration into Palestine should not be closed and that a reasonable number of Europe's persecuted Jews should, in accordance with their wishes, be permitted to resettle there.

I know you are in agreement on the proposition that future peace in Europe depends in large measure upon our finding sound solutions of problems confronting the displaced and formerly persecuted groups of people. No claim is more meritorious than that of the groups who for so many years have known persecution and enslavement.

The main solution appears to lie in the quick evacuation of as many as possible of the non-repatriable Jews, who wish it, to Palestine. If it is to be effective, such action should not be long delayed.

(2) *Statement by the President (Truman) on the Palestine Situation. White House Press Release, October 4, 1946.*[2]

[Excerpts]

. . . .

It will be recalled that, when Mr. Earl Harrison reported on September 29, 1945, concerning the condition of displaced persons in Europe, I

[1] Not reprinted here. For text of Mr. Harrison's report, see *ibid.*, p. 456.
[2] *Ibid.*, XV, p. 669–670.

immediately urged that steps be taken to relieve the situation of these persons to the extent at least of admitting 100,000 Jews into Palestine.[1] In response to this suggestion the British Government invited the Government of the United States to cooperate in setting up a joint Anglo-American Committee of Inquiry, an invitation which this Government was happy to accept in the hope that its participation would help to alleviate the situation of the displaced Jews in Europe and would assist in finding a solution for the difficult and complex problem of Palestine itself. The urgency with which this Government regarded the matter is reflected in the fact that a 120-day limit was set for the completion of the Committee's task.

The unanimous report of the Anglo-American Committee of Inquiry was made on April 20, 1946, and I was gratified to note that among the recommendations contained in the Report was an endorsement of my previous suggestion that 100,000 Jews be admitted into Palestine.[2] The administration immediately concerned itself with devising ways and means for transporting the 100,000 and caring for them upon their arrival. With this in mind, experts were sent to London in June 1946 to work out provisionally the actual travel arrangements. The British Government cooperated with this group but made it clear that in its view the Report must be considered as a whole and that the issue of the 100,000 could not be considered separately.

. . . .

I have, nevertheless, maintained my deep interest in the matter and have repeatedly made known and have urged that steps be taken at the earliest possible moment to admit 100,000 Jewish refugees to Palestine.

In the meantime, this Government was informed of the efforts of the British Government to bring to London representatives of the Arabs and Jews, with a view to finding a solution to this distressing problem. I expressed the hope that as a result of these conversations a fair solution of the Palestine problem could be found. While all the parties invited had not found themselves able to attend, I had hoped that there was still a possibility that representatives of the Jewish Agency might take part. If so, the prospect for an agreed and constructive settlement would have been enhanced.

The British Government presented to the Conference the so-called "Morrison plan" for provincial autonomy and stated that the Conference was open to other proposals. Meanwhile, the Jewish Agency proposed a solution of the Palestine problem by means of the creation of a viable Jewish state in control of its own immigration and economic policies in an adequate area of Palestine instead of in the whole of Palestine. It proposed furthermore the immediate issuance of certificates for 100,000 Jewish immigrants. This proposal received wide-spread attention in the United States, both in the press and in public forums. From the discus-

[1] For text of Mr. Harrison's report, see *ibid.*, XIII, p. 456; for statement of the President, see this volume, p. 903.

[2] For excerpts from the report of the Anglo-American Committee of Inquiry, see *ibid.*, p. 908.

sion which has ensued it is my belief that a solution along these lines would command the support of public opinion in the United States. I cannot believe that the gap between the proposals which have been put forward is too great to be bridged by men of reason and good-will. To such a solution our Government could give its support.

In the light of the situation which has now developed I wish to state my views as succinctly as possible:

1. In view of the fact that winter will come on before the Conference can be resumed I believe and urge that substantial immigration into Palestine cannot await a solution to the Palestine problem and that it should begin at once. Preparations for this movement have already been made by this Government and it is ready to lend its immediate assistance.

2. I state again, as I have on previous occasions, that the immigration laws of other countries, including the United States, should be liberalized with a view to the admission of displaced persons. I am prepared to make such a recommendation to the Congress and to continue as energetically as possible collaboration with other countries on the whole problem of displaced persons.

3. Furthermore, should a workable solution for Palestine be devised, I would be willing to recommend to the Congress a plan for economic assistance for the development of that country.

In the light of the terrible ordeal which the Jewish people of Europe endured during the recent war and the crisis now existing, I cannot believe that a program of immediate action along the lines suggested above could not be worked out with the cooperation of all people concerned. The administration will continue to do everything it can to this end.

(3) *Exchange of Notes between the King of Saudi Arabia (Abdul-Aziz) and the President (Truman).*[1]

(a) *Note from the King of Saudi Arabia to the President, October 15, 1946.*

In my desire to safeguard and strengthen in every way possible the friendship which binds our two countries together and which existed between the late President Roosevelt and which was renewed with Your Excellency, I reiterate my feelings on every occasion when this friendship between the United States on the one hand, and my country and the other Arab countries on the other hand, is endangered, so that all obstacles in the way of that friendship may be removed.

On previous occasions I wrote to the late President Roosevelt and to Your Excellency, and explained the situation in Palestine; how the natural rights of the Arabs therein go back thousands of years and how the Jews are only aggressors, seeking to perpetrate a monstrous injustice, at the beginning, speaking in the name of humanitarianism, but later openly proclaiming their aggressiveness by force and violence as is not unknown to Your Excellency and the American people. Moreover, the designs of the Jews are not limited to Palestine only, but include the neighboring Arab countries within their scope, not even excluding our holy cities.

I was therefore astonished at the latest announcement issued in your name in support of the Jews in Palestine and its demand that floodgates of immigration be opened in such a way as to alter the basic situation in Palestine in contradiction to previous promises.[2] My astonishment was even greater because the state-

[1] Department of State, *Bulletin*, XV, p. 848.   [2] See this volume, p. 903.

ment described to Your Excellency contradicts the Declaration which the American Legation in Jeddah requested our Foreign Office to publish in the Government's official paper *Omm Al-Qura* in the name of the White House, on August 16, 1946, in which it was stated that the Government of the United States had not made any proposals for the solution of the Palestine problem, and in which you expressed your hope that it would be solved through the conversations between the British Government and the Foreign Ministers of the Arab States, on the one hand, and between the British Government and the third party on the other, and in which you expressed the readiness of the United States to assist the displaced persons among whom are Jews. Hence, my great astonishment when I read your Excellency's statement and my incredulity that it could have come from you, because it contradicts previous promises made by the Government of the United States and statements made from the White House.

I am confident that the American people who spent their blood and their money freely to resist aggression, could not possibly support Zionist aggression against a friendly Arab country which has committed no crime except to believe firmly in those principles of justice and equality, for which the United Nations, including the United States, fought, and for which both your predecessor and you exerted great efforts.

My desire to preserve the friendship of the Arab and the East towards the United States of America has obliged me to expound to Your Excellency the injustice which would be visited upon the Arabs by any assistance to Zionist aggression.

I am certain that Your Excellency and the American people cannot support right, justice, and equity and fight for them in the rest of the world while denying them to the Arabs in their country, Palestine, which they have inherited from their ancestors from Ancient Times.

(b) Note from the President to the King of Saudi Arabia, October 28, 1946.

I have just received the letter with regard to Palestine which Your Majesty was good enough to transmit to me through the Saudi Arabian Legation under date of October 15, 1946, and have given careful consideration to the views expressed therein.

I am particularly appreciative of the frank manner in which you expressed yourself in your letter. Your frankness is entirely in keeping with the friendly relations which have long existed between our two countries, and with the personal friendship between Your Majesty and my distinguished predecessor; a friendship which I hope to retain and strengthen. It is precisely the cordial relations between our countries and Your Majesty's own friendly attitude which encourages me to invite your attention to some of the considerations which have prompted this Government to follow the course it has been pursuing with respect to the matter of Palestine and of the displaced Jews in Europe.

I feel certain that Your Majesty will readily agree that the tragic situation of the surviving victims of Nazi persecution in Europe presents a problem of such magnitude and poignancy that it cannot be ignored by people of good will or humanitarian instincts. This problem is worldwide. It seems to me that all of us have a common responsibility for working out a solution which would permit those unfortunates who must leave Europe to find new homes where they may dwell in peace and security.

Among the survivors in the displaced persons centers in Europe are numbers of Jews, whose plight is particularly tragic inasmuch as they represent the pitiful remnants of millions who were deliberately selected by the Nazi leaders for annihilation. Many of these persons look to Palestine as a haven where they hope among people of their own faith to find refuge, to begin to lead peaceful and useful lives, and to assist in the further development of the Jewish National Home.

The Government and people of the United States have given support to the concept of a Jewish National Home in Palestine ever since the termination of the first World War, which resulted in the freeing of a large area of the Near East, including Palestine, and the establishment of a number of independent states which are now members of the United Nations. The United States, which contributed its blood and resources to the winning of that war, could not divest itself of a certain responsibility for the manner in which the freed territories were disposed of, or for the fate of the peoples liberated at that time. It took the position, to which it still adheres, that these peoples should be prepared for self-government and also that a national home for the Jewish people should be established in Palestine. I am happy to note that most of the liberated peoples are now citizens of independent countries. The Jewish National Home, however, has not as yet been fully developed.

It is only natural, therefore, that this Government should favor at this time the entry into Palestine of considerable numbers of displaced Jews in Europe, not only that they may find shelter there, but also that they may contribute their talents and energies to the upbuilding of the Jewish National Home.

It was entirely in keeping with the traditional policies of this Government that over a year ago I began to correspond with the Prime Minister of Great Britain in an effort to expedite the solving of the urgent problem of the Jewish survivors in the displaced persons camps by the transfer of a substantial number of them to Palestine. It was my belief, to which I still adhere, and which is widely shared by the people of this country, that nothing would contribute more effectively to the alleviation of the plight of these Jewish survivors than the authorization of the immediate entry of at least 100,000 of them to Palestine. No decision with respect to this proposal has been reached, but this Government is still hopeful that it may be possible to proceed along the lines which I outlined to the Prime Minister.

At the same time there should, of course, be a concerted effort to open the gates of other lands, including the United States, to those unfortunate persons, who are now entering upon their second winter of homelessness subsequent to the termination of hostilities. I, for my part, have made it known that I am prepared to ask the Congress of the United States, whose cooperation must be enlisted under our Constitution, for special legislation admitting to this country additional numbers of these persons, over and above the immigration quotas fixed by our laws. This Government, moreover, has been actively exploring, in conjunction with other governments, the possibilities of settlement in different countries outside Europe for those displaced persons who are obliged to emigrate from that continent. In this connection it has been most heartening to us to note the statements of various Arab leaders as to the willingness of their countries to share in this humanitarian project by taking a certain number of these persons into their own lands.

I sincerely believe that it will prove possible to arrive at a satisfactory settlement of the refugee problem along the lines which I have mentioned above.

With regard to the possibility envisaged by Your Majesty that force and violence may be used by Jews in aggressive schemes against the neighboring Arab countries, I can assure you that this Government stands opposed to aggression of any kind or to the employment of terrorism for political purposes. I may add, moreover, that I am convinced that responsible Jewish leaders do not contemplate a policy of aggression against the Arab countries adjacent to Palestine.

I cannot agree with Your Majesty that my statement of October 4 is in any way inconsistent with the position taken in the statement issued on my behalf on August 16. In the latter statement the hope was expressed that as a result of the proposed conversations between the British Government and the Jewish and Arab representatives a fair solution of the problem of Palestine could be found and immediate steps could be taken to alleviate the situation of the displaced Jews in Europe. Unfortunately, these hopes have not been realized. The conversations between the British Government and the Arab representatives have, I understand, been adjourned until December without a solution having been found for the problem of Palestine or without any steps having been taken to alleviate the situation of the displaced Jews in Europe.

In this situation it seemed incumbent upon me to state as frankly as possible the urgency of the matter and my views both as to the direction in which a solution based on reason and good will might be reached and the immediate steps which should be taken. This I did in my statement of October 4.

I am at a loss to understand why Your Majesty seems to feel that this statement was in contradiction to previous promises or statements made by this Government. It may be well to recall here that in the past this Government, in outlining its attitude on Palestine, has given assurances that it would not take any action which might prove hostile to the Arab people, and also that in its view there should be no decision with respect to the basic situation in Palestine without prior consultation with both Arabs and Jews.

I do not consider that my urging of the admittance of a considerable number of displaced Jews into Palestine or my statements with regard to the solution of the problem of Palestine in any sense represent an action hostile to the Arab people. My feelings with regard to the Arabs when I made these statements were, and are at the present time, of the most friendly character. I deplore any kind of conflict between Arabs and Jews, and am convinced that if both peoples approach the problems before them in a spirit of conciliation and moderation these problems can be solved to the lasting benefit of all concerned.

I furthermore do not feel that my statements in any way represent a failure on the part of this Government to live up to its assurance that in its view there should be no decision with respect to the basic situation in Palestine without consultation with both Arabs and Jews. During the current year there have been a number of consultations with both Arabs and Jews.

Mindful of the great interest which your country, as well as my own, has in the settlement of the various matters which I have set forth above, I take this opportunity to express my earnest hope that Your Majesty, who occupies a position of such eminence in the Arab world, will use the great influence which you possess to assist in the finding in the immediate future of a just and lasting solution. I am anxious to do all that I can to aid in the matter and I can assure Your Majesty that the Government and people of the United States are continuing to be solicitous of the interests and welfare of the Arabs upon whose historic friendship they place great value.

I also take this occasion to convey to Your Majesty my warm personal greetings and my best wishes for the continued health and welfare of Your Majesty and your people.

2. ANGLO-AMERICAN COMMITTEE OF INQUIRY

(1) *Report of the Anglo-American Committee of Inquiry, Lausanne, Switzerland, April 20, 1946.*[1]

[Excerpts]

The Anglo-American Committee of Inquiry, under the joint chairmanship of Joseph C. Hutcheson (United States) and Sir John Singleton (Great Britain), opened its investigations in Washington, D.C., on January 4, 1946. In the course of its operations, the Committee and its subcommittees journeyed to London, the American Zone of Germany, Czechoslovakia, Paris, the French Zones of Germany and Austria, Berlin, Poland, the British Zone of Germany, Vienna, the American and British Zones of Austria, Italy, Cairo, Palestine, Damascus, Beirut, Baghdad, Riyadh, Amman and Lausanne, Switzerland. At hearings in Washington from January 4 to 17 and in London from January 23 to February 4, 1946, numerous Jewish, Arab and Christian groups were invited to present their views before the Committee undertook its personal investigations. The Committee ended its deliberations at Lausanne, Switzerland, and submitted its report from that city on April 20, 1946.

---

[1] Department of State Publication 2536.

CHAPTER I. RECOMMENDATIONS AND COMMENTS

The European Problem

Recommendation No 1. We have to report that such information as we received about countries other than Palestine gave no hope of substantial assistance in finding homes for Jews wishing or impelled to leave Europe.

But Palestine alone cannot meet the emigration needs of the Jewish victims of Nazi and Fascist persecution; the whole world shares responsibility for them and indeed for the resettlement of all "displaced persons".

We therefore recommend that our Governments together, and in association with other countries, should endeavor immediately to find new homes for all such "displaced persons", irrespective of creed or nationality, whose ties with their former communities have been irreparably broken.

Though emigration will solve the problems of some victims of persecution, the overwhelming majority, including a considerable number of Jews, will continue to live in Europe. We recommend therefore that our Governments endeavor to secure that immediate effect is given to the provision of the United Nations Charter calling for "universal respect for, and observance of, human rights and fundamental freedoms for all without distinction as to race, sex, language, or religion".

Refugee Immigration Into Palestine

Recommendation No 2. We recommend (*a*) that 100,000 certificates be authorized immediately for the admission into Palestine of Jews who have been the victims of Nazi and Fascist persecution; (*b*) that these certificates be awarded as far as possible in 1946 and that actual immigration be pushed forward as rapidly as conditions will permit.

Comment

Since the end of hostilities, little has been done to provide for their resettlement elsewhere. Immigration laws and restrictions bar their entry to most countries and much time must pass before such laws and restrictions can be altered and effect given to the alterations. Some can go to countries where they have relatives; others may secure inclusion in certain quotas. Their number is comparatively small.

We know of no country to which the great majority can go in the immediate future other than Palestine. Furthermore that is where almost all of them want to go. There they are sure that they will receive a welcome denied them elsewhere. There they hope to enjoy peace and rebuild their lives.

We believe it is essential that they should be given an opportunity to do so at the earliest possible time. Furthermore we have the assurances of the leaders of the Jewish Agency that they will be supported and cared for.

We recommend the authorization and issue of 100,000 certificates for these reasons and because we feel that their immediate issue will have a most salutary effect upon the whole situation.

Principles of Government: No Arab, No Jewish State

Recommendation No 3. In order to dispose, once and for all, of the exclusive claims of Jews and Arabs to Palestine, we regard it as essential that a clear statement of the following principles should be made:

I. That Jew shall not dominate Arab and Arab shall not dominate Jew in Palestine. II. That Palestine shall be neither a Jewish state nor an Arab state. III. That the form of government ultimately to be established, shall, under international guarantees, fully protect and preserve the interests in the Holy Land of Christendom and of the Moslem and Jewish faiths.

Thus Palestine must ultimately become a state which guards the rights and interests of Moslems, Jews and Christians alike; and accords to the inhabitants, as a whole, the fullest measure of self-government, consistent with the three paramount principles set forth above.

Comment

. . . . . .

We, therefore, emphatically declare that Palestine is a Holy Land, sacred to Christian, to Jew and to Moslem alike; and because it is a Holy Land, Palestine is not, and can never become, a land which any race or religion can justly claim as its very own.

We further, in the same emphatic way, affirm that the fact that it is the Holy Land, sets Palestine completely apart from other lands, and dedicates it to the precepts and practices of the Brotherhood of Man, not those of narrow nationalism.

For another reason, in the light of its long history, and particularly its history of the last thirty years, Palestine cannot be regarded as either a purely Arab or a purely Jewish land.

. . . . . .

Mandate and United Nations Trusteeship

Recommendation No. 4. We have reached the conclusion that the hostility between Jews and Arabs and, in particular, the determination of each to achieve domination, if necessary by violence, make it almost certain that, now and for some time to come, any attempt to establish either an independent Palestinian State or independent Palestinian States would result in civil strife such as might threaten the peace of the world.

We therefore recommend that, until this hostility disappears, the Government of Palestine be continued as at present under mandate pending the execution of a trusteeship agreement under the United Nations.

Comment

We recognize that in view of the powerful forces both Arab and Jewish, operating from outside Palestine, the task of Great Britain, as Mandatory, has not been easy. The Peel Commission declared in 1937 that the Mandate was unworkable, and the Permanent Mandates Commission of the League of Nations thereupon pointed out that it became almost unworkable once it was publicly declared to be so by such a body. Two years later the British Government, having come to the conclusion that the alternative of partition proposed by the Peel Commission was also unworkable, announced their intention of taking steps to terminate the Mandate by the establishment of an independent Palestine State. Our recommendations are based on what we believe at this stage to be as fair a measure of justice to all as we can find in view of what has gone before and of all that has been done. We recognize that they are not in accord with the claims of either party, and furthermore that they involve a departure from the recent policy of the Mandatory. We recognize that, if they are adopted, they will involve a long period of trusteeship, which will mean a very heavy burden for any single Government to undertake, a burden which would be lightened if the difficulties were appreciated and the Trustee had the support of other members of the United Nations.

Equality of Standards

Recommendation No 5. Looking towards a form of ultimate self-government, consistent with the three principles laid down in Recommendation No. 3, we recommend that the mandatory or trustee should proclaim the principle that Arab economic, educational and political advancement in Palestine is of equal importance with that of the Jews; and should at once prepare measures designed to bridge the gap which now exists and raise the Arab standard of living to that of the Jews; and so bring the two peoples to a full appreciation of their common interest and common destiny in the land where both belong.

Comment

Our examination of conditions in Palestine led us to the conclusion that one of the chief causes of friction is the great disparity between the Jewish and Arab standards of living. Even under conditions of war, which brought considerable financial benefits to the Arabs, this disparity has not been appreciably reduced. Only by a deliberate and carefully planned policy on the part of the Mandatory can the Arab standard of living be raised to that of the Jews. In stressing the need for such a policy we would particularly call attention to the discrepancies between the social services, including hospitals, available in Palestine for Jews and Arabs.

. . . .

Future Immigration Policy

Recommendation No. 6. We recommend that, pending the early reference to the United Nations and the execution of a trusteeship agreement, the mandatory should administer Palestine according to the mandate which declares with regard to immigration that "The administration of Palestine, while ensuring that the rights and position of other sections of the population are not prejudiced, shall facilitate Jewish immigration under suitable conditions".

Comment

We have recommended the admission of 100,000 immigrants, victims of Nazi persecution, as soon as possible. We now deal with the position after the admission of that number. We cannot look far into the future. We cannot construct a yardstick for annual immigration. Until a Trusteeship Agreement is executed it is our clear opinion that Palestine should be administered in accordance with the terms of the Mandate quoted above.

. . . .

We desire, however, to state certain considerations which we agree should be taken into account in determining what number of immigrants there should be in any period. It is the right of every independent nation to determine in the interests of its people the number of immigrants to be admitted to its lands. Similarly it must, we think, be conceded that it should be the right of the Government of Palestine to decide, having regard to the well-being of all the people of Palestine, the number of immigrants to be admitted within any given period.

. . . .

The well-being of all the people of Palestine, be they Jews, Arabs, or neither, must be the governing consideration. We reject the view that there shall be no further Jewish immigration into Palestine without Arab acquiescence, a view which would result in the Arab dominating the Jew. We also reject the insistent Jewish demand that forced Jewish immigration must proceed apace in order to produce as quickly as possible a Jewish majority and a Jewish State. The well-being of the Jews must not be subordinated to that of the Arabs; nor that of the Arabs to the Jews. The well-being of both, the economic situation of Palestine as a whole, the degree of execution of plans for further development, all have to be carefully considered in deciding the number of immigrants for any particular period.

LAND POLICY

Recommendation No. 7. (a) We recommend that the Land Transfers Regulations of 1940 be rescinded and replaced by regulations based on a policy of freedom in the sale, lease or use of land, irrespective of race, community or creed, and providing adequate protection for the interests of small owners and tenant cultivators; (b) We further recommend that steps be taken to render nugatory and to prohibit provisions in conveyances, leases and agreements relating to land which stipulates that only members of one race, community or creed may be employed on or about or in connection therewith; (c) We recommend that the Government should exercise such close supervision over the Holy Places and localities such as the Sea of Galilee and its vicinity as will protect them from desecration and from uses which offend the conscience of religious people, and that such laws as are required for this purpose be enacted forthwith.

Comment

We do not believe that the necessary protection for the Arab can be provided only by confining the Jew to particular portions of Palestine. Such a policy, suggested by the Peel Commission, is consistent with their proposed solution, partition, but scarcely with that put forward by us.

ECONOMIC DEVELOPMENT

Recommendation No. 8. Various plans for large-scale agricultural and industrial development in Palestine have been presented for our consideration; these projects, if successfully carried into effect, could not only greatly enlarge the capacity of the country to support an increasing population but also raise the living standards of Jew and Arab alike.

We are not in a position to assess the soundness of these specific plans; but we cannot state too strongly that, however technically feasible they may be, they will fail unless there is peace in Palestine. Moreover their full success requires the willing cooperation of adjacent Arab states, since they are not merely Palestinian projects. We recommend therefore that the examination, discussion and execution of these plans be conducted, from the start and throughout, in full consultation and cooperation not only with the Jewish Agency but also with the governments of the neighboring Arab States directly affected.

EDUCATION

Recommendation No. 9. We recommend that, in the interests of the conciliation of the two peoples and of general improvement of the Arab standard of living, the educational system of both Jews and Arabs be reformed, including the introduction of compulsory education within a reasonable time.

THE NEED FOR PEACE IN PALESTINE

Recommendation No. 10. We recommend that, if this Report is adopted, it should be made clear beyond all doubt to both Jews and Arabs that any attempt from either side, by threats of violence, by terrorism, or by the organization or use of illegal armies to prevent its execution, will be resolutely suppressed.

Furthermore, we express the view that the Jewish Agency should at once resume active cooperation with the Mandatory in the suppression of terrorism and of illegal immigration, and in the maintenance of that law and order throughout Palestine which is essential for the good of all, including the new immigrants.

* * * * * *

CHAPTER X. GENERAL

1. In view of the dissolution of the League of Nations and of the statement of the Secretary of State for Foreign Affairs in the House of Commons on the 13th November, 1945, we assume that the British Government will in the near future prepare a draft Trusteeship Agreement for eventual submission to the United Nations, and that this Agreement will include the terms under which Palestine will be administered. We do not propose to refer to the existing Mandate in detail; it is set out in Appendix VI.[1]

2. Our views on future immigration policy are contained in Recommendation No. 6 and in the Comments thereunder, and we have nothing to add to them.[2]

3. With regard to the future government of Palestine, we have reviewed the question of a solution by partition.

* * * * * *

We have considered the matter anew and we have heard the views of various witnesses of great experience. Partition has an appeal at first sight as giving a prospect of early independence and self-government to Jews and Arabs, but in our view no partition would have any chance unless it was basically acceptable to Jews and Arabs, and there is no sign of that today. We are accordingly unable to recommend partition as the solution.

4. Palestine is a country unlike any other. It is not merely a place in which Arabs and Jews live. Millions of people throughout the world take a fervent interest in Palestine and in its Holy Places and are deeply grieved by the thought that it has been the seat of trouble for so long and by the fear that it may well become the cockpit of another war. Lord Milner in 1923, having declared himself a strong supporter of pro-Arab policy, said:

"Palestine can never be regarded as a country on the same footing as the other Arab countries. You cannot ignore all history and tradition in the matter. You cannot ignore the fact that this is the cradle of two of the great religions of the world. It is a sacred land to the Arabs, but it is also a sacred land to the Jews and the Christian; and the future of Palestine cannot possibly be left to be determined by the temporary impressions and feelings of the Arab majority in the country of the present day."

The Peel Commission having cited those words wrote (Chapter II, paragraph 51): "The case stated by Lord Milner against an Arab control of Palestine applies equally to a Jewish control." That expresses our view absolutely.

Efforts have been made from time to time to encourage both Arabs and Jews to take part in the Government of the country but these efforts have failed through mutual antagonism; perhaps they might have been pursued further. It is not the case of a backward people going through a period of tutelage; the issue lies between Jews and Arabs.

We believe this can only be met by acceptance of the principle that there shall be no domination of the one by the other, that Palestine shall be neither an Arab nor a Jewish State. The setting up of self-governing institutions is dependent on the will to work together on the part of Jews and Arabs. There has been little sign of that in recent years and yet we hope a change may take place if and when the fear of dominance is removed. We do not think that any good purpose would be served by our going into further detail; once the will to work together appears, representatives of both sides will be of help in framing a constitution; until that happens no step can be taken.

[1] Not reprinted here.   [2] See this volume, p. 911.

Meantime Palestine must remain under some form of Mandate or Trusteeship. We have suggested elsewhere in our Report that much can be done to encourage general advancement by the improvement of educational facilities and measures directed to narrowing the social and economic disparities. We feel, too, that it should be possible to draw the communities closer together, and foster a popular interest in self-government at the local level. Especially in the country districts, a spirit of good neighborliness exists among the common people, Arabs and Jews, despite the general state of political tension in the country. Practical cooperation is evident in day-to-day affairs. We suggest that local administrative areas might be formed, some purely Arab or Jewish in composition, but some of mixed population where a corporate sense of civic responsibility can be encouraged and a new beginning made in the development of self-government.

5. Land questions have been the cause of much friction and dispute between Jews and Arabs. We are opposed to legislation and practices which discriminate against either, and for the reasons already given we recommend the rescission and replacement of the Land Transfers Regulations of 1940 and the prohibition of restrictions limiting employment on certain lands to members of one race, community or creed.

We are aware of the criticisms of the existing Land Ordinances and we do not wish it to be thought that we consider that they afford adequate protection to the Arab small-owners and tenants. In our opinion it should be possible to devise Ordinances furnishing proper protection to such Arabs no matter in what part of Palestine they may reside.

6. We have already stated that the 100,000 certificates for Palestine, the immediate authorization of which we recommend, will provide for only a comparatively small proportion of the total number of Jewish refugees in Europe. The general problem of refugees must, we feel, be dealt with by the United Nations. In our considered opinion it is a matter for regret that this distressing problem has not been dealt with before this time. True the great Powers have had many problems facing them and they have dealt with many displaced persons, but the fact remains that Jews and others have remained in camps or centers for very many months.

We observe that at a recent meeting of the General Assembly of the United Nations the problem of displaced persons and refugees of all categories was recognized to be one of immediate urgency, and it was referred to the Economic and Social Council which has since established a special Committee for its consideration. Without presuming to advise that Committee, and with no desire to go beyond our Terms of Reference, we cannot but observe that international bodies already established for dealing with refugee problems have been unable, through insufficiency of financial resources or other reasons, to fulfill the hopes placed in them at the time of their formation. The world looks forward, we believe, to the birth of a truly effective agency of international collaboration in the humanitarian task of migration and resettlement.

. . . .

C. The Yemen

(1) *Exchange of Notes between the Chief, Special United States Diplomatic Mission to the Yemen (Eddy) and the Deputy Minister of Foreign Affairs of the Yemen (Abdul Karim Mutahhar), Sana'a, May 4, 1946.*[1]

(a) *Note from the Chief, Special United States Diplomatic Mission to the Yemen to the Deputy Minister of Foreign Affairs of the Yemen.*

I have the honor to make the following statement of my Government's understanding of the agreement reached through conversations held at

---

[1] Department of State, *Treaties and Other International Acts Series* 1535.

Sana'a April 14 to May 4 by representatives of the Government of the United States of America and the Government of the Kingdom of the Yemen with reference to diplomatic and consular representation, juridical protection, commerce and navigation as hereafter defined. These two Governments, having in mind the letter dated March 4, 1946, from the President of the United States of America to the Imam Yehya Bin Mohamed Hamid-ud-din, King of the Yemen, by which the United States of America recognized the complete and absolute independence of the Kingdom of the Yemen, and desiring to strengthen the friendly relations happily existing between the two countries, and to respect the rights of this independence recognized by the above-mentioned letter as the basis for all their relations and to maintain the most-favored-nation principle in its unconditional and unlimited form as the basis of their commercial relations, agree to the following provisions:

Article I

The United States of America and the Kingdom of the Yemen will exchange diplomatic representatives and consular officers at a date which shall be fixed by mutual agreement between the two Governments.

Article II

The diplomatic representatives of each Party accredited to the Government of the other Party shall enjoy in the territories of such other Party the rights, privileges, exemptions and immunities accorded under generally recognized principles of international law. The consular officers of each Party who are assigned to the Government of the other Party, and are duly provided with exequaturs, shall be permitted to reside in the territories of such other Party at the places where consular officers are permitted by the applicable laws to reside; they shall enjoy the honorary privileges and the immunities accorded to officers of their rank by general international usage; and they shall not, in any event, be treated in a manner less favorable than similar officers of any third country.

Article III

Subjects of His Majesty the King of the Yemen in the United States of America and nationals of the United States of America in the Kingdom of the Yemen shall be received and treated in accordance with the requirements and practices of generally recognized international law. In respect of their persons, possessions and rights, such subjects or nationals shall enjoy the fullest protection of the laws and authorities of the country, and shall not be treated in any manner less favorable than the nationals of any third country. Subjects of His Majesty in the United States of America and nationals of the United States of America in the Kingdom of the Yemen shall be subject to the local laws and regulations, and shall enjoy the rights and privileges accorded in this third Article.

Article IV

In all matters relating to customs duties and charges of any kind imposed on or in connection with importation or exportation or otherwise affecting commerce and navigation, to the method of levying such duties and charges, to all rules and formalities in connection with importation or exportation, and to transit, warehousing and other facilities, each Party shall accord unconditional and unrestricted most-favored-nation treatment to articles the growth, produce or manufacture of the other Party, from whatever place arriving, or to articles destined for exportation to the territories of such other Party, by whatever route. Any advantage, favor, privilege or immunity with respect to any duty, charge or regulation affecting commerce or navigation now or hereafter accorded by the United States of America or by the Kingdom of the Yemen to any third country will be accorded immediately and unconditionally to the commerce and navigation of the Kingdom of the Yemen and of the United States of America, respectively. The advantages relating to customs duties now or hereafter accorded by the United States of America to the Republic of Cuba shall be excepted from the provisions of this agreement.

Article V

There shall be excepted from the provisions of Article IV of this Agreement advantages now or hereafter accorded: by virtue of a customs union of which either Party may become a member; to adjacent countries in order to facilitate frontier traffic; and by the United States of America or its territories or possessions to one another or to the Panama Canal Zone.

The last clause shall continue to apply in respect of any advantages now or hereafter accorded by the United States of America or its territories or possessions to one another irrespective of any change in the political status of any such territories or possessions. Nothing in this Agreement shall prevent the adoption or enforcement by either Party within the area of its jurisdiction: of measures relating to the importation or exportation of gold or silver or the traffic in arms, ammunition, and implements of war, and, in exceptional circumstances, all other military supplies; of measures necessary in pursuance of obligations for the maintenance of international peace and security or necessary for the protection of the essential interests of such Party in time of national emergency; or of statutes in relation to immigration and travel. Subject to the requirement that, under like circumstances and conditions, there shall be no arbitrary discrimination by either Party against the subjects, nationals, commerce or navigation of the other Party in favor of the subjects, nationals, commerce or navigation of any third country, the provisions of this Agreement shall not extend to prohibitions or restrictions: imposed on moral or humanitarian grounds; designed to protect human, animal, or plant life or health; relating to prison-made goods; or relating to the enforcement of police or revenue law.

Article VI

The provisions of this Agreement shall apply to all territory under the sovereignty or authority of either of the parties, except the Panama Canal Zone.

Article VII

This Agreement shall continue in force until superseded by a more comprehensive commercial agreement, or until thirty days from the date of a written notice of termination given by either party to the other Party, whichever is the earlier. Moreover, either Party may terminate Articles I, II, III, or IV on thirty days written notice.

If the above provisions are acceptable to the Government of the Kingdom of the Yemen this note and the reply signifying assent thereto shall, if agreeable to that Government, be regarded as constituting an agreement between the two Governments which shall become effective on the date of such acceptance.

(b) Note from the Deputy Minister of Foreign Affairs of the Yemen to the Chief, Special United States Diplomatic Mission to the Yemen.

[Translation]

I have the honor to acknowledge receipt of Your Excellency's letter dated May 4, 1946, corresponding to Jamada-al-Thaniya, 3, 1365, the text of which is as follows:—

On behalf of the Government of the Yemen, I declare my government's adherence to the provisions stated in this Agreement which is considered effective on the date of signature.

[Here follows the text of the United States note.]

APPENDIX I

Protocol of Proceedings of the Crimea Conference, February 4–11, 1945. Department of State Press Release, March 24, 1947.[1]

The Crimea Conference of the heads of the Governments of the United States of America, the United Kingdom, and the Union of Soviet Socialist Republics, which took place from February 4 to 11, came to the following conclusions.

I. WORLD ORGANIZATION

It was decided:

1. That a United Nations conference on the proposed world organization should be summoned for Wednesday 25 April, 1945, and should be held in the United States of America.
2. The nations to be invited to this conference should be:
(*a*) The United Nations as they existed on 8 February, 1945; and
(*b*) Such of the Associated Nations as have declared war on the common enemy by 1 March, 1945. (For this purpose, by the term "Associated Nations" was meant the eight Associated Nations and Turkey.) When the conference on world organization is held, the delegates of the United Kingdom and United States of America will support a proposal to admit to original membership two Soviet Socialist Republics, *i.e.*, the Ukraine and White Russia.
3. That the United States Government, on behalf of the three powers, should consult the Government of China and the French Provisional Government in regard to decisions taken at the present conference concerning the proposed world organization.
4. That the text of the invitation to be issued to all the nations which would take part in the United Nations conference should be as follows:

"INVITATION

"The Government of the United States of America, on behalf of itself and of the Governments of the United Kingdom, the Union of Soviet Socialist Republics and the Republic of China and of the Provisional Government of the French Republic, invite the Government of .... to send representatives to a conference of the United Nations to be held on the 25th of April, 1945, or soon thereafter, at San Francisco, in the United States of America, to prepare for a general international organization for the maintenance of international peace and security.

"The above-named Governments suggest that the conference consider as affording a basis for such a Charter the proposals for the establishment of a general international organization which were made public last October as a result of the Dumbarton Oaks conference and which have now been supplemented by the following provisions for Section C of Chapter VI:

"C. VOTING

"1. Each member of the Security Council should have one vote.
"2. Decisions of the Security Council on procedural matters should be made by an affirmative vote of seven members.

[1] *New York Times*, March 25, 1947, p. 14.

"3. Decisions of the Security Council on all matters should be made by an affirmative vote of seven members, including the concurring votes of the permanent members; provided that, in decisions under Chapter VIII, Section A and under the second sentence of Paragraph 1 of Chapter VIII, Section C, a party to a dispute should abstain from voting.

"Further information as to arrangements will be transmitted subsequently.

"In the event that the Government of .... desires in advance of the conference to present views or comments concerning the proposals, the Government of the United States of America will be pleased to transmit such views and comments to the other participating Governments."

Territorial Trusteeship:

It was agreed that the five nations which will have permanent seats on the Security Council should consult each other prior to the United Nations conference on the question of territorial trusteeship.

The acceptance for this recommendation is subject to its being made clear that territorial trusteeship will only apply to (*a*) existing mandates of the League of Nations; (*b*) territories detached from the enemy as a result of the present war; (*c*) any other territory which might voluntarily be placed under trusteeship; and (*d*) no discussion of actual territories is contemplated at the forthcoming United Nations conference or in the preliminary consultations, and it will be a matter for subsequent agreement which territories within the above categories will be placed under trusteeship.

II. DECLARATION OF LIBERATED EUROPE

The following declaration has been approved:

The Premier of the Union of Soviet Socialist Republics, the Prime Minister of the United Kingdom and the President of the United States of America have consulted with each other in the common interests of the peoples of their countries and those of liberated Europe. They jointly declare their mutual agreement to concert during the temporary period of instability in liberated Europe the policies of their three Governments in assisting the peoples liberated from the domination of Nazi Germany and the peoples of the former Axis satellite states of Europe to solve by democratic means their pressing political and economic problems.

The establishment of order in Europe and the rebuilding of national economic life must be achieved by processes which will enable the liberated peoples to destroy the last vestiges of nazism and fascism and to create democratic institutions of their own choice. This is a principle of the Atlantic Charter — the right of all peoples to choose the form of government under which they will live — the restoration of sovereign rights and self-government to those peoples who have been forcibly deprived of them by the aggressor nations.

To foster the conditions in which the liberated peoples may exercise these rights, the three Governments will jointly assist the people in any European liberated state or former Axis satellite state in Europe where, in their judgment, conditions require, (*a*) to establish conditions of internal peace; (*b*) to carry out emergency measures for the relief of distressed peoples; (*c*) to form interim governmental authorities broadly representative of all democratic elements in the population and pledge to the earliest possible establishment through free elections of Governments responsive to the will of the people; and (*d*) to facilitate where necessary the holding of such elections.

The three Governments will consult the other United Nations and provisional authorities or other Governments in Europe when matters of direct interest to them are under consideration.

When, in the opinion of the three Governments, conditions in any European liberated state or any former Axis satellite state in Europe make such action necessary, they will immediately consult together on the measures necessary to discharge the joint responsibilities set forth in this declaration.

By this declaration we reaffirm our faith in the principles of the Atlantic Charter, our pledge in the Declaration by the United Nations and our determination to build in cooperation with other peace-loving nations world order, under law, dedicated to peace, security, freedom and general well-being of all mankind.

In issuing this declaration, the three powers express the hope that the Provisional Government of the French Republic may be associated with them in the procedure suggested.

III. DISMEMBERMENT OF GERMANY

It was agreed that Article 12 (a) of the Surrender Terms for Germany should be amended to read as follows:

"The United Kingdom, the United States of America and the Union of Soviet Socialist Republics shall possess supreme authority with respect to Germany. In the exercise of such authority they will take such steps, including the complete disarmament, demilitarization and dismemberment of Germany as they deem requisite for future peace and security."

The study of the procedure of the dismemberment of Germany was referred to a committee consisting of Mr. [Anthony] Eden [their Foreign Secretary] (chairman), Mr. [John] Winant [of the United States] and Mr. [Fedor T.] Gusev. This body would consider the desirability of associating with it a French representative.

IV. ZONE OF OCCUPATION FOR THE FRENCH AND CONTROL COUNCIL FOR GERMANY

It was agreed that a zone in Germany, to be occupied by the French forces, should be allocated to France. This zone would be formed out of the British and American zones and its extent would be settled by the British and Americans in consultation with the French Provisional Government.

It was also agreed that the French Provisional Government should be invited to become a member of the Allied Control Council for Germany.

V. REPARATION

The following protocol has been approved:

PROTOCOL

ON THE TALKS BETWEEN THE HEADS OF THREE GOVERNMENTS AT THE CRIMEAN CONFERENCE ON THE GERMAN REPARATIONS IN KIND

1. Germany must pay in kind for the losses caused by her to the Allied nations in the course of the war. Reparations are to be received in the first instance those countries which have borne the main burden of the war, have suffered the heaviest losses and have organized victory over the enemy.

2. Reparations in kind is to be exacted from Germany in three following forms:

(a) Removals within two years from the surrender of Germany or the cessation of organized resistance from the national wealth of Germany located on the territory of Germany herself as well as outside her territory (equipment, machine tools, ships, rolling stock, German investments abroad, shares of industrial, transport and other enterprises in Germany, etc.), these removals to be carried out chiefly for purpose of destroying the war potential of Germany.

(b) Annual deliveries of goods from current production for a period to be fixed.

(c) Use of German labor.

3. For the working out on the above principles of a detailed plan for exaction of reparation from Germany an Allied reparation commission will be set up in

Moscow. It will consist of three representatives — one from the Union of Soviet Socialist Republics, one from the United Kingdom and one from the United States of America.

4. With regard to the fixing of the total sum of reparation as well as the distribution of it among the countries which suffered from the German aggression, the Soviet and American delegations agreed as follows:

"The Moscow reparation commission should take in its initial studies as a basis for discussion the suggestion of the Soviet Government that the total sum of the reparation in accordance with the points (a) and (b) of the Paragraph 2 should be 20 billion dollars and that 50 per cent of it should go to the Union of Soviet Socialist Republics."

The British delegation was of the opinion that, pending consideration of the reparation question by the Moscow reparation commission, no figures of reparation should be mentioned.

The above Soviet-American proposal has been passed to the Moscow reparation commission as one of the proposals to be considered by the commission.

VI. MAJOR WAR CRIMINALS

The conference agreed that the question of the major war criminals should be the subject of inquiry by the three Foreign Secretaries for report in due course after the close of the conference.

VII. POLAND

The following declaration on Poland was agreed by the conference:

"A new situation has been created in Poland as a result of her complete liberation by the Red Army. This calls for the establishment of a Polish Provisional Government which can be more broadly based than was possible before the recent liberation of the western part of Poland. The Provisional Government which is now functioning in Poland should therefore be reorganized on a broader democratic basis with the inclusion of democratic leaders from Poland itself and from Poles abroad. This new Government should then be called the Polish Provisional Government of National Unity.

"M. Molotov, Mr. Harriman and Sir A. Clark Kerr are authorized as a commission to consult in the first instance in Moscow with members of the present Provisional Government and with other Polish democratic leaders from within Poland and from abroad, with a view to the reorganization of the present Government along the above lines. This Polish Provisional Government of National Unity shall be pledged to the holding of free and unfettered elections as soon as possible on the basis of universal suffrage and secret ballot. In these elections all democratic and anti-Nazi parties shall have the right to take part and to put forward candidates.

"When a Polish Provisional Government of National Unity has been properly formed in conformity with the above, the Government of the Union of Soviet Socialist Republics, which now maintains diplomatic relations with the present Provisional Government of Poland, and the Government of the United Kingdom and the Government of the United States of America will establish diplomatic relations with the new Polish Provisional Government of National Unity, and will exchange Ambassadors by whose reports the respective Governments will be kept informed about the situation in Poland.

"The three heads of Government consider that the eastern frontier of Poland should follow the Curzon Line with some digressions from it in some regions of five to eight kilometers in favor of Poland. They recognize that Poland must receive substantial accessions of territory in the north and west. They feel that the opinion of the new Polish Provisional Government of National Unity should be sought in due course of the extent of these accessions and that the final delimitation of the western frontier of Poland should thereafter await the peace conference."

VIII. YUGOSLAVIA

It was agreed to recommend to Marshal Tito and to Dr. [Nan] Subasitch:

(a) That the Tito-Subasitch agreement should immediately be put into effect and a new Government formed on the basis of the agreement.

(b) That as soon as the new Government has been formed it should declare:
(I) That the Anti-Fascist Assembly of the National Liberation (AVNOJ) will be extended to include members of the last Yugoslav Skupstina who have not compromised themselves by collaboration with the enemy, thus forming a body to be known as a temporary Parliament and
(II) That legislative acts passed by the Anti-Fascist Assembly of National Liberation (AVNOJ) will be subject to subsequent ratification by a Constituent Assembly; and that this statement should be published in the communiqué of the conference.

IX. ITALO-YUGOSLAV FRONTIER — ITALO-AUSTRIAN FRONTIER

Notes on these subjects were put in by the British delegation, and the American and Soviet delegations agreed to consider them and give their views later.

X. YUGOSLAV-BULGARIAN RELATIONS

There was an exchange of views between the Foreign Secretaries on the question of the desirability of a Yugoslav-Bulgarian pact of alliance. The question at issue was whether a state still under an armistice regime could be allowed to enter into a treaty with another state. Mr. Eden suggested that the Bulgarian and Yugoslav Governments should be informed that this could not be approved. Mr. Stettinius suggested that the British and American Ambassadors should discuss the matter further with Mr. Molotov in Moscow. Mr. Molotov agreed with the proposal of Mr. Stettinius.

XI. SOUTHEASTERN EUROPE

The British delegation put in notes for the consideration of their colleagues on the following subjects:

(a) The Control Commission in Bulgaria.
(b) Greek claims upon Bulgaria, more particularly with reference to reparations.
(c) Oil equipment in Rumania.

XII. IRAN

Mr. Eden, Mr. Stettinius and Mr. Molotov exchanged views on the situation in Iran. It was agreed that this matter should be pursued through the diplomatic channel.

XIII. MEETINGS OF THE THREE FOREIGN SECRETARIES

The conference agreed that permanent machinery should be set up for consultation between the three Foreign Secretaries; they should meet as often as necessary, probably about every three or four months.

These meetings will be held in rotation in the three capitals, the first meeting being held in London.

XIV. THE MONTREUX CONVENTION AND THE STRAITS

It was agreed that at the next meeting of the three Foreign Secretaries to be held in London, they should consider proposals which it was understood the Soviet Government would put forward in relation to the Montreux Convention, and report to their Governments. The Turkish Government should be informed at the appropriate moment.

The foregoing protocol was approved and signed by the three Foreign Secretaries at the Crimean Conference February 11, 1945.

E. R. STETTINIUS, JR.
M. MOLOTOV
ANTHONY EDEN

AGREEMENT REGARDING JAPAN

The leaders of the three great powers — the Soviet Union, the United States of America and Great Britain — have agreed that in two or three months after Germany has surrendered and the war in Europe has terminated, the Soviet Union shall enter into the war against Japan on the side of the Allies on condition that:

1. The status quo in Outer Mongolia (the Mongolian People's Republic) shall be preserved;

2. The former rights of Russia violated by the treacherous attack of Japan in 1904 shall be restored, viz.:

(*a*) The southern part of Sakhalin as well as the islands adjacent to it shall be returned to the Soviet Union;

(*b*) The commercial port of Dairen shall be internationalized, the pre-eminent interests of the Soviet Union in this port being safeguarded, and the lease of Port Arthur as a naval base of the Union of Soviet Socialist Republics restored;

(*c*) The Chinese-Eastern Railroad and the South Manchurian Railroad, which provides an outlet to Dairen, shall be jointly operated by the establishment of a joint Soviet-Chinese company, it being understood that the pre-eminent interests of the Soviet Union shall be safeguarded and that China shall retain full sovereignty in Manchuria.

3. The Kurile Islands shall be handed over to the Soviet Union.

It is understood that the agreement concerning Outer Mongolia and the ports and railroads referred to above will require concurrence of Generalissimo Chiang Kai-shek. The President will take measures in order to obtain this concurrence on advice from Marshall Stalin.

The heads of the three great powers have agreed that these claims of the Soviet Union shall be unquestionably fulfilled after Japan has been defeated.

For its part, the Soviet Union expresses its readiness to conclude with the National Government of China a pact of friendship and alliance between the Union of Soviet Socialist Republics and China in order to render assistance to China with its armed forces for the purpose of liberating China from the Japanese yoke.

JOSEPH V. STALIN
FRANKLIN D. ROOSEVELT
WINSTON S. CHURCHILL

February 11, 1945

APPENDIX II

Protocol of Proceedings of the Berlin Conference, July 17–August 2, 1945. Department of State Press Release, March 24, 1947.[1]

The Berlin conference of the three heads of government of the Union of Soviet Socialist Republics, the United States of America, and United Kingdom, which took place from July 17 to August 2, 1945, came to the following conclusions:

I. ESTABLISHMENT OF A COUNCIL OF FOREIGN MINISTERS

A. The conference reached the following agreement for the establishment of a Council of Foreign Ministers to do the necessary preparatory work for the peace settlements:

1

There shall be established a Council composed of the Foreign Ministers of the United Kingdom, the Union of Soviet Socialist Republics, China, France and the United States.

2

(I) The Council shall normally meet in London, which shall be the permanent seat of the joint secretariat which the Council will form. Each of the Foreign Ministers will be accompanied by a high-ranking deputy, duly authorized to carry on the work of the Council in the absence of his Foreign Minister, and by a small staff of technical advisers.

(II) The first meeting of the Council shall be held in London not later than September 1, 1945. Meetings may be held by common agreement in other capitals as may be agreed from time to time.

3

(I) As its immediate important task the Council shall be authorized to draw up, with a view to their submission to the United Nations, treaties of peace with Italy, Rumania, Bulgaria, Hungary and Finland, and to propose settlements of territorial questions outstanding on the termination of the war in Europe. The Council shall be utilized for the preparation of a peace settlement for Germany to be accepted by the Government of Germany when a Government adequate for the purpose is established.

(II) For the discharge of each of these tasks the Council will be composed of the members representing those states which were signatory to the terms of surrender imposed upon the enemy state concerned. For the purpose of the peace settlement for Italy, France shall be regarded as a signatory to the terms of surrender for Italy. Other members will be invited to participate when matters directly concerning them are under discussion.

(III) Other matters may from time to time be referred to the Council by agreement between the member Governments.

[1] *Ibid.*

4

(I) Whenever the Council is considering a question of direct interest to a state not represented thereon, such state should be invited to send representatives to participate in the discussion and study of that question.

(II) The Council may adapt its procedure to the particular problems under consideration. In some cases it may hold its own preliminary discussions prior to the participation of other interested states. In other cases, the Council may convoke a formal conference of the state chiefly interested in seeking a solution of the particular problem.

B. It was agreed that the three Governments should each address an identical invitation to the Governments of China and France to adopt this text and to join in establishing the Council. The text of the approved invitation was as follows:

COUNCIL OF FOREIGN MINISTERS DRAFT FOR IDENTICAL INVITATION TO BE SENT SEPARATELY BY EACH OF THE THREE GOVERNMENTS TO THE GOVERNMENTS OF CHINA AND FRANCE.

The Governments of the United Kingdom, the United States and the Union of Soviet Socialist Republics consider it necessary to begin without delay the essential preparatory work upon the peace settlements in Europe. To this end they are agreed that there should be established a Council of the Foreign Ministers of the five great powers to prepare treaties of peace with the European enemy states from submission to the United Nations. The Council would also be empowered to propose settlements of outstanding territorial questions in Europe and to consider such other matters as member Governments might agree to refer to it.

The text adopted by the Three Governments is as follows:

(Here insert final agreed text of the proposal.)

"In agreement with the Governments of the United States, His Majesty's Government in the United Kingdom and Union of Soviet Socialist Republics, the United States Government, the United Kingdom and the Soviet Government extend a cordial invitation to the Government of China (France) to adopt the text quoted above and to join in setting up the Council. His Majesty's Government, the United States Government, the Soviet Government attach much importance to the participation of the Chinese Government (French Government) in the proposed arrangements and they hope to receive an early and favorable reply to this invitation."

C. It was understood that the establishment of the Council of Foreign Ministers for the specific purposes named in the text would be without prejudice to the agreement of the Crimea Conference that there should be periodical consultation between the Foreign Secretaries of the United States, the Union of Soviet Socialist Republics and the United Kingdom.

D. The conference also considered the position of the European Advisory Commission in the light of the agreement to establish the Council of Foreign Ministers. It was noted with satisfaction that the Commission had ably discharged its principal tasks by the recommendations that it had furnished for the terms of surrender for Germany, for the zones of occupation in Germany and Austria and for the inter-Allied control machinery in those countries. It was felt that further work of a detailed character for the coordination of Allied policy for the control of Germany and Austria would in future fall within the competence of the Control Council at Berlin and the Allied Commission at Vienna. Accordingly, it was agreed to recommend that the European Advisory Commission be dissolved.

APPENDIX II

II. THE PRINCIPLES TO GOVERN THE TREATMENT OF GERMANY IN THE INITIAL CONTROL

A. Political principles.

[1]

In accordance with the agreement on control machinery in Germany, supreme authority in Germany is exercised, on instructions from their respective Governments, by the commanders in chief of the armed forces of the United States of America, the United Kingdom, the Union of Soviet Socialist Republics and the French Republic, each in his own zone of occupation, and also jointly, in matters affecting Germany as a whole, in their capacity as members of the Control Council.

[2]

So far as is practicable, there shall be uniformity of treatment of the German population throughout Germany.

[3]

The purposes of the occupation of Germany by which the Control Council shall be guided are:
(I) The complete disarmament and demilitarization of Germany and the elimination or control of all German industry that could be used for military production. To these ends:
(*a*) All German land, naval and air forces, the SS, SA, SD and Gestapo, with all their organizations, staffs and institutions, including the general staff, the officers' corps, reserve corps, military schools, war veterans organizations and all other military and semi-military organizations, together with all clubs and associations which serve to keep alive the military tradition in Germany, shall be completely and finally abolished in such manner as permanently to prevent the revival or reorganization of German militarism and nazism;
(*b*) All arms, ammunition and implements of war and all specialized facilities for their production shall be held at the disposal of the Allies or destroyed. The maintenance and production of all aircraft and all arms, ammunition and implements of war shall be prevented.
(II) To convince the German people that they have suffered a total military defeat and that they cannot escape responsibility for what they have brought upon themselves, since their own ruthless warfare and the fanatical Nazi resistance have destroyed German economy and made chaos and suffering inevitable.
(III) To destroy the National Socialist party and its affiliated and supervised organizations, to dissolve all Nazi institutions, to insure that they are not revived in any form and to prevent all Nazi and militarist activity or propaganda.
(IV) To prepare for the eventual reconstruction of German political life on a democratic basis and for eventual peaceful cooperation in international life by Germany.

[4]

All Nazi laws which provide the basis of the Hitler regime or established discriminations on grounds of race, creed or political opinion shall be abolished. No such discriminations, whether legal, administrative or otherwise, shall be tolerated.

[5]

War criminals and those who have participated in planning or carrying out Nazi enterprises involving or resulting in atrocities or war crimes shall be arrested and brought to judgment. Nazi leaders, influential Nazi supporters and high officials of Nazi organizations and institutions and any other persons dangerous to the occupation or its objectives shall be arrested and interned.

[6]

All members of the Nazi party who have been more than nominal participants in its activities and all other persons hostile to Allied purposes shall be removed from public and semi-public office and from positions of responsibility in important private undertakings. Such persons shall be replaced by persons who, by their political and moral qualities, are deemed capable of assisting in developing genuine democratic institutions in Germany.

[7]

German education shall be so controlled as completely to eliminate Nazi and militarist doctrines and to make possible the successful development of democratic ideas.

[8]

The judicial system will be reorganized in accordance with the principles of democracy, of justice under law and of equal rights for all citizens without distinction of race, nationality or religion.

[9]

The administration in Germany should be directed toward the decentralization of the political structure and the development of local responsibility. To this end:

(I) Local self-government shall be restored throughout Germany on democratic principles and in particular through elective councils as rapidly as is consistent with military security and the purposes of military occupation;

(II) All democratic political parties with rights of assembly and of public discussion shall be allowed and encouraged throughout Germany;

(III) Representative and elective principles shall be introduced into regional, provincial and state (Land) administration as rapidly as may be justified by the successful application of these principles in local self-government;

(IV) For the time being, no central German Government shall be established. Notwithstanding this, however, certain essential central German administrative departments, headed by state secretaries, shall be established, particularly in the fields of finance, transport, communications, foreign trade and industry. Such departments will act under the direction of the Control Council.

[10]

Subject to the necessity for maintaining military security, freedom of speech, press and religion shall be permitted, and religious institutions shall be respected. Subject likewise to the maintenance of military security, the formation of free trade unions shall be permitted.

B. *Economic Principles*

[11]

In order to eliminate Germany's war potential, the production of arms, ammunition and implements of war as well as all types of aircraft and sea-going ships shall be prohibited and prevented. Production of metals, chemicals, machinery and other items that are directly necessary to a war economy shall be rigidly controlled and restricted to Germany's approved post-war peacetime needs to meet the objectives stated in Paragraph 15. Productive capacity not needed for permitted production shall be removed in accordance with the reparations plan recommended by the Allied Commission on reparations and approved by the Governments concerned, or if not removed, shall be destroyed.

[12]

At the earliest practicable date, the Germany economy shall be decentralized for the purpose of eliminating the present excessive concentration of economic power as exemplified in particular by cartels, syndicates, trusts and other monopolistic arrangements.

[13]

In organizing the German economy, primary emphasis shall be given to the development of agriculture and peaceful domestic industries.

[14]

During the period of occupation Germany shall be treated as a single economic unit. To this end, common policies shall be established in regard to:
 (a) Mining and industrial production and its allocation;
 (b) Agriculture, forestry and fishing;
 (c) Wages, prices and rationing;
 (d) Import and export programs for Germany as a whole;
 (e) Currency and banking, central taxation and customs;
 (f) Reparation and removal of industrial war potential;
 (g) Transportation and communications.
In applying these policies, account shall be taken, where appropriate, of varying local conditions.

[15]

Allied controls shall be imposed upon the German economy, but only to the extent necessary:
 (a) To carry out programs of industrial disarmament, demilitarization, of reparations and of approved exports and imports.
 (b) To assure the production and maintenance of goods and services required to meet the needs of the occupying forces and displaced persons in Germany and essential to maintain in Germany average living standards not exceeding the average of the standards of living of European countries. (European countries means all European countries, excluding the United Kingdom and the Union of Soviet Socialist Republics.)
 (c) To insure in the manner determined by the Central Council the equitable distribution of essential commodities between the several zones so as to produce a balanced economy throughout Germany and reduce the need for imports.
 (d) To control German industry and all economic and financial international transactions, including exports and imports, with the aim of preventing Germany from developing a war potential and of achieving the other objectives named herein.
 (e) To control all German public and private scientific bodies, research and experimental institutions, laboratories, etc., connected with economic activities.

[16]

In the imposition and maintenance of economic controls established by the Control Council, German administrative machinery shall be created and the German authorities shall be required to the fullest extent practicable to proclaim and assume administration of such controls. Thus it should be brought home to the German people that the responsibility for the administration of such controls and any breakdown in these controls will rest with themselves. Any German controls which may run counter to the objectives of occupation will be prohibited.

[17]

Measures shall be promptly taken:
 (a) To effect essential repair of transport;

(b) To enlarge coal production;
(c) To maximize agricultural output; and
(d) To effect emergency repair of housing and essential utilities.

[18]

Appropriate steps shall be taken by the Control Council to exercise control and the power of disposition over German-owned external assets not already under the control of United Nations which have taken part in the war against Germany.

[19]

Payment of reparations should leave enough resources to enable the German people to subsist without external assistance. In working out the economic balance of Germany, the necessary means must be provided to pay for imports approved by the Control Council in Germany.

The proceeds of exports from current production and stocks shall be available in the first place for payment for such imports.

The above clause will not apply to the equipment and products referred to in Paragraphs 4 (a) and 4 (b) of the reparations agreement.

III. REPARATIONS FROM GERMANY

[1]

Reparation claims of the Union of Soviet Socialist Republics shall be met by removals from the zone of Germany occupied by the Union of Soviet Socialist Republics and from appropriate German external assets.

[2]

The Union of Soviet Socialist Republics undertakes to settle the reparation claims of Poland from its own share of reparations.

[3]

The reparation claims of the United States, the United Kingdom and other countries entitled to reparations shall be met from the Western zones and from appropriate German external assets.

[4]

In addition to the reparations to be taken by the Union of Soviet Socialist Republics from its own zone of occupation, the Union of Soviet Socialist Republics shall receive additionally from the Western zones:

(a) 15 percent of such usable and complete industrial capital equipment, in the first place from the metallurgical, chemical and machine manufacturing industries as is unnecessary for the German peace economy and should be removed from the Western zones of Germany, in exchange for an equivalent value of food, coal, potash, zinc, timber, clay products, petroleum products and such other commodities as may be agreed upon.

(b) 10 percent of such industrial capital equipment as is unnecessary for the German peace economy and should be removed from the Western zones, to be transferred to the Soviet Government on reparations account without payment or exchange of any kind in return. Removals of equipment as provided in (a) and (b) above shall be made simultaneously.

[5]

The amount of equipment to be removed from the Western zones on account of reparations must be determined within six months from now at the latest.

APPENDIX II

[6]

Removals of industrial capital equipment shall begin as soon as possible and shall be completed within two years from the determination specified in Paragraph 5. The delivery of products covered by 4 (a) above shall begin as soon as possible and shall be made by the Union of Soviet Socialist Republics in agreed installments within five years of the date hereof. The determination of the amount and character of the industrial capital equipment unnecessary for the German peace economy and therefore available for reparation shall be made by the Control Council under policies fixed by the Allied Commission on Reparations, with the participation of France, subject to the final approval of the zone commander in the zone from which the equipment is to be removed.

[7]

Prior to the fixing of the total amount of equipment subject to removal, advance deliveries shall be made in respect to such equipment as will be determined to be eligible for delivery in accordance with the procedure set forth in the last sentence of Paragraph 6.

[8]

The Soviet Government renounces all claims in respect of reparations to shares of German enterprises which are located in the Western Zones of Germany as well as to German foreign assets in all countries except those specified in Paragraph 9 below.

[9]

The Governments of the United Kingdom and United States of America renounce all claims in respect of reparations to shares of German enterprises which are located in the Eastern zone of occupation in Germany, as well as to German foreign assets in Bulgaria, Finland, Hungary, Rumania and eastern Austria.

[10]

The Soviet Government makes no claims to gold captured by the Allied troops in Germany.

IV. DISPOSAL OF THE GERMAN NAVY AND MERCHANT MARINE

A. *The following principles for the distribution of the German Navy were agreed:*

1. The total strength of the German surface navy, excluding ships sunk and those taken over from Allied nations, but including ships under construction or repair, shall be divided equally among the Union of Soviet Socialist Republics, United Kingdom and United States of America.

2. Ships under construction or repair mean those ships whose construction or repair may be completed within three to six months, according to the type of ship. Whether such ships under construction or repair shall be complete or repaired shall be determined by the technical commission appointed by the three powers and referred to below, subject to the principle that their completion or repair must be achieved within the time limits above provided, without any increase of skilled employment in the German shipyards and without permitting the reopening of any German shipbuilding or connected industries. Completion date means the date when a ship is able to go out on its first trip, or, under peacetime standards would refer to the customery date of delivery by shipyard to the government.

3. The larger part of the German submarine fleet shall be sunk. Not more than thirty submarines shall be preserved and divided equally between the

Union of Soviet Socialist Republics, United Kingdom and United States of America for experimental and technical purposes.

4. All stocks of armament, ammunition and supplies of the German Navy appertaining to the vessels transferred pursuant to Paragraphs 1 and 3 hereof shall be handed over to the respective powers receiving such ships.

5. The three Governments agree to constitute a tripartite naval commission comprising two representatives for each Government, accompanied by the requisite staff, to submit agreed recommendations to the three Governments for the allocation of specific German warships and handle other detailed matters arising out of the agreement between the three Governments regarding the German fleet. The commission will hold its first meeting not later than 15 August, 1945, in Berlin, which shall be its headquarters. Each delegation on the commission will have the right on the basis of reciprocity to inspect German warships wherever they may be located.

6. The three Governments agreed that transfers, including those of ships under construction and repair, shall be completed as soon as possible, but not later than 15 February 1946. The commission will submit fortnightly reports, including proposals for the progressive allocation of the vessels when agreed by the commission.

B. *The following principles for the distribution of the German merchant marine were agreed:*

1. The German merchant marine, surrendered to the three powers and wherever located, shall be divided equally among the Union of Soviet Socialist Republics, the United Kingdom and the United States of America. The actual transfers of the ships to the respective countries shall take place as soon as practicable after the end of the war against Japan. The United Kingdom and the United States will provide out of their shares of the surrendered German merchant ships appropriate amounts for other allied states whose merchant marines have suffered heavy losses in the common cause against Germany, except that the Soviet Union shall provide out of its share for Poland.

2. The allocation, manning and operation of these ships during the Japanese war period shall fall under the cognizance and authority of the combined shipping adjustment board and the United Maritime Authority.

3. While actual transfer of the ships shall be delayed until after the end of the war with Japan, a tripartite shipping commission shall inventory and value all available ships and recommend a specific distribution in accordance with Paragraph 1.

4. German inland and coastal ships determined to be necessary to the maintenance of the basic German peace economy by the Allied Control Council of Germany shall not be included in the shipping pool thus divided among the three powers.

5. The three Governments agree to constitute a tripartite merchant marine commission comprising two representatives for each Government, accompanied by the requisite staff, to submit agreed recommendations to the three Governments for the allocation of specific German merchant ships and to handle other detailed matters arising out of the agreement between the three Governments regarding the German merchant ships. The commission will hold its first meeting not later than September 1, 1945 in Berlin, which shall be its headquarters. Each delegation on the commission will have the right on the basis of reciprocity to inspect the German merchant ships wherever they may be located.

V. CITY OF KOENIGSBERG AND THE ADJACENT AREA

The conference examined a proposal by the Soviet Government to the effect that, pending the final determination of territorial questions at the peace settlement, the section of the western frontier of the Union of Soviet Socialist Republics which is adjacent to the Baltic Sea should pass from a point on the eastern shore of the Bay of Danzig to the east, north of Braunsberg-Goldap, to the meeting point of the frontiers of Lithuania, the Polish Republic and East Prussia.

The conference has agreed in principle to the proposal of the Soviet Government concerning the ultimate transfer to the Soviet Union of the City of Koenigsberg and the area adjacent to it as described above, subject to expert examination of the actual frontier.

The President of the United States and the British Prime Minister have declared that they will support the proposal of the conference at the forthcoming peace settlement.

VI. WAR CRIMINALS

The three Governments have taken note of the discussions which have been proceeding in recent weeks in London between British, United States, Soviet and French representatives with a view to reaching agreement on the methods of trial of these major war criminals whose crimes under the Moscow declaration of October, 1943, have no particular geographical localization. The three Governments reaffirm their intention to bring these criminals to swift and sure justice. They hope that the negotiations in London will result in speedy agreement being reached for this purpose, and they regard it as a matter of great importance that the trial of these major criminals should begin at the earliest possible date. The first list of defendants will be published before 1 September.

VII. AUSTRIA

The conference examined a proposal by the Soviet Government on the extension of the authority of the Austrian Provisional Government to all of Austria. The three Governments agreed that they were prepared to examine this question after the entry of the British and American forces into the City of Vienna.

It was agreed that reparations should not be exacted from Austria.

VIII. POLAND

A. *Declaration.*

We have taken note with pleasure of the agreement reached among representative Poles from Poland and abroad which has made possible the formation, in accordance with the decisions reached at the Crimea Conference, of a Polish Provisional Government of National Unity recognized by the three powers. The establishment by the British and United States Governments of diplomatic relations with the Polish Provisional Government of National Unity has resulted in the withdrawal of their recognition from the former Polish Government in London, which no longer exists.

The British and United States Governments have taken measures to protect the interest of the Polish Provisional Government of National Unity as the recognized Government of the Polish State in the property belonging to the Polish State located in their territories and under their control, whatever the form of this property may be. They have further taken measures to prevent alienation to third parties of such property. All proper facilities will be given to the Polish Provisional Government of National Unity for the exercise of the ordinary legal remedies for the recovery of any property belonging to the Polish State which may have been wrongfully alienated.

The three powers are anxious to assist the Polish Provisional Government of National Unity in facilitating the return to Poland as soon as practicable of all Poles abroad who wish to go, including members of the Polish armed forces and the merchant marine. They expect that those Poles who return home shall be accorded personal and property rights on the same basis as all Polish citizens.

The three powers note that the Polish Provisional Government of National Unity, in accordance with the decisions of the Crimea Conference, has agreed to the holding of free and unfettered elections as soon as possible on the basis of universal suffrage and secret ballot, in which all democratic and anti-Nazi parties shall have the right to take part and to put forward candidates, and that representatives of the Allied press shall enjoy full freedom to report to the world upon developments in Poland before and during the elections.

In conformity with the agreement on Poland reached at the Crimea Conference, the three heads of Government have sought the opinion of the Polish Provisional Government of National Unity in regard to the accession of territory in the north and west which Poland should receive. The President of the National Council of Poland and members of the Polish Provisional Government of National Unity have been received at the conference and have fully presented their views. The three heads of Government reaffirm their opinion that the final delimitation of the Western frontier of Poland should await the peace settlement.

The three heads of government agree that, pending the final determination of Poland's western frontier, the former German territories east of a line running from the Baltic Sea immediately west of Swinemuende, and thence along the Oder River to the confluence of the Western Niesse River and along the Western Niesse to the Czechoslovak frontier, including that portion of East Prussia not placed under the administration of the Union of Soviet Socialist Republics in accordance with the understanding reached at this conference and including the area of the former Free City of Danzig, shall be under the administration of the Polish state and for such purposes should not be considered as part of the Soviet zone of occupation in Germany.

IX. CONCLUSION OF PEACE TREATIES AND ADMISSION TO THE UNITED NATIONS ORGANIZATION

The three Governments consider it desirable that the present anomalous position of Italy, Bulgaria, Finland, Hungary and Rumania should be terminated by the conclusion of peace treaties. They trust that the other interested Allied Governments will share these views.

For their part, the three Governments have included the preparation for a peace treaty for Italy as the first among the immediate important tasks to be undertaken by the new Council of Foreign Ministers. Italy was the first of the Axis powers to break with Germany, to whose defeat she has made a material contribution, and has now joined with the Allies in the struggle against Japan. Italy has freed herself from the Fascist regime and is making good progress toward re-establishment of a democratic government and institutions. The conclusion of such a peace treaty with a recognized and democratic Italian Government will make it possible for the three Governments to fulfill their desire to support an application from Italy for membership of the United Nations.

The three Governments have also charged the Council of Foreign Ministers with the task of preparing peace treaties for Bulgaria, Finland, Hungary and Rumania. The conclusion of peace treaties with recognized democratic governments in these states will also enable the three Governments to support applications from them for membership of the United Nations. The three Governments agree to examine each separately in the near future, in the light of the conditions then prevailing, the establishment of diplomatic relations with Finland, Rumania, Bulgaria and Hungary to the extent possible prior to the conclusion of peace treaties with those countries.

The three Governments have no doubt that in view of the changed conditions resulting from the termination of the war in Europe, representatives of the Allied press will enjoy full freedom to report to the world upon developments in Rumania, Bulgaria, Hungary and Finland.

As regards the admission of other states into the United Nations Organization, Article 4 of the Charter of the United Nations declares that:

"1. Membership in the United Nations is open to all other peace-loving states who accept the obligations contained in the present Charter and, in the judgment of the organization, are able and willing to carry out these obligations

"2. The admission of any such state to membership in the United Nations will be effected by a decision of the General Assembly upon the recommendation of the Security Council."

The three Governments, so far as they are concerned, will support applications for membership from those states which have remained neutral during the war and which fulfill the qualifications set out above.

The three Governments feel bound, however, to make it clear that they, for their part, would not favor any application for membership put forward by the present Spanish Government, which, having been founded with the support of the Axis powers, does not, in view of its origins, its nature, its record and its close association with the aggressor states, possess the qualifications necessary to justify such membership.

X. TERRITORIAL TRUSTEESHIP

The conference examined a proposal by the Soviet Government on the question of trusteeship territories as defined in the decision of the Crimea Conference and in the Charter of the United Nations Organization.

After an exchange of views on this question, it was decided that the disposition of any former Italian colonial territories was one to be decided in connection with the preparation of a peace treaty for Italy and that the question of Italian colonial territory would be considered by the September Council of Ministers of Foreign Affairs.

XI. REVISED ALLIED CONTROL COMMISSION PROCEDURE IN RUMANIA, BULGARIA AND HUNGARY

The three Governments took note that the Soviet representatives on the Allied Control Commissions in Rumania, Bulgaria and Hungary have communicated to their United Kingdom and United States colleagues proposals for improving the work of the Control Commissions, now that hostilities in Europe have ceased.

The three Governments agreed that the revision of the procedures of the Allied Control Commissions in these countries would now be undertaken, taking into account the interests and responsibilities of the three Governments which together presented the terms of armistice to the respective countries, and accepting as a basis, in respect of all three countries, the Soviet Government's proposals for Hungary as annexed hereto. (Annex I).

XII. ORDERLY TRANSFER OF GERMAN POPULATIONS

The three Governments, having considered the question in all its aspects, recognize that the transfer to Germany of German populations, or elements thereof, remaining in Poland, Czechoslovakia and Hungary will have to be undertaken. They agree that any transfers that take place should be effected in an orderly and humane manner.

Since the influx of a large number of Germans into Germany would increase the burden already resting on the occupying authorities, they consider that the Control Council in Germany should in the first instance examine the problem, with special regard to the question of the equitable distribution of these Germans among the several zones of occupation. They are accordingly instructing their respective representatives on the Control Council to report to their Governments as soon as possible the extent to which such persons have already entered

Germany from Poland, Czechoslovakia and Hungary and to submit an estimate of the time and rate at which further transfers could be carried out, having regard to the present situation in Germany.

The Czechoslovak Government, the Polish Provisional Government and the Control Council in Hungary are at the same time being informed of the above and are being requested meanwhile to suspend further expulsions pending an examination by the Governments concerned of the report from their representatives on the Control Council.

XIII. OIL EQUIPMENT IN RUMANIA

The conference agreed to set up two bilateral commissions of experts, one to be composed of United Kingdom and Soviet members, and one to be composed of United States and Soviet members, to investigate the facts and examine the documents, as a basis for the settlement of questions arising from the removal of oil equipment in Rumania. It was further agreed that these experts shall begin their work within ten days, on the spot.

XIV. IRAN

It was agreed that Allied troops should be withdrawn immediately from Teheran and that further stages of the withdrawal of troops from Iran should be considered at the meeting of the Council of Foreign Ministers to be held in London in September, 1945.

XV. THE INTERNATIONAL ZONE OF TANGIER

A proposal by the Soviet Government was examined and the following decisions were reached:

Having examined the question of the Zone of Tangier, the three Governments have agreed that this zone, which includes the City of Tangier and the area adjacent to it, in view of its special strategic importance, shall remain international.

The question of Tangier will be discussed in the near future at a meeting in Paris of representatives of the Governments of the Union of Soviet Socialist Republics, the United States of America, the United Kingdom and France.

XVI. THE BLACK SEA STRAITS

The three Governments recognize that the convention concluded at Montreux should be revised as failing to meet present-day conditions.

It was agreed that as the next step the matter should be the subject of direct conversations between each of the three Governments and the Turkish Government.

XVII. INTERNATIONAL INLAND WATERWAYS

The conference considered a proposal of the United States delegation on this subject and agreed to refer it for consideration to the forthcoming meeting of the Council of Foreign Ministers in London.

XVIII. EUROPEAN INLAND TRANSPORT CONFERENCE

The British and United States delegations to the conference informed the Soviet delegation of the desire of the British and United States Governments to reconvene the European Inland Transport Conference and stated that they

APPENDIX II

would welcome assurance that the Soviet Government would participate in the work of the reconvened conference. The Soviet Government agreed that it would participate in this conference.

XIX. DIRECTIVES TO MILITARY COMMANDERS ON ALLIED CONTROL COUNCIL FOR GERMANY

The three Governments agreed that each would send a directive to its representative on the Control Council for Germany informing him of all decisions of the conference affecting matters within the scope of his duties.

XX. USE OF ALLIED PROPERTY FOR SATELLITE REPARATIONS OR "WAR TROPHIES"

The proposal (Annex II) presented by the United States delegation was accepted in principle by the conference, but the drafting of an agreement on the matter was left to be worked out through diplomatic channels.

XXI. MILITARY TALKS

During the conference there were meetings between the Chiefs of Staff of the three Governments on military matters of common interest.

ANNEX I

Text of a letter transmitted on July 12 to the representatives of the United States and United Kingdom Governments on the Allied Control Commission in Hungary.

"In view of the changed situation in connection with the termination of the war against Germany, the Soviet Government finds it necessary to establish the following order of work for the Allied Control Commission in Hungary.

"1. During the period up to the conclusion of peace with Hungary the president (or vice president) of the ACC will regularly call conferences with the British and American representatives for the purpose of discussing the most important questions relating to the work of the ACC. The conferences will be called once in ten days, or more frequently in case of need.

"Directives of the ACC on questions of principle will be issued to the Hungarian authorities by the president of the Allied Control Commission after agreement on these directives with the English and American representatives.

"2. The British and American representatives in the ACC will take part in general conferences of heads of divisions and delegates of the ACC, convoked by the president of the ACC, which meetings will be regular in nature. The British and American representatives will also participate personally or through their representatives in appropriate instances in mixed commissions created by the president of the ACC for questions connected with the execution by the ACC of its functions.

"3. Free movement by the American and British representatives in the country will be permitted provided that the ACC is previously informed of the time and route of the journeys.

"4. All questions connected with permission for the entrance and exit of members of the staff of the British and American representatives in Hungary will be decided on the spot by the president of the ACC within a time limit of not more than one week.

"5. The bringing in and sending out by plane of mail, cargoes and diplomatic couriers will be carried out by the British and American representatives on the ACC under arrangements and within time limits established by the ACC, or in special cases by previous coordination with the president of the ACC.

"I consider it necessary to add to the above that in all other points the existing statutes regarding the ACC in Hungary, which was confirmed on January 20, 1945, shall remain in force in the future."

ANNEX II

Use of Allied property for satellite reparations or "war trophies."

1. The burden of reparation and "war trophies" should not fall on Allied nationals.

2. Capital equipment. We object to the removal of such Allied property as reparations, "war trophies" or under any other guise. Loss would accrue to Allied nationals as a result of destruction of plants and the consequent loss of markets and trading connections. Seizure of Allied property makes impossible the fulfillment by the satellite of its obligation under the armistice to restore intact the rights and interests of the Allied nations and their nationals.

The United States looks to the other occupying powers for the return of any equipment already removed and the cessation of removals. Where such equipment will not or cannot be returned, the United States will demand of the satellite adequate, effective and prompt compensation to American nationals and that such compensation have priority equal to that of the reparations payment.

These principles apply to all property wholly or substantially owned by Allied nationals. In the event of removals of property in which the American as well as the entire Allied interest is less than substantial, the United States expects adequate, effective and prompt compensation.

3. Current production. While the United States does not oppose reparation out of current production of Allied investments, the satellite must provide immediate and adequate compensation to the Allied nationals including sufficient foreign exchange or products so that they can recover reasonable foreign currency expenditures and transfer a reasonable return on their investment. Such compensation must also have equal priority with reparations.

We deem it essential that the satellites not conclude treaties, agreements or arrangements which deny to Allied nationals access, on equal terms, to their trade, raw materials and industry; and appropriately modify any existing arrangements which may have that effect.

INDEX

A

Abdul-Aziz, King of Saudi Arabia:
  note on admission of Jewish refugees to Palestine, 905–906
Acheson, Dean:
  Chairman of Secy. of State's Committee on Atomic Energy, 545
  commercial policy toward Czechoslovakia, 875–877
  economic and financial cooperation with Poland, 885–886, 887
  interpretation of Rush-Bagot Agreement, 789
  message to Mazzini Society, 184–185
  position as Under Secy. of State, 49–50, 51
  resignation as Asst. Secy. of State, 57
  revision of Montreux Convention, 863–864
  statements on:
    proposed conference for inter-American peace and security, 768
    St. Lawrence seaway and power project, 784–786
  U.S. food relief commitments, report on, 377–378, 379
  U.S. position on UNRRA, address on, 371–372
  Yugoslav attacks against U.S. military aircraft, 900–902
Act of Chapultepec, 32–33
Administration, Asst. Secy. for, Dept. of State, 56–57
Aerial navigation, international:
  bilateral air-transport agreements:
    Bermuda form, 665–666
    chart of agreements concluded, July 1, 1945–Dec. 31, 1946, 671–672
    Chicago form, 664–665
    U.S.–U.K. Agreement, 666–671
  Convention on International Civil Aviation, 657–662
    ratification by U.S., 657–659
    status of agreements as of Oct. 2, 1946, 660–662
    withdrawal by U.S. from Air-Transport Agreement, 659–660
  Provisional International Civil Aviation Organization, 663–664

validity of presidential agreements, 45–46
Afghanistan:
  admission to UN, 525
Agreements, international, validity of presidential, 47–49
Agriculture and natural resources:
  general:
    Food and Agriculture Organization of United Nations, 697–703
    International Emergency Food Council, 703–704
    U.S. proposal for conference on resource conservation and utilization, 704
  individual commodities:
    coal, 705–707
    coffee, 771–772
    cotton, 707–708
    petroleum, 708–711
    rubber, 712–713
    sugar, 713
    tin, 713
    whaling, 713–714
    wheat, 714–715
    wool, 715–719
Air-Transport Agreement, U.S. withdrawal from, 659–660
Albania:
  admission to UN, 524–525
  withdrawal of U.S. Mission, 871–872
Aldrich, Winthrop W.:
  financing foreign trade, statement on, 611–612
Alien Enemy Control Section, Dept. of State, 359
Aliens, enemy. *See* Enemy aliens.
Allied Commission on Reparations, 221–222. *See also* Inter-Allied Reparations Agency.
Allied Control Council:
  Germany:
    establishment, 224
    failure of, 212–213
    reparations and level of postwar economy, 244–249
    transfer of Germans to occupied zones, 255–256
  Japan:
    establishment, 266, 277–278
American Republic Affairs, Asst. Secy. for, Dept. of State, 60

939

American Republics, U.S. relations with:
　Argentina, 768–769, 775–777
　economic and social cooperation:
　　coffee, 771–772
　　trade, 772–775
　Inter-American Conference on Problems of War and Peace, 16
　Mexico, 777–779
　Panama, 541, 779
　political solidarity and defense:
　　general, 765–768
　　military missions, 768
　　proposed conference for maintenance of peace and security, 768–769
　　proposed program of inter-American military cooperation, 769
　principles of inter-American system, 763–765
Anderson, Clinton P.:
　Chairman, Emergency Food Administration, 377, 378
　report on 1945–1946 famine-relief shipments, 389–393
　Secy. of Agriculture, 703
Andrews, Vice Adm. Adolphus, 172
Andrews, Rep. Walter G., 456
Angell, James W., member of Allied Commission on Reparations, 222, 227
Anglo-American Caribbean Commission. *See* Caribbean Commission.
Anglo-American Financial and Trade Agreement:
　address by Secy. Byrnes, 653–656
　authorization to implement, 656
　joint statement by Pres. Truman and Prime Minister Attlee, 649–651
　negotiations, 643–645
　Pres. Truman's message of transmittal to Congress, 651–652
　text, 645–649
Anglo-American Rice Commission, 378
Anslinger, H. J.:
　control of narcotic drugs in U.S. Zone in Germany, 730–732
Appropriations, State Dept. (1946, 1947), 62
Argentina:
　U.S. relations with, 768–769, 775–777
Armaments, regulation and reduction of:
　debate in UN, 530–532
　resolution submitted by U.S. to UN General Assembly, 536–537
　resolutions on principles, 542–544
　statements of:
　　Sen. Austin, 535–536
　　Secy. of State Byrnes, 540–542
　　Sen. Connally, 537–538
　　Andrei A. Gromyko, 532–533
　　V. M. Molotov, 533–535, 538–540

Armed forces:
　maintenance, 461–469
　procurement of personnel:
　　extension of selective service, 486–495
　　voluntary recruitment, 486
　unification:
　　letter of Pres. Truman to Secys. of War and Navy, 483–485
　　message of Pres. Truman recommending legislation, 469–478
　　prospects of success, 485
　　report of Secys. of War and Navy, 478–483
　universal military training:
　　Advisory Commission, 503
　　Congressional discussion, 495
　　messages of Pres. Truman to Congress, 496–503
Armour, Norman, 891
Arms and Armaments, Policy Committee on, Dept. of State, 61
Army, U.S.:
　enlistment program, 122
　peacetime Military Establishment, 122–123
Army Pearl Harbor Board:
　appointment, 171
　report of, 173–176
Asakura v. *Seattle*, 48
Atlantic Charter, 36
Atomic bomb:
　statement of Pres. Truman, 5–6
Atomic Development Authority:
　functions and powers, 565–570
　proposals, 563–565
Atomic energy (*see also* Defense):
　Bikini tests:
　　first test, 458–459
　　plans and preparations, 455–457
　　postponement of third test, 461
　　second test, 459–461
　　use of naval vessels, 457–458
　development and application:
　　statements of:
　　　Secy. of War Stimson, 413–419
　　　Pres. Truman, 419–421
　international control:
　　declaration by U.S., U.K., and Canada, 547–548
　　initiation, 544–550
　　statement of Pres. Truman, 16–17, 30, 42
　　UN Atomic Energy Commission, 548–576
　national control:
　　Atomic Energy Act of 1946, 422–426, 431–453
　　lands containing radio-active minerals, 426

INDEX 941

letter of Pres. Truman, 429–431
message of Pres. Truman requesting legislation, 426–429
transfer of property and personnel to Atomic Energy Commission, 454–455

Atomic Energy Act of 1946, 422–426, 431–453

Atomic Energy Commission. *See* United Nations Atomic Energy Commission.

Attlee, Clement R.:
address before Congress, Nov. 13, 1945, 843–845
statement on:
Anglo-American Financial and Trade Agreement, 649–651

Austin, Warren R.:
peace goals, address on, 31–35
regulation and reduction of armaments, statement on, 535–536
U.S. representative on Security Council, 37, 518, 531

Australia:
lend-lease settlement agreement, 145–146

Austria:
German assets and reparations:
note of U.S. Military Commissioner, 286–287
problem of, 285–286
Soviet settlement, 287–288
occupation and control:
background material, 288–289
control machinery and zones of occupation, 309–311, 311–317
directive to U.S. commander in chief on military government, 290–309
U.S. recognition of Austrian government, 311
transfer of German population, 256
UNRRA operations, 367
U.S. policy toward, 117–119, 283–285, 317

Aviation. *See* Aerial navigation, international.

Azerbaijan:
evacuation of Soviet troops, 859

Azores:
U.S. military personnel in, 541

B

Bacher, Robert F., 425
Balkan states, 37. *See also* individual countries.
Bard, Ralph A., 419
Barnard, Thurman L., 737
Barnes, Maynard, U.S. Political Representative in Bulgaria, 317
Barrett, Edward W., 737

Barringer, J. Paul, 664
Baruch, Bernard M.:
proposals for International Atomic Development Authority, 557–559
proposals for report of Atomic Energy Commission to Security Council, 570–572
U.S. Representative on Atomic Energy Commission, 545

Belgium:
U.S. relations with:
financial and supply problems, 873–875
lend-lease settlement agreement, 147–148

Benton, William:
Asst. Secy. for Public Affairs, Dept. of State, 57, 737, 757
duties and responsibilities, statement on, 59–60
first General Conference of UNESCO, report on, 743–745
Fulbright Act, statement on, 759–760
International Information Service in conduct of U.S. foreign relations, 753–755

Berle, Adolf A., Jr., 692
Berlin Conference. *See* Potsdam Conference.
Bernard, Chester I., 545
Berry, Burton Y., U.S. Representative in Rumania, 334
Bevin, Ernest, British Foreign Secretary, 578

Bidault, Georges:
central German agencies, creation of, 203–205

Biddle, Francis:
member for U.S. of International Military Tribunal, 342, 344

Bikini tests. *See* Atomic energy.

Bipartisanism:
statements of:
Pres. Truman, 38–39
Sen. Vandenberg, 65
under Roosevelt and Truman, 36–37

Bissell, Maj. Gen. Clayton, 172
Blandy, Vice Adm. William H. P., 423, 455, 456
Bloom, Rep. Sol, 51
Braden, Spruille:
Asst. Secy. for American Republic Affairs, Dept. of State, 60, 359, 775
foreign trade reconstruction in Americas, 772–775
Branch, Harllee, 663
Brand, R. H., 643
Bremen Enclave, 250
Bretton Woods Agreements Act, 608–609, 617

British Cameroons, trusteeship agreement, 573
British Empire. See United Kingdom.
British Togoland, trusteeship agreement, 578
Brophy, Gerald B., 663, 664
Budget, U.S., receipts and expenditures, 1945–1947, 125
Budget and Finance, Office of, Dept. of State, 56–57
Bulgaria:
U.S. policy toward:
enlargement of basis of Government, 319–326
recognition, 317–319
Bulkley, John W., 726
Bunche, Ralph J., 598
Burden, William A. M., 663
Bush, Dr. Vannevar:
Director of Office of Scientific Research and Development, 414, 415, 417, 419, 423, 545
quoted on Federal support for science, 503
Byrnes, James F.:
addresses:
"Neighboring Nations in One World," 7–10
problems of international trade, 10–13
UN and U.S. foreign policy, 21–26
U.S. aims and policies in Europe, 35–38
Austrian draft treaty negotiations, report on, 284
Bulgarian Government, enlargement of basis of, 321–323
Bulgarian national elections, postponement of, 318
central German agencies, establishment of, 201–202
Chairman, interim committee on atomic energy, 419
draft treaty for disarmament and demilitarization of Germany, 205–208
exchange of notes with Swiss Chargé on Japanese offer of surrender, 106–108
inter-American system, principles of, 763–765
member, National Intelligence Authority, 506
military assistance to China, 804
Secy. of State, 49
statements on:
central controls for economic unity of Germany, 208–209
formation of government for Rumania, 335–337
maintenance of defense, 463–465
making of enduring peace, 1
meaning of Potsdam Declaration, 198–201
office of Under Secy. for Economic Affairs, 51–53
opening meeting of Security Council, 26–28
regulation and reduction of armaments, 540–542
treaty on utilization of U.S.-Mexican waters, 778
U.S. interest in Italian elections, 185–186
U.S. postwar economic policy, 601–602
U.S.-Siamese relations, 824–825
State-War-Navy Coordinating Committee, memorandum on, 64
Treaty on Great Lakes Fisheries, report on, 786–788
UNESCO, 738
U.S. policy on Germany, 210–218

C

Cameroons. See British Cameroons; French Cameroons.
Campbell, Sir Roland I., 417
Canada:
U.S. relations with:
disposition of defense installations, 779–783
Great Lakes Fisheries Convention, 786–788
Rush-Bagot Agreement, interpretation of, 788–790
St. Lawrence seaway and power project, 784–786
Cardozo, Justice Benjamin:
quoted on power of precedent, 349
Caribbean Commission, 598–599
Caribbean Tourist Development Association, 598
Caribbean Tourist Trade Conference, Oct. 1, 1946, 598
Case v. Bowles, 48
Casualties:
U.S. battle, World War II, 124
Central Frequency Registration Board, 695–696
Central Intelligence Agency, U.S., 478
Chadwick, Sir James, 417
Chapultepec, Act of, 32–33
Chavez, Sen. Dennis, 721
Chiang Kai-shek, Generalissimo, **797**, 798, 826
Children's Emergency Fund, International, 364, 376
China:
treaty of friendship and alliance with Soviet Union, 826–829

INDEX 943

UNRRA activities, 366–367
U.S. relations with:
    agreement for sale of surplus war property, 163–167
    general policy, 18, 29, 797–799
    statements of Pres. Truman, 799–803
    lend-lease aid, 148–149
    military and financial aid, 803–805
    U.S. troops in, 541
U.S.-Soviet relations in:
    general policy, 825–830
    Manchuria, 830–834
    meeting of Foreign Secretaries, Moscow, Dec., 1945, 829–830
Chistiakov, Gen. Ivan M.:
    letter to Gen. Hodge on U.S.-Soviet Joint Commission in Korea, 839–841
Churchill, Winston S., 37, 179
Chy Lung v. *Freeman*, 49
Civil Aeronautics Act, 45–46
Civil Aeronautics Board, 45–46
Civil aviation. *See* Aerial navigation, international.
Clark, Gen. Mark W.:
    note on German assets in Austria, 286–287
Clark, Tom C.:
    validity of commercial aviation agreements, letter on, 45–46
Clarke, Col. Carter W., 172, 178
Clarke Inquiry, Pearl Harbor attack, 172
Clausen, Maj. Henry C., 172, 178
Clausen Investigation, Pearl Harbor attack, 172
Clay, Lt. Gen. Lucius D., Deputy Military Governor in Germany, 188, 250
Clayton, William L.:
    Dirksen-Amendment to Third Deficiency Appropriation Bill, letter on, 369–371
    statements on:
        UNRRA operations, 365–368
        wool market and foreign economic relations, 715–718
    Under Secy. of State for Economic Affairs, 51, 52–53, 61, 419, 617, 624, 643
    U.S. postwar economic policy, address on, 607–608
Clinton Engineer Works, 415, 416
Coal:
    agreement for establishment of European Coal Organization, 705–707
    production in Ruhr area, 188
Coffee, 771–772
Cohen, Benjamin V.:
    aide-mémoire on Bulgarian Government, 319, 322
    Counselor, Dept. of State, 56

Collado, Emilio G., 617
Colmer, Rep. William M., 602
Combined Food Board, 703
Commerce. *See* Trade.
Commercial aviation. *See* Aerial navigation, international.
Committee for Financing Foreign Trade, 611–612
Common Defense, Dept. of, 478. *See also* Armed forces.
Communication. *See* Transportation and communication.
Communications and Records, Division of, Dept. of State, 56
Communist Party, German, 188
Compton, Dr. Arthur H., 419, 737
Compton, Dr. Karl T., 419, 456, 503
Conant, Dr. James B., 415, 417, 419, 426, 545
Condon, Frank R., 423
Conferences, International, Asst. Secy. for, Dept. of State, 57
Conferences and Congresses:
    Caribbean Tourist Trade, Oct. 1, 1946, 598
    Crimea, protocol of proceedings, 919–924
    Empire-Wide Telecommunications, Nov. 21, 1945, 693
    Four-Power Broadcasting, Paris, Oct. 24, 1946, 694
    German-Owned Patents, July 15–27, 1946, 249–250
    Inter-American, on Problems of War and Peace, 16, 32
    International Civil Aviation, Nov. 1–Dec. 7, 1944, 657
    International, on Trade and Employment, 624–635
    International, on Travel Documents, 395
    International Health, June 19–July 22, 1946, 733
    International Labor, Oct. 15–Nov. 5, 1945, 720–721
    International Labor (Maritime Session, June 6–29, 1946), 678–679
    International Whaling, Nov. 20, 1945, 713–714
    Moscow Telecommunications, Sept. 26, 1946, 693, 694–696
    Potsdam, protocol of proceedings, 925–938
    Reparation, Paris, Nov. 9–Dec. 21, 1945, 227–243
    Second North American Regional Broadcasting Engineering, Feb. 4–25, 1946, 693
    Third Inter-American Radio, Sept. 3, 1945, 692

944 INDEX

Conferences and Congresses — *Continued*
  Twenty-One Nations, Paris, 1946, 65
  UNESCO, 743–745
  U.S. participation, July 1, 1945–Dec. 31, 1946, 76–80
  West Indian, Feb. 21–Mar. 13, 1946, 598
  World High-Frequency Broadcasting, 696

Congress, U.S.:
  Act to establish Office of Under Secy. of State for Economic Affairs, 55
  Act to extend privileges to international organizations, 66–72
  Act to extend Selective Training and Service Act of 1940, 492–495
  Act to provide assistance to China, 804–805
  address by Prime Minister Attlee, Nov. 13, 1945, 843–845
  Bretton Woods Agreements Act, 608–609, 617
  Civil Aeronautics Act, 45–46
  Export-Import Bank Act of 1945, 635
  Foreign Service Act of 1946, 84–101
  foreign surplus disposal, fourth report, letter of transmittal, 167–168
  Fulbright Act, 758–762
  Inter-American Military Cooperation Act, 769–771
  International Organizations Immunities Act, 67–72, 73
  lend-lease operations, twenty-third report, 141–153
    Pres. Truman's letter of transmittal, 140–141
  May-Johnson Bill, 424
  messages of Pres. Truman:
    Anglo-American Financial and Trade Agreement, 651–652
    annual message, Jan. 14, 1946, 13–21, 113–114, 606–607
    extension of selective service, 488–490
    international control of atomic energy, 545–546
    legislation on atomic energy, 426–429
    lend-lease and post-war reconstruction, 126–127
    scientific research and development, 504–506
    unification of armed forces, 469–478
    universal military training, 496–503
  Philippine Rehabilitation Act of 1946, 158, 807–810
  Philippines, Act to provide trade relations with, 810–817
  Philippines Military Assistance Act, 817–819
  Surplus Property Act of 1944, 62
  United Nations Participation Act of 1945, 511–515
  War Powers Act, 471

Congressional Relations, Asst. Secy. for, Dept. of State, 57

Connally, Sen. Tom:
  statements on:
    objectives of Atomic Energy Commission, 550–551
    regulation and reduction of armaments, 537–538
    Secy. Byrnes and administrative unity, 65
    U.S. policy toward Spain, 889–890
    veto question in UN, 526–530

Conservation of resources, 704

Constitutional Law of the United States, The (Willoughby), 48

Control Council:
  establishment of, in Germany, 186–187

Controls, Office of, Dept. of State, 57

Conway, Capt. Granville, Coordinator of Emergency Exports, 379

Cooke, Juan I., 775

Cooperation, international, 9

Coordinator of Emergency Exports, Office of, 379

Coordinator of Inter-American Affairs, Office of, 50

Cotton:
  International Cotton Advisory Committee, 707–708

Counselor, Dept. of State, Office of, 56

Cramer, Lawrence W., 598

Crimea Conference, protocol of proceedings, 919–924

Criminals, war (*see also* Nuremberg Tribunal):
  International Military Tribunal for Europe:
    agreement for prosecution and punishment, 343–344
    appointment of U.S. member and alternate, 344
    formation, jurisdiction, and summary of trials, 341–342
    report of U.S. Chief Counsel, 345–352
  International Military Tribunal for Far East:
    authority of U.S. Chief of Counsel, 352–353
    charter, 354–358
    establishment and jurisdiction, 352, 353–354
  United Nations War Crimes Commission:
    establishment of, 340–341
    summary of trials to Oct. 31, 1946, 341

INDEX 945

Crowley, Leo T., Foreign Economic Administrator, 153, 643, 850
Cultural relations:
  exchange program:
    Fulbright Act, 758–762
    Interdepartmental Committee on Scientific and Cultural Cooperation, 757–758
    International Information Service:
      establishment and activities, 752–753
      role of, in conduct of U.S. foreign relations, 753–755
      summary of projected activities, 755–757
    UNESCO:
      U.S. National Commission, 746–752
      U.S. participation, 737–745
Czechoslovakia:
  transfer of German population, 256
  U.S. relations with:
    commercial policy, 875–877
    general, 875

D

Davies, Joseph E., 503
Davies, Ralph K., 708
Davis, Chester, Chairman, National Famine Emergency Committee, 377, 378
Declaration Regarding the Defeat of Germany, 224
Defense, maintenance of (see also Atomic Energy):
  general statements, 461–469
  procurement of personnel:
    extension of selective service, 486–495
    voluntary recruitment, 486
  unification of armed forces:
    letter of Pres. Truman to Secys. of War and Navy, 483–485
    message of Pres. Truman recommending legislation, 469–478
    prospects of success, 485
    report of Secys. of War and Navy, 478–483
  universal military training:
    Advisory Commission, 503
    Congressional discussion, 495
    messages of Pres. Truman to Congress, 496–503
Defense Act of 1920, 467
Demobilization:
  World War II:
    annual message of Pres. Truman, Jan. 14, 1946, 113–114
    directive of Jan. 15, 1946, 114–116
    statement by Gen. Eisenhower, 116–124

Departmental Administration, Office of, Dept. of State, 56
Dependencies, U.S., 600
Devastated Areas, Temporary Subcommission on the Economic Reconstruction of, 376
Dewey, Bradley, 456
DeWolf, Francis Colt:
  Chief of Telecommunications Division, Dept. of State, 693
  report on Moscow Telecommunications Conference, 694–696
Dill, Field Marshal Sir John, 417
Diplomatic representation. See Foreign Service.
Dirksen Amendment, 364, 369–371
Disarmament, 23–24. See also Armaments.
Displaced persons (see also Refugees):
  admission of, to U.S., 18
  problem of, in Germany, 119
  repatriation of, 393, 395
  treatment of, in U.S. Zone of Germany, 251–255
Documents, custody of captured German, 348–349
Dodd, Morris E.:
  Under Secy. of Agriculture, 697, 698
  U.S. policy on world food proposals, statement on, 699–703
Dodds, Dr. Harold W., 503
Donnell, Sen. Forrest C., 512
Dorr, Russell H., U.S. delegate to Inter-Allied Reparation Agency, 227
Douglas, Justice William O., 48
Doull, Dr. James A., 733
Dreyfus, Louis G., Jr.:
  abrogation of defense agreement with Iceland, 790–792
DuBridge, Lee A., 426
Dulles, John Foster, 39, 578:
  U.S. position on trusteeship system, statement on, 581–584
Dumbarton Oaks Conversations, 9
Dunn, James C., Asst. Secy. of State, 693
DuPont de Nemours Co., E. I., 416

E

Eberstadt, Ferdinand:
  memoranda on proposed Atomic Development Authority, 563–570
Eccles, Marriner S., 643
Economic Affairs, Asst. Secy. for, Dept. of State, 61–62
Economic Affairs, Special Asst. to Asst. Secy., 61
Economic Affairs, Under Secy. for, Dept. of State, 51–55

Economic and Social Council. *See* United Nations Economic and Social Council.
Economic policy, U.S., postwar:
  foreign-lending policy:
    Eighth Report of House Special Committee, 613–614
    general remarks, 612–613
    Report of National Advisory Council on International Monetary and Financial Problems, 614–617
  general principles:
    address by Under Secy. of State Clayton, 607–608
    annual message of Pres. Truman on state of the Union, 606–607
    Eighth Report of House Special Committee, 602–606
    statement of Secy. of State Byrnes, 601–602
  special agencies to implement policy:
    Bretton Woods Agreements Acts, 608–609
    Committee for Financing Foreign Trade, 611–612
    National Advisory Council on International Monetary and Financial Problems, 609–611
Economic Security Policy, Office of, Dept. of State, 61
Eddy, Colonel William A., Special Assistant to Secretary of State, 50
Educational, Scientific, and Cultural Organization. *See* United Nations Educational, Scientific, and Cultural Organization.
Eisenhower, Gen. Dwight D.:
  Jews in U.S. Zone of Germany, report on, 253–255
  problems of demobilization and occupation, statement on, 116–124
Elections:
  Austria, 285, 288
  Bulgaria, 317–318, 322–323, 324–326
  Greece, 878–881
  Italy, 183–186
  Japan, 280–283
  Poland, 882–885
  Rumania, 334–335, 338–339, 340
Emergency Conference on European Cereals, 376, 377, 378
Emergency Economic Committee for Europe, 375
Emergency Food Administration, 377
Emergency Food Council, International, 375, 703–704.
Empire-Wide Telecommunications Conference, Nov. 21, 1945, 693
Employment. *See* International Conference on Trade and Employment.

Enemy aliens:
  treatment of, 358–359
  presidential proclamations on removal of, 359–363
England. *See* United Kingdom.
Erhardt, John G., U.S. Minister to Austria, 317
European Advisory Commission, 63:
  control machinery and zones of occupation in Austria, 309–311, 311–317
European Central Inland Transport Organization, 375, 376, 679–692
European Coal Organization, 375, 705–707
Exchange, foreign. *See* Foreign exchange.
Export-Import Bank:
  credits authorized, July 1, 1945–Dec. 31, 1946, 640–642
  establishment and operations, 635–636
  loans, 371
  loans and authorizations as of Dec. 31, 1946, 638–639
  policy, general statement of, 637–640
Export-Import Bank Act of 1945, 635

F

Fahy, Charles, Legal Adviser of Dept. of State, 62
Famine Emergency Committee. *See* National Famine Emergency Committee.
Far East (*see also* individual countries):
  UNRRA activities, 366–367
  U.S. policy, 28–29, 793–797
  U.S. relations with Soviet Union:
    China, 825–830
    Korea, 834–842
    Manchuria, 830–834
Far Eastern Advisory Commission, 266
Far Eastern Commission:
  establishment of, 266–267, 275–277
  Japanese general election, exchange of correspondence, 280–283
Farrell, Gen. Thomas F., 423
Feller, Abe, 508
Fermi, Dr. Enrico, 419, 426
Figl, Leopold, Austrian Chancellor, 286, 311
Finance. *See* Trade and finance.
Financial Affairs, Deputy on, Dept. of State, 61
Financiers, German, trial of, 347–348
Finland: peace terms, 16
  U.S. relations with, 877–878
FitzGerald, Dr. D. A., Secy.-Gen., International Emergency Food Council, 703
Food (*see also* Agriculture and natural resources):
  distribution of, in U.S. Zone of Germany, 254–255, 260–261

INDEX 947

emergency measures in world crisis, 381–383
famine report by Hoover Mission, 383–389
famine-relief shipments, 1945–1946, 389–393
U.S. exports by destination, 1945–1946, 394
Food and Agriculture Organization. *See* United Nations Food and Agriculture Organization.
Foote, Wilder, 508
Foreign Activity Correlation, Division of, Dept. of State, 57
Foreign exchange, provision of, in impoverished countries, 371–372
Foreign intelligence activities, U.S. (*see also* Defense):
National Intelligence Authority, 506–507
Foreign Liquidation Commissioner:
delegation of authority, 161–162
Office of, Dept. of State, 62
Office of, UNRRA Operations Branch, 56
Foreign policy, U.S. (*see also* subject headings):
general statements on, 1–44
Foreign Policy Association, 32
Foreign relations, U.S.:
conduct of:
Dept. of State, 49–62
diplomatic representation, 81–104
international organizations and conferences, 66–80
other executive departments, 64–66
powers of the president, 45–49
State-War-Navy Coordinating Committee, 63–64
Foreign Service, U.S.:
Act of 1946, 81–102
statement by Pres. Truman, 101–102
Advisory Committee on Commercial Activities, 610–611
changes in Foreign Service posts, 102–104
Foreign surplus disposal. *See* Surplus property disposal.
Foreign Trade. *See* Trade and Finance.
Formosa:
UNRRA operations, 367
Forrestal, James V.:
Pearl Harbor investigation, 171, 172–173
Secy. of the Navy, 424, 506
State-War-Navy Coordinating Committee, memorandum on, 64
unification of armed forces, report on, 478–483

Four-Power Broadcasting Conference, Paris, Oct. 24, 1946, 694
France:
agreements on:
additional requirements for Germany, 189–198
control machinery in Austria, 309–310, 311–317
lend-lease settlement, 142–144
zones of occupation in Austria, 310–311
policy of, in Germany, 259
central German agencies, establishment of, 201–205
U.S. relations with:
commercial policy, 866–868
economic and financial matters, 865–866
settlement of lend-lease, reciprocal aid, surplus war property, and claims, 869–870
Francisco, Don, 737
Frank, Maj. Gen. Walter A., 171
Freedom of Information, Subcommission on, 723–724
French Cameroons, trusteeship agreement, 578
French Togoland, trusteeship agreement, 578
Fulbright, Rep. J. William, 737
Fulbright Act, 758–762

G

Gatch, Rear Adm. T. L., 176
Gaulle, Gen. Charles de, 865
Gavrilovic, Dr. Styoyan, 518
Gehrig, Benjamin, 508
Georgiev, M., Prime Minister of Bulgaria:
note on enlargement of basis of Bulgarian Government, 323–325
German and Austrian Economic Affairs, Division of, Dept. of State, 61
German External Assets Commission, 186, 225–227
Germany:
Allied Control Council:
establishment, 224
failure of, 212–213
reparations and level of postwar economy, 244–249
transfer of Germans to occupied zones, 255–256
assets in Austria, 285–287
Declaration Regarding the Defeat of, 224
refugees and displaced persons:
problem of, 20, 119

948 INDEX

Germany — *Continued*
   repatriation, 393, 395
   treatment of, in U.S. Zone, 251–255
   reparations:
      Allied Commission on, 221–222
      failure of program, 249
      German-owned patents, 249–250
      law on vesting and marshaling external assets, 224–227
      level of postwar economy, 244–249
      Navy, disposal of, 244
      Paris Conference, Final Act and Annex, 227–243
      statement by head of U.S. delegation, 222–224
   U.S. occupation:
      policy, 250–251
      problems of, 117–119
      relations between American forces and German people, 256–263
      relationship of military and civil government, 263–266
   U.S. policy toward:
      agreement with U.K. on economic fusion, 218–221
      agreement with U.K., Soviet Union, and France on additional requirements, 189–198
      central controls for economic unity, 208–209
      central German agencies, establishment of, 201–205
      draft treaty for disarmament and demilitarization, 205–208
      general policy and problems, 186–188, 210–218
      instructions to U.S. Military Governor, 209–210
      Potsdam Declaration, meaning of, for economic issues, 198–201
Germany-Austria Secretariat, Dept. of State, 60
Gerow, Maj. Gen. Leonard T., Pearl Harbor investigation, 174
Gibbons v. *Ogden*, 48
Gibson, Truman K., Jr., 503
Gilbert, Glen A., 663
Gildersleeve, Virginia, 737
Gillem, General, 798
Gold, monetary:
   restitution of, 238
   return of Hungarian by U.S., 327, 329, 331
Goldstein, Dr. Rabbi Israel, 254
Good neighbor policy, 7–8
Goodwin, Robert C., 721
Graves Registration Service, 119
Great Britain. *See* United Kingdom.
Great Lakes Fisheries Convention, 786–788

Greece:
   U.S. relations with:
      economic and financial, 881
      elections, 878–881
      incidents on Greek border, 881–882
Grew, Joseph C.:
   Pearl Harbor investigation, 179
   resignation, 51
   Under Secy. of State, 49
Griffin v. *McCoach*, 49
Gromyko, Andrei A.:
   Allied troops in territory of other states, statement on, 532–533
   draft convention prohibiting weapons based on use of atomic energy, 560–562
   Soviet Representative on UN Security Council, 530–531
Groves, Maj. Gen. Leslie R., 415, 416, 423, 545
Groza, Dr. Petru, Pres. of Rumanian Council of Ministers, 336, 338
Gruber, Dr. Karl, Foreign Minister of Austrian Federal Republic, 284
Grunert, Lt. Gen. George, 171
Gurney, Sen. Chan, 495
Gutt, Camille, Managing Director of International Monetary Fund, 618

H

Hackworth, Green H., 62
Halifax, Earl of, 417, 643
Hall-Patch, E. L., 643
Hanford Engineer Works, 415, 416
Harriman, W. Averell, 337, 338
Harrison, Earl G.:
   U.S. representative on Inter-Governmental Committee on Refugees, 251, 253, 255
Harrison, George L., 419
Hart, Adm. Thomas C., 171, 172, 178
Hart, Sen. Thomas C., 504
Hart Amendment, atomic energy control, 424–425
Hart Inquiry:
   Pearl Harbor attack, 171, 173
Hatch, Sen. Carl, 456, 515
Hawkins, Harry C., 630
Health:
   Pan American Sanitary Bureau, 734–736
   World Health Organization, 732–734
Herter, Rep. Christian A., 515
Hewitt, Adm. H. Kent, 172, 178
Hewitt Inquiry, Pearl Harbor attack, 172–173
Higgins, Judge John P., Member for U.S. of International Military Tribunal, 352

INDEX

Hilldring, Maj. Gen. John H., Asst. Secy. of State for occupied areas, 60, 250, 289
Hines v. *Davidowitz*, 48, 49
Historical Policy Research, Division of, Dept. of State, 59
Hitler Youth, 258, 262
Hocker, John S., 618
Hodge, Lieut. Gen. John R., letters to Gen. Chistiakov on U.S.-Soviet Joint Commission in Korea, 838–839, 841–842
Hodgson, Lt. Col. Joseph V., 341
Holifield, Rep. Chet, 456
Holmes, J. C., Asst. Secy. of State for Occupied Areas, 60
Hoover, Herbert, Honorary Chairman, Famine Emergency Committee, 377, 378
Hoover Mission:
  famine report, 383–389
Howe, C. D., 417
Hull, Cordell, Pearl Harbor investigation, 173, 178, 179
Human Rights, Commission on, 722–723
  proposal for Subcommission on Freedom of Information, 723–724
Humbert II, King of Italy, 183
Hungary:
  Soviet note on economic situation and reparations, 331–334
  transfer of German population, 256
  U.S. policy toward:
    general, 326–327
    request for action to halt economic disintegration, 327–331
Hurley, Patrick J., 797, 798
Hutcheson, Joseph C., 908

I

Iceland:
  admission to UN, 525
  U.S. military personnel in, 541
  U.S. relations with, 790–792
Ickes, Harold L., Secy. of the Interior, 708
Immigration to United States:
  1942–1945, 408
  1946, 406
India:
  lend-lease settlement agreement, 144–145
Industrialists, German, trial of, 347–348
Industry:
  de-Nazification of, in Germany, 261
  German postwar, 244–249
Informal Policy Committee on Germany, 63–64

Inland transport:
  European Central Inland Transport Organization, 375, 376, 679–692
Inter-Allied Declaration on Punishment of War Crimes, 340
Inter-Allied Reparations Agency:
  organization and functions, 187, 222, 227, 235–237
Inter-American Affairs, Office of, 50
Inter-American Arrangement Concerning Telecommunications, 692
Inter-American Coffee Agreement, 771–772
Inter-American Conference on Problems of War and Peace, Feb.–Mar., 1945, 16, 32
Inter-American Military Cooperation Act, 769–771
Inter-American Radio Conference (Third), Sept. 3, 1945, 692
Inter-American system, 7, 9. *See also* American Republics.
Intergovernmental Committee on Refugees, 251, 395
Inter-Governmental Maritime Consultative Organization, 675–678
Interim Foreign Economic and Liquidation Service, Dept. of State, 62
Interim International Information Service, Dept. of State, 57
Interim Research and Intelligence Service, Dept. of State, 50
International agencies, U.S. participation:
  International Bank and Fund:
    address by John W. Snyder, 619–621
    establishment, 617–618
    participation to Oct. 31, 1946, 621–624
  International Trade Organization:
    Preparatory Committee, 629–635
    proposals, 624–628
    suggested charter, 628–629
International agreements, validity of presidential, 47–49
International Atomic Development Authority, proposals for, 557–559. *See also* Atomic energy.
International Bank for Reconstruction and Development, 18, 30, 43, 372
  address by John W. Snyder, 619–621
  establishment, 617–618
  U.S. participation to Oct. 31, 1946, 621–624
International Broadcasting Division, Dept. of State, 58
International Children's Emergency Fund, 364, 376
International Civil Aviation Conference, 657

International Conference on Trade and Employment:
Preparatory Committee, 629–630
address by John G. Winant, 630–631
principles of international trade, address on, 632–635
proposals, 624–628
suggested Charter, 628–629
International Conference on Travel Documents, 395
International cooperation, 9
International Cotton Advisory Committee, 707–708
International Court of Justice:
U.S. acceptance of compulsory jurisdiction, 515–517
International Emergency Food Council, 375, 703–704
International Exchange of Persons, Division of, Dept. of State, 58
International Information and Cultural Affairs, Office of, Dept. of State, 57–58, 752–757
International Information Service:
establishment and activities, 752–753
role of, in U.S. foreign relations, 753–755
summary of projected activities, 755–757
International Labor Conference (Maritime Session, June 6–29, 1946), 678–679
International Labor Organization, 720–721
International Military Tribunal:
Europe:
agreement for prosecution and punishment of major war criminals, 343–344
appointment of U.S. member and alternate, 344
formation, jurisdiction, and summary of trials, 341–342
report of U.S. Chief Counsel, 345–352
Far East:
authority of U.S. Chief of Counsel, 352–353
Charter, 354–358
establishment and jurisdiction, 352, 353–354
International Monetary Fund:
establishment, 617–618
first annual meeting, address by John W. Snyder, 619–621
U.S. participation to Oct. 31, 1946, 621–624
International Motion Pictures Division, Dept. of State, 58
International organizations:
privileges and immunities, 66–73
U.S. participation, 73–76

International Organizations Immunities Act, 67–72, 73
International Press and Publications Division, Dept. of State, 58
International Refugee Organization:
Constitution, 400–406
establishment, 393–396
U.S. position on, 396–400
International Sugar Council, 713
International Telecommunications Union, 694–695
International Telegraph Consulting Committee, 694
International Trade Organization:
Preparatory Committee, 629–630
address by John G. Winant, 630–631
principles of international trade, address on, 632–635
proposals, 624–628
suggested Charter, 628–629
International Whaling Conference, 713–714
International Wheat Council, 714–715
Iran:
retention of Soviet troops, 855–859
withdrawal of foreign troops, 851–854
Ireland:
admission to UN, 525
Italy:
elections, U.S. interest in, 185–186
political and economic developments, 1945–1946, 183–184
supply program, 153
UNRRA operations, 367
U.S. policy toward, 184–185

J

Jackson, Rep. Henry M., 720
Jackson, Justice Robert H.:
Chief Counsel for U.S. of European war trials, 344
final report on prosecution of major Nazi war criminals, 345–352
James, William:
cited on moral equivalent for war, 35
Japan:
democratization, 20
general election:
directive of Supreme Commander for Allied Powers, 280
note from Far Eastern Commission, 280–281
occupation and control:
authority of Gen. MacArthur, 273
establishment of Far Eastern Commission and Allied Council, 275–278
problems of, 120, 266–267
report on first year of occupation, 278–280

statement of Gen. MacArthur, 273–275
U.S. initial post-surrender policy, 267–273
Soviet prosecution of war against, 848–849
surrender:
acceptance of Potsdam Declaration, statement of Pres. Truman, 108
address by Pres. Truman, 110–111
offer of surrender, 106–108
terms, 105–106
text of Instrument of Surrender, 109–110
Japanese and Korean Economic Affairs, Division of, Dept. of State, 61
Japanese-mandated Pacific islands:
disposition of, 584–585
draft trusteeship agreement, 594–597
report of Subcommittee on Pacific Bases, 585–594
statement by Pres. Truman, 594
Japan-Korea Secretariat, Dept. of State, 60
Jews:
treatment of, in U.S. Zone of Germany, 251–255
Johnson, Sen. Edwin, 423
Johnson, Richard, 737
Johnson Bill, control of atomic energy, 423
Joint Chiefs of Staff, U.S., 470, 471
Joint Export-Import Agency (U.S.-U.K.), 218–219
Jones Co., J. A., 416

K

Kalbfus, Adm. Edward C., 172
Keenan, Joseph B., Chief of Counsel for U.S. at Japanese war trials, 352–353
Kefauver, Grayson N., 737
Keith, Gerald:
Polish elections, 884–885
Kellogg, Remington, 714
Kellogg Co., M. W., 416
Kennedy, Donald D., 712
Kent, Tyler, 179
Kerr, Sir A. Clark, 337, 338
Keynes, Lord, 643
Kilgore, Sen. Harley M., 503–504
Kimmel, Adm. Husband E.:
Pearl Harbor investigation, 178, 179
King, Adm. Ernest J., 176, 584
King, W. L. Mackenzie:
note on transfer of defense installations, 780–783
Kleinwaechter, Ludwig, Austrian representative in U.S., 317
Knox, Frank:
Pearl Harbor investigation, 171, 178

Kolaroff, V., Pres. of Bulgaria, 324
Korea:
UNRRA operations, 367
U.S. policy in, 18, 28
U.S.-Soviet relations in:
general policy, 834–836
meeting of Foreign Secretaries, Moscow, Dec., 1945, 836–837
U.S.-Soviet Joint Commission, 837–838
Kotschnig, Walter M., 737
Krupp, Alfried, 348
Kuhn, Ferdinand, Jr., 737
Kuter, Maj. Gen. Lawrence S., 664

L

Labor problems:
International Labor Organization, 720–721
La Guardia, Fiorello H., Director-General of UNRRA, 365, 377
Lane, Arthur Bliss:
Polish elections, 882–883
Lane, Chester T., Lend-Lease Administrator, 151
Lange, Oskar:
note on proposed Polish elections, 884
Langer, William L., Special Asst. to Secy. of State, 50
Lawrence, Dr. E. O., 419
Lawrence, Lord Justice Geoffery, member of Military Tribunal for Europe, 342
League of Nations, 12, 36
Leahy, Fleet Admiral William D., 506
Legal Adviser, Office of, Dept. of State, 62
Lehman, Herbert H., Director-General of UNRRA, 365, 368
Lend-lease and mutual aid:
administration, 139–140, 151–152
by country and category, 154–155
China, 148–149
discontinuance of operations, 126–127
funds available to Sept. 30, 1946, 157–158
Italy:
supply program for, 153
pipeline operations, 149–150
settlements, 127–139, 141–142
Australia, 145–146
Belgium, 147–148
France, 142–144
India, 144–145
New Zealand, 146–147
Turkey, 148
summary of operations, 140–158
Lerch, Maj. Gen. Archibald V., 836
Level of industry plan, 187

952 INDEX

Libraries and Institutes, Division of, Dept. of State, 58
Lie, Trygve, Secretary General, UN, 457
Liechtenstein, Principality of, 896
Lilienthal, David E., 425, 545
Llewellin, Col. J. J., 417
Locke, Edwin A., Jr., 803
Lucas, Sen. Scott, 456
Lundeberg, Harry, 720
Luthringer, George F., 618

M

MacArthur, Gen. Douglas:
  authority of, 273
  directive for Japanese general election, 280
  note to Far Eastern Commission on Japanese general election, 281–283
  proclamation establishing Military Tribunal for Far East, 353–354
  report on first year of occupation of Japan, 278–280
  statement on occupation policy for Japan, 273–275
McCabe, Thomas B., Foreign Liquidation Commissioner, 151, 643, 779, 803
McCarthy, Frank, Asst. Secy. for Administration, Dept. of State, 56
McCloy, John J., Asst. Secy. of War, 153, 545
McCombe, Francis W., 895
McCormack, Col. Alfred, Special Asst. to Secy. of State, 50
McCoy, Maj. Gen. Frank R., 171
McGranery, James P.:
  validity of international agreements executed by Pres., letter on, 47–49
McKellar, Sen. Kenneth, 509
Mackenzie, Dean C. J., 417
MacLeish, Archibald:
  Asst. Secy. for Public Affairs, Dept. of State, 57, 737
  plans for UNESCO, 739–740
McMahon, Sen. Brien, 422, 423, 424, 456, 504
McMahon Bill, control of atomic energy, 422–425
McNarney, Gen. Joseph T.:
  Commanding General of U.S. Forces, European Theater, 250
  instructions to, as U.S. Military Governor in Germany, 209–210
McNutt, Paul V., U.S. High Commissioner to Philippines, 805
Magnuson, Sen. Warren, 503–504
Manchuria:
  U.S.-Soviet relations in:
    general policy, 830
    disposition and control of industrial enterprises, 831–832
    report on industrial conditions, 832–834
Mao Tse-tung, Chinese Communist leader, 797
Marine Corps, U.S., 482–483, 484
Marshall, Gen. George C.:
  address on maintenance of defense, 467–469
  fourth report on foreign surplus disposal, letter of transmittal, 167–168
  Pearl Harbor investigation, 172, 173, 175, 176, 178, 182
  quoted on personnel and national security, 501
  Special Envoy to China, 798
Martin, Rep. Joseph, 495
Martin Resolution, universal military training, 495
May, Rep. Andrew J., 423, 456, 486, 495
May-Johnson Bill, control of atomic energy, 424
Mazzini Society:
  message of Acting Secy. of State Acheson, 184–185
Meany, George, 721
Menthon, François de, 342
Merchant shipping:
  Inter-Governmental Maritime Consultative Organization, 675–678
  International Labor Conference (Maritime Session, June 6–29, 1946), 678–679
  United Maritime Consultative Council, 672–675
Merrow, Rep. Chester E., 737
Messersmith, George, 776
Mexico, U.S., relations with, 777–779
Meyer, Eugene, Pres. of International Bank, 618
Michael, King of Rumania:
  request for advice on reorganization of government, 334, 337
Mikhailovich, Gen. Draja, 899–900
Military cooperation, inter-American, 769–771
Milliken, Sen. Eugene D., 512
Missions, military, naval, and air, to American republics, 768
Molotov, Vyacheslav M.:
  Soviet declaration of war against Japan, 848–849
  Soviet Representative, UN General Assembly, 531
  statements on regulation and reduction of armaments, 533–535, 538–540
Mongolian People's Republic, admission to UN, 524, 525
Monroe Doctrine, 8

INDEX 953

Montreux Convention, revision of, 859–865
Moore, R. Walton, Counselor, Dept. of State, 56
Morlock, George A.:
  U.S. policy on opium, statement on, 726–729
Morrison, Herbert, Lord President of the Council, 378
Morse, David A., Asst. Secy. of Labor, 720
Morse, Sen. Wayne, 515, 516
Moscow Telecommunications Conference, Sept. 26, 1946, 693, 694–696
Murfin, Adm. Orin G., 172
Murray, Sen. James E., 737
Mutual aid. *See* Lend-lease and mutual aid.

N

Nagy, Ferenc, Hungarian Prime Minister, 333
Narcotic drugs:
  control of, 724–726
  in U.S. Zone in Germany, 730–732
  U.S. policy on opium, 726–729
National Advisory Council on International Monetary and Financial Problems, 143
  Report on activities, 609–611, 614–617
National defense. *See* Defense.
National Famine Emergency Committee, 377, 378, 391
National Intelligence Authority, establishment of, 506–507
National Science Foundation, 504
National Security Resources Board, 478
Natural resources. *See* Agriculture and natural resources.
Navigation, international, 30
Navy, disposal of German, Anglo-Soviet-American communiqué, 244
Navy Court of Inquiry, Pearl Harbor attack, 171–172, 173, 178
Navy Dept., U.S. *See* Armed forces.
Nazis (*see also* Criminals, war):
  trial of, 262–263
New Guinea:
  trusteeship agreement, 578
New Zealand:
  lend-lease settlement agreement, 146–147
Newel, William S., 456
Nielsen v. *Johnson*, 49
Nikitchenko, Maj. Gen. I. T., member, Military Tribunal for Europe, 342
Non-intervention, American policy of, 7–8
Normandie, S. S., 144

North American Regional Broadcasting Engineering Conference (Second), Feb. 4–25, 1946, 693
Novikov, Nikolai V.:
  note on U.S. *aide-mémoire* to Bulgarian Government, 320–321
Nuremberg Tribunal (*see also* Criminals, war):
  charter, 41

O

Oak Ridge, Tenn., 415
Occupation:
  Austria:
    background material, 288–289
    control machinery and zones of occupation, 309–311, 311–317
    directive to U.S. commander in chief on military government, 290–309
    U. S. recognition of government, 311
  Germany:
    displaced persons in U.S. Zone, 251–255
    military and civil government in U.S. Zone, 263–266
    relations between American forces and German people, 256–263
    U.S. Zone, policy in, 250–251
  Japan:
    authority of Gen. MacArthur, 273
    establishment of Far Eastern Commission and Allied Council, 275–278
    report on first year, 278–280
    U.S. general policy, 266–267, 273–275
    U.S. initial post-surrender policy, 267–273
  problems of:
    Germany and Austria, 117–119
    Pacific area, 119–121
Occupied Areas, Asst. Secy. for, Dept. of State, 60–61
O'Mahoney, Sen. Joseph C., 718
Operations Crossroads, 456
Opium (*see also* Narcotic drugs):
  U.S. policy on, 726–729
Opium Advisory Commission, 724
Oppenheimer, Dr. J. Robert, 416, 419, 423, 426, 456, 545
Orr, Sir John B., Director-General, FAO, 697–698

P

Pacific area (*see also* countries by name):
  problems of U.S. occupation, 119–121
  U.S. policy in, 793–797
  U.S. trusteeship:
    draft agreement for Japanese-mandated islands, 594–597

954 INDEX

Pacific area (*see also* countries by name) — Continued
    question of annexation, 584–585
    report by Subcommittee on Pacific Bases, 585–594
    statement by Pres. Truman, 594

Palestine:
    U.S. relations with:
        admission of Jewish refugees, 902–908
        report of Anglo-American Committee of Inquiry, 908–914

Panama:
    U.S. relations with, 779
    U.S. troops in, 541

Pan American Sanitary Bureau:
    establishment, 734
    relations with World Health Organization, 734–736

Papen, Franz von:
    acquittal by International Military Tribunal, 342, 347, 349

Paris Conference on Reparation:
    Annex, 240–243
    entry into force and signature, 238–239
    Final Act, 227–240
    German reparation, 228–235
    Inter-Allied Reparation Agency, 235–237
    restitution of monetary gold, 238
    unanimous resolutions, 239–240

Parker, John J., Alternate Member for U.S. of International Military Tribunal, 344

Parran, Dr. Thomas, 732

Patents:
    Conference on German-Owned, 249–250

Patterson, Robert P.:
    extension of selective service, address on, 490–492
    Secy. of War, 506
    statements on:
        maintenance of defense, 461–462
        unification of armed forces, 485
    State-War-Navy Coordinating Committee, memorandum on, 64
    unification of armed forces, report on, 478–483

Pauley, Edwin W.:
    industrial conditions in Manchuria, report on, 832–834
    statements on:
        Allied Commission on Reparations, 222–224
        European reparation program, 249

Pearl Harbor investigation:
    Army Pearl Harbor Board, report of, 173–176
    background of attack, 169–170
    Congressional Committee:
        establishment of, 177
        report of, 178–182
    investigations prior to Congressional inquiry, 170–173

Pennington, Maitland S., 720
Perkins, Frances, 720
Perón, Juan D., Pres. of Argentina, 769, 775, 776
Personnel Procurement Service, U.S., 122
Peterson, Howard C., Asst. Secy. of War, 803

Petroleum:
    Agreement between U.S. and U.K., 708–711

Phelps, D. Maynard, U.S. delegate to Inter-Allied Reparation Agency, 227
Philippine Rehabilitation Act of 1946, 158, 807–810

Philippines:
    U.S. military personnel in, 121, 541
    U.S. relations with:
        Act to provide for trade relations, 810–817
        general, 805–806
        Military Assistance Act, 817–819
        Philippine Rehabilitation Act of 1946, 158, 807–810
        proclamation of independence by Pres. Truman, 819–820
        surplus property, transfer of, 158
        treaty of general relations, 820–823

Picó, Rafael, 598
Pike, Sumner T., 425
Pogue, L. Welch, 663

Poland:
    transfer of German population, 256
    U.S. relations with:
        economic and financial cooperation, 885–887
        elections, 882–885

Poling, Dr. Daniel, 503
Porter, Paul, 881

Portugal:
    admission to UN, 525

Potsdam Agreement:
    meaning of, for economic issues in Germany, 198–201
    U.S. policy in Germany and, 211–218

Potsdam Conference:
    protocol of proceedings, 925–938

Pramoj, M. R. Seni:
    reestablishment of U.S.- Siamese relations, 823–824

President, powers of, 45–49

Price, Byron:
    report on relations between American forces of occupation and German people, 256–263

INDEX 955

Prisoners of war:
 control of, in Germany, 119
 repatriation, 20
Propaganda:
 American, in Germany, 261–262
Property disposal. See Surplus property disposal.
Public Affairs, Asst. Secy. for, Dept. of State, 57–60
Public Liaison, Division of, Dept. of State, 58–59
Public Studies, Division of, Dept. of State, 59
Publications, Division of, Dept. of State, 59
Purnell, Rear Adm. William R., 415

Q

Quislings, apprehension of, 398

R

Rabi, Dr. I. I., 426
Radio:
 supervision of, in U.S. Zone of Germany, 261–262
Rayner, Charles B., 708
Reciprocal aid. See Lend-lease and mutual aid.
Reciprocal trade agreements, 642–643
Recruiting service, U.S., 122
Recruitment, voluntary, U.S. armed forces, 486
Reeves, Rear Adm. Joseph M., 171
Refugees (see also Displaced persons):
 admission to U.S.:
  directive by Pres. Truman, 410–412
  general policy, 406
  statement by Pres. Truman, 407–410
  termination of War Refugee Board, 406–407
 International Refugee Organization:
  Constitution, 400–406
  establishment, 393–396
  U.S. position on, 396–400
 problem of, in Germany, 20
 treatment of, in U.S. Zone of Germany, 251–255
Regional advisory commissions:
 Caribbean Commission, 598–599
Relief:
 action taken by U.S.:
  emergency measures in world food crisis, 381–383
  famine report by Hoover Mission, 383–389
  relief and rehabilitation program, 379–381
  report on 1945–1946 famine-relief food shipments, 389–393
  summary, 376–379
 organizations other than UNRRA, 375–376
 UNRRA:
  Dirksen Amendment, 364, 369–371
  report on operations, Oct. 31–Dec. 31, 1946, 373–375
  status of U.S. appropriations as of Dec. 31, 1946, 374
  subsidiary agencies, 376
  U.S. participation and policy, 364–369, 371–372
Renfrew, Julia H., 726
Renner, Dr. Karl, Pres. of Austrian Federal Republic, 288, 311
Reparations:
 Germany:
  Allied Commission on Reparations, 221–222
  disposal of Navy, 244
  failure of program, 249
  German-owned patents, 249–250
  Inter-Allied Reparations Agency, 187, 222, 227, 235–237
  law on vesting and marshaling external assets, 224–227
  level of postwar economy, 244–249
  Paris Conference, Final Act and Annex, 227–243
  statement by head of U.S. delegation, 222–224
Repatriation. See Displaced persons, Refugees.
Replacements, problem of, in occupied territory, 117, 121–122
Research and Intelligence, Special Asst. for, Dept. of State, 50
Reverse lend-lease (see also Lend-lease and mutual aid):
 by category and country, 156
Richland, Wash., 415
Riddleberger, James J., Chief of Division of Central European Affairs, 289
Ridenour, Dr. Louis N., 423
Roberts, Justice Owen J., 170
Roberts Commission, Pearl Harbor attack, 170–171, 178
Robertson, Walter S., 798
Rockefeller, John D., Jr., 518
Rockefeller, Nelson A., Asst. Secy. for American Republic Affairs, Dept. of State, 60, 775
Rooks, Maj. Gen. Lowell W., Director-General of UNRRA, 365
Roosevelt, Franklin D.:
 Pearl Harbor investigation, 170, 178
 policies, 36–37

Roosevelt, Mrs. Franklin D.:
  Chairman, nuclear Commission on Human Rights, 723
  U.S. position on International Refugee Organization, 396–400
Rose, Hartley, 426
Rosenberg, Mrs. Anna, 503
Rosenman, Samuel I., 503
Ross, John C., 508
Roxas, Manuel A., President of Philippines, 806
Ruanda-Urundi:
  trusteeship agreement, 578
Rubber:
  Rubber Study Group, 712
  termination of purchasing agreements, 712–713
Rubin, Seymour, 895
Rudenko, Gen. R. A., 342
Ruhr:
  coal production, 188
Rumania:
  U.S. policy toward:
    elections, 334–335, 338–339, 340
    formation of democratic government, 335–339
    general, 334–335
    recognition of Government, 339–340
Rush-Bagot Agreement, interpretation of, 788–790
Russell, Donald S., Asst. Secy. for Administration, Dept. of State, 56
Russell, Maj. Gen. Henry D., 171
Russia. *See* Union of Soviet Socialist Republics.

S

St. Lawrence seaway and power project, 784–786
Saltonstall, Sen. Leverett, 456
SAM laboratory, 423
Sandstrom, Justice Emil, 895
Santovincenzo v. *Egan*, 49
Schacht, Hjalmar:
  acquittal by International Military Tribunal, 342, 347, 349
Schoenfeld, H. F. Arthur, U.S. Representative in Hungary, 327
Schwellenbach, Lewis B., Secy. of Labor, 720
Scientific and Cultural Cooperation, Interdepartmental Committee on, 757–758
Scientific research and development (*see also* Defense):
  Congressional discussion, 503–504
  message of Pres. Truman to Congress, 504–506

Scientific Research and Discovery, Office of, 414
Seaborg, Glenn T., 426
Searles, Fred, Jr., 456
Secretary of State, Office of, 49–50
Selective service:
  extension of:
    address by Secy. Patterson, 490–492
    legislation, 486–487, 492–495
    message of Pres. Truman to Congress, 488–490
Self, Sir Henry, 643
Shapley, Harlow, 737
Shawcross, Sir Hartley, 342
Shipping. *See* Transportation and communication.
Shoemaker, T. B., Acting Commissioner of Immigration and Naturalization, 406
Short, Lt. Gen. Walter C., Pearl Harbor investigation, 172, 173, 174, 175–176, 178
Shreveport Case, 48
Siam, U.S. relations with, 823–825
Sikorsky, Maj. Alexander P., 423
Singleton, John C., 908
Smith, Cyril S., 426
Smith, Sen. H. Alexander, 504
Smith, Paul A., 663
Smith, Lt. Gen. Walter Bedell:
  note to Soviet Government on economic disintegration of Hungary, 328–331
  revision of Montreux Convention, 864–865
Snyder, John W.:
  Chairman, Movement Coordinating Committee, 377, 378
  U.S. Government, International Bank and Fund, 618
  address at first meeting, 619–621
Social problems:
  Economic and Social Council:
    activities, 721–722
    Commission on Human Rights, 722–724
    control of narcotic drugs, 724–732
  health:
    Pan American Sanitary Bureau, 734–736
    World Health Organization, 732–734
Southwest Africa, 578
Soviet Union. *See* Union of Soviet Socialist Republics.
Spaak, Paul-Henri, Pres. of UN General Assembly, 532
Spain:
  position of U.S., U.K., and France, 888
  resolution on relations with United Nations, 890–891

INDEX 957

U.S. relations with, 887–888, 889–890
Stalin, Joseph:
   interviewed by London *Sunday Times*, 846–848
Stampar, Dr. Andrija, 704
Standley, Adm. William H., 171
Stanton, Charles I., 663
Stark, Adm. Harold R., Pearl Harbor investigation, 178, 179
State, Dept. of:
   appropriations (1946, 1947), 62
   organization:
      Asst. Secy. for Administration, 56–57
      Asst. Secy. for American Republic Affairs, 60
      Asst. Secy. for Congressional Relations and International Conferences, 57
      Asst. Secy. for Economic Affairs, 61–62
      Asst. Secy. for Occupied Areas, 60–61
      Asst. Secy. for Public Affairs, 57–60
      Counselor, 56
      Legal Adviser, 62
      Secy. of State, 49–50
      Special Asst. for Research and Intelligence, 50
      Under Secy. for Economic Affairs, 51–55
      Under Secy. of State, 51
State-War-Navy Coordinating Committee, 63–64, 250
Stepinac, Archbishop, 900
Stettinius, Edward R., Jr., 49, 508, 722–723
Stevenson, Adlai E., 365, 508
Stimson, Henry L.:
   development and application of atomic energy, statement on, 413–419
   Pearl Harbor investigation, 172, 178, 179
Stoddard, George, 737
Stoichew, Lt. Gen. Vladimir, Bulgarian representative in Washington, 318, 319
Stone, William T., 757
Stone and Webster Engineering Corp., 416
Strategic Services, Office of, termination of, 50
Strauss, Lewis L., 425
Stuart, Dr. J. Leighton, U.S. Ambassador to China, 798
Styer, Lt. Gen. Wilhelm D., 415
Subasitch, Dr. Ivan, Yugoslav Foreign Minister, 897
Sugar:
   International Sugar Council, 713

Supply system, problems of:
   Germany and Austria, 119
   Pacific area, 120
Surplus Property Act of 1944, 62
Surplus Property Administrator, 62
Surplus property disposal:
   Austria, 118, 123
   China:
      U.S. agreement with, 163–167
      Foreign Liquidation Commissioner, 161–162
      fourth report, letter of transmittal, 167–168
   general statement, 158–159
   Germany, 118, 123
   Pacific area, 120, 123
   redistribution of functions, 159–161
   summaries, 169
   U.K.:
      agreement with U.S., 132–134
Sutherland, Justice George, 48
Sweden:
   membership in UN, 525
   U.S. relations with:
      disposition of German assets in Sweden, 894–895
      Swedish-Soviet trade negotiations, 892–894
Switzerland:
   Allied-Swiss negotiations for German external assets, 895–897
Symington, W. Stuart, 643
Szegedy-Maszak, Aladar de, Hungarian Minister to U.S., 327

T

Taft, Sen. Robert A., 512
Tanganyika:
   trusteeship agreement, 578
Tariff. *See* Reciprocal trade agreements.
Tatarescu, G.:
   note on recognition of Rumanian Government, 339
   Rumanian Foreign Minister, 335
Taussig, Charles W., 598
Taylor, Amos E., Director, Bureau of Foreign and Domestic Commerce, 611
Taylor, Brig. Gen. Telford, 347, 348
Telecommunications, international, 692–696. *See also* Transportation and communication.
Tennessee Eastman Company, 416
Thailand. *See* Siam.
Third Deficiency Appropriation Bill, 364, 369
Thomas, Charles A., 545
Thomas, Sen. Elbert D., 515, 516, 720, 721
Thompson, C. Mildred, 737

Thompson, H. E., 423
Thomson, Charles A., 738
Thorp, Willard L., Asst. Secy. for Economic Affairs, Dept. of State, 61
Tin, 713
Tito, Marshal, 897
Togoland. *See* British Togoland; French Togoland.
Tojo, Premier, 170
Tolman, Dr. Richard C., 417
Trade:
  International Trade Organization:
    Preparatory Committee, 629–630
      address by John G. Winant, 630–631
      principles of international trade, address on, 632–635
    proposals, 624–628
    suggested charter, 628–629
  postwar international, 19, 30
    address by Secy. Byrnes, 10–13
Trade and employment. *See* International Conference on Trade and Employment.
Trade and finance:
  Anglo-American Financial and Trade Agreement:
    address by Secy. Byrnes, 653–656
    Authorization to implement, 656
    joint statement by Pres. Truman and Prime Minister Attlee, 649–651
    negotiations, 643–645
    Pres. Truman's message of transmittal to Congress, 651–652
    text, 645–649
  Export-Import Bank:
    credits authorized, July 1, 1945–Dec. 31, 1946, 640–642
    establishment and operations, 635–636
    loans and authorizations as of Dec. 31, 1946, 638–639
    policy, general statement of, 637–640
  participation in international agencies:
    International Bank and Fund, 617–624
    International Trade Organization, 624–635
  principles of postwar economic policy:
    foreign-lending policy, 612–617
    general principles, 601–608
    special agencies to implement policy, 608–612
  reciprocal trade agreements, 642–643
Trans-Jordan:
  admission to UN, 525
Transportation and communication:
  inland transport:
    European Central Inland Transport Organization, 679–692
  international aerial navigation:
    bilateral air-transport agreements, 664–672
    Convention on International Civil Aviation, 657–662
    Provisional International Civil Aviation Organization, 663–664
  international telecommunications, 692–696
  merchant shipping:
    Inter-Governmental Maritime Consultative Organization, 675–678
    International Labor Conference (Maritime Session), 678–679
    United Maritime Consultative Council, 672–675
Travel Documents, International Conference on, 395
Trials, war criminal. *See* Criminals, war.
Tripartite Naval Commission, 244
Truman, Harry S:
  addresses:
    Army Day, Chicago, Apr. 6, 1946, 28–31
    General Assembly of UN, Oct. 24, 1946, 40–44
    maintenance of defense, Apr. 6, 1946, 465–467
    Navy Day, New York, Oct. 27, 1945, 2–6
    surrender of Japan, 110–111
  admission of refugees to U.S., 410–412
  American forces of occupation and German people, letter transmitting report on, 256
  atomic energy, Government control of, letter on, 429–431
  bipartisan policy, 37
  displaced persons in American Zone, letter on, 251–253
  enemy aliens, proclamations on removal of, 359–363
  Executive Orders:
    appointment to International Military Tribunal for Europe, 344
    authority for prosecution of Japanese war criminals, 352–353
    privileges to international organizations, 73
    redistribution of foreign economic functions, 159–161
    termination of War Refugee Board, 407
    transfer of lend-lease fiscal records, 139–140
    transfer of property and personnel to Atomic Energy Commission, 454–455

U.S. lands containing radioactive minerals, 426
FAO, message to delegates, 698–699
Inter-American Military Cooperation Act, letter on, 769–771
International Civil Aviation, ratification of Convention, 657–659
lend-lease operations, report to Congress, 141–153
lend-lease report, letter of transmittal, 140–141
messages to Congress:
  Anglo-American Financial and Trade Agreement, 651–652
  annual, Jan. 14, 1946, 13–21, 113–114, 606–607
  extension of selective service, 488–490
  international control of atomic energy, 545–546
  legislation on atomic energy, 426–429
  lend-lease and postwar reconstruction, 126–127
  scientific research and development, 504–506
  unification of armed forces, 469–478
  universal military training, 496–503
National Intelligence Authority, establishment of, 506–507
proclamation of Philippine independence, 819–820
proclamation terminating hostilities of Second World War, 112
proposed wool program, 718
statements on:
  admission of Jewish refugees to Palestine, 902–905, 906–908
  admission of refugees to U.S., 407–410
  Anglo-American Financial and Trade Agreement, 649–651
  anniversary of V–E Day, May 8, 1946, 31
  bipartisan program for foreign affairs, 38–39
  development and application of atomic energy, 419–421
  Foreign Service Act of 1946, 101–102
  Japanese acceptance of terms of surrender, 108
  relief and rehabilitation program, 379–381
  report of Army Pearl Harbor Board, 176
  resignation of Secy. Wallace, 66
  termination of hostilities of Second World War, 112–113
  UN, U.S. policy in, 519–524
  U.S. policy toward China, 799–803
  U.S. trusteeship in Pacific, 594
  U.S.-U.K. Air-Transport Agreement, 670–671
  world food crisis, 381–383
unification of armed forces, letters on, 483–485
United Nations Charter:
  instrument of U.S. ratification, 511
  transmission to Senate, 509–510
UNRRA, operations, Oct. 31–Dec. 31, 1946, report on, 373–375
West Indian Conference, letter on, 598–599
Trusteeship system, international:
  Trusteeship Council and Agreements:
    memorandum on procedure for dealing with Agreements, 579–580
    preliminary discussion, 577–579
    U.S. position on, 581–584
  U.S. trusteeship in Pacific:
    draft agreement for Japanese-mandated islands, 594–597
    question of annexation, 584–585
    report by Subcommittee on Pacific Bases, 585–594
    statement by Pres. Truman, 594
Tugwell, Rexford G., 598
Tully, Grace, 178
Turkey:
  U.S. relations with:
    lend-lease settlement agreement, 148
    revision of Montreux Convention, 859–865
Tyler Kent case, 179

U

Under Secy. of State, Office of, 51
Unification of armed forces. *See* Armed forces, unification.
Union Carbide and Carbon Co., 416
Union of Soviet Socialist Republics:
  agreements on:
    additional requirements from Germany, 189–198
    control machinery in Austria, 309–310, 311–317
    disposition of lend-lease supplies, 127–132
    zones of occupation in Austria, 310–311
  Anglo-Soviet-American communiqué on German Navy, 244
  German assets in Austria, 287–288
  treaty of friendship and alliance with China, 826–829
  U.S. relations with:
    Bulgaria, 317
    China, 825–830
    financial relations, 849–850
    general, 845–848

960 INDEX

Union of Soviet Socialist Republics — *Continued*
  Hungary, 326–334
  Iran, 851–859
  Korea, 834–842
  Manchuria, 830–834
  prosecution of war against Japan, 848–849
  Rumania, 334
  Turkey, 859–865
United Kingdom:
  address by Prime Minister Attlee before Congress, 843–845
  agreements:
    additional requirements from Germany, 189–198
    control machinery in Austria, 309–310, 311–317
    economic fusion in Germany, 218–221
    lend-lease and reciprocal aid pipelines, 134–139
    zones of occupation in Austria, 310–311
  Anglo-Soviet-American communiqué on German Navy, 244
  settlement of lend-lease, reciprocal aid, surplus war property and claims, 132–134
  U.S. relations with:
    general statement, 843
United Maritime Authority, 672
United Maritime Consultative Council, 672–675
United Nations:
  Charter:
    statement by Secy. Byrnes, 27–28
  General Assembly:
    address by Pres. Truman, Oct. 24, 1946, 40–44
  Security Council:
    statement by Secy. Byrnes, 26–28
  selection of headquarters, 518
  U.S. participation and membership:
    acceptance of compulsory jurisdiction of International Court of Justice, 515–517
    ratification of Charter, 508–511
    United Nations Participation Act of 1945, 511–515
  U.S. policy toward:
    address by Secy. Byrnes, 22–26
    admission of new members, 524–526
    financial support, 517
    general, 518–524
    question of veto, 526–530
United Nations Atomic Energy Commission:
  draft convention prohibiting weapons based on atomic energy, 560–562
  establishment, 422–426, 431–453, 544–545, 548–550, 551–552
  International Atomic Development Authority, proposals for, 557–559
  objectives, 550–551
  proposals for report to Security Council, 570–572
  proposed Atomic Development Authority, 563–570
  report by Board of Consultants to Secy. of State's Committee, 552–557
  report to Security Council, 572–576
United Nations Economic and Social Council:
  activities, 721–722
  Commission on Human Rights, 722–723
  proposal for Subcommission on Freedom of Information, 723–724
  narcotic drugs:
    control of, 724–726
    in U.S. Zone in Germany, 730–732
    U.S. policy on opium, 726–729
United Nations Educational, Scientific, and Cultural Organization:
  U.S. National Commission:
    Report on establishment, 746–748
    report to Secy. Byrnes, 748–752
  U.S. participation:
    admission to membership, 737–743
    report of first General Conference, 743–745
United Nations Emergency Food Fund, 376
United Nations Food and Agriculture Organization:
  establishment and activities, 697–698
  message of Pres. Truman, Oct. 17, 1945, 698–699
  U.S. policy toward, 699–703
United Nations International Children's Emergency Fund, 364, 376
United Nations Participation Act of 1945, 511–515
United Nations Relief and Rehabilitation Administration:
  Dirksen Amendment, 364, 369–371
  refugees and displaced persons, 393–395
  report on operations, Oct. 31–Dec. 31, 1946, 373–375
  status of U.S. appropriations as of Dec. 31, 1946, 374
  transfer of surplus property, 158
  U.S. participation and policy, 364–369, 371–372
United Nations War Crimes Commission:
  establishment of, 340–341
  summary of trials to Oct. 31, 1946, 341

INDEX 961

U.S. Commercial Company, 151
"United States Initial Post-Surrender Policy for Japan," 64
United States v. *Belmont*, 48, 49
United States v. *Curtis-Wright Export Corp.*, 48
United States v. *Pink*, 48, 49
Universal military training:
 Advisory Commission, 503
 Congressional discussion, 495
 messages of Pres. Truman to Congress, 496–503
Urey, Dr. Harold C., 423

V

Vabres, Donnedieu de, member of Military Tribunal for Europe, 342
Vandenberg, Sen. Arthur H., 36, 37, 39, 422, 424
 statements on:
  bipartisan foreign policy, 65
  U.S financial support of UN, 517
Vandenberg, Lt. Gen. Hoyt S., 506
Vandenberg Resolution:
 control of atomic energy, 422
Versailles, Treaty of, 36
Victor Emmanuel III, King of Italy, 183
Vincent, John Carter:
 U.S. policies in Far East, 793–797
Vinson, Rep. Carl, 455, 485
Vinson, Fred M., Secy. of the Treasury, 617, 618, 643
Vinson Resolution:
 Bikini tests, 455, 456
Voluntary recruitment, U.S. armed forces, 486
Vyshinsky, A. Y.:
 position on International Refugee Organization, 397–400
 Soviet Vice Commissar for Foreign Affairs, 322, 328, 337, 338

W

Walker, C. D., 708
Wallace, Henry A., 377, 415, 643
 address, New York, Sept. 12, 1946, 64–65
 resignation as Secy. of Commerce, 66
Walsh, Sen. David I., 456, 485
Walsh, Father E. A., 503
War Crimes Commission. *See* United Nations War Crimes Commission.
War criminals. *See* Criminals, War.
War Department. *See* Armed forces.
War Information, Office of, 50
War Powers Act, 471
War Refugee Board, termination of, 406, 407

War Relocation Camp, Oswego, N.Y., 409
Ware v. *Hylton*, 48
Warner, Dr. Edward, 663
Watt, Robert J., 720
Waymack, William W., 425
Wedemeyer, Lt. Gen. Albert C., 797
Wells v. *United States*, 48
West Indian Conference, Feb. 21–Mar. 13, 1946, 598
Western Samoa:
 trusteeship agreement, 578
Whaling, 713–714
Wheat:
 International Wheat Council, 714–715
Wheeler, Sen. Burton K., 512
Wheeler, Leslie A., Director, Office of Foreign Agricultural Relations, 697, 708, 714
White, Harry D., Asst. Secy. of the Treasury, 617
White Plan, 617
Whitney, John Hay, 737
Wilcox, Clair:
 Director, Office of International Trade Policy, 630
 principles of international trade, address on, 632–635
Wilson, C.E., 503
Wilson, Edwin C.:
 revision of Montreux Convention, 860–861
Wilson, Field Marshal Sir Henry Maitland, 417
Wilson, Woodrow, 12, 36
Winant, John G.:
 Conference on International Trade and Employment, 630–631
 U.S. Representative on Economic and Social Council, 704
Winne, Harry A., 545
Wisconsin R. R. Comm. v. *C., B. & Q. R.R. Co.*, 48
Wool:
 effect of market on foreign economic relations, 715–718
 international talks and proposed Wool Study Group, 718–719
 policy of U.S., 715, 718
World Food Board, 697–698
World Food Programs, Cabinet Committee on, 378
World Health Organization, 43, 364, 732–734
World High Frequency Broadcasting Conference, 696
World War II:
 cessation of hostilities, 111–113
 demobilization, 113–124
 Pearl Harbor investigation, 169–18?

World War II — *Continued*
  requirements and costs:
    lend-lease and mutual aid, 126–158
    national costs, 124–125
  surplus property disposal, 158–169
  surrender of Japan, 105–111
Worthington, Hood, 426
Wrong, Hume:
  interpretation of Rush-Bagot Agreement, 789

Y

Yalta Conference. *See* Crimea Conference.

Yemen:
  U.S. relations with, 914–917
Yugoslavia:
  U.S. relations with:
    general, 899–902
    recognition of Federal People's Republic, 897–899

Z

Zellerbach, David, 720
Zellerbach, James D., 720, 721
Zimmer, Verne A., 721
Zwemer, Raymund L., 757